Video Cases

Eight videos delve into current international business issues and management topics, and include written cases and discussion questions prepared by Charles Hill.

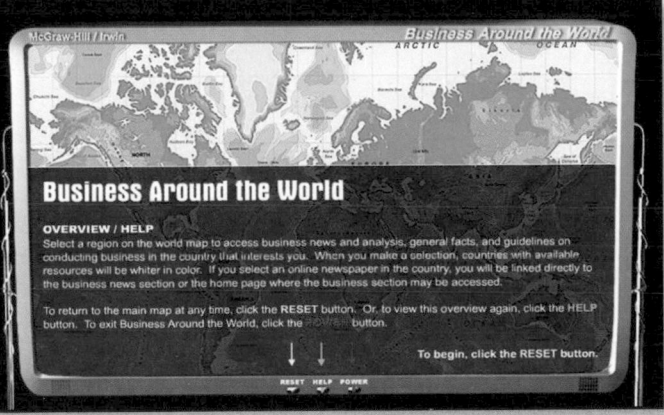

McGraw-Hill's Interactive Maps

- McGraw-Hill/Irwin presents "Business Around the World," an interactive map that allows you to select a list of resources from your favorite regions of interest around the world.

- Test your world geography knowledge with Interactive Maps!

7E International
Business

COMPETING IN THE
GLOBAL MARKETPLACE

Charles W. L. Hill
UNIVERSITY OF WASHINGTON

Boston   Burr Ridge, IL   Dubuque, IA   New York   San Francisco   St. Louis
Bangkok   Bogotá   Caracas   Kuala Lumpur   Lisbon   London   Madrid   Mexico City
Milan   Montreal   New Delhi   Santiago   Seoul   Singapore   Sydney   Taipei   Toronto

INTERNATIONAL BUSINESS: COMPETING IN THE GLOBAL MARKETPLACE

Published by McGraw-Hill/Irwin, a business unit of The McGraw-Hill Companies, Inc., 1221 Avenue of the Americas, New York, NY, 10020. Copyright © 2009, 2007, 2005, 2003, 2000, 1997, 1994 by The McGraw-Hill Companies, Inc. All rights reserved. No part of this publication may be reproduced or distributed in any form or by any means, or stored in a database or retrieval system, without the prior written consent of The McGraw-Hill Companies, Inc., including, but not limited to, in any network or other electronic storage or transmission, or broadcast for distance learning.

Some ancillaries, including electronic and print components, may not be available to customers outside the United States.

This book is printed on acid-free paper.

3 4 5 6 7 8 9 0 DOW/DOW 0 9

ISBN   978-0-07-338134-3
MHID   0-07-338134-9

Editorial director: *Brent Gordon*
Publisher: *Paul Ducham*
Executive editor: *John Weimeister*
Developmental editor: *Megan Richter*
Marketing director: *Krista Bettino*
Project manager: *Jim Labeots*
Lead production supervisor: *Carol A. Bielski*
Design manager: *Kami Carter*
Senior photo research coordinator: *Jeremy Cheshareck*
Photo researcher: *Keri Johnson*
Lead media project manager: *Brian Nacik*
Cover design: *Kami Carter*
Interior design: *Kami Carter*
Typeface: *10.5/12 Goudy*
Compositor: *Aptara, Inc.*
Printer: *R. R. Donnelley*

Library of Congress Cataloging-in-Publication Data

Hill, Charles W. L.
    International business : competing in the global marketplace / Charles W. L. Hill. — 7th ed.
        p. cm.
    Includes index.
    ISBN-13: 978-0-07-338134-3 (alk. paper)
    ISBN-10: 0-07-338134-9 (alk. paper)
    1. International business enterprises—Management. 2. Competition, International.
I. Title.
HD62.4.H55 2009
658'.049—dc22
                                                                        2007045184

www.mhhe.com

For **June** and
Mike Hill, my parents

about the AUTHOR

Charles W. L. Hill   University of Washington

Charles W. L. Hill is the Hughes M. Blake Professor of International Business at the School of Business, University of Washington. Professor Hill received his Ph.D. from the University of Manchester's Institute of Science and Technology (UMIST) in Britain. In addition to the University of Washington, he has served on the faculties of UMIST, Texas A&M University, and Michigan State University.

Professor Hill has published over 40 articles in peer-reviewed academic journals, including the *Academy of Management Journal, Academy of Management Review, Strategic Management Journal,* and *Organization Science.* He has also published two college texts: one on strategic management and the other on international business. Professor Hill has served on the editorial boards of several academic journals, including the *Strategic Management Journal* and *Organization Science.* Between 1993 and 1996 he was consulting editor at the *Academy of Management Review.*

Professor Hill teaches in the MBA, Executive MBA, Management, and Ph.D. programs at the University of Washington. He has received awards for teaching excellence in the MBA, Executive MBA, and Management programs. He has also taught customized executive programs.

Professor Hill works on a consulting basis with a number of organizations. His clients have included ATL, Boeing, BF Goodrich, Hexcel, House of Fraser, Microsoft, Seattle City Light, Tacoma City Light, Thompson Financial Services, and Wizards of the Coast.

brief CONTENTS

part five The Strategy and Structure of International Business

 part six International Business Operations

CONTENTS

part one
Introduction and Overview

part two
Country Differences

part three
The Global Trade and Investment Environment

part four
The Global Monetary System

part five
The Strategy and Structure of
International Business

CHAPTER 12
The Strategy of International Business 418

CHAPTER 13
The Organization of International
Business 448

part six
International Business Operations

list of MAPS

PREFACE

It is now over 17 years since I began work on the first edition of *International Business: Competing in the Global Marketplace*. By the third edition the book was the most widely used international business text in the world. Since then its market share has only increased. I attribute the success of the book to a number of goals I set for myself when I embarked on the first edition of the book. Specifically, I wanted to write a book that (1) was comprehensive and up-to-date, (2) went beyond an uncritical presentation and shallow explanation of the body of knowledge, (3) maintained a tight, integrated flow between chapters, (4) focused on managerial implications, and (5) made important theories accessible and interesting to students.

Over the years, and through seven editions, I have worked hard to adhere to these goals. It has not always been easy. An enormous amount has happened over the last 17 years, both in the real world of economics, politics, and business and in the academic world of theory and empirical research. Often I have had to significantly rewrite chapters, scrap old examples, bring in new ones, incorporate new theory and evidence into the book, and phase out older theories that are increasingly less relevant to the modern and dynamic world of international business. That process continues in the current edition. As noted below, I have made significant changes in this edition, and that will no doubt continue to be the case in the future. In deciding what changes to make, I have been guided not only by my own reading, teaching, and research but also by the invaluable feedback I receive from professors and students around the world who use the book, from reviewers, and from the editorial staff at McGraw-Hill. My thanks go out to all of them.

COMPREHENSIVE AND UP-TO-DATE

To be comprehensive, an international business textbook must

- Explain how and why the world's countries differ.
- Present a thorough review of the economics and politics of international trade and investment.
- Explain the functions and form of the global monetary system.
- Examine the strategies and structures of international businesses.
- Assess the special roles of an international business's various functions.

I have always endeavored to do all of these things in *International Business*. In my view, many other texts paid insufficient attention to the strategies and structures of international businesses and to the implications of international business for firms' various functions. This omission has been a serious deficiency. Many of the students in these international business courses will soon be working in international businesses, and they will be expected to understand the implications of international business for their organization's strategy, structure, and functions. This book pays close attention to these issues.

Comprehensiveness and relevance also require coverage of the major theories. It has always been my goal to incorporate the insights gleaned from recent academic work into the text. Consistent with this goal, over the last seven editions I have added insights from the following research:

- The new trade theory and strategic trade policy.
- The work of Nobel Prize–winning economist Amartya Sen on economic development.
- The work of Hernando de Soto on the link between property rights and economic development.
- Samuel Huntington's influential thesis on the "clash of civilizations."
- The new growth theory of economic development championed by Paul Romer and Gene Grossman.
- Empirical work by Jeffrey Sachs and others on the relationship between international trade and economic growth.
- Michael Porter's theory of the competitive advantage of nations.
- Robert Reich's work on national competitive advantage.
- The work of Nobel Prize–winner Douglas North and others on national institutional structures and the protection of property rights.
- The market imperfections approach to foreign direct investment that has grown out of Ronald Coase and Oliver Williamson's work on transaction cost economics.
- Bartlett and Ghoshal's research on the transnational corporation.

- The writings of C. K. Prahalad and Gary Hamel on core competencies, global competition, and global strategic alliances.

- Insights for international business strategy that can be derived from the resource-based view of the firm.

In addition to including leading edge theory, in light of the fast-changing nature of the international business environment, every effort is being made to ensure that the book is as up-to-date as possible when it goes to press. A significant amount has happened in the world since the first edition of this book was published in 1993. The Uruguay Round of GATT negotiations was successfully concluded and the World Trade Organization was established. In 2001 the WTO embarked upon another major round of talks aimed to reduce barriers to trade, the Doha Round. The European Union moved forward with its post-1992 agenda to achieve a closer economic and monetary union, including the establishment of a common currency in January 1999. The North American Free Trade Agreement passed into law, and Chile indicated its desire to become the next member of the free trade area. The former Communist states of Eastern Europe and Asia continued on the road to economic and political reform. As they did, the euphoric mood that followed the collapse of communism in 1989 was slowly replaced with a growing sense of realism about the hard path ahead for many of these countries. The global money market continued its meteoric growth. By 2007 over $1.8 trillion per day was flowing across national borders. The size of such flows fueled concern about the ability of short-term speculative shifts in global capital markets to destabilize the world economy. The World Wide Web emerged from nowhere to become the backbone of an emerging global network for electronic commerce. The world continued to become more global. Several Asian Pacific economies, including most notably China, continued to grow their economies at a rapid rate. Outsourcing of service functions to places like China and India emerged as a major issue in developed Western nations. New multinationals continued to emerge from developing nations in addition to the world's established industrial powers. Increasingly, the globalization of the world economy affected a wide range of firms of all sizes, from the very large to the very small. And unfortunately, in the wake of the terrorist attacks on the United States that took place on September 11, 2001, global terrorism and the attendant geopolitical risks emerged as a threat to global economic integration and activity.

Reflecting this rapid change, in this edition of the book I have tried to ensure that all material and statistics are as up-to-date as possible as of 2007. However, being absolutely up-to-date is impossible since change is always with us. What is current today may be outdated tomorrow. Accordingly, I have established a home page for this book on the World Wide Web at www.mhhe.com/hill. From this home page the reader can access regular updates of chapter material and reports on topical developments that are relevant to students of international business. I hope readers find this a useful addition to the support material for this book.

BEYOND UNCRITICAL PRESENTATION AND SHALLOW EXPLANATION

Many issues in international business are complex and thus necessitate considerations of pros and cons. To demonstrate this to students, I have adopted a critical approach that presents the arguments for and against economic theories, government policies, business strategies, organizational structures, and so on.

Related to this approach, I have attempted to explain the complexities of the many theories and phenomena unique to international business so the student might fully comprehend the statements of a theory or the reasons a phenomenon is the way it is. I believe this book explains these theories and phenomena in more depth than do competing textbooks, the rationale being that a shallow explanation is little better than no explanation. In international business, a little knowledge is indeed a dangerous thing.

INTEGRATED PROGRESSION OF TOPICS

A weakness of many texts is that they lack a tight, integrated flow of topics from chapter to chapter. This book tells students in Chapter 1 how the book's topics are related to each other. Integration has been achieved by organizing the material so each chapter builds on the material of the previous ones in a logical fashion.

Part One

Chapter 1 provides an overview of the key issues to be addressed and explains the plan of the book.

Part Two

Chapters 2 and 3 focus on national differences in political economy and culture, and Chapter 4 on ethical issues in international business. Most international business textbooks place this material at a later point, but I believe it is vital to discuss national differences first. After all, many of the central issues in international trade and investment, the global monetary system, international business strategy and structure, and international business operations arise out of national differences in political economy and culture. To fully understand these issues, students must first appreciate the differences in countries and cultures. Ethical issues are dealt with at this juncture primarily because many ethical dilemmas flow out of national differences in political systems, economic systems, and culture.

Part Three

Chapters 5 through 8 investigate the political economy of international trade and investment. The purpose of this part is to describe and explain the trade and investment environment in which international business occurs.

Part Four

Chapters 9 through 11 describe and explain the global monetary system, laying out in detail the monetary framework in which international business transactions are conducted.

Part Five

In Chapters 12 through 14 attention shifts from the environment to the firm. Here the book examines the strategies and structures that firms adopt to compete effectively in the international business environment.

Part Six

In Chapters 15 through 20 the focus narrows further to investigate business operations. These chapters explain how firms can perform their key functions—manufacturing, marketing, R&D, human resource management, accounting, and finance—in order to compete and succeed in the international business environment.

Throughout the book, I point out the relationship of new material to topics discussed in earlier chapters to students to reinforce their understanding of how the material comprises an integrated whole.

FOCUS ON MANAGERIAL IMPLICATIONS

I have always believed that it is important to show students how the material covered in the text is relevant to the actual practice of international business. This is explicit in the later chapters of the book, which focus on the practice of international business, but it is not always obvious in the first half of the book, which considered many macroeconomic and political issues, from international trade theory and foreign direct investment flows to the IMF and the influence of inflation rates on foreign exchange quotations. Accordingly, at the end of each chapter in Parts Two, Three, and Four—where the focus is on the environment of international business, as opposed to particular firms—there is a section titled Implications for Business. In this section, the managerial implications of the material discussed in the chapter are clearly explained. For example, Chapter 5, "International Trade Theory," ends with a detailed discussion of the various trade theories' implications for international business management.

In addition, each chapter begins with a *Case* that illustrates the relevance of chapter material for the practice of international business. Chapter 2, "National Differences in Political Economy," for example, opens with a case that describes how the economy of Venezuela has changed under the leadership of Hugo Chavez.

I have also added a *Closing Case* to each chapter. These cases are also designed to illustrate the relevance of chapter material for the practice of international business. The closing case to Chapter 2, for example, looks at the problem of endemic corruption in Indonesia and its impact upon that country's economy.

Another tool that I have used to focus on managerial implications is *Management Focus* boxes. There is at least one Management Focus in each chapter. Like the opening case, the purpose of these boxes is to illustrate the relevance of chapter material for the practice of international business. The Management Focus in Chapter 2, for example, looks at how Starbucks has been able to enforce its trademark in China. This box illustrates the important role that national differences in the protection of intellectual property rights can play in international business.

ACCESSIBLE AND INTERESTING

The international business arena is fascinating and exciting, and I have tried to communicate my enthusiasm for it to the student. Learning is easier and better if the subject matter is communicated in an interesting, informative, and accessible manner. One technique I have used to achieve this is weaving interesting anecdotes into the narrative of the text—stories that illustrate theory. The opening cases and focus boxes are also used to make the theory being discussed in the text both accessible and interesting.

Most chapters have two kinds of focus boxes—a Management Focus box (described above) and a *Country Focus* box. Country Focus boxes provide background on the political, economic, social, or cultural aspects of countries grappling with an international business issue. In Chapter 2, for example, one Country Focus box discusses the steps that India has taken over the last decade to build a dynamic, market-based economic system.

WHAT'S NEW IN THE 7TH EDITION

The success of the first six editions of *International Business* was based in part upon the incorporation of leading-edge research into the text, the use of the up-to-date examples and statistics to illustrate global trends and enterprise strategy, and the discussion of current events within the context of the appropriate theory. Building on these strengths, my goals for the seventh revision have been threefold:

1. Incorporate new insights from recent scholarly research wherever appropriate.

2. Make sure the content of the text covers all appropriate issues.

3. Make sure the text is as up-to-date as possible with regard to current events, statistics, and examples.

As part of the revision process, three major changes have been made.

First, I have added an appendix on international trade and the balance of payments to Chapter 5. I was never entirely happy with the treatment of the balance of payments in prior editions (it was first discussed in the chapter on foreign direct investment theory). Although I do not think the topic warranted an entire chapter, adding extended coverage in the form of an appendix seemed like a reasonable solution to me, and several reviewers agreed.

Second, the two chapters on foreign direct investment in prior editions have been collapsed into a single chapter. Chapter 7 now deals with both the theory of foreign direct investment and government policies toward foreign direct investment (previously two separate chapters). Several reviewers suggested this approach and, moreover, doing so made room for an additional chapter on the global capital market (see below). I believe that Chapter 7 covers all the required material in a more parsimonious manner than prior editions of *International Business*.

Third, as noted, a chapter on global capital markets had been added to the book (Chapter 11). In actual fact, this chapter was in earlier editions of the book, but I removed it to make way for the ethics chapter. It is back by popular demand. Given the growth and importance of global capital markets, I think this is an appropriate decision and I hope it adds value to the book.

As part of the overall revision process, *changes have been made to every chapter in the book.* All statistics have been updated to incorporate the most recently available data. New examples, cases, and boxes have been added and older examples updated to reflect new developments. Almost all of the chapter opening and closing cases are new to this edition. New material has been inserted wherever appropriate to reflect recent academic work or important current events. For example, Chapter 5 has been updated to discuss progress on the current round of talks sponsored by the WTO aimed at reducing barriers to trade, particularly in agriculture (the Doha Round). Chapter 6 now discusses the rebound in foreign direct investment flows that took place in 2005 and 2006 after the slump in 2001–2004. At several places in the book are extended discussions of outsourcing service activities, from software testing and diagnosis of MRI scans to telephone call centers and billing functions, to developing nations such as India and the implications of this development for international business are explored. And so on.

ACKNOWLEDGMENTS

Numerous people deserve to be thanked for their assistance in preparing this book. First, thank you to all the people at McGraw-Hill/Irwin who have worked with me on this project:

Paul Ducham, Publisher

John Weimeister, Executive Editor

Dana Woo, Sponsoring Editor

Megan Richter, Developmental Editor

Krista Bettino, Marketing Director

Michael Gedatus, Marketing Coordinator

James Labeots, Project Manager

Brian Nacik, Media Project Manager

Carol Bielski, Production Supervisor

Kami Carter, Designer

Jeremy Cheshareck, Senior Photo Research Coodinator

Second, my thanks go to the reviewers who provided good feedback that helped shape this book.

Lawrence Beer, Arizona State University–Tempe

Ilgaz Arikan, Georgia State University

Arieh Ullmann, Binghamton University

Ralph Hoffmann, Gwynedd-Mercy College

Kathy Harris, Northwestern Oklahoma State University

David Lum, Lake Forest University

Seymour Schlosser, University of California–Irvine

Ping Deng, Maryville University

Martin Meznar, Arizona State University–West

Amit Sen, Xavier University

Ruth May, University of Dallas

Sesan Kim Sokoya, Middle Tennessee State University

Donald Vest, Clark Atlanta University

David Bruce, Georgia State University

Mike Callow, Morgan State University

Carol Reade, San Jose State University

Jorge Gonzalez, University of Wisconsin–Milwaukee

Andrew Gross, Cleveland State University

Shaomin Li, Old Dominion University

Richard Ajayi, University of Central Florida

Jane Ross, University of Maryland–University College

Joseph Stern, New Jersey City University

Arthur Richardson, Oklahoma City University

Guided Tour

Cases, focus boxes, and exercises throughout the book make theories accessible and interesting and show how theory relates to the practice of international business.

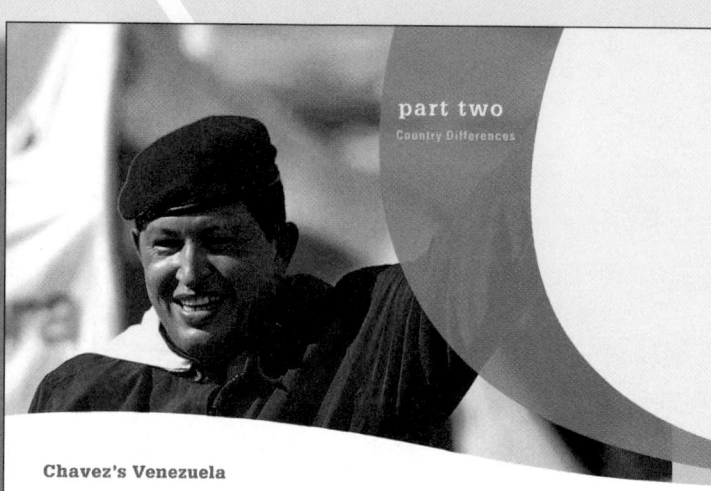

part two
Country Differences

National Differences in Political Economy

LEARNING OBJECTIVES
After you have read this chapter you should:

- LO Understand how the political systems of countries differ.
- LO Understand how the economic systems of countries differ.
- LO Understand how the legal systems of countries differ.
- LO Be able to explain what determines the level of economic development of a nation.
- LO Discuss the macro-political and economic changes taking place worldwide.
- LO Describe how transition economies are moving toward market based systems.
- LO Articulate the implications for management practice of national difference in political economy.

Chavez's Venezuela

Hugo Chavez, a former military officer who was once jailed for engineering a failed coup attempt, was elected president of Venezuela in 1998. Chavez, a self-styled democratic socialist, won the presidential election by campaigning against corruption, economic mismanagement, and the "harsh realities" of global capitalism. When he took office in February 1999, Chavez claimed that he had inherited the worst economic situation in the country's recent history. He wasn't far off the mark. A collapse in the price of oil, which accounted for 70 percent of the country's exports, left Venezuela with a large budget deficit and forced the economy into a deep recession.

Soon after taking office, Chavez proceeded to try to consolidate his hold over the apparatus of government. A constituent assembly, dominated by Chavez followers, drafted a new constitution that strengthened the powers of the presidency and allowed Chavez (if reelected) to stay in office until 2012. Subsequently, the national congress, which was controlled by Chavez supporters, approved a measure allowing the government to remove and appoint Supreme Court justices, effectively increasing Chavez's hold over the judiciary. Chavez also extended government control over the media. By 2006, Freedom House, which annually assesses political and civil liberties worldwide, concluded that Venezuela was only "partly free" and that freedoms were being progressively curtailed.

On the economic front, things remained rough. The economy shrank by 9 percent in 2002 and another 8 percent in 2003. Unemployment remained persistently high at 15 to 17 percent and the poverty rate rose to more than 50 percent of the population. A 2003 study by the World Bank concluded that Venezuela was one of the most regulated economies in the world and that state controls over business activities gave public officials ample opportunities to enrich themselves by demanding bribes in return for permission to expand operations or enter new lines of business. Indeed, despite Chavez's anticorruption rhetoric, Transparency International, which ranks the world's nations according to the extent of public corruption, has noted that corruption has increased under Chavez. In 2006, Transparency International ranked Venezuela 138 out of 163 nations, down from 114 in 2004. Consistent with his socialist rhetoric, Chavez has progressively taken various enterprises into state ownership and has required that other enterprises be restructured as "workers' cooperatives" in return for government loans. In addition, the government has begun to seize large rural farms and ranches that Chavez claims are not sufficiently productive, turning them into state-owned cooperatives.

In 2004, the world oil market bailed Chavez out of mounting economic difficulties. Oil prices surged from the low $20s, reaching $70 a barrel by the spring of 2006, and Venezuela, the world's fifth-largest producer, began to reap a bonanza. On the back of surging oil exports, the economy grew by 18 percent in 2004, 9 percent in 2005 and 10.5 percent in 2006. Chavez's reaction to the oil price increase was to extend government control over foreign oil producers doing business in Venezuela, which he accused of making outsized profits at the expense of a poor nation. In 2005, he increased government royalties on oil sales from 1 percent to 30 percent and the tax rate on sales from 34 to 50 percent. In 2006, he announced plans to reduce foreign companies' stakes in oil projects in the Orinoco regions and to give the state-run oil company, Petroleos de Venezuela SA, a majority position. Riding a wave of popularity at home, in December 2006 Chavez won reelection as president. He celebrated his victory by stepping on the revolutionary accelerator. Parliament gave him the power to legislate by decree for 18 months, and a committee of his supporters started to draft a constitutional reform to turn Venezuela into an avowedly socialist country and to allow the president to stand for reelection indefinitely.[1]

41

Opening Case

Cases

---

erate under during 1947 to 1990? What kind of system is it moving toward today? What are the impediments to completing this transformation?

b. How might widespread public ownership of businesses and extensive government

e. Given what is now occurring in the Indian economy, do you think the country represents an attractive target for inward investment by foreign multinationals selling consumer products? Why?

Indian economy?

Research Task

Use the globalEDGE™ site to complete the following exercises:

1. The definition of words and political ideas can have different meanings in different contexts worldwide. In fact, the *Freedom in the World* survey evaluates the state of political rights and civil liberties around the world. Provide a description of this survey and a ranking (in terms of "freedom") of the leaders and laggards of the world. What factors are taken into consideration in this survey?

2. One way that experts analyze conditions in different emerging markets and cultures in transition

is through the use of economic indictors. Market Potential Indicators (MPI) is an indexing study conducted by the Michigan State University Center for International Business Education and Research (MSU-CIBER) to compare emerging markets on a variety of dimensions. Provide a description of the indicators used in the indexing procedure. Which of the indicators would have greater importance for a company that markets laptop computers? Considering the MPI rankings, which developing countries would you advise this company to enter first?

CLOSING CASE

Indonesia—The Troubled Giant

Indonesia is a vast country. Its 220 million people are spread out over some 17,000 islands that span an arc 3,200 miles long from Sumatra in the west to Irian Jaya in the east. It is the world's most populous Muslim nation—some 85 percent of the population count

themselves as Muslims—but also one of the most ethnically diverse. More than 500 languages are spoken in the country, and separatists are active in a number of provinces. For 30 years, this sprawling nation was held together by the strong arm of President Suharto. Suharto

---

308   Part 3   Cases

Agricultural Subsidies and Development[1]

For decades the rich countries of the developed world have lavished subsidies on their farmers, typically guaranteeing them a minimum price for the products they produce. The aim has been to protect farmers in the developed world from the potentially devastating effects of low commodity prices. Although they are small in numbers, farmers tend to be politically active, and winning their support is important for many politicians. The politicians often claim that their motive is to preserve a historic rural lifestyle, and they see subsidies as a way of doing this.

This logic has resulted in financial support estimated to exceed $300 billion a year for farmers in rich nations. The European Union, for example, has set a minimum price for butter of 3,282 euros per ton. If the world price for butter falls below that amount, the EU will make up the difference to farmers in the form of a direct payment or subsidy. In total, EU dairy farmers receive roughly $15 billion a year in subsidies to produce milk and butter, or about $2 a day for every cow in the EU—a figure that is more than the daily income of half the world's population. According to the OECD, overall EU farmers receive on the order of $134 billion a year in subsidies.

The EU is not alone in this practice. In the United States, a wide range of crop and dairy farmers receive subsidies. Typical is the guarantee that U.S. cotton farmers will receive at least $0.70 for every pound of cotton they harvest. If world cotton prices fall below this level, the

EU market can absorb. The surplus, some 6 million tons per year, is dumped on the world market, where it depresses world prices. Estimates suggest that if the EU stopped dumping its surplus production on world markets, sugar prices would increase by 20 percent. That would make a big difference for developing nations such as South Africa, which exports roughly half of its 2.6 million tons of annual sugar production. With a 20 percent rise in world prices, the South African economy would reap about $40 million more from sugar exports.

American subsidies to cotton farmers have a similar effect. Brazilian officials contend that by creating surplus production in the United States that is then dumped on the world market, U.S. cotton subsidies have depressed world prices for cotton by more than 50 percent since the mid-1990s. Low cotton prices cost Brazil some $600 million in lost export earnings in 2001–2002. India, another big cotton producer, has estimated that U.S. cotton subsidies reduced its export revenue from cotton by some $1 billion in 2001. According to the charitable organization Oxfam, the U.S. government spends about three times as much on cotton subsidies as it does on foreign aid for all of Africa. In 2001, the African nation of Mali lost about $43 million in export revenues due to plunging cotton prices, significantly more than the $37 million in foreign aid it received from the United States that year.

The global rice market is also badly distorted by

---

154   Part 2   Cases

Nike: The Sweatshop Debate

INTRODUCTION

Nike is in many ways the quintessential global corporation. Established in 1972 by former University of Oregon track star, Phil Knight, Nike is now one of the leading marketers of athletic shoes and apparel on the planet. In 2006 the company had $15 billion in annual revenues and sold its products in some 140 countries. Nike does not do any manufacturing. Rather, it designs and markets its products, while contracting for their manufacture from a global network of 600 factories scattered around the globe that employ some 650,000 people.[1] This huge corporation has made founder Phil Knight into one of the richest people in America. Nike's marketing phrase, "Just Do It!" has become as recognizable in popular culture as its "swoosh" logo or the faces of its celebrity sponsors, such as Michael Jordan and Tiger Woods.

For all of its successes, the company was dogged for more than a decade by repeated and persistent accusations that its products were made in "sweatshops" where workers, many of them children, slaved away in hazardous conditions for below-subsistence wages. Nike's wealth, its detractors claimed, was built upon the backs of the world's poor. For many, Nike had become a symbol of the evils of globalization—a rich Western corporation exploiting the world's poor to provide expensive shoes and apparel to the pampered

do not comply with its standards. But for all this effort, the company continues to be a target of protests and a symbol of dissent.

THE CASE AGAINST NIKE

Typical of the exposés against Nike was a CBS *48 Hours* news report that aired on October 17, 1996.[3] Reporter Roberta Basin visited a Nike factory in Vietnam. With a shot of the factory, her commentary begin by saying that

> The signs are everywhere of an American invasion in search of cheap labor. Millions of people who are literate, disciplined, and desperate for jobs. This is Nike Town near what use to be called Saigon, one of four factories Nike doesn't own but subcontracts to make a million shoes a month. 25,000 workers, mostly young women, to "Just Do It."
>
> But the workers here don't share in Nike's huge profits. They work six days a week for only $40 a month, just 20 cents an hour.

Baskin interviews one of the workers in the factory, a young woman named Lap. Baskin tells the listener:

> Her basic wage, even as sewing team leader, still doesn't amount to the minimum wage . . . She's down to 85 pounds. Like most of the young women who make shoes, she has little choice but to accept the low wages and long hours. Nike says that it requires all subcontractors to obey local laws; but Lap has already put in much more

Focus Boxes and Exercises

Country Focus

Each **Country Focus** example provides background on the political, economic, social, or cultural aspects of countries grappling with an international business issue.

COUNTRY FOCUS

Corruption in Nigeria

When Nigeria gained independence from Great Britain in 1960, there were hopes that the country might emerge as an economic heavyweight in Africa. Not only was Nigeria Africa's most populous country, but it also was blessed with abundant natural resources, particularly oil, from which the country earned over $400 billion between 1970 and 2005. Despite this, Nigeria remains one of the poorest countries in the world. According to the United Nations' 2006 Human Development Index, Nigeria ranked 159 out of 177 countries covered. Gross domestic product per capita was just $560, 51 percent of the adult population was illiterate, and life expectancy at birth was only 43 years.

What went wrong? Although there is no simple answer, a number of factors seem to have conspired to damage economic activity in Nigeria. The country is composed of several competing ethnic, tribal, and religious groups, and the conflict among them has limited political stability and led to political strife, including a brutal civil war in the 1970s. With the legitimacy of the government always in question, political leaders often purchased support by legitimizing bribes and by raiding the national treasury to reward allies. Civilian rule after independence was followed by a series of military dictatorships, each of which seemed more corrupt and inept than the last (the country returned to civilian rule in 1999).

During the 1990s, the military dictator, Sani Abacha, openly and systematically plundered the state treasury for his own personal gain. His most blatant scam was the Petroleum Trust Fund, which he set up in the mid-1990s ostensibly to channel extra revenue from an increase in fuel prices into much-needed infrastructure projects and other investments. The fund was not independently audited, and almost none of the money that passed through it was properly accounted for. It was, in fact, a vehicle for Abacha and his supporters to spend at will a sum that in 1996 was equivalent to some 25 percent of the total federal budget. Abacha, aware of his position

as an unpopular and unelected leader, lavished money on personal security and handed out bribes to those whose support he coveted. With examples like this at the very top of the government, it is not surprising that corruption could be found throughout the political and bureaucratic apparatus.

Some of the excesses were simply astounding. In the 1980s an aluminum smelter was built on the orders of the government, which wanted to industrialize Nigeria. The cost of the smelter was $2.4 billion, some 60 to 100 percent higher than the cost of comparable plants elsewhere in the developed world. This high cost was widely interpreted to reflect the bribes that the international contractors who built the plant had to pay to local politicians. The smelter has never operated at more than a fraction of its intended capacity.

Has the situation in Nigeria improved since the country returned to civilian rule in 1999? In 2003, Olusegun Obasanjo was elected president on a platform that included a promise to fight corruption. By some accounts, progress has been seen. His anticorruption chief, Nuhu Ribadu, has claimed that whereas 70 percent of the country's oil revenues were being stolen or wasted in 2002, by 2004 the figure was "only" 40 percent. But in its most recent survey, Transparency International still ranked Nigeria among the most corrupt countries in the world in 2006 (see Figure 2.1), suggesting that the country still has a long way to go. In an effort to move things along, in early 2007 the country's top anticorruption body, the Economic and Financial Crimes Commission, sent letters to political parties listing 130 candidates for upcoming elections who stated would soon be charged with corruption. Several parties responded by removing candidates identified as corrupt from their lists. Others argued that the list was itself influenced by political motives and in particular a desire to strengthen the position of President Obasanjo by blacklisting opponents.[23]

the issuance of permits or licenses, process paperwork, or just get vegetables off the dock and on their way to market. The explanation for this exception to general antibribery provisions is that while grease payments are, technically, bribes, they are distinguishable from (and, apparently, less offensive than) bribes used to obtain or maintain business because they merely facilitate performance of duties that the recipients are already obligated to perform.

53

Management Focus

Management Focus examples further illustrate the relevance of chapter material for the practice of international business.

MANAGEMENT FOCUS

Starbucks Wins Key Trademark Case in China

Starbucks has big plans for China. It believes the fast-growing nation will become the company's second-largest market after the United States. Starbucks entered the country in 1999, and by the end of 2006 it had more than 220 outlets. But in China, copycats of well-established Western brands are commonplace, and Starbucks faced competition from a look alike, Shanghai Xing Ba Ke Coffee Shop, whose stores closely matched the Starbucks format, right down to a green and white Xing Ba Ke circular logo that mimics Starbucks's ubiquitous logo. Moreover, the name mimics the standard Chinese translation for Starbucks: *Xing* means "star" and *Ba Ke* sounds like "bucks."

In 2003, Starbucks decided to sue Xing Ba Ke in Chinese court for trademark violations. Xing Ba Ke's general manager responded by claiming that it was just an accident that the logo and name were so similar to that of Starbucks. Moreover, he claimed the right to use the logo and name because Xing Ba Ke had registered

as a company in Shanghai in 1999, before Starbucks entered the city. "I hadn't heard of Starbucks at the time," claimed the manager, "so how could I imitate its brand and logo?"

However, in January 2006 a Shanghai court ruled that Starbucks had precedence, in part because it had registered its Chinese name in 1998. The court stated that Xing Ba Ke's use of the name and similar logo was "clearly malicious" and constituted improper competition. The court ordered Xing Ba Ke to stop using the name and to pay Starbucks $62,000 in compensation. While the money involved here may be small, the precedent is not. In a country where violation of trademarks has been commonplace, the courts seem to be signaling that a shift toward greater protection of intellectual property rights may be in progress. This is perhaps not surprising, since foreign governments and the World Trade Organization have been pushing China hard recently to start respecting intellectual property rights.[32]

in less developed nations. A boom in product liability suits and awards in the United States resulted in a dramatic increase in the cost of liability insurance. Many business executives argue that the high costs of liability insurance make American businesses less competitive in the global marketplace.

In addition to the competitiveness issue, country differences in product safety and liability laws raise an important ethical issue for firms doing business abroad. When product safety laws are tougher in a firm's home country than in a foreign country or when liability laws are more lax, should a firm doing business in that foreign country follow the more relaxed local standards or should it adhere to the standards of its home country? While the ethical thing to do is undoubtedly to adhere to home-country standards, firms have been known to take advantage of lax safety and liability laws to do business in a manner that would not be allowed at home.

The Determinants of Economic Development

The political, economic, and legal systems of a country can have a profound impact on the level of economic development and hence on the attractiveness of a country as a possible market or production location for a firm. Here we look first at how countries differ in their level of development. Then we look at how political economy affects economic progress.

DIFFERENCES IN ECONOMIC DEVELOPMENT

Different countries have dramatically different levels of economic development. One common measure of economic development is a country's **gross national income (GNI)** per head of population. GNI is regarded as a yardstick for the economic activity of a country; it measures the total annual income received by residents of a nation. Map 2.1

56

Implications for Managers

At the end of each chapter in Parts 2, 3, and 4—where the focus is on the environment of international business, as opposed to particular firms—sections titled **Implications for Managers** clearly explain the managerial implications of material discussed in the chapter.

IMPLICATIONS FOR MANAGERS

The material discussed in this chapter has two broad implications for international business. First, the political, economic, and legal systems of a country raise important ethical issues that have implications for the practice of international business. For example, what ethical implications are associated with doing business in totalitarian countries where citizens are denied basic human rights, corruption is rampant, and bribes are necessary to gain permission to do business? Is it right to operate in such a setting? A full discussion of the ethical implications of country differences in political economy is reserved for Chapter 4, where we explore ethics in international business in much greater depth.

Second, the political, economic, and legal environments of a country clearly influence the attractiveness of that country as a market or investment site. The benefits, costs, and risks associated with doing business in a country are a function of that country's political, economic, and legal systems. The overall attractiveness of a country as a market or investment site depends on balancing the likely long-term benefits of doing business in that country against the likely costs and risks. Below we consider the determinants of benefits, costs, and risks.

BENEFITS

In the most general sense, the long-run monetary benefits of doing business in a country are a function of the size of the market, the present wealth (purchasing power) of consumers in that market, and the likely future wealth of consumers. While some markets are very large when measured by number of consumers (e.g., China and India), low living standards may imply limited purchasing power and therefore a relatively small market when measured in economic terms. International businesses need to be aware of this distinction, but they also need to keep in mind the likely future prospects of a country. In 1960, South Korea was viewed as just another impoverished Third World nation. By 2005 it was the world's eleventh-largest economy, measured in terms of GDP. International firms that recognized South Korea's potential in 1960 and began to do business in that country may have reaped greater benefits than those that wrote off South Korea.

By identifying and investing early in a potential future economic star, international firms may build brand loyalty and gain experience in that country's business practices. These will pay back substantial dividends if that country achieves sustained high economic growth rates. In contrast, late entrants may find that they lack the brand loyalty and experience necessary to achieve a significant presence in the market. In the language of business strategy, early entrants into potential future economic stars may be able to reap substantial first-mover advantages, while late entrants may fall victim to late-mover disadvantages.[70] **First-mover advantages** are the advantages that accrue to early entrants into a market. **Late-mover disadvantages** are the handicaps that late entrants might suffer.) This kind of reasoning has been driving significant inward investment into China, which may become the world's second-largest economy by 2015 if it continues growing at current rates (China is already the world's sixth-largest economy). For more than a decade, China has been the largest recipient of foreign direct investment in the developing world as international businesses ranging from General Motors and Volkswagen to Coca-Cola and Unilever try to establish a sustainable advantage in this nation.

A country's economic system and property rights regime are reasonably good predictors of economic prospects. Countries with free market economies in which property rights are protected tend to achieve greater economic growth rates than command economies or economies where property rights are poorly protected. It follows that a

---

globalEDGE™ Research Task

Using the text and the **globalEDGE™** Web site http://globaledge.msu.edu, students solve realistic international business problems related to each chapter. These exercises expose students to the types of tools and data sources international managers use to make informed business decisions.

---

should be broadened to include more than just economic development. What other factors does Sen think should be included in an assessment of development? How might adoption of Sen's views influence government policy? Do you think Sen is correct that development is about more than just economic development? Explain.

5. You are the CEO of a company that has to choose between making a $100 million investment in Russia or the Czech Republic. Both investments promise the same long-run return, so your choice is driven by risk considerations. Assess the various risks of doing business in each of these nations. Which investment would you favor and why?

6. Read the Country Focus on India in this chapter and answer the following questions:
   a. What kind of economic system did India operate under during 1947 to 1990? What kind of system is it moving toward today? What are the impediments to completing this transformation?
   b. How might widespread public ownership of businesses and extensive government

regulations have impacted (i) the efficiency of state and private businesses, and (ii) the rate of new business formation in India during the 1947–90 time frame? How do you think these factors affected the rate of economic growth in India during this time frame?
   c. How would privatization, deregulation, and the removal of barriers to foreign direct investment affect the efficiency of business, new business formation, and the rate of economic growth in India during the post-1990 time period?
   d. India now has pockets of strengths in key high-technology industries such as software and pharmaceuticals. Why do you think India is developing strength in these areas? How might success in these industries help to generate growth in the other sectors of the Indian economy?
   e. Given what is now occurring in the Indian economy, do you think the country represents an attractive target for inward investment by foreign multinationals selling consumer products? Why?

Research Task globalEDGE

Use the globalEDGE™ site to complete the following exercises:

1. The definition of words and political ideas can have different meanings in different contexts worldwide. In fact, the *Freedom in the World* survey evaluates the state of political rights and civil liberties around the world. Provide a description of this survey and a ranking (in terms of "freedom") of the leaders and laggards of the world. What factors are taken into consideration in this survey?

2. One way that experts analyze conditions in different emerging markets and cultures in transition

is through the use of economic indictors. Market Potential Indicators (MPI) is an indexing study conducted by the Michigan State University Center for International Business Education and Research (MSU-CIBER) to compare emerging markets on a variety of dimensions. Provide a description of the indicators used in the indexing procedure. Which of the indicators would have greater importance for a company that markets laptop computers? Considering the MPI rankings, which developing countries would you advise this company to enter first?

CLOSING CASE

Indonesia—The Troubled Giant

Indonesia is a vast country. Its 220 million people are spread out over some 17,000 islands that span an arc 3,200 miles long from Sumatra in the west to Irian Jaya in the east. It is the world's most populous Muslim nation—some 85 percent of the population count themselves as Muslims—but also one of the most ethnically diverse. More than 500 languages are spoken in the country, and separatists are active in a number of provinces. For 30 years, this sprawling nation was held together by the strong arm of President Suharto. Suharto

Supplements for the Instructor

Instructor's Resource CD

An updated **Instructor's Manual and Video Guide** (prepared by Veronica Horton) includes course outlines, chapter overviews and teaching suggestions, lecture outlines, ideas for student exercises and projects, teaching notes for all cases in the book, and video notes.

Videos

A video collection features original business documentaries as well as footage from sources such as PBS that tie in to cases in the text. Featured titles include "The Politics of Trade in Steel" and "Air Wars."

PowerPoint

Over 500 revamped PowerPoint slides (prepared by Veronica Horton) feature original materials not found in the text in addition to reproduction of key text figures, tables, and maps.

What Is Globalization?

- The world is moving away from self-contained national economies toward an interdependent, integrated global economic system
- Globalization refers to the shift toward a more integrated and interdependent world economy

Globalization has two facets:
  1) the globalization of markets
  2) the globalization of production

1-3

Classroom Performance System (CPS)

Bring more energy and interactivity into your classroom or lecture hall. Our student response system uses wireless connectivity and gives both instructors and students immediate feedback from the entire class. Each of the 20 chapters of the text has 8 to 10 interactive CPS activities (prepared by Jeffrey Kulick of George Mason University) written specifically for *International Business*. Ask your McGraw-Hill/Irwin sales representative for more information.

Test Bank

The **Test Bank** (prepared by Veronica Horton) contains about 120 questions per chapter, each tagged with the level of difficulty, correct answer, and page reference to the text.

For the Student

Wall Street Journal Package

Your students can subscribe to *The Wall Street Journal* for 15 weeks at a special rate of $20.00 in addition to the price of the text. Students will receive a "How to Use the *WSJ*" handbook plus a subscription card shrink-wrapped with their new text. The subscription also gives students access to **www.wsj.com**.

Online Learning Center— www.mhhe.com/hill

A password-protected portion of the book's Web site will be available to adopters of *International Business,* featuring online access to the instructor's manual, PowerPoints, video cases, and globalEDGE answers. Instructors can also view student resources to make more effective supplementary assignments.

For students, this Web site also provides rich interactive resources to help them learn how to practice international business, including chapter quizzes, student PowerPoints, and chapter overviews. Students can also access the text glossary as well as all interactive modules.

Financial Times Package

Your students can subscribe to the *Financial Times* for 15 weeks at a specially priced rate of $10 in addition to the price of the text. Students will receive a subscription card shrink-wrapped with their new text that will activate their subscriptions once they complete and submit the card. The subscription also provides access to **FT.com**.

International Business

Flat Panel Televisions and the Global Economy

They begin as glass panels that are manufactured in high-technology fabrication centers in South Korea, Taiwan, and Japan. Operating sophisticated tooling in environments that must be kept absolutely clean, these factories produce sheets of glass twice as large as king size beds to exacting specifications. From there, the glass panels travel to Mexican plants located alongside the U.S. border. There they are cut to size, combined with electronic components shipped in from Asia and the United States, assembled into finished TVs, and loaded onto trucks bound for retail stores in the United States.

It's a huge business. In 2006, U.S. consumers spent some $26.4 billion on flat panel TVs, a 63 percent increase over the amount spent in 2005. Projections call for U.S. sales to hit $37 billion by 2008—despite the fact that due to intense competition, prices for flat panel displays have been tumbling and are projected to continue doing so. During 2006 alone, prices for 40-inch flat panel TVs fell from $3,000 to $1,600, bringing them within the reach of many more consumers. In 2007, half of all TVs sold in the United States will be flat panel TVs.

The underlying technology for flat panel displays was invented in the United States in the late 1960s by RCA. But after RCA and rivals Westinghouse and Xerox opted not to pursue the technology, the Japanese company Sharp made aggressive investments in flat panel displays. By the early 1990s Sharp was selling the first flat panel screens, but as the Japanese economy plunged into a decade-long recession, investment leadership shifted to South Korean companies such as Samsung. Then the 1997 Asian crisis hit Korea hard, and Taiwanese companies seized leadership. Today, Chinese companies are starting to elbow their way into the flat panel display manufacturing business.

As production for flat panel displays migrates its way around the globe to low-cost locations, clear winners and losers have emerged. One obvious winner has been

Globalization

LEARNING OBJECTIVES

After you have read this chapter you should:

LO¹ Understand what is meant by the term globalization.

LO² Be familiar with the main drivers of globalization.

LO³ Appreciate the changing nature of the global economy.

LO⁴ Understand the main arguments in the debate over the impact of globalization.

LO⁵ Appreciate how the process of globalization is creating opportunities and challenges for business managers.

U.S. consumers, who have benefited from the falling prices of flat panel TVs and are snapping them up. Other winners include efficient manufacturers who have taken advantage of globally dispersed supply chains to make and sell low-cost, high-quality flat panel TVs. Foremost among these has been the California-based company, Vizio. Founded by a Taiwanese immigrant, in just four years sales of Vizio flat panel TVs ballooned from nothing to $700 million in 2006. The company is forecasting sales as high as $2 billion for 2007. Vizio, however, has only 75 employees. These employees focus on final product design, sales, and customer service, while Vizio outsources most of its engineering work, all of its manufacturing, and much of its logistics. For each of its models, Vizio assembles a team of supplier partners strung across the globe. Its 42-inch flat panel TV, for example, contains a panel from South Korea, electronic components from China, and processors from the United States, and it is assembled in Mexico. Vizio's managers scour the globe continually for the cheapest manufacturers of flat panel displays and electronic components. They sell most of their TVs to large discount retailers such as Costco and Sam's Club. Good order visibility from retailers, coupled with tight management of global logistics, allows Vizio to turn over its inventory every three weeks, twice as fast as many of its competitors, which is a major source of cost saving in a business where prices are falling continually.

If Vizio exemplifies the winners in this global industry, the losers include the employees of manufacturers who make traditional cathode ray TVs in high-cost locations. In 2006, for example, Japanese electronics manufacturer Sanyo laid off 300 employees at its U.S. factory, and another Japanese company, Hitachi, closed its TV manufacturing plant in South Carolina, laying off 200 employees. Both Sony and Hitachi, of course, still make TVs, but they are flat panel TVs assembled in Mexico from components manufactured in Asia.[1]

Introduction

A fundamental shift is occurring in the world economy. We are moving away from a world in which national economies were relatively self-contained entities, isolated from each other by barriers to cross-border trade and investment; by distance, time zones, and language; and by national differences in government regulation, culture, and business systems. And we are moving toward a world in which barriers to cross-border trade and investment are declining; perceived distance is shrinking due to advances in transportation and telecommunications technology; material culture is starting to look similar the world over; and national economies are merging into an interdependent, integrated global economic system. The process by which this is occurring is commonly referred to as *globalization*.

What is happening in the flat panel TV industry, which was profiled in the Opening Case, is a classic illustration of the impact of globalization. Production of flat panel TVs is migrating around the globe to low-cost locations. TVs that Vizio sells in the United States, for example, are assembled in Mexico from flat panels manufactured in South Korea, electronic components made in China, and microprocessors made in the United States. By dispersing different activities around the globe to where they can be performed most efficiently, and then coordinating the entire production process, companies like Vizio can deliver flat panel TVs to American consumers at much lower prices than would otherwise be possible. American consumers benefit from the lower prices, as does Vizio and its strategic partners in South Korea, China, the United States, and Mexico. The process of globalization also has losers, however, and the losers in this case are workers in high cost locations who have lost their jobs. As we will see in this book though, most economists argue that the gains outweigh the losses by a wide margin, and that on balance globalization is a very beneficial process.

The flat panel TV industry is hardly alone in exemplifying the process of globalization. In today's interdependent global economy, an American might drive to work in a car designed in Germany that was assembled in Mexico by the American automaker Ford from components made in the United States and Japan that were fabricated from Korean steel and Malaysian rubber. She may have filled the car with gasoline at a BP service station owned by a British multinational company. The gasoline could have been made from oil pumped from a well off the coast of Africa by a French oil company that transported it to the United States in a ship owned by a Greek shipping line. While driving to work, the American might talk to her stockbroker on a Nokia cell phone that was designed in Finland and assembled in Texas using chip sets produced in Taiwan that were designed by Indian engineers working for Texas Instruments. She could tell the stockbroker to purchase shares in Deutsche Telekom, a German telecommunications firm that was transformed from a former state-owned monopoly into a global company by an energetic Israeli CEO. She may turn on the car radio, which was made in Malaysia by a Japanese firm, to hear a popular hip-hop song composed by a Swede and sung by a group of Danes in English who signed a record contract with a French music company to promote their record in America. The driver might pull into a drive-through coffee shop run by a Korean immigrant and order a "single, tall, nonfat latte" and chocolate-covered biscotti. The coffee beans came from Brazil and the chocolate from Peru, while the biscotti was made locally using an old Italian recipe. After the song ends, a news announcer might inform the American listener that antiglobalization protests at a meeting of the World Economic Forum in Davos, Switzerland, have turned violent. One protester has been killed. The announcer then turns to the next item, a story about how fear of interest rate hikes in the United States has sent Japan's Nikkei stock market index down sharply.

This is the world in which we live. It is a world where the volume of goods, services, and investment crossing national borders has expanded faster than world output consistently for more than half a century. It is a world where some $3 *trillion* in foreign exchange transactions are made every day, where $12.06 trillion of goods and $2.71 trillion of services were sold across national borders in 2006.[2] It is a world in which international institutions such as the World Trade Organization and gatherings of leaders from the world's most powerful economies have called for even lower barriers to cross-border trade and investment. It is a world where the symbols of material and popular culture are increasingly global: from Coca-Cola and Starbucks to Sony PlayStations, Nokia cell phones, MTV shows, Disney films, IKEA stores, and Apple iPods. It is a world in which products are made from inputs that come from all over the world. It is a world in which an economic crisis in Asia can cause a recession in the United States, and the threat of higher interest rates in the United States really did help drive Japan's Nikkei index down in the spring of 2006. It is also a world in which vigorous and vocal groups protest against globalization, which they blame for a list of ills, from unemployment in developed nations to environmental degradation and the Americanization of popular culture. And yes, these protests have on occasion turned violent.

For businesses, this process has produced many opportunities. Firms can expand their revenues by selling around the world and/or reduce their costs by producing in nations where key inputs, including labor, are cheap. The global expansion of enterprises has been facilitated by favorable political and economic trends. Since the collapse of communism at the end of the 1980s, the pendulum of public policy in nation after nation has swung toward the free market end of the economic spectrum. Regulatory and administrative barriers to doing business in foreign nations have come down, while those nations have often transformed their economies, privatizing state-owned enterprises, deregulating markets, increasing competition, and welcoming investment by foreign businesses. This has allowed businesses both large and small, from both advanced nations and developing nations, to expand internationally.

At the same time, globalization has created new threats for businesses accustomed to dominating their domestic markets. Foreign companies have entered many formerly protected industries in developing nations, increasing competition and driving down prices. For three decades, U.S. automobile companies have been battling foreign enterprises, as Japanese, European, and now Korean companies have taken business from them. General Motors has seen its U.S. market share decline from more than 50 percent to about 26 percent, while Japan's Toyota has surpassed first Ford and now GM to become the largest automobile company in the world and the second largest producer in the United States behind GM.

As globalization unfolds, it is transforming industries and creating anxiety among those who believed their jobs were protected from foreign competition. Historically, while many workers in manufacturing industries worried about the impact foreign competition might have on their jobs, workers in service industries felt more secure. Now this too is changing. Advances in technology, lower transportation costs, and the rise of skilled workers in developing countries imply that many services no longer need to be performed where they are delivered. For example, accounting work is being outsourced from America to India. In 2005, some 400,000 individual tax returns were compiled in India. Indian accountants, trained in U.S. tax rules, perform work for U.S. accounting firms.[3] They access individual tax returns stored on computers in the United States, perform routine calculations, and save their work so that it can be inspected by a U.S. accountant, who then bills clients. As the best-selling author Thomas Friedman has recently argued, the world is becoming flat.[4] The playing field is no longer tilted in favor of people living in developed nations. Increasingly, enterprising individuals based in India, China, or Brazil have the same opportunities to better themselves as those living in Western Europe, the United States, or Canada.

In this book we will take a close look at the issues introduced here, and at many more besides. We will explore how changes in regulations governing international trade and investment, when coupled with changes in political systems and technology, have dramatically altered the competitive playing field confronting many businesses. We will discuss the resulting opportunities and threats and review the different strategies that managers can pursue to exploit the opportunities and counter the threats. We will consider whether globalization benefits or harms national economies. We will look at what economic theory has to say about the outsourcing of manufacturing and service jobs to places such as India and China and at the benefits and costs of outsourcing, not just to business firms and their employees, but also to entire economies. First, though, we need to get a better overview of the nature and process of globalization, and that is the function of the current chapter.

What Is Globalization?

As used in this book, **globalization** refers to the shift toward a more integrated and interdependent world economy. Globalization has several facets, including the globalization of markets and the globalization of production.

THE GLOBALIZATION OF MARKETS

The **globalization of markets** refers to the merging of historically distinct and separate national markets into one huge global marketplace. Falling barriers to cross-border trade have made it easier to sell internationally. It has been argued for some time that the tastes and preferences of consumers in different nations are beginning to converge on some global norm, thereby helping to create a global market.[5] Consumer products such as Citigroup credit cards, Coca-Cola soft drinks, Sony PlayStation video games, McDonald's hamburgers, Starbucks coffee, and IKEA furniture are frequently identified as prototypical examples of this trend. Firms such as these are more than just benefactors of this trend; they are also facilitators of it. By offering the same basic product worldwide, they help to create a global market.

A company does not have to be the size of these multinational giants to facilitate and benefit from the globalization of markets. In the United States, for example, nearly 90 percent of firms that export are small businesses employing less than 100 people, and their share of total U.S. exports has grown steadily over the last decade to now exceed 20 percent.[6] Firms with less than 500 employees accounted for 97 percent of all U.S. exporters and almost 30 percent of all exports by value.[7] Typical of these is Hytech, a New York–based manufacturer of solar panels that generates 40 percent of its $3 million in annual sales from exports to five countries, or B&S Aircraft Alloys, another New York company whose exports account for 40 percent of its $8 million annual revenues.[8] The situation is similar in several other nations. In Germany, for example, which is the world's largest exporter, a staggering 98 percent of small and mid-sized companies have exposure to international markets, either via exports or international production.[9]

Despite the global prevalence of Citigroup credit cards, McDonald's hamburgers, Starbucks coffee, and IKEA stores, it is important not to push too far the view that national markets are giving way to the global market. As we shall see in later chapters, significant differences still exist among national markets along many relevant dimensions, including consumer tastes and preferences, distribution channels, culturally embedded value systems, business systems, and legal regulations. These differences frequently require companies to customize marketing strategies, product features, and operating practices to best match conditions in a particular country.

The most global markets currently are not markets for consumer products—where national differences in tastes and preferences are still often important enough to act as a brake on globalization—but markets for industrial goods and materials that serve a universal need the world over.

BEIJING, CHINA: Chinese shoppers walk through Beijing's main downtown shopping promenade past a Kentucky Fried Chicken (KFC) franchise. KFC is one of the most successful international businesses in China due to its adaptation and appeal to the Chinese market.

These include the markets for commodities such as aluminum, oil, and wheat; for industrial products such as microprocessors, DRAMs (computer memory chips), and commercial jet aircraft; for computer software; and for financial assets from U.S. Treasury bills to eurobonds and futures on the Nikkei index or the Mexican peso.

In many global markets, the same firms frequently confront each other as competitors in nation after nation. Coca-Cola's rivalry with PepsiCo is a global one, as are the rivalries between General Motors and Toyota, Boeing and Airbus, Caterpillar and Komatsu in earthmoving equipment, and Sony, Nintendo, and Microsoft in video games. If a firm moves into a nation not currently served by its rivals, many of those rivals are sure to follow to prevent their competitor from gaining an advantage.[10] As firms follow each other around the world, they bring with them many of the assets that served them well in other national markets—including their products, operating strategies, marketing strategies, and brand names—creating some homogeneity across markets. Thus, greater uniformity replaces diversity. In an increasing number of industries, it is no longer meaningful to talk about "the German market," "the American market," "the Brazilian market," or "the Japanese market"; for many firms there is only the global market.

THE GLOBALIZATION OF PRODUCTION

The **globalization of production** refers to the sourcing of goods and services from locations around the globe to take advantage of national differences in the cost and quality of **factors of production** (such as labor, energy, land, and capital). By doing this, companies hope to lower their overall cost structure or improve the quality or functionality of their product offering, thereby allowing them to compete more effectively. Consider the Boeing 777, a commercial jet airliner. Eight Japanese suppliers make parts for the fuselage, doors, and wings; a supplier in Singapore makes the doors for the nose landing gear; three suppliers in Italy manufacture wing flaps; and so on.[11] In total, some 30 percent of the 777, by value, is built by foreign companies. For its most recent jet airliner, the 787, Boeing has pushed this trend even further, with some 65 percent of the total value of the aircraft scheduled to be outsourced to foreign companies, 35 percent of which will go to three major Japanese companies.[12]

Boeing's new global product, the 787, rolls out.

Outsourcing American Health Care

Conventional wisdom holds that health care is one of the industries least vulnerable to dislocation from globalization. After all, like many service businesses, health care is delivered where it is purchased, right? If an American goes to a hospital for an MRI scan, won't that scan be read by a local radiologist? And if the MRI scan shows that surgery is required, surely the surgery will be done at a local hospital in the United States. Until recently, this was true, but we are now witnessing the beginnings of globalization in this traditionally most local of industries.

Consider the MRI scan: The United States has a shortage of radiologists, the doctors who specialize in reading and interpreting diagnostic medical images, including X-rays, CT scans, MRI scans, and ultrasounds. Demand for radiologists is reportedly growing twice as fast as the rate at which medical schools are graduating radiologists with the skills and qualifications required to read medical images. This imbalance between supply and demand means that radiologists are expensive; an American radiologist can earn as much as $350,000 a year. In the early 2000s, an Indian radiologist working at the prestigious Massachusetts General Hospital, Dr. Sanjay Saini, thought he had found a clever way to deal with the shortage and expense—send images over the Internet to India where they could be interpreted by radiologists. This would reduce the workload on America's radiologists and also cut costs. A radiologist in India might earn one-tenth of his or her U.S. counterpart. Plus, because India is on the opposite side of the globe, the images could be interpreted while it was nighttime in the United States and be ready for the attending physician when he or she arrived for work the following morning.

As for surgery, here too we are witnessing the beginnings of an outsourcing trend. For example, recently Howard Staab, a 53-year-old uninsured self-employed carpenter from North Carolina, had surgery to repair a leaking heart valve—in India! Mr. Staab flew to New Delhi, had the operation, and afterward toured the Taj Mahal, the price of which was bundled with that of the surgery. The cost, including airfare, totaled $10,000. If Mr. Staab's surgery had been performed in the United States, the cost would have been $60,000 and there would have been no visit to the Taj Mahal. Howard Staab is not alone. According to one estimate, some 150,000 Americans elected to have surgery outside of the United States in 2006, and predictions call for the numbers to grow rapidly. The management consultancy McKinsey & Co. predicts that medical tourism (overseas trips to have medical procedures performed) could be a $2.3 billion industry in India by 2012.

So will demand for American health services soon collapse as work moves offshore to places like India? That seems unlikely. Regulations, personal preferences, and practical considerations mean that the majority of health services will always be performed in the country where the patient resides. Consider the MRI scan: To safeguard patient care, U.S. regulations require that a radiologist be licensed in the state where the image was made and that he or she be certified by the hospital where care is being given. Given that not many radiologists in India have these qualifications, no more than a small fraction of images can be interpreted overseas. Another complication is that the U.S. government-sponsored medical insurance program, Medicare, will not pay for services done outside of the country. Nor will many private insurance plans—not yet anyway. Moreover, most people would prefer to have care delivered close to home, and only in exceptional cases, such as when the procedure is not covered by their medical plan, are they likely to consider the foreign option. Still, most experts believe that the trends now in place will continue. Given that health care costs in America are the highest in the world, it seems likely that increasingly, a small but significant percentage of medical service will be performed in a country that is different from the one where the patient resides. The trend will certainly get a big boost if insurance companies start to offer enrollees the option of getting treatment abroad for expensive surgeries, as some are rumored to be considering.[14]

Part of Boeing's rationale for outsourcing so much production to foreign suppliers is that these suppliers are the best in the world at their particular activity. A global web of suppliers yields a better final product, which enhances the chances of Boeing winning a greater share of total orders for aircraft than its global rival Airbus Industrie. Boeing also outsources some production to foreign countries to increase the chance that it will win significant orders from airlines based in that country.

For another example of a global web of activities, consider again the example of Vizio given in the Opening Case. Vizio, an American company with just 75 employees, has become one of the largest sellers of flat panel TVs in the United States in just four years by coordinating a global web of activities: bringing together components manufactured in South Korea, China, and the United States, arranging for their assembly in Mexico, and then selling them in the United States.

Early outsourcing efforts were primarily confined to manufacturing activities, such as those undertaken by Boeing and Vizio; increasingly, however, companies are taking advantage of modern communications technology, particularly the Internet, to outsource service activities to low-cost producers in other nations. The Internet has allowed hospitals to outsource some radiology work to India; while U.S. physicians sleep, images from MRI scans and the like are read at night and the results are ready in the morning (see the Country Focus for details). Many software companies, including IBM, now use Indian engineers to perform maintenance functions on software designed in the United States. The time difference allows Indian engineers to run debugging tests on software written in the United States when U.S. engineers sleep, and the corrected code is transmitted back to the United States over secure Internet connections so it is ready for U.S. engineers to work on the following day. Dispersing value-creation activities in this way can compress the time and lower the costs required to develop new software programs. Other companies, from computer makers to banks, are outsourcing customer service functions, such as customer call centers, to developing nations where labor is cheaper.

Robert Reich, who served as secretary of labor in the Clinton administration, has argued that as a consequence of the trend exemplified by companies such as Boeing, IBM, and Vizio, in many cases it is becoming irrelevant to talk about American products, Japanese products, German products, or Korean products. Increasingly, according to Reich, outsourcing productive activities to different suppliers results in the creation of products that are global in nature, that is, "global products."[13] But as with the globalization of markets, companies must be careful not to push the globalization of production too far. As we will see in later chapters, substantial impediments still make it difficult for firms to achieve the optimal dispersion of their productive activities to locations around the globe. These impediments include formal and informal barriers to trade between countries, barriers to foreign direct investment, transportation costs, and issues associated with economic and political risk. For example, government regulations ultimately limit the ability of hospitals to outsource the process of interpreting MRI scans to developing nations where radiologists are cheaper.

Nevertheless, the globalization of markets and production will continue. Modern firms are important actors in this trend, their very actions fostering increased globalization. These firms, however, are merely responding in an efficient manner to changing conditions in their operating environment—as well they should.

🌐 The Emergence of Global Institutions

As markets globalize and an increasing proportion of business activity transcends national borders, institutions are needed to help manage, regulate, and police the global marketplace and to promote the establishment of multinational treaties to govern the global business system. Over the past half century, a number of important global institutions have been created to help perform these functions, including the **General Agreement on Tariffs and Trade (GATT)** and its successor, the World Trade Organization (WTO); the International Monetary Fund (IMF) and its sister institution, the World Bank; and the United Nations (UN). All these institutions were created by voluntary agreement between individual nation-states, and their functions are enshrined in international treaties.

The **World Trade Organization** (like the GATT before it) is primarily responsible for policing the world trading system and making sure nation-states adhere to the rules laid down in trade treaties signed by WTO member states. As of 2007, 150 nations that

The United Nations has the important goal of improving the well-being of people around the world.

collectively accounted for 97 percent of world trade were WTO members, thereby giving the organization enormous scope and influence. The WTO is also responsible for facilitating the establishment of additional multinational agreements between WTO member states. Over its entire history, and that of the GATT before it, the WTO has promoted lowering barriers to cross-border trade and investment. In doing so, the WTO has been the instrument of its member states, which have sought to create a more open global business system unencumbered by barriers to trade and investment between countries. Without an institution such as the WTO, the globalization of markets and production is unlikely to have proceeded as far as it has. However, as we shall see in this chapter and in Chapter 6 when we look closely at the WTO, critics charge that the organization is usurping the national sovereignty of individual nation-states.

The **International Monetary Fund** and the **World Bank** were both created in 1944 by 44 nations that met at Bretton Woods, New Hampshire. The IMF was established to maintain order in the international monetary system; the World Bank was set up to promote economic development. In the 65 years since their creation, both institutions have emerged as significant players in the global economy. The World Bank is the less controversial of the two sister institutions. It has focused on making low-interest loans to cash-strapped governments in poor nations that wish to undertake significant infrastructure investments (such as building dams or roads).

The IMF is often seen as the lender of last resort to nation-states whose economies are in turmoil and currencies are losing value against those of other nations. Repeatedly during the past decade, for example, the IMF has lent money to the governments of troubled states, including Argentina, Indonesia, Mexico, Russia, South Korea, Thailand, and Turkey. IMF loans come with strings attached, however; in return for loans, the IMF requires nation-states to adopt specific economic policies aimed at returning their troubled economies to stability and growth. These requirements have sparked controversy. Some critics charge that the IMF's policy recommendations are often inappropriate; others maintain that by telling national governments what economic policies they must adopt, the IMF, like the WTO, is usurping the sovereignty of nation-states. We shall look at the debate over the role of the IMF in Chapter 10.

The **United Nations** was established October 24, 1945, by 51 countries committed to preserving peace through international cooperation and collective security. Today nearly every nation in the world belongs to the United Nations; membership now totals 191 countries.

When states become members of the United Nations, they agree to accept the obligations of the UN Charter, an international treaty that establishes basic principles of international relations. According to the charter, the UN has four purposes: to maintain international peace and security, to develop friendly relations among nations, to cooperate in solving international problems and in promoting respect for human rights, and to be a center for harmonizing the actions of nations. Although the UN is perhaps best known for its peacekeeping role, one of the organization's central mandates is the promotion of higher standards of living, full employment, and conditions of economic and social progress and development—all issues that are central to the creation of a vibrant global economy. As much as 70 percent of the work of the UN system is devoted to accomplishing this mandate. To do so, the UN works closely with other international institutions such as the World Bank. Guiding the work is the belief that eradicating poverty and improving the well-being of people everywhere are necessary steps in creating conditions for lasting world peace.[15]

Drivers of Globalization

Two macro factors underlie the trend toward greater globalization.[16] The first is the decline in barriers to the free flow of goods, services, and capital that has occurred since the end of World War II. The second factor is technological change, particularly the dramatic developments in recent years in communication, information processing, and transportation technologies.

DECLINING TRADE AND INVESTMENT BARRIERS

During the 1920s and 30s many of the world's nation-states erected formidable barriers to international trade and foreign direct investment. **International trade** occurs when a firm exports goods or services to consumers in another country. **Foreign direct investment (FDI)** occurs when a firm invests resources in business activities outside its home country. Many of the barriers to international trade took the form of high tariffs on imports of manufactured goods. The typical aim of such tariffs was to protect domestic industries from foreign competition. One consequence, however, was "beggar thy neighbor" retaliatory trade policies, with countries progressively raising trade barriers against each other. Ultimately, this depressed world demand and contributed to the Great Depression of the 1930s.

Having learned from this experience, the advanced industrial nations of the West committed themselves after World War II to removing barriers to the free flow of goods, services, and capital between nations.[17] This goal was enshrined in the General Agreement on Tariffs and Trade. Under the umbrella of GATT, eight rounds of negotiations among member states (now numbering 150) have worked to lower barriers to the free flow of goods and services. The most recent round of negotiations to be completed, known as the Uruguay Round, was finalized in December 1993. The Uruguay Round further reduced trade barriers; extended GATT to cover services as well as manufactured goods; provided enhanced protection for patents, trademarks, and copyrights; and established the World Trade Organization to police the international trading system.[18] Table 1.1 summarizes the impact of GATT agreements on average tariff rates for manufactured goods. As can be seen, average tariff rates have fallen significantly since 1950 and now stand at about 4 percent.

In late 2001, the WTO launched a new round of talks aimed at further liberalizing the global trade and investment framework. For this meeting, it picked the remote location of Doha in the Persian Gulf state of Qatar. At Doha, the member states of the WTO staked out an agenda. The talks were scheduled to last three years, although it now looks as if they may go on significantly longer. The agenda includes cutting tariffs on industrial goods, services, and agricultural products; phasing out subsidies to agricultural producers; reducing barriers to cross-border investment; and limiting the use of antidumping laws. The biggest gain may come from discussion on agricultural products; average agricultural

TABLE 1.1

Average Tariff Rates on Manufactured Products as Percent of Value

Source: 1913–90 data are from "Who Wants to Be a Giant?" *The Economist: A Survey of the Multinationals*, June 24, 1995, pp. 3–4. Copyright © The Economist Books, Ltd. The 2005 data are from World Trade Organization, *2005 World Trade Report* (Geneva: WTO, 2006).

	1913	**1950**	**1990**	**2005**
France	21%	18%	5.9%	3.9%
Germany	20	26	5.9	3.9
Italy	18	25	5.9	3.9
Japan	30	—	5.3	2.3
Holland	5	11	5.9	3.9
Sweden	20	9	4.4	3.9
Great Britain	—	23	5.9	3.9
United States	44	14	4.8	3.2

tariff rates are still about 40 percent, and rich nations spend some $300 billion a year in subsidies to support their farm sectors. The world's poorer nations have the most to gain from any reduction in agricultural tariffs and subsidies; such reforms would give them access to the markets of the developed world.[19]

In addition to reducing trade barriers, many countries have also been progressively removing restrictions to foreign direct investment. According to the United Nations, some 94 percent of the 2,266 changes made worldwide between 1992 and 2005 in the laws governing foreign direct investment created a more favorable environment for FDI.[20] The desire of governments to facilitate FDI also has been reflected in a dramatic increase in the number of bilateral investment treaties designed to protect and promote investment between two countries. As of 2005, 2,495 such treaties involved more than 160 countries, a 12-fold increase from the 181 treaties that existed in 1980.[21]

Such trends have been driving both the globalization of markets and the globalization of production. Lowering barriers to international trade enables firms to view the world, rather than a single country, as their market. Lowering trade and investment barriers also allows firms to base production at the optimal location for that activity. Thus, a firm might design a product in one country, produce component parts in two other countries, assemble the product in yet another country, and then export the finished product around the world.

The data summarized in Figure 1.1 imply several things. First, more firms are doing what Boeing does with the 777 and 787 and Vizio with flat panel TVs: dispersing parts of their production process to different locations around the globe to drive down production costs and increase product quality. Second, the economies of the world's nation-states are becoming more intertwined. As trade expands, nations are becoming increasingly dependent on each other for important goods and services. Third, the world has become significantly wealthier since 1950, and the implication is that rising trade is the engine that has helped to pull the global economy along.

According to WTO data, the volume of world merchandise trade has grown faster than the world economy since 1950 (see Figure 1.1).[22] From 1970 to 2005, the volume of world merchandise trade expanded 27-fold, outstripping the expansion of world production, which grew about 7.5 times in real terms. (World merchandise trade includes trade in manufactured goods, agricultural goods, and mining products, but *not* services.) What Figure 1.1 does not show is that since the mid-1980s the value of international trade in services has also grown robustly. Trade in services now accounts for almost 20 percent of the value of all international trade. Increasingly, international trade in services has been driven by advances in communications, which allow corporations to outsource service activities to different locations around the globe (see the opening case). Thus, as noted earlier, many corporations in the developed world outsource customer service functions, from software maintenance activities to customer call centers, to developing nations where labor costs are lower.

The evidence also suggests that foreign direct investment is playing an increasing role in the global economy as firms increase their cross-border investments. The average yearly

FIGURE 1.1

Growth in World
Merchandise Trade and
Production, 1950–2005
(average annual %
increase in volume)

Source: Constructed by the
author from World Trade
Organization, *World Trade
Statistics 2006.*

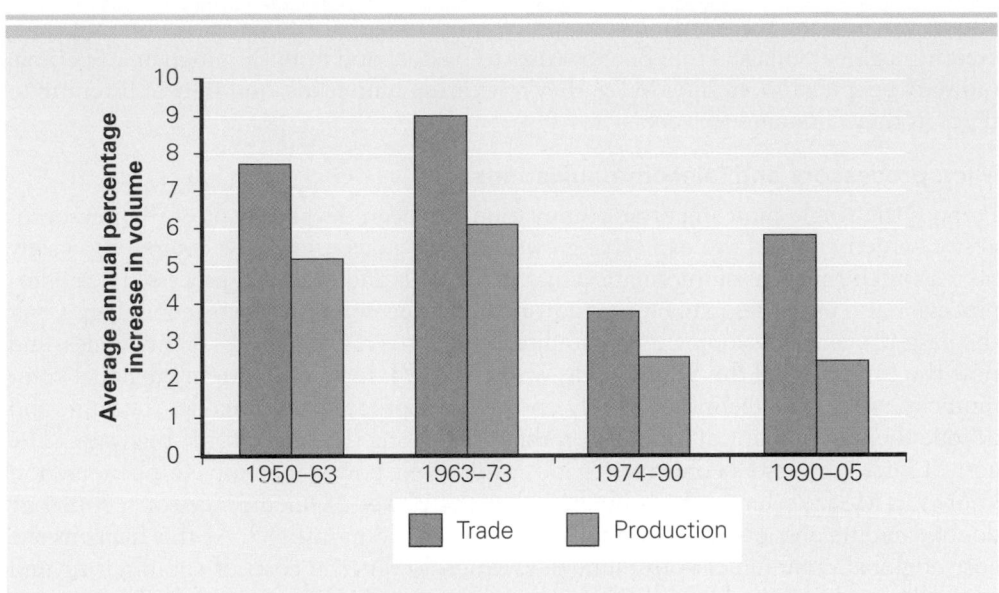

outflow of FDI increased from $25 billion in 1975 to a record $1.2 trillion in 2000. It fell
back in the early 2000s, but by 2006 FDI flows were again around $1.2 trillion.[23] Over
this period, the flow of FDI accelerated faster than the growth in world trade and world
output. For example, between 1992 and 2006, the total flow of FDI from all countries
increased more than sevenfold while world trade by value grew by some 150 percent and
world output by around 45 percent.[24] As a result of the strong FDI flow, by 2005 the global
stock of FDI exceeded $10 trillion. At least 77,000 parent companies had 770,000 affiliates
in foreign markets that collectively employed more than 50 million people abroad and
generated value accounting for about one-tenth of global GDP. The foreign affiliates of
multinationals had an estimated $22 trillion in global sales, much higher than the value
of global exports, which stood at close to $12.6 trillion.[25]

The globalization of markets and production and the resulting growth of world trade,
foreign direct investment, and imports all imply that firms are finding their home markets
under attack from foreign competitors. This is true in Japan, where U.S. companies such
as Kodak, Procter & Gamble, and Merrill Lynch are expanding their presence. It is true
in the United States, where Japanese automobile firms have taken market share away
from General Motors and Ford. And it is true in Europe, where the once-dominant
Dutch company Philips has seen its market share in the consumer electronics industry
taken by Japan's JVC, Matsushita, and Sony, and Korea's Samsung and LG. The growing
integration of the world economy into a single, huge marketplace is increasing the intensity
of competition in a range of manufacturing and service industries.

However, declining barriers to cross-border trade and investment cannot be taken
for granted. As we shall see in subsequent chapters, demands for "protection" from
foreign competitors are still often heard in countries around the world, including the
United States. Although a return to the restrictive trade policies of the 1920s and
30s is unlikely, it is not clear whether the political majority in the industrialized
world favors further reductions in trade barriers. If trade barriers decline no further,
at least for the time being, this will put a brake upon the globalization of both markets and production.

THE ROLE OF TECHNOLOGICAL CHANGE

The lowering of trade barriers made globalization of markets and production a theoretical
possibility. Technological change has made it a tangible reality. Since the end of World
War II, the world has seen major advances in communication, information processing,
and transportation technology, including the explosive emergence of the Internet and

World Wide Web. Telecommunications is creating a global audience. Transportation is creating a global village. From Buenos Aires to Boston, and from Birmingham to Beijing, ordinary people are watching MTV, they're wearing blue jeans, and they're listening to iPods as they commute to work.

Microprocessors and Telecommunications

Perhaps the single most important innovation has been development of the microprocessor, which enabled the explosive growth of high-power, low-cost computing, vastly increasing the amount of information that individuals and firms can process. The microprocessor also underlies many recent advances in telecommunications technology. Over the past 30 years, developments in satellite, optical fiber, and wireless technologies, and now the Internet and the World Wide Web (WWW), have revolutionized global communications. These technologies rely on the microprocessor to encode, transmit, and decode the vast amount of information that flows along these electronic highways. The cost of microprocessors continues to fall, while their power increases (a phenomenon known as **Moore's Law,** which predicts that the power of microprocessor technology doubles and its cost of production falls by half every 18 months).[26] As this happens the cost of global communications plummets, which lowers the costs of coordinating and controlling a global organization. Thus, between 1930 and 1990, the cost of a three-minute phone call between New York and London fell from $244.65 to $3.32.[27] By 1998, it had plunged to just 36 cents for consumers, and much lower rates were available for businesses.[28] Indeed, by using the Internet, the cost of an international phone call is rapidly plummeting toward just a few cents per minute.

The Internet and World Wide Web

The rapid growth of the World Wide Web is the latest expression of this development. In 1990, fewer than 1 million users were connected to the Internet. By 1995, the figure had risen to 50 million. By 2006, the Internet had 747 million users.[29] The WWW has developed into the information backbone of the global economy. In the U.S. alone, some $250 billion of goods and services are expected to be sold online to retail customers in 2007, up from almost nothing in 1997.[30] Viewed globally, the Web is emerging as an equalizer. It rolls back some of the constraints of location, scale, and time zones.[31] The Web makes it much easier for buyers and sellers to find each other, wherever they may be located and whatever their size. It allows businesses, both small and large, to expand their global presence at a lower cost than ever before.

Transportation Technology

In addition to developments in communication technology, several major innovations in transportation technology have occurred since World War II. In economic terms, the most important are probably the development of commercial jet aircraft and superfreighters and the introduction of containerization, which simplifies transshipment from one mode of transport to another. The advent of commercial jet travel, by reducing the time needed to get from one location to another, has effectively shrunk the globe. In terms of travel time, New York is now "closer" to Tokyo than it was to Philadelphia in the Colonial days.

Containerization has revolutionized the transportation business, significantly lowering the costs of shipping goods over long distances. Before the advent of containerization, moving goods from one mode of transport to another was very labor intensive, lengthy, and costly. It could take days and several hundred longshoremen to unload a ship and reload goods onto trucks and trains. With the advent of widespread containerization in the 1970s and 1980s, the whole process can now be executed by a handful of longshoremen in a couple of days. Since 1980, the world's containership fleet has more than quadrupled, reflecting in part the growing volume of international trade and in part the switch to this mode of transportation. As a result of the efficiency gains associated with containerization, transportation costs have plummeted, making it much more economical to ship goods around the globe, thereby helping to drive the globalization of markets and production. Between 1920 and 1990, the average ocean freight and port charges per ton of U.S. export and import cargo fell from $95 to $29 (in 1990 dollars).[32] The cost of shipping freight per ton-mile on railroads in the United States fell from 3.04 cents in 1985 to 2.3 cents in 2000, largely as a result of efficiency gains from the widespread use of containers.[33] An increased share of cargo now goes by air. Between 1955 and 1999, average air transportation revenue per ton-kilometer fell by more than 80 percent.[34] Reflecting the falling cost of airfreight, by the early 2000s air shipments accounted for 28 percent of the value of U.S. trade, up from 7 percent in 1965.[35]

Implications for the Globalization of Production

As transportation costs associated with the globalization of production declined, dispersal of production to geographically separate locations became more economical. As a result of the technological innovations discussed above, the real costs of information processing and communication have fallen dramatically in the past two decades. These developments make it possible for a firm to create and then manage a globally dispersed production system, further facilitating the globalization of production. A worldwide communications network has become essential for many international businesses. For example, Dell uses the Internet to coordinate and control a globally dispersed production system to such an extent that it holds only three days' worth of inventory at its assembly locations. Dell's Internet-based system records orders for computer equipment as they are submitted by customers via the company's Web site, then immediately transmits the resulting orders for components to various suppliers around the world, which have a real-time look at Dell's order flow and can adjust their production schedules accordingly. Given the low cost of airfreight, Dell can use air transportation to speed up the delivery of critical components to meet unanticipated demand shifts without delaying the shipment of final product to consumers. Dell also has used modern communications technology to outsource its customer service operations to India. When U.S. customers call Dell with a service inquiry, they are routed to Bangalore in India, where English-speaking service personnel handle the call.

The Internet has been a major force facilitating international trade in services. It is the Web that allows hospitals in Chicago to send MRI scans to India for analysis, accounting offices in San Francisco to outsource routine tax preparation work to accountants living in the Philippines, and software testers in India to debug code written by developers in Redmond, Washington, the headquarters of Microsoft. We are probably still in the early stages of this development. As Moore's Law continues to advance and telecommunications bandwidth continues to increase, almost any work processes that can be digitalized will be, and this will allow that work to be performed wherever in the world it is most efficient and effective to do so.

The development of commercial jet aircraft has also helped knit together the worldwide operations of many international businesses. Using jet travel, an American manager need spend a day at most traveling to his or her firm's European or Asian operations. This enables the manager to oversee a globally dispersed production system.

Implications for the Globalization of Markets

In addition to the globalization of production, technological innovations have also facilitated the globalization of markets. Low-cost global communications networks such as the World Wide Web are helping to create electronic global marketplaces. As noted above, low-cost transportation has made shipping products around the world more economical, thereby helping to create global markets. For example, due to the tumbling costs of shipping goods by air, roses grown in Ecuador can be sold in New York two days later while they are still fresh. This has given rise to an industry in Ecuador that did not exist 20 years ago and that now supplies a global market for roses. In addition, low-cost jet travel has resulted in the mass movement of people between countries. This has reduced the cultural distance between countries and is bringing about some convergence of consumer tastes and preferences. At the same time, global communication networks and global media are creating a worldwide culture. Many countries now receive U.S. television networks such as CNN, MTV, and HBO, and Hollywood films are shown the world over. In any society, the media are primary conveyors of culture; as global media develop, we must expect the evolution of something akin to a global culture. A logical result of this evolution is the emergence of global markets for consumer products. The first signs of this are already apparent. It is now as easy to find a McDonald's restaurant in Tokyo as it is in New York, to buy an iPod in Rio as it is in Berlin, and to buy Gap jeans in Paris as it is in San Francisco.

Despite these trends, we must be careful not to overemphasize their importance. While modern communication and transportation technologies are ushering in the "global village," significant national differences remain in culture, consumer preferences, and business practices. A firm that ignores differences between countries does so at its peril. We shall stress this point repeatedly throughout this book and elaborate on it in later chapters.

The Changing Demographics of the Global Economy

Hand in hand with the trend toward globalization has been a fairly dramatic change in the demographics of the global economy over the past 30 years. As late as the 1960s, four trends described the demographics of the global economy. The first was U.S. dominance in the world economy and world trade picture. The second was U.S. dominance in world foreign direct investment. Related to this, the third fact was the dominance of large, multinational U.S. firms on the international business scene. The fourth was that roughly half the globe—the centrally planned economies of the Communist world—were off-limits to Western international businesses. As will be explained below, all four of these qualities either have changed or are now changing rapidly.

THE CHANGING WORLD OUTPUT AND WORLD TRADE PICTURE

In the early 1960s, the United States was still by far the world's dominant industrial power. In 1963 the United States accounted for 40.3 percent of world economic activity, measured by Gross Domestic Product (GDP). By 2006, the United States accounted for 19.7 percent of world GDP, still the world's largest industrial power but down significantly in relative size since the 1960s (see Table 1.2). Nor was the United States the only developed nation to see its relative standing slip. The same occurred to Germany, France, and the United Kingdom, all nations that were among the first to industrialize. This change in the U.S. position was not an absolute decline, since the U.S. economy grew at a robust average annual rate of more than 3 percent from 1963 to 2006 (the economies of Germany, France, and the United Kingdom also grew during this time). Rather, it was a relative decline, reflecting the faster economic growth of several other economies, particularly in Asia. For example, as can be seen from Table 1.2, from 1963 to 2006, China's share of world GDP increased from a trivial amount to 15.1 percent. Other countries that markedly increased their share of world output included Japan, Thailand, Malaysia, Taiwan, and South Korea (note that GDP data in Table 1.2 are based on purchasing power parity figures, which adjust the value of GDP to reflect the cost of living in various economies).

By the end of the 1980s, the U.S. position as the world's leading exporter was threatened. Over the past 30 years, U.S. dominance in export markets has waned as Japan, Germany, and a number of newly industrialized countries such as South Korea and China have taken

TABLE 1.2

The Changing
Demographics of
World GDP and Trade

Sources: IMF, *World Economic Outlook*, April 2007. Data for 1963 are from N. Hood and J. Young, *The Economics of the Multinational Enterprise* (New York: Longman, 1973). The GDP data are based on purchasing power parity figures, which adjust the value of GDP to reflect the cost of living in various economies.

Country	Share of World Output, 1963	Share of World GDP, 2006	Share of World Exports, 2006
United States	40.3%	19.7%	9.8%
Germany	9.7	3.9	8.9
France	6.3	2.9	4.3
Italy	3.4	2.7	3.5
United Kingdom	6.5	3.2	4.6
Canada	3.0	1.7	3.1
Japan	5.5	6.3	5.0
China	NA	15.1	7.2

a larger share of world exports. During the 1960s, the United States routinely accounted for 20 percent of world exports of manufactured goods. But as Table 1.2 shows, the U.S. share of world exports of goods and services had slipped to 9.8 percent by 2006. Despite the fall, the United States still remained the world's largest exporter, ahead of Germany, Japan, France, and the fast-rising economic power, China. If China's rapid rise continues, however, it could soon overtake the U.S. as the world's largest economy and largest exporter.

As emerging economies such as China, India, and Brazil continue to grow, a further relative decline in the share of world output and world exports accounted for by the United States and other long-established developed nations seems likely. By itself, this is not bad. The relative decline of the United States reflects the growing economic development and industrialization of the world economy, as opposed to any absolute decline in the health of the U.S. economy, which by many measures is stronger than ever.

Most forecasts now predict a rapid rise in the share of world output accounted for by developing nations such as China, India, Indonesia, Thailand, South Korea, Mexico, and Brazil and a commensurate decline in the share enjoyed by rich industrialized countries such as Great Britain, Germany, Japan, and the United States. If current trends continue, the Chinese economy could be larger than that of the United States on a purchasing power parity basis, while the economy of India will approach that of Germany. The World Bank has estimated that today's developing nations may account for more than 60 percent of world economic activity by 2020, while today's rich nations, which currently account for more than 55 percent of world economic activity, may account for only about 38 percent. Forecasts are not always correct, but these suggest that a shift in the economic geography of the world is now underway, although the magnitude of that shift is not totally evident. For international businesses, the implications of this changing economic geography are clear: Many of tomorrow's economic opportunities may be found in the developing nations of the world, and many of tomorrow's most capable competitors will probably also emerge from these regions. A case in point has been the dramatic expansion of India's software sector, which is profiled in the next Country Focus.

THE CHANGING FOREIGN DIRECT INVESTMENT PICTURE

Reflecting the dominance of the United States in the global economy, U.S. firms accounted for 66.3 percent of worldwide foreign direct investment flows in the 1960s. British firms were second, accounting for 10.5 percent, while Japanese firms were a distant eighth, with only 2 percent. The dominance of U.S. firms was so great that books were written about the economic threat U.S. corporations posed to Europe.[37] Several European governments, most notably France, talked of limiting investment by U.S. firms.

India's Software Sector

Some 25 years ago a number of small software enterprises were established in Bangalore, India. Typical of these enterprises was Infosys Technologies, which seven Indian entrepreneurs started with about $1,000 between them. Infosys now has annual revenues of $22 billion and some 60,000 employees, but it is just one of over a hundred software companies clustered around Bangalore, which has become the epicenter of India's fast-growing information technology sector. From a standing start in the mid-1980s, by 2006 this sector was generating revenues of almost $40 billion, and combined software services, hardware sales, and business process outsourcing exports totaled $31.3 billion. India had also emerged as home to some of the fastest growing software service companies on the planet, including Infosys, Wipro, Tata Consultancy Services, and HCL Technologies.

The growth of the Indian software sector is based on four factors. First, the country has an abundant supply of engineering talent. Every year Indian universities graduate some 400,000 engineers. Second, labor costs in India are low. The cost to hire an Indian graduate is roughly 12 percent of the cost of hiring an American graduate. Third, many Indians are fluent in English, which makes coordination between Western firms and India easier. Fourth, due to time differences, Indians can work while Americans sleep. This means, for example, that software code written in America during the day can be tested in India at night, and shipped back to America via the Internet in time for the start of work the following day. In other words, by utilizing Indian labor and the Internet, software enterprises can create global software development factories that are working 24 hours a day.

Initially Indian software enterprises focused on the low end of the software industry, supplying basic software development and testing services to Western firms. But as the industry has grown in size and sophistication, Indian firms have moved up market. Today the leading Indian companies compete directly with the likes of IBM and EDS for large software development projects, business process outsourcing contracts, and information technology consulting services. These markets are booming. Estimates suggest that global spending on information technology outsourcing will rise from $193 billion in 2004 to $260 billion in 2009, with Indian enterprises capturing a larger slice of the pie. One response of Western firms to this emerging competitive threat has been to invest in India to garner the same kind of economic advantages that Indian firms enjoy. IBM, for example, has invested $2 billion in its Indian operations, and now has 53,000 employees located there, more than in any other country except America. In early 2007 it announced plans to invest another $6 billion over the next few years in India. Microsoft too has made major investments in India, including an R&D center in Hyderabad which employs 900 people and was located there specifically to tap into talented Indian engineers who did not want to move to the United States.[36]

However, as the barriers to the free flow of goods, services, and capital fell, and as other countries increased their shares of world output, non-U.S. firms increasingly began to invest across national borders. The motivation for much of this foreign direct investment by non-U.S. firms was the desire to disperse production activities to optimal locations and to build a direct presence in major foreign markets. Thus, beginning in the 1970s, European and Japanese firms began to shift labor-intensive manufacturing operations from their home markets to developing nations where labor costs were lower. In addition, many Japanese firms invested in North America and Europe—often as a hedge against unfavorable currency movements and the possible imposition of trade barriers. For example, Toyota, the Japanese automobile company, rapidly increased its investment in automobile production facilities in the United States and Europe during the late 1980s and early 1990s. Toyota executives believed that an increasingly strong Japanese yen would price Japanese automobile exports out of foreign markets; therefore, production in the most important foreign markets, as opposed to exports from Japan, made sense. Toyota also undertook these investments to head off growing political pressures in the United States and Europe to restrict Japanese automobile exports into those markets.

FIGURE 1.2

Percentage Share of Total
FDI Stock, 1980–2005

Source: *UNCTAD, World
Investment Report, 2006* (United
Nations, Geneva); UNCTAD
Press release, "Foreign Direct
Investment Rose by 34% in
2006," January 9, 2007.

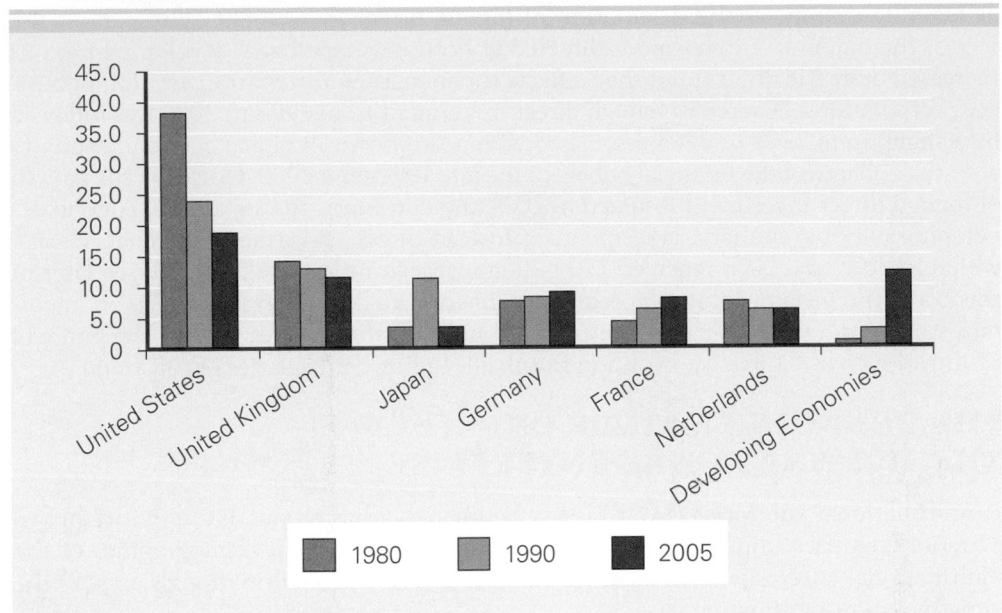

One consequence of these developments is illustrated in Figure 1.2, which shows how the stock of foreign direct investment by the world's six most important national sources—the United States, the United Kingdom, Germany, the Netherlands, France, and Japan—changed between 1980 and 2005. (The **stock of foreign direct investment** refers to the total cumulative value of foreign investments.) Figure 1.2 also shows the stock accounted for by firms from developing economies. The share of the total stock accounted for by U.S. firms declined from about 38 percent in 1980 to 19 percent in 2005. Meanwhile, the shares accounted for by France and the world's developing nations increased markedly. The rise in the share of FDI stock accounted for by developing nations reflects a growing trend for firms from these countries to invest outside their borders. In 2005, firms based in developing nations accounted for 11.9 percent of the stock of foreign direct investment, up from only 1.1 percent in 1980. Firms based in Hong Kong, South Korea, Singapore, Taiwan, India, and mainland China accounted for much of this investment.

Figure 1.3 illustrates two other important trends—the sustained growth in cross-border flows of foreign direct investment that occurred during the 1990s and the importance of

FIGURE 1.3

FDI Inflows, 1988–2006

Source: *UNCTAD, World Invest-
ment Report, 2006* (United
Nations, Geneva); UNCTAD
Press release, "Foreign Direct
Investment Rose by 34% in
2006," January 9, 2007.

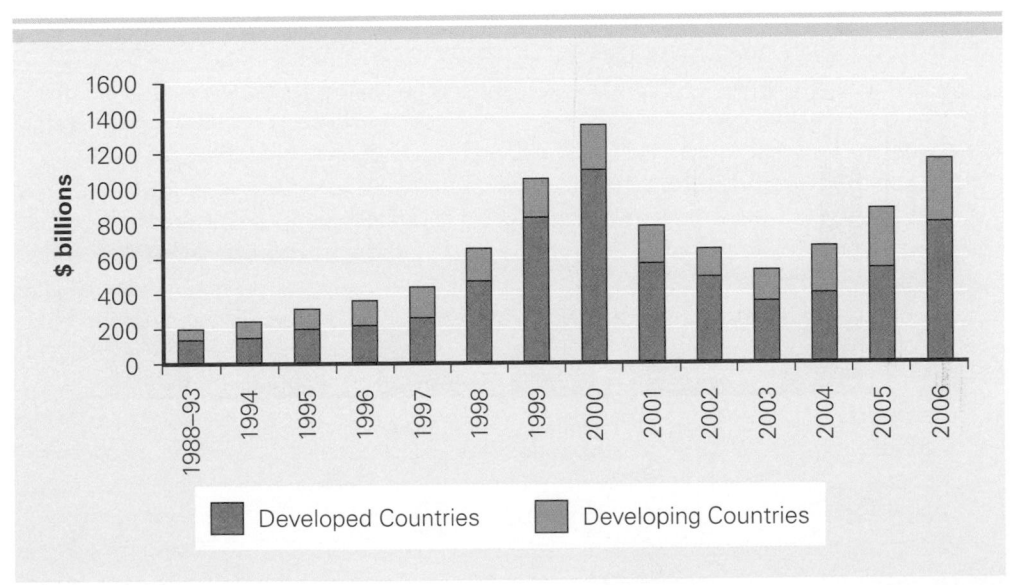

developing nations as the destination of foreign direct investment. Throughout the 1990s, the amount of investment directed at both developed and developing nations increased dramatically, a trend that reflects the increasing internationalization of business corporations. A surge in foreign direct investment from 1998 to 2000 was followed by a slump from 2001 to 2003 associated with a slowdown in global economic activity after the collapse of the financial bubble of the late 1990s and 2000. However, the growth of foreign direct investment resumed in 2004 and continued through 2006. Among developing nations, the largest recipient of foreign direct investment has been China, which in 2005 and 2006 received $70 billion a year in inflows. As we shall see later in this book, the sustained flow of foreign investment into developing nations is an important stimulus for economic growth in those countries, which bodes well for the future of countries such as China, Mexico, and Brazil, all leading beneficiaries of this trend.

THE CHANGING NATURE OF THE MULTINATIONAL ENTERPRISE

A **multinational enterprise** (MNE) is any business that has productive activities in two or more countries. Since the 1960s, two notable trends in the demographics of the multinational enterprise have been (1) the rise of non-U.S. multinationals and (2) the growth of mini-multinationals.

Non-U.S. Multinationals

In the 1960s, large U.S. multinational corporations dominated global business activity. With U.S. firms accounting for about two-thirds of foreign direct investment during the 1960s, one would expect most multinationals to be U.S. enterprises. According to the data summarized in Figure 1.4, in 1973, 48.5 percent of the world's 260 largest multinationals were U.S. firms. The second-largest source country was the United Kingdom, with 18.8 percent of the largest multinationals. Japan accounted for 3.5 percent of the world's largest multinationals at the time. The large number of U.S. multinationals reflected U.S. economic dominance in the three decades after World War II, while the large number of British multinationals reflected that country's industrial dominance in the early decades of the 20th century.

By 2005 things had shifted significantly. Some 27 of the world's 100 largest nonfinancial multinationals were now U.S. enterprises; 15 were French; 13, German; 11, British; and 9, Japanese. In terms of the global stock of foreign direct investment, 21 percent belonged to U.S. firms, 14 percent to British, 8 percent to French firms, 8.5 percent to German

FIGURE 1.4

National Origin of Largest Multinational Enterprises, 1973 and 2005

Source: *UNCTAD, World Investment Report, 2006* (United Nations, Geneva); UNCTAD Press release, "Foreign Direct Investment Rose by 34% in 2006," January 9, 2007.

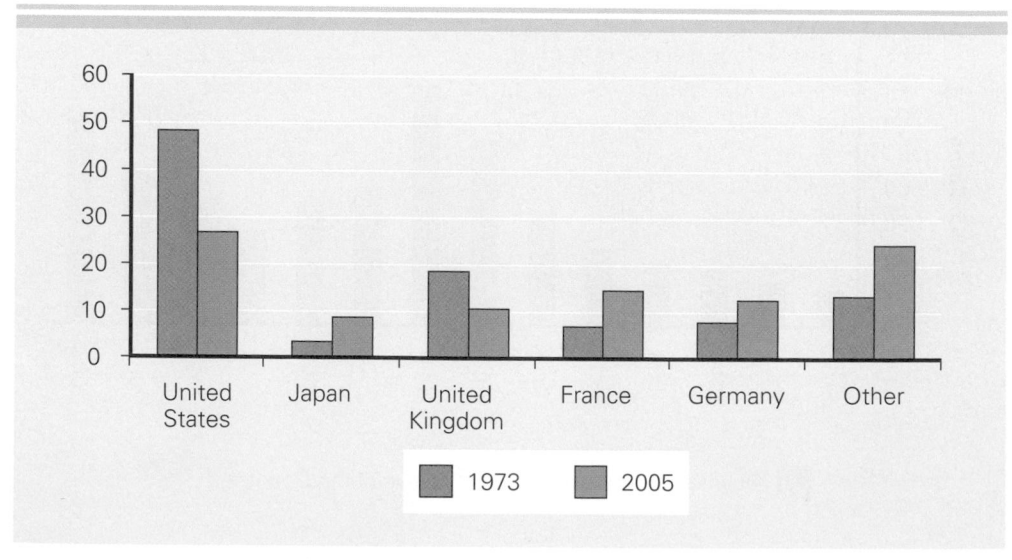

firms, 5.6 percent to Dutch firms, and 4 percent to Japanese.[38] Although the 1973 data are not strictly comparable with the later data, they illustrate the trend (the 1973 figures are based on the largest 260 firms, whereas the later figures are based on the largest 100 multinationals). The globalization of the world economy has resulted in a relative decline in the dominance of U.S. firms in the global marketplace.

According to UN data, the ranks of the world's largest 100 multinationals are still dominated by firms from developed economies.[39] However, five firms from developing economies had entered the UN's list of the 100 largest multinationals by 2005. They were Hutchison Whampoa of Hong Kong, China, which ranked 17 in terms of foreign assets; Singtel of Singapore; Petronas of Malaysia; Samsung of Korea; and CITIC Corp of China.[40] The growth in the number of multinationals from developing economies is evident when we look at smaller firms. By 2005, the largest 50 multinationals from developing economies had foreign sales of $323 billion out of total sales of $738 billion and employed 1.1 million people outside of their home countries. Some 64 percent of the largest 100 multinationals from developing nations came from Hong King, Taiwan, Singapore, and mainland China. Other nations with multiple entries on the list included South Korea, Brazil, Mexico, and Malaysia. We can reasonably expect more growth of new multinational enterprises from the world's developing nations. Firms from developing nations can be expected to emerge as important competitors in global markets, further shifting the axis of the world economy away from North America and Western Europe and threatening the long dominance of Western companies. One such rising competitor, Hisense, one of China's premier manufacturers of consumer appliances and telecommunications equipment, is profiled in the accompanying Management Focus.

The Rise of Mini-Multinationals

Another trend in international business has been the growth of medium-size and small multinationals (mini-multinationals).[42] When people think of international businesses, they tend to think of firms such as Exxon, General Motors, Ford, Fuji, Kodak, Matsushita, Procter & Gamble, Sony, and Unilever—large, complex multinational corporations with operations that span the globe. Although large firms still conduct most international trade and investment, many medium-size and small businesses are becoming increasingly involved in international trade and investment.

For another example, consider Lubricating Systems, Inc., of Kent, Washington. Lubricating Systems, which manufactures lubricating fluids for machine tools, employs 25 people and generates sales of $6.5 million. It's hardly a large, complex multinational, yet exports to a score of countries, including Japan, Israel, and the United Arab Emirates, generate more than $2 million of the company's sales. Lubricating Systems also has set up a joint venture with a German company to serve the European market.[43] Consider also Lixi, Inc., a small U.S. manufacturer of industrial X-ray equipment; 70 percent of Lixi's $4.5 million in revenues comes from exports to Japan.[44] Or take G. W. Barth, a manufacturer of cocoa-bean roasting machinery based in Ludwigsburg, Germany. Employing just 65 people, this small company has captured 70 percent of the global market for cocoa-bean roasting machines.[45] International business is conducted not just by large firms but also by medium-size and small enterprises.

THE CHANGING WORLD ORDER

Between 1989 and 1991 a series of remarkable democratic revolutions swept the Communist world. For reasons that are explored in more detail in Chapter 2, in country after country throughout Eastern Europe and eventually in the Soviet Union itself, Communist Party governments collapsed. The Soviet Union is now receding into history, having been replaced by 15 independent republics. Czechoslovakia has divided itself into two states, while Yugoslavia dissolved into a bloody civil war, now thankfully over, among its five successor states.

China's Hisense—An Emerging Multinational

Hisense is rapidly emerging as one of China's leading multinationals. Like many other Chinese corporations, Hisense traces its origins back to a state-owned manufacturer, in this case Qingdao No 2 Radio Factory, which was established in 1969 with just 10 employees. In the 1970s the state-owned factory diversified into the manufacture of TV sets, and by the 1980s it was one of China's leading manufacturers of color TVs, making sets designed by Matsushita under license. In 1992 a 35-year-old engineer named Zhou Houjian was appointed head of the enterprise. In 1994 the shackles of state ownership were relaxed when the Hisense Company Ltd. was established, with Zhou as CEO (he is now Chairman of the Board).

Under Zhou's leadership, Hisense entered a period of rapid growth, product diversification, and global expansion. By 2006 the company had sales of $3.3 billion and had emerged as one of China's premier makers of TV sets (with an 11 percent share of the domestic market), air conditioners, refrigerators, personal computers, and telecommunications equipment. In 2006, Hisense sold around 10 million TV sets, 3 million air conditioners, 4 million CDMA wireless phones, 6 million refrigerators, and 1 million personal computers. International sales accounted for $490 million, or more than 15 percent of total revenue. The company had established overseas manufacturing subsidiaries in Algeria, Hungary, Iran, Pakistan, and South Africa, and was growing rapidly in developing markets where it was taking share away from long-established consumer electronics and appliance makers.

Hisense ambitions are grand. It seeks to become a global enterprise with a world class consumer brand. It aims to increase revenue to over $12 billion in 2010, a goal that may be attainable following the 2006 acquisition of its troubled Chinese rival, Kelon. What is different about Hisense is that although it is without question a low-cost manufacturer, it believes its core strength is not in low-cost manufacturing but in rapid product innovation. The company believes that the only way to gain leadership in the highly competitive markets in which it competes is to continuously launch advanced, high-quality, and competitively priced products. To this end, Hisense established its first R&D center in China in the mid-1990s. This was followed by a South African R&D center in 1997 and a European R&D center in 2007. The company also has plans for an R&D center in the United States. In 2006 these R&D centers filed for some 534 patents.

Hisense's technological prowess is evident in its digital TV business. It introduced set top boxes in 1999, making it possible to browse the Internet from a TV. In 2002, Hisense introduced its first interactive digital TV set, and in 2005 it developed China's first core digital processing chip for digital TVs, breaking the country's reliance on foreign chip makers for this core technology. In 2006, Hisense launched an innovative line of multimedia TV sets that integrated digital high-definition technology, network technology, and flat panel displays.[41]

Many of the former Communist nations of Europe and Asia seem to share a commitment to democratic politics and free market economics. If this continues, the opportunities for international businesses may be enormous. For half a century, these countries were essentially closed to Western international businesses. Now they present a host of export and investment opportunities. Just how this will play out over the next 10 to 20 years is difficult to say. The economies of many of the former Communist states are still relatively undeveloped, and their continued commitment to democracy and free market economics cannot be taken for granted. Disturbing signs of growing unrest and totalitarian tendencies continue to be seen in several Eastern European and Central Asian states, including Russia, which under the government of Vladimir Putin has shown signs of shifting back toward greater state involvement in economic activity.[46] Thus, the risks involved in doing business in such countries are high, but so may be the returns.

In addition to these changes, more quiet revolutions have been occurring in China, other states in Southeast Asia, and Latin America. Their implications for international businesses may be just as profound as the collapse of communism in Eastern Europe. China suppressed its own pro-democracy movement in the bloody Tiananmen Square massacre of 1989. Despite this, China continues to move progressively toward greater free market reforms. If what is occurring in China continues for two more decades, China may move from Third World status to industrial superpower status even more rapidly than Japan did. If China's gross domestic product (GDP) per capita grows by an average of 6 to 7 percent, which is slower than the 8 percent growth rate achieved during the last decade, then by 2020 this nation of 1.273 billion people could boast an average income per capita of about $13,000, roughly equivalent to that of Spain's today.

The potential consequences for international business are enormous. On the one hand, with more than 1 billion people, China represents a huge and largely untapped market. Reflecting this tremendous potential, between 1983 and 2006, annual foreign direct investment in China increased from less than $2 billion to $70 billion. On the other hand, China's new firms are proving to be very capable competitors, and they could take global market share away from Western and Japanese enterprises (for example, see the Management Focus about Hisense). Thus, the changes in China are creating both opportunities and threats for established international businesses.

As for Latin America, both democracy and free market reforms also seem to have taken hold there. For decades, most Latin American countries were ruled by dictators, many of whom seemed to view Western international businesses as instruments of imperialist domination. Accordingly, they restricted direct investment by foreign firms. In addition, the poorly managed economies of Latin America were characterized by low growth, high debt, and hyperinflation—all of which discouraged investment by international businesses. In the last two decades much of this has changed. Throughout most of Latin America, debt and inflation are down, governments have sold state-owned enterprises to private investors, foreign investment is welcomed, and the region's economies have expanded. Brazil, Mexico, and Chile have led the way here. These changes have increased the attractiveness of Latin America, both as a market for exports and as a site for foreign direct investment. At the same time, given the long history of economic mismanagement in Latin America, there is no guarantee that these favorable trends will continue. Indeed, left-wing governments in Bolivia and Venezuela have led shifts back toward greater state involvement in industry in the last few years, and foreign investment is now less welcome than it was during the 1990s. In both nations, the government has seized control of oil and gas fields from foreign investors and has limited the rights of foreign energy companies to extract oil and gas from their nations. Thus, as in the case of Eastern Europe, substantial opportunities are accompanied by substantial risks.

THE GLOBAL ECONOMY OF THE 21ST CENTURY

As discussed, the past quarter century has seen rapid changes in the global economy. Barriers to the free flow of goods, services, and capital have been coming down. The volume of cross-border trade and investment has been growing more rapidly than global output, indicating that national economies are becoming more closely integrated into a single, interdependent, global economic system. As their economies advance, more nations are joining the ranks of the developed world. A generation ago, South Korea and Taiwan were viewed as second-tier developing nations. Now they boast large economies, and their firms are major players in many global industries, from shipbuilding and steel to electronics and chemicals. The move toward a global economy has been further strengthened by the widespread adoption of liberal economic policies by countries that had firmly opposed them for two generations or more. Thus, in keeping with the normative prescriptions of liberal economic ideology, in country after country we have seen state-owned businesses privatized, widespread deregulation adopted, markets opened to more competition, and commitment increased to removing barriers to cross-border trade and investment. This suggests that over the next few decades, countries such as the Czech Republic, Mexico, Poland, Brazil, China, India, and South Africa may build powerful market-oriented economies. In short, current trends indicate that the world is moving rapidly toward an economic system that is more favorable for international business.

But it is always hazardous to use established trends to predict the future. The world may be moving toward a more global economic system, but globalization is not inevitable. Countries may pull back from the recent commitment to liberal economic ideology if their experiences do not match their expectations. Periodic signs, for example, indicate a retreat from liberal economic ideology in Russia. Russia has experienced considerable economic pain as it tries to shift from a centrally planned economy to a market economy. If Russia's hesitation were to become more permanent and widespread, the liberal vision of a more prosperous global economy based on free market principles might not occur as quickly as many hope. Clearly, this would be a tougher world for international businesses.

Also, greater globalization brings with it risks of its own. This was starkly demonstrated in 1997 and 1998 when a financial crisis in Thailand spread first to other East Asian nations and then in 1998 to Russia and Brazil. Ultimately, the crisis threatened to plunge the economies of the developed world, including the United States, into a recession. We explore the causes and consequences of this and other similar global financial crises in Chapter 10. Even from a purely economic perspective, globalization is not all good. The opportunities for doing business in a global economy may be significantly enhanced, but as we saw in 1997–98, the risks associated with global financial contagion are also greater. Still, as explained later in this book, firms can exploit the opportunities associated with globalization, while at the same time reducing the risks through appropriate hedging strategies.

The Globalization Debate

Is the shift toward a more integrated and interdependent global economy a good thing? Many influential economists, politicians, and business leaders seem to think so.[47] They argue that falling barriers to international trade and investment are the twin engines driving the global economy toward greater prosperity. They say increased international trade and cross-border investment will result in lower prices for goods and services. They believe that globalization stimulates economic growth, raises the incomes of consumers, and helps create jobs in all countries that participate in the global trading system. The arguments of those who support globalization are covered in detail in Chapters 5, 6, and 7. As we shall see, there are good theoretical reasons for believing that declining barriers to international trade and investment do stimulate economic growth, create jobs, and raise income levels. As described in Chapters 6 and 7, empirical evidence lends support to the predictions of this theory. However, despite the existence of a compelling body of theory and evidence, globalization has its critics.[48] Some of these critics have become increasingly vocal and active, taking to the streets to demonstrate their opposition to globalization. Here we look at the nature of protests against globalization and briefly review the main themes of the debate concerning the merits of globalization. In later chapters we elaborate on many of the points mentioned below.

ANTIGLOBALIZATION PROTESTS

Street demonstrations against globalization date to December 1999, when more than 40,000 protesters blocked the streets of Seattle in an attempt to shut down a World Trade Organization meeting being held in the city. The demonstrators were protesting against a wide range of issues, including job losses in industries under attack from foreign competitors, downward pressure on the wage rates of unskilled workers, environmental degradation, and the cultural imperialism of global media and multinational enterprises, which some protesters felt were dominated by what they called the "culturally impoverished" interests and values of the United States. All of these ills, the demonstrators claimed, could be laid at the feet of globalization. The World Trade Organization was meeting to try to launch a new round of talks to cut barriers to cross-border trade and investment. As such, it was seen as a promoter of globalization and a target for the antiglobalization protesters. The protests turned violent, transforming the normally placid streets of Seattle into a running battle between "anarchists" and Seattle's bemused and poorly prepared police

Demonstrators at the WTO meeting in Seattle in December 1999 began looting and rioting in the city's downtown area.

department. Pictures of brick-throwing protesters and armored police wielding their batons were duly recorded by the global media, which then circulated the images around the world. Meanwhile, the World Trade Organization meeting failed to reach agreement, and although the protests outside the meeting halls had little to do with that failure, the impression took hold that the demonstrators had succeeded in derailing the meetings.

Emboldened by the experience in Seattle, antiglobalization protesters now turn up at almost every major meeting of a global institution. Smaller scale protests have occurred in several countries, such as France, where antiglobalization activists destroyed a McDonald's restaurant in August 1999 to protest the impoverishment of French culture by American imperialism (see the Country Focus, "Protesting Globalization in France," for details). While violent protests may give the antiglobalization effort a bad name, it is clear from the scale of the demonstrations that support for the cause goes beyond a core of anarchists. Large segments of the population in many countries believe that globalization has detrimental effects on living standards and the environment, and the media have often fed on this fear. For example, CNN news anchor Lou Dobbs has been highly critical of the trend by American companies to take advantage of globalization and "export jobs" overseas. Both theory and evidence suggest that many of these fears are exaggerated, but this position may not have been communicated clearly and both politicians and businesspeople need to do more to counter these fears. Many protests against globalization are tapping into a general sense of loss at the passing of a world in which barriers of time and distance, and vast differences in economic institutions, political institutions, and the level of development of different nations, produced a world rich in the diversity of human cultures. This world is now passing into history. However, while the rich citizens of the developed world may have the luxury of mourning the fact that they can now see McDonald's restaurants and Starbucks coffeehouses on their vacations to exotic locations such as Thailand, fewer complaints are heard from the citizens of those countries, who welcome the higher living standards that progress brings.

GLOBALIZATION, JOBS, AND INCOME

One concern that globalization opponents frequently voice is that falling barriers to international trade destroy manufacturing jobs in wealthy advanced economies such as the United States and Western Europe. The critics argue that falling trade barriers allow

Protesting Globalization in France

One night in August 1999, 10 men under the leadership of local sheep farmer and rural activist Jose Bove crept into the town of Millau in central France and vandalized a McDonald's restaurant under construction, causing an estimated $150,000 damage. These were no ordinary vandals, however, at least according to their supporters, for the "symbolic dismantling" of the McDonald's outlet had noble aims, or so it was claimed.

The attack was initially presented as a protest against unfair American trade policies. The European Union had banned imports of hormone-treated beef from the United States, primarily because of fears that it might lead to health problems (although EU scientists had concluded there was no evidence of this). After a careful review, the World Trade Organization concluded that the EU ban was not allowed under trading rules that applied to both the European Union and the United States and that the EU would therefore have to lift it or face retaliation. The EU refused to comply, so the U.S. government imposed a 100 percent tariff on imports of certain EU products, including French staples such as foie gras, mustard, and Roquefort cheese. On farms near Millau, Bove and others raised sheep whose milk was used to make Roquefort. They felt incensed by the American tariff and decided to vent their frustrations on McDonald's.

Bove and his compatriots were arrested and charged. They quickly became a focus of the antiglobalization movement in France that was protesting everything from a loss of national sovereignty and "unfair" trade policies that were trying to force hormone-treated beef on French consumers, to the invasion of French culture by alien American values, so aptly symbolized by McDonald's. Lionel Jospin, France's prime minister, called the cause of Jose Bove "just." Allowed to remain free pending his trial, Bove traveled to Seattle in December to protest against the World Trade Organization, where he was feted as a hero of the antiglobalization movement. In France, Bove's July 2000 trial drew some 40,000 supporters to the small town of Millau, where they camped outside the courthouse and waited for the verdict. Bove was found guilty and sentenced to three months in jail,

far less than the maximum possible sentence of five years. His supporters wore T-shirts claiming, "The world is not merchandise, and neither am I."

About the same time in the Languedoc region of France, California winemaker Robert Mondavi had reached agreement with the mayor and council of the village of Aniane and regional authorities to turn 125 acres of wooded hillside belonging to the village into a vineyard. Mondavi planned to invest $7 million in the project and hoped to produce top-quality wine that would sell in Europe and the United States for $60 a bottle. However, local environmentalists objected to the plan, which they claimed would destroy the area's unique ecological heritage. Jose Bove, basking in sudden fame, offered his support to the opponents, and the protests started. In May 2001, the Socialist mayor who had approved the project was defeated in local elections in which the Mondavi project had become the major issue. He was replaced by a Communist, Manuel Diaz, who denounced the project as a capitalist plot designed to enrich wealthy U.S. shareholders at the cost of his villagers and the environment. Following Diaz's victory, Mondavi announced he would pull out of the project. A spokesman noted, "It's a huge waste, but there are clearly personal and political interests at play here that go way beyond us."

So are the French opposed to foreign investment? The experience of McDonald's and Mondavi seems to suggest so, as does the associated news coverage, but look closer and a different reality seems to emerge. McDonald's has more than 800 restaurants in France and continues to do very well there. In fact, France is one of the most profitable markets for McDonald's. France has long been one of the most favored locations for direct foreign investment, receiving over $180 billion of foreign investment between 2004 and 2006, more than any other European nation with the exception of Britain. American companies have always accounted for a significant percentage of this investment. Moreover, French enterprises have also been significant foreign investors; some 1,100 French multinationals account for around 8 percent of the global stock of foreign direct investment.[49]

firms to move manufacturing activities to countries where wage rates are much lower.[50] Indeed, due to the entry of China, India, and states from Eastern Europe into the global trading system, along with global population growth, estimates suggest that the pool of global labor may have quadrupled between 1985 and 2005, with most of the increase taking place after 1990.[51] Other things being equal, one might conclude that this enormous expansion in the global labor force, when coupled with expanding international trade, would have depressed wages in developed nations.

This fear is supported by anecdotes. For example, D. L. Bartlett and J. B. Steele, two journalists for the *Philadelphia Inquirer* who gained notoriety for their attacks on free trade, cite the case of Harwood Industries, a U.S. clothing manufacturer that closed its U.S. operations, where it paid workers $9 per hour, and shifted manufacturing to Honduras, where textile workers receive 48 cents per hour.[52] Because of moves such as this, argue Bartlett and Steele, the wage rates of poorer Americans have fallen significantly over the past quarter of a century.

In the last few years, the same fears have been applied to services, which have increasingly been outsourced to nations with lower labor costs. The popular feeling is that when corporations such as Dell, IBM, or Citigroup outsource service activities to lower-cost foreign suppliers—as all three have done—they are "exporting jobs" to low-wage nations and contributing to higher unemployment and lower living standards in their home nations (in this case, the United States). Some lawmakers in the United States have responded by calling for legal barriers to job outsourcing.

Supporters of globalization reply that critics of these trends miss the essential point about free trade—the benefits outweigh the costs.[53] They argue that free trade will result in countries specializing in the production of those goods and services that they can produce most efficiently, while importing goods and services that they cannot produce as efficiently. When a country embraces free trade, there is always some dislocation—lost textile jobs at Harwood Industries, or lost call center jobs at Dell—but the whole economy is better off as a result. According to this view, it makes little sense for the United States to produce textiles at home when they can be produced at a lower cost in Honduras or China (which, unlike Honduras, is a major source of U.S. textile imports). Importing textiles from China leads to lower prices for clothes in the United States, which enables consumers to spend more of their money on other items. At the same time, the increased income generated in China from textile exports increases income levels in that country, which helps the Chinese purchase more products produced in the United States, such as pharmaceuticals from Amgen, Boeing jets, Intel-based computers, Microsoft software, and Cisco routers.

The same argument can be made to support the outsourcing of services to low-wage countries. By outsourcing its customer service call centers to India, Dell can reduce its cost structure, and thereby its prices for PCs. U.S. consumers benefit from this development. As prices for PCs fall, Americans can spend more of their money on other goods and services. Moreover, the increase in income levels in India allows Indians to purchase more U.S. goods and services, which helps create jobs in the United States. In this manner, supporters of globalization argue that free trade benefits *all* countries that adhere to a free trade regime.

If the critics of globalization are correct, three things must be shown: First, the share of national income received by labor, as opposed to the share received by the owners of capital (e.g., stockholders and bondholders) should have declined in advanced nations as a result of downward pressure on wage rates. Second, even though labor's share of the economic pie may have declined, living standards need not deteriorate if the size of the total pie has increased sufficiently to offset the decline in labor's share—in other words, if economic growth and rising living standards in advanced economies make up for labor's smaller proportion of the whole (this is the position argued by supporters of globalization). Third, the decline in labor's share of national income must be due to moving production to low-wage countries, as opposed to improving production technology and productivity.

So what do the data say? Several recent studies shed light on these questions.[54] First, the data suggest that over the last two decades the share of labor in national income has declined. The decline in share is much more pronounced in Europe and Japan (about 10 percentage points) than in the United States and the United Kingdom (where it is 3–4 percentage points). However, detailed analysis suggests that *skilled labor*'s share of national income has actually *increased*, suggesting that the fall in labor's share has been due to a fall in the share going to *unskilled labor*. For illustration, a study of long-term trends in income distribution in the United States concluded that

> Nationwide, from the late 1970s to the late 1990s, the average income of the lowest-income families fell by over 6 percent after adjustment for inflation, and the average real income of the middle fifth of families grew by about 5 percent. By contrast, the average real income of the highest-income fifth of families increased by over 30 percent.[55]

Another study suggested that the earnings gap between workers in skilled and unskilled sectors has widened by 25 percent over the last two decades.[56] In sum, it is unskilled labor in developed nations that has seen its share of national income decline over the last two decades.

However, this does not mean that the *living standards* of unskilled workers in developed nations have declined. It is possible that economic growth in developed nations has offset the fall in unskilled workers' share of national income, raising their living standards. In fact, evidence suggests that real labor compensation has expanded robustly in most developed nations since the 1980s, including the United States. A study by the Organization for Economic Cooperation and Development, whose members include the 20 richest economies in the world, noted that while the gap between the poorest and richest segments of society in some OECD countries had widened, this trend was by no means universal.[57] Contrary to the results of the study cited above, the OECD study found that while income inequality increased from the mid-1970s to the mid-1980s in the United States, it did not widen further in the next decade. The report also notes that in almost all countries, real income levels rose over the 20-year period studied, including the incomes of the poorest segment of most OECD societies. To add to the mixed research results, a 2002 U.S. study that included data from 1990 to 2000 concluded that during those years, falling unemployment rates brought gains to low-wage workers and fairly broad-based wage growth, especially in the latter half of the 1990s. The income of the worst-paid 10 percent of the population actually rose twice as fast as that of the average worker during 1998–2000.[58] If such trends continued into the 2000s—and they may not have—the argument that globalization leads to growing income inequality may lose some of its punch.

As noted earlier, globalization critics argue that the decline in unskilled wage rates is due to the migration of low-wage manufacturing jobs offshore and a corresponding reduction in demand for unskilled workers. However, supporters of globalization see a more complex picture. They maintain that the apparent decline in real wage rates of unskilled workers owes far more to a technology-induced shift within advanced economies away from jobs where the only qualification was a willingness to turn up for work every day and toward jobs that require significant education and skills. They point out that many advanced economies report a shortage of highly skilled workers and an excess supply of unskilled workers. Thus, growing income inequality is a result of the labor market bidding up wages for skilled workers and discounting the wages for unskilled workers. In fact, recent evidence suggests that technological change has had a bigger impact than globalization on labor's declining share of national income.[59] This indicates that the solution to the problem of stagnant incomes among the unskilled is to be found not in limiting free trade and globalization but in increasing society's investment in education to reduce the supply of unskilled workers.[60]

Finally, it is worth noting that the wage gap between developing and developed nations is closing as developing nations experience rapid economic growth. For example, one estimate suggests that wages in China will approach Western levels in about

30 years.[61] To the extent that this is the case, any migration of unskilled jobs to low-wage countries is a temporary phenomenon representing a structural adjustment on the way to a more tightly integrated global economy.

GLOBALIZATION, LABOR POLICIES, AND THE ENVIRONMENT

A second source of concern is that free trade encourages firms from advanced nations to move manufacturing facilities to less developed countries that lack adequate regulations to protect labor and the environment from abuse by the unscrupulous.[62] Globalization critics often argue that adhering to labor and environmental regulations significantly increases the costs of manufacturing enterprises and puts them at a competitive disadvantage in the global marketplace vis-à-vis firms based in developing nations that do not have to comply with such regulations. Firms deal with this cost disadvantage, the theory goes, by moving their production facilities to nations that do not have such burdensome regulations or that fail to enforce the regulations they have.

If this were the case, one might expect free trade to lead to an increase in pollution and result in firms from advanced nations exploiting the labor of less developed nations.[63] This argument was used repeatedly by those who opposed the 1994 formation of the North American Free Trade Agreement (NAFTA) between Canada, Mexico, and the United States. They painted a picture of U.S. manufacturing firms moving to Mexico in droves so that they would be free to pollute the environment, employ child labor, and ignore workplace safety and health issues, all in the name of higher profits.[64]

Supporters of free trade and greater globalization express doubts about this scenario. They argue that tougher environmental regulations and stricter labor standards go hand in hand with economic progress.[65] In general, as countries get richer, they enact tougher environmental and labor regulations.[66] Because free trade enables developing countries to increase their economic growth rates and become richer, this should lead to tougher environmental and labor laws. In this view, the critics of free trade have got it backward—free trade does not lead to more pollution and labor exploitation, it leads to less. By creating wealth and incentives for enterprises to produce technological innovations, the free market system and free trade could make it easier for the world to cope with pollution and population growth. Indeed, while pollution levels are rising in the world's poorer countries, they have been falling in developed nations. In the United States, for example, the concentration of carbon monoxide and sulphur dioxide pollutants in the atmosphere decreased by 60 percent between 1978 and 1997, while lead concentrations decreased by 98 percent—and these reductions have occurred against a background of sustained economic expansion.[67]

A number of econometric studies have found consistent evidence of a hump-shaped relationship between income levels and pollution levels (see Figure 1.5).[68] As an economy grows and income levels rise, initially pollution levels also rise. However, past some point, rising income levels lead to demands for greater environmental protection, and pollution levels then fall. A seminal study by Grossman and Krueger found that the turning point generally occurred before per capita income levels reached $8,000.[69]

While the hump-shaped relationship depicted in Figure 1.5 seems to hold across a wide range of pollutants—from sulfur dioxide to lead concentrations and water quality—carbon dioxide emissions are an important exception, rising steadily with higher income levels. Given that increased atmospheric carbon dioxide concentrations are a cause of global warming, this should be of serious concern. The solution to the problem, however, is probably not to roll back the trade liberalization efforts that have fostered economic growth and globalization, but to get the nations of the world to agree to tougher standards on limiting carbon emissions. Although UN-sponsored talks have had this as a central aim since the 1992 Earth Summit in Rio de Janeiro, there has been little success

FIGURE 1.5

Income Levels and
Environmental Pollution

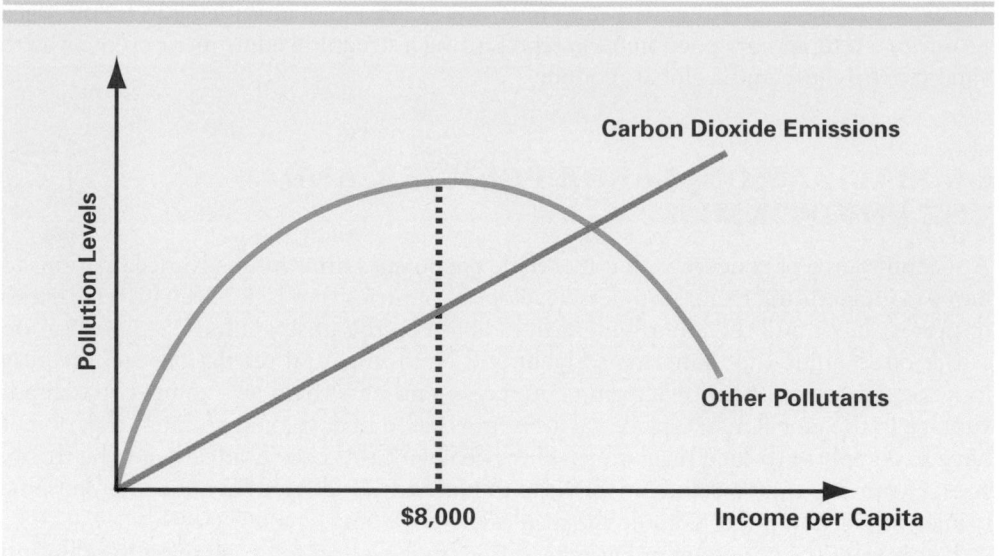

in moving toward the ambitious goals for reducing carbon emissions laid down in the Earth Summit and subsequent talks in Kyoto, Japan, in part because the largest emitter of carbon dioxide, the United States, has refused to sign global agreements that it claims would unreasonably retard economic growth.

Supporters of free trade also point out that it is possible to tie free trade agreements to the implementation of tougher environmental and labor laws in less developed countries. NAFTA, for example, was passed only after side agreements had been negotiated that committed Mexico to tougher enforcement of environmental protection regulations. Thus, supporters of free trade argue that factories based in Mexico are now cleaner than they would have been without the passage of NAFTA.[70]

They also argue that business firms are not the amoral organizations that critics suggest. While there may be some rotten apples, most business enterprises are staffed by managers who are committed to behave in an ethical manner and would be unlikely to move production offshore just so they could pump more pollution into the atmosphere or exploit labor. Furthermore, the relationship between pollution, labor exploitation, and production costs may not be that suggested by critics. In general, a well-treated labor force is productive, and it is productivity rather than base wage rates that often has the greatest influence on costs. The vision of greedy managers who shift production to low-wage countries to exploit their labor force may be misplaced.

GLOBALIZATION AND NATIONAL SOVEREIGNTY

Another concern voiced by critics of globalization is that today's increasingly interdependent global economy shifts economic power away from national governments and toward supranational organizations such as the World Trade Organization, the European Union, and the United Nations. As perceived by critics, unelected bureaucrats now impose policies on the democratically elected governments of nation-states, thereby undermining the sovereignty of those states and limiting the nation's ability to control its own destiny.[71]

The World Trade Organization is a favorite target of those who attack the headlong rush toward a global economy. As noted earlier, the WTO was founded in 1994 to police the world trading system established by the General Agreement on Tariffs and Trade. The WTO arbitrates trade disputes between the 150 states that are signatories to the GATT. The arbitration panel can issue a ruling instructing a member state to change trade policies that violate GATT regulations. If the violator refuses to comply with the ruling, the WTO allows other states to impose appropriate trade sanctions on the transgressor. As a result, according to one prominent critic, U.S. environmentalist, consumer rights advocate, and presidential candidate Ralph Nader,

> Under the new system, many decisions that affect billions of people are no longer made by local or national governments but instead, if challenged by any WTO member nation, would be deferred to a group of unelected bureaucrats sitting behind closed doors in Geneva [which is where the headquarters of the WTO are located]. The bureaucrats can decide whether or not people in California can prevent the destruction of the last virgin forests or determine if carcinogenic pesticides can be banned from their foods; or whether European countries have the right to ban dangerous biotech hormones in meat.... At risk is the very basis of democracy and accountable decision making.[72]

In contrast to Nader's rhetoric, many economists and politicians maintain that the power of supranational organizations such as the WTO is limited to what nation-states collectively agree to grant. They argue that bodies such as the United Nations and the WTO exist to serve the collective interests of member states, not to subvert those interests. Supporters of supranational organizations point out that the power of these bodies rests largely on their ability to persuade member states to follow a certain action. If these bodies fail to serve the collective interests of member states, those states will withdraw their support and the supranational organization will quickly collapse. In this view, real power still resides with individual nation-states, not supranational organizations.

GLOBALIZATION AND THE WORLD'S POOR

Critics of globalization argue that despite the supposed benefits associated with free trade and investment, over the past hundred years or so the gap between the rich and poor nations of the world has gotten wider. In 1870, the average income per capita in the world's 17 richest nations was 2.4 times that of all other countries. In 1990, the same group was 4.5 times as rich as the rest.[73] While recent history has shown that some of the world's poorer nations are capable of rapid periods of economic growth—witness the transformation that has occurred in some Southeast Asian nations such as South Korea, Thailand, and Malaysia—there appear to be strong forces for stagnation among the world's poorest nations. A quarter of the countries with a GDP per capita of less than $1,000 in 1960 had growth rates of less than zero from 1960 to 1995, and a third had growth rates of less than 0.05 percent.[74] Critics argue that if globalization is such a positive development, this divergence between the rich and poor should not have occurred.

Although the reasons for economic stagnation vary, several factors stand out, none of which have anything to do with free trade or globalization.[75] Many of the world's poorest countries have suffered from totalitarian governments, economic policies that destroyed wealth rather than facilitated its creation, endemic corruption, scant protection for property rights, and war. Such factors help explain why countries such as Afghanistan, Cambodia, Cuba, Haiti, Iraq, Libya, Nigeria, Sudan, Vietnam, and Zaire have failed to improve the economic lot of their citizens during recent decades. A complicating factor is the rapidly expanding populations in many of these countries. Without a major change in government, population growth may exacerbate their problems. Promoters of free trade argue that the best way for these countries to improve their lot is to lower their barriers to free trade and investment and to implement economic policies based on free market economics.[76]

Many of the world's poorer nations are being held back by large debt burdens. Of particular concern are the 40 or so "highly indebted poorer countries" (HIPCs), which are home to some 700 million people. Among these countries, the average government debt burden is equivalent to 85 percent of the value of the economy, as measured by gross domestic product, and the annual cost of serving government debt consumes 15 percent of the country's export earnings.[77] Servicing such a heavy debt load leaves the governments of these countries with little left to invest in important public infrastructure projects, such as education, health care, roads, and power. The result is the HIPCs are trapped in a cycle of poverty and debt that inhibits economic development. Free trade alone, some argue, is a necessary but not sufficient prerequisite to help these countries bootstrap

U2's Bono has actively lobbied to have the unpayable debt of poor countries written off.

themselves out of poverty. Instead, large-scale debt relief is needed for the world's poorest nations to give them the opportunity to restructure their economies and start the long climb toward prosperity. Supporters of debt relief also argue that new democratic governments in poor nations should not be forced to honor debts that their corrupt and dictatorial predecessors incurred and mismanaged long ago.

In the late 1990s, a debt relief movement began to gain ground among the political establishment in the world's richer nations.[78] Fueled by high-profile endorsements from Irish rock star Bono (who has been a tireless and increasingly effective advocate for debt relief), Pope John Paul II, the Dalai Lama, and influential Harvard economist Jeffrey Sachs, the debt relief movement was instrumental in persuading the United States to enact legislation in 2000 that provided $435 million in debt relief for HIPCs. More important perhaps, the United States also backed an IMF plan to sell some of its gold reserves and use the proceeds to help with debt relief. The IMF and World Bank have now picked up the banner and have embarked on a systematic debt relief program.

For such a program to have a lasting effect, however, debt relief must be matched by wise investment in public projects that boost economic growth (such as education) and by the adoption of economic policies that facilitate investment and trade. The rich nations of the world also can help by reducing barriers to the importation of products from the world's poorer nations, particularly tariffs on imports of agricultural products and textiles. High tariff barriers and other impediments to trade make it difficult for poor countries to export more of their agricultural production. The World Trade Organization has estimated that if the developed nations of the world eradicated subsidies to their agricultural producers and removed tariff barriers to trade in agriculture this would raise global economic welfare by $128 billion, with $30 billion of that going to developing nations, many of which are highly indebted. The faster growth associated with expanded trade in agriculture could reduce the number of people living in poverty by as much as 13 percent by 2015, according to the WTO.[79]

Managing in the Global Marketplace

Much of this book is concerned with the challenges of managing in an international business. An **international business** is any firm that engages in international trade or investment. A firm does not have to become a multinational enterprise, investing directly in operations in other countries, to engage in international business, although multinational enterprises are international businesses. All a firm has to do is export or import products from other countries. As the world shifts toward a truly integrated global economy, more firms, both large and small, are becoming international businesses. What does this shift toward a global economy mean for managers within an international business?

As their organizations increasingly engage in cross-border trade and investment, managers need to recognize that the task of managing an international business differs from that of managing a purely domestic business in many ways. At the most fundamental level, the differences arise from the simple fact that countries are different. Countries differ in their cultures, political systems, economic systems, legal systems, and levels of economic development. Despite all the talk about the emerging global village, and despite the trend toward globalization of markets and production, as we shall see in this book, many of these differences are very profound and enduring.

Differences between countries require that an international business vary its practices country by country. Marketing a product in Brazil may require a different approach from marketing the product in Germany; managing U.S. workers might require different skills than managing Japanese workers; maintaining close relations with a particular level of government may be very important in Mexico and irrelevant in Great Britain; pursuing a business strategy might be successful in Canada but might not work in South Korea; and so on. Managers in an international business must not only be sensitive to these differences, but they must also adopt the appropriate policies and strategies for coping with them. Much of this book is devoted to explaining the sources of these differences and the methods for successfully coping with them.

A further way in which international business differs from domestic business is the greater complexity of managing an international business. In addition to the problems that arise from the differences between countries, a manager in an international business is confronted with a range of other issues that the manager in a domestic business never confronts. The managers of an international business must decide where in the world to site production activities to minimize costs and to maximize value added. They must decide whether it is ethical to adhere to the lower labor and environmental standards found in many less developed nations. Then they must decide how best to coordinate and control globally dispersed production activities (which, as we shall see later in the book, is not a trivial problem). The managers in an international business also must decide which foreign markets to enter and which to avoid. They must choose the appropriate mode for entering a particular foreign country. Is it best to export its product to the foreign country? Should the firm allow a local company to produce its product under license in that country? Should the firm enter into a joint venture with a local firm to produce its product in that country? Or should the firm set up a wholly owned subsidiary to serve the market in that country? As we shall see, the choice of entry mode is critical because it has major implications for the long-term health of the firm.

Conducting business transactions across national borders requires understanding the rules governing the international trading and investment system. Managers in an international business must also deal with government restrictions on international trade and investment. They must find ways to work within the limits imposed by specific governmental interventions. As this book explains, even though many governments are nominally committed to free trade, they often intervene to regulate cross-border trade and investment. Managers within international businesses must develop strategies and policies for dealing with such interventions.

Cross-border transactions also require that money be converted from the firm's home currency into a foreign currency and vice versa. Because currency exchange rates vary in response to changing economic conditions, managers in an international business must develop policies for dealing with exchange rate movements. A firm that adopts a wrong policy can lose large amounts of money, whereas one that adopts the right policy can increase the profitability of its international transactions.

In sum, managing an international business is different from managing a purely domestic business for at least four reasons: (1) countries are different, (2) the range of problems a manager in an international business confronts is wider and the problems themselves more complex than the problems a manager in a domestic business confronts, (3) an international business must find ways to work within the limits imposed by government intervention in the international trade and investment system, and (4) international transactions involve converting money into different currencies.

In this book we examine all these issues in depth, paying close attention to the different strategies and policies that managers pursue to deal with the various challenges created when a firm becomes an international business. Chapters 2 and 3 explore how countries differ from each other with regard to their political, economic, legal, and cultural institutions. Chapter 4 takes a detailed look at the ethical issues that arise in international business. Chapters 5 to 8 look at the international trade and investment environment within which international businesses must operate. Chapters 9 to 11 review the international monetary system. These chapters focus on the nature of the foreign exchange market and the emerging global monetary system. Chapters 12 to 14 explore the strategy of international businesses. Chapters 15 to 20 look at the management of various functional operations within an international business, including production, marketing, and human relations. By the time you complete this book, you should have a good grasp of the issues that managers working within international business have to grapple with on a daily basis, and you should be familiar with the range of strategies and operating policies available to compete more effectively in today's rapidly emerging global economy.

CHAPTER SUMMARY

This chapter sets the scene for the rest of the book. It shows how the world economy is becoming more global and reviews the main drivers of globalization, arguing that they seem to be thrusting nation-states toward a more tightly integrated global economy. We looked at how the nature of international business is changing in response to the changing global economy; we discussed some concerns raised by rapid globalization; and we reviewed implications of rapid globalization for individual managers. The chapter made the following points:

1. Over the past two decades, we have witnessed the globalization of markets and production.

2. The globalization of markets implies that national markets are merging into one huge marketplace. However, it is important not to push this view too far.

3. The globalization of production implies that firms are basing individual productive activities at the optimal world locations for the particular activities. As a consequence, it is increasingly irrelevant to talk about American products, Japanese products, or German products, since these are being replaced by "global" products.

4. Two factors seem to underlie the trend toward globalization: declining trade barriers and changes in communication, information, and transportation technologies.

5. Since the end of World War II, barriers to the free flow of goods, services, and capital have been lowered significantly. More than anything else, this has facilitated the trend toward the globalization of production and has enabled firms to view the world as a single market.

6. As a consequence of the globalization of production and markets, in the last decade world trade has grown faster than world output, foreign direct investment has surged, imports have penetrated more deeply into the world's industrial nations, and competitive pressures have increased in industry after industry.

7. The development of the microprocessor and related developments in communication and information processing technology have helped firms link their worldwide operations into sophisticated information networks. Jet air travel, by shrinking travel time, has also helped to link the worldwide operations of international businesses. These changes have enabled firms to achieve tight coordination of their worldwide operations and to view the world as a single market.

8. In the 1960s, the U.S. economy was dominant in the world, U.S. firms accounted for most of the foreign direct investment in the world economy, U.S. firms dominated the list of large multinationals, and roughly half the world—the centrally planned economies of the Communist world—was closed to Western businesses.

9. By the mid-1990s, the U.S. share of world output had been cut in half and Western European and Southeast Asian economies accounted for major shares. The U.S. share of worldwide foreign direct investment had also fallen, by about two-thirds. U.S. multinationals were now facing competition from a large number of Japanese and European multinationals. In addition, mini-multinationals emerged.

10. One of the most dramatic developments of the past 20 years has been the collapse of communism in Eastern Europe, which has created enormous long-run opportunities for international businesses. In addition, the move toward free market economies in China and Latin America is creating opportunities (and threats) for Western international businesses.

11. The benefits and costs of the emerging global economy are being hotly debated among businesspeople, economists, and politicians. The debate focuses on the impact of globalization on jobs, wages, the environment, working conditions, and national sovereignty.

12. Managing an international business is different from managing a domestic business for at least four reasons: (*a*) countries are different, (*b*) the range of problems confronted by a manager in an international business is wider and the problems themselves more complex than those confronted by a manager in a domestic business, (*c*) managers in an international business must find ways to work within the limits imposed by governments' intervention in the international trade and investment system, and (*d*) international transactions involve converting money into different currencies.

Critical Thinking and Discussion Questions

1. Describe the shifts in the world economy over the past 30 years. What are the implications of these shifts for international businesses based in Great Britain? North America? Hong Kong?

2. "The study of international business is fine if you are going to work in a large multinational enterprise, but it has no relevance for individuals who are going to work in small firms." Evaluate this statement.

3. How have changes in technology contributed to the globalization of markets and production? Would the globalization of production and markets have been possible without these technological changes?

4. "Ultimately, the study of international business is no different from the study of domestic business. Thus, there is no point in having a separate course on international business." Evaluate this statement.

5. How might the Internet and the associated World Wide Web affect international business activity and the globalization of the world economy?

6. If current trends continue, China may be the world's largest economy by 2020. Discuss the possible implications of such a development for (*a*) the world trading system, (*b*) the world monetary system, (*c*) the business strategy of today's European and U.S. global corporations, and (*d*) global commodity prices.

7. Reread the Country Focus "Outsourcing American Health Care," then answer the following questions:

   a. A decade ago the idea that medical procedures might move offshore was unthinkable. Today it is a reality. What trends have facilitated this process?

   b. Is the globalization of health care good or bad for patients?

   c. Is the globalization of health care good or bad for the American economy?

   d. Who might benefit from the globalization of health care? Who might lose?

   e. Do you think that the U.S. government should restrict the outsourcing of medical procedures to developing nations? What if physicians in those countries are certified by U.S. medical institutions?

Research Task

Use the globalEDGE™ site to complete the following exercises:

1. Your company has developed a new product that has universal appeal across countries and cultures. In fact, it is expected to achieve high penetration rates in all the countries where it is introduced, regardless of the average income of the local populace. Considering the costs of the product launch, the management team has decided to initially introduce the product only in countries that have a sizeable population base. You are required to prepare a preliminary report with the top ten countries in terms of population size. A member of management has indicated that a resource called the "World Population Data Sheet" may be useful for the report. Since growth opportunities are another major concern, the average population growth rates should be listed also for management's consideration.

2. You are working for a company that is considering investing in a foreign country. Investing in countries with different traditions is an important element of your company's long-term strategic goals. As such, management has requested a report regarding the attractiveness of alternative countries based on the potential return of FDI. Accordingly, the ranking of the top 25 countries in terms of FDI attractiveness is a crucial ingredient for your report. A colleague mentioned a potentially useful tool called the "FDI Confidence Index" which is updated periodically. Find this index, and provide additional information regarding how the index is constructed.

CLOSING CASE

IKEA—The Global Retailer

IKEA may be the world's most successful global retailer. Established by Ingvar Kamprad in Sweden in 1943 when he was just 17 years old, today the home-furnishing superstore has grown into a global cult brand with 230 stores in 33 countries that host 410 million shoppers a year and generate sales of €14.8 billion ($17.7 billion). Kamprad himself, who still owns the private company, is rumored to be the world's richest man.

IKEA's target market is the global middle class who are looking for low-priced but attractively designed furniture and household items. The company applies the same basic formula worldwide: Open large warehouse stores festooned in the blue and yellow colors of the Swedish flag that offer 8,000 to 10,000 items, from kitchen cabinets to candlesticks. Use wacky promotions to drive traffic into the stores. Configure the interior of the stores so that customers have to pass through each department to get to the checkout. Add restaurants and child care facilities so that shoppers stay as long as possible. Price the items as low as possible. Make sure that product design reflects the simple, clean Swedish lines that have become IKEA's trademark. And then watch the results—customers who enter the store planning to buy a $40 coffee table and end up spending $500 on everything from storage units to kitchenware.

IKEA aims to reduce the price of its offerings by 2 to 3 percent per year, which requires relentless attention to cost cutting. With a network of 1,300 suppliers in 53 countries, IKEA devotes considerable attention to finding the right manufacturer for each item. Consider the company's best-selling Klippan love seat. Designed in 1980, the Klippan, with its clean lines, bright colors, simple legs, and compact size, has sold some 1.5 million units since its introduction. IKEA originally manufactured the product in Sweden but soon transferred production to lower-cost suppliers in Poland. As demand for the Klippan grew, IKEA then decided that it made more sense to work with suppliers in each of the company's big markets to avoid the costs associated with shipping the product all over the world. Today there are five suppliers of the frames in Europe, plus three in the United States and two in China. To reduce the cost of the cotton slipcovers, IKEA has concentrated production in four core suppliers in China and Europe. The resulting efficiencies from these global sourcing decisions enabled IKEA to reduce the price of the Klippan by some 40 percent between 1999 and 2005.

Despite its standard formula, to achieve global success IKEA had to adapt its offerings to the tastes and preferences of consumers in different nations. IKEA first discovered this in the early 1990s when it entered the United States. The company soon found that its European-style offerings didn't always resonate with American consumers. Beds were measured in centimeters, not the king, queen, and twin sizes with which Americans are familiar. Sofas weren't big enough, wardrobe drawers were not deep enough, glasses were too small, curtains too short, and U.S. size appliances didn't fit in the kitchens. Since then, IKEA has redesigned its U.S. offerings to appeal to American consumers, which has resulted in stronger sales. The same process is now unfolding in China, where the company plans to establish 10 stores by 2010. The store layout in China reflects the layout of many Chinese apartments, and since many Chinese apartments have balconies, IKEA's Chinese stores include a balcony section. IKEA also has had to adapt its locations in China, where car ownership is still not widespread. In the West, IKEA stores are generally located in suburban areas and have lots of parking space. In China, stores are located near public transportation, and IKEA offers delivery services so that Chinese customers can get their purchases home.[80]

Case Discussion Questions

1. How has the globalization of markets benefited IKEA?

2. How has the globalization of production benefited IKEA?

3. What does the IKEA story teach you about the limits of treating the entire world as a single integrated global marketplace?

Notes

1. D. J. Lynch, "Flat Panel TVs Display Effects of Globalization," *USA Today*, May 8, 2007, pp. 1B and 2B; P. Engardio and E. Woyke, "Flat Panels, Thin Margins," *Business Week*, February 26, 2007, p. 50; B. Womack, "Flat TV Seller Vizio Hits $600 Million in Sales, Growing," *Orange County Business Journal*, September 4, 2007, pp. 1, 64.

2. Trade statistics from World Trade Organization, trade statistics database, accessed June 11, 2006 at http://stat.wto.org/Home/WSDBHome.aspx. Foreign exchange statistics from Metrics 2.0 at http://www.metrics2.com/blog/2006/10/06/foreign_exchange_daily_trading_volume_to_hit_3_tri.html, accessed June 12th, 2007.

3. T. L. Friedman, *The World Is Flat* (New York: Farrar, Straus and Giroux, 2005).

4. Ibid.

5. T. Levitt, "The Globalization of Markets," *Harvard Business Review*, May–June 1983, pp. 92–102.

6. U.S. Department of Commerce, "A Profile of U.S. Exporting Companies, 2000–2001," February 2003; report available at www.census.gov/foreign-trade/aip/index.html#profile.

7. Ibid.

8. C. M. Draffen, "Going Global: Export Market Proves Profitable for Region's Small Businesses," *Newsday*, March 19, 2001, p. C18.

9. B. Benoit and R. Milne, "Germany's Best Kept Secret, How Its Exporters Are Betting the World," *Financial Times*, May 19, 2006, p. 11.

10. See F. T. Knickerbocker, *Oligopolistic Reaction and Multinational Enterprise* (Boston: Harvard Business School Press, 1973); and R. E. Caves, "Japanese Investment in the U.S.: Lessons for the Economic Analysis of Foreign Investment," *The World Economy* 16 (1993), pp. 279–300.

11. I. Metthee, "Playing a Large Part," *Seattle Post-Intelligencer*, April 9, 1994, p. 13.

12. D. Pritchard, "Are Federal Tax Laws and State Subsidies for Boeing 787 Selling America Short?" *Aviation Week*, April 12, 2004, pp. 74–75.

13. R. B. Reich, *The Work of Nations* (New York: A. A. Knopf, 1991).

14. Sources: G. Colvin, "Think Your Job Can't Be Sent to India?" *Fortune*, December 13, 2004, p. 80; A. Pollack, "Who's Reading Your X-Ray," *The New York Times*, November 16, 2003, pp. 1, 9; S. Rai, "Low Costs Lure Foreigners to India for Medical Care," *The New York Times*, April 7, 2005, p. C6; J. Solomon, "Traveling Cure: India's New Coup in Outsourcing," *The Wall Street Journal*, April 26, 2004, p. A1; J. Slater, "Increasing Doses in India," *Far Eastern Economic Review*, February 19, 2004, pp. 32–35; U. Kher, "Outsourcing Your Heart," *Time*, May 29, 2006, pp. 44–47; and "Sun, Sand and Scalpels," *The Economist*, March 10, 2007, p. 62.

15. United Nations, "The UN in Brief," www.un.org/Overview/brief.html.

16. J. A. Frankel, "Globalization of the Economy," National Bureau of Economic Research, working paper no. 7858, 2000.

17. J. Bhagwati, *Protectionism* (Cambridge, MA: MIT Press, 1989).

18. F. Williams, "Trade Round Like This May Never Be Seen Again," *Financial Times*, April 15, 1994, p. 8.

19. W. Vieth, "Major Concessions Lead to Success for WTO Talks," *Los Angeles Times*, November 14, 2001, p. A1; and "Seeds Sown for Future Growth," *The Economist*, November 17, 2001, pp. 65–66.

20. United Nations, *World Investment Report*, 2006.

21. Ibid.

22. World Trade Organization, *International Trade Trends and Statistics*, 2006 (Geneva: WTO, 2007).

23. United Nations, *World Investment Report*, 2006; and "Foreign Direct Investment Rose by 34% in 2006," UN Conference on Trade and Development, press release, January 23, 2007.

24. World Trade Organization, *International Trade Statistics*, 2006 (Geneva: WTO, 2006); and United Nations, *World Investment Report*, 2006.

25. United Nations, *World Investment Report*, 2006.

26. Moore's Law is named after Intel founder Gordon Moore.

27. Frankel, "Globalization of the Economy."

28. J. G. Fernald and V. Greenfield, "The Fall and Rise of the Global Economy," *Chicago Fed Letters*, April 2001, pp. 1–4.

29. Data compiled from various sources and listed by CyberAtlas at http://cyberatlas.internet.com/big-picture.

30. From http://www.shop.org/soro07/pr-051407.asp, accessed June 12, 2007.

31. For a counterpoint, see "Geography and the Net: Putting It in Its Place," *The Economist*, August 11, 2001, pp. 18–20.

32. Frankel, "Globalization of the Economy."

33. Data from Bureau of Transportation Statistics, 2001.

34. Fernald and Greenfield, "The Fall and Rise of the Global Economy."

35. Data located at www.bts.gov/publications/us_international_trade_and_freight_transportation_trends/2003/index.html.

36. "America's Pain, India's Gain: Outsourcing," *The Economist*, January 11, 2003, p. 59; "The World Is Our Oyster," *The Economist*, October 7, 2006, pp. 9–10; "IBM and Globalization: Hungry Tiger, Dancing Elephant," *The Economist*, April 7, 2007, pp 67–69.

37. N. Hood and J. Young, *The Economics of the Multinational Enterprise* (New York: Longman, 1973).

38. United Nations, *World Investment Report, 2006*.

39. Ibid.

40. Ibid.

41. H. L. Sirkin, "Someone May Be Gaining on Us," *Barron's*, February 5, 2007, p. 53; "Hisense Plans to Grab More International Sales," *Sino Cast China IT Watch*, November 30, 2006; "Hisense's Wonder Chip," *Financial Times Information Limited—Asian Intelligence Wire*, October 30, 2006; Hisense's Web site, http://www.hisense.com/en/index.jsp, accessed June 14, 2007.

42. S. Chetty, "Explosive International Growth and Problems of Success among Small and Medium Sized Firms," *International Small Business Journal*, February 2003, pp. 5–28.

43. R. A. Mosbacher, "Opening Up Export Doors for Smaller Firms," *Seattle Times*, July 24, 1991, p. A7.

44. "Small Companies Learn How to Sell to the Japanese," *Seattle Times*, March 19, 1992.

45. Holstein, "Why Johann Can Export, but Johnny Can't."

46. N. Buckley and A. Ostrovsky, "Back to Business—How Putin's Allies Are Turning Russia into a Corporate State," *Financial Times*, June 19, 2006, p. 11.

47. J. E. Stiglitz, *Globalization and Its Discontents* (New York: W. W. Norton, 2003); J. Bhagwati, *In Defense of Globalization* (New York: Oxford University Press, 2004); and Friedman, *The World Is Flat*.

48. See, for example, R. Batra, *The Myth of Free Trade* (New York: Touchstone Books, 1993); W. Greider, *One World, Ready or Not: The Manic Logic of Global Capitalism* (New York: Simon and Schuster, 1997); and D. Radrik, *Has*

Globalization Gone Too Far? (Washington, DC: Institution for International Economics, 1997).

49. Sources: "Behind the Bluster," *The Economist*, May 26, 2001; "The French Farmers' Anti-global Hero," *The Economist*, July 8, 2000; C. Trueheart, "France's Golden Arch Enemy?" *Toronto Star*, July 1, 2000; J. Henley, "Grapes of Wrath Scare Off U.S. Firm," *The Economist*, May 18, 2001, p. 11; and United Nations, *World Investment Report, 2006* (New York and Geneva: United Nations, 2006).

50. J. Goldsmith, "The Winners and the Losers," in *The Case against the Global Economy*, eds. J. Mander and E. Goldsmith (San Francisco: Sierra Club, 1996); and Lou Dobbs, *Exporting America* (New York: Time Warner Books, 2004).

51. For an excellent summary see "The Globalization of Labor," Chapter 5 in IMF, *World Economic Outlook 2007* (April 2007). Also see R. Freeman, "Labor Market Imbalances," Harvard University Working Paper, http://www.bos.frb.org/economic/conf/conf51/papers/freeman.pdf, accessed June 14, 2007.

52. D. L. Bartlett and J. B. Steele, "America: Who Stole the Dream," *Philadelphia Inquirer*, September 9, 1996.

53. For example, see Paul Krugman, *Pop Internationalism* (Cambridge, MA: MIT Press, 1996).

54. For example, see B. Milanovic and L. Squire, "Does Tariff Liberalization Increase Wage Inequality?" *National Bureau of Economic Research*, working paper no. 11046, January 2005; and B. Milanovic, "Can We Discern the Effect of Globalization on Income Distribution?" *World Bank Economic Review*, 19, 2005, pp. 21–44. Also see the summary in "The Globalization of Labor."

55. Jared Bernstein, Elizabeth C. McNichol, Lawrence Mishel, and Robert Zahradnik, "Pulling Apart: A State by State Analysis of Income Trends," *Economic Policy Institute*, January 2000.

56. See "The Globalization of Labor."

57. M. Forster and M. Pearson, "Income Distribution and Poverty in the OECD Area," *OECD Economic Studies* 34 (2002).

58. Bernstein et al., "Pulling Apart."

59. See "The Globalization of Labor."

60. See Krugman, *Pop Internationalism*; and D. Belman and T. M. Lee, "International Trade and the Performance of U.S. Labor Markets," in *U.S. Trade Policy and Global Growth*, ed. R. A. Blecker (New York: Economic Policy Institute, 1996).

61. Freeman, "Labor Market Imbalances."

62. E. Goldsmith, "Global Trade and the Environment," in *The Case against the Global Economy*,

eds. J. Mander and E. Goldsmith (San Francisco: Sierra Club, 1996).

63. P. Choate, *Jobs at Risk: Vulnerable U.S. Industries and Jobs under NAFTA* (Washington, DC: Manufacturing Policy Project, 1993).

64. Ibid.

65. B. Lomborg, *The Skeptical Environmentalist* (Cambridge: Cambridge University Press, 2001).

66. H. Nordstrom and S. Vaughan, *Trade and the Environment, World Trade Organization Special Studies No. 4* (Geneva: WTO, 1999).

67. Figures are from "Freedom's Journey: A Survey of the 20th Century. Our Durable Planet," *The Economist*, September 11, 1999, p. 30.

68. For an exhaustive review of the empirical literature, see B. R. Copeland and M. Scott Taylor, "Trade, Growth and the Environment," *Journal of Economic Literature*, March 2004, pp. 7–77.

69. G. M. Grossman and A. B. Krueger, "Economic Growth and the Environment," *Quarterly Journal of Economics* 110 (1995), pp. 353–78.

70. Krugman, *Pop Internationalism*.

71. R. Kuttner, "Managed Trade and Economic Sovereignty," in *U.S. Trade Policy and Global Growth*, ed. R. A. Blecker (New York: Economic Policy Institute, 1996).

72. R. Nader and L. Wallach, "GATT, NAFTA, and the Subversion of the Democratic Process," in *U.S. Trade Policy and Global Growth*, ed. R. A. Blecker (New York: Economic Policy Institute, 1996), pp. 93–94.

73. L. Pritchett, "Divergence, Big Time," *Journal of Economic Perspectives* 11, no. 3 (Summer 1997), pp. 3–18.

74. Ibid.

75. W. Easterly, "How Did Heavily Indebted Poor Countries Become Heavily Indebted?" *World Development*, October 2002, pp. 1677–96; and J. Sachs, *The End of Poverty* (New York, Penguin Books, 2006).

76. See D. Ben-David, H. Nordstrom, and L. A. Winters, "Trade, Income Disparity and Poverty," *World Trade Organization Special Studies No. 5* (Geneva: WTO, 1999).

77. W. Easterly, "Debt Relief," *Foreign Policy*, November–December 2001, pp. 20–26.

78. J. Sachs, "Sachs on Development: Helping the World's Poorest," *The Economist*, August 14, 1999, pp. 17–20.

79. World Trade Organization, *Annual Report 2003* (Geneva: WTO, 2004).

80. Sources: K. Capell, A. Sains, C. Lindblad, and A.T. Palmer, "IKEA," *BusinessWeek*, November 14, 2005, pp. 96–101; K. Capell et al., "What a Sweetheart of a Love Seat," *BusinessWeek*, November 14, 2005, p. 101; P. M. Miller, "IKEA with Chinese Characteristics," *Chinese Business Review*, July–August 2004, pp 36–69; C. Daniels, "Create IKEA, Make Billions, Take Bus," *Fortune*, May 3, 2004, p. 44; and IKEA's Web site, www.ikea.com, accessed June 14, 2007.

Chavez's Venezuela

Hugo Chavez, a former military officer who was once jailed for engineering a failed coup attempt, was elected president of Venezuela in 1998. Chavez, a self-styled democratic socialist, won the presidential election by campaigning against corruption, economic mismanagement, and the "harsh realities" of global capitalism. When he took office in February 1999, Chavez claimed that he had inherited the worst economic situation in the country's recent history. He wasn't far off the mark. A collapse in the price of oil, which accounted for 70 percent of the country's exports, left Venezuela with a large budget deficit and forced the economy into a deep recession.

Soon after taking office, Chavez proceeded to try to consolidate his hold over the apparatus of government. A constituent assembly, dominated by Chavez followers, drafted a new constitution that strengthened the powers of the presidency and allowed Chavez (if reelected) to stay in office until 2012. Subsequently, the national

congress, which was controlled by Chavez supporters, approved a measure allowing the government to remove and appoint Supreme Court justices, effectively increasing Chavez's hold over the judiciary. Chavez also extended government control over the media. By 2006, Freedom House, which annually assesses political and civil liberties worldwide, concluded that Venezuela was only "partly free" and that freedoms were being progressively curtailed.

On the economic front, things remained rough. The economy shrank by 9 percent in 2002 and another 8 percent in 2003. Unemployment remained persistently high at 15 to 17 percent and the poverty rate rose to more than 50 percent of the population. A 2003 study by the World Bank concluded that Venezuela was one of the most regulated economies in the world and that state controls over business activities gave public officials ample opportunities to enrich themselves by demanding bribes in return for permission to expand operations or enter

National Differences in Political Economy

LEARNING OBJECTIVES

After you have read this chapter you should:

LO¹ Understand how the political systems of countries differ.

LO² Understand how the economic systems of countries differ.

LO³ Understand how the legal systems of countries differ.

LO⁴ Be able to explain what determines the level of economic development of a nation.

LO⁵ Discuss the macro-political and economic changes taking place worldwide.

LO⁶ Describe how transition economies are moving toward market based systems.

LO⁷ Articulate the implications for management practice of national difference in political economy.

new lines of business. Indeed, despite Chavez's anti-corruption rhetoric, Transparency International, which ranks the world's nations according to the extent of public corruption, has noted that corruption has increased under Chavez. In 2006, Transparency International ranked Venezuela 138 out of 163 nations, down from 114 in 2004. Consistent with his socialist rhetoric, Chavez has progressively taken various enterprises into state ownership and has required that other enterprises be restructured as "workers' cooperatives" in return for government loans. In addition, the government has begun to seize large rural farms and ranches that Chavez claims are not sufficiently productive, turning them into state-owned cooperatives.

In 2004, the world oil market bailed Chavez out of mounting economic difficulties. Oil prices surged from the low $20s, reaching $70 a barrel by the spring of 2006, and Venezuela, the world's fifth-largest producer, began to reap a bonanza. On the back of surging oil exports, the economy grew by 18 percent in 2004, 9 percent in 2005 and 10.5 percent in 2006. Chavez's reaction to the oil price increase was to extend government control over foreign oil producers doing business in Venezuela, which he accused of making outsized profits at the expense of a poor nation. In 2005, he increased government royalties on oil sales from 1 percent to 30 percent and the tax rate on sales from 34 to 50 percent. In 2006, he announced plans to reduce foreign companies' stakes in oil projects in the Orinoco regions and to give the state-run oil company, Petroleos de Venezuela SA, a majority position. Riding a wave of popularity at home, in December 2006 Chavez won reelection as president. He celebrated his victory by stepping on the revolutionary accelerator. Parliament gave him the power to legislate by decree for 18 months, and a committee of his supporters started to draft a constitutional reform to turn Venezuela into an avowedly socialist country and to allow the president to stand for reelection indefinitely.[1]

Introduction

International business is much more complicated than domestic business because countries differ in many ways. Countries have different political, economic, and legal systems. Cultural practices can vary dramatically, as can the education and skill level of the population, and countries are at different stages of economic development. All these differences can and do have major implications for the practice of international business. They have a profound impact on the benefits, costs, and risks associated with doing business in different countries; the way in which operations in different countries should be managed; and the strategy international firms should pursue in different countries. A main function of this chapter and the next is to develop an awareness of and appreciation for the significance of country differences in political systems, economic systems, legal systems, and national culture. Another function of the two chapters is to describe how the political, economic, legal, and cultural systems of many of the world's nation-states are evolving and to draw out the implications of these changes for the practice of international business.

The opening case illustrates some of the issues covered in this chapter. Under the leadership of Hugo Chavez, Venezuela has shifted to the left. The state has become more involved in business activity, regulation has expanded, and private enterprise is on the defensive, which has hurt economic growth. Corruption, long a problem in the country, has if anything gotten worse, despite the fact that Chavez originally came to power by running on an anticorruption platform. As we shall see in this chapter, corruption also tends to depress economic growth. Moreover, Chavez has unilaterally rewritten the contracts with foreign oil companies that have invested in Venezuela, raising royalty rates and taxes and demanding that the state-run oil company be given a majority stake in all oil projects. While this may increase the government's take in the short run, if foreign enterprises respond by reducing their investments in Venezuela, as some are now doing, it could further constrain the country's economic growth down the road.

This chapter focuses on how the political, economic, and legal systems of countries differ. Collectively we refer to these systems as constituting the political economy of a country. We use the term **political economy** to stress that the political, economic, and legal systems of a country are interdependent; they interact and influence each other, and in doing so they affect the level of economic well-being. In addition to reviewing these systems, we also explore how differences in political economy influence the benefits, costs, and risks associated with doing business in different countries and how they affect management practice and strategy. In the next chapter, we will look at how differences in culture influence the practice of international business. As noted, the political economy and culture of a nation are not independent of each other. As will become apparent in Chapter 3, culture can exert an impact on political economy—on political, economic, and legal systems in a nation—and the converse can also hold true.

Political Systems

The political system of a country shapes its economic and legal systems.[2] As such, we need to understand the nature of different political systems before discussing economic and legal systems. By **political system** we mean the system of government in a nation. Political systems can be assessed according to two dimensions. The first is the degree to which they emphasize collectivism as opposed to individualism. The second is the degree to which they are democratic or totalitarian. These dimensions are interrelated; systems that emphasize collectivism tend toward totalitarianism, whereas those that place a high value on individualism tend to be democratic. However, a large gray area exists in the middle. It is possible to have democratic societies that emphasize a mix of collectivism and individualism. Similarly, it is possible to have totalitarian societies that are not collectivist.

COLLECTIVISM AND INDIVIDUALISM

Collectivism refers to a political system that stresses the primacy of collective goals over individual goals.[3] When collectivism is emphasized, the needs of society as a whole are generally viewed as being more important than individual freedoms. In such circumstances, an individual's right to do something may be restricted on the grounds that it runs counter to "the good of society" or to "the common good." Advocacy of collectivism can be traced to the ancient Greek philosopher Plato (427–347 BC), who argued in *The Republic* that individual rights should be sacrificed for the good of the majority and that property should be owned in common. Plato did not equate collectivism with equality; he believed that society should be stratified into classes, with those best suited to rule (which for Plato, naturally, were philosophers and soldiers) administering society for the benefit of all. In modern times, socialists have picked up the collectivist mantle.

Socialism

Modern **socialists** trace their intellectual roots to Karl Marx (1818–83), although socialist thought clearly predates Marx (elements of it can be traced to Plato). Marx argued that the few benefit at the expense of the many in a capitalist society where individual freedoms are not restricted. While successful capitalists accumulate considerable wealth, Marx postulated that the wages earned by the majority of workers in a capitalist society would be forced down to subsistence levels. He argued that capitalists expropriate for their own use the value created by workers, while paying workers only subsistence wages in return. According to Marx, the pay of workers does not reflect the full value of their labor. To correct this perceived wrong, Marx advocated state ownership of the basic means of production, distribution, and exchange (i.e., businesses). His logic was that if the state owned the means of production, the state could ensure that workers were fully compensated for their labor. Thus, the idea is to manage state-owned enterprise to benefit society as a whole, rather than individual capitalists.[4]

In the early 20th century, the socialist ideology split into two broad camps. The **communists** believed that socialism could be achieved only through violent revolution and totalitarian dictatorship, whereas the **social democrats** committed themselves to achieving socialism by democratic means, turning their backs on violent revolution and dictatorship. Both versions of socialism waxed and waned during the 20th century. The communist version of socialism reached its high point in the late 1970s, when the majority of the world's population lived in communist states. The countries under Communist Party rule at that time included the former Soviet Union; its Eastern European client nations (e.g., Poland, Czechoslovakia, Hungary); China; the Southeast Asian nations of Cambodia, Laos, and Vietnam; various African nations (e.g., Angola and Mozambique); and the Latin American nations of Cuba and Nicaragua. By the mid-1990s, however, communism was in retreat worldwide. The Soviet Union had collapsed and had been replaced by a collection of 15 republics, many of which were at least nominally structured as democracies. The largely bloodless revolutions of 1989 swept Communism out of Eastern Europe. Although China is still nominally a communist state with substantial limits to individual political freedom, in the economic sphere the country has moved sharply away from strict adherence to communist ideology. Other than China, communism hangs on only in some small fringe states, such as North Korea and Cuba.

Social democracy also seems to have passed a high-water mark, although the ideology may prove to be more enduring than communism. Social democracy has had perhaps its greatest influence in a number of democratic Western nations, including Australia, France, Germany, Great Britain, Norway, Spain, and Sweden, where Social Democratic parties have often held political power. Other countries where social democracy has had an important influence include India and Brazil. Consistent with their Marxists roots, many social democratic governments after World War II nationalized private companies in certain industries, transforming them into state-owned enterprises to be run for the "public good rather than private profit." In Great Britain by the end of the 1970s, for example, state-owned companies had a monopoly in the telecommunications, electricity, gas, coal, railway, and shipbuilding industries, as well as substantial interests in the oil, airline, auto, and steel industries.

However, experience demonstrated that state ownership of the means of production ran counter to the public interest. In many countries, state-owned companies performed poorly. Protected from competition by their monopoly position and guaranteed government financial support, many became increasingly inefficient. Individuals paid for the luxury of state ownership through higher prices and higher taxes. As a consequence, a number of Western democracies voted many Social Democratic parties out of office in the late 1970s and early 1980s. They were succeeded by political parties, such as Britain's Conservative Party and Germany's Christian Democratic Party, that were more committed to free market economics. These parties sold state-owned enterprises to private investors (a process referred to as **privatization**). Even where Social Democratic parties have regained power, as in Great Britain in 1997 when the left-leaning Labor Party won control of the government, they too now seem committed to continued private ownership.

Individualism

The opposite of collectivism, **individualism** refers to a philosophy that an individual should have freedom in his or her economic and political pursuits. In contrast to collectivism, individualism stresses that the interests of the individual should take precedence over the interests of the state. Like collectivism, individualism can be traced to an ancient Greek philosopher, in this case Plato's disciple Aristotle (384–322 BC). In contrast to Plato, Aristotle argued that individual diversity and private ownership are desirable. In a passage that might have been taken from a speech by contemporary politicians who adhere to a free market ideology, he argued that private property is more highly productive than communal property and will thus stimulate progress. According to Aristotle, communal property receives little care, whereas property that is owned by an individual will receive the greatest care and therefore be most productive.

Individualism was reborn as an influential political philosophy in the Protestant trading nations of England and the Netherlands during the 16th century. The philosophy was refined in the work of a number of British philosophers, including David Hume (1711–76), Adam Smith (1723–90), and John Stuart Mill (1806–73). Individualism exercised a profound influence on those in the American colonies who sought independence from Great Britain. Indeed, the concept underlies the ideas expressed in the Declaration of Independence. In the 20th century, several Nobel Prize–winning economists, including Milton Friedman, Friedrich von Hayek, and James Buchanan, have championed the philosophy.

Individualism is built on two central tenets. The first is an emphasis on the importance of guaranteeing individual freedom and self-expression. As John Stuart Mill put it,

> The sole end for which mankind are warranted, individually or collectively, in interfering with the liberty of action of any of their number is self-protection. . . . The only purpose for which power can be rightfully exercised over any member of a civilized community, against his will, is to prevent harm to others. His own good, either physical or moral, is not a sufficient warrant. . . . The only part of the conduct of any one, for which he is amenable to society, is that which concerns others. In the part which merely concerns himself, his independence is, of right, absolute. Over himself, over his own body and mind, the individual is sovereign.[5]

The second tenet of individualism is that the welfare of society is best served by letting people pursue their own economic self-interest, as opposed to some collective body (such as government) dictating what is in society's best interest. Or as Adam Smith put it in a famous passage from *The Wealth of Nations*, an individual who intends his own gain is

> led by an invisible hand to promote an end which was no part of his intention. Nor is it always worse for the society that it was no part of it. By pursuing his own interest he frequently promotes that of the society more effectually than when he really intends to promote it. I have never known much good done by those who effect to trade for the public good.[6]

The central message of individualism, therefore, is that individual economic and political freedoms are the ground rules on which a society should be based. This puts individualism in conflict with collectivism. Collectivism asserts the primacy of the collective over the individual; individualism asserts the opposite. This underlying ideological conflict shaped much of the recent history of the world. The Cold War, for example, was in many respects a war between collectivism, championed by the former Soviet Union, and individualism, championed by the United States.

In practical terms, individualism translates into an advocacy for democratic political systems and free market economics. Since the late 1980s, the waning of collectivism has been matched by the ascendancy of individualism. Democratic ideals and free market economics have swept away socialism and communism in many states. The changes of the past 20 years go beyond the revolutions in Eastern Europe and the former Soviet Union to include a move toward greater individualism in Latin America and many of the social democratic states of the West (e.g., Great Britain and Sweden). This is not to claim that individualism has finally won a long battle with collectivism. It has clearly not (indeed, during 2005 and into 2006 there were signs of a swing back toward left-leaning socialist ideas in several countries, most notably in Latin America like Venezuela and Bolivia—see the Opening Case). But as a guiding political philosophy, individualism has been on the ascendancy. This is good news for international business because the pro-business and pro–free trade values of individualism create a favorable environment within which international business can thrive.

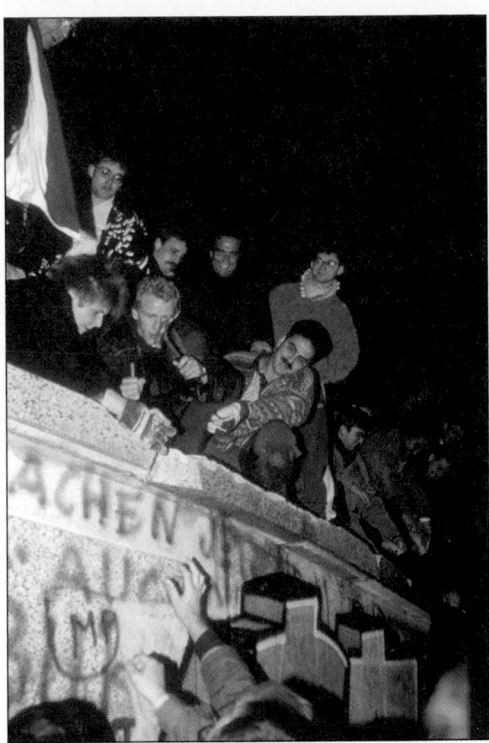

East and West Germans tear down the Berlin Wall on November 9, 1989. Berlin had been politically divided since the end of World War II, with the eastern portion of the city serving as the capital of the German Democratic Republic. The two parts of the city were physically divided in 1961 with the construction of the Berlin Wall.

DEMOCRACY AND TOTALITARIANISM

Democracy and totalitarianism are at different ends of a political dimension. **Democracy** refers to a political system in which government is by the people, exercised either directly or through elected representatives. **Totalitarianism** is a form of government in which one person or political party exercises absolute control over all spheres of human life and prohibits opposing political parties. The democratic–totalitarian dimension is not independent of the collectivism–individualism dimension. Democracy and individualism go hand in hand, as do the communist version of collectivism and totalitarianism. However, gray areas exist; it is possible to have a democratic state in which collective values predominate, and it is possible to have a totalitarian state that is hostile to collectivism and in which some degree of individualism—particularly in the economic sphere—is encouraged. For example, China has moved toward greater individual freedom in the economic sphere, but the country is still ruled by a totalitarian dictatorship that constrains political freedom.

Democracy

The pure form of democracy, as originally practiced by several city-states in ancient Greece, is based on a belief that citizens should be directly involved in decision making. In complex, advanced societies with populations in the tens or hundreds of millions, direct democracy is impractical. Most modern democratic states practice **representative democracy.** In a representative democracy, citizens periodically elect individuals to represent them. These elected representatives then form a government, whose function is to make decisions on behalf of the electorate. In a representative democracy, elected representatives who fail to perform this job adequately will be voted out of office at the next election.

To guarantee that elected representatives can be held accountable for their actions by the electorate, an ideal representative democracy has a number of safeguards that are typically enshrined in constitutional law. These include (1) an individual's right to freedom of expression, opinion, and organization; (2) a free media; (3) regular elections in which all eligible citizens are allowed to vote; (4) universal adult suffrage; (5) limited terms for elected representatives; (6) a fair court system that is independent from the political system; (7) a nonpolitical state bureaucracy; (8) a nonpolitical police force and armed service; and (9) relatively free access to state information.[7]

Totalitarianism

In a totalitarian country, citizens are denied all the constitutional guarantees on which representative democracies are built—an individual's right to freedom of expression and organization, a free media, and regular elections. In most totalitarian states, political repression is widespread, free and fair elections are lacking, media are heavily censored, basic civil liberties are denied, and those who question the right of the rulers to rule are imprisoned, or worse.

Four major forms of totalitarianism exist in the world today. Until recently, the most widespread was **communist totalitarianism.** Communism, however, is in decline worldwide, and most of the Communist Party dictatorships have collapsed since 1989. Exceptions to this trend (so far) are China, Vietnam, Laos, North Korea, and Cuba, although all these states exhibit clear signs that the Communist Party's monopoly on political power is retreating. In many respects, the governments of China, Vietnam, and Laos are communist in name only since those nations now adhere to market-based economic reforms. They remain, however, totalitarian states that deny many basic civil liberties to their populations. On the other hand, there are signs of a swing back toward communist totalitarian ideas in some states, such as Venezuela where the government of Hugo Chavez is starting to display some totalitarian tendencies (see the Opening Case).

A second form of totalitarianism might be labeled **theocratic totalitarianism.** Theocratic totalitarianism is found in states where a party, group, or individual that governs according to religious principles monopolizes political power. The most common form of theocratic totalitarianism is based on Islam and is exemplified by states such as Iran and Saudi Arabia. These states limit freedom of political and religious expression with laws based on Islamic principles.

A third form of totalitarianism might be referred to as **tribal totalitarianism.** Tribal totalitarianism has arisen from time to time in African countries such as Zimbabwe, Tanzania, Uganda, and Kenya. The borders of most African states reflect the administrative boundaries drawn by the old European colonial powers rather than tribal realities. Consequently, the typical African country contains a number of tribes. Tribal totalitarianism occurs when a political party that represents the interests of a particular tribe (and not always the majority tribe) monopolizes power. Such one-party states still exist in Africa.

A fourth major form of totalitarianism might be described as **right-wing totalitarianism.** Right-wing totalitarianism generally permits some individual economic freedom but restricts individual political freedom, frequently on the grounds that it would lead to the rise of communism. A common feature of many right-wing dictatorships is an overt hostility to socialist or communist ideas. Many right-wing totalitarian governments are backed by the military, and in some cases the government may be made up of military officers. The fascist regimes that ruled Germany and Italy in the 1930s and 1940s were right-wing totalitarian states. Until the early 1980s, right-wing dictatorships, many of which were military dictatorships, were common throughout Latin America. They were also found in several Asian countries, particularly South Korea, Taiwan, Singapore, Indonesia, and the Philippines. Since the early 1980s, however, this form of government has been in retreat. Most Latin American countries are now genuine multiparty democracies. Similarly, South Korea, Taiwan, and the Philippines have all become functioning democracies, as has Indonesia (see the closing case).

Economic Systems

It should be clear from the previous section that political ideology and economic systems are connected. In countries where individual goals are given primacy over collective goals, we are more likely to find free market economic systems. In contrast, in countries where collective goals are given preeminence, the state may have taken control over many enterprises; markets in such countries are likely to be restricted rather than free. We can identify three broad types of economic systems—a market economy, a command economy, and a mixed economy.

MARKET ECONOMY

In a pure **market economy,** all productive activities are privately owned, as opposed to being owned by the state. The goods and services that a country produces are not planned by anyone. Production is determined by the interaction of supply and demand and signaled to producers through the price system. If demand for a product exceeds supply, prices will rise, signaling producers to produce more. If supply exceeds demand, prices will fall, signaling producers to produce less. In this system consumers are sovereign. The purchasing patterns of consumers, as signaled to producers through the mechanism of the price system, determine what is produced and in what quantity.

For a market to work in this manner, supply must not be restricted. A supply restriction occurs when a single firm monopolizes a market. In such circumstances, rather than increase output in response to increased demand, a monopolist might restrict output and let prices rise. This allows the monopolist to take a greater profit margin on each unit it sells. Although this is good for the monopolist, it is bad for the consumer, who has to pay higher prices. It also is probably bad for the welfare of society. Since a monopolist has no competitors, it has no incentive to search for ways to lower production costs. Rather, it can simply pass on cost increases to consumers in the form of higher prices. The net result is that the monopolist is likely to become increasingly inefficient, producing high-priced, low-quality goods, and society suffers as a consequence.

Given the dangers inherent in monopoly, the role of government in a market economy is to encourage vigorous free and fair competition between private producers. Governments do this by outlawing monopolies and restrictive business practices designed to monopolize a market (antitrust laws serve this function in the United States). Private ownership also encourages vigorous competition and economic efficiency. Private ownership ensures that entrepreneurs have a right to the profits generated by their own efforts. This gives entrepreneurs an incentive to search for better ways of serving consumer needs. They may introduce new products, develop more efficient production processes, pursue better marketing and after-sale service, or simply manage their businesses more efficiently than their competitors. In turn, the constant improvement in product and process that results from such an incentive, it has been argued, has a major positive impact on economic growth and development.[8]

COMMAND ECONOMY

In a pure **command economy,** the government plans the goods and services that a country produces, the quantity in which they are produced, and the prices at which they are sold. Consistent with the collectivist ideology, the objective of a command economy is for government to allocate resources for "the good of society." In addition, in a pure command economy, all businesses are state owned, the rationale being that the government can then direct them to make investments that are in the best interests of the nation as a whole rather than in the interests of private individuals. Historically, command economies were found in communist countries where collectivist goals were given priority over individual goals. Since the demise of communism in the late 1980s, the number of command economies has fallen dramatically. Some elements of a command economy were also evident in a number of democratic nations led by socialist-inclined governments. France and India both experimented with extensive government planning and state ownership, although government planning has fallen into disfavor in both countries.

While the objective of a command economy is to mobilize economic resources for the public good, the opposite seems to have occurred. In a command economy, state-owned enterprises have little incentive to control costs and be efficient because they cannot go out of business. Also, the abolition of private ownership means there is no incentive for individuals to look for better ways to serve consumer needs; hence, dynamism and innovation are absent from command economies. Instead of growing and becoming more prosperous, such economies tend to stagnate.

MIXED ECONOMY

Between market economies and command economies can be found mixed economies. In a mixed economy, certain sectors of the economy are left to private ownership and free market mechanisms while other sectors have significant state ownership and government planning. Mixed economies were once common throughout much of the world, although they are becoming much less so. Not long ago, Great Britain, France, and Sweden were mixed economies, but extensive privatization has reduced state ownership of businesses in all three nations. A similar trend can be observed in many other countries where there was once a large state sector, such as Brazil, Italy, and India.

In mixed economies, governments also tend to take over troubled firms they consider to be vital to national interests. Consider, for example, the French automobile company Renault. The government took over the company when it ran into serious financial problems. The French government reasoned that the social costs of the unemployment that might result if Renault collapsed were unacceptable, so it nationalized the company to save it from bankruptcy. Renault's competitors weren't thrilled by this move because they had to compete with a company whose costs were subsidized by the state.

🌐 Legal Systems

The **legal system** of a country refers to the rules, or laws, that regulate behavior along with the processes by which the laws are enforced and through which redress for grievances is obtained. The legal system of a country is of immense importance to international business. A country's laws regulate business practice, define the manner in which business transactions are to be executed, and set down the rights and obligations of those involved in business transactions. The legal environments of countries differ in significant ways. As we shall see, differences in legal systems can affect the attractiveness of a country as an investment site or market.

Like the economic system of a country, the legal system is influenced by the prevailing political system (although it is also strongly influenced by historical tradition). The government of a country defines the legal framework within which firms do business—and often the laws that regulate business reflect the rulers' dominant political ideology. For example, collectivist-inclined totalitarian states tend to enact laws that severely restrict private enterprise, whereas the laws enacted by governments in democratic states where individualism is the dominant political philosophy tend to be pro-private enterprise and pro-consumer.

Here we focus on several issues that illustrate how legal systems can vary—and how such variations can affect international business. First, we look at some basic differences in legal systems. Next we look at contract law. Third, we look at the laws governing property rights with particular reference to patents, copyrights, and trademarks. Then we discuss protection of intellectual property. Finally, we look at laws covering product safety and product liability.

DIFFERENT LEGAL SYSTEMS

There are three main types of legal systems—or legal traditions—in use around the world: common law, civil law, and theocratic law.

Common Law

The common law system evolved in England over hundreds of years. It is now found in most of Great Britain's former colonies, including the United States. **Common law** is based on tradition, precedent, and custom. *Tradition* refers to a country's legal history, *precedent* to cases that have come before the courts in the past, and *custom* to the ways in which laws are applied in specific situations. When law courts interpret common law, they do so with regard to these characteristics. This gives a common law system a degree of flexibility that other systems lack. Judges in a common law system have the power to interpret the law so that it applies to the unique circumstances of an individual case. In turn, each new interpretation sets a precedent that may be followed in future cases. As new precedents arise, laws may be altered, clarified, or amended to deal with new situations.

Civil Law

A **civil law system** is based on a detailed set of laws organized into codes. When law courts interpret civil law, they do so with regard to these codes. More than 80 countries, including Germany, France, Japan, and Russia, operate with a civil law system. A civil law system tends to be less adversarial than a common law system, since the judges rely upon detailed legal codes rather than interpreting tradition, precedent, and custom. Judges under a civil law system have less flexibility than those under a common law system. Judges in a common law system have the power to interpret the law, whereas judges in a civil law system have the power only to apply the law.

Theocratic Law

A **theocratic law system** is one in which the law is based on religious teachings. Islamic law is the most widely practiced theocratic legal system in the modern world, although usage of both Hindu and Jewish law persisted into the 20th century. Islamic law is primarily a moral rather than a commercial law and is intended to govern all aspects of life.[9] The foundation for Islamic law is the holy book of Islam, the Koran, along with the Sunnah, or decisions and sayings of the Prophet Muhammad, and the writings of Islamic scholars who have derived rules by analogy from the principles established in the Koran and the Sunnah. Because the Koran and Sunnah are holy documents, the basic foundations of Islamic law cannot be changed. However, in practice Islamic jurists and scholars are constantly debating the application of Islamic law to the modern world. In reality, many Muslim countries have legal systems that are a blend of Islamic law and a common or civil law system.

Although Islamic law is primarily concerned with moral behavior, it has been extended to cover certain commercial activities. An example is the payment or receipt of interest, which is considered usury and outlawed by the Koran. To the devout Muslim, acceptance of interest payments is seen as a grave sin; the giver and the taker are equally damned. This is not just a matter of theology; in several Islamic states it has also become a matter of law. In the 1990s, for example, Pakistan's Federal Shariat Court, the highest Islamic lawmaking body in the country, pronounced interest to be un-Islamic and therefore illegal and demanded that the government amend all financial laws accordingly. In 1999, Pakistan's Supreme Court ruled that Islamic banking methods should be used in the country after July 1, 2001.[10] By 2005, some 300 Islamic financial institutions in the world collectively managed more than $250 billion in assets. In addition to Pakistan, Islamic financial institutions are found in many of the Gulf states, Egypt, and Malaysia.[11]

Islamic law governs all aspects of the Muslims' lives, even commercial activities.

DIFFERENCES IN CONTRACT LAW

The difference between common law and civil law systems can be illustrated by the approach of each to contract law (remember, most theocratic legal systems also have elements of common or civil law). A **contract** is a document that specifies the conditions under which an exchange is to occur and details the rights and obligations of the parties involved. Some form of contract regulates many business transactions. **Contract law** is the body of law that governs contract enforcement. The parties to an agreement normally resort to contract law when one party feels the other has violated either the letter or the spirit of an agreement.

Because common law tends to be relatively ill specified, contracts drafted under a common law framework tend to be very detailed with all contingencies spelled out. In civil law systems, however, contracts tend to be much shorter and less specific because many of the issues are already covered in a civil code. Thus, it is more expensive to draw up contracts in a common law jurisdiction, and resolving contract disputes can be very adversarial in common law systems. But common law systems have the advantage of greater flexibility and allow for judges to interpret a contract dispute in light of the prevailing situation. International businesses need to be sensitive to these differences; approaching a contract dispute in a state with a civil law system as if it had a common law system may backfire, and vice versa.

When contract disputes arise in international trade, there is always the question of which country's laws to apply. To resolve this issue, a number of countries, including the United States, have ratified the **United Nations Convention on Contracts for the International Sale of Goods (CIGS).** The CIGS establishes a uniform set of rules governing certain aspects of making and performing everyday commercial contracts between sellers and buyers who have their places of business in different nations. By adopting the CIGS, a nation signals to other adopters that it will treat the convention's rules as part of its law. The CIGS applies automatically to all contracts for the sale of goods between different firms based in countries that have ratified the convention, unless the parties to the contract explicitly opt out. One problem with the CIGS, however, is that fewer than 70 nations have ratified the convention (the CIGS went into effect in 1988).[12] Many of the world's larger trading nations, including Japan and the United Kingdom, have not ratified the CIGS.

When firms do not wish to accept the CIGS, they often opt for arbitration by a recognized arbitration court to settle contract disputes. The most well known of these courts is the International Court of Arbitration of the International Chamber of Commerce in Paris. In 2005, this court handled some 521 requests for arbitration involving 1,422 parties from 117 countries.[13]

PROPERTY RIGHTS AND CORRUPTION

In a legal sense, the term *property* refers to a resource over which an individual or business holds a legal title; that is, a resource that it owns. Resources include land, buildings, equipment, capital, mineral rights, businesses, and intellectual property (ideas, which are protected by patents, copyrights, and trademarks). **Property rights** refer to the legal rights over the use to which a resource is put and over the use made of any income that may be derived from that resource.[14] Countries differ in the extent to which their legal systems define and protect property rights. Almost all countries now have laws on their books that protect property rights. Even China, still nominally a Communist state despite its booming market economy, finally enacted a law to protect the rights of private property holders in 2007 (the law gives individuals the same legal protection for their property as the state).[15] However, in many countries the authorities do not enforce these laws and property rights are violated (see the opening case). Property rights can be violated in two ways—through private action and through public action.

Private Action

In this context, **private action** refers to theft, piracy, blackmail, and the like by private individuals or groups. Although theft occurs in all countries, a weak legal system allows for a much higher level of criminal action in some than in others. For example, in Russia in the chaotic period following the collapse of communism, an outdated legal system, coupled with a weak police force and judicial system, offered both domestic and foreign businesses scant protection from blackmail by the "Russian Mafia." Successful business owners in Russia often had to pay "protection money" to the Mafia or face violent retribution, including bombings and assassinations (about 500 contract killings of businessmen occurred in 1995 and again in 1996).[16]

Russia is not alone in having Mafia problems (and the situation in Russia has improved significantly since the mid-1990s). The Mafia has a long history in the United States (Chicago in the 1930s was similar to Moscow in the 1990s). In Japan, the local version of the Mafia, known as the *yakuza,* runs protection rackets, particularly in the food and entertainment industries.[17] However, there was a big difference between the magnitude of such activity in Russia in the 1990s and its limited impact in Japan and the United States. This difference arose because the legal enforcement apparatus, such as the police and court system, was so weak in Russia following the collapse of communism. Many other countries from time to time have had problems similar to or even greater than those that Russia experienced.

Public Action and Corruption

Public action to violate property rights occurs when public officials, such as politicians and government bureaucrats, extort income, resources, or the property itself from property holders. This can be done through legal mechanisms such as levying excessive taxation, requiring expensive licenses or permits from property holders, taking assets into state ownership without compensating the owners, or redistributing assets without compensating the prior owners. It can also be done through illegal means, or corruption, by demanding bribes from businesses in return for the rights to operate in a country, industry, or location.[18]

Corruption has been well documented in every society, from the banks of the Congo River to the palace of the Dutch royal family, from Japanese politicians to Brazilian bankers, and from Indonesian government officials to the New York City Police Department. The government of the late Ferdinand Marcos in the Philippines was famous for demanding bribes from foreign businesses wishing to set up operations in that country.[19] The same was true of government officials in Indonesia under the rule of former president Suharto. No society is immune to corruption. However, there are systematic differences in the extent of corruption. In some countries, the rule of law minimizes corruption. Corruption is seen and treated as illegal, and when discovered, violators are punished by the full force of the law. In other countries, the rule of law is weak and corruption by bureaucrats and politicians is rife. Corruption is so endemic in some countries that politicians and bureaucrats regard it as a perk of office and openly flout laws against corruption.

According to Transparency International, an independent nonprofit organization dedicated to exposing and fighting corruption, businesses and individuals spend some $400 billion a year worldwide on bribes related to government procurement contracts alone.[20] Transparency International has also measured the level of corruption among public officials in different countries.[21] As Figure 2.1 shows, the organization rated countries such as Finland and New Zealand as clean; it rated others, such as Russia, India, Indonesia, and Zimbabwe, as corrupt. Haiti ranked last out of all 163 countries in the survey, and Finland ranked first.

Economic evidence suggests that high levels of corruption significantly reduce the foreign direct investment, level of international trade, and economic growth rate in a country.[22] By siphoning off profits, corrupt politicians and bureaucrats reduce the returns

FIGURE 2.1

Rankings of Corruption
by Country, 2006

Source: Transparency International, "Global Corruption Report," 2006.

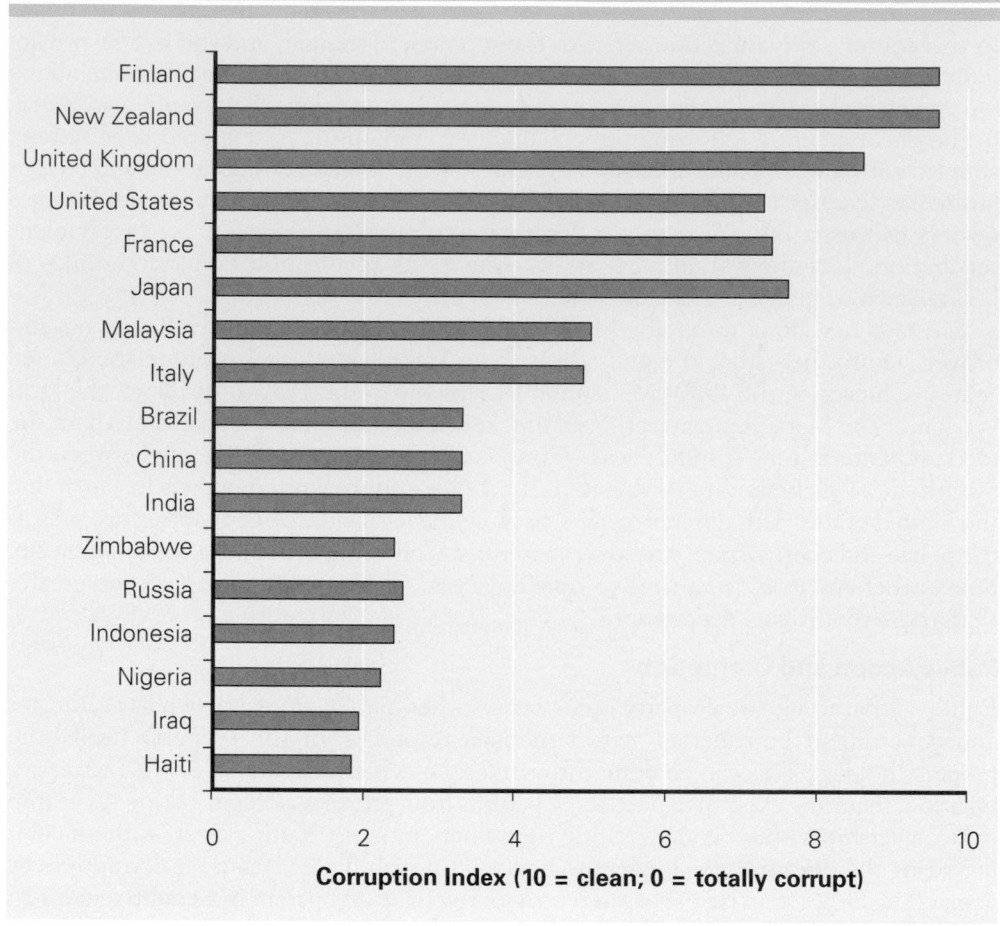

Corruption Index (10 = clean; 0 = totally corrupt)

to business investment and, hence, reduce the incentive of both domestic and foreign businesses to invest in that country. The lower level of investment that results hurts economic growth. Thus, we would expect countries such as Indonesia, Nigeria, and Russia to have a much lower rate of economic growth than might otherwise have been the case. A detailed example of the negative effect that corruption can have on economic progress is given in the accompanying Country Focus, which looks at the impact of corruption on economic growth in Nigeria.

Foreign Corrupt Practices Act

In the 1970s, the United States passed the **Foreign Corrupt Practices Act** following revelations that U.S. companies had bribed government officials in foreign countries in an attempt to win lucrative contracts. This law makes it illegal to bribe a foreign government official to obtain or maintain business over which that foreign official has authority, and it requires all publicly traded companies (whether or not they are involved in international trade) to keep detailed records that would reveal whether a violation of the act has occurred. Along the same lines, in 1997 trade and finance ministers from the member states of the Organization for Economic Cooperation and Development (OECD), an association of the world's 30 most powerful economies, adopted the Convention on Combating Bribery of Foreign Public Officials in International Business Transactions.[24] The convention obliges member states to make the bribery of foreign public officials a criminal offense.

However, both the U.S. law and OECD convention include language that allows for exceptions known as facilitating or expediting payments (also called *grease payments* or *speed money*), the purpose of which is to expedite or to secure the performance of a routine governmental action.[25] For example, they allow for small payments to speed up

Corruption in Nigeria

When Nigeria gained independence from Great Britain in 1960, there were hopes that the country might emerge as an economic heavyweight in Africa. Not only was Nigeria Africa's most populous country, but it also was blessed with abundant natural resources, particularly oil, from which the country earned over $400 billion between 1970 and 2005. Despite this, Nigeria remains one of the poorest countries in the world. According to the United Nations' 2006 Human Development Index, Nigeria ranked 159 out of 177 countries covered. Gross domestic product per capita was just $560, 51 percent of the adult population was illiterate, and life expectancy at birth was only 43 years.

What went wrong? Although there is no simple answer, a number of factors seem to have conspired to damage economic activity in Nigeria. The country is composed of several competing ethnic, tribal, and religious groups, and the conflict among them has limited political stability and led to political strife, including a brutal civil war in the 1970s. With the legitimacy of the government always in question, political leaders often purchased support by legitimizing bribes and by raiding the national treasury to reward allies. Civilian rule after independence was followed by a series of military dictatorships, each of which seemed more corrupt and inept than the last (the country returned to civilian rule in 1999).

During the 1990s, the military dictator, Sani Abacha, openly and systematically plundered the state treasury for his own personal gain. His most blatant scam was the Petroleum Trust Fund, which he set up in the mid-1990s ostensibly to channel extra revenue from an increase in fuel prices into much-needed infrastructure projects and other investments. The fund was not independently audited, and almost none of the money that passed through it was properly accounted for. It was, in fact, a vehicle for Abacha and his supporters to spend at will a sum that in 1996 was equivalent to some 25 percent of the total federal budget. Abacha, aware of his position as an unpopular and unelected leader, lavished money on personal security and handed out bribes to those whose support he coveted. With examples like this at the very top of the government, it is not surprising that corruption could be found throughout the political and bureaucratic apparatus.

Some of the excesses were simply astounding. In the 1980s an aluminum smelter was built on the orders of the government, which wanted to industrialize Nigeria. The cost of the smelter was $2.4 billion, some 60 to 100 percent higher than the cost of comparable plants elsewhere in the developed world. This high cost was widely interpreted to reflect the bribes that the international contractors who built the plant had to pay to local politicians. The smelter has never operated at more than a fraction of its intended capacity.

Has the situation in Nigeria improved since the country returned to civilian rule in 1999? In 2003, Olusegun Obasanjo was elected president on a platform that included a promise to fight corruption. By some accounts, progress has been seen. His anticorruption chief, Nuhu Ribadu, has claimed that whereas 70 percent of the country's oil revenues were being stolen or wasted in 2002, by 2004 the figure was "only" 40 percent. But in its most recent survey, Transparency International still ranked Nigeria among the most corrupt countries in the world in 2006 (see Figure 2.1), suggesting that the country still has a long way to go. In an effort to move things along, in early 2007 the country's top anticorruption body, the Economic and Financial Crimes Commission, sent letters to political parties listing 130 candidates for upcoming elections who it stated would soon be charged with corruption. Several parties responded by removing candidates identified as corrupt from their lists. Others argued that the list was itself influenced by political motives and in particular a desire to strengthen the position of President Obasanjo by blacklisting opponents.[23]

the issuance of permits or licenses, process paperwork, or just get vegetables off the dock and on their way to market. The explanation for this exception to general antibribery provisions is that while grease payments are, technically, bribes, they are distinguishable from (and, apparently, less offensive than) bribes used to obtain or maintain business because they merely facilitate performance of duties that the recipients are already obligated to perform.

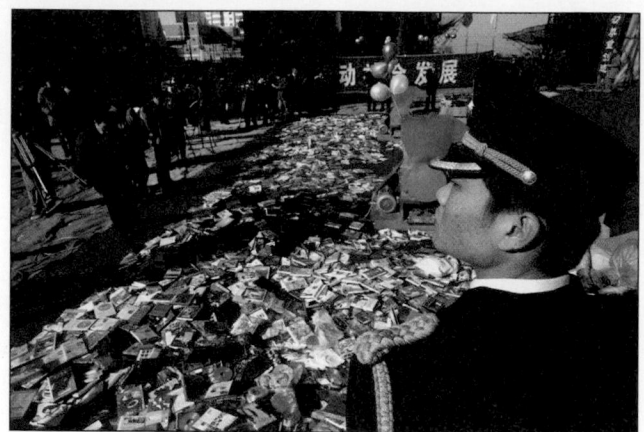

A security guard stands near a pile of pirated CDs and DVDs before they were destroyed at a ceremony in Beijing Saturday, Feb. 26, 2005. Thousands of pirated items were destroyed in the event, one of a number of activities, including an antipiracy pop concert later Saturday, which were staged by China's government to publicize its antipiracy efforts.

THE PROTECTION OF INTELLECTUAL PROPERTY

Intellectual property refers to property that is the product of intellectual activity, such as computer software, a screenplay, a music score, or the chemical formula for a new drug. Patents, copyrights, and trademarks establish ownership rights over intellectual property. A **patent** grants the inventor of a new product or process exclusive rights for a defined period to the manufacture, use, or sale of that invention. **Copyrights** are the exclusive legal rights of authors, composers, playwrights, artists, and publishers to publish and disperse their work as they see fit. **Trademarks** are designs and names, often officially registered, by which merchants or manufacturers designate and differentiate their products (e.g., Christian Dior clothes). In the high-technology "knowledge" economy of the 21st century, intellectual property has become an increasingly important source of economic value for businesses. Protecting intellectual property has also become increasingly problematic, particularly if it can be rendered in a digital form and then copied and distributed at very low cost via pirated CDs or over the Internet (e.g., computer software, music and video recordings).[26]

The philosophy behind intellectual property laws is to reward the originator of a new invention, book, musical record, clothes design, restaurant chain, and the like, for his or her idea and effort. Such laws stimulate innovation and creative work. They provide an incentive for people to search for novel ways of doing things, and they reward creativity. For example, consider innovation in the pharmaceutical industry. A patent will grant the inventor of a new drug a 20-year monopoly in production of that drug. This gives pharmaceutical firms an incentive to undertake the expensive, difficult, and time-consuming basic research required to generate new drugs (it can cost $800 million in R&D and take 12 years to get a new drug on the market). Without the guarantees provided by patents, companies would be unlikely to commit themselves to extensive basic research.[27]

The protection of intellectual property rights differs greatly from country to country. Although many countries have stringent intellectual property regulations on their books, the enforcement of these regulations has often been lax. This has been the case even among many of the 183 countries that are now members of the **World Intellectual Property Organization,** all of which have signed international treaties designed to protect intellectual property, including the oldest such treaty, the **Paris Convention for the Protection of Industrial Property,** which dates to 1883 and has been signed by some 169 nations as of 2006. Weak enforcement encourages the piracy (theft) of intellectual property. China and Thailand have recently been among the worst offenders in Asia. Pirated computer software is widely available in China. Similarly, the streets of Bangkok, Thailand's capital, are lined with stands selling pirated copies of Rolex watches, Levi Strauss jeans, videotapes, and computer software.

Piracy in music recordings is rampant. The International Federation of the Phonographic Industry claims that about one-third of all recorded music products sold worldwide in 2005 were pirated (illegal) copies, suggesting that piracy costs the industry more than $4.5 billion annually.[28] The computer software industry also suffers from lax enforcement of intellectual property rights. Estimates suggest that violations of intellectual property rights cost personal computer software firms revenues equal to $40 billion in 2006.[29] According to the Business Software Alliance, a software industry association, in 2006 some 35 percent of all software applications used in the world were pirated. The worst region was Central and Eastern Europe where the piracy rate was 68 percent (see Figure 2.2). One of the worst countries was China, where the piracy rate in 2006 ran at 82 percent and cost the industry more than $5.42 billion in lost sales, up from $444 million in 1995.

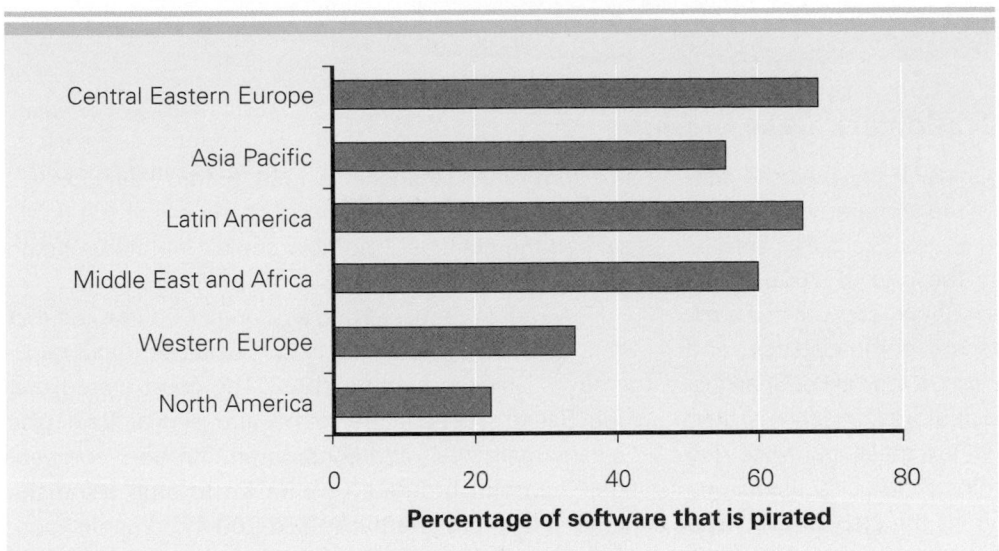

FIGURE 2.2

Regional Piracy Rates for Software, 2006

Source: Business Software Alliance, "Fourth Annual BSA and IDC Global Software Piracy Study," May 2007, www.bsa.org, accessed June 14, 2007.

The piracy rate in the United States was much lower at 21 percent; however, the value of sales lost was more significant because of the size of the U.S. market, reaching an estimated $7.3 billion in 2006.[30]

International businesses have a number of possible responses to violations of their intellectual property. They can lobby their respective governments to push for international agreements to ensure that intellectual property rights are protected and that the law is enforced. Partly as a result of such actions, international laws are being strengthened. As we shall see in Chapter 6, the most recent world trade agreement, signed in 1994, for the first time extends the scope of the General Agreement on Tariffs and Trade to cover intellectual property. The new agreement, known as the Trade Related Aspects of Intellectual Property Rights (or TRIPS), established a council of the World Trade Organization to oversee enforcement of much stricter intellectual property regulations, beginning in 1995. These regulations oblige WTO members to grant and enforce patents lasting at least 20 years and copyrights lasting 50 years. Rich countries had to comply with the rules within a year. Poor countries, in which such protection generally was much weaker, had five years of grace, and the very poorest have 10 years.[31] (For further details of the TRIPS agreement, see Chapter 6.)

In addition to lobbying governments, firms can file lawsuits on their own behalf. For example, Starbucks recently won a landmark trademark copyright case in China against a copycat (see the Management Focus feature for details). Firms may also choose to stay out of countries where intellectual property laws are lax, rather than risk having their ideas stolen by local entrepreneurs. Firms also need to be on the alert to ensure that pirated copies of their products produced in countries with weak intellectual property laws don't turn up in their home market or in third countries. U.S. computer software giant Microsoft, for example, discovered that pirated Microsoft software, produced illegally in Thailand, was being sold worldwide as the real thing.

PRODUCT SAFETY AND PRODUCT LIABILITY

Product safety laws set certain safety standards to which a product must adhere. **Product liability** involves holding a firm and its officers responsible when a product causes injury, death, or damage. Product liability can be much greater if a product does not conform to required safety standards. Both civil and criminal product liability laws exist. Civil laws call for payment and monetary damages. Criminal liability laws result in fines or imprisonment. Both civil and criminal liability laws are probably more extensive in the United States than in any other country, although many other Western nations also have comprehensive liability laws. Liability laws are typically least extensive

MANAGEMENT FOCUS

Starbucks Wins Key Trademark Case in China

Starbucks has big plans for China. It believes the fast-growing nation will become the company's second-largest market after the United States. Starbucks entered the country in 1999, and by the end of 2006 it had more than 220 outlets. But in China, copycats of well-established Western brands are commonplace, and Starbucks faced competition from a look alike, Shanghai Xing Ba Ke Coffee Shop, whose stores closely matched the Starbucks format, right down to a green and white Xing Ba Ke circular logo that mimics Starbuck's ubiquitous logo. Moreover, the name mimics the standard Chinese translation for Starbucks: *Xing* means "star" and *Ba Ke* sounds like "bucks."

In 2003, Starbucks decided to sue Xing Ba Ke in Chinese court for trademark violations. Xing Ba Ke's general manager responded by claiming that it was just an accident that the logo and name were so similar to that of Starbucks. Moreover, he claimed the right to use the logo and name because Xing Ba Ke had registered as a company in Shanghai in 1999, before Starbucks entered the city. "I hadn't heard of Starbucks at the time," claimed the manager, "so how could I imitate its brand and logo?"

However, in January 2006 a Shanghai court ruled that Starbucks had precedence, in part because it had registered its Chinese name in 1998. The court stated that Xing Ba Ke's use of the name and similar logo was "clearly malicious" and constituted improper competition. The court ordered Xing Ba Ke to stop using the name and to pay Starbucks $62,000 in compensation. While the money involved here may be small, the precedent is not. In a country where violation of trademarks has been commonplace, the courts seem to be signaling that a shift toward greater protection of intellectual property rights may be in progress. This is perhaps not surprising, since foreign governments and the World Trade Organization have been pushing China hard recently to start respecting intellectual property rights.[32]

in less developed nations. A boom in product liability suits and awards in the United States resulted in a dramatic increase in the cost of liability insurance. Many business executives argue that the high costs of liability insurance make American businesses less competitive in the global marketplace.

In addition to the competitiveness issue, country differences in product safety and liability laws raise an important ethical issue for firms doing business abroad. When product safety laws are tougher in a firm's home country than in a foreign country or when liability laws are more lax, should a firm doing business in that foreign country follow the more relaxed local standards or should it adhere to the standards of its home country? While the ethical thing to do is undoubtedly to adhere to home-country standards, firms have been known to take advantage of lax safety and liability laws to do business in a manner that would not be allowed at home.

The Determinants of Economic Development

The political, economic, and legal systems of a country can have a profound impact on the level of economic development and hence on the attractiveness of a country as a possible market or production location for a firm. Here we look first at how countries differ in their level of development. Then we look at how political economy affects economic progress.

DIFFERENCES IN ECONOMIC DEVELOPMENT

Different countries have dramatically different levels of economic development. One common measure of economic development is a country's **gross national income (GNI)** per head of population. GNI is regarded as a yardstick for the economic activity of a country; it measures the total annual income received by residents of a nation. Map 2.1

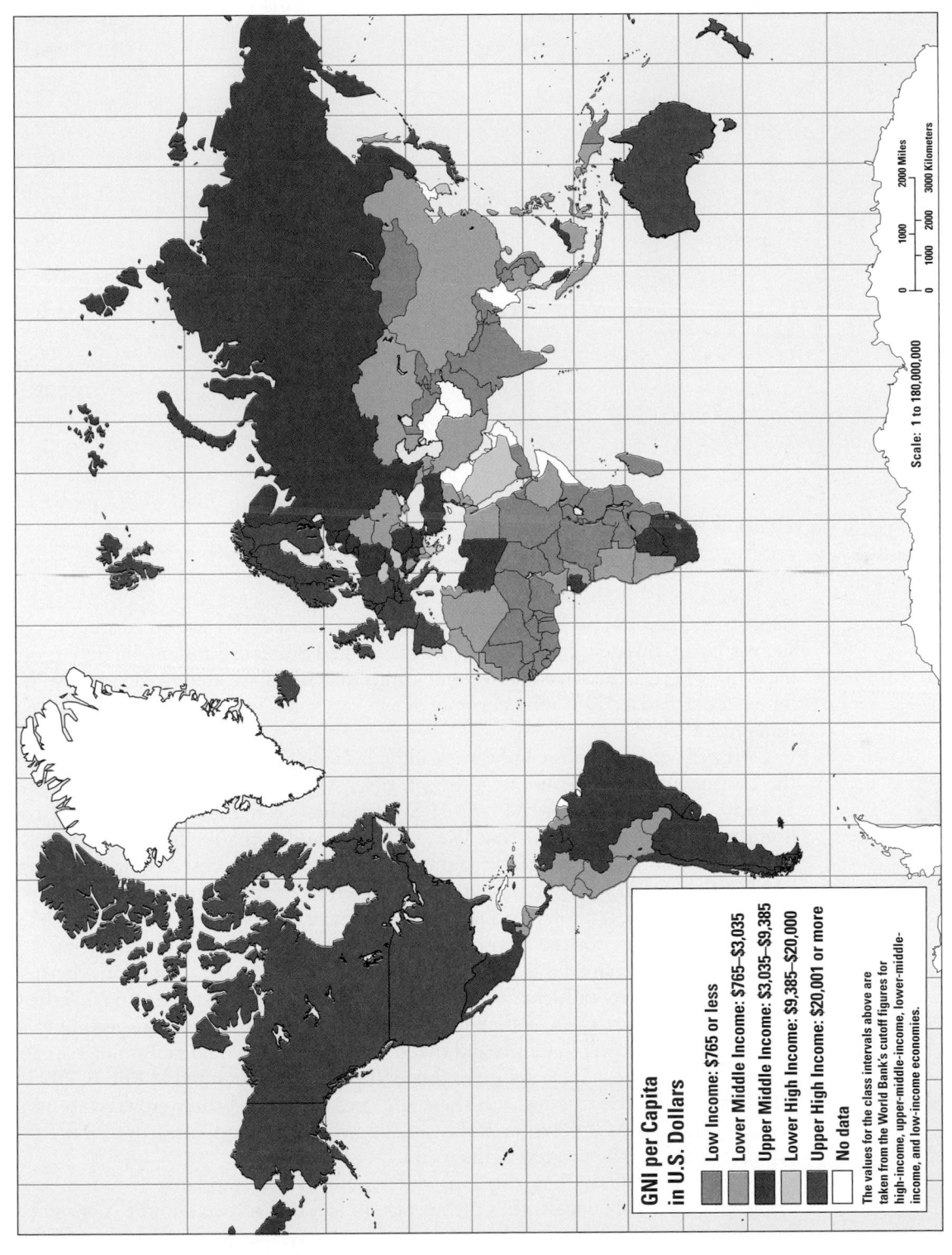

**GNI per Capita
in U.S. Dollars**

Low Income: $765 or less

Lower Middle Income: $765–$3,035

Upper Middle Income: $3,035–$9,385

Lower High Income: $9,385–$20,000

Upper High Income: $20,001 or more

No data

The values for the class intervals above are
taken from the World Bank's cutoff figures for
high-income, upper-middle-income, lower-middle-
income, and low-income economies.

Scale: 1 to 180,000,000

0   1000   2000   3000 Kilometers

0   1000   2000 Miles

MAP 2.1

GNI per Capita, 2005

Country	GNI per Capita, 2005 ($)	GNI PPP per Capita, 2005 ($)	GDP Growth Rate, 1996–2005 (%)	Size of Economy GDP, 2005 ($ billions)
Brazil	3,460	8,230	2.2	794
China	1,740	6,600	9.1	2,229
Germany	34,580	29,210	1.4	2,782
India	720	3,460	6.3	785
Japan	38,950	31,410	1.3	4,560
Nigeria	560	1,040	4.3	99
Poland	7,110	13,490	4.2	299
Russia	4,460	10,640	4.0	764
Switzerland	54,930	37,080	1.5	366
United Kingdom	37,600	32,690	2.7	2,193
United States	43,740	41,950	3.4	12,455

TABLE 2.1

Economic Data for Select Countries

Source: World Development Indicators Online, 2007.

summarizes the GNI per capita of the world's nations in 2005. As can be seen, countries such as Japan, Sweden, Switzerland, and the United States are among the richest on this measure, whereas the large countries of China and India are among the poorest. Japan, for example, had a 2005 GNI per capita of $38,980, but China achieved only $1,740 and India just $720.[33]

GNI per person figures can be misleading because they don't consider differences in the cost of living. For example, although the 2005 GNI per capita of Switzerland, at $54,930, exceeded that of the United States, which was $43,740, the higher cost of living in Switzerland meant that U.S. citizens could actually afford more goods and services than Swiss citizens. To account for differences in the cost of living, one can adjust GNI per capita by purchasing power. Referred to as a **purchasing power parity (PPP)** adjustment, it allows for a more direct comparison of living standards in different countries. The base for the adjustment is the cost of living in the United States. The PPP for different countries is then adjusted (up or down) depending upon whether the cost of living is lower or higher than in the United States. For example, in 2005 the GNI per capita for China was $1,740, but the PPP per capita was $6,660, suggesting that the cost of living was lower in China and that $1,500 in China would buy as much as $6,600 in the United States. Table 2.1 gives the GNI per capita measured at PPP in 2005 for a selection of countries, along with their GNI per capita and their growth rate in gross domestic product (GDP) from 1996 to 2005. Map 2.2 summarizes the GNI PPP per capita in 2005 for the nations of the world.

As can be seen, there are striking differences in the standards of living between countries. Table 2.1 suggests that the average Indian citizen can afford to consume only 8 percent of the goods and services consumed by the average U.S. citizen on a PPP basis. Given this, one might conclude that, despite having a population of 1 billion, India is unlikely to be a very lucrative market for the consumer products produced by many Western international businesses. However, this would be incorrect because India has a fairly wealthy middle class of close to 200 million people, despite its large number of very

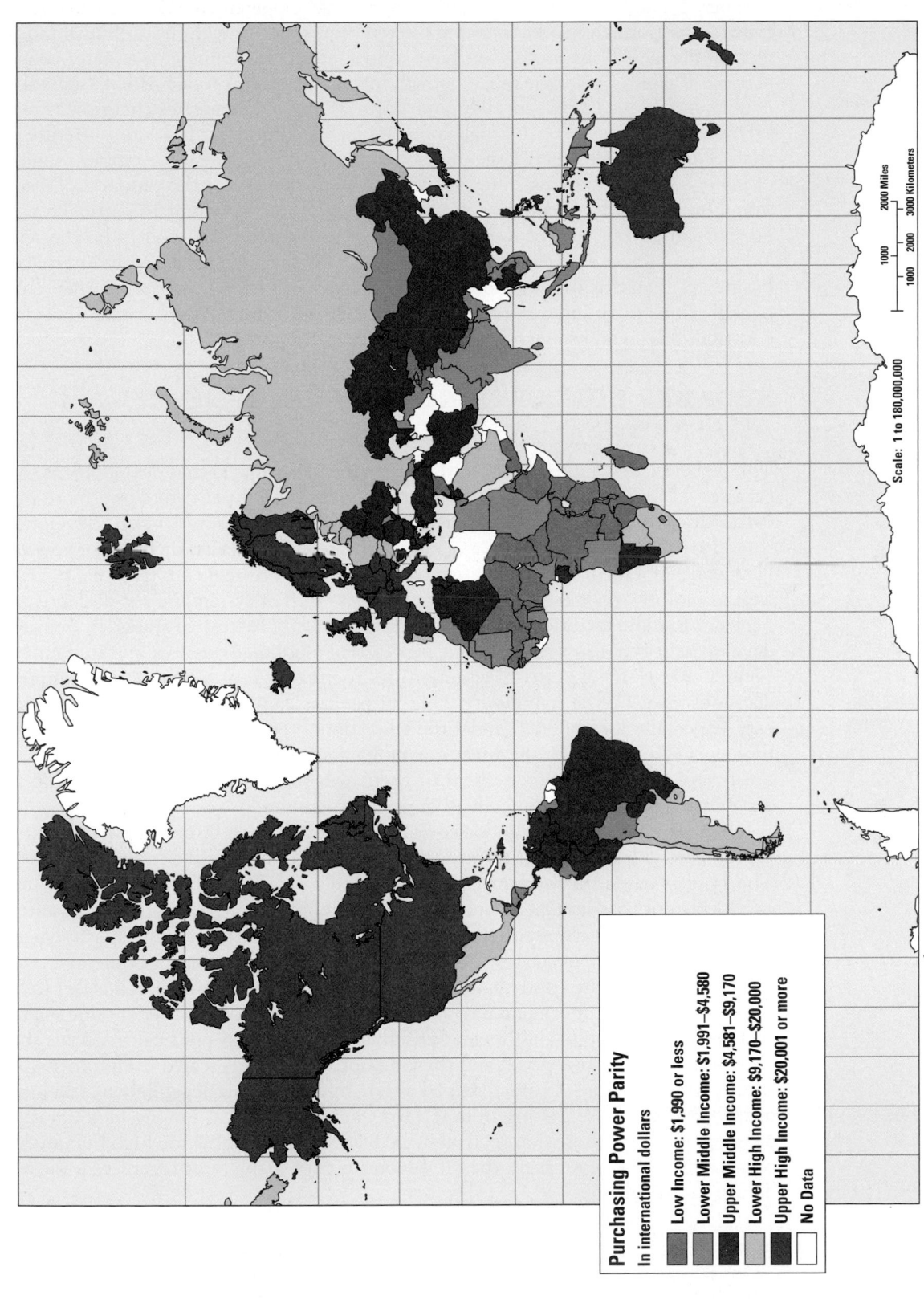

Purchasing Power Parity
In international dollars

- Low Income: $1,990 or less
- Lower Middle Income: $1,991–$4,580
- Upper Middle Income: $4,581–$9,170
- Lower High Income: $9,170–$20,000
- Upper High Income: $20,001 or more
- No Data

Scale: 1 to 180,000,000

1000   2000 Miles
1000 2000 3000 Kilometers

MAP 2.2

GNI Purchasing Power Parity per Capita, 2005

poor. Moreover, in absolute terms the Indian economy is now larger than that of Brazil, Poland, and Russia (see Table 2.1).

The GNI and PPP data give a static picture of development. They tell us, for example, that China is much poorer than the United States, but they do not tell us if China is closing the gap. To assess this, we have to look at the economic growth rates countries achieve. Table 2.1 gives the rate of growth in gross domestic product (GDP) a number of countries achieved between 1996 and 2005. Map 2.3 summarizes the growth rate in GDP from 1996 to 2006. Although countries such as China and India are currently poor, their economies are already large in absolute terms and growing more rapidly than those of many advanced nations. They are already huge markets for the products of international businesses. If it maintains its growth rates, China's economy in particular will be larger than all but that of the United States within a decade, and India too will be among the largest economies in the world. Given that potential, many international businesses are trying to gain a foothold in these markets now. Even though their current contributions to an international firm's revenues might be relatively small, their future contributions could be much larger.

BROADER CONCEPTIONS OF DEVELOPMENT: AMARTYA SEN

The Nobel Prize–winning economist Amartya Sen has argued that development should be assessed less by material output measures such as GNI per capita and more by the capabilities and opportunities that people enjoy.[34] According to Sen, development should be seen as a process of expanding the real freedoms that people experience. Hence, development requires the removal of major impediments to freedom: poverty as well as tyranny, poor economic opportunities as well as systematic social deprivation, neglect of public facilities as well as the intolerance of repressive states. In Sen's view, development is not just an economic process, but a political one too, and it requires the "democratization" of political communities to give citizens a voice in the important decisions made for the community. This perspective leads Sen to emphasize basic health care, especially for children, and basic education, especially for women. Not only are these factors desirable for their instrumental value in helping to achieve higher income levels, but they are also beneficial in their own right. People cannot develop their capabilities if they are chronically ill or woefully ignorant.

The United Nations has endorsed Sen's influential thesis by developing the **Human Development Index (HDI)** to measure the quality of human life in different nations. The HDI is based on three measures: life expectancy at birth (a function of health care), educational attainment (measured by a combination of the adult literacy rate and enrollment in primary, secondary, and tertiary education), and whether average incomes, based on PPP estimates, are sufficient to meet the basic needs of life in a country (adequate food, shelter, and health care). As such, the HDI comes much closer to Sen's conception of how development should be measured than narrow economic measures such as GNI per capita—although Sen's thesis suggests that political freedoms should also be included in the index, and they are not. The HDI is scaled from 0 to 1. Countries scoring less than 0.5 are classified as having low human development (the quality of life is poor); those scoring from 0.5 to 0.8 are classified as having medium human development; and those that score above 0.8 are classified as having high human development. Map 2.4 summarizes the HDI scores for 2004, the most recent year for which data are available.

POLITICAL ECONOMY AND ECONOMIC PROGRESS

It is often argued that a country's economic development is a function of its economic and political systems. What then is the nature of the relationship between political economy and economic progress? This question has been the subject of vigorous debate

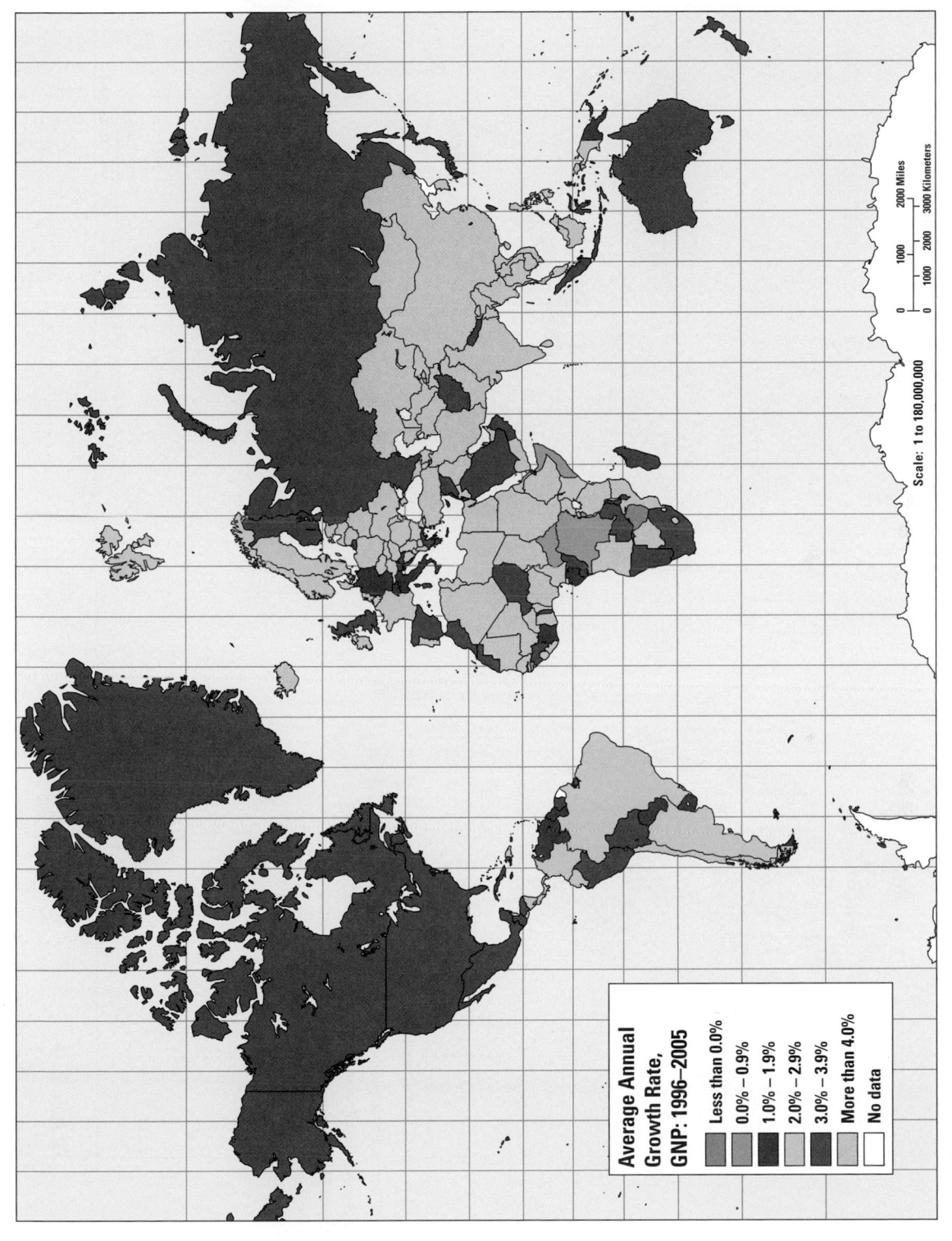

MAP 2.3

Growth Rate in GDP per Capita, 1996–2005

Average Annual Growth Rate, GNP: 1996–2005

Less than 0.0%
0.0% – 0.9%
1.0% – 1.9%
2.0% – 2.9%
3.0% – 3.9%
More than 4.0%
No data

Scale: 1 to 180,000,000

0   1000   2000 Miles
0   1000   2000   3000 Kilometers

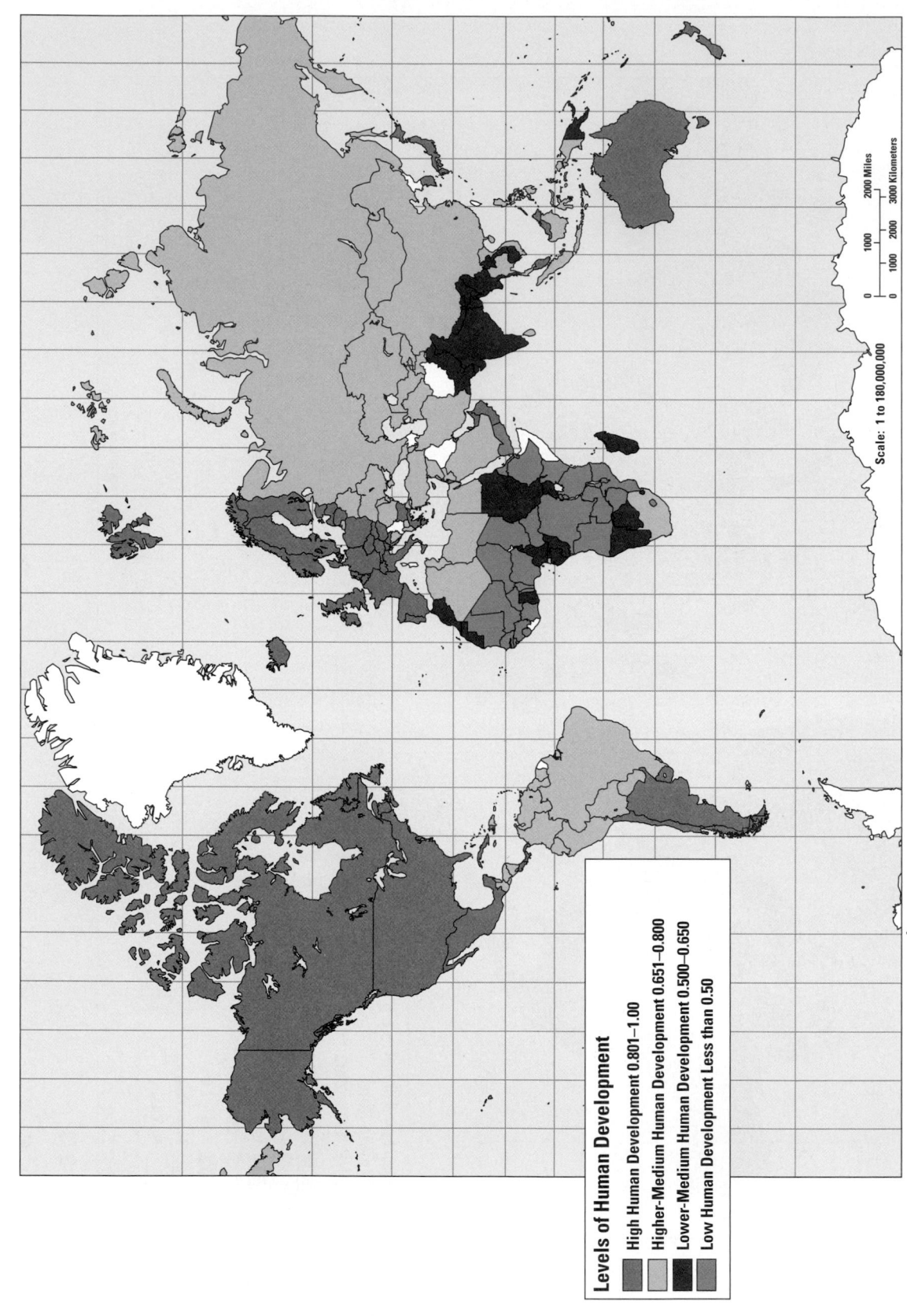

Levels of Human Development

High Human Development 0.801–1.00

Higher-Medium Human Development 0.651–0.800

Lower-Medium Human Development 0.500–0.650

Low Human Development Less than 0.50

Scale: 1 to 180,000,000

0   1000   2000   3000 Kilometers

0   1000   2000 Miles

MAP 2.4

Human Development Indicators, 2004

among academics and policymakers for some time. Despite the long debate, this remains a question for which it is not possible to give an unambiguous answer. However, it is possible to untangle the main threads of the arguments and make a few generalizations as to the nature of the relationship between political economy and economic progress.

Innovation and Entrepreneurship Are the Engines of Growth

There is wide agreement that innovation and entrepreneurial activity are the engines of long-run economic growth.[35] Those who make this argument define **innovation** broadly to include not just new products but also new processes, new organizations, new management practices, and new strategies. Thus, the Toys "R" Us strategy of establishing large warehouse-style toy stores and then engaging in heavy advertising and price discounting to sell the merchandise can be classified as an innovation because it was the first company to pursue this strategy. Innovation and entrepreneurial activity help to increase economic activity by creating new products and markets that did not previously exist. Moreover, innovations in production and business processes lead to an increase in the productivity of labor and capital, which further boosts economic growth rates.[36]

Innovation is also seen as the product of entrepreneurial activity. Often, **entrepreneurs** first commercialize innovative new products and processes, and entrepreneurial activity provides much of the dynamism in an economy. For example, the U.S. economy has benefited greatly from a high level of entrepreneurial activity, which has resulted in rapid innovation in products and process. Firms such as Cisco Systems, Dell, Microsoft, and Oracle were all founded by entrepreneurial individuals to exploit new technology, and all these firms created significant economic value and boosted productivity by helpings to commercialize innovations in products and processes. Thus, one can conclude that if a country's economy is to sustain long-run economic growth, the business environment must be conducive to the consistent production of product and process innovations and to entrepreneurial activity.

Innovation and Entrepreneurship Require a Market Economy

The first conclusion leads logically to a further question: What is required for the business environment of a country to be conducive to innovation and entrepreneurial activity? Those who have considered this issue highlight the advantages of a market economy.[37] It has been argued that the economic freedom associated with a market economy creates greater incentives for innovation and entrepreneurship than either a planned or a mixed economy. In a market economy, any individual who has an innovative idea is free to try to make money out of that idea by starting a business (by engaging in entrepreneurial activity). Similarly, existing businesses are free to improve their operations through innovation. To the extent they are successful, both individual entrepreneurs and established businesses can reap rewards in the form of high profits. Thus, market economies contain enormous incentives to develop innovations.

In a planned economy, the state owns all means of production. Consequently, entrepreneurial individuals have few economic incentives to develop valuable innovations, because it is the state, rather than the individual, that captures most of the gains. The lack of economic freedom and incentives for innovation was probably a main factor in the economic stagnation of many former communist states and led ultimately to their collapse at the end of the 1980s. Similar stagnation occurred in many mixed economies in those sectors where the state had a monopoly (such as health care and telecommunications in Great Britain). This stagnation provided the impetus for the widespread privatization of state-owned enterprises that we witnessed in many mixed economies during the mid-1980s and that is still going on today (*privatization* refers to the process of selling state-owned enterprises to private investors).

A study of 102 countries over a 20-year period provided evidence of a strong relationship between economic freedom (as provided by a market economy) and economic growth.[38] The study found that the more economic freedom a country had between 1975 and

1995, the more economic growth it achieved and the richer its citizens became. The six countries that had persistently high ratings of economic freedom from 1975 to 1995 (Hong Kong, Switzerland, Singapore, the United States, Canada, and Germany) were also all in the top 10 in terms of economic growth rates. In contrast, no country with persistently low economic freedom achieved a respectable growth rate. In the 16 countries for which the index of economic freedom declined the most during 1975 to 1995, gross domestic product fell at an annual rate of 0.6 percent.

Innovation and Entrepreneurship Require Strong Property Rights

Strong legal protection of property rights is another requirement for a business environment to be conducive to innovation, entrepreneurial activity, and hence economic growth.[39] Both individuals and businesses must be given the opportunity to profit from innovative ideas. Without strong property rights protection, businesses and individuals run the risk that the profits from their innovative efforts will be expropriated, either by criminal elements or by the state. The state can expropriate the profits from innovation through legal means, such as excessive taxation, or through illegal means, such as demands from state bureaucrats for kickbacks in return for granting an individual or firm a license to do business in a certain area (i.e., corruption). According to the Nobel Prize–winning economist Douglass North, throughout history many governments have displayed a tendency to engage in such behavior. Inadequately enforced property rights reduce the incentives for innovation and entrepreneurial activity—because the profits from such activity are "stolen"—and hence reduce the rate of economic growth.

The influential Peruvian development economist Hernando de Soto has argued that much of the developing world will fail to reap the benefits of capitalism until property rights are better defined and protected.[40] De Soto's arguments are interesting because he claims that the key problem is not the risk of expropriation but the chronic inability of property owners to establish legal title to the property they own. As an example of the scale of the problem, he cites the situation in Haiti where individuals must take 176 steps over 19 years to own land legally. Because most property in poor countries is informally "owned," the absence of legal proof of ownership means that property holders cannot convert their assets into capital, which could then be used to finance business ventures. Banks will not lend money to the poor to start businesses because the poor possess no proof that they own property, such as farmland, that can be used as collateral for a loan. By de Soto's calculations, the total value of real estate held by the poor in Third World and former communist states amounted to more than $9.3 trillion in 2000. If those assets could be converted into capital, the result could be an economic revolution that would allow the poor to bootstrap their way out of poverty.

Democratic Regimes Are More Conducive to Long-Term Economic Growth

Much debate surrounds which kind of political system best achieves a functioning market economy with strong protection for property rights.[41] People in the West tend to associate a representative democracy with a market economic system, strong property rights protection, and economic progress. Building on this idea, we tend to argue that democracy is good for growth. However, some totalitarian regimes have fostered a market economy and strong property rights protection and have experienced rapid economic growth. Five of the fastest-growing economies of the past 30 years—China, South Korea, Taiwan, Singapore, and Hong Kong—had one thing in common at the start of their economic growth: undemocratic governments. At the same time, countries with stable democratic governments, such as India, experienced sluggish economic growth for long periods. In 1992, Lee Kuan Yew, Singapore's leader for many years, told an audience, "I do not believe that democracy necessarily leads to development. I believe that a country needs to develop discipline more than democracy. The exuberance of democracy leads to undisciplined and disorderly conduct which is inimical to development."[42]

However, those who argue for the value of a totalitarian regime miss an important point: If dictators made countries rich, then much of Africa, Asia, and Latin America should have been growing rapidly during 1960 to 1990, and this was not the case. Only a totalitarian regime that is committed to a free market system and strong protection of property rights is capable of promoting economic growth. Also, there is no guarantee that a dictatorship will continue to pursue such progressive policies. Dictators are rarely so benevolent. Many are tempted to use the apparatus of the state to further their own private ends, violating property rights and stalling economic growth. Therefore, it seems likely that democratic regimes are far more conducive to long-term economic growth than are dictatorships, even benevolent ones. Only in a well-functioning, mature democracy are property rights truly secure.[43] Nor should we forget Amartya Sen's arguments that we reviewed earlier. Totalitarian states, by limiting human freedom, also suppress human development and therefore are detrimental to progress.

Economic Progress Begets Democracy

While it is possible to argue that democracy is not a necessary precondition for a free market economy in which property rights are protected, subsequent economic growth often leads to establishment of a democratic regime. Several of the fastest growing Asian economies adopted more democratic governments during the past two decades, including South Korea and Taiwan. Thus, although democracy may not always be the cause of initial economic progress, it seems to be one consequence of that progress.

A strong belief that economic progress leads to adoption of a democratic regime underlies the fairly permissive attitude that many Western governments have adopted toward human rights violations in China. Although China has a totalitarian government in which human rights are violated, many Western countries have been hesitant to criticize the country too much for fear that foreign criticism might hamper the country's march toward a free market system. The belief is that once China has a free market system, greater individual freedoms and democracy will follow. Whether this optimistic vision comes to pass remains to be seen.

GEOGRAPHY, EDUCATION, AND ECONOMIC DEVELOPMENT

While a country's political and economic systems are probably the big engine driving its rate of economic development, other factors are also important. One that has received attention recently is geography.[44] But the belief that geography can influence economic policy, and hence economic growth rates, goes back to Adam Smith. The influential Harvard University economist Jeffrey Sachs argues

> that throughout history, coastal states, with their long engagements in international trade, have been more supportive of market institutions than landlocked states, which have tended to organize themselves as hierarchical (and often military) societies. Mountainous states, as a result of physical isolation, have often neglected market-based trade. Temperate climes have generally supported higher densities of population and thus a more extensive division of labor than tropical regions.[45]

Sachs's point is that by virtue of favorable geography, certain societies were more likely to engage in trade than others and were thus more likely to be open to and develop market-based economic systems, which in turn would promote faster economic growth. He also argues that, irrespective of the economic and political institutions a country adopts, adverse geographical conditions, such as the high rate of disease, poor soils, and hostile climate that afflict many tropical countries, can have a negative impact on development. Together with colleagues at Harvard's Institute for International Development, Sachs tested for the impact of geography on a country's economic growth rate between 1965 and 1990. He found that the economies of landlocked countries grew more slowly than coastal economies and that being entirely landlocked reduced a country's growth rate by roughly 0.7 percent per year. He also found that tropical countries grew 1.3 percent more slowly each year than countries in the temperate zone.

Education emerges as another important determinant of economic development (a point that Amartya Sen emphasizes). The general assertion is that nations that invest more in education will have higher growth rates because an educated population is a more productive population. Anecdotal comparisons suggest this is true. In 1960, Pakistanis and South Koreans were on equal footing economically. However, just 30 percent of Pakistani children were enrolled in primary schools, while 94 percent of South Koreans were. By the mid-1980s, South Korea's GNP per person was three times that of Pakistan.[46] A survey of 14 statistical studies that looked at the relationship between a country's investment in education and its subsequent growth rates concluded that investment in education did have a positive and statistically significant impact on a country's rate of economic growth.[47] Similarly, the work by Sachs discussed above suggests that investments in education help explain why some countries in Southeast Asia, such as Indonesia, Malaysia, and Singapore, have been able to overcome the disadvantages associated with their tropical geography and grow far more rapidly than tropical nations in Africa and Latin America.

States in Transition

The political economy of many of the world's nation-states has changed radically since the late 1980s. Two trends have been evident. First, during the late 1980s and early 1990s, a wave of democratic revolutions swept the world. Totalitarian governments collapsed and were replaced by democratically elected governments that were typically more committed to free market capitalism than their predecessors had been. Second, there has been a strong move away from centrally planned and mixed economies and toward a more free market economic model. We shall look first at the spread of democracy and then turn our attention to the spread of free market economics.

THE SPREAD OF DEMOCRACY

One notable development of the past 15 years has been the spread of democracy (and, by extension, the decline of totalitarianism). Map 2.5 reports on the extent of totalitarianism in the world as determined by Freedom House.[48] This map charts political freedom in 2006, grouping countries into three broad groupings, free, partly free, and not free. In "free" countries, citizens enjoy a high degree of political and civil freedoms. "Partly free" countries are characterized by some restrictions on political rights and civil liberties, often in the context of corruption, weak rule of law, ethnic strife, or civil war. In "not free" countries, the political process is tightly controlled and basic freedoms are denied.

Freedom House classified some 90 countries as free in 2006, accounting for some 47 percent of the world's population. These countries respect a broad range of political rights. Another 58 countries accounting for 30 percent of the world's population were classified as partly free, while 45 countries representing some 23 percent of the world's population were classified as not free. The number of democracies in the world has increased from 69 nations in 1987 to 123 in 2006, the highest number in history. But not all democracies are free, according to Freedom House, because some democracies still restrict certain political and civil liberties. For example, Russia was rated "not free." According to Freedom House,

> Russia's step backwards into the Not Free category is the culmination of a growing trend under President Vladimir Putin to concentrate political authority, harass and intimidate the media, and politicize the country's law-enforcement system.[49]

Similarly, Freedom House argues that democracy is being restricted in Venezuela under the leadership of Hugo Chavez (see the Opening Case).

Many of the newer democracies are in Eastern Europe and Latin America, although there also have been notable gains in Africa during this time, such as in South Africa.

MAP 2.5

Distribution of Economic Freedom in 2007

Source: Heritage Foundation, http://www.heritage.org/index/

Political Freedom

Free

Partly Free

No Data

Scale: 1 to 180,000,000

0 1000 2000 Miles

0 1000 2000 3000 Kilometers

Entrants into the ranks of the world's democracies include Mexico, which held its first fully free and fair presidential election in 2000 after free and fair parliamentary and state elections in 1997 and 1998; Senegal, where free and fair presidential elections led to a peaceful transfer of power; Yugoslavia, where a democratic election took place despite attempted fraud by the incumbent; and Ukraine, where popular unrest following widespread ballot fraud in the 2004 presidential election resulted in a second election, the victory of a reform candidate, and a marked improvement in civil liberties.

Three main reasons account for the spread of democracy.[50] First, many totalitarian regimes failed to deliver economic progress to the vast bulk of their populations. The collapse of communism in Eastern Europe, for example, was precipitated by the growing gulf between the vibrant and wealthy economies of the West and the stagnant economies of the Communist East. In looking for alternatives to the socialist model, the populations of these countries could not have failed to notice that most of the world's strongest economies were governed by representative democracies. Today, the economic success of many of the newer democracies, such as Poland and the Czech Republic in the former Communist bloc, the Philippines and Taiwan in Asia, and Chile in Latin America, has strengthened the case for democracy as a key component of successful economic advancement.

Second, new information and communication technologies, including shortwave radio, satellite television, fax machines, desktop publishing, and, most important, the Internet, have reduced the state's ability to control access to uncensored information. These technologies have created new conduits for the spread of democratic ideals and information from free societies. Today, the Internet is allowing democratic ideals to penetrate closed societies as never before.[51]

Third, in many countries the economic advances of the past quarter century have led to the emergence of increasingly prosperous middle and working classes who have pushed for democratic reforms. This was certainly a factor in the democratic transformation of South Korea. Entrepreneurs and other business leaders, eager to protect their property rights and ensure the dispassionate enforcement of contracts, are another force pressing for more accountable and open government.

Despite this, it would be naive to conclude that the global spread of democracy will continue unchallenged. Democracy is still rare in large parts of the world. In sub-Saharan Africa in 2006, only 11 countries were considered free, 22 were partly free, and 15 were not free. Among the 27 post-Communist countries in Eastern and Central Europe, 7 are still not electoral democracies and Freedom House classifies only 13 of these states as free (primarily in Eastern Europe). And there are no free states among the 16 Arab nations of the Middle East and North Africa.

THE NEW WORLD ORDER AND GLOBAL TERRORISM

The end of the Cold War and the "new world order" that followed the collapse of communism in Eastern Europe and the former Soviet Union, taken together with the demise of many authoritarian regimes in Latin America, have given rise to intense speculation about the future shape of global geopolitics. Author Francis Fukuyama has argued, "We may be witnessing . . . the end of history as such: that is, the end point of mankind's ideological evolution and the universalization of Western liberal democracy as the final form of human government."[52] Fukuyama goes on to say that the war of ideas may be at an end and that liberal democracy has triumphed.

Others question Fukuyama's vision of a more harmonious world dominated by a universal civilization characterized by democratic regimes and free market capitalism. In a controversial book, the influential political scientist Samuel Huntington argues that there is no "universal" civilization based on widespread acceptance of Western liberal democratic ideals.[53] Huntington maintains that while many societies may be modernizing—they are adopting the material paraphernalia of the modern world, from automobiles to Coca-Cola and

MTV—they are not becoming more Western. On the contrary, Huntington theorizes that modernization in non-Western societies can result in a retreat toward the traditional, such as the resurgence of Islam in many traditionally Muslim societies. He writes,

> The Islamic resurgence is both a product of and an effort to come to grips with modernization. Its underlying causes are those generally responsible for indigenization trends in non-Western societies: urbanization, social mobilization, higher levels of literacy and education, intensified communication and media consumption, and expanded interaction with Western and other cultures. These developments undermine traditional village and clan ties and create alienation and an identity crisis. Islamist symbols, commitments, and beliefs meet these psychological needs, and Islamist welfare organizations, the social, cultural, and economic needs of Muslims caught in the process of modernization. Muslims feel a need to return to Islamic ideas, practices, and institutions to provide the compass and the motor of modernization.[54]

Thus, the rise of Islamic fundamentalism is portrayed as a response to the alienation produced by modernization.

In contrast to Fukuyama, Huntington sees a world that is split into different civilizations, each of which has its own value systems and ideology. In addition to Western civilization, Huntington predicts the emergence of strong Islamic and Sinic (Chinese) civilizations, as well as civilizations based on Japan, Africa, Latin America, Eastern Orthodox Christianity (Russian), and Hinduism (Indian). Huntington also sees the civilizations as headed for conflict, particularly along the "fault lines" that separate them, such as Bosnia (where Muslims and Orthodox Christians have clashed), Kashmir (where Muslims and Hindus clash), and the Sudan (where a bloody war between Christians and Muslims has persisted for decades). Huntington predicts conflict between the West and Islam and between the West and China. He bases his predictions on an analysis of the different value systems and ideology of these civilizations, which in his view tend to bring them into conflict with each other. While some commentators originally dismissed Huntington's thesis, in the aftermath of the terrorist attacks on the United States on September 11, 2001, Huntington's views received new attention.

If Huntington's views are even partly correct—and there is little doubt that the events surrounding September 11 added more weight to his thesis—they have important implications for international business. They suggest many countries may be increasingly difficult places in which to do business, either because they are shot through with violent conflicts or because they are part of a civilization that is in conflict with an enterprise's home country. Huntington's views are speculative and controversial. It is not clear that his predictions will come to pass. More likely is the evolution of a global political system that is positioned somewhere between Fukuyama's universal global civilization based on liberal democratic ideals and Huntington's vision of a fractured world. That would still be a world, however, in which geopolitical forces periodically limit the ability of business enterprises to operate in certain foreign countries.

In Huntington's thesis, global terrorism is a product of the tension between civilizations and the clash of value systems and ideology. Others point to terrorism's roots in long-standing conflicts that seem to defy political resolution, the Palestinian, Kashmir, and Northern Ireland conflicts being obvious examples. It should also be noted that a substantial amount of terrorist activity in some parts of the world, such as Colombia, has been interwoven with the illegal drug trade. The attacks of September 11, 2001, created the impression that global terror is on the rise, although accurate statistics are hard to come by. What we do know is that according to data from the U.S. Department of State, in 2006 there were some 14,388 terrorist attacks worldwide, a 25 percent increase over 2005. These attacks resulted in 20,498 deaths in 2006, a 40 percent increase over 2005. Iraq alone, however, accounted for 45 percent of the attacks and 65 percent of the fatalities.[55] Other global hot spots for terrorist incidents in 2006 included the Sudan, Nigeria, and Afghanistan. As former U.S. secretary of state Colin Powell has maintained, terrorism represents one of the major threats to world peace and economic progress in the 21st century.[56]

THE SPREAD OF MARKET-BASED SYSTEMS

Paralleling the spread of democracy since the 1980s has been the transformation from centrally planned command economies to market-based economies. More than 30 countries that were in the former Soviet Union or the Eastern European Communist bloc have changed their economic systems. A complete list of countries where change is now occurring also would include Asian states such as China and Vietnam, as well as African countries such as Angola, Ethiopia, and Mozambique.[57] There has been a similar shift away from a mixed economy. Many states in Asia, Latin America, and Western Europe have sold state-owned businesses to private investors (privatization) and deregulated their economies to promote greater competition.

The rationale for economic transformation has been the same the world over. In general, command and mixed economies failed to deliver the kind of sustained economic performance that was achieved by countries adopting market-based systems, such as the United States, Switzerland, Hong Kong, and Taiwan. As a consequence, even more states have gravitated toward the market-based model. Map 2.6, based on data from the Heritage Foundation, a politically conservative U.S. research foundation, gives some idea of the degree to which the world has shifted toward market-based economic systems. The Heritage Foundation's index of economic freedom is based on 10 indicators, such as the extent to which the government intervenes in the economy, trade policy, the degree to which property rights are protected, foreign investment regulations, and taxation rules. A country can score between 1 (most free) and 5 (least free) on each of these indicators. The lower a country's average score across all 10 indicators, the more closely its economy represents the pure market model. According to the 2007 index, which is summarized in Map 2.6, the world's freest economies are (in rank order) Hong Kong, Singapore, Australia, United States, New Zealand, United Kingdom, Ireland, Luxembourg, Switzerland, and Canada. Japan came in at 18, France at 45; Mexico, 49; Brazil, 70; India, 104; China, 119; and Russia, 120. The economies of Cuba, Laos, Iran, Venezuela, and North Korea are to be found near the bottom of the rankings.[58]

Economic freedom does not necessarily equate with political freedom, as detailed in Map 2.6. For example, the two top states in the Heritage Foundation index, Hong Kong and Singapore, cannot be classified as politically free. Hong Kong was reabsorbed into Communist China in 1997, and the first thing Beijing did was shut down Hong Kong's freely elected legislature. Singapore is ranked as only partly free on Freedom House's index of political freedom due to practices such as widespread press censorship.

🌐 The Nature of Economic Transformation

The shift toward a market-based economic system often entails a number of steps: deregulation, privatization, and creation of a legal system to safeguard property rights.[59]

DEREGULATION

Deregulation involves removing legal restrictions to the free play of markets, the establishment of private enterprises, and the manner in which private enterprises operate. Before the collapse of communism, the governments in most command economies exercised tight control over prices and output, setting both through detailed state planning. They also prohibited private enterprises from operating in most sectors of the economy, severely restricted direct investment by foreign enterprises, and limited international trade. Deregulation in these cases involved removing price controls, thereby allowing prices to be set by the interplay between demand and supply; abolishing laws regulating the establishment and operation of private enterprises; and relaxing or removing restrictions on direct investment by foreign enterprises and international trade.

MAP 2.6

Economic Freedom in 2006

Economic Freedom

- 80–100% Free
- 70–79.9% Mostly Free
- 60–69.9% Moderately Free
- 50–59.9% Mostly Unfree
- 0–49.9% Repressed
- Not Ranked

Scale: 1 to 180,000,000

In mixed economies, the role of the state was more limited; but here too, in certain sectors the state set prices, owned businesses, limited private enterprise, restricted investment by foreigners, and restricted international trade (for an example, see the Country Focus on India). For these countries, deregulation has involved the same kind of initiatives that we have seen in former command economies, although the transformation has been easier because these countries often had a vibrant private sector.

PRIVATIZATION

Hand in hand with deregulation has come a sharp increase in privatization. Privatization, as we discussed earlier in this chapter, transfers the ownership of state property into the hands of private individuals, frequently by the sale of state assets through an auction.[60] Privatization is seen as a way to stimulate gains in economic efficiency by giving new private owners a powerful incentive—the reward of greater profits—to search for increases in productivity, to enter new markets, and to exit losing ones.[61]

The privatization movement started in Great Britain in the early 1980s when then prime minister Margaret Thatcher started to sell state-owned assets such as the British telephone company, British Telecom (BT). In a pattern that has been repeated around the world, this sale was linked with the deregulation of the British telecommunications industry. By allowing other firms to compete head-to-head with BT, deregulation ensured that privatization did not simply replace a state-owned monopoly with a private monopoly. Since the 1980s, privatization has become a worldwide phenomenon. More than 8,000 acts of privatization were completed around the world between 1995 and 1999.[62] In total, these sales were valued at more than $1 trillion (in 1985 dollars). In the United Kingdom alone, some 139 state-owned enterprises were sold for a total of $130 billion. Some of the most dramatic privatization programs occurred in the economies of the former Soviet Union and its Eastern European satellite states. In the Czech Republic, for example, three-quarters of all state-owned enterprises were privatized between 1989 and 1996, helping to push the share of gross domestic product accounted for by the private sector up from 11 percent in 1989 to 60 percent in 1995.[63]

As privatization has proceeded around the world, it has become clear that simply selling state-owned assets to private investors is not enough to guarantee economic growth. Studies of privatization in central Europe have shown that the process often fails to deliver predicted benefits if the newly privatized firms continue to receive subsidies from the state and if they are protected from foreign competition by barriers to international trade and foreign direct investment.[64] In such cases, the newly privatized firms are sheltered from competition and continue acting like state monopolies. When these circumstances prevail, the newly privatized entities often have little incentive to restructure their operations to become more efficient. For privatization to work, it must also be accompanied by a more general deregulation and opening of the economy. Thus, when Brazil decided to privatize the state-owned telephone monopoly, Telebras Brazil, the government also split the company into four independent units that were to compete with each other and removed barriers to foreign direct investment in telecommunications services. This action ensured that the newly privatized entities would face significant competition and thus would have to improve their operating efficiency to survive.

The ownership structure of newly privatized firms also is important.[65] Many former command economies, for example, lack the legal regulations regarding corporate governance that are found in advanced Western economies. In advanced market economies, boards of directors are appointed by shareholders to make sure managers consider the interests of shareholders when making decisions and try to manage the firm in a manner that is consistent with maximizing the wealth of shareholders. However, some former Communist states still lack laws requiring corporations to establish effective boards. In such cases, managers with a small ownership stake can often gain control over the newly privatized entity and run it for their own benefit, while ignoring the interests of other

Building a Market Economy in India

After gaining independence from Britain in 1947, India adopted a democratic system of government. The economic system that developed in India after 1947 was a mixed economy characterized by a large number of state-owned enterprises, centralized planning, and subsidies. This system constrained the growth of the private sector. Private companies could expand only with government permission. It could take years to get permission to diversify into a new product. Much of heavy industry, such as auto, chemical, and steel production, was reserved for state-owned enterprises. Production quotas and high tariffs on imports also stunted the development of a healthy private sector, as did labor laws that made it difficult to fire employees.

By the early 1990s, it was clear that this system was incapable of delivering the kind of economic progress that many Southeastern Asian nations had started to enjoy. In 1994, India's economy was still smaller than Belgium's, despite having a population of 950 million. Its GDP per capita was a paltry $310; less than half the population could read; only 6 million had access to telephones; only 14 percent had access to clean sanitation; the World Bank estimated that some 40 percent of the world's desperately poor lived in India; and only 2.3 percent of the population had a household income in excess of $2,484.

In 1991, the lack of progress led the government to embark on an ambitious economic reform program. Much of the industrial licensing system was dismantled, and several areas once closed to the private sector were opened, including electricity generation, parts of the oil industry, steelmaking, air transport, and some areas of the telecommunications industry. Investment by foreign enterprises, formerly allowed only grudgingly and subject to arbitrary ceilings, was suddenly welcomed. Across a wide range of sectors, approval was made automatic for foreign equity stakes of up to 51 percent in an Indian enterprise, and 100 percent foreign ownership was allowed under certain circumstances. Raw materials and many industrial goods could be freely imported, and the maximum tariff that could be levied on imports was reduced from 400 percent to 65 percent. The top income tax rate was also reduced, and corporate tax fell from 57.5 percent to 46 percent in 1994, and then to 35 percent in 1997. The government also announced plans to start privatizing India's state-owned businesses, some 40 percent of which were losing money in the early 1990s.

Judged by some measures, the response to these economic reforms has been impressive. The economy expanded at an annual rate of about 6.5 percent from 1994 to 2006. Foreign investment, a key indicator of how attractive foreign companies thought the Indian economy was, jumped from $150 million in 1991 to $9.5 billion in 2006. Some economic sectors have done particularly well, such as the information technology sector, where India has emerged as a vibrant global center for software development with export sales of $23.4 billion in 2006, up from just $150 million in 1990. In pharmaceuticals too, Indian companies are emerging as credible players on the global marketplace, primarily by selling low-cost, generic versions of drugs that have come off patent in the developed world.

However, the country still has a long way to go. Attempts to further reduce import tariffs have been stalled by political opposition from employers, employees, and politicians, who fear that if barriers come down, a flood of inexpensive Chinese products will enter India. The privatization program continues to hit speed bumps—the latest in September 2003 when the Indian Supreme Court ruled that the government could not privatize two state-owned oil companies without explicit approval from the parliament. There has also been strong resistance to reforming many of India's laws that make it difficult for private business to operate efficiently. For example, labor laws make it almost impossible for firms with more than 100 employees to fire workers. Other laws mandate that certain products can be manufactured only by small companies, effectively making it impossible for companies in these industries to attain the scale required to compete internationally, and foreign retailers are banned from selling directly to Indian consumers (although they have found a side door, starting wholesaling and sourcing companies that supply a local retail partner).[68]

shareholders. Sometimes these managers are the same Communist bureaucrats who ran the enterprise before privatization. Because they have been schooled in the old ways of doing things, they often hesitate to take drastic action to increase the efficiency of the enterprise. Instead, they continue to run the firm as a private fiefdom, seeking to extract whatever economic value they can for their own betterment (in the form of perks that are not reported) while doing little to increase the economic efficiency of the enterprise so that shareholders benefit. Such developments seem less likely to occur, however, if a foreign investor takes a stake in the newly privatized entity. The foreign investor, who usually is a major provider of capital, is often able to use control over a critical resource (money) to push through needed change.

LEGAL SYSTEMS

As noted earlier in this chapter, a well-functioning market economy requires laws protecting private property rights and providing mechanisms for contract enforcement. Without a legal system that protects property rights, and without the machinery to enforce that system, the incentive to engage in economic activity can be reduced substantially by private and public entities, including organized crime, that expropriate the profits generated by the efforts of private-sector entrepreneurs. When communism collapsed, many of these countries lacked the legal structure required to protect property rights, all property having been held by the state. Although many nations have made big strides toward instituting the required system, it will be many more years before the legal system is functioning as smoothly as it does in the West. For example, in most Eastern European nations, the title to urban and agricultural property is often uncertain because of incomplete and inaccurate records, multiple pledges on the same property, and unsettled claims resulting from demands for restitution from owners in the pre-Communist era. Also, although most countries have improved their commercial codes, institutional weaknesses still undermine contract enforcement. Court capacity is often inadequate, and procedures for resolving contract disputes out of court are often lacking or poorly developed.[66] Nevertheless, progress is being made. In 2004, for example, China amended its constitution to state that "private property was not to be encroached upon," and in 2007 it enacted a new law on property rights that gave private property holders many of the same protections as those enjoyed by the state.[67]

IMPLICATIONS OF CHANGING POLITICAL ECONOMY

The global changes in political and economic systems discussed above have several implications for international business. The long-standing ideological conflict between collectivism and individualism that defined the twentieth century is less in evidence today. The West won the Cold War, and Western ideology has never been more widespread than it is now. Although command economies remain and totalitarian dictatorships can still be found around the world, the tide has been running in favor of free markets and democracy.

The implications for business are enormous. For nearly 50 years, half of the world was off-limits to Western businesses. Now all that is changing. Many of the national markets of Eastern Europe, Latin America, Africa, and Asia may still be undeveloped and impoverished, but they are potentially enormous. With a population of more than 1.2 billion, the Chinese market alone is potentially bigger than that of the United States, the European Union, and Japan combined. Similarly India, with its nearly 1 billion people, is a potentially huge market. Latin America has another 400 million potential consumers. It is unlikely that China, Russia, Vietnam, or any of the other states now moving toward a free market system will attain the living standards of the West soon. Nevertheless, the upside potential is so large that companies need to consider making inroads now. For example, if China and Japan continue to grow at the

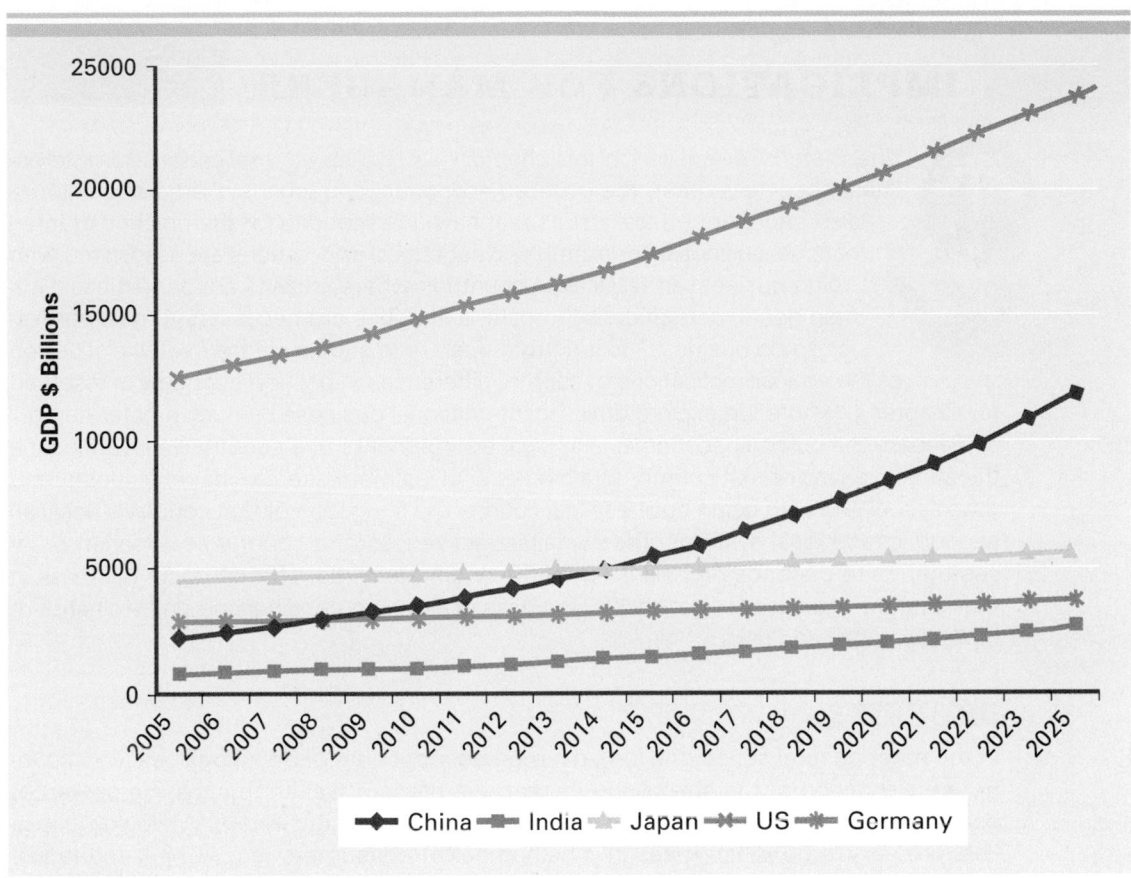

FIGURE 2.3

The World's Largest National Economies, 2005–2025 (GDP $ billions)

Notes: Projections based on nominal GDP, and extrapolate past growth rates into the future.

rate they did during 1996 to 2005, China will surpass Japan and become the world's second largest national economy behind the United States in 2015. Figure 2.3 projects the future size of five major national economies, based on projecting growth rates during the last 10 years forward for another 10. The United States, Japan, and Germany are currently the three largest national economies in the world. As can be seen, China in particular surges, surpassing Germany in 2008 and Japan in 2015, while by 2025 India will be closing in on Germany.[69]

However, just as the potential gains are large, so are the risks. There is no guarantee that democracy will thrive in many of the world's newer democratic states, particularly if these states have to grapple with severe economic setbacks. Totalitarian dictatorships could return, although they are unlikely to be of the communist variety. Although the bipolar world of the Cold War era has vanished, it may be replaced by a multipolar world dominated by a number of civilizations. In such a world, much of the economic promise inherent in the global shift toward market-based economic systems may stall in the face of conflicts between civilizations. While the long-term potential for economic gain from investment in the world's new market economies is large, the risks associated with any such investment are also substantial. It would be foolish to ignore these risks. The financial system in China, for example, is not transparent, and many suspect that Chinese banks hold a high proportion of nonperforming loans on their books. If true, these bad debts could trigger a significant financial crisis during the next decade in China, which would dramatically lower growth rates and render invalid the projections given in Figure 2.3.

IMPLICATIONS FOR MANAGERS

The material discussed in this chapter has two broad implications for international business. First, the political, economic, and legal systems of a country raise important ethical issues that have implications for the practice of international business. For example, what ethical implications are associated with doing business in totalitarian countries where citizens are denied basic human rights, corruption is rampant, and bribes are necessary to gain permission to do business? Is it right to operate in such a setting? A full discussion of the ethical implications of country differences in political economy is reserved for Chapter 4, where we explore ethics in international business in much greater depth.

Second, the political, economic, and legal environments of a country clearly influence the attractiveness of that country as a market or investment site. The benefits, costs, and risks associated with doing business in a country are a function of that country's political, economic, and legal systems. The overall attractiveness of a country as a market or investment site depends on balancing the likely long-term benefits of doing business in that country against the likely costs and risks. Below we consider the determinants of benefits, costs, and risks.

BENEFITS

In the most general sense, the long-run monetary benefits of doing business in a country are a function of the size of the market, the present wealth (purchasing power) of consumers in that market, and the likely future wealth of consumers. While some markets are very large when measured by number of consumers (e.g., China and India), low living standards may imply limited purchasing power and therefore a relatively small market when measured in economic terms. International businesses need to be aware of this distinction, but they also need to keep in mind the likely future prospects of a country. In 1960, South Korea was viewed as just another impoverished Third World nation. By 2005 it was the world's eleventh-largest economy, measured in terms of GDP. International firms that recognized South Korea's potential in 1960 and began to do business in that country may have reaped greater benefits than those that wrote off South Korea.

By identifying and investing early in a potential future economic star, international firms may build brand loyalty and gain experience in that country's business practices. These will pay back substantial dividends if that country achieves sustained high economic growth rates. In contrast, late entrants may find that they lack the brand loyalty and experience necessary to achieve a significant presence in the market. In the language of business strategy, early entrants into potential future economic stars may be able to reap substantial first-mover advantages, while late entrants may fall victim to late-mover disadvantages.[70] (**First-mover advantages** are the advantages that accrue to early entrants into a market. **Late-mover disadvantages** are the handicaps that late entrants might suffer.) This kind of reasoning has been driving significant inward investment into China, which may become the world's second-largest economy by 2015 if it continues growing at current rates (China is already the world's sixth-largest economy). For more than a decade, China has been the largest recipient of foreign direct investment in the developing world as international businesses ranging from General Motors and Volkswagen to Coca-Cola and Unilever try to establish a sustainable advantage in this nation.

A country's economic system and property rights regime are reasonably good predictors of economic prospects. Countries with free market economies in which property rights are protected tend to achieve greater economic growth rates than command economies or economies where property rights are poorly protected. It follows that a country's economic system, property rights regime, and market size (in terms of population) probably constitute reasonably good indicators of the potential long-run benefits of doing business in a country. In contrast, countries where property rights are not well respected and where corruption is rampant tend to have lower levels of economic growth. One must be careful about generalizing too much from this, however, since both China and India have achieved high growth rates despite relatively weak property rights regimes and high levels of corruption. In both countries, the shift toward a market based economic system has produced large gains despite weak property rights and endemic corruption.

COSTS

A number of political, economic, and legal factors determine the costs of doing business in a country. With regard to political factors, a company may have to pay off politically powerful entities in a country before the government allows it to do business there. The need to pay what are essentially bribes is greater in closed totalitarian states than in open democratic societies where politicians are held accountable by the electorate (although this is not a hard-and-fast distinction). Whether a company should actually pay bribes in return for market access should be determined on the basis of the legal and ethical implications of such action. We discuss this consideration in Chapter 4, when we look closely at the issue of business ethics.

With regard to economic factors, one of the most important variables is the sophistication of a country's economy. It may be more costly to do business in relatively primitive or undeveloped economies because of the lack of infrastructure and supporting businesses. At the extreme, an international firm may have to provide its own infrastructure and supporting business, which obviously raises costs. When McDonald's decided to open its first restaurant in Moscow, it found that to serve food and drink indistinguishable from that served in McDonald's restaurants elsewhere, it had to vertically integrate backward to supply its own needs. The quality of Russian-grown potatoes and meat was too poor. Thus, to protect the quality of its product, McDonald's set up its own dairy farms, cattle ranches, vegetable plots, and food processing plants within Russia. This raised the cost of doing business in Russia, relative to the cost in more sophisticated economies where high-quality inputs could be purchased on the open market.

As for legal factors, it can be more costly to do business in a country where local laws and regulations set strict standards with regard to product safety, safety in the workplace, environmental pollution, and the like (since adhering to such regulations is costly). It can also be more costly to do business in a country like the United States, where the absence of a cap on damage awards has meant spiraling liability insurance rates. It can be more costly to do business in a country that lacks well-established laws for regulating business practice (as is the case in many of the former Communist nations). In the absence of a well-developed body of business contract law, international firms may find no satisfactory way to resolve contract disputes and, consequently, routinely face large losses from contract violations. Similarly, local laws that fail to adequately protect intellectual property can lead to the theft of an international business's intellectual property and lost income.

RISKS

As with costs, the risks of doing business in a country are determined by a number of political, economic, and legal factors. **Political risk** has been defined as the likelihood that political forces will cause drastic changes in a country's business environment that adversely affect the profit and other goals of a business enterprise.[71] So defined, political risk tends to be greater in countries experiencing social unrest and disorder or in countries where the underlying nature of a society increases the likelihood of social unrest. Social unrest typically finds expression in strikes, demonstrations, terrorism, and violent conflict. Such unrest is more likely to be found in countries that contain more than one ethnic nationality, in countries where competing ideologies are battling for political control, in countries where economic mismanagement has created high inflation and falling living standards, or in countries that straddle the "fault lines" between civilizations.

Social unrest can result in abrupt changes in government and government policy or, in some cases, in protracted civil strife. Such strife tends to have negative economic implications for the profit goals of business enterprises. For example, in the aftermath of the 1979 Islamic revolution in Iran, the Iranian assets of numerous U.S. companies were seized by the new Iranian government without compensation. Similarly, the violent disintegration of the Yugoslavian federation into warring states, including Bosnia, Croatia, and Serbia, precipitated a collapse in the local economies and in the profitability of investments in those countries.

More generally, a change in political regime can result in the enactment of laws that are less favorable to international business. In Venezuela, for example, the populist socialist politician Hugo Chavez won power in 1998, was reelected as president in 2000, and was reelected in 2006. Chavez has declared himself to be a "Fidelista," a follower of Cuba's Fidel Castro. He has pledged to improve the lot of the poor in Venezuela through government intervention in private business and has frequently railed against American imperialism, all of which is of concern to Western enterprises doing business in the country. Among other actions, he increased the royalties foreign oil companies operating in Venezuela have to pay the government from 1 to 30 percent of sales (see the opening case).

Other risks may arise from a country's mismanagement of its economy. An **economic risk** can be defined as the likelihood that economic mismanagement will cause drastic changes in a country's business environment that hurt the profit and other goals of a particular business enterprise. Economic risks are not independent of political risk. Economic mismanagement may give rise to significant social unrest and hence political risk. Nevertheless, economic risks are worth emphasizing as a separate category because there is not always a one-to-one relationship between economic mismanagement and social unrest. One visible indicator of economic mismanagement tends to be a country's inflation rate. Another is the level of business and government debt in the country.

In Asian states such as Indonesia, Thailand, and South Korea, businesses increased their debt rapidly during the 1990s, often at the bequest of the government, which was encouraging them to invest in industries deemed to be of "strategic importance" to the country. The result was overinvestment, with more industrial (factories) and commercial capacity (office space) being built than could be justified by demand conditions. Many of these investments turned out to be uneconomic. The borrowers failed to generate the profits necessary to service their debt payment obligations. In turn, the banks that had lent money to these businesses suddenly found that they had rapid increases in nonperforming loans on their books. Foreign investors, believing that many local companies and banks might go bankrupt, pulled their money out of these countries, selling local stock, bonds, and currency. This action precipitated the 1997–98 financial crisis in Southeast Asia. The crisis included a precipitous decline in the value of Asian stock markets, which in some cases exceeded 70 percent; a similar collapse in the value of many Asian currencies against the U.S. dollar; an implosion of local demand; and a severe economic recession that will affect many Asian countries for years to come. In short, economic risks were rising throughout Southeast Asia during the 1990s. Astute foreign businesses and investors limited their exposure in this part of the world. More naive businesses and investors lost their shirts.

On the legal front, risks arise when a country's legal system fails to provide adequate safeguards in the case of contract violations or to protect property rights. When legal safeguards are weak, firms are more likely to break contracts or steal intellectual property if they perceive it as being in their interests to do so. Thus, a **legal risk** can be defined as the likelihood that a trading partner will opportunistically break a contract or expropriate property rights. When legal risks in a country are high, an international business might hesitate entering into a long-term contract or joint-venture agreement with a firm in that country. For example, in the 1970s when the Indian government passed a law requiring all foreign investors to enter into joint ventures with Indian companies, U.S. companies such as IBM and Coca-Cola closed their investments in India. They believed that the Indian legal system did not provide for adequate protection of intellectual property rights, creating the very real danger that their Indian partners might expropriate the intellectual property of the American companies—which for IBM and Coca-Cola amounted to the core of their competitive advantage.

OVERALL ATTRACTIVENESS

The overall attractiveness of a country as a potential market or investment site for an international business depends on balancing the benefits, costs, and risks associated with doing business in that country (see Figure 2.4). Generally, the costs and risks associated with doing business in a foreign country are typically lower in economically advanced and politically stable democratic nations and greater in less developed and politically unstable nations. The calculus is complicated, however, because the potential long-run benefits are dependent not only upon a nation's current stage of economic development or political stability but also on likely future economic growth rates. Economic growth appears to be a function of a free market system and a country's capacity for growth (which may be greater in less developed nations). This leads one to conclude that, other things being equal, the benefit–cost–risk trade-off is likely to be most favorable in politically stable developed and developing nations that have free market systems and no dramatic upsurge in either inflation rates or private-sector debt. It is likely to be least favorable in politically unstable developing nations that operate with a mixed or command economy or in developing nations where speculative financial bubbles have led to excess borrowing.

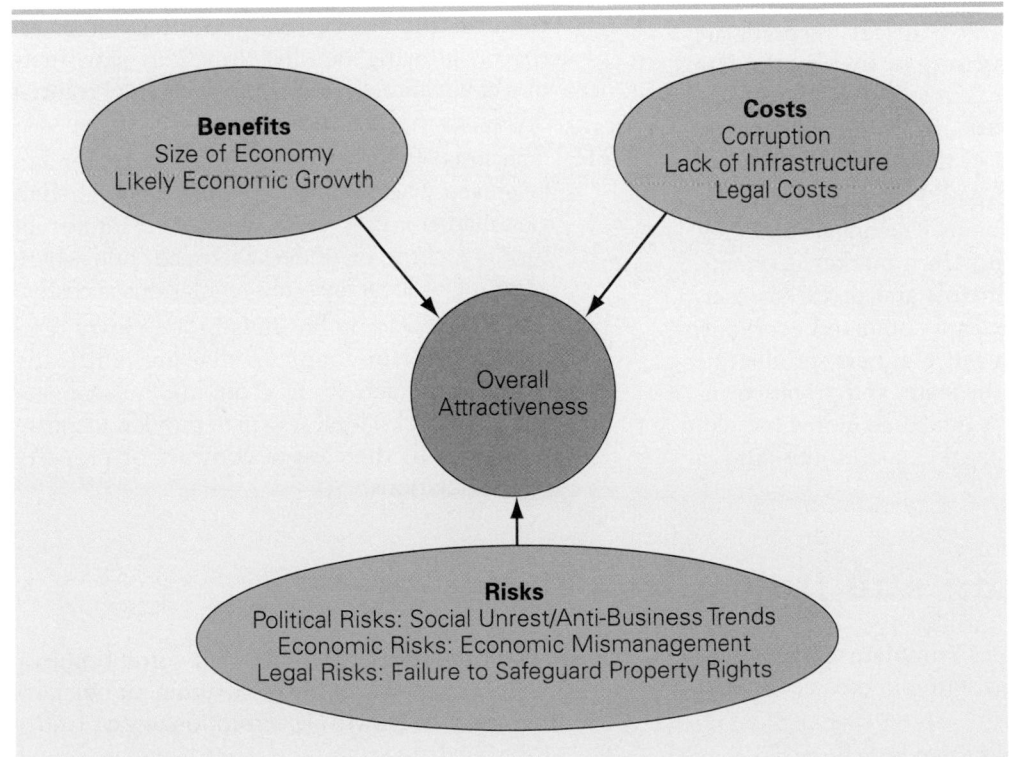

FIGURE 2.4

Country Attractiveness

CHAPTER SUMMARY

This chapter has reviewed how the political, economic, and legal systems of countries vary. The potential benefits, costs, and risks of doing business in a country are a function of its political, economic, and legal systems. The chapter made the following points:

1. Political systems can be assessed according to two dimensions: the degree to which they emphasize collectivism as opposed to individualism, and the degree to which they are democratic or totalitarian.

2. Collectivism is an ideology that views the needs of society as being more important than the needs of the individual. Collectivism translates into an advocacy for state intervention in economic activity and, in the case of communism, a totalitarian dictatorship.

3. Individualism is an ideology that is built on an emphasis of the primacy of an individual's freedoms in the political, economic, and cultural realms. Individualism translates into an advocacy for democratic ideals and free market economics.

4. Democracy and totalitarianism are at different ends of the political spectrum. In a representative democracy, citizens periodically elect individuals to represent them and political freedoms are guaranteed by a constitution. In a totalitarian state, political power is monopolized by a party, group, or individual, and basic political freedoms are denied to citizens of the state.

5. There are three broad types of economic systems: a market economy, a command economy, and a mixed economy. In a market economy, prices are free of controls and private ownership is predominant. In a command economy, prices are set by central planners, productive assets are owned by the state, and private ownership is forbidden. A mixed economy has elements of both a market economy and a command economy.

6. Differences in the structure of law between countries can have important implications for the practice of international business. The degree to which property rights are protected can vary dramatically from country to country, as can product safety and product liability legislation and the nature of contract law.

7. The rate of economic progress in a country seems to depend on the extent to which that country has a well-functioning market economy in which property rights are protected.

8. Many countries are now in a state of transition. There is a marked shift away from totalitarian governments and command or mixed economic systems and toward democratic political institutions and free market economic systems.

9. The attractiveness of a country as a market and/or investment site depends on balancing the likely long-run benefits of doing business in that country against the likely costs and risks.

10. The benefits of doing business in a country are a function of the size of the market (population), its present wealth (purchasing power), and its future growth prospects. By investing early in countries that are currently poor but are nevertheless growing rapidly, firms can gain first-mover advantages that will pay back substantial dividends in the future.

11. The costs of doing business in a country tend to be greater where political payoffs are required to gain market access, where supporting infrastructure is lacking or underdeveloped, and where adhering to local laws and regulations is costly.

12. The risks of doing business in a country tend to be greater in countries that are politically unstable, are subject to economic mismanagement, and lack a legal system to provide adequate safeguards in the case of contract or property rights violations.

Critical Thinking and Discussion Questions

1. Free market economies stimulate greater economic growth, whereas state-directed economies stifle growth. Discuss.

2. A democratic political system is an essential condition for sustained economic progress. Discuss.

3. What is the relationship between corruption in a country (i.e., bribe taking by government officials) and economic growth? Is corruption always bad?

4. The Nobel Prize–winning economist Amartya Sen argues that the concept of development

should be broadened to include more than just economic development. What other factors does Sen think should be included in an assessment of development? How might adoption of Sen's views influence government policy? Do you think Sen is correct that development is about more than just economic development? Explain.

5. You are the CEO of a company that has to choose between making a $100 million investment in Russia or the Czech Republic. Both investments promise the same long-run return, so your choice is driven by risk considerations. Assess the various risks of doing business in each of these nations. Which investment would you favor and why?

6. Read the Country Focus on India in this chapter and answer the following questions:

   a. What kind of economic system did India operate under during 1947 to 1990? What kind of system is it moving toward today? What are the impediments to completing this transformation?

   b. How might widespread public ownership of businesses and extensive government regulations have impacted (*i*) the efficiency of state and private businesses, and (*ii*) the rate of new business formation in India during the 1947–90 time frame? How do you think these factors affected the rate of economic growth in India during this time frame?

   c. How would privatization, deregulation, and the removal of barriers to foreign direct investment affect the efficiency of business, new business formation, and the rate of economic growth in India during the post-1990 time period?

   d. India now has pockets of strengths in key high-technology industries such as software and pharmaceuticals. Why do you think India is developing strength in these areas? How might success in these industries help to generate growth in the other sectors of the Indian economy?

   e. Given what is now occurring in the Indian economy, do you think the country represents an attractive target for inward investment by foreign multinationals selling consumer products? Why?

Research Task

Use the globalEDGE™ site to complete the following exercises:

1. The definition of words and political ideas can have different meanings in different contexts worldwide. In fact, the *Freedom in the World* survey evaluates the state of political rights and civil liberties around the world. Provide a description of this survey and a ranking (in terms of "freedom") of the leaders and laggards of the world. What factors are taken into consideration in this survey?

2. One way that experts analyze conditions in different emerging markets and cultures in transition is through the use of economic indictors. Market Potential Indicators (MPI) is an indexing study conducted by the Michigan State University Center for International Business Education and Research (MSU-CIBER) to compare emerging markets on a variety of dimensions. Provide a description of the indicators used in the indexing procedure. Which of the indicators would have greater importance for a company that markets laptop computers? Considering the MPI rankings, which developing countries would you advise this company to enter first?

CLOSING CASE

Indonesia—The Troubled Giant

Indonesia is a vast country. Its 220 million people are spread out over some 17,000 islands that span an arc 3,200 miles long from Sumatra in the west to Irian Jaya in the east. It is the world's most populous Muslim nation—some 85 percent of the population count themselves as Muslims—but also one of the most ethnically diverse. More than 500 languages are spoken in the country, and separatists are active in a number of provinces. For 30 years, this sprawling nation was held together by the strong arm of President Suharto. Suharto was a virtual dictator who was backed by the military establishment. Under his rule, the Indonesian economy grew steadily, but there was a cost. Suharto brutally repressed internal dissent. He was also famous for "crony capitalism," using his command of the political system to favor the business enterprises of his supporters and family.

In the end, Suharto was overtaken by massive debts that Indonesia had accumulated during the 1990s. In 1997, the Indonesian economy went into a tailspin. The International Monetary Fund stepped in with a $43 billion rescue package. When it was revealed that much of this money found its way into the personal coffers of Suharto and his cronies, people took to the streets in protest and he was forced to resign.

After Suharto, Indonesia moved rapidly toward a vigorous democracy, culminating in October 2004 with the inauguration of Susilo Bambang Yudhoyono, the country's first directly elected president. The economic front has also seen progress. Public debt as a percentage of GDP fell from close to 100 percent in 2000 to less than 60 percent by 2004. Inflation declined from 12 percent annually in 2001 to 6 percent in 2004, and the economy grew by around 4 percent per annum during 2001 to 2005.

But Indonesia lags behind its Southeast Asian neighbors. Its economic growth trails that of China, Malaysia, and Thailand. Unemployment is still high at around 10 percent of the working population. Inflation started to reaccelerate in 2005, hitting 14 percent by year end. Growth in labor productivity has been nonexistent for a decade. Worse still, foreign capital is fleeing the country. Sony made headlines by shutting down an audio equipment factory in 2003, and a number of apparel enterprises have left Indonesia for China and Vietnam. In total, the stock of foreign direct investment in Indonesia fell from $24.8 billion in 2001 to $11.4 billion in 2004 as foreign firms left the nation.

Some observers feel that Indonesia is hobbled by its poor infrastructure. Public infrastructure investment has been declining for years. It was about $3 billion in 2003, down from $16 billion in 1996. The road system is a mess, half the country's population has no access to electricity, the number of brownouts is on the rise as the electricity grid ages, and nearly 99 percent of the population lacks access to modern sewerage facilities. The tsunami that ravaged the coast of Sumatra in

late 2004 only made matters worse. Mirroring the decline in public investment has been a slump in private investment. Investment in the country's all-important oil industry fell from $3.8 billion in 1996 to just $187 million in 2002. Oil production has declined even though oil prices are at record highs. Investment in mining has also fallen from $2.6 billion in 1997 to $177 million in 2003.

According to a World Bank study, business activity in Indonesia is hurt by excessive red tape. It takes 151 days on average to complete the paperwork necessary to start a business, compared to 30 days in Malaysia and just 8 days in Singapore. Another problem is the endemically high level of corruption. Transparency International, which studies corruption around the world, ranks Indonesia among the most corrupt, listing it 137 out of the 158 countries it tracked in 2005. Government bureaucrats, whose salaries are very low, inevitably demand bribes from any company that crosses their path—and Indonesia's penchant for bureaucratic red tape means a long line of officials might require bribes. Abdul Rahman Saleh, the attorney general in Indonesia, has stated that the entire legal system, including the police and the prosecutors, is mired in corruption. The police have been known to throw the executives of foreign enterprises into jail on the flimsiest of pretexts, although some well-placed bribes can secure their release. Even though Indonesia has recently launched an anticorruption drive, critics claim it lacks any teeth. The political elite are reportedly so corrupt that it is not in their interests to do anything meaningful to fix the system.[72]

Case Discussion Questions

1. What political factors explain Indonesia's poor economic performance? What economic factors? Are these two related?

2. Why do you think foreign firms have been exiting Indonesia in recent years? What are the implications for the country? What is required to reverse this trend?

3. Why is corruption so endemic in Indonesia? What are its consequences?

4. What are the risks facing foreign firms that do business in Indonesia? What is required to reduce these risks?

Notes

1. D. Luhnow and P. Millard, "Chavez Plans to Take More Control of Oil away from Foreign Firms," *The Wall Street Journal*, April 24, 2006, p. A1; R. Gallego, "Chavez's Agenda Takes Shape," *The Wall Street Journal*, December 27, 2005, p. A12; "The Sickly Stench of Corruption: Venezuela," *The Economist*, April 1, 2006, p. 50; "Chavez Squeezes the Oil Firms," *The Economist*, November 12, 2005, p. 61; and "Glimpsing the Bottom of the Barrel; Venezuela," *The Economist*, February 3, 2007, p. 51.

2. Although, as we shall see, there is not a strict one-to-one correspondence between political systems and economic systems. A. O. Hirschman, "The On-and-Off Again Connection between Political and Economic Progress," *American Economic Review* 84, no. 2 (1994), pp. 343–48.

3. For a discussion of the roots of collectivism and individualism, see H. W. Spiegel, *The Growth of Economic Thought* (Durham, NC: Duke University Press, 1991). A discussion of collectivism and individualism can be found in M. Friedman and R. Friedman, *Free to Choose* (London: Penguin Books, 1980).

4. For a classic summary of the tenets of Marxism details, see A. Giddens, *Capitalism and Modern Social Theory* (Cambridge: Cambridge University Press, 1971).

5. J. S. Mill, *On Liberty* (London: Longman's, 1865), p. 6.

6. A. Smith, *The Wealth of Nations*, Vol. 1 (London: Penguin Books), p. 325.

7. R. Wesson, *Modern Government—Democracy and Authoritarianism*, 2nd ed. (Englewood Cliffs, NJ: Prentice Hall, 1990).

8. For a detailed but accessible elaboration of this argument, see Friedman and Friedman, *Free to Choose*. Also see P. M. Romer, "The Origins of Endogenous Growth," *Journal of Economic Perspectives* 8, no. 1 (1994), pp. 2–32.

9. T. W. Lippman, *Understanding Islam* (New York: Meridian Books, 1995).

10. "Islam's Interest," *The Economist*, January 18, 1992, pp. 33–34.

11. Rodney Wilson, "Islamic Banking," *Economic Record*, September 2002, pp. 373–74; and M. El Qorchi, "Islamic Finance Gears Up," *Finance and Development*, December 2005, pp 46–50.

12. This information can be found on the UN's Treaty Web site at http://untreaty.un.org/ENGLISH/bible/englishinternetbible/partI/chapterX/treaty17.asp.

13. International Court of Arbitration, www.iccwbo.org/index_court.asp.

14. D. North, *Institutions, Institutional Change, and Economic Performance* (Cambridge: Cambridge University Press, 1991).

15. "China's Next Revolution," *The Economist*, March 10, 2007, p. 9.

16. P. Klebnikov, "Russia's Robber Barons," *Forbes*, November 21, 1994, pp. 74–84; C. Mellow, "Russia: Making Cash from Chaos," *Fortune*, April 17, 1995, pp. 145–51; and "Mr Tatum Checks Out," *The Economist*, November 9, 1996, p. 78.

17. K. van Wolferen, *The Enigma of Japanese Power* (New York: Vintage Books, 1990), pp. 100–5.

18. P. Bardhan, "Corruption and Development: A Review of the Issues," *Journal of Economic Literature*, September 1997, pp. 1320–46.

19. K. M. Murphy, A. Shleifer, and R. Vishny, "Why Is Rent Seeking So Costly to Growth?" *American Economic Review* 83, no. 2 (1993), pp. 409–14.

20. Transparency International, "Global Corruption Report, 2006," www.transparency.org, 2006.

21. www.transparency.org.

22. J. Coolidge and S. Rose Ackerman, "High Level Rent Seeking and Corruption in African Regimes," World Bank policy research working paper no. 1780, June 1997; Murphy et al., "Why Is Rent Seeking So Costly to Growth?"; M. Habib and L. Zurawicki, "Corruption and Foreign Direct Investment," *Journal of International Business Studies* 33 (2002), pp. 291–307; J. E. Anderson and D. Marcouiller, "Insecurity and the Pattern of International Trade," *Review of Economics and Statistics* 84 (2002), pp. 342–52; and T. S. Aidt, "Economic Analysis of Corruption: A Survey," *The Economic Journal* 113 (November 2003), pp. 632–53.

23. Sources: "A Tale of Two Giants," *The Economist*, January 15, 2000, p. 5; J. Coolidge and S. Rose Ackerman, "High Level Rent Seeking and Corruption in African Regimes," World Bank policy research working paper no. 1780, June 1997; D. L. Bevan, P. Collier, and J. W. Gunning, *Nigeria and Indonesia: The Political Economy of Poverty, Equity and Growth* (Oxford: Oxford University Press, 1999); "Democracy and Its Discontents," *The Economist*, January 29, 2005, p. 55; A. Field, "Can Reform Save Nigeria?" *Journal of Commerce*, November 21, 2005, p. 1; and "A Blacklist to Bolster Democracy," *The Economist*, February 17, 2007, p. 59.

24. Details can be found at www.oecd.org/EN/home/0, EN-home-31-nodirectorate-no-nono-31,00.html.

25. Dale Stackhouse and Kenneth Ungar, "The Foreign Corrupt Practices Act: Bribery, Corruption, Record Keeping and More," *Indiana Lawyer*, April 21, 1993.

26. For an interesting discussion of strategies for dealing with the low cost of copying and distributing digital information, see the chapter on rights management in C. Shapiro and H. R. Varian, *Information Rules* (Boston: Harvard Business School Press, 1999). Also see Charles W. L. Hill, "Digital Piracy," *Asian Pacific Journal of Management*, forthcoming, 2007.

27. Douglass North has argued that the correct specification of intellectual property rights is one factor that lowers the cost of doing business and, thereby, stimulates economic growth and development. See North, *Institutions, Institutional Change, and Economic Performance*.

28. International Federation of the Phonographic Industry, *The Commercial Music Industry Global Piracy Report*, 2005, www.ifpi.org.

29. Business Software Alliance, "Fourth Annual BSA and IDC Global Software Piracy Study," May 2007, www.bsa.org, accessed June 14, 2007.

30. Ibid.

31. "Trade Tripwires," *The Economist*, August 27, 1994, p. 61.

32. Sources: M. Dickie, "Starbucks Wins Case against Chinese Copycat," *Financial Times*, January 3, 2006, p. 1; "Starbucks: Chinese Court Backs Company over Trademark Infringement," *The Wall Street Journal*, January 2, 2006, p. A11; and "Starbucks Calls China Its Top Growth Focus," *The Wall Street Journal*, February 14, 2006, p. 1.

33. World Bank, *World Development Indicators Online, 2007*.

34. A. Sen, *Development as Freedom* (New York: Alfred A. Knopf, 1999).

35. G. M. Grossman and E. Helpman, "Endogenous Innovation in the Theory of Growth," *Journal of Economic Perspectives* 8, no. 1 (1994), pp. 23–44; and Romer, "The Origins of Endogenous Growth."

36. W. W. Lewis, *The Power of Productivity* (Chicago: University of Chicago Press, 2004).

37. F. A. Hayek, *The Fatal Conceit: Errors of Socialism* (Chicago: University of Chicago Press, 1989).

38. J. Gwartney, R. Lawson, and W. Block, *Economic Freedom of the World: 1975–1995* (London: Institute of Economic Affairs, 1996).

39. North, *Institutions, Institutional Change, and Economic Performance*. See also Murphy et al., "Why Is Rent Seeking So Costly to Growth?"; and K. E. Maskus, "Intellectual Property Rights in the Global Economy," *Institute for International Economics*, 2000.

40. Hernando de Soto, *The Mystery of Capital: Why Capitalism Triumphs in the West and Fails Everywhere Else* (New York: Basic Books, 2000).

41. Hirschman, "The On-and-Off Again Connection between Political and Economic Progress"; and A. Przeworski and F. Limongi, "Political Regimes and Economic Growth," *Journal of Economic Perspectives* 7, no. 3 (1993), pp. 51–59.

42. Ibid.

43. For details of this argument, see M. Olson, "Dictatorship, Democracy, and Development," *American Political Science Review*, September 1993.

44. For example, see Jared Diamond's Pulitzer Prize–winning book, *Guns, Germs, and Steel* (New York: W. W. Norton, 1997). Also see J. Sachs, "Nature, Nurture and Growth," *The Economist*, June 14, 1997, pp. 19–22; and J. Sachs, *The End of Poverty* (New York: Penguin Books, 2005).

45. Sachs, "Nature, Nurture and Growth."

46. "What Can the Rest of the World Learn from the Classrooms of Asia?" *The Economist*, September 21, 1996, p. 24.

47. J. Fagerberg, "Technology and International Differences in Growth Rates," *Journal of Economic Literature* 32 (September 1994), pp. 1147–75.

48. See The Freedom House Survey Team, "Freedom in the World: 2006" and associated materials, www.freedomhouse.org.

49. "Russia Downgraded to Not Free," Freedom House press release, December 20, 2004, www.freedomhouse.org.

50. Freedom House, "Democracies Century: A Survey of Political Change in the Twentieth Century, 1999," www.freedomhouse.org.

51. L. Conners, "Freedom to Connect," *Wired*, August 1997, pp. 105–6.

52. F. Fukuyama, "The End of History," *The National Interest* 16 (Summer 1989), p. 18.

53. S. P. Huntington, *The Clash of Civilizations and the Remaking of World Order* (New York: Simon & Schuster, 1996).

54. Ibid., p. 116.

55. United States Department of State, Country Reports on Terrorism 2006, archived at http://

www.state.gov/s/ct/rls/crt/2006/82739.htm, accessed June 14, 2007.

56. United States National Counterterrorism Center, *Reports on Incidents of Terrorism*, 2005, April 11, 2006.

57. S. Fisher, R. Sahay, and C. A. Vegh, "Stabilization and the Growth in Transition Economies: the Early Experience," *Journal of Economic Perspectives* 10 (Spring 1996), pp. 45–66.

58. M. Miles et al., 2006 *Index of Economic Freedom* (Washington, DC: Heritage Foundation, 2006).

59. International Monetary Fund, *World Economic Outlook: Focus on Transition Economies* (Geneva: IMF, October 2000).

60. J. C. Brada, "Privatization Is Transition—Is It?" *Journal of Economic Perspectives*, Spring 1996, pp. 67–86.

61. See S. Zahra et al., "Privatization and Entrepreneurial Transformation," *Academy of Management Review* 3, no. 25 (2000), pp. 509–24.

62. N. Brune, G. Garrett, and B. Kogut, "The International Monetary Fund and the Global Spread of Privatization," *IMF Staff Papers* 51, no. 2 (2006), pp. 195–219.

63. Fischer et al., "Stabilization and the Growth in Transition Economies."

64. J. Sachs, C. Zinnes, and Y. Eilat, "The Gains from Privatization in Transition Economies: Is Change of Ownership Enough?" CAER discussion paper no. 63 (Cambridge, MA: Harvard Institute for International Development, 2000).

65. J. Nellis, "Time to Rethink Privatization in Transition Economies?" *Finance and Development* 36, no. 2 (1999), pp. 16–19.

66. M. S. Borish and M. Noel, "Private Sector Development in the Visegrad Countries," *World Bank*, March 1997.

67. "Caught between Right and Left, Town and Country," *The Economist*, March 10, 2007, pp 23–24.

68. Sources: "India's Breakthrough Budget?" *The Economist*, March 3, 2001; Shankar Aiyar, "Reforms: Time to Just Do It," *India Today*, January 24, 2000, p. 47; "America's Pain, India's Gain," *The Economist*, January 11, 2003, p. 57; Joanna Slater, "In Once Socialist India, Privatizations Are Becoming More Like Routine Matters," *The Wall Street Journal*, July 5, 2002, p. A8; "India's Economy: Ready to Roll Again?" *The Economist*, September 20, 2003, pp. 39–40; Joanna Slater, "Indian Pirates Turned Partners," *The Wall Street Journal*, November 13, 2003, p. A14; "The Next Wave: India," *The Economist*, December 17, 2005, p. 67; M. Dell, "The Digital Sector Can Make Poor Nations Prosper," *Financial Times*, May 4, 2006, p. 17; and "Setting Up Shop in India," *The Economist*, November 4, 2006, p. 79.

69. Projections are by the author and are based upon nominal GDP, unadjusted for inflation or purchasing power parity.

70. For a discussion of first-mover advantages, see M. Liberman and D. Montgomery, "First-Mover Advantages," *Strategic Management Journal* 9 (Summer Special Issue, 1988), pp. 41–58.

71. S. H. Robock, "Political Risk: Identification and Assessment," *Columbia Journal of World Business*, July–August 1971, pp. 6–20.

72. Sources: "A Survey of Indonesia: Time to Deliver," *The Economist*, December 11, 2004; "A Survey of Indonesia: Enemies of Promise," *The Economist*, December 11, 2004, pp. 4–5; "A Survey of Indonesia: The Importance of Going Straight," *The Economist*, December 11, 2004, pp. 6–7; World Bank, *World Development Indicators Online*, 2006; Transparency International, *Global Corruption Report*, 2006; and S. Donnan, "Indonesian Workers Mark May Day with Protests at Planned Changes to Labor Laws," *Financial Times*, May 2, 2006, p. 4.

Wal-Mart's Foreign Expansion

Wal-Mart is the world's largest retailer. The company employs some 1.8 million people, operates 3,900 stores in the United States and 2,700 in the rest of the world, and generated sales of $345 billion in the fiscal year ending January 31, 2007. Some $77 billion of these sales were generated in 15 nations outside of the United States. Facing a slowdown in growth in the United States, Wal-Mart began its international expansion in the early 1990s when it entered Mexico, teaming up in a joint venture with Cifra, Mexico's largest retailer, to open a series of super-centers that sell both groceries and general merchandise.

Initially the retailer hit some headwinds in Mexico. It quickly discovered that shopping habits were different. Most people preferred to buy fresh produce at local stores, particularly items like meat, tortillas, and pan dulce, which didn't keep well overnight (many Mexicans lacked large refrigerators). Many consumers also lacked cars, and did not buy in large volumes as in the United States. Wal-Mart adjusted its strategy to meet the local conditions, hiring local managers who understood Mexican culture, letting those managers control merchandising strategy, building smaller stores that people could walk

to, and offering more fresh produce. At the same time, the company believed that it could gradually change the shopping culture in Mexico, educating consumers by showing them the benefits of its American merchandising culture. After all, Wal-Mart's managers reasoned, people once shopped at small stores in the United States, but starting in the 1950s they increasingly gravitated toward large stores like Wal-Mart. As it built up its distribution systems in Mexico, Wal-Mart was able to lower its own costs, which it passed on to Mexican consumers in the form of lower prices. The customization, persistence, and low prices paid off. Mexicans started to change their shopping habits. Today Wal-Mart is Mexico's largest retailer, and the country is widely considered to be the company's most successful foreign venture.

Next Wal-Mart expanded into a number of developed nations, including Britain, Germany, and South Korea. There its experiences have been less successful. In all three countries it found itself going head to head against well-established local rivals who had nicely matched their offerings to local shopping habits and consumer preferences. Moreover, consumers in all three countries seemed to have a preference for higher quality merchandise,

Differences in Culture

3

LEARNING OBJECTIVES

After you have read this chapter you should:

LO¹ Know what is meant by the culture of a society.

LO² Identify the forces that lead to differences in social culture.

LO³ Identify the business and economic implications of differences in culture.

LO⁴ Understand how differences in social culture influence values in the workplace.

LO⁵ Develop an appreciation for the economic and business implications of cultural change.

and they were not as attracted to Wal-Mart's discount strategy as consumers in the United States and Mexico. After years of losses, Wal-Mart pulled out of Germany and South Korea in 2006. At the same time, it continued to look for retailing opportunities elsewhere, particularly in developed nations where it lacked strong local competitors, where it could gradually alter the shopping culture to its advantage, and where its low-price strategy was appealing.

Recently, the centerpiece of its international expansion efforts has been China. Wal-Mart opened its first store in China in 1996, but initially expanded very slowly, and by 2006 had only 66 stores. What Wal-Mart discovered, however, was the Chinese were bargain hunters and open to the low-price strategy and wide selection offered at Wal-Mart stores. Indeed, in terms of their shopping habits, the emerging Chinese middle class seemed more American than European. But to succeed in China, Wal-Mart also found it had to adapt its merchandising and operations strategy so that it meshes with Chinese culture. One of the things that Wal-Mart has learned: Chinese consumers insist that food must be freshly harvested, or even killed in front of them. Wal-Mart initially offended Chinese consumers by trying to sell them dead fish, as well as meat packed in Styrofoam and cellophane. Shoppers turned their noses up at what they saw as old merchandise. So Wal-Mart began to display the meat uncovered, installed fish tanks into which shoppers could plunge fishing nets to pull out their evening meal, and began selling live turtles for turtle soup. Sales soared.

Wal-Mart has also learned that in China, success requires it to embrace unions. Whereas in the United States Wal-Mart has vigorously resisted unionization, it came to the realization that in China unions don't bargain for labor contracts. Instead, they are an arm of the state, providing funding for the Communist Party and (in the government's view) securing social order. In mid-2006 Wal-Mart broke with its long standing antagonism to unions and agreed to allow unions in its Chinese stores. Many believe this set the stage for Wal-Mart's most recent move, the purchase in December 2006 of a 35 percent stake in the Trust-Mart chain, which has 101 hypermarkets in 34 cities across China. Now Wal-Mart has proclaimed that China lies at the center of its growth strategy.[1]

Introduction

As Wal-Mart has discovered, international business is different from domestic business because countries are different. In Chapter 2, we saw how national differences in political, economic, and legal systems influence the benefits, costs, and risks associated with doing business in different countries. In this chapter, we will explore how differences in culture across and within countries can affect international business. Wal-Mart, for example, has had to change the way it displays and sells food to accommodate the culturally embedded tastes and preferences of Chinese consumers.

Several themes run through this chapter. The first theme is that business success in a variety of countries requires cross-cultural literacy. By **cross-cultural literacy,** we mean an understanding of how cultural differences across and within nations can affect the way business is practiced. In these days of global communications, rapid transportation, and worldwide markets, when the era of the global village seems just around the corner, it is easy to forget just how different various cultures really are. Underneath the veneer of modernism, deep cultural differences often remain. Westerners in general, and Americans in particular, are quick to conclude that because people from other parts of the world also wear blue jeans, listen to Western popular music, eat at McDonald's, and drink Coca-Cola, they also accept the basic tenets of Western (or American) culture. However, this is not true. For example, increasingly, the Chinese are embracing the material products of modern society. Anyone who has visited Shanghai cannot fail to be struck by how modern the city seems, with its skyscrapers, department stores, and freeways. Yet beneath the veneer of Western modernism, long-standing cultural traditions rooted in a 2,000-year-old ideology continue to have an important influence on the way business is transacted in China. For example, in China, *guanxi*, or relationships backed by reciprocal obligations, are central to getting business done. Firms that lack sufficient *guanxi* may find themselves at a disadvantage when doing business in China. One of the things that Wal-Mart learned was that to build up *guanxi*, it needed to embrace unions. Once it did this, in 2006 the government opened the way for the company to acquire Trust Mart, one of the biggest operators of hypermarkets in China. The lesson: to succeed in China you have to play by Chinese rules. More generally, in this chapter, we shall argue that it is important for foreign businesses to gain an understanding of the culture that prevails in those countries where they do business, and that success requires a foreign enterprise to adapt to the culture of its host country.[2]

Another theme developed in this chapter is that a relationship may exist between culture and the cost of doing business in a country or region. Different cultures are more or less supportive of the capitalist mode of production and may increase or lower the costs of doing business. For example, some observers have argued that cultural factors lowered the costs of doing business in Japan and helped to explain Japan's rapid economic ascent during the 1960s, 70s, and 80s.[3] Similarly, cultural factors can sometimes raise the costs of doing business. Historically, class divisions were an important aspect of British culture, and for a long time, firms operating in Great Britain found it difficult to achieve cooperation between management and labor. Class divisions led to a high level of industrial disputes in that country during the 1960s and 1970s and raised the costs of doing business relative to the costs in countries such as Switzerland, Norway, Germany, or Japan, where class conflict was historically less prevalent.

The British example, however, brings us to another theme we will explore in this chapter. Culture is not static. It can and does evolve, although the rate at which culture can change is the subject of some dispute. Important aspects of British culture have changed significantly over the past 20 years, and this is reflected in weaker class distinctions and a lower level of industrial disputes. Between 1995 and 2005, the number of days lost per 1,000 workers due to strikes in the United Kingdom was on average 28 each year, significantly less than in the United States (33 each year), Ireland (81), and Canada (168).[4] Finally, it is important to note that multinational enterprises can themselves be engines of cultural change. In Mexico for example, Wal-Mart has helped to change the shopping culture of that nation, drawing them away from small local stores and toward large self-service discount stores. It now hopes to do the same in China.

What Is Culture?

Scholars have never been able to agree on a simple definition of *culture*. In the 1870s, the anthropologist Edward Tylor defined culture as "that complex whole which includes knowledge, belief, art, morals, law, custom, and other capabilities acquired by man as a member of society."[5] Since then hundreds of other definitions have been offered. Geert Hofstede, an expert on cross-cultural differences and management, defined culture as "the collective programming of the mind which distinguishes the members of one human group from another. . . . Culture, in this sense, includes systems of values; and values are among the building blocks of culture."[6] Another definition of culture comes from sociologists Zvi Namenwirth and Robert Weber, who see culture as a system of ideas and argue that these ideas constitute a design for living.[7]

Here we follow both Hofstede and Namenwirth and Weber by viewing **culture** as a system of values and norms that are shared among a group of people and that when taken together constitute a design for living. By **values** we mean abstract ideas about what a group believes to be good, right, and desirable. Put differently, values are shared assumptions about how things ought to be.[8] By **norms** we mean the social rules and guidelines that prescribe appropriate behavior in particular situations. We shall use the term **society** to refer to a group of people who share a common set of values and norms. While a society may be equivalent to a country, some countries harbor several societies (i.e., they support multiple cultures), and some societies embrace more than one country.

VALUES AND NORMS

Values form the bedrock of a culture. They provide the context within which a society's norms are established and justified. They may include a society's attitudes toward such concepts as individual freedom, democracy, truth, justice, honesty, loyalty, social obligations, collective responsibility, the role of women, love, sex, marriage, and so on. Values are not just abstract concepts; they are invested with considerable emotional significance. People argue, fight, and even die over values such as freedom. Values also often are reflected in the political and economic systems of a society. As we saw in Chapter 2, democratic free market capitalism is a reflection of a philosophical value system that emphasizes individual freedom.

Norms are the social rules that govern people's actions toward one another. Norms can be subdivided further into two major categories: folkways and mores. **Folkways** are the routine conventions of everyday life. Generally, folkways are actions of little moral significance. Rather, they are social conventions concerning things such as the appropriate dress code in a particular situation, good social manners, eating with the correct utensils, neighborly behavior, and the like. Although folkways define the way people are expected to behave, violation of them is not normally a serious matter. People who violate folkways may be thought of as eccentric or ill-mannered, but they are not usually considered to be evil or bad. In many countries, foreigners may initially be excused for violating folkways.

A good example of folkways concerns attitudes toward time in different countries. People are keenly aware of the passage of time in the United States and Northern European cultures such as Germany and Britain. Businesspeople are very conscious about scheduling their time and are quickly irritated when their time is wasted because a business associate is late for a meeting or if they are kept waiting. They talk about time as though it were money, as something that can be spent, saved, wasted, and lost.[9] Alternatively, in Arab, Latin, and Mediterranean cultures, time has a more elastic character. Keeping to a schedule is viewed as less important than finishing an interaction with people. For example,

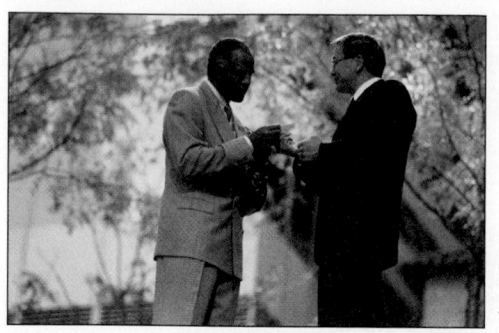

Understanding rituals and symbolic behaviors is essential to doing business in foreign countries.

an American businesswoman might feel slighted if she is kept waiting for 30 minutes outside the office of a Latin American executive before a meeting; but the Latin American may simply be completing an interaction with an associate and view the information gathered from this as more important than sticking to a rigid schedule. The Latin American executive intends no disrespect, but due to a mutual misunderstanding about the importance of time, the American may see things differently. Similarly, Saudi attitudes to time have been shaped by their nomadic Bedouin heritage, in which precise time played no real role and arriving somewhere tomorrow might mean next week. Like Latin Americans, many Saudis are unlikely to understand the American obsession with precise time and schedules, and Americans need to adjust their expectations accordingly.

Folkways include rituals and symbolic behavior. Rituals and symbols are the most visible manifestations of a culture and constitute the outward expression of deeper values. For example, upon meeting a foreign business executive, a Japanese executive will hold his business card in both hands and bow while presenting the card to the foreigner.[10] This ritual behavior is loaded with deep cultural symbolism. The card specifies the rank of the Japanese executive, which is a very important piece of information in a hierarchical society such as Japan (Japanese often have business cards with Japanese printed on one side, and English printed on the other). The bow is a sign of respect, and the deeper the angle of the bow, the greater the reverence one person shows for the other. The person receiving the card is expected to examine it carefully, which is a way of returning respect and acknowledging the card giver's position in the hierarchy. The foreigner is also expected to bow when taking the card, and to return the greeting by presenting the Japanese executive with his own card, similarly bowing in the process. To not do so, and to fail to read the card that he has been given, instead casually placing it in his jacket, violates this important folkway and is considered rude.

Mores are norms that are seen as central to the functioning of a society and to its social life. They have much greater significance than folkways. Accordingly, violating mores can bring serious retribution. Mores include such factors as indictments against theft, adultery, incest, and cannibalism. In many societies, certain mores have been enacted into law. Thus, all advanced societies have laws against theft, incest, and cannibalism. However, there are also many differences between cultures. In America, for example, drinking alcohol is widely accepted, whereas in Saudi Arabia the consumption of alcohol is viewed as violating important social mores and is punishable by imprisonment (as some Western citizens working in Saudi Arabia have discovered).

CULTURE, SOCIETY, AND THE NATION-STATE

We have defined a society as a group of people who share a common set of values and norms; that is, people who are bound together by a common culture. There is not a strict one-to-one correspondence between a society and a nation-state. Nation-states are political creations. They may contain a single culture or several cultures. While the French nation can be thought of as the political embodiment of French culture, the nation of Canada has at least three cultures—an Anglo culture, a French-speaking "Quebecois" culture, and a Native American culture. Similarly, many African nations have important cultural differences between tribal groups, as exhibited in the early 1990s when Rwanda dissolved into a bloody civil war between two tribes, the Tutsis and Hutus. Africa is not alone in this regard. India is composed of many distinct cultural groups. During the first Gulf War, the prevailing view presented to Western audiences was that Iraq was a homogenous Arab nation. However, over the past 15 years, we have learned that several different societies exist within Iraq, each with its own culture. The Kurds in the north do not view themselves as Arabs and have their own distinct history and traditions. There are two Arab societies: the Shiites in the south and the Sunnis who populate the

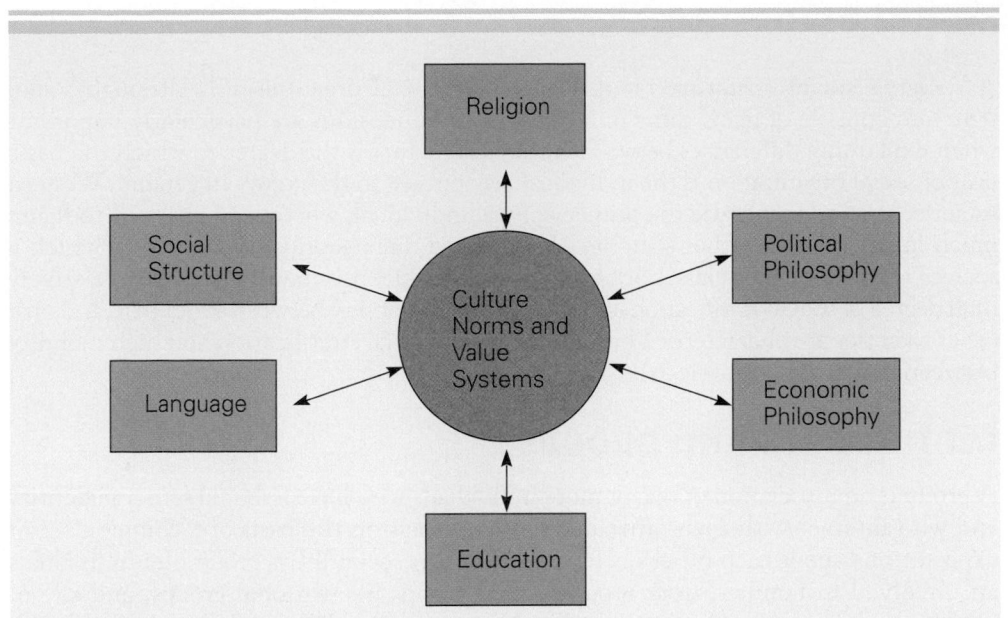

FIGURE 3.1

The Determinants
of Culture

middle of the country and who ruled Iraq under the regime of Saddam Hussein (the terms *Shiites* and *Sunnis* refer to different sects within the religion of Islam). Among the southern Sunnis is another distinct society of 500,000 Marsh Arabs who live at the confluence of the Tigris and Euphrates rivers, pursuing a way of life that dates back 5,000 years.[11]

At the other end of the scale are cultures that embrace several nations. Several scholars argue that we can speak of an Islamic society or culture that the citizens of many different nations in the Middle East, Asia, and Africa share. As you will recall from the last chapter, this view of expansive cultures that embrace several nations underpins Samuel Huntington's view of a world that is fragmented into different civilizations, including Western, Islamic, and Sinic (Chinese).[12]

To complicate things further, it is also possible to talk about culture at different levels. It is reasonable to talk about "American society" and "American culture," but there are several societies within America, each with its own culture. One can talk about African American culture, Cajun culture, Chinese American culture, Hispanic culture, Indian culture, Irish American culture, and Southern culture. The relationship between culture and country is often ambiguous. Even if a country can be characterized as having a single homogenous culture, often that national culture is a mosaic of subcultures.

THE DETERMINANTS OF CULTURE

The values and norms of a culture do not emerge fully formed. They are the evolutionary product of a number of factors, including the prevailing political and economic philosophies, the social structure of a society, and the dominant religion, language, and education (see Figure 3.1). We discussed political and economic philosophies at length in Chapter 2. Such philosophies clearly influence the value systems of a society. For example, the values found in Communist North Korea toward freedom, justice, and individual achievement are clearly different from the values found in the United States, precisely because each society operates according to different political and economic philosophies. Below we will discuss the influence of social structure, religion, language, and education. The chain of causation runs both ways. While factors such as social structure and religion clearly influence the values and norms of a society, the values and norms of a society can also influence social structure and religion.

Social Structure

A society's **social structure** refers to its basic social organization. Although social structure consists of many different aspects, two dimensions are particularly important when explaining differences between cultures. The first is the degree to which the basic unit of social organization is the individual, as opposed to the group. In general, Western societies tend to emphasize the primacy of the individual, whereas groups tend to figure much larger in many other societies. The second dimension is the degree to which a society is stratified into classes or castes. Some societies are characterized by a relatively high degree of social stratification and relatively low mobility between strata (e.g., Indian); other societies are characterized by a low degree of social stratification and high mobility between strata (e.g., American).

INDIVIDUALS AND GROUPS

A **group** is an association of two or more individuals who have a shared sense of identity and who interact with each other in structured ways on the basis of a common set of expectations about each other's behavior.[13] Human social life is group life. Individuals are involved in families, work groups, social groups, recreational groups, and so on. However, while groups are found in all societies, societies differ according to the degree to which the group is viewed as the primary means of social organization.[14] In some societies, individual attributes and achievements are viewed as being more important than group membership; in others the reverse is true.

The Individual

In Chapter 2, we discussed individualism as a political philosophy. However, individualism is more than just an abstract political philosophy. In many Western societies, the individual is the basic building block of social organization. This is reflected not just in the political and economic organization of society but also in the way people perceive themselves and relate to each other in social and business settings. The value systems of many Western societies, for example, emphasize individual achievement. The social standing of individuals is not so much a function of where they work as it is of their individual performance in whatever work setting they choose.

The emphasis on individual performance in many Western societies has both beneficial and harmful aspects. In the United States, the emphasis on individual performance finds expression in an admiration of rugged individualism and entrepreneurship. One benefit of this is the high level of entrepreneurial activity in the United States and other Western societies. New products and new ways of doing business (e.g., personal computers, photocopiers, computer software, biotechnology, supermarkets, and discount retail stores) have repeatedly been created in the United States by entrepreneurial individuals. One can argue that the dynamism of the U.S. economy owes much to the philosophy of individualism.

Individualism also finds expression in a high degree of managerial mobility between companies, and this is not always a good thing. Although moving from company to company may be good for individual managers who are trying to build impressive résumés, it is not necessarily a good thing for American companies. The lack of loyalty and commitment to an individual company, and the tendency to move on for a better offer, can result in managers who have good general skills but lack the knowledge, experience, and network of interpersonal contacts that come from years of working within the same company. An effective manager draws on company-specific experience, knowledge, and a network of contacts to find solutions to current problems, and American companies may suffer if their managers lack these attributes. One positive aspect of high managerial mobility is that executives are exposed to different ways of doing business. The ability to compare business practices helps U.S. executives identify how good practices and techniques developed in one firm might be profitably applied to other firms.

The emphasis on individualism may also make it difficult to build teams within an organization to perform collective tasks. If individuals are always competing with each other on the basis of individual performance, it may be difficult for them to cooperate. A study of U.S. competitiveness by the Massachusetts Institute of Technology concluded that U.S. firms are being hurt in the global economy by a failure to achieve cooperation both within a company (e.g., between functions; between management and labor) and between companies (e.g., between a firm and its suppliers). Given the emphasis on individualism in the American value system, this failure is not surprising.[15] The emphasis on individualism in the United States, while helping to create a dynamic entrepreneurial economy, may raise the costs of doing business due to its adverse impact on managerial stability and cooperation.

The Group

In contrast to the Western emphasis on the individual, the group is the primary unit of social organization in many other societies. For example, in Japan, the social status of an individual is determined as much by the standing of the group to which he or she belongs as by his or her individual performance.[16] In traditional Japanese society, the group was the family or village to which an individual belonged. Today, the group has frequently come to be associated with the individual's work team or business organization. In a now-classic study of Japanese society, Nakane noted how this expresses itself in everyday life:

> When a Japanese faces the outside (confronts another person) and affixes some position to himself socially he is inclined to give precedence to institution over kind of occupation. Rather than saying, "I am a typesetter" or "I am a filing clerk," he is likely to say, "I am from B Publishing Group" or "I belong to S company."[17]

Nakane goes on to observe that the primacy of the group to which an individual belongs often evolves into a deeply emotional attachment in which identification with the group becomes all-important in one's life. One central value of Japanese culture is the importance attached to group membership, which may have beneficial implications for business firms. Strong identification with the group is argued to create pressures for mutual self-help and collective action. If the worth of an individual is closely linked to the achievements of the group (e.g., firm), as Nakane maintains is the case in Japan, this creates a strong incentive for individual members of the group to work together for the common good. Some argue that the success of Japanese enterprises in the global economy has been based partly on their ability to achieve close cooperation between individuals within a company and between companies. This has found expression in the widespread diffusion of self-managing work teams within Japanese organizations, the close cooperation among different functions within Japanese companies (e.g., among manufacturing, marketing, and R&D), and the cooperation between a company and its suppliers on issues such as design, quality control, and inventory reduction.[18] In all of these cases, the need to improve the performance of the group (i.e., the business firm) drives cooperation.

The primacy of the value of group identification also discourages managers and workers from moving from company to company. Lifetime employment in a particular company was long the norm in certain sectors of the Japanese economy (estimates suggest that between 20 and 40 percent of all Japanese employees have formal or informal lifetime employment guarantees). Over the years, managers and workers build up knowledge, experience, and a network of interpersonal business contacts. All these things can help managers perform their jobs more effectively and achieve cooperation with others.

However, the primacy of the group is not always beneficial. Just as U.S. society is characterized by a great deal of dynamism and entrepreneurship, reflecting the primacy of values associated with individualism, some argue that Japanese society is characterized by a corresponding lack of these traits. Although the long-run consequences are unclear, the United States could continue to create more new industries than Japan and to be more successful at pioneering radically new products and new ways of doing business.

SOCIAL STRATIFICATION

All societies are stratified on a hierarchical basis into social categories—that is, into **social strata.** These strata are typically defined on the basis of characteristics such as family background, occupation, and income. Individuals are born into a particular stratum. They become a member of the social category to which their parents belong. Individuals born into a stratum toward the top of the social hierarchy tend to have better life chances than those born into a stratum toward the bottom of the hierarchy. They are likely to have better education, health, standard of living, and work opportunities. Although all societies are stratified to some degree, they differ in two related ways. First, they differ from each other with regard to the degree of mobility between social strata; second, they differ with regard to the significance attached to social strata in business contexts.

Social Mobility

The term **social mobility** refers to the extent to which individuals can move out of the strata into which they are born. Social mobility varies significantly from society to society. The most rigid system of stratification is a caste system. A **caste system** is a closed system of stratification in which social position is determined by the family into which a person is born, and change in that position is usually not possible during an individual's lifetime. Often a caste position carries with it a specific occupation. Members of one caste might be shoemakers, members of another might be butchers, and so on. These occupations are embedded in the caste and passed down through the family to succeeding generations. Although the number of societies with caste systems diminished rapidly during the 20th century, one partial example still remains. India has four main castes and several thousand subcastes. Even though the caste system was officially abolished in 1949, two years after India became independent, it is still a force in rural Indian society where occupation and marital opportunities are still partly related to caste.[19]

A **class system** is a less rigid form of social stratification in which social mobility is possible. It is a form of open stratification in which the position a person has by birth can be changed through his or her own achievements or luck. Individuals born into a class at the bottom of the hierarchy can work their way up; conversely, individuals born into a class at the top of the hierarchy can slip down.

While many societies have class systems, social mobility within a class system varies from society to society. For example, some sociologists have argued that Britain has a more rigid class structure than certain other Western societies, such as the United States.[20] Historically, British society was divided into three main classes: the upper class, which was made up of individuals whose families for generations had wealth, prestige, and occasionally power; the middle class, whose members were involved in professional, managerial, and clerical occupations; and the working class, whose members earned their living from manual occupations. The middle class was further subdivided into the upper-middle class, whose members were involved in important managerial occupations and the prestigious professions (e.g., lawyers, accountants, doctors), and the lower-middle class, whose members were involved in clerical work (e.g., bank tellers) and the less prestigious professions (e.g., schoolteachers).

Historically, the British class system exhibited significant divergence between the life chances of members of different classes. The upper and upper-middle classes typically sent their children to a select group of private schools, where they wouldn't mix with lower-class children, and where they picked up many of the speech accents and social norms that marked them as being from the higher strata of society. These same private schools also had close ties with the most prestigious universities, such as Oxford and Cambridge. Until fairly recently, Oxford and Cambridge guaranteed a certain number of places for the graduates of these private schools. Having been to a prestigious university, the offspring of the upper and upper-middle classes then had an excellent chance of being offered a prestigious job in companies, banks, brokerage firms, and law firms run by members of the upper and upper-middle classes.

In contrast, the members of the British working and lower-middle classes typically went to state schools. The majority left at 16, and those who went on to higher education found it more difficult to get accepted at the best universities. When they did, they found that their lower-class accent and lack of social skills marked them as being from a lower social stratum, which made it more difficult for them to get access to the most prestigious jobs.

Because of this, the class system in Britain perpetuated itself from generation to generation, and mobility was limited. Although upward mobility was possible, it could not normally be achieved in one generation. While an individual from a working-class background may have established an income level that was consistent with membership in the upper-middle class, he or she may not have been accepted as such by others of that class due to accent and background. However, by sending his or her offspring to the "right kind of school," the individual could ensure that his or her children were accepted.

According to many commentators, modern British society is now rapidly leaving this class structure behind and moving toward a classless society. However, sociologists continue to dispute this finding and present evidence that this is not the case. For example, a study reported that in the mid-1990s, state schools in the London suburb of Islington, which has a population of 175,000, had only 79 candidates for university, while one prestigious private school alone, Eton, sent more than that number to Oxford and Cambridge.[21] This, according to the study's authors, implies that "money still begets money." They argue that a good school means a good university, a good university means a good job, and merit has only a limited chance of elbowing its way into this tight little circle.

The class system in the United States is less extreme than in Britain and mobility is greater. Like Britain, the United States has its own upper, middle, and working classes. However, class membership is determined to a much greater degree by individual economic achievements, as opposed to background and schooling. Thus, an individual can, by his or her own economic achievement, move smoothly from the working class to the upper class in a lifetime. Successful individuals from humble origins are highly respected in American society.

Another society where class divisions have historically been of some importance has been China, where there has been a long-standing difference between the life chances of the rural peasantry and urban dwellers. Ironically, this historic division was strengthened during the high point of Communist rule because of a rigid system of household registration that restricted most Chinese to the place of their birth for their lifetime. Bound to collective farming, peasants were cut off from many urban privileges—compulsory education, quality schools, health care, public housing, varieties of foodstuffs, to name only a few—and they largely lived in poverty. Social mobility was thus very limited. This system crumbled following reforms of the late 1970s and early 1980s, and as a consequence, migrant peasant laborers have flooded into China's cities looking for work. Sociologists now hypothesize that a new class system is emerging in China based less on the rural–urban divide and more on urban occupation.[22]

Significance

From a business perspective, the stratification of a society is significant if it affects the operation of business organizations. In American society, the high degree of social mobility and the extreme emphasis on individualism limit the impact of class background on business operations. The same is true in Japan, where most of the population perceives itself to be middle class. In a country such as Great Britain, however, the relative lack of class mobility and the differences between classes have resulted in the emergence of class consciousness. **Class consciousness** refers to a condition where people tend to perceive themselves in terms of their class background, and this shapes their relationships with members of other classes.

Class consciousness has been played out in British society in the traditional hostility between upper-middle-class managers and their working-class employees. Mutual antagonism and lack of respect historically made it difficult to achieve cooperation between management and labor in many British companies and resulted in a relatively high level of industrial disputes. However, as noted earlier, the last two decades have seen a dramatic reduction in industrial disputes, which bolsters the arguments of those who claim that the country is moving toward a classless society (the level of industrial disputes in the United Kingdom is now lower than in the United States). Alternatively, as noted above, class consciousness may be reemerging in urban China, and it may ultimately prove to be significant there.

An antagonistic relationship between management and labor classes, and the resulting lack of cooperation and high level of industrial disruption, tends to raise the costs of production in countries characterized by significant class divisions. In turn, higher costs can make it more difficult for companies based in such countries to establish a competitive advantage in the global economy.

Religious and Ethical Systems

Religion may be defined as a system of shared beliefs and rituals that are concerned with the realm of the sacred.[23] **Ethical systems** refer to a set of moral principles, or values, that are used to guide and shape behavior. Most of the world's ethical systems are the product of religions. Thus, we can talk about Christian ethics and Islamic ethics. However, there is a major exception to the principle that ethical systems are grounded in religion. Confucianism and Confucian ethics influence behavior and shape culture in parts of Asia, yet it is incorrect to characterize Confucianism as a religion.

The relationship among religion, ethics, and society is subtle and complex. Among the thousands of religions in the world today, four dominate in terms of numbers of adherents: Christianity with 1.7 billion adherents, Islam with around 1 billion adherents, Hinduism with 750 million adherents (primarily in India), and Buddhism with 350 million adherents (see Map 3.1). Although many other religions have an important influence in certain parts of the modern world (for example, Judaism, which has 18 million adherents), their numbers pale in comparison with these dominant religions (however, as the precursor of both Christianity and Islam, Judaism has an indirect influence that goes beyond its numbers). We will review these four religions, along with Confucianism, focusing on their business implications. Some scholars have argued that the most important business implications of religion center on the extent to which different religions shape attitudes toward work and entrepreneurship and the degree to which the religious ethics affect the costs of doing business in a country.

It is hazardous to make sweeping generalizations about the nature of the relationship between religion and ethical systems and business practice. While some scholars argue that there is a relationship between religious and ethical systems and business practice in a society, in a world where nations with Catholic, Protestant, Muslim, Hindu, and Buddhist majorities all show evidence of entrepreneurial activity and sustainable economic growth, it is important to view such proposed relationships with a degree of skepticism. The proposed relationships may exist, but their impact is probably small compared to the impact of economic policy. Alternatively, recent research by economists Robert Barro and Rachel McCleary does suggest that strong religious beliefs, and particularly beliefs in heaven, hell, and an afterlife, have a positive impact on economic growth rates, irrespective of the particular religion in question.[24] Barro and McCleary looked at religious beliefs and economic growth rates in 59 countries during the 1980s and 1990s. Their conjecture was that higher religious beliefs stimulate economic growth because they help to sustain aspects of individual behavior that lead to higher productivity.

CHRISTIANITY

Christianity is the most widely practiced religion in the world. Approximately 20 percent of the world's people identify themselves as Christians. The vast majority of Christians live in Europe and the Americas, although their numbers are growing rapidly in Africa. Christianity grew out of Judaism. Like Judaism, it is a monotheistic religion (monotheism is the belief in one god). A religious division in the 11th century led to the establishment of two major Christian organizations—the Roman Catholic Church and the Orthodox Church. Today,

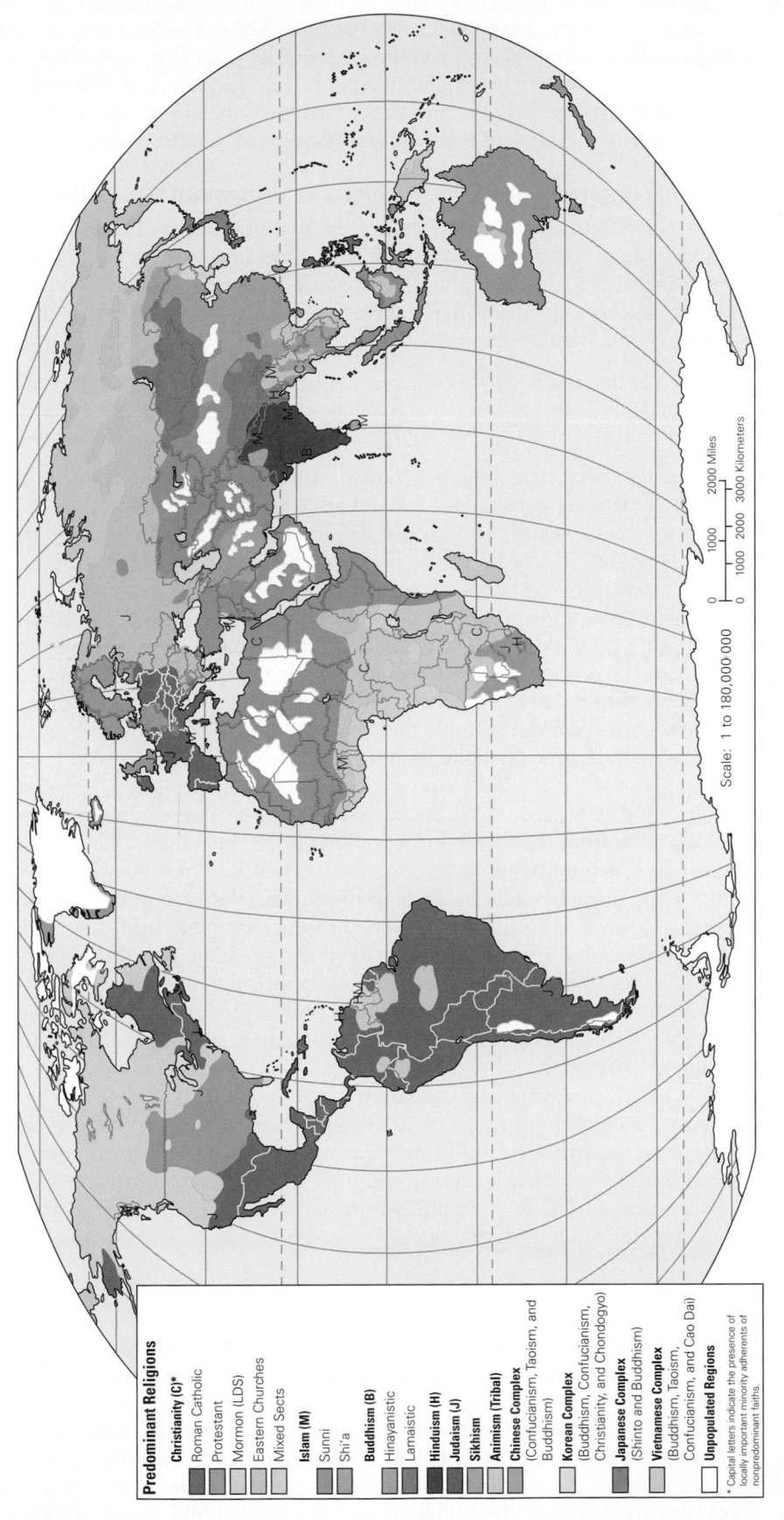

Predominant Religions

Christianity (C)*
- Roman Catholic
- Protestant
- Mormon (LDS)
- Eastern Churches
- Mixed Sects

Islam (M)
- Sunni
- Shi'a

Buddhism (B)
- Hinayanistic
- Lamaistic

Hinduism (H)
Judaism (J)
Sikhism
Animism (Tribal)

Chinese Complex
(Confucianism, Taoism, and Buddhism)

Korean Complex
(Buddhism, Confucianism, Christianity, and Chondogyo)

Japanese Complex
(Shinto and Buddhism)

Vietnamese Complex
(Buddhism, Taoism, Confucianism, and Cao Dai)

Unpopulated Regions

* Capital letters indicate the presence of locally important minority adherents of nonpredominant faiths.

Scale: 1 to 180,000,000

0	1000	2000 Miles
0	1000	2000	3000 Kilometers

MAP 3.1

World Religions

Source: From *Student Atlas of World Geography*, Second Edition, by John L. Allen. Copyright © 2001 by McGraw-Hill Companies. Reprinted by permission of McGraw-Hill Companies, Guilford, CT 06437.

the Roman Catholic Church accounts for more than half of all Christians, most of whom are found in southern Europe and Latin America. The Orthodox Church, while less influential, is still of major importance in several countries (e.g., Greece and Russia). In the 16th century, the Reformation led to a further split with Rome; the result was Protestantism. The nonconformist nature of Protestantism has facilitated the emergence of numerous denominations under the Protestant umbrella (e.g., Baptist, Methodist, Calvinist).

Economic Implications of Christianity: The Protestant Work Ethic

Several sociologists have argued that of the main branches of Christianity—Catholic, Orthodox, and Protestant—the latter has the most important economic implications. In 1904, a German sociologist, Max Weber, made a connection between Protestant ethics and "the spirit of capitalism" that has since become famous.[25] Weber noted that capitalism emerged in Western Europe, where

> business leaders and owners of capital, as well as the higher grades of skilled labor, and even more the higher technically and commercially trained personnel of modern enterprises, are overwhelmingly Protestant.[26]

Weber theorized that there was a relationship between Protestantism and the emergence of modern capitalism. He argued that Protestant ethics emphasize the importance of hard work and wealth creation (for the glory of God) and frugality (abstinence from worldly pleasures). According to Weber, this kind of value system was needed to facilitate the development of capitalism. Protestants worked hard and systematically to accumulate wealth. However, their ascetic beliefs suggested that rather than consuming this wealth by indulging in worldly pleasures, they should invest it in the expansion of capitalist enterprises. Thus, the combination of hard work and the accumulation of capital, which could be used to finance investment and expansion, paved the way for the development of capitalism in Western Europe and subsequently in the United States. In contrast, Weber argued that the Catholic promise of salvation in the next world, rather than this world, did not foster the same kind of work ethic.

Protestantism also may have encouraged capitalism's development in another way. By breaking away from the hierarchical domination of religious and social life that characterized the Catholic Church for much of its history, Protestantism gave individuals significantly more freedom to develop their own relationship with God. The right to freedom of form of worship was central to the nonconformist nature of early Protestantism. This emphasis on individual religious freedom may have paved the way for the subsequent emphasis on individual economic and political freedoms and the development of individualism as an economic and political philosophy. As we saw in Chapter 2, such a philosophy forms the bedrock on which entrepreneurial free market capitalism is based. Building on this, some scholars claim there is a connection between individualism, as inspired by Protestantism, and the extent of entrepreneurial activity in a nation.[27] Again, one must be careful not to generalize too much from this historical sociological view. While nations with a strong Protestant tradition such as Britain, Germany, and the United States were early leaders in the industrial revolution, nations with Catholic or Orthodox majorities show significant and sustained entrepreneurial activity and economic growth in the modern world.

ISLAM

With around 1 billion adherents, Islam is the second largest of the world's major religions. Islam dates back to 610 CE when the prophet Muhammad began spreading the word, although the Muslim calendar begins in 622 CE when, to escape growing opposition, Muhammad left Mecca for the oasis settlement of Yathrib, later known as Medina. Adherents of Islam are referred to as Muslims. Muslims constitute a majority in more than 35 countries and inhabit a nearly contiguous stretch of land from the northwest coast of Africa, through the Middle East, to China and Malaysia in the Far East.

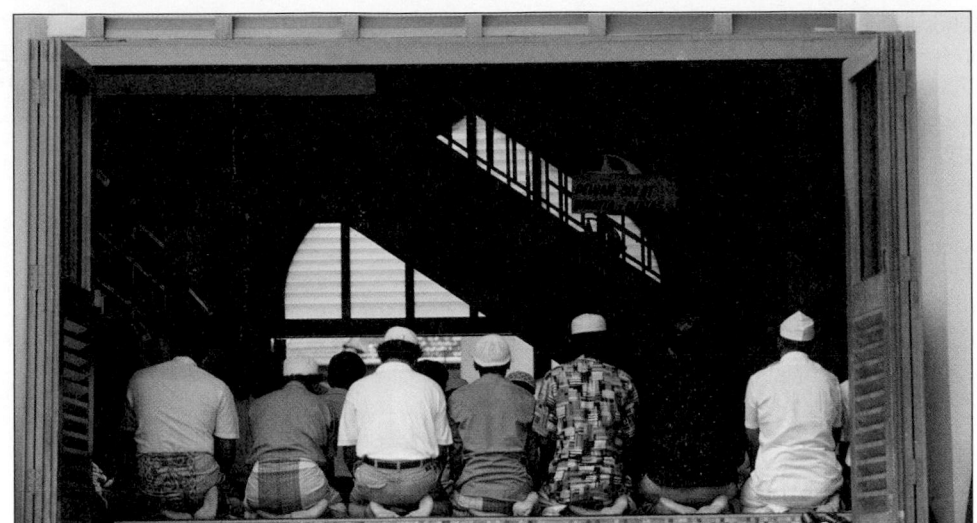

Despite the rise of radical Islamic fundamentalism, the vast majority of the Muslim population supports peace.

Islam has roots in both Judaism and Christianity (Islam views Jesus Christ as one of God's prophets). Like Christianity and Judaism, Islam is a monotheistic religion. The central principle of Islam is that there is but the one true omnipotent God. Islam requires unconditional acceptance of the uniqueness, power, and authority of God and the understanding that the objective of life is to fulfill the dictates of his will in the hope of admission to paradise. According to Islam, worldly gain and temporal power are an illusion. Those who pursue riches on earth may gain them, but those who forgo worldly ambitions to seek the favor of Allah may gain the greater treasure—entry into paradise. Other major principles of Islam include (1) honoring and respecting parents, (2) respecting the rights of others, (3) being generous but not a squanderer, (4) avoiding killing except for justifiable causes, (5) not committing adultery, (6) dealing justly and equitably with others, (7) being of pure heart and mind, (8) safeguarding the possessions of orphans, and (9) being humble and unpretentious.[28] Obvious parallels exist with many of the central principles of both Judaism and Christianity.

Islam is an all-embracing way of life governing the totality of a Muslim's being.[29] As God's surrogate in this world, a Muslim is not a totally free agent but is circumscribed by religious principles—by a code of conduct for interpersonal relations—in social and economic activities. Religion is paramount in all areas of life. The Muslim lives in a social structure that is shaped by Islamic values and norms of moral conduct. The ritual nature of everyday life in a Muslim country is striking to a Western visitor. Among other things, orthodox Muslim ritual requires prayer five times a day (business meetings may be put on hold while the Muslim participants engage in their daily prayer ritual), requires that women should dress in a certain manner, and forbids the consumption of pork and alcohol.

Islamic Fundamentalism

The past three decades have witnessed the growth of a social movement often referred to as Islamic fundamentalism.[30] In the West, Islamic fundamentalism is associated in the media with militants, terrorists, and violent upheavals, such as the bloody conflict occurring in Algeria, the killing of foreign tourists in Egypt, and the September 11, 2001, attacks on the World Trade Center and Pentagon in the United States. This characterization is misleading. Just as Christian fundamentalists are motivated by sincere and deeply held religious values firmly rooted in their faith, so are Islamic fundamentalists. The violence that the Western media associates with Islamic fundamentalism is perpetrated by a small minority of radical "fundamentalists" who have hijacked the religion to further their own political and violent ends. (Some Christian "fundamentalists" have done exactly the same, including Jim Jones and David Koresh.) The vast majority of Muslims point out that Islam teaches peace, justice, and tolerance, not violence and intolerance, and that Islam explicitly repudiates the violence that a radical minority practices.

The rise of fundamentalism has no one cause. In part, it is a response to the social pressures created in traditional Islamic societies by the move toward modernization and by the influence of Western ideas, such as liberal democracy, materialism, equal rights for women, and attitudes toward sex, marriage, and alcohol. In many Muslim countries, modernization has been accompanied by a growing gap between a rich urban minority and an impoverished urban and rural majority. For the impoverished majority, modernization has offered little in the way of tangible economic progress, while threatening the traditional value system. Thus, for a Muslim who cherishes his or her traditions and feels that his or her identity is jeopardized by the encroachment of alien Western values, Islamic fundamentalism has become a cultural anchor.

Fundamentalists demand a rigid commitment to traditional religious beliefs and rituals. The result has been a marked increase in the use of symbolic gestures that confirm Islamic values. In areas where fundamentalism is strong, women have resumed wearing floor-length, long-sleeved dresses and covering their hair; religious studies have increased in universities; the publication of religious tracts has increased; and public religious orations have risen.[31] Also, the sentiments of some fundamentalist groups are often anti-Western. Rightly or wrongly, Western influence is blamed for a range of social ills, and many fundamentalists' actions are directed against Western governments, cultural symbols, businesses, and even individuals.

In several Muslim countries, fundamentalists have gained political power and have used this to try to make Islamic law (as set down in the Koran, the bible of Islam) the law of the land. There are good grounds for this in Islam. Islam makes no distinction between church and state. It is not just a religion; Islam is also the source of law, a guide to statecraft, and an arbiter of social behavior. Muslims believe that every human endeavor is within the purview of the faith—and this includes political activity—because the only purpose of any activity is to do God's will.[32] (Some Christian fundamentalists also share this view.) Muslim fundamentalists have been most successful in Iran, where a fundamentalist party has held power since 1979, but they also have had an influence in many other countries, such as Algeria, Afghanistan (where the Taliban established an extreme fundamentalist state until removed by the U.S.-led coalition in 2002), Egypt, Pakistan, the Sudan, and Saudi Arabia.

Economic Implications of Islam

The Koran establishes some explicit economic principles, many of which are pro–free enterprise.[33] The Koran speaks approvingly of free enterprise and of earning legitimate profit through trade and commerce (the prophet Mohammed was once a trader). The protection of the right to private property is also embedded within Islam, although Islam asserts that all property is a favor from Allah (God), who created and so owns everything. Those who hold property are regarded as trustees rather than owners in the Western sense of the word. As trustees they are entitled to receive profits from the property but are admonished to use it in a righteous, socially beneficial, and prudent manner. This reflects Islam's concern with social justice. Islam is critical of those who earn profit through the exploitation of others. In the Islamic view of the world, humans are part of a collective in which the wealthy and successful have obligations to help the disadvantaged. Put simply, in Muslim countries, it is fine to earn a profit, so long as that profit is justly earned and not based on the exploitation of others for one's own advantage. It also helps if those making profits undertake charitable acts to help the poor. Furthermore, Islam stresses the importance of living up to contractual obligations, keeping one's word, and abstaining from deception. For a closer look at how Islam, capitalism, and globalization can coexist, see the next Country Focus feature on the region around Kayseri in Central Turkey.

Given the Islamic proclivity to favor market-based systems, Muslim countries are likely to be receptive to international businesses as long as those businesses behave in a manner that is consistent with Islamic ethics. Businesses that are perceived as making an

Islamic Capitalism in Turkey

For years now Turkey has been lobbying the European Union to allow it to join the free trade block as a member state. If the EU says yes, it will be the first Muslim state in the Union. Many critics in the EU worry that Islam and Western style capitalism do not mix well, and that as a consequence, allowing Turkey into the EU would be a mistake. However, a close look at what is going on in Turkey suggests that this view may be misplaced. Consider the area around the city of Kayseri in Central Turkey. Many dismiss this poor, largely agricultural region of Turkey as a non-European backwater, far removed from the secular bustle of Istanbul. It is a region where traditional Islamic values hold sway. And yet, it is also a region that has produced so many thriving Muslim enterprises that it is sometimes called the "Anatolian Tiger." Businesses based here include large food manufacturers, textile companies, furniture manufacturers, and engineering enterprises, many of which export a substantial percentage of their production.

Local business leaders attribute the success of companies in the region to an entrepreneurial spirit that they say is part of Islam. They point out that the Prophet Muhammad, who was himself a trader, preached merchant honor and commanded that 90 percent of a Muslim's life be devoted to work in order to put food on the table. Outsider observers have gone further, arguing that what is occurring around Kayseri is an example of Islamic Calvinism, a fusion of traditional Islamic values and the work ethic often associated with Protestantism in general, and Calvinism in particular.

Within Kayseri, the influence of Islam is plain to see. Many companies set aside rooms and time for 15-minute prayer breaks. Most of the older businessmen have been to Mecca on the Haji, the pilgrimage that all Muslims are meant to make at least once in a lifetime. Few of the cafés and restaurants in Kayseri serve alcohol, and most women wear a headscarf.

At the Kayseri sugar factory, one of the most profitable in the region, a senior manager claims that Islam has played a large part in improving the profitability of the enterprise. For a long time the factory bought most of its sugar beets from a single monopoly supplier, who charged a high price. But because Islam preaches equal opportunity in business, managers at the sugar factory decided that the Islamic thing to do was diversify the supply base and encourage small producers to sell beets to them. Today the factory buys sugar beets from 20,000 small growers. Competition between them has lowered prices and boosted the factory's profitability. The same manager also noted that "If you are not a good Muslim, don't pray five times a day and don't have a wife who wears a headscarf, it can be difficult to do business here."

However, not everyone agrees that Islam is the driving force behind the region's success. Saffet Arslan, the managing director of Ipek, the largest furniture producer in the region (which exports to more than 30 countries), claims that another force is at work—globalization. According to Arslan, over the last three decades local Muslims who once eschewed making money in favor of focusing on religion are now making business a priority. They see the Western world, and Western capitalism, as a model, not Islam, and because of globalization and the opportunities associated with it, they want to become successful. At the same time, Arslan is a practicing Muslim who has built a mosque in the basement of Ipec's headquarters building so that people can pray while at work.

If there is a weakness in the Islamic model of business that is emerging in places like Kayseri, some say it can be found in traditional attitudes toward the role of women in the work place, and the low level of female employment in the region. According to a report by the European Stability Initiative, the same group that holds up the Kayseri region as an example of Islamic Calvinism, the low participation of women in the local workforce is the Achilles heel of the economy, and it may stymie the attempts of the region to catch up with the countries of the European Union.[34]

unjust profit through the exploitation of others, by deception, or by breaking contractual obligations are unlikely to be welcomed in an Islamic country. In addition, in Islamic countries where fundamentalism is on the rise, hostility toward Western-owned businesses is likely to increase.

In the previous chapter, we noted that one economic principle of Islam prohibits the payment or receipt of interest, which is considered usury. This is not just a matter of theology;

in several Islamic states, it is also becoming a matter of law. The Koran clearly condemns interest, which is called *riba* in Arabic, as exploitative and unjust. For many years, banks operating in Islamic countries conveniently ignored this condemnation, but starting about 30 years ago with the establishment of an Islamic bank in Egypt, Islamic banks started to open in predominantly Muslim countries. By 2005, some 176 Islamic financial institutions worldwide managed more than $240 billion in assets, making an average return on capital of more than 16 percent. Even conventional banks are entering the market—both Citigroup and HSBC, two of the world's largest financial institutions, now offer Islamic financial services. While only Iran and the Sudan enforce Islamic banking conventions, in an increasing number of countries customers can choose between conventional banks and Islamic banks.

Conventional banks make a profit on the spread between the interest rate they have to pay to depositors and the higher interest rate they charge borrowers. Because Islamic banks cannot pay or charge interest, they must find a different way of making money. Islamic banks have experimented with two different banking methods—the *mudarabah* and the *murabaha*.[35]

A *mudarabah* contract is similar to a profit-sharing scheme. Under *mudarabah*, when an Islamic bank lends money to a business, rather than charging that business interest on the loan, it takes a share in the profits that are derived from the investment. Similarly, when a business (or individual) deposits money at an Islamic bank in a savings account, the deposit is treated as an equity investment in whatever activity the bank uses the capital for. Thus, the depositor receives a share in the profit from the bank's investment (as opposed to interest payments) according to an agreed-on ratio. Some Muslims claim this is a more efficient system than the Western banking system since it encourages both long-term savings and long-term investment. However, there is no hard evidence of this, and many believe that a *mudarabah* system is less efficient than a conventional Western banking system.

The second Islamic banking method, the *murabaha* contract, is the most widely used among the world's Islamic banks, primarily because it is the easiest to implement. In a *murabaha* contract, when a firm wishes to purchase something using a loan—let's say a piece of equipment that costs $1,000—the firm tells the bank after having negotiated the price with the equipment manufacturer. The bank then buys the equipment for $1,000, and the borrower buys it back from the bank at some later date for, say, $1,100, a price that includes a $100 markup for the bank. A cynic might point out that such a markup is functionally equivalent to an interest payment, and it is the similarity between this method and conventional banking that makes it so much easier to adopt.

HINDUISM

Hinduism has approximately 750 million adherents, most of them on the Indian subcontinent. Hinduism began in the Indus Valley in India more than 4,000 years ago, making it the world's oldest major religion. Unlike Christianity and Islam, its founding is not linked to a particular person. Nor does it have an officially sanctioned sacred book such as the Bible or the Koran. Hindus believe that a moral force in society requires the acceptance of certain responsibilities, called *dharma*. Hindus believe in reincarnation, or rebirth into a different body, after death. Hindus also believe in *karma*, the spiritual progression of each person's soul. A person's karma is affected by the way he or she lives. The moral state of an individual's karma determines the challenges he or she will face in the next life. By perfecting the soul in each new life, Hindus believe that an individual can eventually achieve *nirvana*, a state of complete spiritual perfection that renders reincarnation no longer necessary. Many Hindus believe that the way to achieve nirvana is to lead a severe ascetic lifestyle of material and physical self-denial, devoting life to a spiritual rather than material quest.

One of the interesting aspects of Hindu culture is the reverence for the cow, which Hindus see as a gift of the gods to the human race. The sacred status of the cow created some unique problems for McDonald's when it entered India in the 1990s, since devout Hindus do not eat beef (and many are also vegetarians). The accompanying Management Focus looks at how McDonald's dealt with that challenge.

McDonald's and Hindu Culture

In many ways, McDonald's Corporation has written the book on global expansion. Every day, on average, somewhere around the world 4.2 new McDonald's restaurants are opened. The company has some 30,000 restaurants in more than 120 countries that collectively serve close to 50 million customers each day.

One of the latest additions to McDonald's list of countries hosting the famous golden arches is India, where McDonald's started to establish restaurants in the late 1990s. Although India is a poor nation, the large and relatively prosperous middle class, estimated to number around 200 million, attracted McDonald's. India, however, offered McDonald's unique challenges. For thousands of years, India's Hindu culture has revered the cow. Hindu scriptures state that the cow is a gift of the gods to the human race. The cow represents the Divine Mother that sustains all human beings. Cows give birth to bulls that are harnessed to pull plows, cow milk is highly valued and used to produce yogurt and ghee (a form of butter), cow urine has a unique place in traditional Hindu medicine, and cow dung is used as fuel. Some 300 million of these animals roam India, untethered, revered as sacred providers. They are everywhere, ambling down roads, grazing in rubbish dumps, and resting in temples—everywhere, that is, except on your plate, for Hindus do not eat the meat of the sacred cow.

McDonald's is the world's largest user of beef. Since its founding in 1955, countless animals have died to produce Big Macs. How can a company whose fortunes are built upon beef enter a country where the consumption of beef is a grave sin? Use pork instead? However, there are some 140 million Muslims in India, and Muslims don't eat pork. This leaves chicken and mutton. McDonald's responded to this cultural food dilemma by creating an Indian version of its Big Mac—the "Maharaja Mac"—which is made from mutton. Other additions to the menu conform to local sensibilities such as the "McAloo Tikki Burger," which is made from chicken. All foods are strictly segregated into vegetarian and nonvegetarian lines to conform with preferences in a country where many Hindus are vegetarian. According to the head of McDonald's Indian operations, "We had to reinvent ourselves for the Indian palate." Indeed, 75 percent of the menu in McDonald's in India is Indianized.

For a while, this seemed to work. Then in 2001 McDonald's was blindsided by a class-action lawsuit that three Indian businessmen living in Seattle brought against it in the United States. The businessmen, all vegetarians and two of whom were Hindus, sued McDonald's for "fraudulently concealing" the existence of beef in McDonald's French fries! McDonald's had said it used only 100 percent vegetable oil to make French fries, but the company soon admitted that it used a "minuscule" amount of beef extract in the oil. McDonald's settled the suit for $10 million and issued an apology, which read, "McDonald's sincerely apologizes to Hindus, vegetarians, and others for failing to provide the kind of information they needed to make informed dietary decisions at our U.S. restaurants." Going forward, the company pledged to do a better job of labeling the ingredients of its food and to find a substitute for the beef extract used in its oil.

However, news travels fast in the global society of the 21st century, and the revelation that McDonald's used beef extract in its oil was enough to bring Hindu nationalists onto the streets in Delhi, where they vandalized one McDonald's restaurant, causing $45,000 in damage; shouted slogans outside another; picketed the company's headquarters; and called on India's prime minister to close McDonald's stores in the country. McDonald's Indian franchise holders quickly issued denials that they used oil that contained beef extract, and Hindu extremists responded by stating they would submit McDonald's oil to laboratory tests to see if they could detect beef extract.

The negative publicity seemed to have little impact on McDonald's long-term plans in India, however. The company continued to open restaurants, and by 2006 had over 60 restaurants in the country with plans to open another 30 or so. When asked why they frequented McDonald's restaurants, Indian customers noted that their children enjoyed the "American" experience, the food was of a consistent quality, and the toilets were always clean![38]

Economic Implications of Hinduism

Max Weber, famous for expounding on the Protestant work ethic, also argued that the ascetic principles embedded in Hinduism do not encourage the kind of entrepreneurial activity in pursuit of wealth creation that we find in Protestantism.[36] According to Weber, traditional Hindu values emphasize that individuals should be judged not by their material achievements but by their spiritual achievements. Hindus perceive the pursuit of material well-being as making the attainment of nirvana more difficult. Given the emphasis on an ascetic lifestyle, Weber thought that devout Hindus would be less likely to engage in entrepreneurial activity than devout Protestants.

Mahatma Gandhi, the famous Indian nationalist and spiritual leader, was certainly the embodiment of Hindu asceticism. It has been argued that the values of Hindu asceticism and self-reliance that Gandhi advocated had a negative impact on the economic development of postindependence India.[37] But one must be careful not to read too much into Weber's arguments. Modern India is a very dynamic entrepreneurial society, and millions of hard-working entrepreneurs form the economic backbone of the country's rapidly growing economy.

Historically, Hinduism also supported India's caste system. The concept of mobility between castes within an individual's lifetime makes no sense to traditional Hindus. Hindus see mobility between castes as something that is achieved through spiritual progression and reincarnation. An individual can be reborn into a higher caste in his or her next life if he or she achieves spiritual development in this life. Although the caste system has been abolished in India, it still casts a long shadow over Indian life according to many observers. In so far as the caste system limits individuals' opportunities to adopt positions of responsibility and influence in society, the economic consequences of this religious belief are somewhat negative. For example, within a business organization, the most able individuals may find their route to the higher levels of the organization blocked simply because they come from a lower caste. By the same token, individuals may get promoted to higher positions within a firm as much because of their caste background as because of their ability.

BUDDHISM

Buddhism was founded in India in the sixth century BCE by Siddhartha Gautama, an Indian prince who renounced his wealth to pursue an ascetic lifestyle and spiritual perfection. Siddhartha achieved nirvana but decided to remain on earth to teach his followers how they too could achieve this state of spiritual enlightenment. Siddhartha became known as the Buddha (which means "the awakened one"). Today, Buddhism has 350 million followers, most of whom are found in Central and Southeast Asia, China, Korea, and Japan. According to Buddhism, suffering originates in people's desires for pleasure. Cessation of suffering can be achieved by following a path for transformation. Siddhartha offered the Noble Eightfold Path as a route for transformation. The Eightfold Path emphasizes right seeing, thinking, speech, action, living, effort, mindfulness, and meditation. Unlike Hinduism, Buddhism does not support the caste system. Nor does Buddhism advocate the kind of extreme ascetic behavior that Hinduism encourages. Nevertheless, like Hindus, Buddhists stress the afterlife and spiritual achievement rather than involvement in this world.

Economic Implications of Buddhism

The emphasis on wealth creation that is embedded in Protestantism is not found in Buddhism. Buddhist societies have not placed the same kind of historical cultural stress on entrepreneurial behavior that Weber claimed could be found in the Protestant West. But unlike Hinduism, the lack of support for the caste system and extreme ascetic behavior suggests that a Buddhist society may represent a more fertile ground for entrepreneurial activity than a Hindu culture.

CONFUCIANISM

Confucianism was founded in the fifth century BCE by K'ung-Fu-tzu, more generally known as Confucius. For more than 2,000 years until the 1949 Communist revolution, Confucianism was the official ethical system of China. While observance of Confucian ethics has been weakened in China since 1949, more than 200 million people still follow the teachings of Confucius, principally in China, Korea, and Japan. Confucianism teaches the importance of attaining personal salvation through right action. Although not a religion, Confucian ideology has become deeply embedded in the culture of these countries over the centuries, and therefore it has an impact on the lives of many millions more. Confucianism is built around a comprehensive ethical code that sets down guidelines for relationships with others. High moral and ethical conduct and loyalty to others are central to Confucianism. Unlike religions, Confucianism is not concerned with the supernatural and has little to say about the concept of a supreme being or an afterlife.

Economic Implications of Confucianism

Some scholars maintain that Confucianism may have economic implications as profound as those Weber argued were to be found in Protestantism, although they are of a different nature.[39] This basic thesis is that Confucian ethics may help explain the economic success of China, Japan, South Korea, and Taiwan because it lowers the costs of doing business in those countries. In this regard, three values central to the Confucian system of ethics are of particular interest: loyalty, reciprocal obligations, and honesty in dealings with others.

In Confucian thought, loyalty to one's superiors is regarded as a sacred duty—an absolute obligation. In modern organizations based in Confucian cultures, the loyalty that binds employees to the heads of their organization can reduce the conflict between management and labor that we find in more class-conscious societies. Cooperation between management and labor can be achieved at a lower cost in a culture where the value system emphasizes the virtue of loyalty.

However, in a Confucian culture, loyalty to one's superiors, such as a worker's loyalty to management, is not blind loyalty. The concept of reciprocal obligations is important. Confucian ethics stress that superiors are obliged to reward the loyalty of their subordinates by bestowing blessings on them. If these "blessings" are not forthcoming, then neither will be the loyalty. This Confucian ethic is central to the Chinese concept of *guanxi*, which refers to relationship networks supported by reciprocal obligations.[40] *Guanxi* means relationships, although in business settings it can be better understood as connections. Today, Chinese will often cultivate a *guanxiwang*, or "relationship network," for help. Reciprocal obligations are the glue that holds such networks together. If those obligations are not met—if favors done are not paid back or reciprocated—the reputation of the transgressor is tarnished and the person will be less able to draw on his or her *guanxiwang* for help in the future. Thus, the implicit threat of social sanctions is often sufficient to ensure that favors are repaid, obligations are met, and relationships are honored. In a society that lacks a rule-based legal tradition, and thus legal ways of redressing wrongs such as violations of business agreements, *guanxi* is an important mechanism for building long-term business relationships and getting business done in China.

A third concept found in Confucian ethics is the importance attached to honesty. Confucian thinkers emphasize that, although dishonest behavior may yield short-term benefits for the transgressor, dishonesty does not pay in the long run. The importance attached to honesty has major economic implications. When companies can trust each other not to break contractual obligations, the costs of doing business are lowered. Expensive lawyers are not needed to resolve contract disputes. In a Confucian society, people may be less hesitant to commit substantial resources to cooperative ventures than in a society where honesty is less pervasive. When companies adhere to Confucian ethics, they can trust each other not to violate the terms of cooperative agreements. Thus, the costs of achieving cooperation between companies may be lower in societies such as Japan relative to societies where trust is less pervasive.

For example, it has been argued that the close ties between the automobile companies and their component parts suppliers in Japan are facilitated by a combination of trust and reciprocal obligations. These close ties allow the auto companies and their suppliers to work together on a range of issues, including inventory reduction, quality control, and design. The competitive advantage of Japanese auto companies such as Toyota may in part be explained by such factors.[41] Similarly, the combination of trust and reciprocal obligations is central to the workings and persistence of *guanxi* networks in China. Someone seeking and receiving help through a *guanxi* network is then obligated to return the favor and faces social sanctions if that obligation is not reciprocated when it is called upon. If the person does not return the favor, his or her reputation will be tarnished and he or she will be unable to draw on the resources of the network in the future. It is claimed that these relationship-based networks can be more important in helping to enforce agreements between businesses than the Chinese legal system. Some claim, in fact, that *guanxi* networks are a substitute for the legal system.[42]

Language

One obvious way in which countries differ is language. By language, we mean both the spoken and the unspoken means of communication. Language is one of the defining characteristics of a culture.

SPOKEN LANGUAGE

Language does far more than just enable people to communicate with each other. The nature of a language also structures the way we perceive the world. The language of a society can direct the attention of its members to certain features of the world rather than others. The classic illustration of this phenomenon is that whereas the English language has but one word for snow, the language of the Inuit (Eskimos) lacks a general term for it. Instead, because distinguishing different forms of snow is so important in the lives of the Inuit, they have 24 words that describe different types of snow (e.g., powder snow, falling snow, wet snow, drifting snow).[43]

Because language shapes the way people perceive the world, it also helps define culture. Countries with more than one language often have more than one culture. Canada has an English-speaking culture and a French-speaking culture. Tensions between the two can run quite high, with a substantial proportion of the French-speaking minority demanding independence from a Canada "dominated by English speakers." The same phenomenon can be observed in many other countries. Belgium is divided into Flemish and French speakers, and tensions between the two groups exist; in Spain, a Basque-speaking minority with its own distinctive culture has been agitating for independence from the Spanish-speaking majority for decades; on the Mediterranean island of Cyprus, the culturally diverse Greek- and Turkish-speaking populations of the island engaged in open conflict in the 1970s, and the island is now partitioned into two parts. While it does not necessarily follow that language differences create differences in culture and, therefore, separatist pressures (e.g., witness the harmony in Switzerland, where four languages are spoken), there certainly seems to be a tendency in this direction.[44]

Chinese is the mother tongue of the largest number of people, followed by English and Hindi, which is spoken in India. However, the most widely spoken language in the world is English (that is, many people speak English as a second language), followed by French, Spanish, and Chinese. English is increasingly becoming the language of international business. When a Japanese and a German businessperson get together to do business, it is almost certain that they will communicate in English. However, although English is widely used, learning the local language yields considerable advantages. Most people prefer to converse in their own language, and being able to speak the local language can build rapport, which may be very important for a business deal. International businesses that do not understand the local language can make major blunders through improper translation. For example, the Sunbeam Corporation used the English words for its "Mist-Stick" mist-producing hair curling iron when it entered the German market, only to discover after an expensive advertising campaign that *mist* means excrement in German. General Motors was troubled by the lack of enthusiasm among Puerto Rican dealers for its new Chevrolet Nova. When literally translated into Spanish, *nova* means star. However, when spoken it sounds like "no va," which in Spanish means "it doesn't go." General Motors changed the name of the car to Caribe.[45]

UNSPOKEN LANGUAGE

Unspoken language refers to nonverbal communication. We all communicate with each other by a host of nonverbal cues. The raising of eyebrows, for example, is a sign of recognition in most cultures, while a smile is a sign of joy. Many nonverbal cues, however, are culturally bound. A failure to understand the nonverbal cues of another culture can lead to a communication failure. For example, making a circle with the thumb and the forefinger is a friendly gesture in the United States, but it is a vulgar sexual invitation in Greece and Turkey. Similarly, while most Americans and Europeans use the thumbs-up gesture to indicate that "it's all right," in Greece the gesture is obscene.

Another aspect of nonverbal communication is personal space, which is the comfortable amount of distance between you and the person you are talking with. In the United States, the parties in a business discussion customarily choose a distance of three to five feet. Consequently, many North Americans unconsciously feel that Latin Americans are invading their personal space and can be seen backing away from them during a conversation. Indeed, the American may feel that the Latin is being aggressive and pushy. In turn, the Latin American may interpret such backing away as aloofness. The result can be a regrettable lack of rapport between two businesspeople from different cultures.

Education

Formal education plays a key role in a society. Formal education is the medium through which individuals learn many of the language, conceptual, and mathematical skills that are indispensable in a modern society. Formal education also supplements the family's role in socializing the young into the values and norms of a society. Values and norms are taught both directly and indirectly. Schools generally teach basic facts about the social and political nature of a society. They also focus on the fundamental obligations of citizenship. Cultural norms are also taught indirectly at school. Respect for others, obedience to authority, honesty, neatness, being on time, and so on are all part of the "hidden curriculum" of schools. The use of a grading system also teaches children the value of personal achievement and competition.[46]

From an international business perspective, one important aspect of education is its role as a determinant of national competitive advantage.[47] The availability of a pool of skilled and educated workers seems to be a major determinant of the likely economic success of a country. In analyzing the competitive success of Japan since 1945, for example, Michael Porter notes that after the war, Japan had almost nothing except for a pool of skilled and educated human resources:

> With a long tradition of respect for education that borders on reverence, Japan possessed a large pool of literate, educated, and increasingly skilled human resources. . . . Japan has benefited from a large pool of trained engineers. Japanese universities graduate many more engineers per capita than in the United States. . . . A first-rate primary and secondary education system in Japan operates based on high standards and emphasizes math and

science. Primary and secondary education is highly competitive. . . . Japanese education provides most students all over Japan with a sound education for later education and training. A Japanese high school graduate knows as much about math as most American college graduates.[48]

Porter's point is that Japan's excellent education system is an important factor explaining the country's postwar economic success. Not only is a good education system a determinant of national competitive advantage, but it is also an important factor guiding the location choices of international businesses. The recent trend to outsource information technology jobs to India, for example, is partly due to the presence of significant numbers of trained engineers in India, which in turn is a result of the Indian education system. By the same token, it would make little sense to base production facilities that require highly skilled labor in a country where the education system was so poor that a skilled labor pool wasn't available, no matter how attractive the country might seem on other dimensions. It might make sense to base production operations that require only unskilled labor in such a country.

The general education level of a country is also a good index of the kind of products that might sell in a country and of the type of promotional material that should be used. For example, a country where more than 70 percent of the population is illiterate is unlikely to be a good market for popular books. Promotional material containing written descriptions of mass-marketed products is unlikely to have an effect in a country where almost three-quarters of the population cannot read. It is far better to use pictorial promotions in such circumstances.

Culture and the Workplace

Of considerable importance for an international business with operations in different countries is how a society's culture affects the values found in the workplace. Management process and practices may need to vary according to culturally determined work-related values. For example, if the cultures of the United States and France result in different work-related values, an international business with operations in both countries should vary its management process and practices to account for these differences.

Probably the most famous study of how culture relates to values in the workplace was undertaken by Geert Hofstede.[49] As part of his job as a psychologist working for IBM, Hofstede collected data on employee attitudes and values from more than 100,000 individuals from 1967 to 1973. These data enabled him to compare dimensions of culture across 40 countries. Hofstede isolated four dimensions that he claimed summarized different cultures—power distance, uncertainty avoidance, individualism versus collectivism, and masculinity versus femininity.

Hofstede's **power distance** dimension focused on how a society deals with the fact that people are unequal in physical and intellectual capabilities. According to Hofstede, high power distance cultures were found in countries that let inequalities grow over time into inequalities of power and wealth. Low power distance cultures were found in societies that tried to play down such inequalities as much as possible.

The **individualism versus collectivism** dimension focused on the relationship between the individual and his or her fellows. In individualistic societies, the ties between individuals were loose and individual achievement and freedom were highly valued. In societies where collectivism was emphasized, the ties between individuals were tight. In such societies, people were born into collectives, such as extended families, and everyone was supposed to look after the interest of his or her collective.

Hofstede's **uncertainty avoidance** dimension measured the extent to which different cultures socialized their members into accepting ambiguous situations and tolerating uncertainty. Members of high uncertainty avoidance cultures placed a premium on job security, career patterns, retirement benefits, and so on. They also had a strong need for rules and regulations; the manager was expected to issue clear instructions, and subordinates' initiatives were tightly controlled. Lower uncertainty avoidance cultures were characterized by a greater readiness to take risks and less emotional resistance to change.

TABLE 3.1

Work-Related Values for
20 Selected Countries

Source: G. Hofstede, "The Cultural Relativity of Organizational Practices and Theories," *Journal of International Business Studies*, 14 (Fall 1983), pp. 75–89.

	Power Distance	Uncertainty Avoidance	Individualism	Masculinity
Argentina	49	86	46	56
Australia	36	51	90	61
Brazil	69	76	38	49
Canada	39	48	80	52
Denmark	18	23	74	16
France	68	86	71	43
Germany (F.R.)	35	65	67	66
Great Britain	35	35	89	66
India	77	40	48	56
Indonesia	78	48	14	46
Israel	13	81	54	47
Japan	54	92	46	95
Mexico	81	82	30	69
Netherlands	38	53	80	14
Panama	95	86	11	44
Spain	57	86	51	42
Sweden	31	29	71	5
Thailand	64	64	20	34
Turkey	66	85	37	45
United States	40	46	91	62

Hofstede's **masculinity versus femininity** dimension looked at the relationship between gender and work roles. In masculine cultures, sex roles were sharply differentiated and traditional "masculine values," such as achievement and the effective exercise of power, determined cultural ideals. In feminine cultures, sex roles were less sharply distinguished, and little differentiation was made between men and women in the same job.

Hofstede created an index score for each of these four dimensions that ranged from 0 to 100 and scored high for high individualism, high power distance, high uncertainty avoidance, and high masculinity. He averaged the score for all employees from a given country. Table 3.1 summarizes these data for 20 selected countries. Western nations such as the United States, Canada, and Britain score high on the individualism scale and low on the power distance scale. At the other extreme are a group of Latin American and Asian countries that emphasize collectivism over individualism and score high on the power distance scale. Table 3.1 also reveals that Japan's culture has strong uncertainty avoidance and high masculinity. This characterization fits the standard stereotype of Japan as a country that is male dominant and where uncertainty avoidance exhibits itself in the institution of lifetime employment. Sweden and Denmark stand out as countries that have both low uncertainty avoidance and low masculinity (high emphasis on "feminine" values).

Hofstede's results are interesting for what they tell us in a very general way about differences between cultures. Many of Hofstede's findings are consistent with standard Western stereotypes about cultural differences. For example, many people believe Americans are more individualistic and egalitarian than the Japanese (they have a lower power distance), who in turn are more individualistic and egalitarian than Mexicans. Similarly, many might agree that Latin countries such as Mexico place a higher emphasis on masculine value—they are machismo cultures—than the Nordic countries of Denmark and Sweden.

However, one should be careful about reading too much into Hofstede's research. It has been criticized on a number of points.[50] First, Hofstede assumes there is a one-to-one correspondence between culture and the nation-state, but as we saw earlier, many countries have more than one culture. Hofstede's results do not capture this distinction. Second, the research may have been culturally bound. The research team was composed of Europeans and Americans. The questions they asked of IBM employees and their analysis of the answers may have been shaped by their own cultural biases and concerns. So it is not surprising that Hofstede's results confirm Western stereotypes, because it was Westerners who undertook the research.

Third, Hofstede's informants worked not only within a single industry, the computer industry, but also within one company, IBM. At the time, IBM was renowned for its own strong corporate culture and employee selection procedures, making it possible that the employees' values were different in important respects from the values of the cultures from which those employees came. Also, certain social classes (such as unskilled manual workers) were excluded from Hofstede's sample. A final caution is that Hofstede's work is now beginning to look dated. Cultures do not stand still; they evolve, albeit slowly. What was a reasonable characterization in the 1960s and 1970s may not be so today.

Still, just as it should not be accepted without question, Hofstede's work should not be dismissed either. It represents a starting point for managers trying to figure out how cultures differ and what that might mean for management practices. Also, several other scholars have found strong evidence that differences in culture affect values and practices in the workplace, and Hofstede's basic results have been replicated using more diverse samples of individuals in different settings.[51] Still, managers should use the results with caution, for they are not necessarily accurate.

Hofstede subsequently expanded his original research to include a fifth dimension that he argued captured additional cultural differences not brought out in his earlier work.[52] He referred to this dimension as "Confucian dynamism" (sometimes called *long-term orientation*). According to Hofstede, **Confucian dynamism** captures attitudes toward time, persistence, ordering by status, protection of face, respect for tradition, and reciprocation of gifts and favors. The label refers to the derivation of these "values" from Confucian teachings. As might be expected, East Asian countries such as Japan, Hong Kong, and Thailand scored high on Confucian dynamism, while nations such as the United States and Canada scored low. Hofstede and his associates went on to argue that their evidence suggested that nations with higher economic growth rates scored high on Confucian dynamism and low on individualism—the implication being that Confucianism is good for growth. However, subsequent studies have shown that this finding does not hold up under more sophisticated statistical analysis.[53] During the past decade, countries with high individualism and low Confucian dynamics such as the United States have attained high growth rates, while some Confucian cultures such as Japan have had stagnant economic growth. In reality, while culture might influence the economic success of a nation, it is just one of many factors, and while its importance should not be ignored, it should not be overstated either. The factors discussed in Chapter 2—economic, political, and legal systems—are probably more important than culture in explaining differential economic growth rates over time.

Cultural Change

Culture is not a constant; it evolves over time.[54] Changes in value systems can be slow and painful for a society. In the 1960s, for example, American values toward the role of women, love, sex, and marriage underwent significant changes. Much of the social turmoil of that time reflected these changes. Change, however, does occur and can often be quite profound. For example, at the beginning of the 1960s, the idea that women might hold senior management positions in major corporations was not widely accepted. Many scoffed at the idea. Today, it is a reality, and few in the mainstream of American society question the development or the capability of women in the business world. American culture has changed (although it is still more difficult for women to gain senior management positions than men). Similarly, the value systems of many ex-communist states, such as Russia, are undergoing significant changes as those countries move away from values that emphasize collectivism and toward those that emphasize individualism. While social turmoil is an inevitable outcome of such a shift, the shift will still probably occur.

Similarly, some claim that a major cultural shift is occurring in Japan, with a move toward greater individualism.[55] The model Japanese office worker, or "salaryman," is characterized as being loyal to his boss and the organization to the point of giving up evenings, weekends, and vacations to serve the organization, which is the collective of which the employee is a member. However, a new generation of office workers does not seem to fit this model. An individual from the new generation is likely to be more direct than the traditional Japanese. He acts more like a Westerner, a *gaijian*. He does not live for the company and will move on if he gets the offer of a better job. He is not keen on overtime, especially if he has a date. He has his own plans for his free time, and they may not include drinking or playing golf with the boss.[56]

Several studies have suggested that economic advancement and globalization may be important factors in societal change.[57] For example, there is evidence that economic progress is accompanied by a shift in values away from collectivism and toward individualism.[58] Thus, as Japan has become richer, the cultural emphasis on collectivism has declined and greater individualism is being witnessed. One reason for this shift may be that richer societies exhibit less need for social and material support structures built on collectives, whether the collective is the extended family or the paternalistic company. People are better able to take care of their own needs. As a result, the importance attached to collectivism declines, while greater economic freedoms lead to an increase in opportunities for expressing individualism.

The culture of societies may also change as they become richer because economic progress affects a number of other factors, which in turn influence culture. For example, increased urbanization and improvements in the quality and availability of education are both a function of economic progress, and both can lead to declining emphasis on the traditional values associated with poor rural societies. A 25-year study of values in 78 countries, known as the World Values Survey, coordinated by the University of Michigan's Institute for Social Research, has documented how values change. The study linked these changes in values to changes in a country's level of economic development.[59] According to this research, as countries get richer, a shift occurs away from "traditional values" linked to religion, family, and country, and toward "secular rational" values. Traditionalists say religion is important in their lives. They have a strong sense of national pride; they also think that children should be taught to obey and that the first duty of a child is to make his or her parents proud. They say abortion, euthanasia, divorce, and suicide are never justified. At the other end of this spectrum are secular rational values.

Another category in the World Values Survey is quality of life attributes. At one end of this spectrum are "survival values," the values people hold when the struggle for survival is of paramount importance. These values tend to stress that economic and physical security are more important than self-expression. People who cannot take food or safety for granted tend to be xenophobic, are wary of political activity, have authoritarian tendencies, and believe that men make better political leaders than women. "Self-expression" or "well-being" values stress the importance of diversity, belonging, and participation in political processes.

As countries get richer, there seems to be a shift from "traditional" to "secular rational" values, and from "survival values" to "well-being" values. The shift, however, takes time, primarily because individuals are socialized into a set of values when they are young and find it difficult to change as they grow older. Substantial changes in values are linked to generations, with younger people typically being in the vanguard of a significant change in values.

With regard to globalization, some have argued that advances in transportation and communication technologies, the dramatic increase in trade that we have witnessed since World War II, and the rise of global corporations such as Hitachi, Disney, Microsoft, and Levi Strauss, whose products and operations can be found around the globe, are creating conditions for the merging of cultures.[60] With McDonald's hamburgers in China, The Gap in India, iPods in South Africa, and MTV everywhere helping to foster a ubiquitous youth culture, some argue that the conditions for less cultural variation have been created. At the same time, one must not ignore important countertrends, such as the shift toward Islamic fundamentalism in several countries; the separatist movement in Quebec, Canada; or the continuing ethnic strains and separatist movements in Russia. Such countertrends in many ways are a reaction to the pressures for cultural convergence. In an increasingly modern and materialistic world, some societies are trying to reemphasize their cultural roots and uniqueness. Cultural change is not unidirectional, with national cultures converging toward some homogenous global entity. Also, while some elements of culture change quite rapidly—particularly the use of material symbols—other elements change slowly if at all. Thus, just because people the world over wear blue jeans and eat at McDonald's, one should not assume that they have also adopted American values—for more often than not, they have not.

IMPLICATIONS FOR MANAGERS

International business is different from national business because countries and societies are different. In this chapter, we have seen just how different societies can be. Societies differ because their cultures vary. Their cultures vary because of profound differences in social structure, religion, language, education, economic philosophy, and political philosophy. Three important implications for international business flow from these differences. The first is the need to develop cross-cultural literacy. There is a need not only to appreciate that cultural differences exist but also to appreciate what such differences mean for international business. A second implication centers on the connection between culture and national competitive advantage. A third implication looks at the connection between culture and ethics in decision making. In this section, we will explore the first two of these issues in depth. The connection between culture and ethics is explored in the next chapter.

CROSS-CULTURAL LITERACY

One of the biggest dangers confronting a company that goes abroad for the first time is the danger of being ill-informed. International businesses that are ill-informed about the practices of another culture are likely to fail. Doing business in different cultures requires adaptation to conform with the value systems and norms of that culture. Adaptation can embrace all aspects of an international firm's operations in a foreign country. The way in which deals are negotiated, the appropriate incentive pay systems for salespeople, the structure of the organization, the name of a product, the tenor of relations between management and labor, the manner in which the product is promoted, and so on are all sensitive to cultural differences. What works in one culture might not work in another.

To combat the danger of being ill-informed, international businesses should consider employing local citizens to help them do business in a particular culture. They must also ensure that home-country executives are cosmopolitan enough to understand how differences in culture affect the practice of international business. Transferring executives overseas at regular intervals to expose them to different cultures will help build a cadre of cosmopolitan executives. An international business must also be constantly on guard against the dangers of *ethnocentric behavior.* **Ethnocentrism** is a belief in the superiority of one's own ethnic group or culture. Hand in hand with ethnocentrism goes a disregard or contempt for the culture of other countries. Unfortunately, ethnocentrism is all too prevalent; many Americans are guilty of it, as are many French people, Japanese people, British people, and so on. Ugly as it is, ethnocentrism is a fact of life, one that international businesses must be on guard against.

Simple examples illustrate how important cross-cultural literacy can be. Anthropologist Edward T. Hall has described how Americans, who tend to be informal in nature, react strongly to being corrected or reprimanded in public.[61] This can cause problems in Germany, where a cultural tendency toward correcting strangers can shock and offend most Americans. For their part, Germans can be a bit taken aback by the tendency of Americans to call everyone by their first name. This is uncomfortable enough among executives of the same rank, but it can be seen as insulting when a young and junior American executive addresses an older and more senior German manager by his first name without having been invited to do so. Hall concludes it can take a long time to get on a first-name basis with a German; if you rush the process you will be perceived as overfriendly and rude, and that may not be good for business.

Hall also notes that cultural differences in attitude to time can cause a myriad of problems. He notes that in the United States, giving a person a deadline is a way of increasing the urgency or relative importance of a task. However, in the Middle East, giving a deadline can have exactly the opposite effect. The American who insists an Arab business associate make his mind up in a hurry is likely to be perceived as overly demanding and exerting undue pressure. The result may be exactly the opposite of what the American intended, with the Arab going slow as a reaction to the American's arrogance and rudeness. For his part, the American may believe that an Arab associate is being rude if he shows up late to a meeting because he met a friend in the street and stopped to talk. The American, of course, is very concerned about time and scheduling. But for the Arab, who lives in a society where social networks are a major source of information and maintaining relationships is important, finishing the discussion with a friend is more important than adhering to a strict schedule. Indeed, the Arab may be puzzled as to why the American attaches so much importance to time and schedule.

For another example of the consequences of a lack of cultural sensitivity, see the Management Focus feature on cross-cultural illiteracy.

CULTURE AND COMPETITIVE ADVANTAGE

One theme that continually surfaces in this chapter is the relationship between culture and national competitive advantage. Put simply, the value systems and norms of a country influence the costs of doing business in that country. The costs of doing business in a country influence the ability of firms to establish a competitive advantage in the global marketplace. We have seen how attitudes toward cooperation between management and labor, work, and the payment of interest are influenced by social structure and religion. It can be argued that when the class-based conflict between workers and management in class-conscious societies leads to industrial disruption, it raises the costs of doing business in that society. Similarly, we have seen how some sociologists have argued that the ascetic "other-worldly" ethics of Hinduism may not be as supportive of capitalism as the ethics embedded in Protestantism and Confucianism. Also, Islamic laws banning interest payments may raise the costs of doing business by constraining a country's banking system.

Japan presents an interesting case study of how culture can influence competitive advantage. Some scholars have argued that the culture of modern Japan lowers the costs of doing business relative to the costs in most Western nations. Japan's emphasis on

Cross-Cultural Illiteracy

An advertisement for a revolutionary new plane—the Osprey, which can fly like a plane and hover like a helicopter—recently landed the aircraft's makers, Boeing and Bell Helicopter, in a lot of trouble. The ad, which depicted the Osprey hovering above a mosque with soldiers being lowered down on ropes onto the roof, contained the tag lines "It descends from the heavens, ironically it unleashes hell. . . . Consider it a gift from above."

The offending picture initially appeared in the *Armed Forces Journal.* When senior managers at Boeing and Bell saw what their Texas advertising agency had put together, they immediately withdrew it from circulation. For some

reasons, however, the ad was subsequently published in the *National Journal*, causing an outcry from the Council on American Islamic Relations, which feared that the ad conveyed the impression that the war on terror was in fact a war on Islam. Embarrassed by the slip-up, Boeing and Bell issued a press release stating that the ad was ill-conceived, offensive, and should never have been published. Apparently, the Bell executive who cleared the ad for publication was not authorized to do so.

Source: "A Hellish Controversy," *The Economist*, October 8, 2005, p. 73.

group affiliation, loyalty, reciprocal obligations, honesty, and education all boost the competitiveness of Japanese companies. The emphasis on group affiliation and loyalty encourages individuals to identify strongly with the companies in which they work. This tends to foster an ethic of hard work and cooperation between management and labor "for the good of the company." Similarly, reciprocal obligations and honesty help foster an atmosphere of trust between companies and their suppliers. This encourages them to enter into long-term relationships with each other to work on inventory reduction, quality control, and design—all of which have been shown to improve an organization's competitiveness. This level of cooperation has often been lacking in the West, where the relationship between a company and its suppliers tends to be a short-term one structured around competitive bidding rather than one based on long-term mutual commitments. In addition, the availability of a pool of highly skilled labor, particularly engineers, has helped Japanese enterprises develop cost-reducing process innovations that have boosted their productivity.[62] Thus, cultural factors may help explain the competitive advantage many Japanese businesses enjoy in the global marketplace. The rise of Japan as an economic power during the second half of the 20th century may in part be attributed to the economic consequences of its culture.

It also has been argued that the Japanese culture is less supportive of entrepreneurial activity than, say, American society. In many ways, entrepreneurial activity is a product of an individualistic mind-set, not a classic characteristic of the Japanese. This may explain why American enterprises, rather than Japanese corporations, dominate industries where entrepreneurship and innovation are highly valued, such as computer software and biotechnology. Of course, obvious and significant exceptions to this generalization exist. Masayoshi Son recognized the potential of software far faster than any of Japan's corporate giants, set up his company, Softbank, in 1981, and has since built it into Japan's top software distributor. Similarly, dynamic entrepreneurial individuals established major Japanese companies such as Sony and Matsushita. But these examples may be the exceptions that prove the rule, for as yet there has been no surge in entrepreneurial high-technology enterprises in Japan equivalent to what has occurred in the United States.

For the international business, the connection between culture and competitive advantage is important for two reasons. First, the connection suggests which countries are likely to produce the most viable competitors. For example, one might argue that U.S. enterprises are likely to face continued growth in aggressive, cost-efficient competitors from those Pacific Rim nations where a combination of free market economics, Confucian ideology, group-oriented social structures, and advanced education systems can all be found (e.g., South Korea, Taiwan, Japan, and, increasingly, China).

Second, the connection between culture and competitive advantage has important implications for the choice of countries in which to locate production facilities and do business. Consider a hypothetical case when a company has to choose between two countries, A and B, for locating a production facility. Both countries are characterized by low labor costs and good access to world markets. Both countries are of roughly the same size (in terms of population) and both are at a similar stage of economic development. In country A, the education system is undeveloped, the society is characterized by a marked stratification between the upper and lower classes, and there are six major linguistic groups. In country B, the education system is well developed, social stratification is lacking, group identification is valued by the culture, and there is only one linguistic group. Which country makes the best investment site?

Country B probably does. In country A, conflict between management and labor, and between different language groups, can be expected to lead to social and industrial disruption, thereby raising the costs of doing business.[63] The lack of a good education system also can be expected to work against the attainment of business goals.

The same kind of comparison could be made for an international business trying to decide where to push its products, country A or B. Again, country B would be the logical choice because cultural factors suggest that in the long run, country B is the nation most likely to achieve the greatest level of economic growth.

But as important as culture is, it is probably less important than economic, political, and legal systems in explaining differential economic growth between nations. Cultural differences are significant, but we should not overemphasize their importance in the economic sphere. For example, earlier we noted that Max Weber argued that the ascetic principles embedded in Hinduism do not encourage entrepreneurial activity. While this is an interesting academic thesis, recent years have seen an increase in entrepreneurial activity in India, particularly in the information technology sector where India is rapidly becoming an important global player. The ascetic principles of Hinduism and caste-based social stratification have apparently not held back entrepreneurial activity in this sector.

CHAPTER SUMMARY

We have looked at the nature of social culture and studied some implications for business practice. The chapter made the following points:

1. Culture is a complex whole that includes knowledge, beliefs, art, morals, law, customs, and other capabilities people acquire as members of society.

2. Values and norms are the central components of a culture. Values are abstract ideals about what a society believes to be good, right, and desirable. Norms are social rules and guidelines that prescribe appropriate behavior in particular situations.

3. Values and norms are influenced by political and economic philosophy, social structure, religion, language, and education.

4. The social structure of a society refers to its basic social organization. Two main dimensions along which social structures differ are the individual–group dimension and the stratification dimension.

5. In some societies, the individual is the basic building block of social organization. These societies emphasize individual achievements above all else. In other societies, the group is the basic building block of social organization. These societies emphasize group membership and group achievements above all else.

6. All societies are stratified into different classes. Class-conscious societies are characterized by low social mobility and a high degree of stratification. Less class-conscious societies are characterized by high social mobility and a low degree of stratification.

7. Religion may be defined as a system of shared beliefs and rituals that is concerned with the realm of the sacred. Ethical systems refer to a set of

moral principles, or values, that are used to guide and shape behavior. The world's major religions are Christianity, Islam, Hinduism, and Buddhism. Although not a religion, Confucianism has an impact on behavior that is as profound as that of many religions. The value systems of different religious and ethical systems have different implications for business practice.

8. Language is one defining characteristic of a culture. It has both spoken and unspoken dimensions. In countries with more than one spoken language, we tend to find more than one culture.

9. Formal education is the medium through which individuals learn skills and are socialized into the values and norms of a society. Education plays an important role in the determination of national competitive advantage.

10. Geert Hofstede studied how culture relates to values in the workplace. He isolated four dimensions that he claimed summarized different cultures: power distance, uncertainty avoidance, individualism versus collectivism, and masculinity versus femininity.

11. Culture is not a constant; it evolves. Economic progress and globalization seem to be two important engines of cultural change.

12. One danger confronting a company that goes abroad for the first time is being ill-informed. To develop cross-cultural literacy, international businesses need to employ host-country nationals, build a cadre of cosmopolitan executives, and guard against the dangers of ethnocentric behavior.

13. The value systems and norms of a country can affect the costs of doing business in that country.

Critical Thinking and Discussion Questions

1. Outline why the culture of a country might influence the costs of doing business in that country. Illustrate your answer with examples.

2. Do you think that business practices in an Islamic country are likely to differ from business practices in the United States? If so, how?

3. What are the implications for international business of differences in the dominant religion or ethical system of a country?

4. Choose two countries that appear to be culturally diverse. Compare the cultures of those countries and then indicate how cultural differences

influence (*a*) the costs of doing business in each country, (*b*) the likely future economic development of that country, and (*c*) business practices.

5. Reread the Country Focus, "Islamic Capitalism in Turkey." Then answer the following questions:

   a. Can you see anything in the values of Islam that is hostile to business?

   b. What does the experience of the region around Kayseri teach us about the relationship between Islam and business?

   c. What are the implications of Islamic values toward business for the participation of a country like Turkey in the global economy?

6. Reread the case, "McDonald's and Hindu Culture," then answer the following questions:

   a. McDonald's has been reasonably successful in India, despite the country's very different food culture. Why?

   b. Do you think that McDonald's could have and should have foreseen the problems it ran into in India when using beef extract in its oil? What could it have done differently?

Research Task

1. You are preparing for a business trip to Brazil where you will need to interact extensively with local professionals. Therefore, you should consider collecting information regarding local culture and business habits prior to your departure. A colleague from Latin America recommends you visit the "Centre for Intercultural Learning" and read through the country insights provided for Brazil. Prepare a short description of the most striking cultural characteristics that may affect business interactions in this country.

2. Typically, cultural factors drive the differences in business etiquette encountered during international business travel. In fact, Asian cultures exhibit significant differences in business etiquette when compared to Western cultures. For example, in Thailand it is considered offensive to show the sole of the shoe or foot to another. Prior to leaving for your first business trip to Asia, a colleague informed you that a guide called "Business Etiquette Around the World" may help you during your trip. Using the globalEDGE™ Web site, find five tips regarding business etiquette of the Asian country of your choice.

CLOSING CASE

DMG-Shanghai

Back in 1993, New Yorker Dan Mintz moved to China as a freelance film director with no contacts, no advertising experience, and no Mandarin. By 2006, the company he subsequently founded in China, DMG, had emerged as one of China's fastest growing advertising agencies with a client list that includes Budweiser, Unilever, Sony, Nabisco, Audi, Volkswagen, China Mobile, and dozens of other Chinese brands. Mintz attributes his success in part to what the Chinese call *guanxi*.

Guanxi literally means relationships, although in business settings it can be better understood as connections. *Guanxi* has its roots in the Confucian philosophy of valuing social hierarchy and reciprocal obligations. Confucian ideology has a 2,000-year-old history in China. Confucianism stresses the importance of relationships, both within the family and between master and servant. Confucian ideology teaches that people are not created equal. In Confucian thought, loyalty, with its related obligations to one's superiors (or to family), is regarded as a sacred duty, but at the same time, this loyalty has its price. Social superiors are obligated to reward the loyalty of their social inferiors by bestowing "blessings" upon them; thus, the obligations are reciprocal.

Today, Chinese will often cultivate a *guanxiwang*, or "relationship network," for help. Reciprocal obligations are the glue that holds such networks together. If those obligations are not met—if favors done are not paid back or reciprocated—the reputation of the transgressor is tarnished, and he or she will be less able to draw on his or her *guanxiwang* for help in the future. Thus, the implicit threat of social sanctions is often sufficient to ensure that favors are repaid, obligations are met, and relationships are honored. In a society that lacks a strong rule-based legal tradition, and thus legal ways of redressing wrongs such as violations of business agreements, *guanxi* is an important mechanism for building long-term business relationships and getting business done in China. There is a tacit acknowledgment that if you have the right *guanxi*, legal rules can be broken, or at least bent. Mintz, who is now fluent in Mandarin, cultivated his *guanxiwang* by going into business with two young Chinese who had connections, Bing Wu and Peter Xiao. Bing Wu, who works on the production side of the business, was a former national gymnastics champion, which translates into prestige and access to business and government officials. Peter Xiao comes from a military family with major political connections. Together, these three have been able to open doors that long-established Western advertising agencies have not. They have done it in large part by leveraging the contacts of Wu and Xiao, and by backing up their connections with what the Chinese call *shi li*, the ability to do good work.

A case in point was DMG's campaign for Volkswagen, which helped the German company become ubiquitous in China. The ads used traditional Chinese characters, which had been banned by Chairman Mao during the cultural revolution in favor of simplified versions. To get permission to use the characters in film and print ads—a first in modern China—the trio had to draw on high-level government contacts in Beijing. They won over officials by arguing that the old characters should be thought of not as "characters" but as art. Later, they shot TV spots for the ad on Shanghai's famous Bund, a congested boulevard that runs along the waterfront of the old city. Drawing again on government contacts, they were able to shut down the Bund to make the shoot. Steven Spielberg had been able to close down only a portion of the street when he filmed *Empire of the Sun* there in 1986. DMG has also filmed inside Beijing's Forbidden City, even though it is against the law to do so. Using his contacts, Mintz persuaded the government to lift the law for 24 hours. As Mintz has noted, "We don't stop when we come across regulations. There are restrictions everywhere you go. You have to know how to get around them and get things done."[64]

Case Discussion Questions

1. Why do you think that it is so important to cultivate *guanxi* and *guanxiwang* in China?

2. What does the experience of DMG tell us about the way things work in China? What would likely happen to a business that obeyed all the rules and regulations, rather than trying to find a way around them as Dan Mintz apparently does?

3. What are the ethical issues that might arise when drawing upon *guanxiwang* to get things done in China? What does this suggest about the limits of using *guanxiwang* for a Western business committed to high ethical standards?

Notes

1. J. Lyons, "In Mexico Wal-Mart Is Defying Its Critics," *The Wall Street Journal*, March 5, 2007, pp. A1, A9; K. Norton, "The Great Wal-Mart of China," *Newsweek*, October 30, 2006, pp. 50–51; E. Rigby, "Smooth Supply in High Demand," *Financial Times*, February 14, 2007, p. 10.

2. M. Y. Brannen, "When Mickey Loses Face: Recontextualization, Semantic Fit, and the Semiotics of Foreignness," *Academy of Management Review*, 2004, pp. 593–616.

3. See R. Dore, *Taking Japan Seriously* (Stanford, CA: Stanford University Press, 1987).

4. Data come from J. Monger, "International Comparison of Labor Disputes in 2004," *Labor Market Trends*, April 2006, pp. 117–128.

5. E. B. Tylor, *Primitive Culture* (London: Murray, 1871).

6. Geert Hofstede, *Culture's Consequences: International Differences in Work-Related Values* (Beverly Hills, CA: Sage Publications, 1984), p. 21.

7. J. Z. Namenwirth and R. B. Weber, *Dynamics of Culture* (Boston: Allen & Unwin, 1987), p. 8.

8. R. Mead, *International Management: Cross-Cultural Dimensions* (Oxford: Blackwell Business, 1994), p. 7.

9. Edward T. Hall and M. R. Hall, *Understanding Cultural Differences* (Yarmouth, ME: Intercultural Press, 1990).

10. Edward T. Hall and M. R. Hall, *Hidden Differences: Doing Business with the Japanese* (New York: Doubleday, 1987).

11. "Iraq: Down but Not Out," *The Economist*, April 8, 1995, pp. 21–23.

12. S. P. Huntington, *The Clash of Civilizations* (New York: Simon & Schuster, 1996).

13. M. Thompson, R. Ellis, and A. Wildavsky, *Cultural Theory* (Boulder, CO: Westview Press, 1990).

14. M. Douglas, *In the Active Voice* (London: Routledge, 1982), pp. 183–254.

15. M. L. Dertouzos, R. K. Lester, and R. M. Solow, *Made in America* (Cambridge, MA: MIT Press, 1989).

16. C. Nakane, *Japanese Society* (Berkeley: University of California Press, 1970).

17. Ibid.

18. For details, see M. Aoki, *Information, Incentives, and Bargaining in the Japanese Economy* (Cambridge: Cambridge University Press, 1988); and Dertouzos et al., *Made in America*.

19. E. Luce, *The Strange Rise of Modern India* (Boston: Little Brown, 2006); D. Pick and K. Dayaram, "Modernity and Tradition in the Global Era: The Re-invention of Caste in India," *International Journal of Sociology and Social Policy*, 2006, pp. 284–301.

20. For an excellent historical treatment of the evolution of the English class system, see E. P. Thompson, *The Making of the English Working Class* (London: Vintage Books, 1966). See also R. Miliband, *The State in Capitalist Society* (New York: Basic Books, 1969), especially Chapter 2. For more recent studies of class in British societies, see Stephen Brook, *Class: Knowing Your Place in Modern Britain* (London: Victor Gollancz, 1997); A. Adonis and S. Pollard, *A Class Act: The Myth of Britain's Classless Society* (London: Hamish Hamilton, 1997); and J. Gerteis and M. Savage, "The Salience of Class in Britain and America: A Comparative Analysis," *British Journal of Sociology*, June 1998.

21. Adonis and Pollard, *A Class Act*.

22. Y. Bian, "Chinese Social Stratification and Social Mobility," *Annual Review of Sociology* 28 (2002), pp. 91–117.

23. N. Goodman, *An Introduction to Sociology* (New York: HarperCollins, 1991).

24. R. J. Barro and R. McCleary, "Religion and Economic Growth across Countries," *American Sociological Review*, October 2003, pp. 760–82.

25. M. Weber, *The Protestant Ethic and the Spirit of Capitalism* (New York: Charles Scribner's Sons, 1958, original 1904–1905). For an excellent review of Weber's work, see A. Giddens, *Capitalism and Modern Social Theory* (Cambridge: Cambridge University Press, 1971).

26. Weber, *The Protestant Ethic and the Spirit of Capitalism*, p. 35.

27. A. S. Thomas and S. L. Mueller, "The Case for Comparative Entrepreneurship," *Journal of International Business Studies* 31, no. 2 (2000), pp. 287–302; and S. A. Shane, "Why Do Some Societies Invent More than Others?" *Journal of Business Venturing* 7 (1992), pp. 29–46.

28. See S. M. Abbasi, K. W. Hollman, and J. H. Murrey, "Islamic Economics: Foundations and Practices," *International Journal of Social Economics* 16, no. 5 (1990), pp. 5–17; and R. H. Dekmejian, *Islam in Revolution: Fundamentalism in the Arab World* (Syracuse, NY: Syracuse University Press, 1995).

29. T. W. Lippman, *Understanding Islam* (New York: Meridian Books, 1995).

30. Dekmejian, *Islam in Revolution*.

31. M. K. Nydell, *Understanding Arabs* (Yarmouth, ME: Intercultural Press, 1987).

32. Lippman, *Understanding Islam*.

33. The material in this section is based largely on Abbasi et al., "Islamic Economics."

34. Sources: D. Bilefsky, "Turks Knock on Europe's Door with Evidence That Islam and Capitalism Can Coexist," *The New York Times*, August 27, 2006, p. 4; "European Stability Imitative," *Islamic Calvinists*, September 19, 2005, archived at www.esiweb.org.

35. "Forced Devotion," *The Economist*, February 17, 2001, pp. 76–77.

36. For details of Weber's work and views, see Giddens, *Capitalism and Modern Social Theory*.

37. See, for example, the views expressed in "A Survey of India: The Tiger Steps Out," *The Economist*, January 21, 1995.

38. Sources: Luke Harding, "Give Me a Big Mac—But Hold the Beef," *The Guardian*, December 28, 2000, p. 24; Luke Harding, "Indian McAnger," *The Guardian*, May 7, 2001, p. 1; A. Dhillon, "India Has No Beef with Fast Food Chains," *Financial Times*, March 23, 2002, p. 3; "McDonald's

Plans More Outlets in India," *Associated Press Worldstream*, December 24, 2004; and D. Dutta, "The Perishable Food Chain in India," *Just Food*, September 2005, pp. 22–29.

39. See R. Dore, *Taking Japan Seriously*; and C. W. L. Hill, "Transaction Cost Economizing as a Source of Comparative Advantage: The Case of Japan," *Organization Science* 6 (1995).

40. C. C. Chen, Y. R. Chen, and K. Xin, "Guanxi Practices and Trust in Management," *Organization Science* 15, no. 2 (March–April 2004), pp. 200–10.

41. See Aoki, *Information, Incentives, and Bargaining*; and J. P. Womack, D. T. Jones, and D. Roos, *The Machine That Changed the World* (New York: Rawson Associates, 1990).

42. For examples of this line of thinking, see M. W. Peng and P. S. Heath, "The Growth of the Firm in Planned Economies in Transition," *Academy of Management Review* 21 (1996), pp. 492–528; M. W. Peng, *Business Strategies in Transition Economies* (Thousand Oaks, CA: Sage, 2000); and M. W. Peng and Y. Luo, "Managerial Ties and Firm Performance in a Transition Economy," *Academy of Management Journal*, June 2000, pp. 486–501.

43. This hypothesis dates back to two anthropologists, Edward Sapir and Benjamin Lee Whorf. See E. Sapir, "The Status of Linguistics as a Science," *Language* 5 (1929), pp. 207–14; and B. L. Whorf, *Language, Thought, and Reality* (Cambridge, MA: MIT Press, 1956).

44. The tendency has been documented empirically. See A. Annett, "Social Fractionalization, Political Instability, and the Size of Government," *IMF Staff Papers* 48 (2001), pp. 561–92.

45. D. A. Ricks, *Big Business Blunders: Mistakes in Multinational Marketing* (Homewood, IL: Dow Jones-Irwin, 1983).

46. Goodman, *An Introduction to Sociology*.

47. M. E. Porter, *The Competitive Advantage of Nations* (New York: Free Press, 1990).

48. Ibid., pp. 395–97.

49. G. Hofstede, "The Cultural Relativity of Organizational Practices and Theories," *Journal of International Business Studies*, Fall 1983, pp. 75–89; and G. Hofstede, *Cultures and Organizations: Software of the Mind* (New York: McGraw-Hill, 1997).

50. For a more detailed critique, see R. Mead, *International Management: Cross-Cultural Dimensions* (Oxford: Blackwell, 1994), pp. 73–75.

51. For example, see W. J. Bigoness and G. L. Blakely, "A Cross-National Study of Managerial Values," *Journal of International Business Studies*, December 1996, p. 739; D. H. Ralston, D. H. Holt, R. H. Terpstra, and Y. Kai-Cheng, "The Impact of National Culture and Economic Ideology on Managerial Work Values," *Journal of International Business Studies* 28, no. 1 (1997), pp. 177–208; and P. B. Smith, M. F. Peterson, and Z. Ming Wang, "The Manager as a Mediator of Alternative Meanings," *Journal of International Business Studies* 27, no. 1 (1996), pp. 115–37.

52. G. Hofstede and M. H. Bond, "The Confucius Connection," *Organizational Dynamics* 16, no. 4 (1988), pp. 5–12; and G. Hofstede, *Culture's Consequences: Comparing Values, Behaviors, Institutions and Organizations across Nations* (Thousand Oaks, CA: Sage, 2001).

53. R. S. Yeh and J. J. Lawerence, "Individualism and Confucian Dynamism," *Journal of International Business Studies* 26, no. 3 (1995), pp. 655–66.

54. For evidence of this, see R. Inglehart. "Globalization and Postmodern Values," *The Washington Quarterly*, Winter 2000, pp. 215–28.

55. Mead, *International Management*, chap. 17.

56. "Free, Young, and Japanese," *The Economist*, December 21, 1991.

57. Inglehart, "Globalization and Postmodern Values."

58. G. Hofstede, "National Cultures in Four Dimensions," *International Studies of Management and Organization* 13, no. 1, pp. 46–74.

59. See Inglehart, "Globalization and Postmodern Values." For updates, go to http://wvs.isr.umich.edu/index.html.

60. Hofstede, "National Cultures in Four Dimensions."

61. Hall and Hall, *Understanding Cultural Differences*.

62. See Aoki, *Information, Incentives, and Bargaining*; Dertouzos et al., *Made in America*; and Porter, *The Competitive Advantage of Nations*, pp. 395–97.

63. For empirical work supporting such a view, see Annett, "Social Fractionalization, Political Instability, and the Size of Government."

64. Sources: J. Bryan, "The Mintz Dynasty," *Fast Company*, April 2006, pp. 56–62; and M. Graser, "Featured Player," *Variety*, October 18, 2004, p. 6.

新款iPod

00首歌曲。25,000张照片。150小时视频。

Apple's iPod Plant

In mid-2006 news reports surfaced suggesting that there were systematic labor abuses at the factory in China that makes the iconic iPod for Apple Computer. According to the reports, workers at Hongfujin Precision Industries were paid as little as $50 a month to work 15-hour shifts making the iPod. There were also reports of forced overtime and poor living conditions for the workers, many of whom were young women who had migrated in from the countryside to work at the plant and lived in company-owned dormitories. The articles were the work of two Chinese journalists, Wang You and Weng Bao, employed by China Business News, a state-run newspaper. The target of the reports, Hongfujin Precision Industries, was reportedly China's largest export manufacturer in 2005 with overseas sales totaling $14.5 billion. Hongfujin is owned by Foxconn, a large Taiwanese conglomerate, whose customers in addition to Apple include Intel, Dell Computer, and Sony Corporation. The Hongfujin factory

is a small city in its own right, with clinics, recreational facilities, buses, and 13 restaurants that serve the 200,000 employees.

Upon hearing the news, management at Apple responded quickly, pledging to audit the operations to make sure that Hongfujin was complying with Apple's code on labor standards for subcontractors. Managers at Hongfujin took a somewhat different tack—they filed a defamation suit against the two journalists, suing them for $3.8 million in a local court, which promptly froze the journalists' personal assets pending a trial. Clearly, the management of Hongfujin was trying to send a message to the journalist community: criticism would be costly. The suit sent a chill through the Chinese journalist community since Chinese courts have shown a tendency to favor powerful locally based companies in legal proceedings.

Within six weeks, Apple had completed its audit. The company's report suggested that although workers had

Ethics in International Business

4

LEARNING OBJECTIVES:

After you have read this chapter you should:

LO¹ Be familiar with the ethical issues faced by international businesses.

LO² Recognize an ethical dilemma.

LO³ Discuss the causes of unethical behavior by managers.

LO⁴ Be familiar with the different philosophical approaches to ethics.

LO⁵ Know what managers can do to incorporate ethical considerations into their decision making.

not been forced to work overtime, and were earning at least the local minimum wage, many had worked more than the 60 hours a week that Apple allowed, and their housing was substandard. Under pressure from Apple, management at Hongfujin agreed to bring their practices in line with Apple's code, committing themselves to building new housing for employees and limiting work to 60 hours a week.

However, Hongfujin did not immediately withdraw the defamation suit. In an unusually bold move in a country where censorship is still commonplace, Chinese Business News gave its unconditional backing to Wang and Weng. The Shanghai-based news organization issued a statement arguing that what the two journalists did "was not a violation of any rules, laws or journalistic ethics." The Paris-based group, Reporters Without Borders, also took up the case of Wang and Weng, writing a letter to Apple's CEO Steve Jobs that stated, "We believe that all Wang and Weng did was to report the facts and we condemn Foxconn's reaction. We therefore ask you to intercede on behalf of these two journalists so that their assets are unfrozen and the lawsuit is dropped."

Once again, Apple moved quickly, pressuring Foxconn behind the scenes to drop the suit. In early September, Foxconn agreed to do so and issued a "face saving" statement saying that the two sides had agreed to end the dispute after apologizing to each other "for the disturbances brought to both of them by the lawsuit." While the dispute is now over, the experience shed a harsh light on labor conditions in China. At the same time, the response of the Chinese media, and China Business News in particular, points toward the emergence of some journalist freedoms in a nation that has historically seen news organizations as a mouthpiece for the state.[1]

Introduction

As Apple discovered, ethical issues can arise when companies do business in different nations. These issues are often a function of differences in economic development, politics, legal systems, and culture. While managers at Hongfujin were not breaking local laws, their treatment of employees was arguably unethical when judged by Western standards. Moreover, many would argue that it is unethical for a company like Apple to work with a foreign supplier that treats its employees poorly. Managers at Apple had already anticipated this kind of problem and had a code on labor standards in place. When news of the labor conditions at Hongfujin surfaced, Apple management responded appropriately, quickly auditing Hongfujin's operations and requiring that the company change certain practices—although a skeptic might wonder, however, why it took damaging news to get Apple to audit Hongfujin. Apple management should probably have been auditing Hongfujin's operations on a regular basis, which apparently they were not.

As we shall see repeatedly in this chapter, not all companies have been able to deal with ethical problems in as timely a manner as Apple. There are many examples of managers who made poor ethical decisions while engaged in international business. The term *ethics* refers to accepted principles of right or wrong that govern the conduct of a person, the members of a profession, or the actions of an organization. **Business ethics** are the accepted principles of right or wrong governing the conduct of businesspeople, and an **ethical strategy** is a strategy, or course of action, that does not violate these accepted principles. This chapter looks at how ethical issues should be incorporated into decision making in an international business. We start by looking at the source and nature of ethical issues in an international business. Next, we review the reasons for poor ethical decision making. Then we discuss different philosophical approaches to business ethics. We close the chapter by reviewing the different processes managers can adopt to make sure ethical considerations are incorporated into decision making in an international business firm.

Ethical Issues in International Business

Many of the ethical issues in international business are rooted in the fact that political systems, law, economic development, and culture vary significantly from nation to nation. What is considered normal practice in one nation may be considered unethical in another. Because they work for an institution that transcends national borders and cultures, managers in a multinational firm need to be particularly sensitive to these differences. In the international business setting, the most common ethical issues involve employment practices, human rights, environmental regulations, corruption, and the moral obligation of multinational corporations.

EMPLOYMENT PRACTICES

When work conditions in a host nation are clearly inferior to those in a multinational's home nation, what standards should be applied—those of the home nation, those of the host nation, or something in between? While few would suggest that pay and work conditions should be the same across nations, how much divergence is acceptable? For example, while 12-hour workdays, extremely low pay, and a failure to protect workers against toxic chemicals may be common in some developing nations, does this mean it is OK for a multinational to tolerate such working conditions in its subsidiaries there, or to condone it by using local subcontractors?

Like Apple, in the 1990s, Nike found itself the center of a storm of protests when news reports revealed that working conditions at many of its subcontractors were very poor. Typical of the allegations were those detailed in a *48 Hours* program that aired in 1996. The report painted a picture of young women at a Vietnamese subcontractor who worked with toxic materials six days a week in poor conditions for only 20 cents an hour. The report also stated that a living wage in Vietnam was at least $3 a day, an income that could not be achieved at the subcontractor without working substantial overtime. Nike and its subcontractors were not breaking any laws, but this report, and others like it, raised questions about the ethics of using sweatshop labor to make what were essentially fashion accessories. It may have been legal, but was it ethical to use subcontractors who by Western standards clearly exploited their workforce? Nike's critics thought not, and the company found itself the focus of a wave of demonstrations and consumer boycotts. These exposés surrounding Nike's use of subcontractors forced the company to reexamine its policies. Realizing that, even though it was breaking no law, its subcontracting policies were perceived as unethical, Nike's management established a code of conduct for Nike subcontractors and instituted annual monitoring by independent auditors of all subcontractors.[2]

As the Nike and Apple cases demonstrate, a strong argument can be made that it is not OK for a multinational firm to tolerate poor working conditions in its foreign operations, or those of subcontractors. However, this still leaves unanswered the question of what standards should be applied. We shall return to and consider this issue in more detail later in the chapter. For now, note that establishing minimal acceptable standards that safeguard the basic rights and dignity of employees, auditing foreign subsidiaries and subcontractors on a regular basis to make sure those standards are met, and taking corrective action if they are not is a good way to guard against ethical abuses. Another apparel company, Levi Strauss, has long taken such an approach. The company terminated a long-term contract with one of its large suppliers, the Tan family, after discovering that the Tans were allegedly forcing 1,200 Chinese and Filipino women to work 74 hours per week in guarded compounds on the Mariana Islands.[3]

HUMAN RIGHTS

Questions of human rights can arise in international business. Basic human rights still are not respected in many nations. Rights that we take for granted in developed nations, such as freedom of association, freedom of speech, freedom of assembly, freedom of movement, freedom from political repression, and so on, are by no means universally accepted (see Chapter 2 for details). One of the most obvious historic examples was South Africa during the days of white rule and apartheid, which did not end until 1994. The apartheid system denied basic political rights to the majority nonwhite population of South Africa, mandated segregation between whites and nonwhites, reserved certain occupations exclusively for whites, and prohibited blacks from being placed in positions where they would manage whites. Despite the odious nature of this system, Western businesses operated in South Africa. By the 1980s, however, many questioned the ethics of doing so. They argued that inward investment by foreign multinationals, by boosting the South African economy, supported the repressive apartheid regime.

Several Western businesses started to change their policies in the late 1970s and early 1980s.[4] General Motors, which had significant activities in South Africa, was at the forefront of this trend. GM adopted what came to be called the *Sullivan principles*, named after Leon Sullivan, a black Baptist minister and a member of GM's board of directors. Sullivan argued that it was ethically justified for GM to operate in South Africa so long as two conditions were fulfilled. First, the company should not obey the apartheid laws in its own South African operations (a form of passive resistance). Second, the company should do everything within its power to promote the abolition of apartheid laws. Sullivan's principles were widely adopted by U.S. firms operating in South Africa. The South African government, which clearly did not want to antagonize important foreign investors, ignored their violation of the apartheid laws.

However, after 10 years, Leon Sullivan concluded that simply following the principles was not sufficient to break down the apartheid regime and that any American company, even those adhering to his principles, could not ethically justify their continued presence in South Africa. Over the next few years, numerous companies divested their South African operations, including Exxon, General Motors, Kodak, IBM, and Xerox. At the same time, many state pension funds signaled they would no longer hold stock in companies that did business in South Africa, which helped persuade several companies to divest their South African operations. These divestments, coupled with the imposition of economic sanctions from the U.S. and other governments, contributed to the abandonment of white minority rule and apartheid in South Africa and the introduction of democratic elections in 1994. Thus, some argued that adopting an ethical stance helped improve human rights in South Africa.[5]

Although change has come in South Africa, many repressive regimes still exist in the world. Is it ethical for multinationals to do business in them? It is often argued that inward investment by a multinational can be a force for economic, political, and social progress that ultimately improves the rights of people in repressive regimes. This position was first discussed in Chapter 2, when we noted that economic progress in a nation could create pressure for democratization. In general, this belief suggests it is ethical for a multinational to do business in nations that lack the democratic structures and human rights records of developed nations. Investment in China, for example, is frequently justified on the grounds that although human rights groups often question China's human rights record, and although the country is not a democracy, continuing inward investment will help boost economic growth and raise living standards. These developments will ultimately create pressures from the Chinese people for more participative government, political pluralism, and freedom of expression and speech.

However, there is a limit to this argument. As in the case of South Africa, some regimes are so repressive that investment cannot be justified on ethical grounds. A current example would be Myanmar (formally known as Burma). Ruled by a military dictatorship for more than 45 years, Myanmar has one of the worst human rights records in the world. Beginning in the mid-1990s, many Western companies exited Myanmar, judging the human rights violations to be so extreme that doing business there cannot be justified on ethical grounds. (In contrast, the accompanying Management Focus looks at the controversy surrounding one company, Unocal, that chose to stay in Myanmar.) However, a cynic might note that Myanmar has a small economy and that divestment carries no great economic penalty for Western firms, unlike, for example, divestment from China.

Nigeria is another country where serious questions have arisen over the extent to which foreign multinationals doing business in the country have contributed to human rights violations. Most notably, the largest foreign oil producer in the country, Royal Dutch Shell, has been repeatedly criticized.[6] In the early 1990s, several ethnic groups in Nigeria, which was ruled by a military dictatorship, protested against foreign oil companies for causing widespread pollution and failing to invest in the communities from which they extracted oil. Shell reportedly requested the assistance of Nigeria's Mobile Police Force (MPF) to quell the demonstrations. According to the human rights group Amnesty International, the results were bloody. In 1990, the MPF put down protests against Shell in the village of Umuechem, killing 80 people and destroying 495 homes. In 1993, following protests in the Ogoni region of Nigeria that were designed to stop contractors from laying a new pipeline for Shell, the MPF raided the area to quell the unrest. In the chaos that followed, it has been alleged that 27 villages were razed, 80,000 Ogoni people displaced, and 2,000 people killed.

Critics argued that Shell shouldered some of the blame for the massacres. Shell never acknowledged this, and the MPF probably used the demonstrations as a pretext

Nigerian women and children protest Royal Dutch/Shell in April 2004.

Unocal in Myanmar

In 1995, Unocal, an oil and gas enterprise based in California, took a 29 percent stake in a partnership with the French oil company Total and state-owned companies from both Myanmar and Thailand to build a gas pipeline from Myanmar to Thailand. At the time, the $1 billion project was expected to bring Myanmar about $200 million in annual export earnings, a quarter of the country's total export earnings. The gas used domestically would increase Myanmar's generating capacity by 30 percent. Unocal made this investment when a number of other American companies were exiting Myanmar. Myanmar's government, a military dictatorship, had a reputation for brutally suppressing internal dissent. Citing the political climate, the apparel companies Levi Strauss and Eddie Bauer had both withdrawn from the country. However, as far as Unocal's management was concerned, the giant infrastructure project would generate healthy returns for the company and, by boosting economic growth, a better life for Myanmar's 43 million people. Moreover, while Levi Strauss and Eddie Bauer could easily shift production of clothes to another low-cost location, Unocal argued it had to go where the oil and gas were located.

However, Unocal's investment quickly became highly controversial. Under the terms of the contract, the government of Myanmar was contractually obliged to clear a corridor for the pipeline through Myanmar's tropical forests and to protect the pipeline from attacks by the government's enemies. According to human rights groups, the Myanmar army forcibly moved villages and ordered hundreds of local peasants to work on the pipeline in conditions that were no better than slave labor. Those who refused suffered retaliation. News reports cite the case of one woman who was thrown into a fire, along with her baby, after her husband tried to escape from troops forcing him to work on the project. The baby died and she suffered burns. Other villagers report being beaten, tortured, raped, and otherwise mistreated under the alleged slave labor conditions.

In 1996, human rights activists brought a lawsuit against Unocal in the United States on behalf of 15 Myanmar villagers who had fled to refugee camps in Thailand. The suit claimed that Unocal was aware of what was going on, even if it did not participate or condone it, and that awareness was enough to make Unocal in part responsible for the alleged crimes. The presiding judge dismissed the case, arguing that Unocal could not be held liable for the actions of a foreign government against its own people—although the judge did note that Unocal was indeed aware of what was going on in Myanmar. The plaintiffs appealed, and in late 2003 the case wound up at a superior court. In 2005 the case was settled out of court for an undisclosed amount.[11]

---

for punishing an ethnic group that had been agitating against the central government for some time. Nevertheless, these events did prompt Shell to look at its own ethics and to set up internal mechanisms to ensure that its subsidiaries acted in a manner that was consistent with basic human rights.[7] More generally, the question remains, what is the responsibility of a foreign multinational when operating in a country where basic human rights are trampled on? Should the company be there at all, and if it is there, what actions should it take to avoid the situation Shell found itself in?

ENVIRONMENTAL POLLUTION

Ethical issues arise when environmental regulations in host nations are inferior to those in the home nation. Many developed nations have substantial regulations governing the emission of pollutants, the dumping of toxic chemicals, the use of toxic materials in the workplace, and so on. Those regulations are often lacking in developing nations, and according to critics, the result can be higher levels of pollution from the operations of multinationals than would be allowed at home. For example, consider again the case of foreign oil companies in Nigeria. According to a 1992 report prepared by environmental activists in the Niger Delta region of Nigeria,

> Apart from air pollution from the oil industry's emissions and flares day and night, producing poisonous gases that are silently and systematically wiping out vulnerable airborne biota and endangering the life of plants, game, and man himself, we have widespread water pollution and soil/land pollution that results in the death of most aquatic eggs and juvenile stages of the life of fin fish and shell fish on the one hand, whilst, on the other hand, agricultural land contaminated with oil spills becomes dangerous for farming, even where they continue to produce significant yields.[8]

The implication inherent in this description is that the pollution controls foreign companies applied in Nigeria were much more lax than those applied in developed nations.

Should a multinational feel free to pollute in a developing nation? (To do so hardly seems ethical.) Is there a danger that amoral management might move production to a developing nation precisely because costly pollution controls are not required, and the company is therefore free to despoil the environment and perhaps endanger local people in its quest to lower production costs and gain a competitive advantage? What is the right and moral thing to do in such circumstances—pollute to gain an economic advantage, or make sure that foreign subsidiaries adhere to common standards regarding pollution controls?

These questions take on added importance because some parts of the environment are a public good that no one owns, but anyone can despoil. No one owns the atmosphere or the oceans, but polluting both, no matter where the pollution originates, harms all.[9] The atmosphere and oceans can be viewed as a global commons from which everyone benefits but for which no one is specifically responsible. In such cases, a phenomenon known as the *tragedy of the commons* becomes applicable. The tragedy of the commons occurs when individuals overuse a resource held in common by all, but owned by no one, resulting in its degradation. The phenomenon was first named by Garrett Hardin when describing a particular problem in 16th-century England. Large open areas, called commons, were free for all to use as pasture. The poor put out livestock on these commons and supplemented their meager incomes. It was advantageous for each to put out more and more livestock, but the social consequence was far more livestock than the commons could handle. The result was overgrazing, degradation of the commons, and the loss of this much-needed supplement.[10]

In the modern world, corporations can contribute to the global tragedy of the commons by moving production to locations where they are free to pump pollutants into the atmosphere or dump them in oceans or rivers, thereby harming these valuable global commons. While such action may be legal, is it ethical? Again, such actions seem to violate basic societal notions of ethics and social responsibility.

CORRUPTION

As noted in Chapter 2, corruption has been a problem in almost every society in history, and it continues to be one today.[12] There always have been and always will be corrupt government officials. International businesses can and have gained economic advantages by making payments to those officials. A classic example concerns a well-publicized incident in the 1970s. Carl Kotchian, the president of Lockheed, made a $12.5 million payment to Japanese agents and government officials to secure a large order for Lockheed's TriStar jet from Nippon Air. When the payments were discovered, U.S. officials charged Lockheed with falsification of its records and tax violations. Although such payments were supposed to be an accepted business practice in Japan (they might be viewed as an exceptionally lavish form of gift giving), the revelations created a scandal there too. The government ministers in question were criminally charged, one committed suicide, the government fell in disgrace, and the Japanese people were outraged. Apparently, such a payment was not an accepted way of doing business in Japan! The payment was nothing more than a bribe, paid to corrupt officials, to secure a large order that might otherwise have gone to another manufacturer, such as Boeing. Kotchian clearly engaged in unethical behavior, and to argue that the payment was an "acceptable form of doing business in Japan" was self-serving and incorrect.

The Lockheed case was the impetus for the 1977 passage of the **Foreign Corrupt Practices Act** in the United States, which we first discussed in Chapter 2. The act outlawed the paying of bribes to foreign government officials to gain business. Some U.S. businesses immediately objected that the act would put U.S. firms at a competitive disadvantage (there is no evidence that this actually occurred).[13] The act was subsequently amended to allow for "facilitating payments." Sometimes known as speed money or grease payments, facilitating payments are *not* payments to secure contracts that would not otherwise be secured, nor are they payments to obtain exclusive preferential treatment. Rather they are payments to ensure receiving the standard treatment that a business ought to receive from a foreign government, but might not receive due to the obstruction of a foreign official.

In 1997, the trade and finance ministers from the member states of the Organization for Economic Cooperation and Development (OECD) followed the U.S. lead and adopted the **Convention on Combating Bribery of Foreign Public Officials in International Business Transactions.**[14] The convention, which went into force in 1999, obliges member states and other signatories to make the bribery of foreign public officials a criminal offense. The convention excludes facilitating payments made to expedite routine government action from the convention. To date, some 36 countries have signed the convention, six of whom are not OECD members.

While facilitating payments, or speed money, are excluded from both the Foreign Corrupt Practices Act and the OECD convention on bribery, the ethical implications of making such payments are unclear. In many countries, payoffs to government officials in the form of speed money are a part of life. One can argue that not investing because government officials demand speed money ignores the fact that such investment can bring substantial benefits to the local populace in terms of income and jobs. From a pragmatic standpoint, giving bribes, although a little evil, might be the price that must be paid to do a greater good (assuming the investment creates jobs where none existed and assuming the practice is not illegal). Several economists advocate this reasoning, suggesting that in the context of pervasive and cumbersome regulations in developing countries, corruption may improve efficiency and help growth! These economists theorize that in a country where preexisting political structures distort or limit the workings of the market mechanism, corruption in the form of black-marketeering, smuggling, and side payments to government bureaucrats to "speed up" approval for business investments may enhance welfare.[15] Arguments such as this persuaded the U.S. Congress to exempt facilitating payments from the Foreign Corrupt Practices Act.

In contrast, other economists have argued that corruption reduces the returns on business investment and leads to low economic growth.[16] In a country where corruption is common, unproductive bureaucrats who demand side payments for granting the enterprise permission to operate may siphon off the profits from a business activity. This reduces businesses' incentive to invest and may retard a country's economic growth rate. One study of the connection between corruption and economic growth in 70 countries found that corruption had a significant negative impact on a country's growth rate.[17]

Given the debate and the complexity of this issue, one again might conclude that generalization is difficult and the demand for speed money creates a genuine ethical dilemma. Yes, corruption is bad, and yes, it may harm a country's economic development, but yes, there are also cases where side payments to government officials can remove the bureaucratic barriers to investments that create jobs. However, this pragmatic stance ignores the fact that corruption tends to corrupt both the bribe giver and the bribe taker. Corruption feeds on itself, and once an individual starts down the road of corruption, pulling back may be difficult if not impossible. This argument strengthens the ethical case for never engaging in corruption, no matter how compelling the benefits might seem.

Many multinationals have accepted this argument. The large oil multinational, BP, for example, has a zero-tolerance approach toward facilitating payments. Other corporations have a more nuanced approach. For example, consider the following from the code of ethics at Dow Corning:

> Dow Corning employees will not authorize or give payments or gifts to government employees or their beneficiaries or anyone else in order to obtain or retain business. Facilitating payments to expedite the performance of routine services are strongly discouraged. In countries where local business practice dictates such payments and there is no alternative, facilitating payments are to be for the minimum amount necessary and must be accurately documented and recorded.[18]

This statement allows for facilitating payments when "there is no alternative," although they are strongly discouraged.

MORAL OBLIGATIONS

Multinational corporations have power that comes from their control over resources and their ability to move production from country to country. Although that power is constrained not only by laws and regulations but also by the discipline of the market and the competitive process, it is nevertheless substantial. Some moral philosophers argue that with power comes the social responsibility for multinationals to give something back to the societies that enable them to prosper and grow. The concept of **social responsibility** refers to the idea that businesspeople should consider the social consequences of economic actions when making business decisions, and that there should be a presumption in favor of decisions that have both good economic and social consequences.[19] In its purest form, social responsibility can be supported for its own sake simply because it is the right way for a business to behave. Advocates of this approach argue that businesses, particularly large successful businesses, need to recognize their *noblesse oblige* and give something back to the societies that have made their success possible. *Noblesse oblige* is a French term that refers to honorable and benevolent behavior considered the responsibility of people of high (noble) birth. In a business setting, it is taken to mean benevolent behavior that is the responsibility of *successful* enterprises. Businesspeople have long recognized the concept, resulting in a substantial and venerable history of corporate giving to society and social investments designed to enhance the welfare of the communities in which businesses operate.

However, some multinationals have abused their power for private gain. The most famous historic example relates to one of the earliest multinationals, the British East India Company. Established in 1600, the East India Company grew to dominate the entire Indian subcontinent in the 19th century. At the height of its power, the company deployed over 40 warships, possessed the largest standing army in the world, was the de facto ruler of India's 240 million people, and even hired its own church bishops, extending its dominance into the spiritual realm.[20]

Power itself is morally neutral—how power is used is what matters. It can be used in a positive way to increase social welfare, which is ethical, or it can be used in a manner that is ethically and morally suspect. Consider the case of News Corporation, one of the largest media conglomerates in the world, which is profiled in the accompanying Management Focus. The power of media companies derives from their ability to shape public perceptions by the material they choose to publish. News Corporation founder and CEO Rupert Murdoch has long considered China to be one of the most promising media markets in the world and has sought permission to expand News Corporation's operations in China, particularly the satellite broadcasting operations of Star TV. Some critics believe that Murdoch used the power of News Corporation in an unethical way to attain this objective.

Some multinationals have acknowledged a moral obligation to use their power to enhance social welfare in the communities where they do business. BP, one of the world's largest oil companies, has made it part of the company policy to undertake "social investments" in the countries where it does business.[21] In Algeria, BP has been investing in a major project to develop gas fields near the desert town of Salah. When the company noticed the lack of clean water in Salah, it built two desalination plants to provide drinking water for the

News Corporation in China

Rupert Murdoch built News Corporation into one of the largest media conglomerates in the world with interests that include newspapers, publishing, and television broadcasting. According to critics, however, Murdoch abused his power to gain preferential access to the Chinese media market by systematically suppressing media content that was critical of China and publishing material designed to ingratiate the company with the Chinese leadership.

In 1994, News Corporation excluded BBC news broadcasts from Star TV coverage in the region after it had become clear that Chinese politicians were unhappy with the BBC's continual reference to repression in China and, most notably, the 1989 massacre of student protesters for democracy in Beijing's Tiananmen Square. In 1995, News Corporation's book publishing subsidiary, HarperCollins, published a flattering biography of Deng Xiaoping, the former leader of China, written by his daughter. Then in 1998, HarperCollins dropped plans to publish the memoirs of Chris Patten, the last governor of Hong Kong before its transfer to the Chinese. Patten, a critic of Chinese leaders, had aroused their wrath by attempting to introduce a degree of democracy into the administration of the old British territory before its transfer back to China in 1997.

In a 1998 interview in *Vanity Fair*, Murdoch took another opportunity to ingratiate himself with the Chinese leadership when he described the Dalai Lama, the exiled leader of Chinese-occupied Tibet, as "a very political old monk shuffling around in Gucci shoes." On the heels of this, in 2001 Murdoch's son James, who was in charge of running Star TV, made disparaging remarks about Falun Gong, a spiritual movement involving breathing exercises and meditation that had become so popular in China that the Communist regime regarded it

as a political threat and suppressed its activities. According to James Murdoch, Falun Gong was a "dangerous," "apocalyptic cult" that "clearly does not have the success of China at heart."

Critics argued that these events were all part of a deliberate effort on the part of News Corporation to curry favor with the Chinese. The company received its reward in 2001 when Star TV struck an agreement with the Chinese government to launch a Mandarin-language entertainment channel for the affluent southern coastal province of Guangdong. Earlier that year, China's leader, Jiang Zemin, had publicly praised Murdoch and Star TV for their efforts "to present China objectively and to cooperate with the Chinese press."

Once in China, News Corp was soon tugging at the constraints imposed on it by the Chinese government. Starting in 2002, News Corp set up shell companies, owned by News Corp employees, which then resold News Corp programming to local cable TV networks throughout China, in direct violation of Chinese regulations. Payments, sometimes in the form of briefcases stuffed with cash, were channeled to News Corp through the shell companies. One such deal involved selling News Corp programming through a shell company known as Runde Investment Corporation to a nationwide satellite TV channel, Qinghai Satellite, based in the remote Qinghai province of China. Runde was partly owned by the son of the former hard-line Communist Party propaganda minister, Ding Guangen. If News Corp was hoping that its political connections would help it to get away with these actions, it was badly disappointed. In 2005, Chinese authorities raided News Corp's headquarters and seized documents and equipment. They also quickly terminated the deal with Qinghai Satellite.[22]

local community and distributed containers to residents so they could take water from the plants to their homes. There was no economic reason for BP to make this social investment, but the company believes it is morally obligated to use its power in constructive ways. The action, while a small thing for BP, is a very important thing for the local community.

Ethical Dilemmas

The ethical obligations of a multinational corporation toward employment conditions, human rights, corruption, environmental pollution, and the use of power are not always clear-cut. There may be no agreement about accepted ethical principles. From an international business perspective, some argue that what is ethical depends upon one's cultural perspective.[23] In the United States, it is considered acceptable to execute murderers but in many cultures this is not acceptable—execution is viewed as an affront to human dignity and the death penalty is outlawed. Many Americans find this attitude very strange, but many Europeans find the American approach barbaric. For a more business-oriented example, consider the practice of "gift giving" between the parties to a business negotiation. While this is considered right and proper behavior in many Asian cultures, some Westerners view the practice as a form of bribery, and therefore unethical, particularly if the gifts are substantial.

Managers often confront very real ethical dilemmas where the appropriate course of action is not clear. For example, imagine that a visiting American executive finds that a foreign subsidiary in a poor nation has hired a 12-year-old girl to work on a factory floor. Appalled to find that the subsidiary is using child labor in direct violation of the company's own ethical code, the American instructs the local manager to replace the child with an adult. The local manager dutifully complies. The girl, an orphan, who is the only breadwinner for herself and her 6-year-old brother, is unable to find another job, so in desperation she turns to prostitution. Two years later she dies of AIDS. Meanwhile, her brother takes up begging. He encounters the American while begging outside the local McDonald's. Unaware that this was the man responsible for his fate, the boy begs him for money. The American quickens his pace and walks rapidly past the outstretched hand into the McDonald's, where he orders a quarter-pound cheeseburger with fries and a cold milk shake. A year later, the boy contracts tuberculosis and dies.

Had the visiting American understood the gravity of the girl's situation, would he still have requested her replacement? Perhaps not! Would it have been better, therefore, to stick with the status quo and allow the girl to continue working? Probably not, because that would have violated the reasonable prohibition against child labor found in the company's own ethical code. What, then, would have been the right thing to do? What was the obligation of the executive given this ethical dilemma?

There is no easy answer to these questions. That is the nature of **ethical dilemmas**—they are situations in which none of the available alternatives seems ethically acceptable.[24] In this case, employing child labor was not acceptable, but neither was denying the child her only source of income. What the American executive needed, what all managers need, was a moral compass, or perhaps an ethical algorithm, that would guide him through such an ethical dilemma to find an acceptable solution. Later we will outline what such a moral compass, or ethical algorithm, might look like. For now, it is enough to note that ethical dilemmas exist because many real-world decisions are complex, difficult to frame, and involve first-, second-, and third-order consequences that are hard to quantify. Doing the right thing, or even knowing what the right thing might be, is often far from easy.[25]

The Roots of Unethical Behavior

As we have seen, examples abound of managers behaving in a manner that might be judged unethical in an international business setting. Why do managers behave in an unethical manner? There is no simple answer to this question, for the causes are complex, but some generalizations can be made (see Figure 4.1).[26]

PERSONAL ETHICS

Business ethics are not divorced from *personal ethics*, which are the generally accepted principles of right and wrong governing the conduct of individuals. As individuals, we are typically taught that it is wrong to lie and cheat—it is unethical—and that it is right to behave with integrity and honor and to stand up for what we believe to be right. This is generally true across societies. The personal ethical code that guides our behavior comes from a number of sources, including our parents, our schools, our religion, and the media. Our personal ethical code exerts a profound influence on the way we behave as business-people. An individual with a strong sense of personal ethics is less likely to behave in an

FIGURE 4.1

Determinants of Ethical
Behavior

unethical manner in a business setting. It follows that the first step to establishing a strong sense of business ethics is for a society to emphasize strong personal ethics.

Home-country managers working abroad in multinational firms (expatriate managers) may experience more than the usual degree of pressure to violate their personal ethics. They are away from their ordinary social context and supporting culture, and they are psychologically and geographically distant from the parent company. They may be based in a culture that does not place the same value on ethical norms important in the manager's home country, and they may be surrounded by local employees who have less rigorous ethical standards. The parent company may pressure expatriate managers to meet unrealistic goals that can only be fulfilled by cutting corners or acting unethically. For example, to meet centrally mandated performance goals, expatriate managers might give bribes to win contracts or establish working conditions and environmental controls that are below minimal acceptable standards. Local managers might encourage the expatriate to adopt such behavior. Due to its geographical distance, the parent company may be unable to see how expatriate managers are meeting goals, or they may choose not to see how they are doing so, allowing such behavior to flourish and persist.

DECISION-MAKING PROCESSES

Several studies of unethical behavior in a business setting have concluded that businesspeople sometimes do not realize they are behaving unethically, primarily because they simply fail to ask, "Is this decision or action ethical?"[27] Instead, they apply a straightforward business calculus to what they perceive to be a business decision, forgetting that the decision may also have an important ethical dimension. The fault lies in processes that do not incorporate ethical considerations into business decision making. This may have been the case at Nike when managers originally made subcontracting decisions (see the earlier discussion). Those decisions were probably made based on good economic logic. Subcontractors were probably chosen based on business variables such as cost, delivery, and product quality, and the key managers simply failed to ask, "How does this subcontractor treat its workforce?" If they thought about the question at all, they probably reasoned that it was the subcontractor's concern, not theirs. (For another example of a business decision that may have been unethical, see the Management Focus describing Pfizer's decision to test an experimental drug on children suffering from meningitis in Nigeria.)

ORGANIZATION CULTURE

The climate in some businesses does not encourage people to think through the ethical consequences of business decisions. This brings us to the third cause of unethical behavior in businesses—an organizational culture that deemphasizes business ethics, reducing

Pfizer's Drug Testing Strategy in Nigeria

The drug development process is long, risky, and expensive. It can take 10 years and cost in excess of $500 million to develop a new drug. Moreover, between 80 and 90 percent of drug candidates fail in clinical trials. Pharmaceutical companies rely upon a handful of successes to pay for their failures. Among the most successful of the world's pharmaceutical companies is New York–based Pfizer. Given the risks and costs of developing a new drug, pharmaceutical companies will jump at opportunities to reduce them, and in 1996 Pfizer thought it saw one.

Pfizer had been developing a novel antibiotic, Trovan, that was proving to be useful in treating a wide range of bacterial infections. Wall Street analysts were predicting that Trovan could be a blockbuster, one of a handful of drugs capable of generating sales of more than $1 billion a year. In 1996, Pfizer was pushing to submit data on Trovan's efficacy to the Food and Drug Administration (FDA) for review. A favorable review would allow Pfizer to sell the drug in the United States, the world's largest market. Pfizer wanted the drug to be approved for both adults and children, but it was having trouble finding sufficient numbers of sick children in the United States to test the drug on. Then in early 1996, a researcher at Pfizer read about an emerging epidemic of bacterial meningitis in Kano, Nigeria. This seemed like a quick way to test the drug on a large number of sick children.

Within weeks a team of six doctors had flown to Kano and were administering the drug, in oral form, to children with meningitis. Desperate for help, Nigerian authorities allowed Pfizer to give the drug to children (the epidemic would ultimately kill nearly 16,000 people). Over the next few weeks, Pfizer treated 198 children. The protocol called for half the patients to get Trovan and half to get a comparison antibiotic already approved for the treatment of children. After a few weeks, the Pfizer team left, the experiment complete. Trovan seemed to be about as effective and safe as the already approved antibiotic. The data from the trial were put into a package with data from other trials of Trovan and delivered to the FDA.

Questions were soon raised about the nature of Pfizer's experiment. Allegations charged that the Pfizer team kept children on Trovan, even after they failed to show a response to the drug, instead of switching them quickly to another drug. The result, according to critics, was that some children died who might have been saved had they been taken off Trovan sooner. Questions were also raised about the safety of the oral formulation of Trovan, which some doctors feared might lead to arthritis in children. Fifteen children who took Trovan showed signs of joint pain during the experiment, three times the rate of children taking the other antibiotic. Then there were questions about consent. The FDA requires that patient (or parent) consent be given before patients are enrolled in clinical trials, no matter where in the world the trials are conducted. Critics argue that in the rush to get the trial established in Nigeria, Pfizer did not follow proper procedures, and that many parents of the infected children did not know their children were participating in a trial for an experimental drug. Many of the parents were illiterate, could not read the consent forms, and had to rely upon the questionable translation of the Nigerian nursing staff. Pfizer rejected these charges and contends that it did nothing wrong.

Trovan was approved by the FDA for use in adults in 1997, but it was never approved for use in children. Launched in 1998, by 1999 there were reports that up to 140 patients in Europe had suffered liver damage after taking Trovan. The FDA subsequently restricted the use of Trovan to those cases where the benefits of treatment outweighed the risk of liver damage. European regulators banned sales of the drug.[29]

all decisions to the purely economic. The term **organization culture** refers to the values and norms that employees of an organization share. You will recall from Chapter 3 that *values* are abstract ideas about what a group believes to be good, right, and desirable, while *norms* are the social rules and guidelines that prescribe appropriate behavior in particular situations. Just as societies have cultures, so do business organizations. Together, values and norms shape the culture of a business organization, and that culture has an important influence on the ethics of business decision making.

Author Robert Bryce has explained how the organization culture at now-bankrupt multinational energy company Enron was built on values that emphasized greed and deception.[28] According to Bryce, the tone was set by top managers who engaged in self-dealing to enrich themselves and their own families. Bryce tells how former Enron CEO Kenneth Lay made sure his own family benefited handsomely from Enron. Much of Enron's corporate travel business was handled by a travel agency in which Lay's sister was a part-owner. When an internal auditor recommended that the company could do better by using another travel agency, he soon found himself out of a job. In 1997, Enron acquired a company owned by Kenneth Lay's son, Mark Lay, which was trying to establish a business trading paper and pulp products. At the time, Mark Lay and another company he controlled were targets of a federal criminal investigation of bankruptcy fraud and embezzlement. As part of the deal, Enron hired Mark Lay as an executive with a three-year contract that guaranteed him at least $1 million in pay over that period, plus options to purchase about 20,000 shares of Enron. Bryce also details how Lay's grown daughter used an Enron jet to transport her king-sized bed to France. With Kenneth Lay as an example, it is perhaps not surprising that self-dealing soon became endemic at Enron. The most notable example was Chief Financial Officer Andrew Fastow, who set up "off balance sheet" partnerships that not only hid Enron's true financial condition from investors but also paid tens of millions of dollars directly to Fastow. (Fastow was subsequently indicted by the government for criminal fraud and went to jail.)

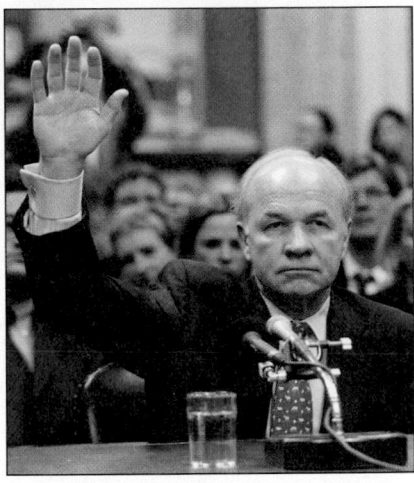

Former Enron CEO Kenneth Lay was charged with a variety of criminal deeds.

UNREALISTIC PERFORMANCE EXPECTATIONS

A fourth cause of unethical behavior has already been hinted at—it is pressure from the parent company to meet unrealistic performance goals that can be attained only by cutting corners or acting in an unethical manner. Again, Bryce discusses how this may have occurred at Enron. Lay's successor as CEO, Jeff Skilling, put a performance evaluation system in place that weeded out 15 percent of underperformers every six months. This created a pressure-cooker culture with a myopic focus on short-run performance, and some executives and energy traders responded to that pressure by falsifying their performance—inflating the value of trades, for example—to make it look as if they were performing better than was actually the case.

The lesson from the Enron debacle is that an organizational culture can legitimize behavior that society would judge as unethical, particularly when the culture is combined with a focus on unrealistic performance goals, such as maximizing short-term economic performance, no matter what the costs. In such circumstances, there is a greater than average probability that managers will violate their own personal ethics and engage in unethical behavior. Conversely, an organization culture can do just the opposite and reinforce the need for ethical behavior. At Hewlett-Packard, for example, Bill Hewlett and David Packard, the company's founders, propagated a set of values known as The HP Way. These values, which shape the way business is conducted both within and by the corporation, have an important ethical component. Among other things, they stress the need for confidence in and respect for people, open communication, and concern for the individual employee.

LEADERSHIP

The Enron and Hewlett-Packard examples suggest a fifth root cause of unethical behavior—leadership. Leaders help to establish the culture of an organization, and they set the example that others follow. Other employees in a business often take their cue from business leaders, and if those leaders do not behave in an ethical manner, they might not either. It is not what leaders say that matters, but what they do. Enron, for example, had a code of ethics that Kenneth Lay himself often referred to, but Lay's own actions to enrich family members spoke louder than any words.

Philosophical Approaches to Ethics

We shall look at several different approaches to business ethics here, beginning with some that can best be described as straw men, which either deny the value of business ethics or apply the concept in a very unsatisfactory way. Having discussed, and dismissed, the straw men, we then move on to consider approaches that most moral philosophers favor and that form the basis for current models of ethical behavior in international businesses.

STRAW MEN

Business ethics scholars discuss some approaches to business ethics primarily to demonstrate that they offer inappropriate guidelines for ethical decision making in a multinational enterprise. Four such approaches to business ethics are commonly discussed in the literature: the Friedman doctrine, cultural relativism, the righteous moralist, and the naive immoralist. All of these approaches have some inherent value, but all are unsatisfactory in important ways. Nevertheless, sometimes companies adopt these approaches.

The Friedman Doctrine

The Nobel Prize–winning economist Milton Friedman wrote an article in 1970 that has since become a classic straw man that business ethics scholars outline only to tear down.[30] Friedman's basic position is that the only social responsibility of business is to increase profits, so long as the company stays within the rules of law. He explicitly rejects the idea that businesses should undertake social expenditures beyond those mandated by the law and required for the efficient running of a business. For example, his arguments suggest that improving working conditions beyond the level required by the law *and* necessary to maximize employee productivity will reduce profits and is therefore not appropriate. His belief is that a firm should maximize its profits because that is the way to maximize the returns that accrue to the owners of the firm, its stockholders. If stockholders then wish to use the proceeds to make social investments, that is their right, according to Friedman, but managers of the firm should not make that decision for them.

Although Friedman is talking about social responsibility, rather than business ethics per se, many business ethics scholars equate social responsibility with ethical behavior and thus believe Friedman is also arguing against business ethics. However, the assumption that Friedman is arguing against ethics is not quite true, for Friedman does state,

> There is one and only one social responsibility of business—to use its resources and engage in activities designed to increase its profits so long as it stays within the rules of the game, which is to say that it engages in open and free competition without deception or fraud.[31]

In other words, Friedman states that businesses should behave in an ethical manner and not use deception and fraud.

Nevertheless, Friedman's arguments do break down under examination. This is particularly true in international business where the "rules of the game" are not well established and differ from country to county. Consider again the case of sweatshop labor. Child labor may not be against the law in a developing nation, and maximizing productivity may not require that a multinational firm stop using child labor in that country, but it is still immoral to use child labor because the practice conflicts with widely held views about what is the right and proper thing to do. Similarly, there may be no rules against pollution in a developed nation and spending money on pollution control may reduce the profit rate of the firm, but generalized notions of morality would hold that it is still unethical to dump toxic pollutants into rivers or foul the air with gas releases. In addition to the local consequences of such pollution, which may have serious health effects for the surrounding population, it also has global consequences as pollutants degrade those two global commons so important to us all—the atmosphere and the oceans.

Cultural Relativism

Another straw man that business ethics scholars often raise is **cultural relativism,** which is the belief that ethics are nothing more than the reflection of a culture—all ethics are culturally determined—and that accordingly, a firm should adopt the ethics of the culture in which it is operating.[32] This approach is often summarized by the maxim *when in Rome do as the Romans do.* As with Friedman's approach, cultural relativism does not stand up to a closer look. At its extreme, cultural relativism suggests that if a culture supports slavery, it is OK to use slave labor in a country. Clearly, it is not! Cultural relativism implicitly rejects the idea that universal notions of morality transcend different cultures, but, as we shall argue later in the chapter, some universal notions of morality are found across cultures.

While dismissing cultural relativism in its most sweeping form, some ethicists argue that there is residual value in this approach.[33] As we noted in Chapter 3, societal values and norms do vary from culture to culture—customs do differ, so it might follow that certain business practices are ethical in one country, but not another. Indeed, the facilitating payments allowed in the Foreign Corrupt Practices Act can be seen as an acknowledgment that in some countries, the payment of speed money to government officials is necessary to get business done, and if not ethically desirable, it is at least ethically acceptable.

However, not all ethicists or companies agree with this pragmatic view. As noted earlier, oil company BP explicitly states it will not make facilitating payments, no matter what the prevailing cultural norms are. In 2002, BP enacted a zero-tolerance policy for facilitation payments, primarily on the basis that such payments are a low-level form of corruption, and thus cannot be justified because corruption corrupts both the bribe giver and the bribe taker and perpetuates the corrupt system. As BP notes on its Web site, because of its zero-tolerance policy:

> Some oil product sales in Vietnam involved inappropriate commission payments to the managers of customers in return for placing orders with BP. These were stopped during 2002 with the result that BP failed to win certain tenders with potential profit totaling $300k. In addition, two sales managers resigned over the issue. The business, however, has recovered using more traditional sales methods and has exceeded its targets at year-end.[34]

BP's experience suggests that companies should not use cultural relativism as an argument for justifying behavior that is clearly based upon suspect ethical grounds, even if that behavior is both legal and routinely accepted in the country where the company is doing business.

The Righteous Moralist

A **righteous moralist** claims that a multinational's home-country standards of ethics are the appropriate ones for companies to follow in foreign countries. This approach is typically associated with managers from developed nations. While this seems reasonable at first blush, the approach can create problems. Consider the following example: An American bank manager was sent to Italy, where he was appalled to learn that the local branch's accounting department recommended grossly underreporting the bank's profits for income tax purposes.[35] The manager insisted that the bank report its earnings accurately, American style. When he was called by the Italian tax department to the firm's tax hearing, he was told the firm owed three times as much tax as it had paid, reflecting the department's standard assumption that each firm underreports its earnings by two-thirds. Despite his protests, the new assessment stood. In this case, the righteous moralist has run into a problem caused by the prevailing cultural norms in the country where he is doing business. How should he respond? The righteous moralist would argue for maintaining the position, while a more pragmatic view might be that in this case, the right thing to do is to follow the prevailing cultural norms, since there is a big penalty for not doing so.

The main criticism of the righteous moralist approach is that its proponents go too far. While there are some universal moral principles that should not be violated, it does not always follow that the appropriate thing to do is adopt home-country standards. For example, U.S. laws set down strict guidelines with regard to minimum wage and working conditions. Does this mean it is ethical to apply the same guidelines in a foreign country, paying people the same as they are paid in the United States, providing the same benefits and working conditions? Probably not, because doing so might nullify the reason for investing in that country and therefore deny locals the benefits of inward investment by the multinational. Clearly, a more nuanced approach is needed.

The Naive Immoralist

A **naive immoralist** asserts that if a manager of a multinational sees that firms from other nations are not following ethical norms in a host nation, that manager should not either. The classic example to illustrate the approach is known as the drug lord problem. In one variant of this problem, an American manager in Colombia routinely pays off the local drug lord to guarantee that his plant will not be bombed and that none of his employees will be kidnapped. The manager argues that such payments are ethically defensible because everyone is doing it.

The objection to the manager's behavior is twofold. First, to say that an action is ethically justified if everyone is doing it is not sufficient. If firms in a country routinely employ 12-year-olds and make them work 10-hour days, is it therefore ethically defensible to do the same? Obviously not, and the company does have a clear choice. It does not have to abide by local practices, and it can decide not to invest in a country where the practices are particularly odious. Second, the multinational must recognize that it does have the ability to change the prevailing practice in a country. It can use its power for a positive moral purpose. This is what BP is doing by adopting a zero-tolerance policy with regard to facilitating payments. BP is stating that the prevailing practice of making facilitating payments is ethically wrong, and it is incumbent upon the company to use its power to try to change the standard. While some might argue that such an approach smells of moral imperialism and a lack of cultural sensitivity, if it is consistent with widely accepted moral standards in the global community, it may be ethically justified.

To return to the drug lord problem, an argument can be made that it is ethically defensible to make such payments, not because everyone else is doing so but because not doing so would cause greater harm (i.e., the drug lord might seek retribution and engage in killings and kidnappings). Another solution to the problem is to refuse to invest in a country where the rule of law is so weak that drug lords can demand protection money. This solution, however, is also imperfect, for it might mean denying the law-abiding citizens of that country the benefits associated with inward investment by the multinational (i.e., jobs, income, greater economic growth and welfare). Clearly, the drug lord problem constitutes one of those intractable ethical dilemmas where there is no obvious right solution, and managers need a moral compass to help them find an acceptable solution to the dilemma.

UTILITARIAN AND KANTIAN ETHICS

In contrast to the straw men just discussed, most moral philosophers see value in utilitarian and Kantian approaches to business ethics. These approaches were developed in the 18th and 19th centuries and although they have been largely superseded by more modern approaches, they form part of the tradition upon which newer approaches have been constructed.

The utilitarian approach to business ethics dates to philosophers such as David Hume (1711–1776), Jeremy Bentham (1784–1832), and John Stuart Mill (1806–1873). **Utilitarian approaches** to ethics hold that the moral worth of actions or practices is determined by their consequences.[36] An action is judged desirable if it leads to the best possible balance of good consequences over bad consequences. Utilitarianism is committed to the maximization of good and the minimization of harm. Utilitarianism recognizes that actions have multiple consequences, some of which are good in a social sense and some of which are harmful. As a philosophy for business ethics, it focuses attention on the need to weigh carefully all the social benefits and costs of a business action and to pursue only those actions where the benefits outweigh the costs. The best decisions, from a utilitarian perspective, are those that produce the greatest good for the greatest number of people.

Many businesses have adopted specific tools such as cost–benefit analysis and risk assessment that are firmly rooted in a utilitarian philosophy. Managers often weigh the benefits and costs of an action before deciding whether to pursue it. An oil company considering drilling in an Alaskan wildlife preserve must weigh the economic benefits of increased oil production and the creation of jobs against the costs of environmental degradation in a fragile ecosystem. An agricultural biotechnology company such as Monsanto must decide whether the benefits of genetically modified crops that produce natural pesticides outweigh the risks. The benefits include increased crop yields and reduced need for chemical fertilizers. The risks include the possibility that Monsanto's insect-resistant crops might make matters worse over time if insects evolve a resistance to the natural pesticides engineered into Monsanto's plants, rendering the plants vulnerable to a new generation of super bugs.

For all of its appeal, utilitarian philosophy does have some serious drawbacks as an approach to business ethics. One problem is measuring the benefits, costs, and risks of a course of action. In the case of an oil company considering drilling in Alaska, how does one measure the potential harm done to the region's ecosystem? In the Monsanto example, how can one quantify the risk that genetically engineered crops might ultimately result in the evolution of super bugs that are resistant to the natural pesticide engineered into the crops? In general, utilitarian philosophers recognize that the measurement of benefits, costs, and risks is often not possible due to limited knowledge.

The second problem with utilitarianism is that the philosophy omits the consideration of justice. The action that produces the greatest good for the greatest number of people may result in the unjustified treatment of a minority. Such action cannot be ethical, precisely because it is unjust. For example, suppose that in the interests of keeping down health insurance costs, the government decides to screen people for the HIV virus and deny insurance coverage to those who are HIV positive. By reducing health costs, such action might produce significant benefits for a large number of people, but the action is unjust because it discriminates unfairly against a minority.

Kantian ethics are based on the philosophy of Immanuel Kant (1724–1804). **Kantian ethics** hold that people should be treated as ends and never purely as *means* to the ends of others. People are not instruments, like a machine. People have dignity and need to be respected as such. Employing people in sweatshops, making them work long hours for low pay in poor working conditions, is a violation of ethics, according to Kantian philosophy, because it treats people as mere cogs in a machine and not as conscious moral beings who have dignity. Although contemporary moral philosophers tend to view Kant's ethical philosophy as incomplete—for example, his system has no place for moral emotions or sentiments such as sympathy or caring—the notion that people should be respected and treated with dignity still resonates in the modern world.

RIGHTS THEORIES

Developed in the 20th century, **rights theories** recognize that human beings have fundamental rights and privileges that transcend national boundaries and cultures. Rights establish a minimum level of morally acceptable behavior. One well-known definition of a fundamental right construes it as something that takes precedence over or "trumps" a collective good. Thus, we might say that the right to free speech is a fundamental right that takes precedence over all but the most compelling collective goals and overrides, for example, the interest of the state in civil harmony or moral consensus.[37] Moral theorists argue that fundamental human rights form the basis for the *moral compass* that managers should navigate by when making decisions that have an ethical component. More precisely, they should not pursue actions that violate these rights.

The notion that there are fundamental rights that transcend national borders and cultures was the underlying motivation for the United Nations' **Universal Declaration of Human Rights,** which has been ratified by almost every country on the planet and lays down basic principles that should always be adhered to irrespective of the culture in which one is doing business.[38] Echoing Kantian ethics, Article 1 of this declaration states:

> Article 1: All human beings are born free and equal in dignity and rights. They are endowed with reason and conscience and should act towards one another in a spirit of brotherhood.

Article 23 of this declaration, which relates directly to employment, states:

> Everyone has the right to work, to free choice of employment, to just and favorable conditions of work, and to protection against unemployment.
> Everyone, without any discrimination, has the right to equal pay for equal work.
> Everyone who works has the right to just and favorable remuneration ensuring for himself and his family an existence worthy of human dignity, and supplemented, if necessary, by other means of social protection.
> Everyone has the right to form and to join trade unions for the protection of his interests.

Clearly, the rights embodied in Article 23 to "just and favorable work conditions," "equal pay for equal work," and remuneration that ensures an "existence worthy of human dignity" imply that it is unethical to employ child labor in sweatshop settings and pay less than subsistence wages, even if that happens to be common practice in some countries. These are fundamental human rights, which transcend national borders.

It is important to note that along with *rights* come *obligations*. Because we have the right to free speech, we are also obligated to make sure that we respect the free speech of others. The notion that people have obligations is stated in Article 29 of the Universal Declaration of Human Rights:

> Article 29: Everyone has duties to the community in which alone the free and full development of his personality is possible.

Within the framework of a theory of rights, certain people or institutions are obligated to provide benefits or services that secure the rights of others. Such obligations also fall upon more than one class of moral agent (a moral agent is any person or institution that is capable of moral action such as a government or corporation).

For example, to escape the high costs of toxic waste disposal in the West, in the late 1980s several firms shipped their waste in bulk to African nations, where it was disposed of at a much lower cost. In 1987, five European ships unloaded toxic waste containing dangerous poisons in Nigeria. Workers wearing sandals and shorts unloaded the barrels for $2.50 a day and placed them in a dirt lot in a residential area. They were not told about the contents of the barrels.[39] Who bears the obligation for protecting the rights of workers and residents to safety in a case like this? According to rights theorists, the obligation rests not on the shoulders of one moral agent, but on the shoulders of all moral agents whose actions might harm or contribute to the harm of the workers and residents. Thus, it was the obligation not just of the Nigerian government but also of the multinational firms that shipped the toxic waste to make sure it did no harm to residents and workers. In this case, both the government and the multinationals apparently failed to recognize their basic obligation to protect the fundamental human rights of others.

JUSTICE THEORIES

Justice theories focus on the attainment of a just distribution of economic goods and services. A **just distribution** is one that is considered fair and equitable. There is no one theory of justice, and several theories of justice conflict with each other in important ways.[40] Here we shall focus on one particular theory of justice that is both very influential and has important ethical implications, the theory attributed to philosopher John Rawls.[41] Rawls argues that all economic goods and services should be distributed equally except when an unequal distribution would work to everyone's advantage.

According to Rawls, valid principles of justice are those with which all persons would agree if they could freely and impartially consider the situation. Impartiality is guaranteed by a conceptual device that Rawls calls the *veil of ignorance*. Under the veil of ignorance, everyone is imagined to be ignorant of all of his or her particular characteristics, for example, race, sex, intelligence, nationality, family background, and special talents. Rawls then asks what system people would design under a veil of ignorance. Under these conditions, people would unanimously agree on two fundamental principles of justice.

The first principle is that each person be permitted the maximum amount of basic liberty compatible with a similar liberty for others. Rawls takes these to be political liberty (e.g., the right to vote), freedom of speech and assembly, liberty of conscience and freedom of thought, the freedom and right to hold personal property, and freedom from arbitrary arrest and seizure.

The second principle is that once equal basic liberty is assured, inequality in basic social goods—such as income and wealth distribution, and opportunities—is to be allowed *only* if such inequalities benefit everyone. Rawls accepts that inequalities can be just if the system that produces inequalities is to the advantage of everyone. More precisely, he formulates what he calls the *difference principle*, which is that inequalities are justified if they benefit the position of the least-advantaged person. So, for example, wide variations in income and wealth can be considered just if the market-based system that produces this unequal distribution also benefits the least-advantaged members of society. One can argue that a well-regulated, market-based economy and free trade, by promoting economic growth, benefit the least-advantaged members of society. In principle at least, the inequalities inherent in such systems are therefore just (in other words, the rising tide of wealth created by a market-based economy and free trade lifts all boats, even those of the most disadvantaged).

In the context of international business ethics, Rawls's theory creates an interesting perspective. Managers could ask themselves whether the policies they adopt in foreign operations would be considered just under Rawls's veil of ignorance. Is it just, for example, to pay foreign workers less than workers in the firm's home country? Rawls's theory would suggest it is, so long as the inequality benefits the least-advantaged members of the global society (which is what economic theory suggests). Alternatively, it is difficult to imagine that managers operating under a veil of ignorance would design a system where foreign employees were paid subsistence wages to work long hours in sweatshop conditions and where they were exposed to toxic materials. Such working conditions are clearly unjust in Rawls's framework, and therefore, it is unethical to adopt them. Similarly, operating under a veil of ignorance, most people would probably design a system that imparts some protection from environmental degradation to important global commons, such as the oceans, atmosphere, and tropical rain forests. To the extent that this is the case, it follows that it is unjust, and by extension unethical, for companies to pursue actions that contribute toward extensive degradation of these commons. Thus, Rawls's veil of ignorance is a conceptual tool that contributes to the moral compass that managers can use to help them navigate through difficult ethical dilemmas.

Ethical Decision Making

What, then, is the best way for managers in a multinational firm to make sure that ethical considerations figure into international business decisions? How do managers decide upon an ethical course of action when confronted with decisions pertaining to working conditions, human rights, corruption, and environmental pollution? From an ethical perspective, how do managers determine the moral obligations that flow from the power of a multinational corporation? In many cases, there are no easy answers to these questions, for many of the most vexing ethical problems arise because very real dilemmas are inherent in them and no correct action is obvious. Nevertheless, managers can and should do many things to make sure they adhere to basic ethical principles and routinely insert ethical issues into international business decisions.

Here we focus on five things that an international business and its managers can do to make sure ethical issues are considered in business decisions. These are to (1) favor hiring and promoting people with a well-grounded sense of personal ethics; (2) build an organizational culture that places a high value on ethical behavior; (3) make sure that leaders within the business not only articulate the rhetoric of ethical behavior but also act in a manner that is consistent with that rhetoric; (4) put decision-making processes in place that require people to consider the ethical dimension of business decisions; and (5) develop moral courage.

HIRING AND PROMOTION

It seems obvious that businesses should strive to hire people who have a strong sense of personal ethics and would not engage in unethical or illegal behavior. Similarly, you would not expect a business to promote people whose behavior does not match generally accepted ethical standards—you might expect the business to fire them. However, actually doing so is very difficult. How do you know that someone has a poor sense of personal ethics? In our society, we have an incentive to hide a lack of personal ethics from public view. Once people realize you are unethical, they will no longer trust you.

Is there anything businesses can do to make sure they do not hire people who subsequently turn out to have poor personal ethics, particularly given that people have an incentive to hide this from public view (indeed, the unethical person may lie about his or her nature)? Businesses can give potential employees psychological tests to try to discern their ethical predisposition, and they can check with prior employers regarding someone's reputation (e.g., by asking for letters of reference and talking to people who have worked with the prospective employee). The latter is common and does influence the hiring process. Promoting people who have displayed poor ethics should not occur in a company where the organization culture values the need for ethical behavior and where leaders act accordingly.

Not only should businesses strive to identify and hire people with a strong sense of personal ethics, but it also is in the interests of prospective employees to find out as much as they can about the ethical climate in an organization. Who wants to work at a multinational such as Enron, which ultimately entered bankruptcy because unethical executives had established risky partnerships that were hidden from public view and that existed in part to enrich those same executives? Table 4.1 lists some questions job seekers might want to ask a prospective employer.

ORGANIZATION CULTURE AND LEADERSHIP

To foster ethical behavior, businesses need to build an organization culture that values ethical behavior. Three things are particularly important in building an organization culture that emphasizes ethical behavior. First, the businesses must explicitly articulate values that emphasize ethical behavior. Many companies now do this by drafting a **code of ethics,** which is a formal statement of the ethical priorities a business adheres to. Often, the code of ethics draws heavily upon documents such as the UN Universal Declaration of Human Rights, which itself is grounded in Kantian and rights-based theories of moral philosophy. Others have incorporated ethical statements into documents that articulate the values or mission of the business. For example, the food and consumer products multinational Unilever has a code of ethics that includes the following points:[42]

Employees: Unilever is committed to diversity in a working environment where there is mutual trust and respect and where everyone feels responsible for the performance and reputation of our company. We will recruit, employ, and promote employees on the sole

Some probing questions to ask about a prospective employer:

1. Is there a formal code of ethics? How widely is it distributed? Is it reinforced in other formal ways such as through decision-making systems?

2. Are workers at all levels trained in ethical decision making? Are they also encouraged to take responsibility for their behavior or to question authority when asked to do something they consider wrong?

3. Do employees have formal channels available to make their concerns known confidentially? Is there a formal committee high in the organization that considers ethical issues?

4. Is misconduct disciplined swiftly and justly within the organization?

5. Is integrity emphasized to new employees?

6. How are senior managers perceived by subordinates in terms of their integrity? How do such leaders model ethical behavior?

TABLE 4.1

A Job Seeker's Ethics Audit

Source: Linda K. Trevino, chair of the Department of Management and Organization, Smeal College of Business, Pennsylvania State University. Reported in K. Maher, "Career Journal. Wanted: Ethical Employer," *The Wall Street Journal*, July 9, 2002, p. B1.

basis of the qualifications and abilities needed for the work to be performed. We are committed to safe and healthy working conditions for all employees. We will not use any form of forced, compulsory, or child labor. We are committed to working with employees to develop and enhance each individual's skills and capabilities. We respect the dignity of the individual and the right of employees to freedom of association. We will maintain good communications with employees through company-based information and consultation procedures.

Business Integrity: Unilever does not give or receive, whether directly or indirectly, bribes or other improper advantages for business or financial gain. No employee may offer, give, or receive any gift or payment which is, or may be construed as being, a bribe. Any demand for, or offer of, a bribe must be rejected immediately and reported to management. Unilever accounting records and supporting documents must accurately describe and reflect the nature of the underlying transactions. No undisclosed or unrecorded account, fund, or asset will be established or maintained.

It is clear from these principles that, among other things, Unilever will not tolerate substandard working conditions, use child labor, or give bribes under any circumstances. Note also the reference to respecting the dignity of employees, a statement that is grounded in Kantian ethics. Unilever's principles send a very clear message about appropriate ethics to managers and employees.

Having articulated values in a code of ethics or some other document, leaders in the business must give life and meaning to those words by repeatedly emphasizing their importance *and then acting on them*. This means using every relevant opportunity to stress the importance of business ethics and making sure that key business decisions not only make good economic sense but also are ethical. Many companies have gone a step further, hiring independent auditors to make sure they are behaving in a manner consistent with their ethical codes. Nike, for example, has hired independent auditors to make sure that the company's subcontractors are living up to Nike's code of conduct.

Finally, building an organization culture that places a high value on ethical behavior requires incentive and reward systems, including promotions that reward people who engage in ethical behavior and sanction those who do not. At General Electric, for example, the former CEO Jack Welch has described how he reviewed the performance of managers, dividing them into several different groups. These included overperformers who displayed the right values and were singled out for advancement and bonuses and overperformers who displayed the wrong values and were let go. Welch was not willing to tolerate leaders within the company who did not act in accordance with the central values of the company, even if they were in all other respects skilled managers.[43]

DECISION-MAKING PROCESSES

In addition to establishing the right kind of ethical culture in an organization, business-people must be able to think through the ethical implications of decisions in a systematic way. To do this, they need a moral compass, and both rights theories and Rawls's theory of justice help to provide such a compass. Beyond these theories, some experts on ethics have proposed a straightforward practical guide—or ethical algorithm—to determine whether a decision is ethical.[44] According to these experts, a decision is acceptable on ethical grounds if a businessperson can answer yes to each of these questions:

- Does my decision fall within the accepted values or standards that typically apply in the organizational environment (as articulated in a code of ethics or some other corporate statement)?
- Am I willing to see the decision communicated to all stakeholders affected by it—for example, by having it reported in newspapers or on television?
- Would the people with whom I have a significant personal relationship, such as family members, friends, or even managers in other businesses, approve of the decision?

Others have recommended a five-step process to think through ethical problems (this is another example of an ethical algorithm).[45] In step 1, businesspeople should identify which stakeholders a decision would affect and in what ways. A firm's **stakeholders** are individuals or groups that have an interest, claim, or stake in the company, what it does, and how well it performs.[46] They can be divided into internal stakeholders and external stakeholders. **Internal stakeholders** are individuals or groups who work for or own the business. They include all employees, the board of directors, and stockholders. **External stakeholders** are all other individuals and groups that have some claim on the firm. Typically, this group comprises customers, suppliers, lenders, governments, unions, local communities and the general public.

All stakeholders are in an exchange relationship with the company. Each stakeholder group supplies the organization with important resources (or contributions), and in exchange each expects its interests to be satisfied (by inducements).[47] For example, employees provide labor, skills, knowledge, and time and in exchange expect commensurate income, job satisfaction, job security, and good working conditions. Customers provide a company with its revenues and in exchange they want quality products that represent value for money. Communities provide businesses with local infrastructure and in exchange they want businesses that are responsible citizens and seek some assurance that the quality of life will be improved as a result of the business firm's existence.

Stakeholder analysis involves a certain amount of what has been called *moral imagination*.[48] This means standing in the shoes of a stakeholder and asking how a proposed decision might impact that stakeholder. For example, when considering outsourcing to subcontractors, managers might need to ask themselves how it might feel to be working under substandard health conditions for long hours.

Step 2 involves judging the ethics of the proposed strategic decision, given the information gained in step 1. Managers need to determine whether a proposed decision would violate the *fundamental rights* of any stakeholders. For example, we might argue that the right to information about health risks in the workplace is a fundamental entitlement of employees. Similarly, the right to know about potentially dangerous features of a product is a fundamental entitlement of customers (something tobacco companies violated when they did not reveal to their customers what they knew about the health risks of smoking). Managers might also want to ask themselves whether they would allow the proposed strategic decision if they were designing a system under Rawls's veil of ignorance. For example, if the issue under consideration was whether to outsource work to a subcontractor with low pay and poor working conditions, managers might want to ask themselves whether they would allow for such action if they were considering it under a veil of ignorance, where they themselves might ultimately be the ones to work for the subcontractor.

The judgment at this stage should be guided by various moral principles that should not be violated. The principles might be those articulated in a corporate code of ethics or other company documents. In addition, certain moral principles that we have adopted as members of society—for instance, the prohibition on stealing—should not be violated. The judgment at this stage will also be guided by the decision rule that is chosen to assess the proposed strategic decision. Although most businesses stress the decision rule of maximizing long-run profitability, it should be applied subject to the constraint that no moral principles are violated—that the business behaves in an ethical manner.

Step 3 requires managers to establish moral intent. This means the business must resolve to place moral concerns ahead of other concerns in cases where either the fundamental rights of stakeholders or key moral principles have been violated. At this stage, input from top management might be particularly valuable. Without the proactive encouragement of top managers, middle-level managers might tend to place the narrow economic interests of the company before the interests of stakeholders. They might do so in the (usually erroneous) belief that top managers favor such an approach.

Step 4 requires the company to engage in ethical behavior. Step 5 requires the business to audit its decisions, reviewing them to make sure they were consistent with ethical principles, such as those stated in the company's code of ethics. This final step is critical and often overlooked. Without auditing past decisions, businesspeople may not know if their decision process is working and if changes should be made to ensure greater compliance with a code of ethics.

ETHICS OFFICERS

To make sure that a business behaves in an ethical manner, a number of firms now have ethics officers. These individuals are responsible for making sure that all employees are trained to be ethically aware, that ethical considerations enter the business decision-making process, and that the company's code of ethics is followed. Ethics officers may also be responsible for auditing decisions to make sure they are consistent with this code. In many businesses, ethics officers act as an internal ombudsperson with responsibility for handling confidential inquiries from employees, investigating complaints from employees or others, reporting findings, and making recommendations for change.

For example, United Technologies, a multinational aerospace company with worldwide revenues of more than $30 billion, has had a formal code of ethics since 1990.[49] The company has some 160 business practice officers (its name for ethics officers) who are responsible for making sure the code is followed. United Technologies also established an ombudsperson program in 1986 that lets employees inquire anonymously about ethics issues. The program has received some 56,000 inquiries since 1986, and ombudspeople have handled 8,000 cases.

MORAL COURAGE

Finally, it is important to recognize that employees in an international business may need significant *moral courage*. Moral courage enables managers to walk away from a decision that is profitable but unethical. Moral courage gives an employee the strength to say no to a superior who instructs her to pursue actions that are unethical. Moral courage gives employees the integrity to go public to the media and blow the whistle on persistent unethical behavior in a company. Moral courage does not come easily; there are well-known cases where individuals have lost their jobs because they blew the whistle on corporate behaviors they thought unethical, telling the media about what was occurring.[50]

However, companies can strengthen the moral courage of employees by committing themselves to not retaliate against employees who exercise moral courage, say no to superiors, or otherwise complain about unethical actions. For example, consider the following extract from Unilever's code of ethics:

> Any breaches of the Code must be reported in accordance with the procedures specified by the Joint Secretaries. The Board of Unilever will not criticize management for any loss of business resulting from adherence to these principles and other mandatory policies and instructions. The Board of Unilever expects employees to bring to their attention, or to that of senior management, any breach or suspected breach of these principles. Provision has been made for employees to be able to report in confidence and no employee will suffer as a consequence of doing so.[51]

This statement gives permission to employees to exercise moral courage. Companies can also set up ethics hotlines, which allow employees to anonymously register a complaint with a corporate ethics officer.

SUMMARY OF DECISION-MAKING STEPS

All the steps discussed here—hiring and promoting people based upon ethical considerations as well as more traditional metrics of performance, establishing an ethical culture in the organization, instituting ethical decision-making processes, appointing ethics officers, and creating an environment that facilitates moral courage—can help ensure that managers are cognizant of the ethical implications of business decisions and do not violate basic ethical prescripts. At the same time, it must be recognized that not all ethical dilemmas have a clean and obvious solution—that is why they are dilemmas. There are clearly things that international businesses should not do and there are things that they should do, but there are also actions that present managers with true dilemmas. In these cases, a premium is placed on managers' ability to make sense out of complex situations and make balanced decisions that are as just as possible.

CHAPTER SUMMARY

This chapter has discussed the source and nature of ethical issues in international businesses, the different philosophical approaches to business ethics, and the steps managers can take to ensure that ethical issues are respected in international business decisions. The chapter made these points:

1. The term *ethics* refers to accepted principles of right or wrong that govern the conduct of a person, the members of a profession, or the actions of an organization. Business ethics are the accepted principles of right or wrong governing the conduct of businesspeople, and an ethical strategy is one that does not violate these accepted principles.

2. Ethical issues and dilemmas in international business are rooted in the variations among political systems, law, economic development, and culture from nation to nation.

3. The most common ethical issues in international business involve employment practices, human rights, environmental regulations,

corruption, and the moral obligation of multinational corporations.

4. Ethical dilemmas are situations in which none of the available alternatives seems ethically acceptable.

5. Unethical behavior is rooted in poor personal ethics, the psychological and geographical distances of a foreign subsidiary from the home office, a failure to incorporate ethical issues into strategic and operational decision making, a dysfunctional culture, and failure of leaders to act in an ethical manner.

6. Moral philosophers contend that approaches to business ethics such as the Friedman doctrine, cultural relativism, the righteous moralist, and the naive immoralist are unsatisfactory in important ways.

7. The Friedman doctrine states that the only social responsibility of business is to increase profits, as long as the company stays within the

rules of law. Cultural relativism contends that one should adopt the ethics of the culture in which one is doing business. The righteous moralist monolithically applies home-country ethics to a foreign situation, while the naive immoralist believes that if a manager of a multinational sees that firms from other nations are not following ethical norms in a host nation, that manager should not either.

8. Utilitarian approaches to ethics hold that the moral worth of actions or practices is determined by their consequences, and the best decisions are those that produce the greatest good for the greatest number of people.

9. Kantian ethics state that people should be treated as ends and never purely as *means* to the ends of others. People are not instruments, like a machine. People have dignity and need to be respected as such.

10. Rights theories recognize that human beings have fundamental rights and privileges that transcend national boundaries and cultures. These rights establish a minimum level of morally acceptable behavior.

11. The concept of justice developed by John Rawls suggests that a decision is just and ethical if people would allow for it when designing a social system under a veil of ignorance.

12. To make sure that ethical issues are considered in international business decisions, managers should (*a*) favor hiring and promoting people with a well-grounded sense of personal ethics; (*b*) build an organization culture that places a high value on ethical behavior; (*c*) make sure that leaders within the business not only articulate the rhetoric of ethical behavior but also act in a manner that is consistent with that rhetoric; (*d*) put decision-making processes in place that require people to consider the ethical dimension of business decisions; and (*e*) be morally courageous and encourage others to do the same.

Critical Thinking and Discussion Questions

1. A visiting American executive finds that a foreign subsidiary in a poor nation has hired a 12-year-old girl to work on a factory floor, in violation of the company's prohibition on child labor. He tells the local manager to replace the child and tell her to go back to school. The local manager tells the American executive that the child is an orphan with no other means of support, and she will probably become a street child if she is denied work. What should the American executive do?

2. Drawing upon John Rawls's concept of the veil of ignorance, develop an ethical code that will (*a*) guide the decisions of a large oil multinational toward environmental protection, and (*b*) influence the policies of a clothing company regarding outsourcing manufacturing process.

3. Under what conditions is it ethically defensible to outsource production to the developing world where labor costs are lower when such actions also involve laying off long-term employees in the firm's home country?

4. Are facilitating payments ethical?

5. A manager from a developing country is overseeing a multinational's operations in a country where drug trafficking and lawlessness are rife. One day, a representative of a local "big man" approaches the manager and asks for a "donation" to help the "big man" provide housing for the poor. The representative tells the manager that in return for the donation, the "big man" will make sure that the manager has a productive stay in his country. No threats are made, but the manager is well aware that the "big man" heads a criminal organization that is engaged in drug trafficking. He also knows that that the big man does indeed help the poor in the run-down neighborhood of the city where he was born. What should the manager do?

6. Reread the Management Focus feature on Unocal and answer the following questions:

   a. Was it ethical for Unocal to enter into a partnership with a brutal military dictatorship for financial gain?

   b. What actions could Unocal have taken, short of not investing at all, to safeguard the human rights of people impacted by the gas pipeline project?

Research Task

Use the globalEDGE™ site to complete the following exercises:

1. Promoting respect for universal human rights is a central dimension of many countries' foreign policy. As history has shown, human rights abuses are an important concern worldwide. Some countries are more ready to work with other governments and civil society organizations to prevent abuses of power. Begun in 1977, the annual Country Reports on Human Rights Practices are designed to assess the state of democracy and human rights around the world, call attention to violations, and—where needed—prompt needed changes in U.S. policies toward particular countries. Find the annual Country Reports on Human Rights Practices and provide information on how the reports are prepared.

2. The level of perceived corruption varies from culture to culture. The *Corruption Perceptions Index (CPI)* is a comparative assessment of a country's integrity performance based on research done in Germany. Provide a description of this index and its ranking. Identify the five countries with the lowest as well as the highest CPI scores. Do you notice any similarities or differences in each group of five countries?

CLOSING CASE

Google in China

Google, the fast growing Internet search engine company, was established with a clear mission in mind: to organize the world's information and make it universally accessible and useful. Google has built a highly profitable advertising business on the back of its search engine, which is by far the most widely used in the world. Under the pay-per-click business model, advertisers pay Google every time a user of its search engine clicks on one of the paid links typically listed on the right hand side of Google's results page.

Google has long operated with the mantra "don't be evil!" When this phrase was originally formulated, the central message was that Google should never compromise the integrity of its search results. For example, Google decided not to let commercial considerations bias its ranking. This is why paid links are not included in its main search results, but listed on the right hand side of the results page. The mantra "don't be evil," however, has become more than that at Google; it has become a central organizing principle of the company and an ethical touchstone by which managers judge all of its strategic decisions.

Google's mission and mantra raised hopes among human rights activities that the search engine would be an unstoppable tool for circumventing government censorship, democratizing information, and allowing people in heavily censored societies to gain access to information that their governments were trying to suppress, including the largest country on earth, China.

Google began a Chinese language service in 2000, although the service was operated from the United States. In 2002, Chinese authorities blocked the site. Would-be users of Google's search engine were directed to a Chinese rival. The blocking took Google's managers totally by surprise. Reportedly, co-founder Sergey Brin immediately ordered half a dozen books on China and quickly read them in an effort to understand this vast country. Two weeks later, for reasons that have never been made clear, Google's service was restored. Google said that it did not change anything about its service, but Chinese users soon found that they could not access politically sensitive sites that appeared in Google's search results, suggesting that the government was censoring more aggressively. (The Chinese government has essentially erected a giant firewall between the Internet in China and the rest of the world, allowing its censors to block sites outside of China that are deemed subversive.)

By late 2004, it was clear to Google that China was a strategically important market. To exploit the opportunities that China offered, however, the company realized it would have to establish operations in China, including its own computer servers and a Chinese home page. Serving Chinese users from the United States was too slow, and the service was badly degraded by the censorship imposed. This created a dilemma for the company given the "don't be evil" mantra. Once it established Chinese operations, it would be subject to Chinese regulations, including those censoring information. For perhaps 18 months, senior managers inside the company debated the pros and cons of entering China directly, as opposed to serving the market from its U.S. site. Ultimately, they decided that the opportunity was too large to ignore. With over 100 million users, and that number growing fast, China promised to become the largest Internet market in the world and a major source of advertising revenue for Google. Moreover, Google was at a competitive disadvantage relative to its U.S. rivals, Yahoo and Microsoft's MSN, which had already established operations in China, and relative to China's homegrown company, Baidu, which leads the market for Internet search in China (in 2006 Baidu had around 40 percent of the market for search in China, compared to Google's 30 percent share).

In mid-2005, Google established a direct sales presence in China. In January 2006, Google rolled out its Chinese home page, which is hosted on servers based in China and maintained by Chinese employees in Beijing and Shanghai. Upon launch, Google stated that its objective was to give Chinese users "the greatest amount of information possible." It was immediately apparent that this was not the same as "access to all information." In accordance with Chinese regulations, Google had decided to engage in self-censorship, excluding results on such politically sensitive topics as democratic reform, Taiwanese independence, the banned Falun Gong movement, and references to the notorious Tiananmen Square massacre of democratic protestors that occurred in 1989. Human rights activists quickly protested, arguing that Google had abandoned its principles in order

to make greater profits. For its part, Google's managers claimed that it was better to give Chinese users access to a limited amount of information, than to none at all, or to serve the market from the United States and allow the government to continue proactively censoring its search results, which would result in a badly degraded service. Sergey Brin justified the Chinese decision by saying that "it will be better for Chinese web users, because ultimately they will get more information, though not quite all of it." Moreover, Google argued that it was the only search engine in China that let users know if search results had been censored (which is done by the inclusion of a bullet at the bottom of the page indicating censorship).[52]

Case Discussion Questions

1. What philosophical principle did Google's managers adopt when deciding that the benefits of operating in China outweighed the costs?

2. Do you think that Google should have entered China and engaged in self-censorship, given the company's long-standing mantra "Don't be evil"? Is it better to engage in self-censorship than have the government censor for you?

3. If all foreign search engine companies declined to invest directly in China due to concerns over censorship, what do you think the results would be? Who would benefit most from this action? Who would lose the most?

Notes

1. E. Kurtenbach, "The Foreign Factory Factor," *Seattle Times*, August 31, 2006, pp. C1, C3; E. Kurtenbach, "Apple Says It's Trying to Resolve Dispute over Labor Conditions at Chinese iPod Factory," *Associated Press Financial Wire*, August 30, 2006; Anonymous, "Chinese iPod Supplier Pulls Suit," *Associated Press Financial Wire*, September 3, 2006.

2. S. Greenhouse, "Nike Shoe Plant in Vietnam Is Called Unsafe for Workers," *The New York Times*, November 8, 1997; and V. Dobnik, "Chinese Workers Abused Making Nikes, Reeboks," *Seattle Times*, September 21, 1997, p. A4.

3. T. Donaldson, "Values in Tension: Ethics Away from Home," *Harvard Business Review*, September–October 1996.

4. R. K. Massie, *Loosing the Bonds: The United States and South Africa in the Apartheid Years* (Doubleday, 1997).

5. Not everyone agrees that the divestment trend had much influence on the South African economy. For a counterview see S. H. Teoh, I. Welch, and C. P. Wazzan, "The Effect of Socially Activist Investing on the Financial Markets: Evidence from South Africa," *The Journal of Business* 72, no. 1 (January 1999), pp. 35–60.

6. A. Rowell, "Trouble Flares in the Delta of Death; Shell Has Polluted More Than Ken Saro Wiwa's Oroniland in Nigeria," *The Guardian*, November 8, 1995, p. 6.

7. H. Hamilton, "Shell's New World Wide View," *Washington Post*, August 2, 1998, p. H1.

8. Rowell, "Trouble Flares in the Delta of Death."

9. P. Singer, *One World: The Ethics of Globalization* (New Haven, CT: Yale University Press, 2002).

10. G. Hardin, "The Tragedy of the Common," *Science* 162, 1, pp. 243–48.

11. Sources: J. Carlton, "Unocal Trial for Slave Labor Claims Is Set to Start Today," *The Wall Street Journal*, December 9, 2003, p. A19; S. Stern, "Big Business Targeted for Rights Abuse," *Christian Science Monitor*, September 4, 2003, p. 2; "Trouble in the Pipeline," *The Economist*, January 18, 1997, p. 39; I. Evelyn, "Feeling the Heat: Unocal Defends Myanmar Gas Pipeline Deal," *Los Angeles Times*, February 20, 1995, p. D1; and "Unocal Settles Myanmar Human Rights Cases," *Business and Environment* 16, February 2005, pp. 14–16.

12. J. Everett, D. Neu, and A. S. Rahaman, "The Global Fight against Corruption," *Journal of Business Ethics* 65 (2006), pp 1–18.

13. R. T. De George, *Competing with Integrity in International Business* (Oxford: Oxford University Press, 1993).

14. Details can be found at www.oecd.org/EN/home/0, EN-home-31-nodirectorate-no-nono-31,00.html.

15. B. Pranab, "Corruption and Development," *Journal of Economic Literature* 36 (September 1997), pp. 1320–46.

16. A. Shleifer and R.W. Vishny, "Corruption," *Quarterly Journal of Economics*, no. 108 (1993), pp. 599–617, and I. Ehrlich and F. Lui, "Bureaucratic Corruption and Endogenous Economic Growth," *Journal of Political Economy* 107 (December 1999), pp. 270–92.

17. P. Mauro, "Corruption and Growth," *Quarterly Journal of Economics*, no. 110 (1995), pp. 681–712.

18. Detailed at www.iit.edu/departments/csep/PublicWWW/codes/coe/Bus_Conduct_Dow_Corning(1996).html.

19. S. A. Waddock and S. B. Graves, "The Corporate Social Performance–Financial Performance Link," *Strategic Management Journal* 8 (1997), pp. 303–19.

20. D. Litvin, *Empires of Profit* (New York: Texere, 2003).

21. Details can be found at BP's Web site, www.bp.com.

22. Source: Litvin, *Empires of Profit*; M. Forney, "Testing Beijing's Limits," *Time*, September 5, 2005, p. 50.

23. This is known as the "when in Rome perspective." Donaldson, "Values in Tension: Ethics Away from Home."

24. De George, *Competing with Integrity in International Business*.

25. For a discussion of the ethics of using child labor, see J. Isern, "Bittersweet Chocolate: The Legacy of Child Labor in Cocoa Production in Cote d'Ivoire," *Journal of Applied Management and Entrepreneurship* 11 (2006), pp 115–132.

26. S. W. Gellerman, "Why Good Managers Make Bad Ethical Choices," in *Ethics in Practice: Managing the Moral Corporation*, ed. Kenneth R. Andrews (Cambridge, MA: Harvard Business School Press, 1989).

27. D. Messick and M. H. Bazerman, "Ethical Leadership and the Psychology of Decision Making," *Sloan Management Review* 37 (Winter 1996), pp. 9–20.

28. R. Bryce, *Pipe Dreams: Greed, Ego and the Death of Enron* (New York: Public Affairs, 2002).

29. Source: J. Stephens, "Where Profits and Lives Hang in the Balance," *Washington Post*, December 17, 2000, p. A1; A. Brichacek, "What Price Corruption?" *Pharmaceutical Executive* 21, no. 11 (November 2001), p. 94; and S. Hensley, "Court Revives Suit against Pfizer on Nigeria Study," *The Wall Street Journal*, October 13, 2004, p. B4.

30. M. Friedman, "The Social Responsibility of Business Is to Increase Profits," *The New York Times Magazine*, September 13, 1970. Reprinted in T. L. Beauchamp and Norman E. Bowie, *Ethical Theory and Business*, 7th ed. (Prentice Hall, 2001).

31. Friedman, "The Social Responsibility of Business Is to Increase Profits," p. 55.

32. For example, see Donaldson, "Values in Tension: Ethics Away from Home." See also N. Bowie, "Relativism and the Moral Obligations of Multination Corporations," in T. L. Beauchamp and N. E. Bowie, *Ethical Theory and Business*.

33. For example, see De George, *Competing with Integrity in International Business*.

34. Details can be found at www.bp.com/sectiongenericarticle.do?category1d=79&contentId=2002369#2014689.

35. This example is often repeated in the literature on international business ethics. It was first outlined by A. Kelly in "Case Study—Italian Style Mores." In T. Donaldson and P. Werhane, *Ethical Issues in Business* (Englewood Cliffs, NJ: Prentice Hall, 1979).

36. See T. L. Beauchamp and N. E. Bowie, *Ethical Theory and Business*.

37. T. Donaldson, *The Ethics of International Business* (Oxford: Oxford University Press, 1989).

38. Found at www.un.org/Overview/rights.html.

39. Donaldson, *The Ethics of International Business*.

40. See Chapter 10 in Beauchamp and Bowie, *Ethical Theory and Business*.

41. J. Rawls, *A Theory of Justice*, rev. ed. (Cambridge, MA: Belknap Press, 1999).

42. Found on Unilever's Web site at www.unilever.com/company/ourprinciples/.

43. J. Bower and J. Dial, "Jack Welch: General Electrics Revolutionary," Harvard Business School Case, Case # 9-394-065, April 1994.

44. For example, see R. Edward Freeman and D. Gilbert, *Corporate Strategy and the Search for Ethics* (Englewood Cliffs, NJ: Prentice Hall, 1988); T. Jones, "Ethical Decision Making by Individuals in Organizations," *Academy of Management Review* 16 (1991), pp. 366–95; and J. R. Rest, *Moral Development: Advances in Research and Theory* (New York: Praeger, 1986).

45. Ibid.

46. See E. Freeman, *Strategic Management: A Stakeholder Approach* (Boston: Pitman Press, 1984);

C. W. L. Hill and T. M. Jones, "Stakeholder-Agency Theory," *Journal of Management Studies* 29 (1992), pp. 131–54; and J. G. March and H. A. Simon, *Organizations* (New York: Wiley, 1958).

47. Hill and Jones, "Stakeholder-Agency Theory," *tional Business*.

48. De George, *Competing with Integrity in International Business*.

49. The code can be accessed at United Technologies Web site, www.utc.com/profile/ethics/index.htm.

50. Colin Grant, "Whistle Blowers: Saints of Secular Culture," *Journal of Business Ethics*, September 2002, pp. 391–400.

51. Found on Unilever's Web site, www.unilever.com/company/ourprinciples/.

52. Sources: A. Kessler, "Sellout.com," *The Wall Street Journal*, January 31, 2006, p. A14; D. Henninger, "Wonderland: Google in China," *The Wall Street Journal*, March 10, 2006, p. A18; J. Dean, "Limited Search: As Google Pushes into China It Faces Clashes with Censors," *The Wall Street Journal*, December 16, 2005, p. A1; "The Party, the People, and the Power of Cyber Talk: China and the Internet," *The Economist*, April 29, 2006, pp. 28–30.

part two
cases

Nike: The Sweatshop Debate

INTRODUCTION

Nike is in many ways the quintessential global corporation. Established in 1972 by former University of Oregon track star Phil Knight, Nike is now one of the leading marketers of athletic shoes and apparel on the planet. In 2006 the company had $15 billion in annual revenues and sold its products in some 140 countries. Nike does not do any manufacturing. Rather, it designs and markets its products, while contracting for their manufacture from a global network of 600 factories scattered around the globe that employ some 650,000 people.[1] This huge corporation has made founder Phil Knight into one of the richest people in America. Nike's marketing phrase, "Just Do It!" has become as recognizable in popular culture as its "swoosh" logo or the faces of its celebrity sponsors, such as Michael Jordan and Tiger Woods.

For all of its successes, the company was dogged for more than a decade by repeated and persistent accusations that its products were made in "sweatshops" where workers, many of them children, slaved away in hazardous conditions for below-subsistence wages. Nike's wealth, its detractors claimed, was built upon the backs of the world's poor. For many, Nike had become a symbol of the evils of globalization—a rich Western corporation exploiting the world's poor to provide expensive shoes and apparel to the pampered consumers of the developed world. Nike's "Niketown" stores became standard targets for antiglobalization protestors. Several nongovernmental organizations, such as San Francisco–based Global Exchange, a human rights organization dedicated to promoting environmental, political, and social justice around the world, targeted Nike for repeated criticism and protests.[2] News organizations such as CBS's 48 Hours hosted by Dan Rather ran exposés on working conditions in foreign factories that supply Nike. Students on the campuses of several major U.S. universities with which Nike has lucrative sponsorship deals protested against the ties, citing Nike's use of sweatshop labor.

For its part, Nike has taken many steps to try to counter the protests. Yes, it admits, there have been problems in some overseas factories. But the company has signaled a commitment to improving working conditions. It requires that foreign subcontractors meet minimum thresholds for working conditions and pay. It has arranged for factories to be examined by independent auditors. It has terminated contracts with factories that

do not comply with its standards. But for all this effort, the company continues to be a target of protests and a symbol of dissent.

THE CASE AGAINST NIKE

Typical of the exposés against Nike was a CBS 48 Hours news report that aired on October 17, 1996.[3] Reporter Roberta Basin visited a Nike factory in Vietnam. With a shot of the factory, her commentary begin by saying that

> The signs are everywhere of an American invasion in search of cheap labor. Millions of people who are literate, disciplined, and desperate for jobs. This is Nike Town near what use to be called Saigon, one of four factories Nike doesn't own but subcontracts to make a million shoes a month. It takes 25,000 workers, mostly young women, to "Just Do It."
> But the workers here don't share in Nike's huge profits. They work six days a week for only $40 a month, just 20 cents an hour.

Baskin interviews one of the workers in the factory, a young woman named Lap. Baskin tells the listener:

> Her basic wage, even as sewing team leader, still doesn't amount to the minimum wage. . . . She's down to 85 pounds. Like most of the young women who make shoes, she has little choice but to accept the low wages and long hours. Nike says that it requires all subcontractors to obey local laws; but Lap has already put in much more overtime than the annual legal limit: 200 hours.

Baskin then asks Lap what would happen if she wanted to leave. If she were sick or had something she needed to take care of such as a sick relative, could she leave the factory? Through a translator, Lap replies:

> It is not possible if you haven't made enough shoes. You have to meet the quota before you can go home.

The clear implication of the story was that Nike was at fault here for allowing such working conditions to persist in the Vietnam factory, which, incidentally, was owned by a Korean company.

Another example of an attack on Nike's subcontracting practices came in June 1996 from Made in the USA, a foundation largely financed by labor unions and domestic apparel manufacturers that oppose free trade with low-wage countries. According to Joel Joseph, chairman of the foundation, a popular line of high-priced Nike sneakers, the "Air Jordans," were put together made by 11-year-olds in Indonesia making 14 cents per hour. A Nike spokeswoman, Donna Gibbs, countered that this statement was

---

[1]From Nike's corporate Web site at www.nikebiz.com.
[2]www.globalexchange.org.

[3]"Boycott Nike" CBS News, 48 Hours, October 17, 1996.

in fact false. According to Gibbs, the average worker made 240,000 rupiah ($103) a month working a maximum 54-hour week, or about 45 cents per hour. Moreover, Gibbs noted that Nike had staff members in each factory monitoring conditions to make sure that they obeyed local minimum wage and child labor laws.[4]

Another example of the criticism against Nike is the following extract from a newsletter published by Global Exchange:[5]

During the 1970s, most Nike shoes were made in South Korea and Taiwan. When workers there gained new freedom to organize and wages began to rise, Nike looked for "greener pastures." It found them in Indonesia and China, where Nike started producing in the 1980s, and most recently in Vietnam. The majority of Nike shoes are made in Indonesia and China, countries with governments that prohibit independent unions and set the minimum wage at rock bottom. The Indonesian government admits that the minimum wage there does not provide enough to supply the basic needs of one person, let alone a family. In early 1997 the entry-level wage was a miserable $2.46 a day. Labor groups estimate that a livable wage in Indonesia is about $4.00 a day.

In Vietnam the pay is even less—20 cents an hour, or a mere $1.60 a day. But in urban Vietnam, three simple meals cost about $2.10 a day, and then of course there is rent, transportation, clothing, health care, and much more. According to Thuyen Nguyen of Vietnam Labor Watch, a living wage in Vietnam is at least $3 a day.

In another attack on Nike's practices, in September 1997 Global Exchange published a report on working conditions in four Nike and Reebok subcontractors in Southern China.[6] Global Exchange, in conjunction with two Hong Kong human rights groups, had interviewed workers at the factories in 1995 and again in 1997. According to Global Exchange, in one factory, owned by a Korean subcontractor for Nike, workers as young as 13 earning as little as 10 cents an hour toiled up to 17 hours daily in enforced silence. Talking during work was not allowed, with violators fined $1.20 to $3.60 according to the report. The practices were in violation of Chinese labor law, which states that no child under 16 may work in a factory, and the Chinese minimum wage requirement of $1.90 for an eight-hour day. Nike condemned the study as "erroneous," stating that it incorrectly stated the wages of workers and made irresponsible accusations.

Global Exchange, however, continued to be a major thorn in Nike's side. In November 1997, the organization

obtained and then leaked a confidential report by Ernst & Young of an audit that Nike had commissioned of a factory in Vietnam owned by a Nike subcontractor.[7] The factory had 9,200 workers and made 400,000 pairs of shoes a month. The Ernst & Young report painted a dismal picture of thousands of young women, most under age 25, laboring 10½ hours a day, six days a week, in excessive heat and noise and in foul air, for slightly more than $10 a week. The report also found that workers with skin or breathing problems had not been transferred to departments free of chemicals and that more than half the workers who dealt with dangerous chemicals did not wear protective masks or gloves. It claimed workers were exposed to carcinogens that exceeded local legal standards by 177 times in parts of the plant and that 77 percent of the employees suffered from respiratory problems.

Put on the defensive yet again, Nike called a news conference and pointed out that it had commissioned the report, and had acted on it.[8] The company stated that it had formulated an action plan to deal with the problems cited in the report, and had slashed overtime, improved safety and ventilation, and reduced the use of toxic chemicals. The company also asserted that the report showed that its internal monitoring system had performed exactly as it should have. According to one spokesman, "This shows our system of monitoring works. . . . We have uncovered these issues clearly before anyone else, and we have moved fairly expeditiously to correct them."

NIKE'S RESPONSES

Unaccustomed to playing defense, over the years Nike formulated a number of strategies and tactics to deal with the problems of subcontractors' working conditions and pay. In 1996, Nike hired one-time U.S. Ambassador to the United Nations and former Atlanta Mayor and Congressional representative Andrew Young to assess working conditions in subcontractors' plants around the world. After completing a two-week tour that involved inspecting 15 factories in three countries, Young released a mildly critical report of Nike in mid-1997. He informed Nike it was doing a good job in treating workers, though it should do better. According to Young, he did not see

sweatshops, or hostile conditions . . . I saw crowded dorms . . . but the workers were eating at least two meals a day on the job and making what I was told were subsistence wages in those cultures.[9]

Young was widely criticized by human rights and labor groups for not taking his own translators and for

[4]D. Jones, "Critics Tie Sweatshop Sneakers to 'Air Jordan,'" *USA Today*, June 6, 1996, p. 1B.
[5]Global Exchange Special Report: "Nike Just Don't Do It," http://www.globalexchange.org/education/publications/newsltr6.97p2.html#nike.
[6] V. Dobnik, "Chinese Workers Abused Making Nikes, Reeboks," *Seattle Times*, September 21, 1997, p. A4.

[7]S. Greenhouse, "Nike Shoeplant in Vietnam Is Called Unsafe for Workers," *The New York Times*, November 8, 1997.
[8]Greenhouse, "Nike Shoeplant in Vietnam Is Called Unsafe for Workers."
[9]Quoted in V. Dobnik, "Chinese Workers Abused Making Nikes, Reeboks," *Seattle Times*, September 21, 1997, p. A4.

doing slipshod inspections, an assertion he repeatedly denied.

In 1996, Nike joined a presidential task force designed to find a way of banishing sweatshops in the shoe and clothing industries. The task force included industry leaders such as Nike, representatives from human rights groups, and labor leaders. In April 1997, the task force announced a workers' rights agreement that U.S. companies could accept when manufacturing abroad. The accord limited the workweek to 60 hours and called for paying at least the local minimum wage in foreign factories. The task force also agreed to establish an independent monitoring association—later named the Fair Labor Association (FLA)—to assess whether companies are abiding by the code.[10]

The FLA now includes among its members the Lawyers Committee for Human Rights, the National Council of Churches, the International Labor Rights Fund, some 135 universities (universities have extensive licensing agreements with sports apparel companies such as Nike), and companies such as Nike, Reebok, and Levi Strauss.

In early 1997, Nike also began to commission independent organizations such as Ernst & Young to audit its subcontractors' factories. In September 1997, Nike tried to show its critics that it was involved in more than just a public relations exercise when it terminated its relationship with four Indonesian subcontractors, stating that these subcontractors had refused to comply with the company's standard for wage levels and working conditions. Nike identified one of the subcontractors, Seyon, which manufactured specialty sports gloves for Nike. Nike said that Seyon refused to meet a 10.7 percent increase in the monthly wage, to $70.30, declared by the Indonesian government in April 1997.[11]

On May 12, 1998, in a speech given at the National Press Club, Phil Knight spelled out in detail a series of initiatives designed to improve working conditions for the 500,000 people that make products for Nike as subcontractors.[12] Among the initiatives Knight highlighted were the following:

- We have effectively changed our minimum age limits from the ILO (International Labor Organization) standards of 15 in most countries and 14 in developing countries to 18 in all footwear manufacturing and 16 in all other types of manufacturing (apparel, accessories and equipment). Existing workers legally employed under the former limits were grand-fathered into the new requirements.

- During the past 13 months we have moved to a 100 percent factory audit scheme, where every Nike contract factory will receive an annual check by PricewaterhouseCoopers teams who are specially trained on our Code of Conduct Owner's Manual and audit/monitoring procedures. To date they have performed about 300 such monitoring visits. In a few instances in apparel factories they have found workers under our age standards. Those factories have been required to raise their standards to 17 years of age, to require three documents certifying age, and to redouble their efforts to ensure workers meet those standards through interviews and records checks.

- Our goal was to ensure workers around the globe are protected by requiring factories to have no workers exposed to levels above those mandated by the permissible exposure limits (PELs) for chemicals prescribed in the OSHA indoor air quality standards.[13]

The business press applauded these moves, but Nike's long-term adversaries in the debate over the use of foreign labor greeted them skeptically. While conceding that's Nike's policies were an improvement, one critic writing in *The New York Times* noted that

> Mr. Knight's child labor initiative is . . . a smokescreen. Child labor has not been a big problem with Nike, and Philip Knight knows that better than anyone. But public relations is public relations. So he announces that he's not going to let the factories hire kids, and suddenly that's the headline.
>
> Mr. Knight is like a three-card monte player. You have to keep a close eye on him at all times.
>
> The biggest problem with Nike is that its overseas workers make wretched, below-subsistence wages. It's not the minimum age that needs raising, it's the minimum wage. Most of the workers in Nike factories in China and Vietnam make less than $2 a day, well below the subsistence levels in those countries. In Indonesia the pay is less than $1 a day.
>
> The company's current strategy is to reshape its public image while doing as little as possible for the workers. Does anyone think it was an accident that Nike set up shop in human rights sinkholes, where labor organizing was viewed as a criminal activity and deeply impoverished workers were willing, even eager, to take their places on assembly lines and work for next to nothing?[14]

Other critics question the value of Nike's auditors, PricewaterhouseCoopers (PwC). Dara O'Rourke, an assistant professor at MIT, followed the PwC auditors

---

[10]W. Bounds and H. Stout, "Sweatshop Pact: Good Fit or Threadbare?" *The Wall Street Journal*, April 10, 1997, p. A2.

[11]"Nike Gives Four Factories the Boot," *Los Angeles Times*, September 23, 1997, p. 20.

[12]Archived at http://www.nikebiz.com/labor/speech_trans.shtml.

[13]OSHA is the United States Occupational Safety and Health Agency.

[14]B. Herbet, "Nike Blinks," *The New York Times*, May 21, 1998.

around several factories in China, Korea, and Vietnam. He concluded that although the auditors found minor violations of labor laws and codes of conduct, they missed major labor practice issues including hazardous working conditions, violations of overtime laws, and violation of wage laws. The problem, according to O'Rourke, was that the auditors had limited training, and relied on factory managers for data and to set up interviews with workers, all of which were performed in the factories. The auditors, in other words, were getting an incomplete and somewhat sanitized view of conditions in the factory.[15]

THE CONTROVERSY CONTINUES

Fueled perhaps by the unforgiving criticisms of Nike that continued after Phil Knight's May 1998 speech, a wave of protests against Nike occurred on many university campuses beginning in 1998 and continuing into 2001. The moving force behind the protests was the United Students Against Sweatshops (USAS). The USAS argued that the Fair Labor Association (FLA), which grew out of the Presidential task force on sweatshops, was an industry tool, and not a truly independent auditor of foreign factories. The USAS set up an alternative independent auditing organization, the Workers Rights Consortium (WRC), which they charged with auditing factories that produce products under collegiate licensing programs (Nike is a high-profile supplier of products under these programs). The WRC is backed, and partly funded, by labor unions and refuses to cooperate with companies, arguing that doing so would jeopardize its independence.

By mid-2000, the WRC had persuaded some 48 universities to join the WRC, including all nine campuses of the University of California systems, the University of Michigan, and the University of Oregon, Phil Knight's alma mater. When Knight heard that the University of Oregon would join the WRC, as opposed to the FLA, he withdrew a planned $30 million donation to the University.[16] Despite Knight's opposition, in November 2000 another major university in the northwest, the University of

Washington, announced that it too would join the WRC, although it would also retain its membership in the FLA.[17]

Nike continued to push forward with its own initiatives, updating progress on its Web site. In April 2000, in response to accusations that it was still hiding conditions, it announced that it would release the complete reports of all independent audits of its subcontractors' plants. Global Exchange continued to criticize the company, arguing in mid-2001 that the company was not living up to Phil Knight's 1998 promises and that it was intimidating workers from speaking out about abuses.[18]

Case Discussion Questions

1. Should Nike be held responsible for working conditions in foreign factories that it does not own, but where subcontractors make products for Nike?

2. What labor standards regarding safety, working conditions, overtime, and the like, should Nike hold foreign factories to: those prevailing in that country or those prevailing in the United States?

3. In Indonesia, an income of $2.28 a day, the base pay of Nike factory workers, is double the daily income of about half the working population. Half of all adults in Indonesia are farmers, who receive less than $1 a day. Given these national standards, is it appropriate to criticize Nike for the low pay rates of its subcontractors in Indonesia?[19]

4. Could Nike have handled the negative publicity over sweatshops better? What might it have done differently, not just from a public relations perspective but also from a policy perspective?

5. Do you think Nike needs to make any changes to its current policy? If so what? Should Nike make changes even if they hinder the ability of the company to compete in the marketplace?

6. Is the WRC right to argue that the FLA is a tool of industry?

7. If sweatshops are a global problem, what might be a global solution to this problem?

Etch-A-Sketch Ethics

The Ohio Art Company is perhaps best known as the producer of one of the top-selling toys of all time, the venerable Etch-A-Sketch. More than 100 million of the

familiar red rectangular drawing toys have been sold since 1960 when it was invented. The late 1990s, however, became a troubled time for the toy's maker. Confronted with

---

[15]Dara O'Rourke, "Monitoring the Monitors: A Critique of the PricewaterhouseCoopers (PwC) Labor Monitoring," Department of Urban Studies and Planning, MIT.

[16]L. Lee and A. Bernstein, "Who Says Student Protests Don't Matter?" *Business Week*, June 12, 2000, pp. 94–96.

[17]R. Deen, "UW to Join Anti-sweatshop Group," *Seattle Post Intelligencer*, November 20, 2000, p. B2.

[18]"Rights Group Says Nike Isn't Fulfilling Promises," *The Wall Street Journal*, May 16, 2001.

[19]Figures from P. Kenel, "The Sweatshop Dilemma," *Christian Science Monitor*, August 21, 1996, p. 20.

sluggish toy sales, the Ohio Art Company lost money for two years. In December 2000, it made the strategic decision to outsource production of the Etch-A-Sketch toys to Kin Ki Industrial, a leading Chinese toy maker, laying off 100 U.S. workers in the process.

The closure of the Etch-A-Sketch line was not unexpected among employees. The company had already moved the production of other toy lines to China, and most employees knew it was just a matter of time before Etch-A-Sketch went too. Still, the decision was a tough one for the company, which did most of its manufacturing in its home base, the small Ohio town of Bryan (population 8,000). As William Killgallon, the CEO of the Ohio Art Company, noted, the employees who made the product "were like family. It was a necessary financial decision we saw coming for some time, and we did it gradually, product by product. But that doesn't mean it's emotionally easy."

In a small town such as Bryan, the cumulative effect of outsourcing to China has been significant. The tax base is eroding from a loss of manufacturing and a population decline. The local paper is full of notices of home foreclosures and auctions. According to former employees, the biggest hole in their lives after Etch-A-Sketch moved came from the death of a community. For many workers, the company was their family, and now that family was gone.

The rationale for the outsourcing was simple enough. Pressured to keep the cost of Etch-A-Sketch under $10 by big retailers such as Wal-Mart and Toys "R" Us, the Ohio Art Company had to get its costs down or lose money. In this case, unionized workers making $1,500 a month were replaced by Chinese factory workers who made $75 a month. However, according to Killgallon, the main savings came not from lower wages but from lower overhead costs for plant, maintenance, electricity, and payroll, and the ability to get out from the soaring costs of providing health benefits to U.S. manufacturing employees.

The choice of Kin Ki as manufacturer for Etch-A-Sketch was easy—the company had been making pocket-sized Etch-A-Sketch toys for nearly a decade and always delivered on cost. To help Kin Ki, the Ohio Art Company shipped some of its best equipment to the company, and it continues to send crucial raw materials, such as aluminum powder, which is hard to get in China.

The story would have ended there had it not been for an exposé in *The New York Times* in December 2003. The *Times* reporter painted a dismal picture of working conditions at the Kin Ki factory that manufactured the Etch-A-Sketch. According to official Kin Ki publications:

> Workers at Kin Ki make a decent salary, rarely work nights or weekends, and often "hang out along the streets, playing Ping Pong and watching TV." They all have work contracts, pensions, and medical benefits. The factory canteen offers tasty food. The dormitories are comfortable.

Not so, according to Joseph Kahn, the *Times* reporter. He alleged that real-world Kin Ki employees, mostly teenage migrants from internal Chinese provinces, work long hours for 40 percent less than the company claims. They are paid 24 cents per hour, below the legal minimum wage of 33 cents an hour in Shenzhen province where Kin Ki is located. Most do not have pensions, medical benefits, or employment contracts. Production starts at 7:30 a.m. and continues until 10 p.m., with breaks only for lunch and dinner. Saturdays and Sundays are treated as normal workdays. This translates into a work week of seven 12-hour days, or 84 hours a week, well above the standard 40-hour week set by authorities in Shenzhen. Local rules also allow for no more than 32 hours of overtime and stipulate that the employees must be paid 1.5 times the standard hourly wage, but Kin Ki's overtime rate is just 1.3 times base pay.

As for the "comfortable dormitories," the workers sleep head to toe in tiny rooms with windows that are covered with chicken wire. To get into and out of the factories, which are surrounded by high walls, workers must enter and leave through a guarded gate. As for the tasty food, it is apparently a mix of boiled vegetables, beans, and rice, with meat or fish served only twice a month.

The workers at Kin Ki have apparently become restless. They went on strike twice in 2003, demanding higher wages and better working conditions. The company responded by raising wages a few cents and allotting an extra dish of food to each worker per day (but still no more meat)! However, Kin Ki simultaneously made "fried squid" of two workers who were ringleaders of the strike ("fried squid" is apparently a popular term for dismissal). Johnson Tao, a senior executive at the company, denies that the two ringleaders were dismissed for organizing the strikes. Rather, he noted that they were well-known troublemakers who left the factory of their own accord. Mr. Tao acknowledges the low wages at the company, stating, "I know that I need to increase wages to comply with the law. I have the intention of doing this and will raise all wages in 2004."

Meanwhile, in Ohio, William Killgallon, Ohio Art Company's CEO, stated to the *Times* reporter that he considered Kin Ki's executives to be honest and that he had no knowledge of labor problems there. But he said he intended to visit China soon to make sure "they understand what we expect."

Case Discussion Questions

1. Was it ethical of the Ohio Art Company to move production to China? What were the economic *and* social costs and benefits of this decision? What would have happened if production had not been moved?

2. Assuming that the description of working conditions given in *The New York Times* is correct, is it ethical for the Ohio Art Company to continue using Kin Ki to manufacture Etch-A-Sketch toys?

3. Is it possible, as Mr. Killgallon claims, that the Ohio Art Company had no knowledge of labor problems at Kin Ki? Do you think company executives had any knowledge of the working conditions?

4. What steps can executives at the Ohio Art Company take to make sure they do not find the company profiled in *The New York Times* again as an enterprise that benefits from sweatshop labor?

Sources

1. Joseph Kahn, "Ruse in Toyland: Chinese Workers' Hidden Woe," *The New York Times*, December 7, 2003, pp. A1, A8.

2. Joseph Kahn, "An Ohio Town Is Hard Hit as Leading Industry Moves to China," *The New York Times*, December 7, 2003, p. A8.

3. Carol Hymowitz, "Toy Maker Survives by Moving an Icon from Ohio to China," *The Wall Street Journal*, October 21, 2003, p. B1.

4. John Seewer, "Etch A Sketch Enters Fourth Decade," *Columbian*, November 22, 2001, p. E3.

Western Drug Companies and the AIDS Epidemic in South Africa

In December 1997, the government of South Africa passed a law that authorized two controversial practices. One, called parallel importing, allowed importers in South Africa to purchase drugs from the cheapest source available, regardless of whether the patent holders had given their approval or not. Thus South Africa asserted its right to import "generic versions" of drugs that are still patent protected. The government did this because it claimed to be unable to afford the high cost of medicines that were patent protected. The other practice, called compulsory licensing, permitted the South African government to license local companies to produce cheaper versions of drugs whose patents are held by foreign companies, irrespective of whether the patent holder agreed.

The law seemed to be in violation of international agreements to protect property rights, including a World Trade Organization agreement on patents to which South Africa is a signatory. South Africa, however, insisted that the law was necessary given its own health crisis and the high cost of patented medicines. By 1997, South Africa was wrestling with an AIDS crisis of enormous proportions. It was estimated that over 3 million of the country's 45 million people were infected with the virus at the time, more than in any other country. However, although the AIDS epidemic in South Africa was seen as primary reason for the new law, the law itself was applied to "communicable diseases" (of which AIDS is just one, albeit a devastating one).

Foreign drug manufacturers saw the law as an unbridled attempt to expropriate their intellectual property rights, and 39 foreign companies quickly filed a lawsuit in the country to try to block implementation of the law. Drug manufacturers were particularly concerned about the applicability of the law to all "communicable diseases." They feared that South Africa was the thin end of the wedge, and if the law were allowed to stand, other countries would follow suit. Many Western companies also feared that if poor countries such as South Africa were allowed to buy low-priced generic versions of patent protected drugs, in violation of intellectual property laws, American and European consumers would soon demand the same.

In defense of their patents, the drug companies argued that because drug development is a very expensive, time-consuming, and risky process, they need the protection of intellectual property laws to maintain the incentive to innovate. It can take $800 million and 12 years to develop a drug and bring it to market. Less than one in five compounds that enter clinical trials actually become marketed drugs—the rest fail in trials due to poor efficacy or unfavorable side effects—and of those that make it to market, only 3 of 10 earn profits that exceed their costs of capital. If drug companies could not count on high prices for their few successful products, the drug development process would dry up.

The drug companies have long recognized that countries such as South Africa face special health challenges and lack the money to pay developed world prices. Accordingly, the industry has a history of pricing drugs low or giving them away in the developing world. For example, many AIDS drugs were already being sold to developing nations at large discounts to their prices in the United States. The South African government thought this practice was not good enough. The government was quickly supported by various human rights and AIDS organizations, which cast the case as an attempt by the prosperous multinational drug companies of the West to maintain their intellectual property rights in the face of desperate attempts by an impoverished government to stem a deadly crisis. For their part, the drug companies stated that the case had little to do with AIDS and was really about the right of South Africa to break international law.

While the drug companies may have had international law on their side, the tie-in with the AIDS epidemic clearly put them on the public relations defensive. After a blizzard of negative publicity, and little support from Western governments who were keen not to touch this political "hot potato," several leading manufacturers of AIDS drugs, while still opposing the South African law, started to change their policies. In May 2000, five large manufacturers of AIDS medicines—Merck, Bristol-Myers Squibb, Roche, Glaxo, and Boehringer Ingelhiem—announced that they would negotiate lower priced AIDS drugs in developing countries, primarily in sub-Saharan Africa (some 25 million of the 36 million people infected with the HIV virus in 2000 lived in that region). Still the protests continued.

In February 2001, an Indian drug company, Cipla Ltd, offered to sell a cocktail of 3 AIDS drugs to poor African nations for $600 per patient per year, and for $350 a year to Doctors without Borders (AIDS is commonly treated with a cocktail that combines up to 10 different antiviral drugs). The patents for these drugs were held by Western companies, but Indian law allowed local companies to produce generic versions of patent protected drugs.

The Cipla announcement seemed to galvanize Western drug companies into further action. In March 2001, Merck announced that it would cut the prices of its two AIDS drugs, Crixivan and Stocrin. Crixivan, which sold for $6,016 per year in the United States, would be sold in developing countries for $600 a year. Stocrin, which cost $4,730 a year in the United States, would be sold for $500. Both drugs were often used together as part of an AIDS cocktail. Officials at Doctors without Borders, the Nobel Peace Prize–winning relief agency, welcomed the announcement, but pointed out that in a region where many people lived on less than a dollar a day, the price was still out of reach of many AIDS patients.

A few days later, Bristol-Myers Squibb went further, announcing that it would sell its AIDS drug Zerit to poor nations in Africa for just $0.15 a day, or $54 a patient per year, which was below Zerit's costs of production. In the United States and Europe, Zerit was selling for $3,589 per patient per year. This move was followed by an announcement from Abbott Labs that it would sell two of its AIDS drugs at "no profit" in sub-Saharan Africa.

None of these moves, however, were enough to satisfy critics. In April 2001, the drug companies seemed to come to the conclusion that they were losing the public relations war, and they agreed to drop their suit against the South African government. This opened the way for South Africa to start importing cheap generic versions of patented medicines from producers such as Cipla of India. The decision to drop the suit was widely interpreted in the media as a defeat for the drug companies and a reaffirmation of the ability of the South Africans to enforce compulsory licensing. At the same time, the pharmaceutical companies appear to have gotten assurances from South Africa that locally produced generic versions of patented drugs would only be sold in sub-Saharan Africa and not exported to other regions of the world.

In 2003, Aspen Pharmaceuticals, a South African drug maker, took advantage of the 1997 law to introduce a generic version of Stavudine, and it asked the South African authorities permission to produce up to six more AIDS drugs. Aspen had licensed the rights to produce this drug, and several others, from Bristol-Myers Squibb and Glaxo, the large British company. Bristol and Glaxo had waved their rights to royalties from sales of the drugs in sub-Saharan Africa. At the same time, the companies noted that Aspen was only able to sell the drugs within the sub-Saharan region.

Despite these moves, critics still urged Western drug companies to do more to fight the global AIDS epidemic, which by 2006 was estimated to afflict some 40 million people. For example, in a *New York Times* Op Ed article, noted playwright and AIDS activist Larry Kramer stated that

> It is incumbent upon every manufacturer of every HIV drug to contribute its patents or its drugs free for the salvation of these people. . . . I believe it is evil for drug companies to possess a means of saving lives and then not provide it to the desperate people who need it. What kind of hideous people have we become? It is time to throw out the selfish notion that these companies have the right not to share their patents.

Meanwhile in South Africa, the AIDS epidemic continued on its relentless course. By 2006 it was estimated that one in nine people in South Africa, or 5.5 million people, were infected with HIV, and 800 people a day were dying from AIDS-related complications. In 2003, the South African government had committed itself to offering antiviral drugs at low or no cost to everyone with AIDS. By working with pharmaceutical companies such as Aspen and three Indian producers of generic drugs, the government was able to purchase a cocktail of antiviral HIV drugs for $65 per patient per month. However, by 2006 only 250,000 people were getting antiviral drugs, while at least 700,000 were in urgent need of the drugs. The problem seems to be distribution and particularly a chronic shortage of clinics, doctors, and nurses. Estimates suggested that it may still be years before cheap AIDS drugs are available to all those who need them in South Africa.

Case Discussion Questions

1. Why is it so important for the drug companies to protect their patents?

2. What should the policy of drug companies be toward the pricing of patent-protected drugs for AIDS in poor developing nations such as South Africa?

3. What should the policy be in developed nations? Is it ethical to charge a high price for drugs that treat a life-threatening condition, such as AIDS?

4. In retrospect, could the large Western pharmaceuticals have responded differently to the 1997 South African law? How might they have better taken the initiative?

5. Is AIDS a special case, or should large drug companies make it normal practice to price low or give away patent protected medicines to those who cannot afford them in poor nations?

Sources

1. H. Cooper, R. Zimmerman, and L. McGinley, "Patents Pending—AIDS Epidemic Traps Drug Firms in a Vise," *The Wall Street Journal*, March 2, 2001, p. A1.

2. R. Block, "Big Drug Firms Defend Right to Patent on AIDS Drugs in South African Courts," *The Wall Street Journal*, March 6, 2001, p. A3.

3. J. Jeter, "Trial Opens in South Africa AIDS Drug Suit," *The Washington Post*, March 6, 2001, p. A1.

4. L. Kramer, "The Plague We Can't Escape," *The New York Times*, March 15, 2003, page A17.

5. J. Norton, "Overcoming the AIDS Hurdle," *Managing Intellectual Property*, June 2002, pp. 39–40.

6. T. Smith, "Mixed View of a Pact for Generic Drugs," *The New York Times*, August 29, 2003, p. C3.

7. C. Timberg, "South Africans with AIDS See a Ray of Hope," *The Washington Post*, November 30, 2004, page A1.

8. Staff Reporter, "Beetroot but No Blushes: South Africa," *The Economist*, August 26, 2006, p. 5.

Matsushita and Japan's Changing Culture

Established in 1920, the consumer electronics giant Matsushita was at the forefront of the rise of Japan to the status of major economic power during the 1970s and 1980s. Like many other long-standing Japanese businesses, Matsushita was regarded as a bastion of traditional Japanese values based on strong group identification, reciprocal obligations, and loyalty to the company. Several commentators attributed Matsushita's success, and that of the Japanese economy, to the existence of Confucian values in the workplace. At Matsushita, the company took care of employees from "cradle to the grave." Matsushita provided them with a wide range of benefits including cheap housing, guaranteed lifetime employment, seniority-based pay systems, and generous retirement bonuses. In return, Matsushita expected, and got, loyalty and hard work from its employees. To Japan's postwar generation, struggling to recover from the humiliation of defeat, it seemed like a fair bargain. The employees worked hard for the greater good of Matsushita, and Matsushita reciprocated by bestowing "blessings" on employees.

However, culture does not stay constant. According to some observers, the generation born after 1964 lacked the same commitment to traditional Japanese values as their parents. They grew up in a world that was richer, where Western ideas were beginning to make themselves felt, and where the possibilities seemed greater. They did not want to be tied to a company for life, to be a "salaryman." These trends came to the fore in the 1990s, when the Japanese economy entered a prolonged economic slump. As the decade progressed, one Japanese firm after another was forced to change its traditional ways of doing business. Slowly at first, troubled companies started to lay off older workers, effectively abandoning lifetime employment guarantees. As younger people saw this happening, they concluded that loyalty to a company might not be reciprocated, effectively undermining one of the central bargains made in postwar Japan.

Matsushita was one of the last companies to turn its back on Japanese traditions, but in 1998, after years of poor performance, it began to modify traditional practices. The principal agents of change were a group of managers who had extensive experience in Matsushita's overseas operations; they included Kunio Nakamura, who became the chief executive of Matsushita in 2000.

First, Matsushita changed the pay scheme for its 11,000 managers. In the past, the traditional twice-a-year bonuses had been based almost entirely on seniority, but now Matsushita said they would be based on performance. In 1999, Matsushita announced this process would be made transparent; managers would be shown what their performance rankings were and how these fed into pay bonuses. As elementary as this might sound in the West, for Matsushita it represented the beginning of a revolution in human resource practices.

About the same time, Matsushita took aim at the lifetime employment system and the associated perks. Under the new system, recruits were given the choice of three employment options. First, they could sign on to the traditional option. Under this, they were eligible to live in subsidized company housing, go free to company-organized social events, and buy subsidized services such as banking from group companies. They also would receive a retirement bonus equal to two years' salary. Under a second scheme, employees could forgo the guaranteed retirement bonus in exchange for higher starting salaries and keep perks such as cheap company housing. Under a third scheme, they would lose both the retirement bonus and the subsidized services, but they would start at a still higher salary. In its first two years of operation, only 3 percent of recruits chose the third option—suggesting there is still a hankering for the traditional paternalistic relationship—but 41 percent took the second option.

In other ways Matsushita's designs are grander still. As the company has moved into new industries such as software engineering and network communications technology, it has begun to praise democratization of employees, and it has sought to encourage individuality, taking initiative, and risk seeking among its younger employees. In 2002 Matsushita also undertook a significant reorganization, dismantling what had become a Byzantine organizational structure under which performance accountability was difficult to establish, and replacing it with 17 stand-alone worldwide business divisions, each focused on a particular product sector.

However, while such changes may be easy to articulate, they are hard to implement. For all its talk, Matsushita has been slow to dismantle its lifetime employment commitment to those hired under the traditional system. This was underlined in early 2001 when, in response to continued poor performance, Matsushita announced it would close 30 factories in Japan, cut 13,000 jobs, including 1,000 management jobs, and sell a "huge amount of assets" over the next three years. While these actions seemed to indicate a final break with the lifetime employment system—it represented the first layoffs in the company's history—the company also said unneeded management staff would not be fired but would instead be transferred to higher growth areas such as health care.

With so many of its managers products of the old way of doing things, a skeptic might question the ability of the company to turn its intentions into reality. As growth has slowed, Matsushita has had to cut back on its hiring, but its continued commitment to long-standing employees means that the average age of its workforce is rising. In the 1960s it was around 25; by the early 2000s it was 35, a trend that might counteract Matsushita's attempts to revolutionize the workplace, for surely those who benefited from the old system will not give way easily to the new. Still, by 2004 it was clear that Matsushita was making progress. After significant losses in 2002, the company broke even in 2003, started to make profits again in 2004, and in 2005 and 2006 recorded record profits. New growth drivers such as sales of DVD equipment and flat screen TVs certainly helped, but so did the cultural and organizational changes that enabled the company to better exploit these new growth opportunities.

Case Discussion Questions

1. What were the triggers of cultural change in Japan during the 1990s? How is cultural change starting to affect traditional values in Japan?

2. How might Japan's changing culture influence the way Japanese businesses operate in the future? What are the potential implications of such changes for the Japanese economy?

3. How did traditional Japanese culture benefit Matsushita during the period from the 1950s to the 1980s? Did traditional values become more of a liability during the 1990s and early 2000s? How so?

4. What is Matsushita trying to achieve with human resource changes it has announced? What are the impediments to successfully implementing these changes? What are the implications for Matsushita if (*a*) the changes are made quickly or (*b*) it takes years or even decades to fully implement the changes?

5. Why do you think Matsushita reorganized itself into stand-alone worldwide business divisions?

6. What does the Matsushita case teach you about the relationship between societal culture and business success?

Sources

1. "Putting the Bounce Back into Matsushita," *The Economist*, May 22, 1999, pp. 67–68.

2. "In Search of the New Japanese Dream," *The Economist*, February 19, 2000, pp. 59–60.

3. P. Landers, "Matsushita to Restructure in Bid to Boost Thin Profits," *The Wall Street Journal*, December 1, 2000, p. A13.

4. M. Tanikawa, "A Pillar of Japan Inc. Finally Turns Around; Work in Progress," *International Herald Tribune*, August 28, 2004, pp. 17–18.

5. M. Nakamoto, "Shift to Digital Drives Growth for Matsushita," *Financial Times*, May 1, 2006, p. 17.

6. Takahior Osada, "Matsushita Electrical: Destruction and Creation," *EDN*, November 2005, p. 118.

Mired in Corruption—Kellogg, Brown & Root in Nigeria

In 1998 the large Texas-based oil and gas service firm, Halliburton, acquired Dresser Industries. Among other businesses, Dresser owned M. W. Kellogg, one of the world's largest general contractors for construction projects in distant parts of the globe. After the acquisition, Kellogg was combined with an existing Halliburton business and renamed Kellogg Brown & Root, or KBR for short. At the time it looked like a good deal for Halliburton. Among other things, Kellogg was involved in a four-firm consortium that was building a series of liquefied natural gas (LNG) plants in Nigeria. By early 2004, the total value of the contracts associated with these plants had exceeded $8 billion.

In early 2005, however, Halliburton put KBR up for sale. The sale was seen as an attempt by Halliburton to distance itself from several scandals that had engulfed KBR. One of these concerned allegations that KBR had systematically overcharged the Pentagon for services it provided to the U.S. military in Iraq. Another scandal, centered on the Nigerian LNG plants, involved KBR employees, several former officials of the Nigerian government, and a mysterious British lawyer called Jeffrey Tesler.

The roots of the Nigerian scandal date back to 1994 when Kellogg and its consortium partners were trying to win an initial contract from the Nigerian government to build two LNG plants. The contract was valued at around $2 billion. Each of the four firms held a 25 percent stake in the consortium, and each had veto power over its decisions. Kellogg employees held many of the top positions at the consortium, and two of the other members, Technip of France and JGC of Japan, have claimed that Kellogg managed the consortium (the fourth member, ENI of Italy, has not made any statement regarding management).

The KBR consortium was one of two to submit a bid on the initial contract, and its bid was the lower of the two. By early 1995 the KBR consortium was deep in final negotiations on the contract. It was at this point that Nigeria's oil minister had a falling out with the country's military dictator, General Abacha, and was replaced by Dan Etete. Mr. Etete proved to be far less accommodating to the KBR consortium, and suddenly the entire deal looked to be in jeopardy. According to some observers, Dan Etete was a tough customer who immediately began to use his influence over the LNG project for personal gain. Whether this is true or not, what is known is that the KBR consortium quickly entered into a contract with the British lawyer, Jeffrey Tesler. The contract, signed by a Kellogg executive, called on Tesler to obtain government permits for the LNG project, maintain good relations with government officials, and provide advice on sales strategy. Tesler's fee for these services was $60 million.

Tesler, it turned out, had long-standing relations with some 20 to 30 senior Nigerian government and military officials. In his capacity as a lawyer, he had handled their London affairs for years, helping the Nigerian officials purchase real estate and set up financial accounts. Kellogg had a relationship with Tesler that dated back to the mid-1980s, when they had employed him to broker the sale of Kellogg's minority interest in a Nigerian fertilizer plant to the Nigerian government.

What happened next is currently the subject of government investigations in France, Nigeria, and the United States. The suspicion is that Tesler promised to funnel big sums to Nigerian government officials if the deal was done. Investigators base these suspicions on a number of factors, including the known corruption of General Abacha's government, the size of the payment to Tesler, which seemed out of proportion to the services he was contracted to provide, and a series of notes turned up by internal investigators at Halliburton. The handwritten notes, taken by Wojciech Chodan, a Kellogg executive, document a meeting between Chodan and Tesler in which they discussed the possibility of channeling $40 million of Tesler's $60 million payment to General Abacha.

It is not known whether a bribe was actually paid. What is known is that in December 1995, Nigeria awarded the $2 billion contract to the KBR consortium. The LNG plant soon became a success. Nigeria contracted to build a second plant in 1999, two more in 2002, and a sixth in July 2004. KBR rehired Jeffrey Tesler in 1999 and again in 2001 to help secure the new contracts, all of which it won. In total, the KBR consortium paid Tesler some $132.3 million from 1994 to early 2004.

Tesler's involvement in the project might have remained unknown were it not for an unrelated event. Georges Krammer, an employee of the French company Technip, which along with KBR was a member of the consortium, was charged by the French government for embezzlement. When Technip refused to defend Krammer, he turned around and aired what he perceived to be Technip's dirty linen. This included the payments to Tesler to secure the Nigeria LNG contracts.

This turn of events led French and Swiss officials to investigate Tesler's Swiss bank accounts. They discovered that Tesler was kicking back some of the funds he received to executives in the consortium and at subcontractors. One of the alleged kickbacks was a transfer of $5 million from Tesler's account to that of Albert J. "Jack" Stanley, who had been head of M. W. Kellogg and then Halliburton's KBR unit. Tesler also transferred some $2.5 million into Swiss bank accounts held under a false name by the Nigerian oil minister, Dan Etete.

Other payments included a $1 million transfer into an account controlled by Wojciech Chodan, the former Kellogg executive whose extensive handwritten notes suggest the payment of a bribe to General Abacha, and $5 million to a German subcontractor on the LNG project in exchange for "information and advice."

After this all came out in June 2004, Halliburton promptly fired Jack Stanley and severed its long-standing relationship with Jeffrey Tesler, asking its three partners in the Nigeria consortium to do the same. The United States Justice Department took things further, establishing a grand jury investigation to determine if Halliburton, through its KBR subsidiary, had been in violation of the Foreign Corrupt Practices Act. In November 2004 the Justice Department widened its investigation to include payments in connection with the Nigeria fertilizer plant that Kellogg had been involved with during the 1980s under the leadership of Jack Stanley. In March 2005, the Justice Department also stated that it was looking at whether Jack Stanley had tried to coordinate bidding with rivals and fix prices on certain foreign construction projects. As of mid-2007, the U.S. investigation was still ongoing.

Case Discussion Questions

1. Could Jeffrey Tesler's alleged payment of bribes to Nigerian government officials be considered "facilitating payments" or "speed money" under the terms of the Foreign Corrupt Practices Act?

2. Irrespective of the legality of any payments that Tesler may have made, do you think it was reasonable for KBR to hire him as an intermediary?

3. Given the known corruption of the Abacha government in Nigeria, should Kellogg and its successor, KBR, have had a policy in place to deal with bribery and corruption? What might that policy have looked like?

4. Should KBR have walked away from the Nigerian LNG project once it became clear that the payment of bribes might be required to secure the contract?

5. There is evidence that Jack Stanley, the former head of M.W. Kellogg and KBR, may have taken kickback payments from Tesler. At least one other former Kellogg employee, Wojciech Chodan, may have taken kickback payments. What does this tell you about the possible nature of the ethical climate at Kellogg and then KBR?

6. Should Halliburton be called to account if it is shown that its KBR unit used bribery to gain business in Nigeria? To what extent should a corporation and its officers be held accountable for ethically suspect activities by the managers in one of its subsidiaries, particularly given that many of those activities were initiated before Halliburton owned the subsidiary?

Sources

1. R. Gold and C. Flemming, "Out of Africa: In Halliburton Nigeria Inquiry, a Search for Bribes to a Dictator," *The Wall Street Journal*, September 29, 2004, p. A1.

2. R. Gold, "Halliburton to Put KBR Unit on Auction Block," *The New York Times*, January 31, 2005, p. A2.

3. T. Sawyer, "Citing Violations, Halliburton Cuts Off Former KBR Chairman," *ENR*, June 28, 2004, p. 16.

4. D. Ivanovich, "Halliburton: Contracts Investigated," *Houston Chronicle*, March 2, 2005, p. 1.

5. Nick Snow, "DOJ, SEC Probe Bonny Island Partners for Violations, *Oil & Gas Journal*, November 13, 2006, pp. 26–28.

The Ecuadorian Rose Industry

It is 6:20 AM, February 7, in the Ecuadorian town of Cayambe, and Maria Pacheco has just been dropped off for work by the company bus. She pulls on thick rubber gloves, wraps an apron over her white, traditional embroidered dress, and grabs her clippers, ready for another long day. Any other time of year, Maria would work until 2 PM, but it's a week before Valentine's Day, and Maria along with her 84 coworkers at the farm are likely to be busy until 5 PM. By then, Maria will have cut more than 1,000 rose stems.

A few days later, after they have been refrigerated and shipped via aircraft, the roses Maria cut will be selling for premium prices in stores from New York to London. Ecuadorian roses are quickly becoming the Rolls Royce of roses. They have huge heads and unusually vibrant colors, including 10 different reds, from bleeding heart crimson to a rosy lover's blush.

Most of Ecuador's 460 or so rose farms are located in the Cayambe and Cotopaxi regions, 10,000 feet up in the Andes about an hour's drive from the capital, Quito. The rose bushes are planted in huge flat fields at the foot of snowcapped volcanoes that rise to more than 20,000 feet. The bushes are protected by 20-foot-high canopies of plastic sheeting. The combination of intense sunlight, fertile volcanic soil, an equatorial location, and high altitude makes for ideal growing conditions, allowing roses to flower almost year-round. Ecuador apparently has a comparative advantage in the production of roses.

Ecuador's rose industry started some 20 years ago and has been expanding rapidly since. Ecuador is now the world's fourth largest producer of roses. Roses are the nation's fifth largest export, with customers all over the world. Rose farms generate $240 million in sales and support tens of thousands of jobs. In Cayambe, the population has increased in 10 years from 10,000 to 70,000, primarily as a result of the rose industry. The revenues and taxes from rose growers have helped to pave roads, build schools, and construct sophisticated irrigation systems.

Maria works Monday to Saturday, and earns $210 a month, which she says is an average wage in Ecuador and substantially above the country's $120 a month

International Trade Theory

5

LEARNING OBJECTIVES:

After you have read this chapter you should:

LO¹ Understand why nations trade with each other.

LO² Be familiar with the different theories explaining trade flows between nations.

LO³ Understand why many economists believe that unrestricted free trade between nations will raise the economic welfare of countries that participate in a free trade system.

LO⁴ Be familiar with the arguments of those who maintain that government can play a proactive role in promoting national competitive advantage in certain industries.

LO⁵ Understand the important implications that international trade theory holds for business practice.

minimum wage. The farm also provides her with health care and a pension. By employing women such as Maria, the industry has fostered a social revolution in which mothers and wives have more control over their family's spending, especially on schooling for their children.

For all of the benefits that roses have bought to Ecuador, where the gross national income per capita is only $1,080 a year, the industry has come under fire from environmentalists. Large growers have been accused of misusing a toxic mixture of pesticides, fungicides, and fumigants to grow and export unblemished pest-free flowers. Reports claim that workers often fumigate roses in street clothes without protective equipment. Some doctors and scientists claim that many of the industry's 50,000 employees have serious health problems as a result of exposure to toxic chemicals. A study by the International Labor Organization claimed that women in the industry had more miscarriages than average and that some 60 percent of all workers suffered from headaches, nausea, blurred vision, and fatigue. Still, the critics acknowledge that

their studies have been hindered by a lack of access to the farms, and they do not know what the true situation is. The International Labor Organization has also claimed that some rose growers in Ecuador use child labor, a claim that has been strenuously rejected by both the growers and Ecuadorian government agencies.

In Europe, consumer groups have urged the European Union to press for improved environmental safeguards. In response, some Ecuadorian growers have joined a voluntary program aimed at helping customers identify responsible growers. The certification signifies that the grower has distributed protective gear, trained workers in using chemicals, and hired doctors to visit workers at least weekly. Other environmental groups have pushed for stronger sanctions, including trade sanctions, against Ecuadorian rose growers that are not environmentally certified by a reputable agency. On February 14, however, most consumers are oblivious to these issues; they simply want to show their appreciation to their wives and girlfriends with a perfect bunch of roses.[1]

Introduction

The Ecuadorian rose industry is a striking example of the benefits of free trade and globalization. Lower barriers to trade have allowed Ecuador to exploit its comparative advantage in the growing of roses and enabled the country to emerge as one of the largest exporters of roses in the world. This benefits Ecuador, where economic growth and personal incomes have been bolstered by the emergence of the rose growing industry. It also benefits consumers in developed nations, who now have access to affordable high-quality roses from Ecuador. February is not exactly the best time for growing roses in New York state, but thanks to free trade, a New Yorker can now buy a bunch of fresh roses for his beloved on February 14 that were picked in Ecuador only 24 hours earlier. It also benefits foreigners who export goods and services to Ecuador, for a stronger Ecuadorian economy can purchase more of those goods and services. If there are losers in this process, they are high-cost rose producers in places like Florida, who have lost business to the Ecuadorians. In the world of international trade, there are always winners and losers, but as economists have long argued, the benefits to the winners outweigh the costs borne by the losers, resulting in a net gain to society. Moreover, economists argue that in the long run free trade stimulates economic growth and raises living standards across the board.

The economic arguments surrounding the benefits and costs of free trade in goods and services are not abstract academic ones. International trade theory has shaped the economic policy of many nations for the past 50 years. It was the driver behind the formation of the World Trade Organization and regional trade blocs such as the European Union and the North American Free Trade Agreement (NAFTA). The 1990s, in particular, saw a global move toward greater free trade. It is crucially important to understand, therefore, what these theories are and why they have been so successful in shaping the economic policy of so many nations and the competitive environment in which international businesses compete.

This chapter has two goals that go to the heart of the debate over the benefits and costs of free trade. The first is to review a number of theories that explain why it is beneficial for a country to engage in international trade. The second goal is to explain the pattern of international trade that we observe in the world economy. With regard to the pattern of trade, we will be primarily concerned with explaining the pattern of exports and imports of goods and services between countries. We will not be concerned with the pattern of foreign direct investment between countries; that is discussed in Chapter 7.

An Overview of Trade Theory

We open this chapter with a discussion of mercantilism. Propagated in the 16th and 17th centuries, mercantilism advocated that countries should simultaneously encourage exports and discourage imports. Although mercantilism is an old and largely discredited doctrine, its echoes remain in modern political debate and in the trade policies of many countries. Next we will look at Adam Smith's theory of absolute advantage. Proposed in 1776, Smith's theory was the first to explain why unrestricted free trade is beneficial to a country. **Free trade** refers to a situation where a government does not attempt to influence through quotas or duties what its citizens can buy from another country, or what they can produce and sell to another country. Smith argued that the invisible hand of the market mechanism, rather than government policy, should determine what a country imports and what it exports. His arguments imply that such a laissez-faire stance toward trade was in the best interests of a country. Building on Smith's work are two additional theories that we shall review. One is the theory of comparative advantage, advanced by the 19th-century English economist David Ricardo. This theory is the intellectual basis of the modern argument for unrestricted free trade. In the 20th century, Ricardo's work was refined by two Swedish economists, Eli Heckscher and Bertil Ohlin, whose theory is known as the Heckscher-Ohlin theory.

THE BENEFITS OF TRADE

The great strength of the theories of Smith, Ricardo, and Heckscher-Ohlin is that they identify with precision the specific benefits of international trade. Common sense suggests that some international trade is beneficial. For example, nobody would suggest that Iceland should grow its own oranges. Iceland can benefit from trade by exchanging some of the products that it can produce at a low cost (fish) for some products that it cannot produce at all (oranges). Thus, by engaging in international trade, Icelanders are able to add oranges to their diet of fish.

The theories of Smith, Ricardo, and Heckscher-Ohlin go beyond this commonsense notion, however, to show why it is beneficial for a country to engage in international trade *even for products it is able to produce for itself*. This is a difficult concept for people to grasp. For example, many people in the United States believe that American consumers should buy products made in the United States by American companies whenever possible to help save American jobs from foreign competition. The same kind of nationalistic sentiments can be observed in many other countries.

However, the theories of Smith, Ricardo, and Heckscher-Ohlin tell us that a country's economy may gain if its citizens buy certain products from other nations that could be produced at home. The gains arise because international trade allows a country to specialize in the manufacture and export of products that can be produced most efficiently in that country, while importing products that can be produced more efficiently in other countries. Thus it may make sense for the United States to specialize in the production and export of commercial jet aircraft since the efficient production of commercial jet aircraft requires resources that are abundant in the United States, such as a highly skilled labor force and cutting-edge technological know-how. On the other hand, it may make sense for the United States to import textiles from China since the efficient production of textiles requires a relatively cheap labor force—and cheap labor is not abundant in the United States.

Of course, this economic argument is often difficult for segments of a country's population to accept. With their future threatened by imports, U.S. textile companies and their employees have tried hard to persuade the government to limit the importation of textiles by demanding quotas and tariffs. Although such import controls may benefit particular groups, such as textile businesses and their employees, the theories of Smith, Ricardo, and Heckscher-Ohlin suggest that such action hurts the economy as a whole. Limits on imports are often in the interests of domestic producers, but not domestic consumers.

THE PATTERN OF INTERNATIONAL TRADE

The theories of Smith, Ricardo, and Heckscher-Ohlin help to explain the pattern of international trade that we observe in the world economy. Some aspects of the pattern are easy to understand. Climate and natural resource endowments explain why Ghana exports cocoa, Brazil exports coffee, Saudi Arabia exports oil, and China exports crawfish. However, much of the observed pattern of international trade is more difficult to explain. For example, why does Japan export automobiles, consumer electronics, and machine tools? Why does Switzerland export chemicals, pharmaceuticals, watches, and jewelry? David Ricardo's theory of comparative advantage offers an explanation in terms of international differences in labor productivity. The more sophisticated Heckscher-Ohlin theory emphasizes the interplay between the proportions in which the factors of production (such as land, labor, and capital) are available in different countries and the proportions in which they are needed for producing particular goods. This explanation rests on the assumption that countries have varying endowments of the various factors of production. Tests of this theory, however, suggest that it is a less powerful explanation of real-world trade patterns than once thought.

One early response to the failure of the Heckscher-Ohlin theory to explain the observed pattern of international trade was the product life-cycle theory. Proposed by

Raymond Vernon, this theory suggests that early in their life cycle, most new products are produced in and exported from the country in which they were developed. As a new product becomes widely accepted internationally, however, production starts in other countries. As a result, the theory suggests, the product may ultimately be exported back to the country of its original innovation.

In a similar vein, during the 1980s economists such as Paul Krugman developed what has come to be known as the new trade theory. **New trade theory** stresses that in some cases countries specialize in the production and export of particular products not because of underlying differences in factor endowments, but because in certain industries the world market can support only a limited number of firms. (This is argued to be the case for the commercial aircraft industry.) In such industries, firms that enter the market first are able to build a competitive advantage that is subsequently difficult to challenge. Thus, the observed pattern of trade between nations may be due in part to the ability of firms within a given nation to capture first-mover advantages. The United States is a major exporter of commercial jet aircraft because American firms such as Boeing were first movers in the world market. Boeing built a competitive advantage that has subsequently been difficult for firms from countries with equally favorable factor endowments to challenge (although Europe's Airbus Industries has succeeded in doing that). In a work related to the new trade theory, Michael Porter developed a theory referred to as the theory of national competitive advantage. This attempts to explain why particular nations achieve international success in particular industries. In addition to factor endowments, Porter points out the importance of country factors such as domestic demand and domestic rivalry in explaining a nation's dominance in the production and export of particular products.

TRADE THEORY AND GOVERNMENT POLICY

Although all these theories agree that international trade is beneficial to a country, they lack agreement in their recommendations for government policy. Mercantilism makes a crude case for government involvement in promoting exports and limiting imports. The theories of Smith, Ricardo, and Heckscher-Ohlin form part of the case for unrestricted free trade. The argument for unrestricted free trade is that both import controls and export incentives (such as subsidies) are self-defeating and result in wasted resources. Both the new trade theory and Porter's theory of national competitive advantage can be interpreted as justifying some limited government intervention to support the development of certain export-oriented industries. We will discuss the pros and cons of this argument, known as strategic trade policy, as well as the pros and cons of the argument for unrestricted free trade, in Chapter 6.

Mercantilism

The first theory of international trade, mercantilism, emerged in England in the mid-16th century. The principal assertion of mercantilism was that gold and silver were the mainstays of national wealth and essential to vigorous commerce. At that time, gold and silver were the currency of trade between countries; a country could earn gold and silver by exporting goods. Conversely, importing goods from other countries would result in an outflow of gold and silver to those countries. The main tenet of **mercantilism** was that it was in a country's best interests to maintain a trade surplus, to export more than it imported. By doing so, a country would accumulate gold and silver and, consequently, increase its national wealth, prestige, and power. As the English mercantilist writer Thomas Mun put it in 1630:

> The ordinary means therefore to increase our wealth and treasure is by foreign trade, wherein we must ever observe this rule: to sell more to strangers yearly than we consume of theirs in value.[2]

Consistent with this belief, the mercantilist doctrine advocated government intervention to achieve a surplus in the balance of trade. The mercantilists saw no virtue in a large volume of trade. Rather, they recommended policies to maximize exports and minimize imports. To achieve this, imports were limited by tariffs and quotas, while exports were subsidized.

The classical economist David Hume pointed out an inherent inconsistency in the mercantilist doctrine in 1752. According to Hume, if England had a balance-of-trade surplus with France (it exported more than it imported), the resulting inflow of gold and silver would swell the domestic money supply and generate inflation in England. In France, however, the outflow of gold and silver would have the opposite effect. France's money supply would contract, and its prices would fall. This change in relative prices between France and England would encourage the French to buy fewer English goods (because they were becoming more expensive) and the English to buy more French goods (because they were becoming cheaper). The result would be deterioration in the English balance of trade and an improvement in France's trade balance, until the English surplus was eliminated. Hence, according to Hume, in the long run no country could sustain a surplus on the balance of trade and so accumulate gold and silver as the mercantilists had envisaged.

The flaw with mercantilism was that it viewed trade as a zero-sum game. (A **zero-sum game** is one in which a gain by one country results in a loss by another.) It was left to Adam Smith and David Ricardo to show the shortsightedness of this approach and to demonstrate that trade is a positive-sum game, or a situation in which all countries can benefit. Unfortunately, the mercantilist doctrine is by no means dead. Neo-mercantilists equate political power with economic power and economic power with a balance-of-trade surplus. Critics argue that many nations have adopted a neo-mercantilist strategy that is designed to simultaneously boost exports and limit imports.[3] For example, critics charge that China is pursuing a neo-mercantilist policy, deliberately keeping its currency value low against the U.S. dollar in order to sell more goods to the United States, and thus amass a trade surplus and foreign exchange reserves (see the Country Focus).

🌐 Absolute Advantage

In his 1776 landmark book *The Wealth of Nations*, Adam Smith attacked the mercantilist assumption that trade is a zero-sum game. Smith argued that countries differ in their ability to produce goods efficiently. In his time, the English, by virtue of their superior manufacturing processes, were the world's most efficient textile manufacturers. Due to the combination of favorable climate, good soils, and accumulated expertise, the French had the world's most efficient wine industry. The English had an *absolute advantage* in the production of textiles, while the French had an *absolute advantage* in the production of wine. Thus, a country has an **absolute advantage** in the production of a product when it is more efficient than any other country in producing it.

According to Smith, countries should specialize in the production of goods for which they have an absolute advantage and then trade these for goods produced by other countries. In Smith's time, this suggested that the English should specialize in the production of textiles while the French should specialize in the production of wine. England could get all the wine it needed by selling its textiles to France and buying wine in exchange. Similarly, France could get all the textiles it needed by selling wine to England and buying textiles in exchange. Smith's basic argument, therefore, is that a country should never produce goods at home that it can buy at a lower cost from other countries. Smith demonstrates that, by specializing in the production of goods in which each has an absolute advantage, both countries benefit by engaging in trade.

Consider the effects of trade between two countries, Ghana and South Korea. The production of any good (output) requires resources (inputs) such as land, labor, and capital. Assume that Ghana and South Korea both have the same amount of resources and that these resources can be used to produce either rice or cocoa. Assume further that 200 units of resources are available in each country. Imagine that in Ghana it takes

Is China a Neo-Mercantilist Nation?

China's rapid rise in economic power has been built on export-led growth. The country has taken raw material imports from other countries and, using its cheap labor, converted them into products that it sells to developed nations like the United States. For years, the country's exports have been growing faster than its imports, leading some critics to claim that China is pursuing a neo-mercantilist policy, trying to amass record trade surpluses and foreign currency that will give it economic power over developed nations. This rhetoric reached new heights in 2006 when China's trade surplus hit a record $210 billion and its foreign exchange reserves exceeded $1 trillion, some 70 percent of which are held in U.S. dollars. Observers worry that if China ever decides to sell its holdings of U.S. currency, this could depress the value of the dollar against other currencies and increase the price of imports into America.

Throughout 2005 and 2006, China's exports grew much faster than its imports, leading some to argue that China was limiting imports by pursuing an import substitution policy, encouraging domestic investment in the production of products like steel, aluminum, and paper, which it had historically imported from other nations. The trade deficit with America has been a particular cause for concern.

In 2006, this reached $214 billion, the largest deficit ever recorded with a single country. At the same time, China has resisted attempts to let its currency float freely against the U.S. dollar. Many claim that China's currency is too cheap, and that this keeps the prices of China's goods artificially low, which fuels the country's exports.

So is China a neo-mercantilist nation that is deliberately discouraging imports and encouraging exports in order to grow its trade surplus and accumulate foreign exchange reserves, which might give it economic power? The jury is out on this issue. Skeptics suggest that the slowdown in imports to China is temporary and that the country will have no choice but to increase its imports of commodities that it lacks, such as oil. They also note that China did start allowing the value of the *renminbi* (China's currency) to appreciate against the dollar in July 2005, although the initial appreciation was limited to just 2.1 percent—hardly enough, say critics. In a sign that pressure on China to change its ways is growing, in late 2006 U.S. Treasury Secretary Henry Paulson visited Beijing and called for the Chinese to allow the renminbi to continue rising against the U.S. dollar. The Chinese responded by making it clear that they had no intention of being hurried on the road to economic reform [4]

FIGURE 5.1

The Theory of Absolute Advantage

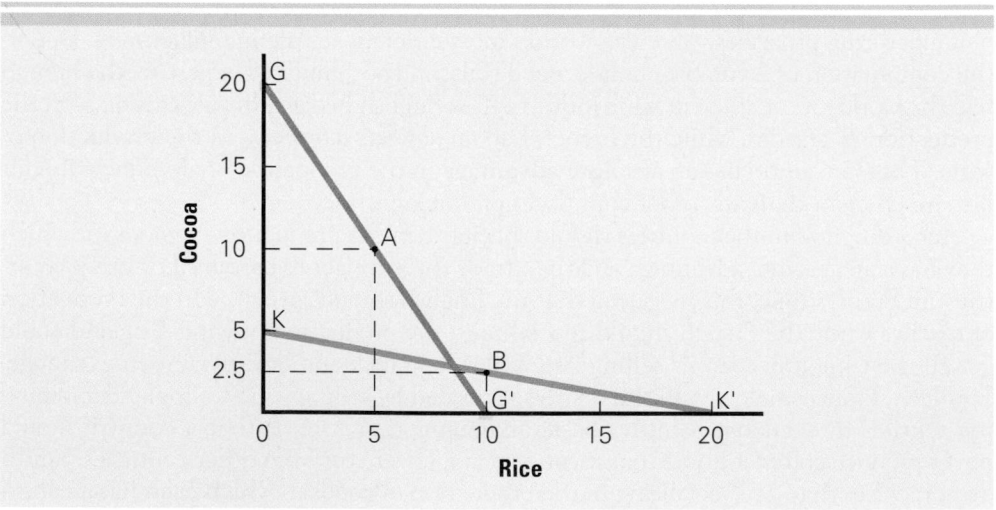

10 resources to produce one ton of cocoa and 20 resources to produce one ton of rice. Thus, Ghana could produce 20 tons of cocoa and no rice, 10 tons of rice and no cocoa, or some combination of rice and cocoa between these two extremes. The different combinations that Ghana could produce are represented by the line GG' in Figure 5.1. This is referred to as Ghana's *production possibility frontier* (PPF). Similarly, imagine that in

South Korea it takes 40 resources to produce 1 ton of cocoa and 10 resources to produce 1 ton of rice. Thus, South Korea could produce 5 tons of cocoa and no rice, 20 tons of rice and no cocoa, or some combination between these two extremes. The different combinations available to South Korea are represented by the line KK′ in Figure 5.1, which is South Korea's PPF. Clearly, Ghana has an absolute advantage in the production of cocoa. (More resources are needed to produce a ton of cocoa in South Korea than in Ghana.) By the same token, South Korea has an absolute advantage in the production of rice.

Now consider a situation in which neither country trades with any other. Each country devotes half its resources to the production of rice and half to the production of cocoa. Each country must also consume what it produces. Ghana would be able to produce 10 tons of cocoa and 5 tons of rice (point A in Figure 5.1), while South Korea would be able to produce 10 tons of rice and 2.5 tons of cocoa. Without trade, the combined production of both countries would be 12.5 tons of cocoa (10 tons in Ghana plus 2.5 tons in South Korea) and 15 tons of rice (5 tons in Ghana and 10 tons in South Korea). If each country were to specialize in producing the good for which it had an absolute advantage and then trade with the other for the good it lacks, Ghana could produce 20 tons of cocoa, and South Korea could produce 20 tons of rice. Thus, by specializing, the production of both goods could be increased. Production of cocoa would increase from 12.5 tons to 20 tons, while production of rice would increase from 15 tons to 20 tons. The increase in production that would result from specialization is therefore 7.5 tons of cocoa and 5 tons of rice. Table 5.1 summarizes these figures.

TABLE 5.1

Absolute Advantage and the Gains from Trade

Resources Required to Produce 1 Ton of Cocoa and Rice

	Cocoa	Rice
Ghana	10	20
South Korea	40	10

Production and Consumption without Trade

	Cocoa	Rice
Ghana	10.0	5.0
South Korea	2.5	10.0
Total production	12.5	15.0

Production with Specialization

	Cocoa	Rice
Ghana	20.0	0.0
South Korea	0.0	20.0
Total production	20.0	20.0

Consumption After Ghana Trades 6 Tons of Cocoa for 6 Tons of South Korean Rice

	Cocoa	Rice
Ghana	14.0	6.0
South Korea	6.0	14.0

Increase in Consumption as a Result of Specialization and Trade

	Cocoa	Rice
Ghana	4.0	1.0
South Korea	3.5	4.0

By engaging in trade and swapping 1 ton of cocoa for 1 ton of rice, producers in both countries could consume more of both cocoa and rice. Imagine that Ghana and South Korea swap cocoa and rice on a one-to-one basis; that is, the price of 1 ton of cocoa is equal to the price of 1 ton of rice. If Ghana decided to export 6 tons of cocoa to South Korea and import 6 tons of rice in return, its final consumption after trade would be 14 tons of cocoa and 6 tons of rice. This is 4 tons more cocoa than it could have consumed before specialization and trade and 1 ton more rice. Similarly, South Korea's final consumption after trade would be 6 tons of cocoa and 14 tons of rice. This is 3.5 tons more cocoa than it could have consumed before specialization and trade and 4 tons more rice. Thus, as a result of specialization and trade, output of both cocoa and rice would be increased, and consumers in both nations would be able to consume more. Thus, we can see that trade is a positive-sum game; it produces net gains for all involved.

🌐 Comparative Advantage

David Ricardo took Adam Smith's theory one step further by exploring what might happen when one country has an absolute advantage in the production of all goods.[5] Smith's theory of absolute advantage suggests that such a country might derive no benefits from international trade. In his 1817 book *Principles of Political Economy*, Ricardo showed that this was not the case. According to Ricardo's theory of comparative advantage, it makes sense for a country to specialize in the production of those goods that it produces most efficiently and to buy the goods that it produces less efficiently from other countries, even if this means buying goods from other countries that it could produce more efficiently itself.[6] While this may seem counterintuitive, the logic can be explained with a simple example.

Assume that Ghana is more efficient in the production of both cocoa and rice; that is, Ghana has an absolute advantage in the production of both products. In Ghana it takes 10 resources to produce 1 ton of cocoa and 13⅓ resources to produce one ton of rice. Thus, given its 200 units of resources, Ghana can produce 20 tons of cocoa and no rice, 15 tons of rice and no cocoa, or any combination in between on its PPF (the line GG' in Figure 5.2). In South Korea it takes 40 resources to produce 1 ton of cocoa and 20 resources to produce one ton of rice. Thus, South Korea can produce 5 tons of cocoa and no rice, 10 tons of rice and no cocoa, or any combination on its PPF (the line KK' in Figure 5.2). Again assume that without trade, each country uses half of its resources to produce rice and half to produce cocoa. Thus, without trade, Ghana will produce 10 tons of cocoa and 7.5 tons of rice (point A in Figure 5.2), while South Korea will produce 2.5 tons of cocoa and 5 tons of rice (point B in Figure 5.2).

In light of Ghana's absolute advantage in the production of both goods, why should it trade with South Korea? Although Ghana has an absolute advantage in the

FIGURE 5.2

The Theory of
Comparative Advantage

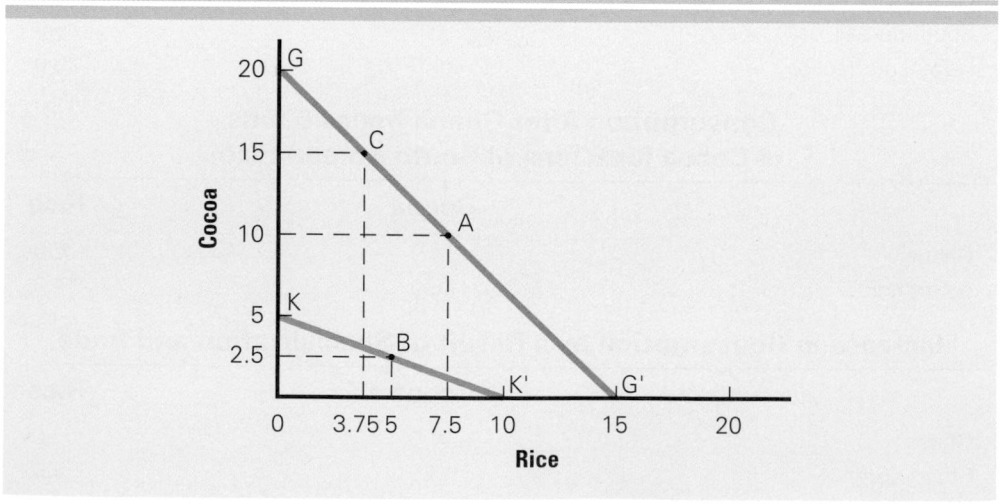

production of both cocoa and rice, it has a comparative advantage only in the production of cocoa: Ghana can produce 4 times as much cocoa as South Korea, but only 1.5 times as much rice. Ghana is *comparatively* more efficient at producing cocoa than it is at producing rice.

Without trade, the combined production of cocoa will be 12.5 tons (10 tons in Ghana and 2.5 in South Korea), and the combined production of rice will also be 12.5 tons (7.5 tons in Ghana and 5 tons in South Korea). Without trade, each country must consume what it produces. By engaging in trade, the two countries can increase their combined production of rice and cocoa, and consumers in both nations can consume more of both goods.

THE GAINS FROM TRADE

Imagine that Ghana exploits its comparative advantage in the production of cocoa to increase its output from 10 tons to 15 tons. This uses up 150 units of resources, leaving the remaining 50 units of resources to use in producing 3.75 tons of rice (point C in Figure 5.2). Meanwhile, South Korea specializes in the production of rice, producing 10 tons. The combined output of both cocoa and rice has now increased. Before specialization, the combined output was 12.5 tons of cocoa and 12.5 tons of rice. Now it is 15 tons of cocoa and 13.75 tons of rice (3.75 tons in Ghana and 10 tons in South Korea). The source of the increase in production is summarized in Table 5.2.

TABLE 5.2

Comparative Advantage and the Gains from Trade

Resources Required to Produce 1 Ton of Cocoa and Rice		
	Cocoa	**Rice**
Ghana	10	13.33
South Korea	40	20

Production and Consumption without Trade		
	Cocoa	**Rice**
Ghana	10.0	7.5
South Korea	2.5	5.0
Total production	12.5	12.5

Production with Specialization		
	Cocoa	**Rice**
Ghana	15.0	3.75
South Korea	0.0	10.0
Total production	15.0	13.75

Consumption After Ghana Trades 6 Tons of Cocoa for 6 Tons of South Korean Rice		
	Cocoa	**Rice**
Ghana	11.0	7.75
South Korea	4.0	6.0

Increase in Consumption as a Result of Specialization and Trade		
	Cocoa	**Rice**
Ghana	1.0	0.25
South Korea	1.5	1.0

Not only is output higher, but both countries also can now benefit from trade. If Ghana and South Korea swap cocoa and rice on a one-to-one basis, with both countries choosing to exchange 4 tons of their export for 4 tons of the import, both countries are able to consume more cocoa and rice than they could before specialization and trade (see Table 5.2). Thus, if Ghana exchanges 4 tons of cocoa with South Korea for 4 tons of rice, it is still left with 11 tons of cocoa, which is 1 ton more than it had before trade. The 4 tons of rice it gets from South Korea in exchange for its 4 tons of cocoa, when added to the 3.75 tons it now produces domestically, leave it with a total of 7.75 tons of rice, which is .25 of a ton more than it had before specialization. Similarly, after swapping 4 tons of rice with Ghana, South Korea still ends up with 6 tons of rice, which is more than it had before specialization. In addition, the 4 tons of cocoa it receives in exchange is 1.5 tons more than it produced before trade. Thus, consumption of cocoa and rice can increase in both countries as a result of specialization and trade.

The basic message of the theory of comparative advantage is that *potential world production is greater with unrestricted free trade than it is with restricted trade*. Ricardo's theory suggests that consumers in all nations can consume more if there are no restrictions on trade. This occurs even in countries that lack an absolute advantage in the production of any good. In other words, to an even greater degree than the theory of absolute advantage, *the theory of comparative advantage suggests that trade is a positive-sum game in which all countries that participate realize economic gains*. As such, this theory provides a strong rationale for encouraging free trade. So powerful is Ricardo's theory that it remains a major intellectual weapon for those who argue for free trade.

QUALIFICATIONS AND ASSUMPTIONS

The conclusion that free trade is universally beneficial is a rather bold one to draw from such a simple model. Our simple model includes many unrealistic assumptions:

1. We have assumed a simple world in which there are only two countries and two goods. In the real world, there are many countries and many goods.
2. We have assumed away transportation costs between countries.
3. We have assumed away differences in the prices of resources in different countries. We have said nothing about exchange rates, simply assuming that cocoa and rice could be swapped on a one-to-one basis.
4. We have assumed that resources can move freely from the production of one good to another within a country. In reality, this is not always the case.
5. We have assumed constant returns to scale; that is, that specialization by Ghana or South Korea has no effect on the amount of resources required to produce 1 ton of cocoa or rice. In reality, both diminishing and increasing returns to specialization exist. The amount of resources required to produce a good might decrease or increase as a nation specializes in production of that good.
6. We have assumed that each country has a fixed stock of resources and that free trade does not change the efficiency with which a country uses its resources. This static assumption makes no allowances for the dynamic changes in a country's stock of resources and in the efficiency with which the country uses its resources that might result from free trade.
7. We have assumed away the effects of trade on income distribution within a country.

Given these assumptions, can the conclusion that free trade is mutually beneficial be extended to the real world of many countries, many goods, positive transportation costs, volatile exchange rates, immobile domestic resources, nonconstant returns to specialization, and dynamic changes? Although a detailed extension of the theory of comparative advantage is beyond the scope of this book, economists have shown that the basic result derived from our simple model can be generalized to a world composed of many countries producing many different goods.[7] Despite the shortcomings of the Ricardian model, research suggests that the basic proposition that countries will export the goods that they are most efficient at producing is borne out by the data.[8]

However, once all the assumptions are dropped, some economists associated with the "new trade theory" argue that the case for unrestricted free trade, while still positive, loses some of its strength.[9] We return to this issue later in this chapter and in the next when we discuss the new trade theory. Moreover, in a recent and widely discussed analysis, the Nobel Prize–winning economist Paul Samuelson argued that contrary to the standard interpretation, in certain circumstances the theory of comparative advantage predicts that a rich country might actually be *worse* off by switching to a free trade regime with a poor nation.[10] We will consider Samuelson's critique in the next section.

EXTENSIONS OF THE RICARDIAN MODEL

Let us explore the effect of relaxing three of the assumptions identified above in the simple comparative advantage model. Below we relax the assumptions that resources move freely from the production of one good to another within a country, that there are constant returns to scale, and that trade does not change a country's stock of resources or the efficiency with which those resources are utilized.

Immobile Resources

In our simple comparative model of Ghana and South Korea, we assumed that producers (farmers) could easily convert land from the production of cocoa to rice, and vice versa. While this assumption may hold for some agricultural products, resources do not always shift quite so easily from producing one good to another. A certain amount of friction is involved. For example, embracing a free trade regime for an advanced economy such as the United States often implies that the country will produce less of some labor-intensive goods, such as textiles, and more of some knowledge-intensive goods, such as computer software or biotechnology products. Although the country as a whole will gain from such a shift, textile producers will lose. A textile worker in South Carolina is probably not qualified to write software for Microsoft. Thus, the shift to free trade may mean that she becomes unemployed or has to accept another less attractive job, such as working at a fast-food restaurant.

Resources do not always move easily from one economic activity to another. The process creates friction and human suffering too. While the theory predicts that the benefits of free trade outweigh the costs by a significant margin, this is of cold comfort to those who bear the costs. Accordingly, political opposition to the adoption of a free trade regime typically comes from those whose jobs are most at risk. In the United States, for example, textile workers and their unions have long opposed the move toward free trade precisely because this group has much to lose from free trade. Governments often ease the transition toward free trade by helping to retrain those who lose their jobs as a result. The pain caused by the movement toward a free trade regime is a short-term phenomenon, while the gains from trade once the transition has been made are both significant and enduring.

Diminishing Returns

The simple comparative advantage model developed above assumes constant returns to specialization. By **constant returns to specialization** we mean the units of resources required to produce a good (cocoa or rice) are assumed to remain constant no matter where one is on a country's production possibility frontier (PPF). Thus, we assumed that it always took Ghana 10 units of resources to produce 1 ton of cocoa. However, it is more realistic to assume diminishing returns to specialization. Diminishing returns to specialization occur when more units of resources are required to produce each additional unit. While 10 units of resources may be sufficient to increase Ghana's output of cocoa from 12 tons to 13 tons, 11 units of resources may be needed to increase output

FIGURE 5.3

Ghana's PPF under
Diminishing Returns

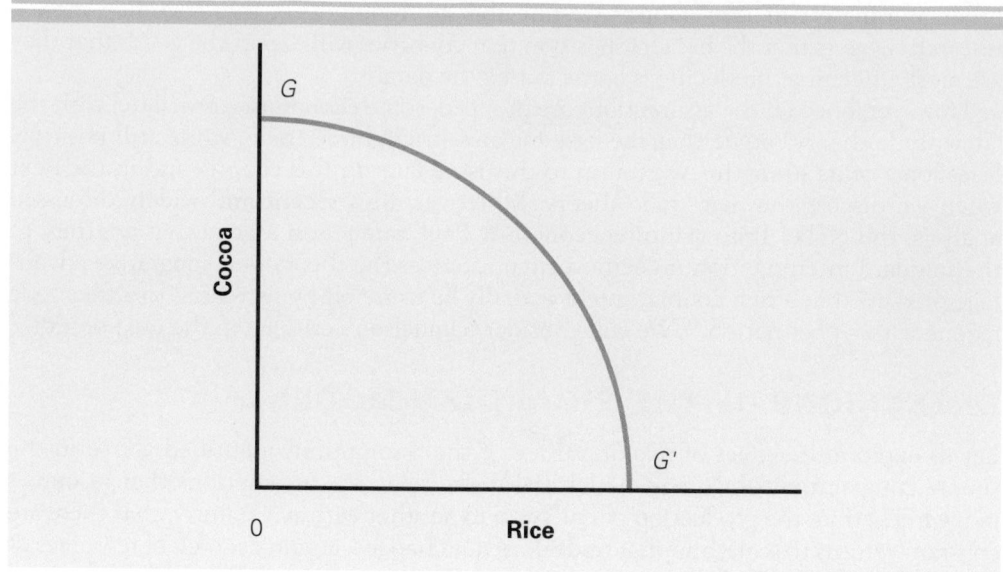

from 13 to 14 tons, 12 units of resources to increase output from 14 tons to 15 tons, and so on. Diminishing returns imply a convex PPF for Ghana (see Figure 5.3), rather than the straight line depicted in Figure 5.2.

It is more realistic to assume diminishing returns for two reasons. First, not all resources are of the same quality. As a country tries to increase its output of a certain good, it is increasingly likely to draw on more marginal resources whose productivity is not as great as those initially employed. The result is that it requires ever more resources to produce an equal increase in output. For example, some land is more productive than other land. As Ghana tries to expand its output of cocoa, it might have to utilize increasingly marginal land that is less fertile than the land it originally used. As yields per acre decline, Ghana must use more land to produce 1 ton of cocoa.

A second reason for diminishing returns is that different goods use resources in different proportions. For example, imagine that growing cocoa uses more land and less labor than growing rice, and that Ghana tries to transfer resources from rice production to cocoa production. The rice industry will release proportionately too much labor and too little land for efficient cocoa production. To absorb the additional resources of labor and land, the cocoa industry will have to shift toward more labor-intensive methods of production. The effect is that the efficiency with which the cocoa industry uses labor will decline, and returns will diminish.

Diminishing returns show that it is not feasible for a country to specialize to the degree suggested by the simple Ricardian model outlined earlier. Diminishing returns to specialization suggest that the gains from specialization are likely to be exhausted before specialization is complete. In reality, most countries do not specialize but, instead, produce a range of goods. However, the theory predicts that it is worthwhile to specialize until that point where diminishing returns outweigh the resulting gains from trade. Thus, the basic conclusion that unrestricted free trade is beneficial still holds, although because of diminishing returns, the gains may not be as great as suggested in the constant returns case.

Dynamic Effects and Economic Growth

The simple comparative advantage model assumed that trade does not change a country's stock of resources or the efficiency with which it utilizes those resources. This static assumption makes no allowances for the dynamic changes that might result from trade. If we relax this assumption, it becomes apparent that opening an economy to trade is

FIGURE 5.4

The Influence of Free Trade on the PPF

likely to generate dynamic gains of two sorts.[11] First, free trade might increase a country's stock of resources as increased supplies of labor and capital from abroad become available for use within the country. For example, more resources have become available in Eastern Europe since the early 1990s since many Western businesses have been investing significant capital in the former Communist countries.

Second, free trade might also increase the efficiency with which a country uses its resources. Gains in the efficiency of resource utilization could arise from a number of factors. For example, economies of large-scale production might become available as trade expands the size of the total market available to domestic firms. Trade might make better technology from abroad available to domestic firms; better technology can increase labor productivity or the productivity of land. (The so-called green revolution had this effect on agricultural outputs in developing countries.) Also, opening an economy to foreign competition might stimulate domestic producers to look for ways to increase their efficiency. Again, this phenomenon has arguably been occurring in the once-protected markets of Eastern Europe, where many former state monopolies have had to increase the efficiency of their operations to survive in the competitive world market.

Dynamic gains in both the stock of a country's resources and the efficiency with which resources are utilized will cause a country's PPF to shift outward. This is illustrated in Figure 5.4, where the shift from PPF$_1$ to PPF$_2$ results from the dynamic gains that arise from free trade. As a consequence of this outward shift, the country in Figure 5.4 can produce more of both goods than it did before introduction of free trade. The theory suggests that opening an economy to free trade not only results in static gains of the type discussed earlier but also results in dynamic gains that stimulate economic growth. If this is so, then one might think that the case for free trade becomes stronger still, and in general it does. However, as noted above, in a recent article one of the leading economic theorists of the 20th century, Paul Samuelson, argued that in some circumstances, dynamic gains can lead to an outcome that is not so beneficial.

The Samuelson Critique

Samuelson's critique looks at what happens when a rich country—the United States —enters into a free trade agreement with a poor country—China—that rapidly improves its productivity after the introduction of a free trade regime (that is, there is a dynamic gain in the efficiency with which resources are used in the poor country). The Samuelson model suggests that in such cases, the lower prices that U.S. consumers pay for goods imported from China following the introduction of a free trade regime *may* not be enough to produce a net gain for the U.S. economy if the dynamic effect of free trade is to lower real wage rates in the United States. As Samuelson stated in a *New York Times* interview, "being able to purchase groceries 20 percent cheaper at Wal-Mart (due to international trade) does not necessarily make up for the wage losses (in America)."[12]

Samuelson goes on to note that he is particularly concerned about the ability to transfer service jobs offshore that traditionally were not internationally mobile, such as software debugging, call center jobs, accounting jobs, and even medical diagnosis of MRI scans (see the next Country Focus for details). Recent advances in communications technology have made this trend possible, effectively expanding the labor market for these jobs to include educated people in places like India, the Philippines, and China. When coupled with rapid advances in the productivity of foreign labor due to better education, the effect on middle class wages in the United States, according to Samuelson, may be similar to mass inward migration into the United States—it will lower the market clearing wage rate, *perhaps* by enough to outweigh the positive benefits of international trade.

Having said this, it should be noted that Samuelson concedes that free trade has historically benefited rich counties (as data discussed below seem to confirm). Moreover, he notes that introducing protectionist measures (e.g., trade barriers) to guard against the theoretical possibility that free trade may harm the United States in the future may produce a situation that is worse than the disease protectionists are trying to prevent. To quote Samuelson: "free trade may turn out pragmatically to be still best for each region in comparison to lobbyist induced tariffs and quotas which involve both a perversion of democracy and non-subtle deadweight distortion losses."[13]

Some economists have been quick to dismiss Samuelson's fears.[14] While not questioning his analysis, they note that as a practical matter developing nations are unlikely to be able to upgrade the skill level of their workforce rapidly enough to give rise to the situation in Samuelson's model. In other words, they will quickly run into diminishing returns. To quote one such rebuttal: "The notion that India and China will quickly educate 300 million of their citizens to acquire sophisticated and complex skills at stake borders on the ludicrous. The educational sectors in these countries face enormous difficulties."[15] Notwithstanding such rebuttals, however, Samuelson's stature is such that his work will undoubtedly be debated for some time to come.

Evidence for the Link between Trade and Growth

Many economic studies have looked at the relationship between trade and economic growth.[17] In general, these studies suggest that, as predicted by the standard theory of comparative advantage, countries that adopt a more open stance toward international trade enjoy higher growth rates than those that close their economies to trade (the opening case provides evidence of the link between trade and growth). Jeffrey Sachs and Andrew Warner created a measure of how "open" to international trade an economy was and then looked at the relationship between "openness" and economic growth for a sample of more than 100 countries from 1970 to 1990.[18] Among other findings, they reported:

> We find a strong association between openness and growth, both within the group of developing and the group of developed countries. Within the group of developing countries, the open economies grew at 4.49 percent per year, and the closed economies grew at 0.69 percent per year. Within the group of developed economies, the open economies grew at 2.29 percent per year, and the closed economies grew at 0.74 percent per year.[19]

A study by Wacziarg and Welch updated the Sachs and Warner data to the late 1990s. They found that over the period 1950–1998, countries that liberalized their trade regimes experienced, on average, increases in their annual growth rates of 1.5 percent compared to periods before liberalization.[20]

Moving U.S. White-Collar Jobs Offshore

Economists have long argued that free trade produces gains for all countries that participate in a free trading system, but as the next wave of globalization sweeps through the U.S. economy, many people are wondering if this is true, particularly those who stand to lose their jobs because of globalization. In the popular imagination for much of the past quarter century, free trade was associated with the movement of low-skill, blue-collar manufacturing jobs out of rich countries such as the United States and toward low-wage countries—textiles to Costa Rica, athletic shoes to the Philippines, steel to Brazil, electronic products to Malaysia, and so on. While many observers bemoaned the "hollowing out" of U.S. manufacturing, economists stated that high-skilled, high-wage white-collar jobs associated with the knowledge-based economy would stay in the United States. Computers might be assembled in Malaysia, so the argument went, but they would continue to be designed in Silicon Valley by highly skilled U.S. engineers.

Recent developments have some people questioning this assumption. As the global economy slowed after 2000 and corporate profits slumped, many American companies responded by moving white-collar "knowledge-based" jobs to developing nations where they could be performed for a fraction of the cost. During the long economic boom of the 1990s, Bank of America had to compete with other organizations for the scarce talents of information technology specialists, driving annual salaries to more than $100,000. However, with business under pressure, between 2002 and early 2003 the bank cut nearly 5,000 jobs from its 25,000-strong, U.S.-based information technology workforce. Some of these jobs were transferred to India, where work that costs $100 an hour in the United States can be done for $20 an hour.

One beneficiary of Bank of America's downsizing is Infosys Technologies Ltd., a Bangalore, India, information technology firm where 250 engineers now develop information technology applications for the bank. Other Infosys employees are busy processing home loan applications for Greenpoint Mortgage of Novato, California. Nearby in the offices of another Indian firm, Wipro Ltd., five radiologists interpret 30 CT scans a day for Massachusetts General Hospital, sent over the Internet. At yet another Bangalore business, engineers earn $10,000 a year designing leading-edge semiconductor chips for Texas Instruments. Nor is India the only beneficiary of these changes. Accenture, a large U.S. management consulting and information technology firm, moved 5,000 jobs in software development and accounting to the Philippines. Also in the Philippines, Procter & Gamble employs 650 professionals who prepare the company's global tax returns. The work used to be done in the United States, but now it is done in Manila, with just final submission to local tax authorities in the United States and other countries handled locally.

Some architectural work also is being outsourced to lower cost locations. Flour Corp., a California-based construction company, employs some 1,200 engineers and draftsmen in the Philippines, Poland, and India to turn layouts of industrial facilities into detailed specifications. For a Saudi Arabian chemical plant Flour is designing, 200 young engineers based in the Philippines earning less than $3,000 a year collaborate in real time over the Internet with elite U.S. and British engineers who make up to $90,000 a year. Why does Flour do this? According to the company, the answer is simple: It reduces the cost of a project by 15 percent, giving the company a cost-based competitive advantage in the global market for construction design.[16]

The message of these studies seems clear: Adopt an open economy and embrace free trade, and your nation will be rewarded with higher economic growth rates. Higher growth will raise income levels and living standards. This last point has been confirmed by a study that looked at the relationship between trade and growth in incomes. The study, undertaken by Jeffrey Frankel and David Romer, found that on average, a 1 percentage point increase in the ratio of a country's trade to its gross domestic product increases income per person by at least .5 percent.[21] For every 10 percent increase in the importance of international trade in an economy, average income levels will rise by at least 5 percent. Despite the short-term adjustment costs associated with adopting a free trade regime, trade would seem to produce greater economic growth and higher living standards in the long run, just as Ricardo's theory would lead us to expect.[22]

Heckscher-Ohlin Theory

Ricardo's theory stresses that comparative advantage arises from differences in productivity. Thus, whether Ghana is more efficient than South Korea in the production of cocoa depends on how productively it uses its resources. Ricardo stressed labor productivity and argued that differences in labor productivity between nations underlie the notion of comparative advantage. Swedish economists Eli Heckscher (in 1919) and Bertil Ohlin (in 1933) put forward a different explanation of comparative advantage. They argued that comparative advantage arises from differences in national factor endowments.[23] By **factor endowments** they meant the extent to which a country is endowed with such resources as land, labor, and capital. Nations have varying factor endowments, and different factor endowments explain differences in factor costs; specifically, the more abundant a factor, the lower its cost. The Heckscher-Ohlin theory predicts that countries will export those goods that make intensive use of factors that are locally abundant, while importing goods that make intensive use of factors that are locally scarce. Thus, the Heckscher-Ohlin theory attempts to explain the pattern of international trade that we observe in the world economy. Like Ricardo's theory, the Heckscher-Ohlin theory argues that free trade is beneficial. Unlike Ricardo's theory, however, the Heckscher-Ohlin theory argues that the pattern of international trade is determined by differences in factor endowments, rather than differences in productivity.

The Heckscher-Ohlin theory has commonsense appeal. For example, the United States has long been a substantial exporter of agricultural goods, reflecting in part its unusual abundance of arable land. In contrast, China excels in the export of goods produced in labor-intensive manufacturing industries, such as textiles and footwear. This reflects China's relative abundance of low-cost labor. The United States, which lacks abundant low-cost labor, has been a primary importer of these goods. Note that it is relative, not absolute, endowments that are important; a country may have larger absolute amounts of land and labor than another country, but be relatively abundant in one of them.

THE LEONTIEF PARADOX

The Heckscher-Ohlin theory has been one of the most influential theoretical ideas in international economics. Most economists prefer the Heckscher-Ohlin theory to Ricardo's theory because it makes fewer simplifying assumptions. Because of its influence, the theory has been subjected to many empirical tests. Beginning with a famous study published in 1953 by Wassily Leontief (winner of the Nobel Prize in economics in 1973), many of these tests have raised questions about its validity.[24] Using the Heckscher-Ohlin theory, Leontief postulated that since the United States was relatively abundant in capital compared to other nations, the United States would be an exporter of capital-intensive goods and an importer of labor-intensive goods. To his surprise, however, he found that U.S. exports were less capital intensive than U.S. imports. Since this result was at variance with the predictions of the theory, it has become known as the Leontief paradox.

No one is quite sure why we observe the Leontief paradox. One possible explanation is that the United States has a special advantage in producing new products or goods made with innovative technologies. Such products may be less capital intensive than products whose technology has had time to mature and become suitable for mass production. Thus, the United States may be exporting goods that heavily use skilled labor and innovative entrepreneurship, such as computer software, while importing heavy manufacturing products that use large amounts of capital. Some empirical studies tend to confirm this.[25] Still, tests of the Heckscher-Ohlin theory using data for a large number of countries tend to confirm the existence of the Leontief paradox.[26]

This leaves economists with a difficult dilemma. They prefer the Heckscher-Ohlin theory on theoretical grounds, but it is a relatively poor predictor of real-world international trade patterns. On the other hand, the theory they regard as being too limited, Ricardo's theory of comparative advantage, actually predicts trade patterns with greater accuracy. The best solution to this dilemma may be to return to the Ricardian idea that trade patterns are largely driven by international differences in productivity. Thus, one might argue that the United States exports commercial aircraft and imports textiles not because its factor endowments are especially suited to aircraft manufacture and not suited to textile manufacture, but because the United States is relatively more efficient at producing aircraft than textiles. A key assumption in the Heckscher-Ohlin theory is that technologies are the same across countries. This may not be the case. Differences in technology may lead to differences in productivity, which, in turn, drive international trade patterns.[27] Thus, Japan's success in exporting automobiles in the 1970s and 1980s was based not just on the relative abundance of capital but also on its development of innovative manufacturing technology that enabled it to achieve higher productivity levels in automobile production than other countries that also had abundant capital. More recent empirical work suggests that this theoretical explanation may be correct.[28] The new research shows that once differences in technology across countries are controlled for, countries do indeed export those goods that make intensive use of factors that are locally abundant, while importing goods that make intensive use of factors that are locally scarce. In other words, once the impact of differences of technology on productivity is controlled for, the Heckscher-Ohlin theory seems to gain predictive power.

The Product Life-Cycle Theory

Raymond Vernon initially proposed the product life-cycle theory in the mid-1960s.[29] Vernon's theory was based on the observation that for most of the 20th century a very large proportion of the world's new products had been developed by U.S. firms and sold first in the U.S. market (e.g., mass-produced automobiles, televisions, instant cameras, photocopiers, personal computers, and semiconductor chips). To explain this, Vernon argued that the wealth and size of the U.S. market gave U.S. firms a strong incentive to develop new consumer products. In addition, the high cost of U.S. labor gave U.S. firms an incentive to develop cost-saving process innovations.

Just because a new product is developed by a U.S. firm and first sold in the U.S. market, it does not follow that the product must be produced in the United States. It could be produced abroad at some low-cost location and then exported back into the United States. However, Vernon argued that most new products were initially produced in America. Apparently, the pioneering firms believed it was better to keep production facilities close to the market and to the firm's center of decision making, given the uncertainty and risks inherent in introducing new products. Also, the demand for most new products tends to be based on non-price factors. Consequently, firms can charge relatively high prices for new products, which obviates the need to look for low-cost production sites in other countries.

Vernon went on to argue that early in the life cycle of a typical new product, while demand is starting to grow rapidly in the United States, demand in other advanced countries is limited to high-income groups. The limited initial demand in other advanced countries does not make it worthwhile for firms in those countries to start producing the new product, but it does necessitate some exports from the United States to those countries.

Over time, demand for the new product starts to grow in other advanced countries (e.g., Great Britain, France, Germany, and Japan). As it does, it becomes worthwhile for foreign producers to begin producing for their home markets. In addition, U.S. firms might set up production facilities in those advanced countries where demand is growing. Consequently, production within other advanced countries begins to limit the potential for exports from the United States.

As the market in the United States and other advanced nations matures, the product becomes more standardized, and price becomes the main competitive weapon. As this occurs, cost considerations start to play a greater role in the competitive process. Producers based in advanced countries where labor costs are lower than in the United States (e.g., Italy, Spain) might now be able to export to the United States. If cost pressures become intense, the process might not stop there. The cycle by which the United States lost its advantage to other advanced countries might be repeated once more, as developing countries (e.g., Thailand) begin to acquire a production advantage over advanced countries. Thus, the locus of global production initially switches from the United States to other advanced nations and then from those nations to developing countries.

The consequence of these trends for the pattern of world trade is that over time the United States switches from being an exporter of the product to an importer of the product as production becomes concentrated in lower-cost foreign locations. Figure 5.5 shows the growth of production and consumption over time in the United States, other advanced countries, and developing countries.

EVALUATING THE PRODUCT LIFE-CYCLE THEORY

Historically, the product life-cycle theory seems to be an accurate explanation of international trade patterns. Consider photocopiers; the product was first developed in the early 1960s by Xerox in the United States and sold initially to U.S. users. Originally Xerox exported photocopiers from the United States, primarily to Japan and the advanced countries of Western Europe. As demand began to grow in those countries, Xerox entered into joint ventures to set up production in Japan (Fuji-Xerox) and Great Britain (Rank-Xerox). In addition, once Xerox's patents on the photocopier process expired, other foreign competitors began to enter the market (e.g., Canon in Japan, Olivetti in Italy). As a consequence, exports from the United States declined, and U.S. users began to buy some of their photocopiers from lower cost foreign sources, particularly Japan. More recently, Japanese companies have found that manufacturing costs are too high in their own country, so they have begun to switch production to developing countries such as Singapore and Thailand. Thus, initially the United States and now other advanced countries (e.g., Japan and Great Britain) have switched from being exporters of photocopiers to importers. This evolution in the pattern of international trade in photocopiers is consistent with the predictions of the product life-cycle theory that mature industries tend to go out of the United States and into low-cost assembly locations.

However, the product life-cycle theory is not without weaknesses. Viewed from an Asian or European perspective, Vernon's argument that most new products are developed and introduced in the United States seems ethnocentric. Although it may be true that during U.S. dominance of the global economy (from 1945 to 1975), most new products were introduced in the United States, there have always been important exceptions. These exceptions appear to have become more common in recent years. Many new products are now first introduced in Japan (e.g., video game consoles) or Europe (new wireless phones). Moreover, with the increased globalization and integration of the world economy discussed in Chapter 1, a growing number of new products (e.g., laptop computers, compact discs, and digital cameras) are now introduced simultaneously in the United States, Japan, and the advanced European nations. Global product introductions may be accompanied by globally dispersed production, with particular components of a new

FIGURE 5.5

The Product Life Cycle
Theory

Source: Adapted from R. Vernon
and L. T. Wells, *The Economic
Environment of International
Business,* 4th ed., © 1986.
Reprinted by permission of
Pearson Education, Inc., Upper
Saddle River, N.J.

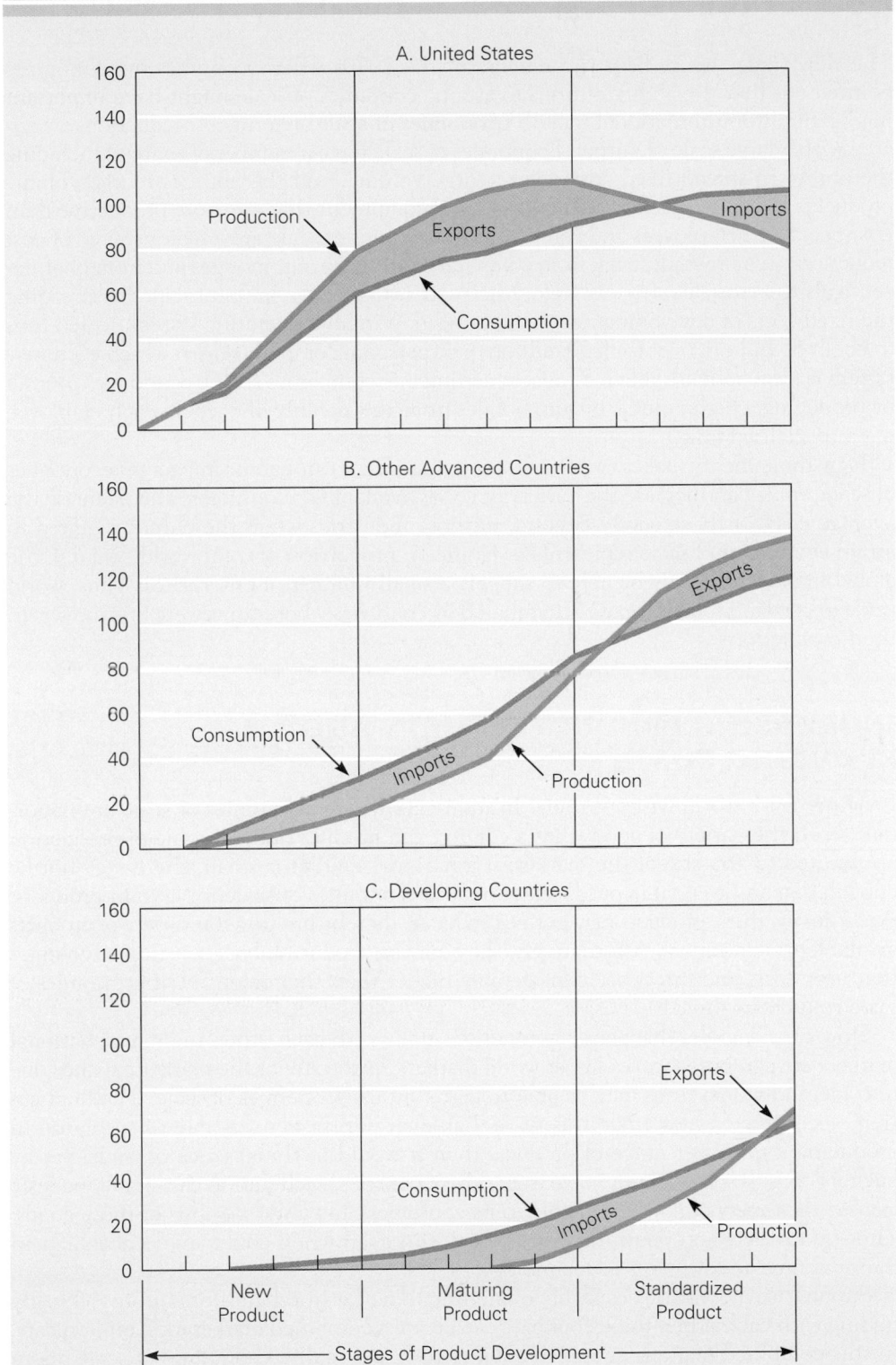

product being produced in those locations around the globe where the mix of factor costs
and skills is most favorable (as predicted by the theory of comparative advantage).
In sum, although Vernon's theory may be useful for explaining the pattern of international trade during the brief period of American global dominance, its relevance in the
modern world seems more limited.

New Trade Theory

The new trade theory began to emerge in the 1970s when a number of economists pointed out that the ability of firms to attain economies of scale might have important implications for international trade.[30] **Economies of scale** are unit cost reductions associated with a large scale of output. Economies of scale have a number of sources, including the ability to spread fixed costs over a large volume, and the ability of large volume producers to utilize specialized employees and equipment that are more productive than less specialized employees and equipment. Economies of scale are a major source of cost reductions in many industries, from computer software to automobiles and from pharmaceuticals to aerospace. For example, Microsoft realizes economies of scale by spreading the fixed costs of developing new versions of its Windows operating system, which runs to about $5 billion, over the 250 million or so personal computers upon which each new system is ultimately installed. Similarly, automobile companies realize economies of scale by producing a high volume of automobiles from an assembly line where each employee has a specialized task.

New trade theory makes two important points: First, through its impact on economies of scale, trade can increase the variety of goods available to consumers and decrease the average costs of those goods. Second, in those industries when the output required to attain economies of scale represents a significant proportion of total world demand, the global market may only be able to support a small number of enterprises. Thus, world trade in certain products may be dominated by countries whose firms were first movers in their production.

INCREASING PRODUCT VARIETY AND REDUCING COSTS

Imagine first a world without trade. In industries where economies of scale are important, both the variety of goods that a country can produce and the scale of production are limited by the size of the market. If a national market is small, there may not be enough demand to enable producers to realize economies of scale for certain products. Accordingly, those products may not be produced, thereby limiting the variety of products available to consumers. Alternatively, they may be produced, but in such low volumes that unit costs and prices are considerably higher than they might be if economies of scale could be realized.

Now consider what happens when nations trade with each other. Individual national markets are combined into a larger world market. As the size of the market expands due to trade, individual firms may be able to better attain economies of scale. The implication, according to new trade theory, is that each nation may be able to specialize in producing a narrower range of products than it would in the absence of trade, yet by buying goods that it does not make from other countries, each nation can simultaneously *increase the variety* of goods available to its consumers and *lower the costs* of those goods. Thus trade offers an opportunity for mutual gain even when countries do not differ in their resource endowments or technology.

Suppose two countries each have an annual market for 1 million automobiles. By trading with each other, these countries can create a combined market for 2 million cars. In this combined market, due to the ability to better realize economies of scale, more varieties (models) of cars can be produced, and cars can be produced at a lower average cost, than in either market alone. For example, demand for a sports car may be limited to 55,000 units in each national market, while a total output of at least 100,000 per year may be required to realize significant scale economies. Similarly, demand for a minivan may be 80,000 units in each national market, and again a total output of at least 100,000 per year may be required to realize significant scale economies. Faced with limited domestic market demand, firms in each nation may decide not to produce a sports car, since the costs of doing so at such low volume are too great. Although they may produce minivans, the cost of doing so will be higher, as will prices, than if significant economies of scale had been attained. Once the two countries decide to trade however, a firm in one nation may specialize in producing sports cars, while a firm in the other nation may produce minivans. The combined demand for 110,000 sports cars and 160,000 minivans allows each firm to realize scale economies. Consumers in this case benefit from having access to a product (sports cars) that was not available before international trade, and from the lower price for a product (minivans) that could not be produced at the most efficient scale before international trade. Trade is thus mutually beneficial because it allows for the specialization of production, the realization of scale economies, the production of a greater variety of products, and lower prices.

ECONOMIES OF SCALE, FIRST MOVER ADVANTAGES, AND THE PATTERN OF TRADE

A second theme in new trade theory is that the pattern of trade we observe in the world economy may be the result of economies of scale and first mover advantages. **First mover advantages** are the economic and strategic advantages that accrue to early entrants into an industry.[31] The ability to capture scale economies ahead of later entrants, and thus benefit from a lower cost structure, is an important first mover advantage. New trade theory argues that for those products where economies of scale are significant and represent a substantial proportion of world demand, the first movers in an industry can gain a scale-based cost advantage that later entrants find almost impossible to match. Thus, the pattern of trade that we observe for such products may reflect first mover advantages. Countries may dominate in the export of certain goods because economies of scale are important in their production, and because firms located in those countries were the first to capture scale economies, giving them a first mover advantage.

For example, consider the commercial aerospace industry. In aerospace there are substantial scale economies that come from the ability to spread the fixed costs of developing a new jet aircraft over a large number of sales. It is costing Airbus some $14 billion to develop its new super-jumbo jet, the 550-seat A380. To recoup those costs and break even, Airbus will have to sell at least 250 A380 planes. If Airbus can sell over 350 A380 planes, it will apparently be a profitable venture. However, total demand over the next 20 years for this class of aircraft is estimated to be somewhere between 400 and 600 units. Thus, the global market can probably only profitably support one producer of jet aircraft in the super-jumbo category. It follows that the European Union might come to dominate in the export of very large jet aircraft, primarily because a European based firm, Airbus, was the first to produce a 550-seat jet aircraft and realize scale economies. Other potential producers, such as Boeing, might be shut out of the market because they will lack the scale economies that Airbus will enjoy. By pioneering this market category, Airbus may have captured a *first mover advantage* based on *scale economies* that will be difficult for rivals to match and that will result in the European Union becoming the *leading exporter* of very large jet aircraft.

IMPLICATIONS OF NEW TRADE THEORY

New trade theory has important implications. The theory suggests that nations may benefit from trade even when they do not differ in resource endowments or technology. Trade allows a nation to specialize in the production of certain products, attaining scale economies and lowering the costs of producing those products, while buying products that it does not produce from other nations that specialize in the production of other products. By this mechanism, the variety of products available to consumers in each nation is increased, while the average costs of those products should fall, as should their price, freeing resources to produce other goods and services.

The theory also suggests that a country may predominate in the export of a good simply because it was lucky enough to have one or more firms among the first to produce that good. Because they are able to gain economies of scale, the first movers in an industry may get a lock on the world market that discourages subsequent entry. First movers' ability to benefit from increasing returns creates a barrier to entry. In the commercial aircraft industry, the fact that Boeing and Airbus are already in the industry and have the benefits of economies of scale discourages new entry and reinforces the dominance of America and Europe in the trade of midsized and large jet aircraft. This dominance is further reinforced because global demand may not be sufficient to profitably support another producer of midsized and large jet aircraft in the industry. So although Japanese firms might be able to compete in the market, they have decided not to enter the industry but to ally themselves as major subcontractors with primary producers (e.g., Mitsubishi Heavy Industries is a major subcontractor for Boeing on the 777 and 787 programs).

New trade theory is at variance with the Heckscher-Ohlin theory, which suggests that a country will predominate in the export of a product when it is particularly well endowed with those factors used intensively in its manufacture. New trade theorists argue that the United States is a major exporter of commercial jet aircraft not because it is better endowed with the factors of production required to manufacture aircraft, but because one of the first movers in the industry, Boeing, was a U.S. firm. The new trade theory is not at variance with the theory of comparative advantage. Economies of scale increase productivity. Thus, the new trade theory identifies an important source of comparative advantage.

This theory is quite useful in explaining trade patterns. Empirical studies seem to support the predictions of the theory that trade increases the specialization of production within an industry, increases the variety of products available to consumers, and results in lower average prices.[32] With regard to first-mover advantages and international trade, a study by Harvard business historian Alfred Chandler suggests that the existence of first-mover advantages is an important factor in explaining the dominance of firms from certain nations in specific industries.[33] The number of firms is very limited in many global industries, including the chemical industry, the heavy construction equipment industry, the heavy truck industry, the tire industry, the consumer electronics industry, the jet engine industry, and the computer software industry.

Perhaps the most contentious implication of the new trade theory is the argument that it generates for government intervention and strategic trade policy.[34] New trade theorists stress the role of luck, entrepreneurship, and innovation in giving a firm first mover advantages. According to this argument, the reason Boeing was the first mover in commercial jet aircraft manufacture—rather than firms like Great Britain's DeHavilland and Hawker Siddley, or Holland's Fokker, all of which could have been—was that Boeing was both lucky and innovative. One way Boeing was lucky is that DeHavilland shot itself in the foot when its Comet jet airliner, introduced two years earlier than Boeing's first jet airliner, the 707, was found to be full of serious technological flaws. Had DeHavilland not made some serious technological mistakes, Great Britain might have become the world's leading exporter of commercial jet aircraft. Boeing's innovativeness was demonstrated by its independent development of the technological know-how required to build a commercial jet airliner. Several new trade theorists have pointed out, however, that the U.S. government largely paid for Boeing's R&D; the 707 was a spin-off from a government-funded military program (the entry of Airbus into the industry was also supported by significant government subsidies). Herein is a rationale for government intervention: By the sophisticated and judicious use of subsidies, could a government increase the chances of its domestic firms becoming first movers in newly emerging industries, as the U.S. government apparently did with Boeing (and the European Union did with Airbus)? If this is possible, and the new trade theory suggests it might be, we have an economic rationale for a proactive trade policy that is at variance with the free trade prescriptions of the trade theories we have reviewed so far. We will consider the policy implications of this issue in Chapter 6.

National Competitive Advantage: Porter's Diamond

In 1990 Michael Porter of the Harvard Business School published the results of an intensive research effort that attempted to determine why some nations succeed and others fail in international competition.[35] Porter and his team looked at 100 industries in 10 nations. Like the work of the new trade theorists, Porter's work was driven by a belief that existing theories of international trade told only part of the story. For Porter, the essential task was to explain why a nation achieves international success in a particular industry. Why does Japan do so well in the automobile industry? Why does Switzerland excel in the production and export of precision instruments and pharmaceuticals? Why do Germany and the United States do so well in the chemical industry? These questions cannot be answered easily by the Heckscher-Ohlin theory, and the theory of comparative advantage offers only a partial explanation. The theory of comparative advantage would say that Switzerland excels in the production and export of precision instruments because it uses its resources very productively in these industries. Although this may be correct, this does not explain why Switzerland is more productive in this industry than Great Britain, Germany, or Spain. Porter tries to solve this puzzle.

Porter theorizes that four broad attributes of a nation shape the environment in which local firms compete, and these attributes promote or impede the creation of competitive advantage (see Figure 5.6). These attributes are

- *Factor endowments*—a nation's position in factors of production such as skilled labor or the infrastructure necessary to compete in a given industry.
- *Demand conditions*—the nature of home demand for the industry's product or service.
- *Relating and supporting industries*—the presence or absence of supplier industries and related industries that are internationally competitive.
- *Firm strategy, structure, and rivalry*—the conditions governing how companies are created, organized, and managed and the nature of domestic rivalry.

Porter speaks of these four attributes as constituting the *diamond*. He argues that firms are most likely to succeed in industries or industry segments where the diamond is most favorable. He also argues that the diamond is a mutually reinforcing system. The effect of one attribute is contingent on the state of others. For example, Porter argues that favorable demand conditions will not result in competitive advantage unless the state of rivalry is sufficient to cause firms to respond to them.

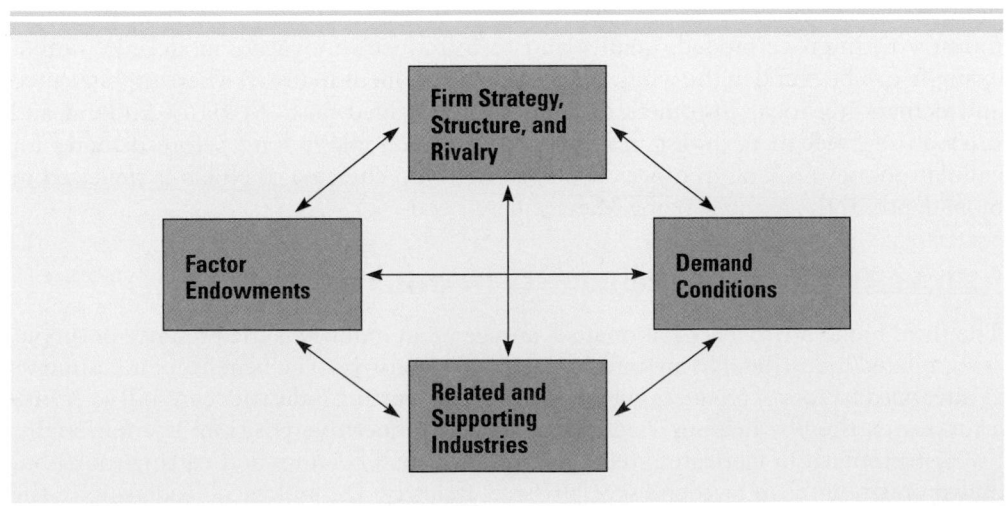

FIGURE 5.6

Determinants of National Competitive Advantage: Porter's Diamond

Porter maintains that two additional variables can influence the national diamond in important ways: chance and government. Chance events, such as major innovations, can reshape industry structure and provide the opportunity for one nation's firms to supplant another's. Government, by its choice of policies, can detract from or improve national advantage. For example, regulation can alter home demand conditions, antitrust policies can influence the intensity of rivalry within an industry, and government investments in education can change factor endowments.

FACTOR ENDOWMENTS

Factor endowments lie at the center of the Heckscher-Ohlin theory. While Porter does not propose anything radically new, he does analyze the characteristics of factors of production. He recognizes hierarchies among factors, distinguishing between *basic factors* (e.g., natural resources, climate, location, and demographics) and *advanced factors* (e.g., communication infrastructure, sophisticated and skilled labor, research facilities, and technological know-how). He argues that advanced factors are the most significant for competitive advantage. Unlike the naturally endowed basic factors, advanced factors are a product of investment by individuals, companies, and governments. Thus, government investments in basic and higher education, by improving the general skill and knowledge level of the population and by stimulating advanced research at higher education institutions, can upgrade a nation's advanced factors.

The relationship between advanced and basic factors is complex. Basic factors can provide an initial advantage that is subsequently reinforced and extended by investment in advanced factors. Conversely, disadvantages in basic factors can create pressures to invest in advanced factors. An obvious example of this phenomenon is Japan, a country that lacks arable land and mineral deposits and yet through investment has built a substantial endowment of advanced factors. Porter notes that Japan's large pool of engineers (reflecting a much higher number of engineering graduates per capita than almost any other nation) has been vital to Japan's success in many manufacturing industries.

DEMAND CONDITIONS

Porter emphasizes the role home demand plays in upgrading competitive advantage. Firms are typically most sensitive to the needs of their closest customers. Thus, the characteristics of home demand are particularly important in shaping the attributes of domestically made products and in creating pressures for innovation and quality. Porter argues that a nation's firms gain competitive advantage if their domestic consumers are sophisticated and demanding. Such consumers pressure local firms to meet high standards of product quality and to produce innovative products. Porter notes that Japan's sophisticated and knowledgeable buyers of cameras helped stimulate the Japanese camera industry to improve product quality and to introduce innovative models. A similar example can be found in the wireless telephone equipment industry, where sophisticated and demanding local customers in Scandinavia helped push Nokia of Finland and Ericsson of Sweden to invest in cellular phone technology long before demand for cellular phones took off in other developed nations. The case of Nokia is reviewed in more depth in the accompanying Management Focus.

RELATED AND SUPPORTING INDUSTRIES

The third broad attribute of national advantage in an industry is the presence of suppliers or related industries that are internationally competitive. The benefits of investments in advanced factors of production by related and supporting industries can spill over into an industry, thereby helping it achieve a strong competitive position internationally. Swedish strength in fabricated steel products (e.g., ball bearings and cutting tools) has drawn on strengths in Sweden's specialty steel industry. Technological leadership in the

U.S. semiconductor industry provided the basis for U.S. success in personal computers and several other technically advanced electronic products. Similarly, Switzerland's success in pharmaceuticals is closely related to its previous international success in the technologically related dye industry.

One consequence of this process is that successful industries within a country tend to be grouped into clusters of related industries. This was one of the most pervasive findings of Porter's study. One such cluster Porter identified was in the German textile and apparel sector, which included high-quality cotton, wool, synthetic fibers, sewing machine needles, and a wide range of textile machinery. Such clusters are important because valuable knowledge can flow between the firms within a geographic cluster, benefiting all within that cluster. Knowledge flows occur when employees move between firms within a region and when national industry associations bring employees from different companies together for regular conferences or workshops.[36]

FIRM STRATEGY, STRUCTURE, AND RIVALRY

The fourth broad attribute of national competitive advantage in Porter's model is the strategy, structure, and rivalry of firms within a nation. Porter makes two important points here. First, different nations are characterized by different management ideologies, which either help them or do not help them to build national competitive advantage. For example, Porter noted the predominance of engineers in top management at German and Japanese firms. He attributed this to these firms' emphasis on improving manufacturing processes and product design. In contrast, Porter noted a predominance of people with finance backgrounds leading many U.S. firms. He linked this to U.S. firms' lack of attention to improving manufacturing processes and product design. He argued that the dominance of finance led to an overemphasis on maximizing short-term financial returns. According to Porter, one consequence of these different management ideologies was a relative loss of U.S. competitiveness in those engineering-based industries where manufacturing processes and product design issues are all-important (e.g., the automobile industry).

Porter's second point is that there is a strong association between vigorous domestic rivalry and the creation and persistence of competitive advantage in an industry. Vigorous domestic rivalry induces firms to look for ways to improve efficiency, which makes them better international competitors. Domestic rivalry creates pressures to innovate, to improve quality, to reduce costs, and to invest in upgrading advanced factors. All this helps to create world-class competitors. Porter cites the case of Japan:

> Nowhere is the role of domestic rivalry more evident than in Japan, where it is all-out warfare in which many companies fail to achieve profitability. With goals that stress market share, Japanese companies engage in a continuing struggle to outdo each other. Shares fluctuate markedly. The process is prominently covered in the business press. Elaborate rankings measure which companies are most popular with university graduates. The rate of new product and process development is breathtaking.[37]

A similar point about the stimulating effects of strong domestic competition can be made with regard to the rise of Nokia of Finland to global preeminence in the market for cellular telephone equipment. For details, see the Management Focus.

Evaluating Porter's Theory

Porter contends that the degree to which a nation is likely to achieve international success in a certain industry is a function of the combined impact of factor endowments, domestic demand conditions, related and supporting industries, and domestic rivalry. He argues that the presence of all four components is usually required for this diamond to boost competitive performance (although there are exceptions). Porter also contends that government can influence each of the four components of the diamond—either

The Rise of Finland's Nokia

The wireless phone market is one of the great growth stories of the last decade. Starting from a very low base in 1990, annual global sales of wireless phones surged to reach around 900 million units in 2006. By the end of 2006, the number of wireless subscribers worldwide was closing in on 2 billion, up from less than 10 million in 1990. Nokia is one of the dominant players in the world market for mobile phones. Nokia's roots are in Finland, not normally a country that comes to mind when one talks about leading-edge technology companies. In the 1980s, Nokia was a rambling Finnish conglomerate with activities that embraced tire manufacturing, paper production, consumer electronics, and telecommunications equipment. By 2006, it had transformed itself into a focused telecommunications equipment manufacturer with a global reach, sales of over $40 billion, earnings of more than $5 billion, and a 34 percent share of the global market for wireless phones. How has this former conglomerate emerged to take a global leadership position in wireless telecommunications equipment? Much of the answer lies in the history, geography, and political economy of Finland and its Nordic neighbors.

In 1981 the Nordic nations cooperated to create the world's first international wireless telephone network. They had good reason to become pioneers: it cost far too much to lay down a traditional wire line telephone service in those sparsely populated and inhospitably cold countries. The same features made telecommunications all the more valuable: people driving through the Arctic winter and owners of remote northern houses needed a telephone to summon help if things went wrong. As a result, Sweden, Norway, and Finland became the first nations in the world to take wireless telecommunications seriously. They found, for example, that although it cost up to $800 per subscriber to bring a traditional wire line service to remote locations, the same locations could be linked by wireless cellular for only $500 per person. As a consequence, 12 percent of people in Scandinavia owned cellular phones by 1994, compared with less than 6 percent in the United States, the world's second most developed market. This lead continued over the next decade. By the end of 2006, 90 percent of the population in Finland owned a wireless phone, compared with 70 percent in the United States.

Nokia, a long-time telecommunications equipment supplier, was well positioned to take advantage of this development from the start, but other forces were also at work that helped Nokia develop its competitive edge. Unlike virtually every other developed nation, Finland has never had a national telephone monopoly. Instead, the country's telephone services have long been provided by about 50 or so autonomous local telephone companies whose elected boards set prices by referendum (which naturally means low prices). This army of independent and cost-conscious telephone service providers prevented Nokia from taking anything for granted in its home country. With typical Finnish pragmatism, its customers were willing to buy from the lowest-cost supplier, whether that was Nokia, Ericsson, Motorola, or some other company. This situation contrasted sharply with that prevailing in most developed nations until the late 1980s and early 1990s, where domestic telephone monopolies typically purchased equipment from a dominant local supplier or made it themselves. Nokia responded to this competitive pressure by doing everything possible to drive down its manufacturing costs while staying at the leading edge of wireless technology.

The consequences of these forces are clear. Nokia is now a leader in digital wireless technology. Many now regard Finland as the lead market for wireless telephone services. If you want to see the future of wireless, you don't go to New York or San Francisco; you go to Helsinki, where Finns use their wireless handsets not just to talk to each other but also to browse the Web, execute e-commerce transactions, control household heating and lighting systems, or purchase Coke from a wireless-enabled vending machine. Nokia has gained this lead because Scandinavia started switching to digital technology five years before the rest of the world.[38]

positively or negatively. Factor endowments can be affected by subsidies, policies toward capital markets, policies toward education, and so on. Government can shape domestic demand through local product standards or with regulations that mandate or influence buyer needs. Government policy can influence supporting and related industries through regulation and influence firm rivalry through such devices as capital market regulation, tax policy, and antitrust laws.

If Porter is correct, we would expect his model to predict the pattern of international trade that we observe in the real world. Countries should be exporting products from those industries where all four components of the diamond are favorable, while importing in those areas where the components are not favorable. Is he correct? We simply do not know. Porter's theory has not been subjected to detailed empirical testing. Much about the theory rings true, but the same can be said for the new trade theory, the theory of comparative advantage, and the Heckscher-Ohlin theory. It may be that each of these theories, which complement each other, explains something about the pattern of international trade.

IMPLICATIONS FOR MANAGERS

Why does all this matter for business? The theories discussed in this chapter have at least three main implications for international businesses: location implications, first-mover implications, and policy implications.

LOCATION

Underlying most of the theories we have discussed is the notion that different countries have particular advantages in different productive activities. Thus, from a profit perspective, it makes sense for a firm to disperse its productive activities to those countries where, according to the theory of international trade, they can be performed most efficiently. If design can be performed most efficiently in France, that is where design facilities should be located; if the manufacture of basic components can be performed most efficiently in Singapore, that is where they should be manufactured; and if final assembly can be performed most efficiently in China, that is where final assembly should be performed. The result is a global web of productive activities, with different activities being performed in different locations around the globe depending on considerations of comparative advantage, factor endowments, and the like. If the firm does not do this, it may find itself at a competitive disadvantage relative to firms that do.

Consider the production of a laptop computer, a process with four major stages: (1) basic research and development of the product design, (2) manufacture of standard electronic components (e.g., memory chips), (3) manufacture of advanced components (e.g., flat-top color display screens and microprocessors), and (4) final assembly. Basic R&D requires a pool of highly skilled and educated workers with good backgrounds in microelectronics. The two countries with a comparative advantage in basic microelectronics R&D and design are Japan and the United States, so most producers of laptop computers locate their R&D facilities in one or both of these countries. (Apple, IBM, Motorola, Texas Instruments, Toshiba, and Sony all have major R&D facilities in both Japan and the United States.)

The manufacture of standard electronic components is a capital-intensive process requiring semiskilled labor, and cost pressures are intense. The best locations for such activities today are places such as Taiwan, Malaysia, and South Korea. These countries have pools of relatively skilled, moderate-cost labor. Thus, many producers of laptop computers manufacture standard components, such as memory chips, at these locations.

The manufacture of advanced components such as microprocessors is a capital-intensive process requiring skilled labor. Because cost pressures are not so intense at this stage, these components can be—and are—manufactured in countries with high labor costs that also have pools of highly skilled labor (e.g., Japan and the United States).

Finally, assembly is a relatively labor-intensive process requiring only low-skilled labor, and cost pressures are intense. As a result, final assembly may be carried out in a country such as Mexico, which has an abundance of low-cost, low-skilled labor. A laptop computer produced by a U.S. manufacturer may be designed in California, have standard components produced in Taiwan and Singapore and advanced components produced in Japan and the United States, be assembled in Mexico, and be sold in the United States or elsewhere in the world. By dispersing production activities to different locations around the globe, the U.S. manufacturer is taking advantage of the differences between countries identified by the various theories of international trade.

FIRST-MOVER ADVANTAGES

According to the new trade theory, firms that establish a first-mover advantage with regard to the production of a particular new product may subsequently dominate global trade in that product. This is particularly true in industries where the global market can profitably support only a limited number of firms, such as the aerospace market, but early commitments also seem to be important in less concentrated industries such as the market for cellular telephone equipment (see the Management Focus on Nokia). For the individual firm, the clear message is that it pays to invest substantial financial resources in trying to build a first-mover, or early-mover, advantage, even if that means several years of losses before a new venture becomes profitable. The idea is to preempt the available demand, gain cost advantages related to volume, build an enduring brand ahead of later competitors, and, consequently, establish a long-term sustainable competitive advantage. Although the details of how to achieve this are beyond the scope of this book, many publications offer strategies for exploiting first-mover advantages and for avoiding the traps associated with pioneering a market (first-mover disadvantages).[39]

GOVERNMENT POLICY

The theories of international trade also matter to international businesses because firms are major players on the international trade scene. Business firms produce exports, and business firms import the products of other countries. Because of their pivotal role in international trade, businesses can exert a strong influence on government trade policy, lobbying to promote free trade or trade restrictions. The theories of international trade claim that promoting free trade is generally in the best interests of a country, although it may not always be in the best interest of an individual firm. Many firms recognize this and lobby for open markets.

For example, when the U.S. government announced its intention to place a tariff on Japanese imports of liquid crystal display (LCD) screens in the 1990s, IBM and Apple Computer protested strongly. Both IBM and Apple pointed out that (1) Japan was the lowest cost source of LCD screens, (2) they used these screens in their own laptop computers, and (3) the proposed tariff, by increasing the cost of LCD screens, would increase the cost of laptop computers produced by IBM and Apple, thus making them less competitive in the world market. In other words, the tariff, designed to protect U.S. firms, would be self-defeating. In response to these pressures, the U.S. government reversed its posture.

Unlike IBM and Apple, however, businesses do not always lobby for free trade. In the United States, for example, restrictions on imports of steel are the result of U.S. firms' direct pressure on the government. In some cases, the government has responded to pressure by getting foreign companies to agree to "voluntary" restrictions on their imports, using the implicit threat of more comprehensive formal trade barriers to get them to adhere to these agreements (historically, this has occurred in the automobile industry). In other cases, the government used what are called "antidumping" actions to justify tariffs on imports from other nations (these mechanisms will be discussed in detail in the next chapter).

As international trade theory predicts, many of these agreements have been self-defeating, such as the voluntary restriction on machine tool imports of 1985. Due to limited import competition from more efficient foreign suppliers, the prices of machine tools in the United States rose to higher levels than would have prevailed under free trade. Because machine tools are used throughout the manufacturing industry, the result was to increase the costs of U.S. manufacturing in general, creating a corresponding loss in world market competitiveness. Shielded from international competition by import barriers, the U.S. machine tool industry had no incentive to increase its efficiency. Consequently, it lost many of its export markets to more efficient foreign competitors. Because of this misguided action, the U.S. machine tool industry shrunk during the period when the agreement was in force. For anyone schooled in international trade theory, this was not surprising.[40] A similar scenario unfolded in the U.S. steel industry, where tariff barriers erected by the government in 2001 raised the cost of steel to important U.S. users, such as automobile companies and appliance makers, making their products less competitive.

Finally, Porter's theory of national competitive advantage also contains policy implications. Porter's theory suggests that it is in the best interest of business for a firm to invest in upgrading advanced factors of production; for example, to invest in better training for its employees and to increase its commitment to research and development. It is also in the best interests of business to lobby the government to adopt policies that have a favorable impact on each component of the national diamond. Thus, according to Porter, businesses should urge government to increase investment in education, infrastructure, and basic research (since all these enhance advanced factors) and to adopt policies that promote strong competition within domestic markets (since this makes firms stronger international competitors, according to Porter's findings).

CHAPTER SUMMARY

This chapter has reviewed a number of theories that explain why it is beneficial for a country to engage in international trade and has explained the pattern of international trade observed in the world economy. We have seen how the theories of Smith, Ricardo, and Heckscher-Ohlin all make strong cases for unrestricted free trade. In contrast, the mercantilist doctrine and, to a lesser extent, the new trade theory can be interpreted to support government intervention to promote exports through subsidies and to limit imports through tariffs and quotas. In explaining the pattern of international trade, the second objective of this chapter, we have seen that with the exception of mercantilism, which is silent on this issue, the different theories offer largely complementary explanations. Although no one theory may explain the apparent pattern of international trade, taken together, the theory of comparative advantage, the Heckscher-Ohlin theory, the product life-cycle theory, the new trade theory, and Porter's theory of national competitive advantage do suggest which factors are important. Comparative advantage tells us that productivity differences are important; Heckscher-Ohlin tells us that factor endowments matter; the product life-cycle

theory tells us that where a new product is introduced is important; the new trade theory tells us that increasing returns to specialization and first-mover advantages matter; and Porter tells us that all these factors may be important insofar as they impact the four components of the national diamond. The chapter made these major points:

1. Mercantilists argued that it was in a country's best interests to run a balance-of-trade surplus. They viewed trade as a zero-sum game, in which one country's gains cause losses for other countries.

2. The theory of absolute advantage suggests that countries differ in their ability to produce goods efficiently. The theory suggests that a country should specialize in producing goods in areas where it has an absolute advantage and import goods in areas where other countries have absolute advantages.

3. The theory of comparative advantage suggests that it makes sense for a country to specialize in producing those goods that it can produce most efficiently, while buying goods that it can

produce relatively less efficiently from other countries—even if that means buying goods from other countries that it could produce more efficiently itself.

4. The theory of comparative advantage suggests that unrestricted free trade brings about increased world production; that is, that trade is a positive-sum game.

5. The theory of comparative advantage also suggests that opening a country to free trade stimulates economic growth, which creates dynamic gains from trade. The empirical evidence seems to be consistent with this claim.

6. The Heckscher-Ohlin theory argues that the pattern of international trade is determined by differences in factor endowments. It predicts that countries will export those goods that make intensive use of locally abundant factors and will import goods that make intensive use of factors that are locally scarce.

7. The product life-cycle theory suggests that trade patterns are influenced by where a new product is introduced. In an increasingly integrated global economy, the product life-cycle theory seems to be less predictive than it once was.

8. New trade theory states that trade allows a nation to specialize in the production of certain goods, attaining scale economies and lowering the costs of producing those goods, while buying goods that it does not produce from other nations that are similarly specialized. By this

mechanism, the variety of goods available to consumers in each nation is increased, while the average costs of those goods should fall.

9. New trade theory also states that in those industries where substantial economies of scale imply that the world market will profitably support only a few firms, countries may predominate in the export of certain products simply because they had a firm that was a first mover in that industry.

10. Some new trade theorists have promoted the idea of strategic trade policy. The argument is that government, by the sophisticated and judicious use of subsidies, might be able to increase the chances of domestic firms becoming first movers in newly emerging industries.

11. Porter's theory of national competitive advantage suggests that the pattern of trade is influenced by four attributes of a nation: (a) factor endowments, (b) domestic demand conditions, (c) relating and supporting industries, and (d) firm strategy, structure, and rivalry.

12. Theories of international trade are important to an individual business firm primarily because they can help the firm decide where to locate its various production activities.

13. Firms involved in international trade can and do exert a strong influence on government policy toward trade. By lobbying government, business firms can promote free trade or trade restrictions.

Critical Thinking and Discussion Questions

1. Mercantilism is a bankrupt theory that has no place in the modern world. Discuss.

2. Is free trade fair? Discuss!

3. Unions in developed nations often oppose imports from low-wage countries and advocate trade barriers to protect jobs from what they often characterize as "unfair" import competition. Is such competition "unfair"? Do you think that this argument is in the best interests of (a) the unions, (b) the people they represent, and/or (c) the country as a whole?

4. What are the potential costs of adopting a free trade regime? Do you think governments should do anything to reduce these costs? What?

5. Reread the Country Focus feature, "Is China a Neo-mercantilist Nation?"

   a. Do you think China is pursuing an economic policy that can be characterized as neo-mercantilist?

   b. What should the United States, and other countries, do about this?

6. Reread the Country Focus feature on moving white collar jobs offshore.

   a. Who benefits from outsourcing skilled white color jobs to developing nations? Who are the losers?

   b. Will developing nations like the United States suffer from the loss of high-skilled and high-paying jobs to countries like India and China?

   c. Is there a difference between transferring high-paying white collar jobs, such as computer programming and accounting, and low-paying blue collar jobs to developing nations? If so, what is the difference, and should government do anything to stop the flow of white collar jobs out of the country to countries like India?

7. Drawing upon the new trade theory and Porter's theory of national competitive advantage, outline the case for government policies that would build national competitive advantage in biotechnology. What kinds of policies would you recommend the government adopt? Are these policies at variance with the basic free trade philosophy?

8. The world's poorest countries are at a competitive disadvantage in every sector of their economies. They have little to export. They have no capital; their land is of poor quality; they often have too many people given available work opportunities; and they are poorly educated. Free trade cannot possibly be in the interests of such nations! Discuss.

Research Task globalEDGE
http://globalEDGE.msu.edu

Use the globalEDGE™ site to complete the following exercises:

1. The *WTO's International Trade Statistics* is an annual report that provides comprehensive, comparable, and updated statistics on trade in merchandise and commercial services. This report allows for an assessment of world trade flows by country, region, and main product or service categories. Using the most recent statistics available, identify the top five countries that lead in the export and import of merchandise, respectively.

2. Food is an integral part of understanding different countries, cultures, and lifestyles. In fact, your company is interested in importing Australian seafood to the United States. As part of the initial analysis, you want to identify the strengths of the Australian seafood industry. One resource you might find useful is the Australian Trade Commission Web site. Provide a short description of the current status of Australian seafood exports by variety, and also a list of the top countries importing Australian seafood.

CLOSING CASE

Trade in Information Technology and U.S. Economic Growth

Entrepreneurial enterprises in the United States invented most of the information technology that we use today, including computer and communications hardware, software, and services. In the 1960s and 1970s, companies like IBM and DEC, which developed first mainframe and then midrange computers, led the information technology sector. In the 1980s, the locus of growth in the sector shifted to personal computers and the innovations of companies like Intel, Apple, IBM, Dell, and Compaq, which helped develop the mass market for the product. Along the way, however, something happened to this uniquely American industry—it started to move the production of hardware offshore.

In the early 1980s production of "commodity components" for computers such as dynamic random access memory chips (DRAMs) migrated to low-cost producers in Japan, and then later to Taiwan and Korea. Soon hard disk drives, display screens, keyboards, computer mice, and a host of other components were outsourced to foreign manufacturers. By the early 2000s, American factories were specializing in making only the highest value

components, such as the microprocessors made by Intel, and in final assembly (Dell, for example, assembles PCs at two North American facilities). Just about every other component was made overseas—because it cost less to do so. There was a lot of hand-wringing among politicians and journalists about the possible negative implication for the U.S. economy of this trend. According to the critics, high-paying manufacturing jobs in the information technology sector were being exported to foreign producers.

Was this trend bad for the U.S. economy, as the critics claimed? According to research, the globalization of production made information technology hardware about 20 percent less expensive than it would otherwise have been. The price declines supported additional investments in information technology by businesses and households. Because they were getting cheaper, computers diffused throughout the United States faster. In turn, the rapid diffusion of information technology translated into faster productivity growth as businesses used computers to streamline process. Between 1995 and 2002, productivity grew by 2.8 percent per annum in the

United States, well above the historic norm. According to calculations by academic researchers, some 0.3 percent per annum of this growth could be attributed directly to the reduced prices of information technology hardware made possible by the move to offshore production. In turn, the 0.3 percent per annum gain in productivity over 1995 to 2002 resulted in an additional $230 billion in accumulated gross domestic product in the United States. In short, some argue that the American economy grew at a faster rate precisely because production of information technology hardware was shifted to foreigners.

There is also evidence that the reduced price for hardware made possible by international trade created a boom in jobs in two related industries—computer software and services. During the 1990s the number of information technology jobs in the United States grew by 22 percent, twice the rate of job creation in the economy as a whole, and this at a time when manufacturing information technology jobs were moving offshore. The growth could partly be attributed to robust demand for computer software and services within the United States, and partly due to demand for software and services from foreigners, including those same foreigners who were now making much of the hardware. In sum,

some argue that buying computer hardware from foreigners, as opposed to making it in the United States, had a significant *positive* impact upon the U.S. economy that outweighed any adverse effects from job losses in the manufacturing sector.[41]

Case Discussion Questions

1. During the 1990s and 2000s computer hardware companies in certain developed nations progressively moved the production of hardware components offshore, often outsourcing them to producers in developing nations. What does international trade theory suggest about the implications of this trend for economic growth in those developed nations?

2. Is the experience of the United States, as described in the case, consistent with the predictions of international trade theory?

3. What are the implications of the theory and data for (a) government policy in advanced nations such as the United States, and (b) the strategy of a firm in the computer industry, such as Dell or Apple Computer?

Notes

1. Sources: G. Thompson, "Behind Roses' Beauty, Poor and Ill Workers," *The New York Times*, February 13, 2003, pp. A1, A27; J. Stuart, "You've Come a Long Way Baby," *The Independent*, February 14, 2003, p. 1; V. Marino, "By Any Other Name, It's Usually a Rosa," *The New York Times*, May 11, 2003, p. A9; A. DePalma, "In Trade Issue, the Pressure Is on Flowers," *The New York Times*, January 24, 2002, p. 1; and "The Search for Roses without Thorns," *The Economist*, February 18, 2006, p. 38.

2. H. W. Spiegel, *The Growth of Economic Thought* (Durham, NC: Duke University Press, 1991).

3. M. Solis, "The Politics of Self-Restraint: FDI Subsidies and Japanese Mercantilism," *The World Economy* 26 (February 2003), pp. 153–70.

4. A. Browne, "China's Wild Swings Can Roil the Global Economy," *The Wall Street Journal*, October 24, 2005, p. A2; S. H. Hanke, "Stop the Mercantilists," *Forbes*, June 20, 2005, p. 164; G. Dyer and A. Balls, "Dollar Threat as China Signals Shift," *Financial Times*, January 6, 2006, p. 1; T. Annett, "Righting the Balance," *The Wall Street Journal*, January 10, 2007, p. 15.

5. S. Hollander, *The Economics of David Ricardo* (Buffalo: The University of Toronto Press, 1979).

6. D. Ricardo, *The Principles of Political Economy and Taxation* (Homewood, IL: Irwin, 1967; first published in 1817).

7. For example, R. Dornbusch, S. Fischer, and P. Samuelson, "Comparative Advantage: Trade and Payments in a Ricardian Model with a Continuum of Goods," *American Economic Review* 67 (December 1977), pp. 823–39.

8. B. Balassa, "An Empirical Demonstration of Classic Comparative Cost Theory," *Review of Economics and Statistics*, 1963, pp. 231–38.

9. See P. R. Krugman, "Is Free Trade Passé?" *Journal of Economic Perspectives* 1 (Fall 1987), pp. 131–44.

10. P. Samuelson, "Where Ricardo and Mill Rebut and Confirm Arguments of Mainstream Economists Supporting Globalization," *Journal of Economic Perspectives* 18(3) (Summer 2004), pp. 135–46.

11. P. Samuelson, "The Gains from International Trade Once Again," *Economic Journal* 72 (1962), pp. 820–29.

12. S. Lohr, "An Elder Challenges Outsourcing's Orthodoxy," *The New York Times*, September 9, 2004, p. C1.

13. P. Samuelson, "Where Ricardo and Mill Rebut and Confirm Arguments of Mainstream Economists Supporting Globalization," *Journal of Economic Perspectives* 18 (3) (Summer 2004), p. 143.

14. See A. Dixit and G. Grossman, "Samuelson Says Nothing about Trade Policy," Princeton University, 2004, accessed from http://www.princeton.edu/~dixitak/home/.

15. J. Bhagwati, A. Panagariya, and T. N. Sirinivasan, "The Muddles over Outsourcing," *Journal of Economic Perspectives* 18(4) (Fall 2004), pp. 93–114.

16. Sources: P. Engardio, A. Bernstein, and M. Kripalani, "Is Your Job Next?" *Business Week*, February 3, 2003, pp. 50–60; "America's Pain, India's Gain," *The Economist*, January 11, 2003, p. 57; M. Schroeder and T. Aeppel, "Skilled Workers Mount Opposition to Free Trade, Swaying Politicians," *The Wall Street Journal*, October 10, 2003, pp. A1, A11.

17. For example, J. D. Sachs and A. Warner, "Economic Reform and the Process of Global Integration," *Brookings Papers on Economic Activity*, 1995, pp. 1–96; J. A. Frankel and D. Romer, "Does Trade Cause Growth?" *American Economic Review* 89, no. 3 (June 1999), pp. 379–99; and D. Dollar and A. Kraay, "Trade, Growth and Poverty," Working Paper, Development Research Group, World Bank, June 2001. Also, for an accessible discussion of the relationship between free trade and economic growth, see T. Taylor, "The Truth about Globalization," *Public Interest*, Spring 2002, pp. 24–44.

18. Sachs and Warner, "Economic Reform and the Process of Global Integration."

19. Ibid., pp. 35–36.

20. R. Wacziarg and K. H. Welch, "Trade Liberalization and Growth: New Evidence," NBER Working Paper Series Number 10152, December 2003.

21. Frankel and Romer, "Does Trade Cause Growth?"

22. A recent skeptical review of the empirical work on the relationship between trade and growth questions these results. See F. Rodriguez and D. Rodrik, "Trade Policy and Economic Growth: A Skeptic's Guide to the Cross-National Evidence," *National Bureau of Economic Research*, Working Paper Series Number 7081, April 1999. Even these authors, however, cannot find any evidence that trade hurts economic growth or income levels.

23. B. Ohlin, *Interregional and International Trade* (Cambridge: Harvard University Press, 1933). For a summary, see R. W. Jones and J. P. Neary, "The Positive Theory of International Trade," in R. W. Jones and P. B. Kenen, eds. *Handbook of International Economics* (Amsterdam: North Holland, 1984).

24. W. Leontief, "Domestic Production and Foreign Trade: The American Capital Position Re-Examined," *Proceedings of the American Philosophical Society* 97 (1953), pp. 331–49.

25. R. M. Stern and K. Maskus, "Determinants of the Structure of U.S. Foreign Trade," *Journal of International Economics* 11 (1981), pp. 207–44.

26. See H. P. Bowen, E. E. Leamer, and L. Sveikayskas, "Multicountry, Multifactor Tests of the Factor Abundance Theory," *American Economic Review* 77 (1987), pp. 791–809.

27. D. Trefler, "The Case of the Missing Trade and Other Mysteries," *American Economic Review* 85 (December 1995), pp. 1029–46.

28. D. R. Davis and D. E. Weinstein, "An Account of Global Factor Trade," *American Economic Review*, December 2001, pp. 1423–52.

29. R. Vernon, "International Investments and International Trade in the Product Life Cycle," *Quarterly Journal of Economics*, May 1966, pp. 190–207, and R. Vernon and L. T. Wells, *The Economic Environment of International Business*, 4th ed. (Englewood Cliffs, NJ: Prentice Hall, 1986).

30. For a good summary of this literature, see E. Helpman and P. Krugman, *Market Structure and Foreign Trade: Increasing Returns, Imperfect Competition, and the International Economy* (Boston: MIT Press, 1985). Also see P. Krugman, "Does the New Trade Theory Require a New Trade Policy? *World Economy*, 15(4), 1992, pp. 423–41.

31. M. B. Lieberman and D. B. Montgomery, "First-Mover Advantages," *Strategic Management Journal* 9 (Summer 1988), pp. 41–58, and W. T. Robinson and Sungwook Min, "Is the First to Market the First to Fail?" *Journal of Marketing Research* 29 (2002), pp. 120–28.

32. J. R. Tybout, "Plant and Firm Level Evidence on New Trade Theories," *National Bureau of Economic Research*, Working Paper Series Number 8418, August 2001, available at http://www.nber.org; S. Deraniyagala and B. Fine, "New Trade Theory versus Old Trade Policy: A Continuing Enigma," *Cambridge Journal of Economics* 25 (November 2001), pp. 809–25.

33. A. D. Chandler, *Scale and Scope* (New York: Free Press, 1990).

34. Krugman, "Does the New Trade Theory Require a New Trade Policy?"

35. M. E. Porter, *The Competitive Advantage of Nations* (New York: Free Press, 1990). For a good review of this book, see R. M. Grant, "Porter's Competitive Advantage of Nations: An Assessment," *Strategic Management Journal* 12 (1991), pp. 535–48.

36. B. Kogut, ed., *Country Competitiveness: Technology and the Organizing of Work* (New York: Oxford University Press, 1993).

37. Porter, *The Competitive Advantage of Nations*, p. 121.

38. Sources: Lessons from the Frozen North," *Economist*, October 8, 1994, pp. 76–77; "A Finnish Fable," *Economist*, October 14, 2000; D. O'Shea and K. Fitchard, "The First 3 Billion Is Always the Hardest," *Wireless Review* 22 (September 2005), pp 25–31; P. Taylor, "Big Names Dominate in Mobile Phones," *Financial Times*, September 29, 2006, p. 26; and Nokia Web site at www.nokia.com.

39. Lieberman and Montgomery, "First-Mover Advantages." See also Robinson and Min, "Is the First to Market the First to Fail?"; W. Boulding and M. Christen, "First Mover Disadvantage," *Harvard Business Review*, October 2001, pp. 20–21; and R. Agarwal and M. Gort, "First Mover Advantage and the Speed of Competitive Entry," *Journal of Law and Economics* 44 (2001), pp. 131–59.

40. C. A. Hamilton, "Building Better Machine Tools," *Journal of Commerce*, October 30, 1991, p. 8, and "Manufacturing Trouble," *The Economist*, October 12, 1991, p. 71.

41. Sources: (1) C. L. Mann, "Globalization of IT Services and White Collar Jobs," International Economic Policy Briefs, *Institute of International Economics*, December 2003. (2) A. Bernstein, "Shaking Up Trade Theory," *Business Week*, December 6, 2004, pp 116–120. (3) "Semiconductor Trade: A Wafer Thin Case," *The Economist*, July 27, 1996, pp. 53–54. (4) K. J. Stiroh, "Information Technology and the U.S. Productivity Revival," *Federal Reserve Bank* of New York, January 2001.

42. J. W. Peters, "U.S. Trade Deficit Grew to Another Record in 06," *The New York Times*, February 14, 2007, p. 1.

43. P. Krugman, *The Age of Diminished Expectations* (Cambridge, MA: MIT Press, 1990).

44. D. Griswold, "Are Trade Deficits a Drag on U.S. Economic Growth," *Free Trade Bulletin*, March 12, 2007, Cato Institute; O. Blanchard, "Current Account Deficits in Rich Countries," NBER Working Paper Number 12925, February 2007.

45. S. Edwards, "The U.S. Current Account Deficit: Gradual Correction or Abrupt Adjustment?" NBER Working Paper Number, 12154, April 2006.

Appendix: International Trade and the Balance of Payments

International trade involves the sale of goods and services to residents in other countries (exports) and the purchase of goods and services from residents in other countries (imports). A country's **balance-of-payments accounts** keep track of the payments to and receipts from other countries for a particular time period. These include payments to foreigners for imports of goods and service, and receipts from foreigners for goods and services exported to them. Table A1 provides a summary copy of the U.S. balance-of-payments accounts for 2006. Any transaction resulting in a payment to other countries is entered in the balance-of-payments accounts as a debit and given a negative (−) sign. Any transaction resulting in a receipt from other countries is entered as a credit and given a positive (+) sign. In this appendix we briefly describe the form of the balance-of-payments accounts, and we discuss whether a current account

deficit, often a cause of much concern in the popular press, is something to worry about.

Balance-of-Payments Accounts

Balance-of-payments accounts are divided into three main sections: the current account, the capital account, and the financial account (to confuse matters, what is now called the *capital account* was until recently part of the current account, and the financial account used to be called the capital account). The **current account** records transactions that pertain to three categories, all of which can be seen in Table A1. The first category, *goods*, refers to the export or import of physical goods (e.g., agricultural foodstuffs, autos, computers, chemicals).

Current Account	$ Millions
Exports of Goods, Services, and Income Receipts	2,058,836
Goods	1,023,689
Services	413,127
Income receipts	622,020
Imports of Goods, Services, and Income Payments	−2,831,369
Goods	−1,859,655
Services	−342,428
Income payments	−629,286
Unilateral Current Transfers (net)	−84,122
Current Account Balance	−856,655
CAPITAL ACCOUNT	
Capital Account Transactions (net)	−3,914
FINANCIAL ACCOUNT	
U.S. Owned Assets Abroad, net	−1,045,760
U.S. official reserve assets	2,374
U.S. government assets	5,219
U.S. private assets	−1,053,353
Foreign Owned Assets in the United States	1,764,909
Foreign official assets in the United States	300,510
Other foreign assets in the United States	1,464,399
Statistical Discrepancy	141,419

TABLE 5.A1

United States Balance-of-Payments Accounts, 2006 ($ millions)

Source: Bureau of Economic Analysis.

The second category is the export or import of *services* (e.g., intangible products such as banking and insurance services). The third category, *income receipts and payments*, refers to income from foreign investments and payments that have to be made to foreigners investing in a country. For example, if a U.S. citizen owns a share of a Finnish company and receives a dividend payment of $5, that payment shows up on the U.S. current account as the receipt of $5 of investment income. Also included in the current account are unilateral current transfers, such as U.S. government grants to foreigners (including foreign aid), and private payments to foreigners (such as when a foreign worker in the United States sends money to his or her home country).

A **current account deficit** occurs when a country imports more goods, services, and income than it exports. A **current account surplus** occurs when a country exports more goods, services, and income than it imports. Table A1 shows that in 2006 the United States ran a current account deficit of −$856,655. This is often a headline grabbing figure that is widely reported in the news media. In recent years the U.S. current account deficit has been getting steadily larger, primarily due to the fact that America imports far more physical goods than it exports (you will notice that America actually runs a surplus on trade in services and is close to balanced on income payments).

Figure A1 shows how the U.S. current account position has changed in recent years. The 2006 current account deficit was the largest on record and was equivalent to around 6.5 percent of the country's GDP. Many people find this figure disturbing, the common assumption being that growing imports of goods displace domestic production, cause unemployment, and reduce the growth of the United States economy. For example, *The New York Times* responded to the record current account deficit in 2006 by stating that

A growing trade deficit acts as a drag on overall economic growth. Economists said that they expect that, in light of the new numbers, the government will have to revise its estimate of the nation's fourth quarter gross domestic product to show slightly slower expansion.[42]

However, the issue is somewhat more complex than implied by statements like this. Fully understanding the implications of a large and persistent deficit requires that we look at the rest of the balance-of-payments accounts.

The **capital account** records one-time changes in the stock of assets. As noted above, until recently this item was included in the current account. The capital account

FIGURE 5.A1

Current Account
Balance and Its
Components

Source: U.S. Bureau of Economic
Analysis (http://www.bea.gov/
international/index.htm).

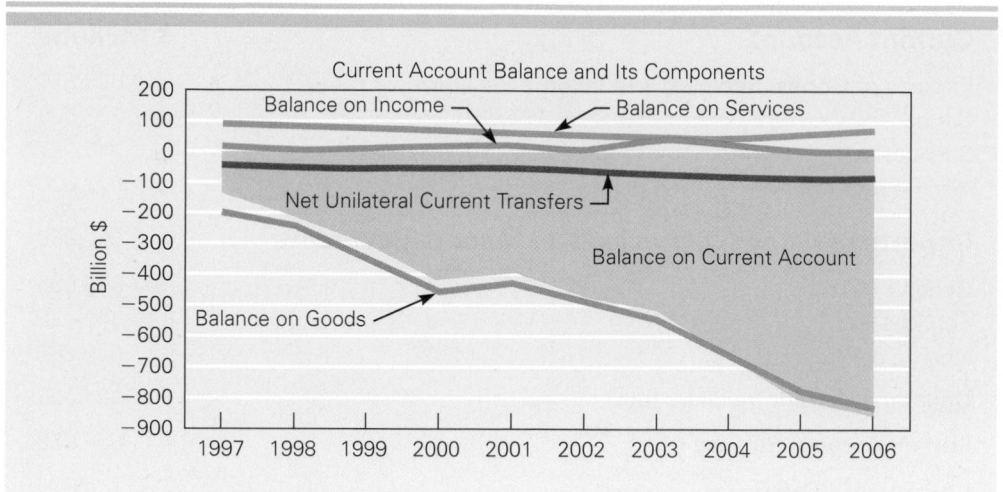

includes capital transfers, such as debt forgiveness and migrants transfers (the goods and financial assets that accompany migrants as they enter or leave the country). In the big scheme of things, this is a relatively small figure amounting to $3.914 billion in 2006.

The **financial account** (formerly the capital account) records transactions that involve the purchase or sale of assets. Thus, when a German firm purchases stock in a U.S. company or buys a U.S. bond, the transaction enters the U.S. balance of payments as a credit on the capital account. This is because capital is flowing into the country. When capital flows out of the United States, it enters the capital account as a debit.

The financial account is comprised of a number of elements. The net change in U.S.-owned assets abroad includes the change in assets owned by the U.S. government (U.S. official reserve assets and U.S. government assets) and the change in assets owned by private individuals and corporations. As can be seen from Table A1, in 2006 there was a −$1,045 billion reduction in U.S. assets owned abroad, primarily due to a $1,053 billion fall in the amount of foreign assets owned by U.S. corporations and individuals. In other words, private entities in the United States were net sellers of foreign assets in 2006, including foreign stocks, bonds, and real estate that they held.

Also included in the financial account are foreign-owned assets in the United States. These are divided into assets owned by foreign governments (foreign official assets) and assets owed by other foreign entities such as corporations and individuals (other foreign assets in the United States). As can be seen, in 2006 foreigners increased their holdings of U.S. assets, including treasury bills, corporate stocks and bonds, and direct investments in the United States, by $1,765 billion. Some $301 billion of this was due to an increase in the holding of U.S. assets by foreign governments, with the remainder

being due to investments by private corporations and individuals in U.S. assets.

It is important at this point to understand that a basic principle of balance-of-payments accounting is double-entry bookkeeping. Every international transaction automatically enters the balance of payments twice—once as a credit and once as a debit. Imagine that you purchase a car produced in Japan by Toyota for $20,000. Since your purchase represents a payment to another country for goods, it will enter the balance of payments as a debit on the current account. Toyota now has the $20,000 and must do something with it. If Toyota deposits the money at a U.S. bank, Toyota has purchased a U.S. asset—a bank deposit worth $20,000—and the transaction will show up as a $20,000 credit on the financial account. Or Toyota might deposit the cash in a Japanese bank in return for Japanese yen. Now the Japanese bank must decide what to do with the $20,000. Any action that it takes will ultimately result in a credit for the U.S. balance of payments. For example, if the bank lends the $20,000 to a Japanese firm that uses it to import personal computers from the United States, then the $20,000 must be credited to the U.S. balance-of-payments current account. Or the Japanese bank might use the $20,000 to purchase U.S. government bonds, in which case it will show up as a credit on the U.S. balance-of-payments financial account.

Thus, any international transaction automatically gives rise to two offsetting entries in the balance of payments. Because of this, *the sum of the current account balance, the capital account, and the financial account balance should always add up to zero*. In practice, this does not always occur due to the existence of "statistical discrepancies," the source of which need not concern us here (note that in 2006 the statistical discrepancy amounted to $141 billion).

Does the Current Account Deficit Matter?

As discussed above, there is some concern when a country is running a deficit on the current account of their balance of payments.[43] In recent years a number of rich countries, including most notably the United States, have run persistent and growing current account deficits. When a country runs a current account deficit, the money that flows to other countries can then be used by those countries to purchase assets in the deficit country. Thus, when the United States runs a trade deficit with China, the Chinese use the money that they receive from U.S. consumers to purchase U.S. assets such as stocks, bonds, and the like. Put another way, a deficit on the current account is financed by selling assets to other countries; that is, by a surplus on the financial account. Thus, the persistent U.S. current account deficit is being financed by a steady sale of U.S. assets (stocks, bonds, real estate, and whole corporations) to other countries. In short, countries that run current account deficits become net debtors.

For example, as a result of financing its current account deficit through asset sales, the United States must deliver a stream of interest payments to foreign bondholders, rents to foreign landowners, and dividends to foreign stockholders. One might argue that such payments to foreigners drain resources from a country and limit the funds available for investment within the country. Since investment within a country is necessary to stimulate economic growth, a persistent current account deficit can choke off a country's future economic growth. This is the basis of the argument that persistent deficits are bad for an economy.

However, things are not this simple. For one thing, in an era of global capital markets money is efficiently directed toward its highest value uses—and over the last quarter of a century many of the highest value uses of capital have been in the United States. So even though capital is flowing out of the United States in the form of payments to foreigners, much of that capital finds its way right back into the country to fund productive investments in the United States. In short, it is not clear that the current account deficit chokes off U.S. economic growth. In fact, the U.S. economy has grown at an impressive rate over the last 25 years, despite running a persistent current account deficit, and despite financing that deficit by selling U.S. assets to foreigners. This is precisely because foreigners reinvest much of the income earned from U.S. assets, and from exports to the United States, right back into the United States. This revisionist view, which has gained in popularity in recent years, suggests that a persistent current account deficit might not be the drag on economic growth it was once thought to be.[44]

Having said this, there is still a nagging fear that at some point the appetite that foreigners have for U.S. assets might decline. If foreigners suddenly reduce their investments in the United States, what would happen? In short, instead of reinvesting the dollars they earn from exports and investment in the United States back into the country, they would sell those dollars for another currency, European euros or Japanese yen for example, and invest in euro- and yen-denominated assets instead. This would lead to a fall in the value of the dollar on foreign exchange markets, which in turn would increase the price of imports, and lower the price of U.S. exports, making them more competitive. This should reduce the overall level of the current account deficit. Thus in the long run the persistent U.S. current account deficit could be correct via a reduction in the value of the U.S. dollar. The concern is that such adjustments may not be smooth. Rather than a controlled decline in the value of the dollar, the dollar might suddenly lose a significant amount of its value in a very short time, precipitating a "dollar crisis."[45] Since the U.S. dollar is the world's major reserve currency, and it is held by many foreign governments and banks, any dollar crisis could deliver a body blow to the world economy and at the very least trigger a global economic slowdown. That would not be a good thing.

United States Cotton Subsidies and World Trade

Way back in the 1930s in the middle of the Great Depression the United States government began providing subsidies to farmers. They have been receiving them ever since. The subsidies are currently running at around $20 billion annually. The largest single recipients have been cotton farmers. In 2005, U.S. cotton farmers received $5 billion in subsidies—and that on a crop that was only worth $4 billion! In total, subsidies to cotton farmers amounted to $19.1 billion between 1995 and 2005. Moreover, these payments are skewed toward large farmers. Between 1995 and 2005 the top 10 percent of recipients received some 81 percent of all payments, or $15.5 billion.

The subsidies for cotton farmers are a testament to the political lobbying power of the National Cotton Council of America, which represents farmers in the cotton producing states. Without the subsidies there is little doubt that many American cotton farmers would not be able to compete in world markets. According to recent data, the average cost to produce a pound of cotton in the United States is almost three times higher than in other major cotton producing countries, such as China, Brazil, and the African nations of Benin and Mali. By shielding U.S. farmers from international competition, critics argue that U.S. cotton subsidies result in overproduction, which depresses the world price for cotton. In the last 10 years, there has been a persistent global surplus of cotton, which has driven down the average price per pound from as high as $1.20 in mid-1995 to only 65 cents a pound in mid-2006, lower than many U.S. cotton farmers' costs of production.

The impact of falling prices on a developing country like the African nations of Benin and Mali can be particularly harsh. One study estimated that in Benin, where 95 percent of rural households live on less than $1 a day, a 40 percent reduction in the price of cotton would reduce income to cotton growers by 21 percent, which in turn would cause an estimated 334,000 people in Benin

The Political Economy of International Trade

LEARNING OBJECTIVES
After you have read this chapter you should:

LO¹ Describe the policy instruments used by governments to influence international trade flows.

LO² Understand why governments sometimes intervene in international trade.

LO³ Articulate the arguments against strategic trade policy.

LO⁴ Describe the development of the world trading system and the current trade issue.

LO⁵ Explain the implications for managers of developments in the world trading system.

to fall below the poverty line. Since the world price of cotton has fallen by almost half since 1995, and assuming that U.S. cotton subsidies caused at least some of that reduction, the data suggest that U.S. subsidies contributed significantly to economic devastation in very poor cotton-producing nations. Indeed, some estimates suggest that Benin's losses due to low cotton prices caused by U.S. subsidies and excess production exceeded the U.S. foreign aid that the country received.

In the early 2000s, Brazil decided to file a complaint against the United States in the World Trade Organization, to which both the United States and Brazil belong (Benin was a third party to the dispute). The Brazilians claimed that U.S. subsidies distorted world trade in cotton and caused harm to efficient producers in Brazil and elsewhere. In a landmark ruling, in March 2005 the World Trade Organization condemned U.S. subsidies and required the U.S. government to remove them. The U.S. responded by removing a program that compensated U.S. cotton mills and exporters for buying U.S. cotton, but the majority of subsidies were left intact. According to Oxfam, a development charity based in the United Kingdom, the U.S. reforms touched programs accounting for less than 10 percent of all the subsidies received by U.S. cotton farmers.

In late 2006, Brazil requested that the World Trade Organization establish a compliance panel to investigate whether the United States scrapped its subsidies as required by the March 2005 ruling. If the WTO finds against the United States, Brazil could seek retaliatory sanctions, imposing duties of up to $3 billion on U.S. goods exported to Brazil. The United States immediately went on the defensive, arguing that "The United States has gone to extraordinary lengths to implement recommendations and rulings. Given all of these changes, there is no basis for Brazil's request for a compliance panel." The WTO, however, overruled American objections and started a formal investigation.[1]

Introduction

Our review of the classical trade theories of Smith, Ricardo, and Heckscher-Ohlin in Chapter 5 showed that in a world without trade barriers, trade patterns are determined by the relative productivity of different factors of production in different countries. Countries will specialize in products that they can make most efficiently, while importing products that they can produce less efficiently. Chapter 5 also laid out the intellectual case for free trade. Remember, **free trade** refers to a situation in which a government does not attempt to restrict what its citizens can buy from or sell to another country. As we saw in Chapter 5, the theories of Smith, Ricardo, and Heckscher-Ohlin predict that the consequences of free trade include both static economic gains (because free trade supports a higher level of domestic consumption and more efficient utilization of resources) and dynamic economic gains (because free trade stimulates economic growth and the creation of wealth).

In this chapter, we look at the political reality of international trade. Although many nations are nominally committed to free trade, they tend to intervene in international trade to protect the interests of politically important groups or promote the interests of key domestic producers. The opening case illustrates the nature of such political realities. In the United States agricultural subsidies have helped to protect relatively inefficient cotton farmers from being exposed to the full forces of competition in the global market-place. The subsidies remain in place due to the political influence that cotton farmers exert on the United States Congress. This is unfortunate, for as the case makes clear, the subsidies given to U.S. cotton producers have stimulated overproduction in the United States, which has driven down the price of cotton on world markets, impoverishing poor nations like Benin and Mali for whom cotton is a major source of foreign income.

In this chapter, we explore the political and economic reasons that governments have for intervening in international trade. When governments intervene, they often do so by restricting imports of goods and services into their nation, while adopting policies that promote domestic production and exports (the subsidies given to American cotton farmers are in a sense an export promotion strategy since the excess U.S. production is typically sold abroad). Normally their motives are to protect domestic producers and jobs from foreign competition while increasing the foreign market for products of domestic producers. However, in recent years, social issues have intruded into the decision-making calculus. In the United States, for example, a movement is growing to ban imports of goods from countries that do not abide by the same labor, health, and environmental regulations as the United States.

We start this chapter by describing the range of policy instruments that governments use to intervene in international trade. This is followed by a detailed review of the various political and economic motives that governments have for intervention. In the third section of this chapter, we consider how the case for free trade stands up in view of the various justifications given for government intervention in international trade. Then we look at the emergence of the modern international trading system, which is based on the General Agreement on Tariffs and Trade and its successor, the WTO. The GATT and WTO are the creations of a series of multinational treaties. The most recent was completed in 1995, involved more than 120 countries, and resulted in the creation of the WTO. The purpose of these treaties has been to lower barriers to the free flow of goods and services between nations. Like the GATT before it, the WTO promotes free trade by limiting the ability of national governments to adopt policies that restrict imports into their nations. In the final section of this chapter, we discuss the implications of this material for management practice.

Instruments of Trade Policy

Trade policy uses seven main instruments: tariffs, subsidies, import quotas, voluntary export restraints, local content requirements, administrative policies, and antidumping duties. Tariffs are the oldest and simplest instrument of trade policy. As we shall see later in this chapter, they are also the instrument that the GATT and WTO have been most successful in limiting. A fall in tariff barriers in recent decades has been accompanied by a rise in nontariff barriers, such as subsidies, quotas, voluntary export restraints, and antidumping duties.

TARIFFS

A **tariff** is a tax levied on imports (or exports). Tariffs fall into two categories. **Specific tariffs** are levied as a fixed charge for each unit of a good imported (for example, $3 per barrel of oil). **Ad valorem tariffs** are levied as a proportion of the value of the imported good. In most cases, tariffs are placed on imports to protect domestic producers from foreign competition by raising the price of imported goods. However, tariffs also produce revenue for the government. Until the income tax was introduced, for example, the U.S. government received most of its revenues from tariffs.

The important thing to understand about an import tariff is who suffers and who gains. The government gains, because the tariff increases government revenues. Domestic producers gain, because the tariff affords them some protection against foreign competitors by increasing the cost of imported foreign goods. Consumers lose because they must pay more for certain imports. For example, in March 2002 the U.S. government placed an ad valorem tariff of 8 percent to 30 percent on imports of foreign steel. The idea was to protect domestic steel producers from cheap imports of foreign steel. The effect, however, was to raise the price of steel products in the United States by between 30 and 50 percent. A number of U.S. steel consumers, ranging from appliance makers to automobile companies, objected that the steel tariffs would raise their costs of production and make it more difficult for them to compete in the global marketplace. Whether the gains to the government and domestic producers exceed the loss to consumers depends on various factors such as the amount of the tariff, the importance of the imported good to domestic consumers, the number of jobs saved in the protected industry, and so on. In the steel case, many argued that the losses to steel consumers apparently outweighed the gains to steel producers. In November 2003, the World Trade Organization declared that the tariffs represented a violation of the WTO treaty, and the United States removed them in December of that year.

In general, two conclusions can be derived from economic analysis of the effect of import tariffs.[2] First, tariffs are unambiguously pro-producer and anticonsumer. While they protect producers from foreign competitors, this restriction of supply also raises domestic prices. For example, a study by Japanese economists calculated that tariffs on imports of foodstuffs, cosmetics, and chemicals into Japan cost the average Japanese consumer about $890 per year in the form of higher prices.[3] Almost all studies find that import tariffs impose significant costs on domestic consumers in the form of higher prices.[4]

Second, import tariffs reduce the overall efficiency of the world economy. They reduce efficiency because a protective tariff encourages domestic firms to produce products at home that, in theory, could be produced more efficiently abroad. The consequence is an inefficient utilization of resources. For example, tariffs on the importation of rice into South Korea have led to an increase in rice production in that country; however, rice farming is an unproductive use of land in South Korea. It would make more sense for the South Koreans to purchase their rice from lower cost foreign producers and to utilize the land now employed in rice production in some other way, such as growing foodstuffs that cannot be produced more efficiently elsewhere or for residential and industrial purposes.

Sometimes tariffs are levied on exports of a product from a country. Export tariffs are far less common than import tariffs. In general, export tariffs have two objectives: first, to raise revenue for the government, and second, to reduce exports from a sector, often for political reasons. For example, in 2004 China imposed a tariff on textile exports. The primary objective was to moderate the growth in exports of textiles from China, thereby alleviating tensions with other trading partners.

SUBSIDIES

A **subsidy** is a government payment to a domestic producer. Subsidies take many forms, including cash grants, low-interest loans, tax breaks, and government equity participation in domestic firms. By lowering production costs, subsidies help domestic producers in two ways: (1) competing against foreign imports and (2) gaining export markets. According to the World Trade Organization, in 2005 countries spent some $300 billion on subsidies, $250 billion of which was spent by 21 developed nations.[5]

Agriculture tends to be one of the largest beneficiaries of subsidies in most countries (see the opening case for an example). In the mid-2000s, the European Union was paying around €44 billion annually ($55 billion) in farm subsidies. Not to be outdone, in May 2002 President George W. Bush signed into law a bill that contained subsidies of more than $180 billion for U.S. farmers spread out over 10 years. In 2005, U.S. subsidies to farmers amounted to some $23 billion. The Japanese also have a long history of supporting inefficient domestic producers with farm subsidies. The accompanying Country Focus looks at subsidies to wheat producers in Japan.

Nonagricultural subsidies are much lower, but they are still significant. For example, subsidies historically were given to Boeing and Airbus to help them lower the cost of developing new commercial jet aircraft. In Boeing's case, subsidies came in the form of tax credits for R&D spending or Pentagon money that was used to develop military technology, which then was transferred to civil aviation projects. In the case of Airbus, subsidies took the form of government loans at below-market interest rates.

The main gains from subsidies accrue to domestic producers, whose international competitiveness is increased as a result. Advocates of strategic trade policy (which, as you will recall from Chapter 5, is an outgrowth of the new trade theory) favor subsidies to help domestic firms achieve a dominant position in those industries in which economies of scale are important and the world market is not large enough to profitably support more than a few firms (aerospace and semiconductors are two such industries). According to this argument, subsidies can help a firm achieve a first-mover advantage in an emerging industry (just as U.S. government subsidies, in the form of substantial R&D grants, allegedly helped Boeing). If this is achieved, further gains to the domestic economy arise from the employment and tax revenues that a major global company can generate. However, government subsidies must be paid for, typically by taxing individuals and corporations.

Whether subsidies generate national benefits that exceed their national costs is debatable. In practice, many subsidies are not that successful at increasing the international competitiveness of domestic producers. Rather, they tend to protect the inefficient and promote excess production. For example, agricultural subsidies, such as the cotton subsidies discussed in the opening case, (1) allow inefficient farmers to stay in business, (2) encourage countries to overproduce heavily subsidized agricultural products, (3) encourage countries to produce products that could be grown more cheaply elsewhere and imported, and therefore (4) reduce international trade in agricultural products. One study estimated that if advanced countries abandoned subsidies to farmers, global trade in agricultural products would be 50 percent higher and the world as a whole would be better off by $160 billion.[6] Another study estimated that removing all barriers to trade in agriculture (both subsidies and tariffs) would raise world income by $182 billion.[7] This increase in wealth arises from the more efficient use of agricultural land. For a specific example, see the Country Focus on wheat subsidies in Japan.

IMPORT QUOTAS AND VOLUNTARY EXPORT RESTRAINTS

An **import quota** is a direct restriction on the quantity of some good that may be imported into a country. The restriction is usually enforced by issuing import licenses to

COUNTRY FOCUS

Subsidized Wheat Production in Japan

Japan is not a particularly good environment for growing wheat. Wheat produced on large fields in the dry climates of North America, Australia, and Argentina is far cheaper and of much higher quality than anything produced in Japan. Indeed, Japan imports some 80 percent of its wheat from foreign producers. Yet tens of thousands of farmers in Japan still grow wheat, usually on small fields where yields are low and costs high, and production is rising. The reason is government subsidies designed to keep inefficient Japanese wheat producers in business. In 2004, Japanese farmers were selling their output at market prices, which were running at $9 per bushel, but they received an average of at least $35 per bushel for their 2004 production! The difference—$26 a bushel—was government subsidies paid to producers. The estimated costs of these subsidies were more than $700 million in 2004.

To finance its production subsidy, Japan operates a tariff rate quota on wheat imports in which a higher tariff rate is imposed once wheat imports exceed the quota level. The in-quota rate tariff is zero, while the over-quota tariff rate for wheat is $500 a ton. The tariff raises the cost so much that it deters over-quota imports, essentially restricting supply and raising the price for wheat inside Japan. The Japanese Ministry of Agriculture, Forestry and Fisheries (MAFF) has the sole right to purchase wheat imports within the quota (and since there are very few over-quota imports, the MAFF is a monopoly buyer on wheat imports into Japan). The MAFF buys wheat at world prices, then resells it to millers in Japan at the artificially high prices that arise due to the restriction on supply engineered by the tariff rate quota. Estimates suggest that in 2003, the world market price for wheat was $5.96 per bushel, but within Japan the average price for imported wheat was $10.23 a bushel. The markup of $4.27 a bushel yielded the MAFF in excess of $450 million in profit. This "profit" was then used to help cover the $700 million cost of subsidies to inefficient wheat farmers, with the rest of the funds coming from general government tax revenues.

Thanks to these policies, the price of wheat in Japan can be anything from 80 to 120 percent higher than the world price, and Japanese wheat production, which exceeded 850,000 tons in 2004, is significantly greater than it would be if a free market were allowed to operate. Indeed, under free market conditions, there would be virtually no wheat production in Japan since the costs of production are simply too high. The beneficiaries of this policy are the thousands of small farmers in Japan who grow wheat. The losers include Japanese consumers, who must pay more for products containing wheat and who must finance wheat subsidies through taxes, and foreign producers, who are denied access to a chunk of the Japanese market by the over-quota tariff rate. Why then does the Japanese government continue to pursue this policy? It continues because small farmers are an important constituency and Japanese politicians want their votes.[8]

a group of individuals or firms. For example, the United States has a quota on cheese imports. The only firms allowed to import cheese are certain trading companies, each of which is allocated the right to import a maximum number of pounds of cheese each year. In some cases, the right to sell is given directly to the governments of exporting countries. Historically this is the case for sugar and textile imports in the United States. However, the international agreement governing the imposition of import quotas on textiles, the Multi-Fiber Agreement, expired in December 2004.

A common hybrid of a quota and a tariff is known as a tariff rate quota. Under a **tariff rate quota,** a lower tariff rate is applied to imports within the quota than those over the quota. For example, as illustrated in Figure 6.1, an ad valorem tariff rate of 10 percent might be levied on rice imports into South Korea of 1 million tons, after which an out-of-quota rate of 80 percent might be applied. Thus, South Korea might import 2 million tons of rice, 1 million at a 10 percent tariff rate and another 1 million at an 80 percent tariff. Tariff rate quotas are common in agriculture, where their goal is to limit imports over quota. The Country Focus on Japanese wheat subsidies illustrates

FIGURE 6.1

Hypothetical Tariff Rate Quota

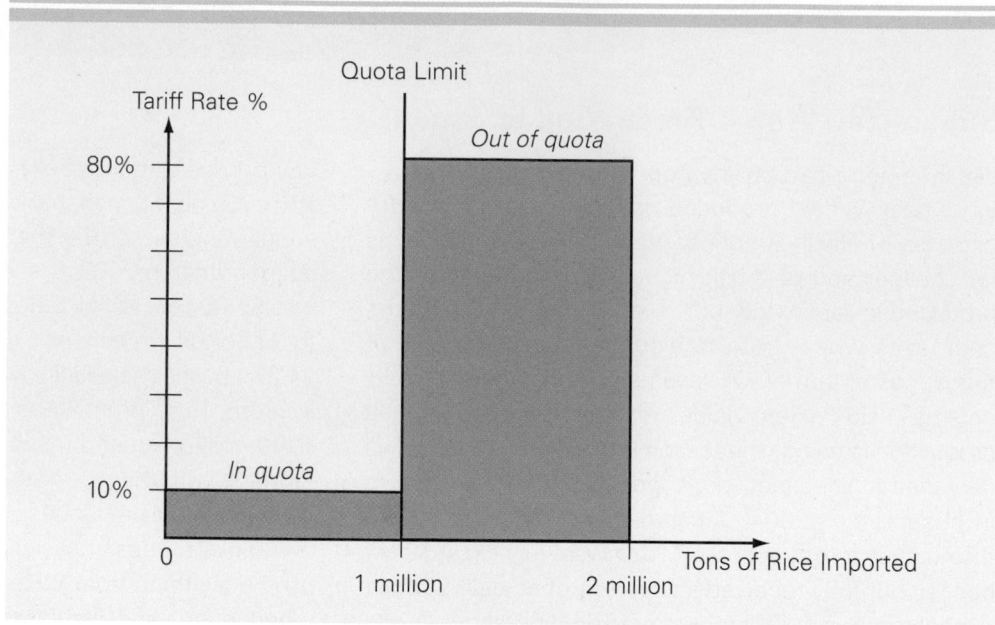

how the combination of a tariff rate quota and subsidies protects inefficient Japanese wheat farmers from foreign competition, for example.

A variant on the import quota is the voluntary export restraint. A **voluntary export restraint (VER)** is a quota on trade imposed by the exporting country, typically at the request of the importing country's government. One of the most famous historical examples is the limitation on auto exports to the United States by Japanese automobile producers in 1981. A response to direct pressure from the U.S. government, this VER limited Japanese imports to no more than 1.68 million vehicles per year. The agreement was revised in 1984 to allow 1.85 million Japanese vehicles per year. The agreement was allowed to lapse in 1985, but the Japanese government indicated its intentions at that time to continue to restrict exports to the United States to 1.85 million vehicles per year.[9] Foreign producers agree to VERs because they fear more damaging punitive tariffs or import quotas might follow if they do not. Agreeing to a VER is seen as a way to make the best of a bad situation by appeasing protectionist pressures in a country.

As with tariffs and subsidies, both import quotas and VERs benefit domestic producers by limiting import competition. As with all restrictions on trade, quotas do not benefit consumers. An import quota or VER always raises the domestic price of an imported good. When imports are limited to a low percentage of the market by a quota or VER, the price is bid up for that limited foreign supply. The automobile industry VER mentioned above increased the price of the limited supply of Japanese imports. According to a study by the U.S. Federal Trade Commission, the automobile VER cost U.S. consumers about $1 billion per year between 1981 and 1985. That $1 billion per year went to Japanese producers in the form of higher prices.[10] The extra profit that producers make when supply is artificially limited by an import quota is referred to as a **quota rent.**

If a domestic industry lacks the capacity to meet demand, an import quota can raise prices for *both* the domestically produced and the imported good. This happened in the U.S. sugar industry, in which a tariff rate quota system has long limited the amount foreign producers can sell in the U.S. market. According to one study, import quotas have caused the price of sugar in the United States to be as much as 40 percent greater than the world price.[11] These higher prices have translated into greater profits for U.S. sugar producers, which have lobbied politicians to keep the lucrative agreement. They argue U.S. jobs in the sugar industry will be lost to foreign producers if the quota system is scrapped.

LOCAL CONTENT REQUIREMENTS

A **local content requirement** is a requirement that some specific fraction of a good be produced domestically. The requirement can be expressed either in physical terms (e.g., 75 percent of component parts for this product must be produced locally) or in value terms (e.g., 75 percent of the value of this product must be produced locally). Developing countries have widely used local content regulations to shift their manufacturing base from the simple assembly of products whose parts are manufactured elsewhere into the local manufacture of component parts. They have also been used in developed countries to try to protect local jobs and industry from foreign competition. For example, a little-known law in the United States, the Buy America Act, specifies that government agencies must give preference to American products when putting contracts for equipment out to bid unless the foreign products have a significant price advantage. The law specifies a product as "American" if 51 percent of the materials by value are produced domestically. This amounts to a local content requirement. If a foreign company, or an American one for that matter, wishes to win a contract from a U.S. government agency to provide some equipment, it must ensure that at least 51 percent of the product by value is manufactured in the United States.

Local content regulations provide protection for a domestic producer of parts in the same way an import quota does: by limiting foreign competition. The aggregate economic effects are also the same; domestic producers benefit, but the restrictions on imports raise the prices of imported components. In turn, higher prices for imported components are passed on to consumers of the final product in the form of higher final prices. So, as with all trade policies, local content regulations tend to benefit producers and not consumers.

ADMINISTRATIVE POLICIES

In addition to the formal instruments of trade policy, governments of all types sometimes use informal or administrative policies to restrict imports and boost exports. **Administrative trade policies** are bureaucratic rules designed to make it difficult for imports to enter a country. It has been argued that the Japanese are the masters of this trade barrier. In recent decades Japan's formal tariff and nontariff barriers have been among the lowest in the world. However, critics charge that the country's informal administrative barriers to imports more than compensate for low tariffs. For example, at one point the Netherlands exported tulip bulbs to almost every country in the world except Japan. In Japan, customs inspectors insisted on checking every tulip bulb by cutting it vertically down the middle, and even Japanese ingenuity could not put them back together. Federal Express also initially had a tough time expanding its global express shipping services into Japan because Japanese customs inspectors insist on opening a large proportion of express packages to check for pornography, a process that delayed an "express" package for days. Japan is not the only country that engages in such policies. France once required that all imported videotape recorders arrive through a small customs entry point that was both remote and poorly staffed. The resulting delays kept Japanese VCRs out of the French market until a VER agreement was negotiated.[12] As with all instruments of trade policy, administrative instruments benefit producers and hurt consumers, who are denied access to possibly superior foreign products.

Antidumping Policies

In the context of international trade, **dumping** is variously defined as selling goods in a foreign market at below their costs of production or as selling goods in a foreign market at below their "fair" market value. There is a difference between these two definitions; the fair market value of a good is normally judged to be greater than the costs of producing that good because the former includes a "fair" profit margin. Dumping is viewed as a method by which firms unload excess production in foreign markets. Some dumping may be the result of predatory behavior, with producers using substantial profits from their home markets to subsidize prices in a foreign market with a view to driving indigenous competitors out of that market. Once this has been achieved, so the argument goes, the predatory firm can raise prices and earn substantial profits.

An alleged example of dumping occurred in 1997, when two South Korean manufacturers of semiconductors, LG Semicon and Hyundai Electronics, were accused of selling dynamic random access memory chips (DRAMs) in the U.S. market at below their costs of production. This action occurred in the middle of a worldwide glut of chip-making capacity. It was alleged that the firms were trying to unload their excess production in the United States.

Antidumping policies are designed to punish foreign firms that engage in dumping. The ultimate objective is to protect domestic producers from unfair foreign competition. Although antidumping policies vary somewhat from country to country, the majority are similar to those used in the United States. If a domestic producer believes that a foreign firm is dumping production in the U.S. market, it can file a petition with two government agencies, the Commerce Department and the International Trade Commission. In the Korean DRAM case, Micron Technology, a U.S. manufacturer of DRAMs, filed the petition. The government agencies then investigate the complaint. If a complaint has merit, the Commerce Department may impose an antidumping duty on the offending foreign imports (antidumping duties are often called **countervailing duties**). These duties, which represent a special tariff, can be fairly substantial and stay in place for up to five years. For example, after reviewing Micron's complaint, the Commerce Department imposed 9 percent and 4 percent countervailing duties on LG Semicon and Hyundai DRAM chips, respectively. The accompanying Management Focus discusses another example of how a firm, U.S. Magnesium, used antidumping legislation to gain protection from unfair foreign competitors.

The Case for Government Intervention

Now that we have reviewed the various instruments of trade policy that governments can use, it is time to look at the case for government intervention in international trade. Arguments for government intervention take two paths: political and economic. Political arguments for intervention are concerned with protecting the interests of certain groups within a nation (normally producers), often at the expense of other groups (normally consumers). Economic arguments for intervention are typically concerned with boosting the overall wealth of a nation (to the benefit of all, both producers and consumers).

POLITICAL ARGUMENTS FOR INTERVENTION

Political arguments for government intervention cover a range of issues, including preserving jobs, protecting industries deemed important for national security, retaliating against unfair foreign competition, protecting consumers from "dangerous" products, furthering the goals of foreign policy, and advancing the human rights of individuals in exporting countries.

Protecting Jobs and Industries

Perhaps the most common political argument for government intervention is that it is necessary for protecting jobs and industries from unfair foreign competition. The tariffs President George W. Bush placed on imports of foreign steel in March 2002 were

U.S. Magnesium Seeks Protection

In February 2004, U.S. Magnesium, the sole surviving U.S. producer of magnesium, a metal that is primarily used in the manufacture of certain automobile parts and aluminum cans, filed a petition with the U.S. International Trade Commission (ITC) contending that a surge in imports had caused material damage to the U.S. industry's employment, sales, market share, and profitability. According to U.S. Magnesium, Russian and Chinese producers had been selling the metal at prices significantly below market value. During 2002 and 2003, imports of magnesium into the United States rose 70 percent, while prices fell by 40 percent and the market share accounted for by imports jumped to 50 percent from 25 percent.

"The United States used to be the largest producer of magnesium in the world," a U.S. Magnesium spokesman said at the time of the filing. "What's really sad is that you can be state of the art and have modern technology, and if the Chinese, who pay people less than 90 cents an hour, want to run you out of business, they can do it. And that's why we are seeking relief."

During a yearlong investigation, the ITC solicited input from various sides in the dispute. Foreign producers and consumers of magnesium in the United States argued that falling prices for magnesium during 2002 and 2003 simply reflected an imbalance between supply and demand due to additional capacity coming on stream not from Russia or China but from a new Canadian plant that opened in 2001 and from a planned Australian plant. The Canadian plant shut down in 2003, the Australian plant never came on stream, and prices for magnesium rose again in 2004.

Magnesium consumers in the United States also argued to the ITC that imposing antidumping duties on foreign imports of magnesium would raise prices in the United States significantly above world levels. A spokesman for Alcoa, which mixes magnesium with aluminum to make alloys for cans, predicted that if antidumping duties were imposed, high magnesium prices in the United States would force Alcoa to move some production out of the United States. Alcoa also noted that in 2003, U.S. Magnesium was unable to supply all of Alcoa's needs, forcing the company to turn to imports. Consumers of magnesium in the automobile industry asserted that high prices in the United States would drive engineers to design magnesium out of automobiles or force manufacturing elsewhere, which would ultimately hurt everyone.

The six members of the ITC were not convinced by these arguments. In March 2005, the ITC ruled that both China and Russia had been dumping magnesium in the United States. The government decided to impose duties ranging from 50 percent to more than 140 percent on imports of magnesium from China. Russian producers face duties ranging from 19 percent to 22 percent. The duties will be levied for five years, after which the ITC will revisit the situation.

According to U.S. Magnesium, the favorable ruling will now allow the company to reap the benefits of nearly $50 million in investments made in its manufacturing plant during the last few years and enable the company to boost its capacity by 28 percent by the end of 2005. Commenting on the favorable ruling, a U.S. Magnesium spokesman noted, "Once unfair trade is removed from the marketplace we'll be able to compete with anyone." U.S. Magnesium's customers and competitors, however, did not view the situation in the 2002–03 period as one of unfair trade. While the imposition of antidumping duties no doubt will help to protect U.S. Magnesium and the 400 people it employs from foreign competition, magnesium consumers in the United States are left wondering if they will be the ultimate losers.[13]

designed to do this (many steel producers were located in states that Bush needed to win reelection in 2004). A political motive also underlay the European Union's establishment of the Common Agricultural Policy (CAP). The CAP was designed to protect the jobs of Europe's politically powerful farmers by restricting imports and guaranteeing prices. However, the higher prices that resulted from the CAP have cost Europe's consumers dearly. This is true of many attempts to protect jobs and industries through government intervention. For example, the imposition of steel tariffs in 2002 raised steel prices for American consumers, such as automobile companies, making them less competitive in the global marketplace.

National Security

Countries sometimes argue that it is necessary to protect certain industries because they are important for national security. Defense-related industries often get this kind of attention (e.g., aerospace, advanced electronics, semiconductors, etc.). Although not as common as it used to be, this argument is still made. Those in favor of protecting the U.S. semiconductor industry from foreign competition, for example, argue that semiconductors are now such important components of defense products that it would be dangerous to rely primarily on foreign producers for them. In 1986, this argument helped persuade the federal government to support Sematech, a consortium of 14 U.S. semiconductor companies that accounted for 90 percent of the U.S. industry's revenues. Sematech's mission was to conduct joint research into manufacturing techniques that can be parceled out to members. The government saw the venture as so critical that it specially protected Sematech from antitrust laws. Initially, the U.S. government provided Sematech with $100 million per year in subsidies. By the mid-1990s, however, the U.S. semiconductor industry had regained its leading market position, largely through the personal computer boom and demand for microprocessor chips made by Intel. In 1994, the consortium's board voted to seek an end to federal funding, and since 1996 the consortium has been funded entirely by private money.[14]

Retaliation

Some argue that governments should use the threat to intervene in trade policy as a bargaining tool to help open foreign markets and force trading partners to "play by the rules of the game." The U.S. government has used the threat of punitive trade sanctions to try to get the Chinese government to enforce its intellectual property laws. Lax enforcement of these laws had given rise to massive copyright infringements in China that had been costing U.S. companies such as Microsoft hundreds of millions of dollars per year in lost sales revenues. After the United States threatened to impose 100 percent tariffs on a range of Chinese imports, and after harsh words between officials from the two countries, the Chinese agreed to tighter enforcement of intellectual property regulations.[15]

If it works, such a politically motivated rationale for government intervention may liberalize trade and bring with it resulting economic gains. It is a risky strategy, however. A country that is being pressured may not back down and instead may respond to the imposition of punitive tariffs by raising trade barriers of its own. This is exactly what the Chinese government threatened to do when pressured by the United States, although it ultimately did back down. If a government does not back down, however, the results could be higher trade barriers all around and an economic loss to all involved.

Protecting Consumers

Many governments have long had regulations to protect consumers from unsafe products. The indirect effect of such regulations often is to limit or ban the importation of such products. For example, in 2003 several countries, including Japan and South Korea, decided to ban imports of American beef after a single case of mad cow disease was found in Washington State. The ban was motivated to protect consumers from what was seen to be an unsafe product. Together, Japan and South Korea accounted for about $2 billion of U.S. beef sales, so the ban had a significant impact on U.S. beef producers. After two years, both countries lifted the ban, although they placed stringent requirements on U.S. beef imports to reduce the risk of importing beef that might be tainted by mad cow disease (for example, Japan required that all beef must come from cattle under 21 months of age).[16]

Trade in Hormone-Treated Beef

Back in the 1970s, scientists discovered how to synthesize certain hormones and use them to accelerate the growth rate of livestock animals, reduce the fat content of meat, and increase milk production. Bovine somatotropin (BST), a growth hormone produced by cattle, was first synthesized by the biotechnology firm Genentech. Injections of BST could be used to supplement an animal's own hormone production and increase its growth rate. These hormones soon became popular among farmers, who found that they could cut costs and help satisfy consumer demands for leaner meat. Although these hormones occurred naturally in animals, consumer groups in several countries soon raised concerns about the practice. They argued that the use of hormone supplements was unnatural and that the health consequences of consuming hormone-treated meat were unknown but might include hormonal irregularities and cancer.

The European Union responded to these concerns in 1989 by banning the use of growth-promoting hormones in the production of livestock and the importation of hormone-treated meat. The ban was controversial because a reasonable consensus existed among scientists that the hormones posed no health risk. Although the EU banned hormone-treated meat, many other countries did not, including big meat-producing countries such as Australia, Canada, New Zealand, and the United States. The use of hormones soon became widespread in these countries. According to trade officials outside the EU, the European ban constituted an unfair restraint on trade. As a result of this ban, exports of meat to the EU fell. For example, U.S. red meat exports to the EU declined from $231 million in 1988 to $98 million in 1994. The complaints of meat exporters were bolstered in 1995 when Codex Alimentarius, the international food standards body of the UN's Food and Agriculture Organization and

the World Health Organization, approved the use of growth hormones. In making this decision, Codex reviewed the scientific literature and found no evidence of a link between the consumption of hormone-treated meat and human health problems, such as cancer.

Fortified by such decisions, in 1995 the United States pressed the EU to drop the import ban on hormone-treated beef. The EU refused, citing "consumer concerns about food safety." In response, both Canada and the United States independently filed formal complaints with the World Trade Organization. A number of other countries joined the United States in its complaint, including Australia and New Zealand. The WTO created a trade panel of three independent experts. After reviewing evidence and hearing from a range of experts and representatives of both parties, the panel in May 1997 ruled that the EU ban on hormone-treated beef was illegal because it had no scientific justification. The EU immediately indicated it would appeal the finding to the WTO court of appeals. The WTO court heard the appeal in November 1997 and in February 1998 agreed with the findings of the trade panel that the EU had not presented any scientific evidence to justify the hormone ban.

This ruling left the EU in a difficult position. Legally, the EU had to lift the ban or face punitive sanctions, but the ban had wide public support in Europe. The EU feared that lifting the ban could produce a consumer backlash. Instead the EU did nothing, so in February 1999 the United States asked the WTO for permission to impose punitive sanctions on the EU. The WTO responded by allowing the United States to impose punitive tariffs valued at $120 million on EU exports to the United States. The EU decided to accept these tariffs rather than lift the ban on hormone-treated beef, and as of 2007, the ban and punitive tariffs were still in place.[20]

The accompanying Country Focus describes how the European Union banned the sale and importation of hormone-treated beef. The ban was motivated by a desire to protect European consumers from the possible health consequences of eating meat from animals treated with growth hormones. The conflict over the importation of hormone-treated beef into the EU may prove to be a taste of things to come. In addition to the use of hormones to promote animal growth and meat production, biotechnology has made it possible to genetically alter many crops so they resist common herbicides, produce proteins that are natural insecticides, grow dramatically improved yields, or withstand inclement weather conditions. A new breed of genetically modified tomatoes has an antifreeze gene inserted into its genome and can thus be grown in colder climates than hitherto possible. Another example is a genetically engineered cotton seed produced by Monsanto. The seed has been engineered to express a protein that protects against three common insect pests: the cotton bollworm, tobacco budworm, and pink bollworm. Use of this seed reduces or eliminates the need for traditional pesticide applications for these pests.

As enticing as such innovations sound, they have met with intense resistance from consumer groups, particularly in Europe. The fear is that the widespread use of genetically altered seed corn could have unanticipated and harmful effects on human health and may result in "genetic pollution." (An example of genetic pollution would be when the widespread use of crops that produce natural pesticides stimulates the evolution of "superbugs" that are resistant to those pesticides.) Such concerns have led Austria and Luxembourg to outlaw the importation, sale, or use of genetically altered organisms. Sentiment against genetically altered organisms also runs strong in several other European countries, most notably Germany and Switzerland. It seems likely, therefore, that the World Trade Organization will be drawn into the conflict between those that want to expand the global market for genetically altered organisms, such as Monsanto, and those that want to limit it, such as Austria and Luxembourg.[17]

Furthering Foreign Policy Objectives

Governments sometimes use trade policy to support their foreign policy objectives.[18] A government may grant preferential trade terms to a country with which it wants to build strong relations. Trade policy has also been used several times to pressure or punish "rogue states" that do not abide by international law or norms. Iraq labored under extensive trade sanctions after the UN coalition defeated the country in the 1991 Gulf War until the 2003 invasion of Iraq by forces led by the United States. The theory is that such pressure might persuade the rogue state to mend its ways, or it might hasten a change of government. In the case of Iraq, the sanctions were seen as a way of forcing that country to comply with several UN resolutions. The United States has maintained long-running trade sanctions against Cuba. Their principal function is to impoverish Cuba in the hope that the resulting economic hardship will lead to the downfall of Cuba's Communist government and its replacement with a more democratically inclined (and pro–United States) regime. The United States also has had trade sanctions in place against Libya and Iran, both of which it accuses of supporting terrorist action against U.S. interests and building weapons of mass destruction. In late 2003, the sanctions against Libya seemed to yield some returns when that country announced it would terminate a program to build nuclear weapons, and the U.S. government responded by relaxing those sanctions.

Other countries can undermine unilateral trade sanctions. The U.S. sanctions against Cuba, for example, have not stopped other Western countries from trading with Cuba. The U.S. sanctions have done little more than help create a vacuum into which other trading nations, such as Canada and Germany, have stepped. In an attempt to halt this and further tighten the screws on Cuba, in 1996 the U.S. Congress passed the **Helms–Burton Act.** This act allows Americans to sue foreign firms that use property in Cuba confiscated from them after the 1959 revolution. Later in 1996, Congress passed a similar law, the **D'Amato Act,** aimed at Libya and Iran.

The passage of Helms–Burton elicited protests from America's trading partners, including the European Union, Canada, and Mexico, all of which claim the law violates their sovereignty and is illegal under World Trade Organization rules. For example, Canadian companies that have been doing business in Cuba for years see no reason they should suddenly be sued in U.S. courts when Canada does not restrict trade with Cuba. They are not violating Canadian law, and they are not U.S. companies, so why should they be subject to U.S. law? Despite such protests, the law is still on the books in the

United States, although the U.S. government has not enforced this act—probably because it is unenforceable.

Protecting Human Rights

Protecting and promoting human rights in other countries is an important element of foreign policy for many democracies. Governments sometimes use trade policy to try to improve the human rights policies of trading partners. For years, the most obvious example of this was the annual debate in the United States over whether to grant most favored nation (MFN) status to China. MFN status allows countries to export goods to the United States under favorable terms. Under MFN rules, the average tariff on Chinese goods imported into the United States was 8 percent. If China's MFN status were rescinded, tariffs could have risen to about 40 percent. Trading partners that are signatories of the World Trade

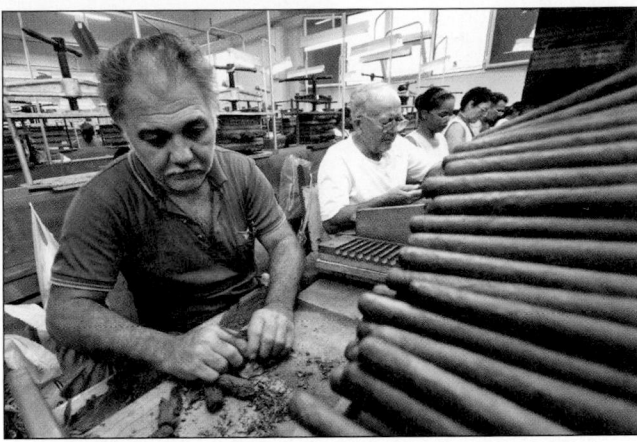

Even though the United States holds trade sanctions with Cuba, other Western countries continue to trade with the island nation.

Organization, as most are, automatically receive MFN status. However, China did not join the WTO until 2001, so historically the decision of whether to grant MFN status to China was a real one. The decision was made more difficult by the perception that China had a poor human rights record. As indications of the country's disregard for human rights, critics of China often point to the 1989 Tiananmen Square massacre, China's continuing subjugation of Tibet (which China occupied in the 1950s), and the squashing of political dissent in China.[19] These critics argue that it was wrong for the United States to grant MFN status to China and that, instead, the United States should withhold MFN status until China showed measurable improvement in its human rights record. The critics argue that trade policy should be used as a political weapon to force China to change its internal policies toward human rights.

Others contend that limiting trade with such countries would make matters worse, not better. They argue that the best way to change the internal human rights stance of a country is to engage it through international trade. At its core, the argument is simple: Growing bilateral trade raises the income levels of both countries, and as a state becomes richer, its people begin to demand, and generally receive, better treatment with regard to their human rights. This is a variant of the argument in Chapter 2 that economic progress begets political progress (if political progress is measured by the adoption of a democratic government that respects human rights). This argument ultimately won the day in 1999 when the Clinton administration blessed China's application to join the WTO and announced that trade and human rights issues should be decoupled.

ECONOMIC ARGUMENTS FOR INTERVENTION

With the development of the new trade theory and strategic trade policy (see Chapter 5), the economic arguments for government intervention have undergone a renaissance in recent years. Until the early 1980s, most economists saw little benefit in government intervention and strongly advocated a free trade policy. This position has changed at the margins with the development of strategic trade policy, although as we will see in the next section, there are still strong economic arguments for sticking to a free trade stance.

The Infant Industry Argument

The **infant industry argument** is by far the oldest economic argument for government intervention. Alexander Hamilton proposed it in 1792. According to this argument, many developing countries have a potential comparative advantage in manufacturing, but new manufacturing industries cannot initially compete with established industries in developed countries. To allow manufacturing to get a toehold, the argument is that governments should temporarily support new industries (with tariffs, import quotas, and subsidies) until they have grown strong enough to meet international competition.

This argument has had substantial appeal for the governments of developing nations during the past 50 years, and the GATT has recognized the infant industry argument as a legitimate reason for protectionism. Nevertheless, many economists remain critical of this argument for two main reasons. First, protection of manufacturing from foreign competition does no good unless the protection helps make the industry efficient. In case after case, however, protection seems to have done little more than foster the development of inefficient industries that have little hope of ever competing in the world market. Brazil, for example, built the world's tenth-largest auto industry behind tariff barriers and quotas. Once those barriers were removed in the late 1980s, however, foreign imports soared, and the industry was forced to face up to the fact that after 30 years of protection, the Brazilian industry was one of the world's most inefficient.[21]

Second, the infant industry argument relies on an assumption that firms are unable to make efficient long-term investments by borrowing money from the domestic or international capital market. Consequently, governments have been required to subsidize long-term investments. Given the development of global capital markets over the past 20 years, this assumption no longer looks as valid as it once did. Today, if a developing country has a potential comparative advantage in a manufacturing industry, firms in that country should be able to borrow money from the capital markets to finance the required investments. Given financial support, firms based in countries with a potential comparative advantage have an incentive to endure the necessary initial losses in order to make long-run gains without requiring government protection. Many Taiwanese and South Korean firms did this in industries such as textiles, semiconductors, machine tools, steel, and shipping. Thus, given efficient global capital markets, the only industries that would require government protection would be those that are not worthwhile.

Strategic Trade Policy

Some new trade theorists have proposed the strategic trade policy argument.[22] We reviewed the basic argument in Chapter 5 when we considered the new trade theory. The new trade theory argues that in industries in which the existence of substantial economies of scale implies that the world market will profitably support only a few firms, countries may predominate in the export of certain products simply because they had firms that were able to capture first-mover advantages. The long-term dominance of Boeing in the commercial aircraft industry has been attributed to such factors.

The **strategic trade policy** argument has two components. First, it is argued that by appropriate actions, a government can help raise national income if it can somehow ensure that the firm or firms that gain first-mover advantages in an industry are domestic rather than foreign enterprises. Thus, according to the strategic trade policy argument, a government should use subsidies to support promising firms that are active in newly emerging industries. Advocates of this argument point out that the substantial R&D grants that the U.S. government gave Boeing in the 1950s and 1960s probably helped tilt the field of competition in the newly emerging market for passenger jets in Boeing's favor. (Boeing's first commercial jet airliner, the 707, was derived from a military plane.) Similar arguments have been made with regard to Japan's dominance in the production of liquid crystal display screens (used in laptop computers). Although these screens were invented in the United States, the Japanese government, in cooperation with major electronics companies, targeted this industry for research support in the late 1970s and early 1980s. The result was that Japanese firms, not U.S. firms, subsequently captured first-mover advantages in this market.

The second component of the strategic trade policy argument is that it might pay a government to intervene in an industry by helping domestic firms overcome the barriers to entry created by foreign firms that have already reaped first-mover advantages. This argument underlies government support of Airbus Industrie, Boeing's major competitor. Formed in 1966 as a consortium of four companies from Great Britain, France, Germany, and Spain, Airbus had less than 5 percent of the world commercial aircraft market when it began production in the mid-1970s. By 2006, it had increased its share to 45 percent, threatening Boeing's long-term dominance of the market. How did Airbus achieve this? According to the U.S. government, the answer is a $15 billion subsidy from the governments of Great Britain, France, Germany, and Spain.[23] Without this subsidy, Airbus would never have been able to break into the world market.

If these arguments are correct, they support a rationale for government intervention in international trade. Governments should target technologies that may be important in the future and use subsidies to support development work aimed at commercializing those technologies. Furthermore, government should provide export subsidies until the domestic firms have established first-mover advantages in the world market. Government support may also be justified if it can help domestic firms overcome the first-mover advantages enjoyed by foreign competitors and emerge as viable competitors in the world market (as in the Airbus and semiconductor examples). In this case, a combination of home-market protection and export-promoting subsidies may be needed.

🌐 The Revised Case for Free Trade

The strategic trade policy arguments of the new trade theorists suggest an economic justification for government intervention in international trade. This justification challenges the rationale for unrestricted free trade found in the work of classic trade theorists such as Adam Smith and David Ricardo. In response to this challenge to economic orthodoxy, a number of economists—including some of those responsible for the development of the new trade theory, such as Paul Krugman—point out that although strategic trade policy looks appealing in theory, in practice it may be unworkable. This response to the strategic trade policy argument constitutes the revised case for free trade.[24]

RETALIATION AND TRADE WAR

Krugman argues that a strategic trade policy aimed at establishing domestic firms in a dominant position in a global industry is a beggar-thy-neighbor policy that boosts national income at the expense of other countries. A country that attempts to use such policies will probably provoke retaliation. In many cases, the resulting trade war between two or more interventionist governments will leave all countries involved worse off than if they had adopted a hands-off approach in the first place. If the U.S. government were to respond to the Airbus subsidy by increasing its own subsidies to Boeing, for example, the result might be that the subsidies would cancel each other out. In the process, both European and U.S. taxpayers would end up supporting an expensive and pointless trade war, and both Europe and the United States would be worse off.

Krugman may be right about the danger of a strategic trade policy leading to a trade war. The problem, however, is how to respond when one's competitors are already being supported by government subsidies; that is, how should Boeing and the United States respond to the subsidization of Airbus? According to Krugman, the answer is probably not to engage in retaliatory action but to help establish rules of the game that minimize the use of trade-distorting subsidies. This is what the World Trade Organization seeks to do.

DOMESTIC POLICIES

Governments do not always act in the national interest when they intervene in the economy; politically important interest groups often influence them. The European Union's support for the Common Agricultural Policy (CAP), which arose because of the political power of French and German farmers, is an example. The CAP benefited inefficient farmers and the politicians who relied on the farm vote, but not consumers in the EU, who ended up paying more for their foodstuffs. Thus, a further reason for not embracing strategic trade policy, according to Krugman, is that such a policy is almost certain to be captured by special-interest groups within the economy, who will distort it to their own ends. Krugman concludes that in the United States,

> To ask the Commerce Department to ignore special-interest politics while formulating detailed policy for many industries is not realistic: To establish a blanket policy of free trade, with exceptions granted only under extreme pressure, may not be the optimal policy according to the theory but may be the best policy that the country is likely to get.[25]

Development of the World Trading System

Strong economic arguments support unrestricted free trade. While many governments have recognized the value of these arguments, they have been unwilling to unilaterally lower their trade barriers for fear that other nations might not follow suit. Consider the problem that two neighboring countries, say, Brazil and Argentina, face when deciding whether to lower trade barriers between them. In principle, the government of Brazil might favor lowering trade barriers, but it might be unwilling to do so for fear that Argentina will not do the same. Instead, the government might fear that the Argentineans will take advantage of Brazil's low barriers to enter the Brazilian market, while at the same time continuing to shut Brazilian products out of their market through high trade barriers. The Argentinean government might believe that it faces the same dilemma. The essence of the problem is a lack of trust. Both governments recognize that their respective nations will benefit from lower trade barriers between them, but neither government is willing to lower barriers for fear that the other might not follow.[26]

Such a deadlock can be resolved if both countries negotiate a set of rules to govern cross-border trade and lower trade barriers. But who is to monitor the governments to make sure they are playing by the trade rules? And who is to impose sanctions on a government that cheats? Both governments could set up an independent body to act as a referee. This referee could monitor trade between the countries, make sure that no side cheats, and impose sanctions on a country if it does cheat in the trade game.

While it might sound unlikely that any government would compromise its national sovereignty by submitting to such an arrangement, since World War II an international trading framework has evolved that has exactly these features. For its first 50 years, this framework was known as the General Agreement on Tariffs and Trade. Since 1995, it has been known as the World Trade Organization. Here we look at the evolution and workings of the GATT and WTO.

FROM SMITH TO THE GREAT DEPRESSION

As noted in Chapter 5, the theoretical case for free trade dates to the late 18th century and the work of Adam Smith and David Ricardo. Free trade as a government policy was first officially embraced by Great Britain in 1846, when the British Parliament repealed the Corn Laws. The Corn Laws placed a high tariff on imports of foreign corn. The objectives of the Corn Laws tariff were to raise government revenues and to protect British corn producers. There had been annual motions in Parliament in favor of free trade since the 1820s when David Ricardo was a member. However, agricultural protection was withdrawn only as a result of a protracted debate when the effects of a harvest failure in Great Britain were compounded by the imminent threat of famine in Ireland. Faced with considerable hardship and suffering among the populace, Parliament narrowly reversed its long-held position.

During the next 80 years or so, Great Britain, as one of the world's dominant trading powers, pushed the case for trade liberalization; but the British government was a voice in the wilderness. Its major trading partners did not reciprocate the British policy of unilateral free trade. The only reason Britain kept this policy for so long was that as the world's largest exporting nation, it had far more to lose from a trade war than did any other country.

By the 1930s, the British attempt to stimulate free trade was buried under the economic rubble of the Great Depression. The Great Depression had roots in the failure of the world economy to mount a sustained economic recovery after the end of World War I in 1918. Things got worse in 1929 with the U.S. stock market collapse and the subsequent run on the U.S. banking system. Economic problems were compounded in 1930 when the U.S. Congress passed the Smoot–Hawley tariff. Aimed at avoiding rising unemployment by protecting domestic industries and diverting consumer demand away from foreign products, the **Smoot–Hawley Act** erected an enormous wall of tariff barriers. Almost every industry was rewarded with its "made-to-order" tariff. A particularly odd aspect of the Smoot–Hawley tariff-raising binge was that the United States was running a balance-of-payment surplus at the time and it was the world's largest creditor nation. The Smoot–Hawley Act had a damaging effect on employment abroad. Other countries reacted to the U.S. action by raising their own tariff barriers. U.S. exports tumbled in response, and the world slid further into the Great Depression.[27]

1947–1979: GATT, TRADE LIBERALIZATION, AND ECONOMIC GROWTH

Economic damage caused by the beggar-thy-neighbor trade policies that the Smoot–Hawley Act ushered in exerted a profound influence on the economic institutions and ideology of the post–World War II world. The United States emerged from the war both victorious and economically dominant. After the debacle of the Great Depression, opinion in the U.S. Congress had swung strongly in favor of free trade. Under U.S. leadership, the GATT was established in 1947.

The GATT was a multilateral agreement whose objective was to liberalize trade by eliminating tariffs, subsidies, import quotas, and the like. From its foundation in 1947 until it was superseded by the WTO, the GATT's membership grew from 19 to more than 120 nations. The GATT did not attempt to liberalize trade restrictions in one fell swoop; that would have been impossible. Rather, tariff reduction was spread over eight rounds. The last, the Uruguay Round, was launched in 1986 and completed in December 1993. In these rounds, mutual tariff reductions were negotiated among all members, who then committed themselves not to raise import tariffs above negotiated rates. GATT regulations were enforced by a mutual monitoring mechanism. If a country believed that one of its trading partners was violating a GATT regulation, it could ask the Geneva-based bureaucracy that administered the GATT to investigate. If GATT investigators found the complaints to be valid, member countries could be asked to pressure the offending party to change its policies. In general, such pressure was sufficient to get an offending country to change its policies. If it were not, the offending country could be expelled from the GATT.

In its early years, the GATT was by most measures very successful. For example, the average tariff declined by nearly 92 percent in the United States between the Geneva Round of 1947 and the Tokyo Round of 1973–79. Consistent with the theoretical arguments first advanced by Ricardo and reviewed in Chapter 5, the move toward free trade under the GATT appeared to stimulate economic growth. From 1953 to 1963, world trade grew at an annual rate of 6.1 percent, and world income grew at an annual rate of 4.3 percent. Performance from 1963 to 1973 was even better; world trade grew at 8.9 percent annually, and world income grew at 5.1 percent annually.[28]

1980–1993: PROTECTIONIST TRENDS

During the 1980s and early 1990s, the world trading system erected by the GATT came under strain as pressures for greater protectionism increased around the world. Three reasons caused the rise in such pressures during the 1980s. First, Japan's economic success strained the world trading system. Japan was in ruins when the GATT was created. By the early 1980s, however, it had become the world's second-largest economy and its largest exporter. Japan's success in such industries as automobiles and semiconductors might have been enough to strain the world trading system. Things were made worse by the widespread perception in the West that despite low tariff rates and subsidies, Japanese markets were closed to imports and foreign investment by administrative trade barriers.

Second, the world trading system was strained by the persistent trade deficit in the world's largest economy, the United States. Although the deficit peaked in 1987 at more than $170 billion, by the end of 1992 the annual rate was still running about $80 billion. From a political perspective, the matter was worsened in 1992 by the $45 billion U.S. trade deficit with Japan, a country perceived as not playing by the rules. The consequences of the U.S. deficit included painful adjustments in industries such as automobiles, machine tools, semiconductors, steel, and textiles, where domestic producers steadily lost market share to foreign competitors. The resulting unemployment gave rise to renewed demands in the U.S. Congress for protection against imports.

A third reason for the trend toward greater protectionism was that many countries found ways to get around GATT regulations. Bilateral voluntary export restraints, or VERs, circumvent GATT agreements, because neither the importing country nor the exporting country complain to the GATT bureaucracy in Geneva—and without a complaint, the GATT bureaucracy can do nothing. Exporting countries agreed to VERs to avoid more damaging punitive tariffs. One of the best-known examples is the automobile VER between Japan and the United States, under which Japanese producers promised to limit their auto imports into the United States as a way of defusing growing trade tensions. According to a World Bank study, 13 percent of the imports of industrialized countries in 1981 were subjected to nontariff trade barriers such as VERs. By 1986, this figure had increased to 16 percent. The most rapid rise was in the United States, where the value of imports affected by nontariff barriers (primarily VERs) increased by 23 percent between 1981 and 1986.[29]

THE URUGUAY ROUND AND THE WORLD TRADE ORGANIZATION

Against the background of rising pressures for protectionism, in 1986 GATT members embarked on their eighth round of negotiations to reduce tariffs, the Uruguay Round (so named because it occurred in Uruguay). This was the most difficult round of negotiations yet, primarily because it was also the most ambitious. Until then, GATT rules had applied only to trade in manufactured goods and commodities. In the Uruguay Round, member countries sought to extend GATT rules to cover trade in services. They also sought to write rules governing the protection of intellectual property, to reduce agricultural subsidies, and to strengthen the GATT's monitoring and enforcement mechanisms.

The Uruguay Round dragged on for seven years before an agreement was reached December 15, 1993. It went into effect July 1, 1995. The Uruguay Round contained the following provisions:

1. Tariffs on industrial goods were to be reduced by more than one-third, and tariffs were to be scrapped on more than 40 percent of manufactured goods.

2. Average tariff rates imposed by developed nations on manufactured goods were to be reduced to less than 4 percent of value, the lowest level in modern history.

3. Agricultural subsidies were to be substantially reduced.

4. GATT fair trade and market access rules were to be extended to cover a wide range of services.

5. GATT rules also were to be extended to provide enhanced protection for patents, copyrights, and trademarks (intellectual property).

6. Barriers on trade in textiles were to be significantly reduced over 10 years.

7. The World Trade Organization was to be created to implement the GATT agreement.

Services and Intellectual Property

In the long run, the extension of GATT rules to cover services and intellectual property may be particularly significant. Until 1995, GATT rules applied only to industrial goods (i.e., manufactured goods and commodities). In 2005, world trade in services amounted to $2,415 billion (compared to world trade in goods of $10,120 billion).[30] Ultimately, extension of GATT rules to this important trading arena could significantly increase both the total share of world trade accounted for by services and the overall volume of world trade. The extension of GATT rules to cover intellectual property will make it much easier for high-technology companies to do business in developing nations where intellectual property rules historically have been poorly enforced (see Chapter 2 for details).

The World Trade Organization

The clarification and strengthening of GATT rules and the creation of the World Trade Organization also hold out the promise of more effective policing and enforcement of GATT rules. The WTO acts as an umbrella organization that encompasses the GATT along with two new sister bodies, one on services and the other on intellectual property. The WTO's General Agreement on Trade in Services (GATS) has taken the lead in extending free trade agreements to services. The WTO's Agreement on Trade-Related Aspects of Intellectual Property Rights (TRIPS) is an attempt to narrow the gaps in the way intellectual property rights are protected around the world and to bring them under common international rules. WTO has taken over responsibility for arbitrating trade disputes and monitoring the trade policies of member countries. While the WTO operates on the basis of consensus as the GATT did, in the area of dispute settlement, member countries are no longer able to block adoption of arbitration reports. The WTO automatically adopts arbitration panel reports on trade disputes between member countries unless there is a consensus to reject them. Countries that the arbitration panel finds in violation of GATT rules may appeal to a permanent appellate body, but its verdict is binding. If offenders fail to comply with the recommendations of the arbitration panel, trading partners have the right to compensation or, in the last resort, to impose (commensurate) trade sanctions. Every stage of the procedure is subject to strict time limits. Thus, the WTO has something that the GATT never had—teeth.[31]

WTO: EXPERIENCE TO DATE

By 2007, the WTO had 150 members, including China, which joined at the end of 2001. Another 25 countries, including the Russian Federation and the Ukraine, were negotiating for membership into the organization. Since its formation, the WTO has remained at the forefront of efforts to promote global free trade. Its creators expressed the hope that the enforcement mechanisms granted to the WTO would make it more effective at policing global trade rules than the GATT had been. The great hope was that the WTO might emerge as an effective advocate and facilitator of future trade deals, particularly in areas such as services. The experience so far has been encouraging, although the collapse of WTO talks in Seattle in late 1999 and slow progress with the next round of trade talks, the Doha Round, have raised a number of questions about the future direction of the WTO.

WTO as Global Police

The first decade in the life of the WTO suggests that its policing and enforcement mechanisms are having a positive effect.[32] Between 1995 and early 2007, more than 360 trade disputes between member countries were brought to the WTO.[33] This record compares with a total of 196 cases handled by the GATT over almost half a century. Of the cases brought to the WTO, three-fourths had been resolved by informal consultations between the disputing countries. Resolving the remainder has involved more formal procedures, but these have been largely successful. In general, countries involved have adopted the WTO's recommendations. The fact that countries are using the WTO represents an important vote of confidence in the organization's dispute resolution procedures.

Expanding Trade Agreements

As explained above, the Uruguay Round of GATT negotiations extended global trading rules to cover trade in services. The WTO was given the role of brokering future agreements to open up global trade in services. The WTO was also encouraged to extend its reach to encompass regulations governing foreign direct investment, something the GATT had never done. Two of the first industries targeted for reform were the global telecommunication and financial services industries.

In February 1997, the WTO brokered a deal to get countries to agree to open their telecommunication markets to competition, allowing foreign operators to purchase ownership stakes in domestic telecommunication providers and establishing a set of common rules for fair competition. Under the pact, 68 countries accounting for more than 90 percent of world telecommunication revenues pledged to start opening their markets to foreign competition and to abide by common rules for fair competition in telecommunications. Most of the world's biggest markets, including the United States, European Union, and Japan, were fully liberalized by January 1, 1998, when the pact went into effect. All forms of basic telecommunication service are covered, including voice telephony, data and fax transmissions, and satellite and radio communications. Many telecommunication companies responded positively to the deal, pointing out that it would give them a much greater ability to offer their business customers one-stop shopping—a global, seamless service for all their corporate needs and a single bill.[34]

This was followed in December 1997 with an agreement to liberalize cross-border trade in financial services.[35] The deal covers more than 95 percent of the world's financial services market. Under the agreement, which took effect at the beginning of March 1999, 102 countries pledged to open to varying degrees their banking, securities, and insurance sectors to foreign competition. In common with the telecommunication deal, the accord covers not just cross-border trade but also foreign direct investment. Seventy countries agreed to dramatically lower or eradicate barriers to foreign direct investment in their financial services sector. The United States and the European Union, with minor exceptions, are fully open to inward investment by foreign banks, insurance, and securities companies. As part of the deal, many Asian countries made important

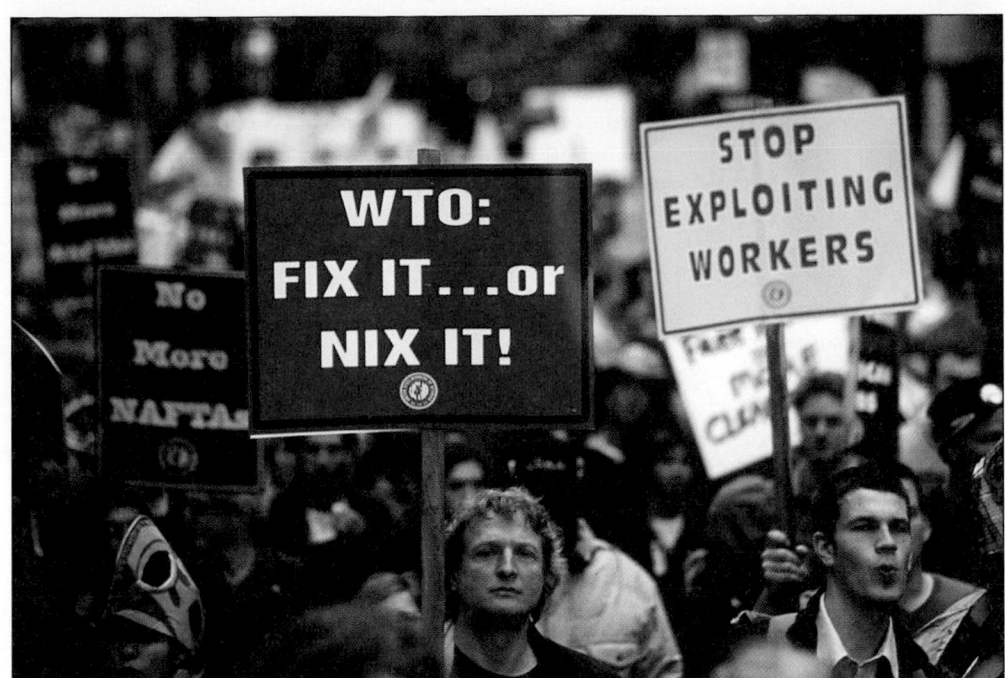

WTO protesters gather in front of the Niketown store at Fifth Avenue and Pike Street in downtown Seattle before the opening of the WTO sessions in Seattle.

concessions that allow significant foreign participation in their financial services sectors for the first time.

The WTO in Seattle: A Watershed?

At the end of November 1999, representatives from the WTO's member states met in Seattle, Washington. The goal of the meeting was to launch a new round of talks—dubbed "the millennium round"—aimed at further reducing barriers to cross-border trade and investment. Prominent on the agenda was an attempt to get the assembled countries to agree to work toward the reduction of barriers to cross-border trade in agricultural products and trade and investment in services.

These expectations were dashed on the rocks of a hard and unexpected reality. The talks ended December 3, 1999, without any agreement being reached. Inside the meeting rooms, the problem was an inability to reach consensus on the primary goals for the next round of talks. A major stumbling block was friction between the United States and the European Union over whether to endorse the aim of ultimately eliminating subsidies to agricultural exporters. The United States wanted the elimination of such subsidies to be a priority. The EU, with its politically powerful farm lobby and long history of farm subsidies, was unwilling to take this step. Another stumbling block was related to efforts by the United States to write "basic labor rights" into the law of the world trading system. The United States wanted the WTO to allow governments to impose tariffs on goods imported from countries that did not abide by what the United States saw as fair labor practices. Representatives from developing nations reacted angrily to this proposal, suggesting it was simply an attempt by the United States to find a legal way of restricting imports from poorer nations.

While the disputes inside the meeting rooms were acrimonious, it was events outside that captured the attention of the world press. The WTO talks proved to be a lightning rod for a diverse collection of organizations from environmentalists and human rights groups to labor unions. For various reasons, these groups oppose free trade. All these organizations argued that the WTO is an undemocratic institution that was usurping the national sovereignty of member states and making decisions of great importance behind closed doors. They took advantage of the Seattle meetings to voice their opposition, which the world press recorded. Environmentalists expressed concern about the impact that free trade in agricultural products might have on the rate of global deforestation. They argued that lower tariffs on imports of lumber from developing nations will stimulate demand and accelerate the rate at which virgin forests are logged, particularly in nations such as Malaysia and Indonesia. They also pointed to the adverse impact that some WTO rulings have had on environmental policies. For example, the WTO had recently blocked a U.S. rule that ordered shrimp nets be equipped with a device that allows endangered sea turtles to escape. The WTO found the rule discriminated against foreign importers who lacked such nets.[36] Environmentalists argued that the rule was necessary to protect the turtles from extinction.

Human rights activists see WTO rules as outlawing the ability of nations to stop imports from countries where child labor is used or working conditions are hazardous. Similarly, labor unions oppose trade laws that allow imports from low-wage countries and result in a loss of jobs in high-wage countries. They buttress their position by arguing that American workers are losing their jobs to imports from developing nations that do not have adequate labor standards.

Supporters of the WTO and free trade dismiss these concerns. They have repeatedly pointed out that the WTO exists to serve the interests of its member states, not subvert them. The WTO lacks the ability to force any member nation to take an action to which it is opposed. The WTO can allow member nations to impose retaliatory tariffs on countries that do not abide by WTO rules, but that is the limit of its power. Furthermore, supporters argue, it is rich countries that pass strict environmental laws and laws governing labor standards, not poor ones. In their view, free trade, by raising living standards in developing nations, will be followed by the passage of such laws in these nations. Using trade regulations to try to impose such practices on developing nations, they believe, will produce a self-defeating backlash.

Many representatives from developing nations, which make up about 110 of the WTO's 150 members, also reject the position taken by environmentalists and advocates of human and labor rights. Poor countries, which depend on exports to boost their economic growth rates and work their way out of poverty, fear that rich countries will use environmental concerns, human rights, and labor-related issues to erect barriers to the products of the developing world. They believe that attempts to incorporate language about the environment or labor standards in future trade agreements will amount to little more than trade barriers by another name.[37] If this were to occur, they argue that the effect would be to trap the developing nations of the world in a grinding cycle of poverty and debt.

These pro-trade arguments fell on deaf ears. As the WTO representatives gathered in Seattle, environmentalists, human rights activists, and labor unions marched in the streets. Some of the more radical elements in these organizations, together with groups of anarchists who were philosophically opposed to "global capitalism" and "the rape of the world by multinationals," succeeded not only in shutting down the opening ceremonies of the WTO but also in sparking violence in the normally peaceful streets of Seattle. A number of demonstrators damaged property and looted; and the police responded with tear gas, rubber bullets, pepper spray, and baton charges. When it was over, 600 demonstrators had been arrested, millions of dollars in property had been damaged in downtown Seattle, and the global news media had their headline: "WTO Talks Collapse amid Violent Demonstrations."

What happened in Seattle is notable because it may have been a watershed of sorts. In the past, previous trade talks were pursued in relative obscurity with only interested economists, politicians, and businesspeople paying much attention. Seattle demonstrated that the issues surrounding the global trend toward free trade have moved to center stage in the popular consciousness. The debate on the merits of free trade and globalization has become mainstream. Whether further liberalization occurs, therefore, may depend on the importance that popular opinion in countries such as the United States attaches

FIGURE 6.2

Antidumping Actions,
1995–2005

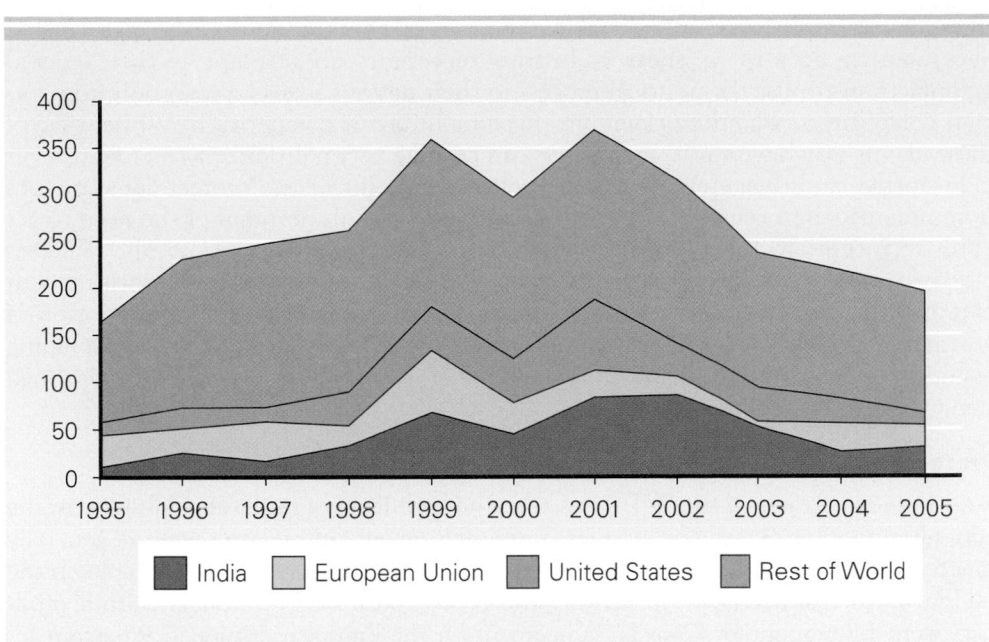

to issues such as human rights and labor standards, job security, environmental policies, and national sovereignty. It will also depend on the ability of advocates of free trade to articulate in a clear and compelling manner the argument that, in the long run, free trade is the best way of promoting adequate labor standards, of providing more jobs, and of protecting the environment.

THE FUTURE OF THE WTO: UNRESOLVED ISSUES AND THE DOHA ROUND

Much remains to be done on the international trade front. Four issues at the forefront of the current agenda of the WTO are the increase in antidumping policies, the high level of protectionism in agriculture, the lack of strong protection for intellectual property rights in many nations, and continued high tariff rates on nonagricultural goods and services in many nations. We shall look at each in turn before discussing the latest round of talks between WTO members aimed at reducing trade barriers, the Doha Round, which began in 2001 and was still ongoing as of 2007.

Antidumping Actions

Antidumping actions proliferated during the 1990s. WTO rules allow countries to impose antidumping duties on foreign goods that are being sold cheaper than at home, or below their cost of production, when domestic producers can show that they are being harmed. Unfortunately, the rather vague definition of what constitutes "dumping" has proven to be a loophole that many countries are exploiting to pursue protectionism.

Between January 1995 and mid-2006, WTO members had reported implementation of some 2,938 antidumping actions to the WTO. India initiated the largest number of antidumping actions, some 448; the EU initiated 345 over the same period, and the United States, 366 (see Figure 6.2). Antidumping actions seem to be concentrated in certain sectors of the economy such as basic metal industries (e.g., aluminum and steel), chemicals, plastics, and machinery and electrical equipment.[38] These sectors account for some 70 percent of all antidumping actions reported to the WTO. These four sectors since 1995 have been characterized by periods of intense competition and excess productive capacity, which have led to low prices and profits (or losses) for firms in those industries. It is not unreasonable, therefore, to hypothesize that the high level of antidumping actions in these industries represents an attempt by beleaguered manufacturers to use the political process in their nations to seek protection from foreign competitors, who they claim are engaging in unfair competition. While some of these claims may have merit, the process can become very politicized as representatives of businesses and their employees lobby government officials to "protect domestic jobs from unfair foreign competition," and government officials, mindful of the need to get votes in future elections, oblige by pushing for antidumping actions. The WTO is clearly worried by this trend, suggesting that it reflects persistent protectionist tendencies and pushing members to strengthen the regulations governing the imposition of antidumping duties. On the other hand, since the WTO signaled that antidumping would be a focus of the Doha Round, the number of antidumping actions has declined somewhat (see Figure 6.2).

Protectionism in Agriculture

Another recent focus of the WTO has been the high level of tariffs and subsidies in the agricultural sector of many economies. Tariff rates on agricultural products are generally much higher than tariff rates on manufactured products or services. For example, in the middle of the first decade of the century, the average tariff rates on nonagricultural products were 4.2 percent for Canada, 3.8 percent for the European Union, 3.9 percent for Japan, and 4.4 percent for the United States. On agricultural products, however, the average tariff rates were 21.2 percent for Canada, 15.9 percent for the European Union, 18.6 percent for Japan, and 10.3 percent for the United States.[39] The implication is that consumers in these countries are paying significantly higher prices than necessary for agricultural products imported from abroad, which leaves them with less money to spend on other goods and services.

The historically high tariff rates on agricultural products reflect a desire to protect domestic agriculture and traditional farming communities from foreign competition. In addition to high tariffs, agricultural producers also benefit from substantial subsidies. According to estimates from the OECD, government subsidies on average account for some 17 percent of the cost of agricultural production in Canada, 21 percent in the United States, 35 percent in the European Union, and 59 percent in Japan.[40] In total, OECD countries spend more than $300 billion a year in subsidies to agricultural producers.

Not surprising, the combination of high tariff barriers and significant subsidies introduces significant distortions into the production of agricultural products and international trade of those products. The net effect is to raise prices to consumers, reduce the volume of agricultural trade, and encourage the overproduction of products that are heavily subsidized (with the government typically buying the surplus). Because global trade in agriculture currently amounts to 10.5 percent of total merchandized trade, or about $750 billion per year, the WTO argues that removing tariff barriers and subsidies could significantly boost the overall level of trade, lower prices to consumers, and raise global economic growth by freeing consumption and investment resources for more productive uses. According to estimates from the International Monetary Fund, removal of tariffs and subsidies on agricultural products would raise global economic welfare by $128 billion annually.[41] Others suggest gains as high as $182 billion.[42]

The biggest defenders of the existing system have been the advanced nations of the world, which want to protect their agricultural sectors from competition by low-cost producers in developing nations. In contrast, developing nations have been pushing hard for reforms that would allow their producers greater access to the protected markets of the developed nations. Estimates suggest that removing all subsidies on agricultural production alone in OECD countries could return to the developing nations of the world three times more than all the foreign aid they currently receive from the OECD nations.[43] In other words, free trade in agriculture could help to jump-start economic growth among the world's poorer nations and alleviate global poverty.

Protecting Intellectual Property

Another issue that has become increasingly important to the WTO has been protecting intellectual property. The 1995 Uruguay agreement that established the WTO also contained an agreement to protect intellectual property (the Trade-Related Aspects of Intellectual Property Rights, or TRIPS, agreement). The TRIPS regulations oblige WTO members to grant and enforce patents lasting at least 20 years and copyrights lasting 50 years. Rich countries had to comply with the rules within a year. Poor countries, in which such protection generally was much weaker, had 5 years' grace, and the very poorest had 10 years. The basis for this agreement was a strong belief among signatory nations that the protection of intellectual property through patents, trademarks, and copyrights must be an essential element of the international trading system. Inadequate protections for intellectual property reduce the incentive for innovation. Because innovation is a central engine of economic growth and rising living standards, the argument has been that a multilateral agreement is needed to protect intellectual property.

Without such an agreement it is feared that producers in a country, let's say India, might market imitations of patented innovations pioneered in a different country, say the United States. This can affect international trade in two ways. First, it reduces the export opportunities in India for the original innovator in the United States. Second, to the extent that the Indian producer is able to export its pirated imitation to additional countries, it also reduces the export opportunities in those countries for the U.S. inventor. Also, one can argue that because the size of the total world market for the innovator is reduced, its incentive to pursue risky and expensive innovations is also reduced. The net effect would be less innovation in the world economy and less economic growth.

Something very similar to this has been occurring in the pharmaceutical industry, with Indian drug companies making copies of patented drugs discovered elsewhere. In 1970, the Indian government stopped recognizing product patents on drugs, but it elected to continue respecting process patents. This permitted Indian companies to reverse-engineer Western pharmaceuticals without paying licensing fees. As a result, foreigners' share of the Indian drug market fell from 75 percent in 1970 to 30 percent in 2000. For example, an Indian company sells a version of Bayer's patented antibiotic Cipro for $0.12 a pill, versus the $5.50 it costs in the United States. Under the WTO TRIPS agreement, India agreed to adopt and enforce the international drug patent regime by 2005.[44]

As noted in Chapter 2, intellectual property rights violation is also an endemic problem in several other industries, most notably computer software and music. The WTO believes that reducing piracy rates in areas such as drugs, software, and music recordings would have a significant impact on the volume of world trade and increase the incentive for producers to invest in the creation of intellectual property. In a world without piracy, more new drugs, computer software, and music recordings would be produced every year. In turn, this would boost economic and social welfare and global economic growth rates. It is thus in the interests of WTO members to make sure that intellectual property rights are respected and enforced. While the 1995 Uruguay agreement that created the WTO did make headway with the TRIPS agreement, some believe these requirements do not go far enough and further commitments are necessary.

Market Access for Nonagricultural Goods and Services

Although the WTO and the GATT have made big strides in reducing the tariff rates on nonagricultural products, much work remains. Although most developed nations have brought their tariff rates on industrial products down to an *average* of 3.8 percent of value, exceptions still remain. In particular, while average tariffs are low, high tariff rates persist on certain imports into developed nations, which limit market access and economic growth. For example, Australia and South Korea, both OECD countries, still

TABLE 6.1

Bound Tariffs on Select Industrial Products— Simple Averages

Source: World Trade Report 2005, WTO, Geneva, 2005.

Country	Metals	Transportation Equipment	Electric Machinery
Canada	2.8%	6.8%	5.2%
United States	1.8	2.7	2.1
Brazil	33.4	33.6	31.9
Mexico	34.7	35.8	34.1
European Union	1.6	4.7	3.3
Australia	4.5	15.1	13.3
Japan	0.9	0.0	0.2
South Korea	7.7	24.6	16.1

have bound tariff rates of 15.1 percent and 24.6 percent, respectively, on imports of transportation equipment (*bound tariff rates* are the highest rate that can be charged, which is often, but not always, the rate that is charged). In contrast, the bound tariff rates on imports of transportation equipment into the United States, EU, and Japan are 2.7 percent, 4.8 percent, and 0 percent, respectively (see Table 6.1). A particular area for concern is high tariff rates on imports of selected goods from developing nations into developed nations.

In addition, tariffs on services remain higher than on industrial goods. The average tariff on business and financial services imported into the United States, for example, is 8.2 percent, into the EU it is 8.5 percent, and into Japan it is 19.7 percent.[45] Given the rising value of cross-border trade in services, reducing these figures can be expected to yield substantial gains.

The WTO would like to bring down tariff rates still further and reduce the scope for the selective use of high tariff rates. The ultimate aim is to reduce tariff rates to zero. Although this might sound ambitious, 40 nations have already moved to zero tariffs on information technology goods, so a precedent exists. Empirical work suggests that further reductions in average tariff rates toward zero would yield substantial gains. One estimate by economists at the World Bank suggests that a broad global trade agreement coming out of the current Doha negotiations could increase world income by $263 billion annually by 2015, of which $109 billion would go to poor countries.[46] Another estimate from the OECD suggests a figure closer to $300 billion annually.[47] See the accompanying Country Focus for estimates of the benefits to the American economy from free trade.

Looking further out, the WTO would like to bring down tariff rates on imports of nonagricultural goods into developing nations. Many of these nations use the infant industry argument to justify the continued imposition of high tariff rates; however, ultimately these rates need to come down for these nations to reap the full benefits of international trade. For example, the bound tariff rates of 53.9 percent on imports of transportation equipment into India and 33.6 percent on imports into Brazil, by raising domestic prices, help to protect inefficient domestic producers and limit economic growth by reducing the real income of consumers who must pay more for transportation equipment and related services.

A New Round of Talks: Doha

Antidumping actions, trade in agricultural products, better enforcement of intellectual property laws, and expanded market access were four of the issues the WTO wanted to tackle at the 1999 meetings in Seattle, but those meetings were derailed. In late 2001, the WTO tried again to launch a new round of talks between member states aimed at

Estimating the Gains from Trade for America

A study published by the Institute for International Economics tried to estimate the gains to the American economy from free trade. According to the study, due to reductions in tariff barriers under the GATT and WTO since 1947, by 2003 the GDP of the United States was 7.3 percent higher than would otherwise have been the case. The benefits of increasing the GDP amount to roughly $1 trillion a year, or $9,000 extra income for each American household per year.

The same study tried to estimate what would happen if America concluded free trade deals with all its trading partners, reducing tariff barriers on all goods and services to zero. Using several methods to estimate the impact, the study concluded that additional annual gains of between $450 billion and $1.3 trillion could be realized. This final march to free trade, according to the authors of the study, could safely be expected to raise incomes of the average American household by an additional $4,500 per year.

The authors also tried to estimate the scale and cost of employment disruption that would be caused by a move to universal free trade. Jobs would be lost in certain sectors and gained in others if the country abolished all tariff barriers. Using historical data as a guide, they estimated that 226,000 jobs would be lost every year due to expanded trade, although some two-thirds of those losing jobs would find reemployment after a year. Reemployment, however, would be at a wage that was 13 to 14 percent lower. The study concluded that the disruption costs would total some $54 billion annually, primarily in the form of lower lifetime wages to those whose jobs were disrupted as a result of free trade. Offset against this, however, must be the higher economic growth resulting from free trade, which creates many new jobs and raises household incomes, creating another $450 billion to $1.3 trillion annually in *net* gains to the economy. In other words, the estimated annual gains from trade are far greater than the estimated annual costs associated with job disruption, and more people benefit than lose as a result of a shift to a universal free trade regime.[48]

further liberalizing the global trade and investment framework. For this meeting, it picked the remote location of Doha in the Persian Gulf state of Qatar, no doubt with an eye on the difficulties that antiglobalization protesters would have in getting there. Unlike the Seattle meetings, at Doha, the member states of the WTO agreed to launch a new round of talks and staked out an agenda. The talks were originally scheduled to last three years, although they have already gone on longer and may not be concluded for a while.

The agenda agreed upon at Doha should be seen as a game plan for negotiations over the next few years. The agenda includes cutting tariffs on industrial goods and services, phasing out subsidies to agricultural producers, reducing barriers to cross-border investment, and limiting the use of antidumping laws. Some difficult compromises were made to reach agreement on this agenda. The EU and Japan had to give significant ground on the issue of agricultural subsidies, which are used extensively by both entities to support politically powerful farmers. The United States bowed to pressure from virtually every other nation to negotiate revisions of antidumping rules, which the United States has used extensively to protect its steel producers from foreign competition. Europe had to scale back its efforts to include environmental policy in the trade talks, primarily because of pressure from developing nations that see environmental protection policies as trade barriers by another name. Excluded from the agenda was any language pertaining to attempts to tie trade to labor standards in a country.

Countries with big pharmaceutical sectors acquiesced to demands from African, Asian, and Latin American nations on the issue of drug patents. Specifically, the language in the agreement declares that WTO regulation on intellectual property "does not and should not prevent members from taking measures to protect public health."

This language was meant to assure the world's poorer nations that they can make or buy generic equivalents to fight such killers as AIDS and malaria.

Clearly, it is one thing to agree to an agenda and quite another to reach a consensus on a new treaty. Nevertheless, this agreement yields some potential winners. These include low-cost agricultural producers in the developing world and developed nations such as Australia and the United States. If the talks are successful, agricultural producers in these nations will ultimately see the global markets for their goods expand. Developing nations also gain from the lack of language on labor standards, which many saw as an attempt by rich nations to erect trade barriers. The sick and poor of the world also benefit from guaranteed access to cheaper medicines. There are also clear losers in this agreement, including EU and Japanese farmers, U.S. steelmakers, environmental activists, and pharmaceutical firms in the developed world. These losers can be expected to lobby their governments hard during the ensuing years to make sure that the final agreement is more in their favor.[49] In general, though, if successful, the Doha Round of negotiations could significantly raise global economic welfare. As noted above, estimates suggest that a successful Doha Round would raise global incomes by as much as $300 billion annually, with 60 percent of the gain going to the world's poorer nations, which would help to pull 150 million people out of poverty.[50]

The talks are currently ongoing, and as seems normal in these cases, they are characterized by halting progress punctuated by significant setbacks and missed deadlines. A September 2003 meeting in Cancun, Mexico, broke down, primarily because there was no agreement on how to proceed with reducing agricultural subsidies and tariffs; the EU, United States, and India, among others, proved less than willing to reduce tariffs and subsidies to their politically important farmers, while countries such as Brazil and certain West African nations wanted free trade as quickly as possible. However, in early 2004, both the United States and the EU made a determined push to start the talks again, and in mid-2004 both seemed to commit themselves to sweeping reductions in agricultural tariffs and subsidies. However, since then little forward progress has been made and the talks are essentially stalled, primarily because of disagreements over how deep the cuts in subsidies to agricultural producers should be. As of early 2007, the goal was to reduce tariffs for manufactured and agricultural goods by 60 percent to 70 percent and to cut subsidies to half of their current level, but getting nations to agree to these goals proved exceedingly difficult.

IMPLICATIONS FOR MANAGERS

What are the implications of all this for business practice? Why should the international manager care about the political economy of free trade or about the relative merits of arguments for free trade and protectionism? There are two answers to this question. The first concerns the impact of trade barriers on a firm's strategy. The second concerns the role that business firms can play in promoting free trade or trade barriers.

TRADE BARRIERS AND FIRM STRATEGY

To understand how trade barriers affect a firm's strategy, consider first the theories of international trade introduced in Chapter 5. We discussed how it makes sense for the firm to disperse its various production activities to those countries around the globe where they can be performed most efficiently. Thus, it may make sense for a firm to design and engineer its product in one country, manufacture components in another, perform final assembly operations in yet another country, and then export the finished product to the rest of the world.

Clearly, trade barriers constrain a firm's ability to disperse its productive activities in such a manner. First and most obvious, tariff barriers raise the costs of exporting products to a country (or of exporting partly finished products between countries). This may put the firm at a competitive disadvantage to indigenous competitors in that country. In response, the firm may then find it economical to locate production facilities in that country so that it can compete on an even footing. Second, quotas may limit a firm's ability to serve a country from locations outside of that country. Again, the response by the firm might be to set up production facilities in that country—even though it may result in higher production costs. Such reasoning was one of the factors behind the rapid expansion of Japanese automaking capacity in the United States during the 1980s and 1990s. This followed the establishment of a VER agreement between the United States and Japan that limited U.S. imports of Japanese automobiles.

Third, to conform to local content regulations, a firm may have to locate more production activities in a given market than it would otherwise. Again, from the firm's perspective, the consequence might be to raise costs above the level that could be achieved if each production activity were dispersed to the optimal location for that activity. And finally, even when trade barriers do not exist, the firm may still want to locate some production activities in a given country to reduce the threat of trade barriers being imposed in the future.

All these effects are likely to raise the firm's costs above the level that could be achieved in a world without trade barriers. The higher costs that result need not translate into a significant competitive disadvantage relative to other foreign firms, however, if the countries imposing trade barriers do so to the imported products of all foreign firms, irrespective of their national origin. But when trade barriers are targeted at exports from a particular nation, firms based in that nation are at a competitive disadvantage to firms of other nations. The firm may deal with such targeted trade barriers by moving production into the country imposing barriers. Another strategy may be to move production to countries whose exports are not targeted by the specific trade barrier.

Finally, the threat of antidumping action limits the ability of a firm to use aggressive pricing to gain market share in a country. Firms in a country also can make strategic use of antidumping measures to limit aggressive competition from low-cost foreign producers. For example, the U.S. steel industry has been very aggressive in bringing antidumping actions against foreign steelmakers, particularly in times of weak global demand for steel and excess capacity. In 1998 and 1999, the United States faced a surge in low-cost steel imports as a severe recession in Asia left producers there with excess capacity. The U.S. producers filed several complaints with the International Trade Commission. One argued that Japanese producers of hot rolled steel were selling it below cost in the United States. The ITC agreed and levied tariffs ranging from 18 percent to 67 percent on imports of certain steel products from Japan (these tariffs are separate from the steel tariffs discussed earlier).[51]

POLICY IMPLICATIONS

As noted in Chapter 5, business firms are major players on the international trade scene. Because of their pivotal role in international trade, firms can and do exert a strong influence on government policy toward trade. This influence can encourage protectionism or it can encourage the government to support the WTO and push for open markets and freer trade among all nations. Government policies with regard to international trade can have a direct impact on business.

Consistent with strategic trade policy, examples can be found of government intervention in the form of tariffs, quotas, antidumping actions, and subsidies helping firms and industries establish a competitive advantage in the world economy. In general, however, the arguments contained in this chapter and in Chapter 5 suggest that government intervention has three drawbacks. Intervention can be self-defeating because it tends to protect the inefficient rather than help firms become efficient global competitors. Intervention is dangerous; it may invite retaliation and trigger a trade war. Finally, intervention is unlikely to be well executed, given the opportunity for such a policy to be captured by special-interest groups. Does this mean that business should simply encourage government to adopt a laissez-faire free trade policy?

Most economists would probably argue that the best interests of international business are served by a free trade stance, but not a laissez-faire stance. It is probably in the best long-run interests of the business community to encourage the government to aggressively promote greater free trade by, for example, strengthening the WTO. Business probably has much more to gain from government efforts to open protected markets to imports and foreign direct investment than from government efforts to support certain domestic industries in a manner consistent with the recommendations of strategic trade policy.

This conclusion is reinforced by a phenomenon we touched on in Chapter 1—the increasing integration of the world economy and internationalization of production that has occurred over the past two decades. We live in a world where many firms of all national origins increasingly depend for their competitive advantage on globally dispersed production systems. Such systems are the result of freer trade. Freer trade has brought great advantages to firms that have exploited it and to consumers who benefit from the resulting lower prices. Given the danger of retaliatory action, business firms that lobby their governments to engage in protectionism must realize that by doing so they may be denying themselves the opportunity to build a competitive advantage by constructing a globally dispersed production system. By encouraging their governments to engage in protectionism, their own activities and sales overseas may be jeopardized if other governments retaliate. This does not mean a firm should never seek protection in the form of antidumping actions and the like, but it should review its options carefully and think through the larger consequences.

CHAPTER SUMMARY

The goal of this chapter was to describe how the reality of international trade deviates from the theoretical ideal of unrestricted free trade reviewed in Chapter 5. In this chapter, we have reported the various instruments of trade policy, reviewed the political and economic arguments for government intervention in international trade, reexamined the economic case for free trade in light of the strategic trade policy argument, and looked at the evolution of the world trading framework. While a policy of free trade may not always be the theoretically optimal policy (given the arguments of the new trade theorists), in practice it is probably the best policy for a government to pursue. In particular, the long-run interests of business and consumers may be best served by strengthening international institutions such as the WTO. Given the danger that isolated protectionism might escalate into a trade war, business probably has far more to gain from government efforts to open protected markets to imports and foreign direct investment (through the WTO) than from government efforts to protect domestic industries from foreign competition. The chapter made the following points:

1. Trade policies, such as tariffs, subsidies, antidumping regulations, and local content requirements tend to be pro-producer and anticonsumer.

Gains accrue to producers (who are protected from foreign competitors), but consumers lose because they must pay more for imports.

2. There are two types of arguments for government intervention in international trade: political and economic. Political arguments for intervention are concerned with protecting the interests of certain groups, often at the expense of other groups, or with promoting goals with regard to foreign policy, human rights, consumer protection, and the like. Economic arguments for intervention are about boosting the overall wealth of a nation.

3. A common political argument for intervention is that it is necessary to protect jobs. However, political intervention often hurts consumers and it can be self-defeating. Countries sometimes argue that it is important to protect certain industries for reasons of national security. Some argue that government should use the threat to intervene in trade policy as a bargaining tool to open foreign markets. This can be a risky policy; if it fails, the result can be higher trade barriers.

4. The infant industry argument for government intervention contends that to let manufacturing

get a toehold, governments should temporarily support new industries. In practice, however, governments often end up protecting the inefficient.

5. Strategic trade policy suggests that with subsidies, government can help domestic firms gain first-mover advantages in global industries where economies of scale are important. Government subsidies may also help domestic firms overcome barriers to entry into such industries.

6. The problems with strategic trade policy are twofold: (*a*) such a policy may invite retaliation, in which case all will lose, and (*b*) strategic trade policy may be captured by special-interest groups, which will distort it to their own ends.

7. The GATT was a product of the postwar free trade movement. The GATT was successful in lowering trade barriers on manufactured goods and commodities. The move toward greater free

trade under the GATT appeared to stimulate economic growth.

8. The completion of the Uruguay Round of GATT talks and the establishment of the World Trade Organization have strengthened the world trading system by extending GATT rules to services, increasing protection for intellectual property, reducing agricultural subsidies, and enhancing monitoring and enforcement mechanisms.

9. Trade barriers act as a constraint on a firm's ability to disperse its various production activities to optimal locations around the globe. One response to trade barriers is to establish more production activities in the protected country.

10. Business may have more to gain from government efforts to open protected markets to imports and foreign direct investment than from government efforts to protect domestic industries from foreign competition.

Critical Thinking and Discussion Questions

1. Do you think governments should consider human rights when granting preferential trading rights to countries? What are the arguments for and against taking such a position?

2. Whose interests should be the paramount concern of government trade policy—the interests of producers (businesses and their employees) or those of consumers?

3. Given the arguments relating to the new trade theory and strategic trade policy, what kind of trade policy should business be pressuring government to adopt?

4. You are an employee of a U.S. firm that produces personal computers in Thailand and then exports them to the United States and other countries for sale. The personal computers were originally

produced in Thailand to take advantage of relatively low labor costs and a skilled workforce. Other possible locations considered at the time were Malaysia and Hong Kong. The U.S. government decides to impose punitive 100 percent ad valorem tariffs on imports of computers from Thailand to punish the country for administrative trade barriers that restrict U.S. exports to Thailand. How should your firm respond? What does this tell you about the use of targeted trade barriers?

5. Reread the Management Focus feature, "U.S. Magnesium Seeks Protection." Who gains most from the antidumping duties levied by the United States on imports of magnesium from China and Russia? Who are the losers? Are these duties in the best national interests of the United States?

Research Task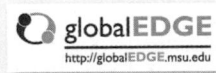

Use the globalEDGE™ site to complete the following exercises:

1. Your company is considering exporting its products to Egypt. Yet, management's current knowledge of this country's trade policies and barriers is limited. However, before your company's management decides to export, a more detailed analysis of the political and economic conditions in Egypt is required. In fact, you

have heard that the *National Trade Estimate Report on Foreign Trade Barriers* may be a good place to start. Begin your search and identify Egypt's current import policies with respect to fundamental issues such as tariffs and restrictions. Prepare an executive summary of your findings.

2. The number of member nations of the World Trade Organization has increased considerably in

recent years. Additionally, some non-member countries have observer status, which requires accession negotiations to begin within five years of attaining this preliminary position. Identify the current total number of WTO members. Also, prepare a list of current observer countries. Do you notice anything in particular about the countries that have observer status?

CLOSING CASE

Trade in Textiles—Holding the Chinese Juggernaut in Check

Since 1974, international trade in textiles has been governed by a system of quotas known as the Multi-Fiber Agreement (MFA). Designed to protect textile producers in developed nations from foreign competition, the MFA assigned countries quotas that specified the amount of textiles they could export. The quotas restrained textile exports from some countries, such as China, but in other cases created a textile industry that might not have existed. Countries such as Bangladesh, Sri Lanka, and Cambodia were able to take advantage of favorable quota allocations to build significant textile industries that generated substantial exports. In 2003, textiles accounted for more than 70 percent of exports from Bangladesh and Cambodia and 50 percent of those from Sri Lanka.

This is now changing. When the World Trade Organization was created in 1995, member countries agreed to let the MFA expire on December 31, 2004. At the time, many textile exporters in the developing world expected to gain from the elimination of the quota system. What they did not anticipate, however, was that China would join the WTO in 2001 and that Chinese textile exports would surge. By 2003, China was making 17 percent of the world's textiles, but this may only be a start. The WTO forecasts that China's share may rise to 50 percent by 2007 as the country's producers take advantage of the removal of quotas to expand their exports to the United States and European Union, displacing exports from many other developing nations. China's gains are due to its comparative advantage in the manufacture of textiles. Not only does the country benefit from low wages and a productive labor force, but China's huge factories also enable its producers to attain economies of scale unimaginable in most developing nations. Also, the country's good infrastructure ensures quick transport of products and a timely turnaround of ships at ports, a critical asset in the clothing industry where fashion trends can result in rapid changes in demand. Chinese producers have been able to reduce the order-to-shipment cycle to as low as 60 days, far below the 90 to 120 days achieved by many other producers in the developing world. In addition, Chinese textile producers have garnered a reputation for reliably delivering on commitments, unlike those in some other countries. Producers in Bangladesh, for example, have a reputation for low quality and poor delivery that offsets their low prices.

Fearful that they will lose market share to China, trade associations from more than 50 other textile-producing nations, many of them low- and middle-income nations, signed the "Istanbul declaration" in 2004 asking the WTO to delay the removal of quotas, but to no avail. Many developing nations now fear that they will lose substantial market share to China. This could conceivably cripple the economies of countries such as Bangladesh, where some 2 million people, most of them women, are employed in the textile industry. Other developing nations, however, think that they might benefit from the removal of the MFA. They believe that buyers in developed nations will need to diversify their supply base as a hedge against disruption in China. Among this second group are Vietnam, India, and Pakistan, all of which expect rising textile exports after 2004. The Indian textile manufacturers group expects Indian textile exports to grow by 18 percent a year after 2004, reaching $40 billion in 2010, or one-third of the country's exports.

In developing nations, too, the prospect of surging imports from China causes unease. In the United States, textile producers lobbied the government to impose quotas on Chinese imports after the MFA expired. Under the terms of China's entry into the WTO, the United States and other major trading nations reserved the right until 2008 to impose annual quotas on Chinese textile imports if they are deemed to be "disruptive."

China tried to head off protectionist pressures in December 2004 by announcing it would impose a tariff on textile exports. By raising the costs of Chinese textiles, the tariff was designed to reduce overseas demand. However, the tariffs are modest, ranging from 2.4 to 6 cents per item, with most at the low end of the range. Many observers see them as little more than a token gesture.

The first eight months of 2005 provided a glimpse of what may be to come. Imports of Chinese textiles into the United States surged 64 percent compared with the same period in 2004 to $15.4 billion. Chinese textile imports into the EU also rose. However, others noted that total textile imports into the U.S. remained flat, and that the surge represented a shift from other producers to China, rather than an absolute increase in the volume of imports. Notwithstanding this, the increase in imports resulted in renewed calls in the United States for quotas on Chinese textile imports. Recognizing reality, in mid-2005 the Chinese entered into bilateral negotiations with the United States to limit imports of Chinese textiles. In November 2005, they reached an agreement that capped the growth in Chinese imports into the United States at around 15 percent per annum until 2008, after which restrictions will be lifted. The EU struck a similar deal with China some months earlier.[52]

Case Discussion Questions

1. Was the removal of the Multi-Fiber Agreement a positive thing for the world economy? Why?

2. As a producer in a developing nation such as Bangladesh that benefited from the MFA agreement, how should you respond to the expiration of the agreement?

3. Do you think China was right to place a tariff on exports of textiles from China? Why? Does such action help or harm the world economy?

4. Whose interests were served by the November 2005 agreement between the United States and China to limit the growth of Chinese textile imports into the United States? Do you think the agreement was a good one for the United States?

5. What kind of trade barrier was erected by the November 2005 agreement between China and the United States?

Notes

1. Sources: K. H. Cross, "King Cotton, Developing Countries and the Peace Clause," *Journal of International Economics and Law* 9 (1) (2006), pp. 149–95; F. Williams, "WTO Plans to Probe US Farm Subsidies," *Financial Times*, September 29, 2006, p. 12; "A Tangle of Troubles: Cotton," *The Economist*, July 22, 2006, p. 53; http://www.unctad.org/infocomm/anglais/cotton/prices.htm, accessed March 23, 2007.

2. For a detailed welfare analysis of the effect of a tariff, see P. R. Krugman and M. Obstfeld, *International Economics: Theory and Policy* (New York: HarperCollins, 2000), chap. 8.

3. Y. Sazanami, S. Urata, and H. Kawai, *Measuring the Costs of Protection in Japan* (Washington, DC: Institute for International Economics, 1994).

4. J. Bhagwati, *Protectionism* (Cambridge, MA: MIT Press, 1988); and "Costs of Protection," *Journal of Commerce*, September 25, 1991, p. 8A.

5. World Trade Organization, *World Trade Report 2006* (Geneva: WTO: 2006).

6. The study was undertaken by Kym Anderson of the University of Adelaide. See "A Not So Perfect Market," *The Economist; Survey of Agriculture and Technology*, March 25, 2000, pp. 8–10.

7. K. Anderson, W. Martin, and D van der Mensbrugghe, "Distortions to World Trade: Impact on Agricultural Markets and Farm Incomes," *Review of Agricultural Economics* 28 (Summer 2006), pp. 168–94.

8. Sources: J. Dyck and H. Fukuda, "Taxes on Imports Subsidize Wheat Production in Japan," *Amber Waves*, February 2005, p. 2; and H. Fukuda, J. Dyck, and J. Stout, "Wheat and Barley Policies in Japan," U.S. Department of Agriculture research report, WHS-04i-01, November 2004.

9. R. W. Crandall, *Regulating the Automobile* (Washington, DC: Brookings Institution, 1986).

10. Krugman and Obstfeld, *International Economics*.

11. G. Hufbauer and Z. A. Elliott, *Measuring the Costs of Protectionism in the United States* (Washington, DC: Institute for International Economics, 1993).

12. Bhagwati, *Protectionism*; and "Japan to Curb VCR Exports," *The New York Times*, November 21, 1983, p. D5.

13. Sources: D. Anderton, "U.S. Magnesium Lands Ruling on Unfair Imports," *Desert News*, October 1, 2004, p. D10; "U.S. Magnesium and Its Largest Consumers Debate before U.S. ITC," *Platt's Metals Week*, February 28, 2005, p. 2; and S. Oberbeck, "U.S. Magnesium Plans Big Utah Production Expansion," *Salt Lake Tribune*, March 30, 2005.

14. Alan Goldstein, "Sematech Members Facing Dues Increase; 30% Jump to Make Up for Loss of Federal Funding," *Dallas Morning News*, July 27, 1996, p. 2F.

15. N. Dunne and R. Waters, "U.S. Waves a Big Stick at Chinese Pirates," *Financial Times*, January 6, 1995, p. 4.

16. B. Tomson, "U.S. Beef Heads Back to China," *Barron's*, December 26, 2005, p. M16.

17. B. Lambrecht, "Monsanto Softens Its Stance on Labeling in Europe," *St. Louis Post-Dispatch*, March 15, 1998, p. E1.

18. P. S. Jordan, "Country Sanctions and the International Business Community," *American Society of International Law Proceedings of the Annual Meeting* 20, no. 9 (1997), pp. 333–42.

19. "Waiting for China; Human Rights and International Trade," *Commonwealth*, March 11, 1994; and "China: The Cost of Putting Business First," *Human Rights Watch*, July 1996.

20. Sources: C. Southey, "Hormones Fuel a Meaty EU Row," *Financial Times*, September 7, 1995, p. 2; E. L. Andrews, "In Victory for U.S., European Ban on Treated Beef Is Ruled Illegal," *The New York Times*, May 9, 1997, p. A1; F. Williams and G. de Jonquieres, "WTO's Beef Rulings Give Europe Food for Thought," *Financial Times*, February 13, 1998, p. 5; R. Baily, "Food and Trade: EU Fear Mongers' Lethal Harvest," *Los Angeles Times*, August 18, 2002, p. M3; "The US–EU Dispute over Hormone Treated Beef," *The Kiplinger Agricultural Letter*, January 10, 2003; and Scott Miller, "EU Trade Sanctions Have Duel Edge," *The Wall Street Journal*, February 26, 2004, p. A3.

21. "Brazil's Auto Industry Struggles to Boost Global Competitiveness," *Journal of Commerce*, October 10, 1991, p. 6A.

22. For reviews, see J. A. Brander, "Rationales for Strategic Trade and Industrial Policy," in *Strategic Trade Policy and the New International Economics*, ed. P. R. Krugman (Cambridge, MA: MIT Press, 1986); P. R. Krugman, "Is Free Trade Passé?" *Journal of Economic Perspectives* 1 (1987), pp. 131–44; and P. R. Krugman, "Does the New Trade Theory Require a New Trade Policy?" *World Economy* 15, no. 4 (1992), pp. 423–41.

23. "Airbus and Boeing: The Jumbo War," *The Economist*, June 15, 1991, pp. 65–66.

24. For details see Krugman, "Is Free Trade Passé?" and Brander, "Rationales for Strategic Trade and Industrial Policy."

25. Krugman, "Is Free Trade Passé?"

26. This dilemma is a variant of the famous prisoner's dilemma, which has become a classic metaphor for the difficulty of achieving cooperation between self-interested and mutually suspicious entities. For a good general introduction, see A. Dixit and B. Nalebuff, *Thinking Strategically: The Competitive Edge in Business, Politics, and Everyday Life* (New York: W. W. Norton & Co., 1991).

27. Note that the Smoot–Hawley Act did not cause the Great Depression. However, the beggar-thy-neighbor trade policies it ushered in certainly made things worse. See Bhagwati, *Protectionism*.

28. Ibid.

29. World Bank, *World Development Report* (New York: Oxford University Press, 1987).

30. World Trade Organization, "World Trade 2005, Prospects 2006," WTO press release, April 11, 2006.

31. Frances Williams, "WTO—New Name Heralds New Powers," *Financial Times*, December 16, 1993, p. 5; and Frances Williams, "Gatt's Successor to Be Given Real Clout," *Financial Times*, April 4, 1994, p. 6.

32. W. J. Davey, "The WTO Dispute Settlement System: The First Ten Years," *Journal of International Economic Law*, March 2005, pp. 17–28.

33. Information provided on WTO Web site, www.wto.org/english/tratop_e/dispu_e/dispu_status_e.htm.

34. Frances Williams, "Telecoms: World Pact Set to Slash Costs of Calls," *Financial Times*, February 17, 1997.

35. G. De Jonquieres, "Happy End to a Cliff Hanger," *Financial Times*, December 15, 1997, p. 15.

36. Jim Carlton, "Greens Target WTO Plan for Lumber," *The Wall Street Journal*, November 24, 1999, p. A2.

37. Kari Huus, "WTO Summit Leaves Only Discontent," MSNBC, December 3, 1999, www.msnbc.com.

38. Data at www.wto.org/english/tratop_e/adp_e/adp_e.htm.

39. *Annual Report by the Director General 2003* (Geneva: World Trade Organization, 2003).

40. Ibid.

41. Ibid.

42. K. Anderson, W. Martin, and D van der Mensbrugghe, "Distortions to World Trade: Impact on Agricultural Markets and Farm Incomes,"

Review of Agricultural Economics 28 (Summer 2006), pp. 168–94.

43. World Trade Organization, *Annual Report 2002* (Geneva: WTO, 2002).

44. A. Tanzer, "Pill Factory to the World," *Forbes*, December 10, 2001, pp. 70–72.

45. S. C. Bradford, P. L. E. Grieco, and G. C. Hufbauer, "The Payoff to America from Global Integration," in *The United States and the World Economy: Foreign Policy for the Next Decade*, C. F. Bergsten, ed. (Washington, DC: Institute for International Economics, 2005).

46. World Bank, *Global Economic Prospects 2005* (Washington, DC: World Bank, 2005).

47. "Doha Development Agenda," *OECD Observer*, Paris, September 2006, pp 64–67.

48. Source: Bradford, Grieco, and Hufbauer, "The Payoff to America."

49. W. Vieth, "Major Concessions Lead to Success for WTO Talks," *Los Angeles Times*, November 14, 2001, p. A1; and "Seeds Sown for Future Growth," *The Economist*, November 17, 2001, pp. 65–66.

50. "The WTO under Fire—The Doha Round," *The Economist*, September 20, 2003, pp. 30–32.

51. "Punitive Tariffs Are Approved on Imports of Japanese Steel," *The New York Times*, June 12, 1999, p. A3.

52. Sources: "The Looming Revolution—The Textile Industry," *The Economist*, November 13, 2004, pp. 92–96; "A New Knot in Textile Trade," *The Economist*, December 18, 2004, p. 138; "Textile Disruption," *The Wall Street Journal*, April 11, 2005, p. A21; M. Fong and W. Echikson, "China Bristles at U.S. Inquiry on Textiles Trade," *The Wall Street Journal*, April 6, 2005, p. A9; and M. Fong, "China, U.S. Sign Three-Year Pact on Textile Trade," *The Wall Street Journal*, November 9, 2005, p. A14.

Starbucks' Foreign Direct Investment

Thirty years ago, Starbucks was a single store in Seattle's Pike Place Market selling premium roasted coffee. Today it is a global roaster and retailer of coffee with some 13,000 stores, more than 3,750 of which are to be found in 38 foreign countries. Starbucks Corporation set out on its current course in the 1980s when the company's director of marketing, Howard Schultz, came back from a trip to Italy enchanted with the Italian coffeehouse experience. Schultz, who later became CEO, persuaded the company's owners to experiment with the coffeehouse format—and the Starbucks experience was born. The strategy was to sell the company's own premium roasted coffee and freshly brewed espresso-style coffee beverages, along with a variety of pastries, coffee accessories, teas, and other products, in a tastefully designed coffeehouse setting. The company also focused on providing superior customer service. Reasoning that motivated employees provide the best customer service, Starbucks' executives devoted a lot of attention to employee hiring and training programs and progressive compensation policies that gave even part-time employees stock option grants and medical benefits. The formula led to spectacular success in the United States, where Starbucks went from obscurity to one of the best-known brands in the country in a decade.

In 1995, with 700 stores across the United States, Starbucks began exploring foreign opportunities. Its first target market was Japan. Although Starbucks had resisted a franchising strategy in North America, where its stores are company owned, Starbucks initially decided to license its format in Japan. However, the company also realized that a pure licensing agreement would not give it the control needed to ensure that the Japanese licensees closely followed Starbucks' successful formula. So the company established a joint venture with a local retailer, Sazaby Inc. Each company held a 50 percent stake in the venture, Starbucks Coffee of Japan. Starbucks initially invested $10 million in this venture, its first foreign direct investment. The Starbucks format was then licensed to the venture, which was charged with taking over responsibility for growing Starbucks' presence in Japan.

To make sure the Japanese operations replicated the "Starbucks experience" in North America, Starbucks transferred some employees to the Japanese operation. The licensing agreement required all Japanese store managers and employees to attend training classes similar to those given to U.S. employees. The agreement also required that stores adhere to the design parameters established in the United States. In 2001, the company

Foreign Direct Investment

7

LEARNING OBJECTIVES
After you have read this chapter you should:

LO¹ Be familiar with current trends regarding FDI in the world economy.

LO² Understand the different theories of foreign direct investment.

LO³ Appreciate how political ideology shapes a government's attitudes toward FDI.

LO⁴ Understand the benefits and costs of FDI to home and host countries.

LO⁵ Be able to discuss the range of policy instruments that governments use to influence FDI.

LO⁶ Articulate the implications for management practice of the theory and government policies associated with FDI.

introduced a stock option plan for all Japanese employees, making it the first company in Japan to do so. Skeptics doubted that Starbucks would be able to replicate its North American success overseas, but by 2006 Starbucks had over 600 stores in Japan and planned to continue opening them at a brisk pace.

After Japan, the company embarked on an aggressive foreign investment program. In 1998, it purchased Seattle Coffee, a British coffee chain with 60 retail stores, for $84 million. An American couple, originally from Seattle, had started Seattle Coffee with the intention of establishing a Starbucks-like chain in Britain. In the late 1990s, Starbucks opened stores in Taiwan, China, Singapore, Thailand, New Zealand, South Korea, and Malaysia.

In Asia, Starbucks' most common strategy was to license its format to a local operator in return for initial licensing fees and royalties on store revenues. As in Japan, Starbucks insisted on an intensive employee training program and strict specifications regarding the format and layout of the store. However, Starbucks became disenchanted with some of the straight licensing arrangements and converted several into joint-venture arrangements or wholly owned subsidiaries. In Thailand,

for example, Starbucks initially entered into a licensing agreement with Coffee Partners, a local Thai company. Under the terms of the licensing agreement, Coffee Partners was required to open at least 20 Starbucks coffee stores in Thailand within five years. However, Coffee Partners found it difficult to raise funds from Thai banks to finance this expansion. In July 2000, Starbucks acquired Coffee Partners for about $12 million. Its goal was to gain tighter control over the expansion strategy in Thailand.

By 2002, Starbucks was pursuing an aggressive expansion in mainland Europe. As its first entry point, Starbucks chose Switzerland. Drawing on its experience in Asia, the company entered into a joint venture with a Swiss company, Bon Appetit Group, Switzerland's largest food service company. Bon Appetit was to hold a majority stake in the venture, and Starbucks would license its format to the Swiss company using a similar agreement to those it had used successfully in Asia. This was followed by a joint venture in other countries. In early 2006, Starbucks announced that it believed there was the potential for up to 15,000 stores outside of the United States, with major opportunities in China, which the company now views as the largest single market opportunity outside the United States.[1]

Introduction

Foreign direct investment (FDI) occurs when a firm invests directly in facilities to produce or market a product in a foreign country. According to the U.S. Department of Commerce, FDI occurs whenever a U.S. citizen, organization, or affiliated group takes an interest of 10 percent or more in a foreign business entity. Once a firm undertakes FDI, it becomes a *multinational enterprise.* The opening case, about Starbucks' expansion, is an example of FDI. Starting in 1995, Starbucks began to move into other nations. By 2007, this FDI had transformed Starbucks into a global brand with operations in 38 countries.

FDI takes on two main forms. The first is a **greenfield investment,** which involves the establishment of a new operation in a foreign country. The second involves acquiring or merging with an existing firm in the foreign country (most of Starbucks' expansion has been in the form of greenfield investments, although it did acquire Britain's Seattle Coffee). Acquisitions can be as a minority (where the foreign firm takes a 10 percent to 49 percent interest in the firm's voting stock), majority (foreign interest of 50 percent to 99 percent), or full outright stake (foreign interest of 100 percent).[2]

We begin this chapter by looking at the importance of foreign direct investment in the world economy. Next, we review the theories that have been used to explain foreign direct investment. The chapter then moves on to look at government policy toward foreign direct investment and closes with a section on implications for business.

Foreign Direct Investment in the World Economy

When discussing foreign direct investment, it is important to distinguish between the flow of FDI and the stock of FDI. The **flow of FDI** refers to the amount of FDI undertaken over a given time period (normally a year). The **stock of FDI** refers to the total accumulated value of foreign-owned assets at a given time. We also talk of **outflows of FDI,** meaning the flow of FDI out of a country, and **inflows of FDI,** the flow of FDI into a country.

TRENDS IN FDI

The past 30 years have seen a marked increase in both the flow and stock of FDI in the world economy. The average yearly outflow of FDI increased from $25 billion in 1975 to a record $1.2 trillion in 2000. It fell back in the early 2000s, but by 2006 FDI flows were again around $1.2 trillion (see Figure 7.1).[3] Over this period, the flow of FDI accelerated faster than the growth in world trade and world output. For example, between 1992 and 2006, the total flow of FDI from all countries increased more than sevenfold while world trade by value grew by some 150 percent and world output by around 45 percent.[4] As a result of the strong FDI flow, by 2005 the global stock of FDI exceeded $10 trillion. At least 77,000 parent companies had 770,000 affiliates in foreign markets that collectively employed more than 50 million people abroad and generated value accounting for about one-tenth of global GDP. The foreign affiliates of multinationals had an estimated $22 trillion in global sales, much higher than the value of global exports, which stood at close to $12.6 trillion.[5]

FDI has grown more rapidly than world trade and world output for several reasons. First, despite the general decline in trade barriers over the past 30 years, business firms still fear protectionist pressures. Executives see FDI as a way of circumventing future trade barriers. Second, much of the recent increase in FDI is being driven by the political and economic changes that have been occurring in many of the world's developing nations. The general shift toward democratic political institutions and free market economies that we discussed in Chapter 2 has encouraged FDI. Across much of Asia, Eastern

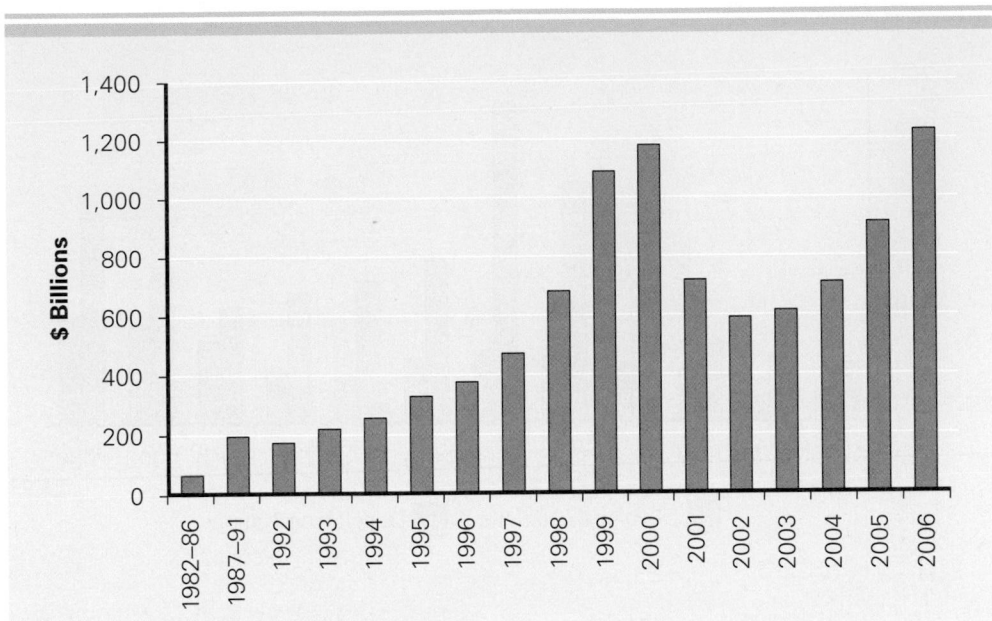

FIGURE 7.1

FDI Outflows, 1982–2006 ($ billions)

Source: Constructed by the author from data in United Nations, *World Investment Report, 2006* (New York and Geneva: United Nations, 2006).

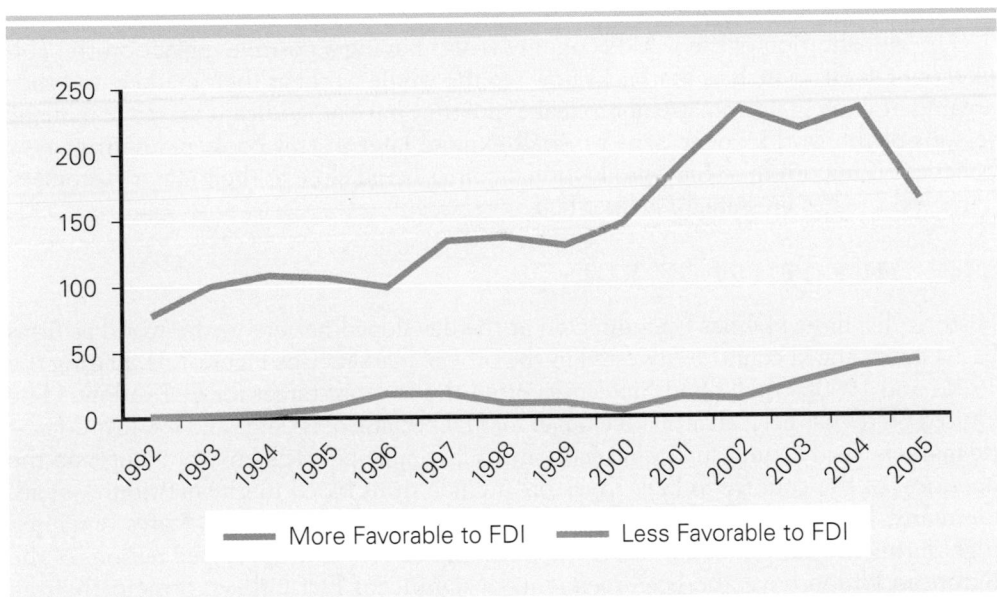

FIGURE 7.2

National Regulatory Changes Governing FDI, 1992–2005

Source: Constructed by the author from data in United Nations, *World Investment Report, 2006* (New York and Geneva: United Nations, 2006).

Europe, and Latin America, economic growth, economic deregulation, privatization programs that are open to foreign investors, and removal of many restrictions on FDI have made these countries more attractive to foreign multinationals. According to the United Nations, between 1992 and 2005 approximately 94 percent of the 2,266 changes made worldwide in the laws governing foreign direct investment created a more favorable environment for FDI (see Figure 7.2).[6] It is noteworthy, however, that since 2002 the number of regulations that are less favorable toward FDI has increased, suggesting that the pendulum may be starting to swing the other way. In Latin America in particular, regulations that are less favorable to FDI have markedly increased; two-thirds of the reported changes in 2005 made the environment for direct investment less welcome.

Notwithstanding recent developments in Latin America, the general desire of governments to facilitate FDI also has been reflected in a dramatic increase in the number

FIGURE 7.3

FDI Inflows by Region
($ billions), 1995–2006

Source: Constructed by the
author from data in United
Nations, *World Investment
Report, 2006* (New York and
Geneva: United Nations, 2006).

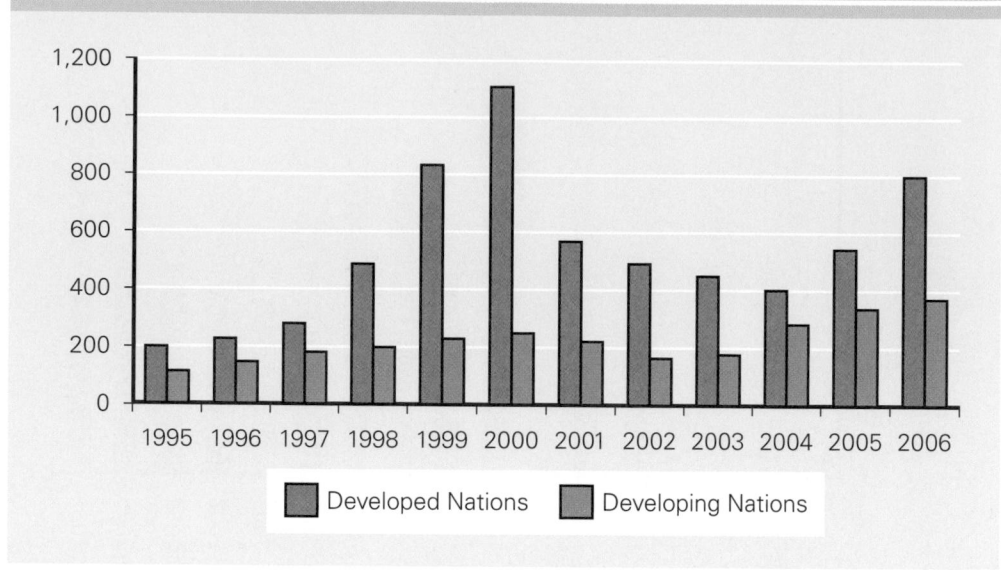

of bilateral investment treaties designed to protect and promote investment between two countries. As of 2005, 2,495 such treaties involved more than 160 countries, a 12-fold increase from the 181 treaties that existed in 1980.[7]

The globalization of the world economy is also having a positive impact on the volume of FDI. Firms such as Starbucks now see the whole world as their market, and they are undertaking FDI in an attempt to make sure they have a significant presence in many regions of the world. For reasons we shall explore later in this book, many firms now believe it is important to have production facilities based close to their major customers. This, too, creates pressure for greater FDI.

THE DIRECTION OF FDI

Historically, most FDI has been directed at the developed nations of the world as firms based in advanced countries invested in the others' markets (see Figure 7.3). During the 1980s and 1990s, the United States was often the favorite target for FDI inflows. The United States has been an attractive target for FDI because of its large and wealthy domestic markets, its dynamic and stable economy, a favorable political environment, and the openness of the country to FDI. Investors include firms based in Great Britain, Japan, Germany, Holland, and France. Inward investment into the United States remained high during the early 2000s, totaling $177 billion in 2006. The developed nations of the European Union have also been recipients of significant FDI inflows, principally from U.S. and Japanese enterprises and from other member states of the EU. In 2006, inward investment into the EU reached a record $549 billion. The United Kingdom was the largest national recipient, with inward investments of some $169 billion.[8]

Even though developed nations still account for the largest share of FDI inflows, FDI into developing nations has increased (see Figure 7.3). From 1985 to 1990, the annual inflow of FDI into developing nations averaged $27.4 billion, or 17.4 percent of the total global flow. In the mid- to late 1990s, the inflow into developing nations was generally between 35 and 40 percent of the total, before falling back to account for about 25 percent of the total in the 2000–2002 period and then rising to 31 to 40 percent between 2004 and 2006. Most recent inflows into developing nations have been targeted at the emerging economies of South, East, and Southeast Asia. Driving much of the increase has been the growing importance of China as a recipient of FDI—China attracted around $60 billion of FDI in 2004 and $70 billion in 2005 and 2006.[9] The reasons for the strong flow of investment into China are discussed in the accompanying Country Focus.

Foreign Direct Investment in China

Beginning in late 1978, China's leadership decided to move the economy away from a centrally planned socialist system to one that was more market driven. The result has been close to three decades of sustained high economic growth rates of around 10 percent annually compounded. This rapid growth has attracted substantial foreign investment. Starting from a tiny base, foreign investment increased to an annual average rate of $2.7 billion between 1985 and 1990 and then surged to $40 billion annually in the late 1990s, making China the second-biggest recipient of FDI inflows in the world after the United States. By the mid-2000s, China was attracting around $70 billion of FDI annually, with another $35 billion a year going into Hong Kong.

Over the past 20 years, this inflow has resulted in establishment of 280,000 foreign-funded enterprises in China. The total stock of FDI in mainland China grew from effectively zero in 1978 to $318 billion in 2005 (another $533 billion of FDI stock was in Hong Kong). FDI amounted to about 10 percent of annualized gross fixed capital formation in China between 1998 and 2005, suggesting that FDI is an important source of economic growth in China.

The reasons for the investment are fairly obvious. With a population of more than 1 billion people, China represents the largest market in the world. Historically, import tariffs made it difficult to serve this market via exports, so FDI was required if a company wanted to tap into the country's huge potential. Although China joined the World Trade Organization in 2001, which will ultimately mean a reduction in import tariffs, this will occur slowly, so this motive for investing in China will persist. Also, many foreign firms believe that doing business in China requires a substantial presence in the country to build *guanxi,* the crucial relationship networks (see Chapter 3 for details). Furthermore, a combination of cheap labor and tax incentives, particularly for enterprises that establish themselves in special economic zones, makes China an attractive base from which to serve Asian or world markets with exports.

Less obvious, at least to begin with, was how difficult it would be for foreign firms to do business in China. Blinded by the size and potential of China's market, many firms have paid scant attention to the complexities of operating a business in this country until after the investment has been made. China may have a huge population, but despite two decades of rapid growth, it is still a poor country. The lack of purchasing power translates into relatively weak markets for many Western consumer goods. Another problem is the lack of a well-developed transportation infrastructure or distribution system outside of major urban areas. PepsiCo discovered this problem at its subsidiary in Chongqing. Perched above the Yangtze River in southwest Sichuan province, Chongqing lies at the heart of China's massive hinterland. The Chongqing municipality, which includes the city and its surrounding regions, contains more than 30 million people, but according to Steve Chen, the manager of the PepsiCo subsidiary, the lack of well-developed road and distribution systems means he can reach only about half of this population with his product.

Other problems include a highly regulated environment, which can make it problematic to conduct business transactions, and shifting tax and regulatory regimes. For example, a few years ago, the Chinese government suddenly scrapped a tax credit scheme that had made it attractive to import capital equipment into China. This immediately made it more expensive to set up operations in the country. Then there are problems with local joint-venture partners that are inexperienced, opportunistic, or simply operate according to different goals. One U.S. manager explained that when he laid off 200 people to reduce costs, his Chinese partner hired them all back the next day. When he inquired why they had been hired back, the executive of the Chinese partner, which was government owned, explained that as an agency of the government, it had an "obligation" to reduce unemployment.

To continue to attract foreign investment, the Chinese government has committed itself to invest more than $800 billion in infrastructure projects over the next 10 years. This should improve the nation's poor highway system. By giving preferential tax breaks to companies that invest in special regions, such as that around Chongqing, the Chinese have created incentives for foreign companies to invest in China's vast interior where markets are underserved. They have been pursuing a macroeconomic policy that includes an emphasis on maintaining steady economic growth, low inflation, and a stable currency, all of which are attractive to foreign investors. Given these developments, it seems likely that the country will continue to be an important magnet for foreign investors well into the future.[11]

FIGURE 7.4

Inward FDI as a Percent of Gross Fixed Capital Formation, 1992–2005

Source: Constructed by the author from data in United Nations, *World Investment Report, 2006* (New York and Geneva: United Nations, 2006).

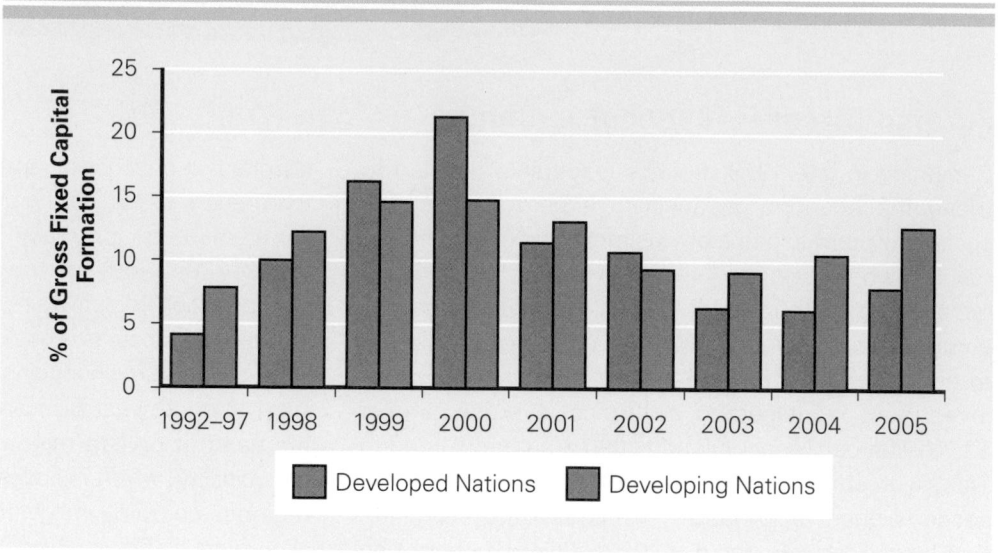

Latin America emerged as the next most important region in the developing world for FDI inflows. In 2006, total inward investments into this region reached about $90 billion. Mexico and Brazil have historically been the two top recipients of inward FDI in Latin America, a trend that continued in 2006. At the other end of the scale, Africa has long received the smallest amount of inward investment, about $39 billion in 2006. The inability of Africa to attract greater investment is in part a reflection of the political unrest, armed conflict, and frequent changes in economic policy in the region.[10]

Another way of looking at the importance of FDI inflows is to express them as a percentage of gross fixed capital formation. **Gross fixed capital formation** summarizes the total amount of capital invested in factories, stores, office buildings, and the like. Other things being equal, the greater the capital investment in an economy, the more favorable its future growth prospects are likely to be. Viewed this way, FDI can be seen as an important source of capital investment and a determinant of the future growth rate of an economy. Figure 7.4 summarizes inward flows of FDI as a percentage of gross fixed capital formation for developed and developing economies for the 1992–2005 period. During the 1992–1997 period, FDI flows accounted for about 4 percent of gross fixed capital formation in developed nations and 8 percent in developing nations. By the 1998–2005 period, the figure was 11.7 percent worldwide, suggesting that FDI had become an increasingly important source of investment in the world's economies.

These gross figures hide important individual country differences. For example, in 2005, inward FDI accounted for some 45 percent of gross fixed capital formation in Britain and 22 percent in Sweden, but only 3.5 percent in India and 0.3 percent in Japan—suggesting that FDI is an important source of investment capital, and thus economic growth, in the first two countries but not the latter two. These differences can be explained by several factors, including the perceived ease and attractiveness of investing in a nation. To the extent that burdensome regulations limit the opportunities for foreign investment in countries such as Japan and India, these nations may be hurting themselves by limiting their access to needed capital investments.

THE SOURCE OF FDI

Since World War II, the United States has been the largest source country for FDI, a position it retained during the late 1990s and early 2000s. Other important source countries include the United Kingdom, France, Germany, the Netherlands, and

FIGURE 7.5

Cumulative FDI Outflows
($ billions), 1998–2005

Note: Share accounted for by the
United States would have been
larger were it not for significant
one-time investment inflows in
2005 due to changes in U.S. tax
laws.

Source: Constructed by the
author from data in United
Nations, *World Investment
Report, 2006* (New York and
Geneva: United Nations, 2006).

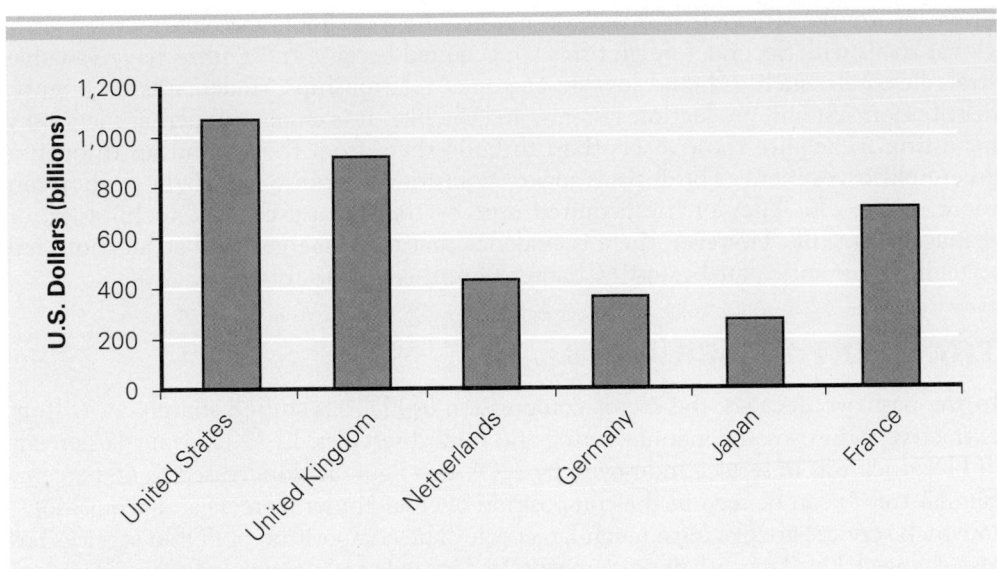

Japan. Collectively, these six countries accounted for 57 percent of all FDI outflows for the 1998–2005 period and 61 percent of the total global stock of FDI in 2006. As might be expected, these countries also predominate in rankings of the world's largest multinationals.

As of 2004, 27 of the world's 100 largest nonfinancial multinationals were U.S. enterprises, 15 were French, 13 German, 12 British, and 9 Japanese. In terms of the global stock of FDI, 19 percent belonged to U.S. firms, 12 percent to British, 8 percent to French firms, 9 percent to German firms, 6 percent to Dutch firms, 3.7 percent to Swiss firms, and 3.6 percent to Japanese.[12] These nations dominate primarily because they were the most developed nations with the largest economies during much of the postwar period and therefore home to many of the largest and best-capitalized enterprises. Many of these countries also had a long history as trading nations and naturally looked to foreign markets to fuel their economic expansion. Thus, it is no surprise that enterprises based there have been at the forefront of foreign investment trends.

THE FORM OF FDI: ACQUISITIONS VERSUS GREENFIELD INVESTMENTS

FDI can take the form of a greenfield investment in a new facility or an acquisition of or a merger with an existing local firm. The data suggest the majority of cross-border investment is in the form of mergers and acquisitions rather than greenfield investments. UN estimates indicate that 40 to 80 percent of all FDI inflows were in the form of mergers and acquisitions between 1998 and 2005. In 2001, for example, mergers and acquisitions accounted for about 78 percent of all FDI inflows. In 2004, the figure was 59 percent, while in 2005 it was back up to 79 percent.[13] However, FDI flows into developed nations differ markedly from those into developing nations. In the case of developing nations, only about one-third of FDI is in the form of cross-border mergers and acquisitions. The lower percentage of mergers and acquisitions may simply reflect the fact that there are fewer target firms to acquire in developing nations.

When contemplating FDI, why do firms apparently prefer to acquire existing assets rather than undertake greenfield investments? We shall consider this question in greater depth in Chapter 14; for now we will make only a few basic observations. First, mergers and acquisitions are quicker to execute than greenfield investments. This is an important consideration in the modern business world where markets evolve very rapidly. Many firms apparently believe that if they do not acquire a desirable target firm, then their global rivals will. Second, foreign firms are acquired because those firms have valuable strategic assets, such as brand loyalty, customer relationships, trademarks or patents, distribution systems, production systems, and the like. It is easier and perhaps less risky for a firm to acquire those assets than to build them from the ground up through a greenfield investment. Third, firms make acquisitions because they believe they can increase the efficiency of the acquired unit by transferring capital, technology, or management skills. However, there is evidence that many mergers and acquisitions fail to realize their anticipated gains.[14] Chapter 14 further studies this issue.

THE SHIFT TO SERVICES

In the past two decades, the sector composition of FDI has shifted sharply away from extractive industries and manufacturing and toward services. In 1990, some 47 percent of FDI stock was in service industries; by 2004, this figure had increased to 66 percent. Similar trends can be seen in the composition of cross-border mergers and acquisitions, in which services are playing a much larger role. The composition of FDI in services has also changed. Until recently it was concentrated in trade and financial services. However, industries such as electricity, water, telecommunications, and business services (such as information technology consulting services) are becoming more prominent.

The shift to services is being driven by four factors that will probably continue to be important for some time. First, the shift reflects the general move in many developed economies away from manufacturing and toward service industries. By the early 2000s, services accounted for 72 percent of the GDP in developed economies and 52 percent in developing economies. Second, many services cannot be traded internationally. They need to be produced where they are consumed. Starbucks, which is a service business, cannot sell hot lattes to Japanese consumers from its Seattle stores—it has to set up shops in Japan. FDI is the principal way to bring services to foreign markets. Third, many countries have liberalized their regimes governing FDI in services (Chapter 6 revealed that the World Trade Organization engineered global deals to remove barriers to cross-border investment in telecommunications and financial services during the late 1990s). This liberalization has made large inflows possible. After Brazil privatized its telecommunications company in the late 1990s and removed restrictions on investment by foreigners in this sector, FDI surged into the Brazilian telecommunications sector.

Finally, the rise of Internet-based global telecommunications networks has allowed some service enterprises to relocate some of their value-creation activities to different nations to take advantage of favorable factor costs. Procter & Gamble, for example, has shifted some of its back-office accounting functions to the Philippines, where accountants trained in U.S. accounting rules can be hired at a much lower salary. Dell has call answering centers in India for the same reason. Similarly, both Microsoft and IBM now have some software development and testing facilities located in India. Software code written at Microsoft during the day can now be transmitted instantly to India and then tested while the code writers at Microsoft sleep. By the time the U.S. code writers arrive for work the next morning, the code has been tested, bugs have been identified, and they can start working on corrections. By locating testing facilities in India, Microsoft can work on its code 24 hours a day, reducing the time it takes to develop new software products.

Theories of Foreign Direct Investment

In this section, we review several theories of foreign direct investment. These theories approach the various phenomena of foreign direct investment from three complementary perspectives. One set of theories seeks to explain why a firm will favor direct investment as a means of entering a foreign market when two other alternatives, exporting and licensing, are open to it. Another set of theories seeks to explain why firms in the same industry often undertake foreign direct investment at the same time, and why they favor certain locations over others as targets for foreign direct investment. Put differently, these theories attempt to explain the observed *pattern* of foreign direct investment flows. A third theoretical perspective, known as the **eclectic paradigm,** attempts to combine the two other perspectives into a single holistic explanation of foreign direct investment (this theoretical perspective is *eclectic* because it combines the best aspects of other theories into a single explanation).

WHY FOREIGN DIRECT INVESTMENT?

Why do firms go to all the trouble of establishing operations abroad through foreign direct investment when two alternatives, exporting and licensing, are available to them for exploiting the profit opportunities in a foreign market? **Exporting** involves producing goods at home and then shipping them to the receiving country for sale. **Licensing** involves granting a foreign entity (the licensee) the right to produce and sell the firm's product in return for a royalty fee on every unit sold. The question is important, given that a cursory examination of the topic suggests that foreign direct investment may be both expensive and risky compared with exporting and licensing. FDI is expensive because a firm must bear the costs of establishing production facilities in a foreign country or of acquiring a foreign enterprise. FDI is risky because of the problems associated with doing business in a different culture where the "rules of the game" may be very different. Relative to indigenous firms, a foreign firm undertaking FDI in a country for the first time will be more likely to make costly mistakes due to ignorance. When a firm exports, it need not bear the costs associated with FDI, and it can reduce the risks associated with selling abroad by using a native sales agent. Similarly, when a firm allows another enterprise to produce its products under license, the licensee bears the costs or risks. So why do so many firms apparently prefer FDI over either exporting or licensing? The answer can be found by examining the limitations of exporting and licensing as means for capitalizing on foreign market opportunities.

Limitations of Exporting

The viability of an exporting strategy is often constrained by transportation costs and trade barriers. When transportation costs are added to production costs, it becomes unprofitable to ship some products over a large distance. This is particularly true of products that have a low value-to-weight ratio and that can be produced in almost any location (e.g., cement, soft drinks, etc.). For such products, the attractiveness of exporting decreases relative to either FDI or licensing. For products with a high value-to-weight ratio, however, transportation costs are normally a minor component of total landed cost (e.g., electronic components, personal computers, medical equipment, computer software, etc.) and have little impact on the relative attractiveness of exporting, licensing, and FDI.

Transportation costs aside, some firms undertake foreign direct investment as a response to actual or threatened trade barriers such as import tariffs or quotas. By placing tariffs on imported goods, governments can increase the cost of exporting relative to foreign direct investment and licensing. Similarly, by limiting imports through quotas, governments increase the attractiveness of FDI and licensing. For example, the wave of FDI by Japanese auto companies in the United States during the 1980s and 1990s was partly driven by protectionist threats from Congress and by quotas on the importation of Japanese cars. For Japanese auto companies, these factors decreased the profitability of exporting and increased that of foreign direct investment. In this context, it is important to understand that trade barriers do not have to be physically in place for FDI to be favored over exporting. Often, the desire to reduce the threat that trade barriers might be imposed is enough to justify foreign direct investment as an alternative to exporting.

Limitations of Licensing

A branch of economic theory known as **internalization theory** seeks to explain why firms often prefer foreign direct investment over licensing as a strategy for entering foreign markets (this approach is also known as the **market imperfections** approach).[15] According to internalization theory, licensing has three major drawbacks as a strategy for exploiting foreign market opportunities. First, *licensing may result in a firm's giving away valuable technological know-how to a potential foreign competitor.* For example, back in the 1960s, RCA licensed its leading-edge color television technology to a number of Japanese companies, including Matsushita and Sony. At the time, RCA saw licensing as a way to earn a good return from its technological know-how in the Japanese market without the costs and risks associated with foreign direct investment. However, Matsushita and Sony quickly assimilated RCA's technology and used it to enter the U.S. market to compete directly against RCA. As a result, RCA is now a minor player in its home market, while Matsushita and Sony have a much bigger market share.

A second problem is that *licensing does not give a firm the tight control over manufacturing, marketing, and strategy in a foreign country that may be required to maximize its profitability.* With licensing, control over manufacturing, marketing, and strategy is granted to a licensee in return for a royalty fee. However, for both strategic and operational reasons, a firm may want to retain control over these functions. The rationale for wanting control over the strategy of a foreign entity is that a firm might want its foreign subsidiary to price and market very aggressively as a way of keeping a foreign competitor in check. Unlike a wholly owned subsidiary, a licensee would probably not accept such an imposition, because it would likely reduce the licensee's profit, or it might even cause the licensee to take a loss.

The rationale for wanting control over the operations of a foreign entity is that the firm might wish to take advantage of differences in factor costs across countries, producing only part of its final product in a given country, while importing other parts from elsewhere where they can be produced at lower cost. Again, a licensee would be unlikely to accept such an arrangement, since it would limit the licensee's autonomy. Thus, for these reasons, when tight control over a foreign entity is desirable, foreign direct investment is preferable to licensing.

A third problem with licensing arises when the firm's competitive advantage is based not as much on its products as on the management, marketing, and manufacturing capabilities that produce those products. The problem here is that *such capabilities are often not amenable to licensing.* While a foreign licensee may be able to physically reproduce the firm's product under license, it often may not be able to do so as efficiently as the firm could itself. As a result, the licensee may not be able to fully exploit the profit potential inherent in a foreign market.

For example, consider Toyota, a company whose competitive advantage in the global auto industry is acknowledged to come from its superior ability to manage the overall process of designing, engineering, manufacturing, and selling automobiles; that is, from its management and organizational capabilities. Indeed, Toyota is credited with pioneering the development of a new production process, known as *lean production,* that enables it to produce higher-quality automobiles at a lower cost than its global rivals.[16] Although Toyota could license certain products, its real competitive advantage comes from its management and process capabilities. These kinds of skills are difficult to articulate or codify; they certainly cannot be written down in a simple licensing contract. They are organizationwide and have been developed over the years. They are not embodied in any one individual but instead are widely dispersed throughout the company. Put another way, Toyota's skills are embedded in its organizational culture, and culture is something that cannot be licensed. Thus, if Toyota were to allow a foreign entity to produce its cars under license, the chances are that the entity could not do so anywhere as near as efficiently as could Toyota. In turn, this would limit the ability of the foreign entity to fully develop the market potential of that product. Such reasoning underlies Toyota's preference for direct investment in foreign markets, as opposed to allowing foreign automobile companies to produce its cars under license.

All of this suggests that when one or more of the following conditions holds, markets fail as a mechanism for selling know-how and FDI is more profitable than licensing: (1) when the firm has valuable know-how that a licensing contract cannot adequately protect; (2) when the firm needs tight control over a foreign entity to maximize its market share and earnings in that country; and (3) when a firm's skills and know-how are not amenable to licensing.

Advantages of Foreign Direct Investment

It follows that a firm will favor foreign direct investment over exporting as an entry strategy when transportation costs or trade barriers make exporting unattractive. Furthermore, the firm will favor foreign direct investment over licensing (or franchising) when it wishes to maintain control over its technological know-how or over its operations and business strategy, or when the firm's capabilities are simply not amenable to licensing, as may often be the case.

THE PATTERN OF FOREIGN DIRECT INVESTMENT

Observation suggests that firms in the same industry often undertake foreign direct investment at around the same time. Moreover, there is a clear tendency for firms to direct their investment activities toward certain locations. The two theories we consider in this section attempt to explain the patterns we observe in FDI flows.

Strategic Behavior

One theory is based on the idea that FDI flows reflect strategic rivalry between firms in the global marketplace. F. T. Knickerbocker, who looked at the relationship between FDI and rivalry in oligopolistic industries, proposed an early variant of this argument.[17] An **oligopoly** is an industry composed of a limited number of large firms (e.g., an industry in which four firms control 80 percent of a domestic market would be defined as an oligopoly). A critical competitive feature of such industries is interdependence of the major players: What one firm does can have an immediate impact on the major competitors, forcing a response in kind. By cutting prices, one firm in an oligopoly can take market share away from its competitors, forcing them to respond with similar price cuts to retain their market share. Thus, the interdependence between firms in an oligopoly leads to imitative behavior; rivals often quickly imitate what a firm does in an oligopoly.

Imitative behavior can take many forms in an oligopoly. One firm raises prices, the others follow; one expands capacity, and the rivals imitate lest they be left at a disadvantage in the future. Knickerbocker argued that the same kind of imitative behavior characterizes FDI. Consider an oligopoly in the United States in which three firms—A, B, and C—dominate the market. Firm A establishes a subsidiary in France. Firms B and C decide that if successful, this new subsidiary may knock out their export business to France and give firm A a first-mover advantage. Furthermore, firm A might discover some competitive asset in France that it could repatriate to the United States to torment firms B and C on their native soil. Given these possibilities, firms B and C decide to follow firm A and establish operations in France.

Studies that looked at FDI by U.S. firms during the 1950s and 1960s show that firms based in oligopolistic industries tended to imitate each other's FDI.[18] The same phenomenon has been observed with regard to FDI undertaken by Japanese firms during the 1980s.[19] For example, Toyota and Nissan responded to investments by Honda in the United States and Europe by undertaking their own FDI in the United States and Europe. More recently, research has shown that models of strategic behavior in a global oligopoly can explain the pattern of FDI in the global tire industry.[20]

Knickerbocker's theory can be extended to embrace the concept of multipoint competition. **Multipoint competition** arises when two or more enterprises encounter each other in different regional markets, national markets, or industries.[21] Economic theory suggests that rather like chess players jockeying for advantage, firms will try to match each other's moves in different markets to try to hold each other in check. The idea is to ensure that a rival does not gain a commanding position in one market and then use the profits generated there to subsidize competitive attacks in other markets. Kodak and Fuji Photo Film Co., for example, compete against each other around the world. If Kodak enters a particular foreign market, Fuji will not be far behind. Fuji feels compelled to follow Kodak to ensure that Kodak does not gain a dominant position in the foreign market that it could then leverage to gain a competitive advantage elsewhere. The converse also holds, with Kodak following Fuji when the Japanese firm is the first to enter a foreign market.

Although Knickerbocker's theory and its extensions can help to explain imitative FDI behavior by firms in oligopolistic industries, it does not explain why the first firm in an oligopoly decides to undertake FDI rather than to export or license. Internalization theory addresses this phenomenon. The imitative theory also does not address the issue of whether FDI is more efficient than exporting or licensing for expanding abroad. Again, internalization theory addresses the efficiency issue. For these reasons, many economists favor internalization theory as an explanation for FDI, although most would agree that the imitative explanation tells an important part of the story.

The Product Life Cycle

Raymond Vernon's product life-cycle theory, described in Chapter 5, also can be used to explain FDI. Vernon argued that often the same firms that pioneer a product in their home markets undertake FDI to produce a product for consumption in foreign markets. Thus, Xerox introduced the photocopier in the United States, and it was Xerox that set up production facilities in Japan (Fuji–Xerox) and Great Britain (Rank–Xerox) to serve those markets. Vernon's view is that firms undertake FDI at particular stages in the life cycle of a product they have pioneered. They invest in other advanced countries when local demand in those countries grows large enough to support local production (as Xerox did). They subsequently shift production to developing countries when product standardization and market saturation give rise to price competition and cost pressures. Investment in developing countries, where labor costs are lower, is seen as the best way to reduce costs.

Vernon's theory has merit. Firms do invest in a foreign country when demand in that country will support local production, and they do invest in low-cost locations (e.g., developing countries) when cost pressures become intense.[22] However, Vernon's theory fails to explain why it is profitable for a firm to undertake FDI at such times, rather than continuing to export from its home base or licensing a foreign firm to produce its product. Just because demand in a foreign country is large enough to support local production, it does not necessarily follow that local production is the most profitable option. It may still be more profitable to produce at home and export to that country (to realize the economies of scale that arise from serving the global market from one location). Alternatively, it may be more profitable for the firm to license a foreign company to produce its product for sale in that country. The product life-cycle theory ignores these options and, instead, simply argues that once a foreign market is large enough to support local production, FDI will occur. The theory's failure to identify when it is profitable to invest abroad limits its explanatory power and its usefulness to business.

THE ECLECTIC PARADIGM

British economist John Dunning has championed the eclectic paradigm.[23] Dunning argues that in addition to the various factors discussed above, location-specific advantages are also of considerable importance in explaining both the rationale for and the direction of foreign direct investment. By **location-specific advantages,** Dunning means the advantages that arise from utilizing resource endowments or assets that are tied to a particular foreign location and that a firm finds valuable to combine with its own unique assets (such as the firm's technological, marketing, or management capabilities). Dunning accepts the argument of internalization theory that it is difficult for a firm to license its own unique capabilities and know-how. Therefore, he argues that combining location-specific assets or resource endowments with the firm's own unique capabilities often requires foreign direct investment. That is, it requires the firm to establish production facilities where those foreign assets or resource endowments are located.

An obvious example of Dunning's arguments is natural resources, such as oil and other minerals, which are by their character specific to certain locations. Dunning suggests that to exploit such foreign resources, a firm must undertake FDI. Clearly, this explains the FDI undertaken by many of the world's oil companies, which have to invest where oil is located in order to combine their technological and managerial capabilities with this valuable location-specific resource. Another obvious example is valuable human resources, such as low-cost,

Silicon Valley has long been known as the epicenter of the computer and semiconductor industry.

highly skilled labor. The cost and skill of labor varies from country to country. Since labor is not internationally mobile, according to Dunning, it makes sense for a firm to locate production facilities in those countries where the cost and skills of local labor are most suited to its particular production processes.

However, Dunning's theory has implications that go beyond basic resources such as minerals and labor. Consider Silicon Valley, which is the world center for the computer and semiconductor industry. Many of the world's major computer and semiconductor companies, such as Apple Computer, Hewlett-Packard, and Intel, are located close to each other in the Silicon Valley region of California. As a result, much of the cutting-edge research and product development in computers and semiconductors takes place there. According to Dunning's arguments, knowledge of the design and manufacture of computers and semiconductors is being generated in Silicon Valley that is available nowhere else in the world. To be sure, as it is commercialized that knowledge diffuses throughout the world, but the leading edge of knowledge generation in the computer and semiconductor industries is to be found in Silicon Valley. In Dunning's language, this means that Silicon Valley has a *location-specific advantage* in the generation of knowledge related to the computer and semiconductor industries. In part, this advantage comes from the sheer concentration of intellectual talent in this area, and in part it arises from a network of informal contacts that allows firms to benefit from each other's knowledge generation. Economists refer to such knowledge "spillovers" as **externalities,** and a well-established theory suggests that firms can benefit from such externalities by locating close to their source.[24]

In so far as this is the case, it makes sense for foreign computer and semiconductor firms to invest in research and, perhaps, production facilities so they too can learn about and utilize valuable new knowledge before those based elsewhere, thereby giving them a competitive advantage in the global marketplace.[25] Evidence suggests that European, Japanese, South Korean, and Taiwanese computer and semiconductor firms are investing in the Silicon Valley region, precisely because they wish to benefit from the externalities that arise there.[26] Others have argued that direct investment by foreign firms in the U.S. biotechnology industry has been motivated by desires to gain access to the unique location-specific technological knowledge of U.S. biotechnology firms.[27] Dunning's theory, therefore, seems to be a useful addition to those outlined above, for it helps explain how location factors affect the direction of FDI.[28]

Political Ideology and Foreign Direct Investment

Historically, political ideology toward FDI within a nation has ranged from a dogmatic radical stance that is hostile to all inward FDI at one extreme to an adherence to the noninterventionist principle of free market economics at the other. Between these two extremes is an approach that might be called *pragmatic nationalism*.

THE RADICAL VIEW

The radical view traces its roots to Marxist political and economic theory. Radical writers argue that the multinational enterprise (MNE) is an instrument of imperialist domination. They see the MNE as a tool for exploiting host countries to the exclusive benefit of their capitalist-imperialist home countries. They argue that MNEs extract profits from the host country and take them to their home country, giving nothing of value to the host country in exchange. They note, for example, that the MNE tightly controls key technology and that important jobs in the MNE's foreign subsidiaries go to home-country nationals rather than to citizens of the host country. Because of this, according to the radical view, FDI by the MNEs of advanced capitalist nations keeps the less developed countries of the world relatively backward and dependent on advanced capitalist nations for investment, jobs, and technology. Thus, according to the extreme version of this view, no country should ever permit foreign corporations to undertake FDI, since they can never be instruments of economic development, only of economic domination. Where MNEs already exist in a country, they should be immediately nationalized.[29]

From 1945 until the 1980s, the radical view was very influential in the world economy. Until the collapse of communism between 1989 and 1991, the countries of Eastern Europe were opposed to FDI. Similarly, communist countries elsewhere, such as China, Cambodia, and Cuba, were all opposed in principle to FDI (although in practice the Chinese started to allow FDI in mainland China in the 1970s). Many socialist countries, particularly in Africa where one of the first actions of many newly independent states was to nationalize foreign-owned enterprises, also embraced the radical position. Countries whose political ideology was more nationalistic than socialistic further embraced the radical position. This was true in Iran and India, for example, both of which adopted tough policies restricting FDI and nationalized many foreign-owned enterprises. Iran is a particularly interesting case because its Islamic government, while rejecting Marxist theory, has essentially embraced the radical view that FDI by MNEs is an instrument of imperialism.

By the end of the 1980s, the radical position was in retreat almost everywhere. There seem to be three reasons for this: (1) the collapse of communism in Eastern Europe; (2) the generally abysmal economic performance of those countries that embraced the radical position, and a growing belief by many of these countries that FDI can be an important source of technology and jobs and can stimulate economic growth; and (3) the strong economic performance of those developing countries that embraced capitalism rather than radical ideology (e.g., Singapore, Hong Kong, and Taiwan).

THE FREE MARKET VIEW

The free market view traces its roots to classical economics and the international trade theories of Adam Smith and David Ricardo (see Chapter 5). The intellectual case for this view has been strengthened by the internalization explanation of FDI. The free market view argues that international production should be distributed among countries according to the theory of comparative advantage. Countries should specialize in the production of those goods and services that they can produce most efficiently. Within this framework, the MNE is an instrument for dispersing the production of goods and services to the most efficient locations around the globe. Viewed this way, FDI by the MNE increases the overall efficiency of the world economy.

Imagine that Dell Computers decided to move assembly operations for many of its personal computers from the United States to Mexico to take advantage of lower labor costs in Mexico. According to the free market view, moves such as this can be seen as increasing the overall efficiency of resource utilization in the world economy. Mexico, due to its lower labor costs, has a comparative advantage in the assembly of PCs. By moving the production of PCs from the United States to Mexico, Dell frees U.S. resources for use in activities in which the United States has a comparative advantage (e.g., the design of computer software, the manufacture of high-value-added components such as microprocessors, or basic R&D). Also, consumers benefit because the PCs cost less than they would if they were produced domestically. In addition, Mexico gains from the technology, skills, and capital that the PC company transfers with its FDI. Contrary to the radical view, the free market view stresses that such resource transfers benefit the host country and stimulate its economic growth. Thus, the free market view argues that FDI is a benefit to both the source country and the host country.

For reasons explored earlier in this book (see Chapter 2), the free market view has been ascendant worldwide in recent years, spurring a global move toward the removal of restrictions on inward and outward foreign direct investment. However, in practice no country has adopted the free market view in its pure form (just as no country has adopted the radical view in its pure form). Countries such as Great Britain and the United States are among the most open to FDI, but the governments of these countries both have still reserved the right to intervene. Britain does so by reserving the right to block foreign takeovers of domestic firms if the takeovers are seen as "contrary to national security interests" or if they have the potential for "reducing competition." (In practice, the UK government has rarely exercised this right.) U.S. controls on FDI are more limited and largely informal. For political reasons, the United States will occasionally restrict U.S. firms from undertaking FDI in certain countries (e.g., Cuba and Iran). In addition, inward FDI meets some limited restrictions. For example, foreigners are prohibited from purchasing more than 25 percent of any U.S. airline or from acquiring a controlling interest in a U.S. television broadcast network. Since 1988, the government has had the right to review the acquisition of a U.S. enterprise by a foreign firm on the grounds of national security. However, of the 1,500 bids the Committee on Foreign Investment in the United States reviewed under this law by 2005, only one has been nullified: the sale of a Seattle-based aircraft parts manufacturer to a Chinese enterprise in the early 1990s.[30]

PRAGMATIC NATIONALISM

In practice, many countries have adopted neither a radical policy nor a free market policy toward FDI, but instead a policy that can best be described as pragmatic nationalism.[31] The pragmatic nationalist view is that FDI has both benefits and costs. FDI can benefit a host country by bringing capital, skills, technology, and jobs, but those benefits come at a cost. When a foreign company rather than a domestic company produces products, the profits from that investment go abroad. Many countries are also concerned that a foreign-owned manufacturing plant may import many components from its home country, which has negative implications for the host country's balance-of-payments position.

Recognizing this, countries adopting a pragmatic stance pursue policies designed to maximize the national benefits and minimize the national costs. According to this view, FDI should be allowed so long as the benefits outweigh the costs. Japan offers an example of pragmatic nationalism. Until the 1980s, Japan's policy was probably one of the most restrictive among countries adopting a pragmatic nationalist stance. This was due to Japan's perception that direct entry of foreign (especially U.S.) firms with ample managerial resources into the Japanese markets could hamper the development and growth of their own industry and technology.[32] This belief led Japan to block the majority of applications to invest in Japan. However, there were always exceptions to this policy. Firms that had important technology were often permitted to undertake FDI if they insisted that they would neither license their technology to a Japanese firm nor enter into a joint venture with a Japanese enterprise. IBM and Texas Instruments were able to set up wholly owned subsidiaries in Japan by adopting this negotiating position. From the perspective of the Japanese government, the benefits of FDI in such cases—the stimulus that these firms might impart to the Japanese economy—outweighed the perceived costs.

Another aspect of pragmatic nationalism is the tendency to aggressively court FDI believed to be in the national interest by, for example, offering subsidies to foreign MNEs in the form of tax breaks or grants. The countries of the European Union often seem to be competing with each other to attract U.S. and Japanese FDI by offering large tax breaks and subsidies. Britain has been the most successful at attracting Japanese investment in the automobile industry. Nissan, Toyota, and Honda now have major assembly plants in Britain and use the country as their base for serving the rest of Europe—with obvious employment and balance-of-payments benefits for Britain.

SHIFTING IDEOLOGY

In recent years the number of countries that adhere to a radical ideology has markedly declined. Although few countries have adopted a pure free market policy stance, an increasing number of countries are gravitating toward the free market end of the spectrum and have liberalized their foreign investment regime. This includes many countries that less than two decades ago were firmly in the radical camp (e.g., the former communist countries of Eastern Europe and many of the socialist countries of Africa) and several countries that until recently could best be described as pragmatic nationalists with regard to FDI (e.g., Japan, South Korea, Italy, Spain, and most Latin American countries). One result has been the surge in the volume of FDI worldwide, which, as we noted earlier, has been growing twice as fast as the growth in world trade. Another result has been an increase in the volume of FDI directed at countries that have recently liberalized their FDI regimes, such as China, India, and Vietnam.

As a counterpoint, there is recent evidence of the beginnings of what might become a shift to a more hostile approach to foreign direct investment. Venezuela and Bolivia have become increasingly hostile to foreign direct investment. In 2005 and 2006, the governments of both nations unilaterally rewrote contracts for oil and gas exploration, raising the royalty rate that foreign enterprises had to pay the government for oil and gas extracted in their territories. Moreover, following his election victory, in 2006 Bolivian president Evo Morales nationalized the nation's gas fields and stated that he would evict foreign firms unless they agreed to pay about 80 percent of their revenues to the state and relinquish production oversight. In some developed nations too, there is increasing evidence of hostile reactions to inward FDI. In Europe in 2006, there was a hostile political reaction to the attempted takeover of Europe's largest steel company, Arcelor, by Mittal Steel, a global company controlled by the Indian entrepreneur Lakshmi Mittal. In mid-2005 China National Offshore Oil Company withdrew a takeover bid for Unocal of the United States after highly negative reaction in Congress about the proposed takeover of a "strategic asset" by a Chinese company. Similarly, as detailed in the next Management Focus feature, in 2006 a Dubai-owned company withdrew its planned takeover of some operations at six U.S. ports after negative political reactions. So far, these countertrends are nothing more than isolated incidents, but if they become more widespread, the 30-year-long movement toward lower barriers to cross-border investment could be in jeopardy.

DP World and the United States

In February 2006, DP World, a ports operator with global reach owned by the government of Dubai, a member of the United Arab Emirates and a staunch U.S. ally, paid $6.8 billion to acquire P&O, a British firm that runs a global network of marine terminals. With P&O came the management operations of six U.S. ports: Miami, Philadelphia, Baltimore, New Orleans, New Jersey, and New York. The acquisition had already been approved by U.S. regulators when it suddenly became front-page news. Upon hearing about the deal, several prominent U.S. senators raised concerns about the acquisition. Their objections were twofold. First, they raised questions about the security risks associated with management operations in key U.S. ports being owned by a foreign enterprise based in the Middle East. The implication was that terrorists could somehow take advantage of the ownership arrangement to infiltrate U.S. ports. Second, they were concerned that DP World was a state-owned enterprise and argued that foreign governments should not be in a position of owning key "U.S. strategic assets."

The Bush administration was quick to defend the takeover, stating that it posed no threat to national security. Others noted that DP World was a respected global firm with an American chief operating officer and an American-educated chairman; the head of the global ports management operation would also be an American. DP World would not own the U.S. ports in question, just manage them, while security issues would remain in the hands of American customs officials and the U.S. Coast Guard. Dubai was also a member of America's Container Security Initiative, which allows American customs officials to inspect cargo in foreign ports before it leaves for the United States. Most of the DP World employees at American ports would be U.S. citizens, and any UAE citizen transferred to DP World would be subject to American visa approval.

These arguments fell on deaf ears. With several U.S. senators threatening to pass legislation to prohibit foreign ownership of U.S. port operations, DP World bowed to the inevitable and announced that it would sell off the right to manage the six U.S. ports for about $750 million. Looking forward however, DP World stated that it would seek an initial public offering in 2007, and that the then-private firm would in all probability continue to look for ways to enter the United States. In the words of the firm's CEO, "this is the world's largest economy. How can you just ignore it?"[33]

Benefits and Costs of FDI

To a greater or lesser degree, many governments can be considered pragmatic nationalists when it comes to FDI. Accordingly, their policy is shaped by a consideration of the costs and benefits of FDI. Here we explore the benefits and costs of FDI, first from the perspective of a host (receiving) country, and then from the perspective of the home (source) country. In the next section, we look at the policy instruments governments use to manage FDI.

HOST-COUNTRY BENEFITS

The main benefits of inward FDI for a host country arise from resource-transfer effects, employment effects, balance-of-payments effects, and effects on competition and economic growth.

Resource-Transfer Effects

Foreign direct investment can make a positive contribution to a host economy by supplying capital, technology, and management resources that would otherwise not be available and thus boost that country's economic growth rate.[34]

With regard to capital, many MNEs, by virtue of their large size and financial strength, have access to financial resources not available to host-country firms. These funds may be available from internal company sources, or, because of their reputation, large MNEs may find it easier to borrow money from capital markets than host-country firms would.

As for technology, you will recall from Chapter 2 that technology can stimulate economic development and industrialization. Technology can take two forms, both of which are valuable. Technology can be incorporated in a production process (e.g., the technology for discovering, extracting, and refining oil) or it can be incorporated in a product (e.g., personal computers). However, many countries lack the research and development resources and skills required to develop their own indigenous product and process technology. This is particularly true in less developed nations. Such countries must rely on advanced industrialized nations for much of the technology required to stimulate economic growth, and FDI can provide it.

Research supports the view that multinational firms often transfer significant technology when they invest in a foreign country.[35] For example, a study of FDI in Sweden found that foreign firms increased both the labor and total factor productivity of Swedish firms that they acquired, suggesting that significant technology transfers had occurred (technology typically boosts productivity).[36] Also, a study of FDI by the Organization for Economic Cooperation and Development (OECD) found that foreign investors invested significant amounts of capital in R&D in the countries in which they had invested, suggesting that not only were they transferring technology to those countries, but they may also have been upgrading existing technology or creating new technology in those countries.[37]

Foreign management skills acquired through FDI may also produce important benefits for the host country. Foreign managers trained in the latest management techniques can often help improve the efficiency of operations in the host country, whether those operations are acquired or greenfield developments. Beneficial spin-off effects may also arise when local personnel who are trained to occupy managerial, financial, and technical posts in the subsidiary of a foreign MNE leave the firm and help establish indigenous firms. Similar benefits may arise if the superior management skills of a foreign MNE stimulate local suppliers, distributors, and competitors to improve their own management skills.

Employment Effects

Another beneficial employment effect claimed for FDI is that it brings jobs to a host country that would otherwise not be created there. The effects of FDI on employment are both direct and indirect. Direct effects arise when a foreign MNE employs a number of host-country citizens. Indirect effects arise when jobs are created in local suppliers as a result of the investment and when jobs are created because of increased local spending by employees of the MNE. The indirect employment effects are often as large as, if not larger than, the direct effects. For example, when Toyota decided to open a new auto plant in France in 1997, estimates suggested that the plant would create 2,000 direct jobs and perhaps another 2,000 jobs in support industries.[38]

Cynics argue that not all the "new jobs" created by FDI represent net additions in employment. In the case of FDI by Japanese auto companies in the United States, some argue that the jobs created by this investment have been more than offset by the jobs lost in U.S.-owned auto companies, which have lost market share to their Japanese competitors. As a consequence of such substitution effects, the net number of new jobs created by FDI may not be as great as initially claimed by an MNE. The issue of the likely net gain in employment may be a major negotiating point between an MNE wishing to undertake FDI and the host government.

When FDI takes the form of an acquisition of an established enterprise in the host economy as opposed to a greenfield investment, the immediate effect may be to reduce employment as the multinational tries to

Job creation is a result of FDI. These French workers assemble cars at Toyota's Valenciennes manufacturing plant.

restructure the operations of the acquired unit to improve its operating efficiency. However, even in such cases, research suggests that once the initial period of restructuring is over, enterprises acquired by foreign firms tend to grow their employment base at a faster rate than domestic rivals. For example, an OECD study found that between 1989 and 1996 foreign firms created new jobs at a faster rate than their domestic counterparts.[39] In America, the workforce of foreign firms grew by 1.4 percent per year, compared with 0.8 percent per year for domestic firms. In Britain and France, the workforce of foreign firms grew at 1.7 percent per year, while employment at domestic firms fell by 2.7 percent. The same study found that foreign firms tended to pay higher wage rates than domestic firms, suggesting that the quality of employment was better. Another study looking at FDI in Eastern European transition economies found that although employment fell following the acquisition of an enterprise by a foreign firm, often those enterprises were in competitive difficulties and would not have survived if they had not been acquired. Also, after an initial period of adjustment and retrenchment, employment downsizing was often followed by new investments, and employment either remained stable or increased.[40]

Balance-of-Payments Effects

FDI's effect on a country's balance-of-payments accounts is an important policy issue for most host governments. A country's **balance-of-payments accounts** track both its payments to and its receipts from other countries. Governments normally are concerned when their country is running a deficit on the current account of their balance of payments. The **current account** tracks the export and import of goods and services. A current account deficit, or trade deficit as it is often called, arises when a country is importing more goods and services than it is exporting. Governments typically prefer to see a current account surplus than a deficit. The only way in which a current account deficit can be supported in the long run is by selling off assets to foreigners (for a detailed explanation of why this is the case, see the Appendix to Chapter 5). For example, the persistent U.S. current account deficit since the 1980s has been financed by a steady sale of U.S. assets (stocks, bonds, real estate, and whole corporations) to foreigners. Since national governments invariably dislike seeing the assets of their country fall into foreign hands, they prefer their nation to run a current account surplus. There are two ways in which FDI can help a country to achieve this goal.

First, if the FDI is a substitute for imports of goods or services, the effect can be to improve the current account of the host country's balance of payments. Much of the FDI by Japanese automobile companies in the United States and Europe, for example, can be seen as substituting for imports from Japan. Thus, the current account of the U.S. balance of payments has improved somewhat because many Japanese companies are now supplying the U.S. market from production facilities in the United States, as opposed to facilities in Japan. Insofar as this has reduced the need to finance a current account deficit by asset sales to foreigners, the United States has clearly benefited.

A second potential benefit arises when the MNE uses a foreign subsidiary to export goods and services to other countries. According to a UN report, inward FDI by foreign multinationals has been a major driver of export-led economic growth in a number of developing and developed nations over the last decade.[41] For example, in China exports increased from $26 billion in 1985 to more than $250 billion by 2001 and $762 billion in 2005. Much of this dramatic export growth was due to the presence of foreign multinationals that invested heavily in China during the 1990s. The subsidiaries of foreign multinationals accounted for 50 percent of all exports from that country in 2001, up from 17 percent in 1991. In mobile phones, for example, the Chinese subsidiaries of foreign multinationals—primarily Nokia, Motorola, Ericsson, and Siemens—accounted for 95 percent of China's exports.

Effect on Competition and Economic Growth

Economic theory tells us that the efficient functioning of markets depends on an adequate level of competition between producers. When FDI takes the form of a greenfield investment, the result is to establish a new enterprise, increasing the number of players in a market and thus consumer choice. In turn, this can increase the level of competition in a national market, thereby driving down prices and increasing consumers' economic welfare. Increased competition tends to stimulate capital investments by firms in plant, equipment, and R&D as they struggle to gain an edge over their rivals. The long-term results may include increased productivity growth, product and process innovations, and greater economic growth.[42] Such beneficial effects seem to have occurred in the South Korean retail sector following the liberalization of FDI regulations in 1996. FDI by large Western discount stores, including Wal-Mart, Costco, Carrefour, and Tesco, seems to have encouraged indigenous discounters such as E-Mart to improve the efficiency of their own operations. The results have included more competition and lower prices, which benefit South Korean consumers.

FDI's impact on competition in domestic markets may be particularly important in the case of services, such as telecommunications, retailing, and many financial services, where exporting is often not an option because the service has to be produced where it is delivered.[43] For example, under a 1997 agreement sponsored by the World Trade Organization, 68 countries accounting for more than 90 percent of world telecommunications revenues pledged to start opening their markets to foreign investment and competition and to abide by common rules for fair competition in telecommunications. Before this agreement, most of the world's telecommunications markets were closed to foreign competitors, and in most countries the market was monopolized by a single carrier, which was often a state-owned enterprise. The agreement has dramatically increased the level of competition in many national telecommunications markets, producing two major benefits. First, inward investment has increased competition and stimulated investment in the modernization of telephone networks around the world, leading to better service. Second, the increased competition has resulted in lower prices.

HOST-COUNTRY COSTS

Three costs of FDI concern host countries. They arise from possible adverse effects on competition within the host nation, adverse effects on the balance of payments, and the perceived loss of national sovereignty and autonomy.

Adverse Effects on Competition

Host governments sometimes worry that the subsidiaries of foreign MNEs may have greater economic power than indigenous competitors. If it is part of a larger international organization, the foreign MNE may be able to draw on funds generated elsewhere to subsidize its costs in the host market, which could drive indigenous companies out of business and allow the firm to monopolize the market. Once the market is monopolized, the foreign MNE could raise prices above those that would prevail in competitive markets, with harmful effects on the economic welfare of the host nation. This concern tends to be greater in countries that have few large firms of their own (generally less developed countries). It tends to be a relatively minor concern in most advanced industrialized nations.

In general, while FDI in the form of greenfield investments should increase competition, it is less clear that this is the case when the FDI takes the form of acquisition of an established enterprise in the host nation, as was the case when Volvo acquired Samsung's excavation division. Because an acquisition does not result in a net increase in the number of players in a market, the effect on competition may be neutral. When a foreign investor acquires two or more firms in a host country and subsequently merges them, the effect may be to reduce the level of competition in that market, create monopoly power for the foreign firm, reduce consumer choice, and raise prices. For example, in India, Hindustan Lever Ltd., the Indian subsidiary of Unilever, acquired its main local rival, Tata Oil Mills, to assume a dominant position in the bath soap (75 percent) and detergents (30 percent) markets. Hindustan Lever also acquired several local companies in other markets, such as the ice cream makers Dollops, Kwality, and Milkfood. By combining these companies, Hindustan Lever's share of the Indian ice cream market went from zero in 1992 to 74 percent in 1997.[44] However, although such cases are of obvious concern, there is little evidence that such developments are widespread. In many nations, domestic competition authorities have the right to review and block any mergers or acquisitions that they view as having a detrimental impact on competition. If such institutions are operating effectively, this should be sufficient to make sure that foreign entities do not monopolize a country's markets.

Adverse Effects on the Balance of Payments

The possible adverse effects of FDI on a host country's balance-of-payments position are twofold. First, the initial capital inflow that comes with FDI must be set against the subsequent outflow of earnings from the foreign subsidiary to its parent company. Such outflows show up as capital outflow on balance-of-payments accounts. Some governments have responded to such outflows by restricting the amount of earnings that can be repatriated to a foreign subsidiary's home country. A second concern arises when a foreign subsidiary imports a substantial number of its inputs from abroad, which results in a debit on the current account of the host country's balance of payments. One criticism leveled against Japanese-owned auto assembly operations in the United States, for example, is that they tend to import many component parts from Japan. Because of this, the favorable impact of this FDI on the current account of the U.S. balance-of-payments position may not be as great as initially supposed. The Japanese auto companies have responded to these criticisms by pledging to purchase 75 percent of their component parts from U.S.-based manufacturers (but not necessarily U.S.-owned manufacturers). When the Japanese auto company Nissan invested in the United Kingdom, Nissan responded to concerns about local content by pledging to increase the proportion of local content to 60 percent and subsequently raising it to more than 80 percent.

National Sovereignty and Autonomy

Some host governments worry that FDI is accompanied by some loss of economic independence. The concern is that key decisions that can affect the host country's economy will be made by a foreign parent that has no real commitment to the host country and over which the host country's government has no real control. Most economists dismiss such concerns as groundless and irrational. Political scientist Robert Reich has noted that such concerns are the product of outmoded thinking because they fail to account for the growing interdependence of the world economy.[45] In a world in which firms from all advanced nations are increasingly investing in each other's markets, it is not possible for one country to hold another to "economic ransom" without hurting itself.

HOME-COUNTRY BENEFITS

The benefits of FDI to the home (source) country arise from three sources. First, the home country's balance of payments benefits from the inward flow of foreign earnings. FDI can also benefit the home country's balance of payments if the foreign subsidiary creates demands for home-country exports of capital equipment, intermediate goods, complementary products, and the like.

Second, benefits to the home country from outward FDI arise from employment effects. As with the balance of payments, positive employment effects arise when the foreign subsidiary creates demand for home-country exports. Thus, Toyota's investment in auto assembly operations in Europe has benefited both the Japanese balance-of-payments position and employment in Japan because Toyota imports some component parts for its European-based auto assembly operations directly from Japan.

Third, benefits arise when the home-country MNE learns valuable skills from its exposure to foreign markets that can subsequently be transferred back to the home country. This amounts to a reverse resource-transfer effect. Through its exposure to a foreign market, an MNE can learn about superior management techniques and superior product and process technologies. These resources can then be transferred back to the home country, contributing to the home country's economic growth rate.[46] For example, one reason General Motors and Ford invested in Japanese automobile companies (GM owns part of Isuzu, and Ford owns part of Mazda) was to learn about their production processes. If GM and Ford are successful in transferring this know-how back to their U.S. operations, the result may be a net gain for the U.S. economy.

HOME-COUNTRY COSTS

Against these benefits must be set the apparent costs of FDI for the home (source) country. The most important concerns center on the balance-of-payments and employment effects of outward FDI. The home country's balance of payments may suffer in three ways. First, the balance of payments suffers from the initial capital outflow required to finance the FDI. This effect, however, is usually more than offset by the subsequent inflow of foreign earnings. Second, the current account of the balance of payments suffers if the purpose of the foreign investment is to serve the home market from a low-cost production location. Third, the current account of the balance of payments suffers if the FDI is a substitute for direct exports. Thus, insofar as Toyota's assembly operations in the United States are intended to substitute for direct exports from Japan, the current account position of Japan will deteriorate.

With regard to employment effects, the most serious concerns arise when FDI is seen as a substitute for domestic production. This was the case with Toyota's investments in the United States and Europe. One obvious result of such FDI is reduced home-country employment. If the labor market in the home country is already tight, with little unemployment, this concern may not be that great. However, if the home country is suffering from unemployment, concern about the export of jobs may arise. For example, one objection frequently raised by U.S. labor leaders to the free trade pact between the United States, Mexico, and Canada (see the next chapter) is that the United States will lose hundreds of thousands of jobs as U.S. firms invest in Mexico to take advantage of cheaper labor and then export back to the United States.[47]

INTERNATIONAL TRADE THEORY AND FDI

When assessing the costs and benefits of FDI to the home country, keep in mind the lessons of international trade theory (see Chapter 5). International trade theory tells us that home-country concerns about the negative economic effects of offshore production may be misplaced. The term **offshore production** refers to FDI undertaken to serve the home market. Far from reducing home-country employment, such FDI may actually stimulate economic growth (and hence employment) in the home country by freeing home-country resources to concentrate on activities where the home country has a comparative advantage. In addition, home-country consumers benefit if the price of the particular product falls as a result of the FDI. Also, if a company were prohibited from making such investments on the grounds of negative employment effects while its international competitors reaped the benefits of low-cost production locations, it would undoubtedly lose market share to its international competitors. Under such a scenario, the adverse long-run economic effects for a country would probably outweigh the relatively minor balance-of-payments and employment effects associated with offshore production

🌐 Government Policy Instruments and FDI

We have now reviewed the costs and benefits of FDI from the perspective of both home country and host country. We now turn our attention to the policy instruments that home (source) countries and host countries can use to regulate FDI.

HOME-COUNTRY POLICIES

Through their choice of policies, home countries can both encourage and restrict FDI by local firms. We look at policies designed to encourage outward FDI first, including foreign risk insurance, capital assistance, tax incentives, and political pressure. Then we will look at policies designed to restrict outward FDI.

Encouraging Outward FDI

Many investor nations now have government-backed insurance programs to cover major types of foreign investment risk. The types of risks insurable through these programs include the risks of expropriation (nationalization), war losses, and the inability to transfer profits back home. Such programs are particularly useful in encouraging firms to undertake investments in politically unstable countries.[48] In addition, several advanced countries also have special funds or banks that make government loans to firms wishing to invest in developing countries. As a further incentive to encourage domestic firms to undertake FDI, many countries have eliminated double taxation of foreign income (i.e., taxation of income in both the host country and the home country). Last, and perhaps most significant, a number of investor countries (including the United States) have used their political influence to persuade host countries to relax their restrictions on inbound FDI. For example, in response to direct U.S. pressure, Japan relaxed many of its formal restrictions on inward FDI in the 1980s. Now, in response to further U.S. pressure, Japan moved toward relaxing its informal barriers to inward FDI. One beneficiary of this trend has been Toys "R" Us, which, after five years of intensive lobbying by company and U.S. government officials, opened its first retail stores in Japan in December 1991. By 2006, Toys "R" Us had more than 148 stores in Japan, and its Japanese operation, in which Toys "R" Us retained a controlling stake, had a listing on the Japanese stock market.

Restricting Outward FDI

Virtually all investor countries, including the United States, have exercised some control over outward FDI from time to time. One policy has been to limit capital outflows out of concern for the country's balance of payments. From the early 1960s until 1979, for example, Britain had exchange-control regulations that limited the amount of capital a firm could take out of the country. Although the main intent of such policies was to improve the British balance of payments, an important secondary intent was to make it more difficult for British firms to undertake FDI.

In addition, countries have occasionally manipulated tax rules to try to encourage their firms to invest at home. The objective behind such policies is to create jobs at home rather than in other nations. At one time, Britain adopted such policies. The British advanced corporation tax system taxed British companies' foreign earnings at a higher rate than their domestic earnings. This tax code created an incentive for British companies to invest at home.

Finally, countries sometimes prohibit national firms from investing in certain countries for political reasons. Such restrictions can be formal or informal. For example, formal U.S. rules prohibited U.S. firms from investing in countries such as Cuba and Iran, whose political ideology and actions are judged to be contrary to U.S. interests. Similarly, during the 1980s, informal pressure was applied to dissuade U.S. firms from investing in South Africa. In this case, the objective was to pressure South Africa to change its apartheid laws, which happened during the early 1990s.

HOST-COUNTRY POLICIES

Host countries adopt policies designed both to restrict and to encourage inward FDI. As noted earlier in this chapter, political ideology has determined the type and scope of these policies in the past. In the last decade of the 20th century, many countries

Because Japan was willing to relax some obstacles to FDI, Toys "R" Us was able to open stores there

moved quickly away from adherence to some version of the radical stance, which prohibited much FDI, and toward a combination of free market objectives and pragmatic nationalism.

Encouraging Inward FDI

It is common for governments to offer incentives to foreign firms to invest in their countries. Such incentives take many forms, but the most common are tax concessions, low-interest loans, and grants or subsidies. Incentives are motivated by a desire to gain from the resource-transfer and employment effects of FDI. They are also motivated by a desire to capture FDI away from other potential host countries. For example, in the mid-1990s, the governments of Britain and France competed with each other on the incentives they offered Toyota to invest in their respective countries. In the United States, state governments often compete with each other to attract FDI. For example, Kentucky offered Toyota an incentive package worth $112 million to persuade it to build its U.S. automobile assembly plants there. The package included tax breaks, new state spending on infrastructure, and low-interest loans.[49]

Restricting Inward FDI

Host governments use a wide range of controls to restrict FDI in one way or another. The two most common are ownership restraints and performance requirements. Ownership restraints can take several forms. In some countries, foreign companies are excluded from specific fields such as tobacco and mining in Sweden and the development of certain natural resources in Brazil, Finland, and Morocco. In other industries, foreign ownership may be permitted although local investors must own a significant proportion of the subsidiary's equity. Foreign ownership is restricted to 25 percent or less of an airline in the United States. In India, foreign firms were prohibited from owning media businesses until 2001, when the rules were relaxed, allowing foreign firms to purchase up to 26 percent of a domestic newspaper.[50]

The rationale underlying ownership restraints seems to be twofold. First, foreign firms are often excluded from certain sectors on the grounds of national security or competition. Particularly in less developed countries, the feeling seems to be that local firms might not be able to develop unless foreign competition is restricted by a combination of import tariffs and controls on FDI. This is a variant of the infant industry argument discussed in Chapter 6.

Second, ownership restraints seem to be based on a belief that local owners can help maximize the resource-transfer and employment benefits of FDI for the host country. Until the early 1980s, the Japanese government prohibited most FDI but allowed joint ventures between Japanese firms and foreign MNEs if the MNE had a valuable technology. The Japanese government clearly believed such an arrangement would speed up the subsequent diffusion of the MNE's valuable technology throughout the Japanese economy.

Performance requirements can also take several forms. Performance requirements are controls over the behavior of the MNE's local subsidiary. The most common performance requirements are related to local content, exports, technology transfer, and local participation in top management. As with certain ownership restrictions, the logic underlying performance requirements is that such rules help maximize the benefits and minimize the costs of FDI for the host country. Many countries employ some form of performance requirements when it suits their objectives. However, performance requirements tend to be more common in less developed countries than in advanced industrialized nations.[51]

INTERNATIONAL INSTITUTIONS AND THE LIBERALIZATION OF FDI

Until the 1990s, multinational institutions were not consistently involved in governing FDI. This changed with the formation of the World Trade Organization in 1995. The WTO promotes international trade in services. Since many services have to be produced where they are sold, exporting is not an option (for example, one cannot export McDonald's hamburgers or consumer banking services). Therefore, the WTO has become involved in regulations governing FDI. As might be expected for an institution created to promote free trade, the thrust of the WTO's efforts has been to push for liberalizing regulations governing FDI, particularly in services. Under the auspices of the WTO, two extensive multinational agreements were reached in 1997 to liberalize trade in telecommunications and financial services. Both these agreements contained detailed clauses that require signatories to liberalize their regulations governing inward FDI, essentially opening their markets to foreign telecommunications and financial services companies.

The WTO has had less success trying to initiate talks aimed at establishing a universal set of rules designed to promote the liberalization of FDI. Led by Malaysia and India, developing nations have so far rejected efforts by the WTO to start such discussions. In an attempt to make some progress on this issue, the Organization for Economic Cooperation and Development (OECD) in 1995 initiated talks between its members. (The OECD is a Paris-based intergovernmental organization of "wealthy" nations whose purpose is to provide its 29 member states with a forum in which governments can compare their experiences, discuss the problems they share, and seek solutions that can then be applied within their own national contexts. The members include most EU countries, the United States, Canada, Japan, and South Korea.) The aim of the talks was to draft a multilateral agreement on investment (MAI) that would make it illegal for signatory states to discriminate against foreign investors. This would liberalize rules governing FDI between OECD states.

These talks broke down in early 1998, primarily because the United States refused to sign the agreement. According to the United States, the proposed agreement contained too many exceptions that would weaken its powers. For example, the proposed agreement would not have barred discriminatory taxation of foreign-owned companies, and it would have allowed countries to restrict foreign television programs and music in the name of preserving culture. Environmental and labor groups also campaigned against the MAI, criticizing the proposed agreement because it contained no binding environmental or labor agreements. Despite such setbacks, negotiations on a revised MAI treaty might restart in the future. Moreover, as noted earlier, many individual nations have continued to liberalize their policies governing FDI to encourage foreign firms to invest in their economies.[52]

IMPLICATIONS FOR MANAGERS

Several implications for business are inherent in the material discussed in this chapter. In this section, we deal first with the implications of the theory and then turn our attention to the implications of government policy.

THE THEORY OF FDI

The implications of the theories of FDI for business practice are straightforward. First, it is worth noting that the location-specific advantages argument associated with John Dunning does help explain the *direction* of FDI. However, the location-specific advantages argument does not explain *why* firms prefer FDI to licensing or to exporting. In this regard, from both an explanatory and a business perspective,

FIGURE 7.6

A Decision Framework

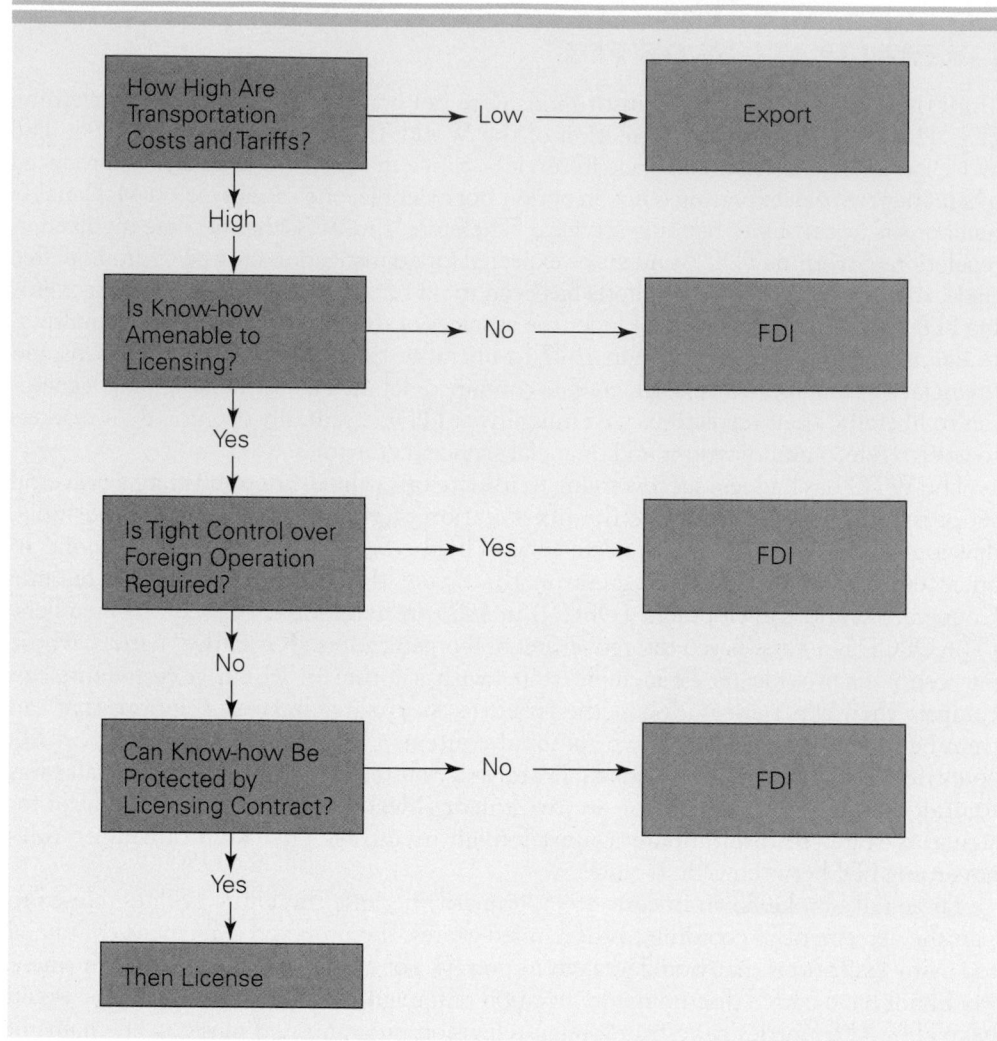

perhaps the most useful theories are those that focus on the limitations of exporting and licensing; that is, internalization theories. These theories are useful because they identify with some precision how the relative profitability of foreign direct investment, exporting, and licensing vary with circumstances. The theories suggest that exporting is preferable to licensing and FDI so long as transportation costs are minor and trade barriers are trivial. As transportation costs or trade barriers increase, exporting becomes unprofitable, and the choice is between FDI and licensing. Since FDI is more costly and more risky than licensing, other things being equal, the theories argue that licensing is preferable to FDI. Other things are seldom equal, however. Although licensing may work, it is not an attractive option when one or more of the following conditions exist: (*a*) the firm has valuable know-how that a licensing contract cannot adequately protect, (*b*) the firm needs tight control over a foreign entity in order to maximize its market share and earnings in that country, and (*c*) a firm's skills and capabilities are not amenable to licensing. Figure 7.6 presents these considerations as a decision tree.

Firms for which licensing is not a good option tend to be clustered in three types of industries:

1.   High-technology industries in which protecting firm-specific expertise is of paramount importance and licensing is hazardous.

2.   Global oligopolies, in which competitive interdependence requires that multinational firms maintain tight control over foreign operations so that they have the

ability to launch coordinated attacks against their global competitors (as Kodak has done with Fuji).

3. Industries in which intense cost pressures require that multinational firms maintain tight control over foreign operations (so they can disperse manufacturing to locations around the globe where factor costs are most favorable in order to minimize costs).

Although empirical evidence is limited, the majority of the evidence seems to support these conjectures.[53] In addition, licensing is not a good option if the competitive advantage of a firm is based upon managerial or marketing knowledge that is embedded in the routines of the firm or the skills of its managers, and that is difficult to codify in a "book of blueprints." This would seem to be the case for firms based in a fairly wide range of industries.

Firms for which licensing is a good option tend to be in industries whose conditions are opposite to those specified above. That is, licensing tends to be more common, and more profitable, in fragmented, low-technology industries in which globally dispersed manufacturing is not an option. A good example is the fast-food industry. McDonald's has expanded globally by using a franchising strategy. Franchising is essentially the service-industry version of licensing, although it normally involves much longer term commitments than licensing. With franchising, the firm licenses its brand name to a foreign firm in return for a percentage of the franchisee's profits. The franchising contract specifies the conditions the franchisee must fulfill if it is to use the franchisor's brand name. Thus McDonald's allows foreign firms to use its brand name so long as they agree to run their restaurants on exactly the same lines as McDonald's restaurants elsewhere in the world. This strategy makes sense for McDonald's because (*a*) like many services, fast food cannot be exported, (*b*) franchising economizes the costs and risks associated with opening up foreign markets, (*c*) unlike technological know-how, brand names are relatively easy to protect using a contract, (*d*) there is no compelling reason for McDonald's to have tight control over franchisees, and (*e*) McDonald's know-how, in terms of how to run a fast-food restaurant, is amenable to being specified in a written contract (e.g., the contract specifies the details of how to run a McDonald's restaurant).

Finally, it should be noted that the product life-cycle theory and Knickerbocker's theory of FDI tend to be less useful from a business perspective. The problem with these two theories is that they are descriptive rather than analytical. They do a good job of describing the historical evolution of FDI, but they do a relatively poor job of identifying the factors that influence the relative profitability of FDI, licensing, and exporting. Indeed, both these theories ignore the issue of licensing as an alternative to FDI.

GOVERNMENT POLICY

A host government's attitude toward FDI should be an important variable in decisions about where to locate foreign production facilities and where to make a foreign direct investment. Other things being equal, investing in countries that have permissive policies toward FDI is clearly preferable to investing in countries that restrict FDI.

However, often the issue is not this straightforward. Despite the move toward a free market stance in recent years, many countries still have a rather pragmatic stance toward FDI. In such cases, a firm considering FDI usually must often negotiate the specific terms of the investment with the country's government. Such negotiations center on two broad issues. If the host government is trying to attract FDI, the central issue is likely to be the kind of incentives the host government is prepared to offer to the MNE and what the firm will commit in exchange. If the host government is uncertain about the benefits of FDI and might choose to restrict access, the central issue is likely to be the concessions that the firm must make in order to be allowed to go forward with a proposed investment.

To a large degree, the outcome of any negotiated agreement depends on the relative bargaining power of both parties. Each side's bargaining power depends on three factors:

• The value each side places on what the other has to offer.

• The number of comparable alternatives available to each side.

• Each party's time horizon.

From the perspective of a firm negotiating the terms of an investment with a host government, the firm's bargaining power is high when the host government places a high value on what the firm has to offer, the number of comparable alternatives open to the firm is greater, and the firm has a long time in which to complete the negotiations. The converse also holds. The firm's bargaining power is low when the host government places a low value on what the firm has to offer, the number of comparable alternatives open to the firm is fewer, and the firm has a short time in which to complete the negotiations.[54]

CHAPTER SUMMARY

The objectives of this chapter were to review theories that attempt to explain the pattern of FDI between countries and to examine the influence of governments on firms' decisions to invest in foreign countries. The following points were made:

1. Any theory seeking to explain FDI must explain why firms go to the trouble of acquiring or establishing operations abroad, when the alternatives of exporting and licensing are available to them.

2. High transportation costs or tariffs imposed on imports help explain why many firms prefer FDI or licensing over exporting.

3. Firms often prefer FDI to licensing when: (a) a firm has valuable know-how that cannot be adequately protected by a licensing contract, (b) a firm needs tight control over a foreign entity in order to maximize its market share and earnings in that country, and (c) a firm's skills and capabilities are not amenable to licensing.

4. Knickerbocker's theory suggests that much FDI is explained by imitative behavior by rival firms in an oligopolistic industry.

5. Vernon's product life-cycle theory suggests that firms undertake FDI at particular stages in the life cycle of products they have pioneered. However, Vernon's theory does not address the issue of whether FDI is more efficient than exporting or licensing for expanding abroad.

6. Dunning has argued that location-specific advantages are of considerable importance in explaining the nature and direction of FDI. According to Dunning, firms undertake FDI to exploit resource endowments or assets that are location specific.

7. Political ideology is an important determinant of government policy toward FDI. Ideology ranges from a radical stance that is hostile to FDI to a noninterventionist, free market stance. Between the two extremes is an approach best described as pragmatic nationalism.

8. Benefits of FDI to a host country arise from resource transfer effects, employment effects, and balance-of-payments effects.

9. The costs of FDI to a host country include adverse effects on competition and balance of payments and a perceived loss of national sovereignty.

10. The benefits of FDI to the home (source) country include improvement in the balance of payments as a result of the inward flow of foreign earnings, positive employment effects when the foreign subsidiary creates demand for home-country exports, and benefits from a reverse resource-transfer effect. A reverse resource-transfer effect arises when the foreign subsidiary learns valuable skills abroad that can be transferred back to the home country.

11. The costs of FDI to the home country include adverse balance-of-payments effects that arise from the initial capital outflow and from the export substitution effects of FDI. Costs also arise when FDI exports jobs abroad.

12. Home countries can adopt policies designed to both encourage and restrict FDI. Host countries try to attract FDI by offering incentives and try to restrict FDI by dictating ownership restraints and requiring that foreign MNEs meet specific performance requirements.

Critical Thinking and Discussion Questions

1. In 2004, inward FDI accounted for some 24 percent of gross fixed capital formation in Ireland, but only 0.6 percent in Japan. What do you think explains this difference in FDI inflows into the two countries?

2. Compare and contrast these explanations of FDI: internalization theory, Vernon's product life-cycle theory, and Knickerbocker's theory of FDI. Which theory do you think offers the best explanation of the historical pattern of FDI? Why?

3. Reread the opening case on Starbucks and then answer the following questions:

   a. Initially Starbucks expanded internationally by licensing its format to foreign operators. It soon became disenchanted with this strategy. Why?

   b. Why do you think Starbucks has now elected to expand internationally primarily through local joint ventures, to whom it licenses its format, as opposed to using a pure licensing strategy?

   c. What are the advantages of a joint-venture entry mode for Starbucks over entering through wholly owned subsidiaries? On occasion, Starbucks has chosen a wholly owned subsidiary to control its foreign expansion (e.g., in Britain and Thailand). Why?

   d. Which theory of FDI best explains the international expansion strategy Starbucks adopted?

4. You are the international manager of a U.S. business that has just developed a revolutionary new personal computer that can perform the same functions as existing PCs but costs only half as much to manufacture. Several patents protect the unique design of this computer. Your CEO has asked you to formulate a recommendation for how to expand into Western Europe. Your options are (*a*) to export from the United States, (*b*) to license a European firm to manufacture and market the computer in Europe, or (*c*) to set up a wholly owned subsidiary in Europe. Evaluate the pros and cons of each alternative and suggest a course of action to your CEO.

Research Task

Use the globalEDGE™ site to complete the following exercises:

1. The *World Investment Report* published annually by UNCTAD provides quick electronic access to comprehensive statistics on foreign direct investment (FDI) and the operations of transnational corporations. Gather a list of the top transnational corporations in terms of foreign direct investment. Also, identify each company's home country (i.e., headquarters country). Provide a commentary about the characteristics of countries that have the greatest number of

transnational firms. Are there any common traits you notice concerning countries with many transnational firms?

2. Your company is considering opening a new factory in Latin America, and management is in the process of evaluating the specific country locations for this direct investment. The pool of candidate countries has been narrowed to Argentina, Mexico, and Brazil. Prepare a short report from a well-known organization's publication of *Country Fact Sheets* to compare the foreign direct investment environment and regulations of these three countries.

CLOSING CASE

Cemex's Foreign Direct Investment

In little more than a decade, Mexico's largest cement manufacturer, Cemex, has transformed itself from a primarily Mexican operation into the third-largest cement company in the world behind Holcim of Switzerland and Lafarge Group of France with 2005 sales of $15 billion and more than $2 billion in net profits. Cemex has long been a powerhouse in Mexico and currently controls more than 60 percent of the market for cement in that country. Cemex's domestic success has been based in large part on an obsession with efficient manufacturing and a focus on customer service that is tops in the industry.

Cemex is a leader in using information technology to match production with consumer demand. The company sells ready-mixed cement that can survive for only about 90 minutes before solidifying, so precise delivery is important. But Cemex can never predict with total certainty what demand will be on any given day, week, or month. To better manage unpredictable demand patterns, Cemex developed a system of seamless information technology, including truck-mounted global positioning systems, radio transmitters, satellites, and computer hardware, that allows it to control the production and distribution of cement like no other company can, responding quickly to unanticipated changes in demand and reducing waste. The results are lower costs and superior customer service, both differentiating factors for Cemex.

The company also pays lavish attention to its distributors—some 5,000 in Mexico alone—who can earn points toward rewards for hitting sales targets. The distributors can then convert those points into Cemex stock. High-volume distributors can purchase trucks and other supplies through Cemex at significant discounts. Cemex also is known for its marketing drives that focus on end users, the builders themselves. For example, Cemex trucks drive around Mexican building sites, and if Cemex cement is being used, the construction crews win soccer balls, caps, and T-shirts.

Cemex's international expansion strategy was driven by a number of factors. First, the company wished to reduce its reliance on the Mexican construction market, which was characterized by very volatile demand. Second, the company realized there was tremendous demand for cement in many developing countries, where significant construction was being undertaken or needed. Third, the company believed that it understood the needs of construction businesses in developing nations better than the established multinational cement companies, all of which were from developed nations. Fourth, Cemex believed that it could create significant value by acquiring inefficient cement companies in other markets and transferring its skills in customer service, marketing, information technology, and production management to those units.

The company embarked in earnest on its international expansion strategy in the early 1990s. Initially, Cemex targeted other developing nations, acquiring established cement makers in Venezuela, Colombia, Indonesia, the Philippines, Egypt, and several other countries. It also purchased two stagnant companies in Spain and turned them around. Bolstered by the success of its Spanish ventures, Cemex began to look for expansion opportunities in developed nations. In 2000, Cemex purchased Houston-based Southland, one of the largest cement

companies in the United States, for $2.5 billion. Following the Southland acquisition, Cemex had 56 cement plants in 30 countries, most of which were gained through acquisitions. In all cases, Cemex devoted great attention to transferring its technological, management, and marketing know-how to acquired units, thereby improving their performance.

In 2004, Cemex made another major foreign investment move, purchasing RMC of Great Britain for $5.8 billion. RMC was a huge multinational cement firm with sales of $8.0 billion, only 22 percent of which were in the United Kingdom, and operations in more than 20 other nations, including many European nations where Cemex had no presence. Finalized in March 2005, the RMC acquisition has transformed Cemex into a global powerhouse in the cement industry with more than $15 billion in annual sales and operations in 50 countries. Only about 15 percent of the company's sales are now generated in Mexico. Following the acquisition of RMC, Cemex found that the RMC plant in Rugby was only running at 70 percent of capacity, partly because repeated production problems kept causing a kiln shutdown. Cemex brought in an international team of specialists to fix the problem, and quickly increased production to 90 percent of capacity.

Going forward, Cemex has made it clear that it will continue to expand and is eyeing opportunities in the fast-growing economies of China and India, where it currently lacks a presence and where its global rivals are already expanding. Still, not all of Cemex's expansions have worked out as planned. In 2006, Cemex announced that it would exit Indonesia after a long-running dispute with the government there. Cemex entered Indonesia in 1998 as part of an IMF-sponsored privatization program by purchasing a 25 percent stake in a government-owned Indonesian cement maker, Semen Gresik. At the time, Indonesia promised to allow Cemex to acquire a majority stake in Semen Gresik in 2001. However, the country never granted that permission, as local vested interests, including politicians and unions, voiced worries about "Indonesian assets falling into foreign hands" and lobbied the central government to block the deal. A frustrated Cemex eventually reached an agreement to sell its 25 percent stake to another Indonesian enterprise.[55]

Case Discussion Questions

1. Which theoretical explanation (or explanations) of FDI best explains Cemex's FDI?

2. What value does Cemex bring to a host economy? Can you see any potential drawbacks of inward investment by Cemex in an economy?

3. Cemex has a strong preference for acquisitions over greenfield ventures as an entry mode. Why?

4. Why do you think Cemex decided to exit Indonesia after failing to gain majority control of Semen Gresik? Why is majority control so important to Cemex?

5. Why do you think politicians in Indonesia tried to block Cemex's attempt to gain majority control over Semen Gresik? Do you think Indonesia's best interests were served by limiting Cemex's FDI in the country?

Notes

1. Sources: Starbucks 10K, various years; C. McLean, "Starbucks Set to Invade Coffee-Loving Continent," *Seattle Times*, October 4, 2000, p. E1; J. Ordonez, "Starbucks to Start Major Expansion in Overseas Market," *The Wall Street Journal*, October 27, 2000, p. B10; S. Homes and D. Bennett, "Planet Starbucks," *BusinessWeek*, September 9, 2002, pp. 99–110; "Starbucks Outlines International Growth Strategy," *Business Wire*, October 14, 2004; and A. Yeh, "Starbucks Aims for New Tier in China," *Financial Times*, February 14, 2006, p. 17.

2. United Nations, *World Investment Report, 2000* (New York and Geneva: United Nations, 2001).

3. United Nations, *World Investment Report, 2006* (New York and Geneva: United Nations, 2006); and "Foreign Direct Investment Rose by 34% in 2006," UN Conference on Trade and Development, press release, January 23, 2007.

4. World Trade Organization, *International Trade Statistics, 2006* (Geneva: WTO, 2006); and United Nations, *World Investment Report, 2006*.

5. United Nations, *World Investment Report, 2006*.

6. Ibid.

7. Ibid.

8. United Nations, *World Investment Report, 2006*; and "Foreign Direct Investment Rose by 34% in 2006."

9. Ibid.

10. Ibid.

11. Sources: Interviews by the author while in China; United Nations, *World Investment Report, 2006*; L. Ng and C. Tuan, "Building a Favorable Investment Environment: Evidence for the Facilitation of FDI in China," *The World Economy*, 2002, pp. 1095–114; and S. Chan and G. Qingyang, "Investment in China Migrates Inland," *Far Eastern Economic Review*, May 2006, pp. 52–57.

12. United Nations, *World Investment Report, 2006*.

13. Ibid.

14. See D. J. Ravenscraft and F. M. Scherer, *Mergers, Selloffs and Economic Efficiency* (Washington, DC: The Brookings Institution, 1987); and A. Seth, K. P. Song, and R. R. Pettit, "Value Creation and Destruction in Cross-Border Acquisitions," *Strategic Management Journal* 23 (2002), pp. 921–40.

15. For example, see S. H. Hymer, *The International Operations of National Firms: A Study of Direct Foreign Investment* (Cambridge, MA: MIT Press, 1976); A. M. Rugman, *Inside the Multinationals: The Economics of Internal Markets* (New York: Columbia University Press, 1981); D. J. Teece, "Multinational Enterprise, Internal Governance, and Industrial Organization," *American Economic Review* 75 (May 1983), pp. 233–38; C. W. L. Hill and W. C. Kim, "Searching for a Dynamic Theory of the Multinational Enterprise: A Transaction Cost Model," *Strategic Management Journal* 9 (special issue, 1988), pp. 93–104; A. Verbeke, "The Evolutionary View of the MNE and the Future of Internalization Theory," *Journal of International Business Studies* 34 (2003), pp. 498–501; and J. H. Dunning, "Some Antecedents of Internalization Theory," *Journal of International Business Studies* 34 (2003), pp. 108–28.

16. J. P. Womack, D. T. Jones, and D. Roos, *The Machine That Changed the World* (New York: Rawson Associates, 1990).

17. The argument is most often associated with F. T. Knickerbocker, *Oligopolistic Reaction and Multinational Enterprise* (Boston: Harvard Business School Press, 1973).

18. The studies are summarized in R. E. Caves, *Multinational Enterprise and Economic Analysis*, 2nd ed. (Cambridge, UK: Cambridge University Press, 1996).

19. See R. E. Caves, "Japanese Investment in the US: Lessons for the Economic Analysis of Foreign Investment," *The World Economy* 16 (1993), pp. 279–300; B. Kogut and S. J. Chang,

"Technological Capabilities and Japanese Direct Investment in the United States," *Review of Economics and Statistics* 73 (1991), pp. 401–43; and J. Anand and B. Kogut, "Technological Capabilities of Countries, Firm Rivalry, and Foreign Direct Investment," *Journal of International Business Studies*, 1997, pp. 445–65.

20. K. Ito and E. L. Rose, "Foreign Direct Investment Location Strategies in the Tire Industry," *Journal of International Business Studies* 33 (2002), pp. 593–602.

21. H. Haveman and L. Nonnemaker, "Competition in Multiple Geographical Markets," *Administrative Science Quarterly* 45 (2000), pp. 232–67; and L. Fuentelsaz and J. Gomez, "Multipoint Competition, Strategic Similarity and Entry into Geographic Markets," *Strategic Management Journal* 27 (2006), pp. 447–57.

22. For the use of Vernon's theory to explain Japanese direct investment in the United States and Europe, see S. Thomsen, "Japanese Direct Investment in the European Community," *The World Economy* 16 (1993), pp. 301–15. Also see Z. Gao and C. Tisdell, "Foreign Investment and Asia, Particularly China's Rise in the Television Industry: The International Product Life Cycle Reconsidered," *Journal of Asia-Pacific Business* 6, no. 3 (2005), pp. 37–50.

23. J. H. Dunning, *Explaining International Production* (London: Unwin Hyman, 1988).

24. P. Krugman. "Increasing Returns and Economic Geography," *Journal of Political Economy* 99, no. 3 (1991), pp. 483–99.

25. J. M. Shaver and F. Flyer, "Agglomeration Economies, Firm Heterogeneity, and Foreign Direct Investment in the United States," *Strategic Management Journal* 21 (2000), pp. 1175–93.

26. J. H. Dunning and R. Narula, "Transpacific Foreign Direct Investment and the Investment Development Path," *South Carolina Essays in International Business*, May 1995.

27. W. Shan and J. Song, "Foreign Direct Investment and the Sourcing of Technological Advantage: Evidence from the Biotechnology Industry," *Journal of International Business Studies*, 1997, pp. 267–84.

28. For some additional evidence see L. E. Brouthers, K. D. Brouthers, and S. Warner, "Is Dunning's Eclectic Framework Descriptive or Normative?" *Journal of International Business Studies* 30 (1999), pp. 831–44.

29. For elaboration, see S. Hood and S. Young, *The Economics of the Multinational Enterprise* (London: Longman, 1979); and P. M. Sweezy and H. Magdoff, "The Dynamics of U.S. Capitalism," *Monthly Review Press*, 1972.

30. C. Forelle and G. Hitt, "IBM Discusses Security Measure in Lenovo Deal," *The Wall Street Journal*, February 25, 2005, p. A2.

31. For an example of this policy as practiced in China, see L. G. Branstetter and R. C. Freenstra, "Trade and Foreign Direct Investment in China: A Political Economy Approach," *Journal of International Economics* 58 (December 2002), pp. 335–58.

32. M. Itoh and K. Kiyono, "Foreign Trade and Direct Investment," in *Industrial Policy of Japan*, ed. R. Komiya, M. Okuno, and K. Suzumura (Tokyo: Academic Press, 1988).

33. Sources: "Trouble at the Waterfront," *The Economist*, February 25, 2006, p. 48; "Paranoia about Dubai Ports Deals Is Needless," *Financial Times*, February 21, 2006, p. 16; and "DP World: We'll Be Back," *Traffic World*, May 29, 2006, p. 1.

34. R. E. Lipsey, "Home and Host Country Effects of FDI," National Bureau of Economic Research, working paper no. 9293, October 2002; and X. Li and X. Liu, "Foreign Direct Investment and Economic Growth," *World Development* 33 (March 2005), pp. 393–413.

35. X. J. Zhan and T. Ozawa, *Business Restructuring in Asia: Cross Border M & As in Crisis Affected Countries* (Copenhagen: Copenhagen Business School, 2000); I. Costa, S. Robles, and R. de Queiroz, "Foreign Direct Investment and Technological Capabilities," *Research Policy* 31 (2002), pp. 1431–43; B. Potterie and F. Lichtenberg, "Does Foreign Direct Investment Transfer Technology across Borders?" *Review of Economics and Statistics* 83 (2001), pp. 490–97; and K. Saggi, "Trade, Foreign Direct Investment and International Technology Transfer," *World Bank Research Observer* 17 (2002), pp. 191–235.

36. K. M. Moden, "Foreign Acquisitions of Swedish Companies: Effects on R&D and Productivity," Stockholm: Research Institute of International Economics, 1998, mimeo.

37. "Foreign Friends," *The Economist*, January 8, 2000, pp. 71–72.

38. A. Jack, "French Go into Overdrive to Win Investors," *Financial Times*, December 10, 1997, p. 6.

39. "Foreign Friends."

40. G. Hunya and K. Kalotay, *Privatization and Foreign Direct Investment in Eastern and Central Europe* (Geneva: UNCTAD, 2001).

41. United Nations, *World Investment Report, 2002* (New York and Geneva: United Nations, 2002).

42. R. Ram and K. H. Zang, "Foreign Direct Investment and Economic Growth," *Economic Development and Cultural Change* 51 (2002), pp. 205–25.

43. United Nations, *World Investment Report, 1998* (New York and Geneva: United Nations, 1997).

44. United Nations, *World Investment Report, 2000.*

45. R. B. Reich, *The Work of Nations: Preparing Ourselves for the 21st Century* (New York: Alfred A. Knopf, 1991).

46. This idea has been articulated, although not quite in this form, by C. A. Bartlett and S. Ghoshal, *Managing across Borders: The Transnational Solution* (Boston: Harvard Business School Press, 1989).

47. P. Magnusson, "The Mexico Pact: Worth the Price?" *BusinessWeek*, May 27, 1991, pp. 32–35.

48. C. Johnston, "Political Risk Insurance," in *Assessing Corporate Political Risk*, ed. D. M. Raddock (Totowa, NJ: Rowan & Littlefield, 1986).

49. M. Tolchin and S. Tolchin, *Buying into America: How Foreign Money Is Changing the Face of Our Nation* (New York: Times Books, 1988).

50. S. Rai, "India to Ease Limits on Foreign Ownership of Media and Tea," *The New York Times*, June 26, 2002, p. W1.

51. L. D. Qiu and Z. Tao, "Export, Foreign Direct Investment and Local Content Requirements," *Journal of Development Economics* 66 (October 2001), pp. 101–25.

52. United Nations, *World Investment Report, 2003*

53. See R. E. Caves, *Multinational Enterprise and Economic Analysis* (Cambridge, UK: Cambridge University Press, 1982).

54. For a good general introduction to negotiation strategy, see M.H. Bazerman, *Negotiating Rationally* (New York: Free Press, 1992); A. Dixit and B. Nalebuff, *Thinking Strategically: The Competitive Edge in Business, Politics, and Everyday Life* (New York: W. W. Norton, 1991); and H. Raiffa, *The Art and Science of Negotiation* (Cambridge, MA: Harvard University Press, 1982).

55. Sources: C. Piggott, "Cemex's Stratospheric Rise," *Latin Finance*, March 2001, p. 76; J. F. Smith, "Making Cement a Household Word," *Los Angeles Times*, January 16, 2000, p. C1; D. Helft, "Cemex Attempts to Cement Its Future," *The Industry Standard*, November 6, 2000; Diane Lindquist, "From Cement to Services," *Chief Executive*, November 2002, pp. 48–50; "Cementing Global Success," *Strategic Direct Investor*, March 2003, p. 1; M. T. Derham, "The Cemex Surprise," *Latin Finance*, November 2004, pp. 1–2; "Holcim Seeks to Acquire Aggregate," *The Wall Street Journal*, January 13, 2005, p. 1; J. Lyons, "Cemex Prowls for Deals in Both China and India," *The Wall Street Journal*, January 27, 2006, p. C4; and S. Donnan, "Cemex Sells 25 Percent Stake in Semen Gresik," *FT.com*, May 4, 2006, p. 1.

The European Energy Market

For several years now the European Union, the largest regional trading bloc in the world, has been trying to liberalize its energy market, replacing the markets of its 27 member states with a single continentwide market for electricity and gas. The first phase of liberalization went into effect in June 2007. When fully implemented, the ability of energy producers to sell electricity and gas across national borders will increase competition, which in turn should lower energy prices, force utilities to become more efficient, and boost economic growth across the region. The road toward the creation of a single EU energy market, however, has been anything but easy. Many national markets are dominated by a single enterprise, often a former state-owned utility. Electricitie de France, for example, has an 87 percent share of that country's electricity market.

Injecting competition into such concentrated markets will prove difficult.

To complicate matters, most of these utilities are vertically integrated, producing, transmitting, and selling power. These vertically integrated producers have little interest in letting other utilities use their transmission grids to sell power to end users or in buying power from other producers. For the full benefits of competition to take hold, the EU recognizes that utilities need to be split into generation, transmission, and marketing companies so that the business of selling energy can be separated from the businesses of producing it and transmitting it. Only then, so the thinking goes, will independent power marketing companies be able to buy energy from the cheapest source, whether it is within national borders or elsewhere in the EU, and resell it to consumers, thereby

Regional Economic Integration

8

LEARNING OBJECTIVES

After you have read this chapter you should:

LO¹ Be able to explain the different levels of regional economic integration.

LO² Understand the economic and political arguments for regional economic integration.

LO³ Understand the economic and political arguments against regional economic integration.

LO⁴ Be familiar with the history, current scope, and future prospects of the world's most important regional economic agreements.

LO⁵ Understand the implications for business that are inherent in regional economic integration agreements.

promoting competition. For now, efforts to mandate the deintegration of utilities are some way off. Indeed, in February 2007 national energy ministers from the different EU states rejected a call from the European Commission, the top administrative body concerned with competition in the EU, to break apart utilities. Instead the energy ministers asked the commission for more details about what such a move would accomplish, thereby effectively delaying any attempt to deintegrate national power companies.

The response of established utilities to the creation of a single continentwide market for energy has been to try to acquire utilities in other EU nations in an effort to build systems that serve more than one country. The underlying logic is that larger utilities should be able to realize economies of scale, which would enable them

to compete more effectively in a liberalized market. However, some cross-border takeover bids have run into fierce opposition from local politicians who resent their "national energy companies" being taken over by foreign entities. Most notably, when E.ON, the largest German utility, made a bid to acquire Endesa, Spain's largest utility, in 2006, Spanish politicians sought to block the acquisition and keep ownership of Endesa in Spanish hands, imposing conditions on the deal which were designed to stop the Germans from acquiring the Spanish company. In response to this outburst of nationalism, the European Commission took the Spanish government to the European Union's highest court, arguing that Madrid had violated the commission's exclusive powers within the EU to scrutinize and approve big cross-border mergers in Europe.[1]

Introduction

In this chapter we will take a close look at the arguments for regional economic integration through the establishment of trading blocs such as the European Union and the North American Free Trade Agreement. We will discuss the difficult process of forming such blocs and using them as an institutional means for lowering the barriers to cross-border trade and investment between member states. The opening case illustrates some of the promise and problems associated with integrating the economies of different nations into regional trading blocs. By promoting free trade in energy across national borders, the EU hopes to increase competition and lower energy prices to consumers. However, as described in the case, so far political opposition and the realities of the existing industry structure have made this a difficult goal to attain.

By **regional economic integration** we mean agreements among countries in a geographic region to reduce, and ultimately remove, tariff and nontariff barriers to the free flow of goods, services, and factors of production between each other. In the last two decades, the proliferation of regional trade blocs that promote regional economic integration has been unprecedented. World Trade Organization members are required to notify the WTO of any regional trade agreements in which they participate. By 2007, nearly all the WTO's members had notified the organization of participation in one or more regional trade agreements. The total number of regional trade agreements currently in force is around 300.[2]

Consistent with the predictions of international trade theory and particularly the theory of comparative advantage (see Chapter 5), agreements designed to promote freer trade within regions are believed to produce gains from trade for all member countries. As we saw in Chapter 6, the General Agreement on Tariffs and Trade and its successor, the World Trade Organization, also seek to reduce trade barriers. With 150 member states, the WTO has a worldwide perspective. By entering into regional agreements, groups of countries aim to reduce trade barriers more rapidly than can be achieved under the auspices of the WTO. Thus while a global market for electricity and gas is a long way off, the EU hopes to have a regional market established and functioning relatively soon.

Nowhere has the movement toward regional economic integration been more successful than in Europe. On January 1, 1993, the European Union (EU) formally removed many barriers to doing business across borders within the EU in an attempt to create a single market with 340 million consumers. However, the EU did not stop there. The member states of the EU have launched a single currency, the euro, and they are moving toward a closer political union. On May 1, 2004, the EU expanded from 15 to 25 countries with a population of 450 million consumers and a gross domestic product approaching that of the United States, and in 2007 two more countries, Bulgaria and Romania, joined the EU.

Similar moves toward regional integration are being pursued elsewhere in the world. Canada, Mexico, and the United States have implemented the North American Free Trade Agreement (NAFTA). Ultimately, this promises to remove all barriers to the free flow of goods and services between the three countries. While the implementation of NAFTA has resulted in job losses in some sectors of the American economy, in aggregate and consistent with the predications of international trade theory, the benefits of greater regional trade are argued to outweigh any costs. South America, too, is moving toward regional integration. In 1991, Argentina, Brazil, Paraguay, and Uruguay implemented an agreement known as MERCOSUR to start reducing barriers to trade between each other, and although progress within MERCOSUR has been slow, the institution is still in place. Active attempts at regional economic integration are also occurring in Central America, the Andean region of South America, Southeast Asia, and parts of Africa.

While the move toward regional economic integration is generally seen as a good thing, some observers worry that it will lead to a world in which regional trade blocs compete against each other. In this possible future scenario, free trade will exist within each bloc, but each bloc will protect its market from outside competition with high tariffs. The specter of the EU and NAFTA turning into economic fortresses that shut out foreign producers with high tariff barriers is worrisome to those who believe in unrestricted free trade. If such a situation were to materialize, the resulting decline in trade between blocs could more than offset the gains from free trade within blocs.

With these issues in mind, this chapter will explore the economic and political debate surrounding regional economic integration, paying particular attention to the economic and political benefits and costs of integration; review progress toward regional economic integration around the world; and map the important implications of regional economic integration for the practice of international business. Before tackling these objectives, we first need to examine the levels of integration that are theoretically possible.

Levels of Economic Integration

Several levels of economic integration are possible in theory (see Figure 8.1). From least integrated to most integrated, they include a free trade area, a customs union, a common market, an economic union, and, finally, a full political union.

In a **free trade area,** all barriers to the trade of goods and services among member countries are removed. In the theoretically ideal free trade area, no discriminatory tariffs, quotas, subsidies, or administrative impediments are allowed to distort trade between members. Each country, however, is allowed to determine its own trade policies with regard to nonmembers. For example, the tariffs placed on the products of nonmember countries may vary from member to member. Free trade agreements are the most popular form of regional economic integration, accounting for almost 90 percent of regional agreements.[3]

The most enduring free trade area in the world is the **European Free Trade Association (EFTA).** Established in January 1960, EFTA currently joins four countries—Norway, Iceland, Liechtenstein, and Switzerland—down from seven in 1995 (three EFTA members, Austria, Finland, and Sweden, joined the EU on January 1, 1996). EFTA was founded by those Western European countries that initially decided not to be part of the European Community (the forerunner of the EU). Its original members included Austria,

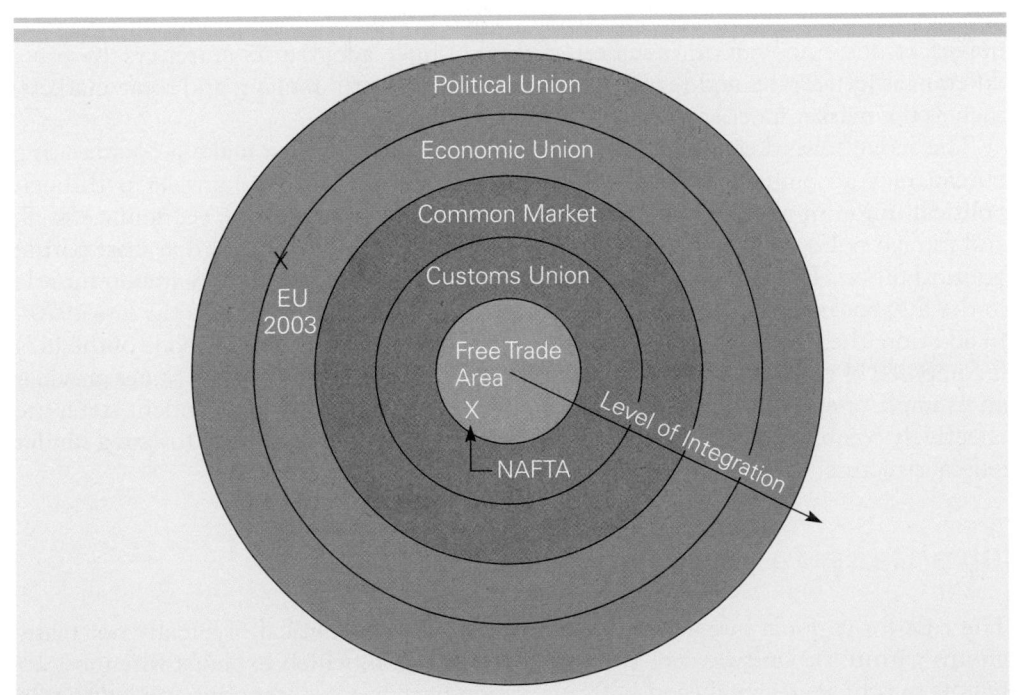

FIGURE 8.1

Levels of Economic Integration

Great Britain, Denmark, Finland, and Sweden, all of which are now members of the EU. The emphasis of EFTA has been on free trade in industrial goods. Agriculture was left out of the arrangement, each member being allowed to determine its own level of support. Members are also free to determine the level of protection applied to goods coming from outside EFTA. Other free trade areas include the North American Free Trade Agreement, which we shall discuss in depth later in the chapter.

The customs union is one step further along the road to full economic and political integration. A **customs union** eliminates trade barriers between member countries and adopts a common external trade policy. Establishment of a common external trade policy necessitates significant administrative machinery to oversee trade relations with nonmembers. Most countries that enter into a customs union desire even greater economic integration down the road. The EU began as a customs union, but has now moved beyond this stage. Other customs unions around the world include the current version of the Andean Community (formally known as the Andean Pact) between Bolivia, Colombia, Ecuador, Peru, and Venezuela. The Andean Community established free trade between member countries and imposes a common tariff of 5 to 20 percent on products imported from outside.[4]

The next level of economic integration, a **common market,** has no barriers to trade between member countries, includes a common external trade policy, and allows factors of production to move freely between members. Labor and capital are free to move because there are no restrictions on immigration, emigration, or cross-border flows of capital between member countries. Establishing a common market demands a significant degree of harmony and cooperation on fiscal, monetary, and employment policies. Achieving this degree of cooperation has proven very difficult. For years, the European Union functioned as a common market, although it has now moved beyond this stage. MERCOSUR, the South American grouping of Argentina, Brazil, Paraguay, Uruguay, and (as of 2006) Venezuela, hopes to eventually establish itself as a common market.

An economic union entails even closer economic integration and cooperation than a common market. Like the common market, an **economic union** involves the free flow of products and factors of production between member countries and the adoption of a common external trade policy, but it also requires a common currency, harmonization of members' tax rates, and a common monetary and fiscal policy. Such a high degree of integration demands a coordinating bureaucracy and the sacrifice of significant amounts of national sovereignty to that bureaucracy. The EU is an economic union, although an imperfect one since not all members of the EU have adopted its currency, the euro, differences in tax rates and regulations across countries still remain, and some markets, such as the market for energy, are still not fully deregulated.

The move toward economic union raises the issue of how to make a coordinating bureaucracy accountable to the citizens of member nations. The answer is through **political union** in which a central political apparatus coordinates the economic, social, and foreign policy of the member states. The EU is on the road toward at least partial political union. The European Parliament, which is playing an ever more important role in the EU, has been directly elected by citizens of the EU countries since the late 1970s. In addition, the Council of Ministers (the controlling, decision-making body of the EU) is composed of government ministers from each EU member. The United States provides an example of even closer political union; in the United States, independent states are effectively combined into a single nation. Ultimately, the EU may move toward a similar federal structure.

The Case for Regional Integration

The case for regional integration is both economic and political. Typically not many groups within a country accept the case for integration, which explains why most attempts to achieve regional economic integration have been contentious and halting. In this section, we examine the economic and political cases for integration and two impediments to it. In the next section, we look at the case against integration.

THE ECONOMIC CASE FOR INTEGRATION

The economic case for regional integration is straightforward. We saw in Chapter 5 how economic theories of international trade predict that unrestricted free trade will allow countries to specialize in the production of goods and services that they can produce most efficiently. The result is greater world production than would be possible with trade restrictions. That chapter also explained how opening a country to free trade stimulates economic growth, which creates dynamic gains from trade. Chapter 7 detailed how foreign direct investment (FDI) can transfer technological, marketing, and managerial know-how to host nations. Given the central role of knowledge in stimulating economic growth, opening a country to FDI also is likely to stimulate economic growth. In sum, economic theories suggest that free trade and investment is a positive-sum game, in which all participating countries stand to gain.

Given this, the theoretical ideal is an absence of barriers to the free flow of goods, services, and factors of production among nations. However, as we saw in Chapters 6 and 7, a case can be made for government intervention in international trade and FDI. Because many governments have accepted part or all of the case for intervention, unrestricted free trade and FDI have proved to be only an ideal. Although international institutions such as the WTO have been moving the world toward a free trade regime, success has been less than total. In a world of many nations and many political ideologies, it is very difficult to get all countries to agree to a common set of rules.

Against this background, regional economic integration can be seen as an attempt to achieve additional gains from the free flow of trade and investment between countries beyond those attainable under international agreements such as the WTO. It is easier to establish a free trade and investment regime among a limited number of adjacent countries than among the world community. Coordination and policy harmonization problems are largely a function of the number of countries that seek agreement. The greater the number of countries involved, the more perspectives that must be reconciled, and the harder it will be to reach agreement. Thus, attempts at regional economic integration are motivated by a desire to exploit the gains from free trade and investment.

THE POLITICAL CASE FOR INTEGRATION

The political case for regional economic integration also has loomed large in several attempts to establish free trade areas, customs unions, and the like. Linking neighboring economies and making them increasingly dependent on each other creates incentives for political cooperation between the neighboring states and reduces the potential for violent conflict. In addition, by grouping their economies, the countries can enhance their political weight in the world.

These considerations underlay the 1957 establishment of the European Community (EC), the forerunner of the EU. Europe had suffered two devastating wars in the first half of the 20th century, both arising out of the unbridled ambitions of nation-states. Those who have sought a united Europe have always had a desire to make another war in Europe unthinkable. Many Europeans also believed that after World War II, the European nation-states were no longer large enough to hold their own in world markets and politics. The need for a united Europe to deal with the United States and the politically alien Soviet Union loomed large in the minds of many of the EC's founders.[5] A longstanding joke in Europe is that the European Commission should erect a statue to Joseph Stalin, for without the aggressive policies of the former dictator of the old Soviet Union, the countries of Western Europe may have lacked the incentive to cooperate and form the EC.

IMPEDIMENTS TO INTEGRATION

Despite the strong economic and political arguments in support, integration has never been easy to achieve or sustain for two main reasons. First, although economic integration aids the majority, it has its costs. While a nation as a whole may benefit significantly from a regional free trade agreement, certain groups may lose. Moving to a free trade regime involves painful adjustments. For example, due to the 1994 establishment of NAFTA, some Canadian and U.S. workers in such industries as textiles, which employ low-cost, low-skilled labor, lost their jobs as Canadian and U.S. firms moved production to Mexico. The promise of significant net benefits to the Canadian and U.S. economies as a whole is little comfort to those who lose as a result of NAFTA. Such groups have been at the forefront of opposition to NAFTA and will continue to oppose any widening of the agreement.

A second impediment to integration arises from concerns over national sovereignty. For example, Mexico's concerns about maintaining control of its oil interests resulted in an agreement with Canada and the United States to exempt the Mexican oil industry from any liberalization of foreign investment regulations achieved under NAFTA. Concerns about national sovereignty arise because close economic integration demands that countries give up some degree of control over such key issues as monetary policy, fiscal policy (e.g., tax policy), and trade policy. This has been a major stumbling block in the EU. To achieve full economic union, the EU introduced a common currency, the euro, controlled by a central EU bank. Although most member states have signed on, Great Britain remains an important holdout. A politically important segment of public opinion in that country opposes a common currency on the grounds that it would require relinquishing control of the country's monetary policy to the EU, which many British perceive as a bureaucracy run by foreigners. In 1992, the British won the right to opt out of any single currency agreement, and as of 2007, the British government had yet to reverse its decision.

The Case against Regional Integration

Although the tide has been running strongly in favor of regional free trade agreements in recent years, some economists have expressed concern that the benefits of regional integration have been oversold, while the costs have often been ignored.[6] They point out that the benefits of regional integration are determined by the extent of trade creation, as opposed to trade diversion. **Trade creation** occurs when low-cost producers within the free trade area replace high-cost domestic producers. It may also occur when lower cost external producers within the free trade area replace higher cost external producers. **Trade diversion** occurs when higher cost suppliers replace lower cost external suppliers within the free trade area. A regional free trade agreement will benefit the world only if the amount of trade it creates exceeds the amount it diverts.

Suppose the United States and Mexico imposed tariffs on imports from all countries, and then they set up a free trade area, scrapping all trade barriers between themselves but maintaining tariffs on imports from the rest of the world. If the United States began to import textiles from Mexico, would this change be for the better? If the United States previously produced all its own textiles at a higher cost than Mexico, then the free trade agreement has shifted production to the cheaper source. According to the theory of comparative advantage, trade has been created within the regional grouping, and there would be no decrease in trade with the rest of the world. Clearly, the change would be for the better. If, however, the United States previously imported textiles from Costa Rica, which produced them more cheaply than either Mexico or the United States, then trade has been diverted from a low-cost source—a change for the worse.

In theory, WTO rules should ensure that a free trade agreement does not result in trade diversion. These rules allow free trade areas to be formed only if the members set tariffs that are not higher or more restrictive to outsiders than the ones previously in effect. However, as we saw in Chapter 6, GATT and the WTO do not cover some nontariff barriers. As a result, regional trade blocs could emerge whose markets are protected from outside competition by high nontariff barriers. In such cases, the trade diversion effects might outweigh the trade creation effects. The only way to guard against this possibility, according to those concerned about this potential, is to increase the scope of the WTO so it covers nontariff barriers to trade. There is no sign that this is going to occur anytime soon, however; so the risk remains that regional economic integration will result in trade diversion.

Regional Economic Integration in Europe

Europe has two trade blocs—the European Union and the European Free Trade Association. Of the two, the EU is by far the more significant, not just in terms of membership (the EU currently has 27 members; the EFTA has 4), but also in terms of economic and political influence in the world economy. Many now see the EU as an emerging economic and political superpower of the same order as the United States and Japan. Accordingly, we will concentrate our attention on the EU.[7]

EVOLUTION OF THE EUROPEAN UNION

The **European Union** (EU) is the product of two political factors: (1) the devastation of Western Europe during two world wars and the desire for a lasting peace, and (2) the European nations' desire to hold their own on the world's political and economic stage. In addition, many Europeans were aware of the potential economic benefits of closer economic integration of the countries.

Belgium, France, West Germany, Italy, Luxembourg, and the Netherlands formed the forerunner of the EU, the European Coal and Steel Community, in 1951. Its objective was to remove barriers to intragroup shipments of coal, iron, steel, and scrap metal. The **Treaty of Rome,** signed in 1957, established the European Community. The name changed again in 1994 when the European Community became the European Union following the ratification of the Maastricht Treaty (discussed later).

The Treaty of Rome provided for the creation of a common market. Article 3 of the treaty laid down the key objectives of the new community, calling for the elimination of internal trade barriers and the creation of a common external tariff and requiring member states to abolish obstacles to the free movement of factors of production among the members. To facilitate the free movement of goods, services, and factors of production, the treaty provided for any necessary harmonization of the member states' laws. Furthermore, the treaty committed the EC to establish common policies in agriculture and transportation.

The community grew in 1973, when Great Britain, Ireland, and Denmark joined. These three were followed in 1981 by Greece, in 1986 by Spain and Portugal, and in 1996 by Austria, Finland, and Sweden, bringing the total membership to 15 (East Germany became part of the EC after the reunification of Germany in 1990). Another 10 countries joined the EU on May 1, 2004, 8 of them from Eastern Europe plus the small Mediterranean nations of Malta and Cyprus, and Bulgaria and Romania joined in 2007, bringing the total number of member states to 27 (see Map 8.1). With a population of over 460 million and a GDP of almost $12 trillion, similar to that of the United States, the EU has become a global superpower through these enlargements.[8]

MAP 8.1

Member States of the European Union in 2007

Source: The EU, www.europarl.org.uk.

POLITICAL STRUCTURE OF THE EUROPEAN UNION

The economic policies of the EU are formulated and implemented by a complex and still-evolving political structure. The four main institutions in this structure are the European Commission, the Council of the European Union, the European Parliament, and the Court of Justice.[9]

The **European Commission** is responsible for proposing EU legislation, implementing it, and monitoring compliance with EU laws by member states. Headquartered in Brussels, Belgium, the commission has more than 24,000 employees. It is run by a group of commissioners appointed by each member country for five-year renewable terms. There are 27 commissioners, one from each member state. Member states choose a president of the commission, and the president then chooses other members in consultation with the states. The entire commission has to be approved by the European Parliament before it can begin work. The commission has a monopoly in proposing European Union legislation. It makes a proposal, which goes to the Council of the European Union and then to the European Parliament. The council cannot legislate without a commission proposal in front of it. The commission is also responsible for implementing aspects of EU law, although in practice much of this must be delegated to member states. Another responsibility of the commission is to monitor member states to make sure they are complying with EU laws. In this policing role, the commission will normally ask a state to comply with any EU laws that are being broken. If this persuasion is not sufficient, the commission can refer a case to the Court of Justice.

The European Commission's role in competition policy has become increasingly important to business in recent years. Since 1990 when the office was formally assigned a role in competition policy, the EU's competition commissioner has been steadily gaining influence as the chief regulator of competition policy in the member nations of the EU. As with antitrust authorities in the United States, which include the Federal Trade Commission and the Department of Justice, the role of the competition commissioner is to ensure that no one enterprise uses its market power to drive out competitors and monopolize markets. The commissioner also reviews proposed mergers and acquisitions to make sure they do not create a dominant enterprise with substantial market power.[10] For example, in 2000 a proposed merger between Time Warner of the United States and EMI of the United Kingdom, both music recording companies, was withdrawn after the commission expressed concerns that the merger would reduce the number of major record companies from five to four and create a dominant player in the $40 billion global music industry. Similarly, the commission blocked a proposed merger between two U.S. telecommunication companies, WorldCom and Sprint, because their combined holdings of Internet infrastructure in Europe would give the merged companies so much market power that the commission argued the combined company would dominate that market. The accompanying Management Focus, which looks at the commission's role in shaping mergers and joint ventures in the media industry, provides another example of the commission's influence over business combinations.

The **Council of the European Union** represents the interests of member states. It is clearly the ultimate controlling authority within the EU since draft legislation from the commission can become EU law only if the council agrees. The council is composed of one representative from the government of each member state. The membership, however, varies depending on the topic being discussed. When agricultural issues are being discussed, the agriculture ministers from each state attend council meetings; when transportation is being discussed, transportation ministers attend, and so on. Before 1993, all council issues had to be decided by unanimous agreement between member states. This often led to marathon council sessions and a failure to make progress or reach agreement on commission proposals. In an attempt to clear the resulting logjams, the Single European Act formalized the use of majority voting rules on issues "which have as their object the establishment and functioning of a single market." Most other issues, however, such as tax regulations and immigration policy, still require unanimity among council members if they are to become law. The votes that a country gets in the council are related to the size of the country. For example, Britain, a large country, has 29 votes, whereas Denmark, a much smaller state, has 7 votes.

The **European Parliament,** which now has 732 members, is directly elected by the populations of the member states. The parliament, which meets in Strasbourg, France, is primarily a consultative rather than legislative body. It debates legislation the commission proposes and the council forwards to it. It can propose amendments to that legislation, which the commission and ultimately the council are not obliged to take up but often will. The power of the parliament recently has been increasing, although not as much as parliamentarians would like. The European Parliament now has the right to vote on the appointment of commissioners as well as to veto some laws (such as the EU budget and single-market legislation). One major debate now being waged in Europe is whether the council or the parliament should ultimately be the most powerful body in the EU. Some in Europe express concern over the democratic accountability of the EU bureaucracy. One side thinks the answer to this apparent democratic deficit lies in increasing the power of the parliament, while others think that true democratic

MANAGEMENT FOCUS

The European Commission and Media Industry Mergers

In late 1999, U.S. Internet giant AOL announced it would merge with the music and publishing conglomerate Time Warner. Both the U.S. companies had substantial operations in Europe. The European commissioner for competition, Mario Monti, announced the commission would investigate the impact of the merger on competition in Europe.

The investigation took on a new twist when Time Warner subsequently announced it would form a joint venture with British-based EMI. Time Warner and EMI are two of the top five music publishing companies in the world. The proposed joint venture would have been three times as large as its nearest global competitor. The European Commission now had two concerns. The first was that the joint venture between EMI and Time Warner would reduce the level of competition in the music publishing industry. The second was that a combined AOL–Time Warner would dominate the emerging market for downloading music over the Internet, particularly given the fact that AOL would be able to gain preferential access to the music libraries of both Warner and EMI. This would potentially put other online service providers at a disadvantage. The commission was also concerned that AOL Europe was a joint venture between AOL and Bertelsmann, a German media company that also had considerable music publishing interests. Accordingly, the commission announced it would undertake a separate investigation of the proposed deal between Time Warner and EMI.

These investigations continued into late 2000 and were resolved by a series of concessions extracted by the European Commission. First, under pressure from the commission, Time Warner and EMI agreed to drop their proposed joint venture, thereby maintaining the level of competition in the music publishing business. Second, AOL and Time Warner agreed to allow rival Internet service providers access to online music on the same terms as AOL would receive from Warner Music Group for the next five years. Third, AOL agreed to sever all ties with Bertelsmann, and the German company agreed to withdraw from AOL Europe. These developments alleviated the commission's concern that the AOL–Time Warner combination would dominate the emerging market for the digital download of music. With these concessions in hand, the commission approved the AOL–Time Warner merger in early October 2000.

By late 2000 the AOL–Time Warner merger had been completed. The shape of the media business, both in Europe and worldwide, now looked very different, and the European Commission had played a pivotal role in determining the outcome. Its demand for concessions altered the strategy of several companies, led to somewhat different combinations from those originally planned, and, the commission believed, preserved competition in the global media business.[11]

legitimacy lies with elected governments, acting through the Council of the European Union.[12]

The **Court of Justice,** which is comprised of one judge from each country, is the supreme appeals court for EU law. Like commissioners, the judges are required to act as independent officials, rather than as representatives of national interests. The commission or a member country can bring other members to the court for failing to meet treaty obligations. Similarly, member countries, companies, or institutions can bring the commission or council to the court for failure to act according to an EU treaty.

THE SINGLE EUROPEAN ACT

Two revolutions occurred in Europe in the late 1980s. The first was the collapse of communism in Eastern Europe. The second revolution was much quieter, but its impact on Europe and the world may have been just as profound as the first. It was the adoption of the **Single European Act** by the member nations of the European Community (EC) in 1987. This act committed member countries to work toward establishment of a single market by December 31, 1992.

The Single European Act was born of a frustration among members that the community was not living up to its promise. By the early 1980s, it was clear that the EC had fallen short of its objectives to remove barriers to the free flow of trade and investment between member countries and to harmonize the wide range of technical and legal standards for doing business. Against this background, many of the EC's prominent businesspeople mounted an energetic campaign in the early 1980s to end the EC's economic divisions. The EC responded by creating the Delors Commission. Under the chairmanship of Jacques Delors, the commission proposed that all impediments to the formation of a single market be eliminated by December 31, 1992. The result was the Single European Act, which was independently ratified by the parliaments of each member country and became EC law in 1987.

The Objectives of the Act

The purpose of the Single European Act was to have one market in place by December 31, 1992. The act proposed the following changes:[13]

- Remove all frontier controls between EC countries, thereby abolishing delays and reducing the resources required for complying with trade bureaucracy.

- Apply the principle of "mutual recognition" to product standards. A standard developed in one EC country should be accepted in another, provided it meets basic requirements in such matters as health and safety.

- Open public procurement to nonnational suppliers, reducing costs directly by allowing lower cost suppliers into national economies and indirectly by forcing national suppliers to compete.

- Lift barriers to competition in the retail banking and insurance businesses, which should drive down the costs of financial services, including borrowing, throughout the EC.

- Remove all restrictions on foreign exchange transactions between member countries by the end of 1992.

- Abolish restrictions on cabotage—the right of foreign truckers to pick up and deliver goods within another member state's borders—by the end of 1992. Estimates suggested this would reduce the cost of haulage within the EC by 10 to 15 percent.

All those changes were predicted to lower the costs of doing business in the EC, but the single-market program was also expected to have more complicated supply-side effects. For example, the expanded market was predicted to give EC firms greater opportunities to exploit economies of scale. In addition, it was thought that the increase in competitive intensity brought about by removing internal barriers to trade and investment would force EC firms to become more efficient. To signify the importance of the Single European Act, the European Community also decided to change its name to the European Union once the act took effect.

Impact

The Single European Act has had a significant impact on the EU economy.[14] The act provided the impetus for restructuring substantial sections of European industry. Many firms have shifted from national to pan-European production and distribution systems in an attempt to realize scale economies and better compete in a single market. The results have included faster economic growth than would otherwise have been the case.

However, 15 years after the formation of a single market, the reality still falls short of the ideal. For example, as the next Country Focus describes, as of 2006 a fully functioning single market for financial services in the EU still was not in place (although much of the groundwork had been completed). Thus, although the EU is undoubtedly moving toward a single marketplace, established legal, cultural, and language differences between nations mean that implementation has been uneven.

Creating a Single European Market in Financial Services

The European Union in 1999 embarked upon an ambitious action plan to create a single market in financial services by January 1, 2005. Launched a few months after the euro, the EU's single currency, the goal was to dismantle barriers to cross-border activity in financial services, creating a continentwide market for banking service, insurance services, and investment products. In this vision of a single Europe, a citizen of France might use a German firm for basic banking services, borrow a home mortgage from an Italian institution, buy auto insurance from a Dutch enterprise, and keep her savings in mutual funds managed by a British company. Similarly, an Italian firm might raise capital from investors across Europe, using a German firm as its lead underwriter to issue stock for sale through stock exchanges in London and Frankfurt.

One main benefit of a single market, according to its advocates, would be greater competition for financial services, which would give consumers more choices and lower prices, and require financial service firms in the EU to become more efficient, thereby increasing their global competitiveness. Another major benefit would be the creation of a single European capital market. The increased liquidity of a larger capital market would make it easier for firms to borrow funds, lowering their cost of capital (the price of money) and stimulating business investment in Europe, which would create more jobs. A European Commission study suggested that the creation of a single market in financial services would increase the EU's gross domestic product by 1.1 percent a year, creating an additional 130 billion euros (€) in wealth over a decade. Total business investment would increase by 6 percent annually in the long run, private consumption by 0.8 percent, and total employment by 0.5 percent a year.

Creating a single market, however, has been anything but easy. The financial markets of different EU member states have historically been segmented from each other, and each has its own regulatory framework. In the past, EU financial services firms rarely did business across national borders because of a host of different national regulations with regard to taxation, oversight, accounting information, cross-border takeovers, and the like, all of which had to be harmonized. To complicate matters, long-standing cultural and linguistic barriers complicated the move toward a single market. While in theory an Italian might benefit by being able to purchase homeowners' insurance from a British company, in practice he might be predisposed to purchase it from a local enterprise, even if the price were higher.

By early 2007 the EU had made significant progress. Some 41 measures designed to create a single market in financial services had become EU law and others were in the pipeline. The new rules embraced issues as diverse as the conduct of business by investment firms, stock exchanges, and banks; disclosure standards for listing companies on public exchanges; and the harmonization of accounting standards across nations. However, there had also been some significant setbacks. Most notably, legislation designed to make it easier for firms to make hostile cross-border acquisitions was defeated, primarily due to opposition from German members of the European Parliament, making it more difficult for financial service firms to build pan-European operations. In addition, national governments have still reserved the right to block even friendly cross-border mergers between financial service firms. For example, Italian banking law still requires the governor of the Bank of Italy to give permission to any foreign enterprise that wishes to purchase more than 5 percent of an Italian bank—and no foreigners have yet to acquire a majority position in an Italian bank, primarily, say critics, due to nationalistic concerns on the part of the Italians.

The critical issue now is enforcement of the rules that have been put in place. Some believe that it will be at least another decade before the benefits of the new regulations become apparent. In the meantime, the changes may impose significant costs on financial institutions as they attempt to deal with the new raft of regulations.[15]

THE ESTABLISHMENT OF THE EURO

In December 1991, EC members signed a treaty (the **Maastricht Treaty**) that committed them to adopting a common currency by January 1, 1999.[16] The euro is now used by 13 of the 27 member states of the European Union; these 13 states are members of what is often referred to as the euro zone. The 10 countries that joined the EU on May 1, 2004, and the two that joined in 2007 will adopt the euro when they fulfill certain economic criteria—a high degree of price stability, a sound fiscal situation, stable exchange rates, and converged long-term interest rates. The current members had to meet the same criteria.

Establishment of the euro has rightly been described as an amazing political feat with few historical precedents. Establishing the euro required participating national governments not only to give up their own currencies but also to give up control over monetary policy. Governments do not routinely sacrifice national sovereignty for the greater good, indicating the importance that the Europeans attach to the euro. By adopting the euro, the EU has created the second largest currency zone in the world after that of the U.S. dollar. Some believe that ultimately the euro could come to rival the dollar as the most important currency in the world.

Three long-term EU members, Great Britain, Denmark, and Sweden, are still sitting on the sidelines. The 13 countries that adopted the euro locked their exchange rates against each other January 1, 1999. Euro notes and coins were not actually issued until January 1, 2002. In the interim, national currencies circulated in each of the 12 countries. However, in each participating state, the national currency stood for a defined amount of euros. After January 1, 2002, euro notes and coins were issued and the national currencies were taken out of circulation. By mid-2002, all prices and routine economic transactions within the euro zone were in euros.

Benefits of the Euro

Europeans decided to establish a single currency in the EU for a number of reasons. First, they believe that businesses and individuals will realize significant savings from handling one currency, rather than many. These savings come from lower foreign exchange and hedging costs. For example, people going from Germany to France will no longer have to pay a commission to a bank to change German deutsche marks into French francs. Instead, they will be able to use euros. According to the European Commission, such savings should amount to 0.5 percent of the European Union's GDP, or about $45 billion a year.

Second, and perhaps more importantly, the adoption of a common currency will make it easier to compare prices across Europe. This should increase competition because it will be much easier for consumers to shop around. For example, if a German finds that cars sell for less in France than Germany, he may be tempted to purchase from a French car dealer rather than his local car dealer. Alternatively, traders may engage in arbitrage to exploit such price differentials, buying cars in France and reselling them in Germany. The only way that German car dealers will be able to hold on to business in the face of such competitive pressures will be to reduce the prices they charge for cars. As a consequence of such pressures, the introduction of a common currency should lead to lower prices. This should translate into substantial gains for European consumers.

Third, faced with lower prices, European producers will be forced to look for ways to reduce their production costs to maintain their profit margins. The introduction of a common currency, by increasing competition, should ultimately produce long-run gains in the economic efficiency of European companies.

Fourth, the introduction of a common currency should give a strong boost to the development of a highly liquid pan-European capital market. The development of such a capital market should lower the cost of capital and lead to an increase in both the level of investment and the efficiency with which investment funds are allocated. This could be especially helpful to smaller companies that have historically had difficulty borrowing money from domestic banks. For example, the capital market of Portugal is very small and illiquid, which makes it extremely difficult for bright Portuguese entrepreneurs with a good idea to borrow money at a reasonable price. However, in theory, such companies should soon be able to tap a much more liquid pan-European capital market. Currently Europe has no continentwide capital market—such as the NASDAQ market in the United States—that funnels investment capital to dynamic young growth companies. The euro's introduction could facilitate establishment of such a market, particularly when coupled with regulations designed to create a single market in financial services (see the Country Focus feature). The long-run benefits of such a development should not be underestimated.

Finally, the development of a pan-European, euro-denominated capital market will increase the range of investment options open to both individuals and institutions. For example, it will now be much easier for individuals and institutions based in, let's say, Holland to invest in Italian or French companies. This will enable European investors to better diversify their risk, which again lowers the cost of capital, and should also increase the efficiency with which capital resources are allocated.[17]

Costs of the Euro

The drawback, for some, of a single currency is that national authorities have lost control over monetary policy. Thus, it is crucial to ensure that the EU's monetary policy is well managed. The Maastricht Treaty called for establishment of the independent European Central Bank (ECB), similar in some respects to the U.S. Federal Reserve, with a clear mandate to manage monetary policy so as to ensure price stability. The ECB, based in Frankfurt, is meant to be independent from political pressure—although critics question this. Among other things, the ECB sets interest rates and determines monetary policy across the euro zone.

The implied loss of national sovereignty to the ECB underlies the decision by Great Britain, Denmark, and Sweden to stay out of the euro zone for now. Many in these countries are suspicious of the ECB's ability to remain free from political pressure and to keep inflation under tight control.

In theory, the design of the ECB should ensure that it remains free of political pressure. The ECB is modeled on the German Bundesbank, which historically has been the most independent and successful central bank in Europe. The Maastricht Treaty prohibits the ECB from taking orders from politicians. The executive board of the bank, which consists of a president, vice president, and four other members, carries out policy by issuing instructions to national central banks. The policy itself is determined by the governing council, which consists of the executive board plus the central bank governors from the 13 euro zone countries. The governing council votes on interest rate changes. Members of the executive board are appointed for eight-year nonrenewable terms, insulating them from political pressures to get reappointed. Nevertheless, the jury is still out on the issue of the ECB's independence, and it will take some time for the bank to establish its credentials.

According to critics, another drawback of the euro is that the EU is not what economists would call an optimal currency area. In an **optimal currency area,** similarities in the underlying structure of economic activity make it feasible to adopt a single currency and use a single exchange rate as an instrument of macroeconomic policy. Many of the European economies in the euro zone, however, are very dissimilar. For example, Finland and Portugal have different wage rates, tax regimes, and business cycles, and they may react very differently to external economic shocks. A change in the euro exchange rate that helps Finland may hurt Portugal. Obviously, such differences complicate macroeconomic policy. For example, when euro economies are not growing in unison, a common monetary policy may mean that interest rates are too high for depressed regions and too low for booming regions. It will be interesting to see how the EU copes with the strains caused by such divergent economic performance.

One way of dealing with such divergent effects within the euro zone might be for the EU to engage in fiscal transfers, taking money from prosperous regions and pumping it into depressed regions. Such a move, however, would open a political can of worms. Would the citizens of Germany forgo their "fair share" of EU funds to create jobs for underemployed Portuguese workers?

Several critics believe that the euro puts the economic cart before the political horse. In their view, a single currency should follow, not precede, political union. They argue that the euro will unleash enormous pressures for tax harmonization and fiscal transfers from the center, both policies that cannot be pursued without the appropriate political structure. The most apocalyptic vision that flows from these negative views is that far from stimulating economic growth, as its advocates claim, the euro will lead to lower economic growth and higher inflation within Europe. To quote one critic:

> Imposing a single exchange rate and an inflexible exchange rate on countries that are characterized by different economic shocks, inflexible wages, low labor mobility, and separate national fiscal systems without significant cross-border fiscal transfers will raise the overall level of cyclical unemployment among EMU members. The shift from national monetary policies dominated by the (German) Bundesbank within the European Monetary System to a European Central Bank governed by majority voting with a politically determined exchange rate policy will almost certainly raise the average future rate of inflation.[18]

The Early Experience

Since its establishment January 1, 1999, the euro has had a volatile trading history against the world's major currency, the U.S. dollar. After starting life in 1999 at €1 = $1.17, the euro steadily fell until it reached a low of €1 = $0.83 in October 2000, leading critics to claim the euro was a failure. A major reason for the fall in the euro's value was that international investors were investing money in booming U.S. stocks and bonds and taking money out of Europe to finance this investment. In other words, they were selling euros to buy dollars so that they could invest in dollar denominated assets. This increased the demand for dollars and decreased the demand for the euro, driving the value of the euro down against the dollar.

The fortunes of the euro began improving in late 2001 when the dollar weakened, and the currency stood at a robust five-year high of €1 = $1.33 in early March 2005. One reason for the rise in the value of the euro was that the flow of capital into the United States had stalled as the U.S. financial markets fell.[19] Many investors were now taking money out of the United States, selling dollar-denominated assets such as U.S. stocks and bonds, and purchasing euro-denominated assets. Falling demand for U.S. dollars and rising demand for euros translated into a fall in the value of the dollar against the euro. Furthermore, in a vote of confidence in both the euro and the ability of the ECB to manage monetary policy within the euro zone, many foreign central banks added more euros to their supply of foreign currencies during 2002–2004. In the first three years of its life, the euro never reached the 13 percent of global reserves made up by the deutsche mark and other former euro zone currencies. The euro didn't jump that hurdle until early 2002, but by 2003 it made up 15 percent of global reserves. Currency specialists expected the growing U.S. current account deficit, which reached 7 percent of GDP in 2005, to drive the dollar down further, and the euro still higher over the next two to four years.[20] So far this has not occurred (in February 2006 the exchange rate was €1 = $1.30). If the euro does appreciate against the dollar, this will be a mixed blessing for the EU. A strengthening euro, while a source of pride, will make it harder for euro zone exporters to sell their goods abroad.

ENLARGEMENT OF THE EUROPEAN UNION

A major issue facing the EU over the past few years has been that of enlargement. Enlargement of the EU into Eastern Europe has been a possibility since the collapse of communism at the end of the 1980s, and by the end of the 1990s, 13 countries had applied to become EU members. To qualify for EU membership the applicants had to privatize state assets, deregulate markets, restructure industries, and tame inflation. They also had to enshrine complex EU laws into their own systems, establish stable democratic governments, and respect human rights.[21] In December 2002, the EU formally agreed to accept the applications of 10 countries, and they joined on May 1, 2004. The new members include the Baltic countries, the Czech Republic, and the larger nations of Hungary and Poland. The only new members not in Eastern Europe are the Mediterranean island nations of Malta and Cyprus. Their inclusion in the EU expanded the union to 25 states, stretching from the Atlantic to the borders of Russia; added 23 percent to the landmass of the EU; brought 75 million new citizens into the EU, resulting in a population of 450 million people; and created a single continental economy with a GDP of close to €11 trillion. In 2007, Bulgaria and Romania joined, bringing total membership to 27 nations.

The new members will not be able to adopt the euro until at least 2007 (and 2010 in the case of the latest entrants), and free movement of labor between the new and existing members will not be allowed until then. Consistent with theories of free trade, the enlargement should create added benefits for all members. However, given the small size of the Eastern European economies (together they amount to only 5 percent of the GDP of current EU members) the initial impact will probably be small. The biggest notable change might be in the EU bureaucracy and decision-making processes, where budget negotiations among 27 nations are bound to prove more problematic than negotiations among 15 nations.

Left standing at the door is Turkey. Turkey, which has long lobbied to join the union, presents the EU with some difficult issues. The country has had a customs union with the EU since 1995, and about half of its international trade is already with the EU. However, full membership has been denied because of concerns over human rights issues (particularly Turkish policies toward its Kurdish minority). In addition, some on the Turk side suspect the EU is not eager to let a primarily Muslim nation of 66 million people, which has one foot in Asia, join the EU. The EU formally indicated in December 2002 that it would allow the Turkish application to proceed with no further delay in December 2004 if the country improved its human rights record to the satisfaction of the EU. In December the EU agreed to allow Turkey to start accession talks in October 2005, but those talks are not moving along rapidly, and the nation might not join until 2010, if at all.

Regional Economic Integration in the Americas

No other attempt at regional economic integration comes close to the EU in its boldness or its potential implications for the world economy, but regional economic integration is on the rise in the Americas. The most significant attempt is the North American Free Trade Agreement. In addition to NAFTA, several other trade blocs are in the offing in the Americas (see Map 8.2), the most significant of which appear to be the Andean Community and MERCOSUR. Also, negotiations are under way to establish a hemispherewide Free Trade Area of the Americas (FTAA), although currently they seem to be stalled.

THE NORTH AMERICAN FREE TRADE AGREEMENT

The governments of the United States and Canada in 1988 agreed to enter into a free trade agreement, which took effect January 1, 1989. The goal of the agreement was to eliminate all tariffs on bilateral trade between Canada and the United States by 1998. This was followed in 1991 by talks among the United States, Canada, and Mexico aimed at establishing a **North American Free Trade Agreement** for the three countries. The talks concluded in August 1992 with an agreement in principle, and the following year the agreement was ratified by the governments of all three countries. The agreement became law January 1, 1994.[22]

NAFTA'S Contents

The contents of NAFTA include the following:

- Abolition by 2004 of tariffs on 99 percent of the goods traded between Mexico, Canada, and the United States.
- Removal of most barriers on the cross-border flow of services, allowing financial institutions, for example, unrestricted access to the Mexican market by 2000.

MAP 8.2

Economic Integration in
the Americas

The Economist, April 21, 2001,
p. 20. Copyright © 2001 the
Economist Newspaper Ltd. All
rights reserved. Reprinted with
permission. Further reproduction
prohibited. www.economist.com.

Continental Commerce

- NAFTA
- MERCOSUR
- Andean community
- Central America
- Caribbean community

- Protection of intellectual property rights.
- Removal of most restrictions on foreign direct investment between the three
  member countries, although special treatment (protection) will be given to
  Mexican energy and railway industries, American airline and radio communications industries, and Canadian culture.
- Application of national environmental standards, provided such standards have
  a scientific basis. Lowering of standards to lure investment is described as being
  inappropriate.
- Establishment of two commissions with the power to impose fines and remove
  trade privileges when environmental standards or legislation involving health
  and safety, minimum wages, or child labor are ignored.

The Case for NAFTA

Proponents of NAFTA have argued that the free trade area should be viewed as an
opportunity to create an enlarged and more efficient productive base for the entire
region. Advocates acknowledge that one effect of NAFTA would be that some U.S.
and Canadian firms would move production to Mexico to take advantage of lower

labor costs. (In 2004, the average hourly labor cost in Mexico was still one-tenth of that in the United States and Canada.) Movement of production to Mexico, they argued, was most likely to occur in low-skilled, labor-intensive manufacturing industries where Mexico might have a comparative advantage (e.g., textiles; see the Opening Case). Advocates of NAFTA argued that many would benefit from such a trend. Mexico would benefit from much-needed inward investment and employment. The United States and Canada would benefit because the increased incomes of the Mexicans would allow them to import more U.S. and Canadian goods, thereby increasing demand and making up for the jobs lost in industries that moved production to Mexico. U.S. and Canadian consumers would benefit from the lower prices of products made in Mexico. In addition, the international competitiveness of U.S. and Canadian firms that move production to Mexico to take advantage of lower labor costs would be enhanced, enabling them to better compete with Asian and European rivals.

The Case against NAFTA

Those who opposed NAFTA claimed that ratification would be followed by a mass exodus of jobs from the United States and Canada into Mexico as employers sought to profit from Mexico's lower wages and less strict environmental and labor laws. According to one extreme opponent, Ross Perot, up to 5.9 million U.S. jobs would be lost to Mexico after NAFTA in what he famously characterized as a "giant sucking sound." Most economists, however, dismissed these numbers as being absurd and alarmist. They argued that Mexico would have to run a bilateral trade surplus with the United States of close to $300 billion for job loss on such a scale to occur—and $300 billion was the size of Mexico's GDP. In other words, such a scenario seemed implausible.

More sober estimates of the impact of NAFTA ranged from a net creation of 170,000 jobs in the United States (due to increased Mexican demand for U.S. goods and services) and an increase of $15 billion per year to the joint U.S. and Mexican GDP, to a net loss of 490,000 U.S. jobs. To put these numbers in perspective, employment in the U.S. economy was predicted to grow by 18 million from 1993 to 2003. As most economists repeatedly stressed, NAFTA would have a small impact on both Canada and the United States. It could hardly be any other way since the Mexican economy was only 5 percent of the size of the U.S. economy. Signing NAFTA required the largest leap of economic faith from Mexico rather than Canada or the United States. Falling trade barriers would expose Mexican firms to highly efficient U.S. and Canadian competitors that, when compared to the average Mexican firm, had far greater capital resources, access to highly educated and skilled workforces, and much greater technological sophistication. The short-run outcome was likely to be painful economic restructuring and unemployment in Mexico. But advocates of NAFTA claimed there would be long-run dynamic gains in the efficiency of Mexican firms as they adjusted to the rigors of a more competitive marketplace. To the extent that this occurred, they argued, Mexico's economic growth rate would accelerate, and Mexico might become a major market for Canadian and U.S. firms.[23]

Environmentalists also voiced concerns about NAFTA. They pointed to the sludge in the Rio Grande River and the smog in the air over Mexico City and warned that Mexico could degrade clean air and toxic waste standards across the continent. They pointed out that the lower Rio Grande was the most polluted river in the United States, and that with NAFTA, chemical waste and sewage would increase along its course from El Paso, Texas, to the Gulf of Mexico.

There was also opposition in Mexico to NAFTA from those who feared a loss of national sovereignty. Mexican critics argued that their country would be dominated by U.S. firms that would not really contribute to Mexico's economic growth, but instead would use Mexico as a low-cost assembly site, while keeping their high-paying, high-skilled jobs north of the border.

NAFTA: The Results So Far

Studies of NAFTA's impact to date suggest its initial effects were at best muted, and both advocates and detractors may have been guilty of exaggeration.[24] On average, studies indicate that NAFTA's overall impact has been small but positive.[25] From 1993 to 2005, trade between NAFTA's partners grew by 250 percent.[26] Canada and Mexico are now the number one and two trade partners of the United States, suggesting the economies of the three NAFTA nations have become more closely integrated. In 1990, U.S. trade with Canada and Mexico accounted for about a quarter of total U.S. trade. By 2005, the figure was close to one-third. Canada's trade with its NAFTA partners increased from about 70 percent to more than 80 percent of all Canadian foreign trade between 1993 and 2005, while Mexico's trade with NAFTA increased from 66 percent to 80 percent over the same period. All three countries also experienced strong productivity growth over this period. In Mexico, labor productivity has increased by 50 percent since 1993, and the passage of NAFTA may have contributed to this. However, estimates suggest that employment effects of NAFTA have been small. The most pessimistic estimates suggest the United States lost 110,000 jobs per year due to NAFTA between 1994 and 2000—though many economists dispute this figure—which is a tiny number compared to the more than 2 million jobs a year created in the United States during the same period. Perhaps the most significant impact of NAFTA has not been economic, but political. Many observers credit NAFTA with helping to create the background for increased political stability in Mexico. Mexico is now viewed as a stable democratic nation with a steadily growing economy, something that is beneficial to the United States, which shares a 2,000-mile border with the country.[27]

Enlargement

One issue confronting NAFTA is that of enlargement. A number of other Latin American countries have indicated their desire to eventually join NAFTA. The governments of both Canada and the United States are adopting a wait-and-see attitude with regard to most countries. Getting NAFTA approved was a bruising political experience, and neither government is eager to repeat the process soon. Nevertheless, the Canadian, Mexican, and U.S. governments began talks in 1995 regarding Chile's possible entry into NAFTA. As of 2007, however, these talks had yielded little progress, partly because of political opposition in the U.S. Congress to expanding NAFTA. In December 2002, however, the United States and Chile did sign a bilateral free trade pact.

THE ANDEAN COMMUNITY

Bolivia, Chile, Ecuador, Colombia, and Peru signed an agreement in 1969 to create the Andean Pact. The **Andean Pact** was largely based on the EU model, but was far less successful at achieving its stated goals. The integration steps begun in 1969 included an internal tariff reduction program, a common external tariff, a transportation policy, a common industrial policy, and special concessions for the smallest members, Bolivia and Ecuador.

By the mid-1980s, the Andean Pact had all but collapsed and had failed to achieve any of its stated objectives. There was no tariff-free trade between member countries, no common external tariff, and no harmonization of economic policies. Political and economic problems seem to have hindered cooperation between member countries. The countries of the Andean Pact have had to deal with low economic growth, hyperinflation, high unemployment, political unrest, and crushing debt burdens. In addition, the dominant political ideology in many of the Andean countries during this period tended toward the radical/socialist end of the political spectrum. Since such an ideology is hostile to the free market economic principles on which the Andean Pact was based, progress toward closer integration could not be expected.

The tide began to turn in the late 1980s when, after years of economic decline, the governments of Latin America began to adopt free market economic policies. In 1990, the heads of the five current members of the Andean Community—Bolivia, Ecuador, Peru, Colombia, and Venezuela—met in the Galápagos Islands. The resulting Galápagos Declaration effectively relaunched the Andean Pact, which was renamed the Andean Community in 1997. The declaration's objectives included the establishment of a free trade area by 1992, a customs union by 1994, and a common market by 1995. This last milestone has not been reached. A customs union was implemented in 1995, although until 2003 Peru opted out and Bolivia received preferential treatment. The Andean Community now operates as a customs union. In December 2003, it signed an agreement with MERCOSUR to restart stalled negotiations on the creation of a free trade area between the two trading blocs. Those negotiations are currently proceeding at a slow pace. In late 2006, Venezuela withdrew from the Andean Community as part of that country's attempts to join MERCOSUR.

MERCOSUR

MERCOSUR originated in 1988 as a free trade pact between Brazil and Argentina. The modest reductions in tariffs and quotas accompanying this pact reportedly helped bring about an 80 percent increase in trade between the two countries in the late 1980s.[28] This success encouraged the expansion of the pact in March 1990 to include Paraguay and Uruguay. In 2005, the pact was further expanded when Venezuela joined MERCOSUR, although it may take years for Venezuela to become fully integrated into the pact.

The initial aim of MERCOSUR was to establish a full free trade area by the end of 1994 and a common market sometime thereafter. In December 1995, MERCOSUR's members agreed to a five-year program under which they hoped to perfect their free trade area and move toward a full customs union—something that has yet to be achieved.[29] For its first eight years or so, MERCOSUR seemed to be making a positive contribution to the economic growth rates of its member states. Trade between MERCOSUR's four core members quadrupled between 1990 and 1998. The combined GDP of the four member states grew at an annual average rate of 3.5 percent between 1990 and 1996, a performance that is significantly better than the four attained during the 1980s.[30]

However, MERCOSUR had its critics, including Alexander Yeats, a senior economist at the World Bank, who wrote a stinging critique of MERCOSUR.[31] According to Yeats, the trade diversion effects of MERCOSUR outweigh its trade creation effects. Yeats pointed out that the fastest growing items in intra-MERCOSUR trade were cars, buses, agricultural equipment, and other capital-intensive goods that are produced relatively inefficiently in the four member countries. In other words, MERCOSUR countries, insulated from outside competition by tariffs that run as high as 70 percent of value on motor vehicles, are investing in factories that build products that are too expensive to sell to anyone but themselves. The result, according to Yeats, is that MERCOSUR countries might not be able to compete globally once the group's external trade barriers come down. In the meantime, capital is being drawn away from more efficient enterprises. In the near term, countries with more efficient manufacturing enterprises lose because MERCOSUR's external trade barriers keep them out of the market.

MERCOSUR hit a significant roadblock in 1998, when its member states slipped into recession and intrabloc trade slumped. Trade fell further in 1999 following a financial crisis in Brazil that led to the devaluation of the Brazilian real, which immediately made the goods of other MERCOSUR members 40 percent more expensive in Brazil, their largest export market. At this point, progress toward establishing a full customs union all but stopped. Things deteriorated further in 2001 when Argentina, beset by economic stresses, suggested that the customs union be temporarily suspended. Argentina wanted to suspend MERCOSUR's tariff so that it could abolish duties on imports of capital equipment, while raising those on consumer goods to 35 percent (MERCOSUR had established a 14 percent import tariff on both sets of goods). Brazil agreed to this request, effectively halting MERCOSUR's quest to become a fully functioning customs union.[32] Hope for a revival arose in 2003 when new Brazilian President Lula da Silva announced his support for a revitalized and expanded MERCOSUR modeled after the EU with a larger membership, a common currency, and a democratically elected MERCOSUR parliament.[33] As of 2007, however, little progress had been made in moving MERCOSUR down that road, and critics felt that the customs union was, if anything, becoming more imperfect over time.[34]

CENTRAL AMERICAN COMMON MARKET, CAFTA, AND CARICOM

Two other trade pacts in the Americas have not made much progress. In the early 1960s, Costa Rica, El Salvador, Guatemala, Honduras, and Nicaragua attempted to set up a **Central American Common Market.** It collapsed in 1969 when war broke out between Honduras and El Salvador after a riot at a soccer match between teams from the two countries. Since then the six member countries have made some progress toward reviving their agreement (the five founding members were joined by the Dominican Republic). The proposed common market was given a boost in 2003 when the United States signaled its intention to enter into bilateral free trade negotiations with the group. These talks culminated in a 2005 agreement to establish a free trade agreement between the six countries and the United States. Known as the **Central America Free Trade Agreement,** or **CAFTA,** the aim is to lower trade barriers between the United States and the six countries for most goods and services.

A customs union was to have been created in 1991 between the English-speaking Caribbean countries under the auspices of the Caribbean Community. Referred to as **CARICOM,** it was established in 1973. However, it repeatedly failed to progress toward economic integration. CARICOM's member states adopted a formal commitment to economic and monetary union in 1984, but since then little progress has been made. In October 1991, the CARICOM governments failed, for the third consecutive time, to meet a deadline for establishing a common external tariff. Despite this, CARICOM expanded to 15 members by 2005. In early 2006, six CARICOM members established the **Caribbean Single Market and Economy** (CSME). Modeled on the EU's single market, the goal of CSME is to lower trade barriers and harmonize macroeconomic and monetary policy between member states.[35]

FREE TRADE AREA OF THE AMERICAS

At a hemispherewide Summit of the Americas in December 1994, a Free Trade Area of the Americas (FTAA) was proposed. It took more than three years for the talks to start, but in April 1998, 34 heads of state traveled to Santiago, Chile, for the second Summit of the Americas where they formally inaugurated talks to establish an FTAA by January 1, 2005—something that didn't occur. The continuing talks have addressed a wide range of economic, political, and environmental issues related to cross-border trade and investment. Although both the United States and Brazil were early advocates of the FTAA, support from both countries seems to be mixed at this point. Because the United States and Brazil have the largest economies in North and South America, respectively, strong U.S. and Brazilian support is a precondition for establishment of the free trade area.

The major stumbling blocks so far have been twofold. First, the United States wants its southern neighbors to agree to tougher enforcement of intellectual property rights and lower manufacturing tariffs, which they do not seem to be eager to embrace.

Second, Brazil and Argentina want the United States to reduce its subsidies to U.S. agricultural producers and scrap tariffs on agricultural imports, which the U.S. government does not seem inclined to do. For progress to be made, most observers agree that the United States and Brazil have to first reach an agreement on these crucial issues.[36] If the FTAA is eventually established, it will have major implications for cross-border trade and investment flows within the hemisphere. The FTAA would open a free trade umbrella over 850 million people and an area with approximately $15 trillion in GDP in 2006.

Currently, however, FTAA is very much a work in progress, and the progress has been slow. The most recent attempt to get talks going again, in November 2005 at a summit of 34 heads of state from North and South America, failed when opponents, led by Venezuela's populist president, Hugo Chavez, blocked efforts by the Bush administration to set an agenda for further talks on FTAA. In voicing his opposition, Chavez condemned the U.S. free trade model as a "perversion" that would unduly benefit the United States, to the detriment of poor people in Latin America whom Chavez claims have not benefited from free trade details.[37] Such views make it unlikely that there will be much progress on establishing an FTAA in the near term.

Regional Economic Integration Elsewhere

Numerous attempts at regional economic integration have been tried throughout Asia and Africa. However, few exist in anything other than name. Perhaps the most significant is the Association of Southeast Asian Nations (ASEAN). In addition, the Asia-Pacific Economic Cooperation (APEC) forum has recently emerged as the seed of a potential free trade region.

ASSOCIATION OF SOUTHEAST ASIAN NATIONS

Formed in 1967, the **Association of Southeast Asian Nations (ASEAN)** includes Brunei, Cambodia, Indonesia, Laos, Malaysia, Myanmar, Philippines, Singapore, Thailand, and Vietnam. Laos, Myanmar, Vietnam, and Cambodia have all joined recently, creating a regional grouping of 500 million people with a combined GDP of some $740 billion (see Map 8.3). The basic objective of ASEAN is to foster freer trade between member countries and to achieve cooperation in their industrial policies. Progress so far has been limited, however.

Until recently only 5 percent of intra-ASEAN trade consisted of goods whose tariffs had been reduced through an ASEAN preferential trade arrangement. This may be changing. In 2003, an ASEAN Free Trade Area (AFTA) between the six original members of ASEAN came into full effect. The AFTA has cut tariffs on manufacturing and agricultural products to less than 5 percent. However, there are some significant exceptions to this tariff reduction. Malaysia, for example, refused to bring down tariffs on imported cars until 2005, and then agreed to lower the tariff to 20 percent, not the 5 percent called for under the AFTA. Malaysia wants to protect its domestically produced compact car, the Proton, made by an inefficient local car maker, from foreign competition. Similarly, the Philippines has refused to lower tariff rates on petrochemicals, and rice, the largest agricultural product in the region, will remain subject to higher tariff rates until at least 2020.[38]

Notwithstanding such issues, ASEAN and AFTA are at least progressing toward establishing a free trade zone. Vietnam joined the AFTA in 2006, Laos and Myanmar in 2008, and Cambodia in 2010. The goal is to reduce import tariffs among the six original members to zero by 2010, and to do so by 2015 for the newer members (although important exceptions to that goal, such as tariffs on rice, will no doubt persist). ASEAN is also pushing for free trade agreements with China, Japan, and South Korea.

MAP 8.3

ASEAN Countries

Source: www.aseansec.org/69.htm.

ASIA-PACIFIC ECONOMIC COOPERATION

Asia-Pacific Economic Cooperation (APEC) was founded in 1990 at the suggestion of Australia. APEC currently has 21 member states including such economic powerhouses as the United States, Japan, and China (see Map 8.4). Collectively, the member states account for about 57 percent of the world's GNP, 46 percent of world trade, and much of the growth in the world economy. The stated aim of APEC is to increase multilateral cooperation in view of the economic rise of the Pacific nations and the growing interdependence within the region. U.S. support for APEC was also based on the belief that it might prove a viable strategy for heading off any moves to create Asian groupings from which it would be excluded.

Interest in APEC was heightened considerably in November 1993 when the heads of APEC member states met for the first time at a two-day conference in Seattle. Debate before the meeting speculated on the likely future role of APEC. One view was that APEC

Rather than producing a product in each of the 27 EU countries or the 3 NAFTA countries, a firm may be able to serve the whole EU or North American market from a single location. This location must be chosen carefully, of course, with an eye on local factor costs and skills.

For example, in response to the changes created by the EU after 1992, the St. Paul–based 3M Company consolidated its European manufacturing and distribution facilities to take advantage of economies of scale. Thus, a plant in Great Britain now produces 3M's printing products and a German factory its reflective traffic control materials for all of the EU. In each case, 3M chose a location for centralized production after carefully considering the likely production costs in alternative locations within the EU. The ultimate goal of 3M is to dispense with all national distinctions, directing R&D, manufacturing, distribution, and marketing for each product group from an EU headquarters.[42] Similarly, Unilever, one of Europe's largest companies, began rationalizing its production in advance of 1992 to attain scale economies. Unilever concentrated its production of dishwashing powder for the EU in one plant, bath soap in another, and so on.[43]

Even after the removal of barriers to trade and investment, enduring differences in culture and competitive practices often limit the ability of companies to realize cost economies by centralizing production in key locations and producing a standardized product for a single multicountry market. Consider the case of Atag Holdings NV, a Dutch maker of kitchen appliances.[44] Atag thought it was well placed to benefit from the single market, but found it tough going. Atag's plant is just one mile from the German border and near the center of the EU's population. The company thought it could cater to both the "potato" and "spaghetti" belts—marketers' terms for consumers in Northern and Southern Europe—by producing two main product lines and selling these standardized "euro-products" to "euro-consumers." The main benefit of such an approach is the economy of scale derived from mass production of a standardized range of products. Atag quickly discovered that the "euro-consumer" was a myth. Consumer preferences vary much more across nations than Atag had thought. Consider ceramic cooktops; Atag planned to market just 2 varieties throughout the EU but has found it needs 11. Belgians, who cook in huge pots, require extra-large burners. Germans like oval pots and burners to fit. The French need small burners and very low temperatures for simmering sauces and broths. Germans like oven knobs on the top; the French want them on the front. Most Germans and French prefer black and white ranges; the British demand a range of colors including peach, pigeon blue, and mint green.

THREATS

Just as the emergence of single markets creates opportunities for business, it also presents a number of threats. For one thing, the business environment within each grouping will become more competitive. Lowering barriers to trade and investment between countries is likely to lead to increased price competition throughout the EU and NAFTA. For example, before 1992 a Volkswagen Golf cost 55 percent more in Great Britain than in Denmark and 29 percent more in Ireland than in Greece.[45] Over time, such price differentials will vanish in a single market. This is a direct threat to any firm doing business in EU or NAFTA countries. To survive in the tougher single-market environment, firms must take advantage of the opportunities offered by the creation of a single market to rationalize their production and reduce their costs. Otherwise, they will be at a severe disadvantage.

A further threat to firms outside these trading blocs arises from the likely long-term improvement in the competitive position of many firms within the areas. This is particularly relevant in the EU, where a high cost structure has historically limited many firms' ability to compete globally with North American and Asian firms. The creation of a single market and the resulting increased competition in the EU is beginning to produce serious attempts by many EU firms to reduce their cost structure by rationalizing production. This is transforming many EU companies into efficient global competitors. The message for non-EU businesses is that they need to prepare for the emergence of more capable European competitors by reducing their own cost structures.

Another threat to firms outside of trading areas is the threat of being shut out of the single market by the creation of a "trade fortress." The charge that regional economic integration might lead to a fortress mentality is most often leveled at the EU. Although the free trade philosophy underpinning the EU theoretically argues against the creation of any fortress in Europe, occasional signs indicate the EU may raise barriers to imports and investment in certain "politically sensitive" areas, such as autos. Non-EU firms might be well advised, therefore, to set up their own EU operations. This could also occur in the NAFTA countries, but it seems less likely.

Finally, the emerging role of the European Commission in competition policy suggests the EU is increasingly willing and able to intervene and impose conditions on companies proposing mergers and acquisitions. This is a threat insofar as it limits the ability of firms to pursue the corporate strategy of their choice. The commission may require significant concessions from businesses as a precondition for allowing proposed mergers and acquisitions to proceed. While this constrains the strategic options for firms, remember that in taking such action, the commission is trying to maintain the level of competition in Europe's single market, which should benefit consumers.

CHAPTER SUMMARY

This chapter pursued three main objectives: to examine the economic and political debate surrounding regional economic integration; to review the progress toward regional economic integration in Europe, the Americas, and elsewhere; and to distinguish the important implications of regional economic integration for the practice of international business. The chapter made the following points:

1. A number of levels of economic integration are possible in theory. In order of increasing integration, they include a free trade area, a customs union, a common market, an economic union, and full political union.

2. In a free trade area, barriers to trade between member countries are removed, but each country determines its own external trade policy. In a customs union, internal barriers to trade are removed and a common external trade policy is adopted. A common market is similar to a customs union, except that a common market also allows factors of production to move freely between countries. An economic union involves even closer integration, including the establishment of a common currency and the harmonization of tax rates. A political union is the logical culmination of attempts to achieve ever closer economic integration.

3. Regional economic integration is an attempt to achieve economic gains from the free flow of trade and investment between neighboring countries.

4. Integration is not easily achieved or sustained. Although integration brings benefits to the majority, it is never without costs for the minority. Concerns over national sovereignty often slow or stop integration attempts.

5. Regional integration will not increase economic welfare if the trade creation effects in the free trade area are outweighed by the trade diversion effects.

6. The Single European Act sought to create a true single market by abolishing administrative barriers to the free flow of trade and investment between EU countries.

7. Thirteen EU members now use a common currency, the euro. The economic gains from a common currency come from reduced exchange costs, reduced risk associated with currency fluctuations, and increased price competition within the EU.

8. Increasingly, the European Commission is taking an activist stance with regard to competition policy, intervening to restrict mergers and acquisitions that it believes will reduce competition in the EU.

9. Although no other attempt at regional economic integration comes close to the EU in terms of potential economic and political significance, various other attempts are being made in the world. The most notable include NAFTA in North America, the Andean Pact and MERCOSUR in Latin America, ASEAN in Southeast Asia, and perhaps APEC.

10. The creation of single markets in the EU and North America means that many markets that were formerly protected from foreign competition are now more open. This creates major investment and export opportunities for firms within and outside these regions.

11. The free movement of goods across borders, the harmonization of product standards, and the simplification of tax regimes make it possible for firms based in a free trade area to realize potentially enormous cost economies by centralizing production in those locations within the area where the mix of factor costs and skills is optimal.

12. Lowering barriers to trade and investment between countries within a trade group will probably be followed by increased price competition.

Critical Thinking and Discussion Questions

1. NAFTA has produced significant net benefits for the Canadian, Mexican, and U.S. economies. Discuss.

2. What are the economic and political arguments for regional economic integration? Given these arguments, why don't we see more substantial examples of integration in the world economy?

3. What effect is creation of a single market and a single currency within the EU likely to have on competition within the EU? Why?

4. Do you think it is correct for the European Commission to restrict mergers between American companies that do business in Europe? (For example, the European Commission vetoed the proposed merger between WorldCom and Sprint, both U.S. companies, and it carefully reviewed the merger between AOL and Time Warner, again both U.S. companies.)

5. How should a U.S. firm that currently exports only to ASEAN countries respond to the creation of a single market in this regional grouping?

6. How should a firm with self-sufficient production facilities in several ASEAN countries respond to the creation of a single market? What are the constraints on its ability to respond in a manner that minimizes production costs?

7. After a promising start, MERCOSUR, the major Latin American trade agreement, has faltered and made little progress since 2000. What problems are hurting MERCOSUR? What can be done to solve these problems?

8. Would establishment of a Free Trade Area of the Americas (FTAA) be good for the two most advanced economies in the hemisphere, the United States and Canada? How might the establishment of the FTAA impact the strategy of North American firms?

9. Reread the Management Focus case, "The European Commission and Media Industry Mergers," then answer the following questions:

    a. Given that both AOL and Time Warner were based in the United States, do you think the European Commission had a right to review and regulate their planned merger?

    b. Were the concessions extracted by the European Commission from AOL and Time Warner reasonable? Whose interests was the commission trying to protect?

    c. What precedent do the actions of the European Commission in this case set? What are the implications for managers of foreign enterprises with substantial operations in Europe?

Research Task   globalEDGE

Use the globalEDGE™ site to complete the following exercises:

1. Your company is considering an expansion by opening new customer representative and sales offices in the European Union (EU). Nevertheless, the size of the investment is significant and top management wishes to have a clearer picture of the current and probable future status of the EU. A colleague who spent some time living in the EU indicated that *Eurostat* might be a comprehensive source to assist in your project.

Prepare an executive summary describing the features you consider as crucial in making such a decision.

2. Trade agreements can impact the cultural interactions between countries. In fact, the establishment of the Free Trade Area of the Americas (FTAA) can be considered a threat as well as an opportunity for your company. Identify the countries participating in negotiations for the FTAA. What are the main themes of the negotiation process?

CLOSING CASE

NAFTA and the U.S. Textile Industry

When the North American Free Trade Agreement (NAFTA) went into effect in 1994, many expressed fears that large job losses in the U.S. textile industry would occur as companies moved production from the United States to Mexico. NAFTA opponents argued passionately, but unsuccessfully, that the treaty should not be adopted because of the negative impact it would have on U.S. employment.

A quick glance at the data available 10 years after the passage of NAFTA suggests the critics had a point. Between 1994 and 2004, production of apparel fell by 40 percent and production of textiles by 20 percent—and this during a period when overall U.S. demand for apparel grew by almost 60 percent. During the same time frame, employment in textile mills in the United Stated dropped from 478,000 to 239,000 and employment in apparel plummeted from 858,000 to 296,000, while exports of apparel from Mexico to the United States surged from $1.26 billion to $3.84 billion. Such data seem to indicate that the job losses have been due to apparel production migrating from the United States to Mexico.

There is anecdotal evidence to support this conclusion. For example, in 1995, Fruit of the Loom Inc., the largest manufacturer of underwear in the United States, said it would close six of its domestic plants and cut back operations at two others, laying off about 3,200 workers, or 12 percent of its U.S. workforce. The company announced the closures were part of its drive to move its operations to cheaper plants abroad, particularly in Mexico. Before the closures, less than 30 percent of its sewing was done outside the United States, but Fruit of the Loom planned to move the majority of that work to Mexico. For textile manufacturers, the advantages of locating in Mexico include cheap labor and inputs. Labor rates in Mexico average between $10 and $20 a day, compared to $10 to $12 an hour for U.S. textile workers.

However, job losses in the U.S. textile industry do not mean that the overall effects of NAFTA have been negative. Clothing prices in the United States have also fallen since 1994 as textile production shifted from high-cost U.S. producers to lower cost Mexican producers. This benefits consumers, who now have more money to spend on other items. The cost of a typical pair of designer jeans, for example, fell from $55 in 1994 to about $48 today. In 1994, blank T-shirts wholesaled for $24 a dozen. Now they sell for $14 a dozen.

In addition to lower prices, the shift in textile production to Mexico also benefited the U.S. economy in other ways. Despite the move of fabric and apparel production to Mexico, exports have surged for U.S. yarn makers, many of which are in the chemical industry. Before the passage of NAFTA, U.S. yarn producers, such as E. I. du Pont, supplied only small amounts of product to Mexico. However, as apparel production moved to Mexico, exports of fabric and yarn to that country have surged. U.S. producers supply 70 percent of the raw material going to Mexican sewing shops. Between 1994 and 2004, U.S. cotton and yarn exports to Mexico grew from $293 million to $1.21 billion. Moreover, although the U.S. textile industry has lost jobs, advocates of NAFTA argue that the U.S. economy has benefited in the form of lower clothing prices and an increase in exports from fabric and yarn producers. NAFTA supporters argue that it has created trade, and U.S. consumers and producers in certain sectors are capturing these gains from trade. As always, the establishment of a free trade area creates winners and losers—and the losers have been employees in the textile industry—but advocates of free trade argue that the gains outweigh the losses.[46]

Case Discussion Questions

1. Why did many textile jobs apparently migrate out of the United States in the years after the establishment of NAFTA?

2. Who gained from the process of readjustment in the textile industry after NAFTA? Who lost?

3. With hindsight, do you think it is better to protect vulnerable industries such as textiles, or to let them adjust to the new situations that follow entering into free trade agreements? What would the benefits of protection be? What would the costs be?

Notes

1. "Power Struggles: European Utilities," *The Economist*, December 2, 2006, p. 74; "Anger Management in Brussels," *Petroleum Economist*, April 2006, pp. 1–3; R. Bream, "Liberalization of EU Market Accelerates Deal-making," *Financial Times*, February 28, 2007, p. 4.

2. Information taken from World Trade Organization Web site and current as of February 2007, www.wto.org.

3. Ibid.

4. The Andean Pact has been through a number of changes since its inception. The latest version was established in 1991. See "Free-Trade Free for All," *The Economist*, January 4, 1991, p. 63.

5. D. Swann, *The Economics of the Common Market*, 6th ed. (London: Penguin Books, 1990).

6. See J. Bhagwati, "Regionalism and Multilateralism: An Overview," Columbia University Discussion Paper 603, Department of Economics, Columbia University, New York; A. de la Torre and M. Kelly, "Regional Trade Arrangements," Occasional Paper 93, Washington, DC: International Monetary Fund, March 1992; J. Bhagwati, "Fast Track to Nowhere," *The Economist*, October 18, 1997, pp. 21–24; Jagdish Bhagwati, *Free Trade Today* (Princeton and Oxford: Princeton University Press, 2002); and B. K. Gordon, "A High Risk Trade Policy," *Foreign Affairs* 82 no. 4 (July/August 2003), pp. 105–15.

7. N. Colchester and D. Buchan, *Europower: The Essential Guide to Europe's Economic Transformation in 1992* (London: The Economist Books, 1990), and Swann, *Economics of the Common Market*.

8. A. S. Posen, "Fleeting Equality, the Relative Size of the EU and US Economies in 2020," The Brookings Institution, September 2004.

9. Swann, *Economics of the Common Market*; Colchester and Buchan, *Europower: The Essential Guide to Europe's Economic Transformation in 1992*; "The European Union: A Survey," *The Economist*, October 22, 1994; "The European Community: A Survey," *The Economist*, July 3, 1993; and the European Union Web site at http://europa.eu.int.

10. E. J. Morgan, "A Decade of EC Merger Control," *International Journal of Economics and Business*, November 2001, pp. 451–73.

11. Sources: W. Drozdiak, "EU Allows Vivendi Media Deal," *Washington Post*, October 14, 2000, p. E2; D. Hargreaves, "Business as Usual in the New Economy," *Financial Times*, October 6, 2000, p. 1; and D. Hargreaves, "Brussels Clears AOL–Time Warner Deal," *Financial Times*, October 12, 2000, p. 12.

12. "The European Community: A Survey."

13. "One Europe, One Economy," *The Economist*, November 30, 1991, pp. 53–54, and "Market Failure: A Survey of Business in Europe," *The Economist*, June 8, 1991, pp. 6–10.

14. Alan Riley, "The Single Market Ten Years On," *European Policy Analyst*, December 2002, pp. 65–72.

15. Sources: C. Randzio-Plath, "Europe Prepares for a Single Financial Market," *Intereconomic*, May–June 2004, pp. 142–46; T. Buck, D. Hargreaves, and P. Norman, "Europe's Single Financial Market," *Financial Times*, January 18, 2005, p. 17; "The Gate-keeper," *The Economist*, February 19, 2005, p. 79; P. Hofheinz, "A Capital Idea: The European Union Has a Grand Plan to Make Its Financial Markets More Efficient," *The Wall Street Journal*, October 14, 2002, p. R4; and "Banking on McCreevy: Europe's Single Market," *The Economist*, November 26, 2005, p. 91.

16. See C. Wyploze, "EMU: Why and How It Might Happen," *Journal of Economic Perspectives* 11 (1997), pp. 3–22, and M. Feldstein, "The Political Economy of the European Economic and Monetary Union," *Journal of Economic Perspectives* 11 (1997), pp. 23–42.

17. "One Europe, One Economy," and Feldstein, "The Political Economy of the European Economic and Monetary Union."

18. Feldstein, "The Political Economy of the European Economic and Monetary Union."

19. "Time for Europhoria?" *The Economist*, January 4, 2003, p. 58.

20. "The Passing of the Buck?" *The Economist*, December 4, 2004, pp. 78–80.

21. Details regarding conditions of membership and the progression of enlargement negotiations can be found at http:europa.eu.int/comm/ enlargement/index.htm.

22. "What Is NAFTA?" *Financial Times*, November 17, 1993, p. 6, and S. Garland, "Sweet Victory," *BusinessWeek*, November 29, 1993, pp. 30–31.

23. "NAFTA: The Showdown," *The Economist*, November 13, 1993, pp. 23–36.

24. N. C. Lustog, "NAFTA: Setting the Record Straight," *The World Economy*, 1997, pp. 605–14; and G. C. Hufbauer and J. J. Scott, *NAFTA Revisited: Achievements and Challenges* (Washington DC: Institute for International Economics, 2005).

25. W. Thorbecke and C. Eigen-Zucchi, "Did NAFTA Cause a Giant Sucking Sound?" *Journal of Labor Research*, Fall 2002, pp. 647–58; G. Gagne, "North American Free Trade, Canada, and U.S. Trade Remedies: An Assessment after Ten Years," *The World Economy*, 2000, pp. 77–91; G. C. Hufbauer and J. J. Schott, *NAFTA Revisited: Achievements and Challenges* (Washington DC: Institute for International Economics, 2005).

26. All trade figures are from U.S. Department of Commerce Trade Stat Express Web site at http://tse.export.gov/.

27. J. Cavanagh et al., "Happy Ever NAFTA?" *Foreign Policy*, September–October 2002, pp. 58–65.

28. "The Business of the American Hemisphere," *The Economist*, August 24, 1991, pp. 37–38.

29. "NAFTA Is Not Alone," *The Economist*, June 18, 1994, pp. 47–48.

30. "Murky MERCOSUR," *The Economist*, July 26, 1997, pp. 66–67.

31. See M. Philips, "South American Trade Pact under Fire," *The Wall Street Journal*, October 23, 1996, p. A2; A. J. Yeats, *Does MERCOSUR's Trade Performance Justify Concerns about the Global Welfare-Reducing Effects of Free Trade Arrangements? Yes!* (Washington, DC: World Bank, 1996); and D. M. Leipziger et al., "MERCOSUR: Integration and Industrial Policy," *The World Economy*, 1997, pp. 585–604.

32. "Another Blow to MERCOSUR," *The Economist*, March 31, 2001, pp. 33–34.

33. "Lula Lays Out MERCOSUR Rescue Mission," *Latin America Newsletters*, February 4, 2003, p. 7.

34. "A Free Trade Tug of War," *The Economist*, December 11, 2004, p. 54.

35. *EIU Views*, "CARICOM Single Market Begins," February 3, 2006.

36. M. Esterl, "Free Trade Area of the Americas Stalls," *The Economist*, January 19, 2005, p. 1.

37. M. Moffett and J. D. McKinnon, "Failed Summit Casts Shadow on Global Trade Talks," *The Wall Street Journal*, November 7, 2005, p. A1.

38. "Every Man for Himself: Trade in Asia," *The Economist*, November 2, 2002, pp. 43–44.

39. "Aimless in Seattle," *The Economist*, November 13, 1993, pp. 35–36.

40. G. de Jonquieres, "APEC Grapples with Market Turmoil," *Financial Times*, November 21, 1997, p. 6, and G. Baker, "Clinton Team Wins Most of the APEC Tricks," *Financial Times*, November 27, 1997, p. 5.

41. M. Turner, "Trio Revives East African Union," *Financial Times*, January 16, 2001, p. 4.

42. P. Davis, "A European Campaign: Local Companies Rush for a Share of EC Market While Barriers Are Down," *Minneapolis–St. Paul City Business*, January 8, 1990, p. 1.

43. "The Business of Europe," *The Economist*, December 7, 1991, pp. 63–64.

44. T. Horwitz, "Europe's Borders Fade," *The Wall Street Journal*, May 18, 1993, pp. A1, A12; "A Singular Market," *The Economist*, October 22, 1994, pp. 10–16; and "Something Dodgy in Europe's Single Market," *The Economist*, May 21, 1994, pp. 69–70.

45. E. G. Friberg, "1992: Moves Europeans Are Making," *Harvard Business Review*, May–June 1989, pp. 85–89.

46. Sources: C. Burritt, "Seven Years into NAFTA, Textile Makers Seek a Payoff in Mexico," *Atlanta Journal-Constitution*, December 17, 2000, p. Q1; I. McAllister, "Trade Agreements: How They Affect U.S. Textile," *Textile World*, March 2000, pp. 50–54; J. Millman, "Mexico Weaves More Ties," *The Wall Street Journal*, August 21, 2000, p. A12; J. R. Giermanski, "A Fresh Look at NAFTA: What Really Happened?" *Logistics*, September 2002, pp. 43–46; G. C. Hufbauer and J. C. Schott, *NAFTA Revisited: Achievements and Challenges*, Institute for International Economics, 2005; O. Cadot et al., "Market Access and Welfare under Free Trade Agreements: Textiles under NAFTA," *The World Bank Economic Review* 19 (2005), pp. 379–405; American Textile Manufactures Institute at www.atmi.org/index.asp; and U.S. Department of Commerce Trade Stat Express Web site at http://tse.export.gov/.

part three
cases

Agricultural Subsidies and Development[1] 🎬

For decades the rich countries of the developed world have lavished subsidies on their farmers, typically guaranteeing them a minimum price for the products they produce. The aim has been to protect farmers in the developed world from the potentially devastating effects of low commodity prices. Although they are small in numbers, farmers tend to be politically active, and winning their support is important for many politicians. The politicians often claim that their motive is to preserve a historic rural lifestyle, and they see subsidies as a way of doing this.

This logic has resulted in financial support estimated to exceed $300 billion a year for farmers in rich nations. The European Union, for example, has set a minimum price for butter of 3,282 euros per ton. If the world price for butter falls below that amount, the EU will make up the difference to farmers in the form of a direct payment or subsidy. In total, EU dairy farmers receive roughly $15 billion a year in subsidies to produce milk and butter, or about $2 a day for every cow in the EU—a figure that is more than the daily income of half the world's population. According to the OECD, overall EU farmers receive on the order of $134 billion a year in subsidies.

The EU is not alone in this practice. In the United States, a wide range of crop and dairy farmers receive subsidies. Typical is the guarantee that U.S. cotton farmers will receive at least $0.70 for every pound of cotton they harvest. If world cotton prices fall below this level, the government makes up the difference, writing a check to the farmers. Some 25,000 United States cotton farmers received some $3.4 billion in annual subsidy checks. Total agricultural subsidies in the United States amount to some $43 billion a year according to OECD figures. Japan is also a large subsidizer, providing some $47.4 billion in subsidies to farmers every year. In relative terms Switzerland, which is not an EU member, spent the most. Subsidies made up a remarkable 68 percent of its farm economy. Iceland was at 67 percent and Norway at 64 percent. European Union subsidies equaled 32 percent of that trading bloc's farm economy, while the United States figure was 16 percent.

One consequence of such subsidies is to create surplus production. That surplus is sold on world markets, where the extra supply depresses prices, making it much harder for producers in the developing world to sell their output at a profit. For example, EU subsidies to sugar beet producers amount to more than $4,000 an acre. With a minimum price guarantee that exceeds their costs of production, EU farmers plant more sugar beets than the

EU market can absorb. The surplus, some 6 million tons per year, is dumped on the world market, where it depresses world prices. Estimates suggest that if the EU stopped dumping its surplus production on world markets, sugar prices would increase by 20 percent. That would make a big difference for developing nations such as South Africa, which exports roughly half of its 2.6 million tons of annual sugar production. With a 20 percent rise in world prices, the South African economy would reap about $40 million more from sugar exports.

American subsidies to cotton farmers have a similar effect. Brazilian officials contend that by creating surplus production in the United States that is then dumped on the world market, U.S. cotton subsidies have depressed world prices for cotton by more than 50 percent since the mid-1990s. Low cotton prices cost Brazil some $600 million in lost export earnings in 2001–2002. India, another big cotton producer, has estimated that U.S. cotton subsidies reduced its export revenue from cotton by some $1 billion in 2001. According to the charitable organization Oxfam, the U.S. government spends about three times as much on cotton subsidies as it does on foreign aid for all of Africa. In 2001, the African nation of Mali lost about $43 million in export revenues due to plunging cotton prices, significantly more than the $37 million in foreign aid it received from the United States that year.

The global rice market is also badly distorted by subsidies, with overproduction of rice in the United States helping to depress world prices. The United States paid its 9,000 rice farmers some $780 million in subsidies in 2006. An average ton of U.S. rice cost $240 to sow, tend, and harvest in 2006, but by the time it had left the United States port subsidies had cut the cost to $205 a ton. This has made it impossible for farmers in Ghana, once one of the largest rice producers in Africa, to survive. It costs farmers in Ghana $230 a ton to produce U.S. quality rice, but with global prices driven down below that by subsidies in developed nations, rice production in Ghana has collapsed. With incomes falling, local farmers do not have the capital to invest in new farming technology, and they risk falling ever further behind mechanized farming in more developed nations.

Overall, the United Nations has estimated that while developed nations give about $50 billion a year in foreign aid to the developing world, agricultural subsidies cost producers in the developing world some $50 billion in lost export revenues, effectively canceling out the effect of the aid. As one UN official has noted, "It's no good building up roads, clinics, and infrastructure in poor areas if you don't give them access to markets and engines for growth." Similarly, Oxfam has taken the unusual position for a charity of coming out strongly in support of the

---

[1]The following PBS video is recommended to accompany this case: http://pbs-newshour.virage.com/cgi-bin/visearch?squery=+ClipID:4++Video-Asset:pbsnh090903&query=Trade&user=pbs-newshour&tid=email

elimination of agricultural subsidies and price supports to developing world producers. By increasing world prices and shifting production from high-cost, protected producers in Europe and America to lower-cost producers in the developing world, Oxfam claims that consumers in rich nations would benefit from lower domestic prices and the elimination of taxes required to pay for the subsidies, while producers in the developing world would gain from fairer competition, expanded markets, and higher world prices. In the long run, the greater economic growth that would occur in agriculturally dependent developing nations would be to everyone's benefit.

Although subsidies have been against the spirit of World Trade Organization rules, under the terms of a 1995 "peace agreement" WTO members agreed not to take each other to court over agricultural subsidies. However, that agreement expired on December 31, 2004. Signs are growing that unless rich countries take steps to cut their subsidies soon, a number of efficient agricultural exporting countries will launch an all-out assault on farm subsidies. Indeed, Brazil did not even wait for the "peace agreement" to expire; in late 2003 it filed a complaint with the World Trade Organization, claiming that the U.S. had retained its position as the second largest cotton grower in the world, and the largest exporter, by paying $12.5 billion in subsidies to its cotton farmers between August 1999 and July 2003. Brazil argued that between 2001 and 2002 alone, the U.S. funneled nearly $4 billion in subsidies to its cotton farmers for a crop worth just $3 billion, which depressed world prices and cost Brazil $600 million in lost sales. In an interim ruling issued in mid-2004, the WTO agreed that U.S. subsidies had artificially lowered cotton prices and harmed Brazilian exporters. The United States appealed and it may be two more years before the issue is resolved.

Case Discussion Questions

1. If agricultural tariffs and subsidies to producers were removed overnight, what would the impact be on the *average* consumer in developed nations such as the Untied States and the EU countries? What would be the impact on the *average* farmer? Do you think the total benefits outweigh the total costs, or vice versa?

2. Which do you think would help the citizens of the world's poorest nations more, increasing foreign aid or removing all agricultural tariffs and subsidies?

3. Why do you think governments in developed nations continue to lavish extensive support on agricultural producers, even though those producers constitute a very small segment of the population?

4. The current Doha Round of trade talks organized by the World Trade Organization is trying to reduce barriers to free trade in agriculture. So far, however, the talks have made little concrete progress on this issue and as of mid-2007 they are stalled. Why do you think this is the case? What other solutions might there be to the problems created by barriers to trade in agriculture?

Sources

1. E. L. Andrews, "Rich Nations Are Criticized for Enforcing Trade Barriers," *The New York Times*, September 30, 2002, p. A1.

2. R. Thurrow and G. Winestock, "Bittersweet: How an Addiction to Sugar Subsidies Hurts Development," *The Wall Street Journal*, September 16, 2002, p. A1.

3. Oxfam, "Milking the CAP," Oxfam Briefing Paper No. 34, 2002, www.maketradefair.com/assets/english/DairyPaper.pdf.

4. N. King, "WTO Rules against U.S. Cotton Aid," *The Wall Street Journal*, April 27, 2004, p. A2.

5. J. V. Reppert-Bismarck, "How Trade Barriers Keep Africans Adrift," *The Wall Street Journal*, December 27, 2006, p. A5.

Boeing versus Airbus: Two Decades of Trade Disputes[1]

INTRODUCTION

For decades the commercial aircraft industry has been an American success story. Until 1980, U.S. manufacturers held a virtual monopoly in the field. Despite the rise of the European-based Airbus Industrie, this dominance persisted to the mid-1990s, when two U.S. firms, Boeing and McDonnell Douglas, accounted for over two-thirds of world market share. In late 1996, many analysts thought that U.S. dominance in this industry would be further strengthened when Boeing announced a decision to acquire McDonnell Douglas for $13.3 billion, creating an aerospace behemoth nearly twice the size of its nearest competitor.

[1]The following PBS video is recommended to accompany this case: http://pbs-newshour.virage.com/cgi-bin/visearch?squery=+ClipID:5++Video-Asset:pbsnh053105&query=Trade&user=pbs-newshour&tid=email

The industry is routinely the largest net contributor to the U.S. balance of trade, and Boeing is the largest U.S. exporter. The U.S. commercial aircraft industry has regularly run a substantial positive trade balance with the rest of the world of $12 to $15 billion per year. The impact of the industry on U.S. employment is also enormous. Boeing directly employs some 57,000 people in the Seattle area alone, and another 100,000 elsewhere in the nation. The company also indirectly supported a further 600,000 jobs nationwide in related industries (e.g., subcontractors) and through the impact of Boeing wages on the general level of economic activity.

Despite Boeing's formidable reach, since the mid-1980s U.S. dominance in the commercial aerospace industry has been threatened by the rise of Airbus Industrie. Founded in 1970, Airbus began as a consortium of four European aircraft manufacturers: one British (20.0 percent ownership stake), one French (37.9 percent ownership), one German (37.9 percent ownership), and one Spanish (4.2 percent ownership). Airbus was initially a marginal competitor and was regarded as unlikely to challenge U.S. dominance. Since 1981, however, Airbus has confounded its critics by progressively gaining market share. By the early 2000s Airbus was consistently gaining a larger share of new orders than Boeing, and in 2003 it surpassed Boeing for the first time in deliveries of aircraft, with 305 deliveries against Boeing's 281. Also, in the early 2000s Airbus made the transition from a consortium to a fully functioning private entity, and it is now a division of the European Aeronautic Defense and Space Company (EADS).

Over the years, many in the United States have responded to the success of Airbus by crying foul. U.S critics repeatedly claim that the governments of Great Britain, France, Germany, and Spain heavily subsidize Airbus. Airbus has responded by pointing out that both Boeing and McDonnell Douglas have benefited for years from hidden U.S. government subsidies. In 1992, the two sides appeared to reach an agreement that put to rest their long-standing trade dispute. The agreement allowed Airbus to receive some launch aid from EU governments and Boeing to benefit from government R&D contracts. However, the dispute broke out again in 1997, when the European Union decided to challenge the merger between Boeing and McDonnell Douglas on the grounds that it limited competition. Although that dispute was settled, trade tensions erupted yet again in 2004 when the United States charged that given Airbus's success in the marketplace, the launch aid that was allowed under the 1992 agreement was no longer appropriate. Airbus responded with accusations that Boeing was still benefiting from subsidies. When negotiations between the United States and EU over this dispute broke down in early 2005, Boeing referred the dispute to the World Trade Organization. This case reviews the history of these trade disputes.

INDUSTRY COMPETITIVE DYNAMICS

Competitive dynamics in the commercial aircraft industry are driven by a number of key factors. Perhaps foremost among these is that the costs of developing a new airliner are enormous. Boeing spent a reported $5 billion developing and tooling up to produce the 777 wide-bodied jetliner that it introduced in 1994. The development costs for Airbus's most recent aircraft, the 555-seat A380 "super-jumbo," which is scheduled to enter service in 2006, are estimated to be anywhere between $10 billion and $15 billion. (The A380 is a direct competitor to Boeing's profitable 747 model line.) Similarly, development costs for Boeing's newest offering, the "super efficient" 787 that will enter service in 2008, are estimated to be in the $7 to $8 billion range.

Given such enormous development costs, a company must capture a significant share of world demand to break even. In the case of the 777, for example, Boeing needed to sell more than 200 aircraft to break even, a figure that represented about 15 percent of predicted industry sales for this class of aircraft between 1994 and 2004. Given the volume of sales required to break even, it can take up to 10 to 14 years of production for an aircraft model to turn a profit and this on top of the 5 to 6 years of negative cash flows during development.

On the manufacturing side, a significant experience curve exists in aircraft production. Due to learning effects, on average, unit cost falls by about 20 percent with each doubling of accumulated output. A company that fails to move along the experience curve faces a significant unit-cost disadvantage. A company that achieves only half of the market share required to break even will suffer a 20 percent unit-cost disadvantage.

Another feature of the industry is that demand for aircraft is highly volatile. This makes long-run planning difficult and raises the risks involved in producing aircraft. The commercial airline business is prone to boom-and-bust cycles. During the early 1990s, and then again in the early 2000s, the major airlines suffered from falling demand and high fuel costs, and many major carriers entered bankruptcy. Orders for aircraft tend to follow these cycles, with order volumes in strong years frequently being two to three times as large as in weak years.

The combination of high development costs, break-even levels that constitute a significant percentage of world demand, substantial experience curve levels, and volatile demand makes for an industry that can support only a few major players. Analysts seem to agree that the large jet commercial aircraft market can profitably support only two, or possibly three, major producers. By the early 2000s there were only two major players in the industry, McDonnell Douglas having been absorbed by Boeing. This, combined with the strong production and order levels reached that year, should have boded well for productivity. However, Boeing's profits were poor during the late 1990s and early 2000s as it struggled to cope with a poorly managed ramp-up of its aircraft production rates, the effects of unexpectedly high manufacturing costs, and intense price competition from an increasingly aggressive Airbus.

TRADE FRICTIONS BEFORE 1992

In the 1980s and early 1990s, both Boeing and McDonnell Douglas argued that Airbus had an unfair competitive advantage due to the level of subsidy it received from the governments of Great Britain, France, Germany, and Spain. They argued that the subsidies allow Airbus to set unrealistically low prices, offer concessions and attractive financing terms to airlines, write off development costs, and use state-owned airlines to obtain orders. In making these claims, Boeing and McDonnell Douglas had the support of the U.S. government. According to a study by the Department of Commerce, Airbus received more than $13.5 billion in government subsidies between 1970 and 1990 ($25.9 billion if commercial interest rates are applied). Most of these subsidies were in the form of loans at below-market interest rates and tax breaks. The subsidies financed research and development and provided attractive financing terms for Airbus's customers. For most of its customers, Airbus is believed to have financed 80 percent of the cost of aircraft for a term of 8 to 10 years at an annual interest rate of approximately 7 percent. In contrast, the U.S. Export–Import Bank required 20 percent down payments from Boeing and McDonnell Douglas customers, financed only 40 percent of the cost of an aircraft directly, and guaranteed the financing of the remaining 40 percent by private banks at an average interest rate of 8.4 percent to 8.5 percent for a period of 10 years.

Airbus's response to these charges was to point out that its success was not due to subsidies but to a good product and a good strategy. Most observers agree that Airbus's aircraft incorporate state-of-the-art technology, particularly in materials applications, systems for flight control and safety, and aerodynamics. Airbus gained ground initially by targeting market segments not served by new aircraft or not served at all. Thus, Airbus took the initiative in targeting two segments of the market with wide-bodied twin-engine aircraft, then in developing a new generation of aircraft for the 150-seat market, and next, going after the market below the 747 for a 250- to 300-seat airliner with its A330 and A340 models (to which Boeing's 777 was a belated but apparently successful competitive response).

Airbus also argued that both Boeing and McDonnell Douglas benefited from U.S. government aid for a long time and that the aid it has received has merely leveled the playing field. In the United States, planes were built under government contract during World War I, and the construction of mail planes was subsidized between the world wars. Almost all production was subsidized during World War II, and subsidies continued at a high level after the war. The Boeing 707, for example, is a derivative of a military transport program that was subsidized by the U.S. government. Boeing's subsidized programs include the B-17, B-29, B-47, B-52, and K-135, just to name a few. Its nonairline programs have included the Minuteman missile, Apollo–Saturn, and space station programs.

A 1991 European Commission study attempted to estimate the amount of subsidies the U.S. industry received. The study contended that Boeing and McDonnell Douglas received $18 billion to $22 billion in indirect government aid between 1976 and 1990. The report claimed that commercial aircraft operations benefited through Defense Department contracts by as much as $6.34 billion during the 1976–1990 period. In addition, the report claims that NASA has pumped at least $8 billion into commercial aircraft production over the same period, and that tax exemptions gave an additional $1.7 billion to Boeing and $1.4 billion to McDonnell Douglas.

Boeing rejected the claims of the European Commission report. The company pointed out that the report's assumption that Boeing receives direct government grants in the form of an additional 5 percent for commercial work with every military or space contract it receives was false. Moreover, the company argued that during the 1980s only 3 percent of Boeing's R&D spending came from Department of Defense funding and only 4 percent from NASA funding. Boeing also argued that since the four companies in the Airbus consortium do twice as much military and space work as Boeing, they must receive much larger indirect subsidies.

THE 1992 AGREEMENT

In mid-1992, the United States and the four European governments involved agreed to a pact that many thought would end the long-standing dispute. The

1992 pact, which was negotiated by the European Union on behalf of the four member states, limited direct government subsidies to 33 percent of the total costs of developing a new aircraft and specified that such subsidies had to be repaid with interest within 17 years. The agreement also limited indirect subsidies, such as government-supported military research that has applications to commercial aircraft, to 3 percent of a country's annual total commercial aerospace revenues, or 4 percent of commercial aircraft revenues of any single company in that country. Although Airbus officials stated that the controversy had now been resolved, Boeing officials argued that they would still be competing for years against subsidized products.

In February 1993, it looked as if the trade dispute was about to reemerge. The newly elected President Clinton repeatedly blasted the European Union for allowing subsidies of Airbus to continue, blamed job losses in the U.S. aerospace industry on the subsidies, and called for the EU to renegotiate the 1992 deal.

To the surprise of the administration, however, this renewed attack on Airbus subsidies was greeted with conspicuous silence from the U.S. industry. Many analysts theorized that this was because a renewed dispute could prompt damaging retaliation from Europe. For one thing, Airbus equips its aircraft with engines made by two U.S. companies—Pratt & Whitney and General Electric—and with avionics made by U.S. companies. In addition, many state-owned airlines in Europe purchase aircraft from Boeing and McDonnell Douglas. Many in the U.S. industry apparently felt that this lucrative business would be put at risk if the government reopened the trade dispute so soon after the 1992 agreement.

A similar cool response from the U.S. industry greeted attempts by two U.S. senators, John C. Danforth of Missouri and Max Baucus of Montana, to reopen the trade dispute with Airbus. In early 1993, Danforth and Baucus cosponsored legislation requiring the U.S. government to launch a trade case against Airbus on charges of unfair subsidies. They also sponsored a bill to create an aerospace industry consortium called Aerotech that would finance aerospace research, with half of the funds coming from industry and half from the U.S. government. Vice President Al Gore called the establishment of Aerotech "an administration priority," but a Boeing spokesman said the company was "very guarded about Aerotech" because it could violate the 1992 accord. Both Danforth/Baucus bills died in committee hearings, and the Clinton administration quietly dropped all talk of reopening the trade dispute.

THE BOEING–MCDONNELL DOUGLAS MERGER

In December 1996, Boeing stunned the aerospace industry by announcing it would merge with longtime rival McDonnell Douglas in a deal estimated to be worth $13.3 billion. The merger, scheduled to be completed by the end of July 1997, was driven by Boeing's desire to strengthen its presence in the defense and space side of the aerospace business areas where McDonnell Douglas was traditionally strong. On the commercial side of the aerospace business, Douglas had been losing market share since the 1970s. By 1996, Douglas accounted for less than 10 percent of production in the large commercial jet aircraft market and only 3 percent of new orders placed that year. The dearth of new orders meant that the long-term outlook for Douglas's commercial business was increasingly murky. With or without the merger, many analysts felt that it was only a matter of time before McDonnell Douglas would be forced to exit from the commercial jet aircraft business. In their view, the merger with Boeing merely accelerated that process. Because the merger would reduce the number of players in the commercial aerospace industry from three to two, it was expected that the antitrust authorities would review the merger.

Boeing and McDonnell Douglas officials expected both the U.S. Federal Trade Commission (FTC) and the Competition Commission of the European Union to investigate the merger to assess its effects on competition. Boeing executives believed that the FTC would approve the proposed merger. Boeing's argument was that the Boeing–McDonnell Douglas combination was necessary to create a strong U.S. competitor in a competitive global marketplace. This is an argument that U.S. antitrust authorities have been sympathetic to in recent years. Moreover, Boeing executives pointed out that since the end of the Cold War, the U.S. government had been arguing for consolidation in the defense industry to eliminate excess capacity. They argued that the Boeing–McDonnell Douglas merger helped to achieve that goal and thus should receive government support.

As for the Europeans, here too Boeing executives believed there would be little opposition to the merger. In the words of Harry Stonecipher, CEO of McDonnell Douglas, "My good friend Jean Pierson, head of Airbus, has been saying at air shows lately, 'Douglas is not a factor in the commercial industry' so the deal is apparently a non-event." Initially, Airbus officials seemed to indicate they agreed with this assessment and would not oppose the merger. However, within days of the merger announcement, Karl Van Miert, the EU competition commissioner, signaled that the EU would launch a probe of the merger. Van Miert stated that the EU would oppose the merger if it thought doing so was necessary to preserve competition. In justifying the probe, he expressed the concern that if the number of players in the market for large commercial jet aircraft were reduced to two, they might engage in tacit collusion, raising prices above the level that would prevail in more competitive market situations.

Van Miert's statements raised hackles in the United States. Government officials and Boeing executives were heard wondering out loud what authority a European body would have over a merger between two U.S. companies that did almost all their manufacturing in the United States and had few assets in Europe. Van Miert stated that EU law required him to evaluate the merger and entitled the EU to block the merger if it was found to be anticompetitive. While Van Miert acknowledged that the EU could not actually stop the merger, under EU competition law the commission could declare the merger illegal, restrict its business in Europe, and fine it up to 10 percent of its estimated $48 billion annual sales. Boeing executives argued that if this were the outcome, it would provoke a trade war between the United States and the EU. Some U.S. politicians claimed that the EU's stance amounted to nothing less than a flagrant violation of U.S. national sovereignty.

Complicating the issue further was Boeing's success in negotiating long-term exclusive supply contracts with three major U.S.-based airlines: American Airlines, Delta, and Continental. The American Airlines deal was signed in late 1996 and the two others in the first half of 1997. All three deals named Boeing the exclusive supplier of each airline's aircraft needs for 20 years. Van Miert argued that these agreements were anticompetitive and reinforced his concerns about the market power of a Boeing–McDonnell Douglas combination. These agreements seemed to promote a change of heart among Airbus executives. After originally stating that they had no objections to the merger, Airbus executives became increasingly vocal in their opposition to it. In March 1997, Jean Pierson, the head of the consortium, warned that the proposed merger could give Boeing a "structural hold" on the industry, spanning the supply of aircraft, servicing, and spare parts. Similarly, commenting on the exclusive supplier deals, Airbus spokesman David Venz argued that the Boeing–McDonnell Douglas combination would "have a locked-in captive customer for 29 years. They have effectively removed choice from the airline who signs those contracts."

In mid-May 1997, the European Commission gave Boeing and McDonnell Douglas its official statement of objections to the planned merger and asked the two U.S. groups to respond before June 12, when hearings on the subject were scheduled to take place in Brussels. The commission stated that the merger raised three principal concerns. First, it would restrict competition in the market for large commercial jet aircraft. Second, McDonnell Douglas's extensive defense and space activities raised the possibility that U.S. government funding for defense and space programs would be used to fund the development of commercial jet aircraft. Third, the sole supplier agreements with American Airlines, Delta, and Continental restricted competition in the commercial aerospace market.

In commenting on these concerns, Boeing CEO Phil Condit noted that since McDonnell Douglas accounted for only 3 percent of commercial sales in 1996, one could hardly argue that the merger would have a restrictive effect on competition. Condit stated that there was no question of defense research funding being used for civil programs since the issue was already regulated by the 1992 bilateral trade agreement. As for the sole supplier agreements, Condit noted that the deals were struck at the initiative of the airlines.

On June 30, 1997, the Federal Trade Commission issued its own ruling on the merger. In a 4-to-1 decision, an FTC panel recommended that the merger be given unconditional approval. Before reaching its decision, the FTC interviewed 40 executives of airlines to find out whether they thought the merger would cause higher prices from Boeing. While some airlines expressed a preference that McDonnell Douglas remain in the bidding, they were virtually unanimous in acknowledging that they were unlikely to buy from that company because it appeared not to be making the investment required to remain viable. In short, the FTC concluded that McDonnell Douglas was no longer a viable competitor in the large commercial jet market, and therefore, the merger would not have a detrimental effect on competition. At the same time, the FTC did note that the sole supplier agreements that Boeing had reached were "potentially troubling." Although the three agreements reached by July 1997 accounted for only 11 percent of the global market, the FTC signaled that it would be concerned if more occurred.

On July 18, senior EU officials stated publicly that they planned to declare the merger illegal, insisting that it would harm competition in Europe. In announcing this intention, Van Miert stated that he was particularly concerned about the exclusive supplier contracts, which unfairly closed Airbus out of an important segment of the global market.

In a last-minute bid to stop the European Commission from declaring the merger illegal, Boeing blinked and stated it would not enforce provisions in the 20-year supplier contracts with American, Delta, and Continental. With this concession in hand, on July 23, a triumphant Van Miert announced that the European Commission would now approve the merger. Across Europe, newspapers sang Van Miert's praise, depicting him as the man who had defeated the American colossus. "You have to hand it to him," stated one EU official, "he took them on and won. He showed them that the European Commission is a force to be reckoned with."

BACK TO THE FUTURE: 2007

In the aftermath of the merger with McDonald Douglas, Boeing went through a period of financial turmoil, the result of congestion in its production system as the company tried to rapidly ramp up deliveries during the late 1990s. By 2002, however, Boeing was back on track and in 2003 it decided to go ahead and build its first new aircraft model in a decade, the 787. The 787, which will be offered in three versions and seat between 200 and 300 people, is to be built using composite materials and super-efficient jet engines that should reduce operating costs by 20 percent. The 787 is capable of flying up to 8,500 miles, making it ideal for long haul "point to point" flights. Boeing believes that as the volume of world air travel grows, more people will fly point to point, as opposed to through congested hubs. Estimates suggest that the new jet will cost some $7 to $8 billion to develop. A trio of three Japanese companies, Mitsubishi Heavy Industries, Kawasaki Heavy Industries, and Fuji Heavy Industries are building 35 percent of the 787 by value, including parts of the fuselage, wings, and landing gear. By July 2007 Boeing had amassed some 642 orders for the 787, a record order book for new planes, indicating strong demand. The first 787 planes are scheduled for delivery in 2008.

Meanwhile, Airbus was pushing ahead with the development of the 555-seat A380 super-jumbo jet. Designed to compete against the aging Boeing 747, the A380 is the largest commercial jet aircraft ever made. With development costs that may run above $15 billion, the A380 represents a huge bet by Airbus that passengers will continue to fly through hubs, rather than point to point as envisioned by Boeing. As of mid-2007, Airbus had some 150 orders for the A380. However, the rate of new orders had dried up as the A380 had become mired in production problems and the launch of the new aircraft had been delayed by nearly two years.

As Boeing started to garner more orders for the 787, however, Airbus began to wonder if it too should not hedge its bets and build a similar-sized super-efficient

long-range aircraft capable of flying point to point. What raised a red flag in the United States was signs from Airbus that it would apply for $1.7 billion in launch aid to help fund the development of the A350. As far as the United States was concerned, this amount of aid was too much. In late 2004 U.S. Trade Representative Robert Zoellick issued a statement formally renouncing the 1992 agreement and calling for an end to launch subsidies. According to Zoellick, "since its creation 35 years ago, some Europeans have justified subsidies to Airbus as necessary to support an infant industry. If that rationalization were ever valid, its time has long passed. Airbus now sells more large civil aircraft than Boeing." Zoellick went on to claim that Airbus has received some $3.7 billion in launch aid for the A380 plus another $2.8 billion in indirect subsidies, including $1.7 billion in taxpayer-funded infrastructure improvements, for a total of $6.5 billion.

Airbus shot back that Boeing too continued to enjoy lavish subsidies, and that the company had received some $12 billion from NASA for development technology, much of which has found its way into commercial jet aircraft. The Europeans also contended that Boeing would receive as much as $3.2 billion in tax breaks from Washington state, where the 787 is to be assembled, and more than $1 billion in loans from the Japanese government to three Japanese suppliers, who will build over one-third of the 787. Moreover, Airbus was quick to point out that a trade war would not benefit either side, and that Airbus purchased some $6 billion a year of supplies from companies in the United States.

In January 2005, both the United States and EU agreed to freeze direct subsidies to the two aircraft makers while talks continued. However, in May 2005 news reports suggested, and Airbus confirmed, that the jet maker had applied to four EU governments for launch aid for the A350 and that the British government would announce some $700 million in aid at the Paris Air Show in mid-2005. Simultaneously, the EU offered to cut launch aid for the A350 by 30 percent. Dissatisfied, the U.S. side decided that the talks were going nowhere, and on May 31 the United States formally filed a request with the World Trade Organization for the establishment of a dispute resolution panel to resolve the issues. The EU quickly responded, filing a countersuit with the WTO claiming that U.S. aid to Boeing exceeded the terms set out in the 1992 agreement. In early 2007 both sides presented their arguments to the World Trade Organization. The EU claimed Boeing was receiving lavish subsidies from federal, state, and local governments in the United States that will amount to $23.7 billion. For its part, Boeing argued that Airbus had received over $100 billion of aid from European governments over its lifetime if the loans it received at below-market interest rates are recalculated at commercial rates. A ruling from the WTO is not expected until mid-2008.

Case Discussion Questions

1. Do you believe Airbus could have become a viable competitor without subsidies?

2. Why do you think the four European governments agreed to subsidize the establishment of Airbus?

3. Is Airbus's position with regard to the long-running dispute over subsidies reasonable?

4. Do you think that the 1992 trade agreement was reasonable?

5. Why do you think that the U.S. industry reacted with caution to attempts by politicians to reopen the trade dispute in 1993?

6. In an era of global competition, what is the case for antitrust authorities to permit the formation of large domestic firms through mergers and acquisitions?

7. Was the threat by EU authorities to declare the Boeing–McDonnell Douglas merger illegal a violation of U.S. national sovereignty?

8. Do you think the EU Commission had a strong case in its attempts to wring concessions from Boeing regarding the merger with McDonnell Douglas? Was Boeing right to make significant concessions to the EU? What might have occurred if the concessions were not made?

9. Why did the U.S. government decide to reopen the long-running trade dispute between Boeing and Airbus in 2004? Do you think the U.S. position is reasonable? What about the EU's countercharges? Are they reasonable?

10. Now that the dispute has gone to the World Trade Organization, what do you think would be a fair and equitable outcome?

Sources

1. B. Barnard, "Battle over Boeing Shifts to Subsidies," *Journal of Commerce*, July 25, 1997, p. 1A.

2. D. Boond and R. Wall, "Irreconcilable Differences," *Aviation Week & Space Technology*, September 6, 2004, pp. 24–30.

3. R. Cohen, "France Pledges Subsidy to Aerospace Group," *The New York Times*, February 3, 1994, p. 5.

4. B. Coleman, "GATT to Rule against German Aid to Airbus," *The Wall Street Journal*, January 16, 1992, p. 5.

5. O. C. Core, "Airbus Arrives," *Seattle Times*, July 21, 1992, pp. C1–C3.

6. B. Davis and B. Ingersoll, "Cloudy Issue," *The Wall Street Journal*, March 8, 1993, p. A1.

7. G. De Jonquieres, "Storm over the Atlantic," *Financial Times*, May 22, 1997, p. 17.

8. M. L. Dertouzos, R. K. Lester, and R. M. Solow, *Made in America*, Cambridge, MA: MIT Press, 1989.

9. "Dissecting Airbus," *The Economist*, February 16, 1991, pp. 51–52.

10. EADS Press Release, "Boeing 787 Trade Issues," May 30, 2005.

11. D. Gow, "Airbus Warns on Sales," *The Guardian*, January 14, 1999, p. 22.

12. J. Grimaldi, "FTC Approves Boeing Merger," *Seattle Times*, July 1, 1997, p. A1.

13. "The Jumbo War," *The Economist*, June 15, 1991, pp. 65–66.

14. M. Kayal, "Boeing May Be Flying into Antitrust Territory," *Journal of Commerce*, March 25, 1997, p. 3A.

15. M. Kayal, "The Boeing–McDonnell Merger Looks Very Different through European Eyes," *Journal of Commerce*, July 21, 1997, p. 1A.

16. G. Klepper, "Entry into the Market for Large Transport Aircraft," *European Economic Review* 34 (1990), pp. 775–803.

17. P. Lane, "Study Complains of Alleged Subsidies," *Seattle Times*, December 4, 1991, p. G2.

18. J. Lunsford and S. Miller, "Hopes Dwindle for U.S.–EU Deal on Aircraft Aid," *The Wall Street Journal*, April 11, 2005, p. 3.

19. J. Mintz, "Boeing to Buy McDonnell Douglas," *Washington Post*, December 16, 1996, p. A1.

20. J. Reppert-Bismarck and W. Echikson, "EU Countersues over U.S. Aid to Boeing," *The Wall Street Journal*, June 1, 2005, p. A2.

21. M. Skapinker, "EU Sets Out Objections to Boeing Merger," *Financial Times*, May 23, 1997, p. 6.

22. M. Stroud, "Worries over a Technology Shift Follow McDonnell-Taiwan Accord," *Investor's Business Daily*, November 21, 1991, p. 36.

23. S. Toy et al., "Zoom! Airbus Comes on Strong," *Business Week*, April 22, 1991, pp. 48–50.

24. E. Tucker, "Van Miert's Finest Hour," *Financial Times*, July 24, 1997, p. 23.

25. United States Trade Representative Press Release, "United States Takes Next Steps in Airbus WTO Litigation," May 30, 2005.

26. Kevin Done, "WTO to Hear of Lavish Boeing Aid," *Financial Times*, March 22, 2007, p. 34.

The Politics of Trade in Steel[1]

In March 2002, President George W. Bush imposed sweeping tariffs ranging from 8 percent to 30 percent on a range of steel imports from foreign producers. The tariffs were scheduled to remain in place until March 2005. The move was an attempt to rescue an industry that has been shrinking for years, but still provides 160,000 jobs in the United States. When the tariffs were announced, 16 American steelmakers were operating under the protection of the bankruptcy court. Leo Gerard, president of the United Steel Workers of America, the industry's main labor union, said the tariffs would protect American jobs by offering the industry a chance for survival. Echoing the union's statement, the managers of steel companies said they needed trade protection to give them time to upgrade their mills so that they could better compete with foreign producers.

This wasn't the first time the U.S. steel industry sought, and got, government protection from foreign producers. In fact, the steel industry has been receiving periodic protection of one sort or another for the past 30 years. Despite this, many producers have continued to suffer as more efficient foreign producers, and perhaps just as importantly, efficient nonunionized U.S. minimills such as Nucor Steel, have taken market share from old-line unionized steel companies. Mini-mills, which utilize electric arc furnaces to smelt scrap steel, now hold 40 percent of the U.S. steel market, up from nothing in the 1960s, and unlike many older steelmakers, most of the mini-mills are profitable.

The main losers of the Bush tariffs appear to have been foreign producers and U.S. consumers. Producers in the European Union were particularly incensed by the tariffs, since more than one-third of their $4 billion worth of steel exports were to be hit by a 30 percent tariff, and they feared that the EU market would be flooded with steel that other foreign producers diverted from the United States. The EU immediately stated it would seek compensation from the United States, as World Trade Organization (WTO) rules allow. If granted, this would raise the costs to the United States of the Bush tariffs.

In the aftermath of the Bush tariffs, U.S. consumers saw the price of steel jump, which raised their costs and made U.S. products less competitive in the global marketplace. In the months following the imposition of tariffs, the price of steel products in the United States rose between 30 percent and 50 percent. Cold rolled steel, which is used by automobile manufacturers among others, was averaging $525 a ton in the United States versus $280 in Japan and $304 in Germany. According to the Institute for International Economics (IIE), this round of price increases was just the latest in a long line of costs that steel tariffs have imposed on U.S. consumers over the last three decades. In total, since the 1970s the IIE estimates that efforts to protect U.S. steel have cost U.S. consumers some $120 billion in the form of higher prices.

In November 2003, the WTO declared the steel tariffs illegal under WTO rules and told the European Union that it could impose some $2.3 billion in retaliatory tariffs on imports from the United States. Initially the Bush administration was defiant, but some economists were quick to point out that the tariffs were counterproductive. By November 2003, the IIE estimated that the costs to steel users of the tariffs, due to higher steel prices, amounted to $600 million in lost profits and 26,000 in lost jobs. According to the IIE, the benefit to U.S. steel producers was only $240 million, with some 5,000 jobs saved.

On December 4, 2003, the Bush administration announced it would lift the 20-month-old tariffs on steel imports. In doing so, President Bush stated the tariffs had served their purpose by giving the U.S. steel industry time to modernize. Democratic Congressman Ted Strickland of Ohio, a large steelmaking state, stated, "The president gave his word that we would have three years of relief from illegal imports. But in the face of pressure from the WTO and the European Union, he walked away from that pledge."

Within minutes of the U.S. announcement, the EU announced it was lifting its threat to impose retaliatory tariffs on U.S. imports. To soften the blow on American steel producers, however, the U.S. government stated it would require importers to obtain licenses from the U.S. Commerce Department. The implication was that the Commerce Department would manage the issuing of licenses to moderate any surge in foreign steel imports following the lifting of tariffs. EU officials noted that although not as bad as tariffs, the mandatory requirement to obtain import licenses was another illegal restriction on trade. As for U.S. steel producers, some indicated they would file antidumping actions against foreign steel producers if they found evidence that steel was being sold below market prices in the United States.

Case Discussion Questions

1. Do you believe the Bush administration was correct in imposing tariffs in March 2002 on a wide range of steel imports?

2. Who are the main beneficiaries of protective tariffs such as those imposed on steel imports? Who are the losers?

---

[1]The following PBS video is suggested as an accompaniment to the case: http://pbs-newshour.virage.com/cgi-bin/visearch?squery=+ClipID:4++VideoAsset:pbsnh111003&query=International+Business&user=pbs-newshour&tid=email.

3. Does the action of the World Trade Organization in this case represent a loss of U.S. national sovereignty? Why do you think the WTO sided with the European Union?

4. If all tariffs on international trade in steel were removed, and subsidies to steel exporters around the world were banned, who would benefit? Who would lose from such action?

Sources

1. N. King and R. Guy Matthews, "Errant Shot? So Far Steel Tariffs Do Little of What President Envisioned," *The Wall Street Journal*, September 13, 2002, p. A1.

2. "Rust Never Sleeps: Steel," *The Economist*, March 9, 2002, pp. 61–62.

3. "Steel, Rolled," *The Economist*, August 31, 2002, pp. 54–55.

4. "Steel's Tariff Addiction," *The Economist*, August 20, 2002, p. A18.

5. "Sparks Fly over Steel: Trade Wars," *The Economist*, November 15, 2003, p. 78.

6. N. King and C. Tejada, "Bush Abandons Steel Tariff Plan," *The Wall Street Journal*, December 5, 2003, p. A3.

7. "Bush Lifts Steel Tariffs," *Journal of Commerce*, December 4, 2003, p. 1.

Dixon Ticonderoga—Victim of Globalization?

Dixon Ticonderoga was one of the oldest public companies in the United States. The company's flagship product is the ubiquitous No. 2 yellow pencil, introduced in 1913, which almost everyone who has gone to school or taken standardized tests in the United States would recognize. With annual revenues of a little over $100 million, Dixon is the second largest pencil manufacturer in the country. For most of its history, Dixon has been a prosperous company, but the 1990s proved to be a very difficult decade. It's not that people are no longer buying pencils—in fact, demand for pencils in the United States has soared. Americans bought an estimated 4.2 billion pencils in 1999, a 53 percent jump from 1991. But an increasing proportion of these pencils have been from China.

The problem began in the early 1990s when Chinese manufacturers entered the market with low-priced pencils. The pencil industry fought back, arguing that the Chinese were dumping pencils on the U.S. market at below cost and lobbying Washington for protection. In 1994, when foreign pencil imports accounted for 16 percent of the market, the United States enacted heavy antidumping duties on Chinese pencils, effectively raising their price. Imports fell dramatically, but the Chinese kept making better, cheaper pencils, and after a couple of years imports returned to the levels attained before the imposition of duties. Nor did it stop there. In 1999, U.S. manufacturers shipped some 2.2 billion pencils domestically, down from 2.4 billion in 1991. During that time, imports jumped from 16 percent to over 50 percent of the market, with China leading the importers. The pencil industry continued to lobby for protection, and in mid-2000, the United States renewed duties on pencil imports from China, imposing import tariffs as high as 53 percent on some brands.

In the meantime, Dixon was not standing still. To try to meet the foreign competition on price, Dixon experimented with cheaper ways to make pencils. The company tried to make pencils out of recycled paper cases, but quickly backed away after the product jammed pencil sharpeners. Then the company looked at the wood used to make pencils—traditionally California incense cedar—and decided it was too expensive for all but the company's premium brand. Now the company uses lower priced Indonesian jelutong wood. As an additional cost reduction measure instituted in the late 1990s, Dixon started to buy the erasers for its pencils from a Korean supplier, rather than its traditional U.S. supplier.

Despite these steps, the company continued to lose share to imports, and by 1999 it was beginning to lose money, too. Realizing that it could bring in finished pencils cheaper than it could manufacture them in the United States, Dixon established a manufacturing operation in Mexico. The original idea behind the Mexican operation was to supplement its U.S. manufacturing, but in late 2000 the company realized it needed to be more aggressive and switched many of its processes from the United States to Mexico, cutting some 40 jobs at its U.S. facility. In another strategic move, in 2000 Dixon created a wholly owned subsidiary in China. This subsidiary manufactures wooden slats for pencil manufacturing. The slats are then sent to Mexico, where they are turned into pencils. The lead for the pencils (carbon) is still made in the United States by Dixon, while the erasers are shipped from Korea. The Chinese subsidiary is also responsible for the production and distribution of certain products that are sold internationally. As a result of these moves, by 2002 Dixon's performance was improving, but the company still needed to cut its cost structure. Accordingly, it decided to shut down its U.S. manufacturing operation at Sandusky, Ohio, in 2003 and move production to either Mexico or China. The company was rewarded in 2004 with its best financial performance in a decade and the company made money after five years of losses. In early 2005 Dixon was acquired by Fabbrica Italiana of Italy, a worldwide manufacturer of writing implements. Fabbrica has stated that it will let Dixon operate as an autonomous division within its organization.

Case Discussion Questions

1. Why do you think that the Chinese apparently have a cost advantage in the production of pencils?

2. Do you think that lobbying the U.S. government to impose antidumping duties on imports of pencils from China is a good way to protect American jobs? Who benefits most from such duties? Who loses? What alternative policy stance might the government take?

3. By establishing facilities in Mexico, Dixon became a multinational company. Why has Dixon become a multinational? What are the economic benefits to Dixon of becoming an international business?

4. Now that Dixon has a production operation in China, why does it not simply import finished pencils from China to the United States, instead of making those pencils in Mexico?

Sources

1. Dixon Ticonderoga, *Form 10K*, 2002.
2. A. Carns, "Point Taken: Hard Hit by Imports, American Pencil Icon Tries to Get a Grip," *The Wall Street Journal*, November 24, 2000, p. B10.
3. "Dixon Decides to Dissect Options," *Mergers and Acquisitions*, November 2000, p. 34.
4. C. Boyd, "Dixon Ticonderoga Promotes Asta to CEO," *Orlando Sentinel*, April 2, 2005, p. C1.

🌐 Drug Development in the European Union

Europe has long produced some of the world's most successful drug companies. However, many of them in recent years have complained that European Union regulations are hurting their ability to develop new proprietary (brand name) drugs and compete in the global marketplace against companies from the United States. Developing innovative new drugs is a very expensive, risky, and time-consuming business. In both the United States and EU it can take as long as 12 years to move a drug from the laboratory, through human clinical trials, and into the marketplace. The failure rate is high, with as many as 85 percent of all drugs entering clinical trials not reaching the market, either because they did not show the predicted efficacy in clinical trials or because they had safety problems due to adverse side effects. Furthermore, it can cost over $800 million to bring a new drug to market. Given the costs and risks, drug companies rely upon a small number of successful new drugs to pay for all of their failures, fund future research, and provide a return to their shareholders. Many European drug companies now believe that EU regulations have made it very difficult for them to earn a sufficient return on their new drugs to do this.

One problem is that extensive price controls on brand name drugs exist throughout the EU. National health care providers set prices, often by negotiation between the providers and drug companies. Because the providers have the objective of reducing health care costs, and thus the tax burden on their citizens, they tend to push for lower drug prices than those found in the United States, where the prices of new brand name drugs are not regulated. This results in a lower return to drug companies in Europe. Also, the extent of price controls varies from country to country. This allows for arbitrage, whereby distributors buy drugs in countries where prices are low and resell them where prices are high. For example, price controls on new drugs are much more stringent in France, Italy, and Spain than they are in Germany or the United Kingdom. This has led to the reexporting of drugs sold for a low price in Spain to Germany where they are sold for less than the price prevailing in that market. Such arbitrage reduces the profits that a pharmaceutical firm can earn from developing a successful new drug. According to industry data, some €6 billion in sales every year can be attributed to arbitrage, and the distributors who practice arbitrage, not the drug companies, capture the profits.

Another issue concerns regulations governing the introduction of a generic version of a brand name drug, which historically have varied from country to country within the EU. Drug companies receive 6 to 10 years of protection from generic competition, depending on the country. The drug companies have long argued that six years is not sufficient to recoup the investment required to bring a new drug to market. (The price of a brand name drug can fall by as much as 80 percent once a generic competitor is introduced.)

The enlargement of the EU from 15 to 25 countries added urgency to this complaint, since eight of the new EU members are in Eastern Europe where protection from generic competition historically lasted for only three years. This led to fears that cheap generic versions of brand name drugs from new EU members would flood the rest of the EU, further reducing returns to drug companies and making it extremely difficult to fund research to develop new drugs. Furthermore, the expansion of the EU into Eastern Europe is also increasing the opportunities for arbitrage, since prices for drugs are as much as 70 percent lower in some Eastern European countries than in Germany or Britain.

Recognizing how serious these issues had become, in 2001 the European Union started to look at the rules governing generic competition. In late December 2003, the European Parliament approved a new set of regulations that established a uniform period of eight years after market introduction before allowing generic drug producers access to data that would help them develop generic versions of brand name pharmaceuticals, and an additional two years before allowing the sale of generic drugs. This was widely seen as a victory for European pharmaceutical companies, which would now be protected from generic competition for 10 years after market introduction of a drug.

Drug companies are attempting to deal with the arbitrage problem through the EU legal system. In 1996, the European Commission found the German drug maker Bayer guilty of restricting the arbitrage of Adalat, a brand name heart medicine. Bayer had struck agreements with French and Spanish wholesalers to dissuade them from taking advantage of price differentials to resell Adalat in Britain, where prices were higher. The European Commission stated that Bayer's actions restricted competition. Bayer appealed the decision, and in early 2004 the European Court of Justice ruled that the European Commission failed to prove that Bayer and the wholesalers had anticompetitive agreements. In a statement released after the judgment, Bayer interpreted the ruling as meaning that pharmaceutical manufacturers are under no obligation to supply the entire EU market from the member state with the lowest state-regulated price. If this ruling is not overturned by legislation in the European Parliament, it might reduce the scope of arbitrage in the European Union, boosting the returns to developing new brand name drugs, and increasing the competitiveness of Europe's drug companies in the global economy.

However, the legal issues surrounding arbitrage have not yet been resolved. On the heels of the Bayer decision,

another large EU drug company, GlaxoSmithKline (GSK), took steps to restrict the supply of three drugs to Greece. Historically GSK had supplied substantially more drugs than were required to Greek wholesalers, only to see the excess reexported to the UK and other countries where prices were higher. Greek wholesalers challenged GSK's decision to limit supplies to Greece and brought the case before the Greek competition authorities. These authorities in turn referred the case to the European Court of Justice. However, in June 2005 Europe's highest court ruled that it did not have the authority to rule in the case and referred the issue back to the Greek competition authorities—an action that was widely seen as plunging the industry once more into legal uncertainty.

Case Discussion Questions

1. To what extent have regulations and institutional arrangements in the EU put European drug companies at a disadvantage vis-à-vis their competitors in the United States?

2. What would the EU have to do to put EU companies on an equal footing with drug companies based in the United States?

3. Who is likely to oppose any attempt to outlaw arbitrage with regard to drugs within the EU? What do you think their arguments will be? How successful might they be?

4. What does this case tell you about the efficacy of the attempt to establish a single market for goods and services within the European Union?

5. If arbitrage in the EU is allowed to continue, what do you think the response of EU drug companies will be?

Sources

1. P. Meller, "Europe Effort to Control Pricing Is Set Back," *The New York Times*, January 7, 2004, p. W1.

2. A. Cowell, "European Union Expansion Has Drug Makers Worried," *The New York Times*, November 20, 2003, pp. W1, W7.

3. "EU Extends Data Exclusivity," *Chemical Market Reporter*, December 22, 2003, p. 5.

4. H. Timmons, "Drug Firms Lose Appeal on Sales Trading Dispute," *International Herald Tribune*, June 1, 2005, p. 11.

Logitech

Best known as one of the world's largest producers of computer mice, Logitech is in many ways the epitome of the modern global corporation. Founded in 1981 in

Apples, Switzerland, by two Italians and a Swiss, the company now generates annual sales of over $1.5 billion, most from products such as mice, keyboards, and low-cost video-cams that cost under $100. Logitech made its name as a technological innovator in the highly competitive business of personal computer peripherals. It was the first company to introduce a mouse that used infrared tracking, rather than a tracking ball, and the first to introduce wireless mice and keyboards. Logitech is differentiated from competitors by its continuing innovation, high brand recognition, and strong retail presence. Less obvious to consumers, but equally important, has been the way the company has configured its global value chain to lower production costs while maintaining the value of those assets that lead to differentiation.

Nowadays Logitech still undertakes basic R&D work (primarily software programming) in Switzerland, where it has 200 employees. Indeed, the company is still legally Swiss, but the corporate headquarters are in Fremont, California, close to many of America's high-technology enterprises, where it has 450 employees. Some R&D work (again, primarily software programming) is also carried out in Fremont. Most significantly though, Fremont is the headquarters for the company's global marketing, finance, and logistics operations. The ergonomic design of Logitech's products—their look and feel—is done in Ireland by an outside design firm. Most of Logitech's products are manufactured in Asia.

Logitech's expansion into Asian manufacturing began in the late 1980s when it opened a factory in Taiwan. At the time, most of its mice were produced in the United States. Logitech was trying to win two of the most prestigious OEM customers—Apple Computer and IBM. Both bought their mice from Alps, a large Japanese firm that supplied Microsoft. To attract discerning customers like Apple, Logitech not only needed the capacity to produce at high volume and low cost, it also had to offer a better designed product. The solution: manufacture in Taiwan. Cost was a factor in the decision, but it was not as significant as might be expected, since direct labor accounted for only 7 percent of the cost of Logitech's mouse. Taiwan offered a well-developed supply base for parts, qualified people, and a rapidly expanding local computer industry. As an inducement to fledgling innovators, Taiwan provided space in its science-based Industrial Park in Hsinchu for the modest fee of $200,000. Assessing the opportunity as a deal that was too good to pass up, Logitech signed the lease. Shortly afterward, Logitech won the OEM contract with Apple. The Taiwanese factory was soon out-producing Logitech's U.S. facility. After the Apple contract, the Taiwan plant also started serving Logitech's other OEM business, and the plant's total capacity increased to 10 million mice per year.

By the late 1990s, Logitech needed more production capacity. This time it turned to China. A wide variety of the company's retail products are now made there. For example, one of Logitech's biggest sellers, a wireless infrared mouse called Wanda, is assembled in Suzhou, China, in a factory that Logitech owns. The factory employs 4,000 people, mostly young women such as Wang Yan, an 18-year-old employee from the impoverished rural province of Anhui. She is paid $75 a month to sit all day at a conveyor belt plugging three tiny bits of metal into circuit boards, which she does about 2,000 times each day. The mouse Wang Yan helps assemble sells to American consumers for about $40. Of this, Logitech takes about $8, which is used to fund R&D, marketing, and corporate overhead. What remains after that is the profit attributable to Logitech's shareholders. Distributors and retailers around the world take a further $15. Another $14 goes to the suppliers who make Wanda's parts. For example, a Motorola plant in Malaysia makes the mouse's chips and another American company, Agilent Technologies, supplies the optical sensors from a plant in the Philippines. That leaves just $3 for the Chinese factory, which is used to cover wages, power, transport and other overhead costs.

Logitech is not alone in exploiting China to manufacture products. According to China's Ministry of Commerce, foreign companies account for three-quarters of China's high-tech exports. China's top 10 exporters include American companies with Chinese operations, such as Motorola and Seagate technologies, a maker of disk drives for computers. Intel now produces some 50 million chips a year in China, the majority of which end up in computers and other goods that are exported to other parts of Asia or back to the United States. Yet Intel's plant in Shanghai doesn't really make chips; it tests and assembles chips from silicon wafers made in Intel plants abroad, mostly in the United States. China adds less than 5 percent of the value. Intel's U.S. operations generate the bulk of the value and profits.

Case Discussion Questions

1. In a world without trade, what would happen to the costs that American consumers would have to pay for Logitech's products?

2. Explain how trade lowers the costs of making computer peripherals such as mice and keyboards.

3. Use the theory of comparative advantage to explain the way in which Logitech has configured its global operations. Why does the company manufacture in China and Taiwan, undertake basic R&D in California and Switzerland, design products in Ireland, and coordinate marketing and operations from California?

4. Who creates more value for Logitech, the 650 people it employs in Fremont and Switzerland, or the 4,000 employees at its Chinese factory? What are

the implications of this observation for the argument that free trade is beneficial?

5. Why do you think the company decided to shift its corporate headquarters from Switzerland to Fremont?

6. To what extent can Porter's diamond help explain the choice of Taiwan as a major manufacturing site for Logitech?

7. Why do you think China is now a favored location for so much high technology manufacturing activity? How will China's increasing involvement in global trade help that country? How will it help the world's developed economies? What potential problems are associated with moving work to China?

Sources

1. V. K. Jolly and K. A. Bechler, "Logitech: The Mouse That Roared," *Planning Review* 20 (6) (1992), pp. 20–34.

2. K. Guerrino, "Lord of the Mice," *Chief Executive* 190 (July 2003), pp. 42–44.

3. A. Higgins, "As China Surges, It Also Proves a Buttress to American Strength," *The Wall Street Journal*, January 30, 2004, pp. A1, A8.

4. J. Fox, "Where Is Your Job Going," *Fortune*, November 24, 2003, pp. 84–88.

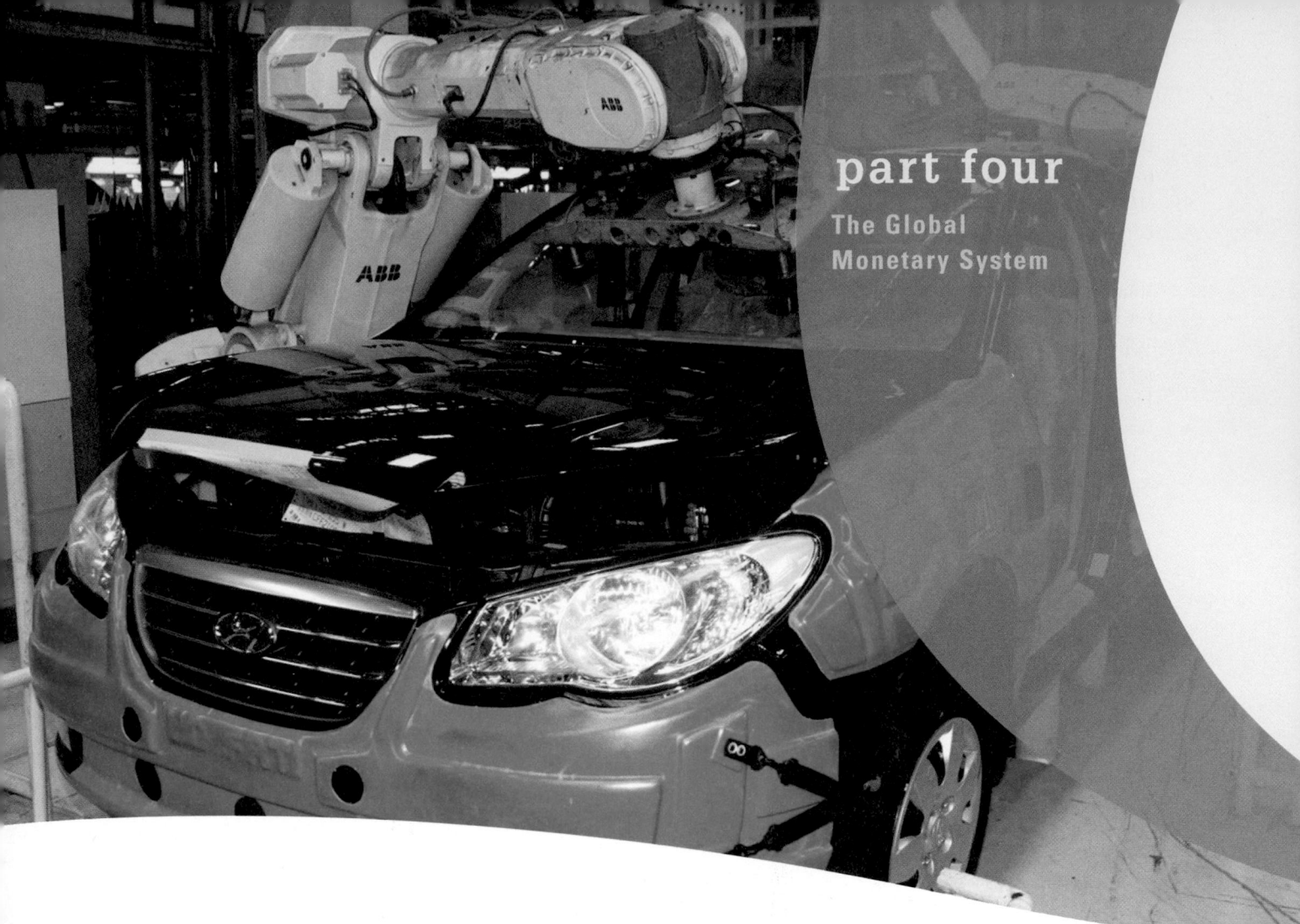

Hyuandai and Kia Face a Strong Won

For several years Hyundai and its affiliate Kia, Korea's fast growing car makers, have benefited from export-led growth. Hyundai sells 60 percent and Kia 80 percent of its production in foreign markets, particularly the United States, where they have been gaining share recently. The two companies currently have about 4.3 percent of the U.S. market, and they plan to double their market share to 8.6 percent by 2010. Their success in foreign markets has been attributed to good product quality, reasonable design, and aggressive pricing. In the United States and EU, they price their cars below the prices of both domestic firms and the major Japanese companies such as Toyota and Honda. This low-price strategy has enabled the two affiliated companies to grow foreign sales, but their profit margins per car are low—as low as 3 percent on cars sold in the United States. This makes them very vulnerable to changes in the value of the Korean currency, the won, against the U.S. dollar.

In 2006, the won rose in value by about 7 percent against the U.S. dollar. A stronger won means that Hyundai and Kia vehicles sold in the United States for dollars are

The Foreign Exchange Market

LEARNING OBJECTIVES

After you have read this chapter you should:

LO¹ Be conversant with the functions of the foreign exchange market.

LO² Understand what is meant by spot exchange rates.

LO³ Appreciate the role that forward exchange rates play in insuring against foreign exchange risk.

LO⁴ Understand the different theories explaining how currency exchange rates are determined and their relative merits.

LO⁵ Be familiar with the merits of different approaches toward exchange rate forecasting.

LO⁶ Understand the differences between translation, transaction, and economic exposure, and what managers can do to manage each type of exposure.

recorded at a lower value when translated back into won, which has hurt the financial performance of both companies. In 2006, despite rising unit sales, profits at Hyundai fell 35 percent, and those at Kia fell some 94 percent. Kia had to sell 15 cars on average in the United States in 2006 to make the same amount of revenue and profit that it got from 14 cars in 2005. If the won continues to gain in value against the dollar going forward, as many analysts predict, Hyundai and Kia may be forced to abandon their low-price strategy, and start to raise prices in the United States.

The possibility that the won will continue to strengthen against the dollar and other major currencies is also a spur to increasing output outside of Korea. Hyundai opened its first U.S. automobile plant in Montgomery, Alabama, in 2005, and recently announced plans to build an engine plant close by. Kia too, is expanding its presence in the United States as a hedge against adverse currency movements. In 2006 the company broke ground on a U.S. manufacturing plant in Georgia that is expected to open in 2009.[1]

Introduction

Like most enterprises in the global economy, Hyundai and its affiliate Kia are impacted by changes in the value of currencies on the foreign exchange market. As detailed in the case at the beginning of the chapter, a rising won has made it more difficult for the two companies to make profits on U.S. sales and forced them to consider changing their long-held low-price strategy. What happens in the foreign exchange market, therefore, can have a fundamental impact on the sales, profits, and strategy of an enterprise. Accordingly, it is very important for managers to understand the working of the foreign exchange market and the potential impact of changes in currency exchange rates for their enterprise. With these needs in mind, the current chapter has three main objectives. The first is to explain how the foreign exchange market works. The second is to examine the forces that determine exchange rates and to discuss the degree to which it is possible to predict future exchange rate movements. The third objective is to map the implications for international business of exchange rate movements. This chapter is the first of two that deal with the international monetary system and its relationship to international business. In the next chapter, we will explore the institutional structure of the international monetary system. The institutional structure is the context within which the foreign exchange market functions. As we shall see, changes in the institutional structure of the international monetary system can exert a profound influence on the development of foreign exchange markets.

The **foreign exchange market** is a market for converting the currency of one country into that of another country. An **exchange rate** is simply the rate at which one currency is converted into another. For example, Kia uses the foreign exchange market to convert the dollars it earns from selling cars in the United States into Korean won. Without the foreign exchange market, international trade and international investment on the scale that we see today would be impossible; companies would have to resort to barter. The foreign exchange market is the lubricant that enables companies based in countries that use different currencies to trade with each other.

We know from earlier chapters that international trade and investment have their risks. As the opening case illustrates, some of these risks exist because future exchange rates cannot be perfectly predicted. The rate at which one currency is converted into another can change over time. For example, in late 2005 one U.S. dollar bought 1,050 Korean won, but by late 2006 one dollar only bought 920 won. The dollar had fallen in value against the won, making Korean goods, such as Kia and Hyundai cars, more expensive in the United States, and U.S. goods cheaper in Korea. The change in exchange rates hurt the profitability of Korean exporters such as Kia and Hyundai. One function of the foreign exchange market is to provide some insurance against the risks that arise from such volatile changes in exchange rates, commonly referred to as foreign exchange risk. Although the foreign exchange market offers some insurance against foreign exchange risk, it cannot provide complete insurance. It is not unusual for international businesses to suffer losses because of unpredicted changes in exchange rates. Currency fluctuations can make seemingly profitable trade and investment deals unprofitable, and vice versa.

We begin this chapter by looking at the functions and the form of the foreign exchange market. This includes distinguishing among spot exchanges, forward exchanges, and currency swaps. Then we will consider the factors that determine exchange rates. We will also look at how foreign trade is conducted when a country's currency cannot be exchanged for other currencies; that is, when its currency is not convertible. The chapter closes with a discussion of these things in terms of their implications for business.

The Functions of the Foreign Exchange Market

The foreign exchange market serves two main functions. The first is to convert the currency of one country into the currency of another. The second is to provide some insurance against **foreign exchange risk,** by which we mean the adverse consequences of unpredictable changes in exchange rates.[2]

The foreign exchange market enables companies based in countries that use different currencies to trade with each other.

CURRENCY CONVERSION

Each country has a currency in which the prices of goods and services are quoted. In the United States, it is the dollar ($); in Great Britain, the pound (£); in France, Germany, and other members of the euro zone it is the euro (€); in Japan, the yen (¥); and so on. In general, within the borders of a particular country, one must use the national currency. A U.S. tourist cannot walk into a store in Edinburgh, Scotland, and use U.S. dollars to buy a bottle of Scotch whisky. Dollars are not recognized as legal tender in Scotland; the tourist must use British pounds. Fortunately, the tourist can go to a bank and exchange her dollars for pounds. Then she can buy the whisky.

When a tourist changes one currency into another, she is participating in the foreign exchange market. The exchange rate is the rate at which the market converts one currency into another. For example, an exchange rate of €1 = $1.30 specifies that one euro buys 1.30 U.S. dollars. The exchange rate allows us to compare the relative prices of goods and services in different countries. Our U.S. tourist wishing to buy a bottle of Scotch whisky in Edinburgh may find that she must pay £30 for the bottle, knowing that the same bottle costs $45 in the United States. Is this a good deal? Imagine the current pound/dollar exchange rate is £1.00 = $1.80 (that is, one British pound buys $1.80). Our intrepid tourist takes out her calculator and converts £30 into dollars. (The calculation is 30 × 1.8). She finds that the bottle of Scotch costs the equivalent of $54. She is surprised that a bottle of Scotch whisky could cost less in the United States than in Scotland (alcohol is taxed heavily in Great Britain).

Tourists are minor participants in the foreign exchange market; companies engaged in international trade and investment are major ones. International businesses have four main uses of foreign exchange markets. First, the payments a company receives for its exports, the income it receives from foreign investments, or the income it receives from licensing agreements with foreign firms may be in foreign currencies. To use those funds in its home country, the company must convert them to its home country's currency. Consider the Scotch distillery that exports its whisky to the United States. The distillery is paid in dollars, but since those dollars cannot be spent in Great Britain, they must be converted into British pounds. Similarly, when Kia sells cars in the United States for dollars, it must convert those dollars into won to use them in Korea.

Second, international businesses use foreign exchange markets when they must pay a foreign company for its products or services in its country's currency. For example, Dell buys many of the components for its computers from Malaysian firms. The Malaysian companies must be paid in Malaysia's currency, the ringgit, so Dell must convert money from dollars into ringgit to pay them.

Third, international businesses use foreign exchange markets when they have spare cash that they wish to invest for short terms in money markets. For example, consider a U.S. company that has $10 million it wants to invest for three months. The best interest rate it can earn on these funds in the United States may be 4 percent. Investing in a South Korean money market account, however, may earn 12 percent. Thus, the company may change its $10 million into Korean won and invest it in South Korea. Note, however, that the rate of return it earns on this investment depends not only on the Korean interest rate but also on the changes in the value of the Korean won against the dollar in the intervening period.

Finally, currency speculation is another use of foreign exchange markets. **Currency speculation** typically involves the short-term movement of funds from one currency to another in the hopes of profiting from shifts in exchange rates. Consider again a U.S. company with $10 million to invest for three months. Suppose the company suspects that the U.S. dollar is overvalued against the Japanese yen. That is, the company expects the value of the dollar to depreciate (fall) against that of the yen. Imagine the current dollar/yen exchange rate is $1 = ¥120. The company exchanges its $10 million into yen, receiving ¥1.2 billion ($10 million × 120 = ¥1.2 billion). Over the next three months, the value of the dollar depreciates against the yen until $1 = ¥100. Now the company exchanges its ¥1.2 billion back into dollars and finds that it has $12 million. The company has made a $2 million profit on currency speculation in three months on an initial investment of $10 million! In general, however, companies should beware, for speculation by definition is a very risky business. The company cannot know for sure what will happen to exchange rates. While a speculator may profit handsomely if his speculation about future currency movements turns out to be correct, he can also lose money if it turns out to be wrong.

INSURING AGAINST FOREIGN EXCHANGE RISK

A second function of the foreign exchange market is to provide insurance against **foreign exchange risk,** which is the possibility that unpredicted changes in future exchange rates will have adverse consequences for the firm. When a firm insures itself against foreign exchange risk, we say that is it engaging in *hedging*. To explain how the market performs this function, we must first distinguish among spot exchange rates, forward exchange rates, and currency swaps.

Spot Exchange Rates

When two parties agree to exchange currency and execute the deal immediately, the transaction is referred to as a spot exchange. Exchange rates governing such "on the spot" trades are referred to as spot exchange rates. The **spot exchange rate** is the rate at which a foreign exchange dealer converts one currency into another currency on a particular day. Thus, when our U.S. tourist in Edinburgh goes to a bank to convert her dollars into pounds, the exchange rate is the spot rate for that day.

Spot exchange rates are reported on a real-time basis on many financial Web sites. Table 9.1 shows the exchange rates for a selection of currencies traded in the New York foreign exchange market as of 4:00 p.m. on February 5, 2007. An exchange rate can be quoted in two ways: as the amount of foreign currency one U.S. dollar will buy, or as the value of a dollar for one unit of foreign currency. Thus, one U.S. dollar bought €0.7735 on February 5, 2007, and one euro bought 1.2928 U.S. dollars.

Spot rates change continually, often on a minute-by-minute basis (although the magnitude of changes over such short periods is usually small). The value of a currency is

Major Currency Cross-Rates February 5, 2007

Currency Last Trade		U.S. $ N/A	Yen 1:22 p.m. ET	Euro 1:20 p.m. ET	Can $ 1:22 p.m. ET	U.K. £ 1:20 p.m. ET	AU $ 1:20 p.m. ET	Swiss Franc 1:22 p.m. ET
1 U.S. $	=	1	120.2750	0.7735	1.1820	0.5105	1.2872	1.2486
1 Yen	=	0.008314	1	0.006431	0.009828	0.004245	0.010702	0.010382
1 Euro	=	1.2928	155.4975	1	1.5282	0.6600	1.6641	1.6143
1 Can $	=	0.8460	101.7512	0.6544	1	0.4319	1.0889	1.0563
1 U.K. £	=	1.9588	235.5945	1.5151	2.3154	1	2.5213	2.4459
1 AU $	=	0.7769	93.4416	0.6009	0.9183	0.3966	1	0.9701
1 Swiss Franc	=	0.8009	96.3240	0.6195	0.9467	0.4089	1.0308	1

TABLE 9.1

Value of the U.S. Dollar against Other Currencies, February 5, 2007

Source: Yahoo Finance.

determined by the interaction between the demand and supply of that currency relative to the demand and supply of other currencies. For example, if lots of people want U.S. dollars and dollars are in short supply, and few people want British pounds and pounds are in plentiful supply, the spot exchange rate for converting dollars into pounds will change. The dollar is likely to appreciate against the pound (or the pound will depreciate against the dollar). Imagine the spot exchange rate is £1 = $1.50 when the market opens. As the day progresses, dealers demand more dollars and fewer pounds. By the end of the day, the spot exchange rate might be £1 = $1.48. Each pound now buys fewer dollars than at the start of the day. The dollar has appreciated, and the pound has depreciated.

Forward Exchange Rates

Changes in spot exchange rates can be problematic for an international business. For example, a U.S. company that imports laptop computers from Japan knows that in 30 days it must pay yen to a Japanese supplier when a shipment arrives. The company will pay the Japanese supplier ¥200,000 for each laptop computer, and the current dollar/yen spot exchange rate is $1 = ¥120. At this rate, each computer costs the importer $1,667 (i.e., 1,667 = 200,000/120). The importer knows she can sell the computers the day they arrive for $2,000 each, which yields a gross profit of $333 on each computer ($2,000 − $1,667). However, the importer will not have the funds to pay the Japanese supplier until the computers have been sold. If over the next 30 days the dollar unexpectedly depreciates against the yen, say, to $1 = ¥95, the importer will still have to pay the Japanese company ¥200,000 per computer, but in dollar terms that would be equivalent to $2,105 per computer, which is more than she can sell the computers for. A depreciation in the value of the dollar against the yen from $1 = ¥120 to $1 = ¥95 would transform a profitable deal into an unprofitable one.

To *insure* or *hedge* against this risk, the U.S. importer might want to engage in a **forward exchange**. A **forward exchange** occurs when two parties agree to exchange currency and execute the deal at some specific date in the future. Exchange rates governing such future transactions are referred to as **forward exchange rates.** For most major currencies, forward exchange rates are quoted for 30 days, 90 days, and 180 days into the future. In some cases, it is possible to get forward exchange rates for several years into the future. Returning to our computer importer example, let us assume the 30-day forward exchange rate for converting dollars into yen is $1 = ¥110. The importer enters into a 30-day forward exchange transaction with a foreign exchange dealer at this rate and is guaranteed that she will have to pay no more than $1,818 for each computer (1,818 = 200,000/110). This guarantees her a profit of $182 per computer ($2,000 − $1,818). She also insures herself against the possibility that an unanticipated change in the dollar/yen exchange rate will turn a profitable deal into an unprofitable one.

In this example, the spot exchange rate ($1 = ¥120) and the 30-day forward rate ($1 = ¥110) differ. Such differences are normal; they reflect the expectations of the foreign exchange market about future currency movements. In our example, the fact that $1 bought more yen with a spot exchange than with a 30-day forward exchange indicates foreign exchange dealers expected the dollar to depreciate against the yen in the next 30 days. When this occurs, we say the dollar is selling at a discount on the 30-day forward market (i.e., it is worth less than on the spot market). Of course, the opposite can also occur. If the 30-day forward exchange rate were $1 = ¥130, for example, $1 would buy more yen with a forward exchange than with a spot exchange. In such a case, we say the dollar is selling at a premium on the 30-day forward market. This reflects the foreign exchange dealers' expectations that the dollar will appreciate against the yen over the next 30 days.

In sum, when a firm enters into a forward exchange contract, it is taking out insurance against the possibility that future exchange rate movements will make a transaction unprofitable by the time that transaction has been executed. Although many firms routinely enter into forward exchange contracts to hedge their foreign exchange risk, there are some spectacular examples of what happens when firms don't take out this insurance. The accompanying Management Focus, which explains how a failure to fully insure against foreign exchange risk cost Volkswagen dearly, provides an example.

Currency Swaps

The above discussion of spot and forward exchange rates might lead you to conclude that the option to buy forward is very important to companies engaged in international trade—and you would be right. By April 2004, the latest date for which information is available, forward instruments accounted for some 65 percent of all foreign exchange transactions, while spot exchanges accounted for 35 percent.[4] However, the vast majority of these forward exchanges were not forward exchanges of the type we have been discussing, but rather a more sophisticated instrument known as currency swaps.

A **currency swap** is the simultaneous purchase and sale of a given amount of foreign exchange for two different value dates. Swaps are transacted between international businesses and their banks, between banks, and between governments when it is desirable to move out of one currency into another for a limited period without incurring foreign exchange risk. A common kind of swap is spot against forward. Consider a company such as Apple Computer. Apple assembles laptop computers in the United States, but the screens are made in Japan. Apple also sells some of the finished laptops in Japan. So, like many companies, Apple both buys from and sells to Japan. Imagine Apple needs to change $1 million into yen to pay its supplier of laptop screens today. Apple knows that in 90 days it will be paid ¥120 million by the Japanese importer that buys its finished laptops. It will want to convert these yen into dollars for use in the United States. Let us say today's spot exchange rate is $1 = ¥120 and the 90-day forward exchange rate is $1 = ¥110. Apple sells $1 million to its bank in return for ¥120 million. Now Apple can pay its Japanese supplier. At the same time, Apple enters into a 90-day forward exchange deal with its bank for converting ¥120 million into dollars. Thus, in 90 days Apple will receive $1.09 million (¥120 million/ 110 = $1.09 million). Since the yen is trading at a premium on the 90-day forward market, Apple ends up with more dollars than it started with (although the opposite could also occur). The swap deal is just like a conventional forward deal in one important respect: It enables Apple to insure itself against foreign exchange risk. By engaging in a swap, Apple knows today that the ¥120 million payment it will receive in 90 days will yield $1.09 million.

Volkswagen's Hedging Strategy

In January 2004 Volkswagen, Europe's largest car maker, reported a 95 percent drop in 2003 fourth-quarter profits, which slumped from €1.05 billion to a mere €50 million. For all of 2003 Volkswagen's operating profit fell by 50 percent from record levels attained in 2002. Although the profit slump had multiple causes, two factors were the focus of much attention—the sharp rise in the value of the euro against the dollar during 2003, and Volkswagen's decision to only hedge 30 percent of its foreign currency exposure, as opposed to the 70 percent it had traditionally hedged. In total, currency losses due to the dollar's rise are estimated to have reduced Volkswagen's operating profits by some €1.2 billion ($1.5 billion).

The rise in the value of the euro during 2003 took many companies by surprise. Since its introduction on January 1, 1999, when it became the currency unit of 12 members of the European Union, the euro had recorded a volatile trading history against the U.S. dollar. In early 1999 the exchange rate stood at €1 = $1.17, but by October 2000 it had slumped to €1 = $0.83. Although it recovered, reaching parity of €1 = $1.00 in late 2002, few analysts predicted a rapid rise in the value of the euro against the dollar during 2003. As so often happens in the foreign exchange markets, the experts were wrong; by late 2003 the exchange rate stood at €1 = $1.25.

For Volkswagen, which made cars in Germany and exported them to the United States, the fall in the value of the dollar against the euro during 2003 was devastating. To understand what happened, consider a Volkswagen Jetta built in Germany for export to the United States. The Jetta costs €14,000 to make in Germany and ship to a dealer in the United States, where it sells for $15,000. With the exchange rate standing at around €1 = $1.00, the $15,000 earned from the sale of a Jetta in the U.S. could be converted into €15,000, giving Volkswagen a profit of €1,000 on every Jetta sold. But if the exchange rate changes during the year, ending up at €1 = $1.25 as it did during 2003, each dollar of revenue will now only buy €0.80 (€1/$1.25 = €0.80), and Volkswagen is squeezed. At an exchange rate of €1 = $1.25, the $15,000 Volkswagen gets for the Jetta is now only worth €12,000 when converted back into euros, meaning the company will lose €2,000 on every Jetta sold (when the exchange rate is €1 = $1.25, $15,000/1.25 = €12,000).

Volkswagen could have insured against this adverse movement in exchange rates by entering the foreign exchange market in late 2002 and buying a *forward contract* for dollars at an exchange rate of around $1 = €1 (a *forward contract* gives the holder the right to exchange one currency for another at some point in the future at a predetermined exchange rate). Called *hedging*, the financial strategy of buying forward guarantees that at some future point, such as 180 days, Volkswagen would have been able to exchange the dollars it got from selling Jettas in the United States into euros at $1 = €1, *irrespective of what the actual exchange rate was at that time*. In 2003 such a strategy would have been good for Volkswagen. However, hedging is not without its costs. For one thing, if the euro had declined in value against the dollar, instead of appreciating as it did, Volkswagen would have made even more profit per car in euros by not hedging (a dollar at the end of 2003 would have bought more euros than a dollar at the end of 2002). For another thing, hedging is expensive since foreign exchange dealers will charge a high commission for selling currency forward. Volkswagen decided to hedge just 30 percent of its anticipated U.S. sales in 2003 though forward contracts, rather than the 70 percent it had historically hedged. The decision cost the company over €1 billion. For 2004, the company announced that it would revert back to hedging 70 percent of its foreign currency exposure.[3]

The Nature of the Foreign Exchange Market

The foreign exchange market is not located in any one place. It is a global network of banks, brokers, and foreign exchange dealers connected by electronic communications systems. When companies wish to convert currencies, they typically go through their own banks rather than entering the market directly. The foreign exchange market has been growing at a rapid pace, reflecting a general growth in the volume of cross-border trade and investment (see Chapter 1). In March 1986, the average total value of global foreign exchange trading was about $200 billion per day. By April 1995, it was more than $1,200 billion per day, and by April 2004 it reached $1.8 trillion per day.[5] The most important trading centers are London (31 percent of activity), New York (19 percent of activity), Tokyo (8 percent of activity), and Singapore (5 percent of activity).[6] Major secondary trading centers include Zurich, Frankfurt, Paris, Hong Kong, and Sydney.

London's dominance in the foreign exchange market is due to both history and geography. As the capital of the world's first major industrial trading nation, London had become the world's largest center for international banking by the end of the 19th century, a position it has retained. Today London's central position between Tokyo and Singapore to the east and New York to the west has made it the critical link between the East Asian and New York markets. Due to the particular differences in time zones, London opens soon after Tokyo closes for the night and is still open for the first few hours of trading in New York.[7]

Two features of the foreign exchange market are of particular note. The first is that the market never sleeps. Tokyo, London, and New York are all shut for only 3 hours out of every 24. During these three hours, trading continues in a number of minor centers, particularly San Francisco and Sydney, Australia. The second feature of the market is the integration of the various trading centers. High-speed computer linkages between trading centers around the globe have effectively created a single market. The integration of financial centers implies there can be no significant difference in exchange rates quoted in the trading centers. For example, if the yen/dollar exchange rate quoted in London at 3:00 p.m. is ¥120 = $1, the yen/dollar exchange rate quoted in New York at the same time (10:00 a.m. New York time) will be identical. If the New York yen/dollar exchange rate were ¥125 = $1, a dealer could make a profit through **arbitrage,** buying a currency low and selling it high. For example, if the prices differed in London and New York as given, a dealer in New York could use $1 million to purchase ¥125 million. She could then immediately sell the ¥125 million for dollars in London, where the transaction would yield $1.046666 million, allowing the trader to book a profit of $46,666 on the transaction. If all dealers tried to cash in on the opportunity, however, the demand for yen in New York would rise, resulting in an appreciation of the yen against the dollar such that the price differential between New York and London would quickly disappear. Because foreign exchange dealers are always watching their computer screens for arbitrage opportunities, the few that arise tend to be small, and they disappear in minutes.

Another feature of the foreign exchange market is the important role played by the U.S. dollar. Although a foreign exchange transaction can involve any two currencies, most transactions involve dollars on one side. This is true even when a dealer wants to sell a nondollar currency and buy another. A dealer wishing to sell Korean won for Brazilian real, for example, will usually sell the won for dollars and then use the dollars to buy real. Although this may seem a roundabout way of doing things, it is actually cheaper than trying to find a holder of real who wants to buy won. Because the volume of international transactions involving dollars is so great, it is not hard to find dealers who wish to trade dollars for won or real.

Due to its central role in so many foreign exchange deals, the dollar is a vehicle currency. In 2004, 89 percent of all foreign exchange transactions involved dollars on one side of the transaction. After the dollar, the most important vehicle currencies were the euro, the Japanese yen, and the British pound—reflecting the importance of these trading entities in the world economy. The euro has replaced the German mark as the world's second most important vehicle currency. The British pound used to be second in importance to the dollar as a vehicle currency, but its importance has diminished in recent years. Despite this, London has retained its leading position in the global foreign exchange market.

Economic Theories of Exchange Rate Determination

At the most basic level, exchange rates are determined by the demand and supply of one currency relative to the demand and supply of another. For example, if the demand for dollars outstrips the supply of them and if the supply of Japanese yen is greater than the demand for them, the dollar/yen exchange rate will change. The dollar will appreciate against the yen (or the yen will depreciate against the dollar). However, while differences in relative demand and supply explain the determination of exchange rates, they do so only in a superficial sense. This simple explanation does not tell us what factors underlie the demand for and supply of a currency. Nor does it tell us when the demand for dollars will exceed the supply (and vice versa) or when the supply of Japanese yen will exceed demand for them (and vice versa). Neither does it tell us under what conditions a currency is in demand or under what conditions it is not demanded. In this section, we will review economic theory's answers to these questions. This will give us a deeper understanding of how exchange rates are determined.

If we understand how exchange rates are determined, we may be able to forecast exchange rate movements. Because future exchange rate movements influence export opportunities, the profitability of international trade and investment deals, and the price competitiveness of foreign imports, this is valuable information for an international business. Unfortunately, there is no simple explanation. The forces that determine exchange rates are complex, and no theoretical consensus exists, even among academic economists who study the phenomenon every day. Nonetheless, most economic theories of exchange rate movements seem to agree that three factors have an important impact on future exchange rate movements in a country's currency: the country's price inflation, interest rate, and market psychology.[8]

PRICES AND EXCHANGE RATES

To understand how prices are related to exchange rate movements, we first need to discuss an economic proposition known as the law of one price. Then we will discuss the theory of purchasing power parity (PPP), which links changes in the exchange rate between two countries' currencies to changes in the countries' price levels.

The Law of One Price

The **law of one price** states that in competitive markets free of transportation costs and barriers to trade (such as tariffs), identical products sold in different countries must sell for the same price when their price is expressed in terms of the same currency.[9] For example, if the exchange rate between the British pound and the dollar is £1 = $1.50, a jacket that retails for $75 in New York should sell for £50 in London (since $75/1.50 = £50). Consider what would happen if the jacket cost £40 in London ($60 in U.S. currency). At this price, it would pay a trader to buy jackets in London and sell them in New York (an example of arbitrage). The company initially could make a profit of $15 on each jacket by purchasing it for £40 ($60) in London and selling it for $75 in New York (we are assuming away transportation costs and trade barriers). However, the increased demand for jackets in London would raise their price in London, and the increased supply of jackets in New York would lower their price there. This would continue until prices were equalized. Thus, prices might equalize when the jacket cost £44 ($66) in London and $66 in New York (assuming no change in the exchange rate of £1 = $1.50).

Purchasing Power Parity

If the law of one price were true for all goods and services, the purchasing power parity (PPP) exchange rate could be found from any individual set of prices. By comparing the prices of identical products in different currencies, it would be possible to determine the "real" or PPP exchange rate that would exist if markets were efficient. (An **efficient market** has no impediments to the free flow of goods and services, such as trade barriers.)

A less extreme version of the PPP theory states that given relatively efficient markets—that is, markets in which few impediments to international trade exist—the price of a "basket of goods" should be roughly equivalent in each country. To express the PPP theory in symbols, let P\$ be the U.S. dollar price of a basket of particular goods and P¥ be the price of the same basket of goods in Japanese yen. The PPP theory predicts that the dollar/yen exchange rate, E\$/¥, should be equivalent to

$$E_{\$/¥} = P_{\$}/P_{¥}$$

Thus, if a basket of goods costs \$200 in the United States and ¥20,000 in Japan, PPP theory predicts that the dollar/yen exchange rate should be \$200/¥20,000 or \$0.01 per Japanese yen (i.e., \$1 = ¥100).

Every year, the newsmagazine *The Economist* publishes its own version of the PPP theorem, which it refers to as the "Big Mac Index." *The Economist* has selected McDonald's Big Mac as a proxy for a "basket of goods" because it is produced according to more or less the same recipe in about 120 countries. The Big Mac PPP is the exchange rate that would have hamburgers costing the same in each country. According to *The Economist*, comparing a country's actual exchange rate with the one predicted by the PPP theorem based on relative prices of Big Macs is a test on whether a currency is undervalued or not. This is not a totally serious exercise, as *The Economist* admits, but it does provide us with a useful illustration of the PPP theorem.

The Big Mac index for February 1, 2007, is reproduced in Table 9.2. To calculate the index, *The Economist* converts the price of a Big Mac in a country into dollars at current exchange rates and divides that by the average price of a Big Mac in America (which is \$3.22). According to the PPP theorem, the prices should be the same. If they are not, it implies that the currency is either overvalued against the dollar or undervalued. For example, the average price of a Big Mac in the euro area was \$3.82 at the euro/dollar exchange rate prevailing on February 1, 2007. Dividing this by the average price of a Big Mac in the United States gives 1.19 (i.e., 3.82/3.22), which suggests that the euro was overvalued by 19 percent against the U.S. dollar.

The next step in the PPP theory is to argue that the exchange rate will change if relative prices change. For example, imagine there is no price inflation in the United States, while prices in Japan are increasing by 10 percent a year. At the beginning of the year, a basket of goods costs \$200 in the United States and ¥20,000 in Japan, so the dollar/yen exchange rate, according to PPP theory, should be \$1 = ¥100. At the end of the year, the basket of goods still costs \$200 in the United States, but it costs ¥22,000 in Japan. PPP theory predicts that the exchange rate should change as a result. More precisely, by the end of the year,

$$E_{\$/¥} = \$200/¥22,000$$

Thus, ¥1 = \$0.0091 (or \$1 = ¥110). Because of 10 percent price inflation, the Japanese yen has depreciated by 10 percent against the dollar. One dollar will buy 10 percent more yen at the end of the year than at the beginning.

Money Supply and Price Inflation

In essence, PPP theory predicts that changes in relative prices will result in a change in exchange rates. Theoretically, a country in which price inflation is running wild should expect to see its currency depreciate against that of countries in which inflation rates are lower. If we can predict what a country's future inflation rate is likely to be, we can also predict how the value of its currency relative to other currencies—its exchange rate—is likely to change. The growth rate of a country's money supply determines its likely future inflation rate.[10] Thus, in theory at least, we can use information about the growth in money supply to forecast exchange rate movements.

Inflation is a monetary phenomenon. It occurs when the quantity of money in circulation rises faster than the stock of goods and services, that is, when the money

	Big Mac Prices		Implied PPP* of the Dollar	Actual Dollar Exchange Rate Jan 31st	Under (−)/Over (+) Valuation against the Dollar, %
	In Local Currency	In Dollars			
United States†	$3.22	3.22			
Argentina	Peso 8.25	2.65	2.56	3.11	−18
Australia	A$3.45	2.67	1.07	1.29	−6
Brazil	Real 6.4	3.01	1.99	2.13	−6
Britain	£1.99	3.90	1.62‡	1.96‡	+21
Canada	C$3.63	3.08	1.13	1.18	−4
Chile	Peso 1,670	3.07	519	544	−5
China	Yuan 11.0	1.41	3.42	7.77	−56
Colombia	Peso 6,900	3.06	2,143	2,254	−5
Costa Rica	Colones 1,130	2.18	351	519	−32
Czech Republic	Koruna 52.1	2.41	16.2	21.6	−25
Denmark	DKr27.75	4.84	8.62	5.74	+50
Egypt	Pound 9.09	1.60	2.82	5.70	−50
Estonia	Kroon 30	2.49	9.32	12.0	−23
Euro area§	€2.94	3.82	1.10**	1.30**	+19
Hong Kong	HK$12.0	1.54	3.73	7.81	−52
Hungary	Forint 590	3.00	183	197	−7
Iceland	Kronur 509	7.44	158	68.4	+131
Indonesia	Rupiah 15,900	1.75	4,938	9,100	−46
Japan	¥280	2.31	87.0	121	−28
Latvia	Lats 1.35	2.52	0.42	0.54	−22
Lithuania	Lias 6.50	2.45	2.02	2.66	−24
Malaysia	Ringgit 5.50	1.57	1.71	3.50	−51
Mexico	Peso 29.0	2.66	9.01	10.9	−17
New Zealand	NZ$4.60	3.16	1.43	1.45	−2
Norway	Kroner 41.5	6.63	12.9	6.26	+106
Pakistan	Rupee 140	2.31	43.5	60.7	−28
Paraguay	Guarani 10,000	1.90	3,106	5,250	−41
Peru	New Sol 9.50	2.97	2.95	3.20	−8
Philippines	Peso 85.0	1.74	26.4	48.9	−46

(continued)

TABLE 9.2

The Big Mac Index, February 1, 2007

Source: *The Economist*, February 1, 2007.

*Purchasing-power parity: local price divided by price in United States
†Average of New York, Atlanta, Chicago, and San Francisco
‡Dollars per pound   §Weighted average of prices in euro area   **Dollars per euro

	Big Mac Prices		Implied PPP* of the Dollar	Actual Dollar Exchange Rate Jan 31st	Under (−)/Over (+) Valuation against the Dollar, %
	In Local Currency	In Dollars			
Poland	Zloty 6.90	2.29	2.14	3.01	−29
Russia	Rouble 49.0	1.85	15.2	26.5	−43
Saudi Arabia	Riyal 9.00	2.40	2.80	3.75	−25
Singapore	S$3.60	2.34	1.12	1.54	−27
Slovakia	Crown 57.98	2.13	18.0	27.2	−34
South Africa	Rand 15.5	2.14	4.81	7.25	−34
South Korea	Won 2,900	3.08	901	942	−4
Sri Lanka	Rupee 190	1.75	59.0	109	−46
Sweden	SKr32.0	4.59	9.94	6.97	+43
Switzerland	SFr6.30	5.05	1.96	1.25	+57
Taiwan	NT$75.0	2.28	23.3	32.9	−29
Thailand	Baht 62.0	1.78	19.3	34.7	−45
Turkey	Lire 4.55	3.22	1.41	1.41	nil
UAE	Dirhams 10.0	2.72	3.11	3.67	−15
Ukraine	Hryvnia 9.00	1.71	2.80	5.27	−47
Uruguay	Peso 55.0	2.17	17.1	25.3	−33
Venezuela	Bolivar 6,800	1.58	2,112	4,307	−51

TABLE 9.2   (concluded)

supply increases faster than output increases. Imagine what would happen if everyone in the country was suddenly given $10,000 by the government. Many people would rush out to spend their extra money on those things they had always wanted—new cars, new furniture, better clothes, and so on. There would be a surge in demand for goods and services. Car dealers, department stores, and other providers of goods and services would respond to this upsurge in demand by raising prices. The result would be price inflation.

A government increasing the money supply is analogous to giving people more money. An increase in the money supply makes it easier for banks to borrow from the government and for individuals and companies to borrow from banks. The resulting increase in credit causes increases in demand for goods and services. Unless the output of goods and services is growing at a rate similar to that of the money supply, the result will be inflation. This relationship has been observed time after time in country after country.

So now we have a connection between the growth in a country's money supply, price inflation, and exchange rate movements. Put simply, *when the growth in a country's money supply is faster than the growth in its output, price inflation is fueled.* The PPP theory tells us that a country with a high inflation rate will see depreciation in its currency exchange rate. In one of the clearest historical examples, in the mid-1980s, Bolivia experienced hyperinflation—an explosive and seemingly uncontrollable price inflation in which money loses value very rapidly. Table 9.3 presents data on Bolivia's money supply and inflation rate, and on its peso's exchange rate with the U.S. dollar during the period of hyperinflation. The exchange rate is actually the "black market" exchange rate, as the Bolivian government prohibited converting the peso to other currencies during the period. The data show that the growth in money supply, the rate of price inflation, and the depreciation of the peso against the dollar all moved in step with each other. This is

Month	Money Supply (billions of pesos)	Price Level Relative to 1982 (average = 1)	Exchange Rate (pesos per dollar)
1984			
April	270	21.1	3,576
May	330	31.1	3,512
June	440	32.3	3,342
July	599	34.0	3,570
August	718	39.1	7,038
September	889	53.7	13,685
October	1,194	85.5	15,205
November	1,495	112.4	18,469
December	3,296	180.9	24,515
1985			
January	4,630	305.3	73,016
February	6,455	863.3	141,101
March	9,089	1,078.6	128,137
April	12,885	1,205.7	167,428
May	21,309	1,635.7	272,375
June	27,778	2,919.1	481,756
July	47,341	4,854.6	885,476
August	74,306	8,081.0	1,182,300
September	103,272	12,647.6	1,087,440
October	132,550	12,411.8	1,120,210

TABLE 9.3

Macroeconomic Data for Bolivia, April 1984–October 1985

Source: Juan-Antino Morales, "Inflation Stabilization in Bolivia," in *Inflation Stabilization: The Experience of Israel, Argentina, Brazil, Bolivia, and Mexico*, ed. Michael Bruno et al. (Cambridge, MA: MIT Press, 1988).

just what PPP theory and monetary economics predict. Between April 1984 and July 1985, Bolivia's money supply increased by 17,433 percent, prices increased by 22,908 percent, and the value of the peso against the dollar fell by 24,662 percent! In October 1985, the Bolivian government instituted a dramatic stabilization plan—which included the introduction of a new currency and tight control of the money supply—and by 1987 the country's annual inflation rate was down to 16 percent.[11]

Another way of looking at the same phenomenon is that an increase in a country's money supply, which increases the amount of currency available, changes the relative demand and supply conditions in the foreign exchange market. If the U.S. money supply is growing more rapidly than U.S. output, dollars will be relatively more plentiful than the currencies of countries where monetary growth is closer to output growth. As a result of this relative increase in the supply of dollars, the dollar will depreciate on the foreign exchange market against the currencies of countries with slower monetary growth.

Government policy determines whether the rate of growth in a country's money supply is greater than the rate of growth in output. A government can increase the money supply simply by telling the country's central bank to issue more money. Governments tend to do this to finance public expenditure (building roads, paying government workers, paying for defense, etc.). A government could finance public expenditure by raising taxes, but since nobody likes paying more taxes and since politicians do not like to be unpopular, they have a natural preference for expanding the money supply. Unfortunately, there is no magic money tree. The inevitable result of excessive growth in money supply is price inflation. However, this has not stopped governments around the world from expanding the money supply, with predictable results. If an international business is attempting to predict future movements in the value of a country's currency on the foreign exchange market, it should examine that country's policy toward monetary growth. If the government seems committed to controlling the rate of growth in money supply, the country's future inflation rate may be low (even if the current rate is high) and its currency should not depreciate too much on the foreign exchange market. If the government seems to lack the political will to control the rate of growth in money supply, the future inflation rate may be high, which is likely to cause its currency to depreciate. Historically, many Latin American governments have fallen into this latter category, including Argentina, Bolivia, and Brazil. More recently, many of the newly democratic states of Eastern Europe made the same mistake.

Empirical Tests of PPP Theory

PPP theory predicts that exchange rates are determined by relative prices, and that changes in relative prices will result in a change in exchange rates. A country in which price inflation is running wild should expect to see its currency depreciate against that of countries with lower inflation rates. This is intuitively appealing, but is it true in practice? There are several good examples of the connection between a country's price inflation and exchange rate position (such as Bolivia). However, extensive empirical testing of PPP theory has yielded mixed results.[12] While PPP theory seems to yield relatively accurate predictions in the long run, it does not appear to be a strong predictor of short-run movements in exchange rates covering time spans of five years or less.[13] In addition, the theory seems to best predict exchange rate changes for countries with high rates of inflation and underdeveloped capital markets. The theory is less useful for predicting short-term exchange rate movements between the currencies of advanced industrialized nations that have relatively small differentials in inflation rates.

The failure to find a strong link between relative inflation rates and exchange rate movements has been referred to as the purchasing power parity puzzle. Several factors may explain the failure of PPP theory to predict exchange rates more accurately.[14] PPP theory assumes away transportation costs and barriers to trade. In practice, these factors are significant and they tend to create significant price differentials between countries. Transportation costs are certainly not trivial for many goods. Moreover, as we saw in Chapter 6, governments routinely intervene in international trade, creating tariff and nontariff barriers to cross-border trade. Barriers to trade limit the ability of traders to use arbitrage to equalize prices for the same product in different countries, which is required for the law of one price to hold. Government intervention in cross-border trade, by violating the assumption of efficient markets, weakens the link between relative price changes and changes in exchange rates predicted by PPP theory.

In addition, the PPP theory may not hold if many national markets are dominated by a handful of multinational enterprises that have sufficient market power to be able to exercise some influence over prices, control distribution channels, and differentiate their product offerings between nations.[15] In fact, this situation seems to prevail in a number of industries. In the detergent industry, two companies, Unilever and Procter & Gamble, dominate the market in nation after nation. In heavy earthmoving equipment, Caterpillar Inc. and Komatsu are global market leaders. In the market for semiconductor equipment, Applied Materials has a commanding market share lead in almost every important national market. Microsoft dominates the market for personal computer operating systems and applications systems around the world, and so on. In such cases, dominant enterprises may be able to exercise a degree of pricing power, setting different prices in different markets to reflect varying demand conditions. This is referred to as price discrimination. For price discrimination to work, arbitrage must be limited. According to this argument, enterprises with some market power may be able to control distribution channels and therefore limit the unauthorized resale (arbitrage) of products purchased in another national market. They may also be able to limit resale (arbitrage) by differentiating otherwise identical products among nations along some line, such as design or packaging.

For example, even though the version of Microsoft Office sold in China may be less expensive than the version sold in the United States, the use of arbitrage to equalize prices may be limited because few Americans would want a version that was based on Chinese characters. The design differentiation between Microsoft Office for China and for the United States means that the law of one price would not work for Microsoft Office, even if transportation costs were trivial and tariff barriers between the United States and China did not exist. If the inability to practice arbitrage were widespread enough, it would break the connection between changes in relative prices and exchange rates predicted by the PPP theorem and help explain the limited empirical support for this theory.

Another factor of some importance is that governments also intervene in the foreign exchange market in attempting to influence the value of their currencies. We will look at why and how they do this in Chapter 10. For now, the important thing to note is that governments regularly intervene in the foreign exchange market, and this further weakens the link between price changes and changes in exchange rates. One more factor explaining the failure of PPP theory to predict short-term movements in foreign exchange rates is the impact of investor psychology and other factors on currency purchasing decisions and exchange rate movements. We will discuss this issue in more detail later in this chapter.

INTEREST RATES AND EXCHANGE RATES

Economic theory tells us that interest rates reflect expectations about likely future inflation rates. In countries where inflation is expected to be high, interest rates also will be high because investors want compensation for the decline in the value of their money. This relationship was first formalized by economist Irvin Fisher and is referred to as the Fisher Effect. The **Fisher Effect** states that a country's "nominal" interest rate (i) is the sum of the required "real" rate of interest (r) and the expected rate of inflation over the period for which the funds are to be lent (I). More formally,

$$i = r + I$$

For example, if the real rate of interest in a country is 5 percent and annual inflation is expected to be 10 percent, the nominal interest rate will be 15 percent. As the Fisher Effect predicts, a strong relationship seems to exist between inflation rates and interest rates.[16]

We can take this one step further and consider how it applies in a world of many countries and unrestricted capital flows. When investors are free to transfer capital between countries, real interest rates will be the same in every country. If differences in real interest rates did emerge between countries, arbitrage would soon equalize them. For example, if the real interest rate in Japan was 10 percent and only 6 percent in the United States, it would pay investors to borrow money in the United States and invest it in Japan. The resulting increase in the demand for money in the United States would raise the real interest rate there, while the increase in the supply of foreign money in Japan would lower the real interest rate there. This would continue until the two sets of real interest rates were equalized.

It follows from the Fisher Effect that if the real interest rate is the same worldwide, any difference in interest rates between countries reflects differing expectations about inflation rates. Thus, if the expected rate of inflation in the United States is greater than that in Japan, U.S. nominal interest rates will be greater than Japanese nominal interest rates.

Since we know from PPP theory that there is a link (in theory at least) between inflation and exchange rates, and since interest rates reflect expectations about inflation, it follows that there must also be a link between interest rates and exchange rates. This link is known as the International Fisher Effect (IFE). The **International Fisher Effect** states that for any two countries, the spot exchange rate should change in an equal amount but in the opposite direction to the difference in nominal interest rates between the two countries. Stated more formally, the change in the spot exchange rate between the United States and Japan, for example, can be modeled as follows:

$$[(S_1 - S_2)/S_2] \times 100 = i_\$ - i_¥$$

where $i_\$$ and $i_¥$ are the respective nominal interest rates in the United States and Japan, S_1 is the spot exchange rate at the beginning of the period, and S_2 is the spot exchange rate at the end of the period. If the U.S. nominal interest rate is higher than Japan's, reflecting greater expected inflation rates, the value of the dollar against the yen should fall by that interest rate differential in the future. So if the interest rate in the United States is 10 percent and in Japan it is 6 percent, we would expect the value of the dollar to depreciate by 4 percent against the Japanese yen.

Do interest rate differentials help predict future currency movements? The evidence is mixed; as in the case of PPP theory, in the long run, there seems to be a relationship between interest rate differentials and subsequent changes in spot exchange rates. However, considerable short-run deviations occur. Like PPP, the International Fisher Effect is not a good predictor of short-run changes in spot exchange rates.[17]

INVESTOR PSYCHOLOGY AND BANDWAGON EFFECTS

Empirical evidence suggests that neither PPP theory nor the International Fisher Effect are particularly good at explaining short-term movements in exchange rates. One reason may be the impact of investor psychology on short-run exchange rate movements. Evidence accumulated over the last decade reveals that various psychological factors play an important role in determining the expectations of market traders as to likely future exchange rates.[18] In turn, expectations have a tendency to become self-fulfilling prophecies.

A good example of this mechanism occurred in September 1992 when the famous international financier George Soros made a huge bet against the British pound. Soros borrowed billions of pounds, using the assets of his investment funds as collateral, and immediately sold those pounds for German deutsche marks (this was before the advent of the euro). This technique, known as short selling, can earn the speculator enormous profits if he can subsequently buy back the pounds he sold at a much better exchange rate and then use those pounds, purchased cheaply, to repay his loan. By selling pounds and buying deutsche marks, Soros helped to start pushing down the value of the pound on the foreign exchange markets. More importantly, when Soros started shorting the British pound, many foreign exchange traders, knowing Soros's reputation, jumped on the bandwagon and did likewise. This triggered a classic **bandwagon effect** with traders moving as a herd in the same direction at the same time. As the bandwagon effect gained momentum, with more traders selling British pounds and purchasing deutsche marks in expectation of a decline in the pound, their expectations became a self-fulfilling prophecy. Massive selling forced down the value of the pound against the deutsche mark. In other words, the pound declined in value not so much because of any major shift in macroeconomic fundamentals but because investors followed a bet placed by a major speculator, George Soros.

According to a number of studies, investor psychology and bandwagon effects play a major role in determining short-run exchange rate movements.[19] However, these effects can be hard to predict. Investor psychology can be influenced by political factors and by microeconomic events, such as the investment decisions of individual firms, many of which are only loosely linked to macroeconomic fundamentals, such as relative inflation rates. Also, bandwagon effects can be both triggered and exacerbated by the idiosyncratic behavior of politicians. Something like this seems to have occurred in Southeast Asia during 1997 when, one after another, the currencies of Thailand, Malaysia, South Korea,

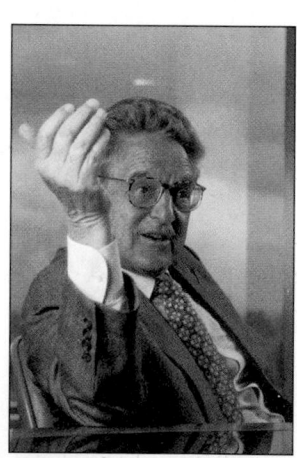

George Soros, whose Quantum Fund has been fantastically successful in managing hedge funds, has been criticized by world leaders because his actions can cause huge changes in currency markets.

and Indonesia lost between 50 percent and 70 percent of their value against the U.S. dollar in a few months. For a detailed look at what occurred in South Korea, see the accompanying Country Focus. The collapse in the value of the Korean currency did not occur because South Korea had a higher inflation rate than the United States. It occurred because of an excessive buildup of dollar-denominated debt among South Korean firms. By mid-1997 it was clear that these companies were having trouble servicing this debt. Foreign investors, fearing a wave of corporate bankruptcies, took their money out of the country, exchanging won for U.S. dollars. As their actions began to depress the exchange rate, currency traders jumped on the bandwagon and speculated against the won (selling it short), and it was this speculation that produced a collapse in the value of the won.

SUMMARY

Relative monetary growth, relative inflation rates, and nominal interest rate differentials are all moderately good predictors of long-run changes in exchange rates. They are poor predictors of short-run changes in exchange rates, however, perhaps because of the impact of psychological factors, investor expectations, and bandwagon effects on short-term currency movements. This information is useful for an international business. Insofar as the long-term profitability of foreign investments, export opportunities, and the price competitiveness of foreign imports are all influenced by long-term movements in exchange rates, international businesses would be advised to pay attention to countries' differing monetary growth, inflation, and interest rates. International businesses that engage in foreign exchange transactions on a day-to-day basis could benefit by knowing some predictors of short-term foreign exchange rate movements. Unfortunately, short-term exchange rate movements are difficult to predict.

Exchange Rate Forecasting

A company's need to predict future exchange rate variations raises the issue of whether it is worthwhile for the company to invest in exchange rate forecasting services to aid decision making. Two schools of thought address this issue. The efficient market school argues that forward exchange rates do the best possible job of forecasting future spot exchange rates, and, therefore, investing in forecasting services would be a waste of money. The other school of thought, the inefficient market school, argues that companies can improve the foreign exchange market's estimate of future exchange rates (as contained in the forward rate) by investing in forecasting services. In other words, this school of thought does not believe the forward exchange rates are the best possible predictors of future spot exchange rates.

THE EFFICIENT MARKET SCHOOL

Forward exchange rates represent market participants' collective predictions of likely spot exchange rates at specified future dates. If forward exchange rates are the best possible predictor of future spot rates, it would make no sense for companies to spend additional money trying to forecast short-run exchange rate movements. Many economists believe the foreign exchange market is efficient at setting forward rates.[21] An **efficient market** is one in which prices reflect all available public information. (If forward rates reflect all available information about likely future changes in exchange rates, a company cannot beat the market by investing in forecasting services.)

If the foreign exchange market is efficient, forward exchange rates should be unbiased predictors of future spot rates. This does not mean the predictions will be accurate in any specific situation. It means inaccuracies will not be consistently above or below future spot rates; they will be random. Many empirical tests have addressed the efficient market hypothesis. Although most of the early work seems to confirm the hypothesis (suggesting that companies should not waste their money on forecasting services), some recent studies

Anatomy of a Currency Crisis

In early 1997, South Korea could look back with pride on a 30-year "economic miracle" that had raised the country from the ranks of the poor and given it the world's 11th largest economy. By the end of 1997, the Korean currency, the won, had lost a staggering 67 percent of its value against the U.S. dollar, the South Korean economy lay in tatters, and the International Monetary Fund was overseeing a $55 billion rescue package. This sudden turn of events had its roots in investments made by South Korea's large industrial conglomerates, or *chaebol,* during the 1990s, often at the bequest of politicians. In 1993, Kim Young-Sam, a populist politician, became president of South Korea. Mr. Kim took office during a mild recession and promised to boost economic growth by encouraging investment in export-oriented industries. He urged the *chaebol* to invest in new factories. South Korea enjoyed an investment-led economic boom in 1994–1995, but at a cost. The *chaebol,* always reliant on heavy borrowing, built up massive debts that were equivalent, on average, to four times their equity.

As the volume of investments ballooned during the 1990s, the quality of many of these investments declined significantly. The investments often were made on the basis of unrealistic projections about future demand conditions. This resulted in significant excess capacity and falling prices. An example is investments made by South Korean *chaebol* in semiconductor factories. Investments in such facilities surged in 1994 and 1995 when a temporary global shortage of dynamic random access memory chips (DRAMs) led to sharp price increases for this product. However, supply shortages had disappeared by 1996 and excess capacity was beginning to make itself felt just as the South Koreans started to bring new DRAM factories onstream. The results were predictable; prices for DRAMs plunged and the earnings of South Korean DRAM manufacturers fell by 90 percent, which meant it was difficult for them to make scheduled payments on the debt they had acquired to build the extra capacity. The risk of corporate bankruptcy increased significantly, and not just in the semiconductor industry. South Korean companies were also investing heavily in a wide range of other industries, including automobiles and steel.

Matters were complicated further because much of the borrowing had been in U.S. dollars, as opposed to Korean won. This had seemed like a smart move at the time. The dollar/won exchange rate had been stable at around $1 = W 850. Interest rates on dollar borrowings were two to three percentage points lower than rates on borrowings in Korean won. Much of this borrowing was in the form of short-term, dollar-denominated debt that had to be paid back to the lending institution within one year. While the borrowing strategy seemed to make sense, it involved risk. If the won were to depreciate against the dollar, the size of the debt burden that South Korean companies would have to service would increase when measured in the local currency. Currency depreciation would raise borrowing costs,

have challenged it.[22] There is some evidence that forward rates are not unbiased predictors of future spot rates and that more accurate predictions of future spot rates can be calculated from publicly available information.[23]

THE INEFFICIENT MARKET SCHOOL

Citing evidence against the efficient market hypothesis, some economists believe the foreign exchange market is inefficient. An **inefficient market** is one in which prices do not reflect all available information. In an inefficient market, forward exchange rates will not be the best possible predictors of future spot exchange rates.

If this is true, it may be worthwhile for international businesses to invest in forecasting services (as many do). The belief is that professional exchange rate forecasts might provide better predictions of future spot rates than forward exchange rates do. However, the track record of professional forecasting services is not that good.[24] For example, depress corporate earnings, and increase the risk of bankruptcy. This is exactly what happened.

By mid-1997, foreign investors had become alarmed at the rising debt levels of South Korean companies, particularly given the emergence of excess capacity and plunging prices in several areas where the companies had made huge investments, including semiconductors, automobiles, and steel. Given increasing speculation that many South Korean companies would not be able to service their debt payments, foreign investors began to withdraw their money from the Korean stock and bond markets. In the process, they sold Korean won and purchased U.S. dollars. The selling of won accelerated in mid-1997 when two of the smaller *chaebol* filed for bankruptcy, citing their inability to meet scheduled debt payments. The increased supply of won and the increased demand for U.S. dollars pushed down the price of won in dollar terms from around W 840 = $1 to W 900 = $1.

At this point, the South Korean central bank stepped into the foreign exchange market to try to keep the exchange rate above W 1,000 = $1. It used dollars that it held in reserve to purchase won. The idea was to try to push up the price of the won in dollar terms and restore investor confidence in the stability of the exchange rate. This action, however, did not address the underlying debt problem faced by South Korean companies. Against a backdrop of more corporate bankruptcies in South Korea and the government's stated intentions to take some troubled companies into state ownership, Standard & Poor's,

the U.S. credit rating agency, downgraded South Korea's sovereign debt. This caused the Korean stock market to plunge 5.5 percent, and the Korean won to fall to W 930 = $1. According to S&P, "The downgrade of . . . ratings reflects the escalating cost to the government of supporting the country's ailing corporate and financial sectors."

The S&P downgrade triggered a sharp sale of the Korean won. In an attempt to protect the won against what was fast becoming a classic bandwagon effect, the South Korean central bank raised short-term interest rates to over 12 percent, more than double the inflation rate. The bank also stepped up its intervention in the currency exchange markets, selling dollars and purchasing won in an attempt to keep the exchange rate above W 1,000 = $1. The main effect of this action, however, was to rapidly deplete South Korea's foreign exchange reserves. These stood at $30 billion on November 1, but fell to only $15 billion two weeks later. With its foreign exchange reserves almost exhausted, the South Korean central bank gave up its defense of the won November 17. Immediately, the price of won in dollars plunged to around W1,500 = $1, effectively increasing by 60 to 70 percent the amount of won heavily indebted Korean companies had to pay to meet scheduled payments on their dollar-denominated debt. These losses, due to adverse changes in foreign exchange rates, depressed the profits of many firms. South Korean firms suffered foreign exchange losses of more than $15 billion in 1997.[20]

forecasting services did not predict the 1997 currency crisis that swept through Southeast Asia.

APPROACHES TO FORECASTING

Assuming the inefficient market school is correct that the foreign exchange market's estimate of future spot rates can be improved, on what basis should forecasts be prepared? Here again, there are two schools of thought. One adheres to fundamental analysis, while the other uses technical analysis.

Fundamental Analysis

Fundamental analysis draws on economic theory to construct sophisticated econometric models for predicting exchange rate movements. The variables contained in these models typically include those we have discussed, such as relative money supply growth rates, inflation rates, and interest rates. In addition, they may include variables related to balance-of-payments positions.

Running a deficit on a balance-of-payments current account (a country is importing more goods and services than it is exporting) creates pressures that may result in the depreciation of the country's currency on the foreign exchange market.[25] Consider what might happen if the United States was running a persistent current account balance-of-payments deficit (as in fact, it has been). Since the United States would be importing more than it was exporting, people in other countries would be increasing their holdings of U.S. dollars. If these people were willing to hold their dollars, the dollar's exchange rate would not be influenced. However, if these people converted their dollars into other currencies, the supply of dollars in the foreign exchange market would increase (as would demand for the other currencies). This shift in demand and supply would create pressures that could lead to the depreciation of the dollar against other currencies.

This argument hinges on whether people in other countries are willing to hold dollars. The answer depends on such factors as U.S. interest rates, the return on holding other dollar-denominated assets such as stocks in U.S. companies, and, most importantly, inflation rates. So, in a sense, the balance-of-payments situation is not a fundamental predictor of future exchange rate movements. For example, between 1998 and 2001, the U.S. dollar appreciated against most major currencies despite a growing balance-of-payments deficit. Relatively high real interest rates in the United States, coupled with low inflation and a booming U.S. stock market that attracted inward investment from foreign capital, made the dollar very attractive to foreigners, so they did not convert their dollars into other currencies. On the contrary, they converted other currencies into dollars to invest in U.S. financial assets, such as bonds and stocks, because they believed they could earn a high return by doing so. Capital flows into the United States fueled by foreigners who wanted to buy U.S. stocks and bonds kept the dollar strong despite the current account deficit. But what makes financial assets such as stocks and bonds attractive? The answer is prevailing interest rates and inflation rates, both of which affect underlying economic growth and the real return to holding U.S. financial assets. Given this, we are back to the argument that the fundamental determinants of exchange rates are monetary growth, inflation rates, and interest rates.

Technical Analysis

Technical analysis uses price and volume data to determine past trends, which are expected to continue into the future. This approach does not rely on a consideration of economic fundamentals. Technical analysis is based on the premise that there are analyzable market trends and waves and that previous trends and waves can be used to predict future trends and waves. Since there is no theoretical rationale for this assumption of predictability, many economists compare technical analysis to fortune-telling. Despite this skepticism, technical analysis has gained favor in recent years.[26]

Currency Convertibility

Until this point we have invalidly assumed that the currencies of various countries are freely convertible into other currencies. Due to government restrictions, a significant number of currencies are not freely convertible into other currencies. A country's currency is said to be **freely convertible** when the country's government allows both residents and nonresidents to purchase unlimited amounts of a foreign currency with it. A currency is said to be **externally convertible** when only nonresidents may convert it into a foreign currency without any limitations. A currency is **nonconvertible** when neither residents nor nonresidents are allowed to convert it into a foreign currency.

Free convertibility is not universal. Many countries place some restrictions on their residents' ability to convert the domestic currency into a foreign currency (a policy of external convertibility). Restrictions range from the relatively minor (such as restricting the amount of foreign currency they may take with them out of the country on trips) to the major (such as restricting domestic businesses' ability to take foreign currency out of the country). External convertibility restrictions can limit domestic companies' ability to invest abroad, but they present few problems for foreign companies wishing to do business in that country. For example, even if the Japanese government tightly controlled the ability of its residents to convert the yen into U.S. dollars, all U.S. businesses with deposits in Japanese banks may at any time convert all their yen into dollars and take them out of the country. Thus, a U.S. company with a subsidiary in Japan is assured that it will be able to convert the profits from its Japanese operation into dollars and take them out of the country.

Serious problems arise, however, under a policy of nonconvertibility. This was the practice of the former Soviet Union, and it continued to be the practice in Russia for several years after the collapse of the Soviet Union. When strictly applied, nonconvertibility means that although a U.S. company doing business in a country such as Russia may be able to generate significant ruble profits, it may not convert those rubles into dollars and take them out of the country. Obviously this is not desirable for international business.

Governments limit convertibility to preserve their foreign exchange reserves. A country needs an adequate supply of these reserves to service its international debt commitments and to purchase imports. Governments typically impose convertibility restrictions on their currency when they fear that free convertibility will lead to a run on their foreign exchange reserves. This occurs when residents and nonresidents rush to convert their holdings of domestic currency into a foreign currency—a phenomenon generally referred to as **capital flight.** Capital flight is most likely to occur when the value of the domestic currency is depreciating rapidly because of hyperinflation or when a country's economic prospects are shaky in other respects. Under such circumstances, both residents and nonresidents tend to believe that their money is more likely to hold its value if it is converted into a foreign currency and invested abroad. Not only will a run on foreign exchange reserves limit the country's ability to service its international debt and pay for imports, but it will also lead to a precipitous depreciation in the exchange rate as residents and nonresidents unload their holdings of domestic currency on the foreign exchange markets (thereby increasing the market supply of the country's currency). Governments fear that the rise in import prices resulting from currency depreciation will lead to further increases in inflation. This fear provides another rationale for limiting convertibility.

Companies can deal with the nonconvertibility problem by engaging in countertrade. **Countertrade** refers to a range of barterlike agreements by which goods and services can be traded for other goods and services. Countertrade can make sense when a country's currency is nonconvertible. For example, consider the deal that General Electric struck with the Romanian government when that country's currency was nonconvertible. When General Electric won a contract for a $150 million generator project in Romania, it agreed to take payment in the form of Romanian goods that could be sold for $150 million on international markets. In a similar case, the Venezuelan government negotiated a contract with Caterpillar under which Venezuela would trade 350,000 tons of iron ore for Caterpillar heavy construction equipment. Caterpillar subsequently traded the iron ore to Romania in exchange for Romanian farm products, which it then sold on international markets for dollars.[27] More recently, in a 2003 deal the government of Indonesia entered into a countertrade with Libya under which Libya agreed to purchase $540 million in Indonesian goods, including textiles, tea, coffee, electronics, plastics, and auto parts, in exchange for 50,000 barrels per day of Libyan crude oil.[28]

How important is countertrade? Twenty years ago, a large number of nonconvertible currencies existed in the world, and countertrade was quite significant. However, in recent years many governments have made their currencies freely convertible, and the percentage of world trade that involves countertrade is probably below 10 percent.[29]

IMPLICATIONS FOR MANAGERS

This chapter contains a number of clear implications for business. First, it is critical that international businesses understand the influence of exchange rates on the profitability of trade and investment deals. Adverse changes in exchange rates can make apparently profitable deals unprofitable. As noted, the risk introduced into international business transactions by changes in exchange rates is referred to as foreign exchange risk. Foreign exchange risk is usually divided into three main categories: transaction exposure, translation exposure, and economic exposure.

TRANSACTION EXPOSURE

Transaction exposure is the extent to which fluctuations in foreign exchange values affect the income from individual transactions. Such exposure includes obligations for the purchase or sale of goods and services at previously agreed prices and the borrowing or lending of funds in foreign currencies. For example, suppose in 2001 an American airline agreed to purchase 10 Airbus 330 aircraft for €120 million each for a total price of €1.20 billion, with delivery scheduled for 2005 and payment due then. When the contract was signed in 2001 the dollar/euro exchange rate stood at $1 = €1.10 so the American airline anticipates paying $1 billion for the 10 aircraft when they are delivered (€1.2 billion/1.1 = $1.09 billion). However, imagine that the value of the dollar depreciates against the euro over the intervening period, so that $1 only buys €0.80 in 2005 when payment is due ($1 = €0.80). Now the total cost in U.S. dollars is $1.5 billion (€1.2 billion/0.80 = $1.5 billion), an increase of $0.41 billion! The transaction exposure here is $0.41 billion, which is the money lost due to an adverse movement in exchange rates between the time when the deal was signed and when the aircraft were paid for.

TRANSLATION EXPOSURE

Translation exposure is the impact of currency exchange rate changes on the reported financial statements of a company. Translation exposure is concerned with the present measurement of past events. The resulting accounting gains or losses are said to be unrealized—they are "paper" gains and losses—but they are still important. Consider a U.S. firm with a subsidiary in Mexico. If the value of the Mexican peso depreciates significantly against the dollar, the dollar value of the Mexican subsidiary's equity would be substantially reduced. In turn, this would reduce the total dollar value of the firm's equity reported in its consolidated balance sheet. This reduced equity would raise the apparent leverage of the firm (its debt ratio), which could increase the firm's cost of borrowing and potentially limit its access to the capital market. Similarly, if the value of the euro depreciates rapidly against that of the dollar over a year, the dollar value of the euro profit made by an American firm's European subsidiary would decline, resulting in negative translation exposure. In fact, many U.S. firms suffered from significant negative translation exposure in Europe during 2000, precisely because the euro did depreciate rapidly against the dollar. In 2002–2004, the euro rose in value against the dollar. This positive translation exposure boosted the dollar profits of American multinationals with significant operations in Europe.

ECONOMIC EXPOSURE

Economic exposure is the extent to which a firm's future international earning power is affected by changes in exchange rates. Economic exposure is concerned with the long-run effect of changes in exchange rates on future prices, sales, and costs. This is distinct from transaction exposure, which is concerned with the effect of exchange rate changes on individual transactions, most of which are short-term affairs that will be executed within a few weeks or months. Consider the effect of wide swings in the value of the dollar on many U.S. firms' international competitiveness. The rapid rise in the value of the dollar on the foreign exchange market in the 1990s hurt the price competitiveness of many U.S. producers in world markets. U.S. manufacturers that relied heavily on exports (such as Caterpillar) saw their export volume and world market share decline. The reverse phenomenon occurred in 2000–2006, when the dollar declined against most major currencies. The fall in the value of the dollar helped increase the price competitiveness of U.S. manufacturers in world markets.

REDUCING TRANSLATION AND TRANSACTION EXPOSURE

A number of tactics can help firms minimize their transaction and translation exposure. These tactics primarily protect short-term cash flows from adverse changes in exchange rates. We have already discussed two of these tactics at length in the chapter, entering into forward exchange rate contracts and buying swaps. In addition to buying forward and using swaps, firms can minimize their foreign exchange exposure through leading and lagging payables and receivables—that is, paying suppliers and collecting payment from customers early or late depending on expected exchange rate movements. A **lead strategy** involves attempting to collect foreign currency receivables (payments from customers) early when a foreign currency is expected to depreciate and paying foreign currency payables (to suppliers) before they are due when a currency is expected to appreciate. A **lag strategy** involves delaying collection of foreign currency receivables if that currency is expected to appreciate and delaying payables if the currency is expected to depreciate. Leading and lagging involve accelerating payments from weak-currency to strong-currency countries and delaying inflows from strong-currency to weak-currency countries.

Lead and lag strategies can be difficult to implement, however. The firm must be in a position to exercise some control over payment terms. Firms do not always have this kind of bargaining power, particularly when they are dealing with important customers who are in a position to dictate payment terms. Also, because lead and lag strategies can put pressure on a weak currency, many governments limit leads and lags. For example, some countries set 180 days as a limit for receiving payments for exports or making payments for imports.

REDUCING ECONOMIC EXPOSURE

Reducing economic exposure requires strategic choices that go beyond the realm of financial management. The key to reducing economic exposure is to distribute the firm's productive assets to various locations so the firm's long-term financial well-being is not severely affected by adverse changes in exchange rates. This is a strategy that firms both large and small sometimes pursue. For example, fearing that the euro will continue to strengthen against the U.S. dollar, some European firms who do significant business in the United States have set up local production facilities in that market to ensure that a rising euro does not put them at a competitive disadvantage relative to their local rivals. Similarly, Toyota has production plants distributed around the world in part to make sure that a rising yen does not price Toyota cars out of local markets. The next Management Focus feature discusses how two German firms tried to reduce economic exposure.

OTHER STEPS FOR MANAGING FOREIGN EXCHANGE RISK

The firm needs to develop a mechanism for ensuring that it maintains an appropriate mix of tactics and strategies for minimizing its foreign exchange exposure. Although there is no universal agreement about the components of this mechanism, a number of common themes stand out.[31] First, central control of exposure is needed to protect resources efficiently and ensure that each subunit adopts the correct mix of tactics and strategies. Many companies have set up in-house foreign exchange centers. Although such centers may not be able to execute all foreign exchange deals—particularly in large, complex multinationals where myriad transactions may be pursued simultaneously—they should at least set guidelines for the firm's subsidiaries to follow.

Second, firms should distinguish between, on one hand, transaction and translation exposure and, on the other, economic exposure. Many companies seem to focus on

MANAGEMENT FOCUS

Dealing with the Rising Euro

Udo Pfeiffer, the CEO of SMS Elotherm, a German manufacturer of machine tools to engineer crankshafts for cars, signed a deal in late November 2004 to supply the U.S. operations of DaimlerChrysler with $1.5 million worth of machines. The machines would be manufactured in Germany and exported to the United States. When the deal was signed, Pfeiffer calculated that at the agreed price, the machines would yield a profit of €30,000 each. Within three days that profit had declined by €8,000! The dollar had slid precipitously against the euro. SMS would be paid in dollars by DaimlerChrysler, but when translated back into euros, the price had declined. Since the company's costs were in euros, the declining revenues when expressed in euros were squeezing profit margins.

With the exchange rate standing at €1 = $1.33 in early December 2004, Pfeiffer was deeply worried. He knew that if the dollar declined further to around €1 = $1.50, SMS would be losing money on its sales to America. He could try to raise the dollar price of his products to compensate for the fall in the value of the dollar, but he knew that was unlikely to work. The market for machine tools was very competitive, and manufacturers were constantly pressuring machine tool companies to lower prices, not raise them.

Another small German supplier to U.S. automobile companies, Keiper, was faring somewhat better. In 2001 Keiper, which manufactures metal frames for automobile seats, opened a plant in London, Ontario, to supply the U.S. operations of DaimlerChrysler. At the time the investment was made, the exchange rate was €1 = $1. Management at Keiper had agonized over whether the investment made sense. Some in the company felt that it was better to continue exporting from Germany. Others argued that Keiper would benefit from being close to a major customer. Now with the euro appreciating every day, it looked like a smart move. Keiper had a real hedge against the rising value of the euro. But the advantages of being based in Canada were tempered by two things; first, the U.S. dollar had also depreciated against the Canadian dollar, although not by as much as its depreciation against the euro. Second, Keiper was still importing parts from Germany, and the euro had also appreciated against the Canadian dollar, raising the costs at Keiper's Ontario plant.[30]

reducing their transaction and translation exposure and pay scant attention to economic exposure, which may have more profound long-term implications.[32] Firms need to develop strategies for dealing with economic exposure. For example, Black & Decker, the maker of power tools, has a strategy for actively managing its economic risk. The key to Black & Decker's strategy is flexible sourcing. In response to foreign exchange movements, Black & Decker can move production from one location to another to offer the most competitive pricing. Black & Decker manufactures in more than a dozen locations around the world—in Europe, Australia, Brazil, Mexico, and Japan. More than 50 percent of the company's productive assets are based outside North America. Although each of Black & Decker's factories focuses on one or two products to achieve economies of scale, there is considerable overlap. On average, the company runs its factories at no more than 80 percent capacity, so most are able to switch rapidly from producing one product to producing another or to add a product. This allows a factory's production to be changed in response to foreign exchange movements. For example, if the dollar depreciates against other currencies, the amount of imports into the United States from overseas subsidiaries can be reduced and the amount of exports from U.S. subsidiaries to other locations can be increased.[33]

Third, the need to forecast future exchange rate movements cannot be overstated, though, as we saw earlier in the chapter, this is a tricky business. No model comes close to perfectly predicting future movements in foreign exchange rates. The best that can be said is that in the short run, forward exchange rates provide the best predictors of exchange rate movements, and in the long run, fundamental economic factors—particularly relative inflation rates—should be watched because they influence exchange rate movements. Some firms attempt to forecast exchange rate movements in-house; others rely on outside forecasters. However, all such forecasts are imperfect attempts to predict the future.

Fourth, firms need to establish good reporting systems so the central finance function (or in-house foreign exchange center) can regularly monitor the firm's exposure positions. Such reporting systems should enable the firm to identify any exposed accounts, the exposed position by currency of each account, and the time periods covered.

Finally, on the basis of the information it receives from exchange rate forecasts and its own regular reporting systems, the firm should produce monthly foreign exchange exposure reports. These reports should identify how cash flows and balance sheet elements might be affected by forecasted changes in exchange rates. The reports can then be used by management as a basis for adopting tactics and strategies to hedge against undue foreign exchange risks.

Surprisingly, some of the largest and most sophisticated firms don't take such precautionary steps, exposing themselves to very large foreign exchange risks. Thus as we have seen in this chapter, Volkswagen suffered significant losses during the early 2000s due to a failure to hedge its foreign exchange exposure.

CHAPTER SUMMARY

This chapter explained how the foreign exchange market works, examined the forces that determine exchange rates, and then discussed the implications of these factors for international business. Given that changes in exchange rates can dramatically alter the profitability of foreign trade and investment deals, this is an area of major interest to international business. The chapter made the following points:

1. One function of the foreign exchange market is to convert the currency of one country into the currency of another. A second function of the foreign exchange market is to provide insurance against foreign exchange risk.

2. The spot exchange rate is the exchange rate at which a dealer converts one currency into another currency on a particular day.

3. Foreign exchange risk can be reduced by using forward exchange rates. A forward exchange rate is an exchange rate governing future transactions. Foreign exchange risk can also be reduced by engaging in currency swaps. A swap is the simultaneous purchase and sale of a given amount of foreign exchange for two different value dates.

4. The law of one price holds that in competitive markets free of transportation costs and barriers to trade, identical products sold in different countries must sell for the same price when their price is expressed in the same currency.

5. Purchasing power parity (PPP) theory states that the price of a basket of particular goods should be roughly equivalent in each country. PPP theory predicts that the exchange rate will change if relative prices change.

6. The rate of change in countries' relative prices depends on their relative inflation rates. A country's inflation rate seems to be a function of the growth in its money supply.

7. The PPP theory of exchange rate changes yields relatively accurate predictions of long-term trends in exchange rates, but not of short-term movements. The failure of PPP theory to predict exchange rate changes more accurately may be due to transportation costs, barriers to trade and investment, and the impact of psychological factors such as bandwagon effects on market movements and short-run exchange rates.

8. Interest rates reflect expectations about inflation. In countries where inflation is expected to be high, interest rates also will be high.

9. The International Fisher Effect states that for any two countries, the spot exchange rate should change in an equal amount but in the opposite direction to the difference in nominal interest rates.

10. The most common approach to exchange rate forecasting is fundamental analysis, which relies on variables such as money supply growth, inflation rates, nominal interest rates, and

balance-of-payments positions to predict future changes in exchange rates.

11. In many countries, government policy restricts the ability of residents and nonresidents to convert local currency into a foreign currency. A government restricts the convertibility of its currency to protect the country's foreign exchange reserves and to halt any capital flight.

12. A policy of nonconvertibility, which prohibits residents and nonresidents from exchanging local currency for foreign currency, is problematic for international business. Nonconvertibility makes it very difficult to engage in international trade and investment in the country. One way of coping with the nonconvertibility problem is to engage in countertrade—to trade goods and services for other goods and services.

13. The three types of exposure to foreign exchange risk are transaction exposure, translation exposure, and economic exposure.

14. Tactics that insure against transaction and translation exposure include buying forward, using currency swaps, leading and lagging payables and receivables, manipulating transfer prices, using local debt financing, accelerating dividend payments, and adjusting capital budgeting to reflect foreign exchange exposure.

15. Reducing a firm's economic exposure requires strategic choices about how the firm's productive assets are distributed around the globe.

16. To manage foreign exchange exposure effectively, the firm must exercise centralized oversight over its foreign exchange hedging activities, recognize the difference between transaction exposure and economic exposure, forecast future exchange rate movements, establish good reporting systems within the firm to monitor exposure positions, and produce regular foreign exchange exposure reports that can be used as a basis for action.

Critical Thinking and Discussion Questions

1. The interest rate on South Korean government securities with one-year maturity is 4 percent, and the expected inflation rate for the coming year is 2 percent. The interest rate on U.S. government securities with one-year maturity is 7 percent, and the expected rate of inflation is 5 percent. The current spot exchange rate for Korean won is $1 = W1,200. Forecast the spot exchange rate one year from today. Explain the logic of your answer.

2. Two countries, Great Britain and the United States, produce just one good: beef. Suppose the price of beef in the United States is $2.80 per pound and in Britain it is £3.70 per pound.
   a. According to PPP theory, what should the dollar/pound spot exchange rate be?
   b. Suppose the price of beef is expected to rise to $3.10 in the United States and to £4.65 in Britain. What should the one-year forward dollar/pound exchange rate be?
   c. Given your answers to parts a and b, and given that the current interest rate in the United States is 10 percent, what would you expect the current interest rate to be in Britain?

3. Reread the Management Focus feature on Volkswagen in this chapter; then answer the following questions:
   a. Why do you think management at Volkswagen decided to hedge only 30 percent

of the company's foreign currency exposure in 2003? What would have happened if they had hedged 70 percent of their exposure?
   b. Why do you think the value of the U.S. dollar declined against that of the euro in 2003?
   c. Apart from hedging through the foreign exchange market, what else can Volkswagen do to reduce its exposure to future declines in the value of the U.S. dollar against the euro?

4. You manufacture wine goblets. In mid-June you receive an order for 10,000 goblets from Japan. Payment of ¥400,000 is due in mid-December. You expect the yen to rise from its present rate of $1 = ¥130 to $1 = ¥100 by December. You can borrow yen at 6 percent a year. What should you do?

5. You are the CFO of a U.S. firm whose wholly owned subsidiary in Mexico manufactures component parts for your U.S. assembly operations. The subsidiary has been financed by bank borrowings in the United States. One of your analysts told you that the Mexican peso is expected to depreciate by 30 percent against the dollar on the foreign exchange markets over the next year. What actions, if any, should you take?

Research Task

Use the globalEDGE™ site to complete the following exercises:

1. One component of learning about another country or region is to understand the relationship of its currency with others on the world currency market. As such, you are assigned the duty of ensuring the availability of 100,000 yen for a payment scheduled for next month. Considering that your company possesses only U.S. dollars, identify the spot and forward exchange rates. What are the factors that influence your decision to use the spot or forward exchange rate? Which one would you choose? How many dollars must you spend to acquire the amount of yen required?

2. Sometimes, analysts use the price of specific products across locations to compare currency valuation and purchasing power. In fact, the Big Mac Index compares the purchasing-power parity of many countries based on the price of a Big Mac. Locate the latest edition of this index that is accessible. Identify the five countries (and the currencies) with the lowest purchasing-power parity according to this classification. Which currencies, if any, are overvalued?

CLOSING CASE

The Curse of the Strong Dollar at STMicro

Europe's STMicro is the world's sixth-largest manufacturer of semiconductor chips, with sales of nearly $9 billion. The company makes chips for mobile phones, printers, and cars, among other things. It counts Nokia, the world's largest maker of wireless handsets, among its customers. Formed in 1987 from a merger between an Italian firm and a French firm, the majority of STMicro's operations have long been in Western Europe. During the early 2000s, when the dollar was strong against the euro, the currency adopted by 12 member states of the European Union, this location worked in STMicro's favor. Some 70 percent of the company's costs were denominated in Europe while semiconductors, like oil, were priced in U.S. dollars. The combination of a weak euro and a strong dollar translated into robust profits for STMicro.

However, in 2003 the euro began to rise against the dollar, rapidly shifting the profit calculus against STMicro. The euro, which traded as low as €1 = $0.83 in October 2000, had reached parity of €1 = $1.00 in late 2002. Few analysts predicted a rapid rise in the value of the euro against the dollar during 2003. As so often happens in the foreign exchange markets, the experts were wrong; by late 2003 the exchange rate stood at €1 = $1.20. The rise continued through 2004, with the exchange rate peaking at €1 = $1.32 in early 2005. It fell back to €1 = $1.20 in early 2006 before rising back to €1 = $1.30 by late 2006.

One cause of the rise in the value of the euro against the dollar was record U.S. foreign trade deficits in 2002–2006. The U.S. economy grew rapidly during 2003–2006, sucking in imports from foreign nations while generating anemic export growth. The result was a flow of dollars out of the United States into the hands of foreigners. Historically, foreigners had reinvested those dollars in the United States, and the return flow had kept the dollar strong despite persistent trade deficits. This didn't happen to the same extent in 2003–2006. Instead, many foreigners sold the dollars they received for other currencies, such as the euro, Japanese yen, or British pound. They did this because they had become increasingly pessimistic about the future value of the dollar and were reducing their dollar holdings accordingly. Their pessimism was itself a function of two factors. First, U.S. government officials stated that they would prefer a weaker dollar in order to increase the competitiveness of U.S. companies in the global marketplace (the theory being that a falling dollar would make U.S. exports more competitive). With the government talking the dollar down, many foreigners decided to reduce their dollar holdings. Second, the U.S. government ran record budget deficits in 2003–2006, and these were projected to remain high for some time. Looking at the situation, some foreigners concluded that the U.S. government might be forced to finance its spending by expanding the supply of dollars (i.e., by printing money), which would lead to inflation and reduce the value of the dollar even further. Thus, they sold dollars and purchased currencies thought to be less inflation prone.

For STMicro, the results of these macroeconomic events were serious. The company does very little currency hedging, so as the dollar fell, the euro value of STMicro's sales compressed, while costs, being largely dominated in euros, stayed high. Although strong global chip sales helped to offset the fall in the value of the dollar, STMicro's profits still slumped in 2004 and 2005. In response, STMicro's CEO, Carlo Bozotti, pledged to take some $500 million out of the company's cost structure, primarily by shutting down some high-cost European operations, cutting 3,000 jobs, and moving production to Asia where it planned to add 1,500 jobs. Mr. Bozotti described the strategy as one of "real hedging" that would allow STMicro to move production from Europe to Asia, and back if necessary, in order to deal with the consequences of shifts in exchange rates against the dollar.[34]

Case Discussion Questions

1. In retrospect, could the fall in the value of the dollar against the Euro have been predicted in 2003?

2. What was the fundamental reason for the decline in the value of the dollar against the euro in 2003–2006? To what extent is the decline in the value of the dollar consistent with the theories of exchange rate determination discussed in this chapter?

3. Why do you think that STMicro did very little currency hedging? Was this wise?

4. What strategy is STMicro now adopting to deal with possible future fluctuations in exchange rates? Is this a smart strategy?

Notes

1. Evan Ramstad, "Won's Rise Hurts Korean Car Makers," *The Wall Street Journal*, December 13, 2006, p. B3.

2. For a good general introduction to the foreign exchange market, see R. Weisweiller, *How the Foreign Exchange Market Works* (New York: New York Institute of Finance, 1990). A detailed description of the economics of foreign exchange markets can be found in P. R. Krugman and M. Obstfeld, *International Economics: Theory and Policy* (New York: HarperCollins, 1994).

3. Sources: M. Landler, "As Exchange Rates Swing, Car Makers Try to Duck," *The New York Times*, January 17, 2004, pp. B1, B4; N. Boudette, "Volkswagen Posts 95% Drop in Net," *The Wall Street Journal*, February 19, 2004, p. A3; "Volkswagen's Financial Mechanic," *Corporate Finance*, June 2003, p. 1.

4. Bank for International Settlements, *Tri-annual Central Bank Survey of Foreign Exchange and Derivatives Market Activity, April 2004* (Basle, Switzerland: BIS, March 2005).

5. Ibid.

6. Ibid.

7. M. Dickson, "Capital Gain: How London Is Thriving as it Takes on the Global Competition," *Financial Times*, March 27, 2006, p. 11.

8. For a comprehensive review see M. Taylor, "The Economics of Exchange Rates," *Journal of Economic Literature* 33 (1995), pp. 13–47.

9. Krugman and Obstfeld, *International Economics: Theory and Policy*.

10. M. Friedman, *Studies in the Quantity Theory of Money* (Chicago: University of Chicago Press, 1956). For an accessible explanation, see M. Friedman and R. Friedman, *Free to Choose* (London: Penguin Books, 1979), chap. 9.

11. Juan-Antino Morales, "Inflation Stabilization in Bolivia," in *Inflation Stabilization: The Experience of Israel, Argentina, Brazil, Bolivia, and Mexico*, ed. Michael Bruno et al. (Cambridge, MA: MIT Press, 1988), and *The Economist, World Book of Vital Statistics* (New York: Random House, 1990).

12. For reviews and recent articles see H. J. Edison, J. E. Gagnon, and W. R. Melick, "Understanding the Empirical Literature on Purchasing Power Parity," *Journal of International Money and Finance* 16 (February 1997), pp. 1–18; J. R. Edison, "Multi-Country Evidence on the Behavior of Purchasing Power Parity under the Current Float," *Journal of International Money and Finance* 16 (February 1997), pp. 19–36; K. Rogoff, "The Purchasing Power Parity Puzzle," *Journal of Economic Literature* 34 (1996), pp. 647–68; D. R. Rapach and M. E. Wohar, "Testing the Monetary Model of Exchange Rate Determination: New Evidence from a Century of Data," *Journal of International Economics*, December 2002, pp. 359–85; and M. P. Taylor, "Purchasing Power Parity," *Review of International Economics*, August 2003, pp. 436–456.

13. M. Obstfeld and K. Rogoff, "The Six Major Puzzles in International Economics," National Bureau of Economic Research Working Paper No. 7777, July 2000.

14. Ibid.

15. See M. Devereux and C. Engel, "Monetary Policy in the Open Economy Revisited: Price Setting and Exchange Rate Flexibility," National Bureau of Economic Research Working Paper No. 7665, April 2000. See also P. Krugman, "Pricing to Market When the Exchange Rate Changes," in *Real Financial Economics*, ed. S. Arndt and J. Richardson (Cambridge, MA: MIT Press, 1987).

16. For a summary of the evidence, see the survey by Taylor, "The Economics of Exchange Rates."

17. R. E. Cumby and M. Obstfeld, "A Note on Exchange Rate Expectations and Nominal Interest Differentials: A Test of the Fisher Hypothesis," *Journal of Finance*, June 1981, pp. 697–703; and L. Coppock and M. Poitras, "Evaluating the Fisher Effect in Long Term Cross Country Averages," *International Review of Economics and Finance* 9 (2000), pp. 181–203.

18. Taylor, "The Economics of Exchange Rates." See also R. K. Lyons, *The Microstructure Approach to Exchange Rates* (Cambridge, MA: MIT Press, 2002).

19. See H. L. Allen and M. P. Taylor, "Charts, Noise, and Fundamentals in the Foreign Exchange Market," *Economic Journal* 100 (1990), pp. 49–59, and T. Ito, "Foreign Exchange Rate Expectations: Micro Survey Data," *American Economic Review* 80 (1990), pp. 434–49.

20. Sources: J. Burton and G. Baker, "The Country That Invested Its Way into Trouble," *Financial Times*, January 15, 1998, p. 8; J. Burton, "South Korea's Credit Rating Is Lowered," *Financial Times*, October 25, 1997, p. 3; J. Burton, "Currency Losses Hit Samsung Electronics," *Financial Times*, March 20, 1998, p. 24; and "Korean Firms' Foreign Exchange Losses Exceed US $15 Billion," *Business Korea*, February 1998, p. 55.

21. For example, see E. Fama, "Forward Rates as Predictors of Future Spot Rates," *Journal of Financial Economics*, October 1976, pp. 361–77.

22. L. Kilian and M. P. Taylor, "Why Is It So Difficult to Beat the Random Walk Forecast of Exchange Rates?" *Journal of International Economics* 20 (May 2003), pp. 85–103, and R. M. Levich, "The Efficiency of Markets for Foreign Exchange," in *International Finance*, ed. G. D. Gay and R. W. Kold (Richmond, VA: Robert F. Dane, Inc., 1983).

23. J. Williamson, *The Exchange Rate System* (Washington, DC: Institute for International Economics, 1983), and R. H. Clarida, L. Sarno, M. P. Taylor, and G. Valente, "The Out of Sample Success of Term Structure Models as Exchange Rate Predictors," *Journal of International Economics* 60 (May 2003), pp. 61–84.

24. Kilian and Taylor, "Why Is It So Difficult to Beat the Random Walk Forecast of Exchange Rates?"

25. Rogoff, "The Purchasing Power Parity Puzzle."

26. C. Engel and J. D. Hamilton, "Long Swings in the Dollar: Are They in the Data and Do Markets Know It?" *American Economic Review*, September 1990, pp. 689–713.

27. J. R. Carter and J. Gagne, "The Do's and Don'ts of International Countertrade," *Sloan Management Review*, Spring 1988, pp. 31–37.

28. "Where There Is a Will," *Trade Finance*, October 2003, pp. 1–2.

29. D. S. Levine, "Got a Spare Destroyer Lying Around?" *World Trade* 10 (June 1997), pp. 34–35, and Dan West, "Countertrade," *Business Credit*, April 2001, pp. 64–67.

30. Sources: Adapted from M. Landler, "Dollar's Fall Drains Profit of European Small Business," *The New York Times*, December 2, 2004, p. C1

31. For details on how various firms manage their foreign exchange exposure, see the articles in the special foreign exchange issue of *Business International Money Report*, December 18, 1989, pp. 401–12.

32. Ibid.

33. S. Arterian, "How Black & Decker Defines Exposure," *Business International Money Report*, December 18, 1989, pp. 404, 405, 409.

34. Sources: M. Pesola, "STMicro Unveils More Job Cuts in Chip Making," *Financial Times*, May 17, 2005, p. 22; B. Lagrotteria and C. Bryan-Low, "Dealing with the Dollar: Strong Euro Bedevils EU Firms," *The Wall Street Journal*, June 21, 2005, p. A14; H. Schoemaker, "STMicro Profit Slips, but 1st Quarter Looks Upbeat," *The Wall Street Journal*, January 26, 2006, p. B5.

Argentina's Monetary Crisis

In the 1990s Argentina was the darling of the international financial community. The country had fixed the exchange rate for the Argentinean peso to the U.S. dollar at $1 = 1 peso. Maintaining the exchange rate had required Argentina to adopt strict anti-inflationary policies, which had succeeded in bringing down Argentina's historically high inflation rate and stimulated economic growth. By 2001, however, the economy was running into trouble. Global economic growth slumped and demand for many of the commodities that Argentina exported fell. Argentina's large neighbor and main trading partner, Brazil, was grappling with a financial crisis of its own and had devalued its currency against the dollar, and thus the peso, effectively pricing many Argentinean goods out of its market. To compound matters, the dollar had appreciated against most major currencies, taking the peso up with it and making Argentinean goods more expensive in other international markets.

Starting in 1999, the Argentinean economy entered into a tailspin that eventually took unemployment up to 25 percent by 2002. Anticipating that the country would have to devalue the peso against the dollar, corporations and individuals started to pull money out of pesos, placing their funds in dollar accounts. As people sold pesos, the Argentinean government used its foreign exchange reserves to buy them back in an effort to maintain the exchange rate at $1 = 1 peso. The government quickly ran down its reserves, and in 2000 the country negotiated a loan from the International Monetary Fund (IMF) to prop up its currency. In return for the loan, which ultimately reached $15 billion, the Argentinean government agreed to adopt a financial

The International Monetary System

LEARNING OBJECTIVES

After you have read this chapter you should:

LO¹ Be familiar with the historical development of the modern global monetary system.

LO² Discuss the role played by the world bank and the IMF in the international monetary system.

LO³ Be familiar with the differences between a fixed and floating exchange rate system.

LO⁴ Know what exchange rate regimes are used in the world today and why countries adopt different exchange rate regimes.

LO⁵ Understand the debate surrounding the role of the IMF in the management of financial crises.

LO⁶ Appreciate the implications of the global monetary system for currency management and business strategy.

austerity program to balance its budget. However, conditions in the country continued to deteriorate, in no small part, some critics claimed, because the strict IMF policies made an already bad recession worse. By late 2001, with government tax revenues plunging as the economy contracted, the Argentinean government defaulted on its debt repayments, effectively rendering $80 billion of government-issued bonds worthless. This created a massive crisis of confidence, which put further pressure on the peso. Throughout 2001 the Argentinean government had been trying to support the value of the peso with the help of the loan from the International Monetary Fund, but it was becoming ever more difficult, and the debt default was the final nail in the coffin. In early 2002, the government bowed to the inevitable and decoupled the peso from the dollar, allowing it to float freely. It immediately fell to $1 = 3.5$ pesos.

The fall in the value of the peso helped revive Argentinean commodity exports, which were now much cheaper for foreign buyers. A rebound in global economic growth after 2001 also helped, as did an economic recovery in neighboring Brazil. By 2003, the economy was once more on a growth path and unemployment was falling. In 2005 Argentina repaid its entire debt to the IMF. Commenting on the debt repayment, Argentinean President Nestor Kirchner criticized the IMF for promoting policies that "provoked poverty and pain on the Argentine people." While that view was popular in Argentina, some outside observers worried that freed from IMF constraints, the Argentinean economy would return to its historic norm of a loose monetary policy and high inflation.[1]

Introduction

What happened in Argentina in the early 2000s goes to the heart of the subject matter covered in this chapter. Here we look at the international monetary system and its role in determining exchange rates. The **international monetary system** refers to the institutional arrangements that govern exchange rates. In Chapter 9 we assumed the foreign exchange market was the primary institution for determining exchange rates and the impersonal market forces of demand and supply determined the relative value of any two currencies (i.e., their exchange rate). Furthermore, we explained that the demand and supply of currencies is influenced by their respective countries' relative inflation rates and interest rates. When the foreign exchange market determines the relative value of a currency, we say that the country is adhering to a **floating exchange rate** regime. The world's four major trading currencies—the U.S. dollar, the European Union's euro, the Japanese yen, and the British pound—are all free to float against each other. Thus, their exchange rates are determined by market forces and fluctuate against each other day to day, if not minute to minute. However, the exchange rates of many currencies are not determined by the free play of market forces; some governments adopt other institutional arrangements.

Many of the world's developing nations peg their currencies, primarily to the dollar or the euro. A **pegged exchange rate** means the value of the currency is fixed relative to a reference currency, such as the U.S. dollar, and then the exchange rate between that currency and other currencies is determined by the reference currency exchange rate. Argentina, for example, pegged its exchange rate to the dollar throughout the 1990s, before allowing it to float in 2002 (as outlined at the beginning of the chapter).

Other countries, while not adopting a formal pegged rate, try to hold the value of their currency within some range against an important reference currency, such as the U.S. dollar, or a "basket" of currencies. This is often referred to as a **dirty float.** It is a float because in theory, the value of the currency is determined by market forces, but it is a *dirty float* (as opposed to a clean float) because the central bank of a country will intervene in the foreign exchange market to try to maintain the value of its currency if it depreciates too rapidly against an important reference currency. The Chinese have adopted this policy since July 2005. The value of the Chinese currency, the yuan, has been linked to a basket of other currencies, including the dollar, yen, and euro, and it is allowed to vary in value against individual currencies, but only within tight limits.

Still other countries have operated with a **fixed exchange rate,** in which the values of a set of currencies are fixed against each other at some mutually agreed-on exchange rate. Before the introduction of the euro in 2000, several member states of the European Union operated with fixed exchange rates within the context of the **European Monetary System (EMS).** For a quarter of a century after World War II, the world's major industrial nations participated in a fixed exchange rate system. Although this system collapsed in 1973, some still argue that the world should attempt to reestablish it.

In this chapter, we will explain how the international monetary system works and point out its implications for international business. To understand how the system works, we must review its evolution. We will begin with a discussion of the gold standard and its breakup during the 1930s. Then we will discuss the 1944 Bretton Woods conference. This established the basic framework for the post–World War II international monetary system. The Bretton Woods system called for fixed exchange rates against the U.S. dollar. Under this fixed exchange rate system, the value of most currencies in terms of U.S. dollars was fixed for long periods and allowed to change only under a specific set of circumstances. The Bretton Woods conference also created two major international institutions that play a role in the international monetary system—the International Monetary Fund (IMF) and the World Bank. The IMF was given the task of maintaining order in the international monetary system; the World Bank's role was to promote development.

Today, both these institutions continue to play major roles in the world economy and in the international monetary system. In 1997 and 1998, for example, the IMF helped several Asian countries deal with the dramatic decline in the value of their currencies that occurred during the Asian financial crisis that started in 1997. The IMF was also actively involved in helping Argentina manage its financial crisis in 2001. By 2005, the IMF had programs in 59 countries, the majority in the developing world, and had some $71 billion in loans to nations.[2] However, there has been a vigorous debate about the role of the IMF and to a lesser extent the World Bank and the appropriateness of their policies for many developing nations. Several prominent critics claim that in some cases, IMF policies make things worse, not better (this was argued to be the case in Argentina, where very restrictive policies may have worsened the crisis). The debate over the role of the IMF took on new urgency given the institution's extensive involvement in the economies of developing countries during the late 1990s and early 2000s. Accordingly, we shall discuss the issue in some depth.

The Bretton Woods system of fixed exchange rates collapsed in 1973. Since then, the world has operated with a mixed system in which some currencies are allowed to float freely, but many are either managed by government intervention or pegged to another currency. We will explain the reasons for the failure of the Bretton Woods system as well as the nature of the present system. We will also discuss how pegged exchange rate systems work. More than three decades after the breakdown of the Bretton Woods system, the debate continues over what kind of exchange rate regime is best for the world. Some economists advocate a system in which major currencies are allowed to float against each other. Others argue for a return to a fixed exchange rate regime similar to the one established at Bretton Woods. This debate is intense and important, and we will examine the arguments of both sides.

Finally, we will discuss the implications of these exchange rate theories and practices for international business. We will see how the exchange rate policy a government adopts can have an important impact on the outlook for business operations in a given country. Pegging the value of the peso to the U.S. dollar, for example, turned out to have serious consequences for the competitiveness of Argentinean businesses. As the dollar appreciated on foreign exchange markets, so did the peso, effectively pricing many Argentinean goods out of world markets and contributing to an economic recession in that nation. If government exchange rate policies result in currency devaluation, exporters based in that country may benefit as their products become more price competitive in foreign markets. This too happened in Argentina after the 2002 devaluation. Alternatively, importers will suffer from an increase in the price of their products, which can trigger inflationary pressure in a nation. We will also look at how the IMF's policies can have an impact on the economic outlook for a country and, accordingly, on the costs and benefits of doing business in that country.

The Gold Standard

The gold standard had its origin in the use of gold coins as a medium of exchange, unit of account, and store of value—a practice that dates to ancient times. When international trade was limited in volume, payment for goods purchased from another country was typically made in gold or silver. However, as the volume of international trade expanded in the wake of the Industrial Revolution, a more convenient means of financing international trade was needed. Shipping large quantities of gold and silver around the world to finance international trade seemed impractical. The solution adopted was to arrange for payment in paper currency and for governments to agree to convert the paper currency into gold on demand at a fixed rate.

MECHANICS OF THE GOLD STANDARD

Pegging currencies to gold and guaranteeing convertibility is known as the **gold standard.** By 1880, most of the world's major trading nations, including Great Britain, Germany, Japan, and the United States, had adopted the gold standard. Given a common gold standard, the value of any currency in units of any other currency (the exchange rate) was easy to determine.

For example, under the gold standard, one U.S. dollar was defined as equivalent to 23.22 grains of "fine" (pure) gold. Thus, one could, in theory, demand that the U.S. government convert that one dollar into 23.22 grains of gold. Since there are 480 grains in an ounce, one ounce of gold cost $20.67 (480/23.22). The amount of a currency needed to purchase one ounce of gold was referred to as the **gold par value.** The British pound was valued at 113 grains of fine gold. In other words, one ounce of gold cost £4.25 (480/113). From the gold par values of pounds and dollars, we can calculate what the exchange rate was for converting pounds into dollars; it was £1 = $4.87 (i.e., $20.67/£4.25).

STRENGTH OF THE GOLD STANDARD

The great strength claimed for the gold standard was that it contained a powerful mechanism for achieving balance-of-trade equilibrium by all countries.[3] A country is said to be in **balance-of-trade equilibrium** when the income its residents earn from exports is equal to the money its residents pay to other countries for imports (the current account of its balance of payments is in balance). Suppose there are only two countries in the world, Japan and the United States. Imagine Japan's trade balance is in surplus because it exports more to the United States than it imports from the United States. Japanese exporters are paid in U.S. dollars, which they exchange for Japanese yen at a Japanese bank. The Japanese bank submits the dollars to the U.S. government and demands payment of gold in return. (This is a simplification of what would occur, but it will make our point.)

Under the gold standard, when Japan has a trade surplus, there will be a net flow of gold from the United States to Japan. These gold flows automatically reduce the U.S. money supply and swell Japan's money supply. As we saw in Chapter 9, there is a close connection between money supply growth and price inflation. An increase in money supply will raise prices in Japan, while a decrease in the U.S. money supply will push U.S. prices downward. The rise in the price of Japanese goods will decrease demand for these goods, while the fall in the price of U.S. goods will increase demand for these goods. Thus, Japan will start to buy more from the United States, and the United States will buy less from Japan, until a balance-of-trade equilibrium is achieved.

This adjustment mechanism seems so simple and attractive that even today, almost 70 years after the final collapse of the gold standard, some people believe the world should return to a gold standard.

THE PERIOD BETWEEN THE WARS: 1918–1939

The gold standard worked reasonably well from the 1870s until the start of World War I in 1914, when it was abandoned. During the war, several governments financed part of their massive military expenditures by printing money. This resulted in inflation, and by the war's end in 1918, price levels were higher everywhere. The United States returned to the gold standard in 1919, Great Britain in 1925, and France in 1928.

Great Britain returned to the gold standard by pegging the pound to gold at the prewar gold parity level of £4.25 per ounce, despite substantial inflation between 1914 and 1925. This priced British goods out of foreign markets, which pushed the country into a deep depression. When foreign holders of pounds lost confidence in Great Britain's commitment to maintaining its currency's value, they began converting their holdings of pounds into gold. The British government saw that it could not satisfy the demand for gold without seriously depleting its gold reserves, so it suspended convertibility in 1931.

The United States followed suit and left the gold standard in 1933 but returned to it in 1934, raising the dollar price of gold from $20.67 per ounce to $35 per ounce. Since more dollars were needed to buy an ounce of gold than before, the implication was that the dollar was worth less. This effectively amounted to a devaluation of the dollar relative to other currencies. Thus, before the devaluation, the pound/dollar exchange rate was £1 = $4.87, but after the devaluation it was £1 = $8.24. By reducing the price of U.S. exports and increasing the price of imports, the government was trying to create employment in the United States by boosting output (the U.S. government was basically using the exchange rate as an instrument of trade policy— something it now accuses China of doing). However, a number of other countries adopted a similar tactic, and in the cycle of competitive devaluations that soon emerged, no country could win.

The net result was the shattering of any remaining confidence in the system. With countries devaluing their currencies at will, one could no longer be certain how much gold a currency could buy. Instead of holding onto another country's currency, people often tried to change it into gold immediately, lest the country devalue its currency in the intervening period. This put pressure on the gold reserves of various countries, forcing them to suspend gold convertibility. By the start of World War II in 1939, the gold standard was dead.

The Bretton Woods System

In 1944, at the height of World War II, representatives from 44 countries met at Bretton Woods, New Hampshire, to design a new international monetary system. With the collapse of the gold standard and the Great Depression of the 1930s fresh in their minds, these statesmen were determined to build an enduring economic order that would facilitate postwar economic growth. There was consensus that fixed exchange rates were desirable. In addition, the conference participants wanted to avoid the senseless competitive devaluations of the 1930s, and they recognized that the gold standard would not ensure this. The major problem with the gold standard as previously constituted was that no multinational institution could stop countries from engaging in competitive devaluations.

The agreement reached at Bretton Woods established two multinational institutions—the International Monetary Fund (IMF) and the World Bank. The task of the IMF would be to maintain order in the international monetary system and that of the World Bank would be to promote general economic development. The Bretton Woods agreement also called for a system of fixed exchange rates that would be policed by the IMF. Under the agreement, all countries were to fix the value of their currency in terms of gold but were not required to exchange their currencies for gold. Only the dollar remained convertible into gold—at a price of $35 per ounce. Each country decided what it wanted its exchange rate to be vis-à-vis the dollar and then calculated the gold par value of the currency based on that selected dollar exchange rate. All participating countries agreed to try to maintain the value of their currencies within 1 percent of the par value by buying or selling currencies (or gold) as needed. For example, if foreign exchange dealers were selling more of a country's currency than demanded, that country's government would intervene in the foreign exchange markets, buying its currency in an attempt to increase demand and maintain its gold par value.

Another aspect of the Bretton Woods agreement was a commitment not to use devaluation as a weapon of competitive trade policy. However, if a currency became too weak to defend, a devaluation of up to 10 percent would be allowed without any formal approval by the IMF. Larger devaluations required IMF approval.

THE ROLE OF THE IMF

The IMF Articles of Agreement were heavily influenced by the worldwide financial collapse, competitive devaluations, trade wars, high unemployment, hyperinflation in Germany and elsewhere, and general economic disintegration that occurred between the two world wars. The aim of the Bretton Woods agreement, of which the IMF was the main custodian, was to try to avoid a repetition of that chaos through a combination of discipline and flexibility.

Discipline

A fixed exchange rate regime imposes discipline in two ways. First, the need to maintain a fixed exchange rate puts a brake on competitive devaluations and brings stability to the world trade environment. Second, a fixed exchange rate regime imposes monetary discipline on countries, thereby curtailing price inflation. For example, consider what would happen under a fixed exchange rate regime if Great Britain rapidly increased its money supply by printing pounds. As explained in Chapter 9, the increase in money supply would lead to price inflation. Given fixed exchange rates, inflation would make British goods uncompetitive in world markets, while the prices of imports would become more attractive in Great Britain. The result would be a widening trade deficit in Great Britain, with the country importing more than it exports. To correct this trade imbalance under a fixed exchange rate regime, Great Britain would be required to restrict the rate of growth in its money supply to bring price inflation back under control. Thus, fixed exchange rates are seen as a mechanism for controlling inflation and imposing economic discipline on countries.

Flexibility

Although monetary discipline was a central objective of the Bretton Woods agreement, it was recognized that a rigid policy of fixed exchange rates would be too inflexible. It would probably break down just as the gold standard had. In some cases, a country's attempts to reduce its money supply growth and correct a persistent balance-of-payments deficit could force the country into recession and create high unemployment. The architects of the Bretton Woods agreement wanted to avoid high unemployment, so they built limited flexibility into the system. Two major features of the IMF Articles of Agreement fostered this flexibility: IMF lending facilities and adjustable parities.

The IMF stood ready to lend foreign currencies to members to tide them over during short periods of balance-of-payments deficits, when a rapid tightening of monetary or fiscal policy would hurt domestic employment. A pool of gold and currencies contributed by IMF members provided the resources for these lending operations. A persistent balance-of-payments deficit can lead to a depletion of a country's reserves of foreign currency, forcing it to devalue its currency. By providing deficit-laden countries with short-term foreign currency loans, IMF funds would buy time for countries to bring down their inflation rates and reduce their balance-of-payments deficits. The belief was that such loans would reduce pressures for devaluation and allow for a more orderly and less painful adjustment.

Countries were to be allowed to borrow a limited amount from the IMF without adhering to any specific agreements. However, extensive drawings from IMF funds would require a country to agree to increasingly stringent IMF supervision of its macroeconomic policies. Heavy borrowers must agree to the IMF's monetary and fiscal conditions, which typically included IMF-mandated targets on domestic money supply growth, exchange rate policy, tax policy, government spending, and so on.

The system of adjustable parities allowed for the devaluation of a country's currency by more than 10 percent if the IMF agreed that a country's balance of payments was in "fundamental disequilibrium." The term *fundamental disequilibrium* was not defined in the IMF's Articles of Agreement, but it was intended to apply to countries that had suffered permanent adverse shifts in the demand for their products. Without devaluation, such a country would experience high unemployment and a persistent trade deficit until the domestic price level had fallen far enough to restore a balance-of-payments equilibrium. The belief was that devaluation could help sidestep a painful adjustment process in such circumstances.

THE ROLE OF THE WORLD BANK

The official name for the World Bank is the International Bank for Reconstruction and Development (IBRD). When the Bretton Woods participants established the World Bank, the need to reconstruct the war-torn economies of Europe was foremost in their minds. The bank's initial mission was to help finance the building of Europe's economy by providing low-interest loans. As it turned out, the World Bank was overshadowed in this role by the Marshall Plan, under which the United States lent money directly to European nations to help them rebuild. So the bank turned its attention to "development" and began lending money to Third World nations. In the 1950s, the bank concentrated on public-sector projects. Power stations, road building, and other transportation investments were much in favor. During the 1960s, the bank also began to lend heavily in support of agriculture, education, population control, and urban development.

The bank lends money under two schemes. Under the IBRD scheme, money is raised through bond sales in the international capital market. Borrowers pay what the bank calls a market rate of interest—the bank's cost of funds plus a margin for expenses. This "market" rate is lower than commercial banks' market rate. Under the IBRD scheme, the bank offers low-interest loans to risky customers whose credit rating is often poor, such as the governments of underdeveloped nations.

A second scheme is overseen by the International Development Association (IDA), an arm of the bank created in 1960. Resources to fund IDA loans are raised through subscriptions from wealthy members such as the United States, Japan, and Germany. IDA loans go only to the poorest countries. Borrowers have 50 years to repay at an interest rate of 1 percent a year. The world's poorest nations receive grants and no-interest loans.

The Collapse of the Fixed Exchange Rate System

The system of fixed exchange rates established at Bretton Woods worked well until the late 1960s, when it began to show signs of strain. The system finally collapsed in 1973, when it was replaced by a managed-float system. To understand why the fixed exchange rate system collapsed, one must appreciate the special role of the U.S. dollar. As the only currency that could be converted into gold, and as the currency that served as the reference point for all others, the dollar occupied a central place in the system. Any pressure on the dollar to devalue could wreak havoc with the system, and that is what occurred.

Most economists trace the breakup of the fixed exchange rate system to the U.S. macroeconomic policy package of 1965–1968.[4] To finance both the Vietnam conflict and his welfare programs, President Lyndon Johnson backed an increase in U.S. government spending that was not financed by an increase in taxes. Instead, it was financed by an increase in the money supply, which led to a rise in price inflation from less than 4 percent in 1966 to close to 9 percent by 1968. At the same time, the rise in government spending had stimulated the economy. With more money in their pockets, people spent more—particularly on imports—and the U.S. trade balance began to deteriorate. (The perceptive reader will note that there are parallels here with the situation prevailing in America in 2002–2005, when once again a government expanded spending to pay for a foreign war and financed that spending through monetary expansion—in essence, more government borrowing—that stimulated the economy and led to a surge in imports. Some observers worry that the implied expansion in the U.S. money supply may ultimately lead to acceleration in the inflation rate in the United States.)

The increase in inflation and the worsening of the U.S. foreign trade position gave rise to speculation in the foreign exchange market that the dollar would be devalued. Things came to a head in the spring of 1971 when U.S. trade figures showed that for the first time since 1945, the United States was importing more than it was exporting. This set off massive purchases of German deutsche marks in the foreign exchange market by speculators who guessed that the mark would be revalued against the dollar. On a single day, May 4, 1971, the Bundesbank (Germany's central bank) had to buy $1 billion to hold the dollar/deutsche mark exchange rate at its fixed exchange rate given the great demand for deutsche marks. On the morning of May 5, the Bundesbank purchased another $1 billion during the first hour of foreign exchange trading! At that point, the Bundesbank faced the inevitable and allowed its currency to float.

In the weeks following the decision to float the deutsche mark, the foreign exchange market became increasingly convinced that the dollar would have to be devalued. However, devaluation of the dollar was no easy matter. Under the Bretton Woods provisions, any other country could change its exchange rates against all currencies simply by fixing its dollar rate at a new level. But as the key currency in the system, the dollar could be devalued only if all countries agreed to simultaneously revalue against the dollar. Many countries did not want to revalue because it would make their products more expensive relative to U.S. products.

To force the issue, President Nixon announced in August 1971 that the dollar was no longer convertible into gold. He also announced that a new 10 percent tax on imports would remain in effect until U.S. trading partners agreed to revalue their currencies against the dollar. This brought the trading partners to the bargaining table, and in December 1971 an agreement was reached to devalue the dollar by about 8 percent against foreign currencies. The import tax was then removed.

The problem was not solved, however. The U.S. balance-of-payments position continued to deteriorate throughout 1972, while the nation's money supply continued to expand at an inflationary rate. Speculation continued to grow that the dollar was still overvalued and that a second devaluation would be necessary. In anticipation, foreign exchange dealers began converting dollars to deutsche marks and other currencies. After a massive wave of speculation in February 1972, which culminated with European central banks spending $3.6 billion on March 1 to try to prevent their currencies from appreciating against the dollar, the foreign exchange market was closed. When the foreign exchange market reopened March 19, the currencies of Japan and most European countries were floating against the dollar, although many developing countries continued to peg their currency to the dollar, and many do to this day. At that time, the switch to a floating system was viewed as a temporary response to unmanageable speculation in the foreign exchange market. But it is now more than 30 years since the Bretton Woods system of fixed exchange rates collapsed, and the temporary solution looks permanent.

The Bretton Woods system had an Achilles' heel: The system could not work if its key currency, the U.S. dollar, was under speculative attack. The Bretton Woods system could work only as long as the U.S. inflation rate remained low and the United States did not run a balance-of-payments deficit. Once these things occurred, the system soon became strained to the breaking point.

🌐 The Floating Exchange Rate Regime

The floating exchange rate regime that followed the collapse of the fixed exchange rate system was formalized in January 1976 when IMF members met in Jamaica and agreed to the rules for the international monetary system that are in place today.

THE JAMAICA AGREEMENT

The Jamaica meeting revised the IMF's Articles of Agreement to reflect the new reality of floating exchange rates. The main elements of the Jamaica agreement include the following:

- Floating rates were declared acceptable. IMF members were permitted to enter the foreign exchange market to even out "unwarranted" speculative fluctuations.
- Gold was abandoned as a reserve asset. The IMF returned its gold reserves to members at the current market price, placing the proceeds in a trust fund to help poor nations. IMF members were permitted to sell their own gold reserves at the market price.
- Total annual IMF quotas—the amount member countries contribute to the IMF—were increased to $41 billion. (Since then they have been increased to $311 billion while the membership of the IMF has been expanded to include 184 countries.) Non–oil-exporting, less developed countries were given greater access to IMF funds.

After Jamaica, the IMF continued its role of helping countries cope with macroeconomic and exchange rate problems, albeit within the context of a radically different exchange rate regime.

EXCHANGE RATES SINCE 1973

Since March 1973, exchange rates have become much more volatile and less predictable than they were between 1945 and 1973.[5] This volatility has been partly due to a number of unexpected shocks to the world monetary system:

- The oil crisis in 1971, when the Organization of Petroleum Exporting Countries (OPEC) quadrupled the price of oil. The harmful effect of this on the U.S. inflation rate and trade position resulted in a further decline in the value of the dollar.
- The loss of confidence in the dollar that followed a sharp rise in the U.S. inflation rate in 1977–1978.
- The oil crisis of 1979, when OPEC once again increased the price of oil dramatically—this time it was doubled.
- The unexpected rise in the dollar between 1980 and 1985, despite a deteriorating balance-of-payments picture.
- The rapid fall of the U.S. dollar against the Japanese yen and German deutsche mark between 1985 and 1987, and against the yen between 1993 and 1995.
- The partial collapse of the European Monetary System in 1992.
- The 1997 Asian currency crisis, when the Asian currencies of several countries, including South Korea, Indonesia, Malaysia, and Thailand, lost between 50 percent and 80 percent of their value against the U.S. dollar in a few months.

Figure 10.1 summarizes how the value of the U.S. dollar has fluctuated against an index of major trading currencies between 1973 and 2006. (The index, which was set equal to 100 in March 1973, is a weighted average of the foreign exchange values of the U.S. dollar against currencies that circulate widely outside the country of issue.) An interesting phenomenon in Figure 10.1 is the rapid rise in the value of the dollar between 1980 and 1985 and its subsequent fall between 1985 and 1988. A similar, though less pronounced, rise and fall in the value of the dollar occurred between 1995 and 2006. We will briefly discuss the rise and fall of the dollar during these periods because it reveals something about how the international monetary system has operated in recent years.[6]

The rise in the value of the dollar between 1980 and 1985 occurred when the United States was running a large and growing trade deficit, importing substantially more than

FIGURE 10.1

Major Currencies Dollar Index, 1973–2006

Source: Constructed by the author from Federal Reserve Board statistics at http://www .federalreserve.gov/releases/H10/ summary/.

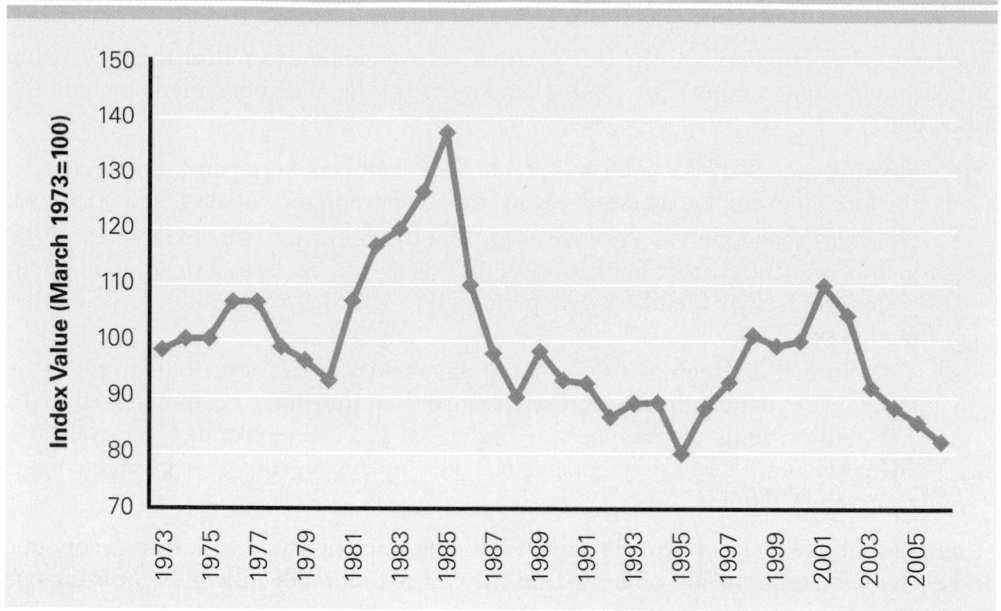

it exported. Conventional wisdom would suggest that the increased supply of dollars in the foreign exchange market as a result of the trade deficit should lead to a reduction in the value of the dollar, but as Figure 10.1 shows, it increased in value. Why?

A number of favorable factors overcame the unfavorable effect of a trade deficit. Strong economic growth in the United States attracted heavy inflows of capital from foreign investors seeking high returns on capital assets. High real interest rates attracted foreign investors seeking high returns on financial assets. At the same time, political turmoil in other parts of the world, along with relatively slow economic growth in the developed countries of Europe, helped create the view that the United States was a good place to invest. These inflows of capital increased the demand for dollars in the foreign exchange market, which pushed the value of the dollar upward against other currencies.

The fall in the value of the dollar between 1985 and 1988 was caused by a combination of government intervention and market forces. The rise in the dollar, which priced U.S. goods out of foreign markets and made imports relatively cheap, had contributed to a dismal trade picture. In 1985, the United States posted a record-high trade deficit of more than $160 billion. This led to growth in demands for protectionism in the United States. In September 1985, the finance ministers and central bank governors of the so-called Group of Five major industrial countries (Great Britain, France, Japan, Germany, and the United States) met at the Plaza Hotel in New York and reached what was later referred to as the Plaza Accord. They announced that it would be desirable for most major currencies to appreciate vis-à-vis the U.S. dollar and pledged to intervene in the foreign exchange markets, selling dollars, to encourage this objective. The dollar had already begun to weaken in the summer of 1985, and this announcement further accelerated the decline.

The dollar continued to decline until 1987. The governments of the Group of Five began to worry that the dollar might decline too far, so the finance ministers of the Group of Five met in Paris in February 1987 and reached a new agreement known as the Louvre Accord. They agreed that exchange rates had been realigned sufficiently and pledged to support the stability of exchange rates around their current levels by intervening in the foreign exchange markets when necessary to buy and sell currency. Although the dollar continued to decline for a few months after the Louvre Accord, the rate of decline slowed, and by early 1988 the decline had ended.

Except for a brief speculative flurry around the time of the Persian Gulf War in 1991, the dollar was relatively stable for the first half of the 1990s. However, in the late 1990s the dollar again began to appreciate against most major currencies, including the euro after its introduction, even though the United States was still running a significant balance-of-payments deficit. Once again, the driving force for the appreciation in the value of the dollar was that foreigners continued to invest in U.S. financial assets, primarily stocks and bonds, and the inflow of money drove up the value of the dollar on foreign exchange markets. The inward investment was due to a belief that U.S. financial assets offered a favorable rate of return.

By 2002, however, foreigners had started to lose their appetite for U.S. stocks and bonds, and the inflow of money into the United States slowed. Instead of reinvesting dollars earned from exports to the United States in U.S. financial assets, they exchanged those dollars for other currencies, particularly euros, to invest them in non–dollar-denominated assets. One reason for this was the continued growth in the U.S. trade deficit, which hit a record $767 billion in 2005. Although the U.S. trade deficits had been hitting records for decades, this deficit was the largest ever when measured as a percentage of the country's GDP (7 percent of GDP in 2005).

The record deficit meant that ever more dollars were flowing out of the United States into foreign hands, and those foreigners were less inclined to reinvest those dollars in the United States at a rate required to keep the dollar stable. This growing reluctance of foreigners to invest in the United States was in turn due to several factors. First, there was a slowdown in U.S. economic activity during 2001–2002, and a somewhat slow recovery thereafter, which made U.S. assets less attractive. Second, the U.S. government's budget deficit expanded rapidly after 2001, hitting a record $318 billion in 2005 before falling back to $248 billion in 2006. This led to fears that ultimately the budget deficit would be financed by an expansionary monetary policy that could lead to higher price inflation. Since inflation would reduce the value of the dollar, foreigners decided to hedge against this risk by holding fewer dollar assets in their investment portfolios. Third, from 2003 onward U.S. government officials began to "talk down" the value of the dollar, in part because the administration believed that a cheaper dollar would increase exports and reduce imports, thereby improving the U.S. balance of trade position.[7] Foreigners saw this as a signal that the U.S. government would not intervene in the foreign exchange markets to prop up the value of the dollar, which increased their reluctance to reinvest dollars earned from export sales in U.S. financial assets. As a result of these factors, demand for dollars weakened and the value of the dollar slid on the foreign exchange markets, hitting an index value of 80.19 in December 2004, the lowest value since the index began in 1973. Although the dollar strengthened a little in 2005 and 2006, many commentators believe that it could resume its fall in coming years, particularly if large holders of U.S. dollars, such as oil producing states, decide to diversify their foreign exchange holdings (see the next Country Focus for a discussion of this possibility).

Thus, we see that in recent history the value of the dollar has been determined by both market forces and government intervention. Under a floating exchange rate regime, market forces have produced a volatile dollar exchange rate. Governments have sometimes responded by intervening in the market—buying and selling dollars—in an attempt to limit the market's volatility and to correct what they see as overvaluation (in 1985) or potential undervaluation (in 1987) of the dollar. In addition to direct intervention, statements from government officials have frequently influenced the value of the dollar. The dollar may not have declined by as much as it did in 2004, for example, had not U.S. government officials publicly ruled out any action to stop the decline. Paradoxically, a signal not to intervene can affect the market. The frequency of government intervention in the foreign exchange market explains why the current system is sometimes thought of as a **managed-float system** or a dirty-float system.

The U.S. Dollar, Oil Prices, and Recycling Petrodollars

Between 2004 and 2006 global oil prices surged. They peaked at over $70 a barrel in mid-2006, up from around $20 in 2001. The rise in oil prices was due to a combination of greater than expected demand for oil, particularly from rapidly developing giants such as China and India, tight supplies, and perceived geopolitical risks in the Middle East, the world's largest oil producing region. With these conditions predicted to persist for some time, oil prices could remain high for the foreseeable future.

The surge in oil prices has been a windfall for oil producing countries. Collectively they earned around $700 billion in oil revenues in 2005 and $900 billion in 2006, some 64 percent of which went to members of OPEC and a major share of that amount to Saudi Arabia, the world's largest oil producer. Since oil is priced in U.S. dollars, the rise in oil prices has translated into a substantial increase in the dollar holdings of oil producers (the dollars earned from the sale of oil are often referred to as *petrodollars*). In essence, rising oil prices represent a net transfer of dollars from oil consumers in countries like the United States to oil producers in Russia, Saudi Arabia, and Venezuela. The question everybody is now asking is, what will they do with those dollars?

One possibility is that the producing countries will spend their petrodollars on public sector infrastructure, such as health services, education, roads, and telecommunications systems. Among other things, this could boost economic growth in those countries and pull in foreign imports, which would help counterbalance the trade surpluses oil producers enjoy and support global economic growth. There is some evidence that spending has picked up in many oil producing countries. However, according to the IMF, OPEC members only spent around 40 percent of their windfall profits from higher oil prices

in 2002–2006. The last time oil prices increased sharply in 1979, oil producers significantly ramped up spending on infrastructure, only to find themselves saddled with excessive debt when oil prices collapsed a few years later. This time they are being more cautious.

Another possibility is that the oil producers will invest a good chunk of the dollars they earn from oil sales in dollar-denominated assets, such as U.S. bonds, stocks, and real estate. So far, this seems to have happened; OPEC members in particular are funneling dollars back into U.S. assets, mostly bonds and stocks. The implication is that by recycling their petrodollars, oil producers are helping to finance the large and growing current account deficit of the United States, enabling it to pay its growing oil import bills.

A third possibility is that oil producers will invest in non–dollar-denominated assets, euro-denominated and yen-denominated assets for example, including European and Japanese bonds and stocks. This too has been happening. Moreover, there has been a trend for some OPEC investors to purchase not just small equity positions, but entire companies. In 2005, for example, Dubai International Capital purchased the Tussauds Group, a British theme-park firm, and DP World of Dubai purchased P&O, Britain's biggest port and ferries group. (As it turns out, P&O held the contract to manage operations at six U.S. ports, and the takeover bid led to a storm of protest in the United States from those who feared that an Arab takeover of P&O might create a security risk.) Despite examples such as these, in 2005 and 2006 at least, the bulk of petrodollars appears to have been recycled into dollar-denominated assets, in large part because U.S. interest rates increased throughout 2004–2006.[8]

Fixed versus Floating Exchange Rates

The breakdown of the Bretton Woods system has not stopped the debate about the relative merits of fixed versus floating exchange rate regimes. Disappointment with the system of floating rates in recent years has led to renewed debate about the merits of fixed exchange rates. In this section, we review the arguments for fixed and floating exchange rate regimes.[9] We will discuss the case for floating rates before discussing why many commentators are disappointed with the experience under floating exchange rates and yearn for a system of fixed rates.

THE CASE FOR FLOATING EXCHANGE RATES

The case in support of floating exchange rates has two main elements: monetary policy autonomy and automatic trade balance adjustments.

Monetary Policy Autonomy

Some analysts argue that under a fixed system, a country's ability to expand or contract its money supply as it sees fit is limited by the need to maintain exchange rate parity. Monetary expansion can lead to inflation, which puts downward pressure on a fixed exchange rate (as predicted by the PPP theory; see Chapter 9). Similarly, monetary contraction requires high interest rates (to reduce the demand for money). Higher interest rates lead to an inflow of money from abroad, which puts upward pressure on a fixed exchange rate. Thus, to maintain exchange rate parity under a fixed system, countries were limited in their ability to use monetary policy to expand or contract their economies.

Advocates of a floating exchange rate regime argue that removal of the obligation to maintain exchange rate parity would restore monetary control to a government. If a government faced with unemployment wanted to increase its money supply to stimulate domestic demand and reduce unemployment, it could do so unencumbered by the need to maintain its exchange rate. Monetary expansion might lead to inflation, which in turn would lead to a depreciation in the country's currency. If PPP theory is correct, the resulting currency depreciation on the foreign exchange markets should offset the effects of inflation. Although domestic inflation would have an impact on the exchange rate under a floating exchange rate regime, it should have no impact on businesses' international cost competitiveness due to exchange rate depreciation. The rise in domestic costs should be exactly offset by the fall in the value of the country's currency on the foreign exchange markets. Similarly, a government could use monetary policy to contract the economy without worrying about the need to maintain parity.

Trade Balance Adjustments

Under the Bretton Woods system, if a country developed a permanent deficit in its balance of trade (importing more than it exported), it could not be corrected by domestic policy; it would require the IMF to agree to a currency devaluation. Critics of this system argue that the adjustment mechanism works much more smoothly under a floating exchange rate regime. They argue that if a country is running a trade deficit, the imbalance between the supply and demand of that country's currency in the foreign exchange markets (supply exceeding demand) will lead to depreciation in its exchange rate. In turn, by making its exports cheaper and its imports more expensive, an exchange rate depreciation should correct the trade deficit.

THE CASE FOR FIXED EXCHANGE RATES

The case for fixed exchange rates rests on arguments about monetary discipline, speculation, uncertainty, and the lack of connection between the trade balance and exchange rates.

Monetary Discipline

We have already discussed the nature of monetary discipline inherent in a fixed exchange rate system when we discussed the Bretton Woods system. The need to maintain a fixed exchange rate parity ensures that governments do not expand their money supplies at inflationary rates. While advocates of floating rates argue that each country should be allowed to choose its own inflation rate (the monetary autonomy argument), advocates of fixed rates argue that governments all too often give in to political pressures and expand the monetary supply far too rapidly, causing unacceptably high price inflation. A fixed exchange rate regime prevents such a situation.

Speculation

Critics of a floating exchange rate regime also argue that speculation can cause fluctuations in exchange rates. They point to the dollar's rapid rise and fall during the 1980s, which they claim had nothing to do with comparative inflation rates and the U.S. trade deficit, but everything to do with speculation. They argue that when foreign exchange dealers see a currency depreciating, they tend to sell the currency in the expectation of future depreciation regardless of the currency's longer term prospects. As more traders jump on the bandwagon, the expectations of depreciation are realized. Such destabilizing speculation tends to accentuate the fluctuations around the exchange rate's long-run value. It can damage a country's economy by distorting export and import prices. Thus, advocates of a fixed exchange rate regime argue that such a system will limit the destabilizing effects of speculation.

Uncertainty

Speculation also adds to the uncertainty surrounding future currency movements that characterizes floating exchange rate regimes. The unpredictability of exchange rate movements in the post–Bretton Woods era has made business planning difficult, and it adds risk to exporting, importing, and foreign investment activities. Given a volatile exchange rate, international businesses do not know how to react to the changes—and often they do not react. Why change plans for exporting, importing, or foreign investment after a 6 percent fall in the dollar this month, when the dollar may rise 6 percent next month? This uncertainty, according to the critics, dampens the growth of international trade and investment. They argue that a fixed exchange rate, by eliminating such uncertainty, promotes the growth of international trade and investment. Advocates of a floating system reply that the forward exchange market insures against the risks associated with exchange rate fluctuations (see Chapter 9), so the adverse impact of uncertainty on the growth of international trade and investment has been overstated.

Trade Balance Adjustments

Those in favor of floating exchange rates argue that floating rates help adjust trade imbalances. Critics question the closeness of the link between the exchange rate and the trade balance. They claim trade deficits are determined by the balance between savings and investment in a country, not by the external value of its currency.[10] They argue that depreciation in a currency will lead to inflation (due to the resulting increase in import prices). This inflation will wipe out any apparent gains in cost competitiveness that arise from currency depreciation. In other words, a depreciating exchange rate will not boost exports and reduce imports, as advocates of floating rates claim; it will simply boost price inflation. In support of this argument, those who favor floating rates point out that the 40 percent drop in the value of the dollar between 1985 and 1988 did not correct the U.S. trade deficit. In reply, opponents of a floating exchange rate regime argue that between 1985 and 1992, the U.S. trade deficit fell from more than $160 billion to about $70 billion, and they attribute this in part to the decline in the value of the dollar.

WHO IS RIGHT?

Which side is right in the vigorous debate between those who favor a fixed exchange rate and those who favor a floating exchange rate? Economists cannot agree. Business, as a major player on the international trade and investment scene, has a large stake in the resolution of the debate. Would international business be better off under a fixed regime, or are flexible rates better? The evidence is not clear.

We do, however, know that a fixed exchange rate regime modeled along the lines of the Bretton Woods system will not work. Speculation ultimately broke the system, a phenomenon that advocates of fixed rate regimes claim is associated with floating exchange rates! Nevertheless, a different kind of fixed exchange rate system might be more enduring and might foster the stability that would facilitate more rapid growth in international trade and investment. In the next section, we look at potential models for such a system and the problems with such systems.

🌐 Exchange Rate Regimes in Practice

Governments around the world pursue a number of different exchange rate policies. These range from a pure "free float" where the exchange rate is determined by market forces to a pegged system that has some aspects of the pre-1973 Bretton Woods system of fixed exchange rates. Figure 10.2 summarizes the exchange rate policies that member states of the IMF adopted in 2006. Some 14 percent of the IMF's members allow their currency to float freely. Another 26 percent intervene in only a limited way (the so-called managed float). A further 28 percent of IMF members now have no separate legal tender of their own. These include the European Union countries that have adopted the euro and effectively given up their own currencies, along with smaller states mostly in Africa or the Caribbean that have no domestic currency and have adopted a foreign currency as legal tender within their borders, typically the U.S. dollar or the euro. The remaining countries use more inflexible systems, including a fixed peg arrangement (26 percent) under which they peg their currencies to other currencies, such as the U.S. dollar, the euro, or a basket of currencies. Other countries have adopted a system under which their exchange rate is allowed to fluctuate against other currencies within a target zone (an adjustable peg system). In this section, we will look more closely at the mechanics and implications of exchange rate regimes that rely on a currency peg or target zone.

PEGGED EXCHANGE RATES

Under a pegged exchange rate regime, a country will peg the value of its currency to that of a major currency so that, for example, as the U.S. dollar rises in value, its own currency rises too. Pegged exchange rates are popular among many of the world's smaller nations. As with a full fixed exchange rate regime, the great virtue claimed for a pegged exchange rate is that it imposes monetary discipline on a country and leads to low inflation. For example, if Belize pegs the value of the Belizean dollar to that of the U.S. dollar so that

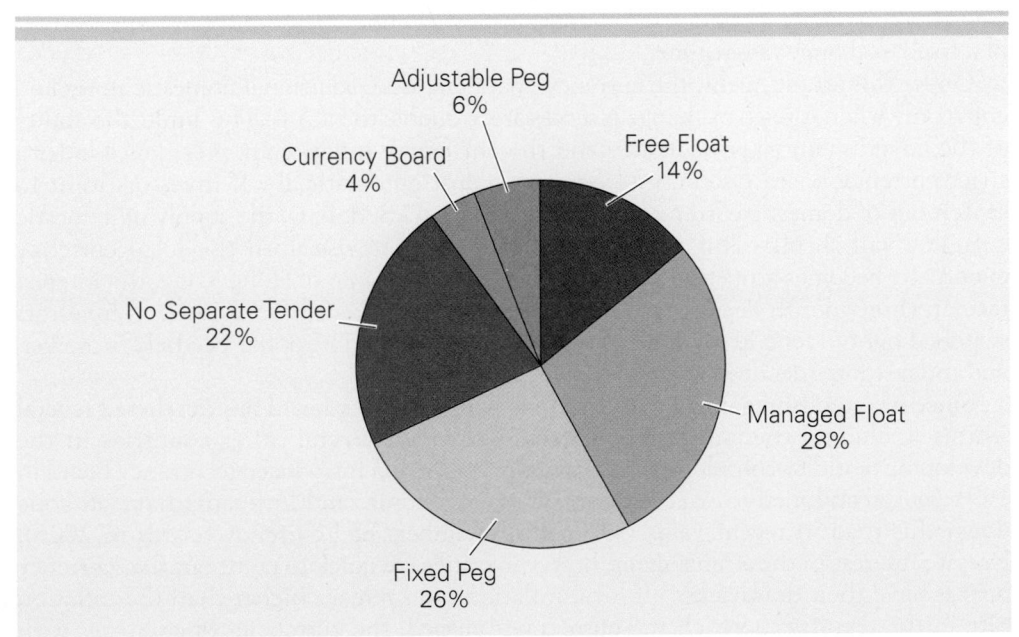

FIGURE 10.2

IMF Members' Exchange Rate Policies, 2006

Source: Constructed by the author from IMF data.

US$1 = B$1.97 (the peg as of 2006), then the Belizean government must make sure the inflation rate in Belize is similar to that in the United States. If the Belizean inflation rate is greater than the U.S. inflation rate, pressure to devalue the Belizean dollar (i.e., to alter the peg) will increase. To maintain the peg, the Belizean government would be required to rein in inflation. Of course, for a pegged exchange rate to impose monetary discipline on a country, the country whose currency is chosen for the peg must also pursue sound monetary policy.

Evidence shows that adopting a pegged exchange rate regime moderates inflationary pressures in a country. An IMF study concluded that countries with pegged exchange rates had an average annual inflation rate of 8 percent, compared with 14 percent for intermediate regimes and 16 percent for floating regimes.[11] However, many countries operate with only a nominal peg and in practice are willing to devalue their currency rather than pursue a tight monetary policy. It can be very difficult for a smaller country to maintain a peg against another currency if capital is flowing out of the country and foreign exchange traders are speculating against the currency. Something like this occurred in 1997 when a combination of adverse capital flows and currency speculation forced several Asian countries, including Thailand and Malaysia, to abandon pegs against the U.S. dollar and let their currencies float freely. Malaysia and Thailand would not have been in this position had they dealt with a number of problems that began to arise in their economies during the 1990s, including excessive private-sector debt and expanding current account trade deficits.

CURRENCY BOARDS

Hong Kong's experience during the 1997 Asian currency crisis added a new dimension to the debate over how to manage a pegged exchange rate. During late 1997 when other Asian currencies were collapsing, Hong Kong maintained the value of its currency against the U.S. dollar at about HK$15 = $7.8 despite several concerted speculative attacks. Hong Kong's currency board has been given credit for this success. A country that introduces a **currency board** commits itself to converting its domestic currency on demand into another currency at a fixed exchange rate. To make this commitment credible, the currency board holds reserves of foreign currency equal at the fixed exchange rate to at least 100 percent of the domestic currency issued. The system used in Hong Kong means its currency must be fully backed by the U.S. dollar at the specified exchange rate. This is still not a true fixed exchange rate regime because the U.S. dollar, and by extension the Hong Kong dollar, floats against other currencies, but it has some features of a fixed exchange rate regime.

Under this arrangement, the currency board can issue additional domestic notes and coins only when foreign exchange reserves are available to back it. This limits the ability of the government to print money and thereby create inflationary pressures. Under a strict currency board system, interest rates adjust automatically. If investors want to switch out of domestic currency into, for example, U.S. dollars, the supply of domestic currency will shrink. This will cause interest rates to rise until the local currency eventually becomes attractive to investors again. In the case of Hong Kong, the interest rate on three-month deposits climbed as high as 20 percent in late 1997, as investors switched out of Hong Kong dollars and into U.S. dollars. The dollar peg held, however, and interest rates declined again.

Since its establishment in 1983, the Hong Kong currency board has weathered several storms, including the latest. This success persuaded several other countries in the developing world to consider a similar system. Argentina introduced a currency board in 1991 (but abandoned it in 2002) and Bulgaria, Estonia, and Lithuania have all gone down this road in recent years (seven IMF members had currency boards in 2006). Despite interest in the arrangement, however, critics are quick to point out that currency boards have their drawbacks.[12] If local inflation rates remain higher than the inflation rate in the country to which the currency is pegged, the currencies of countries with currency boards can become uncompetitive and overvalued (this is what happened in the case of Argentina, which had a currency board, described at the beginning of the chapter). Also, under a currency board system, government lacks the ability to set interest rates. Interest rates in Hong Kong, for example, are effectively set by the U.S. Federal Reserve. In addition, economic collapse in Argentina in 2001 and the subsequent decision to abandon its currency board dampened much of the enthusiasm for this mechanism of managing exchange rates.

Crisis Management by the IMF

Many observers initially believed that the collapse of the Bretton Woods system in 1973 would diminish the role of the IMF within the international monetary system. The IMF's original function was to provide a pool of money from which members could borrow, over the short term, to adjust their balance-of-payments position and maintain their exchange rate. Some believed the demand for short-term loans would be considerably diminished under a floating exchange rate regime. A trade deficit would presumably lead to a decline in a country's exchange rate, which would help reduce imports and boost exports. No temporary IMF adjustment loan would be needed. Consistent with this, after 1973, most industrialized countries tended to let the foreign exchange market determine exchange rates in response to demand and supply. No major industrial country has borrowed funds from the IMF since the mid-1970s, when Great Britain and Italy did. Since the early 1970s, the rapid development of global capital markets has allowed developed countries such as Great Britain and the United States to finance their deficits by borrowing private money, as opposed to drawing on IMF funds. Despite these developments, the activities of the IMF have expanded over the past 30 years. By 2006, the IMF had 189 members, 59 of which had some kind of IMF program in place. In 1997, the institution implemented its largest rescue packages, committing more than $110 billion in short-term loans to three troubled Asian countries—South Korea, Indonesia, and Thailand. These moves were followed by additional IMF rescue packages in Turkey, Russia, Argentina, and Brazil.

The IMF's activities have expanded because periodic financial crises have continued to hit many economies in the post–Bretton Woods era, particularly among the world's developing nations. The IMF has repeatedly lent money to nations experiencing financial crises, requesting in return that the governments enact certain macroeconomic policies. Critics of the IMF claim these policies have not always been as beneficial as the IMF might have hoped and in some cases may have made things worse. Following the IMF loans to several Asian economies, these criticisms reached new levels and a vigorous debate occurred over the appropriate role of the IMF. In this section, we shall discuss some of the main challenges the IMF has had to deal with over the past quarter of a century and review the ongoing debate over the role of the IMF.

FINANCIAL CRISES IN THE POST–BRETTON WOODS ERA

A number of broad types of financial crises have occurred over the past 30 years, many of which have required IMF involvement. A **currency crisis** occurs when a speculative attack on the exchange value of a currency results in a sharp depreciation of its value or forces authorities to expend large volumes of international currency reserves and sharply increase interest rates to defend the prevailing exchange rate. This is what happened in Brazil in 2002, and the IMF stepped in to help stabilize the value of the Brazilian currency on foreign exchange markets. A **banking crisis** refers to a loss of confidence in the banking system that leads to a run on banks, as individuals and companies withdraw their deposits. A **foreign debt crisis** is a situation in which a country cannot service its foreign debt obligations, whether private-sector or government debt.

These crises tend to have common underlying macroeconomic causes: high relative price inflation rates, a widening current account deficit, excessive expansion of domestic borrowing, and asset price inflation (such as sharp increases in stock and property prices).[13] At times, elements of currency, banking, and debt crises may be present simultaneously, as in the 1997 Asian crisis and the 2000–2002 Argentinean crisis.

To assess the frequency of financial crises, the IMF looked at the macroeconomic performance of a group of 53 countries from 1975 to 1997 (22 of these countries were developed nations, and 31 were developing countries).[14] The IMF found that there had been 158 currency crises, including 55 episodes in which a country's currency declined by more than 25 percent. There were also 54 banking crises. The IMF's data suggest that developing nations were more than twice as likely to experience currency and banking crises as developed nations. It is not surprising, therefore, that most of the IMF's loan activities since the mid-1970s have been targeted toward developing nations.

Here we look at two crises that have been of particular significance in terms of IMF involvement since the early 1990s—the 1995 Mexican currency crisis and the 1997 Asian financial crisis. These crises were the result of excessive foreign borrowings, a weak or poorly regulated banking system, and high inflation rates. These factors came together to trigger simultaneous debt and currency crises. Checking the resulting crises required IMF involvement.

MEXICAN CURRENCY CRISIS OF 1995

The Mexican peso had been pegged to the dollar since the early 1980s when the International Monetary Fund made it a condition for lending money to the Mexican government to help bail the country out of a 1982 financial crisis. Under the IMF-brokered arrangement, the peso had been allowed to trade within a tolerance band of plus or minus 3 percent against the dollar. The band was also permitted to "crawl" down daily, allowing for an annual peso depreciation of about 4 percent against the dollar. The IMF believed that the need to maintain the exchange rate within a fairly narrow trading band would force the Mexican government to adopt stringent financial policies to limit the growth in the money supply and contain inflation.

Until the early 1990s, it looked as if the IMF policy had worked. However, strains were beginning to show by 1994. Since the mid-1980s, Mexican producer prices had risen 45 percent more than prices in the United States, and yet there had not been a corresponding adjustment in the exchange rate. By late 1994, Mexico was running a $17 billion trade deficit, which amounted to some 6 percent of the country's gross domestic product, and there had been an uncomfortably rapid expansion in public- and private-sector debt. Despite these strains, Mexican government officials had been stating publicly that they would support the peso's dollar peg at around $1 = 3.5 pesos by adopting appropriate monetary policies and by intervening in the currency markets if necessary. Encouraged by such statements, $64 billion of foreign investment money poured into Mexico between 1990 and 1994 as corporations and money managers sought to take advantage of the booming economy.

However, many currency traders concluded the peso would have to be devalued, and they began to dump pesos on the foreign exchange market. The government tried to hold the line by buying pesos and selling dollars, but it lacked the foreign currency reserves required to halt the speculative tide (Mexico's foreign exchange reserves fell from $6 billion at the beginning of 1994 to less than $3.5 billion at the end of the year). In mid-December 1994, the Mexican government abruptly announced a devaluation. Immediately, much of the short-term investment money that had flowed into Mexican stocks and bonds over the previous year reversed its course, as foreign investors bailed out of peso-denominated financial assets. This exacerbated the sale of the peso and contributed to the rapid 40 percent drop in its value.

The IMF stepped in again, this time arm in arm with the U.S. government and the Bank for International Settlements. Together the three institutions pledged close to $50 billion to help Mexico stabilize the peso and to redeem $47 billion of public- and private-sector debt that was set to mature in 1995. Of this amount, $20 billion came from the U.S. government and another $18 billion came from the IMF (which made Mexico the largest recipient of IMF aid up to that point). Without the aid package, Mexico would probably have defaulted on its debt obligations, and the peso would have gone into free fall. As is normal in such cases, the IMF insisted on tight monetary policies and further cuts in public spending, both of which helped push the country into a deep recession. However, the recession was relatively short-lived, and by 1997 the country was once more on a growth path, had pared down its debt, and had paid back the $20 billion borrowed from the U.S. government ahead of schedule.[15]

THE ASIAN CRISIS

The financial crisis that erupted across Southeast Asia during the fall of 1997 emerged as the biggest challenge to date for the IMF. Holding the crisis in check required IMF loans to help the shattered economies of Indonesia, Thailand, and South Korea stabilize their currencies. In addition, although they did not request IMF loans, the economies of Japan, Malaysia, Singapore, and the Philippines were also hurt by the crisis.

The seeds of this crisis were sown during the previous decade when these countries were experiencing unprecedented economic growth. Although there were and remain important differences between the individual countries, a number of elements were common to most. Exports had long been the engine of economic growth in these countries. From 1990 to 1996, the value of exports from Malaysia had grown by 18 percent annually, Thai exports had grown by 16 percent per year, Singapore's by 15 percent, Hong Kong's by 14 percent, and those of South Korea and Indonesia by 12 percent annually.[16]

The nature of these exports had also shifted in recent years from basic materials and products such as textiles to complex and increasingly high-technology products, such as automobiles, semiconductors, and consumer electronics.

The Investment Boom

The wealth created by export-led growth helped fuel an investment boom in commercial and residential property, industrial assets, and infrastructure. The value of commercial and residential real estate in cities such as Hong Kong and Bangkok started to soar. This fed a building boom the likes of which had never been seen in Asia. Heavy borrowing from banks financed much of this construction. As for industrial assets, the success of Asian exporters encouraged them to make bolder investments in industrial capacity. South Korea's giant diversified conglomerates, or *chaebol*, many of which had ambitions to build a major position in the global automobile and semiconductor industries, exemplified the trend most clearly.

An added factor behind the investment boom in most Southeast Asian economies was the government. In many cases, the governments had embarked on huge infrastructure projects. In Malaysia, for example, a new government administrative center was being constructed in Putrajaya for M$20 billion (U.S. $8 billion at the pre-July 1997 exchange rate), and the government was funding the development of a massive high-technology communications corridor and the huge Bakun dam, which at a cost of M$13.6 billion was to be the most expensive power-generation plant in the country.[17] Throughout the region, governments also encouraged private businesses to invest in certain sectors of the economy in accordance with "national goals" and "industrialization strategy." In South Korea, long a country where the government played a proactive role in private-sector investments, President Kim Young-Sam urged the *chaebol* to invest in new factories as a way of boosting economic growth. South Korea enjoyed an investment-led economic boom in 1994–1995, but at a cost. The *chaebol*, always reliant on heavy borrowings, built up massive debts that were equivalent, on average, to four times their equity.[18]

In Indonesia, President Suharto had long supported investments in a network of an estimated 300 businesses owned by his family and friends in a system known as "crony

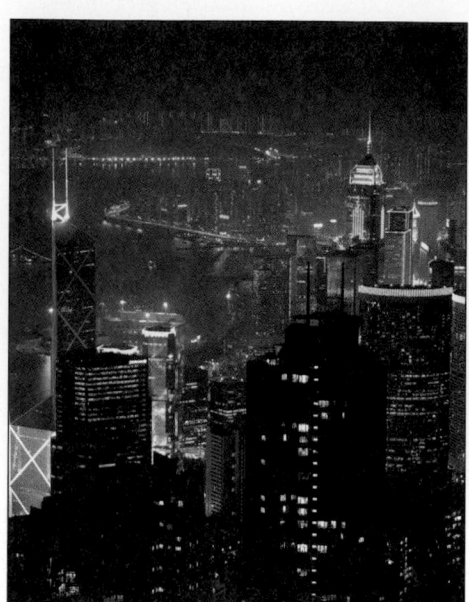

The boom in commercial and residential real estate in Asia in the early 1990s was fueled by export-led growth.

capitalism." The president granted many of these businesses lucrative monopolies. For example, Suharto announced in 1995 that he had decided to manufacture a national car, built by a company owned by one of his sons, Hutomo Mandala Putra, in association with Kia Motors of South Korea. To support the venture, the government "ordered" a consortium of Indonesian banks to offer almost $700 million in start-up loans to the company.[19]

By the mid-1990s, Southeast Asia was in the grips of an unprecedented investment boom, much of it financed with borrowed money. Between 1990 and 1995, gross domestic investment grew by 16.3 percent annually in Indonesia, 16 percent in Malaysia, 15.3 percent in Thailand, and 7.2 percent in South Korea. By comparison, investment grew by 4.1 percent annually over the same period in the United States and 0.8 percent in all high-income economies.[20] And the rate of investment accelerated in 1996. In Malaysia, for example, spending on investment accounted for a remarkable 43 percent of GDP in 1996.[21]

Excess Capacity

As the volume of investments ballooned during the 1990s, often at the bequest of national governments, the quality of many of these investments declined significantly. The investments often were made on the basis of unrealistic projections about future demand conditions. The result was significant excess capacity. For example, South Korean *chaebol* investments in semiconductor factories surged in 1994 and 1995 when a temporary global shortage of dynamic random access memory chips (DRAMs) led to sharp price increases for this product. However, supply shortages had disappeared by 1996 and excess capacity was beginning to appear just as the new South Korean DRAM factories began to produce. The results were predictable: prices for DRAMs plunged, and the earnings of South Korean DRAM manufacturers fell by 90 percent, which meant it was difficult for them to make scheduled payments on the debt they had taken on to build the extra capacity.[22]

In another example, a building boom in Thailand resulted in excess capacity in residential and commercial property. By early 1997, an estimated 365,000 apartment units were unoccupied in Bangkok. With another 100,000 units scheduled to be completed in 1997, years of excess demand in the Thai property market had been replaced by excess supply. By one estimate, Bangkok's building boom had produced enough excess space by 1997 to meet its residential and commercial needs for five years.[23]

The Debt Bomb

By early 1997 what was happening in the South Korean semiconductor industry and the Bangkok property market was being played out elsewhere in the region. Massive investments in industrial assets and property had created excess capacity and plunging prices, while leaving the companies that had made the investments groaning under huge debt burdens that they were now finding it difficult to service.

To make matters worse, much of the borrowing had been in U.S. dollars, as opposed to local currencies. This had originally seemed like a smart move. Throughout the region, local currencies were pegged to the dollar, and interest rates on dollar borrowings were generally lower than rates on borrowings in domestic currency. Thus, it often made economic sense to borrow in dollars if the option was available. However, if the governments could not maintain the dollar peg and their currencies started to depreciate against the dollar, this would increase the size of the debt burden when measured in the local currency. Currency depreciation would raise borrowing costs and could result in companies defaulting on their debt obligations.

Expanding Imports

A final complicating factor was that by the mid-1990s, although exports were still expanding across the region, imports were too. The investments in infrastructure, industrial capacity, and commercial real estate were sucking in foreign goods at unprecedented rates. To build infrastructure, factories, and office buildings, Southeast Asian countries were purchasing capital equipment and materials from America, Europe, and Japan. Many Southeast Asian states saw the current accounts of their balance of payments shift strongly into the red during the mid-1990s. By 1995, Indonesia was running a current account deficit that was equivalent to 3.5 percent of its GDP, Malaysia's was 5.9 percent, and Thailand's was 8.1 percent.[24] With deficits like these, it was increasingly difficult for the governments of these countries to maintain their currencies against the U.S. dollar. If that peg could not be held, the local currency value of dollar-denominated debt would increase, raising the specter of large-scale default on debt service payments. The scene was now set for a potentially rapid economic meltdown.

The Crisis

The Asian meltdown began in mid-1997 in Thailand when it became clear that several key Thai financial institutions were on the verge of default. These institutions had been borrowing dollars from international banks at low interest rates and lending Thai baht at higher interest rates to local property developers. However, due to speculative overbuilding, these developers could not sell their commercial and residential property, forcing them to default on their debt obligations. In turn, the Thai financial institutions seemed increasingly likely to default on their dollar-denominated debt obligations to international banks. Sensing the beginning of the crisis, foreign investors fled the Thai stock market, selling their positions and converting them into U.S. dollars. The increased demand for dollars and increased supply of Thai baht pushed down the dollar/Thai baht exchange rate, while the stock market plunged.

Seeing these developments, foreign exchange dealers and hedge funds started speculating against the baht, selling it short. For the previous 13 years, the Thai baht had been pegged to the U.S. dollar at an exchange rate of about $1 = Bt25. The Thai government tried to defend the peg, but only succeeded in depleting its foreign exchange reserves. On July 2, 1997, the Thai government abandoned its defense and announced it would allow the baht to float freely against the dollar. The baht started a slide that would bring the exchange rate down to $1 = Bt55 by January 1998. As the baht declined, the Thai debt bomb exploded. The 55 percent decline in the value of the baht against the dollar doubled the amount of baht required to serve the dollar-denominated debt commitments of Thai financial institutions and businesses. This increased the probability of corporate bankruptcies and further pushed down the battered Thai stock market. The Thailand Set stock market index ultimately declined from 787 in January 1997 to a low of 337 in December of that year, on top of a 45 percent decline in 1996.

On July 28, the Thai government called in the International Monetary Fund. With its foreign exchange reserves depleted, Thailand lacked the foreign currency needed to finance its international trade and service debt commitments and desperately needed the capital the IMF could provide. It also needed to restore international confidence in its currency and needed the credibility associated with gaining access to IMF funds. Without IMF loans, the baht likely would increase its free fall against the U.S. dollar and the whole country might go into default. The IMF agreed to provide the Thai government with $17.2 billion in loans, but the conditions were restrictive.[25] The IMF required the Thai government to increase taxes, cut public spending, privatize several state-owned businesses, and raise interest rates—all steps designed to cool Thailand's overheated economy. The IMF also required Thailand to close illiquid financial institutions. In December 1997, the government shut 56 financial institutions, laying off 16,000 people and further deepening the recession that now gripped the country.

Following the devaluation of the Thai baht, wave after wave of speculation hit other Asian currencies. One after another in a period of weeks, the Malaysian ringgit, Indonesian rupiah, and the Singaporean dollar were all marked sharply lower. With its foreign exchange reserves down to $28 billion, Malaysia let the ringgit float on July 14, 1997. Before the devaluation, the ringgit was trading at $1 = 2.525 ringgit. Six months later it had declined to $1 = 4.15 ringgit. Singapore followed on July 17, and the Singaporean dollar quickly dropped in value from $1 = S$1.495 before the devaluation to $1 = S$2.68 a few days later. Next up was Indonesia, whose rupiah was allowed to float on August 14. For Indonesia, this was the beginning of a precipitous decline in the value of its currency, which was to fall from $1 = 2,400 rupiah in August 1997 to $1 = 10,000 rupiah on January 6, 1998, a loss of 76 percent.

With the exception of Singapore, whose economy is probably the most stable in the region, these devaluations were driven by factors similar to those behind the earlier devaluation of the Thai baht—a combination of excess investment; high borrowings, much of it in dollar-denominated debt; and a deteriorating balance-of-payments position. Although both Malaysia and Singapore were able to halt the slide in their currencies and stock markets without the help of the IMF, Indonesia was not. Indonesia was struggling with a private-sector, dollar-denominated debt of close to $80 billion. With the rupiah sliding precipitously almost every day, the cost of servicing this debt was exploding, pushing more Indonesian companies into technical default.

On October 31, 1997, the IMF announced it had assembled a $37 billion rescue deal for Indonesia in conjunction with the World Bank and the Asian Development Bank. In return, the Indonesian government agreed to close a number of troubled banks, reduce public spending, remove government subsidies on basic foodstuffs and energy, balance the budget, and unravel the crony capitalism that was so widespread in Indonesia. But the government of President Suharto appeared to backtrack several times on commitments made to the IMF. This precipitated further declines in the Indonesian currency and stock markets. Ultimately, Suharto removed costly government subsidies, only to see the country dissolve into chaos as the populace took to the streets to protest the resulting price increases. The financial strains unleashed a chain of events that led to Suharto's removal from power in May 1998.

The final domino to fall was South Korea. During the 1990s, South Korean companies had built up huge debt loads as they invested heavily in new industrial capacity. Now they found they had too much industrial capacity and could not generate the income required to service their debt. South Korean banks and companies had also made the mistake of borrowing in dollars, much of it in the form of short-term loans that would come due within a year. Thus, when the Korean won started to decline in the fall of 1997 in sympathy with the problems elsewhere in Asia, South Korean companies saw their debt obligations balloon. Several large companies were forced to file for bankruptcy. This triggered a decline in the South Korean currency and stock market that was difficult to halt. The South Korean central bank tried to keep the dollar/won exchange rate above $1 = W1,000 but found that this only depleted its foreign exchange reserves. On November 17, the South Korean central bank gave up the defense of the won, which quickly fell to $1 = W1,500.

With its economy on the verge of collapse, the South Korean government on November 21 requested $20 billion in standby loans from the IMF. As the negotiations progressed, it became apparent that South Korea was going to need far more than $20 billion. Among other problems, the country's short-term foreign debt was found to be twice as large as previously thought, at close to $100 billion, while the country's foreign exchange reserves were down to less than $6 billion. On December 3, 1997, the IMF and South Korean government reached a deal to lend $55 billion to the country. The agreement with the IMF called for the South Koreans to open their economy and banking system to foreign investors. South Korea also pledged to restrain the *chaebol* by reducing their share of bank financing and requiring them to publish consolidated financial statements and undergo annual independent external audits. On trade liberalization, the IMF said South Korea would comply with its commitments to the World Trade Organization to eliminate trade-related subsidies and restrictive import licensing and would streamline its import certification procedures, all of which should open the South Korean economy to greater foreign competition.[26]

EVALUATING THE IMF'S POLICY PRESCRIPTIONS

By 2006, the IMF was committing loans to some 59 countries that were struggling with economic and currency crises. A detailed example of one such program is given in the next Country Focus, which looks at IMF loans to Turkey. All IMF loan packages come with conditions attached. In general, the IMF insists on a combination of tight macroeconomic policies, including cuts in public spending, higher interest rates, and tight monetary policy. It also often pushes for the deregulation of sectors formerly protected from domestic and foreign competition, privatization of state-owned assets, and better financial reporting from the banking sector. These policies are designed to cool overheated economies by reining in inflation and reducing government spending and debt. Recently, this set of policy prescriptions has come in for tough criticisms from many observers.[27]

Inappropriate Policies

One criticism is that the IMF's "one-size-fits-all" approach to macroeconomic policy is inappropriate for many countries. In the case of the Asian crisis, critics argue that the tight macroeconomic policies imposed by the IMF are not well suited to countries that are suffering not from excessive government spending and inflation, but from a private-sector debt crisis with deflationary undertones.[28] In South Korea, for example, the government had been running a budget surplus for years (it was 4 percent of South Korea's GDP in 1994–1996) and inflation was low at about 5 percent. South Korea had the second strongest financial position of any country in the Organization for Economic Cooperation and Development. Despite this, critics say, the IMF insisted on applying the same policies that it applies to countries suffering from high inflation. The IMF required South Korea to maintain an inflation rate of 5 percent. However, given the collapse in the value of its currency and the subsequent rise in price for imports such as oil, critics claimed inflationary pressures would inevitably increase in South Korea. So to hit a 5 percent inflation rate, the South Koreans would be forced to apply an unnecessarily tight monetary policy. Short-term interest rates in South Korea did jump from 12.5 percent to 21 percent immediately after the country signed its initial deal with the IMF. Increasing interest rates made it even more difficult for companies to service their already excessive short-term debt obligations, and critics used this as evidence to argue that the cure prescribed by the IMF may actually increase the probability of widespread corporate defaults, not reduce them.

The IMF rejected this criticism. According to the IMF, the central task was to rebuild confidence in the won. Once this was achieved, the won would recover from its oversold levels, reducing the size of South Korea's dollar-denominated debt burden when expressed in won, making it easier for companies to service their debt. The IMF also argued that by requiring South Korea to remove restrictions on foreign direct investment, foreign capital would flow into the country to take advantage of cheap assets. This, too, would increase demand for the Korean currency and help to improve the dollar/won exchange rate.

Korea did recover fairly quickly from the crisis, supporting the position of the IMF. While the economy contracted by 7 percent in 1998, by 2000 it had rebounded and was growing at a 9 percent rate (measured by growth in GDP). Inflation, which peaked at 8 percent in 1998, fell to 2 percent by 2000, and unemployment fell from 7 percent to 4 percent over the same period. The won hit a low of $1 = W1,812 in early 1998, but by 2000 was back to an exchange rate of around $1 = W1,200, at which it seems to have stabilized.

Moral Hazard

A second criticism of the IMF is that its rescue efforts are exacerbating a problem known to economists as moral hazard. **Moral hazard** arises when people behave recklessly because they know they will be saved if things go wrong. Critics point out that many

Turkey and the IMF

In May 2001, the International Monetary Fund (IMF) agreed to lend $8 billion to Turkey to help the country stabilize its economy and halt a sharp slide in the value of its currency. This was the third time in two years that the international lending institution had put together a loan program for Turkey, and it was the 18th program since Turkey became a member of the IMF in 1958.

Many of Turkey's problems stemmed from a large and inefficient state sector and heavy subsidies to various private sectors of the economy such as agriculture. Although the Turkish government started to privatize state-owned companies in the late 1980s, the programs proceeded at a glacial pace, hamstrung by political opposition within Turkey. Instead of selling state-owned assets to private investors, successive governments increased support to unprofitable state-owned industries and raised the wage rates of state employees. Nor did the government cut subsidies to politically powerful private sectors of the economy, such as agriculture. To support state industries and finance subsidies, Turkey issued significant amounts of government debt. To limit the amount of debt, the government expanded the money supply to finance spending. The result was rampant inflation and high interest rates. During the 1990s, inflation averaged over 80 percent a year while real interest rates rose to more than 50 percent on a number of occasions. Despite this, the Turkish economy continued to grow at a healthy pace of 6 percent annually in real terms, a remarkable achievement given the high inflation rates and interest rates.

By the late 1990s the "Turkish miracle" of sustained growth in the face of high inflation and interest rates was running out of steam. Government debt had risen to 60 percent of gross domestic product, government borrowing was leaving little capital for private enterprises,

and the cost of financing government debt was spiraling out of control. Rampant inflation was putting pressure on the Turkish currency, the lira, which at the time was pegged in value to a basket of other currencies. Realizing that it needed to reform its economy, the Turkish government sat down with the IMF in late 1999 to work out a recovery program, adopted in January 2000.

As with most IMF programs, the focus was on bringing down the inflation rate, stabilizing the value of the Turkish currency, and restructuring the economy to reduce government debt. The Turkish government committed itself to reducing government debt by taking a number of steps. These included an accelerated privatization program that would use the proceeds to pay down debt, the reduction of agricultural subsidies, reform to make it more difficult for people to qualify for public pension programs, and tax increases. The government also agreed to rein in the growth in the money supply to better control inflation. To limit the possibility of speculative attacks on the Turkish currency in the foreign exchange markets, the Turkish government and IMF announced that Turkey would peg the value of the lira against a basket of currencies and devalue the lira by a predetermined amount each month throughout 2000, bringing the total devaluation for the year to 25 percent. To ease the pain, the IMF agreed to provide the Turkish government with $5 billion in loans that could be used to support the value of the lira.

Initially the program seemed to be working. Inflation fell to 35 percent in 2000, while the economy grew by 6 percent. By the end of 2000, however, the program was in trouble. Burdened with nonperforming loans, a number of Turkish banks faced default and the government had taken them into public ownership. When a criminal fraud investigation uncovered evidence that

Japanese and Western banks were far too willing to lend large amounts of capital to overleveraged Asian companies during the boom years of the 1990s. These critics argue that the banks should now be forced to pay the price for their rash lending policies, even if that means some banks must close.[29] Only by taking such drastic action, the argument goes, will banks learn the error of their ways and not engage in rash lending in the future. By providing support to these countries, the IMF is reducing the probability of debt default and in effect bailing out the banks whose loans gave rise to this situation.

This argument ignores two critical points. First, if some Japanese or Western banks with heavy exposure to the troubled Asian economies were forced to write off their loans politicians had pressured several of these banks into providing loans at below-market interest rates, foreign investors, worried that more banks might be involved, started to pull their money out of Turkey. This sent the Turkish stock market into a tailspin and put enormous pressure on the Turkish lira. The government raised Turkish overnight interbank lending rates to as high as 1,950 percent to try to stem the outflow of capital, but it was clear that Turkey alone could not halt the flow.

The IMF stepped once more into the breach on December 6, 2000, announcing a quickly arranged $7.5 billion loan program for the country. In return for the loan, the IMF required the Turkish government to close 10 insolvent banks, speed up its privatization plans (which had once more stalled), and cap any pay increases for government workers. The IMF also reportedly urged the Turkish government to let its currency float freely in the foreign exchange markets, but the government refused, arguing that the result would be a rapid devaluation of the lira, which would raise import prices and fuel price inflation. The government insisted that reducing inflation should be its first priority.

This plan started to come apart in February 2001. A surge in inflation and a rapid slowdown in economic growth once more spooked foreign investors. Into this explosive mix waded Turkey's prime minister and president, who engaged in a highly public argument about economic policy and political corruption. This triggered a rapid outflow of capital. The government raised the overnight interbank lending rate to 7,500 percent to try to persuade foreigners to leave their money in the country, but to no avail. Realizing that it would be unable to keep the lira within its planned monthly devaluation range without raising interest rates to absurd levels or seriously depleting the country's foreign exchange reserves, on February 23, 2001, the Turkish government decided to let the lira float freely. The lira immediately dropped 50 percent in value against the U.S. dollar, but ended the day down some 28 percent.

Over the next two months, the Turkish economy continued to weaken as a global economic slowdown affected the nation. Inflation stayed high, and progress at reforming the country's economy remained bogged down by political considerations. By early April, the lira had fallen 40 percent against the dollar since February 23, and the country was teetering on the brink of an economic meltdown. For the third time in 18 months, the IMF stepped in, arranging for another $8 billion in loans. Once more, the IMF insisted that the Turkish government accelerate privatization, close insolvent banks, deregulate its market, and cut government spending. Critics of the IMF, however, claimed this "austerity program" would only slow the Turkish economy and make matters worse, not better. These critics advocated a mix of sound monetary policy and tax cuts to boost Turkey's economic growth.

By 2006 significant progress had been made. Initially the Turkish government failed to fully comply with IMF mandates on economic policy, causing the institution to hold back a scheduled $1.6 billion in IMF loans until the government passed an "austerity budget," which it did reluctantly in March 2003 after months of public hand-wringing. Since then, things have improved. Inflation fell from a peak of 65 percent in December 2000 to about 8.2 percent for 2005 and 9.6 percent for 2006. Economic growth increased to a robust 9 percent in 2004, followed by 5.9 percent in 2005 and 5.2 percent in 2006. The pace of the privatization program has increased. The government also generated budget surpluses in 2003–2006.[31]

due to widespread debt default, the impact would have been difficult to contain. The failure of large Japanese banks, for example, could have triggered a meltdown in the Japanese financial markets. That would almost inevitably lead to a serious decline in stock markets around the world, which was the very risk the IMF was trying to avoid by stepping in with financial support. Second, it is incorrect to imply that some banks have not had to pay the price for rash lending policies. The IMF has insisted on the closure of banks in South Korea, Thailand, and Indonesia. Circumstances have forced foreign banks with short-term loans outstanding to South Korean enterprises to reschedule those loans at interest rates that do not compensate for the extension of the loan maturity.

Lack of Accountability

The final criticism of the IMF is that it has become too powerful for an institution that lacks any real mechanism for accountability.[30] The IMF has determined macroeconomic policies in those countries, yet according to critics such as noted economist Jeffrey Sachs, the IMF, with a staff of less than 1,000, lacks the expertise required to do a good job. Evidence of this, according to Sachs, can be found in the fact that the IMF was singing the praises of the Thai and South Korean governments only months before both countries lurched into crisis. Then the IMF put together a draconian program for South Korea without having deep knowledge of the country. Sachs's solution to this problem is to reform the IMF so it makes greater use of outside experts and its operations are open to greater outside scrutiny.

Observations

As with many debates about international economics, it is not clear which side has the winning hand about the appropriateness of IMF policies. There are cases where one can argue that IMF policies have been counterproductive or have only had limited success. For example, one might question the success of the IMF's involvement in Turkey given that the country has had to implement some 18 IMF programs since 1958 (see the accompanying Country Focus)! But the IMF can also point to some notable accomplishments, including its success in containing the Asian crisis, which could have rocked the global international monetary system to its core. Similarly, many observers give the IMF credit for its deft handling of politically difficult situations, such as the Mexican peso crisis, and for successfully promoting a free market philosophy.

Several years after the IMF's intervention, the economies of Asia and Mexico recovered. Certainly they all averted the kind of catastrophic implosion that might have occurred had the IMF not stepped in, and although some countries still faced considerable problems, it is not clear that the IMF should take much blame for this. The IMF cannot force countries to adopt the policies required to correct economic mismanagement. While a government may commit to taking corrective action in return for an IMF loan, internal political problems may make it difficult for a government to act on that commitment. In such cases, the IMF is caught between a rock and a hard place, for if it decided to withhold money, it might trigger financial collapse and the kind of contagion it seeks to avoid.

IMPLICATIONS FOR MANAGERS

The implications for international businesses of the material discussed in this chapter fall into three main areas: currency management, business strategy, and corporate–government relations.

CURRENCY MANAGEMENT

An obvious implication with regard to currency management is that companies must recognize that the foreign exchange market does not work quite as depicted in Chapter 9. The current system is a mixed system in which a combination of government intervention and speculative activity can drive the foreign exchange market. Companies engaged in significant foreign exchange activities need to be aware of this and to adjust their foreign exchange transactions accordingly. For example, the currency management unit of Caterpillar claims it made millions of dollars in the hours following the announcement of the Plaza Accord by selling dollars and buying currencies that it expected to appreciate on the foreign exchange market following government intervention.

Under the present system, speculative buying and selling of currencies can create very volatile movements in exchange rates (as exhibited by the rise and fall of the dollar during the 1980s and the Asian currency crisis of the late 1990s). Contrary to the predictions of the purchasing power parity theory (see Chapter 9), exchange rate movements during the 1980s and 1990s often did not seem to be strongly influenced by relative inflation rates. Insofar as volatile exchange rates increase foreign exchange risk, this is not good news for business. On the other hand, as we saw in Chapter 9, the foreign exchange market has developed a number of instruments, such as the forward market and swaps, that can help to insure against foreign exchange risk. Not surprisingly, use of these instruments has increased markedly since the breakdown of the Bretton Woods system in 1973.

BUSINESS STRATEGY

The volatility of the present global exchange rate regime presents a conundrum for international businesses. Exchange rate movements are difficult to predict, and yet their movement can have a major impact on a business's competitive position. For a detailed example, see the accompanying Management Focus on Airbus. Faced with uncertainty about the future value of currencies, firms can utilize the forward exchange market, which Airbus has done. However, the forward exchange market is far from perfect as a predictor of future exchange rates (see Chapter 9). It is also difficult if not impossible to get adequate insurance coverage for exchange rate changes that might occur several years in the future. The forward market tends to offer coverage for exchange rate changes a few months—not years—ahead. Given this, it makes sense to pursue strategies that will increase the company's strategic flexibility in the face of unpredictable exchange rate movements—that is, to pursue strategies that reduce the economic exposure of the firm (which we first discussed in Chapter 9).

Maintaining strategic flexibility can take the form of dispersing production to different locations around the globe as a real hedge against currency fluctuations (this seems to be what Airbus is now considering). Consider the case of Daimler-Benz (now Daimler-Chrysler), Germany's export-oriented automobile and aerospace company. In June 1995, the company stunned the German business community when it announced it expected to post a severe loss in 1995 of about $720 million. The cause was Germany's strong currency, which had appreciated by 4 percent against a basket of major currencies since the beginning of 1995 and had risen by more than 30 percent against the U.S. dollar since late 1994. By mid-1995, the exchange rate against the dollar stood at $1 = DM1.38. Daimler's management believed it could not make money with an exchange rate under $1 = DM1.60. Daimler's senior managers concluded that the appreciation of the mark against the dollar was probably permanent, so they decided to move substantial production outside of Germany and increase purchasing of foreign components. The idea was to reduce the vulnerability of the company to future exchange rate movements. The Mercedes-Benz division has been implementing this move for the last decade. Even before its acquisition of Chrysler Corporation in 1998, Mercedes planned to produce 10 percent of its cars outside of Germany by 2000, mostly in the United States.[32] Similarly, the move by Japanese automobile companies to expand their productive capacity in the United States and Europe can be seen in the context of the increase in the value of the yen between 1985 and 1995, which raised the price of Japanese exports. For the Japanese companies, building production capacity overseas is a hedge against continued appreciation of the yen (as well as against trade barriers).

Another way of building strategic flexibility and reducing economic exposure involves contracting out manufacturing. This allows a company to shift suppliers from country to country in response to changes in relative costs brought about by exchange rate movements. However, this kind of strategy may work only for low-value-added manufacturing (e.g., textiles), in which the individual manufacturers have few if any firm-specific skills that contribute to the value of the product. It may be less appropriate for high-value-added

Airbus and the Euro

Airbus had reason to celebrate in 2003; for the first time in the company's history it delivered more commercial jet aircraft than longtime rival Boeing. Airbus delivered 305 planes in 2003, compared to Boeing's 281. The celebration, however, was muted, for the strength of the euro against the U.S. dollar was casting a cloud over the company's future. Airbus, which is based in Toulouse, France, prices planes in dollars, just as Boeing has always done. But more than half of Airbus's costs are in euros. So as the dollar drops in value against the euro, and it dropped by over 50 percent between 2002 and the end of 2006, Airbus's costs rise in proportion to its revenue, squeezing profits in the process.

In the short run, the fall in the value of the dollar against the euro did not hurt Airbus. The company fully hedged its dollar exposure until 2005 and was mostly hedged for 2006. However, anticipating that the dollar will stay weak against the euro, Airbus has started to take other steps to reduce its economic exposure to a strong European currency. Recognizing that raising prices is not an option given the strong competition from Boeing, Airbus has decided to focus on reducing its costs. As a step toward doing this, Airbus is giving U.S. suppliers a greater share of work on new aircraft models, such

as the A380 super-jumbo and the A350. It is also shifting supply work on some of its older models from European to American-based suppliers. This will increase the proportion of its costs that are in dollars, making profits less vulnerable to a rise in the value of the euro and reducing the costs of building an aircraft when they are converted back into euros.

In addition, Airbus is pushing its European-based suppliers to start pricing in U.S. dollars. Because the costs of many suppliers are in euros, the suppliers are finding that to comply with Airbus's wishes, they too have to move more work to the United States or to countries whose currency is pegged to the U.S. dollar. Thus, one large French-based supplier, Zodiac, announced that it was considering acquisitions in the United States. Not only is Airbus pushing suppliers to price components for commercial jet aircraft in dollars, but the company is also requiring suppliers to its A400M program, a military aircraft that will be sold to European governments and priced in euros, to price components in U.S. dollars. Beyond these steps, the CEO of EADS, Airbus's parent company, has publicly stated that it might be prepared to assemble aircraft in the United States if that helps to win important U.S. contracts.[33]

manufacturing, in which firm-specific technology and skills add significant value to the product (e.g., the heavy equipment industry) and in which switching costs are correspondingly high. For high-value-added manufacturing, switching suppliers will lead to a reduction in the value that is added, which may offset any cost gains arising from exchange rate fluctuations.

The roles of the IMF and the World Bank in the present international monetary system also have implications for business strategy. Increasingly, the IMF has been acting as the macroeconomic police of the world economy, insisting that countries seeking significant borrowings adopt IMF-mandated macroeconomic policies. These policies typically include anti-inflationary monetary policies and reductions in government spending. In the short run, such policies usually result in a sharp contraction of demand. International businesses selling or producing in such countries need to be aware of this and plan accordingly. In the long run, the kind of policies imposed by the IMF can promote economic growth and an expansion of demand, which create opportunities for international business.

CORPORATE–GOVERNMENT RELATIONS

As major players in the international trade and investment environment, businesses can influence government policy toward the international monetary system. For example, intense government lobbying by U.S. exporters helped convince the U.S. government that intervention in the foreign exchange market was necessary. With this in mind, business can and should use its influence to promote an international monetary system that facilitates the growth of international trade and investment. Whether a fixed or floating regime is optimal is a subject for debate. However, exchange rate volatility such as the world experienced during the 1980s and 1990s creates an environment less conducive to international trade and investment than one with more stable exchange rates. Therefore, it would seem to be in the interests of international business to promote an international monetary system that minimizes volatile exchange rate movements, particularly when those movements are unrelated to long-run economic fundamentals.

CHAPTER SUMMARY

This chapter explained the workings of the international monetary system and pointed out its implications for international business. The chapter made the following points:

1. The gold standard is a monetary standard that pegs currencies to gold and guarantees convertibility to gold. It was thought that the gold standard contained an automatic mechanism that contributed to the simultaneous achievement of a balance-of-payments equilibrium by all countries. The gold standard broke down during the 1930s as countries engaged in competitive devaluations.

2. The Bretton Woods system of fixed exchange rates was established in 1944. The U.S. dollar was the central currency of this system; the value of every other currency was pegged to its value. Significant exchange rate devaluations were allowed only with the permission of the IMF. The role of the IMF was to maintain order in the international monetary system to avoid a repetition of the competitive devaluations of the 1930s and to control price inflation by imposing monetary discipline on countries.

3. The fixed exchange rate system collapsed in 1973, primarily due to speculative pressure on the dollar following a rise in U.S. inflation and a growing U.S. balance-of-trade deficit.

4. Since 1973 the world has operated with a floating exchange rate regime, and exchange rates have become more volatile and far less predictable. Volatile exchange rate movements have helped reopen the debate over the merits of fixed and floating systems.

5. The case for a floating exchange rate regime claims that such a system gives countries autonomy regarding their monetary policy and that floating exchange rates facilitate smooth adjustment of trade imbalances.

6. The case for a fixed exchange rate regime claims that the need to maintain a fixed exchange rate imposes monetary discipline on a country; floating exchange rate regimes are vulnerable to speculative pressure; the uncertainty that accompanies floating exchange rates dampens the growth of international trade and investment; and far from correcting trade imbalances, depreciating a currency on the foreign exchange market tends to cause price inflation.

7. In today's international monetary system, some countries have adopted floating exchange rates, some have pegged their currency to another currency such as the U.S. dollar, and some have pegged their currency to a basket of other currencies, allowing their currency to fluctuate within a zone around the basket.

8. In the post–Bretton Woods era, the IMF has continued to play an important role in helping countries navigate their way through financial crises by lending significant capital to embattled governments and by requiring them to adopt certain macroeconomic policies.

9. An important debate is occurring over the appropriateness of IMF-mandated macroeconomic policies. Critics charge that the IMF often imposes inappropriate conditions on developing nations that are the recipients of its loans.

10. The present managed-float system of exchange rate determination has increased the impor-

tance of currency management in international businesses.

11. The volatility of exchange rates under the present managed-float system creates both opportunities and threats. One way of responding to this volatility is for companies to build strategic flexibility and limit their economic exposure by dispersing production to different locations around the globe by contracting out manufacturing (in the case of low-value-added manufacturing) and other means.

Critical Thinking and Discussion Questions

1. Why did the gold standard collapse? Is there a case for returning to some type of gold standard? What is it?

2. What opportunities might current IMF lending policies to developing nations create for international businesses? What threats might they create?

3. Do you think the standard IMF policy prescriptions of tight monetary policy and reduced government spending are always appropriate for developing nations experiencing a currency crisis? How might the IMF change its approach? What would the implications be for international businesses?

4. Debate the relative merits of fixed and floating exchange rate regimes. From the perspective of an international business, what are the most important criteria in a choice between the systems? Which system is the more desirable for an international business?

5. Imagine that Canada, the United States, and Mexico decide to adopt a fixed exchange rate system. What would be the likely consequences of such a system for (a) international businesses and (b) the flow of trade and investment among the three countries?

6. Reread the Country Focus on the U.S. dollar, oil prices, and recycling petrodollars; then answer the following questions:
   a. What will happen to the value of the U.S. dollar if oil producers decide to invest most of their earnings from oil sales in domestic infrastructure projects?
   b. What factors determine the relative attractiveness of assets denominated in dollars, euros, and yen to oil producers flush with petrodollars? What might lead them to direct more funds toward non–dollar-denominated assets?
   c. What will happen to the value of the U.S. dollar if OPEC members decide to invest more of their petrodollars toward non–dollar-denominated assets, such as euro-denominated stocks and bonds?
   d. In addition to oil producers, China is also accumulating a large stock of dollars, currently estimated to total $1,000 billion by the end of 2006. What would happen to the value of the dollar if China and oil producing nations all shifted out of dollar-denominated assets at the same time? What would be the consequence for the United States economy?

Research Task

Use the globalEDGE™ site to complete the following exercises:

1. The quality of life in emerging markets sometimes is impacted by the country's financial and fiscal policies. As such, the *Global Financial Stability Report* is a semi-annual report published by the International Capital Markets division of the International Monetary Fund (IMF). The report aims to provide a regular assessment of global financial markets and to identify potential systemic weaknesses that could lead to crises. Locate and download the latest report to prepare a summary of what the IMF sees as the developments and vulnerabilities facing emerging market countries.

2. An important element to understanding the international monetary system is keeping updated on current growth trends worldwide. A German colleague told you yesterday that Deutsche Bank Research's Megatopics are an effective way to stay informed on important topics in international finance. Find a Megatopics report focusing on global growth centers. Which country (or countries) is included in your report? Is the report on established or emerging economies? What are the key takeaways from your chosen report?

CLOSING CASE

China's Managed Float

In 1994, China pegged the value of its currency, the yuan, to the U.S. dollar at an exchange rate of $1 = 8.28 yuan. For the next 11 years, the value of the yuan moved in lockstep with the value of the U.S. dollar against other currencies. By early 2005, however, pressure was building for China to alter its exchange rate policy and let the yuan float freely against the dollar.

Underlying this pressure were claims that after years of rapid economic growth and foreign capital inflows, the pegged exchange rate undervalued the yuan by as much as 40 percent. In turn, the cheap yuan was helping to fuel a boom in Chinese exports to the West, particularly the United States where the trade deficit with China expanded to a record $160 billion in 2004. Job losses among American manufacturing companies created political pressures in the United States for the government to push the Chinese to let the yuan float freely against the dollar. American manufacturers complained that they could not compete against "artificially cheap" Chinese imports. In early 2005, Senators Charles Schumer and Lindsay Graham tried to get the Senate to impose a 27.5 percent tariff on imports from China unless the Chinese agreed to revalue its currency against the U.S. dollar. Although the move was defeated, Schumer and Graham vowed to revisit the issue. For its part, the Bush administration pressured China from 2003 onwards, urging the government to adopt a more flexible exchange rate policy.

Keeping the yuan pegged to the dollar was also becoming increasingly problematic for the Chinese. The trade surplus with the United States, coupled with strong inflows of foreign investment, led to a surge of dollars into China. To maintain the exchange rate, the Chinese central bank regularly purchased dollars from commercial banks, issuing them yuan at the official exchange rate. As a result, by mid-2005 China's foreign exchange reserves had risen to more than $700 billion. They were forecast to hit $1 trillion by the end of 2006. The Chinese were reportedly buying some $15 billion each month in an attempt to maintain the dollar/yuan exchange rate. When the Chinese central bank issues yuan to mop up excess dollars, the authorities are in effect expanding the domestic money supply. The Chinese banking system is now awash with money and there is growing concern that excessive lending could create a financial bubble and a surge in price inflation, which might destabilize the economy.

On July 25, 2005, the Chinese finally bowed to the pressure. The government announced that it would abandon the peg against the dollar in favor of a "link" to a basket of currencies, which included the euro, yen, and U.S. dollar. Simultaneously, the government announced that it would revalue the yuan against the U.S. dollar by 2.1 percent and allow that value to move by 0.3 percent a day. The yuan was allowed to move by 1.5 percent a day against other currencies.

Many American observers and politicians thought that the Chinese move was too limited. They called for the Chinese to relax further their control over the dollar/yuan exchange rate. The Chinese resisted. By 2006, pressure was increasing on the Chinese to take action. With the U.S. trade deficit with China hitting a new record of $202 billion in 2005, Senators Schumer and Graham once more crafted a Senate bill that would place a 27.5 percent tariff on Chinese imports unless the Chinese allowed the yuan to depreciate further against the dollar. The Chinese responded by inviting the senators to China and convincing them, for now at least, that the country will move progressively toward a more flexible exchange rate policy.[34]

Case Discussion Questions

1. Why do you think the Chinese government originally pegged the value of the yuan against the U.S. dollar? What were the benefits of doing this for China? What were the costs?

2. Over the last decade, many foreign firms have invested in China and used their Chinese factories to produce goods for export. If the yuan is allowed to float freely against the U.S. dollar on the foreign exchange markets and appreciates in value, how might this affect the fortunes of those enterprises?

3. How might a decision to let the yuan float freely affect future foreign direct investment flows into China?

4. Under what circumstances might a decision to let the yuan float freely destabilize the Chinese economy? What might the global implications of this be?

5. Do you think the U.S. government should push the Chinese to let the yuan float freely? Why?

6. What do you think the Chinese government should do—let the yuan float, maintain the peg, or change the peg in some way?

Notes

1. Guillermo Nielsen, "Inside Argentina's Financial Crisis," *Euromoney*, March 2006, pp. 21–28; "Nestor Unbounded: The IMF and Argentina," *The Economist*, December 24, 2005, p. 12; and "Which Is the Victim? Argentina and the IMF," *The Economist*, March 6, 2004, pp. 82–83.

2. Updates can be found at the IMF Web site: www.imf.org/.

3. The argument goes back to 18th-century philosopher David Hume. See D. Hume, "On the Balance of Trade," reprinted in *The Gold Standard in Theory and in History*, ed. B. Eichengreen (London: Methuen, 1985).

4. R. Solomon, *The International Monetary System, 1945–1981* (New York: Harper & Row, 1982).

5. International Monetary Fund, *World Economic Outlook, 2005* (Washington, DC: IMF, May 2005).

6. For an extended discussion of the dollar exchange rate in the 1980s, see B. D. Pauls, "US Exchange Rate Policy: Bretton Woods to the Present," *Federal Reserve Bulletin*, November 1990, pp. 891–908.

7. R. Miller, "Why the Dollar Is Giving Way," *BusinessWeek*, December 6, 2004, pp. 36–37.

8. Sources: *The Economist*, "Recycling the Petrodollars; Oil Producers' Surpluses," November 12, 2005, pp. 101–102; and S. Johnson, "Dollar's Rise Aided by OPEC Holdings," *Financial Times*, December 5, 2005, p. 17.

9. For a feel for the issues contained in this debate, see P. Krugman, *Has the Adjustment Process Worked?* (Washington, DC: Institute for International Economics, 1991); "Time to Tether Currencies," *The Economist*, January 6, 1990, pp. 15–16; P. R. Krugman and M. Obstfeld, *International Economics: Theory and Policy* (New York: HarperCollins, 1994); J. Shelton, *Money Meltdown* (New York: Free Press, 1994); and S. Edwards, "Exchange Rates and the Political Economy of Macroeconomic Discipline," *American Economic Review* 86, no. 2 (May 1996), pp. 159–63.

10. The argument is made by several prominent economists, particularly Stanford's Robert McKinnon. See R. McKinnon, "An International Standard for Monetary Stabilization," *Policy Analyses in International Economics* 8 (1984). The details of this argument are beyond the scope of this book. For a relatively accessible exposition, see P. Krugman, *The Age of Diminished Expectations* (Cambridge, MA: MIT Press, 1990).

11. A. R. Ghosh and A. M. Gulde, "Does the Exchange Rate Regime Matter for Inflation and Growth?" *Economic Issues*, no. 2 (1997).

12. "The ABC of Currency Boards," *The Economist*, November 1, 1997, p. 80.

13. International Monetary Fund, *World Economic Outlook, 1998*.

14. Ibid.

15. See P. Carroll and C. Torres, "Mexico Unveils Program of Harsh Fiscal Medicine," *The Wall Street Journal*, March 10, 1995, pp. A1, A6, and "Putting Mexico Together Again," *The Economist*, February 4, 1995, p. 65.

16. World Trade Organization, *Annual Report, 1997*, vol. II, table III, p. 69.

17. J. Ridding and J. Kynge, "Complacency Gives Way to Contagion," *Financial Times*, January 13, 1998, p. 8.

18. J. Burton and G. Baker, "The Country That Invested Its Way into Trouble," *Financial Times*, January 15, 1998, p. 8.

19. P. Shenon, "The Suharto Billions," *The New York Times*, January 16, 1998, p. 1.

20. World Bank, *1997 World Development Report* (Oxford: Oxford University Press, 1998), Table 11.

21. Ridding and Kynge, "Complacency Gives Way to Contagion."

22. Burton and Baker, "The Country That Invested Its Way into Trouble."

23. "Bitter Pill for the Thais," *Straits Times*, July 5, 1997, p. 46.

24. World Bank, *1997 World Development Report*, Table 2.

25. International Monetary Fund, press release no. 97/37, August 20, 1997.

26. T. S. Shorrock, "Korea Starts Overhaul; IMF Aid Hits $60 Billion," *Journal of Commerce*, December 8, 1997, p. 3A.

27. See J. Sachs, "Economic Transition and Exchange Rate Regime," *American Economic Review* 86, no. 92 (May 1996), pp. 147–52, and J. Sachs, "Power unto Itself," *Financial Times*, December 11, 1997, p. 11.

28. Sachs, "Power unto Itself."

29. Martin Wolf, "Same Old IMF Medicine," *Financial Times*, December 9, 1997, p. 12.

30. Sachs, "Power unto Itself."

31. Sources: P. Blustein, "Turkish Crisis Weakens the Case for Intervention," *Washington Post*, March 2, 2001, p. E1; H. Pope, "Can Turkey Finally Mend Its Economy?" *The Wall Street Journal*, May 22, 2001, p. A18; "Turkish Bath," *The Wall Street Journal*, February 23, 2001, p. A14; E. McBride, "Turkey—Fingers Crossed," *The Economist*, June 10, 2000, pp. SS16–SS17; "Turkey and the IMF," *The Economist*, December 9, 2000, pp. 81–82; G. Chazan, "Turkey's Decision on Aid Is Sinking In," *The Wall Street Journal*, March 6, 2003, p. A11; S. Fittipaldi, "Markets Keep a Wary Eye on Ankara," *Global Finance*, October 2003, p. 88; "Plumper: Turkey," *The Economist*, December 18, 2004, p. 141; and "Turkey: Country Forecast Summary," *The Economist Intelligence Unit*, January 26, 2006.

32. P. Gumbel and B. Coleman, "Daimler Warns of Severe '95 Loss Due to Strong Mark," *The New York Times*, June 29, 1995, pp. 1, 10, and M. Wolf, "Daimler-Benz Announces Major Losses," *Financial Times*, June 29, 1995, p. 1.

33. Sources: D. Michaels, "Airbus Deliveries Top Boeing's, but Several Obstacles Remain," *The Wall Street Journal*, January 16, 2004, p. A9; J. L. Gerondeau, "Airbus Eyes U.S. Suppliers as Euro Gains," *Seattle Times*, February 21, 2004, p. C4; "Euro's Gains Create Worries in Europe," *Houston Chronicle.com*, January 13, 2004, p. 3; and K. Done, "Soft Dollar and A380 Hitches Lead to EADS Losses," *Financial Times*, November 9, 2006, p. 32.

34. Sources: B. Bremner et al., "The Yuan Grows Up," *Business Week*, August 8, 2005, p. 44; "Patching the Basket: The Yuan," *The Economist*, October 1, 2005, p. 83; R. McGregor, "Renminbi Revaluation Will Slow Rise in Foreign Exchange Reserves," *Financial Times*, January 1, 2006, p. 3; and *China Daily*, "Senators Back Off Showdown with China over Yuan," March 29, 2006 (www.chinadaily.com).

Industrial and Commercial Bank of China

In October 2006, the Industrial and Commercial Bank of China, or ICBC, successfully completed the world's largest ever initial public offering (IPO), raising some $21 billion. It beat Japan's 1998 IPO of NTT DoCoMo by a wide margin to earn a place in the record books (NTT raised $18.4 billion in its IPO). The ICBC offering followed the IPOs of a number of other Chinese banks and corporations in recent years. Indeed, Chinese enterprises have been regularly tapping global capital markets for the last decade, as the Chinese have sought to fortify the balance sheets of the country's largest companies, to improve corporate governance and transparency, and to give China's industry leaders global recognition. Since 2000, Chinese companies have raised more than $100 billion from the equity markets. About half of that came in 2005 and 2006, largely from the country's biggest banks. Shares sold by Chinese companies are also accounting for a greater share of global equity sales—around 10 percent in 2006 compared to 2.8 percent in 2001, surpassing the total amount raised by companies in the world's second largest economy, Japan.

To raise this amount of capital, Chinese corporations have been aggressively courting international investors. There is simply not enough capital in the hands of Chinese investors to successfully execute such offerings. In the case of ICBC, it simultaneously listed its IPO shares on the Shanghai stock exchange and the

The Global Capital Market

LEARNING OBJECTIVES

After you have read this chapter you should be able to:

LO¹ Articulate the benefits of the global capital market.

LO² Understand why the global capital market has grown so rapidly over the last quarter century.

LO³ Be familiar with the risks association with the globalization of capital markets.

LO⁴ Appreciate the benefits and risks associated with the eurocurrency market, the global bond market, and global equity markets.

LO⁵ Understand how foreign exchange risk impacts upon the cost of capital.

Hong Kong exchange. The rationale for the Hong Kong listing was that regulations in Hong Kong are in accordance with international standards, while those in Shanghai have some way to go. By listing in Hong Kong, ICBC signaled to potential investors that it would adhere to the strict reporting and governance standards expected of the top global companies.

The ICBC listing attracted considerable interest from foreign investors, who saw it as a way to invest in the Chinese economy. ICBC has a nationwide bank network of more than 18,000, the largest in the nation. It claims 2.5 million corporate customers and 150 million personal accounts. Some 1,000 institutions from across the globe reportedly bid for shares in the IPO.

Total orders from these institutions were equivalent to 40 times the amount of stock offered for sale. In other words, the offering was massively oversubscribed. Indeed, the issue generated total demand of some $430 billion, almost twice the value of Citicorp, the world's largest bank by market capitalization. The listing on the Hong Kong exchange attracted some $350 billion in orders from global investors, more than any other offering in Hong Kong's history. The domestic portion of the stock sales, through the Shanghai exchange, attracted some $80 billion in orders. This massive oversubscription enabled ICBC to raise the issuing price for its shares and reap some $2 billion more than initially planned.[1]

Introduction

The case described at the beginning of the chapter discusses how China's largest bank, ICBC, overcame the limited capital available within China to execute the largest initial public offering in history, raising some $21 billion, much of it from foreign investors who subscribed to its shares through the Hong Kong stock exchange, one of the world's leading stock market exchanges. What ICBC achieved would not have been possible a quarter of a century ago, but the rapid globalization of capital markets now facilitates the free flow of money around the world, enabling individuals and institutions based in one nation to invest in corporations based elsewhere with relative ease.

This represents a sharp break from the practice common during much of the 20th century. In the past, substantial regulatory barriers separated national capital markets from each other. It was often difficult to take capital out of a country and invest it elsewhere. Moreover, corporations lacked the ability to list their shares on stock markets outside of their home nations. These regulatory barriers made it difficult for corporations to attract significant capital from foreign investors. These barriers tumbled fast during the 1980s and 1990s. By the middle of the last decade, a truly global capital market was emerging. This capital market enabled firms to attract capital from international investors, to list their stock on multiple exchanges, and to raise funds by issuing equity or debt around the world. For example, in 1994, Daimler-Benz, Germany's largest industrial company, raised $300 million by issuing new shares not in Germany, but in Singapore.[2] Similarly, in 1996 the German telecommunications provider, Deutsche Telekom, raised some $13.3 billion by simultaneously listing its shares for sale on stock exchanges in Frankfurt, London, New York, and Tokyo. These German companies elected to raise equity through foreign markets because they reasoned that their domestic capital market was too small to supply the requisite funds at a reasonable cost. To lower their cost of capital they tapped into the large and highly liquid global capital market. By 2006 estimates suggested that some $6.5 trillion a year in capital was flowing across national borders and that this figure was growing by 11 percent a year.[3]

We begin this chapter by looking at the benefits associated with the globalization of capital markets. This discussion is followed by a more detailed look at the growth of the international capital market and the macroeconomic risks associated with such growth. Next comes a detailed review of three important segments of the global capital market: the eurocurrency market, the international bond market, and the international equity market. As usual, we close the chapter by pointing out some of the implications for the practice of international business.

Benefits of the Global Capital Market

Although this section is about the global capital market, we open it by discussing the functions of a generic capital market. Then we will look at the limitations of domestic capital markets and discuss the benefits of using global capital markets.

FUNCTIONS OF A GENERIC CAPITAL MARKET

Why do we have capital markets? What is their function? A capital market brings together those who want to invest money and those who want to borrow money (see Figure 11.1). Those who want to invest money include corporations with surplus cash, individuals, and nonbank financial institutions (e.g., pension funds, insurance companies). Those who want to borrow money include individuals, companies, and governments. Between these two groups are the market makers. Market makers are the financial service companies that connect investors and borrowers, either directly or indirectly. They include commercial banks (e.g., Citicorp, U.S. Bank) and investment banks (e.g., Merrill Lynch, Goldman Sachs).

FIGURE 11.1

The Main Players in a
Generic Capital Market

Commercial banks perform an indirect connection function. They take cash deposits from corporations and individuals and pay them a rate of interest in return. They then lend that money to borrowers at a higher rate of interest, making a profit from the difference in interest rates (commonly referred to as the interest rate spread). Investment banks perform a direct connection function. They bring investors and borrowers together and charge commissions for doing so. For example, Merrill Lynch may act as a stockbroker for an individual who wants to invest some money. Its personnel will advise her as to the most attractive purchases and buy stock on her behalf, charging a fee for the service.

Capital market loans to corporations are either equity loans or debt loans. An equity loan is made when a corporation sells stock to investors. The money the corporation receives in return for its stock can be used to purchase plants and equipment, fund R&D projects, pay wages, and so on. A share of stock gives its holder a claim to a firm's profit stream. Ultimately, the corporation honors this claim by paying dividends to the stockholders (although many fast growing young corporations do not start to issue dividends until their business has matured and their growth rate slows down). The amount of the dividends is not fixed in advance. Rather, it is determined by management based on how much profit the corporation is making. Investors purchase stock both for its dividend yield and in anticipation of gains in the price of the stock, which in theory reflect future dividend yields. Stock prices increase when a corporation is projected to have greater earnings in the future, which increases the probability that it will raise future dividend payments.

A debt loan requires the corporation to repay a predetermined portion of the loan amount (the sum of the principal plus the specified interest) at regular intervals regardless of how much profit it is making. Management has no discretion as to the amount it will pay investors. Debt loans include cash loans from banks and funds raised from the sale of corporate bonds to investors. When an investor purchases a corporate bond, he purchases the right to receive a specified fixed stream of income from the corporation for a specified number of years (i.e., until the bond maturity date).

ATTRACTIONS OF THE GLOBAL CAPITAL MARKET

Why do we need a global capital market? Why are domestic capital markets not sufficient? A global capital market benefits both borrowers and investors. It benefits borrowers by increasing the supply of funds available for borrowing and by lowering the cost of capital. It benefits investors by providing a wider range of investment opportunities, thereby allowing them to build portfolios of international investments that diversify their risks.

The Borrower's Perspective: Lower Cost of Capital

In a purely domestic capital market, the pool of investors is limited to residents of the country. This places an upper limit on the supply of funds available to borrowers. In other words, the liquidity of the market is limited. A global capital market, with its much larger pool of investors, provides a larger supply of funds for borrowers to draw on.

Perhaps the most important drawback of the limited liquidity of a purely domestic capital market is that the cost of capital tends to be higher than it is in an international

FIGURE 11.2

Market Liquidity and the
Cost of Capital

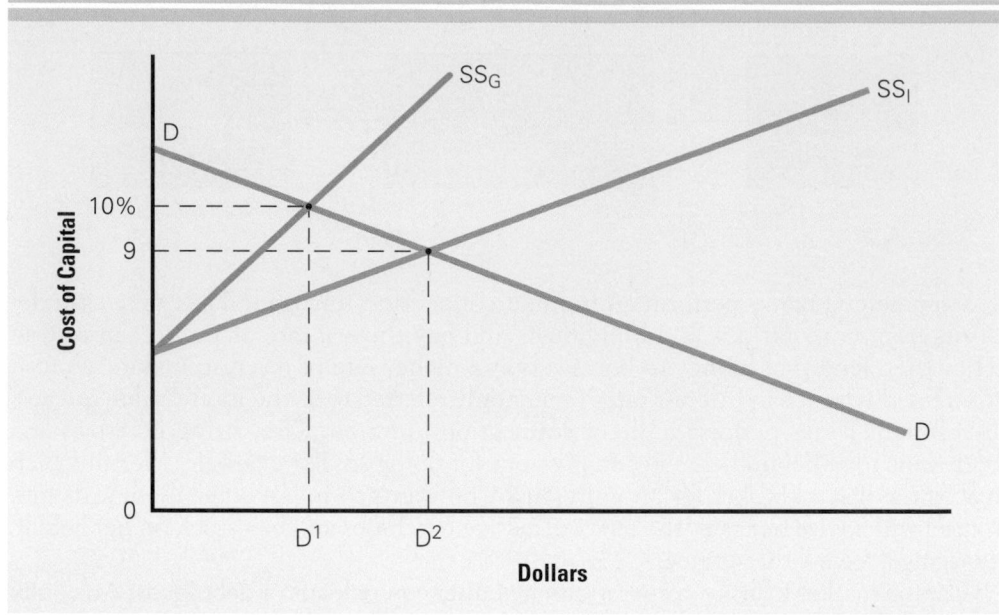

market. The cost of capital is the price of borrowing money, which is the rate of return that borrowers must pay investors. This is the interest rate on debt loans and the dividend yield and expected capital gains on equity loans. In a purely domestic market, the limited pool of investors implies that borrowers must pay more to persuade investors to lend them their money. The larger pool of investors in an international market implies that borrowers will be able to pay less.

The argument is illustrated in Figure 11.2, using Deutsche Telekom as an example (see the Management Focus feature for details). Deutsche Telekom raised over $13 billion by simultaneously offering shares for sale in Frankfurt, New York, London, and Tokyo. The vertical axis in Figure 11.2 is the cost of capital (the price of borrowing money) and the horizontal axis, the amount of money available at varying interest rates. DD is the Deutsche Telekom demand curve for borrowings. Note that the Deutsche Telekom demand for funds varies with the cost of capital; the lower the cost of capital, the more money Deutsche Telekom will borrow. (Money is just like anything else; the lower its price, the more of it people can afford.) SS_G is the supply curve of funds available in the German capital market, and SS_I represents the funds available in the global capital market. Note that Deutsche Telekom can borrow more funds more cheaply on the global capital market. As Figure 11.2 illustrates, the greater pool of resources in the global capital market—the greater liquidity—both lowers the cost of capital and increases the amount Deutsche Telekom can borrow. Thus, the advantage of a global capital market to borrowers is that it lowers the cost of capital.

Problems of limited liquidity are not restricted to less developed nations, which naturally tend to have smaller domestic capital markets. In recent decades, even very large enterprises based in some of the world's most advanced industrialized nations have tapped the international capital markets in their search for greater liquidity and a lower cost of capital, such as Germany's Deutsche Telekom.[4]

The Investor's Perspective: Portfolio Diversification

By using the global capital market, investors have a much wider range of investment opportunities than in a purely domestic capital market. The most significant consequence of this choice is that investors can diversify their portfolios internationally, thereby reducing their risk to below what could be achieved in a purely domestic capital market.

Deutsche Telekom Taps the Global Capital Market

Based in the world's third largest industrial economy, Deutsche Telekom is one of the world's largest telephone companies. Until late 1996, the company was wholly owned by the German government. However, in the mid-1990s, the German government formulated plans to privatize the utility, selling shares to the public. The privatization effort was driven by two factors: (1) a realization that state-owned enterprises tend to be inherently inefficient, and (2) the impending deregulation of the European Union telecommunications industry in 1998, which promised to expose Deutsche Telekom to foreign competition for the first time. Deutsche Telekom realized that, to become more competitive, it needed massive investments in new telecommunications infrastructure, including fiber optics and wireless, lest it start losing share in its home market to more efficient competitors such as AT&T and British Telecom after 1998. Financing such investments from state sources would have been difficult even under the best of circumstances and almost impossible in the late 1990s, when the German government was trying to limit its budget deficit to meet the criteria for membership in the European monetary union. With the active encouragement of the government, Deutsche Telekom hoped to finance its investments in capital equipment through the sale of shares to the public.

From a financial perspective, the privatization looked anything but easy. In 1996, Deutsche Telekom was valued at about $60 billion. If it maintained this valuation as a private company, it would dwarf all others listed on the German stock market. However, many analysts doubted there was anything close to $60 billion available in Germany for investment in Deutsche Telekom stock. One problem was that there was no tradition of retail stock investing in Germany. In 1996, only 1 in 20 German citizens owned shares, compared with 1 in every 4 or 5 in the United States and Britain. This lack of retail interest in stock ownership makes for a relatively illiquid stock market. Nor did banks, the traditional investors in company stocks in Germany, seem enthused about underwriting such a massive privatization effort. A further problem was that a wave of privatizations was already sweeping through Germany and the rest of Europe, so Deutsche Telekom would have to compete with many other state-owned enterprises for investors' attention. Given these factors, probably the only way that Deutsche Telekom could raise $60 billion through the German capital market would have been by promising investors a dividend yield that would raise the company's cost of capital above levels that could be serviced profitably.

Deutsche Telekom managers concluded they had to privatize the company in stages and sell a substantial portion of Deutsche Telekom stock to foreign investors. The company's plans called for an initial public offering (IPO) of 713 million shares of Deutsche Telekom stock, representing 25 percent of the company's total value, for about $18.50 per share. With a total projected value in excess of $13 billion, even this "limited" sale of Deutsche Telekom represented the largest IPO in European history and the second largest in the world after the 1987 sale of shares in Japan's telephone monopoly, NTT, for $15.6 billion. Concluding there was no way the German capital market could absorb even this partial sale of Deutsche Telekom equity, the managers of the company decided to simultaneously list shares and offer them for sale in Frankfurt (where the German stock exchange is located), London, New York, and Tokyo, attracting investors from all over the world. The IPO was successfully executed in November 1996 and raised $13.3 billion for the company.[5]

We will consider how this works in the case of stock holdings, although the same argument could be made for bond holdings.

Consider an investor who buys stock in a biotech firm that has not yet produced a new product. Imagine the price of the stock is very volatile—investors are buying and selling the stock in large numbers in response to information about the firm's prospects. Such stocks are risky investments; investors may win big if the firm produces a marketable product, but investors may also lose all their money if the firm fails to come up with a product that sells. Investors can guard against the risk associated with holding this stock by buying other firms' stocks, particularly those weakly or negatively correlated with the

FIGURE 11.3

Risk Reduction through
Portfolio Diversification

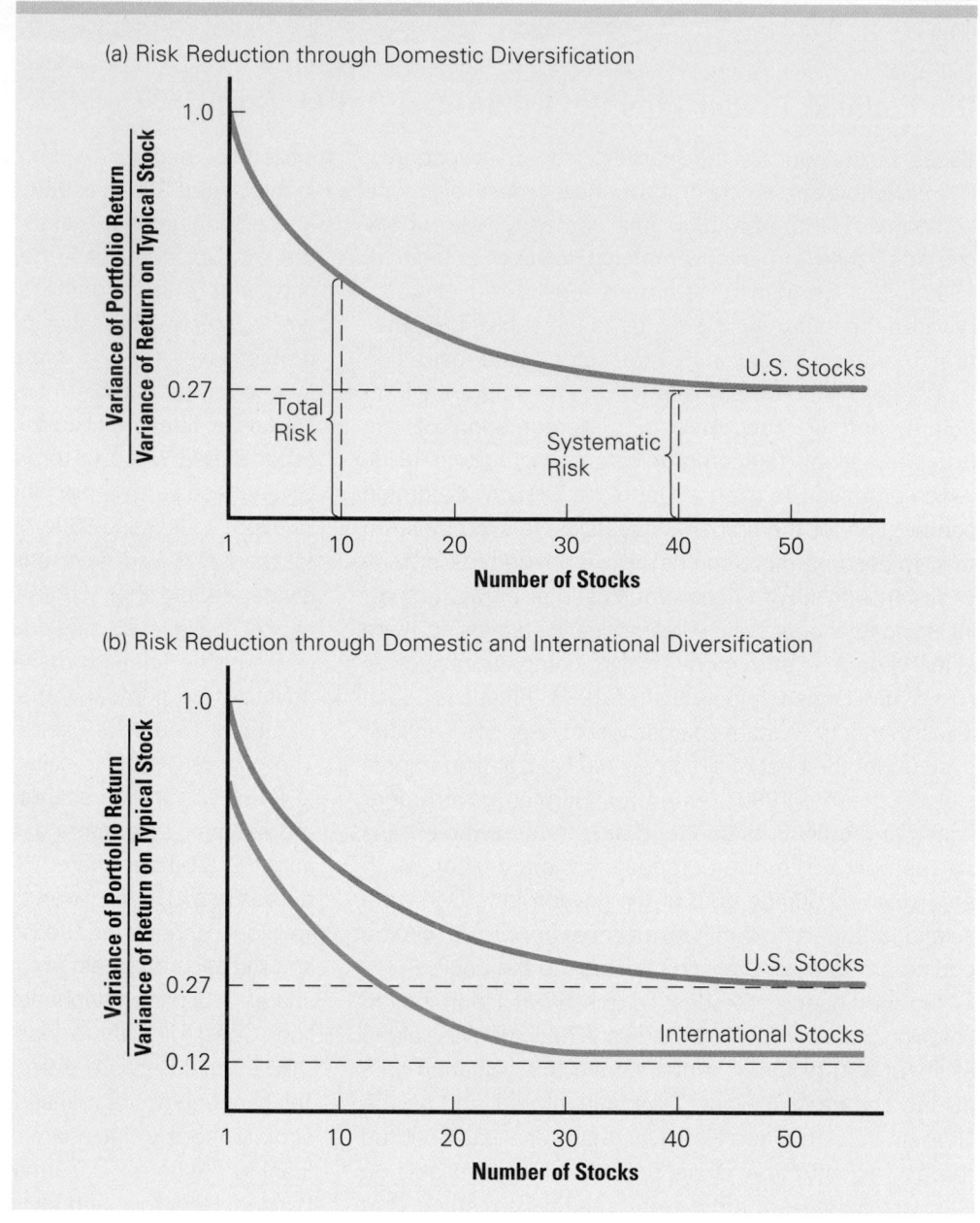

biotech stock. By holding a variety of stocks in a diversified portfolio, the losses incurred
when some stocks fail to live up to their promises are offset by the gains enjoyed when
other stocks exceed their promise.

As an investor increases the number of stocks in her portfolio, the portfolio's risk
declines. At first this decline is rapid. Soon, however, the rate of decline falls off and
asymptotically approaches the systematic risk of the market. Systematic risk refers to
movements in a stock portfolio's value that are attributable to macroeconomic forces
affecting all firms in an economy, rather than factors specific to an individual firm. The
systematic risk is the level of nondiversifiable risk in an economy. Figure 11.3 illustrates
this relationship for the United States using data from a classic study by Solnik.[6] His data
suggested that a fully diversified U.S. portfolio is only about 27 percent as risky as a
typical individual stock.

By diversifying a portfolio internationally, an investor can reduce the level of risk
even further because the movements of stock market prices across countries are not

perfectly correlated. For example, one study looked at the correlation between three stock market indexes. The Standard & Poor's 500 (S&P 500) summarized the movement of large U.S. stocks. The Morgan Stanley Capital International Europe, Australia, and Far East Index (EAFE) summarized stock market movements in other developed nations. The third index, the International Finance Corporation Global Emerging Markets Index (IFC) summarized stock market movements in less developed "emerging economies." From 1981 to 1994, the correlation between the S&P 500 and EAFE indexes was 0.45, suggesting they moved together only about 20 percent of the time (i.e., $0.45 \times 0.45 = 0.2025$). The correlation between the S&P 500 and IFC indexes was even lower at 0.32, suggesting they moved together only a little over 10 percent of the time.[7] More recent studies have confirmed that despite casual observations different national stock markets appear to be only moderately correlated. One study found that between 1972 and 2000 the average pair-wise correlation between the world's four largest equity markets, in the United States, United Kingdom, Germany, and Japan, was 0.475, suggesting that these markets moved in tandem only about 22 percent of the time ($0.475 \times 0.472 = 0.22$ or 22 percent of shared variance).[8]

The relatively low correlation between the movements of stock markets in different countries reflects two basic factors. First, countries pursue different macroeconomic policies and face different economic conditions, so their stock markets respond to different forces and can move in different ways. For example, in 1997, the stock markets of several Asian countries, including South Korea, Malaysia, Indonesia, and Thailand, lost over 50 percent of their value in response to the Asian financial crisis, while at the same time the S&P 500 increased in value by over 20 percent. Second, different stock markets are still somewhat segmented from each other by capital controls—that is, by restrictions on cross-border capital flows (although as noted earlier, such restrictions are declining rapidly). The most common restrictions include limits on the amount of a firm's stock that a foreigner can own and limits on the ability of a country's citizens to invest their money outside that country. For example, until recently it was difficult for foreigners to own more than 30 percent of the equity of South Korean enterprises. Tight restrictions on capital flows make it very hard for Chinese citizens to take money out of their country and invest it in foreign assets. Such barriers to cross-border capital flows limit the ability of capital to roam the world freely in search of the highest risk-adjusted return. Consequently, at any one time, there may be too much capital invested in some markets and too little in others. This will tend to produce differences in rates of return across stock markets.[9] The implication is that by diversifying a portfolio to include foreign stocks, an investor can reduce the level of risk below that incurred by holding just domestic stocks.

Figure 11.3 also illustrates the relationship between international diversification and risk found in the classic study by Bruno Solnik.[10] According to the figure, a fully diversified portfolio that contains stocks from many countries is less than half as risky as a fully diversified portfolio that contains only U.S. stocks. Solnik found that a fully diversified portfolio of international stocks is only about 12 percent as risky as a typical individual stock, whereas a fully diversified portfolio of U.S. stocks is about 27 percent as risky as a typical individual stock.

There is a perception, increasingly common among investment professionals, that in the last 10 years the growing integration of the global economy and the emergence of the global capital market have increased the correlation between different stock markets, reducing the benefits of international diversification.[11] Today, it is argued, if the U.S. economy enters a recession and the U.S. stock market declines rapidly, other markets follow suit. A recent study by Solnik suggests that there may be some truth to this assertion, but that the rate of integration is not occurring as rapidly as the popular perception would lead one to believe. Solnik and his associate looked at the correlation between 15 major stock markets in developed countries between 1971 and 1998. They found that on average, the correlation of monthly stock market returns increased from 0.66 in 1971 to 0.75 in 1998, indicating some convergence over time, but that "the regression results were weak," which suggests that this "average" relationship was not strong, and that there was considerable variation among countries.[12] Similarly, a study published in 2005 confirmed this basic finding, suggesting that even today a portfolio equally diversified across all available markets can reduce portfolio risk to about 35 percent of the volatility associated with a single market (i.e., a 65 percent reduction in risk).[13]

The implication here is that international portfolio diversification can still reduce risk. Moreover, the correlation between stock market movements in developed and emerging markets seems to be much lower, and the rise of stock markets in developing nations, such as China, has given international investors many more opportunities for international portfolio diversification.[14]

The risk-reducing effects of international portfolio diversification would be greater were it not for the volatile exchange rates associated with the current floating exchange rate regime. Floating exchange rates introduce an additional element of risk into invest-ing in foreign assets. As we have said repeatedly, adverse exchange rate movements can transform otherwise profitable investments into unprofitable investments. The uncer-tainty engendered by volatile exchange rates may be acting as a brake on the otherwise rapid growth of the international capital market.

GROWTH OF THE GLOBAL CAPITAL MARKET

According to data from the Bank for International Settlements, the global capital market is growing at a rapid pace.[15] By late 2006 the stock of cross-border bank loans stood at $17,875 billion, compared to $7,859 billion in 2000 and $3,600 billion in 1990. There were $17,561 billion in outstanding international bonds in late 2006, up from $5,908 billion in 2000 and $3,515 billion in 1997. International equity offerings for 2006 exceeded $377 billion, compared to $90 billion in 1997 and some $18 billion in 1990. All the 2006 figures were records. What factors allowed the international capital market to bloom in the 1980s, 1990s, and 2000s? There seem to be two answers—advances in information technology and deregulation by governments.

Information Technology

Financial services is an information-intensive industry. It draws on large volumes of information about markets, risks, exchange rates, interest rates, creditworthiness, and so on. It uses this information to make decisions about what to invest where, how much to charge borrowers, how much interest to pay to depositors, and the value and riskiness of a range of financial assets including corporate bonds, stocks, government securities, and currencies.

Because of this information intensity, the financial services industry has been revolu-tionized more than any other industry by advances in information technology since the 1970s. The growth of international communications technology has facilitated instanta-neous communication between any two points on the globe. At the same time, rapid advances in data processing capabilities have allowed market makers to absorb and process large volumes of information from around the world. According to one study, because of these technological developments, the real cost of recording, transmitting, and processing information fell by 95 percent between 1964 and 1990.[16] With the rapid rise of the Internet and the massive increase in computing power that we have seen since 1990, it seems likely that the cost of recording, transmitting, and processing information has fallen by a similar amount since 1990 and is now trivial.

Such developments have facilitated the emergence of an integrated international capital market. It is now technologically possible for financial services companies to engage in 24-hour-a-day trading, whether it is in stocks, bonds, foreign exchange, or any other financial asset. Due to advances in communications and data processing technology, the international capital market never sleeps. San Francisco closes one hour before Tokyo opens, but during this period trading continues in New Zealand.

The integration facilitated by technology has a dark side.[17] "Shocks" that occur in one financial center now spread around the globe very quickly. The collapse of U.S. stock prices on the notorious Black Monday of October 19, 1987, immediately triggered similar collapses in all the world's major stock markets, wiping billions of dollars off the value of corporate stocks worldwide. Similarly, the Asian financial crisis of 1997 sent shock waves around the world and precipitated a sell-off in world stock markets, although the effects of the shock were short lived. However, most market participants would argue that the benefits of an integrated global capital market far outweigh any potential costs. Moreover, despite the fact that shocks in national financial markets do seem to spill over into other markets, on average the correlation between movements in national equity markets remains relatively low, suggesting that such shocks may have a relative small long-term impact outside of their home market.[18]

Deregulation

In country after country, the financial services industry has historically been the most tightly regulated of all industries. Governments around the world have traditionally kept other countries' financial service firms from entering their capital markets. In some cases, they have also restricted the overseas expansion of their domestic financial services firms. In many countries, the law has also segmented the domestic financial services industry. In the United States, for example, until recently commercial banks were prohibited from performing the functions of investment banks, and vice versa. Historically, many countries have limited the ability of foreign investors to purchase significant equity positions in domestic companies. They have also limited the amount of foreign investment that their citizens could undertake. In the 1970s, for example, capital controls made it very difficult for a British investor to purchase American stocks and bonds.

Many of these restrictions have been crumbling since the early 1980s. In part, this has been a response to the development of the eurocurrency market, which from the beginning was outside of national control. (This is explained later in the chapter.) It has also been a response to pressure from financial services companies, which have long wanted to operate in a less regulated environment. Increasing acceptance of the free market ideology associated with an individualistic political philosophy also has a lot to do with the global trend toward the deregulation of financial markets (see Chapter 2). Whatever the reason, deregulation in a number of key countries has undoubtedly facilitated the growth of the international capital market.

The trend began in the United States in the late 1970s and early 80s with a series of changes that allowed foreign banks to enter the U.S. capital market and domestic banks to expand their operations overseas. In Great Britain, the so-called Big Bang of October 1986 removed barriers that had existed between banks and stockbrokers and allowed foreign financial service companies to enter the British stock market. Restrictions on the entry of foreign securities houses have been relaxed in Japan, and Japanese banks are now allowed to open international banking facilities. In France, the "Little Bang" of 1987 opened the French stock market to outsiders and to foreign and domestic banks. In Germany, foreign banks are now allowed to lend and manage foreign euro issues, subject to reciprocity agreements.[19] All of this has enabled financial services companies to transform themselves from primarily domestic companies into global operations with major offices around the world—a prerequisite for the development of a truly international capital market. As we saw in Chapter 5, in late 1997 the World Trade Organization brokered a deal that removed many of the restrictions on cross-border trade in financial services. This deal facilitated further growth in the size of the global capital market.

In addition to the deregulation of the financial services industry, many countries beginning in the 1970s started to dismantle capital controls, loosening both restrictions on inward investment by foreigners and outward investment by their own citizens and corporations. By the 1980s, this trend spread from developed nations to the emerging economies of the world as countries across Latin America, Asia, and Eastern Europe started to dismantle decades-old restrictions on capital flows.

As of 2007, the trends toward deregulation of financial services and removal of capital controls were still firmly in place. Given the benefits associated with the globalization of capital, the growth of the global capital market can be expected to continue for the foreseeable future. While most commentators see this as a positive development, there are those who believe that the globalization of capital has serious inherent risks.

Global Capital Market Risks

Some analysts are concerned that due to deregulation and reduced controls on cross-border capital flows, individual nations are becoming more vulnerable to speculative capital flows. They see this as having a destabilizing effect on national economies.[20] Harvard economist Martin Feldstein, for example, has argued that most of the capital that moves internationally is pursuing temporary gains, and it shifts in and out of countries as quickly as conditions change.[21] He distinguishes between this short-term capital, or "hot money," and "patient money" that would support long-term cross-border capital flows. To Feldstein, patient money is still relatively rare, primarily because although capital is free to move internationally, its owners and managers still prefer to keep most of it at home. Feldstein supports his arguments with statistics that demonstrate that although vast amounts of money flows through the foreign exchange markets every day, "when the dust settles, most of the savings done in each country stays in that country."[22] Feldstein argues that the lack of patient money is due to the relative paucity of information that investors have about foreign investments. In his view, if investors had better information about foreign assets, the global capital market would work more efficiently and be less subject to short-term speculative capital flows. Feldstein claims that Mexico's economic problems in the mid-1990s were the result of too much hot money flowing in and out of the country and too little patient money. This example is reviewed in detail in the accompanying Country Focus.

A lack of information about the fundamental quality of foreign investments may encourage speculative flows in the global capital market. Faced with a lack of quality information, investors may react to dramatic news events in foreign nations and pull their money out too quickly. Despite advances in information technology, it is still difficult for an investor to get access to the same quantity and quality of information about foreign investment opportunities that he can get about domestic investment opportunities. This information gap is exacerbated by different accounting conventions in different countries, which makes the direct comparison of cross-border investment opportunities difficult for all but the most sophisticated investor (see Chapter 19 for details). For example, German accounting principles are different from those found in the United States and can present quite a different picture of the health of a company. Thus, when the German company Daimler-Benz translated its German financial accounts into U.S.-style accounts in 1993, as it had to do to be listed on the New York Stock Exchange, it found that while it had made a profit of $97 million under German rules, under U.S. rules it had lost $548 million![24]

Given the problems created by differences in the quantity and quality of information, many investors have yet to venture into the world of cross-border investing, and those that do are prone to reverse their decision on the basis of limited (and perhaps inaccurate) information. However, if the international capital market continues to grow, financial intermediaries likely will increasingly provide quality information about foreign investment opportunities. Better information should increase the sophistication of investment decisions and reduce the frequency and size of speculative capital flows. Although concerns about the volume of "hot money" sloshing around in the global capital market increased as a result of the Asian financial crisis, IMF research suggests there has not been an increase in the volatility of financial markets since the 1970s.[25]

Did the Global Capital Markets Fail Mexico?

In early 1994, soon after passage of the North American Free Trade Agreement (NAFTA), Mexico was widely admired among the international community as a shining example of a developing country with a bright economic future. Since the late 1980s, the Mexican government had pursued sound monetary, budget, tax, and trade policies. By historical standards, inflation was low, the country was experiencing solid economic growth, and exports were booming. This robust picture attracted capital from foreign investors; between 1991 and 1993, foreigners invested over $75 billion in the Mexican economy, more than in any other developing nation.

If there was a blot on Mexico's economic report card, it was the country's growing current account (trade) deficit. Mexican exports were booming, but so were its imports. In the 1989–1990 period, the current account deficit was equivalent to about 3 percent of Mexico's gross domestic product. In 1991 it increased to 5 percent, and by 1994 it was running at an annual rate of over 6 percent. Bad as this might seem, it is not unsustainable and should not bring an economy crashing down. The United States has been running a current account deficit for decades with apparently little in the way of ill effects. A current account deficit will not be a problem for a country as long as foreign investors take the money they earn from trade with that country and reinvest it within the country. This has been the case in the United States for years, and during the early 1990s, it was occurring in Mexico too. Thus, companies such as Ford took the pesos they earned from exports to Mexico and reinvested those funds in productive capacity in Mexico, building auto plants to serve the future needs of the Mexican market and to export elsewhere.

Unfortunately for Mexico, much of the $25 billion annual inflow of capital it received during the early 1990s was not the kind of patient long-term money that Ford was putting into Mexico. Rather, according to economist Martin Feldstein, much of the inflow was short-term capital that could flee if economic conditions changed for the worst. This is what seems to have occurred. In February 1994, the U.S. Federal Reserve began to increase U.S. interest rates. This led to a rapid fall in U.S. bond prices. At the same time, the yen began to appreciate sharply against the U.S. dollar. These events resulted in large losses for many managers of short-term capital, such as hedge fund managers and banks, who had been betting on exactly the opposite happening. Many hedge fund managers had anticipated that interest rates would fall, bond prices would rise, and the dollar would appreciate against the yen.

Faced with large losses, money managers tried to reduce the riskiness of their portfolios by pulling out of uncertain situations. About the same time, events took a turn for the worse in Mexico. An armed uprising in the southern state of Chiapas, the assassination of the leading candidate in the presidential election campaign, and an accelerating inflation rate all helped produce a feeling that Mexican investments were riskier than had been assumed. Money managers began to pull many of their short-term investments out of the country.

As hot money flowed out, the Mexican government realized it could not continue to count on capital inflows to finance its current account deficit. The government had assumed the inflow was mainly composed of patient, long-term money. In reality, much of it appeared to be short-term money. As money flowed out of Mexico, the Mexican government had to commit more foreign reserves to defending the value of the peso against the U.S. dollar, which was pegged at 3.5 to the dollar. Currency speculators entered the picture and began to bet against the Mexican government by selling pesos short. Events came to a head in December 1994 when capital flows essentially forced the Mexican government to abandon its support for the peso. Over the next month, the peso lost 40 percent of its value against the dollar, the government was forced to introduce an economic austerity program, and the Mexican economic boom came to an abrupt end.

According to Martin Feldstein, the Mexican economy was brought down not by currency speculation on the foreign exchange market, but by a lack of long-term patient money. He argued that Mexico offered, and still offers, many attractive long-term investment opportunities, but because of the lack of information on long-term investment opportunities in Mexico, most of the capital flowing into the country from 1991 to 1993 was short-term, speculative money, the flow of which could quickly be reversed. If foreign investors had better information, Feldstein argued, Mexico should have been able to finance its current account deficit from inward capital flows because patient capital would naturally gravitate toward attractive Mexican investment opportunities.[23]

The Eurocurrency Market

A **eurocurrency** is any currency banked outside of its country of origin. Eurodollars, which account for about two-thirds of all eurocurrencies, are dollars banked outside of the United States. Other important eurocurrencies include the euroyen, the europound, and the euro-euro! The term *eurocurrency* is actually a misnomer because a eurocurrency can be created anywhere in the world; the persistent *euro-* prefix reflects the European origin of the market. The eurocurrency market has been an important and relatively low-cost source of funds for international businesses.

GENESIS AND GROWTH OF THE MARKET

The eurocurrency market was born in the mid-1950s when Eastern European holders of dollars, including the former Soviet Union, were afraid to deposit their holdings of dollars in the United States lest they be seized by the U.S. government to settle U.S. residents' claims resulting from business losses during the Communist takeover of Eastern Europe.[26] These countries deposited many of their dollar holdings in Europe, particularly in London. Additional dollar deposits came from various Western European central banks and from companies that earned dollars by exporting to the United States. These two groups deposited their dollars in London banks, rather than U.S. banks, because they were able to earn a higher rate of interest (which will be explained).

The eurocurrency market received a major push in 1957 when the British government prohibited British banks from lending British pounds to finance non-British trade, a business that had been very profitable for British banks. British banks began financing the same trade by attracting dollar deposits and lending dollars to companies engaged in international trade and investment. Because of this historical event, London became, and has remained, the leading center of eurocurrency trading.

The eurocurrency market received another push in the 1960s when the U.S. government enacted regulations that discouraged U.S. banks from lending to those who were not U.S. residents. Would-be dollar borrowers outside the United States found it increasingly difficult to borrow dollars in the United States to finance international trade, so they turned to the eurodollar market to obtain the necessary dollar funds.

The U.S. government changed its policies after the 1973 collapse of the Bretton Woods system (see Chapter 10), removing an important impetus to the growth of the eurocurrency market. However, another political event, the oil price increases engineered by OPEC in the 1973–74 and 1979–80 periods, gave the market another big shove. As a result of the oil price increases, the Arab members of OPEC accumulated huge amounts of dollars. They were afraid to place their money in U.S. banks or their European branches, lest the U.S. government attempt to confiscate them. (Their fear was not unfounded; President Carter froze Iranian assets in U.S. banks and their European branches in 1979 after Americans were taken hostage at the U.S. embassy in Tehran.) Instead, these countries deposited their dollars with banks in London, further increasing the supply of eurodollars.

Although these various political events contributed to the growth of the eurocurrency market, they alone were not responsible for it. The market grew because it offered real financial advantages—initially to those who wanted to deposit dollars or borrow dollars and later to those who wanted to deposit and borrow other currencies. We now look at the source of these financial advantages.

ATTRACTIONS OF THE EUROCURRENCY MARKET

The main factor that makes the eurocurrency market attractive to both depositors and borrowers is its lack of government regulation. This allows banks to offer higher interest rates on eurocurrency deposits than on deposits made in the home currency, making eurocurrency deposits attractive to those who have cash to deposit. The lack of regulation

FIGURE 11.4

Interest Rate Spreads
in Domestic and
Eurocurrency Markets

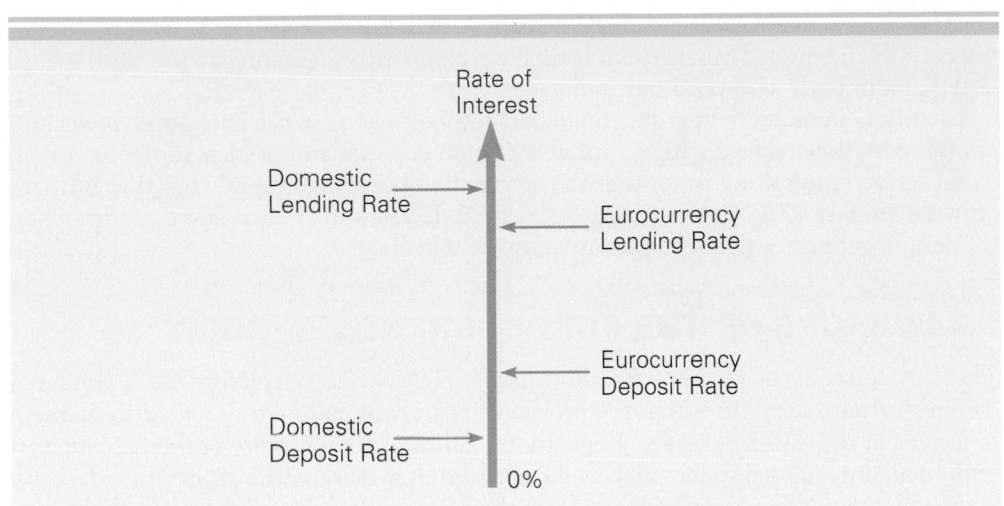

also allows banks to charge borrowers a lower interest rate for eurocurrency borrowings than for borrowings in the home currency, making eurocurrency loans attractive for those who want to borrow money. In other words, the spread between the eurocurrency deposit rate and the eurocurrency lending rate is less than the spread between the domestic deposit and lending rates (see Figure 11.4). To understand why this is so, we must examine how government regulations raise the costs of domestic banking.

Domestic currency deposits are regulated in all industrialized countries. Such regulations ensure that banks have enough liquid funds to satisfy demand if large numbers of domestic depositors should suddenly decide to withdraw their money. All countries operate with certain reserve requirements. For example, each time a U.S. bank accepts a deposit in dollars, it must place some fraction of that deposit in a non-interest-bearing account at a Federal Reserve Bank as part of its required reserves. Similarly, each time a British bank accepts a deposit in pounds sterling, it must place a certain fraction of that deposit with the Bank of England.

Banks are given much more freedom in their dealings in foreign currencies, however. For example, the British government does not impose reserve requirement restrictions on deposits of foreign currencies within its borders. Nor are the London branches of U.S. banks subject to U.S. reserve requirement regulations, provided those deposits are payable only outside the United States. This gives eurobanks a competitive advantage.

For example, suppose a bank based in New York faces a 10 percent reserve requirement. According to this requirement, if the bank receives a $100 deposit, it can lend out no more than $90 of that and it must place the remaining $10 in a non-interest-bearing account at a Federal Reserve bank. Suppose the bank has annual operating costs of $1 per $100 of deposits and that it charges 10 percent interest on loans. The highest interest the New York bank can offer its depositors and still cover its costs is 8 percent per year. Thus, the bank pays the owner of the $100 deposit (0.08 × $100 =) $8, earns (0.10 × $90 =) $9 on the fraction of the deposit it is allowed to lend, and just covers its operating costs.

In contrast, a eurobank can offer a higher interest rate on dollar deposits and still cover its costs. The eurobank, with no reserve requirements regarding dollar deposits, can lend out all of a $100 deposit. Therefore, it can earn 0.10 × $100 = $10 at a loan rate of 10 percent. If the eurobank has the same operating costs as the New York bank ($1 per $100 deposit), it can pay its depositors an interest rate of 9 percent, a full percentage point higher than that paid by the New York bank, and still cover its costs. That is, it can pay out 0.09 × $100 = $9 to its depositor, receive $10 from the borrower, and be left with $1 to cover operating costs. Alternatively, the eurobank might pay the depositor 8.5 percent (which is still above the rate paid by the New York bank), charge borrowers 9.5 percent (still less than the New York bank charges), and cover its operating costs even better. Thus, the eurobank has a competitive advantage vis-à-vis the New York bank in both its deposit rate and its loan rate.

Clearly, companies have strong financial motivations to use the eurocurrency market. By doing so, they receive a higher interest rate on deposits and pay less for loans. Given this, the surprising thing is not that the euromarket has grown rapidly but that it hasn't grown even faster. Why do any depositors hold deposits in their home currency when they could get better yields in the eurocurrency market?

DRAWBACKS OF THE EUROCURRENCY MARKET

The eurocurrency market has two drawbacks. First, when depositors use a regulated banking system, they know that the probability of a bank failure that would cause them to lose their deposits is very low. Regulation maintains the liquidity of the banking system. In an unregulated system such as the eurocurrency market, the probability of a bank failure that would cause depositors to lose their money is greater (although in absolute terms, still low). Thus, the lower interest rate received on home-country deposits reflects the costs of insuring against bank failure. Some depositors are more comfortable with the security of such a system and are willing to pay the price.

Second, borrowing funds internationally can expose a company to foreign exchange risk. For example, consider a U.S. company that uses the eurocurrency market to borrow europounds—perhaps because it can pay a lower interest rate on europound loans than on dollar loans. Imagine, however, that the British pound subsequently appreciates against the dollar. This would increase the dollar cost of repaying the europound loan and thus the company's cost of capital. Using the forward exchange market can insure against this possibility (as we saw in Chapter 9), but the forward exchange market does not offer perfect insurance. Consequently, many companies borrow funds in their domestic currency to avoid foreign exchange risk, even though the eurocurrency markets may offer more attractive interest rates.

The Global Bond Market

The global bond market grew rapidly during the 1980s and 1990s, and has continued to do so in the new century. Bonds are an important means of financing for many companies. The most common kind of bond is a fixed-rate bond. The investor who purchases a fixed-rate bond receives a fixed set of cash payoffs. Each year until the bond matures, the investor gets an interest payment and then at maturity he gets back the face value of the bond.

International bonds are of two types: foreign bonds and eurobonds. **Foreign bonds** are sold outside of the borrower's country and are denominated in the currency of the country in which they are issued. Thus, when Dow Chemical issues bonds in Japanese yen and sells them in Japan, it is issuing foreign bonds. Many foreign bonds have nicknames; foreign bonds sold in the United States are called Yankee bonds, foreign bonds sold in Japan are Samurai bonds, and foreign bonds sold in Great Britain are bulldogs. Companies will issue international bonds if they believe that it will lower their cost of capital. For example, during the late 1990s and early 2000s many companies issued Samurai bonds in Japan to take advantage of the very low interest rates in Japan. In early 2001, 10-year Japanese government bonds yielded 1.24 percent, compared with 5 percent for comparable U.S. government bonds. Against this background, companies found that they could raise debt at a cheaper rate in Japan than the United States.

Eurobonds are normally underwritten by an international syndicate of banks and placed in countries other than the one in whose currency the bond is denominated. For example, a German corporation may issue a bond denominated in U.S. dollars, and an international syndicate of banks may sell it to investors outside of the United States.

Eurobonds are routinely issued by multinational corporations, large domestic corporations, sovereign governments, and international institutions. They are usually offered simultaneously in several national capital markets, but neither in the capital market of the country nor to residents of the country in whose currency they are denominated. Historically, eurobonds accounted for the lion's share of international bond issues, but increasingly they are being eclipsed by foreign bonds.

ATTRACTIONS OF THE EUROBOND MARKET

Three features of the eurobond market make it an appealing alternative to most major domestic bond markets; specifically,

- An absence of regulatory interference.
- Less stringent disclosure requirements than in most domestic bond markets.
- A favorable tax status.

Regulatory Interference

National governments often impose tight controls on domestic and foreign issuers of bonds denominated in the local currency and sold within their national boundaries. These controls tend to raise the cost of issuing bonds. However, government limitations are generally less stringent for securities denominated in foreign currencies and sold to holders of those foreign currencies. Eurobonds fall outside of the regulatory domain of any single nation. As such, they can often be issued at a lower cost to the issuer.

Disclosure Requirements

Eurobond market disclosure requirements tend to be less stringent than those of several national governments. For example, if a firm wishes to issue dollar-denominated bonds within the United States, it must first comply with SEC disclosure requirements. The firm must disclose detailed information about its activities, the salaries and other compensation of its senior executives, stock trades by its senior executives, and the like. In addition, the issuing firm must submit financial accounts that conform to U.S. accounting standards. For non-U.S. firms, redoing their accounts to make them consistent with U.S. standards can be very time consuming and expensive. Therefore, many firms have found it cheaper to issue eurobonds, including those denominated in dollars, than to issue dollar-denominated bonds within the United States.

Favorable Tax Status

Before 1984, U.S. corporations issuing eurobonds were required to withhold up to 30 percent of each interest payment to foreigners for U.S. income tax. This did not encourage foreigners to hold bonds issued by U.S. corporations. Similar tax laws were operational in many countries at that time, and they limited market demand for eurobonds. U.S. laws were revised in 1984 to exempt foreign holders of bonds issued by U.S. corporations from any withholding tax. As a result, U.S. corporations found it feasible for the first time to sell eurobonds directly to foreigners. Repeal of the U.S. laws caused other governments—including those of France, Germany, and Japan—to liberalize their tax laws likewise to avoid outflows of capital from their markets. The consequence was an upsurge in demand for eurobonds from investors who wanted to take advantage of their tax benefits.

🌐 The Global Equity Market

Although we have talked about the growth of the global equity market, strictly speaking there is no international equity market in the sense that there are international currency and bond markets. Rather, many countries have their own domestic equity markets in which corporate stock is traded. The largest of these domestic equity markets are to be found in the United States, Britain, and Japan. Although each domestic equity market is still dominated by investors who are citizens of that country and companies incorporated in that country, developments are internationalizing the world equity market. Investors are spending heavily in foreign equity markets to diversify their portfolios. Facilitated by deregulation and advances in information technology, this trend seems to be here to stay.

An interesting consequence of the trend toward international equity investment is the internationalization of corporate ownership. Today it is still generally possible to talk about U.S. corporations, British corporations, and Japanese corporations, primarily because the majority of stockholders (owners) of these corporations are of the respective nationality. However, this is changing. Increasingly, U.S. citizens are buying stock in companies incorporated abroad, and foreigners are buying stock in companies incorporated in the United States. Looking into the future, Robert Reich has mused about "the coming irrelevance of corporate nationality."[27]

A second development internationalizing the world equity market is that companies with historic roots in one nation are broadening their stock ownership by listing their stock in the equity markets of other nations. The reasons are primarily financial. Listing stock on a foreign market is often a prelude to issuing stock in that market to raise capital. The idea is to tap into the liquidity of foreign markets, thereby increasing the funds available for investment and lowering the firm's cost of capital. (The relationship between liquidity and the cost of capital was discussed earlier in the chapter.) Firms also often list their stock on foreign equity markets to facilitate future acquisitions of foreign companies. Other reasons for listing a company's stock on a foreign equity market are that the company's stock and stock options can be used to compensate local management and employees, it satisfies the desire for local ownership, and it increases the company's visibility with local employees, customers, suppliers, and bankers. Although firms based in developed nations were the first to start listing their stock on foreign exchanges, increasingly firms from developing countries who find their own growth limited by an illiquid domestic capital market are exploiting this opportunity. For example, firms from the Czech Republic have turned to the London stock exchange to raise equity capital (see the next Country Focus feature).

🌐 Foreign Exchange Risk and the Cost of Capital

We have emphasized repeatedly that a firm can borrow funds at a lower cost on the global capital market than on the domestic capital market. However, we have also mentioned that under a floating exchange rate regime, foreign exchange risk complicates this picture. Adverse movements in foreign exchange rates can substantially increase the cost of foreign currency loans, which is what happened to many Asian companies during the 1997–1998 Asian financial crisis.

Consider a South Korean firm that wants to borrow 1 billion Korean won for one year to fund a capital investment project. The company can borrow this money from a Korean bank at an interest rate of 10 percent, and at the end of the year pay back the loan plus interest, for a total of W1.10 billion. Or the firm could borrow dollars from an international bank at a 6 percent interest rate. At the prevailing exchange rate of $1 = W1,000, the firm would borrow $1 million and the total loan cost would be $1.06 million, or W1.06 billion. By borrowing dollars, the firm could reduce its cost of capital by 4 percent, or W40 million. However, this saving is predicated on the assumption that during the year of the loan, the dollar/won exchange rate stays constant. Instead, imagine that the won depreciates sharply against the U.S. dollar during the year and ends the year at $1 = W1,500. (This occurred in late 1997 when the won declined in value from $1 = W1,000 to $1 = W1,500 in two months.) The firm still has to pay the international bank $1.06 million at the end of the year, but now this costs the company W1.59 billion

The Search for Capital in the Czech Republic

Following the collapse of communism and the shift toward a more market-oriented system, the Czech Republic initially emerged as one of the more vibrant and market-driven economies in Eastern Europe. By early 1998, however, the economic development of the Czech Republic was constrained by a shortage of capital. The problem was rooted in macroeconomic conditions and institutional problems.

On the macroeconomic front, adverse developments in 1997 included a combination of a rise in inflation, a growing government deficit, and a speculative attack on the Czech currency that forced the government to abandon its fixed exchange rate policy for a floating exchange rate system. After the shift to a floating exchange rate system, the Czech currency declined by about 10 percent against the German deutsche mark and over 15 percent against the U.S. dollar. Since many internationally traded commodities, such as oil, are traded in dollars, this devaluation added to the Czech Republic's escalating inflation rate. The government responded by tightening monetary policy, raising interest rates to around 16 percent.

These macroeconomic problems had a predictably negative effect on the Prague stock market. The PX50, the key index of Czech shares listed on the Prague exchange, declined from around 520 to a low of 430 by June 1998. Much of the decline was due to foreign investment capital leaving the country for more attractive investment opportunities in neighboring Hungary and Poland, where macroeconomic conditions were more favorable and where local stock markets were performing better.

But that wasn't the only problem for the Prague stock market. Many Western investors had been discouraged from investing in Czech stocks by the poor reputation of the Prague stock exchange. That institution is reportedly rife with stock manipulation by insiders, insider trading that would be illegal in more developed markets, a lack of protection for minority stockholders, poor corporate reporting, and fraud. Also, most state-owned enterprises in the Czech Republic were privatized through a voucher scheme that has left the majority of shareholdings in the hands of institutions and groups that are preoccupied with maintaining control over their companies and opposed to any attempt to raise capital through new equity issues. Consequently, the Prague stock market is small and liquidity is very limited. These factors have combined to increase the cost of capital for individual Czech enterprises.

Traditionally, many Czech firms forged tight relationships with banks and borrowed money from them. However, with interest rates at 16 percent and many banks reining in credit to make up for past largesse, it was increasingly expensive for Czech companies to raise capital through borrowings. As for the Czech stock market, its poor reputation and low liquidity made it almost impossible to raise capital by issuing new shares. In mid-1997, one of the Czech Republic's most dynamic and profitable new enterprises, Bonton, a film and music company, attempted to raise $30 to $40 million through an initial public offering on the Prague exchange. This would have been only the second IPO in the history of the Prague exchange, and the only one of any significance. A successful IPO would have helped to legitimize the market, but Bonton canceled the IPO when the Prague market declined to yearlong lows in the wake of the Asian financial crisis.

Despite all these problems, most agree that the Czech economy has a bright future. However, this future cannot be realized unless Czech companies can raise the capital to invest in the necessary plants and equipment. A number of prominent Czech companies in 1998 announced their intentions to make international equity issues. At the beginning of 1997, only two Czech companies had foreign listings, both of them large banks. However, another five significant companies sought listings on the London stock exchange in 1998. The first to list was Ceske Radiokomunikace, a state-owned radio, television, and telecommunications company that successfully raised $134 million in equity by listing global depository receipts on the London exchange, increasing its equity by 36 percent and decreasing the state holding in the company to around 51 percent.[28]

(i.e., $1.06 = W1,500). As a result of the depreciation in the value of the won, the cost of borrowing in U.S. dollars has soared from 6 percent to 59 percent, a huge rise in the firm's cost of capital. Although this may seem like an extreme example, it happened to many South Korean firms in 1997 at the height of the Asian financial crisis. Not surprisingly, many of them were pushed into technical default on their loans.

Unpredictable movements in exchange rates can inject risk into foreign currency borrowing, making something that initially seems less expensive ultimately much more expensive. The borrower can hedge against such a possibility by entering into a forward contract to purchase the required amount of the currency being borrowed at a predetermined exchange rate when the loan comes due (see Chapter 9 for details). Although this will raise the borrower's cost of capital, the added insurance limits the risk involved in such a transaction. Unfortunately, many Asian borrowers did not hedge their dollar-denominated short-term debt, so when their currencies collapsed against the dollar in 1997, many saw a sharp increase in their cost of capital.

When a firm borrows funds from the global capital market, it must weigh the benefits of a lower interest rate against the risks of an increase in the real cost of capital due to adverse exchange rate movements. Although using forward exchange markets may lower foreign exchange risk with short-term borrowings, it cannot remove the risk. Most importantly, the forward exchange market does not provide adequate coverage for long-term borrowings.

IMPLICATIONS FOR MANAGERS

The implications of the material discussed in this chapter for international business are quite straightforward but no less important for being obvious. The growth of the global capital market has created opportunities for international businesses that wish to borrow and/or invest money. On the borrowing side, by using the global capital market, firms can often borrow funds at a lower cost than is possible in a purely domestic capital market. This conclusion holds no matter what form of borrowing a firm uses—equity, bonds, or cash loans. The lower cost of capital on the global market reflects their greater liquidity and the general absence of government regulation. Government regulation tends to raise the cost of capital in most domestic capital markets. The global market, being transnational, escapes regulation. Balanced against this, however, is the foreign exchange risk associated with borrowing in a foreign currency.

On the investment side, the growth of the global capital market is providing opportunities for firms, institutions, and individuals to diversify their investments to limit risk. By holding a diverse portfolio of stocks and bonds in different nations, an investor can reduce total risk to a lower level than can be achieved in a purely domestic setting. Once again, however, foreign exchange risk is a complicating factor.

The trends noted in this chapter seem likely to continue, with the global capital market continuing to increase in both importance and degree of integration over the next decade. Perhaps the most significant development will be the emergence of a unified capital market and common currency within the EU by the end of the decade as those countries continue toward economic and monetary union. Since Europe's capital markets are currently fragmented and relatively introspective (with the major exception of Britain's capital market), such a development could pave the way for even more rapid internationalization of the capital market in the early years of the next century. If this occurs, the implications for business are likely to be positive.

CHAPTER SUMMARY

This chapter explained the functions and form of the global capital market and defined the implications of these for international business practice. This chapter made the following points:

1. The function of a capital market is to bring those who want to invest money together with those who want to borrow money.

2. Relative to a domestic capital market, the global capital market has a greater supply of funds available for borrowing, and this makes for a lower cost of capital for borrowers.

3. Relative to a domestic capital market, the global capital market allows investors to diversify portfolios of holdings internationally, thereby reducing risk.

4. The growth of the global capital market during recent decades can be attributed to advances in information technology, the widespread deregulation of financial services, and the relaxation of regulations governing cross-border capital flows.

5. A eurocurrency is any currency banked outside its country of origin. The lack of government regulations makes the eurocurrency market attractive to both depositors and borrowers. Due to the absence of regulation, the spread between the eurocurrency deposit and lending rates is less than the spread between the domestic deposit and lending rates. This gives eurobanks a competitive advantage.

6. The global bond market has two classifications: the foreign bond market and the eurobond market. Foreign bonds are sold outside of the borrower's country and are denominated in the currency of the country in which they are issued. A eurobond issue is normally underwritten by an international syndicate of banks and placed in countries other than the one in whose currency the bond is denominated. Eurobonds account for the lion's share of international bond issues.

7. The eurobond market is an attractive way for companies to raise funds due to the absence of regulatory interference, less stringent disclosure requirements, and eurobonds' favorable tax status.

8. Foreign investors are investing in other countries' equity markets to reduce risk by diversifying their stock holdings among nations.

9. Many companies are now listing their stock in the equity markets of other nations, primarily as a prelude to issuing stock in those markets to raise additional capital. Other reasons for listing stock in another country's exchange are to facilitate future stock swaps; to enable the company to use its stock and stock options for compensating local management and employees; to satisfy local ownership desires; and to increase the company's visibility among its local employees, customers, suppliers, and bankers.

10. When borrowing funds from the global capital market, companies must weigh the benefits of a lower interest rate against the risks of greater real costs of capital due to adverse exchange rate movements.

11. One major implication of the global capital market for international business is that companies can often borrow funds at a lower cost of capital in the international capital market than they can in the domestic capital market.

12. The global capital market provides greater opportunities for businesses and individuals to build a truly diversified portfolio of international investments in financial assets, which lowers risk.

Critical Thinking and Discussion Questions

1. Why has the global capital market grown so rapidly in recent decades? Do you think this growth will continue throughout the next decade? Why?

2. Reread the Country Focus on the search for capital in the Czech Republic. What are the advantages to Czech firms of listing their equity on the London stock exchange? Can you see any disadvantages?

3. A firm based in Mexico has found that its growth is restricted by the limited liquidity of the Mexican capital market. List the firm's options for raising money on the global capital market. Discuss the pros and cons of each option, and

make a recommendation. How might your recommended options be affected if the Mexican peso depreciates significantly on the foreign exchange markets over the next two years?

4. Happy Company wants to raise $2 million with debt financing. The funds are needed to finance working capital, and the firm will repay them with interest in one year. Happy Company's treasurer is considering three options:

    a. Borrowing U.S. dollars from Security Pacific Bank at 8 percent.

    b. Borrowing British pounds from Midland Bank at 14 percent.

    c. Borrowing Japanese yen from Sanwa bank at 5 percent.

    If Happy borrows foreign currency, it will not cover the currency; that is, it will simply change foreign currency for dollars at today's spot rate and buy the same foreign currency a year later at the spot rate then in effect. Happy Company estimates the pound will depreciate by 5 percent relative to the dollar and the yen will appreciate 3 percent relative to the dollar in the next year. From which bank should Happy Company borrow?

Research Task

Use the globalEDGE™ site to complete the following exercises:

1. The top management of your company is looking for somebody to analyze the current position of the United States in world trade. Remembering that you learned about the dynamics of the balance of payments in your studies, you decide to prepare the analysis of the latest state of U.S. trade.

2. The Bureau of Economic Analysis is an agency of the U.S. Department of Commerce. It lists data about the U.S. International Accounts, including current investment positions and the amount of direct investment by multinational corporations. Prepare a brief report regarding the direct investments of other countries in the United States. Which are the leading countries in foreign direct investment?

CLOSING CASE

China Mobile

China Mobile (Hong Kong) Ltd. is a Hong Kong–based provider of wireless telephone service and one of the largest providers of mobile telephone service in the world. In 1996 the company was spun out of China Mobile Communications Corporation, a state-owned provider of mobile telephone service in Mainland China, which retained a 75 percent ownership stake in China Mobile (Hong Kong) Ltd. The spin-out was part of the Chinese government's strategy for privatizing its telecommunications network. China Mobile was given the right to expand into Mainland China. By September 2000 the company was the largest provider of mobile communications in China with 23.9 million subscribers and a market leadership position in six provinces.

In late 2000, China was finishing up negotiations to enter the World Trade Organization. Under the terms of the WTO agreement, China would have to progressively open up its telecommunications market to foreign telecommunications service providers. Galvanized by the impending threat of new competition in this fast-growing market, China Mobile realized that it needed to accelerate its expansion into Mainland China in order to preempt foreign competitors. Accordingly, in October 2000 China Mobile reached an agreement to purchase mobile networks in an additional seven provinces from its state-owned parent company. The purchase of these networks would give China Mobile an additional 15.4 million subscribers. It would also give the Hong Kong company a geographically contiguous market covering all of the coastal regions of Mainland China, a 56 percent share of all cellular subscribers in Mainland China, and service coverage of approximately 48.0 percent of the total population.

The price tag for this deal was $32.8 billion. For China Mobile, a critical question was how to finance the deal. It could issue additional equity or debt in Hong Kong, but Hong Kong's capital market might not be big enough to absorb a multibillion-dollar offering without driving up the price of the capital to an unacceptably high level. For example, China Mobile might be required to pay a relatively high interest rate in order to sell sufficient bonds in Hong Kong to finance part of its acquisition of the provincial networks, thereby raising its cost of capital. After consulting its underwriters, which included the U.S. companies Goldman Sachs and Merrill Lynch, China Mobile opted for an international offering of equity and debt. The shares of China Mobile were already listed on the New York Stock Exchange as American Depository Receipts (ADRs). Each ADR represented and controlled five shares in the Hong Kong company. China Mobile opted to sell ADRs worth approximately $6.6 billion and, in addition, to raise a further $600 million from the sales of five-year convertible bonds. (Convertible bonds are bonds that can be converted into equity at some future date, in this case after five years. They are considered to be a hybrid between conventional stock and bonds.) In addition, China Mobile agreed to sell a 2 percent stake in the company to Vodafone PLC, Europe's largest wireless service provider, for $2.5 billion. The remainder of the $32.8 billion purchase price for the mainland wireless networks was to be financed by issuing new shares to state-owned China Mobile Communications Corporation, which would retain for now its 75 percent stake in the company despite the issuing of new equity.

A significant portion of the ADRs would be offered for sale in New York. However, the underwriters also planned to offer ADRs in Asia and Europe. Similarly, the convertible bond issue would be priced in U.S. dollars and offered to global investors. The equity and bond offerings were closed in November 2000. Both offerings were substantially oversubscribed. The equity portion of the offering was 2.6 times oversubscribed. This was a remarkable achievement for what was at the time the largest ever Asian equity issue outside of Japan. In total, China Mobile raised some $8.24 billion, over $1 billion more than planned for. Some $690 million came from the sale of convertible bonds, and the remainder from the sale of equity. The convertible bonds carried a 2.25 percent interest rate, significantly less than the 2.75 percent rate initially targeted (as bond prices are bid up, the interest rate offered by the bond goes down). This lowered China Mobile's cost of capital. The oversubscription of the equity portion of the offering had a similar effect. Moreover, the offering was truly global in nature. While 55 percent of the placement was in the United States, another 25 percent went to Asian investors, and 20 percent to European investors.[29]

Case Discussion Questions

1. Why did China Mobile feel it was necessary to issue equity in markets outside of its home base in Hong Kong? What are the advantages of such a move?

2. Why did China Mobile price the bond issue in U.S. dollars instead of Hong Kong dollars?

3. Can you see any downside to China Mobile's international equity and bond issue?

Notes

1. K. Linebaugh, "Record IPO Could Have Been Even Bigger," *The Wall Street Journal*, October 21, 2006, p. B3; "Deals That Changed the Market in 2006: ICBC's Initial Public Offering," *Euromoney*, February 7, 2007, p. 1; and T. Mitchell, "ICBC Discovers That Good Things Come to Those Who Wait," *Financial Times*, October 26, 2006, p. 40.

2. D. Waller, "Daimler in $250m Singapore Placing," *Financial Times*, May 10, 1994, p. 17.

3. A. Rawi, *Capital Rules* (Harvard University Press, Boston, 2006); and M. Rees, "Why Money Can Now Make Its Way around the World," *The Wall Street Journal*, February 14, 2007, p. D12.

4. Waller, "Daimler in $250m Singapore Placing."

5. Sources: J. O. Jackson, "The Selling of the Big Pink," *Time*, December 2, 1996, p. 46; S. Ascarelli, "Privatization Is Worrying Deutsche Telekom," *The Wall Street Journal*, February 3, 1995, p. A1; "Plunging into Foreign Markets," *The Economist*, September 17, 1994, pp. 86–87; and A. Raghavan and M. R. Sesit, "Financing Boom: Foreign Firms Raise More and More Money in the U.S. Market," *The Wall Street Journal*, October 5, 1993, p. A1.

6. B. Solnik, "Why Not Diversify Internationally Rather than Domestically?" *Financial Analysts Journal*, July 1974, p. 17.

7. C. G. Luck and R. Choudhury, "International Equity Diversification for Pension Funds," *Journal of Investing* 5, no. 2 (1996), pp. 43–53.

8. W. N. Goetzmann, L. Li, and K. G. Rouwenhorst, "Long Term Global Market Correlations," *The Journal of Business*, January 2005, pp. 78–126.

9. I. Domowitz, J. Glen, and A. Madhavan, "Market Segmentation and Stock Prices: Evidence from an Emerging Market," *Journal of Finance* 3, no. 3 (1997), pp. 1059–68.

10. B. Solnik, "Why Not Diversify Internationally Rather than Domestically?" *Financial Analysts Journal*, July 1974, p. 17.

11. A Lavine, "With Overseas Markets Now Moving in Sync with U.S. Markets, It's Getting Harder to Find True Diversification Abroad," *Financial Planning*, December 1, 2000, pp. 37–40.

12. B. Solnik and J. Roulet, "Dispersion as Cross Sectional Correlation," *Financial Analysts Journal*, 56(1), 2000, pp. 54–61.

13. W. N. Goetzmann, L. Li, and K. G. Rouwenhorst, "Long Term Global Market Correlations," *The Journal of Business*, January 2005, pp. 78–126.

14. Ibid.

15. Bank for International Settlements, *BIS Quarterly Review*, March 2007, Basle, Switzerland.

16. T. F. Huertas, "U.S. Multinational Banking: History and Prospects," in *Banks as Multinationals*, ed. G. Jones (London: Routledge, 1990).

17. G. J. Millman, *The Vandals' Crown* (New York: Free Press, 1995).

18. Goetzmann, Li, and Rouwenhorst, "Long Term Global Market Correlations."

19. P. Dicken, *Global Shift: The Internationalization of Economic Activity* (London: The Guilford Press, 1992).

20. Ibid.

21. Martin Feldstein, "Global Capital Flows: Too Little, Not Too Much," *The Economist*, June 24, 1995, pp. 72–73.

22. Ibid., p. 73.

23. Sources: Feldstein, "Global Capital Flows"; R. Dornbusch, "We Have Salinas to Thank for the Peso Debacle," *Business Week*, January 16, 1995, p. 20; P. Carroll and C. Torres, "Mexico Unveils Program of Harsh Fiscal Medicine," *The Wall Street Journal*, March 10, 1995, pp. A1, A6. See also M. Feldstein and C. Horioka, "Domestic Savings and International Capital Flows," *Economic Journal* 90 (1980), pp. 314–29.

24. D. Duffy and L. Murry, "The Wooing of American Investors," *The Wall Street Journal*, February 25, 1994, p. A14

25. International Monetary Fund, *World Economic Outlook* (Washington, DC: IMF, 1998).

26. C. Schenk, "The Origins of the Eurodollar Market in London, 1955–1963," *Explorations in Economic History*, Vol. 35 (1998), pp. 221–39.

27. R. Reich, *The Work of Nations* (New York: Alfred A. Knopf, 1991).

28. Sources: R. Anderson, "Czech Groups Cast Their Net Abroad in Search of Funds," *Financial Times*, May 26, 1997, p. 27; V. Boland, "The Czech Stockmarket: Looking Beyond Recent Turmoil," *Financial Times*, December 1, 1997, p. 4; and "Ceske Radiokomunikace Equity Offer Raises $134 Million," *Financial Times*, May 27, 1998, p. 38.

29. Sources: China Mobile Hong Kong Ltd., SEC Form F-3, filed October 30, 2000; M. Johnson, "Deal of the Month," *Corporate Finance*, December 2000, p. 10; "Jumbo Equity Raid Elevates China Mobile to Big League," *Euroweek*, November 3, 2000, pp. 1, 13.

part four
cases

The Tragedy of the Congo

The Democratic Republic of the Congo, formerly known as Zaire, gained its independence from Belgium in 1960. The central African nation, rich in natural resources such as copper, seemed to have a promising future. If the country had simply sustained its preindependence economic growth rate, its gross national product (GNP) would have been $1,400 per capita by 1997, making it one of the richest countries in Africa. Instead, by 1997, the country was a wreck. Battered by a brutal civil war that led to the ousting of the country's longtime dictator, Mobutu Sese Seko, the economy had shrunk to its 1958 level with a GNP per capita below $100. The annual inflation rate was in excess of 750 percent, an improvement from the 9,800 percent inflation rate recorded in 1994. Consequently, the local currency was almost worthless. Most transactions were made by barter or, for the lucky few, with U.S. dollars. Infant mortality stood at a dismal 106 per 1,000 live births and life expectancy at 47 years, roughly comparable to that of Europe in the Middle Ages.

What were the underlying causes of the economic, political, and social collapse of Zaire? While the story is a complex one, according to several influential critics, some of the blame must be placed at the feet of two multinational lending institutions, the International Monetary Fund (IMF) and the World Bank. Both institutions were established in 1944 at the famous Bretton Woods conference, which paved the way for the post–World War II international monetary system. The IMF was given the task of maintaining order in the international monetary system, while the role of the World Bank was to promote general economic development, particularly among the world's poorer nations.

The IMF and the World Bank were major donors to postindependence Zaire. The IMF's involvement with Zaire dates to 1967, when the IMF approved Zaire's first economic stabilization plan, backed by a $27 million line of credit. About the same time, the World Bank began to make low-interest infrastructure loans to the government of Mobutu Sese Seko. This was followed by a series of further plans and loans between 1976 and 1981. At the urging of the IMF, Zaire's currency was devalued five times during this period to help boost exports and reduce imports, while taxes were raised in an effort to balance Zaire's budget. IMF and other Western officials were also placed in key positions at the Zairian central bank, finance ministry, and office of debt management.

Despite all this help, Zaire's economy continued to deteriorate. By 1982, after 15 years of IMF assistance, Zaire had a lower GNP than in 1967 and faced default on its debt. Some critics, including Jeffrey Sachs, the noted development economist from Harvard University, claim that this poor performance could in part be attributed to the policies imposed by the IMF, which included tax hikes, cuts in government subsidies, and periodic competitive currency devaluations. These policies, claim critics, were ill suited to such a poor country and created a vicious cycle of economic decline. The tax hikes simply drove work into the "underground economy" or created a disincentive to work. As a consequence, government tax revenues dwindled and the budget deficit expanded, making it difficult for the government to service its debt obligations. By raising import prices, the devaluations helped fuel the phenomenon the IMF was trying to control: inflation. In turn, high inflation of both prices and wages soon brought ordinary Zairians into high tax brackets, which drove even more work into the underground economy and further shrank government tax revenues.

Others point to corruption to explain Zaire's malaise. In 1982, a senior IMF official in Zaire reported that President Mobutu Sese Seko and his cronies were systematically stealing IMF and World Bank loans. Later news reports suggest that Mobutu accumulated a personal fortune of $4 billion by the mid-1980s, making him one of the richest men in the world at that time.

In 1982, Zaire was initially suspended from further use of its IMF credit line. However, the position was reversed in 1983 when a new agreement was negotiated that included an additional $356 million in IMF loans. The loans were linked to a further devaluation of the Zairian currency, more tax hikes, and cuts in government subsidies. The IMF's decision to turn a blind eye to the corruption problem and extend new loans was influenced by pressure from Western politicians who saw Mobutu's pro-Western regime as a bulwark against the spread of Marxism in Africa. By ignoring the corruption, the IMF could claim it was abiding by IMF rules, which stated the institution should offer only economic advice and stay out of internal political issues. The IMF's decision lent credence to Mobutu Sese Seko's government and enabled Zaire to attract more foreign loans. As a consequence, the country's overall foreign debt increased to $5 billion by the mid-1980s, up from $3 billion in 1978.

Unfortunately, the new loans and IMF policies did little to improve Zaire's economic performance, which continued to deteriorate. In 1987, Zaire was forced to abandon its agreement with the IMF due to food riots. The IMF negotiated another agreement for 1989–1991, which included further currency devaluation. This also failed to produce any tangible progress. The Zairian economy continued to implode while the country's civil war flared. In 1993, Zaire suspended its debt repayments, effectively going into default. In 1994, the World Bank announced it would shut down its operations in the country. About the same time, the IMF suspended Zaire's membership in the institution, making Zaire ineligible for further loans.

In 1997, after a long civil war, Mobutu Sese Seko was deposed. The new government inherited $14.6 billion of external debt, including debt arrears exceeding $1 billion. At a formal meeting chaired by the World Bank to discuss rescheduling the country's debt, delegates from the new government claimed that the World Bank, IMF, and other institutions acted irresponsibly by lending money to Mobutu's regime despite evidence of both substantial corruption and Zaire's inability to service such a high level of debt. In an implicit acknowledgment that this may have been the case, the IMF and World Bank began telling debtor countries to stamp out corruption or lose access to IMF and World Bank loans.

Case Discussion Questions

1. What was the goal of the policies that the (*a*) IMF and (*b*) World Bank adopted toward Zaire? Do you think these policies were appropriate for an impoverished nation? In what ways may IMF policies have contributed to economic problems in Zaire?

2. Do you think the IMF and World Bank should lend money to countries such as Zaire where there is systematic evidence of widespread government corruption?

3. What alternative policies could the IMF and World Bank have adopted in Zaire? How might these policies have helped the country avert the economic and political chaos of the 1990s, which includes a prolonged civil war and economic disintegration?

Sources

1. G. Fossedal, "The IMF's Role in Zaire's Decline," *The Wall Street Journal*, May 15, 1997, p. 22.

2. J. Burns and M. Holman, "Mobutu Built a Fortune of $4 Billion from Looted Aid," *Financial Times*, May 12, 1997, p. 1.

3. J. D. Sachs and R. I. Rotberg, "Help Congo Now," *The New York Times*, May 29, 1997, p. 21.

4. H. Dunphy, "IMF, World Bank Now Make Political Judgments," *Journal of Commerce*, August 21, 1997, p. 3A.

5. CIA *World Factbook* (Washington, DC: CIA, 1998).

The Russian Ruble Crisis and Its Aftermath

PRELUDE

In the early 1990s, following the collapse of Communism and the dissolution of the Soviet Union, the Russian government implemented an economic reform program designed to transform the country's crumbling centrally planned economy into a dynamic market economy. A central element of this plan was an end to price controls on January 1, 1992. Once controls were removed, however, prices surged. Inflation was soon running at a monthly rate of about 30 percent. For the whole of 1992, the inflation rate in Russia was 3,000 percent. The annual rate for 1993 was approximately 900 percent.

Several factors contributed to the spike in Russia's inflation rate. State planners during the Communist era had held prices at artificially low levels. At the same time there were shortages of many basic goods, so with nothing to spend their money on, many Russians simply hoarded rubles. After the liberalization of price controls, the country was suddenly awash in rubles chasing a still limited supply of goods. The result was to rapidly bid up prices. The inflationary fires that followed price liberalization were stoked by the Russian government itself. Unwilling to face the social consequences of the massive unemployment that would follow if many state-owned enterprises were privatized quickly, the government continued to subsidize the operations of many money-losing establishments. The result was a surge in the government's budget deficit. In the first quarter of 1992, the budget deficit amounted to 1.5 percent of the country's GDP. By the end of 1992, it had risen to 17 percent. Unable or unwilling to finance this deficit by raising taxes, the government found another solution—it printed money, which added fuel to the inflation fire.

With inflation rising, the ruble tumbled in value against the dollar and other major currencies. In January

1992 the exchange rate stood at $1 = R125. By the end of 1992 it was $1 = R480 and by late 1993, it was $1 = R1,500. As 1994 progressed, it became increasingly evident that due to vigorous political opposition, the Russian government would not be able to bring down its budget deficit as quickly as had been thought. By September the monthly inflation rate was accelerating. October started badly, with the ruble sliding more than 10 percent in value against the U.S. dollar in the first 10 days of the month. On October 11, the ruble plunged 21.5 percent against the dollar, reaching a value of $1 = R3,926 by the time the foreign exchange market closed!

Despite the announcement of a tough budget plan that placed tight controls on the money supply, the ruble continued to slide and by April 1995 the exchange rate stood at $1 = R5,120. However, by mid-1995 inflation was again on the way down. In June 1995 the *monthly* inflation rate was at a yearly low of 6.7 percent. Also, the ruble had recovered to stand at $1 = R4,559 by July 6. On that day the Russian government announced it would intervene in the currency market to keep the ruble in a trading range of R4,300 to R4,900 against the dollar. The Russian government believed that it was essential to maintain a relatively stable currency. Government officials announced that the central bank would be able to draw on $10 billion in foreign exchange reserves to defend the ruble against any speculative selling in Russia's relatively small foreign exchange market.

In the world of international finance, $10 billion is small change and it wasn't long before Russia found that its foreign exchange reserves were being depleted. It was at this point that the Russian government requested IMF loans. In February 1996, the IMF obliged with its second largest rescue effort ever, a loan of $10 billion. In return for the loan, Russia agreed to limit the growth in its money supply, reduce public-sector debt, increase government tax revenues, and peg the ruble to the dollar. Russia also rebased the value of the ruble, making one ruble equivalent to 1,000 old rubles.

Initially the package seemed to have the desired effect. Inflation declined from nearly 50 percent in 1996 to about 15 percent in 1997; the exchange rate stayed within its predetermined band of 4.3 to 4.8 rubles per dollar; and the balance-of-payments situation remained broadly favorable. In 1997, the Russian economy grew for the first time since the breakup of the former Soviet Union, if only by a modest half of 1 percent of GDP. However, the public-sector debt situation did not improve. The Russian government continued to spend more than it agreed to under IMF targets, while government tax revenues were much lower than projected. Low tax revenues were in part due to falling oil prices (the government collected tax on oil sales), in part due to the difficulties of collecting tax in an economy where so much economic activity was in the "underground economy," and partly due to a complex tax system that was peppered with loopholes. In 1997, Russian federal government spending amounted to 18.3 percent of GDP, while revenues were only 10.8 percent of GDP, implying a deficit of 7.5 percent of GDP, which was financed by an expansion in public debt.

CRISIS

Dismayed by the failure of Russia to meet its targets, the IMF responded by suspending its scheduled payment to Russia in early 1998, pending reform of Russia's complex tax system and a sustained attempt by the Russian government to cut public spending. This put further pressure on the Russian ruble, forcing the Russian central bank to raise interest rates on overnight loans to 150 percent. In June 1998, the U.S. government indicated it would support a new IMF bailout. The IMF was more circumspect, insisting instead that the Russian government push through a package of corporate tax increases and public spending cuts to balance the budget. The Russian government indicated it would do so, and the IMF released a tranche of $640 million that had been suspended. The IMF followed this with an additional $11.2 billion loan designed to preserve the ruble's stability.

Almost as soon as the funding was announced, however, it began to unravel. The IMF loan required the Russian government to take concrete steps to raise personal tax rates, improve tax collections, and cut government spending. A bill containing the required legislative changes was sent to the Russian parliament, where it was emasculated by antigovernment forces. The IMF responded by withholding $800 million of its first $5.6 billion tranche, undermining the credibility of its own program. The Russian stock market plummeted on the news, closing 6.5 percent down. Selling of rubles accelerated. The central bank began hemorrhaging foreign exchange reserves as it tried to maintain the value of the ruble. Foreign exchange reserves fell by $1.4 billion in the first week of August alone, to $17 billion, while interest rates surged again.

Against this background, on the weekend of August 15–16, top Russian officials huddled to develop a response to the most recent crisis. Their options were limited. The patience of the IMF had been exhausted. Foreign currency reserves were being rapidly depleted. Social tensions in the country were running high. The government faced upcoming redemptions on $18 billion of domestic bonds, with no idea of where the money would come from.

On Monday, August 17, Prime Minister Sergei Kiriyenko announced the results of the weekend's conclave. He said Russia would restructure the domestic debt market, unilaterally transforming short-term debt into long-term debt. In other words, the government had decided to default on its debt commitments. The government also announced a 90-day moratorium on the repayment of private foreign debt and stated it would allow the ruble to decline by 34 percent against the U.S. dollar. In short, Russia had turned its back on the IMF plan. The effect was immediate. Overnight, shops marked up the price of goods by 20 percent. As the ruble plummeted, currency exchange points were only prepared to sell dollars at a rate of 9 rubles per dollar, rather than the new official exchange rate of 6.43 rubles to the dollar. As for Russian government debt, it lost 85 percent of its value in a matter of hours, leaving foreign and Russian holders of debt alike suddenly gaping at a huge black hole in their financial assets

AFTERMATH

In the aftermath of Russia's default on government debt, the IMF effectively turned its back on the Russian government, leaving the country to fix its own financial mess. With no more IMF loans in the offing, the government had to find some other way to manage its large public sector deficit. The government took a two-pronged approach; first, it slashed government spending, and second, it reformed the tax system. With regard to the tax system, the government of Vladimir Putin ignored the advice of the IMF, which wanted Russia to raise tax rates and focus on tougher enforcement. Instead, the government replaced Russia's complex income tax code, which had a top marginal rate of 30 percent, with a 13 percent flat tax. Corporate tax rates were also slashed from 35 percent to 24 percent, and the tax code was simplified, closing many loopholes. Paradoxically, the cut in tax rates led to a surge in government revenues as individuals and corporations decided it was easier to pay taxes than go to the trouble of avoiding them—which they had long done.

In addition to these government actions, a sharp rise in commodity prices, and particularly world oil prices, helped the Russian economy enormously. Russia is now the world's largest oil exporter, ahead of even Saudi Arabia. In addition, it exports significant amounts of natural gas, metals, and timber, all of which have seen sharp price increases since 1998. The country now runs a large current account surplus with the rest of the world (in 2004 it hit $46 billion).

As a result of these changes, the Russian economy grew at an average annual rate of 6.5 percent between 1998 and 2004. Foreign debt declined from 90 percent of GDP in 1998 to around 28 percent in 2004, while foreign reserves increased tenfold to $120 billion. The government has been running a budget surplus since 1999. In 2004 it took in some $13.1 billion more than it spent. Moreover, in January 2005 the Russian government repaid its entire obligations to the IMF ahead of schedule.

Despite these positive developments, the Russian economy still has numerous structural weaknesses. The country is now very dependent on commodity prices, and if they should fall, the economy will suffer a sharp pullback. The banking system remains weak, the manufacturing infrastructure is poor, the country is still rife with corruption, there is widespread mistrust in the institutions of government, and foreign investment is relatively low.

Case Discussion Questions

1. What were the causes of the surge in inflation in Russia during the early 1990s? Could this have been avoided? How?

2. What does the decline in the value of the ruble against the dollar between 1992 and 1998 teach you about the relationship between inflation rates and currency values?

3. During the mid-1990s, the IMF wanted Russia to raise tax rates, close loopholes in the tax system, and cut public spending. Russia was unable to do this. Why?

4. In the early 2000s Russia cut tax rates for individuals and corporations, and government tax revenues surged. Why? Does this result suggest that the IMF policy prescriptions were wrong?

Sources

1. S. Erlanger, "Russia Will Test a Trading Band for the Ruble," *The New York Times*, July 7, 1995, p. 1.

2. C. Freeland, "Russia to Introduce a Trading Band for Ruble against Dollar," *Financial Times*, July 7, 1995, p. 1.

3. J. Thornhill, "Russians Bemused by 'Black Tuesday,'" *Financial Times*, October 12, 1994, p. 4.

4. R. Sikorski, "Mirage of Numbers," *The Wall Street Journal*, May 18, 1994, p. 14.

5. "Can Russia Fight Back?" *The Economist*, June 6, 1998, pp. 47–48.

6. J. Thornhill, "Russia's Shrinking Options," *Financial Times*, August 19, 1998, p. 19.
7. *CIA World Fact Book, Russia, 2005*. On the web at https://www.cia.gov/library/publications/the-world-factbook/index.html.
8. "Change Those Light Bulbs: The Russian Economy," *The Economist*, February 8, 2003, p. 43.
9. "The Kremlin Repents, Maybe: Russia's Economy," *The Economist*, April 9, 2005, p. 32.

🌐 Japan's Surging Samurai Bond Market

Following the implosion of Japan's stock market and real estate bubbles in the early 1990s, the country had to contend with a decade of poor economic performance. The economy seemingly teetered constantly on the brink of a serious recession, and sustained growth remained elusive. In an effort to keep the bleak economic clouds at bay, the Bank of Japan repeatedly lowered interest rates to try to encourage corporate and consumer spending. As a result, by early 2001 Japan had the lowest interest rates in the world. In March 2001 10-year Japanese government bonds yielded 1.24 percent, compared with 5 percent for comparable U.S. government debt. Despite these low interest rates, many Japanese corporations continue to focus on restructuring and downsizing rather than investing in new capacity, as they struggle with the sustained hangover from the boom years of the 1980s and early 1990s. Consequently, Japanese corporations have not taken advantage of the low interest rates to issue additional debt. Nor have consumers responded to the lower interest rates by increasing their consumption. Instead, the personal savings rate in Japan remains stubbornly high, even though many Japanese hold the majority of their savings in post office accounts that pay very low interest rates.

However, there is a silver lining to this bleak economic outlook—for foreign corporations and governments that is. Increasingly, they have been taking advantage of Japan's low interest rate to issue yen-denominated debt. With the yen/dollar exchange rate relatively stable, this seems like a shrewd economic bet. Moreover, yield-hungry retail investors, who are looking for better returns than the 1 to 2 percent they get on post office savings accounts, have snapped up foreign debt offerings in Japan. As the equivalent of some $1 trillion in Japanese postal savings reached maturity between April 2000 and April 2002, a huge wave of retail money entered the market looking for higher returns. Japan's equity markets have been flirting with 10-year lows, and with the economy near recession, few retail investors are putting their money in Japanese stocks. With Japanese corporations issuing only a few bonds, few investment opportunities are available there. This leaves foreign bonds as one of the few attractive investment opportunities for retail investors looking for higher yields.

An increasing number of foreigners took advantage of this opportunity. The number of Samurai bond issues increased from less than 20 in 1998 to over 120 in 2000, and seemed set to exceed that number in 2001. In 2001, foreigners issuing yen-denominated debt raised some $24 billion in the Japanese bond market, up from $9 billion in 1998. Countries including Croatia, Uruguay, and Brazil have raised money for their treasuries by issuing Samurai bonds. For example, in February 2002 the government of Uruguay issued ¥30 billion of five-year bonds. The interest rate it had to pay on those bonds was just 2.2 percent. In contrast, Uruguay had to pay 7.6 percent for five-year dollar borrowings. Similarly, an increasing number of corporations have been issuing Samurai bonds. In late 2000, Citigroup completed an offering of ¥155 billion ($1.43 billion) in Samurai bonds. Several U.S. investment banks, including Morgan Stanley, Merrill Lynch, and Lehman Brothers, also issued Samurai bonds in 2000. In early 2001, the trend continued with a major Samurai bond issue placed by Deutsche Telekom, which offered ¥500 billion ($4.5 billion) in bonds. In addition, Posco, Korea's largest steel company, came to the market with a ¥30 billion five-year offering. In both cases, these companies chose to raise debt in Japan as opposed to other markets because even factoring in the costs of hedging against fluctuations in the value of the Japanese yen, they could significantly reduce their cost of capital by doing so.

Case Discussion Questions

1. What were the macroeconomic underpinnings of the increase in Samurai bond issues?

2. How might an increase in Japan's rate of economic growth affect the vitality of the Samurai bond market?

3. For a company like Deutsche Telekom, which issues yen-denominated debt to raise funds for investments outside of Japan, the lower interest rate must be offset against higher costs. What

are these higher costs, and what determines their magnitude?

4. What would happen to activity in the Samurai bond market if the yen started to appreciate significantly against the dollar, but interest rate differentials between the United States and Japan stayed constant? What would happen if the yen depreciated against the dollar? What does this tell you about the risks of issuing foreign bonds?

Sources

1. "Posco to Return to Samurai Market as Yen Offers Cheap Alternative to Dollar Funding," *Euroweek*, January 19, 2001, p. 13.

2. J. Singer, "Japan's Woes Benefit World's Borrowers," *The Wall Street Journal*, March 8, 2001, p. A17.

3. "Samurai Market to Scale New Heights," *Asiamoney*, October 2000.

MTV Networks

MTV Networks has become a symbol of globalization. Established in 1981, the U.S.-based music TV network has been expanding outside of its North American base since 1987 when it opened MTV Europe. Today MTV Networks figures that every second of every day over 2 million people are watching MTV around the world, the majority outside the United States. Despite its international success, MTV's global expansion got off to a weak start. In the 1980s it piped a single feed across Europe almost entirely composed of American programming with English-speaking veejays. Naively, the network's U.S. managers thought Europeans would flock to the American programming. But while viewers in Europe shared a common interest in a handful of global superstars, their tastes turned out to be surprisingly local. What was popular in Germany might not be popular in Great Britain. Many staples of the American music scene left Europeans cold. MTV suffered as a result. Soon local copycat stations were springing up in Europe that focused on the music scene in individual countries. They took viewers and advertisers away from MTV. As Tom Freston, chairman of MTV Networks, explained, "We were going for the most shallow layer of what united viewers and brought them together. It didn't go over too well."

MTV changed it strategy in the 1990s. It broke its service into "feeds" aimed at national or regional markets, first in Europe, and then in the rest of the world. Thus today MTV offers local feeds for the United Kingdom

The Strategy of International Business

LEARNING OBJECTIVES

After you have read this chapter you should be able to:

LO¹ Explain the concept of strategy.

LO² Understand how firms can profit by expanding globally.

LO³ Understand how pressures for cost reductions and pressures for local responsiveness influence strategic choice.

LO⁴ Be familiar with different strategies for competing globally and their pros and cons.

---

and Ireland; another for Germany, Austria, and Switzerland; one for Scandinavia; one for Italy; one for France; one for Spain; one for Holland; and so on. In Asia, MTV has an English–Hindi channel for India, separate Mandarin feeds for China and Taiwan, a Korean feed for South Korea, a Bahasa-language feed for Indonesia, Japanese feed for Japan, and so on. Digital and satellite technology have made the localization of programming cheaper and easier. MTV Networks can now beam half a dozen feeds off one satellite transponder.

While MTV Networks exercises creative control over these different feeds, and while all the channels have the same familiar frenetic look and feel of MTV in the United States, a significant share of the programming and content is now local. Moreover, an increasing share of programming is local in conception. Although a lot of programming ideas still originate in the United States, with equivalents of staples such as *The Real World* in different countries, an increasing share of programming is local in conception. In Italy, *MTV Kitchen* combines cooking with a music countdown. *Erotica*, which features a panel of youngsters discussing sex, airs in Brazil. The Indian channel produces 21 homegrown shows hosted by local veejays who speak "Hinglish," a city-bred cross of Hindi and English. And of course, each feed prominently features music videos by locally popular performers. This localization push has produced big benefits for MTV, allowing the network to capture viewers back from local imitators.[1]

Introduction

MTV Networks offers a preview of some issues that we will explore in this chapter. Like many other companies, MTV moved into other countries because it saw huge growth opportunities there, and it thought it could create value by transferring its business model and American style music programming to foreign markets. MTV initially treated foreign markets much like the United States, right down to airing the same music videos worldwide, but it soon found that this was not the correct approach. Many American music stars drew big yawns in Europe and Asia, where most of the stars were local. These national differences in customer tastes and preferences required MTV to change its approach to programming. It moved away from its one-size-fits-all strategy of global standardization and became more local in its orientation, adapting its programming to different markets by airing different music videos and programs in different markets. At the same time, MTV's foreign affiliates still have the same look, feel, and overall programming philosophy of the U.S. parent. Striking the right balance between global standardization and local responsiveness let MTV reap big dividends, enabling the network to gain viewers and advertisers at the expense of competitors. As we shall see, many other enterprises have sought to do the same thing.

As the MTV example suggests, in this chapter we are switching focus from aspects of the larger environment in which international businesses compete to the firm itself. As we have described it in the preceding chapters, this environment has included the different political, economic, and cultural institutions of nations, the international trade and investment framework, and the international monetary system. Now our focus shifts to the actions managers can take to compete more effectively as an international business. In this chapter, we look at how firms can increase their profitability by expanding their operations in foreign markets. We discuss the different strategies that firms pursue when competing internationally. We consider the pros and cons of these strategies. Finally, we also discuss the various factors that affect a firm's choice of strategy.

Strategy and the Firm

Before we discuss the strategies that managers in the multinational enterprise can pursue, we need to review some basic principles of strategy. A firm's **strategy** can be defined as the actions that managers take to attain the goals of the firm. For most firms, the preeminent goal is to maximize the value of the firm for its owners, its shareholders (subject to the very important constraint that this is done in a legal, ethical, and socially responsible manner—see Chapter 5 for details). To maximize the value of a firm, managers must pursue strategies that increase the *profitability* of the enterprise and its rate of *profit growth* over time (see Figure 12.1). **Profitability** can be measured in a number of ways, but for consistency, we shall define it as the rate of return that the firm makes on its invested capital (ROIC), which is calculated by dividing the net profits of the firm by total invested capital.[2] **Profit growth** is measured by the percentage increase in net profits over time. In general, higher profitability and a higher rate of profit growth will increase the value of an enterprise and thus the returns garnered by its owners, the shareholders.[3] For a formal exposition of profit growth, see the appendix at the end of this chapter.

Managers can increase the profitability of the firm by pursuing strategies that lower costs or by pursuing strategies that add value to the firm's products, either of which enables the firm to raise prices. Managers can increase the rate at which the firm's profits grow over time by pursuing strategies to sell more products in existing markets or by pursuing strategies to enter new markets. As we shall see, expanding internationally can help managers boost the firm's profitability *and* increase the rate of profit growth over time.

FIGURE 12.1

Determinants of
Enterprise Value

FIGURE 12.2

Value Creation

VALUE CREATION

The way to increase the profitability of a firm is to create more value. The amount of value a firm creates is measured by the difference between its costs of production and the value that consumers perceive in its products. In general, the more value customers place on a firm's products, the higher the price the firm can charge for those products. However, the price a firm charges for a good or service is typically less than the value the customer places on that good or service. This is because the customer captures some of that value in the form of what economists call a consumer surplus.[4] The customer is able to do this because the firm is competing with other firms for the customer's business, so the firm must charge a lower price than it could if it were a monopoly supplier. Also, it is normally impossible to segment the market to such a degree that the firm can charge each customer a price that reflects that individual's assessment of the value of a product, which economists refer to as a customer's reservation price. For these reasons, the price that gets charged tends to be less than the value many customers place on the product.

Figure 12.2 illustrates these concepts. The value of a product to an *average* consumer is V; the average price that the firm can charge a consumer for that product given competitive pressures and its ability to segment the market is P; and the average unit cost of producing that product is C (C comprises all relevant costs, including the firm's cost of capital). The firm's profit per unit sold (π) is equal to P − C, while the consumer surplus per unit is equal to V − P (another way of thinking of the consumer surplus is as "value for the money";

the greater the consumer surplus, the greater the value for the money the consumer gets). The firm makes a profit so long as P is greater than C, and its profit will be greater the lower C is *relative* to P. The difference between V and P is in part determined by the intensity of competitive pressure in the marketplace; the lower the intensity of competitive pressure, the higher the price charged relative to V.[5] In general, the higher the firm's profit per unit sold is, the greater its profitability will be, all else being equal.

The firm's **value creation** is measured by the difference between V and C (V − C); a company creates value by converting inputs that cost C into a product on which consumers place a value of V. A company can create more value (V − C) either by lowering production costs, C, or by making the product more attractive through superior design, styling, functionality, features, reliability, after-sales service, and the like, so that consumers place a greater value on it (V increases) and, consequently, are willing to pay a higher price (P increases). This discussion suggests that *a firm has high profits when it creates more value for its customers and does so at a lower cost.* We refer to a strategy that focuses primarily on lowering production costs as a *low-cost strategy*. We refer to a strategy that focuses primarily on increasing the attractiveness of a product as a *differentiation strategy.*[6] MTV primarily focuses on the differentiation side of this equation—it tried to differentiate itself from rivals through more compelling programming.

Michael Porter has argued that *low cost* and *differentiation* are two basic strategies for creating value and attaining a competitive advantage in an industry.[7] According to Porter, superior profitability goes to those firms that can create superior value, and the way to create superior value is to drive down the cost structure of the business and/or differentiate the product in some way so that consumers value it more and are prepared to pay a premium price. Superior value creation relative to rivals does not necessarily require a firm to have the lowest cost structure in an industry or to create the most valuable product in the eyes of consumers. However, it does require that the gap between value (V) and cost of production (C) be greater than the gap attained by competitors.

STRATEGIC POSITIONING

Porter notes that it is important for a firm to be explicit about its choice of strategic emphasis with regard to value creation (differentiation) and low cost and to configure its internal operations to support that strategic emphasis.[8] Figure 12.3 illustrates his point. The convex curve in Figure 12.3 is what economists refer to as an efficiency frontier. The efficiency frontier shows all the different positions a firm can adopt toward adding value to the product (V) and low cost (C) assuming that its internal operations are configured efficiently to support a particular position (note that the horizontal axis in Figure 12.3 is reverse scaled—moving along the axis to the right implies lower costs). The efficiency

FIGURE 12.3

Strategic Choice in the International Hotel Industry

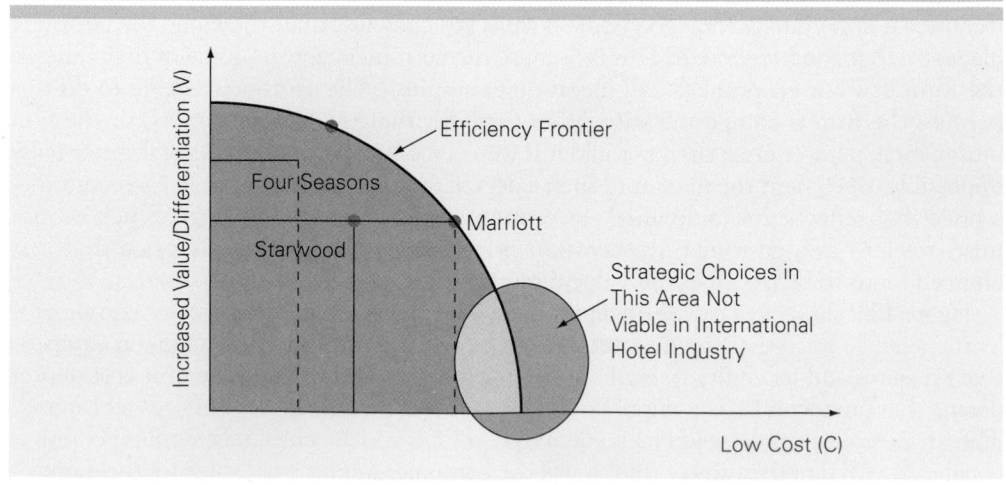

frontier has a convex shape because of diminishing returns. Diminishing returns imply that when a firm already has significant value built into its product offering, increasing value by a relatively small amount requires significant additional costs. The converse also holds: when a firm already has a low-cost structure, it has to give up a lot of value in its product offering to get additional cost reductions.

Figure 12.3 plots three hotel firms with a global presence that cater to international travelers—Four Seasons, Marriott International, and Starwood (Starwood owns the Sheraton and Westin chains). Four Seasons positions itself as a luxury chain and emphasizes the value of its product offering, which drives up its costs of operations. Marriott and Starwood are positioned more in the middle of the market. Both emphasize sufficient value to attract international business travelers, but are not luxury chains like Four Seasons. In Figure 12.3, Four Seasons and Marriott are shown to be on the efficiency frontier, indicating that their internal operations are well configured to their strategy and run efficiently. Starwood is inside the frontier, indicating that its operations are not running as efficiently as they might be and that its costs are too high. This implies that Starwood is less profitable than Four Seasons and Marriott and that its managers must take steps to improve the company's performance.

Porter emphasizes that it is very important for management to decide where the company wants to be positioned with regard to value (V) and cost (C), to configure operations accordingly, and to manage them efficiently to make sure the firm is operating on the efficiency frontier. However, not all positions on the efficiency frontier are viable. In the international hotel industry, for example, there might not be enough demand to support a chain that emphasizes very low cost and strips all the value out of its product offering (see Figure 12.3). International travelers are relatively affluent and expect a degree of comfort (value) when they travel away from home.

A central tenet of the basic strategy paradigm is that to maximize its profitability, a firm must do three things: (a) pick a position on the efficiency frontier that is viable in the sense that there is enough demand to support that choice; (b) configure its internal operations, such as manufacturing, marketing, logistics, information systems, human resources, and so on, so that they support that position; and (c) make sure that the firm has the right organization structure in place to execute its strategy. *The strategy, operations, and organization of the firm must all be consistent with each other if it is to attain a competitive advantage and garner superior profitability.* By **operations** we mean the different value creation activities a firm undertakes, which we shall review next.

OPERATIONS: THE FIRM AS A VALUE CHAIN

The operations of a firm can be thought of as a value chain composed of a series of distinct value creation activities including production, marketing and sales, materials management, R&D, human resources, information systems, and the firm infrastructure. We can categorize these value creation activities, or operations, as primary activities and support activities (see Figure 12.4).[9] As noted above, if a firm is to implement its strategy efficiently and position itself on the efficiency frontier shown in Figure 12.3, it must manage these activities effectively and in a manner that is consistent with its strategy.

Primary Activities

Primary activities have to do with the design, creation, and delivery of the product; its marketing; and its support and after-sale service. Following normal practice, in the value chain illustrated in Figure 12.4, the primary activities are divided into four functions: research and development, production, marketing and sales, and customer service.

Research and development (R&D) is concerned with the design of products and production processes. Although we think of R&D as being associated with the design of physical products and production processes in manufacturing enterprises, many service companies also undertake R&D. For example, banks compete with each other by developing new financial products and new ways of delivering those products to customers.

FIGURE 12.4

The Value Chain

Online banking and smart debit cards are two examples of product development in the banking industry. Earlier examples of innovation in the banking industry included automated teller machines, credit cards, and debit cards. Through superior product design, R&D can increase the functionality of products, which makes them more attractive to consumers (raising V). Alternatively, R&D may result in more efficient production processes, thereby cutting production costs (lowering C). Either way, the R&D function can create value.

Production is concerned with the creation of a good or service. For physical products, when we talk about production we generally mean manufacturing. Thus, we can talk about the production of an automobile. For services such as banking or health care, "production" typically occurs when the service is delivered to the customer (for example, when a bank originates a loan for a customer, it is engaged in "production" of the loan). For a retailer such as Wal-Mart, "production" is concerned with selecting the merchandise, stocking the store, and ringing up the sale at the cash register. For MTV, production is concerned with the creation, programming, and broadcasting of content, such as music videos and thematic shows. The production activity of a firm creates value by performing its activities efficiently so lower costs result (lower C) and/or by performing them in such a way that a higher quality product is produced (which results in higher V).

The marketing and sales functions of a firm can help create value in several ways. Through brand positioning and advertising, the marketing function can increase the value (V) that consumers perceive in a firm's product. If these create a favorable impression of the firm's product in the minds of consumers, they increase the price that can be charged for it. For example, Ford has produced a high-value version of its Ford Expedition SUV. Sold as the Lincoln Navigator and priced around $10,000 higher, the Navigator has the same body, engine, chassis, and design as the Expedition, but through skilled advertising and marketing, supported by some fairly minor features changes (e.g., more accessories and the addition of a Lincoln-style engine grille and nameplate), Ford has fostered the perception that the Navigator is a "luxury SUV." This marketing strategy has increased the perceived value (V) of the Navigator relative to the Expedition, and enables Ford to charge a higher price for the car (P).

Marketing and sales can also create value by discovering consumer needs and communicating them back to the R&D function of the company, which can then design products that better match those needs. For example, the allocation of research budgets at Pfizer, the world's largest pharmaceutical company, is determined by the marketing function's assessment of the potential market size associated with solving unmet medical needs. Thus, Pfizer is currently directing significant monies to R&D efforts aimed at

Perception is everything! Even though the Ford Expedition (left) and the Lincoln Navigator (right) share many of the same attributes such as the body and engine, customers are willing to pay about $10,000 more for the Navigator's "little extras."

finding treatments for Alzheimer's disease, principally because marketing has identified the treatment of Alzheimer's as a major unmet medical need in nations around the world where the population is aging.

The role of the enterprise's service activity is to provide after-sale service and support. This function can create a perception of superior value (V) in the minds of consumers by solving customer problems and supporting customers after they have purchased the product. Caterpillar, the U.S.-based manufacturer of heavy earthmoving equipment, can get spare parts to any point in the world within 24 hours, thereby minimizing the amount of downtime its customers have to suffer if their Caterpillar equipment malfunctions. This is an extremely valuable capability in an industry where downtime is very expensive. It has helped to increase the value that customers associate with Caterpillar products and thus the price that Caterpillar can charge.

Support Activities

The support activities of the value chain provide inputs that allow the primary activities to occur (see Figure 12.4). In terms of attaining a competitive advantage, support activities can be as important as, if not more important than, the "primary" activities of the firm. Consider information systems—the electronic systems for managing inventory, tracking sales, pricing products, selling products, dealing with customer service inquiries, and so on. Information systems, when coupled with the communications features of the Internet, can alter the efficiency and effectiveness with which a firm manages its other value creation activities. Dell Computer, for example, has used its information systems to attain a competitive advantage over rivals. When customers place an order for a Dell product over the firm's Web site, that information is immediately transmitted, via the Internet, to suppliers, who then configure their production schedules to produce and ship that product so that it arrives at the right assembly plant at the right time. These systems have reduced the amount of inventory that Dell holds at its factories to under two days, which is a major source of cost savings.

The logistics function controls the transmission of physical materials through the value chain, from procurement through production and into distribution. The efficiency with which this is carried out can significantly reduce cost (lower C), thereby creating more value. The combination of logistics systems and information systems is a particularly potent source of cost savings in many enterprises, such as Dell, where information systems tell Dell on a real time basis where in its global logistics network parts are, when they will arrive at an assembly plant, and thus how production should be scheduled.

The human resource function can help create more value in a number of ways. It ensures that the company has the right mix of skilled people to perform its value creation activities effectively. The human resource function also ensures that people are adequately trained, motivated, and compensated to perform their value creation tasks. In a multinational enterprise, one of the things human resources can do to boost the competitive position of the firm is to take advantage of its transnational reach to identify, recruit, and develop a cadre of skilled managers, regardless of their nationality, who can be groomed to take on senior management positions. They can find the very best, wherever they are in the world. Indeed, the senior management ranks of many multinationals are becoming increasingly diverse, as managers from a variety of national backgrounds have ascended to senior leadership positions. Japan's Sony, for example, is now headed not by a Japanese national, but by Howard Stringer, a Welshman.

The final support activity is the company infrastructure, or the context within which all the other value creation activities occur. The infrastructure includes the organizational structure, control systems, and culture of the firm. Because top management can exert considerable influence in shaping these aspects of a firm, top management should also be viewed as part of the firm's infrastructure. Through strong leadership, top management can consciously shape the infrastructure of a firm and through that the performance of all its value creation activities.

🌐 Global Expansion, Profitability, and Profit Growth

Expanding globally allows firms to increase their profitability and rate of profit growth in ways not available to purely domestic enterprises.[10] Firms that operate internationally are able to

1. Expand the market for their domestic product offerings by selling those products in international markets.
2. Realize location economies by dispersing individual value creation activities to those locations around the globe where they can be performed most efficiently and effectively.
3. Realize greater cost economies from experience effects by serving an expanded global market from a central location, thereby reducing the costs of value creation.
4. Earn a greater return by leveraging any valuable skills developed in foreign operations and transferring them to other entities within the firm's global network of operations.

As we will see, however, a firm's ability to increase its profitability and profit growth by pursuing these strategies is constrained by the need to customize its product offering, marketing strategy, and business strategy to differing national conditions; that is, by the imperative of localization.

EXPANDING THE MARKET: LEVERAGING PRODUCTS AND COMPETENCIES

A company can increase its growth rate by taking goods or services developed at home and selling them internationally. Almost all multinationals started out doing just this. Procter and Gamble, for example, developed most of its best-selling products such as Pampers disposable diapers and Ivory soap in the United States and subsequently sold them around the world. Similarly, although Microsoft developed its software in the United States, from its earliest days the company has always focused on selling that software in international markets. Automobile companies such as Volkswagen and Toyota also grew by developing products at home and then selling them in international markets. The returns from such a strategy are likely to be greater if indigenous competitors in the nations a company enters lack comparable products. Thus, Toyota has increased its profits by entering the large automobile markets of North America and Europe, offering products that differ from those of their local rivals (Ford and GM) because of their superior quality and reliability.

The success of many multinational companies that expand in this manner is based not just upon the goods or services that they sell in foreign nations but also upon the core competencies that underlie the development, production, and marketing of those goods or services. The term **core competence** refers to skills within the firm that competitors cannot easily match or imitate.[11] These skills may exist in any of the firm's value creation activities—production, marketing, R&D, human resources, logistics, general management, and so on. Such skills are typically expressed in product offerings that other firms find difficult to match or imitate. Core competencies are the bedrock of a firm's competitive advantage. They enable a firm to reduce the costs of value creation and/or to create perceived value in such a way that premium pricing is possible. For example, Toyota has a core competence in the production of cars. It is able to produce high-quality, well-designed cars at a lower delivered cost than any other firm in the world. The competencies that enable Toyota to do this seem to reside primarily in the firm's production and logistics functions.[12] McDonald's has a core competence in managing fast-food operations (it seems to be one of the most skilled firms in the world in this industry); Procter & Gamble has a core competence in developing and marketing name brand consumer products (it is one of the most skilled firms in the world in this business); Starbucks has a core competence in the management of retail outlets selling high volumes of freshly brewed coffee-based drinks.

Since core competencies are by definition the source of a firm's competitive advantage, the successful global expansion by manufacturing companies such as Toyota and P&G was based not just on leveraging products and selling them in foreign markets but also on the transfer of core competencies to foreign markets where indigenous competitors lacked them. The same can be said of companies engaged in the service sectors of an economy, such as financial institutions, retailers, restaurant chains, and hotels. Expanding the market for their services often means replicating their business model in foreign nations (albeit with some changes to account for local differences, which we will discuss in more detail shortly). Starbucks, for example, is expanding rapidly outside of the United States by taking the basic business model it developed at home and using that as a blueprint for establishing international operations. MTV has done the same thing, and now serves 140 nations. Similarly, McDonald's is famous for its international expansion strategy, which has taken the company into more than 120 nations that collectively generate over half of the company's revenues.

LOCATION ECONOMIES

We know from earlier chapters that countries differ along a range of dimensions, including the economic, political, legal, and cultural, and that these differences can either raise or lower the costs of doing business in a country. The theory of international trade also teaches us that due to differences in factor costs, certain countries have a comparative advantage in the production of certain products. Japan might excel in the production of automobiles and consumer electronics; the United States in the production of computer software, pharmaceuticals, biotechnology products, and financial services; Switzerland in the production of precision instruments and pharmaceuticals; South Korea in the production of semiconductors; and China in the production of apparel.[13]

For a firm that is trying to survive in a competitive global market, this implies that *trade barriers and transportation costs* permitting, the firm will benefit by basing each value creation activity it performs at that location where economic, political, and cultural conditions, including relative factor costs, are most conducive to its performance. Thus, if the best designers for a product live in France, a firm should base its design operations in France. If the most productive labor force for assembly operations is in Mexico, assembly operations should be based in Mexico. If the best marketers are in the United States, the marketing strategy should be formulated in the United States.

Firms that pursue such a strategy can realize what we refer to as **location economies,** which are the economies that arise from performing a value creation activity in the optimal location for that activity, wherever in the world that might be (transportation costs and trade barriers permitting). Locating a value creation activity in the optimal location for that activity can have one of two effects. *It can lower the costs of value creation and help the firm achieve a low-cost position, and/or it can enable a firm to differentiate its product offering from those of competitors.* In terms of Figure 12.2, it can lower C and/or increase V (which in general supports higher pricing), both of which boost the profitability of the enterprise.

For an example of how this works in an international business, consider Clear Vision, a manufacturer and distributor of eyewear. Started by David Glassman, the firm now generates annual gross revenues of more than $100 million. Not exactly small, but no corporate giant either, Clear Vision is a multinational firm with production facilities on three continents and customers around the world. Clear Vision began its move toward becoming a multinational in the 1990s. The strong dollar at that time made U.S.-based manufacturing very expensive. Low-priced imports were taking an ever-larger share of the U.S. eyewear market, and Clear Vision realized it could not survive unless it also began to import. Initially the firm bought from independent overseas manufacturers, primarily in Hong Kong. However, the firm became dissatisfied with these suppliers' product quality and delivery. As Clear Vision's volume of imports increased, Glassman decided the best way to guarantee quality and delivery was to set up Clear Vision's own manufacturing operation overseas. Accordingly, Clear Vision found a Chinese partner, and together they opened a manufacturing facility in Hong Kong, with Clear Vision being the majority shareholder.

The choice of the Hong Kong location was influenced by its combination of low labor costs, a skilled workforce, and tax breaks given by the Hong Kong government. The firm's objective at this point was to lower production costs by locating value creation activities at an appropriate location. After a few years, however, Hong Kong's increasing industrialization and growing labor shortage had pushed up wage rates to the extent that it was no longer a low-cost location. In response, Glassman and his Chinese partner moved part of their manufacturing to a plant in mainland China to take advantage of the lower wage rates there. Again, the goal was to lower production costs. The parts for eyewear frames manufactured at this plant are shipped to the Hong Kong factory for final assembly and then distributed to markets in North and South America. The Hong Kong factory now employs 80 people and the China plant between 300 and 400.

At the same time, Clear Vision was looking for opportunities to invest in foreign eyewear firms with reputations for fashionable design and high quality. Its objective was not to reduce production costs but to launch a line of high-quality differentiated, "designer" eyewear. Clear Vision did not have the design capability in-house to support such a line, but Glassman knew that certain foreign manufacturers did. As a result, Clear Vision invested in factories in Japan, France, and Italy, holding a minority shareholding in each case. These factories now supply eyewear for Clear Vision's Status Eye division, which markets high-priced designer eyewear.[14]

Thus, to deal with a threat from foreign competition, Clear Vision adopted a strategy intended to lower its cost structure (lower C): shifting its production from a high-cost location, the United States, to a low-cost location, first Hong Kong and later China. Then Clear Vision adopted a strategy intended to increase the perceived value of its product (increase V) so it could charge a premium price (P). Reasoning that premium pricing in eyewear depended on superior design, its strategy involved investing capital in French, Italian, and Japanese factories that had reputations for superior design. In sum, Clear Vision's strategies included some actions intended to reduce its costs of creating value and other actions intended to add perceived value to its product through differentiation. The overall goal was to increase the value created by Clear Vision and thus the profitability of the enterprise. To the extent that these strategies were successful, the firm should have attained a higher profit margin and greater profitability than if it had remained a U.S.-based manufacturer of eyewear.

Creating a Global Web

Generalizing from the Clear Vision example, one result of this kind of thinking is the creation of a **global web** of value creation activities, dispersing different stages of the value chain to those locations around the globe where perceived value is maximized or where the costs of value creation are minimized.[15] Consider Lenova's ThinkPad laptop computers (Lenova is the Chinese computer company that purchased IBM's personal computer operations in 2005).[16] Engineers in the United States design this product because Lenova believes the United States is the best location in the world to do the basic design work. The case, keyboard, and hard drive are made in Thailand; the display screen and memory in South Korea; the built-in wireless card in Malaysia; and the microprocessor in the United States. In each case, Lenova manufactures and sources components from the optimal location given current factor costs. It then ships the components to an assembly operation in Mexico, which assembles the product before shipping it to the United States for final sale. Lenova assembles the ThinkPad in Mexico because managers have calculated that due to low labor costs, the costs of assembly can be minimized there. Personnel in the United States develop the marketing and sales strategy for North America, primarily because managers believe that due to their knowledge of the local marketplace, U.S. personnel add more value to the product through their marketing efforts than personnel based elsewhere.

In theory, a firm that realizes location economies by dispersing each of its value creation activities to its optimal location should have a competitive advantage vis-à-vis a firm that bases all of its value creation activities at a single location. It should be able to better differentiate its product offering (thereby raising perceived value, V) and lower its cost structure (C) than its single-location competitor. In a world where competitive pressures are increasing, such a strategy may become an imperative for survival.

Some Caveats

Introducing transportation costs and trade barriers complicates this picture. Due to favorable factor endowments, New Zealand may have a comparative advantage for automobile assembly operations, but high transportation costs would make it an uneconomical location from which to serve global markets. Another caveat concerns the importance of assessing political and economic risks when making location decisions. Even if a country looks very attractive as a production location when measured against all the standard criteria, if its government is unstable or totalitarian, the firm might be advised not to base production there. (Political risk is discussed in Chapter 2.) Similarly, if the government appears to be pursuing inappropriate economic policies that could lead to foreign exchange risk, that might be another reason for not basing production in that location, even if other factors look favorable.

EXPERIENCE EFFECTS

The **experience curve** refers to systematic reductions in production costs that have been observed to occur over the life of a product.[17] A number of studies have observed that a product's production costs decline by some quantity about each time *cumulative* output doubles. The relationship was first observed in the aircraft industry, where each time cumulative output of airframes was doubled, unit costs typically declined to 80 percent of their previous level.[18] Thus, production cost for the 4th airframe would be 80 percent of production cost for the 2nd airframe, the 8th airframe's production costs 80 percent of the 4th's, the 16th's 80 percent of the 8th's, and so on. Figure 12.5 illustrates this experience curve relationship between unit production costs and *cumulative* output (the relationship is for *cumulative* output over time, and *not* output in any one period, such as a year). Two things explain this: learning effects and economies of scale.

Learning Effects

Learning effects refer to cost savings that come from learning by doing. Labor, for example, learns by repetition how to carry out a task, such as assembling airframes, most efficiently. Labor productivity increases over time as individuals learn the most efficient ways to perform particular tasks. Equally important, in new production facilities management typically learns how to manage the new operation more efficiently over time.

FIGURE 12.5

The Experience Curve

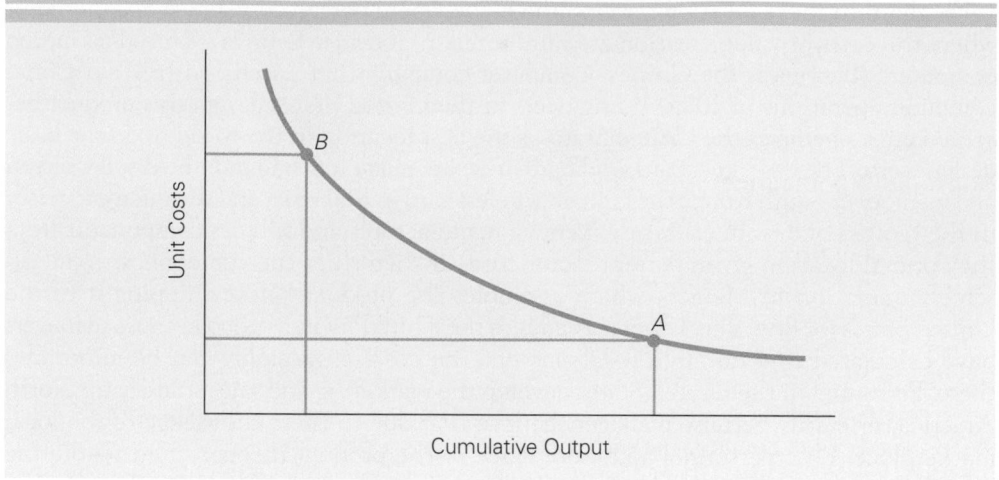

Hence, production costs decline due to increasing labor productivity and management efficiency, which increases the firm's profitability.

Learning effects tend to be more significant when a technologically complex task is repeated because there is more that can be learned about the task. Thus, learning effects will be more significant in an assembly process involving 1,000 complex steps than in one of only 100 simple steps. No matter how complex the task, however, learning effects typically disappear after a while. It has been suggested that they are important only during the start-up period of a new process and that they cease after two or three years.[19] Any decline in the experience curve after such a point is due to economies of scale.

Economies of Scale

Economies of scale refer to the reductions in unit cost achieved by producing a large volume of a product. Attaining economies of scale lowers a firm's unit costs and increases its profitability. Economies of scale have a number of sources. One is the ability to spread fixed costs over a large volume.[20] Fixed costs are the costs required to set up a production facility, develop a new product, and the like. They can be substantial. For example, the fixed cost of establishing a new production line to manufacture semiconductor chips now exceeds $1 billion. Similarly, according to one estimate, developing a new drug and bringing it to market costs about $800 million and takes about 12 years.[21] The only way to recoup such high fixed costs may be to sell the product worldwide, which reduces average unit costs by spreading fixed costs over a larger volume. The more rapidly that cumulative sales volume is built up, the more rapidly fixed costs can be amortized over a large production volume, and the more rapidly unit costs will fall.

Second, a firm may not be able to attain an efficient scale of production unless it serves global markets. In the automobile industry, for example, an efficiently scaled factory is one designed to produce about 200,000 units a year. Automobile firms would prefer to produce a single model from each factory since this eliminates the costs associated with switching production from one model to another. If domestic demand for a particular model is only 100,000 units a year, the inability to attain a 200,000-unit output will drive up average unit costs. By serving international markets as well, however, the firm may be able to push production volume up to 200,000 units a year, thereby reaping greater scale economies, lowering unit costs, and boosting profitability. By serving domestic and international markets from its production facilities, a firm may be able to utilize those facilities more intensively. For example, if Intel sold microprocessors only in the United States, it may only be able to keep its factories open for one shift, five days a week. By serving international markets from the same factories, Intel can utilize its productive assets more intensively, which translates into higher capital productivity and greater profitability.

Finally, as global sales increase the size of the enterprise, so its bargaining power with suppliers increases, which may allow it to attain economies of scale in purchasing, bargaining down the cost of key inputs and boosting profitability that way. For example, Wal-Mart has been able to use its enormous sales volume as a lever to bargain down the price it pays suppliers for merchandise it sells.

Strategic Significance

The strategic significance of the experience curve is clear. Moving down the experience curve allows a firm to reduce its cost of creating value (to lower C in Figure 12.2) and increase its profitability. The firm that moves down the experience curve most rapidly will have a cost advantage vis-à-vis its competitors. Firm A in Figure 12.5, because it is farther down the experience curve, has a clear cost advantage over firm B.

Many of the underlying sources of experience-based cost economies are plant based. This is true for most learning effects as well as for the economies of scale derived by spreading the fixed costs of building productive capacity over a large output, attaining an efficient scale of output, and utilizing a plant more intensively. Thus, one key to progressing downward on the experience curve as rapidly as possible is to increase the volume produced by a single plant as rapidly as possible. Because global markets are larger than domestic markets, a firm that serves a global market from a single location is likely to build accumulated volume more quickly than a firm that serves only its home market or that serves multiple markets from multiple production locations. Thus, serving a global market from a single location is consistent with moving down the experience curve and establishing a low-cost position. In addition, to get down the experience curve rapidly, a firm may need to price and market aggressively so demand will expand rapidly. It will also need to build sufficient production capacity for serving a global market. Also, the cost advantages of serving the world market from a single location will be even more significant if that location is the optimal one for performing the particular value creation activity.

Once a firm has established a low-cost position, it can act as a barrier to new competition. Specifically, an established firm that is well down the experience curve, such as firm A in Figure 12.5, can price so that it is still making a profit while new entrants, which are farther up the curve, are suffering losses.

The classic example of the successful pursuit of such a strategy concerns the Japanese consumer electronics company Matsushita. Along with Sony and Philips, Matsushita was in the race to develop a commercially viable videocassette recorder in the 1970s. Although Matsushita initially lagged behind Philips and Sony, it was able to get its VHS format accepted as the world standard and to reap enormous experience curve–based cost economies in the process. This cost advantage subsequently constituted a formidable barrier to new competition. Matsushita's strategy was to build global volume as rapidly as possible. To ensure it could accommodate worldwide demand, the firm increased its production capacity 33-fold from 205,000 units in 1977 to 6.8 million units by 1984. By serving the world market from a single location in Japan, Matsushita was able to realize significant learning effects and economies of scale. These allowed Matsushita to drop its prices 50 percent within five years of selling its first VHS-format VCR. As a result, Matsushita was the world's major VCR producer by 1983, accounting for about 45 percent of world production and enjoying a significant cost advantage over its competitors. The next largest firm, Hitachi, accounted for only 11.1 percent of world production in 1983.[22] Today, firms such as Intel are the masters of this kind of strategy. The costs of building a state-of-the-art facility to manufacture microprocessors are so large (now in excess of $2 billion) that to make this investment pay Intel *must* pursue experience curve effects, serving world markets from a limited number of plants to maximize the cost economies that derive from scale and learning effects.

LEVERAGING SUBSIDIARY SKILLS

Implicit in our earlier discussion of core competencies is the idea that valuable skills are developed first at home and then transferred to foreign operations. Thus, MTV developed its programming skills in the United States before transferring them to foreign locations.

However, for more mature multinationals that have already established a network of subsidiary operations in foreign markets, the development of valuable skills can just as well occur in foreign subsidiaries.[23] Skills can be created anywhere within a multinational's global network of operations, wherever people have the opportunity and incentive to try new ways of doing things. The creation of skills that help to lower the costs of production, or to enhance perceived value and support higher product pricing, is not the monopoly of the corporate center.

Leveraging the skills created within subsidiaries and applying them to other operations within the firm's global network may create value. For example, McDonald's increasingly is finding that its foreign franchisees are a source of valuable new ideas. Faced with slow growth in France, its local franchisees have begun to experiment not only with the menu but also with the layout and theme of restaurants. Gone are the ubiquitous golden arches; gone too are many of the utilitarian chairs and tables and other plastic features of the fast-food giant. Many McDonald's restaurants in France now have hardwood floors, exposed brick walls, and even armchairs. Half of the 930 or so outlets in France have been upgraded to a level that would make them unrecognizable to an American. The menu, too, has been changed to include premier sandwiches, such as chicken on focaccia bread, priced some 30 percent higher than the average hamburger. In France at least, the strategy seems to be working. Following the change, increases in same-store sales rose from 1 percent annually to 3.4 percent. Impressed with the impact, McDonald's executives are now considering adopting similar changes at other McDonald's restaurants in markets where same-store sales growth is sluggish, including the United States.[24]

For the managers of the multinational enterprise, this phenomenon creates important new challenges. First, they must have the humility to recognize that valuable skills that lead to competencies can arise anywhere within the firm's global network, not just at the corporate center. Second, they must establish an incentive system that encourages local employees to acquire new skills. This is not as easy as it sounds. Creating new skills involves a degree of risk. Not all new skills add value. For every valuable idea created by a McDonald's subsidiary in a foreign country, there may be several failures. The management of the multinational must install incentives that encourage employees to take the necessary risks. The company must reward people for successes and not sanction them unnecessarily for taking risks that did not pan out. Third, managers must have a process for identifying when valuable new skills have been created in a subsidiary. And finally, they need to act as facilitators, helping to transfer valuable skills within the firm.

GLOBAL EXPANSION ISSUES—A SUMMARY

We have seen how firms that expand globally can increase their profitability and profit growth by entering new markets where indigenous competitors lack similar competencies, by lowering costs and adding value to their product offering through the attainment of location economies, by exploiting experience curve effects, and by transferring valuable skills between their global network of subsidiaries. For completeness it should be noted that strategies that increase profitability may also expand a firm's business and thus enable it to attain a higher rate of profit growth. For example, by simultaneously realizing location economies and experience effects a firm may be able to produce a more highly valued product at a lower unit cost, thereby boosting profitability. The increase in the perceived value of the product may also attract more customers, thereby growing revenues and profits as well. Furthermore, rather than raising prices to reflect the higher perceived value of the product, the firm's managers may elect to hold prices low in order to increase global market share and attain greater scale economies (in other words, they may elect to offer consumers better "value for money"). Such a strategy could increase the firm's rate of profit growth even further since consumers will be attracted by prices that are low relative to value. The strategy might also increase profitability if the scale economies that result from market share gains are substantial. In sum, managers need to keep in mind the complex relationship between profitability and profit growth when making strategic decisions about pricing.

Cost Pressures and Pressures for Local Responsiveness

Firms that compete in the global marketplace typically face two types of competitive pressure that affect their ability to realize location economies and experience effects, to leverage products and transfer competencies and skills within the enterprise. They face *pressures for cost reductions* and *pressures to be locally responsive* (see Figure 12.6).[25] These competitive pressures place conflicting demands on a firm. Responding to pressures for cost reductions requires that a firm try to minimize its unit costs. But responding to pressures to be locally responsive requires that a firm differentiate its product offering and marketing strategy from country to country in an effort to accommodate the diverse demands arising from national differences in consumer tastes and preferences, business practices, distribution channels, competitive conditions, and government policies. Because differentiation across countries can involve significant duplication and a lack of product standardization, it may raise costs.

While some enterprises, such as firm A in Figure 12.6, face high pressures for cost reductions and low pressures for local responsiveness, and others, such as firm B, face low pressures for cost reductions and high pressures for local responsiveness, many companies are in the position of firm C. They face high pressures for *both* cost reductions and local responsiveness. Dealing with these conflicting and contradictory pressures is a difficult strategic challenge, primarily because being locally responsive tends to raise costs.

PRESSURES FOR COST REDUCTIONS

In competitive global markets, international businesses often face pressures for cost reductions. Responding to pressures for cost reduction requires a firm to try to lower the costs of value creation. A manufacturer, for example, might mass-produce a standardized product at the optimal location in the world, wherever that might be, to realize economies of scale, learning effects, and location economies. Alternatively, a firm might outsource certain functions to low-cost foreign suppliers in an attempt to reduce costs. Thus, many computer companies have outsourced their telephone-based customer service functions to India, where qualified technicians who speak English can be hired for a lower wage rate than in the United States. In the same manner, a retailer such as Wal-Mart might push its

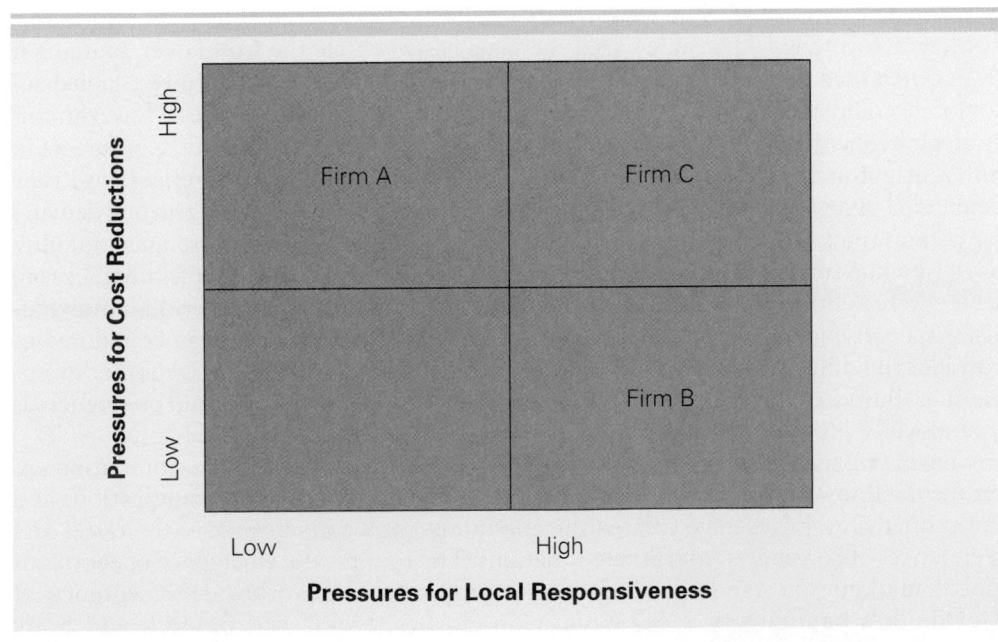

FIGURE 12.6

Pressures for Cost Reductions and Local Responsiveness

suppliers (manufacturers) to do the same. (The pressure that Wal-Mart has placed on its suppliers to reduce prices has been cited as a major cause of the trend among North American manufacturers to shift production to China.)[26] A service business such as a bank might respond to cost pressures by moving some back-office functions, such as information processing, to developing nations where wage rates are lower.

Pressures for cost reduction can be particularly intense in industries producing commodity-type products where meaningful differentiation on nonprice factors is difficult and price is the main competitive weapon. This tends to be the case for products that serve universal needs. **Universal needs** exist when the tastes and preferences of consumers in different nations are similar if not identical. This is the case for conventional commodity products such as bulk chemicals, petroleum, steel, sugar, and the like. It also tends to be the case for many industrial and consumer products; for example, handheld calculators, semiconductor chips, personal computers, and liquid crystal display screens. Pressures for cost reductions are also intense in industries where major competitors are based in low-cost locations, where there is persistent excess capacity, and where consumers are powerful and face low switching costs. The liberalization of the world trade and investment environment in recent decades, by facilitating greater international competition, has generally increased cost pressures.[27]

PRESSURES FOR LOCAL RESPONSIVENESS

Pressures for local responsiveness arise from national differences in consumer tastes and preferences, infrastructure, accepted business practices, distribution channels, and host-government demands. Responding to pressures to be locally responsive requires a firm to differentiate its products and marketing strategy from country to country to accommodate these factors, all of which tends to raise the firm's cost structure.

Differences in Customer Tastes and Preferences

Strong pressures for local responsiveness emerge when customer tastes and preferences differ significantly between countries, as they often do for deeply embedded historic or cultural reasons. In such cases, a multinational's products and marketing message have to be customized to appeal to the tastes and preferences of local customers. This typically creates pressure to delegate production and marketing responsibilities and functions to a firm's overseas subsidiaries.

For example, the automobile industry in the 1980s and early 1990s moved toward the creation of "world cars." The idea was that global companies such as General Motors, Ford, and Toyota would be able to sell the same basic vehicle the world over, sourcing it from centralized production locations. If successful, the strategy would have enabled automobile companies to reap significant gains from global scale economies. However, this strategy frequently ran aground upon the hard rocks of consumer reality. Consumers in different automobile markets seem to have different tastes and preferences, and they demanded different types of vehicles. North American consumers show a strong demand for pickup trucks. This is particularly true in the South and West where many families have a pickup truck as a second or third car. But in European countries, pickup trucks are seen purely as utility vehicles and are purchased primarily by firms rather than individuals. As a consequence, the product mix and marketing message needs to be tailored to consider the different nature of demand in North America and Europe. Another example that illustrates the need to respond to national differences in tastes and preferences is that of MTV Networks, which we discussed in the introduction to the chapter.

Some commentators have argued that customer demands for local customization are on the decline worldwide.[28] According to this argument, modern communications and transport technologies have created the conditions for a convergence of the tastes and preferences of consumers from different nations. The result is the emergence of enormous global markets for standardized consumer products. The worldwide acceptance of McDonald's hamburgers, Coca-Cola, Gap clothes, Nokia cell phones, and Sony

PlayStations, all of which are sold globally as standardized products, is often cited as evidence of the increasing homogeneity of the global marketplace.

However, as illustrated by the MTV example, this argument seems somewhat naive. Significant differences in consumer tastes and preferences still exist across nations and cultures. Managers in international businesses do not yet have the luxury of being able to ignore these differences, and they may not for a long time to come. Even in a modern industry such as the cell phone business, important national differences in consumer usage patterns can be observed. Americans, for example, tend to think of cell phones primarily as devices for talking, and not as devices that can also send e-mails and browse the Web. Consequently, when selling to U.S. consumers, cell phone manufacturers focus more on slim good looks and less on advanced functions and features. This is in direct contrast to Asia and Europe, where text messaging and Web browsing functions have been much more widely embraced. A cultural issue seems to be at work here. People in Europe and Asia often have more time to browse the Web on their phones because they spend more time commuting on trains, while Americans tend to spend more time in cars, where their hands are occupied.[29]

Differences in Infrastructure and Traditional Practices

Pressures for local responsiveness arise from differences in infrastructure or traditional practices among countries, which create a need to customize products accordingly. Fulfilling this need may require delegating manufacturing and production functions to foreign subsidiaries. For example, in North America, consumer electrical systems are based on 110 volts, whereas in some European countries, 240-volt systems are standard. Thus, domestic electrical appliances have to be customized for this difference in infrastructure. Traditional practices also often vary across nations. For example, in Britain, people drive on the left-hand side of the road, creating a demand for right-hand-drive cars, whereas in France (and the rest of Europe), people drive on the right-hand side of the road and therefore want left-hand-drive cars. Obviously, automobiles have to be customized to accommodate this difference in traditional practice.

Although many national differences in infrastructure are rooted in history, some are quite recent. For example, in the wireless telecommunications industry different technical standards exist in different parts of the world. A technical standard known as GSM is common in Europe, and an alternative standard, CDMA, is more common in the United States and parts of Asia. Equipment designed for GSM will not work on a CDMA network, and vice versa. Thus, companies such as Nokia, Motorola, and Ericsson, which manufacture wireless handsets and infrastructure such as switches, need to customize their product offering according to the technical standard prevailing in a given country.

Differences in Distribution Channels

A firm's marketing strategies may have to be responsive to differences in distribution channels among countries, which may necessitate the delegation of marketing functions to national subsidiaries. In the pharmaceutical industry, for example, the British and Japanese distribution systems are radically different from the U.S. system. British and Japanese doctors will not accept or respond favorably to a U.S.-style high-pressure sales force. Thus, pharmaceutical companies have to adopt different marketing practices in Britain and Japan compared with the United States—soft sell versus hard sell. Similarly, Poland, Brazil, and Russia all have similar per capita income on a purchasing power parity basis, but there are big differences in distribution systems across the three countries. In Brazil, supermarkets account for 36 percent of food retailing, in Poland for 18 percent, and in Russia for less than 1 percent.[30] These differences in channels require that companies adapt their own distribution and sales strategy.

Host-Government Demands

Economic and political demands imposed by host-country governments may require local responsiveness. For example, pharmaceutical companies are subject to local clinical testing, registration procedures, and pricing restrictions, all of which make it necessary that the manufacturing and marketing of a drug should meet local requirements. Because governments and government agencies control a significant proportion of the health care budget in most countries, they are in a powerful position to demand a high level of local responsiveness.

More generally, threats of protectionism, economic nationalism, and local content rules (which require that a certain percentage of a product should be manufactured locally) dictate that international businesses manufacture locally. For example, consider Bombardier, the Canadian-based manufacturer of railcars, aircraft, jet boats, and snowmobiles. Bombardier has 12 railcar factories across Europe. Critics of the company argue that the resulting duplication of manufacturing facilities leads to high costs and helps explain why Bombardier makes lower profit margins on its railcar operations than on its other business lines. In reply, managers at Bombardier argue that in Europe, informal rules with regard to local content favor people who use local workers. To sell railcars in Germany, they claim, you must manufacture in Germany. The same goes for Belgium, Austria, and France. To try to address its cost structure in Europe, Bombardier has centralized its engineering and purchasing functions, but it has no plans to centralize manufacturing.[31]

Choosing a Strategy

Pressures for local responsiveness imply that it may not be possible for a firm to realize the full benefits from economies of scale, learning effects, and location economies. It may not be possible to serve the global marketplace from a single low-cost location, producing a globally standardized product and marketing it worldwide to attain the cost reductions associated with experience effects. The need to customize the product offering for local conditions may work against the implementation of such a strategy. For example, automobile firms have found that Japanese, American, and European consumers demand different kinds of cars, which necessitates producing products that are customized for local markets. In response, firms such as Honda, Ford, and Toyota are pursuing a strategy of establishing top-to-bottom design and production facilities in each of these regions so that they can better serve local demands. Although such customization brings benefits, it also limits the ability of a firm to realize significant scale economies and location economies.

In addition, pressures for local responsiveness imply that it may not be possible to leverage skills and products associated with a firm's core competencies wholesale from one nation to another. Concessions often have to be made to local conditions. Despite being depicted as the "poster boy" for the proliferation of standardized global products, even McDonald's has found that it has to customize its product offerings (i.e., its menu) to account for national differences in tastes and preferences.

How do differences in the strength of pressures for cost reductions versus those for local responsiveness affect the firm's choice of strategy? Firms typically choose among four main strategic postures when competing internationally. These can be characterized as a global standardization strategy, a localization strategy, a transnational strategy, and an international strategy.[32] The appropriateness of each strategy varies given the extent of pressures for cost reductions and local responsiveness. Figure 12.7 illustrates the conditions under which each of these strategies is most appropriate.

GLOBAL STANDARDIZATION STRATEGY

Firms that pursue a **global standardization strategy** focus on increasing profitability and profit growth by reaping the cost reductions that come from economies of scale, learning effects, and location economies; that is, their strategic goal is to pursue a low-cost strategy on a global scale. The production, marketing, and R&D activities of firms pursuing a global standardization strategy are concentrated in a few favorable locations. Firms pursuing a global standardization strategy try not to customize their product offering and marketing strategy to local conditions because customization involves shorter production

FIGURE 12.7

Four Basic Strategies

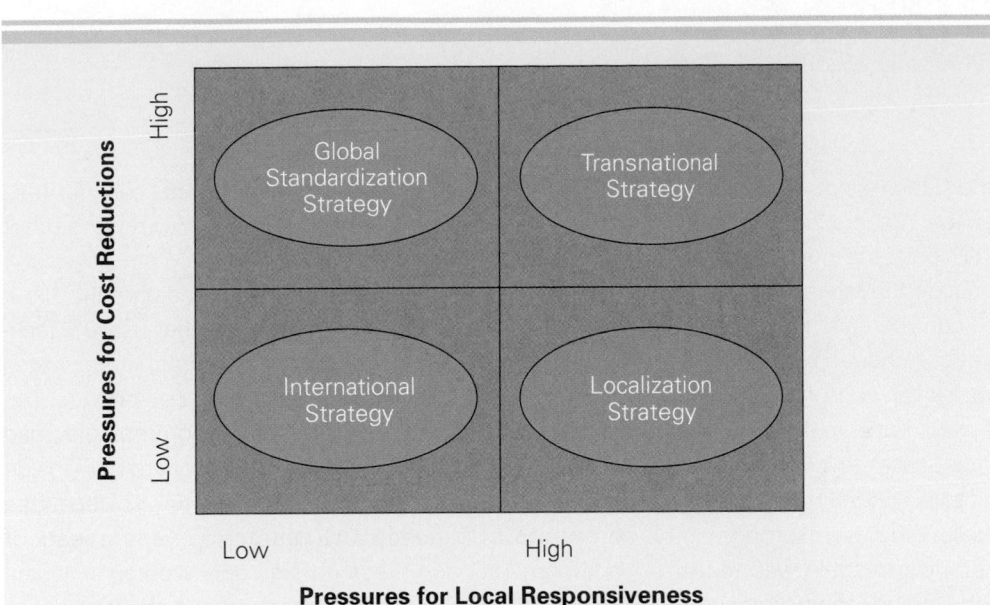

runs and the duplication of functions, which tend to raise costs. Instead, they prefer to market a standardized product worldwide so that they can reap the maximum benefits from economies of scale and learning effects. They also tend to use their cost advantage to support aggressive pricing in world markets.

This strategy makes most sense when there are strong pressures for cost reductions and minimal demands for local responsiveness. Increasingly, these conditions prevail in many industrial goods industries, whose products often serve universal needs. In the semiconductor industry, for example, global standards have emerged, creating enormous demands for standardized global products. Accordingly, companies such as Intel, Texas Instruments, and Motorola all pursue a global standardization strategy. However, these conditions are not yet found in many consumer goods markets, where demands for local responsiveness remain high. The strategy is inappropriate when demands for local responsiveness are high. The experience of Vodafone, which is discussed in the next Management Focus feature, illustrates what can happen when a global standardization strategy does not match market realities.

LOCALIZATION STRATEGY

A **localization strategy** focuses on increasing profitability by customizing the firm's goods or services so they provide a good match to tastes and preferences in different national markets. Localization is most appropriate where consumer tastes and preferences differ substantially across nations and cost pressures are not too intense. By customizing the product offering to local demands, the firm increases the value of that product in the local market. On the downside, because it involves some duplication of functions and smaller production runs, customization limits the ability of the firm to capture the cost reductions associated with mass-producing a standardized product for global consumption. The strategy may make sense, however, if the added value associated with local customization supports higher pricing, which enables the firm to recoup its higher costs, or if it leads to substantially greater local demand, enabling the firm to reduce costs through the attainment of some scale economies in the local market.

MTV is a good example of a company that has had to pursue a localization strategy. If MTV had not localized its programming to match the demands of viewers in different nations, it would have lost market share to local competitors, its advertising revenues would have fallen, and its profitability would have declined. Thus, even though it raised costs, localization was a strategic imperative at MTV. Procter & Gamble, which is

MANAGEMENT FOCUS

Vodafone in Japan

In 2002 Vodafone Group of the UK, the world's largest provider of wireless telephone service, made a big splash by paying $14 billion to acquire J-Phone, the number three player in Japan's fast growing market for wireless communications services. J-Phone was considered a hot property, having just launched Japan's first cell phones with embedded digital cameras, which won over large numbers of young people who wanted to e-mail photos to their friends. Four years later, after losing market share to local competitors, Vodafone sold J-Phone and took an $8.6 billion charge against earnings related to the sale. What went wrong?

According to analysts, Vodafone's mistake was to focus too much on building a global brand, and not enough upon local market conditions in Japan. In the early 2000s, Vodafone's vision was to offer consumers in different countries the same technology, so that they could take their phones with them when they traveled across international borders. The problem, however, was that Japan's most active cell phone users, many of them young

people who don't regularly travel abroad, care far less about this capability than about game playing and other embedded features.

Vodafone's emphasis on global services meant that it delayed its launch in Japan of phones that use 3G technology, which allows users to do things such as watch video clips and teleconference on their cell phones. The company, in line with its global branding ambitions, had decided to launch 3G cell phones that worked both inside and outside Japan. The delay was costly. Its Japanese competitors launched 3G phones a year ahead of Vodafone. Although these phones only worked in Japan, they rapidly gained share as consumers adopted these leading edge devices. Moreover, when Vodafone did finally introduce a 3G phone, design problems associated with making a phone that worked globally meant that the supply of phones was limited, and the launch fizzled despite strong product reviews simply because consumers could not get the phones.[33]

---

discussed in the next Management Focus feature, is another good example of a firm that historically pursued a localization strategy.

Of course, even though localization can increase costs, firms such as MTV and Procter & Gamble still have to keep an eye on costs. Firms pursuing a localization strategy still need to be efficient and, whenever possible, to capture some scale economies from their global reach. As noted earlier, many automobile companies have found that they have to customize some of their product offerings to local market demands—for example, producing large pickup trucks for U.S. consumers and small fuel-efficient cars for Europeans and Japanese. At the same time, these multinationals try to get some scale economies from their global volume by using common vehicle platforms and components across many different models and manufacturing those platforms and components at efficiently scaled factories that are optimally located. By designing their products in this way, these companies have been able to localize their product offering, yet simultaneously capture some scale economies, learning effects, and location economies.

TRANSNATIONAL STRATEGY

We have argued that a global standardization strategy makes most sense when cost pressures are intense and demands for local responsiveness limited. Conversely, a localization strategy makes most sense when demands for local responsiveness are high, but cost pressures are moderate or low. What happens, however, when the firm simultaneously faces both strong cost pressures and strong pressures for local responsiveness? How can managers balance the competing and inconsistent demands such divergent pressures place on the firm? According to some researchers, the answer is to pursue what has been called a transnational strategy.

Two of these researchers, Christopher Bartlett and Sumantra Ghoshal, argue that in today's global environment, competitive conditions are so intense that to survive, firms must do all they can to respond to pressures for cost reductions and local responsiveness.

Evolution of Strategy at Procter & Gamble

Founded in 1837, Cincinnati-based Procter & Gamble has long been one of the world's most international companies. Today P&G is a global colossus in the consumer products business with annual sales in excess of $50 billion, some 54 percent of which are generated outside of the United States. P&G sells more than 300 brands—including Ivory soap, Tide, Pampers, IAM pet food, Crisco, and Folgers—to consumers in 160 countries. Historically the strategy at P&G was well established. The company developed new products in Cincinnati and then relied on semiautonomous foreign subsidiaries to manufacture, market, and distribute those products in different nations. In many cases, foreign subsidiaries had their own production facilities and tailored the packaging, brand name, and marketing message to local tastes and preferences. For years this strategy delivered a steady stream of new products and reliable growth in sales and profits. By the 1990s, however, profit growth at P&G was slowing.

The essence of the problem was simple; P&G's costs were too high because of extensive duplication of manufacturing, marketing, and administrative facilities in different national subsidiaries. The duplication of assets made sense in the world of the 1960s, when national markets were segmented from each other by barriers to cross-border trade. Products produced in Great Britain, for example, could not be sold economically in Germany due to high tariff duties levied on imports into Germany. By the 1980s, however, barriers to cross-border trade were falling rapidly worldwide and fragmented national markets were merging into larger regional or global markets. Also, the retailers through which P&G distributed its products were growing larger and more global, such as Wal-Mart, Tesco from the United Kingdom, and Carrefour from France. These emerging global retailers were demanding price discounts from P&G.

In the 1990s P&G embarked on a major reorganization in an attempt to control its cost structure and recognize the new reality of emerging global markets. The company shut down some 30 manufacturing plants around the globe, laid off 13,000 employees, and concentrated production in fewer plants that could better realize economies of scale and serve regional markets. It wasn't enough. Profit growth remained sluggish, so in 1999 P&G launched its second reorganization of the decade. Named "Organization 2005," the goal was to transform P&G into a truly global company. The company tore up its old organization, which was based on countries and regions, and replaced it with one based on seven self-contained global business units, ranging from baby care to food products. Each business unit was given complete responsibility for generating profits from its products and for manufacturing, marketing, and product development. Each business unit was told to rationalize production, concentrating it in fewer larger facilities; to try to build global brands wherever possible, thereby eliminating marketing difference between countries; and to accelerate the development and launch of new products. P&G announced that as a result of this initiative, it would close another 10 factories and lay off 15,000 employees, mostly in Europe where there was still extensive duplication of assets. The annual cost savings were estimated to be about $800 million. P&G planned to use the savings to cut prices and increase marketing spending in an effort to gain market share, and thus further lower costs through the attainment of scale economies. This time the strategy seemed to be working. Between 2003 and 2006 P&G reported strong growth in both sales and profits. Significantly, P&G's global competitors, such as Unilever, Kimberly-Clark, and Colgate-Palmolive, were struggling in 2003 to 2006.[34]

They must try to realize location economies and experience effects, to leverage products internationally, to transfer core competencies and skills within the company, and to simultaneously pay attention to pressures for local responsiveness.[35] Bartlett and Ghoshal note that in the modern multinational enterprise, core competencies and skills do not reside just in the home country but can develop in any of the firm's worldwide operations. Thus, they maintain that the flow of skills and product offerings should not be all one way, from home country to foreign subsidiary. Rather, the flow should also be from foreign subsidiary to home country and from foreign subsidiary to foreign subsidiary. Transnational enterprises, in other words, must also focus on leveraging subsidiary skills.

In essence, firms that pursue a **transnational strategy** are trying to simultaneously achieve low costs through location economies, economies of scale, and learning effects;

differentiate their product offering across geographic markets to account for local differences; and foster a multidirectional flow of skills between different subsidiaries in the firm's global network of operations. As attractive as this may sound in theory, the strategy is not an easy one to pursue since it places conflicting demands on the company. Differentiating the product to respond to local demands in different geographic markets raises costs, which runs counter to the goal of reducing costs. Companies such as Ford and ABB (one of the world's largest engineering conglomerates) have tried to embrace a transnational strategy and found it difficult to implement.

How best to implement a transnational strategy is one of the most complex questions that large multinationals are grappling with today. Few if any enterprises have perfected this strategic posture. But some clues as to the right approach can be derived from a number of companies. For example, consider the case of Caterpillar. The need to compete with low-cost competitors such as Komatsu of Japan forced Caterpillar to look for greater cost economies. However, variations in construction practices and government regulations across countries mean that Caterpillar also has to be responsive to local demands. Therefore, Caterpillar confronted significant pressures for cost reductions *and* for local responsiveness.

To deal with cost pressures, Caterpillar redesigned its products to use many identical components and invested in a few large-scale component manufacturing facilities, sited at favorable locations, to fill global demand and realize scale economies. At the same time, the company augments the centralized manufacturing of components with assembly plants in each of its major global markets. At these plants, Caterpillar adds local product features, tailoring the finished product to local needs. Thus, Caterpillar is able to realize many of the benefits of global manufacturing while reacting to pressures for local responsiveness by differentiating its product among national markets.[36] By pursuing this strategy Caterpillar succeeded in doubling output per employee, significantly reducing its overall cost structure in the process. Meanwhile, Komatsu and Hitachi, which are still wedded to a Japan-centric global strategy, have seen their cost advantages evaporate and have been steadily losing market share to Caterpillar.

Changing a firm's strategic posture to build an organization capable of supporting a transnational strategy is a complex and challenging task. Some would say it is too complex, because the strategy implementation problems of creating a viable organizational structure and control systems to manage this strategy are immense.

INTERNATIONAL STRATEGY

Sometimes it is possible to identify multinational firms that find themselves in the fortunate position of being confronted with low cost pressures and low pressures for local responsiveness. Many of these enterprises have pursued an **international strategy,** taking products first produced for their domestic market and selling them internationally with only minimal local customization. The distinguishing feature of many such firms is that they are selling a product that serves universal needs, but they do not face significant competitors, and thus unlike firms pursuing a global standardization strategy, they are not confronted with pressures to reduce their cost structure. Xerox found itself in this position in the 1960s after its invention and commercialization of the photocopier. The technology underlying the photocopier was protected by strong patents, so for several years Xerox did not face competitors—it had a monopoly. The product serves universal needs, and it was highly valued in most developed nations. Thus, Xerox was able to sell the same basic product the world over, charging a relatively high price for that product. Since Xerox did not face direct competitors, it did not have to deal with strong pressures to minimize its cost structure.

Enterprises pursuing an international strategy have followed a similar developmental pattern as they expanded into foreign markets. They tend to centralize product development functions such as R&D at home. However, they also tend to establish manufacturing and marketing functions in each major country or geographic region in which they do business. The resulting duplication can raise costs, but this is less of an issue if the firm does not face strong pressures for cost reductions. Although they may undertake some local customization of product offering and marketing strategy, it tends to be rather limited in scope. Ultimately, in most firms that pursue an international strategy, the head office retains fairly tight control over marketing and product strategy.

Other firms that have pursued this strategy include Procter & Gamble and Microsoft. Historically, Procter & Gamble developed innovative new products in Cincinnati and then transferred them wholesale to local markets (see the Management Focus feature). Similarly, the bulk of Microsoft's product development work takes place in Redmond, Washington, where the company is headquartered. Although some localization work is undertaken elsewhere, it is limited to producing foreign-language versions of popular Microsoft programs.

THE EVOLUTION OF STRATEGY

The Achilles' heel of the international strategy is that over time, competitors inevitably emerge, and if managers do not take proactive steps to reduce their firm's cost structure, efficient global competitors will rapidly outflank it. This is exactly what happened to Xerox. Japanese companies such as Canon ultimately invented their way around Xerox's patents, produced their own photocopiers in very efficient manufacturing plants, priced them below Xerox's products, and rapidly took global market share from Xerox. In the final analysis, Xerox's demise was not due to the emergence of competitors, for ultimately that was bound to occur, but due to its failure to proactively reduce its cost structure in advance of the emergence of efficient global competitors. The message in this story is that an international strategy may not be viable in the long term, and to survive, firms need to shift toward a global standardization strategy or a transnational strategy in advance of competitors (see Figure 12.8).

The same can be said about a localization strategy. Localization may give a firm a competitive edge, but if it is simultaneously facing aggressive competitors, the company will also have to reduce its cost structure, and the only way to do that may be to shift toward a transnational strategy. This is what Procter & Gamble has been doing (see the Management Focus). Thus, as competition intensifies, international and localization strategies tend to become less viable, and managers need to orientate their companies toward either a global standardization strategy or a transnational strategy.

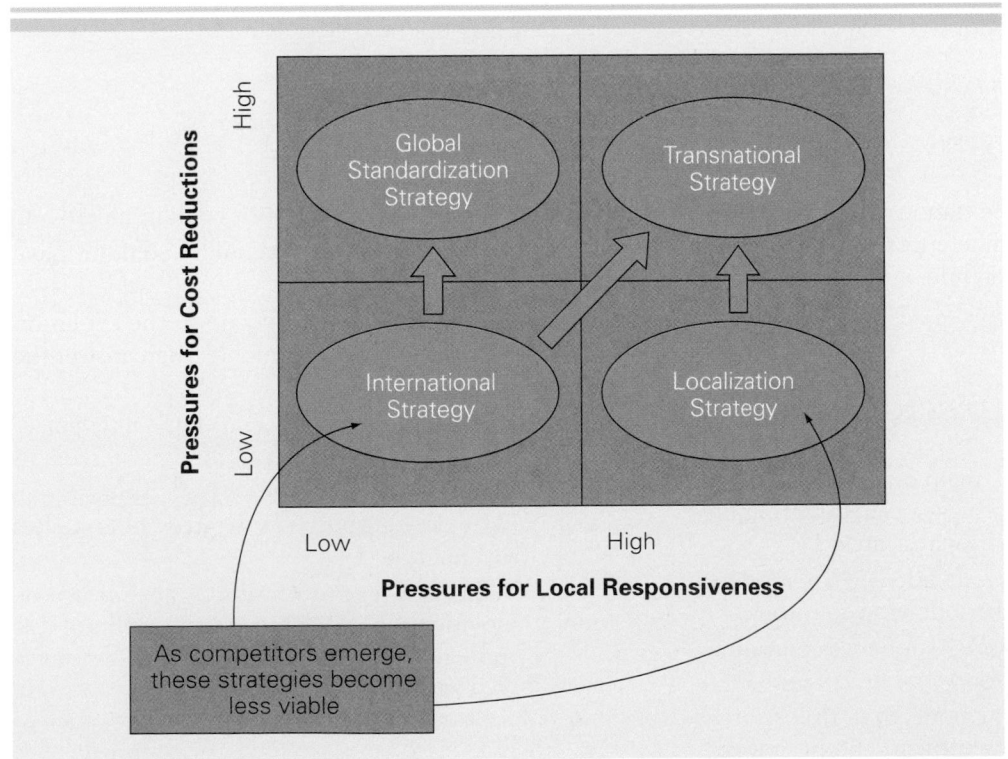

FIGURE 12.8

Changes in Strategy over Time

CHAPTER SUMMARY

In this chapter we reviewed basic principles of strategy and the various ways in which firms can profit from global expansion, and we looked at the strategies firms that compete globally can adopt. The chapter made these major points:

1. A strategy can be defined as the actions managers take to attain the goals of the firm. For most firms, the preeminent goal is to maximize shareholder value. Maximizing shareholder value requires firms to focus on increasing their profitability and the growth rate of profits over time.

2. International expansion may enable a firm to earn greater returns by transferring the product offerings derived from its core competencies to markets where indigenous competitors lack those product offerings and competencies.

3. It may pay a firm to base each value creation activity it performs at that location where factor conditions are most conducive to the performance of that activity. We refer to this strategy as focusing on the attainment of location economies.

4. By rapidly building sales volume for a standardized product, international expansion can assist a firm in moving down the experience curve by realizing learning effects and economies of scale.

5. A multinational firm can create additional value by identifying valuable skills created within its foreign subsidiaries and leveraging those skills within its global network of operations.

6. The best strategy for a firm to pursue often depends on a consideration of the pressures for cost reductions and for local responsiveness.

7. Firms pursuing an international strategy transfer the products derived from core competencies to foreign markets, while undertaking some limited local customization.

8. Firms pursuing a localization strategy customize their product offering, marketing strategy, and business strategy to national conditions.

9. Firms pursuing a global standardization strategy focus on reaping the cost reductions that come from experience curve effects and location economies.

10. Many industries are now so competitive that firms must adopt a transnational strategy. This involves a simultaneous focus on reducing costs, transferring skills and products, and boosting local responsiveness. Implementing such a strategy may not be easy.

Critical Thinking and Discussion Questions

1. In a world of zero transportation costs, no trade barriers, and nontrivial differences between nations with regard to factor conditions, firms must expand internationally if they are to survive. Discuss.

2. Plot the position of the following firms on Figure 12.8: Procter & Gamble, IBM, Nokia, Coca-Cola, Dow Chemical, US Steel, McDonald's. In each case, justify your answer.

3. What do you see as the main organizational problems that are likely to be associated with implementation of a transnational strategy?

4. Reread the Management Focus, "Vodafone in Japan," then answer the following questions:
   a. Why do you think Vodafone was pursuing a global standardization strategy?
   b. How did the firm hope that this strategy would boost profitability and profit growth?

   c. Why did the strategy not work in Japan?
   d. In retrospect, what should Vodafone have done differently?

5. Reread the Management Focus on the evolution of strategy at Procter & Gamble, then answer the following questions:
   a. What strategy was Procter & Gamble pursuing when it first entered foreign markets in the period up until the early 1990s?
   b. Why do you think this strategy became less viable in the 1990s?
   c. What strategy does P&G appear to be moving toward? What are the benefits of this strategy? What are the potential risks associated with it?

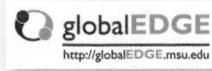

Research Task

Use the globalEDGE™ site to complete the following exercises:

1. The globalization of multinational corporations impacts the product and service choices available to customers. As such, several classifications and rankings of multinational corporations are prepared by a variety of sources. Find one such ranking system and identify the criteria used in ranking top global companies. Although some of these rankings require subscriptions, find a freely available listing and extract the ranking of the top 25 companies paying particular attention to their home countries.

2. The top management of your company, a manufacturer and marketer of laptop computers, has decided to pursue international expansion opportunities in Eastern Europe. In order to achieve some economies of scale, your management is aiming for a strategy of minimum local adaptation. Focusing on an Eastern European country of your choice, prepare an executive summary that features aspects of the product where standardization will simply not work, and adaptation to local conditions will be essential.

CLOSING CASE

Wal-Mart's Global Expansion

Established in Arkansas in 1962 by Sam Walton, over the last four decades Wal-Mart has grown rapidly to become the largest retailer in the world with sales of $330 billion, 1.8 million associates (Wal-Mart's term for employees), and almost 7,000 stores. Until 1991, Wal-Mart's operations were confined to the United States. There it established a competitive advantage based upon a combination of efficient merchandising, buying power, and human relations policies. Among other things, Wal-Mart was a leader in the implementation of information systems to track product sales and inventory, developed one of the most efficient distribution systems in the world, and was one of the first companies to promote widespread stock ownership among employees. These practices led to high productivity that enabled Wal-Mart to drive down its operating costs, which it passed on to consumers in the form of everyday low prices, a strategy that enabled the company to gain market share first in general merchandising, where it now dominates, and later in food retailing, where it is taking market share from established supermarkets.

By 1990, however, Wal-Mart realized that its opportunities for growth in the United States were becoming more limited. Management calculated that by the early 2000s, domestic growth opportunities would be constrained due to market saturation. So the company decided to expand globally. Initially, the critics scoffed. Wal-Mart, they said, was too American a company. While its retailing practices were well suited to America, they would not work in other countries where infrastructure was different, consumer tastes and preferences vary, and where established retailers already dominated.

Unperturbed, in 1991 Wal-Mart started to expand internationally with the opening of its first stores in Mexico. The Mexican operation was established as a joint venture with Cifera, the largest local retailer. Initially, Wal-Mart made a number of missteps that seemed to prove the critics right. Wal-Mart had problems replicating its efficient distribution system in Mexico. Poor infrastructure, crowded roads, and a lack of leverage with local suppliers, many of which could not or would not deliver directly to Wal-Mart's stores or distribution centers, resulted in stocking problems and raised costs and prices. Initially, prices at Wal-Mart in Mexico were some 20 percent above prices for comparable products in the company's U.S. stores, which limited Wal-Mart's ability to gain market share. There were also problems with merchandise selection. Many of the stores in Mexico carried items that were popular in the United States. These included ice skates, riding lawn mowers, leaf blowers, and fishing tackle. Not surprisingly, these items did not sell well in Mexico, so managers would slash prices to move inventory, only to find that the company's automated information systems would immediately order more inventory to replenish the depleted stock.

By the mid-1990s, however, Wal-Mart had learned from its early mistakes and adapted its Mexican operations to match the local environment. A partnership with a Mexican trucking company dramatically improved the distribution system, while more careful stocking practices meant that the Mexican stores sold merchandise that appealed more to local tastes and preferences. As Wal-Mart's presence grew, many of Wal-Mart's suppliers built factories near its Mexican distribution centers so that they could better serve the company, which helped to further drive down inventory and logistics costs. Today, Mexico is a leading light in Wal-Mart's international operations. In 1998, Wal-Mart acquired a controlling interest in Cifera. By 2005, Wal-Mart was more than twice the size of its nearest rival in Mexico with some 700 stores and revenues of $12.5 billion.

The Mexican experience proved to Wal-Mart that it could compete outside of the United States. It has subsequently expanded into thirteen other countries. Wal-Mart entered Canada, Great Britain, Germany, Japan, and South Korea, by acquiring existing retailers and then transferring its information systems, logistics, and management expertise. In other nations Wal-Mart established its own stores. As a result of these moves, by mid-2006 the company had over 2,700 stores outside the United States, employed some 500,000 associates, and generated international revenues of more than $62 billion.

In addition to greater growth, expanding internationally has bought Wal-Mart two other major benefits. First, Wal-Mart has also been able to reap significant economies of scale from its global buying power. Many of Wal-Mart's key suppliers have long been international companies; for example, GE (appliances), Unilever (food products), and Procter & Gamble (personal care products) are all major Wal-Mart suppliers that have long had their own global operations. By building international reach, Wal-Mart has used its enhanced size to demand deeper discounts from the local operations of its global suppliers, increasing the company's ability to lower prices to consumers, gain market share, and ultimately earn greater profits. Second, Wal-Mart has found that it is benefiting from the flow of ideas across the 14 countries in which it now competes. For

example, a two-level store in New York State came about because of the success of multilevel stores in South Korea. Other ideas, such as wine departments in its stores in Argentina, have now been integrated into layouts worldwide.

Wal-Mart realized that if it didn't expand internationally, other global retailers would beat it to the punch. Wal-Mart faces significant global competition from Carrefour of France, Ahold of Holland, and Tesco from the United Kingdom. Carrefour, the world's second largest retailer, is perhaps the most global of the lot. The pioneer of the hypermarket concept now operates in 26 countries and generates more than 50 percent of its sales outside France. Compared to this, Wal-Mart is a laggard with less than 20 percent of its sales in 2006 generated from international operations. However, there is room for significant global expansion. The global retailing market is still very fragmented. The top 25 retailers controlled less than 20 percent of worldwide retail sales in 2006, although forecasts suggest the figure could reach 40 percent by 2010, with Latin America, Southeast Asia, and Eastern Europe being the main battlegrounds.[37]

Case Discussion Questions

1. How does expanding internationally benefit Wal-Mart?

2. What are the risks that Wal-Mart faces when entering other retail markets? How can these risks be mitigated?

3. Why do you think that Wal-Mart first entered Mexico via a joint venture? Why did it purchase its Mexican joint venture partner in 1998?

4. What strategy is Wal-Mart pursuing—a global strategy, localization strategy, international strategy, or transnational strategy? Does this strategic choice make sense? Why?

Notes

1. Sources: M. Gunther, "MTV's Passage to India," *Fortune*, August 9, 2004, pp. 117–122; B. Pulley and A. Tanzer, "Sumner's Gemstone," *Forbes*, February 21, 2000, pp. 107–11; K. Hoffman, "Youth TV's Old Hand Prepares for the Digital Challenge," *Financial Times*, February 18, 2000, p. 8; presentation by Sumner M. Redstone, chairman and CEO, Viacom Inc., delivered to Salomon Smith Barney 11th Annual Global Entertainment Media, Telecommunications Conference, Scottsdale, AZ, January 8, 2001, archived at www.viacom.com; and Viacom 10K Statement, 2005.

2. More formally, ROIC = Net profit after tax/ Capital, where capital includes the sum of the firm's equity and debt. This way of calculating profitability is highly correlated with return on assets. For details, see the appendix to this chapter.

3. T. Copeland, T. Koller, and J. Murrin. *Valuation: Measuring and Managing the Value of Companies* (New York: John Wiley & Sons, 2000).

4. The concept of consumer surplus is an important one in economics. For a more detailed exposition, see D. Besanko, D. Dranove, and M. Shanley, *Economics of Strategy* (New York: John Wiley & Sons, 1996).

5. However, P = V only in the special case where the company has a perfect monopoly, and where it can charge each customer a unique price that reflects the value of the product to that customer (i.e., where perfect price discrimination is possible). More generally, except in the limiting case of perfect price discrimination, even a monopolist will see most consumers capture some of the value of a product in the form of a consumer surplus.

6. This point is central to the work of Michael Porter, *Competitive Advantage* (New York: Free Press, 1985). See also Chapter 4 in P. Ghemawat, *Commitment: The Dynamic of Strategy* (New York: Free Press, 1991).

7. Porter, *Competitive Strategy*.

8. M. E. Porter, "What Is Strategy?" *Harvard Business Review*, On-point Enhanced Edition article, February 1, 2000.

9. Porter, *Competitive Advantage*.

10. Empirical evidence does seem to indicate that, on average, international expansion is linked to greater firm profitability. For some recent examples, see M. A. Hitt, R. E. Hoskisson, and H. Kim, "International Diversification, Effects on Innovation and Firm Performance," *Academy of Management Journal* 40, no. 4 (1997), pp. 767–98, and S. Tallman and J. Li, "Effects of International Diversity and Product Diversity on the Performance of Multinational Firms," *Academy of Management Journal* 39, no. 1 (1996), pp. 179–96.

11. This concept has been popularized by G. Hamel and C. K. Prahalad, *Competing for the Future* (Boston: Harvard Business School Press, 1994). The concept is grounded in the resource-based view of the firm; for a summary, see J. B. Barney, "Firm Resources and Sustained Competitive Advantage," *Journal of Management* 17 (1991), pp. 99–120, and K. R. Conner, "A Historical Comparison of Resource-Based Theory and Five Schools of Thought within Industrial Organization Economics: Do We Have a New Theory of the Firm?" *Journal of Management* 17 (1991), pp. 121–54.

12. J. P. Womack, D. T. Jones, and D. Roos, *The Machine That Changed the World* (New York: Rawson Associates, 1990).

13. M. E. Porter, *The Competitive Advantage of Nations* (New York: Free Press, 1990).

14. Example is based on C. S. Trager, "Enter the Mini-Multinational," *Northeast International Business*, March 1989, pp. 13–14.

15. See: R. B. Reich, *The Work of Nations* (New York: Alfred A. Knopf, 1991); and P. J. Buckley and N. Hashai, "A Global System View of Firm Boundaries," *Journal of International Business Studies*, January 2004, pp. 33–50.

16. D. Barboza, "An Unknown Giant Flexes Its Muscles," *The New York Times*, December 4, 2004, pp. B1, B3.

17. G. Hall and S. Howell, "The Experience Curve from an Economist's Perspective," *Strategic Management Journal* 6 (1985), pp. 197–212.

18. A. A. Alchain, "Reliability of Progress Curves in Airframe Production," *Econometrica* 31 (1963), pp. 697–93.

19. Hall and Howell, "The Experience Curve from an Economist's Perspective."

20. For a full discussion of the source of scale economies, see D. Besanko, D. Dranove, and M. Shanley, *Economics of Strategy* (New York: John Wiley & Sons, 1996).

21. This estimate was provided by the Pharmaceutical Manufacturers Association.

22. "Matsushita Electrical Industrial in 1987," in *Transnational Management*, eds. C. A. Bartlett and S. Ghoshal (Homewood, IL: Richard D. Irwin, 1992).

23. See J. Birkinshaw and N. Hood, "Multinational Subsidiary Evolution: Capability and Charter Change in Foreign Owned Subsidiary Companies," *Academy of Management Review* 23 (October 1998), pp. 773–95; A. K. Gupta and V. J. Govindarajan, "Knowledge Flows within Multinational Corporations," *Strategic Management Journal* 21 (2000), pp. 473–96; V. J. Govindarajan and A. K. Gupta, *The Quest for Global Dominance* (San Francisco: Jossey Bass, 2001); T. S. Frost, J. M. Birkinshaw, and P. C. Ensign, "Centers of Excellence in Multinational Corporations," *Strategic Management Journal* 23 (2002), pp. 997–1018; and U. Andersson, M. Forsgren, and U. Holm, "The Strategic Impact of External Networks," *Strategic Management Journal* 23 (2002), pp. 979–96.

24. S. Leung, "Armchairs, TVs and Espresso: Is It McDonald's?" *The Wall Street Journal*, August 30, 2002, pp. A1, A6.

25. C. K. Prahalad and Yves L. Doz, *The Multinational Mission: Balancing Local Demands and Global Vision* (New York: Free Press, 1987). Also see J. Birkinshaw, A. Morrison, and J. Hulland,

"Structural and Competitive Determinants of a Global Integration Strategy," *Strategic Management Journal* 16 (1995), pp. 637–55.

26. J. E. Garten, "Wal-Mart Gives Globalization a Bad Name," *BusinessWeek*, March 8, 2004, p. 24.

27. Prahalad and Doz, *The Multinational Mission: Balancing Local Demands and Global Vision*. Prahalad and Doz actually talk about local responsiveness rather than local customization.

28. T. Levitt, "The Globalization of Markets," *Harvard Business Review*, May–June 1983, pp. 92–102.

29. K. Belson, "In U.S., Cell Phone Users Are Often All Talk," *The New York Times*, December 13, 2004, pp. C1, C4.

30. W. W. Lewis, *The Power of Productivity* (Chicago, University of Chicago Press, 2004).

31. C. J. Chipello, "Local Presence Is Key to European Deals," *The Wall Street Journal*, June 30, 1998, p. A15.

32. Bartlett and Ghoshal, *Managing across Borders*.

33. Sources: C. Bryan-Low, "Vodafone's Global Ambitions Got Hung Up in Japan," *The Wall Street Journal*, March 18, 2006, p. A1; G. Parket, "Going Global Can Hit Snags Vodafone Finds," *The Wall Street Journal*, June 16, 2004, p. B1.

34. Sources: J. Neff, "P&G Outpacing Unilever in Five-Year Battle," *Advertising Age*, November

3, 2003, pp. 1–3; G. Strauss, "Firm Restructuring into Truly Global Company," *USA Today*, September 10, 1999, p. B2; *Procter & Gamble 10K Report, 2005*; and M. Kolbasuk McGee, "P&G Jump-Starts Corporate Change," *Information Week*, November 1, 1999, pp. 30–34.

35. Ibid.

36. T. Hout, M. E. Porter, and E. Rudden, "How Global Companies Win Out," *Harvard Business Review*, September–October 1982, pp. 98–108.

37. Sources: A. Lillo, "Wal-Mart Says Global Going Good," *Home Textiles Today*, September 15, 2003, pp. 12–13; A. de Rocha and L. A. Dib, "The Entry of Wal-Mart into Brazil," *International Journal of Retail and Distribution Management* 30 (2002), pp. 61–73; "Wal-Mart: Mexico's Biggest Retailer," *Chain Store Age*, June 2001, pp. 52–54; M. N. Hamilton, "Global Food Fight," *Washington Post*, November 19, 2000, p. H1; "Global Strategy—Why Tesco Will Beat Carrefour," *Retail Week*, April 6, 2001, p. 14; "Shopping All over the World," *The Economist*, June 19, 1999, pp. 59–61; G. Samor, C. Rohwedder, and A. Zimmerman, "Innocents Abroad?" *Wall Street Journal*, May 16, 2006, p. B1; and Wal-Mart Web site, accessed June 2006.

Appendix: Profitability, Growth, and Valuation

The ultimate goal of strategy is to maximize the value of a company to its shareholders (subject to the important constraints that this is done in a legal, ethical and socially responsible manner). The two main drivers of enterprise valuation are profitability, as measured by the company's return on invested capital (**ROIC**) and the growth rate of profits, g.[1]

ROIC is defined as net operating profits less adjusted taxes (NOPLAT) over the invested capital of the enterprise (IC), where IC is the sum of the company's equity and debt (the method for calculating adjusted taxes need not concern us here). That is:

$$ROIC = NOPLAT/IC$$

where

$$
\begin{aligned}
NOPLAT = \ &\text{Revenues} - \text{Cost of goods sold} \\
&- \text{Operating expenses} - \text{Depreciation charges} \\
&- \text{Adjusted taxes}
\end{aligned}
$$

$$IC = \text{Value of shareholders equity} + \text{Value of debt}$$

The growth rate of profits, g, can be defined as the percentage increase in net operating profits (NOPLAT) over a given time period. More precisely:

$$g = [(NOPLAT_{t+1} - NOPLAT_t)/NOPLAT_t] \times 100$$

The valuation of a company can be calculated using discounted cash flow analysis and applying it to future expected free cash flows (free cash flow in a period is defined

---

[1] C. Y. Baldwin, *Fundamental Enterprise Valuation: Return on Invested Capital*, Harvard Business School Note 9-801-125, July 3, 2004, and T. Copeland et al., *Valuation: Measuring and Managing the Value of Companies* (New York: Wiley, 2000).

TABLE 12.A1

ROIC, Growth, and Valuation

NOPLAT Growth g	ROIC 7.5%	ROIC 10.0%	ROIC 12.5%	ROIC 15.0%	ROIC 20%
3%	887	1000	1058	1113	1170
6%	708	1000	1117	1295	1442
9%	410	1000	1354	1591	1886

as NOPLAT − net investments). It can be shown that the valuation of a company so calculated is related to the company's weighted average cost of capital (WACC), which is the cost of the equity and debt that the firm uses to finance its business, and the company's ROIC. Specifically:

- If ROIC > WACC the company is earning more than its cost of capital and it is creating value.
- If ROIC = WACC the company is earning its cost of capital and its valuation will be stable.
- If ROIC < WACC the company is earning less than its cost of capital and it is therefore destroying value.

A company that earns more than its cost of capital is even more valuable if it can grow its net operating profits less adjusted taxes (NOPLAT) over time. Conversely, a firm that is not earning its cost of capital destroys value if it grows its NOPLAT. This critical relationship between ROIC, g, and value is shown in Table A1.

In Table A1, the figures in the cells of the matrix represent the discounted present values of future free cash flows for a company that has a starting NOPLAT of $100, invested capital of $1,000, cost of capital of 10 percent, and a 25-year time horizon after which ROIC equals the cost of capital.

The important points revealed by this exercise are as follows:

- A company with an already high ROIC can create more value by increasing its profit growth rate rather than pushing for an even higher ROIC. Thus a company with an ROIC of 15 percent and a 3 percent growth rate can create more value by increasing its profit growth rate from 3 percent to 9 percent than it can by increasing ROIC to 20 percent.
- A company with a low ROIC destroys value if it grows. Thus, if ROIC equals 7.5 percent, a 9 percent growth rate for 25 years will produce less value than a 3 percent growth rate. This is because unprofitable growth requires capital investments, the cost of which cannot be covered.
- Unprofitable growth destroys value.

The best of both worlds is high ROIC and high growth.

Very few companies are able to maintain ROIC greater than WACC and grow NOPLAT over time, but there are some notable examples including Dell, Microsoft, and Wal-Mart—all of which have increased their profitability and their growth rates by expanding internationally. Because these companies have generally been able to fund their capital investment needs from internally generated cash flows, they have not had to issue more shares to raise capital. Thus growth in NOPLAT has translated directly into higher earning per share for these companies, making their shares more attractive to investors and leading to substantial share price appreciation. By successfully pursuing strategies that result in a high ROIC and growing NOPLAT, these firms have maximized shareholder value.

Nestlé

For years Nestlé, the world's largest food and beverage company, operated with a highly decentralized organization. This organization reflected the company's belief that there is no such thing as a global consumer in the food and beverage business, and that the need to customize product offerings to local tastes and preferences required the creation of highly autonomous national subsidiaries. Recently, however, Nestlé has begun to move away from this structure. The catalysts have been falling trade barriers and the rise of more integrated regional and global markets in which it faces aggressive competitors, such as Unilever and Procter & Gamble.

Faced with increasing competition, Nestlé has realized that it needs to adapt its organization structure so it can maintain local responsiveness, while at the same time realizing the cost savings that come from eliminating duplication of activities across subsidiaries. Progressively, the company has moved toward the creation of

The Organization of International Business

LEARNING OBJECTIVES

After you have read this chapter you should be able to:

LO1 Understand what is meant by organization architecture.

LO2 Be familiar with the different organizational choices that can be made in an international business.

LO3 Explain how organization can be matched to strategy to improve the performance of an international business.

LO4 Be able to discuss what is required for an international business to change its organization so that it better matches its strategy.

global business units that oversee the strategy for major product lines and realized cost economies by centralizing key functions such as purchasing, production, and R&D at favorable locations. At the same time, marketing and sales remain decentralized to national subsidiaries, where local managers configure the marketing and sales mix so that it best matches consumer needs and local distribution systems. Nestlé has now adopted this structure for its water business, which includes the Perrier and San Pellegrino brands, and for its nutrition business, which includes the company's infant formula brands. The water business, for example, has centralized production in France and Italy to realize economies of scale. It has also developed a global brand positioning strategy. At the same time, Nestlé gives national subsidiaries the ability to develop programs for implementing the global brand strategy in their own geographical regions, customizing their approach to local conditions.[1]

Introduction

As the Nestlé example suggests, this chapter is concerned with identifying the organization architecture that international businesses use to manage and direct their global operations. By **organizational architecture** we mean the totality of a firm's organization, including formal organization structure, control systems and incentives, processes, organizational culture, and people. The core argument this chapter outlines is that superior enterprise profitability requires three conditions to be fulfilled. First, the different elements of a firm's organizational architecture must be internally consistent. For example, the control and incentive systems the firm uses must be consistent with the structure of the enterprise. Second, the organizational architecture must match or fit the strategy of the firm—strategy and architecture must be consistent. For example, if a firm is pursuing a global standardization strategy but it has the wrong kind of organization architecture in place, it is unlikely that it will be able to execute that strategy effectively and poor performance may result. Third, the strategy and architecture of the firm must not only be consistent with each other, but they also must be consistent with competitive conditions prevailing in the firm's markets—strategy, architecture, and competitive environment must all be consistent.

For example, a firm pursuing a localization strategy might have the right kind of organizational architecture in place for that strategy. However, if it competes in markets where cost pressures are intense and demands for local responsiveness are low, it will still have inferior performance because a global standardization strategy is more appropriate in such an environment. The example of Nestlé touches on some of the important issues here. Historically Nestlé has competed in markets where local responsiveness has been very important. The production and marketing of food and beverages have traditionally been tailored to the tastes and preferences of consumers in different nations. Nestlé satisfied this environmental demand for local responsiveness by pursuing a localization strategy. Its organizational architecture reflected this strategy. Nestlé operated with a decentralized structure that delegated responsibility for production, marketing, sales, and distribution decisions to autonomous national operating companies. This allowed local managers to configure product offerings and marketing and sales activities to the conditions prevailing in a particular nation. For a long time, this fit between strategy and architecture served Nestlé well, helping it become a dominant consumer products enterprise.

However, by the early 1990s the competitive environment was changing. Trade barriers between countries were falling. This made it possible to manufacture certain items, such as infant formula and bottled water, at favorable central locations to realize the benefits associated with location and experience curve economies. Some of Nestlé's competitors moved rapidly to exploit this change in the competitive environment and Nestlé found itself disadvantaged by a high-cost structure (caused by the duplication of manufacturing operations) and an inability to introduce new products in several national markets at once. In other words, the competitive environment changed, but Nestlé did not change with it.

Nestlé has come to the realization that it needs to change both its strategy and its organizational architecture to better match the new competitive realities. Nestlé has begun to shift toward a more transnational strategic orientation, seeking to balance local responsiveness in marketing and sales with the centralization of manufacturing and product development activities to realize scale economies and execute global brand strategies and product launches. To implement this strategy, Nestlé has progressively introduced a new organizational architecture based on global business units, each of which has worldwide responsibility for the strategy and performance of key product lines. At the same time, recognizing that local responsiveness remains important, it has retained its national subsidiaries and granted managers in them the autonomy to develop programs for marketing and sales that best match local needs. What Nestlé is trying to do through these changes is to establish the right fit between strategy, architecture, and environment by reconfiguring its organization and operations to match new competitive realities.

To explore the issues illustrated by examples such as Nestlé, we open the current chapter by discussing in more detail the concepts of organizational architecture and fit. Next we turn to a more detailed exploration of various components of architecture—structure, control systems and incentives, organization culture, and processes—and explain how these components must be internally consistent. (We discuss the "people" component of architecture in Chapter 18, when we discuss human resource strategy in the multinational firm.) After reviewing the various components of architecture, we look at the ways in which architecture can be matched to strategy and the competitive environment to achieve high performance. The chapter closes with a discussion of organizational change, for as the Nestlé example illustrates, periodically firms have to change their organization so it matches new strategic and competitive realities.

Organizational Architecture

As noted in the introduction, the term *organizational architecture* refers to the totality of a firm's organization, including formal organizational structure, control systems and incentives, organizational culture, processes, and people.[2] Figure 13.1 illustrates these different elements. By **organizational structure,** we mean three things: First, the formal division of the organization into subunits such as product divisions, national operations, and functions (most organizational charts display this aspect of structure); second, the location of decision-making responsibilities within that structure (e.g., centralized or decentralized); and third, the establishment of integrating mechanisms to coordinate the activities of subunits including cross-functional teams and/or pan-regional committees.

Control systems are the metrics used to measure the performance of subunits and make judgments about how well managers are running those subunits. For example, historically Unilever measured the performance of national operating subsidiary companies according to profitability—profitability was the metric. **Incentives** are the devices used to reward appropriate managerial behavior. Incentives are very closely tied to performance metrics. For example, the incentives of a manager in charge of a national operating subsidiary might be linked to the performance of that company. Specifically, she might receive a bonus if her subsidiary exceeds its performance targets.

Processes are the manner in which decisions are made and work is performed within the organization. Examples are the processes for formulating strategy, for deciding how to

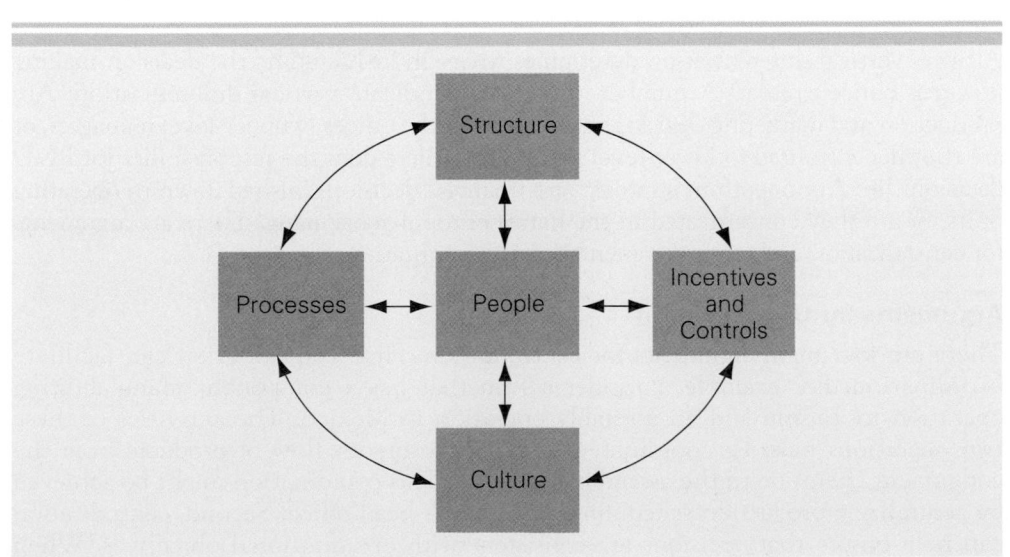

FIGURE 13.1

Organization Architecture

allocate resources within a firm, or for evaluating the performance of managers and giving feedback. Processes are conceptually distinct from the location of decision-making responsibilities within an organization, although both involve decisions. While the CEO might have ultimate responsibility for deciding what the strategy of the firm should be (that is, the decision-making responsibility is centralized), the process he or she uses to make that decision might include the solicitation of ideas and criticism from lower-level managers.

Organizational culture refers to the norms and value systems that the employees of an organization share. Just as societies have cultures (see Chapter 3 for details), so do organizations. Organizations are societies of individuals who come together to perform collective tasks. They have their own distinctive patterns of culture and subculture.[3] As we shall see, organizational culture can have a profound impact on how a firm performs. Finally, by **people** we mean not just the employees of the organization but also the strategy used to recruit, compensate, and retain those individuals and the type of people they are in terms of their skills, values, and orientation (discussed in depth in Chapter 18).

As the arrows in Figure 13.1 illustrate, the various components of an organization's architecture are not independent of each other: Each component shapes, and is shaped by, other components of architecture. An obvious example is the strategy regarding people. A firm can choose a proactive strategy, hiring individuals whose internal values are consistent with those that the firm wishes to emphasize in its organization culture. Thus, the people component of architecture can be used to reinforce (or not) the prevailing culture of the organization. For example, Unilever has historically made an effort to hire managers who were sociable and placed a high value on consensus and cooperation, values that the enterprise wished to emphasize in its own culture.[4] To maximize profitability, a firm must pay close attention to achieving internal consistency between the various components of its architecture.

Organizational Structure

Organizational structure can be thought of in terms of three dimensions: (1) **vertical differentiation,** which refers to the location of decision-making responsibilities within a structure; (2) **horizontal differentiation,** which refers to the formal division of the organization into subunits; and (3) the establishment of **integrating mechanisms,** which are mechanisms for coordinating subunits. We begin by discussing vertical differentiation, then horizontal differentiation, and then integrating mechanisms.

VERTICAL DIFFERENTIATION: CENTRALIZATION AND DECENTRALIZATION

A firm's vertical differentiation determines where in its hierarchy the decision-making power is concentrated.[5] A number of questions indicate vertical differentiation: Are production and marketing decisions centralized in the offices of upper-level managers, or are they decentralized to lower-level managers? Where does the responsibility for R&D decisions lie? Are important strategic and financial decisions pushed down to operating units, or are they concentrated in the hands of top management? There are arguments for centralization and other arguments for decentralization.

Arguments for Centralization

There are four main arguments for centralization. First, centralization can facilitate coordination. For example, consider a firm that has a component manufacturing operation in Taiwan and an assembly operation in Mexico. The activities of these two operations must be coordinated to ensure a smooth flow of products from the component operation to the assembly operation. This coordination might be achieved by centralizing production scheduling at the firm's head office. Second, centralization can help ensure that decisions are consistent with organizational objectives. When decisions are decentralized to lower-level managers, those managers may make decisions at variance with top management's goals. Centralization of important decisions minimizes the chance of this inconsistency occurring.

Third, by concentrating power and authority in one individual or a management team, centralization can give top-level managers the means to bring about needed major organizational changes. Fourth, centralization can avoid the duplication of activities that occurs when various subunits within the organization carry on similar activities. For example, many international firms centralize their R&D functions at one or two locations to ensure that R&D work is not duplicated. Production activities may be centralized at key locations for the same reason.

Arguments for Decentralization

There are five main arguments for decentralization. First, top management can become overburdened when decision-making authority is centralized, and this can result in poor decisions. Decentralization gives top management time to focus on critical issues by delegating more routine issues to lower-level managers. Second, motivational research favors decentralization. Behavioral scientists have long argued that people are willing to give more to their jobs when they have a greater degree of individual freedom and control over their work. Third, decentralization permits greater flexibility—more rapid response to environmental changes—because decisions do not have to be "referred up the hierarchy" unless they are exceptional in nature. Fourth, decentralization can result in better decisions. In a decentralized structure, decisions are made closer to the spot by individuals who (presumably) have better information than managers several levels up in a hierarchy (for an example of decentralization to achieve this goal, see the Management Focus on Wal-Mart's International Division). Fifth, decentralization can increase control. Decentralization can be used to establish relatively autonomous, self-contained subunits within an organization. Subunit managers can then be held accountable for subunit performance. The more responsibility subunit managers have for decisions that impact subunit performance, the fewer excuses they have for poor performance.

Strategy and Centralization in an International Business

The choice between centralization and decentralization is not absolute. Frequently it makes sense to centralize some decisions and to decentralize others, depending on the type of decision and the firm's strategy. Decisions regarding overall firm strategy, major financial expenditures, financial objectives, and legal issues are typically centralized at the firm's headquarters. However, operating decisions, such as those relating to production, marketing, R&D, and human resource management, may or may not be centralized depending on the firm's strategy.

Consider firms pursuing a global standardization strategy. They must decide how to disperse the various value creation activities around the globe so location and experience economies can be realized. The head office must make the decisions about where to locate R&D, production, marketing, and so on. In addition, the globally dispersed web of value creation activities that facilitates a global strategy must be coordinated. All of this creates pressures for centralizing some operating decisions.

In contrast, the emphasis on local responsiveness in firms pursuing a localization strategy creates strong pressures for decentralizing operating decisions to foreign subsidiaries. Firms pursuing an international strategy also tend to maintain centralized control over their core competency and to decentralize other decisions to foreign subsidiaries. Typically, such firms centralize control over R&D in their home country, but decentralize operating decisions to foreign subsidiaries. For example, Microsoft Corporation, which fits the international mode, centralizes its product development activities (where its core competencies lie) at its Redmond, Washington, headquarters and decentralizes marketing activity to various foreign subsidiaries. Thus, while products are developed at home, managers in the various foreign subsidiaries have significant latitude for formulating strategies to market those products in their particular settings.[6]

The International Division at Wal-Mart

When Wal-Mart started to expand internationally in the early 1990s, it decided to set up an international division to oversee the process. The International Division was based in Bentonville, Arkansas, at the company head-quarters. Today the division oversees operations in fourteen countries that collectively generate over $60 billion in sales. In terms of reporting structure, the division is divided into three regions—Europe, Asia, and the Americas, with the CEO of each region reporting to the CEO of the International Division, who in turn reports to the CEO of Wal-Mart.

Initially, the senior management of the International Division exerted tight centralized control over merchandising strategy and operations in different countries. The reasoning was straightforward; Wal-Mart's managers wanted to make sure that international stores copied the format for stores, merchandising, and operations that had served the company so well in the United States. They believed, naively perhaps, that centralized control over merchandising strategy and operations was the way to make sure operations would be standard.

By the late 1990s, with the International Division approaching $20 billion in sales, Wal-Mart's managers concluded that this centralized approach was not serving them well. Country managers had to get permission from their superiors in Bentonville before changing strategy and operations, and this was slowing decision making. Centralization also produced information over-load at headquarters and led to some poor decisions. Wal-Mart found that managers in Bentonville were not necessarily the best ones to decide on store layout in Mexico, merchandising strategy in Argentina, or compensation policy in the United Kingdom. The need to adapt merchandising strategy and operations to local conditions argued strongly for greater decentralization.

The pivotal event that led to a change in policy at Wal-Mart was the company's 1999 acquisition of Britain's ASDA supermarket chain. The ASDA acquisition added a mature and successful $14 billion operation to Wal-Mart's International Division. The company realized that it was not appropriate for managers in Bentonville to be making all important decisions for ASDA. Accordingly, over the next few months, John Menzer, CEO of the International Division, reduced the number of staff located in Bentonville who were devoted to international operations by 50 percent. Country leaders were given greater responsibility, especially in the area of merchandising and operations. In Menzer's own words, "We were at the point where it was time to break away a little bit. . . . You can't run the world from one place. The countries have to drive the business. . . . The change has sent a strong message [to country managers] that they no longer have to wait for approval from Bentonville."

Although Wal-Mart has now decentralized decisions within the International Division, it is still struggling to find the right formula for managing global procurement. Ideally, the company would like to centralize procurement in Bentonville so that it could use its enormous purchasing power to bargain down the prices it pays suppliers. As a practical matter, however, this has not been easy to attain given that the product mix in Wal-Mart stores has to be tailored to conditions prevailing in the local market. Currently, significant responsibility for procurement remains at the country and regional level. However, Wal-Mart would like to have a global procurement strategy so it can negotiate on a global basis with key suppliers and can simultaneously introduce new merchandise into its stores around the world.

As merchandising and operating decisions have been decentralized, the International Division has increasingly taken on a new role—that of identifying best practices and transferring them between countries. For example, the division has developed a knowledge management system whereby stores in one country, let's say Argentina, can quickly communicate pictures of items, sales data, and ideas on how to market and promote products to stores in another country, such as Japan. The division is also starting to move personnel between stores in different countries as a way of facilitating the flow of best practices across national borders. Finally, the division is at the cutting edge of moving Wal-Mart away from its U.S.-centric mentality, and it is showing the organization that ideas implemented in foreign operations might also be used to improve the efficiency and effectiveness of Wal-Mart's operations at home.[8]

The situation in firms pursuing a transnational strategy is more complex. The need to realize location and experience curve economies requires some degree of centralized control over global production centers. However, the need for local responsiveness dictates the decentralization of many operating decisions, particularly for marketing, to foreign subsidiaries. Thus, in firms pursuing a transnational strategy, some operating decisions are relatively centralized, while others are relatively decentralized. In addition, global learning based on the multidirectional transfer of skills between subsidiaries, and between subsidiaries and the corporate center, is a central feature of a firm pursuing a transnational strategy. The concept of global learning is predicated on the notion that foreign subsidiaries within a multinational firm have significant freedom to develop their own skills and competencies. Only then can these be leveraged to benefit other parts of the organization. A substantial degree of decentralization is required if subsidiaries are going to have the freedom to do this. For this reason too, the pursuit of a transnational strategy requires a high degree of decentralization.[7]

HORIZONTAL DIFFERENTIATION: THE DESIGN OF STRUCTURE

Horizontal differentiation is concerned with how the firm decides to divide itself into subunits.[9] The decision is normally made on the basis of function, type of business, or geographical area. In many firms, just one of these factors predominates, but more complex solutions are adopted in others. This is particularly likely in the case of multinational firms, where the conflicting demands to organize the company around different products (to realize location and experience curve economies) and different national markets (to remain locally responsive) must be reconciled.

The Structure of Domestic Firms

Most firms begin with no formal structure and are run by a single entrepreneur or a small team of individuals. As they grow, the demands of management become too great for one individual or a small team to handle. At this point the organization is split into functions reflecting the firm's value creation activities (e.g., production, marketing, R&D, sales). Top management typically coordinates and controls these functions (see Figure 13.2). Decision making in this functional structure tends to be centralized.

Further horizontal differentiation may be required if the firm significantly diversifies its product offering, which takes the firm into different business areas. For example, Dutch multinational Philips NV began as a lighting company, but diversification took the company into consumer electronics (e.g., visual and audio equipment), industrial electronics (integrated circuits and other electronic components), and medical systems (MRI scanners and ultrasound systems). In such circumstances, a functional structure can be too clumsy. Problems of coordination and control arise when different business areas are managed within the framework of a functional structure.[10] For one thing, it

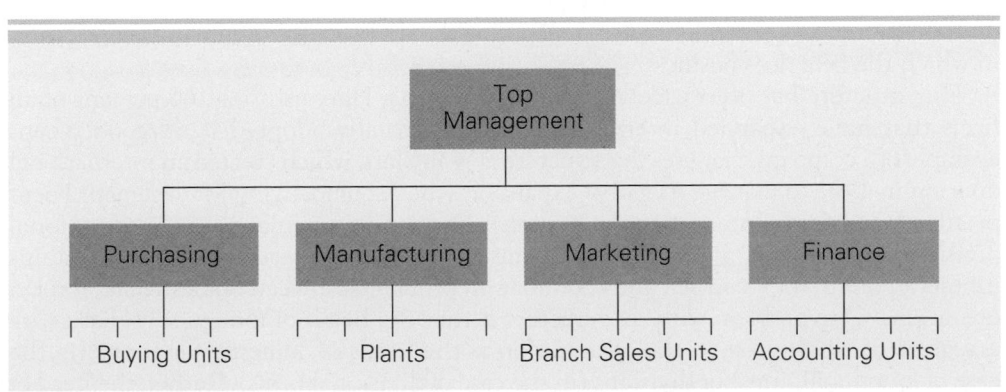

FIGURE 13.2

A Typical Functional Structure

FIGURE 13.3

A Typical Product
Divisional Structure

becomes difficult to identify the profitability of each distinct business area. For another, it is difficult to run a functional department, such as production or marketing, if it is supervising the value creation activities of several business areas.

To solve the problems of coordination and control, at this stage most firms switch to a product divisional structure (see Figure 13.3). With a product divisional structure, each division is responsible for a distinct product line (business area). Thus, Philips created divisions for lighting, consumer electronics, industrial electronics, and medical systems. Each product division is set up as a self-contained, largely autonomous entity with its own functions. The responsibility for operating decisions is typically decentralized to product divisions, which are then held accountable for their performance. Headquarters is responsible for the overall strategic development of the firm and for the financial control of the various divisions.

The International Division

When firms initially expand abroad, they often group all their international activities into an **international division.** This has tended to be the case for firms organized on the basis of functions and for firms organized on the basis of product divisions. Regardless of the firm's domestic structure, its international division tends to be organized on geography. Figure 13.4 illustrates this for a firm whose domestic organization is based on product divisions.

Many manufacturing firms expanded internationally by exporting the product manufactured at home to foreign subsidiaries to sell. Thus, in the firm illustrated in Figure 13.4, the subsidiaries in countries 1 and 2 would sell the products manufactured by divisions A, B, and C. In time, however, it might prove viable to manufacture the product in each country, and so production facilities would be added on a country-by-country basis. For firms with a functional structure at home, this might mean replicating the functional structure in every country in which the firm does business. For firms with a divisional structure, this might mean replicating the divisional structure in every country in which the firm does business.

This structure has been widely used; according to a Harvard study, 60 percent of all firms that have expanded internationally have initially adopted it. A good recent example of a company that uses this structure is Wal-Mart, which created an international division in 1991 to manage its global expansion (the accompanying Management Focus profiles Wal-Mart's International Division). Despite its popularity, an international division structure can give rise to problems.[11] The dual structure it creates contains inherent potential for conflict and coordination problems between domestic and foreign operations. One problem with the structure is that the heads of foreign subsidiaries are not given as much voice in the organization as the heads of domestic functions (in the case of functional firms) or divisions (in the case of divisional firms). Rather, the head of the international division is presumed to be able to represent the interests of all countries

FIGURE 13.4

One Company's International Divisional Structure

to headquarters. This effectively relegates each country's manager to the second tier of the firm's hierarchy, which is inconsistent with a strategy of trying to expand internationally and build a true multinational organization.

Another problem is the implied lack of coordination between domestic operations and foreign operations, which are isolated from each other in separate parts of the structural hierarchy. This can inhibit the worldwide introduction of new products, the transfer of core competencies between domestic and foreign operations, and the consolidation of global production at key locations so as to realize location and experience curve economies.

As a result of such problems, many firms that continue to expand internationally abandon this structure and adopt one of the worldwide structures we discuss next. The two initial choices are a worldwide product divisional structure, which diversified firms that have domestic product divisions tend to adopt, and a worldwide area structure, which undiversified firms whose domestic structures are based on functions tend to favor. Figure 13.5 illustrates these two alternative paths of development. John Stopford and Louis Wells developed the model in the figure, which is referred to as the international structural stages model.[12]

Worldwide Area Structure

Firms with a low degree of diversification and a domestic structure based on functions tend to favor a **worldwide area structure** (see Figure 13.6). Under this structure, the world is divided into geographic areas. An area may be a country (if the market is large enough) or a group of countries. Each area tends to be a self-contained, largely autonomous entity with its own set of value creation activities (e.g., its own production, marketing, R&D, human resources, and finance functions). Operations authority and strategic decisions relating to each of these activities are typically decentralized to each area, with headquarters retaining authority for the overall strategic direction of the firm and financial control.

This structure facilitates local responsiveness. Because decision-making responsibilities are decentralized, each area can customize product offerings, marketing strategy, and

FIGURE 13.5

The International
Structural Stages Model

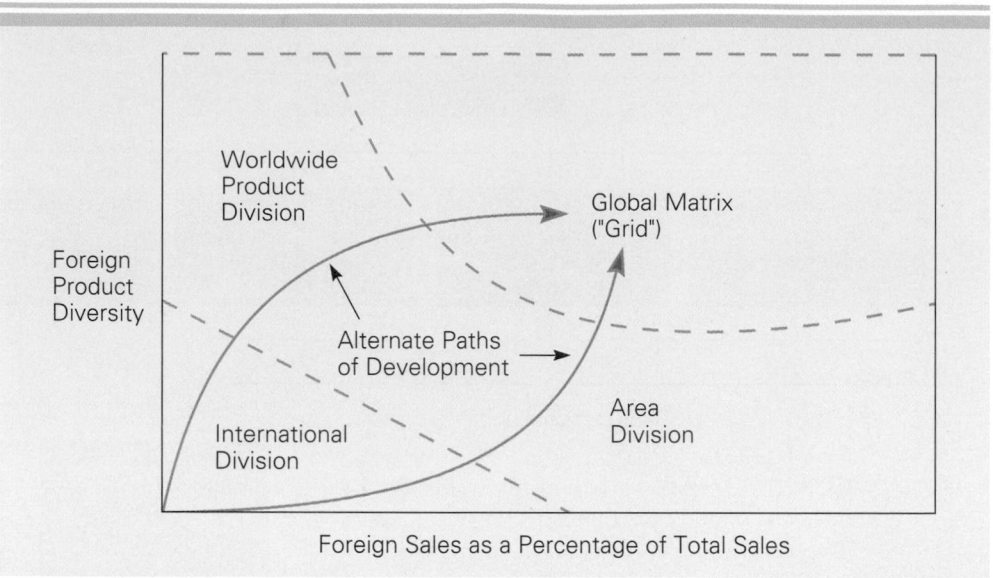

FIGURE 13.6

A Worldwide Product
Divisional Structure

business strategy to the local conditions. However, this structure encourages fragmentation of the organization into highly autonomous entities. This can make it difficult to transfer core competencies and skills between areas and to realize location and experience curve economies. In other words, the structure is consistent with a localization strategy, but may make it difficult to realize gains associated with global standardization. Firms structured on this basis may encounter significant problems if local responsiveness is less critical than reducing costs or transferring core competencies for establishing a competitive advantage.

Worldwide Product Divisional Structure

Firms that are reasonably diversified and, accordingly, originally have domestic structures based on product divisions tend to adopt a **worldwide product division structure.** As with the domestic product divisional structure, each division is a self-contained, largely autonomous entity with full responsibility for its own value creation activities. The headquarters retains responsibility for the overall strategic development and financial control of the firm (see Figure 13.6).

Underpinning the organization is a belief that each product division should coordinate its value creation activities worldwide. Thus, the worldwide product divisional structure is designed to help overcome the coordination problems that arise with the international division and worldwide area structures. This structure provides an organizational context that enhances the consolidation of value creation activities at key locations necessary for realizing location and experience curve economies. It also facilitates the transfer of core competencies within a division's worldwide operations and the simultaneous worldwide introduction of new products. The main problem with the structure is the limited voice it gives to area or country managers, since it makes them subservient to product division managers. The result can be a lack of local responsiveness, which, as we saw in Chapter 12, can lead to performance problems.

Global Matrix Structure

Both the worldwide area structure and the worldwide product divisional structure have strengths and weaknesses. The worldwide area structure facilitates local responsiveness, but it can inhibit the realization of location and experience curve economies and the transfer of core competencies between areas. The worldwide product division structure provides a better framework for pursuing location and experience curve economies and for transferring core competencies, but it is weak in local responsiveness. Other things being equal, this suggests that a worldwide area structure is more appropriate if the firm is pursuing a localization strategy, while a worldwide product divisional structure is more appropriate for firms pursuing global standardization or international strategies. However, as we saw in Chapter 12, other things are not equal. As Bartlett and Ghoshal have argued, to survive in some industries, firms must adopt a transnational strategy. That is, they must focus simultaneously on realizing location and experience curve economies, on local responsiveness, and on the internal transfer of core competencies (worldwide learning).[13]

Some firms have attempted to cope with the conflicting demands of a transnational strategy by using a matrix structure. In the classic **global matrix structure,** horizontal differentiation proceeds along two dimensions: product division and geographic area (see Figure 13.7). The philosophy is that responsibility for operating decisions pertaining to a particular product should be shared by the product division and various areas of the firm. Thus, the nature of the product offering, the marketing strategy, and the business strategy to be pursued in area 1 for the products produced by division A are determined by conciliation between division A and area 1 management. It is believed that this dual

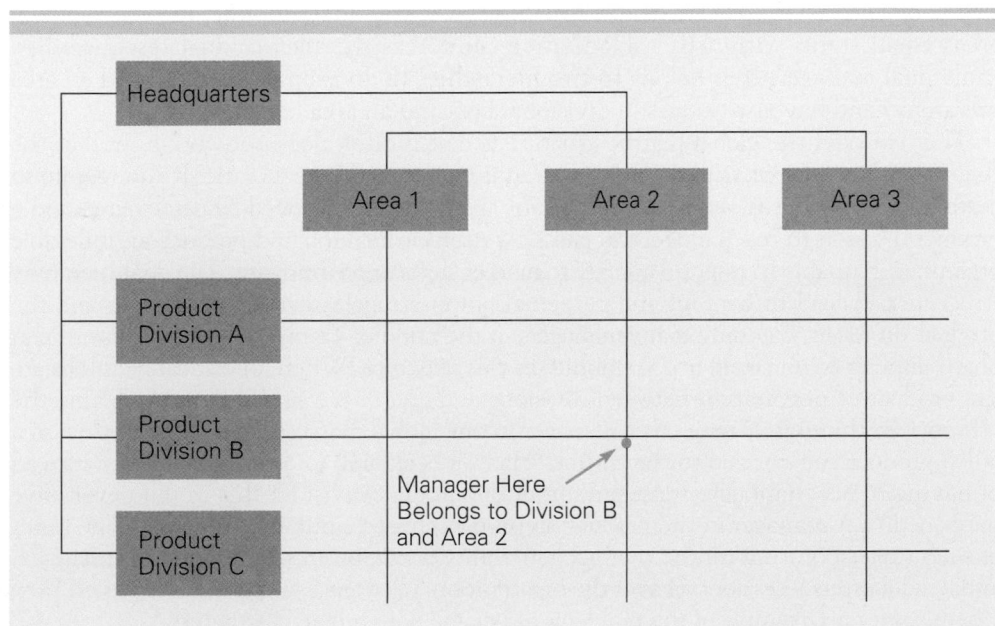

FIGURE 13.7

A Global Matrix Structure

The Rise and Fall of Dow Chemical's Matrix Structure

A handful of major players compete head-to-head around the world in the chemical industry. These companies are Dow Chemical and Du Pont of the United States, Great Britain's ICI, and the German trio of BASF, Hoechst AG, and Bayer. The barriers to the free flow of chemical products between nations largely disappeared in the 1970s. This along with the commodity nature of most bulk chemicals has ushered in a prolonged period of intense price competition. In such an environment, the company that wins the competitive race is the one with the lowest costs. Dow Chemical was long among the cost leaders.

For years, Dow's managers insisted that part of the credit should be placed at the feet of its "matrix" organization. Dow's organizational matrix had three interacting elements: functions (e.g., R&D, manufacturing, marketing), businesses (e.g., ethylene, plastics, pharmaceuticals), and geography (e.g., Spain, Germany, Brazil). Managers' job titles incorporated all three elements—for example, plastics marketing manager for Spain—and most managers reported to at least two bosses. The plastics marketing manager in Spain might report to both the head of the worldwide plastics business and the head of the Spanish operations. The intent of the matrix was to make Dow operations responsive to both local market needs and corporate objectives. Thus, the plastics business might be charged with minimizing Dow's global plastics production costs, while the Spanish operation might be charged with determining how best to sell plastics in the Spanish market.

When Dow introduced this structure, the results were less than promising; multiple reporting channels led to confusion and conflict. The large number of bosses made for an unwieldy bureaucracy. The overlapping responsibilities resulted in turf battles and a lack of accountability. Area managers disagreed with managers overseeing business sectors about which plants should be built and where. In short, the structure didn't work. Instead of abandoning the structure, however, Dow decided to see if it could be made more flexible.

Dow's decision to keep its matrix structure was prompted by its move into the pharmaceuticals industry. The company realized that the pharmaceutical business is very different from the bulk chemicals business. In bulk chemicals, the big returns come from achieving economies of scale in production. This dictates establishing large plants in key locations from which regional or global markets can be served. But in pharmaceuticals,

decision-making responsibility should enable the firm to simultaneously achieve its particular objectives. In a classic matrix structure, giving product divisions and geographical areas equal status within the organization reinforces the idea of dual responsibility. Individual managers thus belong to two hierarchies (a divisional hierarchy and an area hierarchy) and have two bosses (a divisional boss and an area boss).

The reality of the global matrix structure is that it often does not work as well as the theory predicts. In practice, the matrix often is clumsy and bureaucratic. It can require so many meetings that it is difficult to get any work done. The need to get an area and a product division to reach a decision can slow decision making and produce an inflexible organization unable to respond quickly to market shifts or to innovate. The dual-hierarchy structure can lead to conflict and perpetual power struggles between the areas and the product divisions, catching many managers in the middle. To make matters worse, it can prove difficult to ascertain accountability in this structure. When all critical decisions are the product of negotiation between divisions and areas, one side can always blame the other when things go wrong. As a manager in one global matrix structure, reflecting on a failed product launch, said to the author, "Had we been able to do things our way, instead of having to accommodate those guys from the product division, this would never have happened." (A manager in the product division expressed similar sentiments.) The result of such finger-pointing can be that accountability is compromised, conflict is enhanced, and headquarters loses control over the organization. (See the Management Focus on Dow Chemical for an example of the problems associated with a matrix structure.)

regulatory and marketing requirements for drugs vary so much from country to country that local needs are far more important than reducing manufacturing costs through scale economies. A high degree of local responsiveness is essential. Dow realized its pharmaceutical business would never thrive if it were managed by the same priorities as its mainstream chemical operations.

Accordingly, instead of abandoning its matrix, Dow decided to make it more flexible so it could better accommodate the different businesses, each with its own priorities, within a single management system. A small team of senior executives at headquarters helped set the priorities for each type of business. After the team identified priorities for each business sector, it gave one of the three elements of the matrix—function, business, or geographic area—primary authority in decision making. Which element took the lead varied according to the type of decision and the market or location in which the company was competing. Such flexibility required that all employees understand what was occurring in the rest of the matrix. Although this may seem confusing, for years Dow claimed this flexible system worked well and credited much of its success to the quality of the decisions it facilitated.

By the mid-1990s, however, Dow had refocused its business on the chemicals industry, divesting itself of its pharmaceutical activities where the company's performance had been unsatisfactory. Reflecting the change in corporate strategy, in 1995 Dow decided to abandon its matrix structure in favor of a more streamlined structure based on global business divisions. The change was also driven by realization that the matrix structure was just too complex and costly to manage in the intense competitive environment of the 1990s, particularly given the company's renewed focus on its commodity chemicals where competitive advantage often went to the low-cost producer. As Dow's then CEO put it in a 1999 interview, "We were an organization that was matrixed and depended on teamwork, but there was no one in charge. When things went well, we didn't know whom to reward; and when things went poorly, we didn't know whom to blame. So we created a global divisional structure, and cut out layers of management. There used to be 11 layers of management between me and the lowest level employees, now there are five." In short, Dow ultimately found that a matrix structure was unsuited to a company that was competing in very cost-competitive global industries, and it had to abandon its matrix to drive down operating costs.[14]

In light of these problems, many firms that pursue a transnational strategy have tried to build "flexible" matrix structures based more on enterprisewide management knowledge networks and a shared culture and vision than on a rigid hierarchical arrangement. Within such companies the informal structure plays a greater role than the formal structure. We discuss this issue when we consider informal integrating mechanisms in the next section.

INTEGRATING MECHANISMS

In the previous section, we explained that firms divide themselves into subunits. Now we need to examine some means of coordinating those subunits. One way of achieving coordination is through centralization. If the coordination task is complex, however, centralization may not be very effective. Higher-level managers responsible for achieving coordination can soon become overwhelmed by the volume of work required to coordinate the activities of various subunits, particularly if the subunits are large, diverse, and/or geographically dispersed. When this is the case, firms look toward integrating mechanisms, both formal and informal, to help achieve coordination. In this section, we introduce the various integrating mechanisms that international businesses can use. Before doing so, however, let us explore the need for coordination in international firms and some impediments to coordination.

Strategy and Coordination in the International Business

The need for coordination between subunits varies with the strategy of the firm. The need for coordination is lowest in firms pursuing a localization strategy, is higher in international companies, higher still in global companies, and highest of all in transnational companies. Firms pursuing a localization strategy are primarily concerned with local responsiveness. Such firms are likely to operate with a worldwide area structure in which each area has considerable autonomy and its own set of value creation functions. Because each area is established as a stand-alone entity, the need for coordination between areas is minimized.

The need for coordination is greater in firms pursuing an international strategy and trying to profit from the transfer of core competencies and skills between units at home and abroad. Coordination is necessary to support the transfer of skills and product offerings between units. The need for coordination is also great in firms trying to profit from location and experience curve economies; that is, in firms pursuing global standardization strategies. Achieving location and experience economies involves dispersing value creation activities to various locations around the globe. The resulting global web of activities must be coordinated to ensure the smooth flow of inputs into the value chain, the smooth flow of semifinished products through the value chain, and the smooth flow of finished products to markets around the world.

The need for coordination is greatest in transnational firms, which simultaneously pursue location and experience curve economies, local responsiveness, and the multidirectional transfer of core competencies and skills among all of the firm's subunits (referred to as global learning). As with a global standardization strategy, coordination is required to ensure the smooth flow of products through the global value chain. As with an international strategy, coordination is required for ensuring the transfer of core competencies to subunits. However, the transnational goal of achieving multidirectional transfer of competencies requires much greater coordination than in firms pursuing an international strategy. In addition, a transnational strategy requires coordination between foreign subunits and the firm's globally dispersed value creation activities (e.g., production, R&D, marketing) to ensure that any product offering and marketing strategy is sufficiently customized to local conditions.

Impediments to Coordination

Managers of the various subunits have different orientations, partly because they have different tasks. For example, production managers are typically concerned with production issues such as capacity utilization, cost control, and quality control, whereas marketing managers are concerned with marketing issues such as pricing, promotions, distribution, and market share. These differences can inhibit communication between the managers. Quite simply, these managers often do not even "speak the same language." There may also be a lack of respect between subunits (e.g., marketing managers "looking down on" production managers, and vice versa), which further inhibits the communication required to achieve cooperation and coordination.

Differences in subunits' orientations also arise from their differing goals. For example, worldwide product divisions of a multinational firm may be committed to cost goals that require global production of a standardized product, whereas a foreign subsidiary may be committed to increasing its market share in its country, which will require a nonstandard product. These different goals can lead to conflict.

Such impediments to coordination are not unusual in any firm, but they can be particularly problematic in the multinational enterprise with its profusion of subunits at home and abroad. Differences in subunit orientation are often reinforced in multinationals by the separations of time zone, distance, and nationality between managers of the subunits.

For example, until recently the Dutch company Philips had an organization comprising worldwide product divisions and largely autonomous national organizations. The company has long had problems getting its product divisions and national organizations to cooperate on such things as new-product introductions. When Philips developed a VCR format, the V2000 system, it could not get its North American subsidiary to introduce the product. Rather, the North American unit adopted the rival VHS format produced

FIGURE 13.8

Formal Integrating
Mechanisms

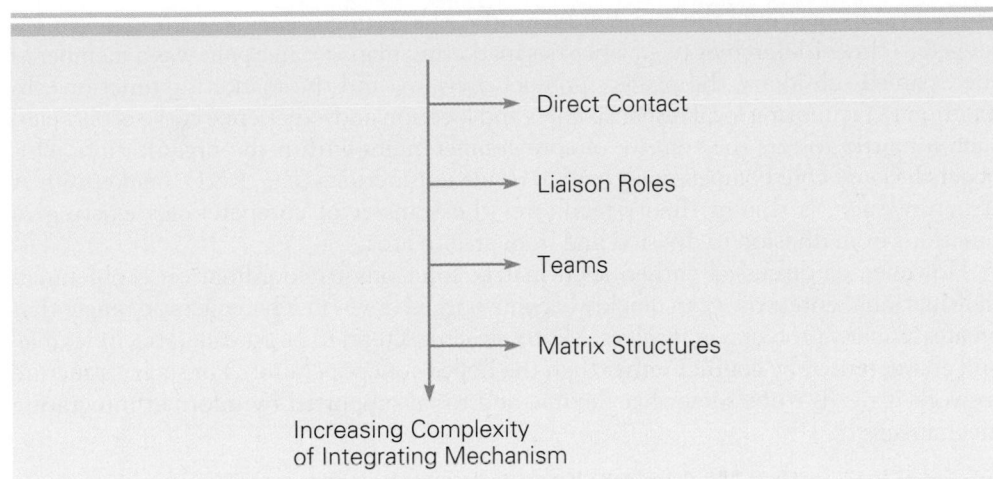

by Philip's global competitor, Matsushita. Unilever experienced a similar problem in its detergents business. The need to resolve disputes between Unilever's many national organizations and its product divisions extended the time necessary for introducing a new product across Europe to several years. This denied Unilever the first-mover advantage crucial to building a strong market position.

Formal Integrating Mechanisms

The formal mechanisms used to integrate subunits vary in complexity from simple direct contact and liaison roles, to teams, to a matrix structure (see Figure 13.8). In general, the greater the need for coordination, the more complex the formal integrating mechanisms need to be.[15]

Direct contact between subunit managers is the simplest integrating mechanism. By this "mechanism," managers of the various subunits simply contact each other whenever they have a common concern. Direct contact may not be effective if the managers have differing orientations that act to impede coordination, as pointed out in the previous subsection.

Liaison roles are a bit more complex. When the volume of contacts between subunits increases, coordination can be improved by giving a person in each subunit responsibility for coordinating with another subunit on a regular basis. Through these roles, the people involved establish a permanent relationship, which helps attenuate the impediments to coordination discussed in the previous subsection.

When the need for coordination is greater still, firms tend to use temporary or permanent teams composed of individuals from the subunits that need to achieve coordination. They typically coordinate product development and introduction, but they are useful when any aspect of operations or strategy requires the cooperation of two or more subunits. Product development and introduction teams are typically composed of personnel from R&D, production, and marketing. The resulting coordination aids the development of products that are tailored to consumer needs and that can be produced at a reasonable cost (design for manufacturing).

When the need for integration is very high, firms may institute a matrix structure, in which all roles are viewed as integrating roles. The structure is designed to facilitate maximum integration among subunits. The most common matrix in multinational firms is based on geographical areas and worldwide product divisions. This achieves a high level of integration between the product divisions and the areas so that, in theory, the firm can pay close attention to both local responsiveness and the pursuit of location and experience curve economies.

In some multinationals, the matrix is more complex still, structuring the firm into geographical areas, worldwide product divisions, and functions, all of which report directly to headquarters. Thus, within a company such as Dow Chemical before it abandoned its matrix in the mid-1990s (see the Management Focus), each manager belonged to three hierarchies (e.g., a plastics marketing manager in Spain was a member of the Spanish subsidiary, the plastics product division, and the marketing function). In addition to facilitating local responsiveness and location and experience curve economies, such a matrix fosters the transfer of core competencies within the organization. This occurs because core competencies tend to reside in functions (e.g., R&D, marketing). A structure such as this in theory facilitates the transfer of competencies existing in functions from division to division and from area to area.

However, as discussed earlier, such matrix solutions to coordination problems in multinational enterprises can quickly become bogged down in a bureaucratic tangle that creates as many problems as it solves. Matrix structures tend to be bureaucratic, inflexible, and characterized by conflict rather than the hoped-for cooperation. For such a structure to work it needs to be somewhat flexible and to be supported by informal integrating mechanisms.[16]

Informal Integrating Mechanism: Knowledge Networks

In attempting to alleviate or avoid the problems associated with formal integrating mechanisms in general, and matrix structures in particular, firms with a high need for integration have been experimenting with an informal integrating mechanism: knowledge networks that are supported by an organization culture that values teamwork and cross-unit cooperation.[17] A **knowledge network** is a network for transmitting information within an organization that is based not on formal organization structure, but on informal contacts between managers within an enterprise and on distributed information systems.[18] The great strength of such a network is that it can be used as a nonbureaucratic conduit for knowledge flows within a multinational enterprise.[19] For a network to exist, managers at different locations within the organization must be linked to each other at least indirectly. For example, Figure 13.9 shows the simple network relationships between seven managers within a multinational firm. Managers A, B, and C all know each other personally, as do managers D, E, and F. Although manager B does not know manager F personally, they are linked through common acquaintances (managers C and D). Thus, we can say that managers A through F are all part of the network, and also that manager G is not.

Imagine manager B is a marketing manager in Spain and needs to know the solution to a technical problem to better serve an important European customer. Manager F, an R&D manager in the United States, has the solution to manager B's problem. Manager B mentions her problem to all of her contacts, including manager C, and asks if they know of anyone who might be able to provide a solution. Manager C asks manager D, who tells manager F, who then calls manager B with the solution. In this way, coordination is achieved informally through the network, rather than by formal integrating mechanisms such as teams or a matrix structure.

FIGURE 13.9

A Simple Management Network

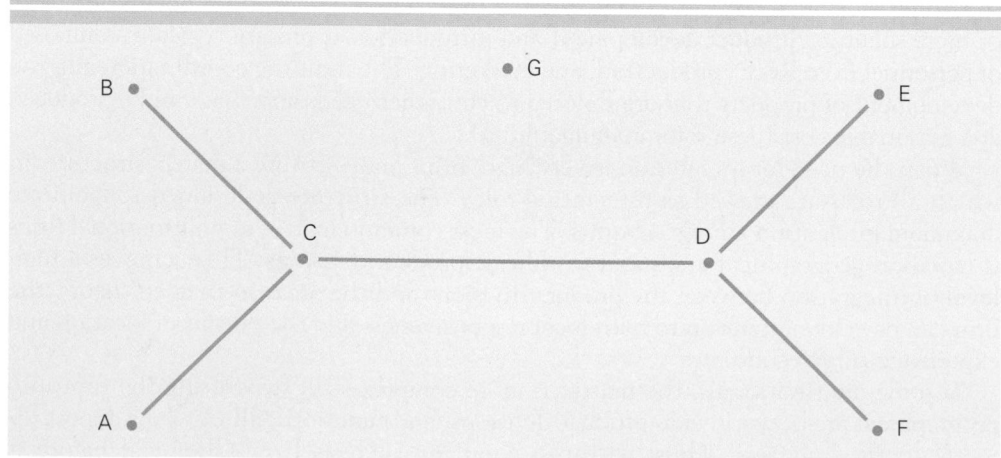

For such a network to function effectively, however, it must embrace as many managers as possible. For example, if manager G had a problem similar to manager B's, he would not be able to utilize the informal network to find a solution; he would have to resort to more formal mechanisms. Establishing firmwide knowledge networks is difficult, and although network enthusiasts speak of networks as the "glue" that binds multinational companies together, it is far from clear how successful firms have been at building companywide networks. Two techniques being used to establish networks are information systems and management development policies.

Firms are using their distributed computer and telecommunications information systems to provide the foundation for informal knowledge networks.[20] Electronic mail, videoconferencing, high-bandwidth data systems, and Web-based search engines make it much easier for managers scattered over the globe to get to know each other, to identify contacts that might help to solve a particular problem, and to publicize and share best practices within the organization. Wal-Mart, for example, now uses its intranet system to communicate ideas about merchandising strategy between stores located in different countries.

Firms are also using their management development programs to build informal networks. Tactics include rotating managers through various subunits on a regular basis so they build their own informal network and using management education programs to bring managers of subunits together in a single location so they can become acquainted.

Knowledge networks by themselves may not be sufficient to achieve coordination if subunit managers persist in pursuing subgoals that are at variance with firmwide goals. For a knowledge network to function properly—and for a formal matrix structure to work also—managers must share a strong commitment to the same goals. To appreciate the nature of the problem, consider again the case of manager B and manager F. As before, manager F hears about manager B's problem through the network. However, solving manager B's problem would require manager F to devote considerable time to the task. Insofar as this would divert manager F away from his own regular tasks—and the pursuit of subgoals that differ from those of manager B—he may be unwilling to do it. Thus, manager F may not call manager B, and the informal network would fail to provide a solution to manager B's problem.

To eliminate this flaw, organization's managers must adhere to a common set of norms and values that override differing subunit orientations.[21] In other words, the firm must have a strong organizational culture that promotes teamwork and cooperation. When this is the case, a manager is willing and able to set aside the interests of his own subunit when doing so benefits the firm as a whole. If manager B and manager F are committed to the same organizational norms and value systems, and if these organizational norms and values place the interests of the firm as a whole above the interests of any individual subunit, manager F should be willing to cooperate with manager B on solving her subunit's problems.

Summary

The message contained in this section is crucial to understanding the problems of managing the multinational firm. Multinationals need integration—particularly if they are pursuing global standardization, international, or transnational strategies—but it can be difficult to achieve due to the impediments to coordination we discussed. Firms traditionally have tried to achieve coordination by adopting formal integrating mechanisms. These do not always work, however, since they tend to be bureaucratic and do not necessarily address the problems that arise from differing subunit orientations. This is particularly likely with a complex matrix structure, and yet, a complex matrix structure is required for simultaneously achieving location and experience curve economies, local responsiveness, and the multidirectional transfer of core competencies within the organization. The solution to this dilemma seems twofold. First, the firm must try to establish an informal knowledge network that can do much of the work previously undertaken by a formal matrix structure. Second, the firm must build a common culture. Neither of these partial solutions, however, is easy to achieve.[22]

Control Systems and Incentives

A major task of a firm's leadership is to control the various subunits of the firm—whether they be defined on the basis of function, product division, or geographic area—to ensure their actions are consistent with the firm's overall strategic and financial objectives. Firms achieve this with various control and incentive systems. In this section, we first review the various types of control systems firms use to control their subunits. Then we briefly discuss incentive systems. Then we will look at how the appropriate control and incentive systems vary according to the strategy of the multinational enterprise.

TYPES OF CONTROL SYSTEMS

Multinational firms use four main types of control systems: personal controls, bureaucratic controls, output controls, and cultural controls. Most firms use all four, but their relative emphasis varies with the strategy of the firm.

Personal Controls

Personal control is control by personal contact with subordinates. This type of control tends to be most widely used in small firms, where it is seen in the direct supervision of subordinates' actions. However, it also structures the relationships between managers at different levels in multinational enterprises. For example, the CEO may use a great deal of personal control to influence the behavior of his or her immediate subordinates, such as the heads of worldwide product divisions or major geographic areas. In turn, these heads may use personal control to influence the behavior of their subordinates, and so on down through the organization. Jack Welch, the longtime CEO of General Electric who retired in 2001, had regular one-on-one meetings with the heads of all GE's major businesses (most of which are international).[23] He used these meetings to probe the managers about the strategy, structure, and financial performance of their operations. In doing so, he essentially exercised personal control over these managers and, undoubtedly, over the strategies that they favored.

Bureaucratic Controls

Bureaucratic control is control through a system of rules and procedures that directs the actions of subunits. The most important bureaucratic controls in subunits within multinational firms are budgets and capital spending rules. Budgets are essentially a set of rules for allocating a firm's financial resources. A subunit's budget specifies with some precision how much the subunit may spend. Headquarters uses budgets to influence the behavior of subunits. For example, the R&D budget normally specifies how much cash the R&D unit may spend on product development. R&D managers know that if they spend too much on one project, they will have less to spend on other projects, so they modify their behavior to stay within the budget. Most budgets are set by negotiation between headquarters management and subunit management. Headquarters management can encourage the growth of certain subunits and restrict the growth of others by manipulating their budgets.

Capital spending rules require headquarters management to approve any capital expenditure by a subunit that exceeds a certain amount. A budget allows headquarters to specify the amount a subunit can spend in a given year, and capital spending rules give headquarters additional control over how the money is spent. Headquarters can be expected to deny approval for capital spending requests that are at variance with overall firm objectives and to approve those that are congruent with firm objectives.

Output Controls

Output controls involve setting goals for subunits to achieve and expressing those goals in terms of relatively objective performance metrics such as profitability, productivity, growth, market share, and quality. The performance of subunit managers is then judged by their ability to achieve the goals.[24] If goals are met or exceeded, subunit managers will be rewarded. If goals are not met, top management will normally intervene to find out why and take appropriate corrective action. Thus, control is achieved by comparing actual performance against targets and intervening selectively to take corrective action. Subunits' goals depend on their role in the firm. Self-contained product divisions or national subsidiaries are typically given goals for profitability, sales growth, and market share. Functions are more likely to be given goals related to their particular activity. Thus, R&D will be given product development goals, production will be given productivity and quality goals, marketing will be given market share goals, and so on.

As with budgets, goals are normally established through negotiation between subunits and headquarters. Generally, headquarters tries to set goals that are challenging but realistic, so subunit managers are forced to look for ways to improve their operations but are not so pressured that they will resort to dysfunctional activities to do so (such as short-run profit maximization). Output controls foster a system of "management by exception," in that so long as subunits meet their goals, they are left alone. If a subunit fails to attain its goals, however, headquarters managers are likely to ask some tough questions. If they don't get satisfactory answers, they are likely to intervene proactively in a subunit, replacing top management and looking for ways to improve efficiency.

Cultural Controls

Cultural controls exist when employees "buy into" the norms and value systems of the firm. When this occurs, employees tend to control their own behavior, which reduces the need for direct supervision. In a firm with a strong culture, self-control can reduce the need for other control systems. We shall discuss organizational culture later. McDonald's actively promotes organizational norms and values, referring to its franchisees and suppliers as partners and emphasizing its long-term commitment to them. This commitment is not just a public relations exercise; it is backed by actions, including a willingness to help suppliers and franchisees improve their operations by providing capital and/or management assistance when needed. In response, McDonald's franchisees and suppliers are integrated into the firm's culture and thus become committed to helping McDonald's succeed. One result is that McDonald's can devote less time than would otherwise be necessary to controlling its franchisees and suppliers.

INCENTIVE SYSTEMS

Incentives refer to the devices used to reward appropriate employee behavior. Many employees receive incentives in the form of annual bonus pay. Incentives are usually closely tied to the performance metrics used for output controls. For example, setting targets linked to profitability might be used to measure the performance of a subunit, such as a global product division. To create positive incentives for employees to work hard to exceed those targets, they may be given a share of any profits above those targeted. If a subunit has set a goal of attaining a 15 percent return on investment and it actually attains a 20 percent return, unit employees may be given a share in the profits generated in excess of the 15 percent target in the form of bonus pay. We shall return to the topic of incentive systems in Chapter 18 when we discuss human resource strategy in the multinational firm. For now, however, several important points need to be made. First, the type of incentive used often varies depending on the employees and their tasks. Incentives for employees working on the factory floor may be very different from the incentives used for senior managers. The incentives used must be matched to the type of work being performed. The employees on the factory floor of a manufacturing plant may be broken into teams of 20 to 30 individuals, and they may have their bonus pay tied to the ability of their team to hit or exceed targets for output and product quality. In contrast, the senior managers of the plant may be rewarded according to metrics linked to the output of the entire operation. The basic principle is to make sure the incentive scheme for an individual employee is linked to an output target that he or she has some control over and can influence. The individual employees on the factory floor may not be able to exercise much influence over the performance of the entire operation, but they can influence the performance of their team, so incentive pay is tied to output at this level.

Second, the successful execution of strategy in the multinational firm often requires significant cooperation between managers in different subunits. For example, as noted earlier, some multinational firms operate with matrix structures where a country subsidiary might be responsible for marketing and sales in a nation, while a global product division might be responsible for manufacturing and product development. The managers of these different units need to cooperate closely with each other if the firm is to be successful. One way of encouraging the managers to cooperate is to link incentives to performance at a higher level in the organization. Thus, the senior managers of the country subsidiaries and global product divisions might be rewarded according to the profitability of the entire firm. The thinking here is that boosting the profitability of the entire firm requires managers in the country subsidiaries and product divisions to cooperate with each other on strategy implementation, and linking incentive systems to the next level up in the hierarchy encourages this. Most firms use a formula for incentives that links a portion of incentive pay to the performance of the subunit in which a manager or employee works and a portion to the performance of the entire firm, or some other higher-level organizational unit. The goal is to encourage employees to improve the efficiency of their unit and to cooperate with other units in the organization.

Third, the incentive systems a multinational enterprise uses often have to be adjusted to account for national differences in institutions and culture. Incentive systems that work in the United States might not work, or even be allowed, in other countries. For example, Lincoln Electric, a leader in the manufacture of arc welding equipment, has used an incentive system for its employees based on piecework rates in its American factories (under a piecework system, employees are paid according to the amount they produce). While this system has worked very well in the United States, Lincoln has found that the system is difficult to introduce in other countries. In some countries, such as Germany, piecework systems are illegal, while in others the prevailing national culture is antagonistic to a system where performance is so closely tied to individual effort.

Finally, it is important for managers to recognize that incentive systems can have unintended consequences. Managers need to carefully think through exactly what behavior certain incentives encourage. For example, if employees in a factory are rewarded solely on the basis of how many units of output they produce, with no attention paid to the quality of that output, they may produce as many units as possible to boost their incentive pay, but the quality of those units may be poor.

CONTROL SYSTEMS, INCENTIVES, AND STRATEGY IN THE INTERNATIONAL BUSINESS

The key to understanding the relationship between international strategy, control systems, and incentive systems is the concept of performance ambiguity.

Performance Ambiguity

Performance ambiguity exists when the causes of a subunit's poor performance are not clear. This is not uncommon when a subunit's performance is partly dependent on the performance of other subunits; that is, when there is a high degree of interdependence between subunits within the organization. Consider the case of a French subsidiary of a U.S. firm that depends on another subsidiary, a manufacturer based in Italy, for the products it sells. The French subsidiary is failing to achieve its sales goals, and the U.S. management asks the managers to explain. They reply that they are receiving poor-quality goods from the Italian subsidiary. The U.S. management asks the managers of the Italian operation what the problem is. They reply that their product quality is excellent—the best in the industry, in fact—and that the French simply don't know how to sell a good product. Who is right, the French or the Italians? Without more information, top management cannot tell. Because they are dependent on the Italians for their product, the French have an alibi for poor performance. U.S. management needs to have more information to determine who is correct. Collecting this information is expensive and time consuming and will divert attention away from other issues. In other words, performance ambiguity raises the costs of control.

Consider how different things would be if the French operation were self-contained, with its own manufacturing, marketing, and R&D facilities. The French operation would lack a convenient alibi for its poor performance; the French managers would stand or fall on their own merits. They could not blame the Italians for their poor sales. The level of performance ambiguity, therefore, is a function of the interdependence of subunits in an organization.

Strategy, Interdependence, and Ambiguity

Now let us consider the relationships between strategy, interdependence, and performance ambiguity. In firms pursuing a localization strategy, each national operation is a stand-alone entity and can be judged on its own merits. The level of performance ambiguity is low. In an international firm, the level of interdependence is somewhat higher. Integration is required to facilitate the transfer of core competencies and skills. Since the success of a foreign operation is partly dependent on the quality of the competency transferred from the home country, performance ambiguity can exist.

In firms pursuing a global standardization strategy, the situation is still more complex. Recall that in a pure global firm the pursuit of location and experience curve economies leads to the development of a global web of value creation activities. Many of the activities in a global firm are interdependent. A French subsidiary's ability to sell a product does depend on how well other operations in other countries perform their value creation activities. Thus, the levels of interdependence and performance ambiguity are high in global companies.

The level of performance ambiguity is highest of all in transnational firms. Transnational firms suffer from the same performance ambiguity problems that global firms do. In addition, since they emphasize the multidirectional transfer of core competencies, they also suffer from the problems characteristic of firms pursuing an international strategy. The extremely high level of integration within transnational firms implies a high degree of joint decision making, and the resulting interdependencies create plenty of alibis for poor performance. There is lots of room for finger-pointing in transnational firms.

Implications for Control and Incentives

The arguments of the previous section, along with the implications for the costs of control, are summarized in Table 13.1. The costs of control can be defined as the amount of time top management must devote to monitoring and evaluating subunits' performance. This is greater when the amount of performance ambiguity is greater. When performance ambiguity is low, management can use output controls and a system of management by exception; when it is high, managers have no such luxury. Output controls do not provide totally unambiguous signals of a subunit's efficiency

Strategy	Interdependence	Performance Ambiguity	Costs of Control
Localization	Low	Low	Low
International	Moderate	Moderate	Moderate
Global	High	High	High
Transnational	Very High	Very High	Very High

TABLE 13.1

Interdependence, Performance Ambiguity, and the Costs of Control for the Four International Business Strategies when the performance of that subunit is dependent on the performance of another subunit within the organization. Thus, management must devote time to resolving the problems that arise from performance ambiguity, with a corresponding rise in the costs of control.

Table 13.1 reveals a paradox. We saw in Chapter 12 that a transnational strategy is desirable because it gives a firm more ways to profit from international expansion than do localization, international, and global standardization strategies. But now we see that due to the high level of interdependence, the costs of controlling transnational firms are higher than the costs of controlling firms that pursue other strategies. Unless there is some way of reducing these costs, the higher profitability associated with a transnational strategy could be canceled out by the higher costs of control. The same point, although to a lesser extent, can be made with regard to firms pursuing a global standardization strategy. Although firms pursuing a global standardization strategy can reap the cost benefits of location and experience curve economies, they must cope with a higher level of performance ambiguity, which raises the costs of control (in comparison with firms pursuing an international or localization strategy).

This is where control systems and incentives come in. When we survey the systems that corporations use to control their subunits, we find that irrespective of their strategy, multinational firms all use output and bureaucratic controls. However, in firms pursuing either global or transnational strategies, the usefulness of output controls is limited by substantial performance ambiguities. As a result, these firms place greater emphasis on cultural controls. Cultural control—by encouraging managers to want to assume the organization's norms and value systems—gives managers of interdependent subunits an incentive to look for ways to work out problems that arise between them. The result is a reduction in finger-pointing and, accordingly, in the costs of control. The development of cultural controls may be a precondition for the successful pursuit of a transnational strategy and perhaps of a global strategy as well.[25] As for incentives, the material discussed earlier suggests that the conflict between different subunits can be reduced and the potential for cooperation enhanced, if incentive systems are tied in some way to a higher level in the hierarchy. When performance ambiguity makes it difficult to judge the performance of subunits as stand-alone entities, linking the incentive pay of senior managers to the entity to which both subunits belong can reduce the resulting problems.

rocesses

We defined processes as the manner in which decisions are made and work is performed within the organization.[26] Processes can be found at many different levels within an organization. There are processes for formulating strategy, processes for allocating resources, processes for evaluating new-product ideas, processes for handling customer inquiries and complaints, processes for improving product quality, processes for evaluating employee performance, and so on. Often, the core competencies or valuable skills of a firm are embedded in its processes. Efficient and effective processes can lower the costs of value creation and add additional value to a product. For example, the global success of many Japanese manufacturing enterprises in the 1980s was based in part on their early adoption of processes for improving product quality and operating efficiency, including total quality management and just-in-time inventory systems. Today, the competitive success of General Electric can in part be attributed to a number of processes that have been widely promoted within the company. These include the company's Six Sigma process for quality improvement, its process for "digitalization" of business (using corporate intranets and the Internet to automate activities and reduce operating costs), and its process for idea generation, referred to within the company as "workouts," where managers and employees get together for intensive sessions over several days to identify and commit to ideas for improving productivity.

An organization's processes can be summarized by means of a flow chart, which illustrates the various steps and decision points involved in performing work. Many processes cut across functions or divisions and require cooperation between individuals in different subunits. For example, product development processes require employees from R&D, manufacturing, and marketing to work together in a cooperative manner to make sure new products are developed with market needs in mind and designed in such a way that they can be manufactured at a low cost. Because they cut across organizational boundaries, performing processes effectively often requires the establishment of formal integrating mechanisms and incentives for cross-unit cooperation (see above).

A detailed consideration of the nature of processes and strategies for process improvement and reengineering is beyond the scope of this book. However, it is important to make two basic remarks about managing processes, particularly in the context of an international business.[27] The first is that in a multinational enterprise, many processes cut not only across organizational boundaries, embracing several different subunits, but also across national boundaries. Designing a new product may require the cooperation of R&D personnel located in California, production people located in Taiwan, and marketing located in Europe, America, and Asia. The chances of pulling this off are greatly enhanced if the processes are embedded in an organizational culture that promotes cooperation between individuals from different subunits and nations, if the incentive systems of the organization explicitly reward such cooperation, and if formal and informal integrating mechanisms are used to facilitate coordination between subunits.

Second, it is particularly important for a multinational enterprise to recognize that valuable new processes that might lead to a competitive advantage can be developed anywhere within the organization's global network of operations.[28] New processes may be developed by a local operating subsidiary in response to conditions pertaining to its market. Those processes might then have value to other parts of the multinational enterprise. For example, in response to competition in Japan and a local obsession with product quality, Japanese firms were at the leading edge of developing processes for total quality management (TQM) in the 1970s. Because few American firms had Japanese subsidiaries at the time, they were relatively ignorant of the trend until the 1980s when high-quality Japanese products began to make big inroads into the United States. An exception to this generalization was Hewlett-Packard, which had a very successful operating company in Japan, Yokogwa Hewlett-Packard (YHP). YHP was a pioneer of the total quality management process in Japan and won the prestigious Deming Prize for its achievements in improving product quality. Through YHP, Hewlett-Packard learned about the quality movement ahead of many of its U.S. peers and was one of the first Western companies to introduce TQM processes into its worldwide operations. Not only did Hewlett-Packard's Japanese operation give the company access to a valuable process, but the company also transferred this knowledge within its global network of operations, raising the performance of the entire company. The ability to create valuable processes matters, but it is also important to leverage those processes. This requires both formal and informal integrating mechanisms such as knowledge networks.

⊕ Organizational Culture

Chapter 3 applied the concept of culture to nation-states. Culture, however, is a social construct ascribed to societies, including organizations.[29] Thus, we can speak of organizational culture and organizational subculture. The basic definition of culture remains the same, whether we are applying it to a large society such as a nation-state or a small society such as an organization or one of its subunits. Culture refers to a system of values and norms that are shared among people. Values are abstract ideas about what a group believes to be good, right, and desirable. Norms mean the social rules and guidelines that prescribe appropriate behavior in particular situations. Values and norms express themselves as the behavior patterns or style of an organization that new employees are automatically encouraged to follow by their fellow employees. Although an organization's culture is rarely static, it tends to change relatively slowly.

CREATING AND MAINTAINING ORGANIZATIONAL CULTURE

An organization's culture comes from several sources. First, there seems to be wide agreement that founders or important leaders can have a profound impact on an organization's culture, often imprinting their own values on the culture.[30] A famous example of a strong founder effect concerns the Japanese firm Matsushita. Konosuke Matsushita's almost Zen-like personal business philosophy was codified in the "Seven Spiritual Values" of Matsushita that all new employees still learn today. These values are (1) national service through industry, (2) fairness, (3) harmony and cooperation, (4) struggle for betterment, (5) courtesy and humility, (6) adjustment and assimilation, and (7) gratitude. A leader does not have to be the founder to have a profound influence on organizational culture. Jack Welch is widely credited with having changed the culture of GE, primarily by emphasizing a countercultural set of values, such as risk taking, entrepreneurship, stewardship, and boundaryless behavior, when he first became CEO. It is more difficult for a leader, however forceful, to change an established organizational culture than it is to create one from scratch in a new venture.

Another important influence on organizational culture is the broader social culture of the nation where the firm was founded. In the United States, for example, the competitive ethic of individualism looms large and there is enormous social stress on producing winners. Many American firms find ways of rewarding and motivating individuals so that they see themselves as winners.[31] The values of American firms often reflect the values of American culture. Similarly, the cooperative values found in many Japanese firms have been argued to reflect the values of traditional Japanese society, with its emphasis on group cooperation, reciprocal obligations, and harmony.[32] Thus, although it may be a generalization, there may be something to the argument that organizational culture is influenced by national culture.

A third influence on organizational culture is the history of the enterprise, which over time may come to shape the values of the organization. In the language of historians, organizational culture is the path-dependent product of where the organization has been through time. For example, Philips NV, the Dutch multinational, long operated with a culture that placed a high value on the independence of national operating companies. This culture was shaped by the history of the company. During World War II, Holland was occupied by the Germans. With the head office in occupied territories, power devolved by default to various foreign operating companies, such as Philips subsidiaries in the United States and Great Britain. After the war ended, these subsidiaries continued to operate in a highly autonomous fashion. A belief that this was the right thing to do became a core value of the company.

Decisions that subsequently result in high performance tend to become institutionalized in the values of a firm. In the 1920s, 3M was primarily a manufacturer of sandpaper. Richard Drew, who was a young laboratory assistant at the time, came up with what he thought would be a great new product—a glue-covered strip of paper, which he called "sticky tape." Drew saw applications for the product in the automobile industry, where it could be used to mask parts of a vehicle during painting. He presented the idea to the company's president, William McKnight. An unimpressed McKnight suggested that Drew drop the research. Drew didn't; instead he developed the "sticky tape" and then went out and got endorsements from potential customers in the auto industry. Armed with this information, he approached McKnight again. A chastened McKnight reversed his position and gave Drew the go-ahead to start developing what was to become one of 3M's main product lines—sticky tape—a business it dominates to this day.[33] From then on, McKnight emphasized the importance of giving researchers at 3M free rein to explore their own ideas and experiment with product offerings. This soon became a core value at 3M and was enshrined in the company's famous "15 percent rule," which stated that researchers could spend 15 percent of the company time working on ideas of their own choosing. Today, new employees are often told the Drew story, which is used to illustrate the value of allowing individuals to explore their own ideas.

Culture is maintained by a variety of mechanisms. These include (1) hiring and promotional practices of the organization, (2) reward strategies, (3) socialization processes, and (4) communication strategy. The goal is to recruit people whose values are consistent with those of the company. To further reinforce values, a company may promote individuals whose behavior is consistent with the core values of the organization. Merit review processes may also be linked to a company's values, which further reinforces cultural norms.

Socialization can be formal, such as training programs for employees that educate them in the core values of the organization. Informal socialization may be friendly advice from peers or bosses or may be implicit in the actions of peers and superiors toward new employees. As for communication strategy, many companies with strong cultures devote a lot of attention to framing their key values in corporate mission statements, communicating them often to employees, and using them to guide difficult decisions. Stories and symbols are often used to reinforce important values (e.g., the Drew and McKnight story at 3M).

3M's famous Post-it note was an idea that stuck. Innovation continues to be a hallmark of the company to this day.

ORGANIZATIONAL CULTURE AND PERFORMANCE IN THE INTERNATIONAL BUSINESS

Management authors often talk about "strong cultures."[34] In a strong culture, almost all managers share a relatively consistent set of values and norms that have a clear impact on the way work is performed. New employees adopt these values very quickly, and employees that do not fit in with the core values tend to leave. In such a culture, a new executive is just as likely to be corrected by his subordinates as by his superiors if he violates the values and norms of the organizational culture. Outsiders normally see firms with a strong culture as having a certain style or way of doing things. Lincoln Electric, pioneered in the Part Five Cases, is an example of a firm with a strong culture.

Strong does not necessarily mean good. A culture can be strong but bad. The culture of the Nazi Party in Germany was certainly strong, but it was most definitely not good. Nor does it follow that a strong culture leads to high performance. One study found that in the 1980s General Motors had a "strong culture," but it was a strong culture that discouraged lower-level employees from demonstrating initiative and taking risks, which the authors argued was dysfunctional and led to low performance at GM.[35] Also, a strong culture might be beneficial at one point, leading to high performance, but inappropriate at another time. The appropriateness of the culture depends on the context. In the 1980s, when IBM was performing very well, several management authors sang the praises of its strong culture, which among other things placed a high value on consensus-based decision making.[36] These authors argued that such a decision-making process was appropriate given the substantial financial investments that IBM routinely made in new technology. However, this process turned out to be a weakness in the fast-moving computer industry of the late 1980s and 1990s. Consensus-based decision making was slow, bureaucratic, and not particularly conducive to corporate risk taking. While this was fine in the 1970s, IBM needed rapid decision making and entrepreneurial risk taking in the 1990s, but its culture discouraged such behavior. IBM found itself outflanked by then-small enterprises such as Microsoft.

One academic study concluded that firms that exhibited high performance over a prolonged period tended to have strong but adaptive cultures. According to this study, in an adaptive culture most managers care deeply about and value customers, stockholders, and employees. They also strongly value people and processes that create useful change in a firm.[37] While this is interesting, it does reduce the issue to a very high level of abstraction; after all, what company would say that it doesn't care deeply about customers, stockholders, and employees? A somewhat different perspective is to argue that the culture of the firm must match the rest of the architecture of the organization, the firm's strategy, and the demands of the competitive environment to attain superior performance. All these elements must be consistent with each other. Lincoln Electric provides another useful example (see Part Five Cases). Lincoln competes in a business that is very competitive, where cost minimization is a key source of competitive advantage. Lincoln's culture and incentive systems both encourage employees to strive for high levels of productivity, which translates into the low costs that are critical for Lincoln's success. The Lincoln example also demonstrates another important point for international businesses: A culture that leads to high performance in the firm's home nation may not be easy to impose on foreign subsidiaries! Lincoln's culture has clearly helped the firm achieve superior performance in the U.S. market, but this same culture is very "American" in its form and difficult to implement in other countries. The managers and employees of several of Lincoln's European subsidiaries found the culture to be alien to their own values and were reluctant to adopt it. The result was that Lincoln found it very difficult to replicate in foreign markets the success it has had in the United States. Lincoln compounded the problem by acquiring established enterprises that already had their own organizational cultures. Thus, in trying to impose its culture on foreign operating subsidiaries, Lincoln had to deal with two problems: how to change the established organizational culture of those units, and how to introduce an organizational culture whose key values might be alien to the values members of that society held. These problems are not unique to Lincoln; many international businesses have to deal with exactly the same problems.

The solution Lincoln has adopted is to establish new subsidiaries, rather than acquiring and trying to transform an enterprise with its own culture. It is much easier to establish a set of values in a new enterprise than it is to change the values of an established enterprise. A second solution is to devote a lot of time and attention to transmitting the firm's organizational culture to its foreign operations. This was something Lincoln originally omitted. Other firms make this an important part of their strategy for internationalization. When MTV Networks opens an operation in a new country, it initially staffs that operation with several expatriates. The job of these expatriates is to hire local employees whose values are consistent with the MTV culture and to socialize those individuals into values and norms that underpin MTV's unique way of doing things. Once this has been achieved, the expatriates move on to their next assignment, and local employees run the operation. A third solution is to recognize that it may be necessary to change some aspects of a firm's culture so that it better fits the culture of the host nation. For example, many Japanese firms use symbolic behavior, such as company songs and morning group exercise sessions, to reinforce cooperative values and norms. However, such symbolic behavior is seen as odd in Western cultures, so many Japanese firms have not used such practices in Western subsidiaries.

The need for a common organizational culture that is the same across a multinational's global network of subsidiaries probably varies with the strategy of the firm. Shared norms and values can facilitate coordination and cooperation between individuals from different subunits.[38] A strong common culture may lead to goal congruence and can attenuate the problems that arise from interdependence, performance ambiguities, and conflict among managers from different subsidiaries. As noted earlier, a shared culture may help informal integrating mechanisms such as knowledge networks to operate more effectively. As such, a common culture may be of greater value in a multinational that is pursuing a strategy that requires cooperation and coordination between globally dispersed subsidiaries. This suggests that it is more important to have a common culture in firms employing a transnational strategy than a localization strategy, with global and international strategies falling between these two extremes.

Synthesis: Strategy and Architecture

In Chapter 12, we identified four basic strategies that multinational firms pursue: localization strategies, international strategies, global strategies, and transnational strategies. So far in this chapter we have looked at several aspects of organization architecture, and we have discussed the interrelationships between these dimensions and strategies. Now it is time to synthesize this material.

LOCALIZATION STRATEGY

Firms pursuing a localization strategy focus on local responsiveness. Table 13.2 shows that such firms tend to operate with worldwide area structures, within which operating decisions are decentralized to functionally self-contained country subsidiaries. The need for coordination between subunits (areas and country subsidiaries) is low. This suggests that firms pursuing a localization strategy do not have a high need for integrating mechanisms, either formal or informal, to knit together different national operations. The lack of interdependence implies that the level of performance ambiguity in such enterprises is low, as (by extension) are the costs of control. Thus, headquarters can manage foreign operations by relying primarily on output and bureaucratic controls and a policy of management by exception. Incentives can be linked to performance metrics at the level of country subsidiaries. Since the need for integration and coordination is low, the need for common processes and organization culture is also quite low. Were it not for the fact that these firms are unable to profit from the realization of location and experience curve economies, or from the transfer of core competencies, their organizational simplicity would make this an attractive strategy.

INTERNATIONAL STRATEGY

Firms pursuing an international strategy attempt to create value by transferring core competencies from home to foreign subsidiaries. If they are diverse, as most of them are,

Structure and Controls	Strategy			
	Localization	**International**	**Global Standardization**	**Transnational**
Vertical differentiation	Decentralized	Core competency more centralized; rest decentralized	Some centralization	Mixed centralization and decentralization
Horizontal differentiation	Worldwide area structure	Worldwide product divisions	Worldwide product divisions	Informal matrix
Need for coordination	Low	Moderate	High	Very High
Integrating mechanisms	None	Few	Many	Very many
Performance ambiguity	Low	Moderate	High	Very high
Need for cultural controls	Low	Moderate	High	Very high

TABLE 13.2

A Synthesis of Strategy, Structure, and Control Systems

these firms operate with a worldwide product division structure. Headquarters typically maintains centralized control over the source of the firm's core competency, which is most typically found in the R&D and/or marketing functions of the firm. All other operating decisions are decentralized within the firm to subsidiary operations in each country (which in diverse firms report to worldwide product divisions).

The need for coordination is moderate in such firms, reflecting the need to transfer core competencies. Thus, although such firms operate with some integrating mechanisms, they are not that extensive. The relatively low level of interdependence that results translates into a relatively low level of performance ambiguity. These firms can generally get by with output and bureaucratic controls and with incentives that are focused on performance metrics at the level of country subsidiaries. The need for a common organizational culture and common processes is not that great. An important exception is when the core skills or competencies of the firm are embedded in processes and culture, in which case the firm needs to pay close attention to transferring those processes and associated culture from the corporate center to country subsidiaries. Overall, although the organization required for an international strategy is more complex than that of firms pursuing a localization strategy, the increase in the level of complexity is not that great.

GLOBAL STANDARDIZATION STRATEGY

Firms pursuing a global standardization strategy focus on the realization of location and experience curve economies. If they are diversified, as many of them are, these firms operate with a worldwide product division structure. To coordinate the firm's globally dispersed web of value creation activities, headquarters typically maintains ultimate control over most operating decisions. In general, such firms are more centralized than enterprises pursuing a localization or international strategy. Reflecting the need for coordination of the various stages of the firms' globally dispersed value chains, the need for integration in these firms also is high. Thus, these firms tend to operate with an array of formal and informal integrating mechanisms. The resulting interdependencies can lead to significant performance ambiguities. As a result, in addition to output and bureaucratic controls, firms pursuing a global standardization strategy tend to stress the need to build a strong organizational culture that can facilitate coordination and cooperation. They also tend to use incentive systems that are linked to performance metrics at the corporate level, giving the managers of different operations a strong incentive to cooperate with each other to increase the performance of the entire corporation. On average, the organization of such firms is more complex than that of firms pursuing a localization or international strategy.

TRANSNATIONAL STRATEGY

Firms pursuing a transnational strategy focus on the simultaneous attainment of location and experience curve economies, local responsiveness, and global learning (the multidirectional transfer of core competencies or skills). These firms may operate with matrix-type structures in which both product divisions and geographic areas have significant influence. The need to coordinate a globally dispersed value chain and to transfer core competencies creates pressures for centralizing some operating decisions (particularly production and R&D). At the same time, the need to be locally responsive creates pressures for decentralizing other operating decisions to national operations (particularly marketing). Consequently, these firms tend to mix relatively high degrees of centralization for some operating decisions with relative high degrees of decentralization for other operating decisions.

The need for coordination is high in transnational firms. This is reflected in the use of an array of formal and informal integrating mechanisms, including formal matrix structures and informal management networks. The high level of interdependence of subunits implied by such integration can result in significant performance ambiguities, which raise the costs of control. To reduce these, in addition to output and bureaucratic controls, firms pursuing a transnational strategy need to cultivate a strong culture and to establish incentives that promote cooperation between subunits.

ENVIRONMENT, STRATEGY, ARCHITECTURE, AND PERFORMANCE

Underlying the scheme outlined in Table 13.2 is the notion that a "fit" between strategy and architecture is necessary for a firm to achieve high performance. For a firm to succeed, two conditions must be fulfilled. First, the firm's strategy must be consistent with the environment in which the firm operates. We discussed this issue in Chapter 12 and noted that in some industries a global standardization strategy is most viable, in others an international or transnational strategy may be most viable, and in still others a localization strategy may be most viable. Second, the firm's organization architecture must be consistent with its strategy.

If the strategy does not fit the environment, the firm is likely to experience significant performance problems. If the architecture does not fit the strategy, the firm is also likely to experience performance problems. Therefore, to survive, a firm must strive to achieve a fit of its environment, its strategy, and its organizational architecture. You will recall that we saw the importance of this concept in the opening case. Philips NV, the Dutch electronics firm, provides another illustration of the need for this fit. For reasons rooted in the history of the firm, Philips operated until recently with an organization typical of an enterprise pursuing localization; operating decisions were decentralized to largely autonomous foreign subsidiaries. Historically, electronics markets were segmented from each other by high trade barriers, so an organization consistent with a localization strategy made sense. However, by the mid-1980s, the industry in which Philips competed had been revolutionized by declining trade barriers, technological change, and the emergence of low-cost Japanese competitors that utilized a global strategy. To survive, Philips needed to adopt a global standardization strategy itself. The firm recognized this and tried to adopt a global posture, but it did little to change its organizational architecture. The firm nominally adopted a matrix structure based on worldwide product divisions and national areas. In reality, however, the national areas continued to dominate the organization, and the product divisions had little more than an advisory role. As a result, Philips's architecture did not fit the strategy, and by the early 1990s Philips was losing money. It was only after four years of wrenching change and large losses that Philips was finally able to tilt the balance of power in its matrix toward the product divisions. By the mid-1990s, the fruits of this effort to realign the company's strategy and architecture with the demands of its operating environment were beginning to show up in improved financial performance.[39]

Organizational Change

Multinational firms periodically have to alter their architecture so that it conforms to the changes in the environment in which they are competing and the strategy they are pursuing. To be profitable, Philips NV had to alter its strategy and architecture in the 1990s so that both matched the demands of the competitive environment in the electronics industry, which had shifted from localization and toward a global industry. While a detailed consideration of organizational change is beyond the scope of this book, a few comments are warranted regarding the sources of organization inertia and the strategies and tactics for implementing organizational change.

ORGANIZATIONAL INERTIA

Organizations are difficult to change. Within most organizations are strong inertia forces. These forces come from a number of sources. One source of inertia is the existing distribution of power and influence within an organization.[40] The power and influence individual managers enjoy is in part a function of their role in the organizational hierarchy, as defined by structural position. By definition, most substantive changes in an organization require a change in structure and, by extension, a change in the distribution of power and influence within the organization. Some individuals will see their power and influence increase as a result of organizational change, and some will see the converse. For example, in the 1990s, Philips NV increased the roles and responsibilities of its global product divisions and decreased the roles and responsibilities of its foreign subsidiary companies. This meant the managers running the global product divisions saw their power and influence increase, while the managers running the foreign subsidiary companies saw their power and influence decline. As might be expected, some managers of foreign subsidiary companies did not like this change and resisted it, which slowed the pace of change. Those whose power and influence are reduced as a consequence of organizational change can be expected to resist it, primarily by arguing that the change might not work. To the extent that they are successful, this constitutes a source of organizational inertia that might slow or stop change.

Another source of organizational inertia is the existing culture, as expressed in norms and value systems. Value systems reflect deeply held beliefs, and as such, they can be very hard to change. If the formal and informal socialization mechanisms within an organization have been emphasizing a consistent set of values for a prolonged period, and if hiring, promotion, and incentive systems have all reinforced these values, then suddenly announcing that those values are no longer appropriate and need to be changed can produce resistance and dissonance among employees. For example, Philips NV historically placed a very high value on local autonomy. The changes of the 1990s implied a reduction in the autonomy foreign subsidiaries enjoy, which was counter to the established values of the company and thus resisted.

Organizational inertia might also derive from senior managers' preconceptions about the appropriate business model or paradigm. When a given paradigm has worked well in the past, managers might have trouble accepting that it is no longer appropriate. At Philips, granting considerable autonomy to foreign subsidiaries had worked very well in the past, allowing local managers to tailor product and business strategy to the conditions prevailing in a given country. Since this paradigm had worked so well, it was difficult for many managers to understand why it no longer applied. Consequently, they had difficulty accepting a new business model and tended to fall back on their established paradigm and ways of doing things. This change required managers to let go of long-held assumptions about what worked and what didn't work, which was something many of them couldn't do.

Institutional constraints might also act as a source of inertia. National regulations including local content rules and policies pertaining to layoffs might make it difficult for a multinational to alter its global value chain. A multinational might wish to take control for manufacturing away from local subsidiaries, transfer that control to global product divisions, and consolidate manufacturing at a few choice locations. However, if local content rules (see Chapter 5) require some degree of local production and if regulations regarding layoffs make it difficult or expensive for a multinational to close operations in a country, a multinational may find that these constraints make it very difficult to adopt the most effective strategy and architecture.

IMPLEMENTING ORGANIZATIONAL CHANGE

Although all organizations suffer from inertia, the complexity and global spread of many multinationals might make it particularly difficult for them to change their strategy and architecture to match new organizational realities. Yet at the same time, the trend toward globalization in many industries has made it more critical than ever that many multinationals do just that. In industry after industry, declining barriers to cross-border trade and investment have led to a change in the nature of the competitive environment. Cost pressures have increased, requiring multinationals to respond by streamlining their operations to realize economic benefits associated with location and experience curve economies and with the transfer of competencies and skills within the organization. At the same time, local responsiveness remains an important source of differentiation. To survive in this emerging competitive environment, multinationals must change not only their strategy but also their architecture so that it matches strategy in discriminating ways. The basic principles for successful organizational change can be summarized as follows: (1) unfreeze the organization through shock therapy, (2) move the organization to a new state through proactive change in the architecture, and (3) refreeze the organization in its new state.

Unfreezing the Organization

Because of inertia forces, incremental change is often no change. Those whose power is threatened by change can too easily resist incremental change. This leads to the big bang theory of change, which maintains that effective change requires taking bold action early to "unfreeze" the established culture of an organization and to change the distribution of power and influence. Shock therapy to unfreeze the organization might include the closure of plants deemed uneconomic or the announcement of a dramatic structural reorganization. It is also important to realize that change will not occur unless senior managers are committed to it. Senior managers must clearly articulate the need for change so employees understand both why it is being pursued and the benefits that will flow from successful change. Senior managers must also practice what they preach and take the necessary bold steps. If employees see senior managers preaching the need for change but not changing their own behavior or making substantive changes in the organization, they will soon lose faith in the change effort, which then will flounder.

Moving to the New State

Once an organization has been unfrozen, it must be moved to its new state. Movement requires taking action—closing operations; reorganizing the structure; reassigning responsibilities; changing control, incentive, and reward systems; redesigning processes; and letting people go who are seen as an impediment to change. In other words, movement requires a substantial change in the form of a multinational organization's architecture so that it matches the desired new strategic posture. For movement to be successful, it must be done with sufficient speed. Involving employees in the change effort is an excellent way to get them to appreciate and buy into the needs for change and to help with rapid movement. For example, a firm might delegate substantial responsibility for designing operating processes to lower-level employees. If enough of their recommendations are then acted on, the employees will see the consequences of their efforts and consequently buy into the notion that change is really occurring.

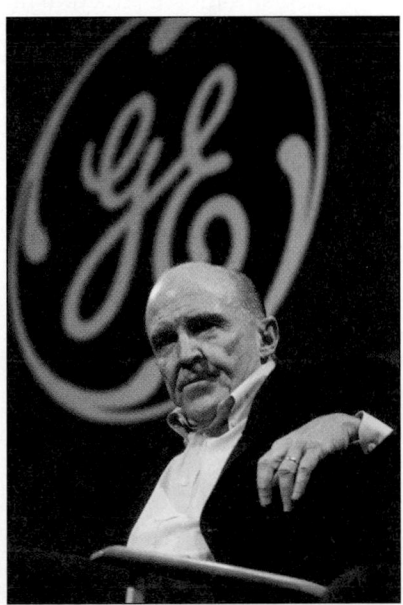

Refreezing the Organization

Refreezing the organization takes longer. It may require that a new culture be established, while the old one is being dismantled. Thus, refreezing requires that employees be socialized into the new way of doing things. Companies will often use management education programs to achieve this. At General Electric, where longtime CEO Jack Welch instituted a major change in the culture of the company, management education programs were used as a proactive tool to communicate new values to organization members. On their own, however, management education programs are not enough. Hiring policies must be changed to reflect the new realities, with an emphasis on hiring individuals whose own values are consistent with that of the new culture the firm is trying to build. Similarly, control and incentive systems must be consistent with the new realities of the organization, or change will never take. Senior management must recognize that changing culture takes a long time. Any letup in the pressure to change may allow the old culture to reemerge as employees fall back into familiar ways of doing things. The communication task facing senior managers, therefore, is a long-term endeavor that requires managers to be

Jack Welch, General Electric's legendary former CEO, is an individual who set a benchmark for embracing change.

relentless and persistent in their pursuit of change. One striking feature of Jack Welch's two-decade tenure at GE, for example, is that he never stopped pushing his change agenda. It was a consistent theme of his tenure. He was always thinking up new programs and initiatives to keep pushing the culture of the organization along the desired trajectory.

CHAPTER SUMMARY

This chapter identified the organizational architecture that multinational enterprises use to manage and direct their global operations. A central theme of the chapter was that different strategies require different architectures; strategy is implemented through architecture. To succeed, a firm must match its architecture to its strategy in discriminating ways. Firms whose architecture does not fit their strategic requirements will experience performance problems. It is also necessary for the different components of architecture to be consistent with each other. The chapter made the following points:

1. Superior enterprise profitability requires three conditions to be fulfilled: the different elements of a firm's organizational architecture must be internally consistent, the organizational architecture must fit the strategy of the firm, and the strategy and architecture of the firm must be consistent with competitive conditions prevailing in the firm's markets.

2. Organizational structure means three things: the formal division of the organization into subunits (horizontal differentiation), the location of decision-making responsibilities within that structure (vertical differentiation), and the establishment of integrating mechanisms.

3. Control systems are the metrics used to measure the performance of subunits and make judgments about how well managers are running those subunits.

4. Incentives refer to the devices used to reward appropriate employee behavior. Many employees receive incentives in the form of annual bonus pay. Incentives are usually closely tied to the performance metrics used for output controls.

5. Processes refer to the manner in which decisions are made and work is performed within the organization. Processes can be found at many different levels within an organization. The core competencies or valuable skills of a firm are often embedded in its processes. Efficient and effective processes can help lower the costs of value creation and add additional value to a product.

6. Organizational culture refers to a system of values and norms that is shared among employees. Values and norms express themselves as the behavior patterns or style of an organization that new employees are automatically encouraged to follow by their fellow employees.

7. Firms pursuing different strategies must adopt a different architecture to implement those strategies successfully. Firms pursuing localization, global, international, and transnational strategies all must adopt an organizational architecture that matches their strategy.

8. While all organizations suffer from inertia, the complexity and global spread of many multinationals might make it particularly difficult for them to change their strategy and architecture to match new organizational realities. At the same time, the trend toward globalization in many industries has made it more critical than ever that many multinationals do just that.

Critical Thinking and Discussion Questions

1. "The choice of strategy for a multinational firm must depend on a comparison of the benefits of that strategy (in terms of value creation) with the costs of implementing it (as defined by organizational architecture necessary for implementation). On this basis, it may be logical for some firms to pursue a localization strategy, others a global or international strategy, and still others a transnational strategy." Is this statement correct?

2. Discuss this statement: "An understanding of the causes and consequences of performance ambiguity is central to the issue of organizational design in multinational firms."

3. Describe the organizational architecture a transnational firm might adopt to reduce the costs of control.

4. What is the most appropriate organizational architecture for a firm that is competing in an industry where a global strategy is most appropriate?

5. If a firm is changing its strategy from an international to a transnational strategy, what are the most important challenges it is likely to face in implementing this change? How can the firm overcome these challenges?

6. Reread the Management Focus on Wal-Mart's International Division and answer the following questions:

    a. Why did the centralization of decisions at the headquarters of Wal-Mart's international division create problems for the company's different national operations? Has Wal-Mart's response been appropriate?

    b. Do you think that having an international division is the best structure for managing Wal-Mart's foreign operations? What

problems might arise with this structure? What other structure might work?

7. Reread the Management Focus on the rise and fall of the matrix structure at Dow Chemical, then answer the following questions:

    a. Why did Dow first adopt a matrix structure? What were the problems with this structure? Do you think these problems are typical of matrix structures?

    b. What drove the shift away from the matrix structure in the late 1990s? Does Dow's structure now make sense given the nature of its businesses and the competitive environment in which it competes?

8. Read the Part 5 Case on Incentives and Culture at Lincoln Electric, then answer the following questions:

    a. To what extent are the organization culture and incentive systems of Lincoln Electric aligned with the firm's strategy?

    b. How was the culture at Lincoln Electric created and nurtured over time?

    c. Why did the culture and incentive systems work well in the United States? Why did it not take in other nations?

Research Task

Use the globalEDGE™ site to complete the following exercises:

1. *Fortune* conducts an annual survey and publishes the rankings of its Global Most Admired Companies. Locate the most recent ranking available and focus on the methodology used to determine which companies are most admired. Prepare an executive summary of the strategic and organizational success factors involved in this survey.

2. Globalization can present many challenges for companies, cultures, and countries. In fact, the globalEDGE™ Web site presents selected articles from the business media under its "news & views" section. Locate the "in depth look" section and find an article that provides insights about the challenges facing firms in the globalization process. Prepare a description of these challenges and any solutions that the authors may recommend.

CLOSING CASE

A Decade of Organizational Change at Unilever

Unilever is one of the world's oldest multinational corporations with extensive product offerings in the food, detergent, and personal care businesses. It generates annual revenues in excess of $50 billion and a wide range of branded products in virtually every country.

Detergents, which account for about 25 percent of corporate revenues, include well-known names such as Omo, which is sold in more than 50 countries. Personal care products, which account for about 15 percent of sales, include Calvin Klein Cosmetics, Pepsodent toothpaste brands, Faberge hair care products, and Vaseline skin lotions. Food products account for the remaining 60 percent of sales and include strong offerings in margarine (where Unilever's market share in most countries exceeds 70 percent), tea, ice cream, frozen foods, and bakery products.

Historically, Unilever was organized on a decentralized basis. Subsidiary companies in each major national market were responsible for the production, marketing, sales, and distribution of products in that market. In Western Europe, for example, the company had 17 subsidiaries in the early 1990s, each focused on a different national market. Each was a profit center and each was held accountable for its own performance. This decentralization was viewed as a source of strength. The structure allowed local managers to match product offerings and marketing strategy to local tastes and preferences and to alter sales and distribution strategies to fit the prevailing retail systems. To drive the localization, Unilever recruited local managers to run local organizations; the U.S. subsidiary (Lever Brothers) was run by Americans, the Indian subsidiary by Indians, and so on.

By the mid-1990s, this decentralized structure was increasingly out of step with a rapidly changing competitive environment. Unilever's global competitors, which include the Swiss firm Nestlé and Procter & Gamble from the United States, had been more successful than Unilever on several fronts—building global brands, reducing cost structure by consolidating manufacturing operations at a few choice locations, and executing simultaneous product launches in several national markets. Unilever's decentralized structure worked against efforts to build global or regional brands. It also meant lots of duplication, particularly in manufacturing; a lack of scale economies; and a high-cost structure. Unilever also found that it was falling behind rivals in the race to bring new products to market. In Europe, for example, while Nestlé and Procter & Gamble moved toward pan-European product launches, it could take Unilever four to five years to "persuade" its 17 European operations to adopt a new product.

Unilever began to change all this in the mid-1990s. In 1996, it introduced a new structure based on regional business groups. Within each business group were a number of divisions, each focusing on a specific category of products. Thus, in the European Business Group, a division focused on detergents, another on ice cream and frozen foods, and so on. These groups and divisions coordinated the activities of national subsidiaries within their region to drive down operating costs and speed up the process of developing and introducing new products.

For example, Lever Europe was established to consolidate the company's detergent operations. The 17 European companies reported directly to Lever Europe. Using its newfound organizational clout, Lever Europe consolidated the production of detergents in Europe in a few key locations to reduce costs and speed up new product introduction. Implicit in this new approach was a bargain: the 17 companies relinquished autonomy in their traditional markets in exchange for opportunities to help develop and execute a unified pan-European strategy. The number of European plants manufacturing soap was cut from 10 to 2, and some new products were manufactured at only one site. Product sizing and packaging were harmonized to cut purchasing costs and to accommodate unified pan-European advertising. By taking these steps, Unilever estimated it saved as much as $400 million a year in its European detergent operations.

By 2000, however, Unilever found that it was still lagging its competitors, so the company embarked upon another reorganization. This time the goal was to cut the number of brands that Unilever sold from 1,600 to just 400 that could be marketed on a regional or global scale. To support this new focus, the company planned to reduce the number of manufacturing plants from 380 to about 280 by 2004. The company also established a new organization based on just two global product divisions—a food division and a home personal care division. Within each division are a number of regional business groups that focus on developing, manufacturing, and marketing either food or personal care products within a given region. For example, Unilever Bestfoods Europe, which is headquartered in Rotterdam, focuses on selling food brands across Western and Eastern Europe, while Unilever Home and Personal Care Europe does the same for home and personal care products. A similar structure can be found in North America, Latin America, and Asia. Thus, Bestfoods North America, headquartered in New Jersey, has a similar charter to Bestfoods Europe, but in keeping with differences in local history, many of the food brands Unilever markets in North America are different from those it markets in Europe.[41]

Case Discussion Questions

1. Why did Unilever's decentralization make sense in the 1950s–1970s? Why did this structure start to create problems for the company in the 1980s?

2. What was Unilever trying to do when it introduced a new structure based on business groups in the mid-1990s? Why do you think this structure failed to cure Unilever's ills?

3. In the 2000s Unilever has switched to a structure based on global product divisions. What do you think is the underlying logic for this shift? Does the structure make sense given the nature of competition in the detergents and food business?

Notes

1. C. Busco et al., "Integrating Global Organizations through Performance Measurement Systems," *Strategic Finance,* January 2006, pp. 30–36; P. Brabeck-Letmathe, Address to shareholders at 139th Annual General Meeting, Lausanne, Switzerland, April 6, 2006.

2. D. Naidler, M. Gerstein, and R. Shaw, *Organization Architecture* (San Francisco: Jossey-Bass, 1992).

3. G. Morgan, *Images of Organization* (Beverly Hills, CA: Sage Publications, 1986).

4. "Unilever: A Networked Organization," *Harvard Business Review,* November–December 1996, p. 138.

5. The material in this section draws on John Child, *Organizations* (London: Harper & Row, 1984).

6. Allan Cane, "Microsoft Reorganizes to Meet Market Challenges," *Financial Times,* March 16, 1994, p. 1. Interviews by Charles Hill.

7. For research evidence that is related to this issue, see J. Birkinshaw, "Entrepreneurship in the Multinational Corporation: The Characteristics of Subsidiary Initiatives," *Strategic Management Journal* 18 (1997), pp. 207–29; J. Birkinshaw, N. Hood, and S. Jonsson, "Building Firm Specific Advantages in Multinational Corporations: The Role of Subsidiary Initiatives," *Strategic Management Journal* 19 (1998), pp. 221–41; and I. Bjorkman, W. Barner-Rasussen, and L. Li, "Managing Knowledge Transfer in MNCs: The Impact of Headquarters Control Mechanisms," *Journal of International Business* 35 (2004), pp. 443–60.

8. Sources: M. Troy, "Wal-Mart Braces for International Growth with Personnel Moves," *DSN Retailing Today,* February 9, 2004, pp. 5–7; "Division Heads Let Numbers Do the Talking," *DSN Retailing Today,* June 21, 2004, pp. 26–28; and "The Division That Defines the Future," *DSN Retailing Today,* June 2001, pp. 4–7.

9. For more detail, see S. M. Davis, "Managing and Organizing Multinational Corporations," in C. A. Bartlett and S. Ghoshal, *Transnational Management* (Homewood, IL: Richard D. Irwin, 1992). Also see J. Wolf and W. G. Egelhoff, "A Reexamination and Extension of International Strategy-Structure Theory," *Strategic Management Journal* 23 (2002), pp. 181–89.

10. A. D. Chandler, *Strategy and Structure: Chapters in the History of the Industrial Enterprise* (Cambridge, MA: MIT Press, 1962).

11. Davis, "Managing and Organizing Multinational Corporations."

12. J. M. Stopford and L. T. Wells, *Strategy and Structure of the Multinational Enterprise* (New York: Basic Books, 1972).

13. C. A. Bartlett and S. Ghoshal, *Managing across Borders* (Boston: Harvard Business School Press, 1989).

14. Sources: "Dow Draws Its Matrix Again, and Again, and Again," *The Economist,* August 5, 1989, pp. 55–56; "Dow Goes for Global Structure," *Chemical Marketing Reporter,* December 11, 1995, pp. 4–5; and R. M. Hodgetts, "Dow Chemical CEO William Stavropoulos on Structure and Decision Making," *Academy of Management Executive,* November 1999, pp. 29–35.

15. See J. R. Galbraith, *Designing Complex Organizations* (Reading, MA: Addison-Wesley, 1977).

16. M. Goold and A. Campbell, "Structured Networks: Towards the Well Designed Matrix," *Long Range Planning,* October 2003, pp. 427–60.

17. Bartlett and Ghoshal, *Managing across Borders;* F. V. Guterl, "Goodbye, Old Matrix," *Business Month,* February 1989, pp. 32–38; and Bjorkman, Barner-Rasussen, and Li, "Managing Knowledge Transfer in MNCs."

18. M. S. Granovetter, "The Strength of Weak Ties," *American Journal of Sociology* 78 (1973), pp. 1360–80.

19. A. K. Gupta and V. J. Govindarajan, "Knowledge Flows within Multinational Corporations," *Strategic Management Journal* 21, no. 4 (2000), pp. 473–96; V. J. Govindarajan and A. K. Gupta, *The Quest for Global Dominance* (San Francisco: Jossey-Bass, 2001); and U. Andersson, M. Forsgren, and U. Holm, "The Strategic Impact of External Networks: Subsidiary Performance and Competence Development in the Multinational Corporation," *Strategic Management Journal* 23 (2002), pp. 979–96.

20. For examples, see W. H. Davidow and M. S. Malone, *The Virtual Corporation* (New York: HarperCollins, 1992).

21. W. G. Ouchi, "Markets, Bureaucracies, and Clans," *Administrative Science Quarterly* 25 (1980), pp. 129–44.

22. For some empirical work that addresses this issue, see T. P. Murtha, S. A. Lenway, and R. P. Bagozzi, "Global Mind Sets and Cognitive Shift in a

Complex Multinational Corporation," *Strategic Management Journal* 19 (1998), pp. 97–114.

23. J. Welch and J. Byrne, *Jack: Straight from the Gut* (Warner Books: New York, 2001).

24. C. W. L. Hill, M. E. Hitt, and R. E. Hoskisson, "Cooperative versus Competitive Structures in Related and Unrelated Diversified Firms," *Organization Science* 3 (1992), pp. 501–21.

25. Murtha, Lenway, and Bagozzi, "Global Mind Sets."

26. M. Hammer and J. Champy, *Reengineering the Corporation* (New York: Harper Business, 1993).

27. T. Kostova, "Transnational Transfer of Strategic Organizational Practices: A Contextual Perspective," *Academy of Management Review* 24, no. 2 (1999), pp. 308–24.

28. Andersson, Forsgren, and Holm, "The Strategic Impact of External Networks: Subsidiary Performance and Competence Development in the Multinational Corporation."

29. E. H. Schein, "What Is Culture?" in P. J. Frost et al., *Reframing Organizational Culture* (Newbury Park, CA: Sage, 1991).

30. E. H. Schein, *Organizational Culture and Leadership*, 2nd ed. (San Francisco: Jossey-Bass, 1992).

31. G. Morgan, *Images of Organization* (Beverly Hills, CA: Sage, 1986).

32. R. Dore, *British Factory, Japanese Factory* (London: Allen & Unwin, 1973).

33. M. Dickson, "Back to the Future," *Financial Times*, May 30, 1994, p. 7.

34. See J. P. Kotter and J. L. Heskett, *Corporate Culture and Performance* (New York: Free Press,

1992), and M. L. Tushman and C. A. O'Reilly, *Winning through Innovation* (Boston: Harvard Business School Press, 1997).

35. Kotter and Heskett, *Corporate Culture and Performance*.

36. The classic song of praise was produced by T. Peters and R. H. Waterman, *In Search of Excellence* (New York: Harper & Row, 1982). Ironically, IBM's decline began shortly after Peters and Waterman's book was published.

37. Kotter and Heskett, *Corporate Culture and Performance*.

38. Bartlett and Ghoshal, *Managing across Borders*.

39. See F. J. Aguilar and M. Y. Yoshino, "The Philips Group: 1987," Harvard Business School Case No. 388-050, 1987; "Philips Fights Flab," *The Economist*, April 7, 1990, pp. 73–74; and R. Van de Krol, "Philips Wins Back Old Friends," *Financial Times*, July 14, 1995, p. 14.

40. J. Pfeffer, *Managing with Power: Politics and Influence within Organizations* (Boston: Harvard Business School Press, 1992).

41. H. Connon, "Unilever's Got the Nineties Licked," *The Guardian*, May 24, 1998, p. 5; "Unilever: A Networked Organization," *Harvard Business Review*, November–December 1996, p. 138; C. Christensen and J. Zobel, "Unilever's Butter Beater: Innovation for Global Diversity," Harvard Business School Case No. 9-698-017, March 1998; M. Mayer, A. Smith, and R. Whittington, "Restructuring Roulette," *Financial Times*, November 8, 2002, p. 8; and Unilever's Web site at www.unilever.com.

JCB in India

In 1979, JCB, the large British manufacturer of construction equipment, entered into a joint venture with Escorts, an Indian engineering conglomerate, to manufacture backhoe loaders for sale in India. Escorts held a majority 60 percent stake in the venture, and JCB 40 percent. The joint venture was a first for JCB, which historically had exported as much as two-thirds of its production from Britain to a wide range of nations. The decision to enter into a joint venture in India was driven by a number of factors. First, high tariff barriers made direct exports to India difficult. Second, although JCB would have preferred to go it alone in India, government regulations at the time required foreign investors to create joint ventures with local companies. Third, JCB felt that the Indian construction market was ripe for growth, and that looking forward it could become very large indeed. The company's managers believed that it was better to get a

foothold in the nation, thereby gaining an advantage over global competitors, rather than wait until the growth potential was realized.

Twenty years later, some of JCB's foresight had been rewarded. The joint venture was selling some 2,000 backhoes in India, and had an 80 percent share of the Indian market. Moreover, after years of deregulation, the Indian economy was booming. However, JCB felt that the joint venture limited its ability to expand. For one thing, much of JCB's global success was based upon the utilization of leading edge manufacturing technologies and relentless product innovation, but the company was very hesitant about transferring this know-how to a venture where it did not have a majority stake, and therefore lacked control. The last thing JCB wanted was for these valuable technologies to leak out of the joint venture into Escorts, which was one of the largest

Entry Strategy and Strategic Alliances

14

LEARNING OBJECTIVES

After you have read this chapter you should be able to:

LO¹ Explain the three basic decisions that firms contemplating foreign expansion must make: which markets to enter, when to enter those markets, and on what scale.

LO² Outline the advantages and disadvantages of the different modes that firms use to enter foreign markets.

LO³ Identify the factors that influence a firm's choice of entry mode.

LO⁴ Evaluate the pros and cons of acquisitions versus greenfield ventures as an entry strategy.

LO⁵ Evaluate the pros and cons of using strategic alliances with foreign competitors to achieve the firm's objectives in a global marketplace.

manufacturers of tractors in India and might conceivably become a direct competitor in the future. Moreover, JCB was unwilling to make the investment in India required to take the joint venture to the next level unless it could capture more of the long-run returns. Accordingly, in 1999 JCB took advantage of changes in government regulations to renegotiate the terms of the venture with Escorts, purchasing 20 percent of its partner's equity to give JCB majority control. In 2002, JCB took this to its logical end when it responded to further relaxation of government regulations on foreign investment to purchase all of Escorts' remaining equity, transforming the joint venture into a wholly owned subsidiary. Around the same time, JCB also invested in wholly owned factories in the United States and Brazil.

Having gained full control, in early 2005 JCB increased its investment in India, announcing that it would build a second factory that it would use to serve the fast growing Indian market. At the same time, JCB also announced that it would set up another wholly owned factory in China to serve that market. The strategy was clear; India and China, the two most populous nations in the world, were growing rapidly, construction was booming, and JCB, then the world's fifth largest manufacturer of construction equipment, was eager to expand its presence in order to match its global rivals, particularly Caterpillar, Komatsu, and Volvo, who were also expanding aggressively in these markets. By mid-2006 there were signs that JCB's foreign investment was starting to bear fruit. The product line had been expanded from 120 machines in 2001 to some 257 in 2006. JCB's sales approached £1.5 billion, earnings were a record £110 million, and the company had moved up to number four in the industry with almost 10 percent of global market share.[1]

Introduction

This chapter is concerned with two closely related topics: (1) the decision of which foreign markets to enter, when to enter them, and on what scale; and (2) the choice of entry mode. Any firm contemplating foreign expansion must first struggle with the issue of which foreign markets to enter and the timing and scale of entry. The choice of which markets to enter should be driven by an assessment of relative long-run growth and profit potential. In the opening case, for example, we saw that JCB's original decision to enter the Indian market through a joint venture was based upon a favorable outlook for growth in demand.

The choice of mode for entering a foreign market is another major issue with which international businesses must wrestle. The various modes for serving foreign markets are exporting, licensing, or franchising to host-country firms, establishing joint ventures with a host-country firm, setting up a new wholly owned subsidiary in a host country to serve its market, or acquiring an established enterprise in the host nation to serve that market. Each of these options has advantages and disadvantages. The magnitude of the advantages and disadvantages associated with each entry mode is determined by a number of factors, including transport costs, trade barriers, political risks, economic risks, business risks, and firm strategy. The optimal entry mode varies by situation, depending on these factors. Thus, whereas some firms may best serve a given market by exporting, other firms may better serve the market by setting up a new wholly owned subsidiary or by acquiring an established enterprise.

As discussed in the opening case, JCB originally entered the Indian market through a joint venture, primarily because tariff barriers made exporting difficult and government regulations required foreign investors to enter joint ventures with local partners. However, JCB was never entirely happy with this arrangement, and when regulations permitted, the company acquired a majority stake in the venture, and then purchased all of the remaining equity in 2005. Its quest for full control of the Indian venture was a strategic decision, based upon an assessment of the business risks of transferring technology to a venture that was partially owned by a potential competitor. As we shall see, many firms prefer a wholly owned subsidiary for precisely this reason.

Basic Entry Decisions

A firm contemplating foreign expansion must make three basic decisions: which markets to enter, when to enter those markets, and on what scale.[2]

WHICH FOREIGN MARKETS?

There are more than 200 nation-states in the world. They do not all hold the same profit potential for a firm contemplating foreign expansion. Ultimately, the choice must be based on an assessment of a nation's long-run profit potential. This potential is a function of several factors, many of which we have studied in earlier chapters. In Chapter 2, we looked in detail at the economic and political factors that influence the potential attractiveness of a foreign market. There we noted that the attractiveness of a country as a potential market for an international business depends on balancing the benefits, costs, and risks associated with doing business in that country.

Chapter 2 also noted that the long-run economic benefits of doing business in a country are a function of factors such as the size of the market (in terms of demographics), the present wealth (purchasing power) of consumers in that market, and the likely future wealth of consumers, which depends upon economic growth rates. Although some markets are very large when measured by number of consumers (e.g., China, India, and Indonesia), businesses must also consider living standards and economic growth. On this basis, China and, to a lesser extent, India, while relatively poor, are growing so rapidly that they are attractive targets for inward investment. Alternatively, weak growth in Indonesia implies that this populous nation is a far less attractive target for inward investment. As we saw in Chapter 2, likely future economic growth rates appear to be a function of a free market system and a country's capacity for growth (which may be greater in less developed nations). We also argued in Chapter 2 that the costs and risks associated with doing business in a foreign country are typically lower in economically advanced and politically stable democratic nations, and they are greater in less developed and politically unstable nations.

The discussion in Chapter 2 suggests that, other things being equal, the benefit–cost–risk trade-off is likely to be most favorable in politically stable developed and developing nations that have free market systems, and where there is not a dramatic upsurge in either inflation rates or private-sector debt. The trade-off is likely to be least favorable in politically unstable developing nations that operate with a mixed or command economy or in developing nations where speculative financial bubbles have led to excess borrowing (see Chapter 2 for further details).

Another important factor is the value an international business can create in a foreign market. Value depends on the suitability of its product offering to that market and the nature of indigenous competition.[3] If the international business can offer a product that has not been widely available in that market and that satisfies an unmet need, the value of that product to consumers is likely to be much greater than if the international business simply offers the same type of product that indigenous competitors and other foreign entrants are already offering. Greater value translates into an ability to charge higher prices or to build sales volume more rapidly.

By considering such factors, a firm can rank countries in terms of their attractiveness and long-run profit potential. Preference is then given to entering markets that rank highly. For example, in the case of Citigroup, entering China made sense given the strong underlying growth trends and the move by Citigroup's global rivals into the same markets.

TIMING OF ENTRY

Once the firm has identified attractive markets, it must consider the **timing of entry.** We say that entry is early when an international business enters a foreign market before other foreign firms and late when it enters after other international businesses have already established themselves. The advantages frequently associated with entering a market early are commonly known as **first-mover advantages.**[4] One first-mover advantage is the ability to preempt rivals and capture demand by establishing a strong brand name. A second advantage is the ability to build sales volume in that country and ride down the experience curve ahead of rivals, giving the early entrant a cost advantage over later entrants. This cost advantage may enable the early entrant to cut prices below that of later entrants, thereby driving them out of the market. A third advantage is the ability of early entrants to create switching costs that tie customers into their products or services. Such switching costs make it difficult for later entrants to win business.

There can also be disadvantages associated with entering a foreign market before other international businesses. These are often referred to as **first-mover disadvantages.**[5] A primary disadvantage is that an early entry may entail **pioneering costs,** costs that the firm has to bear that a later entrant can avoid. Pioneering costs arise when the business system in a foreign country is so different from that in a firm's home market that the enterprise has to devote considerable effort, time, and expense to learning the rules of the game. Pioneering costs include the costs of business failure if the firm, due to its ignorance of the foreign environment, makes some major mistakes. A certain liability is associated with being a foreigner, and this liability is greater for foreign firms that enter a national market early.[6] Research seems to confirm that the probability of survival increases if an international business enters a national market after several other foreign firms have already done so.[7] The late entrant may benefit by observing and learning from the mistakes made by early entrants.

Pioneering costs also include the costs of promoting and establishing a product offering, including the costs of educating customers. These can be significant when the product being promoted is unfamiliar to local consumers. In contrast, later entrants may be able to

MANAGEMENT FOCUS

International Expansion at ING Group

ING Group was formed in 1991 from the merger between the third-largest bank in the Netherlands and the country's largest insurance company. Since then, the company has grown rapidly to become one of the top 10 financial services firms in the world, with operations in 65 countries and a wide range of products in banking, insurance, and asset management. ING's strategy has been to expand rapidly across national borders, primarily through a series of careful acquisitions. Its formula has been to pick a target that has good managers and a strong local presence, take a small stake in the company, win the trust of managers, and then propose a takeover. After the deal, ING leaves the management and products of the acquired companies largely intact, but requires them to sell ING products alongside their own. ING's big push has been the selling of insurance, banking, and investment products, something it has been doing in Holland since the original 1991 merger (in Holland, some 20 percent of ING's insurance products are sold through banks).

Two changes in the regulatory environment have helped ING pursue this strategy. One has been a trend to remove regulatory barriers that traditionally kept different parts of the financial services industry separate. In the United States, for example, a Depression-era law, the Glass-Steagall Act, disallowed insurance companies, banks, and asset managers such as mutual fund companies from selling each other's products. The U.S. Congress repealed this act in 1999, opening the way for the consolidation of the U.S. financial services industry. Many other countries that had similar regulations removed them in the 1990s. Another significant regulatory development occurred in 1997 when the World Trade Organization struck a deal between its member nations that effectively removed barriers to cross-border investment in financial services. This made it much easier for a company such as ING to build a global financial services business.

ING's expansion was initially centered on Europe, where its largest acquisitions have included banks in Germany and Belgium. More recently the centerpiece of ING's strategy has been its aggressive moves into the United States. The big push into the United States began with the 1997 acquisition of Equitable Life Insurance Company of Iowa. This was followed by the acquisitions of Furman Selz, a New York investment bank, whose activities complement those of Barings, a British-based investment bank with significant U.S. activities that ING acquired in 1995. In 2000, ING acquired ReliaStar Financial Services and the non–health insurance units of Aetna Financial Services. These acquisitions combined to make ING one of the top 10 financial services companies in the United States.

ride on an early entrant's investments in learning and customer education by watching how the early entrant proceeded in the market, by avoiding the early entrant's costly mistakes, and by exploiting the market potential created by the early entrant's investments in customer education. For example, KFC introduced the Chinese to American-style fast food, but a later entrant, McDonald's, has capitalized on the market in China.

An early entrant may be put at a severe disadvantage, relative to a later entrant, if regulations change in a way that diminishes the value of an early entrant's investments. This is a serious risk in many developing nations where the rules that govern business practices are still evolving. Early entrants can find themselves at a disadvantage if a subsequent change in regulations invalidates prior assumptions about the best business model for operating in that country.

SCALE OF ENTRY AND STRATEGIC COMMITMENTS

Another issue that an international business needs to consider when contemplating market entry is the scale of entry. Entering a market on a large scale involves the commitment of significant resources; it also implies rapid entry. Consider the entry of the Dutch insurance company ING into the U.S. insurance market in 1999 (described in detail in the accompanying Management Focus). ING had to spend several billion

In 2000, ING established ING Direct in the United States, a consumer bank that offers two main products—a savings account and a mortgage—primarily over the Internet. Unlike its insurance and investment banking businesses, which were based on acquisitions, ING Direct was a greenfield investment established from the ground up in the United States. From a standing start, ING Direct has grown to become the fourth largest savings bank in the United States with more than 4 million customers and over $60 billion in assets as of 2006.

ING found several factors of the U.S. market attractive. The United States is by far the world's largest financial services market, so any company aspiring to be a global player must have a significant presence there. Deregulation made ING's strategy of cross-selling financial service products feasible in the United States. Despite some state-by-state regulation of insurance, ING says it is easier to do business in the United States than in the European Union, where the patchwork of languages and cultures makes it difficult to build a pan-European business with a single identity. Another lure is that with more and more Americans responsible for managing their own retirement with 401(k) plans and the like rather than traditional pensions, the personal investment business in the United States is booming, which has increased ING's appetite for U.S. financial services firms. In contrast, national governments are still primarily responsible for pensions in Europe. Furthermore, in recent years U.S. insurance companies have traded at relatively low price–earnings ratios, making them seem like bargains compared to their European counterparts, which trade at higher valuations. Building a substantial U.S. presence also brings with it the benefits of geographic diversification, allowing ING to offset any revenue or profit shortfalls in one region with earnings elsewhere in the world.

Finally, ING has found it somewhat easier to make acquisitions in the United States than in Europe, where national pride has made it difficult for ING to acquire local companies. ING's initial attempt to acquire a Belgian bank in 1992 was rebuffed, primarily due to nationalistic concerns, and it took ING until 1997 to make the acquisition. Similarly, a 1999 attempt to acquire a major French bank, Credit Commercial de France, in which it already held a 19 percent stake, was turned down. According to news reports, French regulators had expressed concerns over what would have been the first foreign acquisition of a French bank, and the board of CCF believed the acquisition should not proceed without the regulators' blessing.[10]

dollars to acquire its U.S. operations. Not all firms have the resources necessary to enter on a large scale, and even some large firms prefer to enter foreign markets on a small scale and then build slowly as they become more familiar with the market.

The consequences of entering on a significant scale—entering rapidly—are associated with the value of the resulting **strategic commitments.**[8] A strategic commitment has a long-term impact and is difficult to reverse. Deciding to enter a foreign market on a significant scale is a major strategic commitment. Strategic commitments, such as rapid large-scale market entry, can have an important influence on the nature of competition in a market. For example, by entering the U.S. financial services market on a significant scale, ING has signaled its commitment to the market (see the Management Focus). This will have several effects. On the positive side, it will make it easier for the company to attract customers and distributors (such as insurance agents). The scale of entry gives both customers and distributors reasons for believing that ING will remain in the market for the long run. The scale of entry may also give other foreign institutions considering entry into the United States pause; now they will have to compete against not only indigenous institutions in the United States but also an aggressive and successful European institution. On the negative side, by committing itself heavily to the United States, ING may have fewer resources available to support expansion in other desirable markets, such as Japan. The commitment to the United States limits the company's strategic flexibility.

Being the first in an industry to enter a developing nation such as India is risky, but potentially rewarding.

As the ING example suggests, significant strategic commitments are neither unambiguously good nor bad. Rather, they tend to change the competitive playing field and unleash a number of changes, some of which may be desirable and some of which will not be. It is important for a firm to think through the implications of large-scale entry into a market and act accordingly. Of particular relevance is trying to identify how actual and potential competitors might react to large-scale entry into a market. Also, the large-scale entrant is more likely than the small-scale entrant to be able to capture first-mover advantages associated with demand preemption, economies of scale, and switching costs.

The value of the commitments that flow from rapid large-scale entry into a foreign market must be balanced against the resulting risks and lack of flexibility associated with significant commitments. But strategic inflexibility can also have value. A famous example from military history illustrates the value of inflexibility. When Hernán Cortés landed in Mexico, he ordered his men to burn all but one of his ships. Cortés reasoned that by eliminating their only method of retreat, his men had no choice but to fight hard to win against the Aztecs—and ultimately they did.[9]

Balanced against the value and risks of the commitments associated with large-scale entry are the benefits of a small-scale entry. Small-scale entry allows a firm to learn about a foreign market while limiting the firm's exposure to that market. Small-scale entry is a way to gather information about a foreign market before deciding whether to enter on a significant scale and how best to enter. By giving the firm time to collect information, small-scale entry reduces the risks associated with a subsequent large-scale entry. But the lack of commitment associated with small-scale entry may make it more difficult for the small-scale entrant to build market share and to capture first-mover or early-mover advantages. The risk-averse firm that enters a foreign market on a small scale may limit its potential losses, but it may also miss the chance to capture first-mover advantages.

SUMMARY

There are no "right" decisions here, just decisions that are associated with different levels of risk and reward. Entering a large developing nation such as China or India before most other international businesses in the firm's industry, and entering on a large scale, will be associated with high levels of risk. In such cases, the liability of being foreign is increased by the absence of prior foreign entrants whose experience can be a useful guide. At the same time, the potential long-term rewards associated with such a strategy are great. The early large-scale entrant into a major developing nation may be able to capture significant first-mover advantages that will bolster its long-run position in that market.[11] In contrast, entering developed nations such as Australia or Canada after other international businesses in the firm's industry, and entering on a small scale to first learn more about those markets, will be associated with much lower levels of risk. However, the potential long-term rewards are also likely to be lower because the firm is essentially forgoing the opportunity to capture first-mover advantages and because the lack of commitment signaled by small-scale entry may limit its future growth potential.

This section has been written largely from the perspective of a business based in a developed country considering entry into foreign markets. Christopher Bartlett and Sumantra Ghoshal have pointed out that businesses based in developing nations also have the opportunity to enter foreign markets and become global players.[12] Although such firms tend to be late entrants into foreign markets, and although their resources may be limited, Bartlett and Ghoshal argue that such late movers can still succeed against well-established global competitors by pursuing appropriate strategies. In particular, they argue that companies based in developing nations should use the entry of foreign multinationals as an opportunity to learn from these competitors by benchmarking their operations and performance against them. Furthermore, they suggest that the local company may be able to find ways to differentiate itself from a foreign multinational, for example, by focusing on market niches that the multinational ignores or is unable to serve effectively if it has a standardized global product offering. Having improved its performance through learning and differentiated its product offering, the firm from a developing nation may then be able to pursue its own international expansion strategy. Even though the firm may be a late entrant into many countries, by benchmarking and then differentiating itself from early movers in global markets, the firm from the developing nation may still be able to build a strong international business presence. A good example of how this can work is given in the accompanying Management Focus, which looks at how Jollibee, a Philippines-based fast-food chain, has started to build a global presence in a market dominated by U.S. multinationals such as McDonald's and KFC.

Entry Modes

Once a firm decides to enter a foreign market, the question arises as to the best mode of entry. Firms can use six different modes to enter foreign markets: exporting, turnkey projects, licensing, franchising, establishing joint ventures with a host-country firm, or setting up a new wholly owned subsidiary in the host country. Each entry mode has advantages and disadvantages. Managers need to consider these carefully when deciding which to use.[14]

EXPORTING

Many manufacturing firms begin their global expansion as exporters and only later switch to another mode for serving a foreign market. We take a close look at the mechanics of exporting in the next chapter. Here we focus on the advantages and disadvantages of exporting as an entry mode.

Advantages

Exporting has two distinct advantages. First, it avoids the often substantial costs of establishing manufacturing operations in the host country. Second, exporting may help a firm achieve experience curve and location economies (see Chapter 12). By manufacturing the product in a centralized location and exporting it to other national markets, the firm may realize substantial scale economies from its global sales volume. This is how Sony came to dominate the global TV market, how Matsushita came to dominate the VCR market, how many Japanese automakers made inroads into the U.S. market, and how South Korean firms such as Samsung gained market share in computer memory chips.

Disadvantages

Exporting has a number of drawbacks. First, exporting from the firm's home base may not be appropriate if lower cost locations for manufacturing the product can be found abroad (i.e., if the firm can realize location economies by moving production elsewhere). Thus, particularly for firms pursuing global standardization or transnational strategies, it may be preferable to manufacture where the mix of factor conditions is most favorable from a value-creation perspective and to export to the rest of the world from that location. This is not so much an argument against exporting as an argument against exporting from the firm's home country. Many U.S. electronics firms have moved some

The Jollibee Phenomenon—A Philippine Multinational

Jollibee is one of the Philippines' phenomenal business success stories. Jollibee, which stands for "Jolly Bee," began operations in 1975 as a two-branch ice cream parlor. It later expanded its menu to include hot sandwiches and other meals. Encouraged by early success, Jollibee Foods Corporation was incorporated in 1978, with a network that had grown to seven outlets. In 1981, when Jollibee had 11 stores, McDonald's began to open stores in Manila. Many observers thought Jollibee would have difficulty competing against McDonald's. However, Jollibee saw this as an opportunity to learn from a very successful global competitor. Jollibee benchmarked its performance against that of McDonald's and started to adopt operational systems similar to those used at McDonald's to control its quality, cost, and service at the store level. This helped Jollibee improve its performance.

As it came to better understand McDonald's business model, Jollibee began to look for a weakness in McDonald's global strategy. Jollibee executives concluded that McDonald's fare was too standardized for many locals, and that the local firm could gain share by tailoring its menu to local tastes. Jollibee's hamburgers were set apart by a secret mix of spices blended into the ground beef to make the burgers sweeter than those produced by McDonald's, appealing more to Philippine tastes. It also offered local fare including various rice dishes, pineapple burgers, and banana *langka* and peach mango pies for desserts. By pursuing this strategy, Jollibee maintained a leadership position over the global giant. By 2006, Jollibee had over 540 stores in the Philippines, a market share of more than 60 percent, and revenues in excess of $600 million. McDonald's, in contrast, had around 250 stores.

In the mid-1980s, Jollibee had gained enough confidence to expand internationally. Its initial ventures were into neighboring Asian countries such as Indonesia, where it pursued the strategy of localizing the menu to better match local tastes, thereby differentiating itself from McDonald's. In 1987, Jollibee entered the Middle East, where a large contingent of expatriate Filipino workers provided a ready-made market for the company. The strategy of focusing on expatriates worked so well that in the late 1990s Jollibee decided to enter another foreign market where there was a large Filipino population—the United States. Between 1999 and 2004, Jollibee opened eight stores in the United States, all in California. Even though many believe the U.S. fast-food market is saturated, the stores have performed well. While the initial clientele was strongly biased toward the expatriate Filipino community, where Jollibee's brand awareness is high, non-Filipinos increasingly are coming to the restaurant. In the San Francisco store, which has been open the longest, more than half the customers

of their manufacturing to the Far East because of the availability of low-cost, highly skilled labor there. They then export from that location to the rest of the world, including the United States.

A second drawback to exporting is that high transportation costs can make exporting uneconomical, particularly for bulk products. One way of getting around this is to manufacture bulk products regionally. This strategy enables the firm to realize some economies from large-scale production and at the same time to limit its transportation costs. For example, many multinational chemical firms manufacture their products regionally, serving several countries from one facility.

Another drawback is that tariff barriers can make exporting uneconomical. Similarly, the threat of tariff barriers by the host-country government can make it very risky. A fourth drawback to exporting arises when a firm delegates its marketing, sales, and service in each country where it does business to another company. This is a common approach for manufacturing firms that are just beginning to expand internationally. The other company may be a local agent, or it may be another multinational with extensive international distribution operations. Local agents often carry the products of competing firms and so have divided loyalties. In such cases, the local agent may not do as good a are now non-Filipino. Today, Jollibee has 37 international stores and a potentially bright future as a niche player in a market that has historically been dominated by U.S. multinationals.

Recently Jollibee has focused its attentions on two international markets, mainland China and India. It has over 100 stores in China, which operate under the Yonghe brand name (and serve Chinese-style fast food). While it does not yet have a presence in India, the company is reported to be considering its options for entering that nation in 2007 and, for the first time, is reported to be considering acquiring an Indian fast-food chain.[13]

Jollibee may be heading your way! Unlike many fast-food chains that have their roots within the United States, the Jollibee chain originated in the Philippines using McDonald's as a role model.

job as the firm would if it managed its marketing itself. Similar problems can occur when another multinational takes on distribution.

The way around such problems is to set up wholly owned subsidiaries in foreign nations to handle local marketing, sales, and service. By doing this, the firm can exercise tight control over marketing and sales in the country while reaping the cost advantages of manufacturing the product in a single location, or a few choice locations.

TURNKEY PROJECTS

Firms that specialize in the design, construction, and start-up of turnkey plants are common in some industries. In a **turnkey project,** the contractor agrees to handle every detail of the project for a foreign client, including the training of operating personnel. At completion of the contract, the foreign client is handed the "key" to a plant that is ready for full operation—hence, the term *turnkey*. This is a means of exporting process technology to other countries. Turnkey projects are most common in the chemical, pharmaceutical, petroleum refining, and metal refining industries, all of which use complex, expensive production technologies.

Advantages

The know-how required to assemble and run a technologically complex process, such as refining petroleum or steel, is a valuable asset. Turnkey projects are a way of earning great economic returns from that asset. The strategy is particularly useful where foreign direct investment (FDI) is limited by host-government regulations. For example, the governments of many oil-rich countries have set out to build their own petroleum refining industries, so they restrict FDI in their oil and refining sectors. But because many of these countries lack petroleum-refining technology, they gain it by entering into turnkey projects with foreign firms that have the technology. Such deals are often attractive to the selling firm because without them, they would have no way to earn a return on their valuable know-how in that country. A turnkey strategy can also be less risky than conventional FDI. In a country with unstable political and economic environments, a longer-term investment might expose the firm to unacceptable political or economic risks (e.g., the risk of nationalization or of economic collapse).

Disadvantages

Three main drawbacks are associated with a turnkey strategy. First, the firm that enters into a turnkey deal will have no long-term interest in the foreign country. This can be a disadvantage if that country subsequently proves to be a major market for the output of the process that has been exported. One way around this is to take a minority equity interest in the operation. Second, the firm that enters into a turnkey project with a foreign enterprise may inadvertently create a competitor. For example, many of the Western firms that sold oil-refining technology to firms in Saudi Arabia, Kuwait, and other Gulf states now find themselves competing with these firms in the world oil market. Third, if the firm's process technology is a source of competitive advantage, then selling this technology through a turnkey project is also selling competitive advantage to potential or actual competitors.

LICENSING

A **licensing agreement** is an arrangement whereby a licensor grants the rights to intangible property to another entity (the licensee) for a specified period, and in return, the licensor receives a royalty fee from the licensee.[15] Intangible property includes patents, inventions, formulas, processes, designs, copyrights, and trademarks. For example, to enter the Japanese market, Xerox, inventor of the photocopier, established a joint venture with Fuji Photo that is known as Fuji–Xerox. Xerox then licensed its xerographic know-how to Fuji–Xerox. In return, Fuji–Xerox paid Xerox a royalty fee equal to 5 percent of the net sales revenue that Fuji–Xerox earned from the sales of photocopiers based on Xerox's patented know-how. In the Fuji–Xerox case, the license was originally granted for 10 years, and it has been renegotiated and extended several times since. The licensing agreement between Xerox and Fuji–Xerox also limited Fuji–Xerox's direct sales to the Asian Pacific region (although Fuji–Xerox does supply Xerox with photocopiers that are sold in North America under the Xerox label).[16]

Advantages

In the typical international licensing deal, the licensee puts up most of the capital necessary to get the overseas operation going. Thus, a primary advantage of licensing is that the firm does not have to bear the development costs and risks associated with opening a foreign market. Licensing is attractive for firms lacking the capital to develop operations overseas. In addition, licensing can be attractive when a firm is unwilling to commit substantial financial resources to an unfamiliar or politically volatile foreign market. A firm may use licensing when it wishes to participate in a foreign market but is prohibited from doing so by barriers to investment. This was one of the original reasons for the formation of the Fuji–Xerox joint venture in 1962. Xerox wanted to participate in the Japanese market but was prohibited from setting up a wholly owned subsidiary by the Japanese government. So Xerox set up the joint venture with Fuji and then licensed its know-how to the joint venture.

Finally, licensing is frequently used when a firm possesses some intangible property that might have business applications, but it does not want to develop those applications itself. For example, Bell Laboratories at AT&T originally invented the transistor circuit in the 1950s, but AT&T decided it did not want to produce transistors, so it licensed the technology to a number of other companies, such as Texas Instruments. Similarly, Coca-Cola has licensed its famous trademark to clothing manufacturers, which have incorporated the design into clothing.

Disadvantages

Licensing has three serious drawbacks. First, it does not give a firm the tight control over manufacturing, marketing, and strategy that is required for realizing experience curve and location economies. Licensing typically involves each licensee setting up its own production operations. This severely limits the firm's ability to realize experience curve and location economies by producing its product in a centralized location. When these economies are important, licensing may not be the best way to expand overseas.

Second, competing in a global market may require a firm to coordinate strategic moves across countries by using profits earned in one country to support competitive attacks in another. By its very nature, licensing limits a firm's ability to utilize a coordinated strategy. A licensee is unlikely to allow a multinational firm to use its profits (beyond those due in the form of royalty payments) to support a different licensee operating in another country.

A third problem with licensing is one that we encountered in Chapter 7 when we reviewed the economic theory of FDI. This is the risk associated with licensing technological know-how to foreign companies. Technological know-how constitutes the basis of many multinational firms' competitive advantage. Most firms wish to maintain control over how their know-how is used, and a firm can quickly lose control over its technology by licensing it. Many firms have made the mistake of thinking they could maintain control over their know-how within the framework of a licensing agreement. RCA Corporation, for example, once licensed its color TV technology to Japanese firms including Matsushita and Sony. The Japanese firms quickly assimilated the technology, improved on it, and used it to enter the U.S. market, taking substantial market share away from RCA.

There are ways of reducing this risk. One way is to enter into a **cross-licensing agreement** with a foreign firm. Under a cross-licensing agreement, a firm might license some valuable intangible property to a foreign partner, but in addition to a royalty payment, the firm might also request that the foreign partner license some of its valuable know-how to the firm. Such agreements may reduce the risks associated with licensing technological know-how because the licensee realizes that if it violates the licensing contract (by using the knowledge obtained to compete directly with the licensor), the licensor can do the same to it. Cross-licensing agreements enable firms to hold each other hostage, which reduces the probability that they will behave opportunistically toward each other.[17] Such cross-licensing agreements are increasingly common in high-technology industries. For example, the U.S. biotechnology firm Amgen licensed one of its key drugs, Nuprogene, to Kirin, the Japanese pharmaceutical company. The license gives Kirin the right to sell Nuprogene in Japan. In return, Amgen receives a royalty payment and, through a licensing agreement, gained the right to sell some of Kirin's products in the United States.

Another way of reducing the risk associated with licensing is to follow the Fuji–Xerox model and link an agreement to license know-how with the formation of a joint venture in which the licensor and licensee take important equity stakes. Such an approach aligns the interests of licensor and licensee, because both have a stake in ensuring that the venture is successful. Thus, the risk that Fuji Photo might appropriate Xerox's technological know-how, and then compete directly against Xerox in the global photocopier market, was reduced by the establishment of a joint venture in which both Xerox and Fuji Photo had an important stake.

FRANCHISING

Franchising is similar to licensing, although franchising tends to involve longer-term commitments than licensing. **Franchising** is basically a specialized form of licensing in which the franchiser not only sells intangible property (normally a trademark) to the franchisee but also insists that the franchisee agree to abide by strict rules as to how it does business. The franchiser will also often assist the franchisee to run the business on an ongoing basis. As with licensing, the franchiser typically receives a royalty payment, which amounts to some percentage of the franchisee's revenues. Whereas licensing is pursued primarily by manufacturing firms, franchising is employed primarily by service firms.[18] McDonald's is a good example of a firm that has grown by using a franchising strategy. McDonald's strict rules as to how franchisees should operate a restaurant extend to control over the menu, cooking methods, staffing policies, and design and location. McDonald's also organizes the supply chain for its franchisees and provides management training and financial assistance.[19]

Advantages

The advantages of franchising as an entry mode are similar to those of licensing. The firm is relieved of many of the costs and risks of opening a foreign market on its own. Instead, the franchisee typically assumes those costs and risks. This creates a good incentive for the franchisee to build a profitable operation as quickly as possible. Thus, using a franchising strategy, a service firm can build a global presence quickly and at a relatively low cost and risk, as McDonald's has.

Disadvantages

The disadvantages of franchising can be less pronounced than in the case of licensing. Many service companies, such as hotels, use franchising; in such instances, the firm has no reason to consider the need for coordination of manufacturing to achieve experience curve and location economies. But franchising may inhibit the firm's ability to take profits out of one country to support competitive attacks in another. A more significant disadvantage of franchising is quality control. The foundation of franchising arrangements is that the firm's brand name conveys a message to consumers about the quality of the firm's product. Thus, a business traveler checking in at a Four Seasons hotel in Hong Kong can reasonably expect the same quality of room, food, and service that she would receive in New York. The Four Seasons name is supposed to guarantee consistent product quality. This presents a problem in that foreign franchisees may not be as concerned about quality as they are supposed to be, and the result of poor quality can extend beyond lost sales in a particular foreign market to a decline in the firm's worldwide reputation. For example, if the business traveler has a bad experience at the Four Seasons in Hong Kong, she may never go to another Four Seasons hotel and may urge her colleagues to do likewise. The geographical distance of the firm from its foreign franchisees can make poor quality difficult to detect. In addition, the sheer numbers of franchisees—in the case of McDonald's, tens of thousands—can make quality control difficult. Due to these factors, quality problems may persist.

One way around this disadvantage is to set up a subsidiary in each country in which the firm expands. The subsidiary might be wholly owned by the company or a joint venture with a foreign company. The subsidiary assumes the rights and obligations to establish franchises throughout the particular country or region. McDonald's, for example, establishes a master franchisee in many countries. Typically, this master franchisee is a joint venture between McDonald's and a local firm. The proximity and the smaller number of franchises to oversee reduce

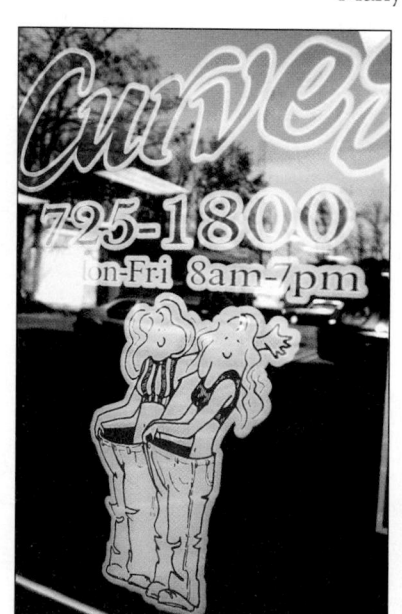

Curves is the largest fitness franchise in the world, with fitness centers in the United States, Europe, Mexico, and Canada, and was ranked the number two franchise in 2004 by *Entrepreneur* magazine.

the quality control challenge. In addition, because the firm at least partially owns the subsidiary (or master franchisee), it can place its own managers there to help ensure that it is doing a good job of monitoring the franchises. This organizational arrangement has proven very satisfactory for McDonald's, KFC, and others.

JOINT VENTURES

A **joint venture** entails establishing a firm that is jointly owned by two or more otherwise independent firms. Fuji–Xerox, for example, was set up as a joint venture between Xerox and Fuji Photo. Establishing a joint venture with a foreign firm has long been a popular mode for entering a new market. The most typical joint venture is a 50/50 venture, in which there are two parties, each of which holds a 50 percent ownership stake and contributes a team of managers to share operating control (this was the case with the Fuji–Xerox joint venture until 2001; it is now a 25/75 venture, with Xerox holding 25 percent). Some firms, however, have sought joint ventures in which they have a majority share and thus tighter control.[20]

Advantages

Joint ventures have a number of advantages. First, a firm benefits from a local partner's knowledge of the host country's competitive conditions, culture, language, political systems, and business systems. Thus, for many U.S. firms, joint ventures have involved the U.S. company providing technological know-how and products and the local partner providing the marketing expertise and the local knowledge necessary for competing in that country. Second, when the development costs or risks of opening a foreign market are high, a firm might gain by sharing these costs and or risks with a local partner. Third, in many countries, political considerations make joint ventures the only feasible entry mode (for an example, this was the case with JCB's entry into India, outlined at the beginning of the chapter). Research suggests joint ventures with local partners face a low risk of being subject to nationalization or other forms of adverse government interference.[21] This appears to be because local equity partners, who may have some influence on host-government policy, have a vested interest in speaking out against nationalization or government interference.

Disadvantages

Despite these advantages, joint ventures have major disadvantages. First, as with licensing, a firm that enters into a joint venture risks giving control of its technology to its partner. Thus, a proposed joint venture in 2002 between Boeing and Mitsubishi Heavy Industries to build a new wide-body jet raised fears that Boeing might unwittingly give away its commercial airline technology to the Japanese. However, joint-venture agreements can be constructed to minimize this risk. One option is to hold majority ownership in the venture. This allows the dominant partner to exercise greater control over its technology. But it can be difficult to find a foreign partner who is willing to settle for minority ownership. Another option is to "wall off" from a partner technology that is central to the core competence of the firm, while sharing other technology.

A second disadvantage is that a joint venture does not give a firm the tight control over subsidiaries that it might need to realize experience curve or location economies. Nor does it give a firm the tight control over a foreign subsidiary that it might need for engaging in coordinated global attacks against its rivals. Consider the entry of Texas Instruments (TI) into the Japanese semiconductor market. When TI established semiconductor facilities in Japan, it did so for the dual purpose of checking Japanese manufacturers' market share and limiting their cash available for invading TI's global market. In other words, TI was engaging in global strategic coordination. To implement this strategy, TI's subsidiary in Japan had to be prepared to take instructions from corporate headquarters regarding competitive strategy. The strategy also required the Japanese subsidiary to run at a loss if necessary. Few if any potential joint-venture partners would have been willing to accept such conditions, since it would have necessitated a willingness to accept a negative return on investment. Indeed, many joint ventures establish a degree of autonomy that would make such direct control over strategic decisions all but impossible to establish.[22] Thus, to implement this strategy, TI set up a wholly owned subsidiary in Japan.

A third disadvantage with joint ventures is that the shared ownership arrangement can lead to conflicts and battles for control between the investing firms if their goals and objectives change or if they take different views as to what the strategy should be. This was apparently not a problem with the Fuji–Xerox joint venture. According to Yotaro Kobayashi, currently the chairman of Fuji–Xerox, a primary reason is that both Xerox and Fuji Photo adopted an arm's-length relationship with Fuji–Xerox, giving the venture's management considerable freedom to determine its own strategy.[23] However, a great deal of research indicates that conflicts of interest over strategy and goals often arise in joint ventures. These conflicts tend to be greater when the venture is between firms of different nationalities, and they often end in the dissolution of the venture.[24] Such conflicts tend to be triggered by shifts in the relative bargaining power of venture partners. For example, in the case of ventures between a foreign firm and a local firm, as a foreign partner's knowledge about local market conditions increases, it depends less on the expertise of a local partner. This increases the bargaining power of the foreign partner and ultimately leads to conflicts over control of the venture's strategy and goals.[25] Some firms have sought to limit such problems by entering into joint ventures in which one partner has a controlling interest.

WHOLLY OWNED SUBSIDIARIES

In a **wholly owned subsidiary,** the firm owns 100 percent of the stock. Establishing a wholly owned subsidiary in a foreign market can be done in two ways. The firm either can set up a new operation in that country, often referred to as a *greenfield venture*, or it can acquire an established firm in that host nation and use that firm to promote its products.[26] For example, as we saw in the Management Focus, ING's strategy for entering the U.S. market was to acquire established U.S. enterprises rather than try to build an operation from the ground floor.

Advantages

Wholly owned subsidiaries have several clear advantages. First, when a firm's competitive advantage is based on technological competence, a wholly owned subsidiary will often be the preferred entry mode because it reduces the risk of losing control over that competence. (See Chapter 7 for more details.) Many high-tech firms prefer this entry mode for overseas expansion (e.g., firms in the semiconductor, electronics, and pharmaceutical industries). As discussed in the chapter's opening case, for example, JCB was unwilling to transfer key technology to its Indian joint venture with Escorts and only did so once it had purchased its venture partner. Second, a wholly owned subsidiary gives a firm tight control over operations in different countries. This control is necessary for engaging in global strategic coordination (i.e., using profits from one country to support competitive attacks in another).

Third, a wholly owned subsidiary may be required if a firm is trying to realize location and experience curve economies (as firms pursuing global and transnational strategies try to do). As we saw in Chapter 12, when cost pressures are intense, it may pay a firm to configure its value chain in such a way that the value added at each stage is maximized. Thus, a national subsidiary may specialize in manufacturing only part of the product line or certain components of the end product, exchanging parts and products with other subsidiaries in the firm's global system. Establishing such a global production system requires a high degree of control over the operations of each affiliate. The various operations must be prepared to accept centrally determined decisions as to how they will produce, how much they will produce, and how their output will be priced for transfer to the next operation. Because licensees or joint-venture partners are unlikely to accept such a subservient role, establishing wholly owned subsidiaries may be necessary. Finally, establishing a wholly owed subsidiary gives the firm a 100 percent share in the profits generated in a foreign market.

Disadvantages

Establishing a wholly owned subsidiary is generally the most costly method of serving a foreign market from a capital investment standpoint. Firms doing this must bear the full capital costs and risks of setting up overseas operations. The risks associated with learning to do business in a new culture are less if the firm acquires an established host-country enterprise. However, acquisitions raise additional problems, including those associated with trying to marry divergent corporate cultures. These problems may more than offset any benefits derived by acquiring an established operation. Because the choice between greenfield ventures and acquisitions is such an important one, we shall discuss it in more detail later in the chapter.

Selecting an Entry Mode

As the preceding discussion demonstrated, all the entry modes have advantages and disadvantages, as summarized in Table 14.1. Thus, trade-offs are inevitable when selecting an entry mode. For example, when considering entry into an unfamiliar country with a track record for discriminating against foreign-owned enterprises when awarding

Entry Mode	Advantages	Disadvantages
Exporting	Ability to realize location and experience curve economies	High transport costs Trade barriers Problems with local marketing agents
Turnkey contracts	Ability to earn returns from process technology skills in countries where FDI is restricted	Creating efficient competitors Lack of long-term market presence
Licensing	Low development costs and risks	Lack of control over technology Inability to realize location and experience curve economies Inability to engage in global strategic coordination
Franchising	Low development costs and risks	Lack of control over quality Inability to engage in global strategic coordination
Joint ventures	Access to local partner's knowledge Sharing development costs and risks Politically acceptable	Lack of control over technology Inability to engage in global strategic coordination Inability to realize location and experience economies
Wholly owned subsidiaries	Protection of technology Ability to engage in global strategic coordination Ability to realize location and experience economies	High costs and risks

TABLE 14.1

Advantages and Disadvantages of Entry Modes

government contracts, a firm might favor a joint venture with a local enterprise. Its rationale might be that the local partner will help it establish operations in an unfamiliar environment and will help the company win government contracts. However, if the firm's core competence is based on proprietary technology, entering a joint venture might risk losing control of that technology to the joint-venture partner, in which case the strategy may seem unattractive. Despite the existence of such trade-offs, it is possible to make some generalizations about the optimal choice of entry mode.[27]

CORE COMPETENCIES AND ENTRY MODE

As we saw in Chapter 12, often firms expand internationally to earn greater returns from their core competencies, transferring the skills and products derived from their core competencies to foreign markets where indigenous competitors lack those skills. The optimal entry mode for these firms depends to some degree on the nature of their core competencies. A distinction can be drawn between firms whose core competency is in technological know-how and those whose core competency is in management know-how.

Technological Know-How

As observed in Chapter 7, if a firm's competitive advantage (its core competency) is based on control over proprietary technological know-how, it should avoid licensing and joint-venture arrangements if possible to minimize the risk of losing control over that technology. Thus, if a high-tech firm sets up operations in a foreign country to profit from a core competency in technological know-how, it will probably do so through a wholly owned subsidiary. This rule should not be viewed as hard and fast, however. Sometimes a licensing or joint-venture arrangement can be structured to reduce the risk of the licensee's or joint-venture partner's expropriation of technological know-how. Another exception exists when a firm perceives its technological advantage to be only transitory, when it expects rapid imitation of its core technology by competitors. In such cases, the firm might want to license its technology as rapidly as possible to foreign firms to gain global acceptance for its technology before the imitation occurs.[28] Such a strategy has some advantages. By licensing its technology to competitors, the firm may deter them from developing their own, possibly superior, technology. Further, by licensing its technology, the firm may establish its technology as the dominant design in the industry (as Matsushita did with its VHS format for VCRs). This may ensure a steady stream of royalty payments. However, the attractions of licensing are frequently outweighed by the risks of losing control over technology, and if this is a risk, the firm should avoid licensing.

Management Know-How

The competitive advantage of many service firms is based on management know-how (e.g., McDonald's). For such firms, the risk of losing control over the management skills to franchisees or joint-venture partners is not that great. These firms' valuable asset is their brand name, and brand names are generally well protected by international laws pertaining to trademarks. Given this, many of the issues arising in the case of technological know-how are of less concern here. As a result, many service firms favor a combination of franchising and subsidiaries to control the franchises within particular countries or regions. The subsidiaries may be wholly owned or joint ventures, but most service firms have found that joint ventures with local partners work best for the controlling subsidiaries. A joint venture is often politically more acceptable and brings a degree of local knowledge to the subsidiary.

PRESSURES FOR COST REDUCTIONS AND ENTRY MODE

The greater the pressures for cost reductions are, the more likely a firm will want to pursue some combination of exporting and wholly owned subsidiaries. By manufacturing in those locations where factor conditions are optimal and then exporting to the rest of the world, a firm may be able to realize substantial location and experience curve economies. The firm might then want to export the finished product to marketing subsidiaries based in various countries. These subsidiaries will typically be wholly owned and have the responsibility for overseeing distribution in their particular countries. Setting up wholly owned marketing subsidiaries is preferable to joint-venture arrangements and to using foreign marketing agents because it gives the firm tight control that might be required for coordinating a globally dispersed value chain. It also gives the firm the ability to use the profits generated in one market to improve its competitive position in another market. In other words, firms pursuing global standardization or transnational strategies tend to prefer establishing wholly owned subsidiaries.

Greenfield Ventures or Acquisitions?

A firm can establish a wholly owned subsidiary in a country by building a subsidiary from the ground up, the so-called greenfield strategy, or by acquiring an enterprise in the target market.[29] The volume of cross-border acquisitions has been growing at a rapid rate for two decades. Over the last decade, between 50 and 80 percent of all FDI inflows have been in the form of mergers and acquisitions. In 2001, for example, mergers and acquisitions accounted for 80 percent of all FDI inflows. In 2005 the figure was 78 percent, or some $716 billion.[30]

PROS AND CONS OF ACQUISITIONS

Acquisitions have three major points in their favor. First, they are quick to execute. By acquiring an established enterprise, a firm can rapidly build its presence in the target foreign market. When the German automobile company Daimler-Benz decided it needed a bigger presence in the U.S. automobile market, it did not increase that presence by building new factories to serve the United States, a process that would have taken years. Instead, it acquired the number three U.S. automobile company, Chrysler, and merged the two operations to form DaimlerChrysler. When the Spanish telecommunications service provider Telefonica wanted to build a service presence in Latin America, it did so through a series of acquisitions, purchasing telecommunications companies in Brazil and Argentina. In these cases, the firms made acquisitions because they knew that was the quickest way to establish a sizable presence in the target market.

Second, in many cases firms make acquisitions to preempt their competitors. The need for preemption is particularly great in markets that are rapidly globalizing, such as telecommunications, where a combination of deregulation within nations and liberalization of regulations governing cross-border foreign direct investment has made it much easier for enterprises to enter foreign markets through acquisitions. Such markets may see concentrated waves of acquisitions as firms race each other to attain global scale. In the telecommunications industry, for example, regulatory changes triggered what can be called a feeding frenzy, with firms entering each other's markets via acquisitions to establish a global presence. These included the $60 billion acquisition of Air Touch Communications in the United States by the British company Vodafone, which was the largest acquisition ever; the $13 billion acquisition of One 2 One in Britain by the German company Deutsche Telekom; and the $6.4 billion acquisition of Excel Communications in the United States by Teleglobe of Canada, all of which occurred in 1998 and 1999.[31] A similar wave of cross-border acquisitions occurred in the global automobile industry over the same time period, with Daimler acquiring Chrysler, Ford acquiring Volvo, and Renault acquiring Nissan.

Third, managers may believe acquisitions to be less risky than greenfield ventures. When a firm makes an acquisition, it buys a set of assets that are producing a known revenue and profit stream. In contrast, the revenue and profit stream that a greenfield venture might generate is uncertain because it does not yet exist. When a firm makes an acquisition in a foreign market, it not only acquires a set of tangible assets, such as factories, logistics systems, customer service systems, and so on, but it also acquires valuable intangible assets including a local brand name and managers' knowledge of the business environment in that nation. Such knowledge can reduce the risk of mistakes caused by ignorance of the national culture.

Despite the arguments for making acquisitions, acquisitions often produce disappointing results.[32] For example, a study by Mercer Management Consulting looked at 150 acquisitions worth more than $500 million each that were undertaken between January 1990 and July 1995.[33] The Mercer study concluded that 50 percent of these acquisitions eroded shareholder value, while another 33 percent created only marginal returns. Only 17 percent were judged to be successful. Similarly, a study by KPMG, an accounting and management consulting company, looked at 700 large acquisitions between 1996 and 1998. The study found that while some 30 percent of these actually created value for the acquiring company, 31 percent destroyed value, and the remainder had little impact.[34] A similar study by McKenzie & Co. estimated that some 70 percent of mergers and acquisitions failed to achieve expected revenue synergies.[35] In a seminal study of the postacquisition performance of acquired companies, David Ravenscraft and Mike Scherer concluded that on average the profits and market shares of acquired companies declined following acquisition.[36] They also noted that a smaller but substantial subset of those companies experienced traumatic difficulties, which ultimately led to the acquiring company selling them. Ravenscraft and Scherer's evidence suggests that many acquisitions destroy rather than create value. Most of this research has looked at domestic acquisitions; however, the findings probably also apply to cross-border acquisitions.[37]

Why Do Acquisitions Fail?

Acquisitions fail for several reasons. First, the acquiring firms often overpay for the assets of the acquired firm. The price of the target firm can get bid up if more than one firm is interested in its purchase, as is often the case. In addition, the management of the acquiring firm is often too optimistic about the value that can be created via an acquisition and is thus willing to pay a significant premium over a target firm's market capitalization. This is called the *hubris hypothesis* of why acquisitions fail. The hubris hypothesis postulates that top managers typically overestimate their ability to create value from an acquisition, primarily because rising to the top of a corporation has given them an exaggerated sense of their own capabilities.[38] For example, Daimler acquired Chrysler in 1998 for $40 billion, a premium of 40 percent over the market value of Chrysler before the takeover bid. Daimler paid this much because it thought it could use Chrysler to help it grow market share in the United States. At the time, Daimler's management issued bold announcements about the "synergies" that would be created from combining the operations of the two companies. Executives believed they could attain greater economies of scale from the global presence, take costs out of the German and U.S. operations, and boost the profitability of the combined entity. However, within a year of the acquisition, Daimler's German management faced a crisis at Chrysler, which was suddenly losing money because of weak sales in the United States. In retrospect, Daimler's management had been far too optimistic about the potential for future demand in the U.S. auto market and about the opportunities for creating value from synergies. Daimler acquired Chrysler at the end of a multiyear boom in U.S. auto sales and paid a large premium over Chrysler's market value just before demand slumped.[39]

Second, many acquisitions fail because of a clash between the cultures of the acquiring and acquired firms. After an acquisition, many acquired companies experience high management turnover, possibly because their employees do not like the acquiring company's way of doing things.[40] This happened at DaimlerChrysler; many senior managers left Chrysler in the first year after the merger. Apparently, Chrysler executives disliked the dominance in decision making by Daimler's German managers, while the Germans resented that Chrysler's American managers were paid two to three times as much as their German counterparts. These cultural differences created tensions, which ultimately exhibited themselves in high management turnover at Chrysler.[41] The loss of management talent and expertise can materially harm the performance of the acquired unit.[42] This may be particularly problematic in an international business, where management of the acquired unit may have valuable local knowledge that can be difficult to replace.

Third, many acquisitions fail because attempts to realize synergies by integrating the operations of the acquired and acquiring entities often run into roadblocks and take much longer than forecast. Differences in management philosophy and company culture can slow the integration of operations. Differences in national culture may exacerbate these problems. Bureaucratic haggling between managers also complicates the process. Again, this reportedly occurred at DaimlerChrysler, where grand plans to integrate the operations of the two companies were bogged down by endless committee meetings and by simple logistical considerations such as the six-hour time difference between Detroit and Germany. By the time an integration plan had been worked out, Chrysler was losing money, and Daimler's German managers had a crisis on their hands.

Finally, many acquisitions fail due to inadequate preacquisition screening.[43] Many firms decide to acquire other firms without thoroughly analyzing the potential benefits and costs. They often move with undue haste to execute the acquisition, perhaps because they fear another competitor may preempt them. After the acquisition, however, many acquiring firms discover that instead of buying a well-run business, they have purchased a troubled organization. This may be a particular problem in cross-border acquisitions because the acquiring firm may not fully understand the target firm's national culture and business system.

Reducing the Risks of Failure

A firm can overcome all these problems if it is careful about its acquisition strategy.[44] Screening of the foreign enterprise to be acquired, including a detailed auditing of operations, financial position, and management culture, can help to make sure the firm (1) does not pay too much for the acquired unit, (2) does not uncover any nasty surprises after the acquisition, and (3) acquires a firm whose organization culture is not antagonistic to that of the acquiring enterprise. It is also important for the acquirer to allay any concerns that management in the acquired enterprise might have. The objective should be to reduce unwanted management attrition after the acquisition. Finally, managers must move rapidly after an acquisition to put an integration plan in place and to act on that plan. Some people in both the acquiring and acquired units will try to slow or stop any integration efforts, particularly when losses of employment or management power are involved, and managers should have a plan for dealing with such impediments before they arise.

PROS AND CONS OF GREENFIELD VENTURES

The big advantage of establishing a greenfield venture in a foreign country is that it gives the firm a much greater ability to build the kind of subsidiary company that it wants. For example, it is much easier to build an organization culture from scratch than it is to change the culture of an acquired unit. Similarly, it is much easier to establish a set of operating routines in a new subsidiary than it is to convert the operating routines of an acquired unit. This is a very important advantage for many international businesses, where transferring products, competencies, skills, and know-how from the established operations of the firm to the new subsidiary are principal ways of creating value. For example, when Lincoln Electric, the U.S. manufacturer of arc welding equipment, first ventured overseas in the mid-1980s, it did so by acquisitions, purchasing arc welding equipment companies in Europe. However, Lincoln's competitive advantage in the United States was based on a strong organizational culture and a unique set of incentives that encouraged its employees to do everything possible to increase productivity. Lincoln found through bitter experience that it was almost impossible to transfer its organizational culture and incentives to acquired firms, which had their own distinct organizational cultures and incentives. As a result, the firm switched its entry strategy in the mid-1990s and began to enter foreign countries by establishing greenfield ventures, building operations from the ground up. While this strategy takes more time to execute, Lincoln has found that it yields greater long-run returns than the acquisition strategy.

Set against this significant advantage are the disadvantages of establishing a greenfield venture. Greenfield ventures are slower to establish. They are also risky. As with any new venture, a degree of uncertainty is associated with future revenue and profit prospects. However, if the firm has already been successful in other foreign markets and understands what it takes to do business in other countries, these risks may not be that great. For example, having already gained substantial knowledge about operating internationally, the risk to McDonald's of entering yet another country is probably not that great. Also, greenfield ventures are less risky than acquisitions in the sense that there is less potential for unpleasant surprises. A final disadvantage is the possibility of being preempted by more aggressive global competitors that enter via acquisitions and build a big market presence that limits the market potential for the greenfield venture.

GREENFIELD OR ACQUISITION?

The choice between making an acquisition or establishing a greenfield venture is not an easy one. Both modes have their advantages and disadvantages. In general, the choice will depend on the circumstances confronting the firm. If the firm is seeking to enter a market in which there are already well-established incumbent enterprises, and in which global competitors are also interested in establishing a presence, acquisition may be the better mode of entry. In such circumstances, a greenfield venture may be too slow to establish a sizable presence. However, if the firm is going to make an acquisition, its management should be cognizant of the risks discussed earlier and consider these when determining which firms to purchase. It may be better to enter by the slower route of a greenfield venture than to make a bad acquisition.

If the firm is considering entering a country in which there are no incumbent competitors to be acquired, then a greenfield venture may be the only mode. Even when incumbents exist, if the competitive advantage of the firm is based on the transfer of organizationally embedded competencies, skills, routines, and culture, it may still be preferable to enter via a greenfield venture. Things such as skills and organizational culture, which are based on significant knowledge that is difficult to articulate and codify, are much easier to embed in a new venture than they are in an acquired entity, where the firm may have to overcome the established routines and culture of the acquired firm. Thus, as our earlier examples suggest, firms such as McDonald's and Lincoln Electric prefer to enter foreign markets by establishing greenfield ventures.

Strategic Alliances

Strategic alliances refer to cooperative agreements between potential or actual competitors. In this section, we are concerned specifically with strategic alliances between firms from different countries. Strategic alliances run the range from formal joint ventures, in which two or more firms have equity stakes (e.g., Fuji–Xerox), to short-term contractual agreements, in which two companies agree to cooperate on a particular task (such as developing a new product). Collaboration between competitors is fashionable; recent decades have seen an explosion in the number of strategic alliances.

THE ADVANTAGES OF STRATEGIC ALLIANCES

Firms ally themselves with actual or potential competitors for various strategic purposes.[45] First, strategic alliances may facilitate entry into a foreign market. For example, many firms feel that if they are to successfully enter the Chinese market, they need a local

Cisco and Fujitsu

In late 2004, Cisco Systems, the world's largest manufacturer of Internet routers, entered into an alliance with Fujitsu, the Japanese computer, electronics, and telecommunications equipment firm. The stated purpose of the alliance was to jointly develop next-generation high-end routers for sales in Japan. Routers are the digital switches that sit at the heart of the Internet and direct traffic; they are, in effect, the traffic cops of the Internet. Although Cisco has long held the leading share in the market for routers—indeed, it pioneered the original router technology—it faces increasing competition from other firms such as Juniper Technologies and China's fast-growing Huawei Technologies. At the same time, demand in the market is shifting as more and more telecommunications companies adopt Internet-based telecommunications services. Although Cisco has long had a strong global presence, management felt that the company needed to have a better presence in Japan, which is shifting rapidly to second-generation high-speed Internet-based telecommunications networks.

By entering into an alliance with Fujitsu, Cisco feels it can achieve a number of goals. First, both firms can pool their R&D efforts, which will enable them to share

complementary technology and develop products quicker, thereby gaining an advantage over competitors. Second, by combining Cisco's proprietary leading-edge router technology with Fujitsu's production expertise, the companies believe that they can produce products that are more reliable than those currently on offer. Third, Fujitsu will give Cisco a stronger sales presence in Japan. Fujitsu has good links with Japan's telecommunications companies and a well-earned reputation for reliability. It will leverage these assets to sell the routers the alliance produces, which will be co-branded as Fujitsu–Cisco products. Fourth, sales may be further enhanced by bundling the co-branded routers together with other telecommunications equipment that Fujitsu sells and marketing an entire solution to customers. Fujitsu sells many telecommunications products, but it lacks a strong presence in routers. Cisco is strong in routers, but it lacks strong offerings elsewhere. The combination of the two companies' products will enable Fujitsu to offer Japan's telecommunications companies end-to-end communications solutions. Since many companies prefer to purchase their equipment from a single provider, this should drive sales. The alliance introduced its first products in May 2006.[50]

partner who understands business conditions and who has good connections (or *guanxi*—see Chapter 3). Thus, in 2004 Warner Brothers entered into a joint venture with two Chinese partners to produce and distribute films in China. As a foreign film company, Warner found that if it wanted to produce films on its own for the Chinese market it had to go through a complex approval process for every film, and it had to farm out distribution to a local company, which made doing business in China very difficult. Due to the participation of Chinese firms, however, the joint-venture films will go through a streamlined approval process, and the venture will be able to distribute any films it produces. Moreover, the joint venture will be able to produce films for Chinese TV, something that foreign firms are not allowed to do.[46]

Second, strategic alliances allow firms to share the fixed costs (and associated risks) of developing new products or processes. An alliance between Boeing and a number of Japanese companies to build Boeing's latest commercial jetliner, the 787, was motivated by Boeing's desire to share the estimated $8 billion investment required to develop the aircraft. For another example of cost sharing, see the accompanying Management Focus, which discusses the strategic alliances between Cisco and Fujitsu.

Third, an alliance is a way to bring together complementary skills and assets that neither company could easily develop on its own.[47] In 2003, for example, Microsoft and Toshiba established an alliance aimed at developing embedded microprocessors (essentially tiny computers) that can perform a variety of entertainment functions in an automobile (e.g., run a backseat DVD player or a wireless Internet connection). The processors will run a version of Microsoft's Windows CE operating system. Microsoft brings its software engineering skills to the alliance and Toshiba its skills in developing microprocessors.[48] The alliance between Cisco and Fujitsu was also formed to share know-how (see the Management Focus).

Fourth, it can make sense to form an alliance that will help the firm establish technological standards for the industry that will benefit the firm. For example, in 1999 Palm Computer, the leading maker of personal digital assistants (PDAs), entered into an alliance with Sony under which Sony agreed to license and use Palm's operating system in Sony PDAs. The motivation for the alliance was in part to help establish Palm's operating system as the industry standard for PDAs, as opposed to a rival Windows-based operating system from Microsoft.[49]

THE DISADVANTAGES OF STRATEGIC ALLIANCES

The advantages we have discussed can be significant. Despite this, some commentators have criticized strategic alliances on the grounds that they give competitors a low-cost route to new technology and markets.[51] For example, a few years ago some commentators argued that many strategic alliances between U.S. and Japanese firms were part of an implicit Japanese strategy to keep high-paying, high-value-added jobs in Japan while gaining the project engineering and production process skills that underlie the competitive success of many U.S. companies.[52] They argued that Japanese success in the machine tool and semiconductor industries was built on U.S. technology acquired through strategic alliances. And they argued that U.S. managers were aiding the Japanese by entering alliances that channel new inventions to Japan and provide a U.S. sales and distribution network for the resulting products. Although such deals may generate short-term profits, so the argument goes, in the long run the result is to "hollow out" U.S. firms, leaving them with no competitive advantage in the global marketplace.

These critics have a point; alliances have risks. Unless a firm is careful, it can give away more than it receives. But there are so many examples of apparently successful alliances between firms—including alliances between U.S. and Japanese firms—that their position seems extreme. It is difficult to see how the Microsoft–Toshiba alliance, the Boeing–Mitsubishi alliance for the 787, or the Fuji–Xerox alliance fit the critics' thesis. In these cases, both partners seem to have gained from the alliance. Why do some alliances benefit both firms while others benefit one firm and hurt the other? The next section provides an answer to this question.

MAKING ALLIANCES WORK

The failure rate for international strategic alliances seems to be high. One study of 49 international strategic alliances found that two-thirds run into serious managerial and financial troubles within two years of their formation, and that although many of these problems are solved, 33 percent are ultimately rated as failures by the parties involved.[53] The success of an alliance seems to be a function of three main factors: partner selection, alliance structure, and the manner in which the alliance is managed.

Partner Selection

One key to making a strategic alliance work is to select the right ally. A good ally, or partner, has three characteristics. First, a good partner helps the firm achieve its strategic goals, whether they are market access, sharing the costs and risks of product development, or gaining access to critical core competencies. The partner must have capabilities that the firm lacks and that it values. Second, a good partner shares the firm's vision for the purpose of the alliance. If two firms approach an alliance with radically different agendas, the chances are great that the relationship will not be harmonious, will not flourish, and will end in divorce. Third, a good partner is unlikely to try to opportunistically exploit the alliance for its own ends; that is, to expropriate the firm's technological know-how while giving away little in return. In this respect, firms with reputations for fair play to maintain probably make the best allies. For example, IBM is involved in so many strategic alliances that it would not pay the company to trample over individual alliance partners (in early 2003, IBM reportedly had more than 150 major strategic alliances).[54] This would tarnish IBM's reputation of being a good ally and would make it more difficult for the company to attract alliance partners. Because IBM attaches great importance to its alliances, it is unlikely to engage in the kind of opportunistic behavior that critics highlight. Similarly, their reputations make it less likely (but by no means impossible) that such Japanese firms as Sony, Toshiba, and Fuji, which have histories of alliances with non-Japanese firms, would opportunistically exploit an alliance partner.

To select a partner with these three characteristics, a firm needs to conduct comprehensive research on potential alliance candidates. To increase the probability of selecting a good partner, the firm should

1. Collect as much pertinent, publicly available information on potential allies as possible.
2. Gather data from informed third parties, including firms that have had alliances with the potential partners, investment bankers who have had dealings with them, and former employees.
3. Get to know the potential partner as well as possible before committing to an alliance. This process should include face-to-face meetings between senior managers (and perhaps middle-level managers) to ensure that the chemistry is right.

Alliance Structure

Once a partner has been selected, the alliance should be structured so that the firm's risks of giving too much away to the partner are reduced to an acceptable level. First, alliances can be designed to make it difficult, if not impossible, to transfer technology not meant to be transferred. The design, development, manufacture, and service of a product manufactured by an alliance can be structured so as to wall off sensitive technologies to prevent their leakage to the other participant. In an alliance between General Electric and Snecma to build commercial aircraft engines, for example, GE reduced the risk of excess transfer by walling off certain sections of the production process. The modularization effectively cut off the transfer of what GE regarded as key competitive technology, while permitting Snecma access to final assembly. Similarly, in the alliance between Boeing and the Japanese to build the 767, Boeing walled off research, design, and marketing functions considered central to its competitive position, while allowing the Japanese to share in production technology. Boeing also walled off new technologies not required for 767 production.[55]

Second, contractual safeguards can be written into an alliance agreement to guard against the risk of opportunism by a partner. (Opportunism includes the theft of technology or markets.) For example, TRW, Inc., has three strategic alliances with large Japanese auto component suppliers to produce seat belts, engine valves, and steering gears for sale to Japanese-owned auto assembly plants in the United States. TRW has clauses in each of its alliance contracts that bar the Japanese firms from competing with TRW to supply U.S.-owned auto companies with component parts. By doing this, TRW protects itself against the possibility that the Japanese companies are entering into the alliances merely to gain access to the North American market to compete with TRW in its home market.

Third, both parties to an alliance can agree in advance to swap skills and technologies that the other covets, thereby ensuring a chance for equitable gain. Cross-licensing agreements are one way to achieve this goal. Fourth, the risk of an alliance partner's opportunism can be reduced if the firm extracts a significant credible commitment from its partner in advance. The long-term alliance between Xerox and Fuji to build photocopiers for the Asian market perhaps best illustrates this. Rather than enter into an informal agreement or a licensing arrangement (which Fuji Photo initially wanted), Xerox insisted that Fuji invest in a 50/50 joint venture to serve Japan and East Asia. This venture constituted such a significant investment in people, equipment, and facilities that Fuji was committed from the outset to making the alliance work in order to earn a return on its investment. By agreeing to the joint venture, Fuji essentially made a credible commitment to the alliance. Given this commitment, Xerox felt secure in transferring its photocopier technology to Fuji.[56]

Managing the Alliance

Once a firm has selected a partner and the parties have agreed on an appropriate alliance structure, the task facing each is to maximize the benefits it gains from the alliance. As in all international business deals, an important factor is sensitivity to cultural differences (see Chapter 3). Many differences in management style are attributable to cultural differences, and managers need to make allowances for these in dealing with their partner. Beyond this, maximizing the benefits from an alliance seems to involve building trust between partners and learning from partners.[57]

Managing an alliance successfully requires building interpersonal relationships between the firms' managers, or what is sometimes referred to as *relational capital*.[58] This is one lesson that can be drawn from a successful strategic alliance between Ford and Mazda. The two companies set up a framework of meetings within which their managers not only discuss matters pertaining to the alliance but also have time to get to know each other better. The belief is that the resulting friendships help build trust and facilitate harmonious relations between the two firms. Personal relationships also foster an informal management network between the firms. This network can then be used to help solve problems arising in more formal contexts (such as in joint committee meetings between personnel from the two firms).

Academics have argued that a major determinant of how much knowledge a company gains from an alliance is its ability to learn from its alliance partner.[59] For example, in a five-year study of 15 strategic alliances between major multinationals, Gary Hamel, Yves Doz, and C. K. Prahalad focused on a number of alliances between Japanese companies and Western (European or American) partners.[60] In every case in which a Japanese company emerged from an alliance stronger than its Western partner, the Japanese company had made a greater effort to learn. Few Western companies studied seemed to want to learn from their Japanese partners. They tended to regard the alliance purely as a cost-sharing or risk-sharing device, rather than as an opportunity to learn how a potential competitor does business.

Consider the alliance formed between General Motors and Toyota in 1985 to build the Chevrolet Nova. This alliance was structured as a formal joint venture, called New United Motor Manufacturing, Inc., and each party had a 50 percent equity stake. The venture owned an auto plant in Fremont, California. According to one Japanese manager, Toyota quickly achieved most of its objectives from the alliance: "We learned about U.S. supply and transportation. And we got the confidence to manage U.S. workers."[61] All that knowledge was then transferred to Georgetown, Kentucky, where Toyota opened its own plant in 1988. Possibly all GM got was a new product, the Chevrolet Nova. Some GM managers complained that the knowledge they gained through the alliance with Toyota has never been put to good use inside GM. They believe they should have been kept together as a team to educate GM's engineers and workers about the Japanese system. Instead, they were dispersed to various GM subsidiaries.

To maximize the learning benefits of an alliance, a firm must try to learn from its partner and then apply the knowledge within its own organization. It has been suggested that all operating employees should be well briefed on the partner's strengths and weaknesses and should understand how acquiring particular skills will bolster their firm's competitive position. Hamel, Doz, and Prahalad note that this is already standard practice among Japanese companies. They made this observation:

We accompanied a Japanese development engineer on a tour through a partner's factory. This engineer dutifully took notes on plant layout, the number of production stages, the rate at which the line was running, and the number of employees. He recorded all this despite the fact that he had no manufacturing responsibility in his own company, and that the alliance did not encompass joint manufacturing. Such dedication greatly enhances learning.[62]

For such learning to be of value, it must be diffused throughout the organization (as was seemingly not the case at GM after the GM–Toyota joint venture). To diffuse learning, the managers involved in the alliance should educate their colleagues about the skills of the alliance partner.

CHAPTER SUMMARY

The chapter made the following points:

1. Basic entry decisions include identifying which markets to enter, when to enter those markets, and on what scale.

2. The most attractive foreign markets tend to be found in politically stable developed and developing nations that have free market systems and where there is not a dramatic upsurge in either inflation rates or private-sector debt.

3. Several advantages are associated with entering a national market early, before other international businesses have established themselves. These advantages must be balanced against the pioneering costs that early entrants often have to bear, including the greater risk of business failure.

4. Large-scale entry into a national market constitutes a major strategic commitment that is likely to change the nature of competition in that market and limit the entrant's future strategic flexibility. Although making major strategic commitments can yield many benefits, risks are also associated with such a strategy.

5. A firm can enter a foreign market in six ways: exporting, creating turnkey projects, licensing, franchising, establishing joint ventures, and setting up a wholly owned subsidiary.

6. Exporting has the advantages of facilitating the realization of experience curve economies and of avoiding the costs of setting up manufacturing operations in another country. Disadvantages include high transportation costs, trade barriers, and problems with local marketing agents.

7. Turnkey projects allow firms to export their process know-how to countries where FDI might be prohibited, thereby enabling the firm to earn a greater return from this asset. The disadvantage is that the firm may inadvertently create efficient global competitors in the process.

8. The main advantage of licensing is that the licensee bears the costs and risks of opening a foreign market. Disadvantages include the risk of losing technological know-how to the licensee and a lack of tight control over licensees.

9. The main advantage of franchising is that the franchisee bears the costs and risks of opening a foreign market. Disadvantages center on problems of quality control of distant franchisees.

10. Joint ventures have the advantages of sharing the costs and risks of opening a foreign market and of gaining local knowledge and political influence. Disadvantages include the risk of losing control over technology and a lack of tight control.

11. The advantages of wholly owned subsidiaries include tight control over technological know-how. The main disadvantage is that the firm must bear all the costs and risks of opening a foreign market.

12. The optimal choice of entry mode depends on the firm's strategy. When technological know-how constitutes a firm's core competence, wholly owned subsidiaries are preferred, since they best control technology. When management know-how constitutes a firm's core competence, foreign franchises controlled by joint ventures seem to be optimal. When the firm is pursuing a global standardization or transnational strategy, the need for tight control over operations to realize location and experience curve economies suggests wholly owned subsidiaries are the best entry mode.

13. When establishing a wholly owned subsidiary in a country, a firm must decide whether to do so by a greenfield venture strategy or by acquiring an established enterprise in the target market.

14. Acquisitions are quick to execute, may enable a firm to preempt its global competitors, and involve buying a known revenue and profit stream. Acquisitions may fail when the acquiring firm overpays for the target, when the cultures of the acquiring and acquired firms clash, when there is a high level of management attrition after the acquisition, and when there is a failure to integrate the operations of the acquiring and acquired firms.

15. The advantage of a greenfield venture in a foreign country is that it gives the firm a much greater ability to build the kind of subsidiary company that it wants. For example, it is much easier to build an organization culture from scratch than it is to change the culture of an acquired unit.

16. Strategic alliances are cooperative agreements between actual or potential competitors. The advantages of alliances are that they facilitate entry into foreign markets, enable partners to share the fixed costs and risks associated with new products and processes, facilitate the transfer of complementary skills between companies, and help firms establish technical standards.

17. The disadvantage of a strategic alliance is that the firm risks giving away technological know-how and market access to its alliance partner.

18. The disadvantages associated with alliances can be reduced if the firm selects partners carefully, paying close attention to the firm's reputation and the structure of the alliance so as to avoid unintended transfers of know-how.

19. Two keys to making alliances work seem to be building trust and informal communications networks between partners and taking proactive steps to learn from alliance partners.

Critical Thinking and Discussion Questions

1. Licensing proprietary technology to foreign competitors is the best way to give up a firm's competitive advantage. Discuss.

2. Discuss how the need for control over foreign operations varies with firms' strategies and core competencies. What are the implications for the choice of entry mode?

3. Under what circumstances are joint ventures to be preferred to wholly owned subsidiaries as the most appropriate mode for entering foreign nations?

4. In recent years the number of cross-border mergers and acquisitions has ballooned. What are the risks associated with the popularity of this vehicle for entering foreign markets? Can you find an example in recent press reports of such risks? How can these risks be reduced?

5. A small Canadian firm that has developed some valuable new medical products using its unique biotechnology know-how is trying to decide how best to serve the European Union. Its choices are given below. The cost of investment in manufacturing facilities will be a major one for the Canadian firm, but it is not outside its reach. If these are the firm's only options, which one would you advise it to choose? Why?

   a. Manufacture the product at home and let foreign sales agents handle marketing.

   b. Manufacture the product at home and set up a wholly owned subsidiary in Europe to handle marketing.

   c. Enter into an alliance with a large European pharmaceutical firm. The product would be manufactured in Europe by the 50/50 joint venture and marketed by the European firm.

6. Reread the Management Focus on international expansion at the ING Group and then answer the following questions:

   a. Why did ING focus on entering the U.S. market rather than, for example, emerging markets such as China and India?

   b. What explains the timing of ING's entry into the U.S. market?

   c. ING entered the U.S. insurance and investment banking market through acquisitions, rather than beginning from scratch. Why do you think the company chose this entry mode? What are the advantages and disadvantages?

   d. Why do you think ING opted to begin its Internet bank, ING Direct, from scratch in the United States?

7. Reread the Management Focus on the Jollibee phenomenon; then answer the following questions:

a. What explains the pattern of Jollibee's international expansion? Why do you think it entered the countries it did?

b. Jollibee's expansion into the United States has been quite limited. Why might this be so?

c. Jollibee now seems to be focusing on India and China for oversees growth. Why are these countries attractive to Jollibee?

d. Why is Jollibee considering entering India via an acquisition?

8. Reread the case about JCB at the beginning of the chapter, then answer the following questions:

a. Do you think entering India via a joint venture was JCB's optimal choice in 1979? What other options did it have?

b. Why do you think JCB picked India for its first direct foreign investment?

c. Was JCB right to take full control of its Indian joint venture in the 2000s?

9. Reread the Management Focus on Cisco and Fujitsu; then answer the following questions:

a. What are the benefits of Cisco's alliance with Fujitsu? What are the risks and associated costs?

b. Given your assessment of the benefits, risks, and cost associated with this alliance, did it make sense for Cisco to enter the alliance?

c. How might Cisco mitigate the risks associated with the alliance?

Research Task

Use the globalEDGE™ site to complete the following exercises:

1. A vital element in a successful international market entry strategy is an appropriate fit of skills and capabilities between partners. As such, the *Entrepreneur* magazine annually publishes a ranking of America's top 200 franchisors seeking international franchisees. Provide a list of the top 10 companies that pursue franchising as a mode of international expansion. Study one of these companies in detail and provide a description of its business model, its international expansion pattern, desirable qualifications in possible franchisees, and the support and training typically provided by the franchisor.

2. The U.S. Commercial Service prepares reports known as the "Country Commercial Guide" for countries of interest to U.S. investors. Utilize the Country Commercial Guide for Brazil to gather information on this country. Considering that your company is producing laptop computers and is considering entering this country, select the most appropriate entry method, supporting your decision with the information collected.

CLOSING CASE

Tesco Goes Global

Tesco is the largest grocery retailer in the United Kingdom, with a 25 percent share of the local market. In its home market, the company's strengths are reputed to come from strong competencies in marketing and store site selection, logistics and inventory management, and its own label product offerings. By the early 1990s, these competencies had already given the company a leading position in the United Kingdom. The company was generating strong cash flows, and senior management had to decide how to use that cash. One strategy they settled on was overseas expansion. As they looked at international markets, they soon concluded that the best opportunities were not in established markets, such as those in North America and Western Europe, where strong local competitors already existed, but in the emerging markets of Eastern Europe and Asia where there were few capable competitors but strong underlying growth trends.

Tesco's first international foray was into Hungary in 1994, when it acquired an initial 51 percent stake in Global, a 43-store, state-owned grocery chain. By 2004, Tesco was the market leader in Hungary, with some 60 stores and a 14 percent market share. In 1995, Tesco acquired 31 stores in Poland from Stavia; a year later it added 13 stores purchased from Kmart in the Czech Republic and Slovakia; and the following year it entered the Republic of Ireland.

Tesco's Asian expansion began in 1998 in Thailand when it purchased 75 percent of Lotus, a local food retailer with 13 stores. Building on that base, Tesco had 64 stores in Thailand by 2004. In 1999, the company entered South Korea, where it partnered with Samsung to develop a chain of hypermarkets. This was followed by entry into Taiwan in 2000, Malaysia in 2002, and China in 2004. The move into China came after three years of careful research and discussions with potential partners. Like many other Western companies, Tesco was attracted to the Chinese market by its large size and rapid growth. In the end, Tesco settled on a 50/50 joint venture with Hymall, a hypermarket chain that is controlled by Ting Hsin, a Taiwanese group that had been operating in China for six years. Currently, Hymall has 25 stores in China, and it plans to open another 10 each year. Ting Hsin is a well-capitalized enterprise in its own right, and it will match Tesco's investments, reducing the risks Tesco faces in China.

As a result of these moves, by early 2005 Tesco had 814 stores outside the United Kingdom, which generated £9.2 billion in annual revenues. In the United Kingdom, Tesco had some 1,900 stores, generating £32 billion. The addition of international stores has helped to make Tesco the fourth-largest company in the global grocery market behind Wal-Mart, Carrefore of France, and Ahold of Holland. Of the four, however, Tesco may be the most successful internationally. By 2005, all of its foreign ventures were making money.

In explaining the company's success, Tesco's managers have detailed a number of important factors. First, the company devotes considerable attention to transferring its core capabilities in retailing to its new ventures. At the same time, it does not send in an army of expatriate managers to run local operations, preferring to hire local managers and support them with a few operational experts from the United Kingdom. Second, the company believes that its partnering strategy in Asia has been a great asset. Tesco has teamed up with good companies that have a deep understanding of the markets in which they are participating, but that lack Tesco's financial strength and retailing capabilities. Consequently, both Tesco and its partners have brought useful assets to the venture, which have increased the probability of success. As the venture becomes established, Tesco has typically increased its ownership stake in its partner. Thus, under current plans, by 2011 Tesco will own 99 percent of Homeplus, its South Korean hypermarket chain. When the venture was established, Tesco owned 51 percent. Third, the company has focused on markets with good growth potential but that lack strong indigenous competitors, which provides Tesco with ripe ground for expansion.

In March 2006, Tesco took its international expansion strategy to the next level when it announced it would enter the crowded United States grocery market with its Tesco Express concept. Currently running in five countries, Tesco Express stores are smaller, high-quality neighborhood grocery outlets that feature a large selection of prepared and healthy foods. Tesco will initially enter on the West Coast, investing some £250 million per year, with breakeven expected in the second year of operation. Although some question the wisdom of this move, others point out that in the United Kingdom Tesco has consistently outperformed the ASDA chain, which is owned by Wal-Mart. Moreover, the Tesco Express format is not something found in the United States.[63]

Case Discussion Questions

1. Why did Tesco's initial international expansion strategy focus on developing nations?

2. How does Tesco create value in its international operations?

3. In Asia, Tesco has a long history of entering into joint venture agreements with local partners. What are the benefits of doing this for Tesco? What are the risks? How are those risks mitigated?

4. In March 2006, Tesco announced that it would enter the United States. This represents a departure from its historic strategy of focusing on developing nations. Why do you think Tesco made this decision? How is the U.S. market different from others Tesco has entered? What are the risks here? How do you think Tesco will do?

Notes

1. Sources: P. Marsh, "Partnerships Feel the Indian Heat," *Financial Times*, June 22, 2006, p. 11; P. Marsh, "JCB Targets Asia to Spread Production," *Financial Times*, March 16, 2005, p. 26; D. Jones, "Profits Jump at JCB," *Daily Post*, June 20, 2006, p. 21; R. Bentley, "Still Optimistic about Asia," *Asian Business Review*, October 1, 1999, p. 1.

2. For interesting empirical studies that deal with the issues of timing and resource commitments, see T. Isobe, S. Makino, and D. B. Montgomery, "Resource Commitment, Entry Timing, and Market Performance of Foreign Direct Investments in Emerging Economies," *Academy of Management Journal* 43, no. 3 (2000), pp. 468–84; and Y. Pan and P. S. K. Chi, "Financial Performance and Survival of Multinational Corporations in China," *Strategic Management Journal* 20, no. 4 (1999), pp. 359–74. A complementary theoretical perspective on this issue can be found in V. Govindarjan and A. K. Gupta, *The Quest for Global Dominance* (San Francisco: Jossey-Bass, 2001). Also see F. Vermeulen and H. Barkeme, "Pace, Rhythm and Scope: Process Dependence in Building a Profitable Multinational Corporation," *Strategic Management Journal* 23 (2002), pp. 637–54.

3. This can be reconceptualized as the resource base of the entrant, relative to indigenous competitors. For work that focuses on this issue, see W. C. Bogenr, H. Thomas, and J. McGee, "A Longitudinal Study of the Competitive Positions and Entry Paths of European Firms in the U.S. Pharmaceutical Market," *Strategic Management Journal* 17 (1996), pp. 85–107; D. Collis, "A Resource-Based Analysis of Global Competition," *Strategic Management Journal* 12 (1991), pp. 49–68; and S. Tallman, "Strategic Management Models and Resource-Based Strategies among MNEs in a Host Market," *Strategic Management Journal* 12 (1991), pp. 69–82.

4. For a discussion of first-mover advantages, see M. Lieberman and D. Montgomery, "First-Mover Advantages," *Strategic Management Journal* 9 (summer 1988, special issue), pp. 41–58.

5. J. M. Shaver, W. Mitchell, and B. Yeung, "The Effect of Own Firm and Other Firm Experience on Foreign Direct Investment Survival in the United States, 1987–92," *Strategic Management Journal* 18 (1997), pp. 811–24.

6. S. Zaheer and E. Mosakowski, "The Dynamics of the Liability of Foreignness: A Global Study of Survival in the Financial Services Industry," *Strategic Management Journal* 18 (1997), pp. 439–64.

7. Shaver, Mitchell, and Yeung, "The Effect of Own Firm and Other Firm Experience on Foreign Direct Investment Survival in the United States."

8. P. Ghemawat, *Commitment: The Dynamics of Strategy* (New York: Free Press, 1991).

9. R. Luecke, *Scuttle Your Ships before Advancing* (Oxford: Oxford University Press, 1994).

10. Sources: J. Carreyrou, "Dutch Financial Giant Maps Its U.S. Invasion," *The Wall Street Journal*, June 22, 2000, p. A17; J. B. Treaster, "ING Group Makes Its Move in Virtual Banking and Insurance," *The New York Times*, August 26, 2000, p. C1; "The Lion's Friendly Approach," *The Economist*, December 18, 2000; S. Kirsner, "Would You Like a Mortgage with Your Mocha?" *Fast Company*, March 2003, pp. 110–14; O. O'Sullivan, "Tough Love Bank Thrives," *ABA Banking Journal*, December 2003, p. 12; L. Bielski, "Bucking the Back to Bricks Trend," *ABA Banking Journal*, November 2004, pp. 25–32; I. Bickerton, "ING Permanently Watching for Deals," *Financial Times*, May 3, 2006, p. 27; and Steve Bergsman, "The Orange Mortgage," *Mortgage Banking*, June 2006, pp 48–54.

11. Isobe and Montgomery, "Resource Commitment, Entry Timing, and Market Performance"; Pan and Chi, "Financial Performance and Survival of Multinational Corporations in China"; and Govindarjan and Gupta, *The Quest for Global Dominance*.

12. Christopher Bartlett and Sumantra Ghoshal, "Going Global: Lessons from Late Movers," *Harvard Business Review*, March–April 2000, pp. 132–45.

13. Sources: C. Bartlett and Sumantra Ghoshal, "Going Global: Lessons from Late Movers," *Harvard Business Review*, March–April 2000, pp. 132–45; "Jollibee Battles Burger Giants in US Market," *Philippine Daily Inquirer*, July 13, 2000; M. Ballon, "Jollibee Struggling to Expand in U.S.," *Los Angeles Times*, September 16, 2002, p. C1; J. Hookway, "Burgers and Beer," *Far Eastern Economic Review*, December 2003, pp. 72–74; S. E. Lockyer, "Coming to America," *Nation's Restaurant News*, February 14, 2005, pp. 33–35; Erik de la Cruz, "Jollibee to Open

120 New Stores This Year, Plans India," *Inquirer Money,* July 5, 2006 (www.business.inquirer.net); and www.jollibee.com.ph.

14. This section draws on numerous studies, including C. W. L. Hill, P. Hwang, and W. C. Kim, "An Eclectic Theory of the Choice of International Entry Mode," *Strategic Management Journal* 11 (1990), pp. 117–28; C. W. L. Hill and W. C. Kim, "Searching for a Dynamic Theory of the Multinational Enterprise: A Transaction Cost Model," *Strategic Management Journal* 9 (special issue on strategy content, 1988), pp. 93–104; E. Anderson and H. Gatignon, "Modes of Foreign Entry: A Transaction Cost Analysis and Propositions," *Journal of International Business Studies* 17 (1986), pp. 1–26; F. R. Root, *Entry Strategies for International Markets* (Lexington, MA: D. C. Heath, 1980); A. Madhok, "Cost, Value and Foreign Market Entry: The Transaction and the Firm," *Strategic Management Journal* 18 (1997), pp. 39–61; K. D. Brouthers and L. B. Brouthers, "Acquisition or Greenfield Start-Up?" *Strategic Management Journal* 21, no. 1 (2000), pp. 89–97; X. Martin and R. Salmon, "Knowledge Transfer Capacity and Its Implications for the Theory of the Multinational Enterprise," *Journal of International Business Studies,* July 2003, p. 356; and A. Verbeke, "The Evolutionary View of the MNE and the Future of Internalization Theory," *Journal of International Business Studies,* November 2003, pp. 498–515.

15. For a general discussion of licensing, see F. J. Contractor, "The Role of Licensing in International Strategy," *Columbia Journal of World Business,* Winter 1982, pp. 73–83.

16. See E. Terazono and C. Lorenz, "An Angry Young Warrior," *Financial Times,* September 19, 1994, p. 11; and K. McQuade and B. Gomes-Casseres, "Xerox and Fuji–Xerox," Harvard Business School case no. 9-391-156.

17. O. E. Williamson, *The Economic Institutions of Capitalism* (New York: Free Press, 1985).

18. J. H. Dunning and M. McQueen, "The Eclectic Theory of International Production: A Case Study of the International Hotel Industry," *Managerial and Decision Economics* 2 (1981), pp. 197–210.

19. Andrew E. Serwer, "McDonald's Conquers the World," *Fortune,* October 17, 1994, pp. 103–16.

20. For an excellent review of the basic theoretical literature of joint ventures, see B. Kogut, "Joint Ventures: Theoretical and Empirical Perspectives," *Strategic Management Journal* 9 (1988), pp. 319–32.

More recent studies include T. Chi, "Option to Acquire or Divest a Joint Venture," *Strategic Management Journal* 21, no. 6 (2000), pp. 665–88; H. Merchant and D. Schendel, "How Do International Joint Ventures Create Shareholder Value?" *Strategic Management Journal* 21, no. 7 (2000), pp. 723–37; H. K. Steensma and M. A. Lyles, "Explaining IJV Survival in a Transitional Economy through Social Exchange and Knowledge Based Perspectives," *Strategic Management Journal* 21, no. 8 (2000), pp. 831–51; and J. F. Hennart and M. Zeng, "Cross Cultural Differences and Joint Venture Longevity," *Journal of International Business Studies,* December 2002, pp. 699–717.

21. D. G. Bradley, "Managing against Expropriation," *Harvard Business Review,* July–August 1977, pp. 78–90.

22. J. A. Robins, S. Tallman, and K. Fladmoe-Lindquist, "Autonomy and Dependence of International Cooperative Ventures," *Strategic Management Journal,* October 2002, pp. 881–902.

23. Speech given by Tony Kobayashi at the University of Washington Business School, October 1992.

24. A. C. Inkpen and P. W. Beamish, "Knowledge, Bargaining Power, and the Instability of International Joint Ventures," *Academy of Management Review* 22 (1997), pp. 177–202; and S. H. Park and G. R. Ungson, "The Effect of National Culture, Organizational Complementarity, and Economic Motivation on Joint Venture Dissolution," *Academy of Management Journal* 40 (1997), pp. 279–307.

25. Inkpen and Beamish, "Knowledge, Bargaining Power, and the Instability of International Joint Ventures."

26. See Brouthers and Brouthers, "Acquisition or Greenfield Start-Up?"; and J. F. Hennart and Y. R. Park, "Greenfield versus Acquisition: The Strategy of Japanese Investors in the United States," *Management Science,* 1993, pp. 1054–70.

27. This section draws on Hill, Hwang, and Kim, "An Eclectic Theory of the Choice of International Entry Mode."

28. C. W. L. Hill, "Strategies for Exploiting Technological Innovations: When and When Not to License," *Organization Science* 3 (1992), pp. 428–41.

29. See Brouthers and Brouthers, "Acquisition or Greenfield Start-Up?"; and J. Anand and A. Delios, "Absolute and Relative Resources as Determinants of International Acquisitions,"

Strategic Management Journal, February 2002, pp. 119–34.

30. United Nations, *World Investment Report, 2006* (New York and Geneva: United Nations, 2006).

31. Ibid.

32. For evidence on acquisitions and performance, see R. E. Caves, "Mergers, Takeovers, and Economic Efficiency," *International Journal of Industrial Organization* 7 (1989), pp. 151–74; M. C. Jensen and R. S. Ruback, "The Market for Corporate Control: The Scientific Evidence," *Journal of Financial Economics* 11 (1983), pp. 5–50; R. Roll, "Empirical Evidence on Takeover Activity and Shareholder Wealth," in *Knights, Raiders and Targets*, ed. J. C. Coffee, L. Lowenstein, and S. Rose (Oxford: Oxford University Press, 1989); A. Schleifer and R. W. Vishny, "Takeovers in the 60s and 80s: Evidence and Implications," *Strategic Management Journal* 12 (Winter 1991, special issue), pp. 51–60; T. H. Brush, "Predicted Changes in Operational Synergy and Post-Acquisition Performance of Acquired Businesses," *Strategic Management Journal* 17 (1996), pp. 1–24; and A. Seth, K. P. Song, and R. R. Pettit, "Value Creation and Destruction in Cross-Border Acquisitions," *Strategic Management Journal* 23 (October 2002), pp. 921–40.

33. J. Warner, J. Templeman, and R. Horn, "The Case against Mergers," *BusinessWeek*, October 30, 1995, pp. 122–34.

34. "Few Takeovers Pay Off for Big Buyers," *Investors Business Daily*, May 25, 2001, p. 1.

35. S. A. Christofferson, R. S. McNish, and D. L. Sias, "Where Mergers Go Wrong," *The McKinsey Quarterly* 2 (2004), pp. 92–110.

36. D. J. Ravenscraft and F. M. Scherer, *Mergers, Selloffs, and Economic Efficiency* (Washington, DC: Brookings Institution, 1987).

37. See P. Ghemawat and F. Ghadar, "The Dubious Logic of Global Mega-mergers," *Harvard Business Review*, July–August 2000, pp. 65–72.

38. R. Roll, "The Hubris Hypothesis of Corporate Takeovers," *Journal of Business* 59 (1986), pp. 197–216.

39. "Marital Problems," *The Economist*, October 14, 2000.

40. See J. P. Walsh, "Top Management Turnover following Mergers and Acquisitions," *Strategic Management Journal* 9 (1988), pp. 173–83.

41. B. Vlasic and B. A. Stertz, *Taken for a Ride: How Daimler-Benz Drove Off with Chrysler* (New York: HarperCollins, 2000).

42. See A. A. Cannella and D. C. Hambrick, "Executive Departure and Acquisition Performance," *Strategic Management Journal* 14 (1993), pp. 137–52.

43. P. Haspeslagh and D. Jemison, *Managing Acquisitions* (New York: Free Press, 1991).

44. Ibid.

45. See K. Ohmae, "The Global Logic of Strategic Alliances," *Harvard Business Review*, March–April 1989, pp. 143–54; G. Hamel, Y. L. Doz, and C. K. Prahalad, "Collaborate with Your Competitors and Win!" *Harvard Business Review*, January–February 1989, pp. 133–39; W. Burgers, C. W. L. Hill, and W. C. Kim, "Alliances in the Global Auto Industry," *Strategic Management Journal* 14 (1993), pp. 419–32; and P. Kale, H. Singh, H. Perlmutter, "Learning and Protection of Proprietary Assets in Strategic Alliances: Building Relational Capital," *Strategic Management Journal* 21 (2000), pp. 217–37.

46. L. T. Chang, "China Eases Foreign Film Rules," *The Wall Street Journal*, October 15, 2004, p. B2.

47. B. L. Simonin, "Transfer of Marketing Know-How in International Strategic Alliances," *Journal of International Business Studies*, 1999, pp. 463–91; and J. W. Spencer, "Firms' Knowledge Sharing Strategies in the Global Innovation System," *Strategic Management Journal* 24 (2003), pp. 217–33.

48. C. Souza, "Microsoft Teams with MIPS, Toshiba," *EBN*, February 10, 2003, p. 4.

49. M. Frankel, "Now Sony Is Giving Palm a Hand," *BusinessWeek*, November 29, 2000, p. 50.

50. Sources: "Fujitsu, Cisco Systems to Develop High-End Routers for Web Traffic," *Knight Ridder Tribune Business News*, December 6, 2004, p. 1; and "Fujitsu and Cisco Introduce New High-Performance Routers for IP Next Generation Networks," *JCN Newswire*, May 25, 2006.

51. P. Kale, H. Singh, and H. Perlmutter, "Learning and Protection of Proprietary Assets in Strategic Alliances: Building Relational Capital," *Strategic Management Journal* 21 (2000), pp. 217–37.

52. R. B. Reich and E. D. Mankin, "Joint Ventures with Japan Give Away Our Future," *Harvard Business Review*, March–April 1986, pp. 78–90.

53. J. Bleeke and D. Ernst, "The Way to Win in Cross-Border Alliances," *Harvard Business Review*, November–December 1991, pp. 127–35.

54. E. Booker and C. Krol, "IBM Finds Strength in Alliances," *B to B*, February 10, 2003, pp. 3, 27.

55. W. Roehl and J. F. Truitt, "Stormy Open Marriages Are Better," *Columbia Journal of World Business*, Summer 1987, pp. 87–95.

56. McQuade and Gomes-Casseres, "Xerox and Fuji-Xerox."

57. See T. Khanna, R. Gulati, and N. Nohria, "The Dynamics of Learning Alliances: Competition, Cooperation, and Relative Scope," *Strategic Management Journal* 19 (1998), pp. 193–210; and Kale, Singh, and Perlmutter, "Learning and Protection of Proprietary Assets in Strategic Alliances."

58. Kale, Singh, and Perlmutter, "Learning and Protection of Proprietary Assets in Strategic Alliances."

59. Hamel, Doz, and Prahalad, "Collaborate with Your Competitors"; Khanna, Gulati, and Nohria, "The Dynamics of Learning Alliances"; and E. W. K. Tang, "Acquiring Knowledge by Foreign Partners from International Joint Ventures in a Transition Economy: Learning by Doing and Learning Myopia," *Strategic Management Journal* 23 (2002), pp. 835–54.

60. Hamel, Doz, and Prahalad, "Collaborate with Your Competitors."

61. B. Wysocki, "Cross-Border Alliances Become Favorite Way to Crack New Markets," *The Wall Street Journal*, March 4, 1990, p. A1.

62. Hamel, Doz, and Prahalad, "Collaborate with Competitors," p. 138.

63. Sources: P. N. Child, "Taking Tesco Global," *The McKenzie Quarterly*, no. 3 (2002); H. Keers, "Global Tesco Sets Out Its Stall in China," *Daily Telegraph*, July 15, 2004, p. 31; K. Burgess, "Tesco Spends Pounds 140m on Chinese Partnership," *Financial Times*, July 15, 2004, p. 22; J. McTaggart, "Industry Awaits Tesco Invasion," *Progressive Grocer*, March 1, 2006, pp. 8–10; and Tesco's annual reports, archived at www.tesco.com.

part five
cases

Toyota: The Rise of a Global Corporation

INTRODUCTION

The growth of Toyota has been one of the great success stories of Japanese industry during the last half century. In 1947, the company was a little-known domestic manufacturer producing around 100,000 vehicles a year. In 2006, Toyota surpassed General Motors to become the largest automobile company in the world, selling 8.81 million vehicles, compared to GM's 8.68 million. The company's goal is to gain a 15 percent share of the global automobile market by 2010, up from 11.5 percent in 2006.[1]

This case describes the rise of Toyota from an obscure Japanese automobile company into the giant of today. It explains how the revolutionary production system developed at Toyota during the quarter of a century after 1950 paved the way for the company's current success. The case closes with a look at the challenges and opportunities Toyota now faces.

THE ORIGINS OF TOYOTA

The original idea behind the founding of the Toyota Motor Company came from the fertile mind of Toyoda Sakichi.[2] The son of a carpenter, Sakichi was an entrepreneur and inventor whose primary interest lay in the textile industry, but he had been intrigued by automobiles since a visit to the United States in 1910. Sakichi's principal achievement was the invention of an automatic loom that held out the promise of being able to lower the costs of weaving high-quality cloth. In 1926 Sakichi set up Toyoda Automatic Loom to manufacture this product. In 1930 Sakichi sold the patent rights to a British textile concern, Platt Brothers, for about 1 million yen, a considerable sum in those days. Sakichi urged his son, Toyoda Kiichiro, to use this money to study the possibility of manufacturing automobiles in Japan. A mechanical engineer with a degree from the University of Tokyo, in 1930 Kiichiro became managing director of loom production at Toyoda Automatic Loom.

Kiichiro was at first reluctant to invest in automobile production. The Japanese market was at that time dominated by Ford and General Motors, both of which imported knock-down car kits from the United States and assembled them in Japan. Given this, the board of Toyoda Automatic Loom, including Kiichiro's brother-in-law and the company's president, Kodama Risaburo, opposed the investment on the grounds that it was too risky. Kiichiro probably would not have pursued the issue further had not his father made a deathbed request in 1930 that Kiichiro explore the possibilities of automobile production. Kiichiro had to push, but in 1933 he was able to get permission to set up an automobile department within Toyoda Automatic Loom.

Kiichiro's belief was that he would be able to figure out how to manufacture automobiles by taking apart U.S.-made vehicles and examining them piece by piece. He also felt that it should be possible to adapt U.S. mass-production technology to manufacture cost-efficiently at lower volumes. His confidence was based in large part upon the already considerable engineering skills and capabilities at his disposal through Toyoda Automatic Loom. Many of the precision engineering and manufacturing skills needed in automobile production were similar to the skills required to manufacture looms.

Kiichiro produced his first 20 vehicles in 1935, and in 1936 the automobile department produced 1,142 vehicles—910 trucks, 100 cars, and 132 buses. At this time, however, the production system was essentially craft-based rather than a modern assembly line. Despite some progress, the struggle might still have been uphill had not fate intervened in the form of the Japanese military. Japan had invaded Manchuria in 1931 and quickly found American-made trucks useful for moving men and equipment. As a result, the military felt that it was strategically important for Japan to have its own automobile industry. The result was the passage of an automobile manufacturing law in 1936 which required companies producing more than 3,000 vehicles per year in Japan to get a license from the government. Moreover, to get a license over 50 percent of the stock had to be owned by Japanese investors. The law also placed a duty on imported cars, including the knock-down kits that Ford and GM brought into Japan. As a direct result of this legislation, both GM and Ford exited from the Japanese market in 1939.

Once the Japanese government passed this law, Kodama Risaburo decided that the automobile venture could be profitable and switched from opposing to proactively supporting Kiichiro (in fact, Risaburo's wife, who was Kiichiro's elder sister, had been urging him to take this step for some time). The first priority was to attract the funds necessary to build a mass-production facility. In 1937 Risaburo and Kiichiro decided to incorporate the automobile department as a separate company in order to attract outside investors—which they were successful in doing. Kiichiro Toyoda was appointed president of the new company. The company was named the Toyota Motor Company. (The founding family's name, "Toyoda," means "abundant rice field" in Japanese. The new name had no meaning in Japanese.)

Upon incorporation, Risaburo and Kiichiro's vision was that Toyota should expand its passenger car production as quickly as possible. However, once again fate intervened in the form of the Japanese military. Toyota had barely begun passenger car production when war broke out; in 1939 the Japanese government, on advice from the military, prohibited passenger car production and demanded that the company specialize in the production of military trucks.

THE EVOLUTION OF TOYOTA

After the end of World War II, Kiichiro was determined that Toyota should reestablish itself as a manufacturer of automobiles.[3] Toyota, however, faced a number of problems in doing this:

1. The Japanese domestic market was too small to support efficient-scale mass-production facilities such as those common in America by that time.

2. The Japanese economy was starved of capital, which made it difficult to raise funds to finance new investments.

3. New labor laws introduced by the American occupiers increased the bargaining power of labor and made it difficult for companies to lay off workers.

4. North America and Western Europe were full of large auto manufacturers eager to establish operations in Japan.

In response to the last point, in 1950 the new Japanese government prohibited direct foreign investment in the automobile industry and imposed high tariffs on the importation of foreign cars. This protection, however, did little to solve the other problems facing the company at this time.

Limitations of Mass Production

At this juncture a remarkable mechanical engineer entered the scene: Ohno Taiichi. More than anyone else, it was Ohno who was to work out a response to the above problems. Ohno had joined Toyoda Spinning and Weaving in 1932 as a production engineer in cotton thread manufacture and entered Toyota when the former company was absorbed into the latter in 1943. Ohno worked in auto production for two years, was promoted and managed auto assembly and machine shops between 1945 and 1953, and in 1954 was appointed a company director.

When Ohno Taiichi joined Toyota the mass-production methods pioneered by Ford had become the accepted method of manufacturing automobiles. The basic philosophy behind mass production was to produce a limited product line in massive quantities to gain maximum economies of scale. The economies came from spreading the fixed costs involved in setting up the specialized equipment required to stamp body parts and manufacture components over as large a production run as possible. Since setting up much of the equipment could take a full day or more, the economies involved in long production runs were reckoned to be considerable. Thus, for example, Ford would stamp 500,000 right-hand door panels in a single production run and then store the parts in warehouses until they were needed in the assembly plant, rather than stamp just those door panels that were needed immediately and then change the settings and stamp out left-hand door panels, or other body parts.

A second feature of mass production was that each assembly worker should perform only a single task, rather than a variety of tasks. The idea here was that as the worker became completely familiar with a single task, he could perform it much faster, thereby increasing labor productivity. Assembly line workers were overseen by a foreman who did not perform any assembly tasks himself, but instead ensured that the workers followed orders. In addition, a number of specialists were employed to perform nonassembly operations such as tool repair, die changes, quality inspection, and general "housecleaning."

After working in Toyota for five years and visiting Ford's U.S. plants, Ohno became convinced that the basic mass-production philosophy was flawed. He saw five problems with the mass-production system:

1. Long production runs created massive inventories that had to be stored in large warehouses. This was expensive both because of the cost of warehousing and because inventories tied up capital in unproductive uses.

2. If the initial machine settings were wrong, long production runs resulted in the production of a large number of defects.

3. The sheer monotony of assigning assembly line workers to a single task generated defects, since workers became lax about quality control. In addition, since assembly line workers were not responsible for quality control, they had little incentive to minimize defects.

4. The extreme division of labor resulted in the employment of specialists such as foremen, quality inspectors, and tooling specialists, whose jobs logically could be performed by assembly line workers.

5. The mass-production system was unable to accommodate consumer preferences for product diversity.

In addition to these flaws, Ohno knew that the small domestic market in Japan and the lack of capital for investing in mass-production facilities made the American model unsuitable for Toyota.

Reducing Setup Times

Given these flaws and the constraints that Toyota faced, Ohno decided to take a fresh look at the techniques used for automobile production. His first goal was to try to make it economical to manufacture auto body parts in small batches. To do this, he needed to reduce the time it took to set up the machines for stamping out body parts. Ohno and his engineers began to experiment with a number of techniques to speed up the time it took to change the dies in stamping equipment. This included using rollers to move dies in and out of position along with a number of simple mechanized adjustment mechanisms to fine-tune the settings. These techniques were relatively simple to master, so Ohno directed production workers to perform the die changes themselves. This in itself reduced the need for specialists and eliminated the idle time that workers previously had enjoyed while waiting for the dies to be changed.

Through a process of trial and error, Ohno succeeded in reducing the time required to change dies on stamping equipment from a full day to fifteen minutes by 1962, and to as little as three minutes by 1971. By comparison, even in the early 1980s many American and European plants required anywhere between two and six hours to change dies on stamping equipment. As a consequence, American and European plants found it economical to manufacture in lots equivalent to 10 to 30 days' supply and to reset equipment only every other day. In contrast, since Toyota could change the dies on stamping equipment in a matter of minutes, it manufactured in lots equivalent to just one day's supply, while resetting equipment three times per day.

Not only did these innovations make small production runs economical, but they also had the added benefit of reducing inventories and improving product quality. Making small batches eliminated the need to hold large inventories, thereby reducing warehousing costs and freeing up scarce capital for investment elsewhere. Small production runs and the lack of inventory also meant that defective parts were produced only in small numbers and entered the assembly process almost immediately. This had the added effect of making those in the stamping shops far more concerned about quality. In addition, once it became economical to manufacture small batches of components, much greater variety could be included into the final product at little or no cost penalty.

Organization of the Workplace

One of Ohno's first innovations was to group the workforce into teams. Each team was given a set of assembly tasks to perform, and team members were trained to perform each task that the team was responsible for. Each team had a leader who was himself an assembly line worker. In addition to coordinating the team, the team leader was expected to perform basic assembly line tasks and to fill in for any absent worker. The teams were given the job of housecleaning, minor tool repair, and quality inspection (along with the training required to perform these tasks). Time was also set aside for team members to discuss ways to improve the production process (the practice now referred to as "quality circles").

The immediate effect of this approach was to reduce the need for specialists in the workplace and to create a more flexible workforce in which individual assembly line workers were not treated simply as human machines. All of this resulted in increased worker productivity.

None of this would have been possible, however, had it not been for an agreement management and labor reached after a 1950 strike. The strike was brought on by management's attempt to cut the workforce by 25 percent (in response to a recession in Japan). After lengthy negotiations, Toyota and the union worked out a compromise. The workforce was cut by 25 percent as originally proposed, but the remaining employees were given two guarantees, one for lifetime employment and the other for pay graded by seniority and tied to company profitability through bonus payments. In exchange for these guarantees, the employees agreed to be flexible in work assignments. In turn, this allowed for the introduction of the team concept.

Improving Quality

One of the standard practices in the mass-production automobile assembly plants was to fix any errors that occurred during assembly in a rework area at the end of the assembly line. Errors routinely occurred in most assembly plants either because bad parts were installed or because good parts were installed incorrectly. The belief was that stopping an assembly line to fix such errors would cause enormous bottlenecks in the production system. Thus it was thought to be more efficient to correct errors at the end of the line.

Ohno viewed this system as wasteful for three reasons: (1) since workers understood that any errors would be fixed at the end of the line, they had little incentive to correct errors themselves; (2) once a defective part had been embedded in a complex vehicle, an enormous amount of rework might be required to fix it; and (3) since defective parts were often not discovered until the end of the line when the finished cars were tested, a large number of cars containing the same defect may have been built before the problem was found.

In an attempt to get away from this practice, Ohno decided to look for ways to reduce the amount of rework at the end of the line. His approach involved two elements. First, he placed a cord above every workstation and instructed workers to stop the assembly line if a problem emerged that could not be fixed. It then became the responsibility of the whole team to come over and work on the problem. Second, team members were taught to trace every defect back to its ultimate cause and then to ensure that the problem was fixed so that it would not reoccur.

Initially, this system produced enormous disruption. The production line was stopping all the time and workers became discouraged. However, as team members began to gain experience in identifying problems and tracing them back to their root cause, the number of errors began to drop dramatically and stops in the line became much rarer, so that today in most Toyota plants the line virtually never stops.

Developing the Kanban System

Once reduced setup times had made small production runs economical, Ohno began to look for ways to coordinate the flow of production within the Toyota manufacturing system so that the amount of inventory in the system could be reduced to a minimum. Toyota produced about 25 percent of its major components in-house (the rest were contracted out to independent suppliers). Ohno's initial goal was to arrange for components and/or subassemblies manufactured in-house to be delivered to the assembly floor only when they were needed, and not before (this goal was later extended to include independent suppliers).

To achieve this, in 1953 Ohno began experimenting with what came to be known as the kanban system. Under the kanban system, component parts are delivered to the assembly line in containers. As each container is emptied, it is sent back to the previous step in the manufacturing process. This then becomes the signal to make more parts. The system minimizes work in progress by increasing inventory turnover. The elimination of buffer inventories also means that defective components show up immediately in the next process. This speeds up the processes of tracing defects back to their source and facilitates correction of the problem before too many defects are made. Moreover, the elimination of buffer stocks, by removing all safety nets, makes it imperative that problems be solved before they become serious enough to jam up the production process, thereby creating a strong incentive for workers to ensure that errors are corrected as quickly as possible. In addition, by decentralizing responsibility for coordinating the manufacturing process to lower-level employees, the kanban system does away with the need for extensive centralized management to coordinate the flow of parts between the various stages of production.

After perfecting the kanban system in one of Toyota's machine shops, Ohno had a chance to apply the system broadly in 1960 when he was made general manager of the Motomachi assembly plant. Ohno already had

converted the machining, body stamping, and body shops to the kanban system, but since many parts came from shops that had yet to adopt the system, or from outside suppliers, the impact on inventories was initially minimal. However, by 1962 he had extended the kanban to forging and casting, and between 1962 and 1965 he began to bring independent suppliers into the system.

Organizing Suppliers

Assembly of components into a final vehicle accounts for only about 15 percent of the total manufacturing process in automobile manufacture. The remaining 85 percent of the process involves manufacturing more than 10,000 individual parts and assembling them into about 100 major components, such as engines, suspension systems, transaxles, and so on. Coordinating this process so that everything comes together at the right time has always been a problem for auto manufacturers. Historically, the response at Ford and GM to this problem was massive vertical integration. The belief was that control over the supply chain would allow management to coordinate the flow of component parts into the final assembly plant. In addition, American firms held the view that vertical integration made them more efficient by reducing their dependence on other firms for materials and components and by limiting their vulnerability to opportunistic overcharging.

As a consequence of this philosophy, even as late as the mid-1990s General Motors made 68 percent of its own components in-house, while Ford made 50 percent (in the late 1990s both GM and Ford deintegrated, spinning out much of their in-house supply operations as independent enterprises). Where they didn't vertically integrate, U.S. auto companies historically tried to reduce procurement costs through competitive bidding—asking a number of companies to submit contracts and giving orders to suppliers offering the lowest price.

Under the leadership of Kiichiro Toyoda during the 1930s and 1940s, Toyota followed the American model and pursued extensive vertical integration into the manufacture of component parts. In fact, Toyota had little choice in this matter, since only a handful of Japanese companies were able to make the necessary components. However, the low volume of production during this period meant that the scale of integration was relatively small. In the 1950s, however, the volume of auto production began to increase dramatically. This presented Toyota with a dilemma: Should the company increase its capacity to manufacture components in-house in line with the growth in production of autos, or should the company contract out?

In contrast to American practice, the company decided that while it should increase in-house capacity for essential subassemblies and bodies, it would do better to contract out for most components. Four reasons seem to bolster this decision:

1. Toyota wanted to avoid the capital expenditures required to expand capacity to manufacture a wide variety of components.

2. Toyota wanted to reduce risk by maintaining a low factory capacity in case factory sales slumped.

3. Toyota wanted to take advantage of the lower wage scales in smaller firms.

4. Toyota managers realized that in-house manufacturing offered few benefits if it was possible to find stable, high-quality, and low-cost external sources of component supply.

At the same time, Toyota managers felt that the American practice of inviting competitive bids from suppliers was self-defeating. While competitive bidding might achieve the lowest short-run costs, the practice of playing suppliers off against each other did not guarantee stable supplies, high quality, or cooperation beyond existing contracts to solve design or engineering problems. Ohno and other Toyota managers believed that real efficiencies could be achieved if the company entered into long-term relationships with major suppliers. This would allow them to introduce the kanban system, thereby further reducing inventory holding costs and realizing the same kind of quality benefits that Toyota was already beginning to encounter with its in-house supply operations. In addition, Ohno wanted to bring suppliers into the design process since he believed that suppliers might be able to suggest ways of improving the design of component parts based upon their own manufacturing experience.

As it evolved during the 1950s and 1960s, Toyota's strategy toward its suppliers had several elements. The company spun off some of its own in-house supply operations into quasi-independent entities in which it took a minority stake, typically holding between 20 percent and 40 percent of the stock. It then recruited a number of independent companies with a view to establishing a long-term relationship with them for the supply of critical components. Sometimes, but not always, Toyota took a minority stake in these companies as well. All of these companies were designated as "first-tier suppliers." First-tier suppliers were responsible for working with Toyota as an integral part of the new product development team. Each first tier was responsible for the formation of a "second tier" of suppliers under its direction. Companies in the second tier were given the job of fabricating individual parts. Both first- and second-tier suppliers were formed into supplier associations.

By 1986 Toyota had three regional supply organizations in Japan with 62, 135, and 25 first-tier suppliers. A major function of the supplier associations was to share information regarding new manufacturing, design, or materials management techniques among themselves. Concepts such as statistical process control, total quality control, and computer-aided design were rapidly diffused among suppliers by this means.

Toyota also worked closely with its suppliers, providing them with management expertise, engineering expertise, and sometimes capital to finance new investments. A critical feature of this relationship was the incentives that Toyota established to encourage its suppliers to focus on realizing continuous process improvements. The basic contract for a component would be for four to five years, with the price being agreed in advance. If by joint efforts the supplier and Toyota succeeded in reducing the costs of manufacturing the components, then the additional profit would be shared between the two. If the supplier by its own efforts came up with an innovation that reduced costs, the supplier would keep the additional profit that the innovation generated for the lifetime of the contract.

As a consequence of this strategy, Toyota outsourced more production than almost any other major auto manufacturer. By the late 1980s Toyota was responsible for only about 27 percent of the value going into a finished automobile, with the remainder coming from outside suppliers. In contrast, at the time General Motors was responsible for about 70 percent of the value going into a finished automobile. Other consequences included long-term improvements in productivity and quality among Toyota's suppliers that were comparable to the improvements achieved by Toyota itself. In particular, the extension of the kanban system to include suppliers eliminated buffer inventory stocks, in essence forcing suppliers to focus more explicitly on the quality of their product.

Consequences

The consequences of Toyota's production system included a surge in labor productivity and a decline in the number of defects per car. Exhibit 1 compares the number of vehicles produced per worker at General Motors, Ford, Nissan, and Toyota between 1965 and 1983.

These figures are adjusted for the degree of vertical integration pursued by each company. As can be seen, in 1960 productivity at Toyota already outstripped that of Ford, General Motors, and its main Japanese competitor, Nissan. As Toyota refined its production system over the next 18 years, productivity doubled. In comparison, productivity essentially stood still at General Motors and Ford during the same period.

EXHIBIT 1

Vehicles Produced per Worker (adjusted for vertical integration), 1965–1983

Source: M. A. Cusumano, *The Japanese Automotive Industry* (Cambridge, Mass.: Harvard University Press, 1989), Table 48, p. 197.

Year	General Motors	Ford	Nissan	Toyota Motors
1965	5.0	4.4	4.3	8.0
1970	3.7	4.3	8.8	13.4
1975	4.4	4.0	9.0	15.1
1979	4.5	4.2	11.1	18.4
1980	4.1	3.7	12.2	17.8
1983	4.8	4.7	11.0	15.0

	GM Framingham	Toyota Takaoka
Assembly hours per car	31	16
Assembly defects per 100 cars	135	45
Inventory of parts	2 weeks	2 hours

EXHIBIT 2

General Motors' Framingham Plant versus Toyota's Takaoka Plant, 1987

Source: J. P. Womack, D. T. Jones, and D. Roos, *The Machines That Changed the World* (New York: Macmillan, 1990), Figure 4.2, p. 83.

Exhibit 2 provides another way to assess the superiority of Toyota's production system. Here the performance of Toyota's Takaoka plant is compared with that of General Motors' Framingham plant in 1987. As can be seen, the Toyota plant was more productive, produced far fewer defects per 100 cars, and kept far less inventory on hand.

A further aspect of Toyota's production system is that the short setup times made it economical to manufacture a much wider range of models than is feasible at a traditional mass-production assembly plant. In essence, Toyota soon found that it could supply much greater product variety than its competitors with little in the way of a cost penalty. In 1990 Toyota was offering consumers around the world roughly as many products as General Motors (about 150), even though Toyota was still only half GM's size. Moreover, it could do this at a lower cost than GM.

Distribution and Customer Relations

Toyota's approach to its distributors and customers as it evolved during the 1950s and 1960s was in many ways just as radical as its approach toward suppliers. In 1950 Toyota formed a subsidiary, Toyota Motor Sales, to handle distribution and sales. The new subsidiary was headed by Kaymiya Shotaro from its inception until 1975. Kaymiya's philosophy was that dealers should be treated as "equal partners" in the Toyota family. To back this up, he had Toyota Motor Sales provide a wide range of sales training and service training for dealership personnel.

Kaymiya then used the dealers to build long-term ties with Toyota's customers. The ultimate aim was to bring customers into the Toyota design and production process. To this end, through its dealers, Toyota Motor Sales assembled a huge database on customer preferences. Much of these data came from monthly or semiannual surveys conducted by dealers. These asked Toyota customers their preferences for styling, model types, colors, prices, and other features. Toyota also used these surveys to estimate the potential demand for new models. This information was then fed directly into the design process.

Kaymiya began this process in 1952 when the company was redesigning its Toyopet model. The Toyopet was primarily used by urban taxi drivers. Toyota Motor Sales surveyed taxi drivers to try to find out what type of vehicle they preferred. They wanted something reliable, inexpensive, and with good city fuel mileage—which Toyota engineers then set about designing. In 1956 Kaymiya formalized this process when he created a unified department for planning and market research whose function was to coordinate the marketing strategies developed by researchers at Toyota Motor Sales with product planning by Toyota's design engineers. From this time on, marketing information played a critical role in the design of Toyota's cars and in the company's strategy. In particular, it was the research department at Toyota Motor Sales that provided the initial stimulus for Toyota to start exporting during the late 1960s after predicting, correctly, that growth in domestic sales would slow down considerably during the 1970s.

Expanding Internationally

Large-scale overseas expansion did not become feasible at Toyota until the late 1960s for one principal reason: despite the rapid improvement in productivity, Japanese cars were still not competitive.[4] In 1957, for example, the Toyota Corona sold in Japan for the equivalent of $1,694. At the same time the Volkswagen Beetle sold for $1,111 in West Germany, while Britain's Austin company was selling its basic model for the equivalent of $1,389 in Britain. Foreign companies were effectively kept out of the Japanese market, however, by a 40 percent value-added tax and shipping costs.

Despite these disadvantages, Toyota tried to enter the United States market in the late 1950s. The company set up a U.S. subsidiary in California in October 1957 and began to sell cars in early 1958, hoping to capture the American small car market (which at that time was poorly served by the U.S. automobile companies). The result was a disaster. Toyota's cars performed poorly in road tests on U.S. highways. The basic problem was that the engines of Toyota's cars were too small for prolonged high-speed driving and tended to overheat and burn oil, while poorly designed chassis resulted in excessive vibration. Sales were slow and in 1964 Toyota closed down its U.S. subsidiary and withdrew from the market.

The company was determined to learn from its U.S. experience and quickly redesigned several of its models based on feedback from American consumer surveys and U.S. road tests. As a result, by 1967 the picture had changed considerably. The quality of Toyota's cars was now sufficient to make an impact in the U.S. market, while production costs and retail prices had continued to fall and were now comparable with international competitors in the small car market.

In the late 1960s Toyota reentered the U.S. market. Although sales were initially slow, they increased steadily. Then the OPEC-engineered fourfold increase in oil prices that followed the 1973 Israeli/Arab conflict gave Toyota an unexpected boost. U.S. consumers began to turn to small fuel-efficient cars in droves, and Toyota was one of the main beneficiaries. Driven primarily by a surge in U.S. demand, worldwide exports of Toyota cars increased from 157,882 units in 1967 to 856,352 units by 1974 and 1,800,923 units by 1984. Put another way, in 1967 exports accounted for 19 percent of Toyota's total output. By 1984 they accounted for 52.5 percent.

Success brought its own problems. By the early 1980s political pressures and talk of local content regulations in the United States and Europe were forcing an initially reluctant Toyota to rethink its exporting strategy. Toyota already had agreed to "voluntary" import quotas with the United States in 1981. The consequence for Toyota was stagnant export growth between 1981 and 1984. Against this background, in the early 1980s Toyota began to think seriously about setting up manufacturing operations overseas.

Transplant Operations

Toyota's first overseas operation was a 50/50 joint venture with General Motors established in February 1983 under the name New United Motor Manufacturing, Inc. (NUMMI). NUMMI, which is based in Fremont, California, began producing Chevrolet Nova cars for GM in December 1984.[5] The maximum capacity of the Fremont plant is about 250,000 cars per year.

For Toyota, the joint venture provided a chance to find out whether it could build quality cars in the United States using American workers and American suppliers. It also provided Toyota with experience dealing with an American union (the United Auto Workers Union) and with a means of circumventing "voluntary" import restrictions. For General Motors, the venture provided an opportunity to observe in full detail the Japanese approach to manufacturing. While General Motors' role was marketing and distributing the plant's output, Toyota designed the product and designed, equipped, and operated the plant. At the venture's start, Toyota loaned 34 executives to NUMMI, and General Motors 16. The chief executive and chief operating officer were both Toyota personnel.

By the fall of 1986 the NUMMI plant was running at full capacity and the early indications were that the NUMMI plant was achieving productivity and quality levels close to those achieved at Toyota's major Takaoka plant in Japan. For example, in 1987 it took the NUMMI plant 19 assembly hours to build a car, compared to 16 hours at Takaoka, while the number of defects per 100 cars was the same at NUMMI as at Takaoka—45.[6]

Encouraged by its success at NUMMI, in December 1985 Toyota announced that it would build an automobile manufacturing plant in Georgetown, Kentucky. The plant, which came on stream in May 1988, officially had the capacity to produce 200,000 Toyota Camrys a year. Such was the success of this plant, however, that by early 1990 it was producing the equivalent of 220,000 cars per year. This success was followed by an announcement in December 1990 that Toyota would build a second plant in Georgetown with a capacity to produce a further 200,000 vehicles per year.[7]

By 2006, Toyota had invested $16.8 billion in U.S.-based operations and had assembly plants in Kentucky, California, Indiana, Texas, and Ontario, Canada, that collectively produced 1.5 million vehicles a year, or 60 percent of its total North American sales. Toyota's U.S. employees totaled more than 38,000 by this time. In 2003 it opened a plant in Alabama and in 2004 one in Mexico; it opened another plant in Texas in 2006. Toyota plans to be able to produce 1.8 million vehicles in the United States by 2008 and 2.2 million by 2010.

Similar investments have been made in Europe. As with the United States, the European investment was triggered by a desire to get around import barriers. Also, with Europe moving rapidly toward a single market, Toyota felt that it needed a manufacturing presence in the region. In 1989, it established a manufacturing plant in the United Kingdom capable of producing 200,000 cars a year. Output from the plant was sold in the United Kingdom and exported to Europe. This was followed in 1997 by a decision to invest $640 million in a production facility in France. The choice of France was made despite intense lobbying from the British government, which wanted Toyota to invest in additional facilities in the United Kingdom, thereby generating employment and export earnings for the United Kingdom. According to news reports, Toyota picked France in part because of subsidies from French authorities in the form of tax breaks and aid for training workers that totaled 10 percent of the value of the investment. In 2002, Toyota decided to build a third European production facility in the Czech Republic. The U.K. and French investments were wholly owned by Toyota; however, the Czech investment, which will ultimately total $1.3 billion, is a 50/50 joint venture with French carmaker Peugeot. This plant is scheduled to start producing cars in 2005.

Going forward, the company will be making larger direct investments in China, now the world's fastest growing car market. Toyota's production in China began in 2001 with a joint venture with government-owned Tianjin Automotive. After deciding that Tianjin was not the best partner, Toyota engineered a takeover of Tianjin by another government-owned automaker, First Automotive, and committed to investing hundreds of millions of dollars in the joint venture. By 2005, Toyota and its partner were producing over 400,000 cars in China, and plans call for a million to be sold in the country by 2010, the majority coming from local manufacturing plants.

Despite Toyota's apparent commitment to expand foreign operations, it has not all been smooth sailing. One problem has been building an overseas supplier network comparable to Toyota's Japanese network. For example, in a 1990 meeting of Toyota's North American suppliers' association, Toyota executives informed their North American suppliers that the defect ratio for parts produced by 75 North American and European suppliers was 100 times greater than the defect ratio for parts supplied by 147 Japanese suppliers—1,000 defects per million parts versus 10 defects per million among Toyota's Japanese suppliers. Moreover, Toyota executives pointed out that parts manufactured by North American and European suppliers tend to be significantly more expensive than comparable parts manufactured in Japan.

Because of these problems, Toyota had to import many parts from Japan for its U.S. assembly operations. However, for political reasons Toyota was being pushed to increase the local content of cars assembled in North America. The company's plan was for 50 percent of the value of Toyota cars assembled in the United States to be locally produced by January 1991. By the early 2000s, the local content of cars produced in North America was over 70 percent. To improve the efficiency of its U.S.-based suppliers, Toyota embarked upon an aggressive supplier education process. In 1992, it established the Toyota Supplier Support Center to teach its suppliers the basics of the Toyota production system. By 2001, 89 supplier companies had been through the center. Many have reportedly seen double- and triple-digit productivity growth as a result, as well as dramatic reductions in inventory levels.[8]

Product Strategy

Toyota's initial production was aimed at the small car/basic transportation end of the automobile market. This was true both in Japan and of its export sales to North America and Europe. During the 1980s, however, Toyota progressively moved up-market and abandoned much of the lower end of the market to new entrants such as the South Koreans. Thus, the company's Camry and Corolla models, which initially were positioned toward the bottom of the market, have been constantly upgraded and now are aimed at the middle-income segments of the market. This upgrading reflects two factors: (1) the rising level of incomes in Japan and the commensurate increase in the ability of Japanese consumers to purchase midrange and luxury cars and (2) a desire to hold onto its U.S. consumers, many of whom initially purchased inexpensive Toyotas in their early 20s and have since traded up to more expensive models.

The constant upgrading of Toyota's models reached a logical conclusion in September 1989 when the company's Lexus division began marketing luxury cars to compete with Jaguars, BMWs, and the like. Although the Lexus brand initially got off to a slow start—in large part due to an economic recession—by 2001 Toyota was selling over 200,000 Lexus models a year in the United States, making it the best-selling luxury brand in the country.

Another addition to Toyota's product range in the late 1980s was a minivan. This vehicle was aimed at the North American market, where the minivan segment had grown rapidly. Toyota first introduced a minivan in 1986, but it flopped. The company dispatched product planners and design engineers to showrooms to find out why. Among the problems they identified were that the minivans lacked an aisle down the center, the short wheelbase gave them a pitchy ride, and the engine was not easy to service. Based on this feedback, Toyota designers completely redesigned the vehicle and reintroduced it in April 1990 as the Previa minivan, and sales soon exceeded expectations.[9]

TOYOTA IN 2006

As 2006 drew to a close, Toyota was enjoying one of its best years ever. By some measures the company had overtaken General Motors to become the largest automobile company in the world. Its goal of attaining a 15 percent share of the global market seemed attainable. Toyota was now a truly international company. Its overseas operations had grown from 11 production facilities in 9 countries in 1980 to 52 production facilities in 26 countries around the world by 2006.[10] In the important United States market, the world's largest, Toyota held a 14.9 percent share of passenger car sales in 2006, up from 11 percent in 2000.[11]

The company was very profitable. In the financial year ending March 2007 it earned $11 billion net profits on sales of $152 billion. It had more profits than General Motors, Ford, and Daimler Chrysler combined and ended the year with some $35 billion in cash and short-term investments.

According to data from J.D. Power, Toyota was still the quality leader in the United States market. For cars that had been on the market for over three years, Toyota led the pack with 207 problems per 100 vehicles, compared to an industry average of 269 problems per 100 vehicles. Toyota also had the best record in the industry when measured by problems reported in the first 90 days after a sale—101 problems per 100 cars versus an industry average of 119 problems per 100 cars.[12]

J.D. Power also found that Toyota led the market in Japan. A survey found that for vehicles purchased in 2002, Toyota had 89 problems per 100 vehicles compared to an industry average of 104. Honda was next with 91 problems per 100 vehicles, followed by Nissan with 108 problems per 100 vehicles.[13]

Furthermore, Toyota seemed to be maintaining a high level of productivity. In its American assembly operations, Toyota took 20.6 employee hours to build a car. This compares to 23.6 hours at General Motors, 25.4 hours at Ford, and 26.0 hours at Daimler Chrysler. However, both Nissan and Honda had more productive factories in the United States. Indeed, Nissan took 17.32 employee hours to build a car at its North American factories.[14] On the other hand, according to J.D. Power, Toyota has the three most efficient assembly plants in the world, all of which are located in Japan.[15]

Toyota's ability to stay on top of productivity and quality rankings can be attributed to a companywide obsession with continuing to improve the efficiency and effectiveness of its manufacturing operations. Toyota

President Fujio Cho initiated the latest round of these in 2000. Cho, who worked for a while under Toyota's legendary engineer, Taichi Ohno, introduced an initiative known as "Construction of Cost Competitiveness for the 21st Century", or CCC21. The initiative has a goal of slashing component part costs by 30 percent on all new models. Attaining this goal necessitated Toyota working closely with suppliers—something it has long done.

According to news reports, by 2004 Toyota was close to attaining its CCC21 goal. In implementing CCC21, no detail has been too small. For example, Toyota took a close look at the grip handles mounted above the doors inside most cars. By working closely with suppliers, they managed to reduce the number of parts in these handles from 34 to 5, which cut procurement costs by 40 percent and reduced the time needed for installation from 12 seconds to 3 seconds.[16]

More generally, Toyota continues to refine its lean production system. For example, in die making, by 2004 Toyota had reduced the lead time to engineer and manufacture die sets for large body panels to 1.7 months, down from 3 months in 2002. By reducing lead time, Toyota reduces the start-up costs associated with producing a new model, and the development time.[17]

In welding, Toyota has developed and installed a simplified assembly process known as the "Global Body Line" or GBL. First developed in a low-volume Vietnamese assembly plant in 1996, and introduced into its first Japanese plant in 1998, by 2004 the GBL was operating in some 20 of the company's 52 assembly plants and was scheduled to be found in all 52 by 2007. The GBL system replaced Toyota's Flexible Body Line assembly philosophy that has been in place since 1985. The GBL system is based upon a series of programmable robotic welding tools. Under the old FBL system each car required three pallets to hold body parts in place during the welding process, each gripping either a major body side assembly or the roof assembly. The GBL system replaces these three pallets with a single pallet that holds all three major body panels in place from the inside as welding proceeds.[18]

According to Toyota, the GBL system has the following consequences:

- 30 percent reduction in the time a vehicle spends in the body shop.
- 70 percent reduction in the time required to complete a major body change.
- 50 percent cut in the cost to add or switch models.
- 50 percent reduction in the investment to set up a line for a new model.
- 50 percent reduction in assembly line footprint.

The floor space freed up by the GBL allows two assembly lines to be placed in the space traditionally required for one, effectively doubling plant capacity. Moreover, using GBL technology as many as eight different models can be produced on a single assembly line. To achieve this, Toyota has pushed for consistency in design across model ranges, particularly with regard to the "hard points" that the single master pallet grasps.

Meanwhile, Toyota has also been accelerating the process of moving toward fewer vehicle platforms, the goal being to build a wide range of models on a limited range of platforms that use many of the same component parts or modules. The company is reportedly working toward a goal of having just 10 platforms, down from over 20 in 2000.[19]

While Toyota is undoubtedly making progress refining its manufacturing efficiency, the fact remains that the productivity and quality gap between Toyota and its global competitors has narrowed. General Motors and Ford have both made significant strides in improving their quality and productivity in recent years. Moreover, in the American market at least, Toyota has suffered from the perception that its product offerings lack design flair and are not always as well attuned to consumer tastes as they might be. Here too, however, there are signs that Toyota is improving matters, interestingly enough, by listening more to its American designers and engineers.

A pivotal event in the changing relationship between Toyota and its American designers occurred in the late 1990s. Japanese managers had resisted their U.S. colleagues' idea that the company should produce a V8 pickup truck for the American market. To change their minds, the U.S. executives flew their Japanese counterparts over from Japan and took them to a Dallas Cowboys football game—with a pit stop in the Texas Stadium parking lot. There the Japanese saw row upon row of full-size pickups. Finally, it dawned on them that Americans see the pickup as more than a commercial vehicle, considering it primary transportation. The result of this was Toyota's best-selling V8 pickup truck, the Toyota Tundra.[20]

American designers also pushed Toyota to redesign the Prius, its hybrid car first introduced in Japan in 1997. The Americans wanted a futuristic design change so that people would notice the technology. The result, the new Prius, has become a surprise hit with Toyota forecasting global sales of 300,000 units in 2005.[21]

Toyota's Americanization runs deeper than just product design issues. On the sales front, the company now sells more cars and trucks in North America than it does in Japan, and over 60 percent of Toyota's global profits come from North America. On the personnel front, President Cho himself made his reputation by opening Toyota's first U.S. production plant in Georgetown, Kentucky, in 1988. His likely successor,

Yoshi Inaba, spent eight years in the U.S. and has an MBA from Northwestern University. Americans are also starting to make their way into Toyota's top ranks. Two Americans from Toyota's U.S. subsidiary now rank among Toyota's top 42 executives, and each spends one to two weeks a month in Japan.[22]

Another concern of Toyota has been the aging of its customer base. According to J.D. Power, the average Toyota customer is 44 years old, compared with 38 for Volkswagen and 41 for Honda. Concerned that it was loosing its cache with the younger generation, some 60 million of whom will reach driving age over the next few years, Toyota introduced a new car brand, the Scion, into America in June 2004. Currently the brand has three models, all priced in the $13,000–$17,000 range. The cars are targeted at young entry-level buyers and can be purchased over the Web in addition to through traditional Toyota dealers. Early sales results suggest that the brand is doing well. Toyota's initial sales goals for the brand were 100,000 cars in 2005, but in October 2004 it raised that target to 170,000. The average buyer in the months following launch was 31 years old.[23]

As Toyota entered 2007, the key question facing management was whether the company was doing enough to attain its goal of capturing 15 percent of the global marketplace, particularly given the renewed efforts by its global rivals to close the quality and productivity gap between themselves and Toyota.

Case Discussion Questions

1. Compare and contrast Toyota's revolutionary lean production system with the traditional mass production system for making automobiles. How is Toyota's system superior?

2. Compare and contrast the arm's-length relationships that Toyota used to manage suppliers in Japan with the approach traditionally taken by U.S. automobile manufacturers. What were the benefits of the Toyota system? Can you see any drawbacks?

3. What drove the development of Toyota's revolutionary "lean production system" during the 1950s to1980s? To what extent were factors unique to Japan during this time frame responsible for the development of the lean production system?

4. Why did Toyota enter into the NUMMI joint venture with General Motors in 1984? What were the benefits of this venture to Toyota?

5. What drove Toyota's subsequent expansion of production facilities in the United States and Europe?

6. In general, Toyota's foreign plants have achieved productivity levels similar to those in Japan. What conclusion can you draw from this about

the role of national culture in shaping Toyota's lean production system?

7. What evidence is there in the case that Toyota is becoming more of a global corporation? What are the implications of this for the long term competitive advantage of the company?

Notes

1. J. Sapsford, "Toyota Aims to Rival GM in Production," *The Wall Street Journal*, November 2, 2004, p. A3; "Toyota Surpasses General Motors in 2006 Global Sales," *Financial Wire*, June 13, 2007, p. 1.

2. This section is based primarily on the account given in M. A. Cusumano, *The Japanese Automobile Industry* (Cambridge, Mass: Harvard University Press, 1989).

3. The material in this section is drawn from three main sources: M. A. Cusumano, *The Japanese Automobile Industry*; Ohno Taiichi, *Toyota Production System* (Cambridge, Mass.: Productivity Press, 1990; Japanese Edition, 1978); and J. P. Womack, D. T. Jones, and D. Roos, *The Machine That Changed the World* (New York: Macmillan, 1990).

4. The material in this section is based on M. A. Cusumano, *The Japanese Automobile Industry*.

5. Niland Powell, "U.S.–Japanese Joint Venture: New United Motor Manufacturing, Inc.," *Planning Review*, January–February 1989, pp. 40–45.

6. From J. P. Womack, D. T. Jones, and D. Roos, *The Machine That Changed the World*.

7. J. B. Treece, "Just What Detroit Needs: 200,000 More Toyotas a Year," *Business Week*, December 10, 1990, p. 29.

8. P. Strozniak, "Toyota Alters the Face of Production," *Industry Week*, August 13, 2001, pp. 46–48.

9. J. Flint, "The New Number Three?" *Forbes*, June 11, 1990, pp. 136–140.

10. Toyota Web site http://www.toyota.co.jp/en/about_toyota/outline/index.html, accessed July 11, 2007.

11. Standard & Poor's Industry Surveys, *Auto and Auto Parts*, June 24, 2007.

12. J. D. Power Press Release, April 28, 2004, "Korean Branded Vehicles Overtake Europeans and Domestics in Initial Quality"; J. D. Power Press Release June 29, 2004, "Toyota Motor Sales Capture Top Corporate Rankings in Vehicle Dependability."

13. J. D. Power Press Release, "Toyota Ranks Highest in Japans First Long Term Vehicle Dependability Study," September 2, 2004.

14. Data reported in J. Palmer, "Can Anyone Stop Toyota," *Barron's*, September 13, 2004, pp.25–29.

15. J. D. Power Press Release, "Toyota Ranks Highest in Japans First Long Term Vehicle Dependability Study," September 2, 2004.

16. B. Bremner and C. Dawson, "Can Anything Stop Toyota," *Business Week*, November 17, 2003, pp. 114–117.

17. M. Hara, "Moving Target," *Automotive Industries*, June 2004, pp. 26–29.

18. B. Visnic, "Toyota Adopts New Flexible Assembly Process," *Wards Auto World*, November 2002, pp. 30–31; M. Bursa, "A Review of Flexible Automotive Manufacturing," *Just Auto*, May 2004, page 15.

19. M. Hara, "Moving Target" *Automotive Industries*, June 2004, pp. 26–29.

20. C. Dawson and L. Armstrong, "The Americanization of Toyota," *Business Week*, April 15, 2002, pp. 52–54.

21. A. Taylor, "Toyota's Secret Weapon," *Fortune*, August 23, 2004, pp. 65–66.

22. A. Taylor, "The Americanization of Toyota," *Fortune*, December 8, 2004, p. 165.

23. N. Shirouzu, "Scion Plays Hip-Hop Impresario to Impress Young Drivers," *The Wall Street Journal*, October 5, 2004, p. B1.

Nestlé: Global Strategy

INTRODUCTION

Nestlé is one of the oldest of all multinational businesses. The company was founded in Switzerland in 1866 by Heinrich Nestlé, who established Nestlé to distribute "milk food," a type of infant food he had invented that was made from powdered milk, baked food, and sugar. From its very early days, the company looked to other countries for growth opportunities, establishing its first foreign offices in London in 1868. In 1905, the company merged with the Anglo Swiss Condensed Milk, thereby broadening the company's product line to include both condensed milk and infant formulas. Forced by Switzerland's small size to look outside its borders for growth opportunities, Nestlé established condensed milk and infant food processing plants in the United States and Great Britain in the late 19th century and in Australia, South America, Africa, and Asia in the first three decades of the 20th century.

In 1929, Nestlé moved into the chocolate business when it acquired a Swiss chocolate maker. This was followed in 1938 by the development of Nestlé's most revolutionary product, Nescafe, the world's first soluble coffee drink. After World War II, Nestlé continued to expand into other areas of the food business, primarily through a series of acquisitions that included Maggi (1947), Cross & Blackwell (1960), Findus (1962), Libby's (1970), Stouffer's (1973), Carnation (1985), Rowntree (1988), and Perrier (1992).

By the late 1990s, Nestlé had 500 factories in 76 countries and sold its products in a staggering 193 nations—almost every country in the world. In 1998, the company generated sales of close to SWF 72 billion ($51 billion), only 1 percent of which occurred in its home country. Similarly, only 3 percent of its 210,000 employees were located in Switzerland. Nestlé was the world's biggest maker of infant formula, powdered milk, chocolates, instant coffee, soups, and mineral waters. It was number two in ice cream, breakfast cereals, and pet food. Roughly 38 percent of its food sales were made in Europe, 32 percent in the Americas, and 20 percent in Africa and Asia.

A GROWTH STRATEGY FOR THE 21ST CENTURY

Despite its undisputed success, Nestlé realized by the early 1990s that it faced significant challenges in maintaining its growth rate. The large Western European and North American markets were sature. In several countries, population growth had stagnated and in some there had been a small decline in food consumption. The retail environment in many Western nations had become increasingly challenging, and the balance of power was shifting away from the large-scale manufacturers of branded foods and beverages and toward nationwide supermarket and discount chains. Increasingly, retailers found themselves in the unfamiliar position of playing off against each other manufacturers of branded foods, thus bargaining down prices. Particularly in Europe, this trend was enhanced by the successful introduction of private-label brands by several of Europe's leading supermarket chains. The results included increased price competition in several key segments of the food and beverage market, such as cereals, coffee, and soft drinks.

At Nestlé, one response has been to look toward emerging markets in Eastern Europe, Asia, and Latin America for growth possibilities. The logic is simple and obvious—a combination of economic and population growth, when coupled with the widespread adoption of market-oriented economic policies by the governments of many developing nations, makes for attractive business opportunities. Many of these countries are still relatively poor, but their economies are growing rapidly. For example, if current economic growth forecasts occur, by 2010 there will be 700 million people in China and India that have income levels approaching those of Spain in the mid 1990s. As income levels rise, it is increasingly likely that consumers in these nations will start to substitute branded food products for basic foodstuffs, creating a large market opportunity for companies such as Nestlé.

In general, the company's strategy has been to enter emerging markets early—before competitors—and build a substantial position by selling basic food items that appeal to the local population base, such as infant formula, condensed milk, noodles, and tofu. By narrowing its initial market focus to just a handful of strategic brands, Nestlé claims it can simplify life, reduce risk, and concentrate its marketing resources and managerial effort on a limited number of key niches. The goal is to build a commanding market position in each of these niches. By pursuing such a strategy, Nestlé has taken as much as 85 percent of the market for instant coffee in Mexico, 66 percent of the market for powdered milk in the Philippines, and 70 percent of the market for soups in Chile. As income levels rise, the company progressively moves out from these niches, introducing more upscale items, such as mineral water, chocolate, cookies and prepared foodstuffs.

Although the company is known worldwide for several key brands, such as Nescafe, it uses local brands in many markets. The company owns 8,500 brands, but only 750 of them are registered in more than one country, and only 80 are registered in more than 10 countries. While the company will use the same "global brands" in multiple developed markets, in the developing world it focuses on trying to optimize ingredients and processing technology to local conditions and then using a brand name that resonates locally. Customization rather than globalization is the key to the company's strategy in emerging markets.

EXECUTING THE STRATEGY

Successful execution of the strategy for developing markets requires a degree of flexibility, an ability to adapt in often unforeseen ways to local conditions, and a long-term perspective that puts building a sustainable business before short-term profitability. In Nigeria, for example, a crumbling road system, aging trucks, and the danger of violence forced the company to rethink its traditional distribution methods. Instead of operating a central warehouse, as is its preference in most nations, the company built a network of small warehouses around the country. For safety reasons, trucks carrying Nestlé goods are allowed to travel only during the day and frequently under armed guard. Marketing also poses challenges in Nigeria. With little opportunity for typical Western-style advertising on television or billboards, the company hired local singers to go to towns and villages offering a mix of entertainment and product demonstrations.

China provides another interesting example of local adaptation and a long-term focus. After 13 years of talks, Nestlé was formally invited into China in 1987 by the government of Heilongjiang province. Nestlé opened a plant to produce powdered milk and infant formula there in 1990, but quickly realized that the local rail and road infrastructure was inadequate and inhibited the collection of milk and delivery of finished products. Rather than make do with the local infrastructure, Nestlé embarked on an ambitious plan to establish its own distribution network, known as milk roads, between 27 villages in the region and factory collection points, called chilling centers. Farmers brought their milk—often on bicycles or carts—to the centers where it was weighed and analyzed. Unlike the government, Nestlé paid the farmers promptly. Suddenly the farmers had an incentive to produce milk, and many bought a second cow, increasing the cow population in the district by 3,000, to 9,000, in 18 months. Area managers then organized a delivery system that used dedicated vans to deliver the milk to Nestlé's factory.

Although at first glance this might seem to be a very costly solution; Nestlé calculated that the long-term benefits would be substantial. Nestlé's strategy is similar to that undertaken by many European and American companies during the first waves of industrialization in those countries. Companies often had to invest in infrastructure that we now take for granted to get production off the ground. Once the infrastructure was in place in China, Nestlé's production took off. In 1990, 316 tons of powdered milk and infant formula were produced. By 1994, output exceeded 10,000 tons, and the company decided to triple capacity. Based on this experience, Nestlé decided to build another two powdered milk factories in China and was aiming to generate sales of $700 million by 2000.

Nestlé is pursuing a similar long-term bet in the Middle East, an area in which most multinational food companies have little presence. Collectively, the Middle East accounts for only about 2 percent of Nestlé's worldwide sales, and the individual markets are very small. However, Nestlé's long-term strategy is based on the assumption that regional conflicts will subside and intraregional trade will expand as trade barriers between countries in the region come down. Once that happens, Nestlé's factories in the Middle East should be able to sell throughout the region, thereby realizing scale economies. In anticipation of this development, Nestlé has established a network of factories in five countries in hopes that each will someday supply the entire region with different products. The company currently makes ice cream in Dubai, soups and cereals in Saudi Arabia, yogurt and bouillon in Egypt, chocolate in Turkey, and ketchup and instant noodles in Syria. For the present, Nestlé can survive in these markets by using local materials and focusing on local demand. The Syrian factory, for example, relies on products that use tomatoes, a major local agricultural product. Syria also produces wheat, which is the main ingredient in instant noodles. Even if trade barriers don't come down soon, Nestlé has indicated it will remain committed to the region. By using local inputs and focusing on local consumer needs, it has earned a good rate of return in the region, even though the individual markets are small.

Despite its successes in places such as China and parts of the Middle East, not all of Nestlé's moves have worked out so well. Like several other Western companies, Nestlé has had its problems in Japan, where a failure to adapt its coffee brand to local conditions meant the loss of a significant market opportunity to another Western company, Coca-Cola. For years, Nestlé's instant coffee brand was the dominant coffee product in Japan. In the 1960s, cold canned coffee (which can be purchased from soda vending machines) started to gain a following in Japan. Nestlé dismissed the product as just a coffee-flavored drink, rather than the real thing, and declined to enter the market. Nestlé's local partner at the time, Kirin Beer, was so incensed at Nestlé's refusal to enter the canned coffee market that it broke off its relationship with the company. In contrast, Coca-Cola entered the market with Georgia, a product developed specifically for this segment of the Japanese market. By leveraging its existing distribution channel. Coca-Cola captured a 40 percent share of the $4 billion a year market for canned coffee in Japan. Nestlé, which failed to enter the market until the 1980s, has only a 4 percent share.

While Nestlé has built businesses from the ground up in many emerging markets, such as Nigeria and China, in others it will purchase local companies if suitable candidates can be found. The company pursued such a strategy in Poland, which it entered in 1994 by purchasing Goplana, the country's second largest chocolate manufacturer. With the collapse of communism and the opening of the Polish market, income levels in Poland have started to rise and so has chocolate consumption. Once a scarce item, the market grew by 8 percent a year throughout the 1990s. To take advantage of this opportunity, Nestlé has pursued a strategy of evolution, rather than revolution. It has kept the top management of the company staffed with locals—as it does in most of its operations around the world—and carefully adjusted Goplana's product line to better match local opportunities. At the same time, it has pumped money into Goplana's marketing, which has enabled the unit to gain share from several other chocolate makers in the country. Still, competition in the market is intense. Eight companies, including several foreign-owned enterprises, such as the market leader, Wedel, which is owned by PepsiCo, are vying for market share, and this has depressed prices and profit margins, despite the healthy volume growth.

MANAGEMENT STRUCTURE

Nestlé is a decentralized organization. Responsibility for operating decisions is pushed down to local units, which typically enjoy a high degree of autonomy with regard to decisions involving pricing, distribution, marketing, human resources, and so on. At the same time, the company is organized into seven worldwide strategic business units (SBUs) that have responsibility for high-level strategic decisions and business development. For example, a strategic business unit focuses on coffee and beverages. Another one focuses on confectionery and ice cream. These SBUs engage in overall strategy development, including acquisitions and market entry strategy. In recent years, two-thirds of Nestlé's growth has come from acquisitions, so this is a critical function. Running in parallel to this structure is a regional organization that divides the world into five major geographical zones, such as Europe, North America, and Asia. The regional organizations assist in the overall strategy development process and are responsible for developing regional strategies (an example would be Nestlé's strategy in the Middle East, which was discussed earlier). Neither the SBU nor regional managers, however, get involved in local operating or strategic decisions on anything other than an exceptional basis.

Although Nestlé makes intensive use of local managers, to knit its diverse worldwide operations together the company relies on its "expatriate army." This consists of about 700 managers who spend the bulk of their careers on foreign assignments, moving from one country to the next. Selected primarily on the basis of their ability, drive, and willingness to live a quasi-nomadic lifestyle, these individuals often work in half a dozen nations, during their careers. Nestlé also uses management development programs as a strategic tool for creating an *esprit de corps* among managers. At Rive-Reine, the company's international training center in Switzerland, the company brings together managers from around the world, at different stages in their careers, for specially targeted development programs of two to three weeks duration. The objective of these programs is to give the managers a better understanding of Nestlé's culture and strategy and to give them access to the company's top management.

The research and development operation has a special place within Nestlé, which is not surprising for a company that was established to commercialize innovative foodstuffs. The R&D function comprises 18 different groups that operate in 11 countries throughout the world. Nestlé spends approximately 1 percent of its annual sales revenue on R&D and has 3,100 employees dedicated to the function. Around 70 percent of the R&D budget is spent on development initiatives. These initiatives focus on developing products and processes that fulfill market needs, as identified by the SBUs, in concert with regional and local managers. For example, Nestlé instant noodle products were originally developed by the R&D group in response to the perceived needs of local operating companies through the Asian region. The company also has longer-term development projects that focus on developing new technological platforms, such as nonanimal protein sources or agricultural biotechnology products.

Case Discussion Questions

1. Does it make sense for Nestlé to focus its growth efforts on emerging markets? Why?

2. What is the company's strategy with regard to business development in emerging markets? Does this strategy make sense?

3. From an organizational perspective, what is required for this strategy to work effectively?

4. How would you describe Nestlé's strategic posture at the corporate level; is it pursuing a global strategy, a multidomestic strategy, an international strategy, or a transnational strategy?

5. Does this overall strategic posture make sense given the markets and countries that Nestlé participates in? Why?

6. Is Nestlé's management structure and philosophy aligned with its overall strategic posture?

Sources

1. Hall, W. "Strength of Brands Is Key to Success," *Financial Times*, November 30, 1998, p. 2.

2. "How to Conquer China (and the World) with Instant Noodles," *The Economist*, June 17, 1995.

3. Lorenz, C. "Sugar Daddy," *Financial Times*, April 20, 1994, p. 19.

4. Michaels, D. "Chocolate Giants Worldwide Find Themselves Sweet on Polish Market," *The Wall Street Journal*, December 12, 1997.

5. Nestlé. "Key Facts and History," At http://www.nestle.com.

6. Rapoport, C. "Nestlé's Brand Building Machine," *Fortune*, September 19, 1994, p. 147.

7. Steinmetz, G., and T. Parker-Rope. "All Over the Map." *The Wall Street Journal*, September 26, 1996, p. R4.

8. Sullivan, M. "Nestlé Is Looking to Coffee Market in Russia for Sales," *The Wall Street Journal*, August 7, 1998, p. B7A.

🌐 Strategic and Organization Change at Black & Decker

Known primarily for its power tools, Black & Decker is one of the world's older multinational corporations. The company was founded in Baltimore, Maryland, in 1910, and by the end of the 1920s had become a small multinational company with operations in Canada and Britain. Today the company has two well-known brands,

Black & Decker consumer power tools and its DeWalt brand of professional power tools. It sells its products in over 100 nations, and has revenues in excess of $5 billion, more than half of which are generated outside of the United States.

The company grew rapidly during the 1950s and 1960s due to its strong brand name and near monopoly share of the consumer and professional power tools markets. This monopoly was based on Black & Decker's pioneering development of handheld power tools. It was during this period that Black & Decker expanded rapidly in international markets, typically by setting up wholly owned subsidiaries in a nation and giving them the right to develop, manufacture, and market the company's power tools. As a result, by the early 1980s, the company had 23 wholly owned subsidiaries in foreign nations and two joint ventures.

During its period of rapid international expansion, Black & Decker operated with a decentralized organization. In its 1979 annual report, the company described how "In order to be effective in the marketplace, Black & Decker follows a decentralized organizational approach. All business functions (marketing, engineering, manufacturing, etc.) are kept as close as possible to the market to be served." In effect, each wholly owned subsidiary was granted considerable autonomy to run its own business.

By the mid-1980s, however, this structure was starting to become untenable. New competitors had emerged in the power tool business, including Bosch, Makita, and Panasonic. As a result, Black & Decker's monopoly position had eroded. Throughout the 1980s, the company pursued a strategy of rationalization. Factories were closed and the company consolidated production in fewer, more efficient production facilities. This process was particularly evident in Europe, where different national operating companies had traditionally had their own production facilities. As the company noted in its 1985 annual report, "Globalization remains a key strategic objective. In 1985, sound progress was made in designing and marketing products for a worldwide market, rather than just regional ones. Focused design centers will ensure a greater number of global products for the future. . . . Global purchasing programs have been established, and cost benefits are being realized."

During this period, while the company maintained a number of design centers, it cut the number of basic R&D centers from eight to just two. The autonomy of individual factories also started to decrease. The factories that remained after the round of closures had to compete with each other for the right to produce a product for the world market. Major decisions about where to produce products to serve world markets were now being made by managers at the corporate headquarters. Even so, national subsidiaries still maintained a fair degree of autonomy. For example, if a national subsidiary

developed a new product, it was still likely that it would get the mandate to produce that product for the world market. Also, if a national subsidiary performed well, corporate management was likely to leave it alone.

By the 1990s, however, it was clear that this change had not gone far enough. The rise of powerful retailers such as Home Depot and Lowe's in the United States had further pressured prices in the power tools market. Blacker & Decker responded by looking for ways to garner additional manufacturing efficiencies. During this period, Black & Decker shut down several more factories in its long-established subsidiaries and started to shift production to new facilities that it opened in Mexico and China. As this process proceeded, any remaining autonomy the managers of local factories enjoyed was virtually eliminated. Corporate managers became much more aggressive about allocating products to different factories based on a consideration of operating costs. In effect, Black & Decker's factories now had to compete with each other for the right to make products, and those factories that did not do well in this process were shut down.

In 2001, Black & Decker announced yet another restructuring initiative. Among other things, the initiative involved reducing the workforce by 700 people, to 4,500, shutting long-established factories in the United States and Britain, and shifting production to low-cost facilities. By 2004 this process reached a logical conclusion when the company reorganized its power tools business into two separate global divisions—one that was charged with the global development, manufacture, and marketing of Black & Decker power tools, and another that was charged with the same for the company's professional DeWalt brand. At this point, the company operated some 36 manufacturing facilities, 18 outside of the United States in Mexico, China, the Czech Republic, Germany, Italy, and Britain. It had seven design centers, and two basic R&D centers, one in the United States and one in Britain. Increasingly, the design and R&D centers in the United States and Britain took on responsibility for new-product development for the global market. Throughout the early 2000s, successively larger shares of production were allocated to factories in just three nations, China, Mexico, and the Czech Republic, and in its 2004 annual report, Black & Decker indicated that this process was likely to continue.

Case Discussion Questions

1. How would you characterize Black & Decker's international expansion during the 1950s and 1960s? What strategy was the company pursuing? What was the key feature of the international organization structure that Black & Decker operated with at this time? Did Black & Decker's strategy and structure make sense given the competitive environment at that time?

2. How did the competitive environment confronting Black & Decker change during the 1980s and 1990s? What changes did Black & Decker make in its (a) strategy and (b) structure to compete more effectively in this new environment?

3. By the 2000s, what strategy was Black & Decker pursuing in the global marketplace? How would you characterize its structure? Did the structure fit the strategy and environment?

4. Why do you think it took nearly two decades for Black & Decker to effect a change in strategy and structure?

Sources

1. N. A. Phelps and P. Waley, "Capital versus the Districts: A Tale of One Multinational Company's Attempt to Disembed Itself," *Economic Geography* 80 (2004), pp. 191–214.

2. T. Walton, "The Black & Decker Corporation," *Design Management Institute Case Study*, October 1997.

3. "Black & Decker Reorganizes Power Tools and Accessories Business," Black & Decker press release, March 1, 2004.

4. *Black & Decker 10K Report*, 2003.

Organizational Culture and Incentives at Lincoln Electric

Lincoln Electric is one of the leading companies in the global market for arc welding equipment. Lincoln's success has been based on extremely high levels of employee productivity. The company attributes its productivity to a strong organizational culture and an incentive scheme based on piecework. Lincoln's organizational culture dates back to James Lincoln, who in 1907 joined the company that his brother had established a few years earlier. Lincoln had a strong respect for the ability of the individual and believed that, correctly motivated, ordinary people could achieve extraordinary performance. He emphasized that Lincoln should be a meritocracy where people were rewarded for their individual effort. Strongly egalitarian, Lincoln removed barriers to communication between "workers" and "managers," practicing an open-door policy. He made sure that all who worked for the company were treated equally; for example, everyone ate in the same cafeteria, there were no reserved parking places for "managers," and so on. Lincoln also believed that any gains in productivity should be shared with consumers in the form of lower prices, with employees in the form of higher pay, and with shareholders in the form of higher dividends.

The company's incentive system reinforces the organizational culture that grew out of James Lincoln's beliefs. Production workers receive no base salary but are paid according to the number of pieces they produce. The piecework rates at the company enable an employee working at a normal pace to earn an income equivalent to the average wage for manufacturing workers in the area where a factory is based. Workers have responsibility for the quality of their output and must repair any defects spotted by quality inspectors before the pieces are included in the piecework calculation. Since 1934, production workers have been awarded a semiannual bonus based on merit ratings. These ratings are based on objective criteria (such as an employee's level and quality of output) and subjective criteria (such as an employee's attitude toward cooperation and his or her dependability). These systems give Lincoln's employees an incentive to work hard and to generate innovations that boost productivity, for doing so influences their level of pay. Lincoln's factory workers have been able to earn a base pay that often exceeds the average manufacturing wage in the area by more than 50 percent and receive a bonus on top of this that in good years could double their base pay. Indeed, employees at Lincoln's U.S. plants consistently rank among the highest paid factory workers in the world. Despite high employee compensation, the workers are so productive that Lincoln has a lower cost structure than its competitors.

Lincoln's unique culture and incentive systems enabled it to operate with a very flat organizational structure. The supervisor to worker ratio in Lincoln's main U.S. plant is 1 to 100. In a typical factory in the United States the ratio is more like 1 to 25, and in some auto plants it is 1 to 10. Motivated by the incentive system, Lincoln's employees often work long hours. The average workweek in Lincoln's U.S. plants is between 43 and 58 hours, and the company is able to ask people to work longer hours on short notice.

While this organizational culture and set of incentives works well in the United States, where it is compatible with the individualistic culture of the country, and the tradition of hard work for more money, it did not translate easily into foreign operations. In the 1980s and early 1990s, Lincoln expanded into international markets. It did consider exporting from the United States, but was told by foreign distributors that American equipment would not sell well in Europe, so instead the company decided to set up wholly owned subsidiaries to make the equipment locally. Lincoln acquired seven arc welding manufacturers in Europe and one in Mexico, and established greenfield plants in Japan, Venezuela, and Brazil. The total investment amounted to $325 million, a substantial amount for Lincoln. Lincoln's aggressive expansion represented a sharp break in the history of the company. Up until that point its foreign operations had been minimal. The company's senior management, most of whom were hired straight out of college and promoted from within, had almost no experience running businesses outside of the United States. They were, however, proud of their unique incentive system and the high productivity it created, and they believed that applying this system to foreign factories would be a source of competitive advantage enabling Lincoln to grow its foreign sales and profits.

For the acquisitions, Lincoln left local managers in place, believing that they knew local conditions better than Americans who had little international experience. However, the local managers had little working knowledge of Lincoln's strong organizational culture and were unable or unwilling to impose that culture on their units, which had their own long-established organizational cultures. Nevertheless, Lincoln told local managers to introduce its incentive systems in acquired companies. They frequently ran into legal and cultural roadblocks.

In many countries, piecework is viewed as an exploitive compensation system that forces employees to work ever harder. In Germany, where Lincoln made an acquisition, it is illegal. In Brazil, a bonus paid for more than two years becomes a legal entitlement! In many other countries, both managers and workers were opposed to the idea of piecework. Lincoln found that many European workers valued extra leisure more highly than extra income and were not prepared to work as hard as their American counterparts. For example, in Germany the average workweek was 35 hours, as opposed to the 43–58 hours that Lincoln employees worked in the United States. Many of the acquired companies were also unionized, and the local unions vigorously opposed the introduction of piecework. As a result, Lincoln was not able to replicate the high level of employee productivity that it had achieved in the United States, and its expansion pulled down the performance of the entire company. To make matters worse, the entry into Europe was soon followed by a recession that hit the industry hard, and many of Lincoln's foreign plants were working at only half their capacity.

Ultimately Lincoln scaled back operations in Europe, shut down its German plant, and closed plants in Brazil, Japan, and Venezuela, taking a restructuring charge of $70 million. The company also shifted its strategy, electing to export U.S. made machines to foreign markets like Germany, rather than build them locally, a strategy that soon turned out to be surprisingly successful. Indeed, in Germany the company gained an advantage by thumbing its nose at one local tradition—the norm that trade shows should not be used for selling products, but for entertaining customers and conducting public relations. Lincoln flew over three planeloads of arc welding equipment from the United States, and set itself a target of selling 1,200 welding machines at an eight-day industry trade show. It sold 1,762 and discovered that contrary to what it had been told, American equipment would sell very well in Germany. From that point on, Lincoln emphasized exports.

The one foreign venture that did do relatively well was in Mexico. Acquired in 1990, the Mexican venture was unionized and piecework ran against the Mexican culture. However, the local manager tried to introduce the incentive system gradually. In a plant of 175 employees he asked 2 of them to take a chance on piecework. He also guaranteed them a minimum income, to reduce the risks associated with piecework. After they started to make more money than their counterparts, other people started to ask if they could go into the system. It took two years, but eventually the entire labor force converted to a piecework system.

Reflecting on the problems it encountered when expanding internationally, the CEO of the company noted that "Our managers didn't know how to run foreign operations; nor did they understand foreign cultures. Consequently, we had to rely upon people in our foreign companies, people we didn't know and people who did not know us."

Case Discussion Questions

1. What is the source of Lincoln's long-standing competitive advantage in the United States market for arc welding equipment?

2. Why did Lincoln enter foreign markets through acquisitions and greenfield ventures, rather than through exporting?

3. Why did Lincoln's foreign ventures fail to deliver the gains forecasted?

4. In retrospect, what might Lincoln have done differently to avoid the financial crisis it found itself in?

5. What lessons can be gleaned from the Mexican venture?

Sources

1. J. O'Connell, "Lincoln Electric: Venturing Abroad," Harvard Business School Case No. 9-398-095, April 1998.

2. Company information at www.lincolnelectric.com (accessed July 11, 2007).

3. D. F. Hastings "Lincoln Electric's Harsh Lessons from International Expansion," Harvard Business Review, May–June 1999, pp. 3–11.

4. P. Marsh, "Change to Global Approach," Financial Times, February 13, 1998, p. 13.

5. R. M. Hodgetts, "A Conversation with Donald F. Hastings," Organizational Dynamics, Winter 1977, pp. 68–75.

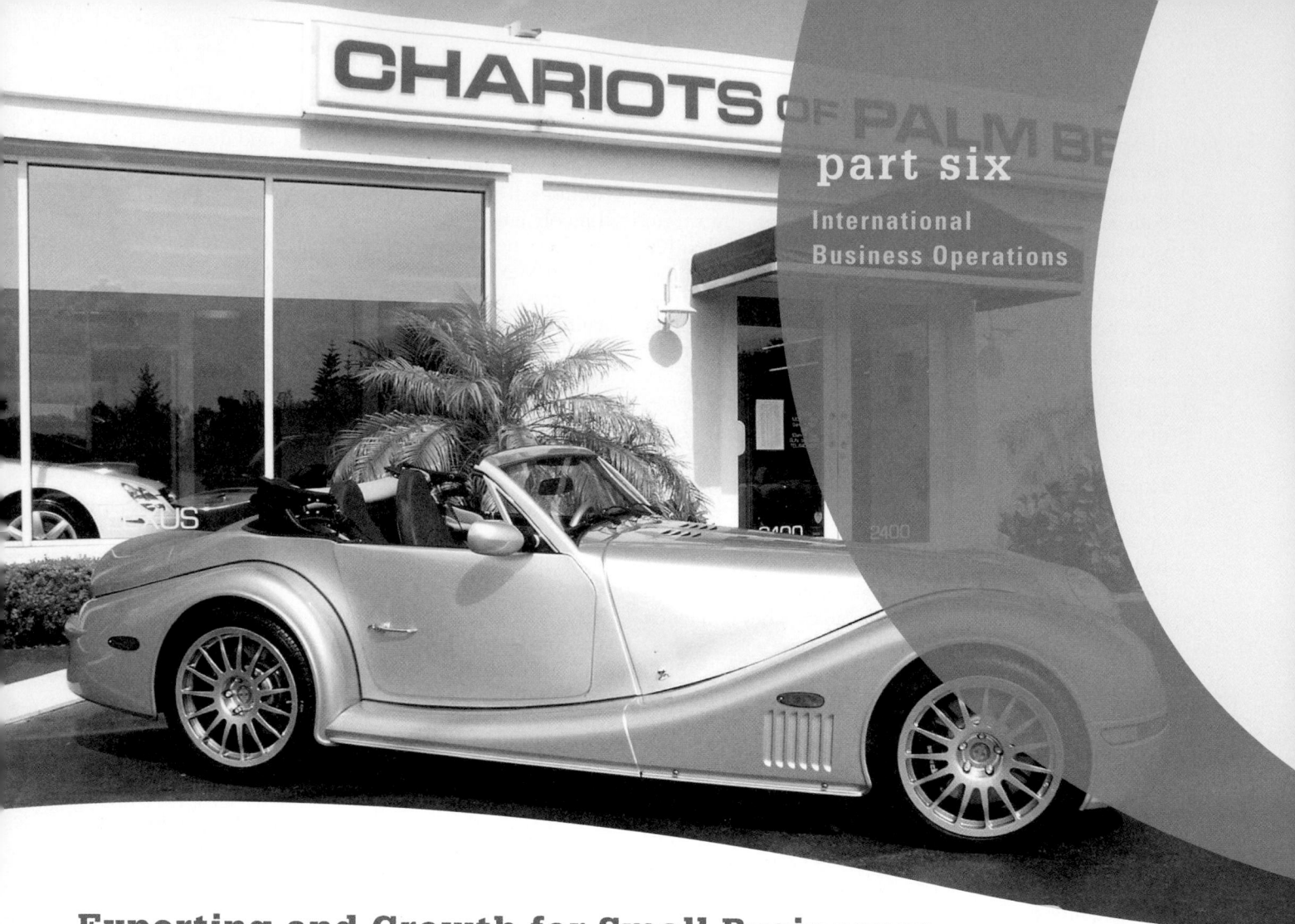

Exporting and Growth for Small Businesses

Morgan Motor Co. is one of the iconic small businesses of the United Kingdom. The company has been making its classic sports cars since 1909. Today some 150 employees build up to 700 cars a year, each of which sells for $80,000 to $120,000. However, Morgan's niche is so small that it could not survive if it did not export. Today some 70 percent of its production is shipped overseas, primarily to the United States and Europe. Moreover, the modern Morgan car, although looking every bit the British sports car, contains major components that are imported from foreign manufacturers, such as engines from BMW and components

for ABS braking systems from Bosch. For Morgan, exporting and importing represent the very lifeblood of the company.

Morgan is not alone. Many other small businesses have found that exports can drive growth. Another success story is Wadia, a Michigan-based manufacturer of high-end premium-priced compact disc players for audiophiles. Wadia, which has annual sales of $8 million, gets some 70 to 80 percent of its sales from overseas. Around 35 to 45 percent comes from Asia, with both Japan and China accounting for as much as 15 percent of sales volume in any one year. Like Morgan, Wadia

Exporting, Importing, and Countertrade

15

LEARNING OBJECTIVES

After you have read this chapter you should be able to:

LO¹ Explain the promises and risks associated with exporting.

LO² Outline the steps managers can take to improve their firm's export performance.

LO³ Identify information sources and government programs that exist to help exporters.

LO⁴ Grasp the basic steps involved in export financing.

LO⁵ Articulate how countertrade can be used to facilitate exporting.

---

produces a high-end product that is so specialized it could not survive on sales in its home country alone.

Exporting, however, is not easy, particularly for smaller enterprises like Morgan and Wadia. Many succeed only after tapping into help from government export agencies and export financing institutions. Consider Malden Mills, the United States manufacturer of Polartech®, a high-technology textile material used in premium-priced outdoor wear. Facing limited growth opportunities in the United States, Malden Mills contracted with the South Carolina Export Consortium, a state agency, to perform an international market analysis to determine the sales potential of its

portfolio of high-tech fabrics. Malden Mills used the consortium's research to identify new opportunities for its materials, forecast future demand trends, and secure a $20 million working capital loan guarantee from the U.S. Export–Import Bank (which was later raised to $35 million). The resulting expansion in export sales to France, Korea, and the United Kingdom allowed Malden Mills to better utilize its capacity and to continue to make textile products in the United States, despite the fact that the industry as a whole has been in rapid decline due to globalization and the rise of low-cost manufacturers in developing nations. By 2006 over half of Malden Mills' $48 million in sales were due to exports.[1]

Introduction

Whereas we take it for granted that many large businesses export or produce overseas, as discussed in this chapter's opening case, numerous small businesses do too, often with major benefit. The volume of export activity in the world economy is increasing as exporting has become easier. The gradual decline in trade barriers under the umbrella of GATT and now the WTO (see Chapter 6), along with regional economic agreements such as the European Union and the North American Free Trade Agreement (see Chapter 8), has significantly increased export opportunities. At the same time, modern communication and transportation technologies have alleviated the logistical problems associated with exporting. Firms are increasingly using the Internet, toll-free 800 phone numbers, and international air express services to reduce the costs of exporting. Consequently, it is no longer unusual to find small companies that are thriving as exporters.

Nevertheless, exporting remains a challenge for many firms. Smaller enterprises can find the process intimidating. The firm wishing to export must identify foreign market opportunities, avoid a host of unanticipated problems that are often associated with doing business in a foreign market, familiarize itself with the mechanics of export and import financing, learn where it can get financing and export credit insurance, and learn how it should deal with foreign exchange risk. The process can be made more problematic by currencies that are not freely convertible. Arranging payment for exports to countries with weak currencies can be a problem. This brings us to the topic of countertrade, by which payment for exports is received in goods and services rather than money. In this chapter, we will discuss all these issues with the exception of foreign exchange risk, which was covered in Chapter 10. We open the chapter by considering the promise and pitfalls of exporting.

The Promise and Pitfalls of Exporting

The great promise of exporting is that large revenue and profit opportunities are to be found in foreign markets for most firms in most industries. The international market is normally so much larger than the firm's domestic market that exporting is nearly always a way to increase the revenue and profit base of a company. By expanding the size of the market, exporting can enable a firm to achieve economies of scale, thereby lowering its unit costs. Firms that do not export often lose out on significant opportunities for growth and cost reduction.[2]

Studies have shown that while many large firms tend to be proactive about seeking opportunities for profitable exporting, systematically scanning foreign markets to see where the opportunities lie for leveraging their technology, products, and marketing skills in foreign countries, many medium-sized and small firms are very reactive.[3] Typically, such reactive firms do not even consider exporting until their domestic market is saturated and the emergence of excess productive capacity at home forces them to look for growth opportunities in foreign markets. Also, many small and medium-sized firms tend to wait for the world to come to them, rather than going out into the world to seek opportunities. Even when the world does come to them, they may not respond. An example is MMO Music Group, which makes sing-along tapes for karaoke machines. Foreign sales accounted for about 15 percent of MMO's revenues of $8 million, but the firm's CEO admits that this figure would probably have been much higher had he paid attention to building international sales. Unanswered faxes and phone messages from Asia and Europe often piled up while he was trying to manage the burgeoning domestic side of the business. By the time MMO did turn its attention to foreign markets, other competitors had stepped into the breach and MMO found it tough going to build export volume.[4]

MMO's experience is common, and it suggests a need for firms to become more proactive about seeking export opportunities. One reason more firms are not proactive is that they are unfamiliar with foreign market opportunities; they simply do not know how big the opportunities actually are or where they might lie. Simple ignorance of the potential opportunities is a huge barrier to exporting.[5] Also, many would-be exporters, particularly smaller firms, are often intimidated by the complexities and mechanics of exporting to countries where business practices, language, culture, legal systems, and currency are very different from the home market.[6] This combination of unfamiliarity and intimidation probably explains why exporters still account for only a tiny percentage of U.S. firms, less than 5 percent of firms with fewer than 500 employees, according to the Small Business Administration.[7]

To make matters worse, many neophyte exporters run into significant problems when first trying to do business abroad, and this sours them on future exporting ventures. Common pitfalls include poor market analysis, a poor understanding of competitive conditions in the foreign market, a failure to customize the product offering to the needs of foreign customers, lack of an effective distribution program, a poorly executed promotional campaign, and problems securing financing.[8] Novice exporters tend to underestimate the time and expertise needed to cultivate business in foreign countries.[9] Few realize the amount of management resources that have to be dedicated to this activity. Many foreign customers require face-to-face negotiations on their home turf. An exporter may have to spend months learning about a country's trade regulations, business practices, and more before a deal can be closed. The next Management Focus feature, which documents the experience of FCX Systems in China, suggests that it may take years before foreigners are comfortable enough to purchase in significant quantities.

Exporters often face voluminous paperwork, complex formalities, and many potential delays and errors. According to a UN report on trade and development, a typical international trade transaction may involve 30 parties, 60 original documents, and 360 document copies, all of which have to be checked, transmitted, reentered into various information systems, processed, and filed. The United Nations has calculated that the time involved in preparing documentation, along with the costs of common errors in paperwork, often amounts to 10 percent of the final value of goods exported.[10]

Improving Export Performance

Inexperienced exporters have a number of ways to gain information about foreign market opportunities and avoid common pitfalls that tend to discourage and frustrate novice exporters.[12] In this section, we look at information sources for exporters to increase their knowledge of foreign market opportunities, we consider the pros and cons of using export management companies (EMCs) to assist in the export process, and we review various exporting strategies that can increase the probability of successful exporting. We begin, however, with a look at how several nations try to help domestic firms export.

AN INTERNATIONAL COMPARISON

One big impediment to exporting is the simple lack of knowledge of the opportunities available. Often there are many markets for a firm's product, but because they are in countries separated from the firm's home base by culture, language, distance, and time, the firm does not know of them. Identifying export opportunities is made even more complex because more than 200 countries with widely differing cultures compose the world of potential opportunities. Faced with such complexity and diversity, firms sometimes hesitate to seek export opportunities.

The way to overcome ignorance is to collect information. In Germany, one of the world's most successful exporting nations, trade associations, government agencies, and commercial banks gather information, helping small firms identify export opportunities. The Japanese Ministry of International Trade and Industry (**MITI**), which is always on the lookout for export opportunities, provides similar services. In addition, many

FCX Systems

Founded in 1987 with the help of a $20,000 loan from the Small Business Administration, FCX Systems is an American exporting success story. FCX makes power converters for the aerospace industry. These devices convert common electric utility frequencies into the higher frequencies used in aircraft systems and are primarily used to provide power to aircraft while they are on the ground. Today the West Virginia enterprise generates over half of its $20 million in annual sales from exports to more than 50 countries. FCX's prowess in opening up foreign markets has earned the company several awards for export excellence, including a 1999 presidential award for achieving extraordinary growth in export sales.

FCX initially got into exporting because it found that foreigners were often more receptive to the company's products than potential American customers. According to Don Gallion, president of FCX, "In the overseas market, they were looking for a good technical product, preferably made in the U.S., but they weren't asking questions about 'How long have you been in business? Are you still going to be here tomorrow?' They were just anxious to get the product."

In 1989, FCX signed on with an international distribution company to help with exporting, but Gallion became disillusioned with that company, and in 1994 FCX started to handle the exporting process on its own. At the time, exports represented 12 percent of sales, but by 1997 they had jumped to over 50 percent of the total, where they have stayed since.

In explaining the company's export success, Gallion cites a number of factors. One was the extensive assistance that FCX has received over the years from a number of federal and state agencies, including the U.S. Department of Commerce and the Development Office of West Virginia. These agencies demystified the process of exporting and provided FCX with good contacts. Finding a good local representative to help work through local regulations and customs is another critical factor, according to Gallion, who says, "A good rep will keep you out of trouble when it comes to customs and what you should and shouldn't do." Persistence is also very important, says Gallion, particularly when trying to break into markets where personal relationships are crucial, such as China.

China has been an interesting story for FCX. In 2004, the company booked $2 million in sales to China, but it took years to get to this point. China had been on Gallion's radar screen since the early 1990s, primarily because of the country's rapid modernization and its plans to build or remodel some 179 airports between 1998 and 2008. This constituted a potentially large market opportunity for FCX, particularly compared with the United States where perhaps only three new airports would be built during the same period. Despite the scale of the opportunity, progress was very slow. The company had to identify airports and airline projects, government agencies, customers, and decision makers, as well as work through different languages—and make friends. According to Gallion, "Only after they consider you a friend will they buy a product. They believe a friend would never cheat you." To make friends in China, Gallion estimates he had to make more than 100 trips to China since 1990, but now that the network has been established, it is starting to pay dividends.[11]

Japanese firms are affiliated in some way with the *sogo shosha,* Japan's great trading houses. The *sogo shosha* have offices all over the world, and they proactively and continuously seek export opportunities for their affiliated companies, large and small.[13]

German and Japanese firms can draw on the large reservoirs of experience, skills, information, and other resources of their respective export-oriented institutions. Unlike their German and Japanese competitors, many U.S. firms are relatively blind when they seek export opportunities; they are information disadvantaged. In part, this reflects historical differences. Both Germany and Japan have long made their living as trading nations, whereas until recently the United States has been a relatively self-contained continental economy in which international trade played a minor role. This is changing; both imports and exports now play a greater role in the U.S. economy than they did

20 years ago. However, the United States has not yet evolved an institutional structure for promoting exports similar to that of either Germany or Japan.

INFORMATION SOURCES

Despite institutional disadvantages, U.S. firms can increase their awareness of export opportunities. The most comprehensive source of information is the U.S. Department of Commerce and its district offices all over the country. Within that department are two organizations dedicated to providing businesses with intelligence and assistance for attacking foreign markets: the International Trade Administration and the United States and Foreign Commercial Service Agency.

These agencies provide the potential exporter with a "best prospects" list, which gives the names and addresses of potential distributors in foreign markets along with businesses they are in, the products they handle, and their contact person. In addition, the Department of Commerce has assembled a "comparison shopping service" for 14 countries that are major markets for U.S. exports. For a small fee, a firm can receive a customized market research survey on a product of its choice. This survey provides information on marketability, the competition, comparative prices, distribution channels, and names of potential sales representatives. Each study is conducted on-site by an officer of the Department of Commerce.

The Department of Commerce also organizes trade events that help potential exporters make foreign contacts and explore export opportunities. The department organizes exhibitions at international trade fairs, which are held regularly in major cities worldwide. The department also has a matchmaker program, in which department representatives accompany groups of U.S. businesspeople abroad to meet with qualified agents, distributors, and customers.

Another government organization, the Small Business Administration (SBA), can help potential exporters (see the accompanying Management Focus for examples of the SBA's work). The SBA employs 76 district international trade officers and 10 regional international trade officers throughout the United States as well as a 10-person international trade staff in Washington, D.C. Through its Service Corps of Retired Executives (SCORE) program, the SBA also oversees some 850 volunteers with international trade experience to provide one-on-one counseling to active and new-to-export businesses. The SBA also coordinates the Export Legal Assistance Network (ELAN), a nationwide group of international trade attorneys who provide free initial consultations to small businesses on export-related matters.

In addition to the Department of Commerce and SBA, nearly every state and many large cities maintain active trade commissions whose purpose is to promote exports. Most of these provide business counseling, information gathering, technical assistance, and financing. Unfortunately, many have fallen victim to budget cuts or to turf battles for political and financial support with other export agencies.

A number of private organizations are also beginning to provide more assistance to would-be exporters. Commercial banks and major accounting firms are more willing to assist small firms in starting export operations than they were a decade ago. In addition, large multinationals that have been successful in the global arena are typically willing to discuss opportunities overseas with the owners or managers of small firms.[14]

UTILIZING EXPORT MANAGEMENT COMPANIES

One way for first-time exporters to identify the opportunities associated with exporting and to avoid many of the associated pitfalls is to hire an **export management company** (EMC). EMCs are export specialists who act as the export marketing department or international department for their client firms. EMCs normally accept two types of export assignments. They start exporting operations for a firm with the understanding that the firm will take over operations after they are well established. In the other type of service, the EMC performs start-up services with the understanding that the EMC will have continuing responsibility for selling the firm's products. Many EMCs specialize in

Exporting with a Little Government Help

Exporting can seem like a daunting prospect, but the reality is that in the United States, as in many other countries, many small enterprises have built profitable export businesses. For example, Landmark Systems of Virginia had virtually no domestic sales before it entered the European market. Landmark had developed a software program for IBM mainframe computers and located an independent distributor in Europe to represent its product. In the first year, 80 percent of sales were attributed to exporting. In the second year, sales jumped from $100,000 to $1.4 million—with 70 percent attributable to exports. Landmark is not alone; government data suggest that in the United States nearly 89 percent of firms that export are small businesses that employ fewer than 100 people. Their share of total U.S. exports has grown steadily over the last decade, reaching 21 percent by the early 2000s. Firms with less than 500 employees account for 97 percent of all U.S. exporters and almost 30 percent of all exports by value.

To help jump-start the exporting process, many small companies have drawn on the expertise of government agencies, financial institutions, and export management companies. Consider the case of Novi, Inc., a California-based business. Company President Michael Stoff tells how he utilized the services of the U.S. Small Business Administration (SBA) Office of International Trade to start exporting: "When I began my business venture, Novi, Inc., I knew that my Tune-Tote (a stereo system for bicycles) had the potential to be successful in international markets. Although I had no prior experience in this area, I began researching and collecting information on international markets. I was willing to learn, and by targeting key sources for information and guidance, I was able to penetrate international markets in a short period of time. One vital source I used from the beginning was the SBA. Through the SBA I was directed to a program that dealt specifically with business development—the Service Corps of Retired Executives (SCORE). I was assigned an adviser who had run his own import/export business for 30 years. The services of SCORE are provided on a continual basis and are free.

"As I began to pursue exporting, my first step was a thorough marketing evaluation. I targeted trade shows with a good presence of international buyers. I also went to DOC (Department of Commerce) for counseling and information about the rules and regulations of exporting. I advertised my product in 'Commercial News USA,' distributed through U.S. embassies to buyers worldwide. I utilized DOC's World Traders Data Reports to get background information on potential foreign buyers. As a result, I received 60 to 70 inquiries about Tune-Tote from around the world. Once I completed my research and evaluation of potential buyers, I decided which ones would be most suitable to market my product internationally. Then I decided to grant exclusive distributorship. In order to effectively communicate with my international customers, I invested in a fax. I chose a U.S. bank to handle international transactions. The bank also provided guidance on methods of payment and how best to receive and transmit money. This is essential know-how for anyone wanting to be successful in foreign markets."

In just one year of exporting, export sales at Novi topped $1 million and increased 40 percent in the second year of operations. Today, Novi, Inc., is a large distributor of wireless intercom systems that exports to more than 10 countries.[15]

---

serving firms in particular industries and in particular areas of the world. Thus, one EMC may specialize in selling agricultural products in the Asian market, while another may focus on exporting electronics products to Eastern Europe.

In theory, the advantage of EMCs is that they are experienced specialists who can help the neophyte exporter identify opportunities and avoid common pitfalls. A good EMC will have a network of contacts in potential markets, have multilingual employees, have a good knowledge of different business mores, and be fully conversant with the ins and outs of the exporting process and with local business regulations. However, the quality of EMCs varies.[16] While some perform their functions very well, others appear to add little value to the exporting company. Therefore, an exporter should review carefully a number of EMCs and check references. One drawback of relying on EMCs is that the company can fail to develop its own exporting capabilities.

Export Strategy at 3M

The Minnesota Mining and Manufacturing Co. (3M), which makes more than 40,000 products including tape, sandpaper, medical products, and the ever-present Post-it notes, is one of the world's great multinational operations. In 2006, the firm generated 61 percent of its $23 billion in revenues outside the United States. Although the bulk of these revenues came from foreign-based operations, 3M remains a major exporter with over $2 billion in exports. The company often uses its exports to establish an initial presence in a foreign market, only building foreign production facilities once sales volume rises to a level that justifies local production.

The export strategy is built around simple principles. One is known as "FIDO," which stands for First In (to a new market) Defeats Others. The essence of FIDO is to gain an advantage over other exporters by getting into a market first and learning about that country and how to sell there before others do. A second principle is "make a little, sell a little," which is the idea of entering on a small scale with a very modest investment and pushing one basic product, such as reflective sheeting for traffic signs in Russia or scouring pads in Hungary. Once 3M believes it has learned enough about the market to reduce the risk of failure to reasonable levels, it adds additional products.

A third principle at 3M is to hire local employees to sell the firm's products. The company normally sets up a local sales subsidiary to handle its export activities in a country. It then staffs this subsidiary with local hires because it believes they are likely to have a much better idea of how to sell in their own country than American expatriates. Because of the implementation of this principle, just 160 of 3M's 39,500 foreign employees are U.S. expatriates.

Another common practice at 3M is to formulate global strategic plans for the export and eventual overseas production of its products. Within the context of these plans, 3M gives local managers considerable autonomy to find the best way to sell the product within their country. Thus, when 3M first exported its Post-it notes, it planned to "sample the daylights" out of the product, but it also told local managers to find the best way of doing this. Local managers hired office cleaning crews to pass out samples in Great Britain and Germany; in Italy, they used office products distributors to pass out free samples; while in Malaysia, local managers employed young women to go from office to office handing out samples of the product. In typical 3M fashion, when the volume of Post-it notes was sufficient to justify it, local production replaced exports from the United States. Thus, after several years 3M found it worthwhile to set up production facilities in France to produce Post-it notes for the European market.[19]

EXPORT STRATEGY

In addition to using EMCs, a firm can reduce the risks associated with exporting if it is careful about its choice of export strategy.[17] A few guidelines can help firms improve their odds of success. For example, one of the most successful exporting firms in the world, the Minnesota Mining and Manufacturing Co. (3M), has built its export success on three main principles—enter on a small scale to reduce risks, add additional product lines once the exporting operations start to become successful, and hire locals to promote the firm's products (3M's export strategy is profiled in the accompanying Management Focus). Another successful exporter, Red Spot Paint & Varnish, emphasizes the importance of cultivating personal relationships when trying to build an export business (see the next Management Focus).

The probability of exporting successfully can be increased dramatically by taking a handful of simple strategic steps. First, particularly for the novice exporter, it helps to hire an EMC or at least an experienced export consultant to help identify opportunities and navigate the paperwork and regulations so often involved in exporting. Second, it often makes sense to focus initially on one market or a handful of markets. Learn what is required to succeed in those markets before moving on to other markets. The firm that enters many markets at once runs the risk of spreading its limited management resources too thin. The result of such

Red Spot Paint & Varnish

Established in 1903 in Evansville, Indiana, Red Spot Paint & Varnish Company is in many ways typical of the companies that can be found in the small towns of America's heartland. The closely held company, whose CEO, Charles Storms, is the great-grandson of the founder, has 500 employees and annual sales of close to $90 million. The company's main product is paint for plastic components used in the automobile industry. Red Spot products are seen on automobile bumpers, wheel covers, grilles, headlights, instrument panels, door inserts, radio buttons, and other components. Unlike many other companies of a similar size and location, however, Red Spot has a thriving international business. International sales (which include exports and local production by licensees) now account for between 15 percent and 25 percent of revenue in any one year, and Red Spot does business in about 15 countries.

Red Spot Paint & Varnish's international business accounts for up to 25 percent of its revenue.

Red Spot has long had some international sales and once won an export award. To further its international business, Red Spot hired a Central Michigan University professor, Bryan Williams. Williams, who was hired because of his foreign-language skills (he speaks German, Japanese, and some Chinese), was the first employee at Red Spot whose exclusive focus was international marketing and sales. His first challenge was the lack of staff skilled in the business of exporting. He found that it was difficult to build an international business without in-house expertise in the basic mechanics of exporting.

According to Williams, Red Spot needed people who understood the nuts and bolts of exporting—letters of credit, payment terms, bills of lading, and so on. As might be expected for a business based in the heartland of America, no ready supply of such individuals was in the vicinity. It took Williams several years to solve this problem. Now Red Spot has a full-time staff of two who have been trained in the principles of exporting and international operations.

A second problem that Williams encountered was the clash between the quarter-to-quarter mentality that frequently pervades management practice in the United States and the long-term perspective that is often necessary to build a successful international business. Williams has found that building long-term personal relationships with potential foreign customers is often the key to getting business. When foreign customers visit Evansville, Williams often invites them home for dinner. His young children even started calling one visitor from Hong Kong "Uncle." Even with such efforts, however, the business may not come quickly. Meeting with potential foreign customers yields no direct business 90 percent of the time, although Williams points out that it often yields benefits in terms of competitive information and relationship building. He has found that perseverance pays. For example, Williams and Storms called on a major German automobile parts manufacturer for seven years before finally landing some business from the company.[20]

a shotgun approach to exporting may be a failure to become established in any one market. Third, as with 3M, it often makes sense to enter a foreign market on a small scale to reduce the costs of any subsequent failure. Most importantly, entering on a small scale provides the time and opportunity to learn about the foreign country before making significant capital commitments to that market. Fourth, the exporter needs to recognize the time and managerial commitment involved in building export sales and should hire additional personnel to oversee this activity. Fifth, in many countries, it is important to devote a lot of attention to building strong and enduring relationships with local distributors and/or customers (see the Management Focus on Red Spot Paint for an example). Sixth, as 3M often does, it is important to hire local personnel to help the firm establish itself in a foreign market. Local people are likely to have a much better sense of how to do business in a given country than a manager from an exporting firm who has never previously set foot in that country. Seventh, several studies have suggested that the firm needs to be proactive about seeking export opportunities.[18] Armchair exporting does not work! The world will not normally beat a pathway to your door. Finally, it is important for the exporter to retain the option of local production. Once exports reach a sufficient volume to justify cost-efficient local production, the exporting firm should consider establishing production facilities in the foreign market. Such localization helps foster good relations with the foreign country and can lead to greater market acceptance. Exporting is often not an end in itself, but merely a step on the road toward establishment of foreign production (again, 3M provides an example of this philosophy).

Export and Import Financing

Mechanisms for financing exports and imports have evolved over the centuries in response to a problem that can be particularly acute in international trade: the lack of trust that exists when one must put faith in a stranger. In this section, we examine the financial devices that have evolved to cope with this problem in the context of international trade: the letter of credit, the draft (or bill of exchange), and the bill of lading. Then we will trace the 14 steps of a typical export–import transaction.

LACK OF TRUST

Firms engaged in international trade have to trust someone they may have never seen, who lives in a different country, who speaks a different language, who abides by (or does not abide by) a different legal system, and who could be very difficult to track down if he or she defaults on an obligation. Consider a U.S. firm exporting to a distributor in France. The U.S. businessman might be concerned that if he ships the products to France before he receives payment from the French businesswoman, she might take delivery of the products and not pay him. Conversely, the French importer might worry that if she pays for the products before they are shipped, the U.S. firm might keep the money and never ship the products or might ship defective products. Neither party to the exchange completely trusts the other. This lack of trust is exacerbated by the distance between the two parties—in space, language, and culture—and by the problems of using an underdeveloped international legal system to enforce contractual obligations.

Due to the (quite reasonable) lack of trust between the two parties, each has his or her own preferences as to how the transaction should be configured. To make sure he is paid, the manager of the U.S. firm would prefer the French distributor to pay for the products before he ships them (see Figure 15.1). Alternatively, to ensure she

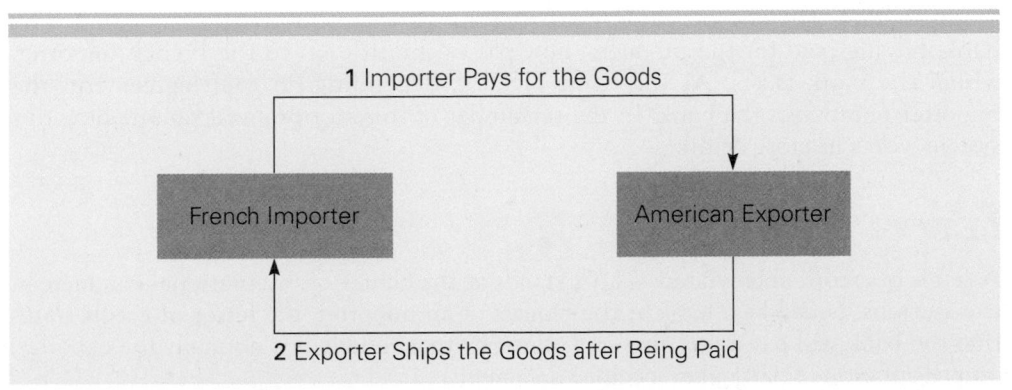

FIGURE 15.1

Preference of the U. S. Exporter

FIGURE 15.2

Preference of the
French Importer

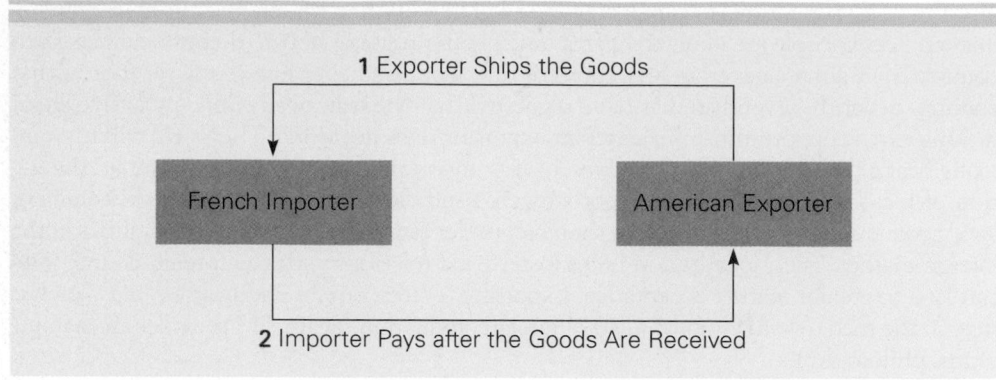

FIGURE 15.3

The Use of a Third Party

receives the products, the French distributor would prefer not to pay for them until they arrive (see Figure 15.2). Thus, each party has a different set of preferences. Unless there is some way of establishing trust between the parties, the transaction might never occur.

Using a third party trusted by both—normally a reputable bank—to act as an intermediary solves the problem. What happens can be summarized as follows (see Figure 15.3). First, the French importer obtains the bank's promise to pay on her behalf, knowing the U.S. exporter will trust the bank. This promise is known as a letter of credit. Having seen the letter of credit, the U.S. exporter now ships the products to France. Title to the products is given to the bank in the form of a document called a bill of lading. In return, the U.S. exporter tells the bank to pay for the products, which the bank does. The document for requesting this payment is referred to as a draft. The bank, having paid for the products, now passes the title on to the French importer, whom the bank trusts. At that time or later, depending on their agreement, the importer reimburses the bank. In the remainder of this section, we examine how this system works in more detail.

LETTER OF CREDIT

A letter of credit, abbreviated as L/C, stands at the center of international commercial transactions. Issued by a bank at the request of an importer, the **letter of credit** states that the bank will pay a specified sum of money to a beneficiary, normally the exporter, on presentation of particular, specified documents.

Consider again the example of the U.S. exporter and the French importer. The French importer applies to her local bank, say, the Bank of Paris, for the issuance of a letter of credit. The Bank of Paris then undertakes a credit check of the importer. If the Bank of Paris is satisfied with her creditworthiness, it will issue a letter of credit. However, the Bank of Paris might require a cash deposit or some other form of collateral from her first. In addition, the Bank of Paris will charge the importer a fee for this service. Typically this amounts to between 0.5 percent and 2 percent of the value of the letter of credit, depending on the importer's creditworthiness and the size of the transaction. (As a rule, the larger the transaction, the lower the percentage.)

Assume the Bank of Paris is satisfied with the French importer's creditworthiness and agrees to issue a letter of credit. The letter states that the Bank of Paris will pay the U.S. exporter for the merchandise as long as it is shipped in accordance with specified instructions and conditions. At this point, the letter of credit becomes a financial contract between the Bank of Paris and the U.S. exporter. The Bank of Paris then sends the letter of credit to the U.S. exporter's bank, say, the Bank of New York. The Bank of New York tells the exporter that it has received a letter of credit and that he can ship the merchandise. After the exporter has shipped the merchandise, he draws a draft against the Bank of Paris in accordance with the terms of the letter of credit, attaches the required documents, and presents the draft to his own bank, the Bank of New York, for payment. The Bank of New York then forwards the letter of credit and associated documents to the Bank of Paris. If all the terms and conditions contained in the letter of credit have been complied with, the Bank of Paris will honor the draft and will send payment to the Bank of New York. When the Bank of New York receives the funds, it will pay the U.S. exporter.

As for the Bank of Paris, once it has transferred the funds to the Bank of New York, it will collect payment from the French importer. Alternatively, the Bank of Paris may allow the importer some time to resell the merchandise before requiring payment. This is not unusual, particularly when the importer is a distributor and not the final consumer of the merchandise, since it helps the importer's cash flow. The Bank of Paris will treat such an extension of the payment period as a loan to the importer and will charge an appropriate rate of interest.

The great advantage of this system is that both the French importer and the U.S. exporter are likely to trust reputable banks, even if they do not trust each other. Once the U.S. exporter has seen a letter of credit, he knows that he is guaranteed payment and will ship the merchandise. Also, an exporter may find that having a letter of credit will facilitate obtaining preexport financing. For example, having seen the letter of credit, the Bank of New York might be willing to lend the exporter funds to process and prepare the merchandise for shipping to France. This loan may not have to be repaid until the exporter has received his payment for the merchandise. As for the French importer, she does not have to pay for the merchandise until the documents have arrived and unless all conditions stated in the letter of credit have been satisfied. The drawback for the importer is the fee she must pay the Bank of Paris for the letter of credit. In addition, since the letter of credit is a financial liability against her, it may reduce her ability to borrow funds for other purposes.

DRAFT

A draft, sometimes referred to as a **bill of exchange,** is the instrument normally used in international commerce to effect payment. A **draft** is simply an order written by an exporter instructing an importer, or an importer's agent, to pay a specified amount of money at a specified time. In the example of the U.S. exporter and the French importer, the exporter writes a draft that instructs the Bank of Paris, the French importer's agent, to pay for the merchandise shipped to France. The person or business initiating the draft is known as the maker (in this case, the U.S. exporter). The party to whom the draft is presented is known as the drawee (in this case, the Bank of Paris).

International practice is to use drafts to settle trade transactions. This differs from domestic practice in which a seller usually ships merchandise on an open account, followed by a commercial invoice that specifies the amount due and the terms of payment. In domestic transactions, the buyer can often obtain possession of the merchandise without signing a formal document acknowledging his or her obligation to pay. In contrast, due to the lack of trust in international transactions, payment or a formal promise to pay is required before the buyer can obtain the merchandise.

Drafts fall into two categories, sight drafts and time drafts. A **sight draft** is payable on presentation to the drawee. A **time draft** allows for a delay in payment—normally 30, 60, 90, or 120 days. It is presented to the drawee, who signifies acceptance of it by writing or stamping a notice of acceptance on its face. Once accepted, the time draft becomes a promise to pay by the accepting party. When a bank accepts and draws on a time draft, it is called a banker's acceptance. When a business firm accepts and draws on it, it is called a trade acceptance.

Time drafts are negotiable instruments; that is, once the draft is stamped with an acceptance, the maker can sell the draft to an investor at a discount from its face value. Imagine that the agreement between the U.S. exporter and the French importer calls for the exporter to present the Bank of Paris (through the Bank of New York) with a time draft requiring payment 120 days after presentation. The Bank of Paris stamps the time draft with an acceptance. Imagine further that the draft is for $100,000. The exporter can either hold onto the accepted time draft and receive $100,000 in 120 days or he can sell it to an investor, say, the Bank of New York, for a discount from the face value. If the prevailing discount rate is 7 percent, the exporter could receive $97,700 by selling it immediately (7 percent per year discount rate for 120 days for $100,000 equals $2,300, and $100,000 − $2,300 = $97,700). The Bank of New York would then collect the full $100,000 from the Bank of Paris in 120 days. The exporter might sell the accepted time draft immediately if he needed the funds to finance merchandise in transit and/or to cover cash flow shortfalls.

BILL OF LADING

The third key document for financing international trade is the bill of lading. The common carrier transporting the merchandise issues the **bill of lading** to the exporter. It serves three purposes: it is a receipt, a contract, and a document of title. As a receipt, the bill of lading indicates that the carrier has received the merchandise described on the face of the document. As a contract, it specifies that the carrier is obligated to provide a transportation service in return for a certain charge. As a document of title, it can be used to obtain payment or a written promise of payment before the merchandise is released to the importer. The bill of lading can also function as collateral against which funds may be advanced to the exporter by its local bank before or during shipment and before final payment by the importer.

A TYPICAL INTERNATIONAL TRADE TRANSACTION

Now that we have reviewed the elements of an international trade transaction, let us see how the process works in a typical case, sticking with the example of the U.S. exporter and the French importer. The typical transaction involves 14 steps (see Figure 15.4).

1. The French importer places an order with the U.S. exporter and asks the American if he would be willing to ship under a letter of credit.
2. The U.S. exporter agrees to ship under a letter of credit and specifies relevant information such as prices and delivery terms.
3. The French importer applies to the Bank of Paris for a letter of credit to be issued in favor of the U.S. exporter for the merchandise the importer wishes to buy.

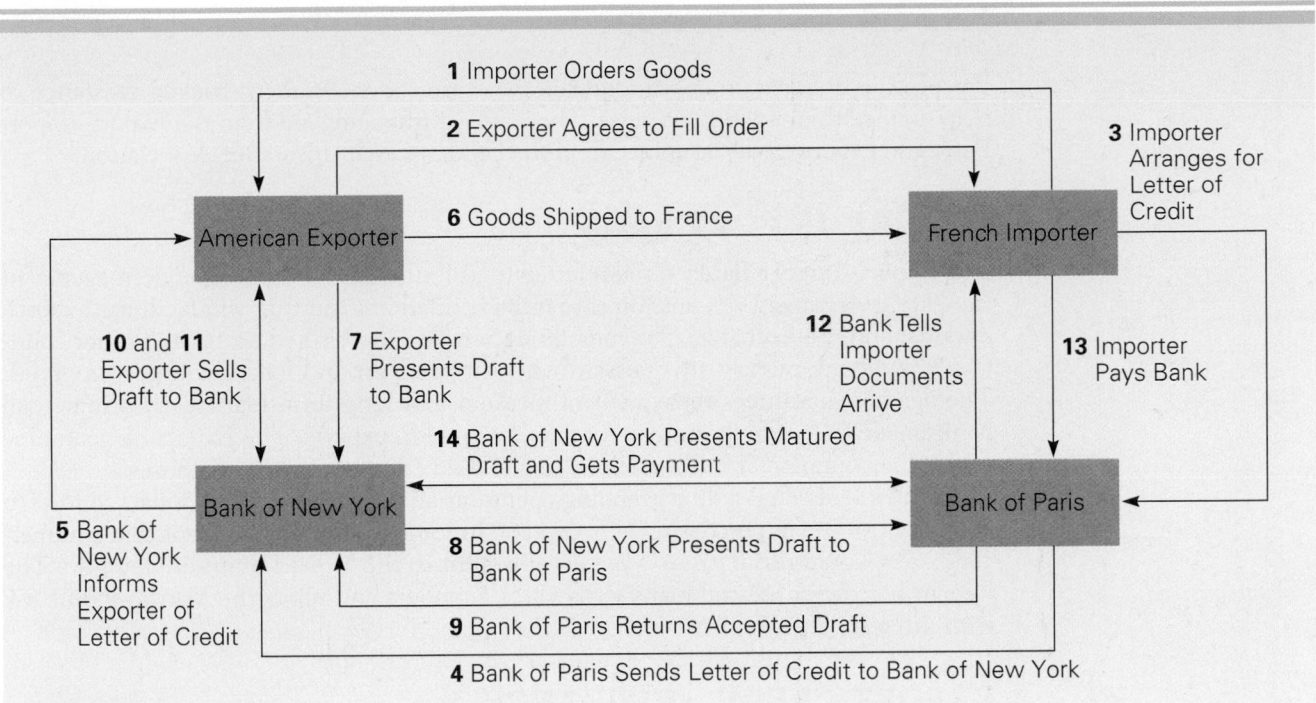

FIGURE 15.4

A Typical International Trade Transaction

4. The Bank of Paris issues a letter of credit in the French importer's favor and sends it to the U.S. exporter's bank, the Bank of New York.

5. The Bank of New York advises the exporter of the opening of a letter of credit in his favor.

6. The U.S. exporter ships the goods to the French importer on a common carrier. An official of the carrier gives the exporter a bill of lading.

7. The U.S. exporter presents a 90-day time draft drawn on the Bank of Paris in accordance with its letter of credit and the bill of lading to the Bank of New York. The exporter endorses the bill of lading so title to the goods is transferred to the Bank of New York.

8. The Bank of New York sends the draft and bill of lading to the Bank of Paris. The Bank of Paris accepts the draft, taking possession of the documents and promising to pay the now-accepted draft in 90 days.

9. The Bank of Paris returns the accepted draft to the Bank of New York.

10. The Bank of New York tells the U.S. exporter that it has received the accepted bank draft, which is payable in 90 days.

11. The exporter sells the draft to the Bank of New York at a discount from its face value and receives the discounted cash value of the draft in return.

12. The Bank of Paris notifies the French importer of the arrival of the documents. She agrees to pay the Bank of Paris in 90 days. The Bank of Paris releases the documents so the importer can take possession of the shipment.

13. In 90 days, the Bank of Paris receives the importer's payment, so it has funds to pay the maturing draft.

14. In 90 days, the holder of the matured acceptance (in this case, the Bank of New York) presents it to the Bank of Paris for payment. The Bank of Paris pays.

Export Assistance

Prospective U.S. exporters can draw on two forms of government-backed assistance to help finance their export programs. They can get financing aid from the Export–Import Bank and export credit insurance from the Foreign Credit Insurance Association.

EXPORT–IMPORT BANK

The **Export–Import Bank,** often referred to as Eximbank, is an independent agency of the U.S. government. Its mission is to provide financing aid that will facilitate exports, imports, and the exchange of commodities between the United States and other countries. Eximbank pursues this mission with various loan and loan-guarantee programs. The agency guarantees repayment of medium and long-term loans U.S. commercial banks make to foreign borrowers for purchasing U.S. exports. The Eximbank guarantee makes the commercial banks more willing to lend cash to foreign enterprises.

Eximbank also has a direct lending operation under which it lends dollars to foreign borrowers for use in purchasing U.S. exports. In some cases, it grants loans that commercial banks would not if it sees a potential benefit to the United States in doing so. The foreign borrowers use the loans to pay U.S. suppliers and repay the loan to Eximbank with interest.

EXPORT CREDIT INSURANCE

For reasons outlined earlier, exporters clearly prefer to get letters of credit from importers. However, sometimes an exporter who insists on a letter of credit will lose an order to one who does not require a letter of credit. Thus, when the importer is in a strong bargaining position and able to play competing suppliers against each other, an exporter may have to forgo a letter of credit.[21] The lack of a letter of credit exposes the exporter

Eximbank provides financing aid to companies, such as the example below, that require assistance with imports, exports, and the exchange of commodities.

to the risk that the foreign importer will default on payment. The exporter can insure against this possibility by buying export credit insurance. If the customer defaults, the insurance firm will cover a major portion of the loss.

In the United States, the Foreign Credit Insurance Association (FCIA), an association of private commercial institutions operating under the guidance of the Export–Import Bank, provides export credit insurance. The FCIA provides coverage against commercial and political risks. Losses due to commercial risk result from the buyer's insolvency or payment default. Political losses arise from actions of governments that are beyond the control of either buyer or seller.

Countertrade

Countertrade is an alternative means of structuring an international sale when conventional means of payment are difficult, costly, or nonexistent. We first encountered countertrade in Chapter 10 in our discussion of currency convertibility. A government may restrict the convertibility of its currency to preserve its foreign exchange reserves to use to service international debt commitments and purchase crucial imports.[22] This is problematic for exporters. Nonconvertibility implies that the exporter may not be paid in his or her home currency; and few exporters would desire payment in a currency that is not convertible.[23] **Countertrade** denotes a whole range of barterlike agreements; its principle is to trade goods and services for other goods and services when they cannot be traded for money. Some examples of countertrade are included in the following situations:

- An Italian company that manufactures power-generating equipment, ABB SAE Sadelmi SpA, was awarded a 720 million baht ($17.7 million) contract by the Electricity Generating Authority of Thailand. The contract specified that the company had to accept 218 million baht ($5.4 million) of Thai farm products as part of the payment.
- Saudi Arabia agreed to buy 10 747 jets from Boeing with payment in crude oil, discounted at 10 percent below posted world oil prices.
- General Electric won a contract for a $150 million electric generator project in Romania by agreeing to market $150 million of Romanian products in markets to which Romania did not have access.
- The Venezuelan government negotiated a contract with Caterpillar under which Venezuela would trade 350,000 tons of iron ore for Caterpillar earth-moving equipment.
- Albania offered such items as spring water, tomato juice, and chrome ore in exchange for a $60 million fertilizer and methanol complex.
- Philip Morris ships cigarettes to Russia, for which it receives chemicals that can be used to make fertilizer. Philip Morris ships the chemicals to China, and in return, China ships glassware to North America for retail sale by Philip Morris.[24]

THE INCIDENCE OF COUNTERTRADE

In the modern era, countertrade arose in the 1960s as a way for the Soviet Union and the Communist states of Eastern Europe, whose currencies were generally nonconvertible, to purchase imports. During the 1980s, the technique grew in popularity among many developing nations that lacked the foreign exchange reserves required to purchase necessary imports. Today, reflecting their own shortages of foreign exchange reserves, some successor states to the former Soviet Union and the Eastern European Communist nations periodically engage in countertrade to purchase their imports.

Estimates of the percentage of world trade covered by some sort of countertrade agreement range from highs of 8 and 10 percent by value to lows of around 2 percent.[25] The precise figure is unknown but it may well be at the low end of these estimates given the increasing liquidity of international financial markets and wider currency convertibility. However, a short-term spike in the volume of countertrade can follow periodic financial crises. For example, countertrade activity increased notably after the Asian financial crisis of 1997. That crisis left many Asian nations with little hard currency to finance international trade. In the tight monetary regime that followed the crisis in 1997, many Asian firms found it very difficult to get access to export credits to finance their own international trade. Thus they turned to the only option available to them—countertrade.

Given that countertrade is a means of financing international trade, albeit a relatively minor one, prospective exporters may have to engage in this technique from time to time to gain access to certain international markets. The governments of developing nations sometimes insist on a certain amount of countertrade.[26] For example, all foreign companies contracted by Thai state agencies for work costing more than 500 million baht ($12.3 million) are required to accept at least 30 percent of their payment in Thai agricultural products. Between 1994 and mid-1998, foreign firms purchased 21 billion baht ($517 million) in Thai goods under countertrade deals.[27]

TYPES OF COUNTERTRADE

With its roots in the simple trading of goods and services for other goods and services, countertrade has evolved into a diverse set of activities that can be categorized as five distinct types of trading arrangements: barter, counterpurchase, offset, switch trading, and compensation or buyback.[28] Many countertrade deals involve not just one arrangement, but elements of two or more.

Barter

Barter is the direct exchange of goods and/or services between two parties without a cash transaction. Although barter is the simplest arrangement, it is not common. Its problems are twofold. First, if goods are not exchanged simultaneously, one party ends up financing the other for a period. Second, firms engaged in barter run the risk of having to accept goods they do not want, cannot use, or have difficulty reselling at a reasonable price. For these reasons, barter is viewed as the most restrictive countertrade arrangement. It is primarily used for one-time-only deals in transactions with trading partners who are not creditworthy or trustworthy.

Counterpurchase

Counterpurchase is a reciprocal buying agreement. It occurs when a firm agrees to purchase a certain amount of materials back from a country to which a sale is made. Suppose a U.S. firm sells some products to China. China pays the U.S. firm in dollars, but in exchange, the U.S. firm agrees to spend some of its proceeds from the sale on textiles produced by China. Thus, although China must draw on its foreign exchange reserves to pay the U.S. firm, it knows it will receive some of those dollars back because of the counterpurchase agreement. In one counterpurchase agreement, Rolls-Royce sold jet parts to Finland. As part of the deal, Rolls-Royce agreed to use some of the proceeds from the sale to purchase Finnish-manufactured TV sets that it would then sell in Great Britain.

Offset

An **offset** is similar to a counterpurchase insofar as one party agrees to purchase goods and services with a specified percentage of the proceeds from the original sale. The difference is that this party can fulfill the obligation with any firm in the country to which the sale is being made. From an exporter's perspective, this is more attractive than a straight counterpurchase agreement because it gives the exporter greater flexibility to choose the goods that it wishes to purchase.

Switch Trading

The term **switch trading** refers to the use of a specialized third-party trading house in a countertrade arrangement. When a firm enters a counterpurchase or offset agreement with a country, it often ends up with what are called counterpurchase credits, which can be used to purchase goods from that country. Switch trading occurs when a third-party trading house buys the firm's counterpurchase credits and sells them to another firm that can better use them. For example, a U.S. firm concludes a counterpurchase agreement with Poland for which it receives some number of counterpurchase credits for purchasing Polish goods. The U.S. firm cannot use and does not want any Polish goods, however, so it sells the credits to a third-party trading house at a discount. The trading house finds a firm that can use the credits and sells them at a profit.

In one example of switch trading, Poland and Greece had a counterpurchase agreement that called for Poland to buy the same U.S.-dollar value of goods from Greece that it sold to Greece. However, Poland could not find enough Greek goods that it required, so it ended up with a dollar-denominated counterpurchase balance in Greece that it was unwilling to use. A switch trader bought the right to 250,000 counterpurchase dollars from Poland for $225,000 and sold them to a European sultana (grape) merchant for $235,000, who used them to purchase sultanas from Greece.

Compensation or Buybacks

A **buyback** occurs when a firm builds a plant in a country—or supplies technology, equipment, training, or other services to the country—and agrees to take a certain percentage of the plant's output as partial payment for the contract. For example, Occidental Petroleum negotiated a deal with Russia under which Occidental would build several ammonia plants in Russia and as partial payment receive ammonia over a 20-year period.

THE PROS AND CONS OF COUNTERTRADE

Countertrade's main attraction is that it can give a firm a way to finance an export deal when other means are not available. Given the problems that many developing nations have in raising the foreign exchange necessary to pay for imports, countertrade may be the only option available when doing business in these countries. Even when countertrade is not the only option for structuring an export transaction, many countries prefer countertrade to cash deals. Thus, if a firm is unwilling to enter a countertrade agreement, it may lose an export opportunity to a competitor that is willing to make a countertrade agreement.

In addition, the government of a country to which a firm is exporting goods or services may require a countertrade agreement. Boeing often has to agree to counterpurchase agreements to capture orders for its commercial jet aircraft. For example, in exchange for gaining an order from Air India, Boeing may be required to purchase certain component parts, such as aircraft doors, from an Indian company. Taking this one step further, Boeing can use its willingness to enter into a counterpurchase agreement as a way of winning orders in the face of intense competition from its global rival, Airbus Industrie. Thus, countertrade can become a strategic marketing weapon.

However, the drawbacks of countertrade agreements are substantial. Other things being equal, firms would normally prefer to be paid in hard currency. Countertrade contracts may involve the exchange of unusable or poor-quality goods that the firm cannot dispose of profitably. For example, a few years ago, one U.S. firm got burned when 50 percent of the television sets it received in a countertrade agreement with

Hungary were defective and could not be sold. In addition, even if the goods it receives are of high quality, the firm still needs to dispose of them profitably. To do this, countertrade requires the firm to invest in an in-house trading department dedicated to arranging and managing countertrade deals. This can be expensive and time-consuming.

Given these drawbacks, countertrade is most attractive to large, diverse multinational enterprises that can use their worldwide network of contacts to dispose of goods acquired in countertrading. The masters of countertrade are Japan's giant trading firms, the *sogo shosha*, which use their vast networks of affiliated companies to profitably dispose of goods acquired through countertrade agreements. The trading firm of Mitsui & Company, for example, has about 120 affiliated companies in almost every sector of the manufacturing and service industries. If one of Mitsui's affiliates receives goods in a countertrade agreement that it cannot consume, Mitsui & Company will normally be able to find another affiliate that can profitably use them. Firms affiliated with one of Japan's *sogo shosha* often have a competitive advantage in countries where countertrade agreements are preferred.

Western firms that are large, diverse, and have a global reach (e.g., General Electric, Philip Morris, and 3M) have similar profit advantages from countertrade agreements. Indeed, 3M has established its own trading company—3M Global Trading, Inc.—to develop and manage the company's international countertrade programs. Unless there is no alternative, small and medium-sized exporters should probably try to avoid countertrade deals because they lack the worldwide network of operations that may be required to profitably utilize or dispose of goods acquired through them.[29]

CHAPTER SUMMARY

In this chapter, we examined the steps firms must take to establish themselves as exporters. The chapter made the following points:

1. One big impediment to exporting is ignorance of foreign market opportunities.

2. Neophyte exporters often become discouraged or frustrated with the exporting process because they encounter many problems, delays, and pitfalls.

3. The way to overcome ignorance is to gather information. In the United States, a number of institutions, most important of which is the Department of Commerce, can help firms gather information in the matchmaking process. Export management companies can also help identify export opportunities.

4. Many of the pitfalls associated with exporting can be avoided if a company hires an experienced export management company, or export consultant, and if it adopts the appropriate export strategy.

5. Firms engaged in international trade must do business with people they cannot trust and people who may be difficult to track down if they default on an obligation. Due to the lack of trust, each party to an international transaction has a different set of preferences regarding the configuration of the transaction.

6. The problems arising from lack of trust between exporters and importers can be solved by using a third party that both trust, normally a reputable bank.

7. A letter of credit is issued by a bank at the request of an importer. It states that the bank promises to pay a beneficiary, normally the exporter, on presentation of documents specified in the letter.

8. A draft is the instrument normally used in international commerce to effect payment. It is an order written by an exporter instructing an importer, or an importer's agent, to pay a specified amount of money at a specified time.

9. Drafts are either sight drafts or time drafts. Time drafts are negotiable instruments.

10. A bill of lading is issued to the exporter by the common carrier transporting the merchandise. It serves as a receipt, a contract, and a document of title.

11. U.S. exporters can draw on two types of government-backed assistance to help finance their exports: loans from the Export–Import Bank and export credit insurance from the FCIA.

12. Countertrade includes a range of barterlike agreements. It is primarily used when a firm exports to a country whose currency is not freely convertible and may lack the foreign exchange reserves required to purchase the imports.

13. The main attraction of countertrade is that it gives a firm a way to finance an export deal when other means are not available. A firm that insists on being paid in hard currency may be at a competitive disadvantage vis-à-vis one that is willing to engage in countertrade.

14. The main disadvantage of countertrade is that the firm may receive unusable or poor-quality goods that cannot be disposed of profitably.

Critical Thinking and Discussion Questions

1. A firm based in Washington State wants to export a shipload of finished lumber to the Philippines. The would-be importer cannot get sufficient credit from domestic sources to pay for the shipment but insists that the finished lumber can quickly be resold in the Philippines for a profit. Outline the steps the exporter should take to effect this export to the Philippines.

2. You are the assistant to the CEO of a small textile firm that manufactures quality, premium-priced, stylish clothing. The CEO has decided to see what the opportunities are for exporting and has asked you for advice as to the steps the company should take. What advice would you give the CEO?

3. An alternative to using a letter of credit is export credit insurance. What are the advantages and disadvantages of using export credit insurance rather than a letter of credit for exporting (a) a luxury yacht from California to Canada, and (b) machine tools from New York to Ukraine?

4. How do you explain the continued existence of countertrade? Under what scenarios might its

popularity increase still further by 2010? Under what scenarios might its popularity decline?

5. How might a company make strategic use of countertrade schemes as a marketing weapon to generate export revenues? What are the risks associated with pursuing such a strategy?

6. Reread the Management Focus on FCX Systems, then answer the following questions:

   a. What lessons about the requirements for export success can be drawn from the story of FCX?

   b. Why do you think FCX terminated its relationship with an international distribution company and started to export on its own?

   c. What does the story of FCX tell you about the importance of foreign markets for the growth of a small enterprise?

7. Reread the Management focus on Red Spot Paint and Varnish. What basic lessons about exporting strategy can be drawn from the example of Red Spot Paint and Varnish?

Research Task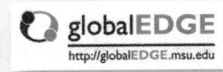

Use the globalEDGE™ site to complete the following exercises:

1. Exporting is an important way for small and large companies to introduce products and develop new markets. In fact, the Internet is rich with resources that provide guidance to companies wishing to expand their markets through exporting. globalEDGE™ provides links to these tutorial Web sites. Identify five sources and provide a description of the services available for new exporters through each source.

2. Understanding the specific terminology used in the export process is necessary prior to your company's first export venture. Utilize the globalEDGE™ Glossary of International Business Terms to identify the definitions of the following exporting terms: air waybill, certificate of inspection, certificate of product origin, wharfage charge, and export broker.

CLOSING CASE

Megahertz Communications

Established in 1982, U.K.-based Megahertz Communications quickly became one of Great Britain's leading independent broadcasting system builders. The company's core skill is in the design, manufacture, and installation of TV and radio broadcast systems, including broadcast and news-gathering vehicles with satellite links. In 1998, Megahertz's managing director, Ashley Coles, set up a subsidiary company, Megahertz International, to sell products to the Middle East, Africa, and Eastern Europe.

While the EU market for media and broadcasting is both mature and well served by large established companies, the Middle East, Africa, and Eastern Europe are growth markets with significant long-term potential for media and broadcasting. At the time, they were not well served by other companies, and all three regions lacked an adequate supply of local broadcast engineers.

Megahertz International's export strategy was simple. The company aimed to provide a turnkey solution to emerging broadcast and media entities in Africa, the Middle East, and Eastern Europe, offering to custom design, manufacture, install, and test broadcasting systems. To gain access to customers, Megahertz hired salespeople with significant experience in these regions and opened a foreign sales office in Italy. Megahertz also exhibited at a number of exhibitions that focused on the targeted regions, sent mailings and e-mail messages to local broadcasters, and set up a Web page, which drew a number of international inquiries.

The response was swift. By early 2000, Megahertz had already been involved in projects in Namibia, Oman, Romania, Russia, Nigeria, Poland, South Africa, Iceland, and Ethiopia. The international operations had expanded to a staff of 75 and were generating £10 million annually. The average order size was about £250,000, and the largest £500,000. In recognition of the company's success, in January 2000 the British government picked Megahertz to receive a Small Business Export Award.

Despite the company's early success, it was not all smooth sailing. According to Managing Director Coles, preshipment financing became a major headache. Coles described his working life as a juggling act, with as much as 20 percent of his time spent chasing money. Due to financing problems, one week Megahertz could have next to nothing in the bank; the next it might have £300,000. The main problem was getting money to finance an order. Megahertz needed additional working capital to finance the purchase of component parts that go into the systems it builds for customers. The company found that banks were very cautious, particularly when they heard that the customers for the order were in Africa or Eastern Europe. The banks worried that Megahertz would not get paid on time, or at all, or that currency fluctuations would reduce the value of payments to Megahertz. Even when Megahertz had a letter of credit from the customer's bank and export insurance documentation, many lenders still saw the risks as too great and declined to lend bridging funds to Megahertz. As a partial solution, Megahertz turned to lending companies that specialize in financing international trade, but many of these companies charged interest rates significantly greater than those charged by banks, thereby squeezing Megahertz's profit margins.

Coles hoped these financing problems were temporary. Once Megahertz established a more sustained cash flow from its international operations, and once banks better appreciated the ability of Coles and his team to secure payment from foreign customers, he hoped that they would become more amenable to lending capital to Megahertz at rates that would help to protect the company's profit margins. By 2002, however, it was clear that the company's growth was too slow to achieve these goals anytime soon. As an alternative solution, in 2003 Coles agreed to sell Megahertz Communications to AZCAR of Canada. AZCAR acquired Megahertz to gain access to the expanding EU market and Megahertz's contacts in the Middle East. For Megahertz, the acquisition gave the company additional working capital that enabled it to take full advantage of export opportunities.[30]

Case Discussion Questions

1. What was the motivation for Megahertz's shift toward a strategy of export-led growth? Why do you think the opportunities for growth might be greater in foreign markets? Do you think that developing countries are likely to be a major market opportunity for Megahertz? Why?

2. Does Megahertz's strategy for building exports make sense given the nature of the broadcast industry? Why?

3. Why do you think Megahertz found it difficult to raise the working capital required to finance its

international trade activities? What does the experience of Megahertz tell you about the problems facing small firms that wish to export?

4. Megahertz solved its financing problem by selling the company to AZCAR of Canada. What other solutions might the company have adopted?

Notes

1. J. Moules, "Morgan: A Member of the Family, Jonathan Moules Meets the Manufacturer of the First and Last Real Sports Cars," *Financial Times*, August 19, 2006, p. 18; S. Rutberg, "Small Business Growing by Going against the Grain," *The Secured Lender*, November/December 2006, pp. 64–67; G. Hilton, "Knocking Down Export Barriers to Smaller Firms," *Business and Economic Review*, July–September 2005, pp. 18–21.

2. R. A. Pope, "Why Small Firms Export: Another Look," *Journal of Small Business Management* 40 (2002), pp. 17–26.

3. S. T. Cavusgil, "Global Dimensions of Marketing," in *Marketing*, ed. P. E. Murphy and B. M. Enis (Glenview, IL: Scott Foresman, 1985), pp. 577–99.

4. S. M. Mehta, "Enterprise: Small Companies Look to Cultivate Foreign Business," *The Wall Street Journal*, July 7, 1994, p. B2.

5. P. A. Julien and C. Ramagelahy, "Competitive Strategy and Performance of Exporting SMEs," *Entrepreneurship Theory and Practice*, 2003, pp. 227–94.

6. W. J. Burpitt and D. A. Rondinelli, "Small Firms' Motivations for Exporting: To Earn and Learn?" *Journal of Small Business Management*, October 2000, pp. 1–14; and J. D. Mittelstaedt, G. N. Harben, and W. A. Ward, "How Small Is Too Small?" *Journal of Small Business Management* 41 (2003), pp. 68–85.

7. Small Business Administration, "The State of Small Business 1999–2000: Report to the President," 2001, at www.sba.gov/advo/stats/stateofsb99_00.pdf.

8. A. O. Ogbuehi and T. A. Longfellow, "Perceptions of U.S. Manufacturing Companies Concerning Exporting," *Journal of Small Business Management*, October 1994, pp. 37–59, and U.S. Small Business Administration, "Guide to Exporting," www.sba.gov/oit/info/Guide-toExporting/index.html.

9. R. W. Haigh, "Thinking of Exporting?" *Columbia Journal of World Business* 29 (December 1994), pp. 66–86.

10. F. Williams, "The Quest for More Efficient commerce," *Financial Times*, October 13, 1994, p. 7.

11. Sources: J. Sparshott, "Businesses Must Export to Compete," *The Washington Times*, September 1, 2004, p. C8; "Entrepreneur of the Year 2001: Donald Gallion, FCX Systems," *The State Journal*, June 18, 2001, p. S10; and T. Pierro, "Exporting Powers Growth of FCX Systems," *The State Journal*, April 6, 1998, p. 1.

12. See Burpitt and Rondinelli, "Small Firms' Motivations for Exporting," and C. S. Katsikeas, L. C. Leonidou, and N. A. Morgan, "Firm Level Export Performance Assessment," *Academy of Marketing Science* 28 (2000), pp. 493–511.

13. M. Y. Yoshino and T. B. Lifson, *The Invisible Link* (Cambridge, MA: MIT Press, 1986).

14. L. W. Tuller, *Going Global* (Homewood, IL: Business One-Irwin, 1991).

15. Sources: Small Business Administration Office of International Trade, "Guide to Exporting," www.sba.gov/oit/info/Guide-ToExporting/index.html, and U.S. Department of Commerce, "A Profile of U.S. Exporting Companies, 2000–2001," February 2003. Report available at www.census.gov/foreign-trade/aip/index.html#profile.

16. Haigh, "Thinking of Exporting?"

17. M. A. Raymond, J. Kim, and A. T. Shao. "Export Strategy and Performance," *Journal of Global Marketing* 15 (2001), pp. 5–29, and P. S. Aulakh, M. Kotabe, and H. Teegen, "Export Strategies and Performance of Firms from Emerging Economies," *Academy of Management Journal* 43 (2000), pp. 342–61.

18. J. Francis and C. Collins-Dodd, "The Impact of Firms' Export Orientation on the Export Performance of High-Tech Small and Medium Sized Enterprises," *Journal of International Marketing* 8, no. 3 (2000), pp. 84–103.

19. Sources: R. L. Rose, "Success Abroad," *The Wall Street Journal*, March 29, 1991, p. A1; T. Eiben, "US Exporters Keep On Rolling," *Fortune*, June 14, 1994, pp. 128–31; 3M Company, *A Century on Innovation*, 3M, 2002; and 2005 10K form archived at 3M's Web site at www.mmm.com.

20. Sources: R. L. Rose and C. Quintanilla, "More Small U.S. Firms Take Up Exporting with Much Success," *The Wall Street Journal*, December 20, 1996, pp. A1, A10, and interview with Bryan Williams of Red Spot Paint.

21. For a review of the conditions under which a buyer has power over a supplier, see M. E. Porter, *Competitive Strategy* (New York: Free Press, 1980).

22. *Exchange Agreements and Exchange Restrictions* (Washington, DC: International Monetary Fund, 1989).

23. It's also sometimes argued that countertrade is a way of reducing the risks inherent in a traditional money-for-goods transaction, particularly with entities from emerging economies. See C. J. Choi, S. H. Lee, and J. B. Kim, "A Note of Countertrade: Contractual Uncertainty and Transactional Governance in Emerging Economies," *Journal of International Business Studies* 30, no. 1 (1999), pp. 189–202.

24. J. R. Carter and J. Gagne, "The Do's and Don'ts of International Countertrade," *Sloan Management Review*, Spring 1988, pp. 31–37, and W. Maneerungsee, "Countertrade: Farm Goods Swapped for Italian Electricity," *Bangkok Post*, July 23, 1998.

25. Estimate from the American Countertrade Association at www.countertrade.org/index.htm. See also D. West, "Countertrade," *Business Credit* 104, no. 4 (2001), pp. 64–67, and B. Meyer, "The Original Meaning of Trade Meets the Future of Barter," *World Trade* 13 (January 2000), pp. 46–50.

26. Carter and Gagne, "The Do's and Don'ts of International Countertrade."

27. Maneerungsee, "Countertrade: Farm Goods Swapped for Italian Electricity."

28. For details, see Carter and Gagne, "Do's and Don'ts"; J. F. Hennart, "Some Empirical Dimensions of Countertrade," *Journal of International Business Studies*, 1990, pp. 240–60; and West, "Countertrade."

29. D. J. Lecraw, "The Management of Countertrade: Factors Influencing Success," *Journal of International Business Studies*, Spring 1989, pp. 41–59.

30. Sources: www.megahertz.co.uk; W. Smith, "Today Batley, Tomorrow the World?" *Director*, January 2000, pp. 42–49; and "AZCAR Acquires 80% of Megahertz Broadcast Systems," Canadian Corporate Newswire, March 31, 2003.

Li & Fung

Established in 1906, Hong Kong–based Li & Fung is now one of the largest multinational trading companies in the developing world, with annual sales forecasted to hit $10 billion in 2007, up from just $1.2 billion in 2000. The company, which is still run by the grandsons of the founder, Victor and William Fung, does not see itself as a traditional trading enterprise. Rather, it sees itself as an expert in supply chain management for its 500 or so customers. These customers are a diverse group and include clothing retailers and consumer electronics companies. Li & Fung takes orders from customers and then sifts through its network of 7,500 independent suppliers located in 40 countries to find the right manufacturing enterprises to produce the product for customers at the most attractive combination of cost and quality. Attaining this goal frequently requires Li & Fung to break up the value chain and disperse different productive activities to manufacturers located in different countries depending on an assessment of factors such as labor costs, trade barriers, transportation costs, and so on. Li & Fung then coordinates the whole process, managing the logistics and arranging for the shipment of the finished product to the customer.

Typical of its customers is The Limited, Inc., a large chain of retail clothing stores based in the United States. The Limited outsources much of its manufacturing and logistics functions to Li & Fung. The process starts when The Limited comes to Li & Fung with designer sketches of clothes for the next fashion season. Li & Fung takes the basic product concepts and researches the market to find the right kind of yarn, dye, buttons, and so on. Then Li & Fung assembles these into prototypes that The Limited can inspect. Once The Limited has settled on a prototype, it will give Li & Fung an order and ask for delivery within five weeks. The short time between an order and requested delivery is necessitated by the rapid rate of product obsolescence in the fashion clothing industry.

With order in hand, Li & Fung distributes the various aspects of the overall manufacturing process to different producers depending on their capabilities and costs. For example, Li & Fung might decide to purchase yarn from

Global Production, Outsourcing, and Logistics

LEARNING OBJECTIVES

After you have read this chapter you should be able to:

LO1 Explain why production and logistics decisions are of central importance to many multinational businesses.

LO2 Explain how country differences, production technology, and product features all affect the choice of where to locate production activities.

LO3 Discuss how the role of foreign subsidiaries in production can be enhanced over time as they accumulate knowledge.

LO4 Identify the factors that influence a firm's decision of whether to source supplies from within the company or from foreign suppliers.

LO5 Articulate what is required to efficiently coordinate a globally dispersed production system.

---

a Korean company but have it woven and dyed in Taiwan. So Li & Fung will arrange for the yarn to be picked up from Korea and shipped to Taiwan. The Japanese might have the best zippers and buttons, but they manufacture them mostly in China. So Li & Fung will go to YKK, a big Japanese zipper manufacturer, and order the right zippers from their Chinese plants. Then Li & Fung might decide that due to constraints imposed by export quotas and labor costs, the best place to make the final garments might be in Thailand. So everything will be shipped to Thailand. In addition, because The Limited, like many retail customers, needs quick delivery, Li & Fung might divide the order across five factories in Thailand. Five weeks after the order has been received, the garments will arrive on the shelves of The Limited, all looking like they came from one factory, with colors perfectly matched. The result is a product that may have a label that says "Made in Thailand," but is a global product.

To better serve the needs of its customers, Li & Fung is divided into numerous small, customer-focused divisions.

There is a theme store division that serves a handful of customers such as Warner Brothers; there is a division for The Limited and another for Gymboree, a U.S. children's clothing store. Walk into one of these divisions, such as the Gymboree division, and you will see that every one of the 40 or so people in the division is focused solely on meeting Gymboree's needs. On every desk is a computer with a direct software link to Gymboree. The staff is organized into specialized teams in areas such as design, technical support, merchandising, raw material purchasing, quality assurance, and shipping. These teams also have direct electronic links to dedicated staff in Li & Fung's branch offices in various countries where Gymboree buys in volume, such as China, Indonesia, and the Philippines. Thus, Li & Fung uses information systems to manage, coordinate, and control the globally dispersed design, production, and shipping process to ensure that the time between receipt of an order and delivery is minimized, as are overall costs.[1]

Introduction

As trade barriers fall and global markets develop, many firms increasingly confront a set of interrelated issues. First, where in the world should production activities be located? Should they be concentrated in a single country, or should they be dispersed around the globe, matching the type of activity with country differences in factor costs, tariff barriers, political risks, and the like to minimize costs and maximize value added? Second, what should be the long-term strategic role of foreign production sites? Should the firm abandon a foreign site if factor costs change, moving production to another more favorable location, or is there value to maintaining an operation at a given location even if underlying economic conditions change? Third, should the firm own foreign production activities, or is it better to outsource those activities to independent vendors? Fourth, how should a globally dispersed supply chain be managed, and what is the role of Internet-based information technology in the management of global logistics? Fifth, should the firm manage global logistics itself, or should it outsource the management to enterprises that specialize in this activity?

Li & Fung, which we reviewed in the case that opened the chapter, is an excellent example of a enterprise that has grown rapidly by taking over the global logistics activities of other companies, such as Warner Brothers, The Limited, and Toys R Us. As a logistics specialist, Li & Fung deals with a number of issues that many other firms competing in today's global economy also have had to deal with. To serve the needs of its customers, Li & Fung has to decide how best to distribute manufacturing activities among operations based in various countries so as to minimize costs, produce products that have an acceptable level of quality, and deliver goods in a timely manner. Li & Fung scans its global network of some 7,500 suppliers located in 40 countries to make these decisions, weighing factors such as labor costs, trade barriers, transportation costs, and product quality, and only then deciding what should be produced where and in what quantities. Li & Fung often unbundles the value chain associated with producing a product, dispersing various parts of the chain to different locations depending on an assessment of the value that performing an activity in a particular location can create. Li & Fung must then coordinate and control the globally dispersed value chain so that it minimizes the time between receipt of an order and delivery of the finished product.

Strategy, Production, and Logistics

In Chapter 12, we introduced the concept of the value chain and discussed a number of value creation activities, including production, marketing, logistics, R&D, human resources, and information systems. In this chapter, we will focus on two of these activities—**production** and **logistics**—and attempt to clarify how they might be performed internationally to (1) lower the costs of value creation and (2) add value by better serving customer needs. We will discuss the contributions of information technology to these activities, which has become particularly important in the era of the Internet. In later chapters, we will look at other value creation activities in this international context (marketing, R&D, and human resource management).

In Chapter 12, we defined *production* as "the activities involved in creating a product." We used the term *production* to denote both service and manufacturing activities, since one can produce a service or produce a physical product. Although in this chapter we focus more on the production of physical goods, one should not forget that the term can also be applied to services. This has become more evident in recent years with the trend among U.S. firms to outsource the "production" of certain service activities to developing nations where labor costs are lower (for example, the trend among many U.S. companies to outsource customer care services to places such as India, where English is widely spoken and labor costs are much lower). **Logistics** is the activity that controls the transmission of physical materials through the value chain, from procurement through

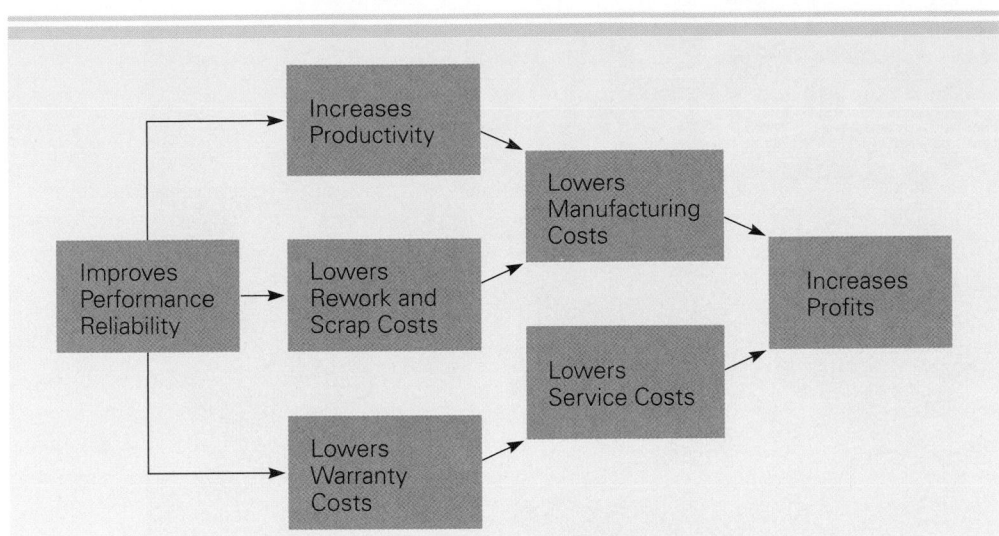

FIGURE 16.1

The Relationship between Quality and Costs

Source: Reprinted from "What Does Product Quality Really Mean?" by David A. Garvin, *Sloan Management Review* 26 (Fall 1984), Figure 1, p. 37, by permission of the publisher. Copyright 1984 by Massachusetts Institute of Technology. All rights reserved.

production and into distribution. Production and logistics are closely linked since a firm's ability to perform its production activities efficiently depends on a timely supply of high-quality material inputs, for which logistics is responsible.

The production and logistics functions of an international firm have a number of important strategic objectives.[2] One is to lower costs. Dispersing production activities to various locations around the globe where each activity can be performed most efficiently can lower costs. Costs can also be cut by managing the global supply chain efficiently so as to better match supply and demand. Efficient supply chain management reduces the amount of inventory in the system and increases inventory turnover, which means the firm has to invest less working capital in inventory and is less likely to find excess inventory on hand that cannot be sold and has to be written off.

A second strategic objective that production and logistics share is to increase product quality by eliminating defective products from both the supply chain and the manufacturing process.[3] (In this context, *quality* means *reliability*, implying that the product has no defects and performs well.) The objectives of reducing costs and increasing quality are not independent of each other. As illustrated in Figure 16.1, the firm that improves its quality control will also reduce its costs of value creation. Improved quality control reduces costs by

- Increasing productivity because time is not wasted producing poor-quality products that cannot be sold, leading to a direct reduction in unit costs.
- Lowering rework and scrap costs associated with defective products.
- Reducing the warranty costs and time associated with fixing defective products.

The effect is to lower the costs of value creation by reducing both production and after-sales service costs.

The principal tool that most managers now use to increase the reliability of their product offering is the Six Sigma quality improvement methodology. The Six Sigma methodology is a direct descendant of the **total quality management** (TQM) philosophy that was widely adopted, first by Japanese companies and then American companies, during the 1980s and early 1990s.[4] The TQM philosophy was developed by a number of American consultants such as W. Edward Deming, Joseph Juran, and A. V. Feigenbaum.[5] Deming identified a number of steps that should be part of any TQM program. He argued that management should embrace the philosophy that mistakes, defects, and poor-quality materials are not acceptable and should be eliminated. He suggested that the quality of supervision should be improved by allowing more time for supervisors to work with

General Electric is one of the major corporations that has embraced Six Sigma. Its commitment to quality is evident in all its industries, from retail to insurance to aviation.

employees and by providing them with the tools they need to do the job. Deming recommended that management should create an environment in which employees will not fear reporting problems or recommending improvements. He believed that work standards should not only be defined as numbers or quotas but should also include some notion of quality to promote the production of defect-free output. He argued that management has the responsibility to train employees in new skills to keep pace with changes in the workplace. In addition, he believed that achieving better quality requires the commitment of everyone in the company.

Six Sigma, the modern successor to TQM, is a statistically based philosophy that aims to reduce defects, boost productivity, eliminate waste, and cut costs throughout a company. Several major corporations, such as Motorola, General Electric, and Allied Signal, have adopted Six Sigma programs. Sigma comes from the Greek letter that statisticians use to represent a standard deviation from a mean, the higher the number of "sigmas" the smaller the number of errors. At six sigma, a production process would be 99.99966 percent accurate, with just 3.4 defects per million units. While it is almost impossible for a company to achieve such perfection, Six Sigma quality is a goal that some strive toward to try to boost their product quality and productivity.[6]

The growth of international standards has also focused greater attention on the importance of product quality. In Europe, for example, the European Union requires that the quality of a firm's manufacturing processes and products be certified under a quality standard known as **ISO 9000** before the firm is allowed access to the EU marketplace. Although the ISO 9000 certification process has proved to be somewhat bureaucratic and costly for many firms, it does focus management attention on the need to improve the quality of products and processes.[7]

In addition to lowering costs and improving quality, two other objectives have particular importance in international businesses. First, production and logistics functions must be able to accommodate demands for local responsiveness. As we saw in Chapter 12, demands for local responsiveness arise from national differences in consumer tastes and preferences, infrastructure, distribution channels, and host-government demands. Demands for local responsiveness create pressures to decentralize production activities to the major national or regional markets in which the firm does business or to implement flexible manufacturing processes that enable the firm to customize the product coming out of a factory according to the market in which it is to be sold.

Second, production and logistics must be able to respond quickly to shifts in customer demand. In recent years, time-based competition has grown more important.[8] When consumer demand is prone to large and unpredictable shifts, the firm that can adapt most quickly to these shifts will gain an advantage. As we shall see, both production and logistics play critical roles here. Part of the competitive advantage of Li & Fung, for example, is based on its ability to use real-time information about ordering patterns and inventory to bring demand and supply into alignment, thereby quickly satisfying customer needs and taking excess inventory out of the supply chain (see the opening case).

Where to Produce

An essential decision facing an international firm is where to locate its production activities to best minimize costs and improve product quality. For the firm contemplating international production, a number of factors must be considered. These factors can be grouped under three broad headings: country factors, technological factors, and product factors.[9]

COUNTRY FACTORS

We reviewed country-specific factors in some detail earlier in the book. Political economy, culture, and relative factor costs differ from country to country. In Chapter 5, we saw that due to differences in factor costs, some countries have a comparative advantage for producing certain products. In Chapters 2 and 3, we saw how differences in political economy and national culture influence the benefits, costs, and risks of doing business in a country. Other things being equal, a firm should locate its various manufacturing activities where the economic, political, and cultural conditions, including relative factor costs, are conducive to the performance of those activities (for an example, see the accompanying Management Focus, which looks at the Philips NV investment in China). In Chapter 12, we referred to the benefits derived from such a strategy as location economies. We argued that one result of the strategy is the creation of a global web of value creation activities.

Also important in some industries is the presence of global concentrations of activities at certain locations. In Chapter 7, we discussed the role of location externalities in influencing foreign direct investment decisions. Externalities include the presence of an appropriately skilled labor pool and supporting industries.[10] Such externalities can play an important role in deciding where to locate manufacturing activities. For example, because of a cluster of semiconductor manufacturing plants in Taiwan, a pool of labor with experience in the semiconductor business has developed. In addition, the plants have attracted a number of supporting industries, such as the manufacturers of semiconductor capital equipment and silicon, which have established facilities in Taiwan to be near their customers. This implies that there are real benefits to locating in Taiwan, as opposed to another location that lacks such externalities. Other things being equal, the externalities make Taiwan an attractive location for semiconductor manufacturing facilities.

Of course, other things are not equal. Differences in relative factor costs, political economy, culture, and location externalities are important, but other factors also loom large. Formal and informal trade barriers obviously influence location decisions (see Chapter 6), as do transportation costs and rules and regulations regarding foreign direct investment (see Chapter 7). For example, although relative factor costs may make a country look attractive as a location for performing a manufacturing activity, regulations prohibiting foreign direct investment may eliminate this option. Similarly, a consideration of factor costs might suggest that a firm should source production of a certain component from a particular country, but trade barriers could make this uneconomical.

Another country factor is expected future movements in its exchange rate (see Chapters 9 and 10). Adverse changes in exchange rates can quickly alter a country's attractiveness as a manufacturing base. Currency appreciation can transform a low-cost

Philips in China

The Dutch consumer electronics, lighting, semiconductor, and medical equipment conglomerate Philips NV has been operating factories in China since 1985 when the country first opened its markets to foreign investors. Then China was seen as the land of unlimited demand, and Philips, like many other Western companies, dreamed of Chinese consumers snapping up its products by the millions. But the company soon found out that one of the big reasons the company liked China—the low wage rates—also meant that few Chinese workers could afford to buy the products they were producing. Chinese wage rates are currently one-third of those in Mexico and Hungary, and 5 percent of those in the United States or Japan. So Philips hit on a new strategy: keep the factories in China but export most of the goods to the United States and elsewhere.

By 2003, Philips had invested some $2.5 billion in China. The company now operates 25 wholly owned subsidiaries and joint ventures in China. Together they employ some 30,000 people. Philips exports nearly two-thirds of the $7 billion in products that the factories produce every year. Philips accelerated its Chinese investment in anticipation of China's entry into the World Trade Organization. The company plans to move even more production to China over the next few years. In 2003, Philips announced it would phase out production of electronic razors in the Netherlands, lay off 2,000 Dutch employees, and move production to China by 2005. A week earlier, Philips had stated that it would expand capacity at its semiconductor factories in China, while phasing out production in higher-cost locations elsewhere.

The attractions of China to Philips include continuing low wage rates, an educated workforce, a robust Chinese economy, a stable exchange rate that is linked to the U.S. dollar (it has a managed float), a rapidly expanding industrial base that includes many other Western and Chinese companies that Philips uses as suppliers, and easier access to world markets given China's entry into the WTO. Philips has stated that ultimately its goal is to turn China into a global supply base from which the company's products will be exported around the world. Today more than 25 percent of everything Philips makes worldwide comes from China, and executives say the figure is rising rapidly. Several products, such as CD and DVD players, are now made only in China. Philips is also starting to give its Chinese factories a greater role in product development. In the TV business, for example, basic development used to occur in Holland but was moved to Singapore in the early 1990s. In the early 2000s Philips transferred TV development work to Suzhou near Shanghai. Similarly, basic product development work on LCD screens for cell phones was recently shifted to Shanghai.

Philips is hardly alone in this process. By the mid-2000s more than half of all exports from China came from foreign manufacturers or their joint ventures in China. China was the source of more than 80 percent of the DVD players sold worldwide, 50 percent of the cameras, 40 percent of all microwave ovens, 30 percent of the air conditioners, 25 percent of the washing machines, and 20 percent of all refrigerators.

Some observers worry that Philips and companies pursuing a similar strategy might be overdoing it. Too much dependence on China could be dangerous if political, economic, or other problems disrupt production and the company's ability to supply global markets. Some observers believe that it might be better if the manufacturing facilities of companies were more geographically diverse as a hedge against problems in China. These critics' fears gained some substance in early 2003 when an outbreak of the pneumonia-like SARS (severe acute respiratory syndrome) virus in China resulted in the temporary shutdown of several plants operated by foreign companies and disrupted their global supply chains. Although Philips was not directly affected, it did restrict travel by its managers and engineers to its Chinese plants.[11]

location into a high-cost location. Many Japanese corporations had to grapple with this problem during the 1990s and early 2000s. The relatively low value of the yen on foreign exchange markets between 1950 and 1980 helped strengthen Japan's position as a low-cost location for manufacturing. Between 1980 and the mid-1990s, however, the yen's steady appreciation against the dollar increased the dollar cost of products exported from Japan, making Japan less attractive as a manufacturing location. In response, many Japanese firms moved their manufacturing offshore to lower-cost locations in East Asia.

TECHNOLOGICAL FACTORS

The type of technology a firm uses to perform specific manufacturing activities can be pivotal in location decisions. For example, because of technological constraints, in some cases it is necessary to perform certain manufacturing activities in only one location and serve the world market from there. In other cases, the technology may make it feasible to perform an activity in multiple locations. Three characteristics of a manufacturing technology are of interest here: the level of fixed costs, the minimum efficient scale, and the flexibility of the technology.

Fixed Costs

As we noted in Chapter 12, in some cases the fixed costs of setting up a production plant are so high that a firm must serve the world market from a single location or from a very few locations. For example, it now costs more than $1 billion to set up a state-of-the-art plant to manufacture semiconductor chips. Given this, other things being equal, serving the world market from a single plant sited at a single (optimal) location can make sense.

Conversely, a relatively low level of fixed costs can make it economical to perform a particular activity in several locations at once. This allows the firm to better accommodate demands for local responsiveness. Manufacturing in multiple locations may also help the firm avoid becoming too dependent on one location. Being too dependent on one location is particularly risky in a world of floating exchange rates. Many firms disperse their manufacturing plants to different locations as a "real hedge" against potentially adverse moves in currencies.

Minimum Efficient Scale

The concept of economies of scale tells us that as plant output expands, unit costs decrease. The reasons include the greater utilization of capital equipment and the productivity gains that come with specialization of employees within the plant.[12] However, beyond a certain level of output, few additional scale economies are available. Thus, the "unit cost curve" declines with output until a certain output level is reached, at which point further increases in output realize little reduction in unit costs. The level of output at which most plant-level scale economies are exhausted is referred to as the **minimum efficient scale** of output. This is the scale of output a plant must operate to realize all major plant-level scale economies (see Figure 16.2).

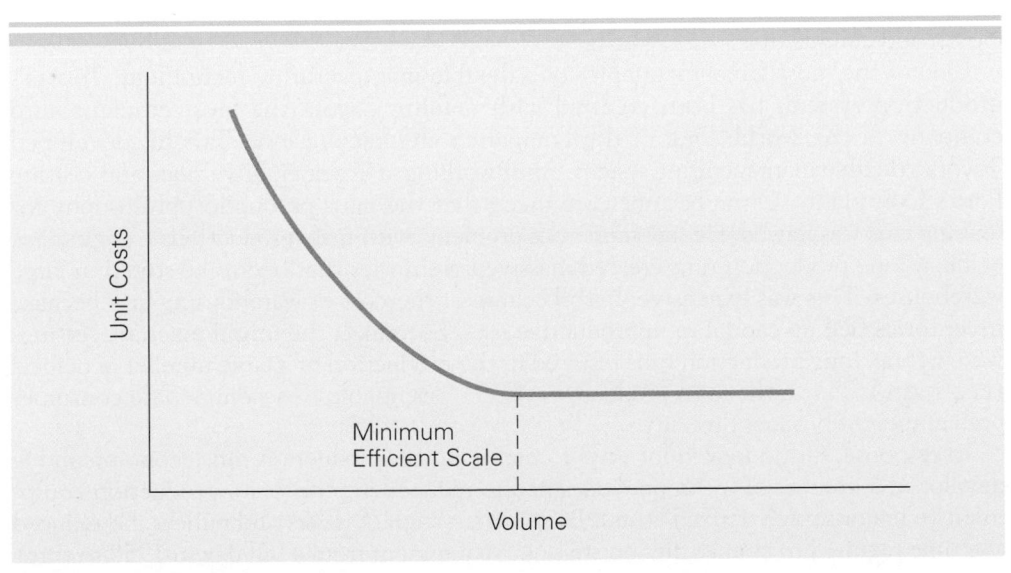

FIGURE 16.2

A Typical Unit Cost Curve

The implications of this concept are as follows: The larger the minimum efficient scale of a plant relative to total global demand, the greater the argument for centralizing production in a single location or a limited number of locations. Alternatively, when the minimum efficient scale of production is low relative to global demand, it may be economical to manufacture a product at several locations. For example, the minimum efficient scale for a plant to manufacture personal computers is about 250,000 units a year, while the total global demand exceeds 35 million units a year. The low level of minimum efficient scale in relation to total global demand makes it economically feasible for a company such as Dell to manufacture PCs in six locations.

As in the case of low fixed costs, the advantages of a low minimum efficient scale include allowing the firm to accommodate demands for local responsiveness or to hedge against currency risk by manufacturing the same product in several locations.

Flexible Manufacturing and Mass Customization

Central to the concept of economies of scale is the idea that the best way to achieve high efficiency, and hence low unit costs, is through the mass production of a standardized output. The trade-off implicit in this idea is between unit costs and product variety. Producing greater product variety from a factory implies shorter production runs, which in turn implies an inability to realize economies of scale. That is, wide product variety makes it difficult for a company to increase its production efficiency and thus reduce its unit costs. According to this logic, the way to increase efficiency and drive down unit costs is to limit product variety and produce a standardized product in large volumes.

The rise of flexible manufacturing technologies has challenged this view of production efficiency. The term **flexible manufacturing technology**—or **lean production,** as it is often called—covers a range of manufacturing technologies designed to (1) reduce setup times for complex equipment, (2) increase the utilization of individual machines through better scheduling, and (3) improve quality control at all stages of the manufacturing process.[13] Flexible manufacturing technologies allow the company to produce a wider variety of end products at a unit cost that at one time could be achieved only through the mass production of a standardized output. Research suggests the adoption of flexible manufacturing technologies may actually increase efficiency and lower unit costs relative to what can be achieved by the mass production of a standardized output, while at the same time enabling the company to customize its product offering to a much greater extent than was once thought possible. The term **mass customization** has been coined to describe the ability of companies to use flexible manufacturing technology to reconcile two goals that were once thought to be incompatible—low cost and product customization.[14] Flexible manufacturing technologies vary in their sophistication and complexity.

One of the most famous examples of a flexible manufacturing technology, Toyota's production system, has been credited with making Toyota the most efficient auto company in the world. One of the company's engineers, Ohno Taiichi, developed Toyota's flexible manufacturing system. After working at Toyota for five years and visiting Ford's U.S. plants, Ohno became convinced that the mass production philosophy for making cars was flawed. He saw numerous problems with mass production.

First, long production runs created massive inventories that had to be stored in large warehouses. This was expensive, both because of the cost of warehousing and because inventories tied up capital in unproductive uses. Second, if the initial machine settings were wrong, long production runs resulted in the production of a large number of defects (i.e., waste). Third, the mass production system was unable to accommodate consumer preferences for product diversity.

In response, Ohno looked for ways to make shorter production runs economical. He developed a number of techniques designed to reduce setup times for production equipment (a major source of fixed costs). By using a system of levers and pulleys, he reduced the time required to change dies on stamping equipment from a full day in 1950 to three

In 2004, Ford Motor Company renovated its oldest plant in Chicago, allowing for flexible manufacturing. What other industries could benefit from flexible manufacturing?

minutes by 1971. This made small production runs economical, which allowed Toyota to respond better to consumer demands for product diversity. Small production runs also eliminated the need to hold large inventories, thereby reducing warehousing costs. Plus, small product runs and the lack of inventory meant that defective parts were produced only in small numbers and entered the assembly process immediately. This reduced waste and helped trace defects back to their source to fix the problem. In sum, these innovations enabled Toyota to produce a more diverse product range at a lower unit cost than was possible with conventional mass production.[15]

Flexible machine cells are another common flexible manufacturing technology. A flexible machine cell is a grouping of various types of machinery, a common materials handler, and a centralized cell controller (computer). Each cell normally contains four to six machines capable of performing a variety of operations. The typical cell is dedicated to the production of a family of parts or products. The settings on machines are computer controlled, which allows each cell to switch quickly between the production of different parts or products.

Improved capacity utilization and reductions in work in progress (that is, stockpiles of partly finished products) and waste are major efficiency benefits of flexible machine cells. Improved capacity utilization arises from the reduction in setup times and from the computer-controlled coordination of production flow between machines, which eliminates bottlenecks. The tight coordination between machines also reduces work-in-progress inventory. Reductions in waste are due to the ability of computer-controlled machinery to identify ways to transform inputs into outputs while producing a minimum of unusable waste material. While freestanding machines might be in use 50 percent of the time, the same machines when grouped into a cell can be used more than 80 percent of the time and produce the same end product with half the waste. This increases efficiency and results in lower costs.

The effects of installing flexible manufacturing technology on a company's cost structure can be dramatic. Ford Motor Company is currently introducing flexible manufacturing technologies into its automotive plants around the world. These new technologies should allow Ford to produce multiple models from the same line and to switch production from one model to another much more quickly than in the past. In total, Ford hopes to take $2 billion out of its cost structure by 2010.[16]

Besides improving efficiency and lowering costs, flexible manufacturing technologies also enable companies to customize products to the demands of small consumer groups—at a cost that at one time could be achieved only by mass-producing a standardized output. Thus, the technologies help a company achieve mass customization, which increases its customer responsiveness. Most important for international business, flexible manufacturing technologies can help a firm to customize products for different national markets. The importance of this advantage cannot be overstated. When flexible manufacturing technologies are available, a firm can manufacture products customized to various national markets at a single factory sited at the optimal location. And it can do this without absorbing a significant cost penalty. Thus, firms no longer need to establish manufacturing facilities in each major national market to provide products that satisfy specific consumer tastes and preferences, part of the rationale for a localization strategy (Chapter 12).

Summary

A number of technological factors support the economic arguments for concentrating production facilities in a few choice locations or even in a single location. Other things being equal, when fixed costs are substantial, the minimum efficient scale of production is high, and/or flexible manufacturing technologies are available, the arguments for concentrating production at a few choice locations are strong. This is true even when substantial differences in consumer tastes and preferences exist between national markets because flexible manufacturing technologies allow the firm to customize products to national differences at a single facility. Alternatively, when fixed costs are low, the minimum efficient scale of production is low, and flexible manufacturing technologies are not available, the arguments for concentrating production at one or a few locations are not as compelling. In such cases, it may make more sense to manufacture in each major market in which the firm is active if this helps the firm better respond to local demands. This holds only if the increased local responsiveness more than offsets the cost disadvantages of not concentrating manufacturing. With the advent of flexible manufacturing technologies and mass customization, such a strategy is becoming less attractive. In sum, technological factors are making it feasible, and necessary, for firms to concentrate manufacturing facilities at optimal locations. Trade barriers and transportation costs are major brakes on this trend.

PRODUCT FACTORS

Two product features affect location decisions. The first is the product's *value-to-weight* ratio because of its influence on transportation costs. Many electronic components and pharmaceuticals have high value-to-weight ratios; they are expensive and they do not weigh very much. Thus, even if they are shipped halfway around the world, their transportation costs account for a very small percentage of total costs. Given this, other things being equal, there is great pressure to produce these products in the optimal location and to serve the world market from there. The opposite holds for products with low value-to-weight ratios. Refined sugar, certain bulk chemicals, paint, and petroleum products all have low value-to-weight ratios; they are relatively inexpensive products that weigh a lot. Accordingly, when they are shipped long distances, transportation costs account for a large percentage of total costs. Thus, other things being equal, there is great pressure to make these products in multiple locations close to major markets to reduce transportation costs.

The other product feature that can influence location decisions is whether the product serves universal needs, needs that are the same all over the world. Examples include many industrial products (e.g., industrial electronics, steel, bulk chemicals) and modern consumer products (e.g., handheld calculators, personal computers, video game consoles). Because there are few national differences in consumer taste and preference for such products, the need for local responsiveness is reduced. This increases the attractiveness of concentrating production at an optimal location.

TABLE 16.1

Location Strategy and
Production

	Concentrated Production Favored	Decentralized Production Favored
Country Factors		
Differences in political economy	Substantial	Few
Differences in culture	Substantial	Few
Differences in factor costs	Substantial	Few
Trade barriers	Few	Substantial
Location externalities	Important in industry	Not important in industry
Exchange rates	Stable	Volatile
Technological Factors		
Fixed costs	High	Low
Minimum efficient scale	High	Low
Flexible manufacturing technology	Available	Not available
Product Factors		
Value-to-weight ratio	High	Low
Serves universal needs	Yes	No

LOCATING PRODUCTION FACILITIES

There are two basic strategies for locating production facilities: concentrating them in a centralized location and serving the world market from there, or decentralizing them in various regional or national locations that are close to major markets. The appropriate strategic choice is determined by the various country-specific, technological, and product factors that we have discussed in this section and are summarized in Table 16.1.

As Table 16.1 shows, concentration of production makes most sense when

- Differences between countries in factor costs, political economy, and culture have a substantial impact on the costs of manufacturing in various countries.
- Trade barriers are low.
- Externalities arising from the concentration of like enterprises favor certain locations.
- Important exchange rates are expected to remain relatively stable.
- The production technology has high fixed costs and high minimum efficient scale relative to global demand, or flexible manufacturing technology exists.
- The product's value-to-weight ratio is high.
- The product serves universal needs.

Alternatively, decentralization of production is appropriate when

- Differences between countries in factor costs, political economy, and culture do not have a substantial impact on the costs of manufacturing in various countries.
- Trade barriers are high.
- Location externalities are not important.
- Volatility in important exchange rates is expected.
- The production technology has low fixed costs and low minimum efficient scale, and flexible manufacturing technology is not available.

- The product's value-to-weight ratio is low.
- The product does not serve universal needs (that is, significant differences in consumer tastes and preferences exist between nations).

In practice, location decisions are seldom clear-cut. For example, it is not unusual for differences in factor costs, technological factors, and product factors to point toward concentrated production while a combination of trade barriers and volatile exchange rates points toward decentralized production. This seems to be the case in the world automobile industry. Although the availability of flexible manufacturing and cars' relatively high value-to-weight ratios suggest concentrated manufacturing, the combination of formal and informal trade barriers and the uncertainties of the world's current floating exchange rate regime (see Chapter 10) have inhibited firms' ability to pursue this strategy. For these reasons, several automobile companies have established "top-to-bottom" manufacturing operations in three major regional markets: Asia, North America, and Western Europe.

The Strategic Role of Foreign Factories

Whatever the rationale behind establishing a foreign production facility, the strategic role of foreign factories can evolve over time.[17] Initially, many foreign factories are established where labor costs are low. Their strategic role typically is to produce labor-intensive products at as low a cost as possible. For example, beginning in the 1970s, many U.S. firms in the computer and telecommunication equipment businesses established factories across Southeast Asia to manufacture electronic components, such as circuit boards and semiconductors, at the lowest possible cost. They located their factories in countries such as Malaysia, Thailand, and Singapore precisely because each of these countries offered an attractive combination of low labor costs, adequate infrastructure, and favorable tax and trade regimes. Initially, the components produced by these factories were designed elsewhere and the final product was assembled elsewhere. Over time, however, the strategic role of some of these factories has expanded; they have become important centers for the design and final assembly of products for the global marketplace. For example, Hewlett-Packard's operation in Singapore was established as a low-cost location for the production of circuit boards, but the facility has become the center for the design and final assembly of portable ink-jet printers for the global marketplace (see the accompanying Management Focus). A similar process seems to be occurring at some of the factories that Philips has established in China (see the Management Focus on Philips).

Such upward migration in the strategic role of foreign factories arises because many foreign factories upgrade their own capabilities.[18] This improvement comes from two sources. First, pressure from the center to improve a factory's cost structure and/or customize a product to the demands of consumers in a particular nation can start a chain of events that ultimately leads to development of additional capabilities at that factory. For example, to meet centrally mandated directions to drive down costs, engineers at HP's Singapore factory argued that they needed to redesign products so they could be manufactured at a lower cost. This led to the establishment of a design center in Singapore. As this design center proved its worth, HP executives realized the importance of co-locating design and manufacturing operations. They increasingly transferred more design responsibilities to the Singapore factory. In addition, the Singapore factory ultimately became the center for the design of products tailored to the needs of the Asian market. This made good strategic sense because it meant products were being designed by engineers who were close to the Asian market and probably had a good understanding of the needs of that market, as opposed to engineers located in the United States.

A second source of improvement in the capabilities of a foreign factory can be the increasing abundance of advanced factors of production in the nation in which the

Hewlett-Packard in Singapore

In the late 1960s, Hewlett-Packard was looking around Asia for a low-cost location to produce electronic components that were to be manufactured using labor-intensive processes. The company looked at several Asian locations and eventually settled on Singapore, opening its first factory there in 1970. Although Singapore did not have the lowest labor costs in the region, costs were low relative to North America. Plus, the Singapore location had several important benefits that could not be found at many other locations in Asia. The education level of the local workforce was high. English was widely spoken. The government of Singapore seemed stable and committed to economic development, and the city-state had one of the better infrastructures in the region, including good communication and transportation networks and a rapidly developing industrial and commercial base. HP also extracted favorable terms from the Singapore government with regard to taxes, tariffs, and subsidies.

At its start, the plant manufactured only basic components. The combination of low labor costs and a favorable tax regime helped make this plant profitable early. In 1973, HP transferred the manufacture of one of its basic handheld calculators from the United States to Singapore. The objective was to reduce manufacturing costs, which the Singapore factory was quickly able to do. Increasingly confident in the capability of the Singapore factory to handle entire products, as opposed to just components, HP's management transferred other products to Singapore over the next few years including keyboards, solid-state displays, and integrated circuits. However, all these products were still designed, developed, and initially produced in the United States.

The plant's status shifted in the early 1980s when HP embarked on a worldwide campaign to boost product quality and reduce costs. HP transferred the production of its HP41C handheld calculator to Singapore. The managers at the Singapore plant were given the goal of substantially reducing manufacturing costs. They argued

that this could be achieved only if they were allowed to redesign the product so it could be manufactured at a lower overall cost. HP's central management agreed, and 20 engineers from the Singapore facility were transferred to the United States for one year to learn how to design application-specific integrated circuits. They then brought this expertise back to Singapore and set about redesigning the HP41C.

The results were a huge success. By redesigning the product, the Singapore engineers reduced manufacturing costs for the HP41C by 50 percent. Using this newly acquired capability for product design, the Singapore facility then set about redesigning other products it produced. HP's corporate managers were so impressed with the progress made at the factory that they transferred production of the entire calculator line to Singapore in 1983. This was followed by the partial transfer of ink-jet production to Singapore in 1984 and keyboard production in 1986. In all cases, the facility redesigned the products and often reduced unit manufacturing costs by more than 30 percent. The initial development and design of all these products, however, still occurred in the United States.

In the 1990s, the Singapore plant assumed added responsibilities, particularly in the ink-jet printer business. First the factory was given the job of redesigning an HP ink-jet printer for the Japanese market. Although the initial product redesign was a market failure, the managers at Singapore pushed to be allowed to try again, and they were given the job of redesigning HP's DeskJet 505 printer for the Japanese market. This time the redesigned product was a success, garnering significant sales in Japan. Emboldened by this success, the plant has continued to take on additional design responsibilities. Today, it is viewed as a "lead plant" within HP's global network, with primary responsibility not just for manufacturing but also for the development and design of a family of small ink-jet printers targeted at the Asian market.[21]

factory is located. Many nations that were considered economic backwaters a generation ago have been experiencing rapid economic development during the past 20 years. Their communication and transportation infrastructures and the education level of the population have improved. While these countries once lacked the advanced infrastructure required to support sophisticated design, development, and manufacturing operations, this is often no longer the case. This has made it much easier for factories based in these nations to take on a greater strategic role.

Because of such developments, many international businesses are moving away from a system in which their foreign factories were viewed as nothing more than low-cost manufacturing facilities and toward one where foreign factories are viewed as globally dispersed centers of excellence.[19] In this new model, foreign factories take the lead role for the design and manufacture of products to serve important national or regional markets or even the global market. The development of such dispersed centers of excellence is consistent with the concept of a transnational strategy, introduced in Chapter 12. A major aspect of a transnational strategy is a belief in **global learning**—the idea that valuable knowledge does not reside just in a firm's domestic operations; it may also be found in its foreign subsidiaries. Foreign factories that upgrade their capabilities over time are creating valuable knowledge that might benefit the whole corporation.

Managers of international businesses need to remember that foreign factories can improve their capabilities over time, and this can be of immense strategic benefit to the firm. Rather than viewing foreign factories simply as sweatshops where unskilled labor churns out low-cost goods, managers need to see them as potential centers of excellence and to encourage and foster attempts by local managers to upgrade the capabilities of their factories and thereby enhance their strategic standing within the corporation.

Such a process does imply that once a foreign factory has been established and valuable skills have been accumulated, it may not be wise to switch production to another location simply because some underlying variable, such as wage rates, has changed.[20] HP has kept its facility in Singapore rather than switching production to a location where wage rates are now much lower, such as Vietnam, because it recognizes that the Singapore factory has accumulated valuable skills that more than make up for the higher wage rates. Thus, when reviewing the location of production facilities, the international manager must consider the valuable skills that may have been accumulated at various locations, and the impact of those skills on factors such as productivity and product design.

Outsourcing Production: Make-or-Buy Decisions

International businesses frequently face **make-or-buy decisions,** decisions about whether they should perform a certain value creation activity themselves or outsource it to another entity. Historically, most outsourcing decisions have involved the manufacture of physical products. Most manufacturing firms have done their own final assembly, but have had to decide whether to vertically integrate and manufacture their own component parts or outsource the production of such parts, purchasing them from independent suppliers. Such make-or-buy decisions are an important aspect of the strategy of many firms. In the automobile industry, for example, the typical car contains more than 10,000 components, so automobile firms constantly face make-or-buy decisions. Toyota produces less than 30 percent of the value of cars that roll off its assembly lines. The remaining 70 percent, mainly accounted for by component parts and complex subassemblies, comes from independent suppliers. In the athletic shoe industry, the make-or-buy issue has been taken to an extreme with companies such as Nike and Reebok having no involvement in manufacturing; all production has been outsourced, primarily to manufacturers based in low-wage countries.

In recent years, the outsourcing decision has gone beyond the manufacture of physical products to embrace the production of service activities. For example, many U.S.-based companies, from credit card issuers to computer companies, have outsourced their customer call centers to India. They are "buying" the customer call center function, while "making" other parts of the product in house. Similarly, many information technology companies have been outsourcing some parts of the software development process, such as testing computer code written in the United States, to independent providers based in India. Such companies are "making" (writing) most of the code in-house, but "buying," or outsourcing, part of the production process—testing—to independent companies. India is often the focus of such outsourcing because English is widely spoken there; the nation has a well-educated workforce, particularly in engineering fields; and the pay is much lower than in the United States (a call center worker in India earns about $200 to $300 a month, about one-tenth of the comparable U.S. wage).[22]

Outsourcing decisions pose plenty of problems for purely domestic businesses but even more problems for international businesses. These decisions in the international arena are complicated by the volatility of countries' political economies, exchange rate movements, changes in relative factor costs, and the like. In this section, we examine the arguments for making products in-house and for buying them, and we consider the trade-offs involved in such a decision. Then we discuss strategic alliances as an alternative to producing all or part of a product within the company.

THE ADVANTAGES OF MAKE

The arguments that support making all or part of a product in-house—vertical integration—are fourfold. Vertical integration may be associated with lower costs, facilitate investments in highly specialized assets, protect proprietary product technology, and ease the scheduling of adjacent processes.

Nike relies on outsourcing to manufacture its products; however, the company has received worldwide criticism for turning its back on social responsibility for the sake of profit.

Lowering Costs

It may pay a firm to continue manufacturing a product or component part in-house if the firm is more efficient at that production activity than any other enterprise. Boeing, for example, has looked closely at its make-or-buy decisions with regard to commercial jet aircraft (see the accompanying Management Focus). It decided to outsource the production of some component parts but keep the design and final integration of aircraft. Boeing's rationale was that it has a core competence in large systems integration, and it is more efficient at this activity than any other comparable enterprise in the world. Therefore, it makes little sense for Boeing to outsource this particular activity.

Facilitating Specialized Investments

Sometimes firms have to invest in specialized assets in order to do business with another enterprise.[23] A **specialized asset** is an asset whose value is contingent upon a particular relationship persisting. For example, imagine that Ford of Europe has developed a new, high-performance, high-quality, and uniquely designed fuel injection system. The increased fuel efficiency will help sell Ford cars. Ford must decide whether to make the system in-house or to contract out the manufacturing to an independent supplier. Manufacturing these uniquely designed systems requires investments in equipment that can be used only for this purpose; it cannot be used to make fuel injection systems for any other auto firm. Thus, investment in this equipment constitutes an investment in specialized assets. When, as in this situation, one firm must invest in specialized assets to supply another, mutual dependency is created. In such circumstances, each party might fear the other will abuse the relationship by seeking more favorable terms.

To appreciate this, let us first examine this situation from the perspective of an independent supplier whom Ford has asked to make this investment. The supplier might reason that once it has made the investment, it will become dependent on Ford for

MANAGEMENT FOCUS

Outsourcing at the Boeing Company

The Boeing Company is one of the two premier manufacturers of commercial jet aircraft in the world, holding around half of the global market for large commercial jet aircraft. Despite its market share, over the last decade Boeing found it tough going. The company's problems are twofold. First, Boeing faces an aggressive competitor in Europe's Airbus Industrie. The dogfight between Boeing and Airbus for market share has enabled major airlines to play the two companies off against each other in an attempt to bargain down the price for commercial jet aircraft. Second, the airline business is quite cyclical, and airlines sharply reduce orders for new aircraft when their own business is in a downturn. This occurred in the early 1990s and again after the events of September 11, 2001, hit the airline industry hard, and resulted in slumping orders for Boeing and Airbus.

During downturns, some of which can be lengthy, intense price competition often occurs between Airbus and Boeing as they struggle to maintain market share and order volume in the face of falling demand. Given these pricing pressures, the only way Boeing can maintain its profitability is to reduce its own manufacturing costs. With this in mind, Boeing is constantly studying make-or-buy decisions. The objective is to identify activities that can be outsourced to subcontractors, both in the United States and abroad, to reduce production costs.

When making outsourcing decisions, Boeing applies a number of criteria. First, Boeing looks at the basic economics. The central issue is whether an activity could be performed more cost-effectively by an outside manufacturer or by Boeing. Second, Boeing considers the strategic risk associated with outsourcing an activity. Boeing has decided it will not outsource any activity deemed to be part of its long-term competitive

advantage, particularly design work and final integration and assembly. Third, Boeing looks at the operational risk associated with outsourcing an activity. The basic objective is to make sure Boeing does not become too dependent on a single outside supplier for critical components. Boeing's philosophy is to hedge operational risk by purchasing from two or more suppliers. Finally, Boeing considers whether it makes sense to outsource certain activities to a supplier in a given country to help secure orders for commercial jet aircraft from that country. This practice is known as offsetting, and it is common in many industries. For example, Boeing decided to outsource the production of certain components to China. This decision was influenced by forecasts suggesting that the Chinese will purchase more than $100 billion worth of commercial jets over the next 20 years. Boeing's hope is that pushing some subcontracting work China's way will help Boeing gain a larger share of this market than its global competitor, Airbus.

By 2006, Boeing was outsourcing around two-thirds of the work involved in building a commercial jet aircraft, up from half a percent a decade earlier, with companies in Japan, Italy, and elsewhere shipping fuselage sections or even entire wings to Boeing. For its part, Boeing has decided to focus its efforts on design, final manufacturing integration and assembly, and marketing and sales. Every other activity can be potentially outsourced. Boeing will outsource substantially more work than ever when making its latest jet, the 787, a "super-efficient" wide-body jet scheduled for market introduction in 2008. Much of the wing and fuselage will come from subcontractors in Japan, Australia, and Canada; the passenger doors and landing gear will come from France; the cargo doors from Sweden; the horizontal stabilizer from Italy; and the wing tips from South Korea.[26]

business since Ford is the only possible customer for the output of this equipment. The supplier perceives this as putting Ford in a strong bargaining position and worries that once the specialized investment has been made, Ford might use it to squeeze down prices for the systems. Given this risk, the supplier declines to make the investment in specialized equipment.

Now take the position of Ford. Ford might reason that if it contracts out production of these systems to an independent supplier, it might become too dependent on that supplier for a vital input. Because specialized equipment is required to produce the fuel injection systems, Ford cannot easily switch its orders to other suppliers who lack that equipment (it would face high switching costs). Ford perceives this as increasing the bargaining power of the supplier and worries that the supplier might use its bargaining strength to demand higher prices.

Thus, the mutual dependency that outsourcing would create makes Ford nervous and scares away potential suppliers. The problem here is lack of trust. Neither party completely trusts the other to play fair. Consequently, Ford might reason that the only safe way to get the new fuel injection systems is to manufacture them itself. It may be unable to persuade any independent supplier to manufacture them. Thus, Ford decides to make rather than buy.

In general, we can predict that when substantial investments in specialized assets are required to manufacture a component, the firm will prefer to make the component internally rather than contract it out to a supplier. Substantial empirical evidence supports this prediction.[24]

Protecting Proprietary Product Technology

Proprietary product technology is unique to a firm. If it enables the firm to produce a product containing superior features, proprietary technology can give the firm a competitive advantage. The firm would not want competitors to get this technology. If the firm outsources the production of entire products or components containing proprietary technology, it runs the risk that those suppliers will expropriate the technology for their own use or that they will sell it to the firm's competitors. Thus, to maintain control over its technology, the firm might prefer to make such products or component parts in-house. An example of a firm that has made such decisions is given in the accompanying Management Focus, which looks at make-or-buy decisions at Boeing. While Boeing has decided to outsource a number of important components that go toward the production of an aircraft, it has explicitly decided not to outsource the manufacture of cockpits because it believes that doing so would give away key technology to potential competitors.

Improving Scheduling

Another argument for producing all or part of a product in-house is that production cost savings result because it makes planning, coordination, and scheduling of adjacent processes easier.[25] This is particularly important in firms with just-in-time inventory systems (discussed later in the chapter). In the 1920s, for example, Ford profited from tight coordination and scheduling made possible by backward vertical integration into steel foundries, iron ore shipping, and mining. Deliveries at Ford's foundries on the Great Lakes were coordinated so well that ore was turned into engine blocks within 24 hours. This substantially reduced Ford's production costs by eliminating the need to hold excessive ore inventories.

For international businesses that source worldwide, scheduling problems can be exacerbated by the time and distance between the firm and its suppliers. This is true whether the firms use their own subunits as suppliers or use independent suppliers. However, ownership of upstream production facilities is not the issue here. By using information technology, firms can attain tight coordination between different stages in the production process.

THE ADVANTAGES OF BUY

Buying component parts, or an entire product, from independent suppliers can give the firm greater flexibility, can help drive down the firm's cost structure, and may help the firm capture orders from international customers.

Strategic Flexibility

The great advantage of buying component parts, or even an entire product, from independent suppliers is that the firm can maintain its flexibility, switching orders between suppliers as circumstances dictate. This is particularly important internationally, where changes in exchange rates and trade barriers can alter the attractiveness of supply sources. One year Hong Kong might offer the lowest cost for a particular component, and the next year Mexico may. Many firms source the same products from suppliers based in two countries, primarily as a hedge against adverse movements in factor costs, exchange rates, and the like. Li & Fung, which we discussed at the beginning of the chapter, specialized in sourcing products from producers based in different countries, switching orders from nation to nation in order to get the best deal.

Sourcing products from independent suppliers can also be advantageous when the optimal location for manufacturing a product is beset by political risks. Under such circumstances, foreign direct investment to establish a component manufacturing operation in that country would expose the firm to those risks. The firm can avoid many of these risks by buying from an independent supplier in that country, thereby maintaining the flexibility to switch sourcing to another country if a war, revolution, or other political change alters that country's attractiveness as a supply source.

However, maintaining strategic flexibility has its downside. If a supplier perceives that the firm will change suppliers in response to changes in exchange rates, trade barriers, or general political circumstances, that supplier might not be willing to make investments in specialized plants and equipment that would ultimately benefit the firm.

Lower Costs

Although making a product or component part in-house—vertical integration—is often undertaken to lower costs, it may have the opposite effect. When this is the case, outsourcing may lower the firm's cost structure. Making all or part of a product in-house increases an organization's scope, and the resulting increase in organizational complexity can raise a firm's cost structure. There are three reasons for this.

First, the greater the number of subunits in an organization, the more problems coordinating and controlling those units. Coordinating and controlling subunits requires top management to process large amounts of information about subunit activities. The greater the number of subunits, the more information top management must process and the harder it is to do that well. Theoretically, when the firm becomes involved in too many activities, headquarters management will be unable to effectively control all of them, and the resulting inefficiencies will more than offset any advantages derived from vertical integration.[27] This can be particularly serious in an international business, where distance and differences in time, language, and culture exacerbate the problem of controlling subunits.

Second, the firm that vertically integrates into component part manufacture may find that because its internal suppliers have a captive customer in the firm, they lack an incentive to reduce costs. The fact that they do not have to compete for orders with other suppliers may result in high operating costs. The managers of the supply operation may be tempted to pass on cost increases to other parts of the firm in the form of higher transfer prices, rather than looking for ways to reduce those costs.

Third, vertically integrated firms have to determine appropriate prices for goods transferred to subunits within the firm. This is a challenge in any firm, but it is even more complex in international businesses. Different tax regimes, exchange rate movements, and headquarters' ignorance about local conditions all increase the complexity of transfer pricing decisions. This complexity enhances internal suppliers' ability to manipulate transfer prices to their advantage, passing cost increases downstream rather than looking for ways to reduce costs.

The firm that buys its components from independent suppliers can avoid all these problems and the associated costs. The firm that sources from independent suppliers has fewer subunits to control. The incentive problems that occur with internal suppliers do not arise with independent suppliers. Independent suppliers know they must continue to be efficient if they are to win business from the firm. Also, because independent suppliers' prices are set by market forces, the transfer pricing problem does not exist. In sum, buying component parts from independent suppliers avoids the bureaucratic inefficiencies and resulting costs that can arise when firms vertically integrate backward and produce their own components.

Offsets

Another reason for outsourcing some manufacturing to independent suppliers based in other countries is that it may help the firm capture more orders from that country. As the Management Focus on Boeing notes, offsets are common in the commercial aerospace industry. For example, before Air India places a large order with Boeing, the Indian government might ask Boeing to push some subcontracting work toward Indian manufacturers. This is not unusual in international business. Representatives of the U.S. government have repeatedly urged Japanese automobile companies to purchase more component parts from U.S. suppliers to partially offset the large volume of automobile imports from Japan in the United States.

TRADE-OFFS

Clearly there are trade-offs in make-or-buy decisions. The benefits of making all or part of a product in-house seem to be greatest when highly specialized assets are involved, when vertical integration is necessary for protecting proprietary technology, or when the firm is simply more efficient than external suppliers at performing a particular activity. When these conditions are not present, the risk of strategic inflexibility and organizational problems suggests it may be better to contract out some or all production to independent suppliers. Because issues of strategic flexibility and organizational control loom even larger for international businesses than purely domestic ones, an international business should be particularly wary of vertical integration into component part manufacture. In addition, some outsourcing in the form of offsets may help a firm gain larger orders in the future.

STRATEGIC ALLIANCES WITH SUPPLIERS

Several international businesses have tried to reap some benefits of vertical integration without the associated organizational problems by entering strategic alliances with essential suppliers. For example, there is an alliance between Kodak and Canon, under which Canon builds photocopiers for sale by Kodak; an alliance between Apple and Sony, under which Sony builds laptop computers for Apple; and an alliance between Microsoft and Flextronics, under which Flextronics builds the Xbox for Microsoft. By these alliances, Kodak, Apple, and Microsoft have committed themselves to long-term relationships with these suppliers, which has encouraged the suppliers to undertake specialized investments. Strategic alliances build trust between the firm and its suppliers. Trust results when a firm makes a credible commitment to continue purchasing from a supplier on reasonable terms. For example, the firm may invest money in a supplier—perhaps by taking a minority shareholding—to signal its intention to build a productive, mutually beneficial long-term relationship.

This kind of arrangement between the firm and its parts suppliers was pioneered in Japan by large auto companies such as Toyota. Many Japanese automakers have cooperative relationships with their suppliers that go back decades. In these relationships, the auto companies and their suppliers collaborate on ways to increase value added by, for example, implementing just-in-time inventory systems or cooperating in the design of component parts to improve quality and reduce assembly costs. These relationships were formalized when the auto firms acquired minority shareholdings in many of their essential suppliers to symbolize their desire for long-term cooperative relationships with them.

At the same time, the relationship between the firm and each essential supplier remains market mediated and terminable if the supplier fails to perform. By pursuing such a strategy, the Japanese automakers capture many of the benefits of vertical integration, particularly those arising from investments in specialized assets, without suffering the organizational problems that come with formal vertical integration. The parts suppliers also benefit from these relationships because they grow with the firm they supply and share in its success.[28]

In general, the trends toward just-in-time inventory systems (JIT), computer-aided design (CAD), and computer-aided manufacturing (CAM) seem to have increased pressures for firms to establish long-term relationships with their suppliers. JIT, CAD, and CAM systems all rely on close links between firms and their suppliers supported by substantial specialized investment in equipment and information systems hardware. To get a supplier to agree to adopt such systems, a firm must make a credible commitment to an enduring relationship with the supplier—it must build trust with the supplier. It can do this within the framework of a strategic alliance.

Alliances are not all good. Like formal vertical integration, a firm that enters long-term alliances may limit its strategic flexibility by the commitments it makes to its alliance partners. As we saw in Chapter 12 when we considered alliances between competitors, a firm that allies itself with another firm risks giving away key technological know-how to a potential competitor.

Managing a Global Supply Chain

Logistics encompasses the activities necessary to get materials from suppliers to a manufacturing facility, through the manufacturing process, and out through a distribution system to the end user.[29] In the international business, the logistics function manages the global supply chain. The twin objectives of logistics are to manage a firm's global supply chain at the lowest possible cost and in a way that best serves customer needs, thereby lowering the costs of value creation and helping the firm establish a competitive advantage through superior customer service.

The potential for reducing costs through more efficient logistics is enormous. For the typical manufacturing enterprise, material costs account for between 50 and 70 percent of revenues, depending on the industry. Even a small reduction in these costs can have a substantial impact on profitability. According to one estimate, for a firm with revenues of $1 million, a return on investment rate of 5 percent, and materials costs that are 50 percent of sales revenues, a $15,000 increase in total profits could be achieved either by increasing sales revenues 30 percent or by reducing materials costs by 3 percent.[30] In a saturated market, it would be much easier to reduce materials costs by 3 percent than to increase sales revenues by 30 percent.

THE ROLE OF JUST-IN-TIME INVENTORY

Pioneered by Japanese firms during the 1950s and 60s, just-in-time inventory systems now play a major role in most manufacturing firms. The basic philosophy behind **just-in-time (JIT)** systems is to economize on inventory holding costs by having materials arrive at a manufacturing plant just in time to enter the production process and not before. The major cost saving comes from speeding up inventory turnover. This reduces inventory holding costs, such as warehousing and storage costs. It means the company can reduce the amount of working capital it needs to finance inventory, freeing capital for other uses and/or lowering the total capital requirements of the enterprise. Other things being equal, this will boost the company's profitability as measured by return on capital invested. It also means the company is less likely to have excess unsold inventory that it has to write off against earnings or price low to sell.

In addition to the cost benefits, JIT systems can also help firms improve product quality. Under a JIT system, parts enter the manufacturing process immediately; they are not warehoused. This allows defective inputs to be spotted right away. The problem can then be traced to the supply source and fixed before more defective parts are produced. Under a more traditional system, warehousing parts for weeks before they are used allows many defective parts to be produced before a problem is recognized.

The drawback of a JIT system is that it leaves a firm without a buffer stock of inventory. Although buffer stocks are expensive to store, they can help a firm respond quickly to increases in demand and tide a firm over shortages brought about by disruption among suppliers. Such a disruption occurred after the September 11, 2001, attacks on the World Trade Center, when the subsequent shutdown of international air travel and shipping left many firms that relied upon globally dispersed suppliers and tightly managed "just-in-time" supply chains without a buffer stock of inventory. A less pronounced but similar situation occurred again in April 2003 when the outbreak of the pneumonia-like SARS (severe acute respiratory syndrome) virus in China resulted in the temporary shutdown of several plants operated by foreign companies and disrupted their global supply chains. Similarly, in late 2004, record imports into the United States left several major West Coast shipping ports clogged with too many ships from Asia that could not be unloaded fast enough, and disrupted the finely tuned supply chains of several major U.S. enterprises.[31]

There are ways of reducing the risks associated with a global supply chain that operates on just-in-time principles. To reduce the risks associated with depending on one supplier for an important input, some firms source these inputs from several suppliers located in different countries. While this does not help in the case of an event with global ramifications, such as September 11, 2001, it does help manage country-specific supply disruptions, which are more common.

THE ROLE OF INFORMATION TECHNOLOGY AND THE INTERNET

Web-based information systems play a crucial role in modern materials management. By tracking component parts as they make their way across the globe toward an assembly plant, information systems enable a firm to optimize its production scheduling according to when components are expected to arrive. By locating component parts in the supply chain precisely, good information systems allow the firm to accelerate production when needed by pulling key components out of the regular supply chain and having them flown to the manufacturing plant.

Firms increasingly use electronic data interchange (EDI) to coordinate the flow of materials into manufacturing, through manufacturing, and out to customers. EDI systems require computer links between a firm, its suppliers, and its shippers. Sometimes customers also are integrated into the system. These electronic links are then used to place orders with suppliers, to register parts leaving a supplier, to track them as they travel toward a manufacturing plant, and to register their arrival. Suppliers typically use an EDI link to send invoices to the purchasing firm. One consequence of an EDI system is that suppliers, shippers, and the purchasing firm can communicate with each other with no time delay, which increases the flexibility and responsiveness of the whole global supply system. A second consequence is that much of the paperwork between suppliers, shippers, and the purchasing firm is eliminated. Good EDI systems can help a firm decentralize materials management decisions to the plant level by giving corporate-level managers the information they need for coordinating and controlling decentralized materials management groups.

Before the emergence of the Internet as a major communication medium, firms and their suppliers normally had to purchase expensive proprietary software solutions to implement EDI systems. The ubiquity of the Internet and the availability of Web-based applications have made most of these proprietary solutions obsolete. Less expensive Web-based systems that are much easier to install and manage now dominate the market for global supply chain management software. These Web-based systems are rapidly transforming the management of globally dispersed supply chains,

allowing even small firms to achieve a much better balance between supply and demand, thereby reducing the inventory in their systems and reaping the associated economic benefits. With increasing numbers of firms adopting these systems, those that don't may find themselves at a significant competitive disadvantage.

CHAPTER SUMMARY

This chapter explained how efficient production and logistics functions can improve an international business's competitive position by lowering the costs of value creation and by performing value creation activities so as to enhance customer service and maximize value added. We looked closely at three issues central to international production and logistics: where to produce, what to make and what to buy, and how to coordinate a globally dispersed manufacturing and supply system. The chapter made the following points:

1. The choice of an optimal production location must consider country factors, technological factors, and product factors.

2. Country factors include the influence of factor costs, political economy, and national culture on production costs, along with the presence of location externalities.

3. Technological factors include the fixed costs of setting up production facilities, the minimum efficient scale of production, and the availability of flexible manufacturing technologies that allow for mass customization.

4. Product factors include the value-to-weight ratio of the product and whether the product serves universal needs.

5. Location strategies either concentrate or decentralize manufacturing. The choice should be made in light of country, technological, and product factors. All location decisions involve trade-offs.

6. Foreign factories can improve their capabilities over time, and this can be of immense strategic benefit to the firm. Managers need to view foreign factories as potential centers of excellence and to encourage and foster attempts by local managers to upgrade factory capabilities.

7. An essential issue in many international businesses is determining which component parts should be manufactured in-house and which should be outsourced to independent suppliers.

8. Making components in-house facilitates investments in specialized assets and helps the firm protect its proprietary technology. It may also improve scheduling between adjacent stages in the value chain. In-house production also makes sense if the firm is an efficient, low-cost producer of a technology.

9. Buying components from independent suppliers facilitates strategic flexibility and helps the firm avoid the organizational problems associated with extensive vertical integration. Outsourcing might also be employed as part of an "offset" policy, which is designed to win more orders for the firm from a country by pushing some subcontracting work to that country.

10. Several firms have tried to attain the benefits of vertical integration and avoid its associated organizational problems by entering long-term strategic alliances with essential suppliers.

11. Although alliances with suppliers can give a firm the benefits of vertical integration without dispensing entirely with the benefits of a market relationship, alliances have drawbacks. The firm that enters a strategic alliance may find its strategic flexibility limited by commitments to alliance partners.

12. Logistics encompasses all the activities that move materials to a production facility, through the production process, and out through a distribution system to the end user. The logistics function is complicated in an international business by distance, time, exchange rates, custom barriers, and other things.

13. Just-in-time systems generate major cost savings from reducing warehousing and inventory holding costs and from reducing the need to write off excess inventory. In addition, JIT systems help the firm spot defective parts and remove them from the manufacturing process quickly, thereby improving product quality.

14. Information technology, particularly Internet-based electronic data interchange, plays a major role in materials management. EDI facilitates the tracking of inputs, allows the firm to optimize its production schedule, lets the firm and its suppliers communicate in real time, and eliminates the flow of paperwork between a firm and its suppliers.

Critical Thinking and Discussion Questions

1. An electronics firm is considering how best to supply the world market for microprocessors used in consumer and industrial electronic products. A manufacturing plant costs about $500 million to construct and requires a highly skilled workforce. The total value of the world market for this product over the next 10 years is estimated to be between $10 billion and $15 billion. The tariffs prevailing in this industry are currently low. Should the firm adopt a concentrated or decentralized manufacturing strategy? What kind of location(s) should the firm favor for its plant(s)?

2. A chemical firm is considering how best to supply the world market for sulfuric acid. A manufacturing plant costs about $20 million to construct and requires a moderately skilled workforce. The total value of the world market for this product over the next 10 years is estimated to be between $20 billion and $30 billion. The tariffs prevailing in this industry are moderate. Should the firm favor concentrated manufacturing or decentralized manufacturing? What kind of location(s) should the firm seek for its plant(s)?

3. Reread the Management Focus on Philips in China; then answer the following questions:

   a. What are the benefits to Philips of shifting so much of its global production to China?

   b. What are the risks associated with a heavy concentration of manufacturing assets in China?

   c. What strategies might Philips adopt to maximize the benefits and mitigate the risks associated with moving so much product development and production activity to developing nations like China?

4. A firm must decide whether to make a component part in-house or to contract it out to an independent supplier. Manufacturing the part requires a nonrecoverable investment in specialized assets. The most efficient suppliers are located in countries with currencies that many foreign exchange analysts expect to appreciate substantially over the next decade. What are the pros and cons of (a) manufacturing the component in-house and (b) outsourcing manufacturing to an independent supplier? Which option would you recommend? Why?

5. Explain how an efficient logistics function can help an international business compete more effectively in the global marketplace.

Research Task

Use the globalEDGE™ site to complete the following exercises:

1. The globalization of production makes many people more aware of the differences in manufacturing costs worldwide. The U.S. Department of Labor's Bureau of International Labor Affairs publishes a *Chartbook of International Labor Comparisons*. Locate the latest edition of this report and identify the hourly compensation costs for manufacturing workers in the U.S., Japan, Korea, Taiwan, Germany, and the U.K.

2. The internationalization of manufacturing has become much more predominant in recent years. In fact, the *Industry Week* magazine ranks the world's largest manufacturing companies by sales revenue. Identify the largest Chinese manufacturing companies as provided in the most recent ranking by paying special attention to the industries these companies operate in.

CLOSING CASE

Microsoft—Outsourcing Xbox Production

When Microsoft decided to enter the video game market with its Xbox gaming console it faced a crucial strategic decision: Should it manufacture the Xbox or outsource manufacturing to a third party, and if it chose outsourcing, to whom? Although Microsoft is primarily known as a software company, it has long had a small but important hardware business selling computer mice, keyboards, and joysticks under the Microsoft brand name. However, Xbox was different. This was not a simple computer peripheral; it was a fully functional specialized computer, with multiple components including microprocessors, memory chips, graphics chips, and an internal hard drive.

Microsoft quickly decided that it lacked the manufacturing and logistics capabilities to make the Xbox itself and manage a global supply chain. After reviewing potential suppliers, it decided to outsource assembly and significant logistics functions to Flextronics, a Singapore-based contract manufacturer. Flextronics has global sales in excess of $13 billion and more than 100,000 employees. In addition to Microsoft, customers include Dell, Ericsson Telecom AB, Hewlett-Packard Company, Siemens AG, Sony-Ericsson, and Xerox Corporation. The company manufactures products for these companies in 28 countries. Its largest concentration of activities is in China, where it has 35,000 employees.

Microsoft had already contracted out the manufacture of computer mice to Flextronics, so it knew something about how the company operated and was happy with the cost and quality of Flextronics products. In looking for a supplier, Microsoft wanted a partner that could manufacture the Xbox at a low cost, maintain very high product quality, respond quickly to shifts in demand, and share detailed information on production schedules, product quality, and inventory with Microsoft on a real-time basis. Flextronics seemed to fit the bill for a number of reasons.

First, Flextronics had been pursuing an "industrial park" strategy that enabled the company to tightly manage its own supply chain, reduce the chances of supply disruptions, and lower costs, which could then be passed on to Microsoft in the form of lower prices for the Xbox. Flextronics' industrial park strategy requires key suppliers to site their factories next to a Flextronics assembly plant at low-cost locations near customers' end markets. Flextronics has large industrial parks in Brazil, China, Hungary, Mexico, and Poland.

In addition to a Flextronics factory, each park contains manufacturers of printed circuit boards, components, cables, plastics, and metal parts needed for assembly of a product such as Xbox. The co-location of Flextronics and its suppliers at an industrial park minimizes logistics costs by facilitating just-in-time inventory systems and reducing transportation costs. Co-location also minimizes supply problems that might arise from a breakdown in globally dispersed supply chains—as occurred after September 11, 2001, and again in 2003 due to the SARS epidemic.

Second, Flextronics' global presence enables the company to shift production from location to location as cost and demand conditions warrant, something that Microsoft wanted. Initially, the Xbox was produced in Hungary (for sale in Europe) and Mexico (for sale in North America and Asia). Within a year, however, Flextronics shifted production from Hungary to China, where labor costs were a fraction of those in Hungary. In 2003, it also moved Xbox production from Mexico to China, for the same reason. Today all Xbox production is in China. Flextronics can execute production shifts very quickly—the company says within three weeks—since all of the relevant manufacturing data are stored in centralized information systems. Thus, if China proves to be a suboptimal location for Xbox production in the future, Flextronics can shift production elsewhere.

Third, using Web-based information systems, Flextronics and Microsoft have the ability to share information in real time with each other. Microsoft feeds information on demand conditions to Flextronics, which enables Flextronics to configure its own production schedules to minimize inventory and closely match supply with demand. In addition, Microsoft has access to real-time information from Flextronics regarding production schedules, inventory, and product quality. This is crucially important because Microsoft handles the overall management of about 40 strategic suppliers for Xbox, including the manufacturers of microprocessors, graphics chips, hard drives, and flash memory (Flextronics handles the supply of commodity-like inputs, such as circuit boards and plastic molding). The information exchange between Microsoft and Flextronics ensures that production schedules between all of the players in the supply chain are tightly coordinated so that inventory is minimized, shortages are avoided, and demand and supply are balanced.

Finally, Microsoft trusted Flextronics. Microsoft had worked with the company for years, and there were strong personal relationships between employees of the two companies. This helped cement the business transaction. To facilitate joint design, which is important for reducing manufacturing costs, some Microsoft people are located at the Flextronics U.S. operations center in San Jose, California, and some Flextronics people are located at Microsoft's headquarters in Redmond, Washington. The two companies had worked together on product design before, and Microsoft knew that could be replicated with the Xbox. Microsoft also believed that Flextronics could deliver production of Xbox on time, even though assembly of the product was far more complex than the assembly of a computer mouse.[32]

Case Discussion Questions

1. What was the strategic advantage to Microsoft of outsourcing Xbox production to Flextronics?

2. What were the risks associated with outsourcing to Flextronics? Did Microsoft mitigate these risks? Do you think Microsoft would have been better off making the Xbox itself?

3. How did Flextronics' industrial park strategy enable the company to respond to national changes in relative factor costs?

4. How important are Web-based information systems to the relationship between Microsoft and Flextronics? What are the economic advantages of real-time information flows between Microsoft, Flextronics, and Flextronics' own subcontractors?

Notes

1. Sources: J. Magretta, "Fast, Global, and Entrepreneurial: Supply Chain Management Hong Kong Style," *Harvard Business Review*, September–October 1998, pp. 102–114; J. Ridding, "A Multinational Trading Group with Chinese Characteristics," *Financial Times*, November 7, 1997, p. 16; J. Ridding, "The Family in the Frame," *Financial Times*, October 28, 1996, p. 12; and J. Lo, "Second Half Doubts Shadow Li & Fung Strength in Interims," *South China Morning Post*, August 27, 1998, p. 3; R. Meredith, "At the Crossroads," *Forbes*, April 17, 2006, pp. 31–32; and "Li & Fung Profit Increases 23% on Improving Margins," *The Wall Street Journal*, March 22, 2007, p. C7.

2. B. C. Arntzen, G. G. Brown, T. P. Harrison, and L. L. Trafton, "Global Supply Chain Management at Digital Equipment Corporation," *Interfaces* 25 (1995), pp. 69–93; and Diana Farrell, "Beyond Offshoring," *Harvard Business Review*, December 2004, pp. 1–8.

3. D. A. Garvin, "What Does Product Quality Really Mean," *Sloan Management Review* 26 (Fall 1984), pp. 25–44.

4. See the articles published in the special issue of the *Academy of Management Review on Total Quality Management* 19, no. 3 (1994). The following article provides a good overview of many of the issues involved from an academic perspective: J. W. Dean and D. E. Bowen, "Management Theory and Total Quality," *Academy of Management Review* 19 (1994),

pp. 392–418. Also see T. C. Powell, "Total Quality Management as Competitive Advantage," *Strategic Management Journal* 16 (1995), pp. 15–37.

5. For general background information, see "How to Build Quality," *The Economist*, September 23, 1989, pp. 91–92; A. Gabor, *The Man Who Discovered Quality* (New York: Penguin, 1990); P. B. Crosby, *Quality Is Free* (New York: Mentor, 1980); and M. Elliot et al., "A Quality World, a Quality Life," *Industrial Engineer*, January 2003, pp. 26–33.

6. G. T. Lucier and S. Seshadri, "GE Takes Six Sigma beyond the Bottom Line," *Strategic Finance*, May 2001, pp. 40–46.

7. M. Saunders, "U.S. Firms Doing Business in Europe Have Options in Registering for ISO 9000 Quality Standards," *Business America*, June 14, 1993, p. 7.

8. G. Stalk and T. M. Hout, *Competing against Time* (New York: Free Press, 1990).

9. Diana Farrell, "Beyond Offshoring," *Harvard Business Review*, December 2004, pp. 1–8, and M. A. Cohen and H. L. Lee, "Resource Deployment Analysis of Global Manufacturing and Distribution Networks," *Journal of Manufacturing and Operations Management* 2 (1989), pp. 81–104.

10. P. Krugman, "Increasing Returns and Economic Geography," *Journal of Political Economy* 99, no. 3 (1991), pp. 483–99, and J. M. Shaver and

F. Flyer, "Agglomeration Economies, Firm Heterogeneity, and Foreign Direct Investment in the United States," *Strategic Management Journal* 21 (2000), pp. 1175–93.

11. Sources: B. Einhorn. "Philips' Expanding Asia Connections," *BusinessWeek Online*, November 27, 2003; K. Leggett and P. Wonacott, "The World's Factory: A Surge in Exports from China Jolts the Global Industry," *The Wall Street Journal*, October 10, 2002, p. A1; "Philips NV: China Will Be Production Site for Electronic Razors," *The Wall Street Journal*, April 8, 2003, p. B12; "Philips Plans China Expansion," *The Wall Street Journal*, September 25, 2003, p. B13; and M. Saunderson, "Eight out of 10 DVD Players Will Be Made in China," *Dealerscope*, July 2004, p. 28.

12. For a review of the technical arguments, see D. A. Hay and D. J. Morris, *Industrial Economics: Theory and Evidence* (Oxford: Oxford University Press, 1979). See also C. W. L. Hill and G. R. Jones, *Strategic Management: An Integrated Approach* (Boston: Houghton Mifflin, 2004).

13. See P. Nemetz and L. Fry, "Flexible Manufacturing Organizations: Implications for Strategy Formulation," *Academy of Management Review* 13 (1988), pp. 627–38; N. Greenwood, *Implementing Flexible Manufacturing Systems* (New York: Halstead Press, 1986); J. P. Womack, D. T. Jones, and D. Roos, *The Machine That Changed the World* (New York: Rawson Associates, 1990); and R. Parthasarthy and S. P. Seith, "The Impact of Flexible Automation on Business Strategy and Organizational Structure," *Academy of Management Review* 17 (1992), pp. 86–111.

14. B. J. Pine, *Mass Customization: The New Frontier in Business Competition* (Boston: Harvard Business School Press, 1993); S. Kotha, "Mass Customization: Implementing the Emerging Paradigm for Competitive Advantage," *Strategic Management Journal* 16 (1995), pp. 21–42; and J. H. Gilmore and B. J. Pine II, "The Four Faces of Mass Customization," *Harvard Business Review*, January–February 1997, pp. 91–101.

15. M. A. Cusumano, *The Japanese Automobile Industry* (Cambridge, MA: Harvard University Press, 1989); T. Ohno, *Toyota Production System* (Cambridge, MA: Productivity Press, 1990); and Womack, Jones, and Roos, *The Machine That Changed the World*.

16. P. Waurzyniak, "Ford's Flexible Push," *Manufacturing Engineering*, September 2003, pp. 47–50.

17. K. Ferdows, "Making the Most of Foreign Facto-

ries," *Harvard Business Review*, March–April 1997, pp. 73–88.

18. This argument represents a simple extension of the dynamic capabilities research stream in the strategic management literature. See D. J. Teece, G. Pisano, and A. Shuen, "Dynamic Capabilities and Strategic Management," *Strategic Management Journal* 18 (1997), pp. 509–33.

19. T. S. Frost, J. M. Birkinshaw, and P. C. Ensign, "Centers of Excellence in Multinational Corporations," *Strategic Management Journal* 23 (November 2002), pp. 997–1018.

20. C. W. L. Hill, "Globalization, the Myth of the Nomadic Multinational Enterprise, and the Advantages of Location Persistence," Working Paper, School of Business, University of Washington, 2001.

21. Sources: K. Ferdows, "Making the Most of Foreign Factories," *Harvard Business Review*, March–April 1997, pp. 73–88; and "Hewlett-Packard: Singapore," Harvard Business School, Case No. 694–035.

22. J. Solomon and E. Cherney, "A Global Report: Outsourcing to India Sees a Twist," *The Wall Street Journal*, April 1, 2004, p. A2.

23. The material in this section is based primarily on the transaction cost literature of vertical integration; for example, O. E. Williamson, *The Economic Institutions of Capitalism* (New York: The Free Press, 1985).

24. For a review of the evidence, see Williamson, *The Economic Institutions of Capitalism*. See also L. Poppo and T. Zenger, "Testing Alternative Theories of the Firm: Transaction Cost, Knowledge Based, and Measurement Explanations for Make or Buy Decisions in Information Services," *Strategic Management Journal* 19 (1998), pp. 853–78.

25. A. D. Chandler, *The Visible Hand* (Cambridge, MA: Harvard University Press, 1977).

26. Sources: D. Gates, "Boeing Buzzes about 'Source' of Work," *Seattle Times*, March 9, 2003, p. A1; S. Wilhelm, "Tough Contest Ahead over 7E7," *Puget Sound Business Journal*, April 11, 2002, p. 50; interviews between Charles Hill and senior management personnel at Boeing; and M. Tatge, "Global Gamble," *Forbes*, April 17, 2006, pp. 78–79.

27. For a review of these arguments, see C. W. L. Hill and R. E. Hoskisson, "Strategy and Structure in the Multiproduct Firm," *Academy of Management Review* 12 (1987), pp. 331–41.

28. C. W. L. Hill, "Cooperation, Opportunism, and the Invisible Hand," *Academy of Management Review* 15 (1990), pp. 500–13.

29. See R. Narasimhan and J. R. Carter, "Organization, Communication and Coordination of International Sourcing," *International Marketing Review* 7 (1990), pp. 6–20, and Arntzen, Brown, Harrison, and Trafton, "Global Supply Chain Management at Digital Equipment Corporation."

30. H. F. Busch, "Integrated Materials Management," *IJPD & MM* 18 (1990), pp. 28–39.

31. T. Aeppel, "Manufacturers Cope with the Costs of Strained Global Supply Lines," *The Wall Street Journal*, December 8, 2004, p. A1.

32. Sources: J. Carborne, "Outsourcing the Xbox," *Purchasing*, August 15, 2002, pp. 22–25; H. B. Hayes, "Outsourcing Xbox Manufacturing," *Pharmaceutical Technology North America*, November 2002, pp. 88–91; "Weathering the Tech Storm," *BusinessWeek*, May 2, 2003, pp. 24–25; and Flextronics *10K Report 2003*.

Levi Strauss Goes Local

It's been a tough few years for Levi Strauss, the iconic manufacturer of blue jeans. Sales at the company, whose 501 jeans became the global symbol of the baby boom generation and were sold in more than 100 countries, dropped from a peak of $7.1 billion in 1996 to just $4.0 billion in 2004. Fashion trends had moved on, its critics charged, and Levi Strauss, hamstrung by high costs and a stagnant product line, was looking more faded than a well-worn pair of 501s. Perhaps so, but 2005 and 2006 bought signs that a turnaround was in progress. Sales increased for the first time in eight years, and after a string of losses the company started to register profits again in 2006.

There were three parts to this turnaround. First, Levi's made cost reductions at home. Levi's closed its last remaining American factories and moved production offshore where jeans could be produced more cheaply.

Second, the company broadened its product line, introducing the Levi's Signature brand that could be sold through lower-priced outlets in markets that were more competitive, including the core American market where Wal-Mart had driven down prices. Third, the company decided in the late 1990s to give more responsibility to national managers, allowing them to better tailor the product offering and marketing mix to local conditions. Prior to this, Levi's had basically sold the same product worldwide, often using the same advertising message. The old strategy was designed to enable Levi's to realize economies of scale in production and advertising, but it wasn't working.

Under the new strategy, variations between national markets have become more pronounced. Jeans have been tailored to different body types. In Asia, shorter leg lengths are common, whereas in South Africa, women's

Global Marketing and R&D

LEARNING OBJECTIVES

After you have read this chapter you should be able to:

LO1 Explain why it might make sense to vary the attributes of a product from country to country.

LO2 Articulate why and how a firm's distribution strategy might vary among countries.

LO3 Identify why and how advertising and promotional strategies might vary among countries.

LO4 Explain why and how a firm's pricing strategy might vary among countries.

LO5 Discuss how the globalization of the world economy is affecting new product development within the international business firm.

jeans need to be roomier in the back, so Levi's has customized the product offering to account for these physical differences. Then there are sociocultural differences: In Japan, tight-fitting black jeans are popular, whereas in Islamic countries, women are discouraged from wearing tight-fitting jeans so Levi's offerings in countries like Turkey are roomier. Climate also has an effect on product design. In northern Europe, standard-weight jeans are sold, whereas in hotter countries lighter denim is used, along with brighter colors that are not washed out by the tropical sun.

Levi's ads, which used to be global, have also been tailored to regional differences. In Europe, the ads now talk about the cool fit. In Asia, they talk about the rebirth of an original. In the United States, the ads show real people who are themselves originals: ranchers, surfers, great musicians.

Levi's has also differentiated distribution channels and pricing strategy. In the fiercely competitive American market, prices are as low as $25 and Levi's are sold through mass-market discount retailers, such as Wal-Mart. In India, strong sales growth is being driven by Levi's low-priced Signature brand. In Spain, jeans are seen as higher fashion items and are being sold for $50 in higher quality outlets. In the United Kingdom too, prices for 501s are much higher than in the United States, reflecting a more benign competitive environment.

This variation is marketing mix seems to be reaping dividends; although demand in the United States and Europe remains sluggish, growth in many other countries is strong. Turkey, South Korea, and South Africa all recorded growth rates in excess of 20 percent in the 2004–05 period. Looking forward, Levi's expects 60 percent of its growth to come from emerging markets.[1]

Introduction

In the previous chapter, we looked at the roles of global production and logistics in an international business. In this chapter, we continue our focus on specific business functions by examining the roles of marketing and research and development (R&D) in an international business. We focus on how marketing and R&D can be performed so they will reduce the costs of value creation and add value by better serving customer needs.

In Chapter 12 we spoke of the tension in most international businesses between the needs to reduce costs and at the same time to respond to local conditions, which tends to raise costs. This tension continues to be a persistent theme in this chapter. A global marketing strategy that views the world's consumers as similar in their tastes and preferences is consistent with the mass production of a standardized output. By mass-producing a standardized output, the firm can realize substantial unit cost reductions from experience curve and other economies of scale. This is basically the strategy that Levi Strauss adopted until the late 1990s, but as the opening case makes clear, by then it was no longer working. Ignoring country differences in consumer tastes and preferences can lead to failure. Thus, an international business's marketing function must determine when product standardization is appropriate and when it is not, and adjust the marketing strategy accordingly. Moreover, even if product standardization is appropriate, the way in which a product is positioned in a market, and the promotions and messages used to sell that product, may still have to be customized to resonate with local consumers. Similarly, the firm's R&D function must be able to develop globally standardized products when appropriate, as well as products customized to local requirements when that makes most sense.[2]

We consider marketing and R&D within the same chapter because of their close relationship. A critical aspect of the marketing function is identifying gaps in the market so the firm can develop new products to fill those gaps. Developing new products requires R&D—thus the linkage between marketing and R&D. A firm should develop new products with market needs in mind, and only marketing can define those needs for R&D personnel. Also, only marketing can tell R&D whether to produce globally standardized or locally customized products. Research has long maintained that a major contributor to the success of new-product introductions is a close relationship between marketing and R&D.[3]

In this chapter, we begin by reviewing the debate on the globalization of markets. Then we discuss the issue of market segmentation. Next we look at four elements that constitute a firm's marketing mix: product attributes, distribution strategy, communication strategy, and pricing strategy. The **marketing mix** is the set of choices the firm offers to its targeted markets. Many firms vary their marketing mix from country to country, depending on differences in national culture, economic development, product standards, distribution channels, and so on. In the opening case, for example, we saw how Levi Strauss has adjusted its marketing mix from country to country, changing product design, distribution strategy, pricing, and promotion strategy to better match local conditions. In the case of Levi Strauss, varying the marketing mix to take local differences into account has been a good thing: The firm has stopped the erosion of its sales and has started to gain market share again.

The chapter closes with a look at new-product development in an international business and at its implications for the organization of the firm's R&D function.

The Globalization of Markets and Brands

In a now-classic *Harvard Business Review* article, Theodore Levitt wrote lyrically about the globalization of world markets. Levitt's arguments have become something of a lightning rod in the debate about the extent of globalization. According to Levitt,

> A powerful force drives the world toward a converging commonalty, and that force is technology. It has proletarianized communication, transport, and travel. The result is a new commercial reality—the emergence of global markets for standardized consumer products on a previously unimagined scale of magnitude.

Gone are accustomed differences in national or regional preferences. The globalization of markets is at hand. With that, the multinational commercial world nears its end, and so does the multinational corporation. The multinational corporation operates in a number of countries and adjusts its products and practices to each—at high relative costs. The global corporation operates with resolute consistency—at low relative cost—as if the entire world were a single entity; it sells the same thing in the same way everywhere.

Commercially, nothing confirms this as much as the success of McDonald's from the Champs Élysées to the Ginza, of Coca-Cola in Bahrain and Pepsi-Cola in Moscow, and of rock music, Greek salad, Hollywood movies, Revlon cosmetics, Sony television, and Levi's jeans everywhere.

Ancient differences in national tastes or modes of doing business disappear. The commonalty of preference leads inescapably to the standardization of products, manufacturing, and the institutions of trade and commerce.[4]

This is eloquent and evocative writing, but is Levitt correct? The rise of global media phenomenon from CNN to MTV, and the ability of such media to help shape a global culture, would seem to lend weight to Levitt's argument. If Levitt is correct, his argument has major implications for the marketing strategies pursued by international business. However, the consensus among academics is that Levitt overstates his case.[5] Although Levitt may have a point when it comes to many basic industrial products, such as steel, bulk chemicals, and semiconductor chips, globalization in the sense Levitt uses it seems to be the exception rather than the rule in many consumer goods markets and industrial markets. Even a firm such as McDonald's, which Levitt holds up as the archetypal example of a consumer products firm that sells a standardized product worldwide, modifies its menu from country to country in light of local consumer preferences. In the Middle East, for example, McDonald's sells the McArabia, a chicken sandwich on Arabian style bread, and in France, the Croque McDo, a hot ham and cheese sandwich.[6] In addition, as we saw in the opening case, despite its strong global brand, Levi's has had to adapt its marketing mix in order to succeed in foreign nations.

On the other hand, Levitt is probably correct to assert that modern transportation and communications technologies are facilitating a convergence of certain tastes and preferences among consumers in the more advanced countries of the world. The popularity of sushi in Los Angeles, hamburgers in Tokyo, hip-hop music, and global media phenomena such as MTV all support this. In the long run, such technological forces may lead to the evolution of a global culture. At present, however, the continuing persistence of cultural and economic differences between nations acts as a brake on any trend toward the standardization of consumer tastes and preferences across nations. Indeed, standardizing tastes may never occur. Some writers have argued that the rise of global culture doesn't mean that consumers share the same tastes and preferences.[7] Rather, people in different nations, often with conflicting viewpoints, are increasingly participating in a shared "global" conversation, drawing upon shared symbols that include global brands from Nike and Kodak to Coca-Cola and Sony. But the way in which these brands are perceived, promoted, and used still varies from country to country, depending upon local differences in tastes and preferences. Furthermore, trade barriers and differences in product and technical standards also constrain a firm's ability to sell a standardized product to a global market using a standardized marketing strategy. We discuss the sources of these differences in subsequent sections when we look at how products must be altered from country to country. In short, Levitt's globally standardized markets seem a long way off in many industries.

Market Segmentation

Market segmentation refers to identifying distinct groups of consumers whose purchasing behavior differs from others in important ways. Markets can be segmented in numerous ways: by geography, demography (sex, age, income, race, education level, etc.), sociocultural factors (social class, values, religion, lifestyle choices), and psychological factors (personality). Because different segments exhibit different patterns of purchasing behavior, firms often adjust their marketing mix from segment to segment. They may vary the

Marketing to Black Brazil

Brazil is home to the largest black population outside of Nigeria. Nearly half of the 160 million people in Brazil are of African or mixed race origin. Despite these numbers, until recently businesses have made little effort to target this large segment. Part of the reason is rooted in economics. Black Brazilians have historically been poorer than Brazilians of European origin and thus have not received the same attention as whites. But after a decade of relatively strong economic performance in Brazil, an emerging black middle class is beginning to command the attention of consumer product companies. To take advantage of this, companies such as Unilever have introduced a range of skin care products and cosmetics aimed at black Brazilians, and Brazil's largest toy company recently introduced a black Barbie-like doll, Susi Olodum, sales of which quickly caught up with sales of a similar white doll.

But there is more to the issue than simple economics. Unlike the United States, where a protracted history of racial discrimination gave birth to the civil rights movement, fostered black awareness, and produced an identifiable subculture in U.S. society, the history of blacks in Brazil has been very different. Although Brazil did not abolish slavery until 1888, racism in Brazil has historically been much subtler than in the United States. Brazil has never excluded blacks from voting or had a tradition of segregating the races. Historically, too, the government encouraged intermarriage between whites and blacks in order to "bleach" society. Partly due to this more benign history, Brazil has not had a black rights movement similar to that in the United States, and racial self-identification is much weaker. Surveys routinely find that African Brazilian consumers decline to categorize themselves as either black or white; instead they choose one of dozens of skin tones and see themselves as being part of a culture that transcends race.

This subtler racial dynamic has important implications for market segmentation and tailoring the marketing mix in Brazil. Unilever had to face this issue when launching a Vaseline Intensive Care lotion for black consumers in Brazil. The company learned in focus groups that for the product to resonate with nonwhite women, its promotions had to feature women of different skin tones, excluding neither whites nor blacks. The campaign Unilever devised features three women with different skin shades at a fitness center. The bottle says the lotion is for "tan and black skin," a description that could include many white women considering that much of the population lives near the beach. Unilever learned that the segment exists, but it is more difficult to define and requires more subtle marketing messages than the African American segment in the United States or middle-class segments in Africa.[10]

precise design of a product, the pricing strategy, the distribution channels used, and the choice of communication strategy from segment to segment. The goal is to optimize the fit between the purchasing behavior of consumers in a given segment and the marketing mix, thereby maximizing sales to that segment. Automobile companies, for example, use a different marketing mix to sell cars to different socioeconomic segments. Toyota uses its Lexus division to sell high-priced luxury cars to high-income consumers, while selling its entry-level models, such as the Toyota Corolla, to lower-income consumers. Similarly, personal computer manufacturers will offer different computer models, embodying different combinations of product attributes and price points, precisely to appeal to consumers from different market segments (e.g., business users and home users).

When managers in an international business consider market segmentation in foreign countries, they need to be cognizant of two main issues: the differences between countries in the structure of market segments and the existence of segments that transcend national borders. The structure of market segments may differ significantly from country to country. An important market segment in a foreign country may have no parallel in the firm's home country, and vice versa. The firm may have to develop a unique marketing mix to appeal to the purchasing behavior of a certain segment in a given country. The accompanying Management Focus provides an example of such a market segment, the African Brazilian market segment in Brazil, which as you will see is very different from the African American segment in the United States. In another example, a research project identified a segment of consumers in China in the 45 to 55 age range that has few parallels in other countries.[8] This group came of age during China's Cultural Revolution in the late 1960s and early 1970s, and the group's values have been shaped by their experiences during the Cultural Revolution. They tend to be highly sensitive to price and respond negatively to new products and most forms of marketing. Thus, firms doing business in China may need to customize their marketing mix to address the unique values and purchasing behavior of the group. The existence of such a segment constrains the ability of firms to standardize their global marketing strategy.

In contrast, the existence of market segments that transcend national borders clearly enhances the ability of an international business to view the global marketplace as a single entity and pursue a global strategy, selling a standardized product worldwide and using the same basic marketing mix to help position and sell that product in a variety of national markets. For a segment to transcend national borders, consumers in that segment must have some compelling similarities along important dimensions—such as age, values, and lifestyle choices—and those similarities must translate into similar purchasing behavior. Although such segments clearly exist in certain industrial markets, they are somewhat rarer in consumer markets. One emerging global segment that is attracting the attention of international marketers of consumer goods is the so-called global youth segment. Global media are paving the way for a global youth segment. Evidence that such a segment exists comes from a study of the cultural attitudes and purchasing behavior of more than 6,500 teenagers in 26 countries.[9] The findings suggest that teens around the world are increasingly living parallel lives that share many common values. It follows that they are likely to purchase the same kind of consumer goods and for the same reasons.

Product Attributes

A product can be viewed as a bundle of attributes.[11] For example, the attributes that make up a car include power, design, quality, performance, fuel consumption, and comfort; the attributes of a hamburger include taste, texture, and size; a hotel's attributes include atmosphere, quality, comfort, and service. Products sell well when their attributes match consumer needs (and when their prices are appropriate). BMW cars sell well to people who have high needs for luxury, quality, and performance, precisely because BMW builds those attributes into its cars. If consumer needs were the same the world over, a firm could simply sell the same product worldwide. However, consumer needs vary from country to country, depending on culture and the level of economic development. A firm's ability to sell the same product worldwide is further constrained by countries' differing product standards. In this section, we review each of these issues and discuss how they influence product attributes.

CULTURAL DIFFERENCES

We discussed countries' cultural differences in Chapter 3. Countries differ along a whole range of dimensions, including social structure, language, religion, and education. These differences have important implications for marketing strategy. For example, hamburgers do not sell well in Islamic countries, where Islamic law forbids the consumption of ham. The most important aspect of cultural differences is probably the impact of tradition. Tradition is particularly important in foodstuffs and beverages. For example, reflecting differences in traditional eating habits, the Findus frozen food division of Nestlé, the Swiss food giant, markets fish cakes and fish fingers in Great Britain, but beef bourguignon and coq au vin in France and vitéllo con funghi and braviola in Italy. In addition to its normal range of products, Coca-Cola in Japan markets Georgia, a cold coffee in a can, and Aquarius, a tonic drink, both of which appeal to traditional Japanese tastes.

Tastes and preferences vary from country to country. Coca-Cola has a wide variety of products to suit its global customers, such as Aquarius and Georgia (shown), which are sold in Japan.

For historical and idiosyncratic reasons, a range of other cultural differences exist between countries. For example, scent preferences differ from one country to another. SC Johnson, a manufacturer of waxes and polishes, encountered resistance to its lemon-scented Pledge furniture polish among older consumers in Japan. Careful market research revealed that the polish smelled similar to a latrine disinfectant used widely in Japan in the 1950s. Sales rose sharply after the scent was adjusted.[12] In another example, Cheetos, the bright orange and cheesy-tasting snack from PepsiCo's Frito-Lay unit, do not have a cheese taste in China. Chinese consumers generally do not like the taste of cheese because it has never been part of traditional cuisine and because many Chinese are lactose-intolerant.[13]

There is some evidence of the trends Levitt talked about, however. Tastes and preferences are becoming more cosmopolitan. Coffee is gaining ground against tea in Japan and Great Britain, while American-style frozen dinners have become popular in Europe (with some fine-tuning to local tastes). Taking advantage of these trends, Nestlé has found that it can market its instant coffee, spaghetti bolognese, and Lean Cuisine frozen dinners in essentially the same manner in both North America and Western Europe. However, there is no market for Lean Cuisine dinners in most of the rest of the world, and there may not be for years or decades. Although some cultural convergence has occurred, particularly among the advanced industrial nations of North America and Western Europe, Levitt's global culture characterized by standardized tastes and preferences is still a long way off.

ECONOMIC DEVELOPMENT

Just as important as differences in culture are differences in the level of economic development. We discussed the extent of country differences in economic development in Chapter 2. Consumer behavior is influenced by the level of economic development of a country. Firms based in highly developed countries such as the United States tend to build a lot of extra performance attributes into their products. Consumers in less-developed countries do not usually demand these extra attributes; their preference is for more basic products. Thus, cars sold in less-developed nations typically lack many of the features found in those sold in developed nations, such as air-conditioning, power steering, power windows, radios, and cassette players. For most consumer durables, product reliability may be a more important attribute in less-developed nations, where such a purchase may account for a major proportion of a consumer's income, than it is in advanced nations.

Contrary to Levitt's suggestions, consumers in the most developed countries are often not willing to sacrifice their preferred attributes for lower prices. Consumers in the most advanced countries often shun globally standardized products that have been developed with the lowest common denominator in mind. They are willing to pay more for products that have additional features and attributes customized to their tastes and preferences. For example, demand for top-of-the-line four-wheel-drive sport utility vehicles, such as Chrysler's Jeep, Ford's Explorer, and Toyota's Land Cruiser, is largely restricted to the United States. This is due to a combination of factors, including the high income level of U.S. consumers, the country's vast distances, the relatively low cost of gasoline, and the culturally grounded "outdoor" theme of American life.

PRODUCT AND TECHNICAL STANDARDS

Even with the forces that are creating some convergence of consumer tastes and preferences among advanced, industrialized nations, Levitt's vision of global markets may still be a long way off because of national differences in product and technological standards.

Differing government-mandated product standards can rule out mass production and marketing of a standardized product. Differences in technical standards also constrain the globalization of markets. Some of these differences result from idiosyncratic decisions made long ago rather than from government actions, but their long-term effects are profound. For example, DVD equipment manufactured for sale in the United States will not play DVDs recorded on equipment manufactured for sale in Great Britain, Germany, and France (and vice versa). Different technical standards for television signal frequency emerged in the 1950s that require television and video equipment to be customized to prevailing standards. RCA stumbled in the 1970s when it failed to account for this in its marketing of TVs in Asia. Although several Asian countries adopted the U.S. standard, Singapore, Hong Kong, and Malaysia adopted the British standard. People who bought RCA TVs in those countries could receive a picture but no sound![14]

Distribution Strategy

A critical element of a firm's marketing mix is its distribution strategy: the means it chooses for delivering the product to the consumer. The way the product is delivered is determined by the firm's entry strategy, discussed in Chapter 12. In this section, we examine a typical distribution system, discuss how its structure varies between countries, and look at how appropriate distribution strategies vary from country to country.

Figure 17.1 illustrates a typical distribution system consisting of a channel that includes a wholesale distributor and a retailer. If the firm manufactures its product in the particular country, it can sell directly to the consumer, to the retailer, or to the wholesaler. The same options are available to a firm that manufactures outside the country. Plus, this firm may decide to sell to an import agent, which then deals with the wholesale distributor, the retailer, or the consumer. Later in the chapter we will consider the factors that determine the firm's choice of channel.

DIFFERENCES BETWEEN COUNTRIES

The four main differences between distribution systems are retail concentration, channel length, channel exclusivity, and channel quality.

Retail Concentration

In some countries, the retail system is very concentrated, but it is fragmented in others. In a **concentrated retail system,** a few retailers supply most of the market. A **fragmented retail system** is one in which there are many retailers, no one of which has a major share

FIGURE 17.1

A Typical Distribution System

of the market. Many of the differences in concentration are rooted in history and tradition. In the United States, the importance of the automobile and the relative youth of many urban areas have resulted in a retail system centered on large stores or shopping malls to which people can drive. This has facilitated system concentration. Japan, with a much greater population density and a large number of urban centers that grew up before the automobile has a more fragmented retail system, with many small stores serving local neighborhoods, to which people frequently walk. In addition, the Japanese legal system protects small retailers. Small retailers can try to block the establishment of a large retail outlet by petitioning their local government.

There is a tendency for greater retail concentration in developed countries. Three factors that contribute to this are the increases in car ownership, number of households with refrigerators and freezers, and number of two-income households. All these factors have changed shopping habits and facilitated the growth of large retail establishments sited away from traditional shopping areas. The last decade has seen consolidation in the global retail industry, with companies such as Wal-Mart and Carrefour attempting to become global retailers by acquiring retailers in different countries. This has increased retail concentration.

In contrast, retail systems are very fragmented in many developing countries, which can make for interesting distribution challenges. In rural China, large areas of the country can be reached only by traveling rutted dirt roads. In India, Unilever has to sell to retailers in 600,000 rural villages, many of which cannot be accessed via paved roads, which means products can reach their destination only by bullock, bicycle, or cart (see the Management Focus on Unilever in this chapter). In neighboring Nepal, the terrain is so rugged that even bicycles and carts are not practical, and businesses rely on yak trains and the human back to deliver products to thousands of small retailers.

Channel Length

Channel length refers to the number of intermediaries between the producer (or manufacturer) and the consumer. If the producer sells directly to the consumer, the channel is very short. If the producer sells through an import agent, a wholesaler, and a retailer, a long channel exists. The choice of a short or long channel is in part a strategic decision for the producing firm. However, some countries have longer distribution channels than others. The most important determinant of channel length is the degree to which the retail system is fragmented. Fragmented retail systems tend to promote the growth of wholesalers to serve retailers, which lengthens channels.

The more fragmented the retail system, the more expensive it is for a firm to make contact with each individual retailer. Imagine a firm that sells toothpaste in a country where there are more than a million small retailers, as in rural India and China. To sell directly to the retailers, the firm would have to build a huge sales force. This would be very expensive, particularly since each sales call would yield a very small order. But suppose a few hundred wholesalers in the country supply retailers not only with toothpaste but also with all other personal care and household products. Because these wholesalers carry a wide range of products, they get bigger orders with each sales call, making it worthwhile for them to deal directly with the retailers. Accordingly, it makes economic sense for the firm to sell to the wholesalers and the wholesalers to deal with the retailers.

Because of such factors, countries with fragmented retail systems also tend to have long channels of distribution, sometimes with multiple layers. The classic example is Japan, where there are often two or three layers of wholesalers between the firm and retail outlets. In countries such as Great Britain, Germany, and the United States where the retail system is far more concentrated, channels are much shorter. When the retail sector is very concentrated, it makes sense for the firm to deal directly with retailers, cutting out wholesalers. A relatively small sales force is required to deal with a concentrated retail sector, and the orders generated from each sales call can be large. Such circumstances tend to prevail in the United States, where large food companies may sell directly to supermarkets rather than going through wholesale distributors.

The rapid development of the Internet in recent years has helped to shorten channel length. For example, the Seattle-based outdoor equipment retailer REI sells its products in Japan via a Japanese-language Web site, thereby eliminating the need for a retail presence on the ground in Japan, which obviously shortens the channel length between REI and its customers. However, there are definite drawbacks with such a strategy. In the case of REI, consumers cannot receive the same level of advice over the Web as in physical retail stores, where salespeople can help customers choose the right gear for their needs. So although REI benefits from a short channel in Japan, it may lose significant sales due to the lack of point-of-sale service.

Another factor that is shortening channel length in some countries is the entry of large discount superstores, such as Carrefour, Wal-Mart, and Tesco. The business model of these retailers is in part based upon the idea that in an attempt to lower prices, they cut out wholesalers and instead deal directly with manufacturers. Thus, when Wal-Mart entered Mexico, its policy of dealing directly with manufacturers, instead of buying merchandise through wholesalers, helped shorten distribution channels in that nation. Similarly, Japan's historically long distribution channels are now being shortened by the rise of large retailers, some of them foreign owned, such as Toys "R" Us, and some of them indigenous enterprises that are imitating the American model, all of which are progressively cutting out wholesalers and dealing directly with manufacturers.

Channel Exclusivity

An **exclusive distribution channel** is one that is difficult for outsiders to access. For example, it is often difficult for a new firm to get access to shelf space in supermarkets. This occurs because retailers tend to prefer to carry the products of established foodstuff manufacturers with national reputations rather than gamble on the products of unknown firms. The exclusivity of a distribution system varies between countries. Japan's system is often held up as an example of a very exclusive system. In Japan, relationships between manufacturers, wholesalers, and retailers often go back decades. Many of these relationships are based on the understanding that distributors will not carry the products of competing firms. In return, the manufacturer guarantees the distributors an attractive markup. As many U.S. and European manufacturers have learned, the close ties that result from this arrangement can make access to the Japanese market difficult. However, it is possible to break into the Japanese market with a new consumer product. Procter & Gamble did so during the 1990s with its Joy brand of dish soap. P&G was able to overcome a tradition of exclusivity for two reasons. First, after a decade of lackluster economic performance, Japan is changing. In their search for profits, retailers are far more willing than they have been historically to violate the old norms of exclusivity. Second, P&G has been in Japan long enough and has a broad enough portfolio of consumer products to give it considerable leverage with distributors, enabling it to push new products out through the distribution channel.

Channel Quality

Channel quality refers to the expertise, competencies, and skills of established retailers in a nation, and their ability to sell and support the products of international businesses. Although the quality of retailers is good in most developed nations, in emerging markets and less-developed nations from Russia to Indonesia channel quality is variable at best. The lack of a high-quality channel may impede market entry, particularly in the case of new or sophisticated products that require significant point of sale assistance and after-sales services and support. When channel quality is poor, an international business may have to devote considerable attention to upgrading the channel, for example, by providing extensive education and support to existing retailers and, in extreme cases, by establishing its own channel. Thus, after pioneering its Apple retail store concept in the United States, Apple is now opening up retail stores in several nations, such as the United Kingdom, in order to provide point-of-sales education, service, and support for its popular iPod and computer products. Apple believes that this strategy will help it gain market share in these nations.

CHOOSING A DISTRIBUTION STRATEGY

A choice of distribution strategy determines which channel the firm will use to reach potential consumers. Should the firm try to sell directly to the consumer or should it go through retailers; should it go through a wholesaler; should it use an import agent; or should it invest in establishing its own channel? The optimal strategy is determined by the relative costs and benefits of each alternative, which vary from country to country, depending on the four factors we have just discussed: retail concentration, channel length, channel exclusivity, and channel quality.

Because each intermediary in a channel adds its own markup to the products, there is generally a critical link between channel length, the final selling price, and the firm's profit margin. The longer a channel, the greater is the aggregate markup, and the higher the price that consumers are charged for the final product. To ensure that prices do not get too high as a result of markups by multiple intermediaries, a firm might be forced to operate with lower profit margins. Thus, if price is an important competitive weapon, and if the firm does not want to see its profit margins squeezed, other things being equal, the firm would prefer to use a shorter channel.

However, the benefits of using a longer channel may outweigh these drawbacks. As we have seen, one benefit of a longer channel is that it cuts selling costs when the retail sector is very fragmented. Thus, it makes sense for an international business to use longer channels in countries where the retail sector is fragmented and shorter channels in countries where the retail sector is concentrated. Another benefit of using a longer channel is market access—the ability to enter an exclusive channel. Import agents may have long-term relationships with wholesalers, retailers, or important consumers and thus be better able to win orders and get access to a distribution system. Similarly, wholesalers may have long-standing relationships with retailers and be better able to persuade them to carry the firm's product than the firm itself would.

Import agents are not limited to independent trading houses; any firm with a strong local reputation could serve as well. For example, to break down channel exclusivity and gain greater access to the Japanese market, Apple Computer signed distribution agreements with five large Japanese firms, including business equipment giant Brother Industries, stationery leader Kokuyo, Mitsubishi, Sharp, and Minolta. These firms use their own long-established distribution relationships with consumers, retailers, and wholesalers to push Apple computers through the Japanese distribution system. As a result, Apple's share of the Japanese market increased from less than 1 percent to 13 percent in the four years following the signing of the agreements.[15]

If such an arrangement is not possible, the firm might want to consider other, less traditional alternatives to gaining market access. Frustrated by channel exclusivity in Japan, some foreign manufacturers of consumer goods have attempted to sell directly to Japanese consumers using direct mail and catalogs. REI had trouble persuading Japanese wholesalers and retailers to carry its products, so it began a direct-mail campaign and then a Web-based strategy to enter Japan that is proving successful.

Finally, if channel quality is poor, a firm should consider what steps it could take to upgrade the quality of the channel, including establishing its own distribution channel.

Communication Strategy

Another critical element in the marketing mix is communicating the attributes of the product to prospective customers. A number of communication channels are available to a firm, including direct selling, sales promotion, direct marketing, and advertising. A firm's communication strategy is partly defined by its choice of channel. Some firms rely primarily on direct selling, others on point-of-sale promotions or direct marketing, and others on mass advertising; still others use several channels simultaneously to communicate their message to prospective customers. In this section, we will look first at the barriers to international communication. Then we will survey the various factors that determine which communication strategy is most appropriate in a particular country. After that we discuss global advertising.

BARRIERS TO INTERNATIONAL COMMUNICATION

International communication occurs whenever a firm uses a marketing message to sell its products in another country. The effectiveness of a firm's international communication can be jeopardized by three potentially critical variables: cultural barriers, source effects, and noise levels.

Cultural Barriers

Cultural barriers can make it difficult to communicate messages across cultures. We discussed some sources and consequences of cultural differences between nations in Chapter 3 and in the previous section of this chapter. Because of cultural differences, a message that means one thing in one country may mean something quite different in another. For example, when Procter & Gamble promoted its Camay soap in Japan in the 1980s it ran into unexpected trouble. In a TV commercial, a Japanese man walked into the bathroom while his wife was bathing. The woman began telling her husband all about her new soap, but the husband, stroking her shoulder, hinted that suds were not on his mind. This ad had been popular in Europe, but it flopped in Japan because it is considered bad manners there for a man to intrude on his wife.[16]

Benetton, the Italian clothing manufacturer and retailer, is another firm that has run into cultural problems with its advertising. The company launched a worldwide advertising campaign with the theme "United Colors of Benetton" that had won awards in France. One of its ads featured a black woman breast-feeding a white baby, and another one showed a black man and a white man handcuffed together. Benetton was surprised when U.S. civil rights groups attacked the ads for promoting white racial domination. Benetton withdrew its ads and fired its advertising agency, Eldorado of France.

You may not be able to recognize its products on the street, but Benetton has become famous for controversial advertising, which countries frequently refuse to run because they are deemed offensive or inappropriate.

The best way for a firm to overcome cultural barriers is to develop cross-cultural literacy (see Chapter 3). In addition, it should use local input, such as a local advertising agency, in developing its marketing message. If the firm uses direct selling rather than advertising to communicate its message, it should develop a local sales force whenever possible. Cultural differences limit a firm's ability to use the same marketing message and selling approach worldwide. What works well in one country may be offensive in another. The accompanying Management Focus, which profiles Procter & Gamble's strategy for selling Tampax tampons internationally, demonstrates how cultural factors can influence the choice of communication strategy.

Source and Country of Origin Effects

Source effects occur when the receiver of the message (the potential consumer in this case) evaluates the message on the basis of status or image of the sender. Source effects can be damaging for an international business when potential consumers in a target country have a bias against foreign firms. For example, a wave of "Japan bashing" swept the United States in the early 1990s. Worried that U.S. consumers might view its products negatively, Honda responded by creating ads that emphasized the U.S. content of its cars to show how "American" the company had become.

Many international businesses try to counter negative source effects by deemphasizing their foreign origins. When the French antiglobalization protestor Jose Bove was hailed as a hero by some in France for razing a partly built McDonald's in 1999, the French McDonald's franchisee responded with an ad depicting a fat, ignorant American who could not understand why McDonald's France used locally produced food that wasn't genetically modified. The edgy ad worked, and McDonald's French operations are now among the most robust in the company's global network.[17] Similarly, when British Petroleum acquired Mobil Oil's extensive network of U.S. gas stations, it changed its name to BP, diverting attention away from the fact that one of the biggest operators of gas stations in the United States is a British firm.

A subset of source effects is referred to as **country of origin effects,** or the extent to which the place of manufacturing influences product evaluations. Research suggests that

Overcoming Cultural Barriers to Selling Tampons

In 1997, Procter & Gamble purchased Tambrands, the manufacturer of Tampax tampons, for $1.87 billion. P&G's goal was to make Tampax a global brand. At the time of the acquisition, some 70 percent of women in North America and a significant majority in northwestern Europe used tampons. However, usage elsewhere was very low, ranging from single digits in countries such as Spain and Japan to less than 2 percent throughout Latin America. P&G believed that it could use its global marketing skills and distribution networks to grow the product, particularly in underserved markets such as Latin America and southern Europe. But P&G has found it tough going.

A big part of the problem has been religious and cultural taboos. A persistent myth in many countries holds that if a girl uses a tampon, she might lose her virginity. This concern seems to crop up most often in countries that are predominantly Catholic. Although the Roman Catholic Church states it has no official position on tampons, some priests have spoken out against the product, associating it with birth control and sexual activities that the church prohibits! Women must also understand their bodies to use a tampon. P&G is finding that in countries where school health education is limited, that understanding is difficult to foster.

After failed attempts to market the product in India and Brazil using conventional marketing strategies, such as print media advertising and retail distribution, P&G has decided to change to an approach based on direct selling and relationship marketing. It tested this model in Monterrey, Mexico. A centerpiece of the strategy has been the hiring of a sales force of counselors. These young women must first promise to become regular tampon users. Most have never tried a tampon. P&G trains each woman and observes her early classes. After passing a written test, the women are equipped with anatomy charts, a blue foam model of a woman's reproductive system, and a box of samples. In navy pantsuits or a doctor's white coat embroidered with the Tampax logo, the counselors are dispatched to speak in stores, schools, gyms, and anywhere women gather. The counselors talk to about 60 women a day, explaining how the product works with the aid of flip charts. About one-third of those women end up buying the product.

The counselors also use these meetings as an opportunity to recruit young women to host gatherings in their homes. Modeled on Tupperware parties, about 20 women typically attend these "bonding sessions" where the counselor explains the product and how it is used, answers questions, and dispenses free samples. About 40 percent of women who attend these gatherings go on to host one.

P&G also found that about half of all doctors in Monterrey thought that tampons were bad for women. The company believes that this is based on ignorance; most of the doctors are men and they simply do not understand how the product works. To combat this, P&G used its sales force, which already called on doctors to sell products such as Pepto-Bismol and Metamucil, to give away tampons and explain how the product works. As a result, P&G believes it has reduced resistance among doctors to less than 10 percent.

Would this selling strategy work? The early signs were encouraging. In just a few months, sales of tampons grew from 2 percent to 4 percent of the total feminine hygiene market in Monterrey, and sales of the Tampax brand tripled. On the basis of these results, P&G decided to launch its first full campaign in Venezuela in early 2001, with several other Latin American countries following soon after.[19]

---

the consumer may use country of origin as a cue when evaluating a product, particularly if he or she lacks more detailed knowledge of the product. For example, one study found that Japanese consumers tended to rate Japanese products more favorably than U.S. products across multiple dimensions, even when independent analysis showed that they were actually inferior.[18] When a negative country of origin effect exists, an international business may have to work hard to counteract this effect by, for example, using promotional messages that stress the positive performance attributes of its product. Thus, the South Korean automobile company Hyundai tried to overcome negative perceptions about the quality of its vehicle in the United States by running advertisements that favorably compare the company's cars to more prestigious brands.

Source effects and country of origin effects are not always negative. French wine, Italian clothes, and German luxury cars benefit from nearly universal positive source effects. In such cases, it may pay a firm to emphasize its foreign origins. In Japan, for example, there is strong demand for high-quality foreign goods, particularly those from Europe. It has become chic to carry a Gucci handbag, sport a Rolex watch, drink expensive French wine, and drive a BMW.

Noise Levels

Noise tends to reduce the probability of effective communication. **Noise** refers to the amount of other messages competing for a potential consumer's attention, and this too varies across countries. In highly developed countries such as the United States, noise is extremely high. Fewer firms vie for the attention of prospective customers in developing countries, and thus the noise level is lower.

PUSH VERSUS PULL STRATEGIES

The main decision with regard to communications strategy is the choice between a push strategy and a pull strategy. A **push strategy** emphasizes personal selling rather than mass media advertising in the promotional mix. Although effective as a promotional tool, personal selling requires intensive use of a sales force and is relatively costly. A **pull strategy** depends more on mass media advertising to communicate the marketing message to potential consumers.

Although some firms employ only a pull strategy and others only a push strategy, still other firms combine direct selling with mass advertising to maximize communication effectiveness. Factors that determine the relative attractiveness of push and pull strategies include product type relative to consumer sophistication, channel length, and media availability.

Product Type and Consumer Sophistication

Firms in consumer goods industries that are trying to sell to a large segment of the market generally favor a pull strategy. Mass communication has cost advantages for such firms; thus they rarely use direct selling. Exceptions can be found in poorer nations with low literacy levels, where direct selling may be the only way to reach consumers (see the Management Focus on Unilever). Firms that sell industrial products or other complex products favor a push strategy. Direct selling allows the firm to educate potential consumers about the features of the product. This may not be necessary in advanced nations where a complex product has been in use for some time, where the product's attributes are well understood, where consumers are sophisticated, and where high-quality channels exist that can provide point-of-sale assistance. However, customer education may be important when consumers have less sophistication toward the product, which can be the case in developing nations or in advanced nations when a new complex product is being introduced, or where high-quality channels are absent or scarce.

Channel Length

The longer the distribution channel, the more intermediaries there are that must be persuaded to carry the product for it to reach the consumer. This can lead to inertia in the channel, which can make entry difficult. Using direct selling to push a product through many layers of a distribution channel can be expensive. In such circumstances, a firm may try to pull its product through the channels by using mass advertising to create consumer demand—once demand is created, intermediaries will feel obliged to carry the product.

In Japan, products often pass through two, three, or even four wholesalers before they reach the final retail outlet. This can make it difficult for foreign firms to break into the Japanese market. Not only must the foreign firm persuade a Japanese retailer to carry its

Unilever—Selling to India's Poor

One of the world's largest and oldest consumer products companies, Unilever has long had a substantial presence in many of the world's poorer nations, such as India. Outside of major urban areas, low income, unsophisticated consumers, illiteracy, fragmented retail distribution systems, and the lack of paved roads have made for difficult marketing challenges. Despite this, Unilever has built a significant presence among impoverished rural populations by adopting innovative selling strategies.

Take India as an example. The country's large rural population is dispersed among some 600,000 villages, more than 500,000 of which cannot be reached by a motor vehicle. Some 91 percent of the rural population lives in villages of fewer than 2,000 people, and of necessity, rural retail stores are very small and carry limited stock. The population is desperately poor, making perhaps a dollar a day, and two-thirds of that income is spent on food, leaving about 30 cents a day for other items. Literacy levels are low, and TVs are rare, making traditional media ineffective. Despite these drawbacks, Hindustan Lever, Unilever's Indian subsidiary, has made a concerted effort to reach the rural poor. Although the revenues generated from rural sales are small, Unilever hopes that as the country develops and income levels rise, the population will continue to purchase the Unilever brands that they are familiar with, giving the company a long-term competitive advantage.

To contact rural consumers, Hindustan Lever tries to establish a physical presence wherever people frequently gather in numbers. This means ensuring that advertisements are seen in places where people congregate and make purchases, such as at village wells and weekly rural markets, and where they consume products, such as at riverbanks where people gather to wash their clothes using (the company hopes) Unilever soap. It is not uncommon to see the villages well plastered with advertisements for Unilever products. The company also takes part in weekly rural events, such as market day, at which farm produce is sold and family provisions purchased. Hindustan Lever salesmen will visit these gatherings, display their products, explain how they work, give away some free samples, make a few sales, and seed the market for future demand.

The backbone of Hindustan Lever's selling effort, however, is a rural distribution network that encompasses 100 factories, 7,500 distributors, and an estimated 3 million retail stores, many of which are little more than a hole in a wall or a stall at a market. The total stock of Unilever products in these stores may be no more than a few sachets of shampoo and half a dozen bars of soap. A depot in each of India's states feeds products to major wholesalers, which then sell directly to retailers in thousands of small towns and villages that can be reached by motor vehicles. If access via motor vehicles is not possible, the major wholesalers sell to smaller second-tier wholesalers, which then handle distribution to India's 500,000 inaccessible rural villages, reaching them by bicycle, bullock, cart, or baskets carried on a human back.[20]

product, but it may also have to persuade every intermediary in the chain to carry the product. Mass advertising may be one way to break down channel resistance in such circumstances. However, in countries such as India, which has a very long distribution channel to serve its massive rural population, mass advertising may not work because of low literacy levels, in which case the firm may need to fall back on direct selling or rely on the goodwill of distributors (see the Management Focus on Unilever).

Media Availability

A pull strategy relies on access to advertising media. In the United States, a large number of media are available, including print media (newspapers and magazines), broadcasting media (television and radio), and the Internet. The rise of cable television in the United States has facilitated extremely focused advertising (e.g., MTV for teens and young adults, Lifetime for women, ESPN for sports enthusiasts). The same is true of the Internet, with different Web sites attracting different kinds of users. While this level of media sophistication is found in some other developed countries, it is not universal.

Even many advanced nations have far fewer electronic media available for advertising than the United States. In Scandinavia, for example, no commercial television or radio stations existed until recently; all electronic media were state owned and carried no commercials, although this has now changed with the advent of satellite television deregulation. In many developing nations, the situation is even more restrictive because mass media of all types are typically more limited. A firm's ability to use a pull strategy is limited in some countries by media availability. In such circumstances, a push strategy is more attractive. For example, Unilever uses a push strategy to sell consumer products in rural India, where few mass media are available (see the Management Focus).

Media availability is limited by law in some cases. Few countries allow advertisements for tobacco and alcohol products on television and radio, though they are usually permitted in print media. When the leading Japanese whiskey distiller, Suntory, entered the U.S. market, it had to do so without television, its preferred medium. The firm spends about $50 million annually on television advertising in Japan. Similarly, while advertising pharmaceutical products directly to consumers is allowed in the United States, it is prohibited in many other advanced nations. In such cases, pharmaceutical firms must rely heavily upon advertising and direct-sales efforts focused specifically at doctors in order to have their products prescribed.

The Push–Pull Mix

The optimal mix between push and pull strategies depends on product type and consumer sophistication, channel length, and media sophistication. Push strategies tend to be emphasized

- For industrial products or complex new products.
- When distribution channels are short.
- When few print or electronic media are available.

Pull strategies tend to be emphasized

- For consumer goods.
- When distribution channels are long.
- When sufficient print and electronic media are available to carry the marketing message.

GLOBAL ADVERTISING

In recent years, largely inspired by the work of visionaries such as Theodore Levitt, there has been much discussion about the pros and cons of standardizing advertising worldwide.[21] One of the most successful standardized campaigns in history was Philip Morris's promotion of Marlboro cigarettes. The campaign was instituted in the 1950s, when the brand was repositioned, to assure smokers that the flavor would be unchanged by the addition of a filter. The campaign theme of "Come to where the flavor is: Come to Marlboro country" was a worldwide success. Marlboro built on this when it introduced "the Marlboro man," a rugged cowboy smoking his Marlboro while riding his horse through the great outdoors. This ad proved successful in almost every major market around the world, and it helped propel Marlboro to the top of the world market. Arguments have been made both for and against standardized advertising.

For Standardized Advertising

The support for global advertising is threefold. First, it has significant economic advantages. Standardized advertising lowers the costs of value creation by spreading the fixed costs of developing the advertisements over many countries. For example, Levi Strauss paid an advertising agency $550,000 to produce a series of TV commercials. By reusing this series in many countries, rather than developing a series for each country, the company enjoyed significant cost savings. Similarly, Coca-Cola's advertising agency, McCann-Erickson, claims to have saved Coca-Cola $90 million over 20 years by using certain elements of its campaigns globally.

Second, because of concerns about the scarcity of creative talent, some feel that one large effort to develop a campaign will produce better results than 40 or 50 smaller efforts. A third justification for a standardized approach is that many brand names are global. With the substantial amount of international travel today and the considerable overlap in media across national borders, many international firms want to project a single brand image to avoid confusion caused by local campaigns. This is particularly important in regions such as Western Europe, where travel across borders is almost as common as travel across state lines in the United States.

Against Standardized Advertising

There are two main arguments against globally standardized advertising. First, as we have seen repeatedly in this chapter and in Chapter 3, cultural differences between nations are such that a message that works in one nation can fail miserably in another. Cultural diversity makes it extremely difficult to develop a single advertising theme that is effective worldwide. Messages directed at the culture of a given country may be more effective than global messages.

Second, advertising regulations may block implementation of standardized advertising. For example, Kellogg could not use a television commercial it produced in Great Britain to promote its cornflakes in many other European countries. A reference to the iron and vitamin content of its cornflakes was not permissible in the Netherlands, where claims relating to health and medical benefits are outlawed. A child wearing a Kellogg T-shirt had to be edited out of the commercial before it could be used in France, because French law forbids the use of children in product endorsements. The key line "Kellogg's makes their cornflakes the best they have ever been" was disallowed in Germany because of a prohibition against competitive claims.[22] Similarly, American Express ran afoul of regulatory authorities in Germany when it launched a promotional scheme that had proved successful in other countries. The scheme advertised the offer of "bonus points" every time American Express cardholders used their cards. According to the advertisements, these bonus points could be used toward air travel with three airlines and hotel accommodations. American Express was charged with breaking Germany's competition law, which prevents an offer of free gifts in connection with the sale of goods, and the firm had to withdraw the advertisements at considerable cost.[23]

Dealing with Country Differences

Some firms are experimenting with capturing benefits of global standardization while recognizing differences in countries' cultural and legal environments. A firm may select some features to include in all its advertising campaigns and localize other features. By doing so, it may be able to save on some costs and build international brand recognition and yet customize its advertisements to different cultures.

Nokia, the Finnish cell phone manufacturer, has been trying to do this. Historically, Nokia had used a different advertising campaign in different markets. In 2004, however, the company launched a global advertising campaign that used the slogan "1001 reasons to have a Nokia imaging phone." Nokia did this to reduce advertising costs and capture some economies of scale. In addition, in an increasingly integrated world the company believes that there is value in trying to establish a consistent global brand image. At the same time, Nokia is tweaking the advertisements for different cultures. The campaign uses actors from the region where the ad runs to reflect the local population, though they say the same lines. Local settings are also modified when showcasing the phones by, for example, using a marketplace when advertising in Italy or a bazaar when advertising in the Middle East.[24]

Pricing Strategy

International pricing strategy is an important component of the overall international marketing mix.[25] In this section, we look at three aspects of international pricing strategy. First, we examine the case for pursuing price discrimination, charging different prices for the same product in different countries. Second, we look at what might be called strategic pricing. Third, we review some regulatory factors, such as government-mandated price controls and antidumping regulations, that limit a firm's ability to charge the prices it would prefer in a country.

PRICE DISCRIMINATION

Price discrimination exists whenever consumers in different countries are charged different prices for the same product.[26] Price discrimination involves charging whatever the market will bear; in a competitive market, prices may have to be lower than in a market where the firm has a monopoly. Price discrimination can help a company maximize its profits. It makes economic sense to charge different prices in different countries.

Two conditions are necessary for profitable price discrimination. First, the firm must be able to keep its national markets separate. If it cannot do this, individuals or businesses may undercut its attempt at price discrimination by engaging in arbitrage. Arbitrage occurs when an individual or business capitalizes on a price differential for a firm's product between two countries by purchasing the product in the country where prices are lower and reselling it in the country where prices are higher. For example, many automobile firms have long practiced price discrimination in Europe. A Ford Escort once cost $2,000 more in Germany than it did in Belgium. This policy broke down when car dealers bought Escorts in Belgium and drove them to Germany, where they sold them at a profit for slightly less than Ford was selling Escorts in Germany. To protect the market share of its German auto dealers, Ford had to bring its German prices into line with those being charged in Belgium. Ford could not keep these markets separate.

However, Ford still practices price discrimination between Great Britain and Belgium. A Ford car can cost up to $3,000 more in Great Britain than in Belgium. In this case, arbitrage has not been able to equalize the price because right-hand-drive cars are sold in Great Britain and left-hand-drive cars in the rest of Europe. Because there is no market for left-hand-drive cars in Great Britain, Ford has been able to keep the markets separate.

The second necessary condition for profitable price discrimination is different price elasticities of demand in different countries. The **price elasticity of demand** is a measure of the responsiveness of demand for a product to change in price. Demand is said to be **elastic** when a small change in price produces a large change in demand; it is said to be **inelastic** when a large change in price produces only a small change in demand. Figure 17.2 illustrates elastic and inelastic demand curves. Generally, a firm can charge a higher price in a country where demand is inelastic.

The elasticity of demand for a product in a given country is determined by a number of factors, of which income level and competitive conditions are the two most important. Price elasticity tends to be greater in countries with low income levels. Consumers with limited incomes tend to be very price conscious; they have less to spend, so they look much more closely at price. Thus, price elasticities for products such as television sets are greater in countries such as India, where a television set is still a luxury item, than in the United States, where it is considered a necessity.

In general, the more competitors there are, the greater consumers' bargaining power will be and the more likely consumers will be to buy from the firm that charges the lowest price. Thus, many competitors cause high elasticity of demand. In such circumstances, if a firm raises its prices above those of its competitors, consumers will switch to the competitors' products. The opposite is true when a firm faces few competitors. When competitors are limited, consumers' bargaining power is weaker and price is less

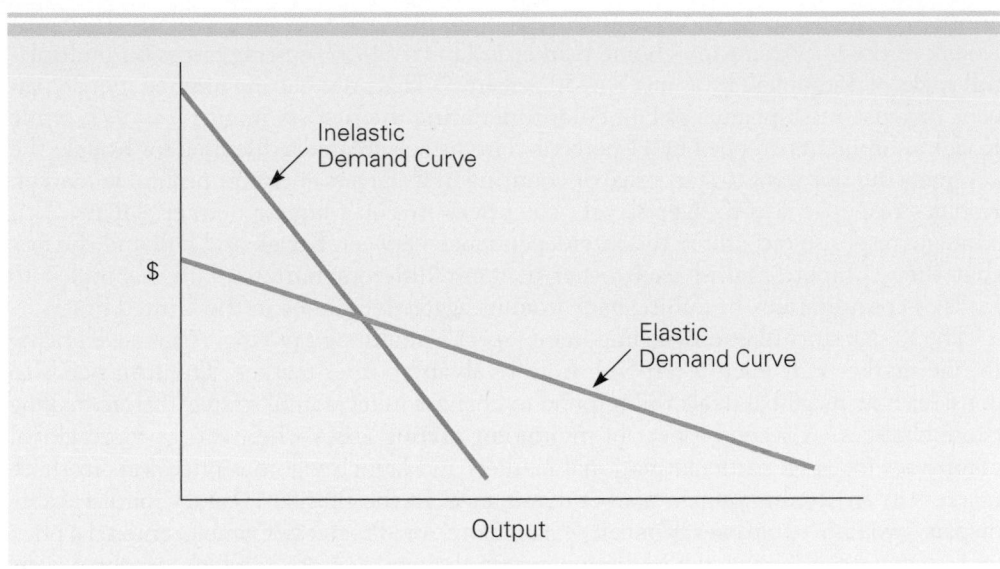

FIGURE 17.2

Elastic and Inelastic Demand Curves

important as a competitive weapon. Thus, a firm may charge a higher price for its product in a country where competition is limited than in one where competition is intense.

STRATEGIC PRICING

The concept of **strategic pricing** has three aspects, which we will refer to as predatory pricing, multipoint pricing, and experience curve pricing. Both predatory pricing and experience curve pricing may violate antidumping regulations. After we review predatory, multipoint, and experience curve pricing, we will look at antidumping rules and other regulatory policies.

Predatory Pricing

Predatory pricing is the use of price as a competitive weapon to drive weaker competitors out of a national market. Once the competitors have left the market, the firm can raise prices and enjoy high profits. For such a pricing strategy to work, the firm must normally have a profitable position in another national market, which it can use to subsidize aggressive pricing in the market it is trying to monopolize. Historically, many Japanese firms were accused of pursuing such a policy. The argument ran like this: Because the Japanese market was protected from foreign competition by high informal trade barriers, Japanese firms could charge high prices and earn high profits at home. They then used these profits to subsidize aggressive pricing overseas, with the goal of driving competitors out of those markets. Once this had occurred, so this argument claims, the Japanese firms then raised prices. Matsushita was accused of using this strategy to enter the U.S. TV market. As one of the major TV producers in Japan, Matsushita earned high profits at home. It then used these profits to subsidize the losses it made in the United States during its early years there, when it priced low to increase its market penetration. Ultimately, Matsushita became the world's largest manufacturer of TVs.[27]

Multipoint Pricing Strategy

Multipoint pricing becomes an issue when two or more international businesses compete against each other in two or more national markets. For example, multipoint pricing has been an issue for Kodak and Fuji Photo because the companies have long competed against each other around the world.[28] **Multipoint pricing** refers to the impact a firm's pricing strategy in one market may have on its rivals' pricing strategy in another market. Aggressive pricing in one market may elicit a competitive response from a rival in another market. For example, Fuji launched an aggressive competitive attack against Kodak in the U.S. company's home market in January 1997, cutting prices on multiple-roll packs of 35mm film by as much as 50 percent.[29] This price cutting resulted in a 28 percent increase in shipments of Fuji color film during the first six months of 1997, while Kodak's shipments dropped by 11 percent. This attack created a dilemma for Kodak; the company did not want to start price discounting in its largest and most profitable market. Kodak's response was to aggressively cut prices in Fuji's largest market, Japan. This strategic response recognized the interdependence between Kodak and Fuji and the fact that they compete against each other in many different nations. Fuji responded to Kodak's counterattack by pulling back from its aggressive stance in the United States.

The Kodak story illustrates an important aspect of multipoint pricing: Aggressive pricing in one market may elicit a response from rivals in another market. The firm needs to consider how its global rivals will respond to changes in its pricing strategy before making those changes. A second aspect of multipoint pricing arises when two or more global companies focus on particular national markets and launch vigorous price wars in those markets in an attempt to gain market dominance. In the Brazilian market for disposable diapers, two U.S. companies, Kimberly-Clark Corp. and Procter & Gamble, entered a price war as each struggled to establish dominance in the market.[30] As a result, over three years the cost of disposable diapers fell from $1 per diaper to 33 cents per diaper, while several other competitors, including indigenous Brazilian firms, were driven out of the market. Kimberly-Clark and Procter & Gamble are engaged in a global struggle for market share and dominance, and Brazil is one of their battlegrounds. Both companies can afford to engage in this behavior, even though it reduces their profits in Brazil, because they have profitable operations elsewhere in the world that can subsidize these losses.

Pricing decisions around the world must be centrally monitored. It is tempting to delegate full responsibility for pricing decisions to the managers of various national subsidiaries, thereby reaping the benefits of decentralization. However, because pricing strategy in one part of the world can elicit a competitive response in another, central management needs to at least monitor and approve pricing decisions in a given national market, and local managers need to recognize that their actions can affect competitive conditions in other countries.

Experience Curve Pricing

We first encountered the experience curve in Chapter 12. As a firm builds its accumulated production volume over time, unit costs fall due to experience effects. Learning effects and economies of scale underlie the experience curve. Price comes into the picture because aggressive pricing (along with aggressive promotion and advertising) can build accumulated sales volume rapidly and thus move production down the experience curve. Firms further down the experience curve have a cost advantage vis-à-vis those further up the curve.

Many firms pursuing an **experience curve pricing** strategy on an international scale will price low worldwide in attempting to build global sales volume as rapidly as possible, even if this means taking large losses initially. Such a firm believes that in several years, when it has moved down the experience curve, it will be making substantial profits and have a cost advantage over its less-aggressive competitors.

REGULATORY INFLUENCES ON PRICES

The ability to engage in either price discrimination or strategic pricing may be limited by national or international regulations. Most important, a firm's freedom to set its own prices is constrained by antidumping regulations and competition policy.

Antidumping Regulations

Both predatory pricing and experience curve pricing can run afoul of antidumping regulations. Dumping occurs whenever a firm sells a product for a price that is less than the cost of producing it. Most regulations, however, define dumping more vaguely. For example, a country is allowed to bring antidumping actions against an importer under Article 6 of GATT as long as two criteria are met: sales at "less than fair value" and "material injury to a domestic industry." The problem with this terminology is that it does not indicate what a fair value is. The ambiguity has led some to argue that selling abroad at prices below those in the country of origin, as opposed to below cost, is dumping.

Such logic led the Bush administration to place a 20 percent duty on imports of foreign steel in 2001. Foreign manufacturers protested that they were not selling below cost. Admitting that their prices were lower in the United States than some other countries, they argued that this simply reflected the intensely competitive nature of the U.S. market (i.e., different price elasticities).

Antidumping rules set a floor under export prices and limit firms' ability to pursue strategic pricing. The rather vague terminology used in most antidumping actions suggests that a firm's ability to engage in price discrimination also may be challenged under antidumping legislation.

Competition Policy

Most developed nations have regulations designed to promote competition and to restrict monopoly practices. These regulations can be used to limit the prices a firm can charge in a given country. For example, at one time the Swiss pharmaceutical manufacturer Hoffmann-LaRoche had a monopoly on the supply of Valium and Librium tranquilizers. The British Monopolies and Mergers Commission, which is responsible for promoting fair competition in Great Britain, investigated the company. The commission found that Hoffmann-LaRoche was overcharging for its tranquilizers and ordered the company to reduce its prices 35 to 40 percent. Hoffmann-LaRoche maintained unsuccessfully that it was merely engaging in price discrimination. The German cartel office and the Dutch and Danish governments later brought similar actions against Hoffmann-LaRoche.[31]

Configuring the Marketing Mix

A firm might vary aspects of its marketing mix from country to country to take into account local differences in culture, economic conditions, competitive conditions, product and technical standards, distribution systems, government regulations, and the like. Such differences may require variation in product attributes, distribution strategy, communications strategy, and pricing strategy. The cumulative effect of these factors makes it rare for a firm to adopt the same marketing mix worldwide.

For example, the financial service industry is often thought of as one in which global standardization of the marketing mix is the norm. However, while a financial services company such as American Express may sell the same basic charge card service worldwide, utilize the same basic fee structure for that product, and adopt the same basic global advertising message ("don't leave home without it"), differences in national regulations still mean that it has to vary aspects of its communications strategy from country to country (as pointed out earlier, the promotional strategy it had developed in the United States was illegal in Germany). Similarly, while McDonald's is often thought of as the quintessential example of a firm that sells the same basic standardized product worldwide, in reality it varies one important aspect of its marketing mix—its menu—from country to country. McDonald's also varies its distribution strategy. In Canada and the United States, most McDonald's are located in areas that are easily accessible by car, whereas in more densely populated and less automobile-reliant societies of the world, such as Japan and Great Britain, location decisions are driven by the accessibility of a restaurant to pedestrian traffic. Because countries typically still differ along one or more of the dimensions discussed above, some customization of the marketing mix is normal.

However, there are often significant opportunities for standardization along one or more elements of the marketing mix.[32] Firms may find that it is possible and desirable to

MANAGEMENT FOCUS

Castrol Oil in Vietnam

Castrol is the lubricants division of the British chemical, oil, and gas concern Burmah Castrol. In Europe and in the United States, where Castrol has a 15 percent share of the do-it-yourself lubricants market, Castrol targets motorists who want to cosset their engine by paying a bit more for Castrol's high-margin GTX brand rather than for a standard lubricant. The company supports this differentiated positioning strategy by sponsoring Formula 1 racing and the Indy car series in the United States and by heavy spending on television and in automobile magazines in both Europe and the United States.

Some of Castrol's most notable successes in recent years, however, have been in the developing nations of Asia, where Castrol reaps only one-sixth of its sales but more than one-quarter of its operating profits. In Vietnam, automobiles are still relatively rare, so Castrol has targeted motorcycle owners. Castrol's strategy is to target people who want to take care of their new motorcycles. The long-term goal is to build brand loyalty, so that when automobile ownership becomes common in Vietnam, as Castrol believes it will, former motorcycle owners will stick with Castrol when they trade up to cars. This strategy has already worked in Thailand. Castrol has held the leading share of the motorcycle market in Thailand since the early 1980s, and it now holds the leading share in that country's rapidly growing automobile market.

Unlike its practice in more developed countries, Castrol's communications strategy in Vietnam does not focus on television and glossy print media (there is relatively little of either in Vietnam). Rather, Castrol focuses on building consumer awareness through extensive use of billboards, car stickers, and some 4,000 signs at Vietnam's ubiquitous roadside garages and motorcycle cleaning shops. Castrol also developed a unique slogan that has a rhythmic quality in Vietnamese—*Dau nhot tot nhat*, or "best-quality lubricants"—and sticks in consumers' minds. Castrol's researchers say the slogan is now recognized by a remarkable 99 percent of people in Ho Chi Minh City.

At the same time, Castrol is starting to leverage some of its international promotional strategies and use them in Vietnam. In 2003, the company developed a global advertising campaign that featured English soccer star David Beckham, who is probably the most recognizable athlete in the world outside of the United States. As part of the campaign, Beckham visited several Asian nations, including Vietnam, where he attended a soccer tournament sponsored by Castrol.

As elsewhere, Castrol has adopted a premium pricing strategy in Vietnam, which is consistent with the company's attempt to build a global brand image of high quality. Castrol oil costs about $1.5 per liter in Vietnam, about three times as much as the price of cheaper oil imported from Taiwan and Thailand. Despite the high price of its product, Castrol claims it is gaining share in Vietnam as its branding strategy wins converts.

Castrol has had to tailor its distribution strategy to Vietnam's unique conditions. In most countries where it operates, Castrol divides the country into regions and has a single distributor in each region. In Vietnam, however, Castrol will often have two distinct distributors in a region—one to deal with state-owned customers, of which there are still many in this nominally Communist country, and one to deal with private customers. Castrol acknowledges the system is costly but says it is the only way to operate in a country where there is still some tension between state and private entities.[33]

standardize their global advertising message or core product attributes to realize substantial cost economies. They may find it desirable to customize their distribution and pricing strategy to take advantage of local differences. In reality, the "customization versus standardization" debate is not an all or nothing issue; it frequently makes sense to standardize some aspects of the marketing mix and customize others, depending on conditions in various national marketplaces. The accompanying Management Focus provides an explicit example, that of Castrol Oil. Castrol sells a standardized product worldwide—lubricating oil—yet it varies other aspects of its marketing mix from country to country, depending on economic conditions, competitive conditions, and distribution systems. Decisions about what to customize and what to standardize should be driven by a detailed examination of the costs and benefits of doing so for each element in the marketing mix.

New-Product Development

Firms that successfully develop and market new products can earn enormous returns. Examples include Du Pont, which has produced a steady stream of successful innovations such as cellophane, nylon, Freon, and Teflon (nonstick pans); Sony, whose successes include the Walkman, the compact disc, and the PlayStation; Pfizer, the drug company that during the 1990s produced several major new drugs, including Viagra; 3M, which has applied its core competency in tapes and adhesives to developing a wide range of new products; Intel, which has consistently managed to lead in the development of innovative microprocessors to run personal computers; and Cisco Systems, which developed the routers that sit at the hubs of Internet connections, directing the flow of digital traffic.

In today's world, competition is as much about technological innovation as anything else. The pace of technological change has accelerated since the Industrial Revolution in the 18th century, and it continues to do so today. The result has been a dramatic shortening of product life cycles. Technological innovation is both creative and destructive.[34] An innovation can make established products obsolete overnight. But an innovation can also make a host of new products possible. Witness recent changes in the electronics industry. For 40 years before the early 1950s, vacuum tubes were a major component in radios and then in record players and early computers. The advent of transistors destroyed the market for vacuum tubes, but at the same time it created new opportunities connected with transistors. Transistors took up far less space than vacuum tubes, creating a trend toward miniaturization that continues today. The transistor held its position as the major component in the electronics industry for just a decade. Microprocessors were developed in the 1970s, and the market for transistors declined rapidly. The microprocessor created yet another set of new-product opportunities: handheld calculators (which destroyed the market for slide rules), compact disc players (which destroyed the market for analog record players), personal computers (which destroyed the market for typewriters), and cell phones (which may ultimately replace land line phones), to name a few.

This "creative destruction" unleashed by technological change makes it critical that a firm stay on the leading edge of technology, lest it lose out to a competitor's innovations. As we explain in the next subsection, this not only creates a need for the firm to invest in R&D, but it also requires the firm to establish R&D activities at those locations where expertise is concentrated. As we shall see, leading-edge technology on its own is not enough to guarantee a firm's survival. The firm must also apply that technology to developing products that satisfy consumer needs, and it must design the product so that it can be manufactured in a cost-effective manner. To do that, the firm needs to build close links between R&D, marketing, and manufacturing. This is difficult enough for the domestic firm, but it is even more problematic for the international business competing in an industry where consumer tastes and preferences differ from country to country.[35] With all of this in mind, we move on to examine locating R&D activities and building links between R&D, marketing, and manufacturing.

THE LOCATION OF R&D

The interactions of scientific research, demand conditions, and competitive conditions stimulate ideas for new products. Other things being equal, the rate of new-product development seems to be greater in countries where

- More money is spent on basic and applied research and development.
- Underlying demand is strong.
- Consumers are affluent.
- Competition is intense.[36]

Basic and applied research and development discovers new technologies and then commercializes them. Strong demand and affluent consumers create a potential market for new products. Intense competition between firms stimulates innovation as the firms try to beat their competitors and reap potentially enormous first-mover advantages that result from successful innovation.

For most of the post–World War II period, the country that ranked highest on these criteria was the United States. The United States devoted a greater proportion of its gross domestic product to R&D than any other country did. Its scientific establishment was the largest and most active in the world. U.S. consumers were the most affluent, the market was large, and competition among U.S. firms was brisk. Due to these factors, the United States was the market where most new products were developed and introduced. Accordingly, it was the best location for R&D activities; it was where the action was.

Over the past 20 years, things have been changing quickly. The U.S. monopoly on new-product development has weakened considerably. Although U.S. firms are still at the leading edge of many new technologies, Asian and European firms are also strong players, with companies such as Sony, Sharp, Samsung, Ericsson, Nokia, and Philips NV driving product innovation in their respective industries. In addition, both Japan and the European Union are large, affluent markets, and the wealth gap between them and the United States is closing.

As a result, it is often no longer appropriate to consider the United States as the lead market. In video games, for example, Japan is often the lead market, with companies like Sony and Nintendo introducing their latest video game players in Japan some six months before they introduce them in the United States. In wireless telecommunications, Europe is generally reckoned to be ahead of the United States. Some of the most advanced applications of wireless telecommunications services are being pioneered not in the United States but in Finland, where more than 90 percent of the population has wireless telephones, compared with 65 percent of the U.S. population. However, it often is questionable whether any developed nation can be considered the lead market. To succeed in today's high-technology industries, it is often necessary to simultaneously introduce new products in all major industrialized markets. When Intel introduces a new microprocessor, for example, it does not first introduce it in the United States and then roll it out in Europe a year later. It introduces it simultaneously around the world.

Because leading-edge research is now carried out in many locations around the world, the argument for centralizing R&D activity in the United States is now much weaker than it was two decades ago. (It used to be argued that centralized R&D eliminated duplication.) Much leading-edge research is now occurring in Japan and Europe. Dispersing R&D activities to those locations allows a firm to stay close to the center of leading-edge activity to gather scientific and competitive information and to draw on local scientific resources.[37] This may result in some duplication of R&D activities, but the cost disadvantages of duplication are outweighed by the advantages of dispersion.

For example, to expose themselves to the research and new-product development work being done in Japan, many U.S. firms have set up satellite R&D centers in Japan. Kodak's R&D center in Japan employs about 200 people. The company hired about 100 Japanese researchers and directed the lab to concentrate on electronic imaging technology. U.S. firms that have established R&D facilities in Japan include Corning, Texas Instruments, IBM, Digital Equipment, Procter & Gamble, Upjohn, Pfizer, Du Pont, Monsanto, and Microsoft.[38] The National Science Foundation (NSF) has documented a sharp increase in the proportion of total R&D spending by U.S. firms that is now done abroad.[39] For example, Motorola now has 14 dedicated R&D facilities located in seven countries, and Bristol-Myers Squibb has 12 facilities in six countries. At the same time, to internationalize their own research and gain access to U.S. talent, many European and Japanese firms are investing in U.S.-based research facilities, according to the NSF.

INTEGRATING R&D, MARKETING, AND PRODUCTION

Although a firm that is successful at developing new products may earn enormous returns, new-product development has a high failure rate. One study of product development in

16 companies in the chemical, drug, petroleum, and electronics industries suggested that only about 20 percent of R&D projects result in commercially successful products or processes.[40] Another in-depth case study of product development in three companies (one in chemicals and two in drugs) reported that about 60 percent of R&D projects reached technical completion, 30 percent were commercialized, and only 12 percent earned an economic profit that exceeded the company's cost of capital.[41] Along the same lines, another study concluded that one in nine major R&D projects, or about 11 percent, produced commercially successful products.[42] In sum, the evidence suggests that only 10 to 20 percent of major R&D projects give rise to commercially successful products. Well-publicized product failures include Apple Computer's Newton personal digital assistant, Sony's Betamax format in the video player and recorder market, and Sega's Dreamcast video game console.

The reasons for such high failure rates are various and include development of a technology for which demand is limited, failure to adequately commercialize promising technology, and inability to manufacture a new product cost-effectively. Firms can reduce the probability of making such mistakes by insisting on tight cross-functional coordination and integration between three core functions involved in the development of new products: R&D, marketing, and production.[43] Tight cross-functional integration between R&D, production, and marketing can help a company to ensure that

1. Product development projects are driven by customer needs.
2. New products are designed for ease of manufacture.
3. Development costs are kept in check.
4. Time to market is minimized.

Close integration between R&D and marketing is required to ensure that the needs of customers drive product development projects. A company's customers can be a primary source of new-product ideas. Identification of customer needs, particularly unmet needs, can set the context within which successful product innovation occurs. As the point of contact with customers, the marketing function of a company can provide valuable information in this regard. Integration of R&D and marketing is crucial if a new product is to be properly commercialized. Without integration of R&D and marketing, a company runs the risk of developing products for which there is little or no demand.

Integration between R&D and production can help a company design products with manufacturing requirements in mind. Designing for manufacturing can lower costs and increase product quality. Integrating R&D and production can also help lower development costs and speed products to market. If a new product is not designed with manufacturing capabilities in mind, it may prove too difficult to build. Then the product will have to be redesigned, and both overall development costs and the time it takes to bring the product to market may increase significantly. Making design changes during product planning could increase overall development costs by 50 percent and add 25 percent to the time it takes to bring the product to market.[44] Many quantum product innovations require new processes to manufacture them, which makes it all the more important to achieve close integration between R&D and production. Minimizing time to market and development costs may require the simultaneous development of new products and new processes.[45]

CROSS-FUNCTIONAL TEAMS

One way to achieve cross-functional integration is to establish cross-functional product development teams composed of representatives from R&D, marketing, and production. Because these functions may be located in different countries, the team will sometimes have a multinational membership. The objective of a team should be to take a product development project from the initial concept development to market introduction. A number of attributes seem to be important for a product development team to function effectively and meet all its development milestones.[46]

First, the team should be led by a "heavyweight" project manager who has high status within the organization and who has the power and authority required to get the financial and human resources the team needs to succeed. The leader should be dedicated primarily, if not entirely, to the project. He or she should be someone who believes in the project (a champion) and who is skilled at integrating the perspectives of different functions and at helping personnel from different functions and countries work together for a common goal. The leader should also be able to act as an advocate of the team to senior management.

Second, the team should be composed of at least one member from each key function. The team members should have a number of attributes, including an ability to contribute functional expertise, high standing within their function, a willingness to share responsibility for team results, and an ability to put functional and national advocacy aside. It is generally preferable if core team members are 100 percent dedicated to the project for its duration. This ensures their focus on the project, not on the ongoing work of their function.

Third, the team members should physically be in one location if possible to create a sense of camaraderie and to facilitate communication. This presents problems if the team members are drawn from facilities in different nations. One solution is to transfer key individuals to one location for the duration of a product development project. Fourth, the team should have a clear plan and clear goals, particularly with regard to critical development milestones and development budgets. The team should have incentives to attain those goals, such as receiving pay bonuses when major development milestones are hit. Fifth, each team needs to develop its own processes for communication and conflict resolution. For example, one product development team at Quantum Corporation, a California-based manufacturer of disk drives for personal computers, instituted a rule that all major decisions would be made and conflicts resolved at meetings that were held every Monday afternoon. This simple rule helped the team meet its development goals. In this case, it was also common for team members to fly in from Japan, where the product was to be manufactured, to the U.S. development center for the Monday morning meetings.[47]

BUILDING GLOBAL R&D CAPABILITIES

The need to integrate R&D and marketing to adequately commercialize new technologies poses special problems in the international business because commercialization may require different versions of a new product to be produced for various countries.[48] To do this, the firm must build close links between its R&D centers and its various country operations. A similar argument applies to the need to integrate R&D and production, particularly in those international businesses that have dispersed production activities to different locations around the globe in consideration of relative factor costs and the like.

Integrating R&D, marketing, and production in an international business may require R&D centers in North America, Asia, and Europe that are linked by formal and informal integrating mechanisms with marketing operations in each country in their regions and with the various manufacturing facilities. In addition, the international business may have to establish cross-functional teams whose members are dispersed around the globe. This complex endeavor requires the company to utilize formal and informal integrating mechanisms to knit its far-flung operations together so they can produce new products in an effective and timely manner.

While there is no one best model for allocating product development responsibilities to various centers, one solution many international businesses adopt involves establishing a global network of R&D centers. In this model, fundamental research is undertaken at basic research centers around the globe. These centers are normally located in regions or cities where valuable scientific knowledge is being created and where there is a pool of skilled research talent (e.g., Silicon Valley in the United States, Cambridge in England, Kobe in Japan, Singapore). These centers are the innovation engines of the firm. Their job is to develop the basic technologies that become new products.

These technologies are picked up by R&D units attached to global product divisions and used to generate new products to serve the global marketplace. At this level, commercialization of the technology and design for manufacturing are emphasized. If further customization is needed so the product appeals to the tastes and preferences of consumers in individual markets, an R&D group based in a subsidiary in that country or at a regional center that customizes products for several countries in the region will undertake it.

Hewlett-Packard has four basic research centers located in Palo Alto, California; Bristol, England; Haifa, Israel; and Tokyo, Japan.[49] These labs are the seedbeds for technologies that ultimately become new products and businesses. They are the company's innovation engines. The Palo Alto center, for example, pioneered HP's thermal ink-jet technology. R&D centers associated with HP's global product divisions develop the product ideas. Thus, the Consumer Products Group, which has its worldwide headquarters in San Diego, California, designs, develops, and manufactures a range of imaging products using HP-pioneered thermal ink-jet technology. Subsidiaries might then customize the product so that it best matches the needs of important national markets. HP's subsidiary in Singapore, for example, is responsible for the design and production of thermal ink-jet printers for Japan and other Asian markets. This subsidiary takes products originally developed in San Diego and redesigns them for the Asian market. In addition, the Singapore subsidiary has taken the lead from San Diego in the design and development of certain portable thermal ink-jet printers. HP delegated this responsibility to Singapore because this subsidiary has acquired important competencies in the design and production of thermal ink-jet products, so it has become the best place in the world to undertake this activity.

Microsoft offers a similar example. The company has basic research sites in Redmond, Washington (its headquarters); Silicon Valley, California; Cambridge, England; Tokyo, Japan; Beijing, China; and Bangalore, India. Staff at these research sites work on the fundamental problems that underlie the design of future products. For example, a group at Redmond is working on natural language recognition software, while another works on artificial intelligence. These research centers don't produce new products; rather, they produce the technology that is used to enhance existing products or help produce new products. Dedicated product groups (e.g., desktop operating systems, applications) produce the products themselves, and local subsidiaries sometimes customize the products to match the needs of local markets. Thus, the Chinese subsidiary will do some basic customization of programs such as Microsoft Office, adding Chinese characters and customizing the interface.

CHAPTER SUMMARY

This chapter discussed the marketing and R&D functions in international business. A persistent theme of the chapter is the tension that exists between the need to reduce costs and the need to be responsive to local conditions, which raises costs. The chapter made these major points:

1. Theodore Levitt argued that due to the advent of modern communications and transport technologies, consumer tastes and preferences are becoming global, which is creating global markets for standardized consumer products. However, many commentators regard this position as extreme, arguing that substantial differences still exist between countries.

2. Market segmentation refers to the process of identifying distinct groups of consumers whose purchasing behavior differs from each other in important ways. Managers in an international business need to be aware of two main issues relating to segmentation: the extent to which there are differences between countries in the structure of market segments, and the existence of segments that transcend national borders.

3. A product can be viewed as a bundle of attributes. Product attributes must be varied from country to country to satisfy different consumer tastes and preferences.

4. Country differences in consumer tastes and preferences are due to differences in culture and economic development. In addition, differences in product and technical standards may require the firm to customize product attributes from country to country.

5. A distribution strategy decision is an attempt to define the optimal channel for delivering a product to the consumer.

6. Significant country differences exist in distribution systems. In some countries, the retail system is concentrated; in others, it is fragmented. In some countries, channel length is short; in others, it is long. Access to distribution channels is difficult to achieve in some countries, and the quality of the channel may be poor.

7. A critical element in the marketing mix is communication strategy, which defines the process the firm will use in communicating the attributes of its product to prospective customers.

8. Barriers to international communication include cultural differences, source effects, and noise levels.

9. A communication strategy is either a push strategy or a pull strategy. A push strategy emphasizes personal selling, and a pull strategy emphasizes mass media advertising. Whether a push strategy or a pull strategy is optimal depends on the type of product, consumer sophistication, channel length, and media availability.

10. A globally standardized advertising campaign, which uses the same marketing message all over the world, has economic advantages, but it fails to account for differences in culture and advertising regulations.

11. Price discrimination exists when consumers in different countries are charged different prices for the same product. Price discrimination can help a firm maximize its profits. For price discrimination to be effective, the national markets must be separate and their price elasticities of demand must differ.

12. Predatory pricing is the use of profit gained in one market to support aggressive pricing in another market to drive competitors out of that market.

13. Multipoint pricing refers to the fact that a firm's pricing strategy in one market may affect rivals' pricing strategies in another market. Aggressive pricing in one market may elicit a competitive response from a rival in another market that is important to the firm.

14. Experience curve pricing is the use of aggressive pricing to build accumulated volume as rapidly as possible to quickly move the firm down the experience curve.

15. New-product development is a high-risk, potentially high-return activity. To build a competency in new-product development, an international business must do two things: disperse R&D activities to those countries where new products are being pioneered, and integrate R&D with marketing and manufacturing.

16. Achieving tight integration among R&D, marketing, and manufacturing requires the use of cross-functional teams.

Critical Thinking and Discussion Questions

1. Imagine you are the marketing manager for a U.S. manufacturer of disposable diapers. Your firm is considering entering the Brazilian market. Your CEO believes the advertising message that has been effective in the United States will suffice in Brazil. Outline some possible objections to her belief. Your CEO also believes that the pricing decisions in Brazil can be delegated to local managers. Why might she be wrong?

2. Within 20 years, we will have seen the emergence of enormous global markets for standardized consumer products. Do you agree with this statement? Justify your answer.

3. You are the marketing manager of a food products company that is considering entering the Indian market. The retail system in India tends to be very fragmented. Also, retailers and wholesalers tend to have long-term ties with Indian food companies, which makes access to distribution channels difficult. What distribution strategy would you advise the company to pursue? Why?

4. Price discrimination is indistinguishable from dumping. Discuss the accuracy of this statement.

5. You work for a company that designs and manufactures personal computers. Your company's

R&D center is in North Dakota. The computers are manufactured under contract in Taiwan. Marketing strategy is delegated to the heads of three regional groups: a North American group (based in Chicago), a European group (based in Paris), and an Asian group (based in Singapore). Each regional group develops the marketing approach within its region. In order of importance, the largest markets for your products are North America, Germany, Great Britain, China, and Australia. Your company is experiencing problems in its product development and commercialization process. Products are late to market, the manufacturing quality is poor, costs are higher than projected, and market acceptance of new products is less than hoped for. What might be the source of these problems? How would you fix them?

Research Task

Use the globalEDGE™ site to complete the following exercises:

1. The consumer purchase of specific brands is an indication of the relationship that develops over time between a company and its customers. Locate and retrieve the most current ranking of global brands. Identify the criteria that are utilized. Which country (or countries) appears to dominate the top 100 global brands list? Why do you think this is the case? Prepare a short report identifying the countries that possess global brands and the potential reasons for success.

2. Some regions of the world are more widely known for their innovation efforts than others. Identify the fifteen organizations with the highest research and development (R&D) expenditures in the world. A colleague mentioned that the *Technology Review* is a particularly informative source on innovation topics. Prepare a short report regarding the country of origin of the companies with the most R&D spending, as well as the distribution of R&D expenditures by industry.

CLOSING CASE

Kodak in Russia

In the early 1990s, Kodak entered Russia. At the time, the country was deep in the middle of a turbulent transition from a Communist-run command economy to a fledgling democracy that was committed to pushing through the privatization of state-owned enterprises and economic reforms designed to establish competitive markets. Kodak's entry into this market posed a number of challenges. Russian consumers had little knowledge of Kodak's products, and the consumer market for photography was very underdeveloped. Moreover, apart from state-run stores that were generally poorly run, there was little or no infrastructure in place for distributing photographic equipment and films and for processing film. To compound matters, Russian consumers were poor and unlikely to be able to afford all but the most inexpensive cameras and films.

A decade later, Kodak's entry into Russia is widely regarded as a major success. Russia accounts for a significant proportion of the $2.59 billion in international sales in emerging markets that Kodak registered in 2004; and with a growth rate of 26 percent over the prior year, Russia is the fastest-growing emerging market for Kodak, outstripping even China. How did Kodak do it?

First, Kodak had a clear and consistent marketing message that it communicated to Russian consumers through a number of media, including radio, television, and print advertising. The marketing message was based upon the idea of "saving memories" by taking pictures in a quick and easy way. "You press the button and we will do the rest" the ads stated. As it turned out, this was the perfect message for a consumer market that was not used to photography. To complement the core marketing message, Kodak spent heavily on promotional campaigns, exhibitions, conventions, sponsored events, and the like, in an attempt to educate consumers and raise awareness of the Kodak brand name. For example, in addition to standard media advertising, Kodak owns a traveling photo park with a fleet of hot air balloons that have become very popular in Russia.

Kodak has also invested heavily in promoting a corporate image as a firm that takes a stand against corruption and black market practices. The company has been very clear about its business practices and about its refusal to engage in shady dealings. In a country where such practices were once commonplace, and still persist to a degree, this stance has been well received by consumers and has helped to build the company's brand image as an enterprise that can be trusted—which, as it turns out, has been good for business. Kodak also boosted its corporate image by opening a factory in Russia to produce cameras, film, and chemicals for film processing. In addition to the public relations benefit, this move also helped Kodak lower its costs by utilizing cheap Russian labor and by avoiding tariffs on imports of photographic products into Russia.

Recognizing the limited income of Russian consumers, Kodak's product strategy has been to sell lower-end film and cameras in Russia. Kodak offers simple cameras for around $20 to Russian consumers, something that the company can afford to do because the cameras are made locally. It does not sell disposable cameras in Russia, since at $10 each the cost would be too high. Instead of trying to sell top-quality Kodak Gold film, which is popular in the West, the cheaper brand, Kodak Color Plus, is marketed heavily in Russia.

Another of Kodak's marketing tactics has been to try to build demand for its products by encouraging major enterprises to give cameras to valued employees, rather than the traditional bottle of vodka. Kodak has also worked closely with travel agents, giving them cameras to give away to their customers. Kodak's hope, of course, has been that consumers will purchase Kodak film to use in these cameras, and to a large degree, that seems to have occurred.

Finally, Kodak realized that it needed to build a distribution channel for its products. Rather than invest directly in its own stores, the company set up a franchising program to open Kodak Express stores throughout Russia to sell its products and develop film. These owner-operated stores adhere to strict business guidelines Kodak set down in its master franchise agreement. The stores are clean, attractively designed, have a consistent appearance that helps promote the Kodak brand, and are staffed by friendly and polite employees. These stores rapidly set a new standard for retailing in Russia. Within three years, more than 350 Kodak Express outlets had opened in Russia, and today there are several thousand.[50]

Case Discussion Questions

1. How did the Russian market differ from markets in developed Western nations? How were these differences likely to impact upon demand for photographic products?

2. How did Kodak adjust its marketing mix in Russia to match local requirements? Do you think this was the right thing to do?

3. Kodak's traditional film business is now under attack from digital photography (in which Kodak is also a leader). Should Kodak adjust its marketing mix for digital products to the Russian market? Why?

Notes

1. Sources: "How Levi Strauss Rekindled the Allure of Brand America," *World Trade*, March 2005, p. 28; "Levi Strauss Walks with a Swagger into New Markets," *Africa News*, March 17, 2005; "Levi's Adaptable Standards," *Strategic Direction*, June 2005, pp. 14–16; A. Benady, "Levi's Looks to the Bottom Line," *Financial Times*, February 15, 2005, p. 14; and R. A. Smith, "At Levi Strauss Dockers Are In," *The Wall Street Journal*, February 14, 2007, p. A14.

2. For evidence on the importance of marketing and R&D in the performance of a multinational firm, see M. Kotabe, S. Srinivasan, and P. S. Aulakh, "Multinationality and Firm Performance: The Moderating Role of R&D and Marketing Capabilities," *Journal of International Business Studies* 33, no. 1 (2002), pp. 79–97.

3. See R. W. Ruekert and O. C. Walker, "Interactions between Marketing and R&D Departments in Implementing Different Business-Level Strategies," *Strategic Management Journal* 8 (1987), pp. 233–48; and K. B. Clark and S. C. Wheelwright, *Managing New Product and Process Development* (New York: Free Press, 1993).

4. T. Levitt, "The Globalization of Markets," *Harvard Business Review*, May–June 1983, pp. 92–102. Reprinted by permission of *Harvard Business Review*, an excerpt from "The Globalization of Markets," by Theodore Levitt, May–June 1983. Copyright © 1983 by the President and Fellows of Harvard College. All rights reserved.

5. For example, see S. P. Douglas and Y. Wind, "The Myth of Globalization," *Columbia Journal of World Business*, Winter 1987, pp. 19–29;

C. A. Bartlett and S. Ghoshal, *Managing across Borders: The Transnational Solution* (Boston: Harvard Business School Press, 1989); V. J. Govindarajan and A. K. Gupta, *The Quest for Global Dominance* (San Francisco: Jossey Bass, 2001); and J. Quelch, "The Return of the Global Brand," *Harvard Business Review*, August 2003, pp. 1–3.

6. J. Tagliabue, "U.S. Brands Are Feeling Global Tension," *The New York Times*, March 15, 2003, p. C3.

7. D. B. Holt, J. A. Quelch, and E. L. Taylor, "How Global Brands Compete," *Harvard Business Review*, September 2004.

8. J. T. Landry, "Emerging Markets: Are Chinese Consumers Coming of Age?" *Harvard Business Review*, May–June 1998, pp. 17–20.

9. C. Miller, "Teens Seen as the First Truly Global Consumers," *Marketing News*, March 27, 1995, p. 9.

10. Source: M. Jordan, "Marketers Discover Black Brazil," *The Wall Street Journal*, November 24, 2000, pp. A11, A14. Copyright 2000 by Dow Jones & Co. Inc. Reproduced with permission from Dow Jones & Co. Inc. in the format textbook by the Copyright Clearance Center.

11. This approach was originally developed in K. Lancaster, "A New Approach to Demand Theory," *Journal of Political Economy* 74 (1965), pp. 132–57.

12. V. R. Alden, "Who Says You Can't Crack Japanese Markets?" *Harvard Business Review*, January–February 1987, pp. 52–56.

13. T. Parker-Pope, "Custom Made," *The Wall Street Journal*, September 26, 1996, p. 22.

14. "RCA's New Vista: The Bottom Line," *BusinessWeek*, July 4, 1987, p. 44.

15. N. Gross and K. Rebello, "Apple? Japan Can't Say No," *BusinessWeek*, June 29, 1992, pp. 32–33.

16. "After Early Stumbles P&G Is Making Inroads Overseas," *The Wall Street Journal*, February 6, 1989, p. B1.

17. C. Matlack and P. Gogoi, "What's This? The French Love McDonald's?" *BusinessWeek*, January 13, 2003, pp. 50–51.

18. Z. Gurhan-Cvanli and D. Maheswaran, "Cultural Variation in Country of Origin Effects," *Journal of Marketing Research*, August 2000, pp. 309–17.

19. Sources: E. Nelson and M. Jordan, "Seeking New Markets for Tampons, P&G Faces Cultural Barriers," *The Wall Street Journal*, December 8, 2000, pp. A1, A8. Copyright 2000 by *The Wall Street Journal*. Reproduced with permission of Dow Jones & Company, Inc., in the format textbook by the Copyright Clearance Center.

20. Sources: K. Merchant, "Striving for Success—One Sachet at a Time," *Financial Times*, December 11, 2000, p. 14; M. Turner, "Bicycle Brigade Takes Unilever to the People," *Financial Times*, August 17, 2000, p. 8; and "Brands Thinking Positively," *Brand Strategy*, December 2003, pp. 28–29.

21. See M. Laroche, V. H. Kirpalani, F. Pons, and L. Zhou, "A Model of Advertising Standardization in Multinational Corporations," *Journal of International Business Studies* 32 (2001), pp. 249–66; and D. A. Aaker and E. Joachimsthaler, "The Lure of Global Branding," *Harvard Business Review*, November–December 1999, pp. 137–44.

22. "Advertising in a Single Market," *The Economist*, March 24, 1990, p. 64.

23. D. Waller, "Charged Up over Competition Law," *Financial Times*, June 23, 1994, p. 14.

24. R. G. Matthews and D. Pringle, "Nokia Bets One Global Message Will Ring True in Many Markets," *The Wall Street Journal*, September 27, 2004, p. B6.

25. R. J. Dolan and H. Simon, *Power Pricing* (New York: Free Press, 1999).

26. B. Stottinger, "Strategic Export Pricing: A Long Winding Road," *Journal of International Marketing* 9 (2001), pp. 40–63; and S. Gil-Pareja, "Export Process Discrimination in Europe and Exchange Rates," *Review of International Economics*, May 2002, pp. 299–312.

27. These allegations were made on a PBS *Frontline* documentary telecast in the United States in May 1992.

28. Y. Tsurumi and H. Tsurumi, "Fujifilm–Kodak Duopolistic Competition in Japan and the United States," *Journal of International Business Studies* 30 (1999), pp. 813–30.

29. G. Smith and B. Wolverton, "A Dark Moment for Kodak," *BusinessWeek*, August 4, 1997, pp. 30–31.

30. R. Narisette and J. Friedland, "Disposable Income: Diaper Wars of P&G and Kimberly-Clark Now Heat Up in Brazil," *The Wall Street Journal*, June 4, 1997, p. A1.

31. J. F. Pickering, *Industrial Structure and Market Conduct* (London: Martin Robertson, 1974).

32. S. P. Douglas, C. Samuel Craig, and E. J. Nijissen, "Integrating Branding Strategy across Markets," *Journal of International Marketing* 9, no. 2 (2001), pp. 97–114.

33. Sources: V. Mallet, "Climbing the Slippery Slope," *Financial Times,* July 28, 1994, p. 7; A. Bolger, "Growth by Successful Targeting," *Financial Times,* June 21, 1994, p. 27; "A Decade in Lubricants," *Vietnam Investment Review,* August 27, 2001; and V. Bao, "England's Beckham to Visit Vietnam Despite Broken Wrist," *Saigon Times,* May 26, 2003.

34. The phrase was first used by economist Joseph Schumpeter in *Capitalism, Socialism, and Democracy* (New York: Harper Brothers, 1942).

35. S. Kotabe, S. Srinivasan, and P. S. Aulakh. "Multinationality and Firm Performance: The Moderating Role of R&D and Marketing," *Journal of International Business Studies* 33 (2002), pp. 79–97.

36. See D. C. Mowery and N. Rosenberg, *Technology and the Pursuit of Economic Growth* (Cambridge, UK: Cambridge University Press, 1989); and M. E. Porter, *The Competitive Advantage of Nations* (New York: Free Press, 1990).

37. W. Kuemmerle, "Building Effective R&D Capabilities Abroad," *Harvard Business Review,* March–April 1997, pp. 61–70; and C. Le Bas and C. Sierra, "Location versus Home Country Advantages in R&D Activities," *Research Policy* 31 (2002), pp. 589–609.

38. "When the Corporate Lab Goes to Japan," *The New York Times,* April 28, 1991, sec. 3, p. 1.

39. D. Shapley, "Globalization Prompts Exodus," *Financial Times,* March 17, 1994, p. 10.

40. E. Mansfield. "How Economists See R&D," *Harvard Business Review,* November–December, 1981, pp. 98–106.

41. Ibid.

42. G. A. Stevens and J. Burley, "Piloting the Rocket of Radical Innovation," *Research Technology Management* 46 (2003), pp. 16–26.

43. K. B. Clark and S. C. Wheelwright, *Managing New Product and Process Development* (New York: Free Press, 1993); and M. A. Shilling and C. W. L. Hill, "Managing the New Product Development Process," *Academy of Management Executive* 12, no. 3 (1998), pp. 67–81.

44. O. Port, "Moving Past the Assembly Line," *BusinessWeek Special Issue: Reinventing America,* 1992, pp. 177–80.

45. K. B. Clark and T. Fujimoto, "The Power of Product Integrity," *Harvard Business Review,* November–December 1990, pp. 107–18; Clark and Wheelwright, *Managing New Product and Process Development*; S. L. Brown and K. M. Eisenhardt, "Product Development: Past Research, Present Findings, and Future Directions," *Academy of Management Review* 20 (1995), pp. 348–78; and G. Stalk and T. M. Hout, *Competing against Time* (New York: Free Press, 1990).

46. Shilling and Hill, "Managing the New Product Development Process."

47. C. Christensen. "Quantum Corporation—Business and Product Teams," Harvard Business School case no. 9-692-023.

48. R. Nobel and J. Birkinshaw, "Innovation in Multinational Corporations: Control and Communication Patterns in International R&D Operations," *Strategic Management Journal* 19 (1998), pp. 479–96.

49. Information comes from the company's Web site; also see K. Ferdows, "Making the Most of Foreign Factories," *Harvard Business Review,* March–April 1997, pp. 73–88.

50. Sources: G. C. Anders and D. A. Usachev, "Strategic Elements of Eastman Kodak's Successful Market Entry in Russia," *Thunderbird International Business Review* 45, no. 2 (March–April 2003), pp. 171–83; S. McNamara, "Kodak Stores Set U.S. Standards in Russia," *USA Today,* December 21, 1998, p. 12B; and "Making Foreign Policy Work with Kodak and Norske Skog," *Strategic Direction* 19, no. 11 (November–December 2003), pp. 27–30.

Lenovo

In late 2004 IBM announced that it was getting out of the personal computer business, and would sell its entire PC operations to Lenovo, the fast-growing Chinese manufacturer of personal computers, for $1.75 billion. The acquisition turned Lenovo into the world's third-largest PC firm. It also raised many questions about how a Chinese enterprise with little global exposure would manage the assets of an American firm that had 2,400 employees in the United States, 4,000 in foreign manufacturing facilities, and 3,600 sales and distribution centers in over 60 countries around the world.

Lenovo moved quickly to reassure employees that it was committed to building a truly global enterprise with a truly global workforce. Less than 24 hours after the two companies announced the acquisition, the human resources department at IBM's PC division released a memo to all employees made up of 59 questions and answers that informed them they would become employees of Lenovo, their compensation and benefits would remain identical or fully comparable to their IBM package, and they would not be asked to relocate. The memo also made it clear that employees could accept employment at Lenovo or leave, with no separation pay. IBM would not consider them for a transfer within IBM or recruit or hire the new Lenovo employees for two years.

Global Human Resource Management

LEARNING OBJECTIVES

After you have read this chapter you should be able to:

LO¹ Articulate the strategic role of human resource management in the international business.

LO² Discuss the pros and cons of different approaches to staffing policy in the international business.

LO³ Explain why managers may fail to thrive in foreign postings.

LO⁴ Articulate how management development and training programs can increase the value of human capital in the international business firm.

LO⁵ Explain how and why performance appraisal systems might vary across nations.

LO⁶ Explain how and why compensation systems might vary across nations.

What really surprised many observers, however, was the composition of the top management team at the new Lenovo and the location of its global headquarters. Top executives at Lenovo were smart enough to realize that the acquisition would have little value if IBM's managers, engineers, and salespeople left the company, so they moved Lenovo's global headquarters to New York! Moreover, the former head of IBM's PC division, Stephen Ward, was appointed CEO of Lenovo, while Yang Yuanqing, the former CEO of Lenovo, became chairman, and Lenovo's Mary Ma became CFO. The 30-member top management team was split down the middle—half Chinese, half American—and boasted more women than men. English was declared the company's new business language. The goal, according to Yang, is to transform Lenovo into a truly global corporation with a global workforce that is capable of going head-to-head with Dell in the battle for dominance in the global PC business. The choice of Ward for CEO, for example, was based on the presumption that none of the Chinese executives had the experience and capabilities required to manage a truly global enterprise. For Lenovo, when deciding who should hold management positions, the national origin of a candidate is not an issue. Rather, the decision focuses upon whether the person has the skills and capabilities required for working in a global enterprise. Lenovo is committed to hiring the very best people, wherever they might come from.[1]

Introduction

This chapter continues our survey of specific functions within an international business by looking at international human resource management (HRM). **Human resource management** refers to the activities an organization carries out to use its human resources effectively.[2] These activities include determining the firm's human resource strategy, staffing, performance evaluation, management development, compensation, and labor relations. None of these activities is performed in a vacuum; all are related to the strategy of the firm. As we will see, HRM has an important strategic component.[3] Through its influence on the character, development, quality, and productivity of the firm's human resources, the HRM function can help the firm achieve its primary strategic goals of reducing the costs of value creation and adding value by better serving customer needs.

Take Lenovo as an example. Lenovo's goal is to become a major player in the global personal computer industry. To that end it is trying to distance itself from its Chinese origins and to become a truly global enterprise with a global workforce. Within this context, the strategic role of HRM is to make sure that it hires the very best people for job openings, irrespective of their national origin. Lenovo sent a very clear signal of its approach when the company appointed an American as its CEO and moved its global headquarters to the United States.

Irrespective of the desire of companies like Lenovo to build a truly global enterprise with a global workforce, the reality is that HRM practices still have to be modified to national context. The strategic role of HRM is complex enough in a purely domestic firm, but it is more complex in an international business, where profound differences between countries in labor markets, culture, legal systems, economic systems, and the like complicate staffing, management development, performance evaluation, and compensation activities (see Chapters 2 and 3). For example,

- Compensation practices may vary from country to country, depending on prevailing management customs.
- Labor laws may prohibit union organization in one country and mandate it in another.
- Equal employment legislation may be strongly pursued in one country and not in another.

If it is to build a cadre of managers capable of managing a multinational enterprise, the HRM function must deal with a host of issues. It must decide how to staff key management posts in the company, how to develop managers so they are familiar with the nuances of doing business in different countries, how to compensate people in different nations, and how to evaluate the performance of managers based in different countries. HRM must also deal with a host of issues related to expatriate managers. (An **expatriate manager** is a citizen of one country who is working abroad in one of the firm's subsidiaries.) It must decide when to use expatriates, determine whom to send on expatriate postings, be clear about why they are doing it, compensate expatriates appropriately, and make sure that they are adequately debriefed and reoriented once they return home.

In this chapter, we will look closely at the role of HRM in an international business. We begin by briefly discussing the strategic role of HRM. Then we turn our attention to four major tasks of the HRM function: staffing policy, management training and development, performance appraisal, and compensation policy. We will point out the strategic implications of each of these tasks. The chapter closes with a look at international labor relations and the relationship between the firm's management of labor relations and its overall strategy.

The Strategic Role of International HRM

A large and expanding body of academic research suggests that a strong fit between human resources practices and strategy is required for high profitability.[4] You will recall from Chapter 12 that superior performance requires not only the right strategy, but the

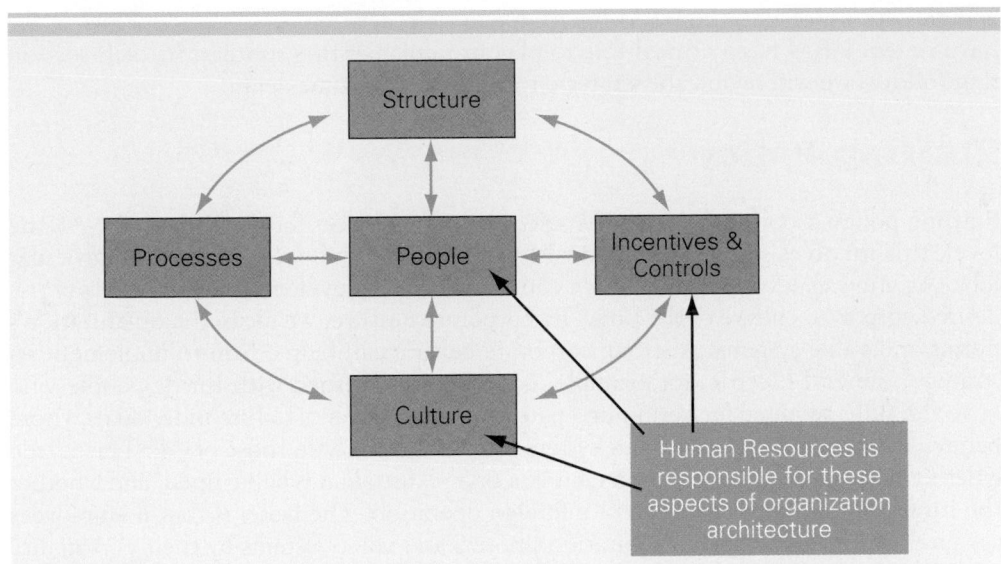

strategy must also be supported by the right organization architecture. Strategy is implemented through organization. As shown in Figure 18.1 (which is based on Figure 13.1), people are the linchpin of a firm's organization architecture. For a firm to outperform its rivals in the global marketplace, it must have the right people in the right postings. Those people must be trained appropriately so they have the skill sets required to perform their jobs effectively and so they behave in a manner that is congruent with the desired culture of the firm. Their compensation packages must create incentives for them to take actions that are consistent with the strategy of the firm, and the performance appraisal systems the firm uses must measure the behavior that the firm wants to encourage.

As indicated in Figure 18.1, the HRM function, through its staffing, training, compensation, and performance appraisal activities, has a critical impact upon the people, culture, incentive, and control system elements of the firm's organization architecture (performance appraisal systems are part of the control systems in an enterprise). Thus, HRM professionals have a critically important strategic role. It is incumbent upon them to shape these elements of a firm's organization architecture in a manner that is consistent with the strategy of the enterprise, so that the firm can effectively implement its strategy.

In short, superior human resource management can be a sustained source of high productivity and competitive advantage in the global economy. At the same time, research suggests that many international businesses have room for improving the effectiveness of their HRM function. In one study of competitiveness among 326 large multinationals, the authors found that human resource management was one of the weakest capabilities in most firms, suggesting that improving the effectiveness of international HRM practices might have substantial performance benefits.[5]

In Chapter 12, we examined four strategies pursued by international businesses: localization strategy, international strategy, global standardization strategy, and transnational strategy. Firms that emphasize localization try to create value by emphasizing local responsiveness; international firms, by transferring products and competencies overseas; global firms, by realizing experience curve and location economies; and transnational firms, by doing all these things simultaneously. In this chapter, we will see that success also requires HRM policies to be congruent with the firm's strategy. For example, a transnational strategy imposes different requirements for staffing, management development, and compensation practices than a localization strategy. Firms pursuing a transnational strategy need to build a strong corporate culture and an informal management network for transmitting information and knowledge within the organization. Through its employee selection, management development, performance appraisal, and compensation policies, the HRM function can help develop these things. Thus, as we have noted, HRM has a critical role to play in implementing strategy. In each section that follows, we will review the strategic role of HRM in some detail.

Staffing Policy

Staffing policy is concerned with the selection of employees for particular jobs. At one level, this involves selecting individuals who have the skills required to do particular jobs. At another level, staffing policy can be a tool for developing and promoting the desired corporate culture of the firm.[6] By **corporate culture,** we mean the organization's norms and value systems. A strong corporate culture can help a firm to implement its strategy. General Electric, for example, is not just concerned with hiring people who have the skills required for performing particular jobs; it wants to hire individuals whose behavioral styles, beliefs, and value systems are consistent with those of GE. This is true whether an American, an Italian, a German, or an Australian is being hired, and whether the hiring is for a U.S. operation or a foreign operation. The belief is that if employees are predisposed toward the organization's norms and value systems by their personality type, the firm will be able to attain higher performance.

TYPES OF STAFFING POLICY

Research has identified three types of staffing policies in international businesses: the ethnocentric approach, the polycentric approach, and the geocentric approach.[7] We will review each policy and link it to the firm's strategy. The most attractive staffing policy is probably the geocentric approach, although there are several impediments to adopting it.

The Ethnocentric Approach

An **ethnocentric staffing policy** is one in which parent-country nationals fill all key management positions. This practice was widespread at one time. Firms such as Procter & Gamble, Philips NV, and Matsushita originally followed it. In the Dutch firm Philips, for example, all important positions in most foreign subsidiaries were at one time held by Dutch nationals, who were referred to by their non-Dutch colleagues as the Dutch Mafia. In many Japanese and South Korean firms, such as Toyota, Matsushita, and Samsung, key positions in international operations have often been held by home-country nationals. According to the Japanese Overseas Enterprise Association, in 1996 only 29 percent of foreign subsidiaries of Japanese companies had presidents who were not Japanese. In contrast, 66 percent of the Japanese subsidiaries of foreign companies had Japanese presidents.[8]

Firms pursue an ethnocentric staffing policy for three reasons. First, the firm may believe the host country lacks qualified individuals to fill senior management positions. This argument is heard most often when the firm has operations in less-developed countries. Second, the firm may see an ethnocentric staffing policy as the best way to maintain a unified corporate culture. Many Japanese firms, for example, prefer expatriate Japanese managers to head their foreign operations because these managers have been socialized into the firm's culture while employed in Japan.[9] Procter & Gamble until recently preferred to staff important management positions in its foreign subsidiaries with U.S. nationals who had been socialized into P&G's corporate culture by years of employment in its U.S. operations. Such reasoning tends to predominate when a firm places a high value on its corporate culture.

Third, if the firm is trying to create value by transferring core competencies to a foreign operation, as firms pursuing an international strategy are, it may believe that the best way to accomplish this goal is to transfer parent-country nationals who have knowledge of that competency to the foreign operation. Imagine what might occur if a firm tried to transfer a core competency in marketing to a foreign subsidiary without a corresponding transfer of home-country marketing management personnel. The transfer would probably fail to produce the anticipated benefits because the knowledge underlying a core competency cannot easily be articulated and written down. Such knowledge often has a significant tacit dimension; it is acquired through experience. Just like the great tennis player who cannot instruct others how to become great tennis players simply by writing a handbook, the firm that has a core competency in marketing, or anything else, cannot just write a handbook that tells a foreign subsidiary how to build the firm's core competency anew in a foreign setting. It must also transfer management personnel to the foreign operation to show foreign managers how to become good marketers, for example. The need to transfer managers overseas arises because the knowledge that underlies the firm's core competency resides in the heads of its domestic managers and was acquired through years of experience, not by reading a handbook. Thus, if a firm is to transfer a core competency to a foreign subsidiary, it must also transfer the appropriate managers.

Despite this rationale for pursuing an ethnocentric staffing policy, the policy is now on the wane in most international businesses for two reasons. First, an ethnocentric staffing policy limits advancement opportunities for host-country nationals. This can lead to resentment, lower productivity, and increased turnover among that group. Resentment can be greater still if, as often occurs, expatriate managers are paid significantly more than home-country nationals.

Second, an ethnocentric policy can lead to *cultural myopia*, the firm's failure to understand host-country cultural differences that require different approaches to marketing and management. The adaptation of expatriate managers can take a long time, during which they may make major mistakes. For example, expatriate managers may fail to appreciate how product attributes, distribution strategy, communications strategy, and pricing strategy should be adapted to host-country conditions. The result may be costly blunders. They may also make decisions that are ethically suspect simply because they do not understand the culture in which they are managing.[10] In one highly publicized case in the United States, the federal Equal Employment Opportunity Commission sued Mitsubishi Motors for tolerating extensive and systematic sexual harassment in a plant in Illinois. The plant's top management, all Japanese expatriates, denied the charges. The Japanese managers may have failed to realize that behavior that would be viewed as acceptable in Japan was not acceptable in the United States.[11]

The Polycentric Approach

A **polycentric staffing policy** requires host-country nationals to be recruited to manage subsidiaries, while parent-country nationals occupy key positions at corporate headquarters. In many respects, a polycentric approach is a response to the shortcomings of an ethnocentric approach. One advantage of adopting a polycentric approach is that the firm is less likely to suffer from cultural myopia. Host-country managers are unlikely to make the mistakes arising from cultural misunderstandings to which expatriate managers are vulnerable. A second advantage is that a polycentric approach may be less expensive to implement, reducing the costs of value creation. Expatriate managers can be expensive to maintain.

A polycentric approach also has its drawbacks. Host-country nationals have limited opportunities to gain experience outside their own country and thus cannot progress beyond senior positions in their own subsidiary. As in the case of an ethnocentric policy, this may cause resentment. Perhaps the major drawback with a polycentric approach, however, is the gap that can form between host-country managers and parent-country managers. Language barriers, national loyalties, and a range of cultural differences may isolate the corporate headquarters staff from the various foreign subsidiaries. The lack of management transfers from home to host countries, and vice versa, can exacerbate this isolation and lead to a lack of integration between corporate headquarters and foreign subsidiaries. The result can be a "federation" of largely independent national units with only nominal links to the corporate headquarters. Within such a federation, the coordination required to transfer core competencies or to pursue experience curve and location economies may be difficult to achieve. Thus, although a polycentric approach may be effective for firms pursuing a localization strategy, it is inappropriate for other strategies.

The federation that may result from a polycentric approach can also be a force for inertia within the firm. After decades of pursuing a polycentric staffing policy, food and detergents giant Unilever found that shifting from a strategic posture that emphasized localization to a transnational posture was very difficult. Unilever's foreign subsidiaries had evolved into quasi-autonomous operations, each with its own strong national identity. These "little kingdoms" objected strenuously to corporate headquarters' attempts to limit their autonomy and to rationalize global manufacturing.[12]

The Geocentric Approach

A **geocentric staffing policy** seeks the best people for key jobs throughout the organization, regardless of nationality. This is the staffing policy that Lenovo has adopted. This policy has a number of advantages. First, it enables the firm to make the best use of its human resources. Second, and perhaps more important, a geocentric policy enables the firm to build a cadre of international executives who feel at home working in a number of cultures. Creation of such a cadre may be a critical first step toward building a strong unifying corporate culture and an informal management network, both of which are required for global standardization and transnational strategies.[13] Firms pursuing a geocentric staffing policy may be better able to create value from the pursuit of experience curve and location economies and from the multidirectional transfer of core competencies than firms pursuing other staffing policies. In addition, the multinational composition of the management team that results from geocentric staffing tends to reduce cultural myopia and to enhance local responsiveness. Thus, other things being equal, a geocentric staffing policy seems the most attractive.

A number of problems limit the firm's ability to pursue a geocentric policy. Many countries want foreign subsidiaries to employ their citizens. To achieve this goal, they use immigration laws to require the employment of host-country nationals if they are available in adequate numbers and have the necessary skills. Most countries, including the United States, require firms to provide extensive documentation if they wish to hire a foreign national instead of a local national. This documentation can be time consuming, expensive, and at times futile. A geocentric staffing policy also can be expensive to implement. Training and relocation costs increase when transferring managers from country to country. The company may also need a compensation structure with a standardized international base pay level higher than national levels in many countries. In addition, the higher pay managers on an international fast track enjoy may be a source of resentment within a firm.

Summary

Table 18.1 summarizes the advantages and disadvantages of the three approaches to staffing policy. Broadly speaking, an ethnocentric approach is compatible with an international strategy, a polycentric approach is compatible with a localization strategy, and a geocentric approach is compatible with both global standardization and transnational strategies. (See Chapter 12 for details of the strategies.)

While the staffing policies described here are well known and widely used among both practitioners and scholars of international businesses, some critics have claimed that the typology is too simplistic and that it obscures the internal differentiation of management practices within international businesses. The critics claim that within some international businesses, staffing policies vary significantly from national subsidiary to national subsidiary; while some are managed on an ethnocentric basis, others are managed in a polycentric or geocentric manner.[14] Other critics note that the staffing policy adopted by a firm is primarily driven by its geographic scope, as opposed to its strategic orientation. Firms that have a broad geographic scope are the most likely to have a geocentric mind-set.[15]

TABLE 18.1

Comparison of Staffing Approaches

Staffing Approach	Strategic Appropriateness	Advantages	Disadvantages
Ethnocentric	International	Overcomes lack of qualified managers in host nation Unified culture Helps transfer core competencies	Produces resentment in host country Can lead to cultural myopia
Polycentric	Localization	Alleviates cultural myopia Inexpensive to implement	Limits career mobility Isolates headquarters from foreign subsidiaries
Geocentric	Global standardization and transnational	Uses human resources efficiently Helps build strong culture and informal management networks	National immigration policies may limit implementation Expensive

EXPATRIATE MANAGERS

Two of the three staffing policies we have discussed—the ethnocentric and the geocentric—rely on extensive use of expatriate managers. As defined earlier, expatriates are citizens of one country who are working in another country. Sometimes the term *inpatriates* is used to identify a subset of expatriates who are citizens of a foreign country working in the home country of their multinational employer.[16] Thus, a citizen of Japan who moves to the United States to work at Microsoft would be classified as an inpatriate. With an ethnocentric policy, the expatriates are all home-country nationals who are transferred abroad. With a geocentric approach, the expatriates need not be home-country nationals; the firm does not base transfer decisions on nationality. A prominent issue in the international staffing literature is **expatriate failure**—the premature return of an expatriate manager to his or her home country.[17] Here we briefly review the evidence on expatriate failure before discussing a number of ways to minimize the failure rate.

Expatriate Failure Rates

Expatriate failure represents a failure of the firm's selection policies to identify individuals who will not thrive abroad.[18] The consequences include premature return from a foreign posting and high resignation rates, with expatriates leaving their company at about twice the rate of domestic managements.[19] Research suggests that between 16 and 40 percent of all American employees sent abroad to developed nations return from their assignments early, and almost 70 percent of employees sent to developing nations return home early.[20] Although detailed data are not available for most nationalities, one suspects that high expatriate failure is a universal problem. Some 28 percent of British expatriates, for example, are estimated to fail in their overseas postings.[21] The costs of expatriate failure are high. One estimate is that the average cost per failure to the parent firm can be as high as three times the expatriate's annual domestic salary plus the cost of relocation (which is affected by currency exchange rates and location of assignment). Estimates of the costs of each failure run between $250,000 and $1 million.[22] In addition,

TABLE 18.2

Expatriate Failure Rates

Source: Data from R. L. Tung, "Selection and Training Procedures of U.S., European, and Japanese Multinationals," pp. 51–71. Copyright © by The Regents of the University of California. Reprinted from the *California Management Review* 1.25, no. 1, by permission from The Regents.

Recall Rate Percent	Percent of Companies
U.S. multinationals	
20–40%	7%
10–20	69
<10	24
European multinationals	
11–15%	3%
6–10	38
<5	59
Japanese multinationals	
11–19%	14%
6–10	10
<5	76

approximately 30 to 50 percent of American expatriates, whose average annual compensation package runs to $250,000, stay at their international assignments but are considered ineffective or marginally effective by their firms.[23] In a seminal study, R. L. Tung surveyed a number of U.S., European, and Japanese multinationals.[24] Her results, summarized in Table 18.2, show that 76 percent of U.S. multinationals experienced expatriate failure rates of 10 percent or more, and 7 percent experienced a failure rate of more than 20 percent. Tung's work also suggests that U.S.-based multinationals experience a much higher expatriate failure rate than either European or Japanese multinationals.

Tung asked her sample of multinational managers to indicate reasons for expatriate failure. For U.S. multinationals, the reasons, in order of importance, were

1. Inability of spouse to adjust.
2. Manager's inability to adjust.
3. Other family problems.
4. Manager's personal or emotional maturity.
5. Inability to cope with larger overseas responsibilities.

Managers of European firms gave only one reason consistently to explain expatriate failure: the inability of the manager's spouse to adjust to a new environment. For the Japanese firms, the reasons for failure were

1. Inability to cope with larger overseas responsibilities.
2. Difficulties with new environment.
3. Personal or emotional problems.
4. Lack of technical competence.
5. Inability of spouse to adjust.

The most striking difference between these lists is that "inability of spouse to adjust" was the top reason for expatriate failure among U.S. and European multinationals but only the number five reason among Japanese multinationals. Tung comments that this difference is not surprising, given the role and status to which Japanese society tradition-ally relegates the wife and the fact that most of the Japanese expatriate managers in the study were men.

Since Tung's study, a number of other studies have consistently confirmed that the inability of a spouse to adjust, the inability of the manager to adjust, or other family problems remain major reasons for continuing high levels of expatriate failure. One study by International Orientation Resources, an HRM consulting firm, found that 60 percent of expatriate failures occur due to these three reasons.[25] Another study found that the most common reason for assignment failure is lack of partner (spouse) satisfaction, which was listed by 27 percent of respondents.[26] The inability of expatriate managers to adjust to foreign postings seems to be caused by a lack of cultural skills on the part of the manager being transferred. According to one HRM consulting firm, this is because the expatriate selection process at many firms is fundamentally flawed. "Expatriate assignments rarely fail because the person cannot accommodate to the technical demands of the job. Typically, the expatriate selections are made by line managers based on technical competence. They fail because of family and personal issues and lack of cultural skills that haven't been part of the selection process."[27]

The failure of spouses to adjust to a foreign posting seems to be related to a number of factors. Often spouses find themselves in a foreign country without the familiar network of family and friends. Language differences make it difficult for them to make new friends. While this may not be a problem for the manager, who can make friends at work, it can be difficult for the spouse, who might feel trapped at home. The problem is often exacerbated by immigration regulations prohibiting the spouse from taking employment. With the recent rise of two-career families in many developed nations, this issue has become much more important. One survey found that 69 percent of expatriates are married, with spouses accompanying them 77 percent of the time. Of those spouses, 49 percent were employed before an assignment and only 11 percent were employed during an assignment.[28] Research suggests that a main reason managers now turn down international assignments is concern over the impact such an assignment might have on their spouse's career.[29] The accompanying Management Focus examines how one large multinational company, Royal Dutch/Shell, has tried to come to grips with this issue.

Expatriate Selection

One way to reduce expatriate failure rates is by improving selection procedures to screen out inappropriate candidates. In a review of the research on this issue, Mendenhall and Oddou state that a major problem in many firms is that HRM managers tend to equate domestic performance with overseas performance potential.[31] Domestic performance and overseas performance potential are *not* the same thing. An executive who performs well in a domestic setting may not be able to adapt to managing in a different cultural setting. From their review of the research, Mendenhall and Oddou identified four dimensions that seem to predict success in a foreign posting: self-orientation, others-orientation, perceptual ability, and cultural toughness.

Self-Orientation. The attributes of this dimension strengthen the expatriate's self-esteem, self-confidence, and mental well-being. Expatriates with high self-esteem, self-confidence, and mental well-being were more likely to succeed in foreign postings. Mendenhall and Oddou concluded that such individuals were able to adapt their interests in food, sport, and music; had interests outside of work that could be pursued (e.g., hobbies); and were technically competent.

Others-Orientation. The attributes of this dimension enhance the expatriate's ability to interact effectively with host-country nationals. The more effectively the expatriate interacts with host-country nationals, the more likely he or she is to succeed. Two factors seem to be particularly important here: relationship development and willingness to communicate. Relationship development refers to the ability to develop long-lasting friendships with host-country nationals. Willingness to communicate refers to the expatriate's willingness to use the host-country language. Although language fluency helps, an expatriate need not be fluent to show willingness to communicate. Making the effort to use the language is what is important. Such gestures tend to be rewarded with greater cooperation by host-country nationals.

MANAGEMENT FOCUS

Managing Expatriates at Royal Dutch/Shell

Royal Dutch/Shell is a global petroleum company with joint headquarters in both London and The Hague in the Netherlands. The company employs more than 100,000 people, approximately 5,500 of whom are living and working as expatriates at any one time. The expatriates at Shell are a diverse group, made up of over 70 nationalities and located in more than 100 countries. Shell, as a global corporation, has long recognized that the international mobility of its workforce is essential to its success. By the early 1990s, however, Shell was finding it harder to recruit key personnel for foreign postings. To discover why, the company interviewed more than 200 expatriate employees and their spouses to determine their biggest concerns. The data were then used to construct a survey that was sent to 17,000 current and former expatriate employees, expatriates' spouses, and employees who had declined international assignments.

The survey registered a phenomenal 70 percent response rate, clearly indicating that many employees thought this was an important issue. According to the survey, five issues had the greatest impact on the willingness of an employee to accept an international assignment. In order of importance, these were (1) separation from children during their secondary education (the children of British and Dutch expatriates were often sent to boarding schools in their home countries while their parents worked abroad), (2) harm done to a spouse's career and employment, (3) failure to recognize and involve a spouse in the relocation decision, (4) failure to provide adequate information and assistance regarding relocation, and (5) health issues. The underlying message was that the family is the

basic unit of expatriation, not the individual, and Shell needed to do more to recognize this.

To deal with these issues, Shell implemented a number of programs designed to address some of these problems. To help with the education of children, Shell built elementary schools for Shell employees where there was a heavy concentration of expatriates. As for secondary school education, it worked with local schools, often providing grants, to help them upgrade their educational offerings. It also offered an education supplement to help expatriates send their children to private schools in the host country.

Helping spouses with their careers is a more vexing problem. According to the survey data, half the spouses accompanying Shell staff on assignment were employed until the transfer. When expatriated, only 12 percent were able to secure employment, while a further 33 percent wished to be employed. Shell set up a spouse employment center to address the problem. The center provides career counseling and assistance in locating employment opportunities both during and immediately after an international assignment. The company also agreed to reimburse up to 80 percent of the costs of vocational training, further education, or reaccreditation, up to $4,400 per assignment.

Shell also set up a global information and advice network known as "The Outpost" to provide support for families contemplating a foreign posting. The Outpost has its headquarters in The Hague and now runs 40 information centers in more than 30 countries. The center recommends schools and medical facilities and provides housing advice and up-to-date information on employment, study, self-employment, and volunteer work.[30]

Perceptual Ability. This is the ability to understand why people of other countries behave the way they do; that is, the ability to empathize. This dimension seems critical for managing host-country nationals. Expatriate managers who lack this ability tend to treat foreign nationals as if they were home-country nationals. As a result, they may experience significant management problems and considerable frustration. As one expatriate executive from Hewlett-Packard observed, "It took me six months to accept the fact that my staff meetings would start 30 minutes late, and that it would bother no one but me." According to Mendenhall and Oddou, well-adjusted expatriates tend to be nonjudgmental and nonevaluative in interpreting the behavior of host-country nationals and willing to be flexible in their management style, adjusting it as cultural conditions warrant.

Cultural Toughness. This dimension refers to the relationship between the country of assignment and how well an expatriate adjusts to a particular posting. Some countries are much tougher postings than others because their cultures are more unfamiliar and uncomfortable. For example, many Americans regard Great Britain as a relatively easy foreign posting, and for good reason—the two cultures have much in common. But many Americans find postings in non-Western cultures, such as India, Southeast Asia, and the Middle East, to be more difficult.[32] The reasons are many, including poor health care and housing standards, inhospitable climate, lack of Western entertainment, and language difficulties. Also, many cultures are extremely male-dominated and may be particularly difficult postings for female Western managers.

THE GLOBAL MIND-SET

Some researchers suggest that a global mind-set, one characterized by cognitive complexity and a cosmopolitan outlook, is the fundamental attribute of a global manager. Such managers can deal with high levels of complexity and ambiguity and are open to the world. How do you develop these attributes? Often they are gained in early life from a family that is bicultural, lives in foreign countries, or learns foreign languages as a regular part of family life.

Mendenhall and Oddou note that standard psychological tests can be used to assess the first three of these dimensions, whereas a comparison of cultures can give managers a feeling for the fourth dimension. They contend that these four dimensions, in addition to domestic performance, should be considered when selecting a manager for foreign posting. However, practice does not often conform to Mendenhall and Oddou's recommendations. Tung's research, for example, showed that only 5 percent of the firms in her sample used formal procedures and psychological tests to assess the personality traits and relational abilities of potential expatriates.[33] Research by International Orientation Resources suggests that when selecting employees for foreign assignments, only 10 percent of the 50 *Fortune* 500 firms they surveyed tested for important psychological traits such as cultural sensitivity, interpersonal skills, adaptability, and flexibility. Instead, 90 percent of the time employees were selected on the basis of their technical expertise, not their cross-cultural fluency.[34]

Mendenhall and Oddou do not address the problem of expatriate failure due to a spouse's inability to adjust. According to a number of other researchers, a review of the family situation should be part of the expatriate selection process (see the Management Focus on Royal Dutch/Shell for an example).[35] A survey by Windam International, another international HRM consulting firm, found that spouses were included in preselection interviews for foreign postings only 21 percent of the time, and that only half of them received any cross-cultural training. The rise of dual-career families has added an additional and difficult dimension to this long-standing problem.[36] Increasingly, spouses wonder why they should have to sacrifice their own career to further that of their partner.[37]

⊕ Training and Management Development

Selection is just the first step in matching a manager with a job. The next step is training the manager to do the specific job. For example, an intensive training program might be used to give expatriate managers the skills required for success in a foreign posting. However, management development is a much broader concept. It is intended to develop the manager's skills over his or her career with the firm. Thus, as part of a management development program, a manager might be sent on several foreign postings over a number of years to build his or her cross-cultural sensitivity and experience. At the same time, along with other managers in the firm, the person might attend management education programs at regular intervals. The thinking behind job transfers is that broad international experience will enhance the management and leadership skills of executives. Research suggests this may be the case.[38]

Historically, most international businesses have been more concerned with training than with management development. In addition, they tended to focus their training efforts on preparing home-country nationals for foreign postings. Recently, however, the shift toward greater global competition and the rise of transnational firms have changed this. It is increasingly common for firms to provide general management development programs in addition to training for particular posts. In many international businesses, the explicit purpose of these management development programs is strategic. Management development is seen as a tool to help the firm achieve its strategic goals, not only by giving managers the required skill set but also by helping to reinforce the desired culture of the firm and by facilitating the creation of an informal network for sharing knowledge within the multinational enterprise.

With this distinction between training and management development in mind, we first examine the types of training managers receive for foreign postings. Then we discuss the connection between management development and strategy in the international business.

TRAINING FOR EXPATRIATE MANAGERS

Earlier in the chapter we saw that the two most common reasons for expatriate failure were the inability of a manager's spouse to adjust to a foreign environment and the manager's own inability to adjust to a foreign environment. Training can help the manager and spouse cope with both these problems. Cultural training, language training, and practical training all seem to reduce expatriate failure. We discuss each of these kinds of training here.[39] Despite the usefulness of these kinds of training, evidence suggests that many managers receive no training before they are sent on foreign postings. One study found that only about 30 percent of managers sent on one- to five-year expatriate assignments received training before their departure.[40]

Cultural Training

Cultural training seeks to foster an appreciation for the host country's culture. The belief is that understanding a host country's culture will help the manager empathize with the culture, which will enhance his or her effectiveness in dealing with host-country nationals. It has been suggested that expatriates should receive training in the host country's culture, history, politics, economy, religion, and social and business practices.[41] If possible, it is also advisable to arrange for a familiarization trip to the host country before the formal transfer, as this seems to ease culture shock. Given the problems related to spouse adaptation, it is important that the spouse, and perhaps the whole family, be included in cultural training programs.

Language Training

English is the language of world business; it is quite possible to conduct business all over the world using only English (note that Lenovo decided that English was to be the official language of the company, even though it is a Chinese enterprise; see the opening case). Notwithstanding the prevalence of English, however, an exclusive reliance on English diminishes an expatriate manager's ability to interact with host-country nationals. As noted earlier, a willingness to communicate in the language of the host country, even if the expatriate is far from fluent, can help build rapport with local employees and improve the manager's effectiveness. Despite this, one study of 74 executives of U.S. multinationals found that only 23 believed knowledge of foreign languages was necessary for conducting business abroad.[42] Those firms that did offer foreign language training for expatriates believed it improved their employees' effectiveness and enabled them to relate more easily to a foreign culture, which fostered a better image of the firm in the host country.

Practical Training

Practical training is aimed at helping the expatriate manager and family ease themselves into day-to-day life in the host country. The sooner a routine is established, the better are the prospects that the expatriate and his or her family will adapt successfully. One critical need is for a support network of friends for the expatriate. Where an expatriate community exists, firms often devote considerable effort to ensuring the new expatriate family is quickly integrated into that group. The expatriate community can be a useful source of support and information and can be invaluable in helping the family adapt to a foreign culture.

REPATRIATION OF EXPATRIATES

At Caterpillar, expatriate managers and their families receive culture and language training, as well as relocation assistance, before relocating to one of Caterpillar's global facilities.

A largely overlooked but critically important issue in the training and development of expatriate managers is to prepare them for reentry into their home-country organization.[43] Repatriation should be seen as the final link in an integrated, circular process that connects good selection and cross-cultural training of expatriate managers with completion of their term abroad and reintegration into their national organization. However, instead of having employees come home to share their knowledge and encourage other high-performing managers to take the same international career track, expatriates too often face a different scenario.[44]

Often when they return home after a stint abroad—where they have typically been autonomous, well-compensated, and celebrated as a big fish in a little pond—they face an organization that doesn't know what they have done for the last few years, doesn't know how to use their new knowledge, and doesn't particularly care. In the worst cases, reentering employees have to scrounge for jobs, or firms will create standby positions that don't use the expatriate's skills and capabilities and fail to make the most of the business investment the firm has made in that individual.

Research illustrates the extent of this problem. According to one study of repatriated employees, 60 to 70 percent didn't know what their position would be when they returned home. Also, 60 percent said their organizations were vague about repatriation, about their new roles, and about their future career progression within the company; 77 percent of those surveyed took jobs at a lower level in their home organization than in their international assignments.[45] Not surprising, 15 percent of returning expatriates leave their firms within a year of arriving home, and 40 percent leave within three years.[46]

The key to solving this problem is good human resource planning. Just as the HRM function needs to develop good selection and training programs for its expatriates, it also needs to develop good programs for reintegrating expatriates back into work life within their home-country organization, for preparing them for changes in their physical and professional landscape, and for utilizing the knowledge they acquired while abroad. For an example of the kind of program that might be used, see the accompanying Management Focus that looks at Monsanto's repatriation program.

MANAGEMENT DEVELOPMENT AND STRATEGY

Management development programs are designed to increase managers' overall skill levels through a mix of ongoing management education and rotation through a number of jobs within the firm to give them varied experiences. They are attempts to improve the overall productivity and quality of the firm's management resources.

International businesses increasingly are using management development as a strategic tool. This is particularly true in firms pursuing a transnational strategy, as increasing

Monsanto's Repatriation Program

Monsanto is a global provider of agricultural products with revenues of $5 billion and 10,000 employees. At any one time, the company will have 100 mid- and higher-level managers on extended postings abroad. Two-thirds of these are Americans posted overseas; the remainder are foreign nationals employed in the United States. At Monsanto, managing expatriates and their repatriation begins with a rigorous selection process and intensive cross-cultural training, both for the managers and for their families. As at many other global companies, the idea is to build an internationally minded cadre of highly capable managers who will lead the organization in the future.

One of the strongest features of this program is that employees and their sending and receiving managers, or sponsors, develop an agreement about how this assignment will fit into the firm's business objectives. The focus is on why employees are going abroad to do the job and what their contribution to Monsanto will be when they return. Sponsoring managers are expected to be explicit about the kind of job opportunities the expatriates will have once they return home.

Once they arrive back in their home country, expatriate managers meet with cross-cultural trainers during debriefing sessions. They are also given the opportunity to showcase their experiences to their peers, subordinates, and superiors in special information exchanges.

However, Monsanto's repatriation program focuses on more than just business; it also attends to the family's reentry. Monsanto has found that difficulties with repatriation often have more to do with personal and family-related issues than with work-related issues. But the personal matters obviously affect an employee's on-the-job performance, so it is important for the company to pay attention to such issues.

This is why Monsanto offers returning employees an opportunity to work through personal difficulties. About three months after they return home, expatriates meet for three hours at work with several colleagues of their choice. The debriefing session is a conversation aided by a trained facilitator who has an outline to help the expatriate cover all the important aspects of the repatriation. The debriefing allows the employee to share important experiences and to enlighten managers, colleagues, and friends about his or her expertise so others within the organization can use some of the global knowledge. According to one participant, "It sounds silly, but it's such a hectic time in the family's life, you don't have time to sit down and take stock of what's happening. You're going through the move, transitioning to a new job, a new house, and the children may be going to a new school. This is a kind of oasis; a time to talk and put your feelings on the table." Apparently it works; since the program was introduced, the attrition rate among returning expatriates has dropped sharply.[50]

---

numbers are. Such firms need a strong unifying corporate culture and informal management networks to assist in coordination and control. In addition, transnational firm managers need to be able to detect pressures for local responsiveness, and that requires them to understand the culture of a host country.

Management development programs help build a unifying corporate culture by socializing new managers into the norms and value systems of the firm. In-house company training programs and intense interaction during off-site training can foster esprit de corps—shared experiences, informal networks, perhaps a company language or jargon—as well as develop technical competencies. These training events often include songs, picnics, and sporting events that promote feelings of togetherness. These rites of integration may include "initiation rites" wherein personal culture is stripped, company uniforms are donned (e.g., T-shirts bearing the company logo), and humiliation is inflicted (e.g., a pie in the face). All these activities aim to strengthen a manager's identification with the company.[47]

Bringing managers together in one location for extended periods and rotating them through different jobs in several countries help the firm build an informal management network. Such a network can then be used as a conduit for exchanging valuable performance-enhancing knowledge within the organization.[48] Consider the Swedish telecommunications company L. M. Ericsson. Interunit cooperation is extremely important at Ericsson, particularly for transferring know-how and core competencies from the parent to foreign subsidiaries, from foreign subsidiaries to the parent, and between foreign subsidiaries. To facilitate cooperation, Ericsson transfers large numbers of people back and forth between headquarters and subsidiaries. Ericsson sends a team of 50 to 100 engineers and managers from one unit to another for a year or two. This establishes a network of interpersonal contacts. This policy is effective for both solidifying a common culture in the company and coordinating the company's globally dispersed operations.[49]

Performance Appraisal

Performance appraisal systems are used to evaluate the performance of managers against some criteria that the firm judges to be important for the implementation of strategy and the attainment of a competitive advantage. A firm's performance appraisal systems are an important element of its control systems, which is a central component of organization architecture (see Figure 18.1). A particularly thorny issue in many international businesses is how best to evaluate the performance of expatriate managers.[51] In this section, we look at this issue and consider some guidelines for appraising expatriate performance.

PERFORMANCE APPRAISAL PROBLEMS

Unintentional bias makes it difficult to evaluate the performance of expatriate managers objectively. In many cases, two groups evaluate the performance of expatriate managers—host-nation managers and home-office managers—and both are subject to bias. The host-nation managers may be biased by their own cultural frame of reference and expectations. For example, Oddou and Mendenhall report the case of a U.S. manager who introduced participative decision making while working in an Indian subsidiary.[52] The manager subsequently received a negative evaluation from host-country managers because in India, the strong social stratification means managers are seen as experts who should not have to ask subordinates for help. The local employees apparently viewed the U.S. manager's attempt at participatory management as an indication that he was incompetent and did not know his job.

Home-country managers' appraisals may be biased by distance and by their own lack of experience working abroad. Home-office managers are often not aware of what is going on in a foreign operation. Accordingly, they tend to rely on hard data in evaluating an expatriate's performance, such as the subunit's productivity, profitability, or market share. Such criteria may reflect factors outside the expatriate manager's control (e.g., adverse changes in exchange rates, economic downturns). Also, hard data do not take into account many less-visible soft variables that are also important, such as an expatriate's ability to develop cross-cultural awareness and to work productively with local managers. Due to such biases, many expatriate managers believe that headquarters management evaluates them unfairly and does not fully appreciate the value of their skills and experience. This could be one reason many expatriates believe a foreign posting does not benefit their careers. In one study of personnel managers in U.S. multinationals, 56 percent of the managers surveyed stated that a foreign assignment is either detrimental or immaterial to one's career.[53]

GUIDELINES FOR PERFORMANCE APPRAISAL

Several things can reduce bias in the performance appraisal process.[54] First, most expatriates appear to believe more weight should be given to an on-site manager's appraisal than to an off-site manager's appraisal. Due to proximity, an on-site manager is more likely to evaluate the soft variables that are important aspects of an expatriate's performance. The evaluation may be especially valid when the on-site manager is of the same nationality as the expatriate, since cultural bias should be alleviated. In practice, home-office managers often write performance evaluations after receiving input from on-site managers. When this is the case, most experts recommend that a former expatriate who served in the same location should be involved in the appraisal to help reduce bias. Finally, when the policy is for foreign on-site managers to write performance evaluations, home-office managers should be consulted before an on-site manager completes a formal termination evaluation. This gives the home-office manager the opportunity to balance what could be a very hostile evaluation based on a cultural misunderstanding.

🌐 Compensation

Two issues are raised in every discussion of compensation practices in an international business. One is how compensation should be adjusted to reflect national differences in economic circumstances and compensation practices. The other issue is how expatriate managers should be paid. From a strategic perspective, the important point is that whatever compensation system is used, it should reward managers for taking actions that are consistent with the strategy of the enterprise.

NATIONAL DIFFERENCES IN COMPENSATION

Substantial differences exist in the compensation of executives at the same level in various countries. The results of a survey by Towers Perrin are summarized in Table 18.3. Among other things, this survey looked at average compensation for top human resource executives across 26 countries in the 2005–06 period for companies with annual sales of around $500 million.[55] The figures include both base compensation and performance-related pay bonuses, but they do not include stock options. As can be seen, wide variations exist across countries. The average compensation for top HR executives in the United States was $525,923, compared with $278,697 in Japan and $158,146 in Taiwan. According to Towers Perrin, similar pay differences can be seen across other job categories, including the CEO and CFO positions. These figures underestimate the true differential because many U.S. executives earn considerable sums of money from stock option grants.

National differences in compensation raise a perplexing question for an international business: Should the firm pay executives in different countries according to the prevailing standards in each country, or should it equalize pay on a global basis? The problem does not arise in firms pursuing ethnocentric or polycentric staffing policies. In ethnocentric firms, the issue can be reduced to that of how much home-country expatriates should be paid (which we will consider later). As for polycentric firms, the lack of managers' mobility among national operations implies that pay can and should be kept country-specific. There would seem to be no point in paying executives in Great Britain the same as U.S. executives if they never work side by side.

However, this problem is very real in firms with geocentric staffing policies. A geocentric staffing policy is consistent with a transnational strategy. One aspect of this policy is the need for a cadre of international managers that may include many different nationalities. Should all members of such a cadre be paid the same salary and the same incentive pay? For a U.S.-based firm, this would mean raising the compensation of foreign nationals to U.S. levels, which could be expensive. If the firm does not equalize pay, it could cause considerable resentment among foreign nationals who are members of the international cadre and work with U.S. nationals. If a firm is serious about building an international cadre, it may have to pay its international executives the same basic

Country	HR Executive Total Compensation ($)
Argentina	212,879
Australia	293,782
Belgium	446,624
Brazil	356,733
Canada	307,053
China (Hong Kong)	268,158
China (Shanghai)	85,393
France	384,904
Germany	456,665
India	146,384
Italy	432,569
Japan	278,697
Malaysia	140,587
Mexico	382,334
Netherlands	287,247
Poland	120,410
Singapore	230,281
South Africa	371,781
South Korea	182,716
Spain	305,519
Sweden	302,473
Switzerland	447,563
Taiwan	158,146
United Kingdom	494,519
United States	525,923
Venezuela	225,317

salary irrespective of their country of origin or assignment. Currently, however, this practice is not widespread.

What has occurred over the last 10 years is that many firms have moved toward a compensation structure based upon consistent global standards, with employees being evaluated by the same grading system and having access to the same bonus pay and benefits structure irrespective of where they work. Indeed, some 85 percent of the companies in a recent survey by Mercer Management Consulting have stated that they now have a global compensation strategy in place.[56] McDonald's, which is featured in the next Management Focus, is one such enterprise. Another survey found that two-thirds of multinationals now exercise central control over the benefit plans offered in different nations.[57] However, except for a relatively small cadre of internationally mobile executives, base pay in most firms is set with regard to local market conditions.

Global Compensation Practices at McDonald's

With more than 400,000 managers and senior staff employees in 118 countries around the world, by the early 2000s McDonald's had to develop a consistent global compensation and performance appraisal strategy. In 2003, McDonald's launched an initiative designed to do just that. After months of consultation with managers all over the world, in 2004 the company began to roll out its new global compensation program.

One important element of this program calls for the corporate head office to provide local country managers with a menu of business principles to focus on in the coming year. These principles include areas like customer service, marketing, and restaurant reimaging. Each country manager then picks three to five areas they need to focus on for success in their local market. For example, if France is introducing a new menu item, it might create business targets around that for the year. Human resource managers then submit their business cases and targets to senior executives at the headquarters for approval. At the end of the year, the country's annual incentive pool is based on how the region met its targets, as well as on the business unit's operating income. A portion of each employee's annual bonus is based upon that mix.

The other portion of an employee's annual incentives is based on individual performance. McDonald's has always had a performance rating system, but in 2004 the company introduced global guidelines that suggest that 20 percent of employees receive the highest rating, 70 percent the middle, and 10 percent the bottom. By providing guidelines rather than forced ranking, McDonald's hopes to encourage differentiation of performance while allowing for some local flexibility. By providing principles and guidance, and yet allowing local managers to customize their compensation programs to meet local market demands, McDonald's also claims that it has seen a reduction in turnover. The company's own internal surveys suggest that more employees now believe that their compensation is fair and reflects local market conditions.[58]

EXPATRIATE PAY

The most common approach to expatriate pay is the balance sheet approach. According to Organizational Resources Consulting, some 80 percent of the 781 companies it surveyed in 2002 use this approach.[59] This approach equalizes purchasing power across countries so employees can enjoy the same living standard in their foreign posting that they enjoyed at home. In addition, the approach provides financial incentives to offset qualitative differences between assignment locations.[60] Figure 18.2 shows a typical balance sheet. Note that home-country outlays for the employee are designated as income taxes, housing expenses, expenditures for goods and services (food, clothing, entertainment, etc.), and reserves (savings, pension contributions, etc.). The balance sheet approach attempts to provide expatriates with the same standard of living in their host countries that they enjoy at home plus a financial inducement (i.e., premium, incentive) for accepting an overseas assignment.

The components of the typical expatriate compensation package are a base salary, a foreign service premium, allowances of various types, tax differentials, and benefits. We shall briefly review each of these components.[61] An expatriate's total compensation package may amount to three times what he or she would cost the firm in a home-country posting. Because of the high cost of expatriates, many firms have reduced their use in recent years. However, a firm's ability to reduce its use of expatriates may be limited, particularly if it is pursuing an ethnocentric or geocentric staffing policy.

Base Salary

An expatriate's base salary is normally in the same range as the base salary for a similar position in the home country. The base salary is normally paid in either the home-country currency or the local currency.

FIGURE 18.2

The Balance Sheet

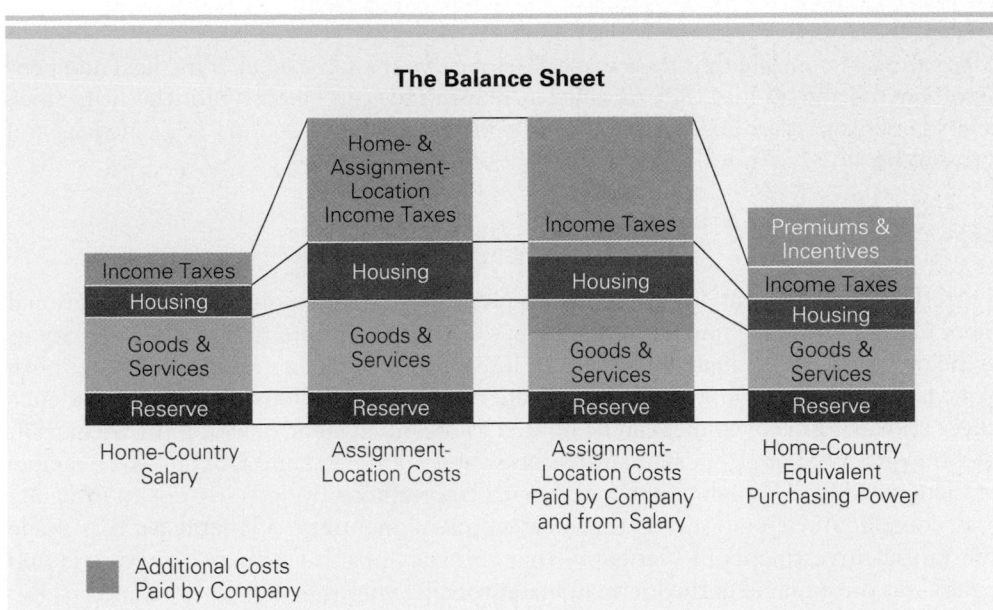

The Balance Sheet

Foreign Service Premium

A foreign service premium is extra pay the expatriate receives for working outside his or her country of origin. It is offered as an inducement to accept foreign postings. It compensates the expatriate for having to live in an unfamiliar country isolated from family and friends, deal with a new culture and language, and adapt to new work habits and practices. Many firms pay foreign service premiums as a percentage of base salary, ranging from 10 to 30 percent after tax, with 16 percent being the average premium.[62]

Allowances

Four types of allowances are often included in an expatriate's compensation package: hardship allowances, housing allowances, cost-of-living allowances, and education allowances. A hardship allowance is paid when the expatriate is being sent to a difficult location, usually defined as one where such basic amenities as health care, schools, and retail stores are grossly deficient by the standards of the expatriate's home country. A housing allowance is normally given to ensure that the expatriate can afford the same quality of housing in the foreign country as at home. In locations where housing is expensive (e.g., London, Tokyo), this allowance can be substantial—as much as 10 to 30 percent of the expatriate's total compensation package. A cost-of-living allowance ensures that the expatriate will enjoy the same standard of living in the foreign posting as at home. An education allowance ensures that an expatriate's children receive adequate schooling (by home-country standards). Host-country public schools are sometimes not suitable for an expatriate's children, in which case they must attend a private school.

Taxation

Unless a host country has a reciprocal tax treaty with the expatriate's home country, the expatriate may have to pay income tax to both the home- and host-country governments. When a reciprocal tax treaty is not in force, the firm typically pays the expatriate's income tax in the host country. In addition, firms normally make up the difference when a higher income tax rate in a host country reduces an expatriate's take-home pay.

Benefits

Many firms also ensure that their expatriates receive the same level of medical and pension benefits abroad that they received at home. This can be costly for the firm, since many benefits that are tax deductible for the firm in the home country (e.g., medical and pension benefits) may not be deductible out of the country.

International Labor Relations

The HRM function of an international business is typically responsible for international labor relations. From a strategic perspective, the key issue in international labor relations is the degree to which organized labor can limit the choices of an international business. A firm's ability to integrate and consolidate its global operations to realize experience curve and location economies can be limited by organized labor, constraining the pursuit of a transnational or global standardization strategy. Prahalad and Doz cite the example of General Motors, which gained peace with labor unions by agreeing not to integrate and consolidate operations in the most efficient manner.[63] General Motors made substantial investments in Germany—matching its new investments in Austria and Spain—at the demand of the German metalworkers' unions.

One task of the HRM function is to foster harmony and minimize conflict between the firm and organized labor. With this in mind, this section is divided into three parts. First, we review organized labor's concerns about multinational enterprises. Second, we look at how organized labor has tried to deal with these concerns. And third, we look at how international businesses manage their labor relations to minimize labor disputes.

THE CONCERNS OF ORGANIZED LABOR

Labor unions generally try to get better pay, greater job security, and better working conditions for their members through collective bargaining with management. Unions' bargaining power is derived largely from their ability to threaten to disrupt production, either by a strike or some other form of work protest (e.g., refusing to work overtime). This threat is credible, however, only insofar as management has no alternative but to employ union labor.

A principal concern of domestic unions about multinational firms is that the company can counter its bargaining power with the power to move production to another country. Ford, for example, clearly threatened British unions with a plan to move manufacturing to Continental Europe unless British workers abandoned work rules that limited productivity, showed restraint in negotiating for wage increases, and curtailed strikes and other work disruptions.[64]

Another concern of organized labor is that an international business will keep highly skilled tasks in its home country and farm out only low-skilled tasks to foreign plants. Such a practice makes it relatively easy for an international business to switch production from one location to another as economic conditions warrant. Consequently, the bargaining power of organized labor is once more reduced.

A final union concern arises when an international business attempts to import employment practices and contractual agreements from its home country. When these practices are alien to the host country, organized labor fears the change will reduce its influence and power. This concern has surfaced in response to Japanese multinationals that have been trying to export their style of labor relations to other countries. For example, much to the annoyance of the United Auto Workers (UAW), many Japanese auto plants in the United States are not unionized. As a result, union influence in the auto industry is declining.

THE STRATEGY OF ORGANIZED LABOR

Organized labor has responded to the increased bargaining power of multinational corporations by taking three actions: (1) trying to establish international labor organizations,

(2) lobbying for national legislation to restrict multinationals, and (3) trying to achieve international regulations on multinationals through such organizations as the United Nations. These efforts have not been very successful.

In the 1960s, organized labor began to establish international trade secretariats (ITSs) to provide worldwide links for national unions in particular industries. The long-term goal was to be able to bargain transnationally with multinational firms. Organized labor believed that by coordinating union action across countries through an ITS, it could counter the power of a multinational corporation by threatening to disrupt production on an international scale. For example, Ford's threat to move production from Great Britain to other European locations would not have been credible if the unions in various European countries had united to oppose it.

However, the ITSs have had virtually no real success. Although national unions may want to cooperate, they also compete with each other to attract investment from international businesses, and hence jobs for their members. For example, in attempting to gain new jobs for their members, national unions in the auto industry often court auto firms that are seeking locations for new plants. One reason Nissan chose to build its European production facilities in Great Britain rather than Spain was that the British unions agreed to greater concessions than the Spanish unions did. As a result of such competition between national unions, cooperation is difficult to establish.

A further impediment to cooperation has been the wide variation in union structure. Trade unions developed independently in each country. As a result, the structure and ideology of unions tend to vary significantly from country to country, as does the nature of collective bargaining. For example, in Great Britain, France, and Italy, many unions are controlled by left-wing socialists, who view collective bargaining through the lens of "class conflict." In contrast, most union leaders in Germany, the Netherlands, Scandinavia, and Switzerland are far more moderate politically. The ideological gap between union leaders in different countries has made cooperation difficult. Divergent ideologies are reflected in radically different views about the role of a union in society and the stance unions should take toward multinationals.

Organized labor has also met with only limited success in its efforts to get national and international bodies to regulate multinationals. Such international organizations as the International Labor Organization (ILO) and the Organization for Economic Cooperation and Development (OECD) have adopted codes of conduct for multinational firms to follow in labor relations. However, these guidelines are not as far-reaching as many unions would like. They also do not provide any enforcement mechanisms. Many researchers report that such guidelines are of only limited effectiveness.[65]

APPROACHES TO LABOR RELATIONS

International businesses differ markedly in their approaches to international labor relations. The main difference is the degree to which labor relations activities are centralized or decentralized. Historically, most international businesses have decentralized international labor relations activities to their foreign subsidiaries because labor laws, union power, and the nature of collective bargaining varied so much from country to country. It made sense to decentralize the labor relations function to local managers. The belief was that there was no way central management could effectively handle the complexity of simultaneously managing labor relations in a number of different environments.

Although this logic still holds, there is now a trend toward greater centralized control. This trend reflects international firms' attempts to rationalize their global operations. The general rise in competitive pressure in industry after industry has made it more important for firms to control their costs. Because labor costs account for such a large percentage of total costs, many firms are now using the threat to move production to another country in their negotiations with unions to change work rules and limit wage increases (as Ford did in Europe). Because such a move would involve major new investments and plant closures, this bargaining tactic requires the input of headquarters management. Thus, the level of centralized input into labor relations is increasing.

In addition, the realization is growing that the way work is organized within a plant can be a major source of competitive advantage. Much of the competitive advantage of Japanese automakers, for example, has been attributed to the use of self-managing teams, job rotation, cross-training, and the like in their Japanese plants.[66] To replicate their domestic performance in foreign plants, the Japanese firms have tried to replicate their work practices there. This often brings them into direct conflict with traditional work practices in those countries, as sanctioned by the local labor unions, so the Japanese firms have often made their foreign investments contingent on the local union accepting a radical change in work practices. To achieve this, the headquarters of many Japanese firms bargains directly with local unions to get union agreement to changes in work rules before committing to an investment. For example, before Nissan decided to invest in northern England, it got a commitment from British unions to agree to a change in traditional work practices. By its very nature, pursuing such a strategy requires centralized control over the labor relations function.

CHAPTER SUMMARY

This chapter focused on human resource management in international businesses. HRM activities include human resource strategy, staffing, performance evaluation, management development, compensation, and labor relations. None of these activities is performed in a vacuum; all must be appropriate to the firm's strategy. The chapter made these major points:

1. Firm success requires HRM policies to be congruent with the firm's strategy and with its formal and informal structure and controls.

2. Staffing policy is concerned with selecting employees who have the skills required to perform particular jobs. Staffing policy can be a tool for developing and promoting a corporate culture.

3. An ethnocentric approach to staffing policy fills all key management positions in an international business with parent-country nationals. The policy is congruent with an international strategy. A drawback is that ethnocentric staffing can result in cultural myopia.

4. A polycentric staffing policy uses host-country nationals to manage foreign subsidiaries and parent-country nationals for the key positions at corporate headquarters. This approach can minimize the dangers of cultural myopia, but it can create a gap between home- and host-country operations. The policy is best suited to a localization strategy.

5. A geocentric staffing policy seeks the best people for key jobs throughout the organization, regardless of their nationality. This approach is consistent with building a strong unifying culture and informal management network and is well suited to both global standardization and transnational strategies. Immigration policies of national governments may limit a firm's ability to pursue this policy.

6. A prominent issue in the international staffing literature is expatriate failure, defined as the premature return of an expatriate manager to his or her home country. The costs of expatriate failure can be substantial.

7. Expatriate failure can be reduced by selection procedures that screen out inappropriate candidates. The most successful expatriates seem to be those who have high self-esteem and self-confidence, can get along well with others, are willing to attempt to communicate in a foreign language, and can empathize with people of other cultures.

8. Training can lower the probability of expatriate failure. It should include cultural training, language training, and practical training, and it should be provided to both the expatriate manager and the spouse.

9. Management development programs attempt to increase the overall skill levels of managers

through a mix of ongoing management education and rotation of managers through different jobs within the firm to give them varied experiences. Management development is often used as a strategic tool to build a strong unifying culture and informal management network, both of which support transnational and global standardization strategies.

10. It can be difficult to evaluate the performance of expatriate managers objectively because of unintentional bias. A firm can take a number of steps to reduce this bias.

11. Country differences in compensation practices raise a difficult question for an international business: Should the firm pay executives in different countries according to the standards in each country or equalize pay on a global basis?

12. The most common approach to expatriate pay is the balance sheet approach. This approach

aims to equalize purchasing power so employees can enjoy the same living standard in their foreign posting that they had at home.

13. A key issue in international labor relations is the degree to which organized labor can limit the choices available to an international business. A firm's ability to pursue a transnational or global standardization strategy can be significantly constrained by the actions of labor unions.

14. A principal concern of organized labor is that the multinational can counter union bargaining power with threats to move production to another country.

15. Organized labor has tried to counter the bargaining power of multinationals by forming international labor organizations. In general, these efforts have not been effective.

Critical Thinking and Discussion Questions

1. What are the main advantages and disadvantages of the ethnocentric, polycentric, and geocentric approaches to staffing policy? When is each approach appropriate?

2. Research suggests that many expatriate employees encounter problems that limit both their effectiveness in a foreign posting and their contribution to the company when they return home. What are the main causes and consequences of these problems, and how might a firm reduce the occurrence of such problems?

3. What is the link between an international business's strategy and its human resource

management policies, particularly with regard to the use of expatriate employees and their pay scale?

4. In what ways can organized labor constrain the strategic choices of an international business? How can an international business limit these constraints?

5. Reread the Management Focus on McDonald's global compensation practices. How does McDonald's approach help the company take local differences into account when reviewing the performance of different country managers and awarding bonus pay?

Research Task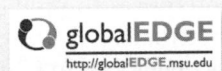

Use the globalEDGE™ site to complete the following exercises:

1. Living costs can vary considerably from country to country. The U.S. Department of State prepares a series of reports called *Quarterly Reports for Living Costs Abroad*. Using the most current report, identify the countries that are regarded as having a high cost of living and those that are perceived as risky. What are the living allowances and hardship differentials

determined by the U.S. Department of State for those countries?

2. You work in the human resources department at the headquarters of a multinational corporation. Your company is about to send several American managers overseas as expatriates (or expats). Utilize resources available on the globalEDGE™ Web site regarding "expat" life to compile a short checklist of concerns and steps for your company to go through before sending these managers overseas.

XCO China

It had been a bad morning for John Ross, the general manager of XCO's Chinese joint venture. He had just got off the phone with his boss in St Louis, Phil Smith, who was demanding to know why the joint venture's return on investment was still in the low single digits four years after Ross had taken over the top post in the operation. "We had expected much better performance by now," said Smith, "particularly given your record of achievement; you need to fix this Phil. Our patience is not infinite. You know the corporate goal is for a 20 percent return on investment for operating units, and your unit is not even close to that." Ross had a bad feeling that Smith had just fired a warning shot across his bow. There was an implicit threat underlying Smith's demands for improved performance. For the first time in his 20-year career at XCO, Ross felt that his job was on the line.

XCO was a U.S.-based multinational electronics enterprise with sales of $2 billion and operations in more than 10 countries. XCO China specialized in the mass production of printed circuit boards for companies in the cell phone and computer industries. It was a joint venture with Shanghai Electronic Corporation, a former state-owned enterprise that held 40 percent of the joint-venture equity (XCO held the rest). Although XCO held a majority of the equity, the company had to consult with its partner before making major investments or changing employment levels.

John Ross had been running XCO China for the past four years. He had arrived at XCO China after a successful career at XCO, which included extended postings in Mexico and Hungary. When he took the China position, Ross thought that if he succeeded he would probably be in line for one of the top jobs at corporate within a few years. He had known that he was taking on a challenge with XCO China, but nothing prepared him for what he found there. The joint venture was a mess. Operations were horribly inefficient. Despite very low wage rates, productivity was being killed by poor product quality and lax inventory controls. The venture probably employed too many people, but XCO's Chinese partner seemed to view the venture as a job-creation program and repeatedly objected to any plans for cutting the workforce. To make matters worse, XCO China had failed to keep up with the latest developments in manufacturing technology, and it was falling behind competitors. Ross was determined to change this, but it had not been easy.

To improve operations, Ross had put in a request to corporate HR for two specialists from the United States to work with the Chinese production employees. It had been a disaster. One had lasted just three months before requesting a transfer home for personal reasons. Apparently, his spouse hated China. The other had stayed on for a year, but he had interacted so poorly with the local Chinese employees that he had to be sent back to the States. Ross wished that XCO's corporate HR department had done a better job of selecting and then training these employees for a difficult foreign posting, but in retrospect he had to admit that he wasn't surprised at the lack of cultural training—after all, he had never been given any.

After this failure, Ross had taken a different tack. He had picked four of his best Chinese production employees and sent them over to XCO's U.S. operations, along with a translator, for a two-month training program focusing on the latest production techniques. This had worked out much better. The Chinese had visited efficient XCO factories in the United States, Mexico, and Brazil and had seen what was possible. They had returned home fired up to improve operations at XCO China. Within a year they had introduced a Six Sigma quality control program and improved the flow of inventory through XCO's factory. Ross could now walk through the factory without being appalled by the sight of large quantities of inventory stacked on the floor, or bins full of discarded circuit boards that had failed postassembly quality tests. Productivity had improved, and after three tough years, XCO China had finally turned a profit.

Apparently, this was not good enough for corporate headquarters. Ross knew that improving performance further would be very difficult. The market in China had become very competitive. XCO was vying with many other enterprises to produce printed circuit boards for large multinational customers who themselves had assembly operations in China. The customers were constantly demanding lower prices, and it seemed to Ross that prices were falling almost as fast as XCO's costs. Moreover, Ross was limited in his ability to cut the workforce by the demands of his Chinese joint-venture partner. He had tried to explain all of this to Phil Smith, but Smith didn't seem to get it. "The man is just a number cruncher," thought Ross, "he has no sense of the market in China. He has no idea how hard it is to do business here. I have worked damn hard to turn this operation around, and I am getting no credit for it, none at all."[67]

Case Discussion Questions

1. Why do you think John Ross' prior expatriate experience failed to prepare him for the task of managing XCO China?

2. What does the experience of XCO with American expatriates tell you about the problems of working abroad and about the difficulties of using home-country employees to transfer valuable knowledge with a multinational firm?

3. In order to transfer valuable knowledge, why was it apparently more effective to take Chinese employees to the United States, and then transfer them back home, than it was to use U.S. expatriates?

4. How might XCO's performance appraisal system be adjusted so that Ross gets credit, if it is deserved, for the difficult work that he is doing in China, work that is not reflected in a level of performance at XCO China that matches XCO's operations elsewhere?

Notes

1. Sources: D. Barboza, "An Unknown Giant Flexes Its Muscles," *The New York Times*, December 4, 2004, pp. B1, B3; D. Roberts and L. Lee, "East Meets West," *BusinessWeek*, May 9, 2005, pp. 1–4; and C. Forelle, "How IBM's Ward Will Lead China's Largest PC Company," *The Wall Street Journal*, April 21, 2005, p. B1; and F. Hansen, "International Business Machine," *Workforce Management*, July 2005, pp. 36–44.

2. P. J. Dowling and R. S. Schuler, *International Dimensions of Human Resource Management* (Boston: PSW-Kent, 1990).

3. J. Millman, M. A. von Glinow, and M. Nathan, "Organizational Life Cycles and Strategic International Human Resource Management in Multinational Companies," *Academy of Management Review* 16 (1991), pp. 318–39.

4. See P. Bamberger and I. Meshoulam, *Human Resource Strategy: Formulation, Implementation, and Impact* (Thousand Oaks, CA: Sage, 2000); P. M. Wright and S. Snell, "Towards a Unifying Framework for Exploring Fit and Flexibility in Human Resource Management," *Academy of Management Review* 23 (October 1998), pp. 756–72; and B. A. Colbert, "The Complex Resource-Based View: Implications for Theory and Practice in Strategic Human Resource Management," *Academy of Management Review* 29 (July 2004), pp. 341–60.

5. R. Colman, "HR Management Lags Behind at World Class Firms," *CMA Management*, July–August 2002, p. 9.

6. E. H. Schein, *Organizational Culture and Leadership* (San Francisco: Jossey-Bass, 1985).

7. H. V. Perlmutter, "The Tortuous Evolution of the Multinational Corporation," *Columbia Journal of World Business* 4 (1969), pp. 9–18; D. A. Heenan and H.V. Perlmutter, *Multinational Organizational Development* (Reading, MA: Addison-Wesley, 1979); D. A. Ondrack, "International Human Resources Management in European and North American Firms," *International Studies of Management and Organization* 15 (1985), pp. 6–32; and T. Jackson, "The Management of People across Cultures: Valuing People Differently," *Human Resource Management* 41 (2002), pp. 455–75.

8. V. Reitman and M. Schuman, "Men's Club: Japanese and Korean Companies Rarely Look Outside for People to Run Their Overseas Operations," *The Wall Street Journal*, September 26, 1996, p. 17.

9. S. Beechler and J. Z. Yang, "The Transfer of Japanese Style Management to American Subsidiaries," *Journal of International Business Studies* 25 (1994), pp. 467–91. See also R. Konopaske, S. Warner, and K. E. Neupert, "Entry Mode Strategy and Performance: The Role of FDI Staffing," *Journal of Business Research*, September 2002, pp. 759–70.

10. M. Banai and L. M. Sama, "Ethical Dilemma in MNCs' International Staffing Policies," *Journal of Business Ethics*, June 2000, pp. 221–35.

11. Reitman and Schuman, "Men's Club."

12. C. A. Bartlett and S. Ghoshal, *Managing across Borders: The Transnational Solution* (Boston: Harvard Business School Press, 1989).

13. S. J. Kobrin, "Geocentric Mindset and Multinational Strategy," *Journal of International Business Studies* 25 (1994), pp. 493–511.

14. P. M. Rosenzweig and N. Nohria, "Influences on Human Resource Management Practices in Multinational Corporations," *Journal of International Business Studies* 25 (1994), pp. 229–51.

15. Kobrin, "Geocentric Mindset and Multinational Strategy."

16. M. Harvey and H. Fung, "Inpatriate Managers: The Need for Realistic Relocation Reviews," *International Journal of Management* 17 (2000), pp. 151–59.

17. S. Black, M. Mendenhall, and G. Oddou, "Toward a Comprehensive Model of International Adjustment," *Academy of Management Review* 16 (1991), pp. 291–317; J. Shay and T. J. Bruce, "Expatriate Managers," *Cornell Hotel & Restaurant Administration Quarterly,* February 1997, pp. 30–40; and Y. Baruch and Y. Altman, "Expatriation and Repatriation in MNCs— A Taxonomy," *Human Resource Management* 41 (2002), pp. 239–59.

18. M. G. Harvey, "The Multinational Corporation's Expatriate Problem: An Application of Murphy's Law," *Business Horizons* 26 (1983), pp. 71–78.

19. J. Barbian, "Return to Sender," *Training,* January 2002, pp. 40–43.

20. Shay and Bruce, "Expatriate Managers." Also see J. S. Black and H. Gregersen, "The Right Way to Manage Expatriates," *Harvard Business Review,* March–April 1999, pp. 52–63; and Baruch and Altman, "Expatriation and Repatriation in MNCs."

21. N. Foster, "The Persistent Myth of High Expatriate Failure Rates," *Journal of Human Resource Management* 8 (1997), pp. 177–205.

22. Barbian, "Return to Sender."

23. Black, Mendenhall, and Oddou, "Toward a Comprehensive Model of International Adjustment."

24. R. L. Tung, "Selection and Training Procedures of U.S., European, and Japanese Multinationals," *California Management Review* 25 (1982), pp. 57–71.

25. C. M. Solomon, "Success Abroad Depends upon More than Job Skills," *Personnel Journal,* April 1994, pp. 51–58.

26. C. M. Solomon, "Unhappy Trails," *Workforce,* August 2000, pp. 36–41.

27. Solomon, "Success Abroad."

28. Solomon, "Unhappy Trails."

29. M. Harvey, "Addressing the Dual-Career Expatriation Dilemma," *Human Resource Planning* 19, no. 4 (1996), pp. 18–32.

30. Sources: E. Smockum, "Don't Forget the Trailing Spouse," *Financial Times,* May 6, 1998, p. 22; V. Frazee, "Tearing Down Roadblocks," *Workforce* 77, no. 2 (1998), pp. 50–54; C. Sievers, "Expatriate Management," *HR Focus* 75, no. 3 (1998), pp. 75–76; and J. Barbian, "Return to Sender," *Training,* January 2002, pp. 40–43.

31. M. Mendenhall and G. Oddou, "The Dimensions of Expatriate Acculturation: A Review," *Academy of Management Review* 10 (1985), pp. 39–47.

32. I. Torbiorin, *Living Abroad: Personal Adjustment and Personnel Policy in the Overseas Setting* (New York: John Wiley & Sons, 1982).

33. R. L. Tung, "Selection and Training of Personnel for Overseas Assignments," *Columbia Journal of World Business* 16 (1981), pp. 68–78.

34. Solomon, "Success Abroad."

35. S. Ronen, "Training and International Assignee," in *Training and Career Development,* ed. I. Goldstein (San Francisco: Jossey-Bass, 1985); and Tung, "Selection and Training of Personnel for Overseas Assignments."

36. Solomon, "Success Abroad."

37. Harvey, "Addressing the Dual-Career Expatriation Dilemma"; and J. W. Hunt, "The Perils of Foreign Postings for Two," *Financial Times,* May 6, 1998, p. 22.

38. C. M. Daily, S. T. Certo, and D. R. Dalton, "International Experience in the Executive Suite: A Path to Prosperity?" *Strategic Management Journal* 21 (2000), pp. 515–23.

39. Dowling and Schuler, *International Dimensions of Human Resource Management.*

40. Ibid.

41. G. Baliga and J. C. Baker, "Multinational Corporate Policies for Expatriate Managers: Selection, Training, and Evaluation," *Advanced Management Journal,* Autumn 1985, pp. 31–38.

42. J. C. Baker, "Foreign Language and Departure Training in U.S. Multinational Firms," *Personnel Administrator,* July 1984, pp. 68–70.

43. A 1997 study by the Conference Board looked at this in depth. For a summary, see L. Grant, "That Overseas Job Could Derail Your Career," *Fortune,* April 14, 1997, p. 166. Also see J. S. Black and H. Gregersen, "The Right Way to Manage Expatriates," *Harvard Business Review,* March–April 1999, pp. 52–63.

44. J. S. Black and M. E. Mendenhall, *Global Assignments: Successfully Expatriating and*

Repatriating International Managers (San Francisco: Jossey-Bass, 1992); and K. Vermond, "Expatriates Come Home," *CMA Management*, October 2001, pp. 30–33.

45. Ibid.

46. Figures from the Conference Board study. For a summary, see Grant, "That Overseas Job Could Derail Your Career."

47. S. C. Schneider, "National v. Corporate Culture: Implications for Human Resource Management," *Human Resource Management* 27 (Summer 1988), pp. 231–46.

48. I. M. Manve and W. B. Stevenson, "Nationality, Cultural Distance and Expatriate Status," *Journal of International Business Studies* 32 (2001), pp. 285–303; and D. Minbaeva et al., "MNC Knowledge Transfer, Subsidiary Absorptive Capacity, and HRM," *Journal of International Business Studies* 34, no. 6 (2003), pp. 586–604.

49. Bartlett and Ghoshal, *Managing across Borders*.

50. Sources: C. M. Solomon, "Repatriation: Up, Down, or Out?" *Personnel Journal*, January 1995, pp. 28–34; and J. Schaefer, E. Hannibal, and J. O'Neill, "How Strategy, Culture and Improved Service Delivery Reshape Monsanto's International Assignment Program," *Journal of Organizational Excellence* 22, no. 3 (2003), pp. 35–40.

51. See G. Oddou and M. Mendenhall, "Expatriate Performance Appraisal: Problems and Solutions," in *International Human Resource Management*, ed. Mendenhall and Oddou (Boston: PWS-Kent, 1991); Dowling and Schuler, *International Dimensions*; R. S. Schuler and G.W. Florkowski, "International Human Resource Management," in *Handbook for International Management Research*, ed. B. J. Punnett and O. Shenkar (Oxford: Blackwell, 1996); and K. Roth and S. O'Donnell, "Foreign Subsidiary Compensation Strategy: An Agency Theory Perspective," *Academy of Management Journal* 39, no. 3 (1996), pp. 678–703.

52. Oddou and Mendenhall, "Expatriate Performance Appraisal."

53. "Expatriates Often See Little Benefit to Careers in Foreign Stints, Indifference at Home," *The Wall Street Journal*, December 11, 1989, p. B1.

54. Oddou and Mendenhall, "Expatriate Performance Appraisal"; and Schuler and Florkowski, "International Human Resource Management."

55. Towers Perrin, *Towers Perrin Worldwide Total Remuneration Study, 2005–2006*, www.towersperrin.com.

56. J. Cummings and L. Brannen, "The New World of Compensation," *Business Finance*, June 2005, p. 8.

57. Staff Reporter, "Multinationals Tighten Control of Benefit Plans," *Workforce Management*, May 2005, p. 5.

58. J. Marquez, "McDonald's Rewards Program Leaves Some Room for Local Flavor," *Workforce Management*, April 10, 2006, p. 26.

59. Organizational Resource Counselors, *2002 Survey of International Assignment Policies and Practices*, March 2003.

60. C. Reynolds, "Compensation of Overseas Personnel," in *Handbook of Human Resource Administration*, ed. J. J. Famularo (New York: McGraw-Hill, 1986).

61. M. Helms, "International Executive Compensation Practices," in *International Human Resource Management*, ed. M. Mendenhall and G. Oddou (Boston: PWS-Kent, 1991).

62. G. W. Latta, "Expatriate Incentives," *HR Focus* 75, no. 3 (March 1998), p. S3.

63. C. K. Prahalad and Y. L. Doz, *The Multinational Mission* (New York: Free Press, 1987).

64. Ibid.

65. Schuler and Florkowski, "International Human Resource Management."

66. See J. P. Womack, D. T. Jones, and D. Roos, *The Machine That Changed the World* (New York: Rawson Associates, 1990).

67. This is a disguised case based on interviews undertaken by Charles Hill.

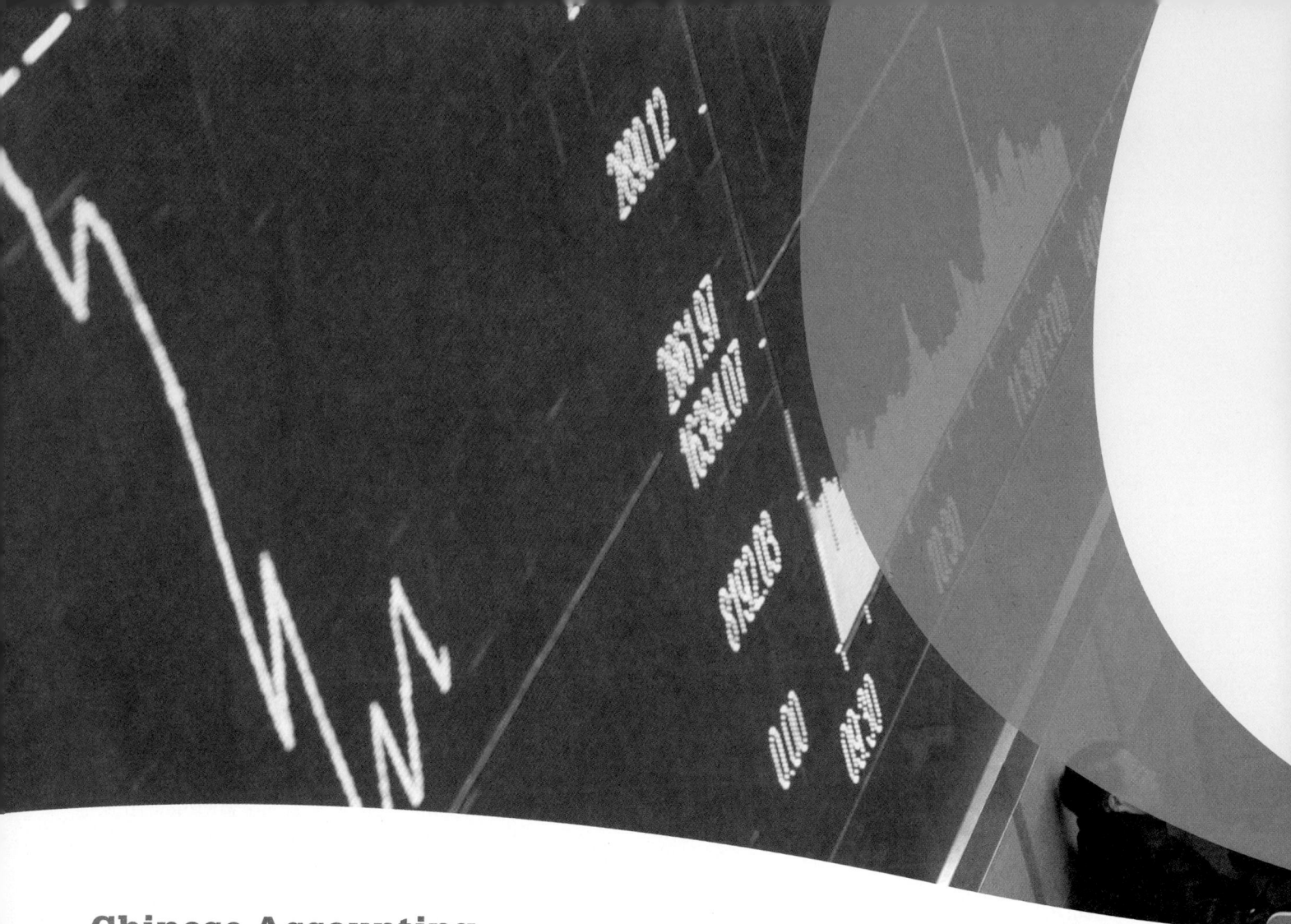

Chinese Accounting

Over the last decade, more and more Chinese companies have been tapping global capital markets and more foreigners have been investing in Chinese companies through the Shanghai stock exchange. Foreign investors, quite naturally, want to be assured that the financial picture they are getting of Chinese enterprises is reliable. So far, that has not always been the case. In December 2003, for example, China Life Insurance successfully listed its stock on the Hong Kong and New York stock exchanges, raising some $3.4 billion. However, in January 2004, the head of China's National Audit Office let it slip that a routine audit of China Life's state-owned parent company had uncovered $652 million in financial irregularities in 2003! The stock immediately fell, and China Life found itself the target of a class action lawsuit on behalf of U.S. investors claiming financial fraud. Shortly afterwards, plans to list China Minsheng Banking Corp., China's largest private bank, on the New York Stock Exchange were put on hold after the company admitted

that it had faked a shareholder meeting in 2000. The stock of another successful Chinese offering in New York, that of Semiconductor Manufacturing International, slid in 2004 when its chief financial officer made statements that contradicted those contained in filings with the United States Securities and Exchange Commission.

The core of the problem here is that accounting rules in China are not consistent with international standards, making it very difficult for investors to accurately value Chinese companies. Accounting in China has traditionally been rooted in information gathering and compliance reporting designed to measure the government's production and tax goals. The Chinese system was based on the old Soviet system, which had little to do with profit. Although the system has been changing rapidly, many problems associated with the old order still remain. Indeed, it is often said, only half in jest, that Chinese firms keep several sets of books—one for the government, one

Accounting in the International Business

LEARNING OBJECTIVES

After you have read this chapter you should be able to:

LO¹ Discuss the source of country differences in accounting standards.

LO² Discuss the consequences of national differences in accounting standards.

LO³ Explain the implications of the rise of international accounting standards.

LO⁴ Understand the accounting implications of currency translation.

LO⁵ Explain how accounting systems impact upon control systems within the multinational enterprise.

for company records, one for foreigners, and one to report what is actually going on.

To bring its rules into closer alignment with international standards, China has signaled that it will move toward adopting standards developed by the International Accounting Standards Board (IASB). In 2001, China adopted a new regulation, called the "Accounting System for Business Enterprises," that was largely based on ISAB standards. The system is now used to regulate both local and foreign companies operating in China. In 2005, the Chinese went further still, mandating that on January 1, 2007, the largest 1,200 firms listed on the Shanghai and Shenzhen stock exchanges adopt a broad set of accounting rules that are based on, but not identical to, IASB standards. It remains to be seen whether adoption of these new rules will make the financial performance of Chinese companies more transparent.

Complicating matters, China has a severe shortage of accountants, financial managers, and auditors, especially those experienced with market economy transactions and international accounting practices. Estimates suggest that China needs some 600,000 accountants, but as of 2006 there were still only 70,000 in the country. Chinese enterprises, including equity and cooperative joint ventures with foreign firms, must be audited by Chinese accounting firms, which are regulated by the state. Traditionally, many experienced auditors have audited only state-owned enterprises, working through the local province or city authorities and the state audit bureau to report to the government entity overseeing the audited firm. In response to the shortage of accountants schooled in the principles of private sector accounting, several large international auditing firms have established joint ventures with emerging Chinese accounting and auditing firms to meet the growing need for international accounting, tax, and securities expertise. Still, the current lack of experienced auditors in China raises questions about how accurate the financial statements of Chinese companies actually are, even under the new rules.[1]

Introduction

Accounting has often been referred to as "the language of business."[2] This language finds expression in profit-and-loss statements, balance sheets, budgets, investment analysis, and tax analysis. Accounting information is the means by which firms communicate their financial position to the providers of capital—investors, creditors, and government. It enables the providers of capital to assess the value of their investments or the security of their loans and to make decisions about future resource allocations (see Figure 19.1). Accounting information is also the means by which firms report their income to the government so the government can assess how much tax the firm owes. It is also the means by which the firm can evaluate its performance, control its internal expenditures, and plan for future expenditures and income. Thus, a good accounting function is critical to the smooth running of the firm and to a nation's financial system.

International businesses are confronted with a number of accounting problems that do not confront purely domestic businesses. The opening case on accounting in China draws attention to one of these problems—the lack of consistency in the accounting standards of different countries. The accounting rules currently used in China are not the same as those used in more developed markets (although as the case explains, the Chinese are pushing companies toward the adoption of international accounting standards). This makes it very difficult for international investors to accurately value Chinese firms, and it opens up the possibility that firms that seem to be profitable and financially strong are in fact not.

We begin this chapter by looking at the source of country differences in accounting standards. Then we shift our attention to attempts by the International Accounting Standards Board (IASB) to establish international accounting and auditing standards and discuss the progress that has been made. Next we examine the problems arising when an international business with operations in more than one country must produce consolidated financial statements. As we will see, these firms face special problems because, for example, the accounts for their operations in Brazil will be in *real*, in Korea they will be in *won*, and in Japan they will be in *yen*. If the firm is based in the United States, it will have to decide what basis to use for translating all these accounts into U.S. dollars. The last issue we discuss is control in an international business. We touched on the issue of control in Chapter 13 in rather abstract terms. Here we look at control from an accounting perspective.

Country Differences in Accounting Standards

Accounting is shaped by the environment in which it operates. Just as different countries have different political systems, economic systems, and cultures, historically they have also had different accounting systems.[3] In each country, the accounting system has evolved in response to the demands for accounting information.

FIGURE 19.1

Accounting Information and Capital Flows

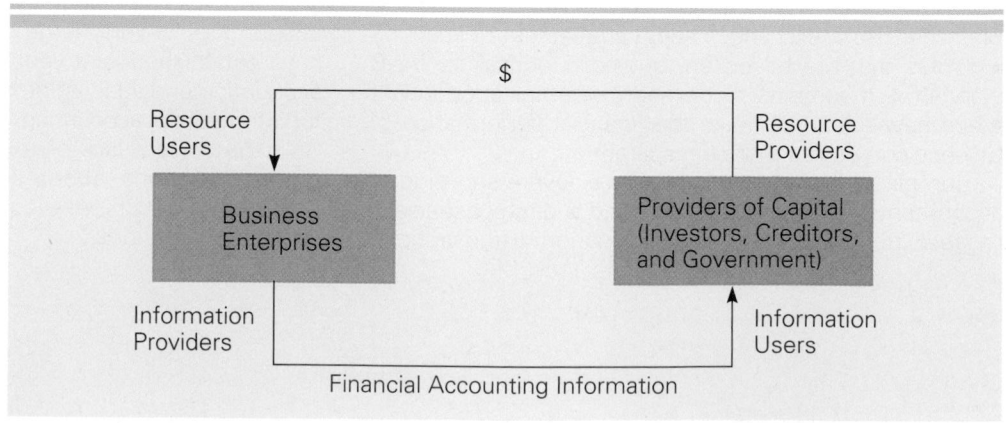

An example of differences in accounting conventions concerns employee disclosures. In many European countries, government regulations require firms to publish detailed information about their training and employment policies, but there is no such requirement in the United States. Another difference is in the treatment of goodwill. A firm's goodwill is any advantage, such as a trademark or brand name (e.g., the Coca-Cola brand name), that enables a firm to earn higher profits than its competitors. When one company acquires another in a takeover, the value of the goodwill is calculated as the amount paid for a firm above its book value, which is often substantial. Under accounting rules that have prevailed in many countries, acquiring firms have been allowed to deduct the value of goodwill from the amount of equity or net worth reported on their balance sheet. In the United States, until recently goodwill has had to be deducted from the profits of the acquiring firm over as much as 40 years. If two equally profitable firms, one German and one American, acquired comparable firms that had identical goodwill, the U.S. firm would have reported a much lower profit than the German firm because of differences in accounting conventions regarding goodwill.[4] (Interestingly, in 2001 the U.S. changed the way it treated goodwill, no longer requiring that goodwill associated with acquisitions had to be amortized against earnings. This change brought the United States more into line with emerging international standards, although some important differences in the treatment of goodwill still remain.)[5]

Despite attempts to harmonize standards by developing internationally acceptable accounting conventions (more on this later), differences between national accounting systems still remain. A study tried to quantify the extent of these differences by comparing various accounting measures and profitability ratios across 22 developed nations, including Australia, Britain, France, Germany, Hong Kong, Japan, Spain, and South Korea.[6] The study found that among the 22 countries, there were 76 differences in the way cost of goods sold was assessed, 65 differences in the assessment of return on assets, 54 differences in the measurement of research and development expenses as a percentage of sales, and 20 differences in the calculation of net profit margin. These differences make it very difficult to compare the financial performance of firms based in different nation-states.

Although many factors can influence the development of a country's accounting system, there appear to be five main variables:[7]

1. The relationship between business and the providers of capital.
2. Political and economic ties with other countries.
3. The level of inflation.
4. The level of a country's economic development.
5. The prevailing culture in a country.

Figure 19.2 illustrates these variables. We will review each in turn.

RELATIONSHIP BETWEEN BUSINESS AND PROVIDERS OF CAPITAL

The three main external sources of capital for business enterprises are individual investors, banks, and government. In most advanced countries, all three sources are important. In the United States, for example, business firms can raise capital by selling shares and bonds to individual investors through the stock market and the bond market. They can also borrow capital from banks and, in rather limited cases (particularly to support investments in defense-related R&D), from the government. The importance of each source of capital varies from country to country. In some countries, such as the United States, individual investors are the major source of capital; in others, banks play a greater role; in still others, the government is the major provider of capital. A country's accounting system tends to reflect the relative importance of these three constituencies as providers of capital.

FIGURE 19.2

Determinants of
National Accounting
Standards

Consider the case of the United States and Great Britain. Both have well-developed stock and bond markets in which firms can raise capital by selling stocks and bonds to individual investors. Most individual investors purchase only a very small proportion of a firm's total outstanding stocks or bonds. As such, they have no desire to be involved in the day-to-day management of the firms in which they invest; they leave that task to professional managers. But because of their lack of contact with the management of the firms in which they invest, individual investors may not have the information required to assess how well the companies are performing. Because of their small stake in firms, individual investors generally lack the ability to get information on demand from management. The financial accounting system in both Great Britain and the United States evolved to cope with this problem. In both countries, the financial accounting system is oriented toward providing individual investors with the information they need to make decisions about purchasing or selling corporate stocks and bonds.

In countries such as Switzerland, Germany, and Japan, historically a few large banks satisfied most of the capital needs of business enterprises. Individual investors have until recently played a relatively minor role. In these countries, the role of the banks has been so important that a bank's officers often have seats on the boards of firms to which it lends capital. In such circumstances, the information needs of the capital providers are satisfied in a relatively straightforward way—through personal contacts, direct visits, and information provided at board meetings. Consequently, although firms do prepare financial reports because government regulations in these countries mandate some public disclosure of a firm's financial position, the reports have historically tended to contain less information than those of British or U.S. firms. Because banks are the major providers of capital, financial accounting practices are oriented toward protecting a bank's investment. Thus, assets are valued conservatively and liabilities are overvalued (in contrast to U.S. practice) to provide a cushion for the bank in the event of default.

In still other countries, the national government has historically been an important provider of capital, which has influenced accounting practices. This is the case in France and Sweden, where the national government has often stepped in to make loans or to invest in firms whose activities are deemed in the "national interest." In these countries, financial accounting practices tend to be oriented toward the needs of government planners.

POLITICAL AND ECONOMIC TIES WITH OTHER COUNTRIES

Similarities in the accounting systems of countries are sometimes due to the countries' close political and/or economic ties. For example, the U.S. system has influenced accounting practices in Canada and Mexico, and since passage of NAFTA, the accounting systems in these three countries seem set to converge on a common set of norms. U.S.-style accounting systems are also used in the Philippines, which was once a U.S. protectorate. Another significant force in accounting worldwide has been the British system. The vast majority of former colonies of the British Empire have accounting practices modeled after Great Britain's. Similarly, the European Union has been attempting to harmonize accounting practices in its member countries. The accounting systems of EU members such as Great Britain, Germany, and France have been quite different, but under EU rules, they are now in the process of converging on International Accounting Standards norms.

INFLATION ACCOUNTING

In many countries, including Germany, Japan, and the United States, accounting has been based on the **historic cost principle.** This principle assumes the currency unit used to report financial results is not losing its value due to inflation. Firms record sales, purchases, and the like at the original transaction price and make no adjustments in the amounts later. The historic cost principle affects accounting most significantly in the area of asset valuation. If inflation is high, the historic cost principle underestimates a firm's assets, so the depreciation charges based on these underestimates can be inadequate for replacing assets when they wear out or become obsolete.

The appropriateness of this principle varies inversely with the level of inflation in a country. The high level of price inflation in many industrialized countries during the 1970s and 1980s created a need for accounting methods that adjust for inflation. A number of industrialized countries adopted new practices. Great Britain adopted one of the most far-reaching approaches in 1980. Called current cost accounting, it adjusts all items in a financial statement—assets, liabilities, costs, and revenues—to factor out the effects of inflation. The method uses a general price index to convert historic figures into current values. The standard was not made compulsory, however, and once Great Britain's inflation rate fell in the 1980s, most firms stopped providing the data.

LEVEL OF DEVELOPMENT

Developed nations tend to have large, complex organizations, whose accounting problems are far more difficult than those of small organizations. Developed nations also tend to have sophisticated capital markets in which business organizations raise funds from investors and banks. These providers of capital require that the organizations they invest in and lend to provide comprehensive reports of their financial activities. The workforces of developed nations tend to be highly educated and skilled and can perform complex accounting functions. For all these reasons, accounting in developed countries tends to be far more sophisticated than it is in less-developed countries, where the accounting standards may be fairly primitive. In much of the developing world, the accounting system was inherited from former colonial powers. Many African nations, for example, have accounting practices based on either the British or French models, depending on which was the former colonial power. These models may not apply very well to small businesses in a poorly developed economy. Another problem in many of the world's poorer countries is a simple lack of trained accountants.[8]

CULTURE

A number of academic accountants have argued that the culture of a country has an important impact upon the nature of its accounting system.[9] Using the cultural typologies developed by Hofstede,[10] which we reviewed in Chapter 3, researchers have found that the extent to which a culture is characterized by uncertainty avoidance seems to have an impact on accounting systems.[11] **Uncertainty avoidance** refers to the extent to which cultures socialize their members to accept ambiguous situations and tolerate uncertainty. Members of high uncertainty avoidance cultures place a premium on job security, career patterns, retirement benefits, and so on. They also have a strong need for rules and regulations; the manager is expected to issue clear instructions, and subordinates' initiatives are tightly controlled. Lower uncertainty avoidance cultures are characterized by a greater readiness to take risks and less emotional resistance to change. According to Hofstede, countries such as Britain, the United States, and Sweden are characterized by low uncertainty avoidance, while countries such as Japan, Mexico, and Greece have higher uncertainty avoidance. Research suggests that countries with low uncertainty avoidance cultures tend to have strong independent auditing professions that audit a firm's accounts to make sure they comply with generally accepted accounting regulations.[12]

National and International Standards

The diverse accounting practices discussed in the previous section have been enshrined in national accounting and auditing standards. **Accounting standards** are rules for preparing financial statements; they define what is useful accounting information. **Auditing standards** specify the rules for performing an audit—the technical process by which an independent person (the auditor) gathers evidence for determining if financial accounts conform to required accounting standards and if they are also reliable.

LACK OF COMPARABILITY

Historically, the result of national differences in accounting and auditing standards has been a general lack of comparability of financial reports from one country to another (something that is now in the process of changing). For example, until recently, the following has been true:

- Dutch standards favored the use of current values for replacement assets; Japanese law generally prohibited revaluation and prescribes historic cost.
- Capitalization of financial leases was required practice in Great Britain, but not practiced in France.
- Research and development costs must be written off in the year they are incurred in the United States, but in Spain they could be deferred as an asset and need not be amortized as long as benefits that will cover them are expected to arise in the future.
- German accountants have treated depreciation as a liability, whereas British companies have deducted it from assets.

Such differences would not matter much if there was little need for a firm headquartered in one country to report its financial results to citizens of another country. However, one striking development of the past two decades has been the development of global capital markets. We have seen the growth of both transnational financing and transnational investment.

Transnational financing occurs when a firm based in one country enters another country's capital market to raise capital from the sale of stocks or bonds. A German firm raising capital by selling stock through the London Stock Exchange is an example of transnational financing. In point of fact, over the last decade large firms have been increasing their use of transnational financing by gaining listings, and ultimately issuing stock, on foreign stock exchanges, and particularly the New York and London stock exchanges (we shall discuss this practice in more depth in the next chapters).

Transnational investment occurs when an investor based in one country enters the capital market of another nation to invest in the stocks or bonds of a firm based in that country. An investor based in Great Britain buying General Motors stock through the New York Stock Exchange would be an example of transnational investment. As with transnational financing, transnational investment has been on the rise in recent years (see the next chapter).

The rapid expansion of transnational financing and investment in recent years has been accompanied by a corresponding growth in transnational financial reporting. For example, in addition to its Danish financial reports, the Danish firm raising capital in London must issue financial reports that serve the needs of its British investors. Similarly, the U.S. firm with a large number of Japanese investors might wish to issue reports that serve the needs of those investors. However, the lack of comparability between accounting standards in different nations can lead to confusion. For example, the German firm that issues two sets of financial reports, one set prepared under German standards and the other under U.S. standards, may find that its financial position looks significantly different in the two reports, and its investors may have difficulty identifying the firm's true worth. Some examples of the confusion that can arise from this lack of comparability appear in the accompanying Management Focus.

In addition to the problems this lack of comparability gives investors, it can give the firm major headaches. The firm has to explain to its investors why its financial position looks so different in the two accountings. Also, an international business may find it difficult to assess the financial positions of important foreign customers, suppliers, and competitors.

INTERNATIONAL STANDARDS

Substantial efforts have been made in recent years to harmonize accounting standards across countries.[14] The rise of global capital markets during the last two decades has added some urgency to this endeavor. Today, many companies raise money from providers of capital outside of their national borders. Those providers are demanding consistency in the way in which financial results are reported so they can make more informed investment decisions. Moreover, the realization has grown that adoption of common accounting standards will facilitate the development of global capital markets, since more investors will be willing to invest across borders, and the end result will be to lower the cost of capital and stimulate economic growth. Thus it is increasingly accepted that the standardization of accounting practices across national borders is in the best interests of all participants in the world economy.

The International Accounting Standards Board (IASB) has emerged as a major proponent of standardization. The IASB was formed in March 2001 to replace the International Accounting Standards Committee (IASC), which had been established in 1973. The IASB has 14 members who are responsible for the formulation of new international financial reporting standards. By 2006 the IASB and its predecessor, the IASC, had issued around 45 international accounting standards.[15] To issue a new standard, 75 percent of the 14 members of the board must agree. It can be difficult to get three-quarters agreement, particularly since members come from different cultures and legal systems. To get around this problem, most IASB statements provide two acceptable alternatives. As Arthur Wyatt, former chairman of the IASB, once said, "It's not much of a standard if you have two alternatives, but it's better than having six. If you can get agreement on two alternatives, you can capture the 11 required votes and eliminate some of the less used practices."[16]

The Consequences of Different Accounting Standards

In 1999, two major drug firms, Zeneca and Astra, merged to form AstraZeneca. Based in the UK, in 2000 the profit of AstraZeneca was $865 million under U.S. accounting rules, but $3,318 million under British accounting rules. The largest difference between the two sets of accounts was $1,756 million, which related to amortization and other acquisition-related costs. Under rules then prevailing in the United States, the combination of Astra and Zeneca was treated as an acquisition, which required goodwill to be recognized with consequent amortization. Under British rules, any amortization was avoided as the combination was treated as a merger and so no goodwill arose.

U.S.-based SmithKline Beckman (SKB) merged with the British company Beecham Group in 1989. After the merger, SKB had quotations on both the London and New York stock exchanges, so it had to prepare financial reports in accordance with both U.S. and British standards. SKB's postmerger earnings, properly prepared in accordance with British accounting standards, were £130 million—quite a bit more than the £87 million reported in SKB's statement prepared in accordance with U.S. accounting standards. The difference resulted primarily from treating the merger as a pooling of assets for British purposes and as a purchase of assets for U.S. purposes. Even more confusing, the differences resulted in a shareholders' equity of £3.5 billion in the United States, but a negative £300 million in Great Britain! Not surprisingly, after these figures were released, SKB's stock traded 17 percent lower on the London Stock Exchange than on the New York Stock Exchange.

In the mid-1980s, Telefonica, Spain's largest industrial company, was the first company in the world to float a multicountry stock offering simultaneously. In 1990, it reported net income under U.S. accounting standards of 176 billion pesetas, more than twice the 76 billion pesetas it reported under Spanish accounting standards. The difference was mainly due to an "add-back" of the incremental depreciation on assets carried at historic cost in the United States but reflecting more recent market value in the Spanish report. The effect of this difference on shareholders' equity was in the opposite direction; the equity reported in the U.S. accounts was 15 percent less than the equity reported in the Spanish accounts.

In 2000, British Airways reported a loss under British accounting rules of £21 million, but under U.S. rules, its loss was £412 million. Most of the difference could be attributed to adjustments for a number of relatively small items such as depreciation and amortization, pensions, and deferred taxation. The largest adjustment was due to a reduction in revenue reported in the U.S. accounts of £136 million. This reduced revenue was related to frequent flyer miles, which under U.S. rules have to be deferred until the miles are redeemed. Apparently, this is not the case under British rules.

A final example is more hypothetical in nature, but just as revealing. Two college professors set up a computer model to evaluate the reported net profits of an imaginary company with gross operating profits of $1.5 million. This imaginary company operated in three different countries—the United States, Britain, and Australia. The professors found that holding all else equal (such as national differences in interest rates on the firm's debt), when different accounting standards were applied the firm made a net profit of $34,600 in the United States, $260,600 in Britain, and $240,600 in Australia.[13]

Another hindrance to the development of international accounting standards is that compliance is voluntary; the IASB has no power to enforce its standards. Even so, support for the IASB and recognition of its standards has been growing. Increasingly, the IASB is regarded as an effective voice for defining acceptable worldwide accounting principles. Japan, for example, began requiring financial statements to be prepared on a consolidated basis after the IASB issued its initial standards on the topic, and in 2004 Japanese accounting authorities started working closely with the IASB to harmonize standards. Russia and China have also stated their intention to adopt emerging international standards (see the opening case). Indeed, by early 2007 more than

100 nations had either adopted the IASB standards or permitted their use to report financial results.

To date, the impact of the IASB standards has probably been least noticeable in the United States because most of the IASB standards have been consistent with opinions already articulated by the U.S. Financial Accounting Standards Board (FASB). The FASB writes the generally accepted accounting principles (GAAP) by which the financial statements of U.S. firms must be prepared. Nevertheless, differences between IASB and FASB standards remain, although the IASB and FASB have a goal of convergence by 2008. Moreover, in April 2007 the U.S. Securities and Exchange Commission stated that it was considering whether to allow U.S. public companies to use IASB standards, rather than GAAP, to report their results, a move that some believe could ultimately spell the end of U.S. GAAP.[17]

Another body that is having a substantial influence on the harmonization of accounting standards is the European Union (EU). In accordance with its plans for closer economic and political union, the EU has mandated harmonization of the accounting principles of its member countries. The EU does this by issuing directives that the member states are obligated to incorporate into their own national laws. Because EU directives have the power of law, we might assume the EU has a better chance of achieving harmonization than the IASB does. The EU has required that from January 1, 2005, onward, financial accounts issued by some 7,000 publicly listed companies in the EU were to be in accordance with IASB standards. The Europeans hope that this requirement, by making it easier to compare the financial position of companies from different EU member states, will facilitate the development of a pan-European capital market and ultimately lower the cost of capital for EU firms.

Given the harmonization in the EU, and given that countries like Japan, China, and Russia may follow suit, as they have signaled that they will, by late 2010 there could be only two major accounting bodies with dominant influence on global reporting: FASB in the United States and IASB elsewhere. Moreover, under an agreement reached in 2002, these two bodies are trying to align their standards by 2008, suggesting that over time differences in accounting standards across countries may well disappear.

In a move that indicates the trend toward adoption of acceptable international accounting standards is accelerating, the IASB has developed accounting standards for firms seeking stock listings in global markets. Also, the FASB has joined forces with accounting standard setters in Canada, Mexico, and Chile to explore areas in which the four countries can harmonize their accounting standards (Canada, Mexico, and the United States are members of NAFTA, and Chile may join in the near future). The Securities and Exchange Commission has also dropped many of its objections to international standards, which could accelerate their adoption. A taste of what is to come if increasing numbers of international firms jump on the bandwagon and adopt IASB principles can be found in the accompanying Management Focus, which details the impact of adopting these standards on Ciba, the Swiss pharmaceuticals and chemicals group.

Multinational Consolidation and Currency Translation

A consolidated financial statement combines the separate financial statements of two or more companies to yield a single set of financial statements as if the individual companies were really one. Most multinational firms are composed of a parent company and a number of subsidiary companies located in various other countries. Such firms typically issue consolidated financial statements, which merge the accounts of all the companies, rather than issuing individual financial statements for the parent company and each subsidiary. In this section we examine the consolidated financial statements and then look at the related issue of foreign currency translation.

MANAGEMENT FOCUS

Novartis Joins the International Accounting Club

Switzerland does not have a history of very detailed accounting rules. As a result, published financial statements by major Swiss firms such as Novartis, Roche Group, and Nestlé often obscured as much as they revealed. The standard set of accounts from a Swiss firm was viewed as being very unusual and difficult for international investors to understand and described as being more like a statistical summary than the result of an integrated accounting system.

Swiss firms began to move toward adoption of IASC accounting principles in the 1990s. The catalyst was increasing interest by foreign investors in the stock of major Swiss corporations. By the early 1990s, foreign investors owned up to 40 percent of the stock of many of these firms. As a group these investors were demanding more detailed financial statements that were comparable to those issued by other multinational enterprises.

One of the first firms to respond to these pressures was Ciba, Switzerland's largest pharmaceuticals and chemicals firm and a major multinational enterprise with operations around the globe (Ciba subsequently became Novartis after it merged with another Swiss pharmaceutical company, Sandoz, in 1998). In 1993, the company announced that its 1994 financial statements would be in accordance with IASC guidelines. At the same time, it restated its 1992 results in line with IASC guidelines. The effect was to increase post-tax profits by 18 percent while raising inventories, cash, and marketable securities. Ciba's decision was motivated by a desire to appease foreign stockholders, who in 1994 held over one-third of Ciba's stock, and to position itself for the possibility of listings on the London and New York stock markets.

Ciba also decided to use the same international standards for internal financial reporting. Ciba set up a small international team to develop and implement its new system. While there were some preliminary problems in development of the system, including a figure on the insurance value of fixed assets that was off by $690 million, the new system is now running smoothly and seems to have produced several major benefits.

Ciba discovered large savings as a result of the change, including tighter cash management, more efficient capital investment, a different approach to acquisitions, and more rigid asset management, which has reportedly reduced the value of inventories by 6 percent. The new system also enabled Ciba to benchmark its performance for the first time against its global competitors.

One big difference between the new and old systems was the move from the arguably more informative current cost accounting method, which Ciba has used for over 25 years and which regularly updates asset values to account for inflation, to historic cost accounting under international standards. However, Ciba's management admits this drawback is not serious given the low inflation rate in Switzerland and the offsetting gains produced by the switch to a new system.

In 2000, Novartis decided that it needed to become more aggressive about attracting U.S. investors. Although Novartis already listed its shares as American Depositary Receipts (ADRs) on the American Stock Exchange, it decided to switch the listing to the more visible New York Stock Exchange and to double the amount of ADRs offered. Accompanying this shift, Novartis also decided that in addition to presenting its rules based on IASC principles, it needed to adopt full U.S. accounting principles. Novartis published its first complete set of U.S. accounts in 2002.[18]

CONSOLIDATED FINANCIAL STATEMENTS

Many firms find it advantageous to organize as a set of separate legal entities (companies). For example, a firm may separately incorporate the various components of its business to limit its total legal liability or to take advantage of corporate tax regulations. Multinationals are often required by the countries in which they do business to set up a separate company. Thus, the typical multinational comprises a parent company and a number of subsidiary companies located in different countries, most of which are wholly owned by the parent. However, although the subsidiaries may be separate legal entities, they are not separate economic entities. Economically, all the companies in a corporate group are interdependent. For example, if the Brazilian subsidiary of a U.S. parent company experiences substantial financial losses that suck up corporate funds, the cash available for investment in that subsidiary, the U.S. parent company, and other subsidiary companies will be limited. Thus, the purpose of consolidated financial statements is to provide accounting information about a group of companies that recognize their economic interdependence.

Transactions among the members of a corporate family are not included in consolidated financial statements; only assets, liabilities, revenues, and expenses with external third parties are shown. By law, however, separate legal entities are required to keep their own accounting records and to prepare their own financial statements. Thus, transactions with other members of a corporate group must be identified in the separate statements so they can be excluded when the consolidated statements are prepared. The process involves adding up the individual assets, liabilities, revenues, and expenses reported on the separate financial statements and then eliminating the intragroup ones. For example, consider these items selected from the individual financial statements of a parent company and one of its foreign subsidiaries:

	Parent	Foreign Subsidiary
Cash	1,000	250
Receivables	3,000*	900
Payables	300	500*
Revenues	7,000†	5,000
Expenses	2,000	3,000†

Notes: *Subsidiary owes parent $300.

†Subsidiary pays parent $1,000 in royalties for products licensed from parent.

The $300 receivable that the parent includes on its financial statements and the $300 payable that the subsidiary includes on its statements represent an intragroup item. These items cancel each other out and thus are not included in consolidated financial statements. Similarly, the $1,000 the subsidiary owes the parent in royalty payments is an intragroup item that will not appear in the consolidated accounts. The adjustments are as follows:

			Eliminations		
	Parent	**Subsidiary**	**Debit**	**Credit**	**Consolidated**
Cash	$1,000	$250			$1,250
Receivables	3,000*	900		$ 300	3,600
Payables	300	500*	$ 300		500
Revenues	7,000†	5,000		1,000	11,000
Expenses	2,000	3,000†	1,000		4,000

Notes: *Subsidiary owes parent $300.

†Subsidiary pays parent $1,000 in royalties for products licensed from parent.

Thus, while simply adding the two sets of accounts would suggest that the group of companies has revenues of $12,000 and receivables of $3,900, once intragroup transactions are removed from the picture, these figures drop to $11,000 and $3,600, respectively.

Preparing consolidated financial statements is becoming the norm for multinational firms. Investors realize that without consolidated financial statements, a multinational firm could conceal losses in an unconsolidated subsidiary, thereby hiding the economic status of the entire group. For example, the parent company in our illustration could increase its profit merely by charging the subsidiary company higher royalty fees. Since this has no effect on the group's overall profits, it amounts to little more than window dressing, making the parent company look good. If the parent does not issue a consolidated financial statement, however, the true economic status of the group is obscured by such a practice. With this in mind, the IASB has issued two standards requiring firms to prepare consolidated financial statements, and in most industrialized countries this is now required.

CURRENCY TRANSLATION

Foreign subsidiaries of multinational firms normally keep their accounting records and prepare their financial statements in the currency of the country in which they are located. Thus, the Japanese subsidiary of a U.S. firm will prepare its accounts in yen, a Brazilian subsidiary in real, a Korean subsidiary in won, and so on. When a multinational prepares consolidated accounts, it must convert all these financial statements into the currency of its home country. As we saw in Chapter 10, however, exchange rates vary in response to changes in economic circumstances. Companies can use two main methods to determine what exchange rate should be used when translating financial statement currencies—the current rate method and the temporal method.

The Current Rate Method

Under the current rate method, the exchange rate at the balance sheet date is used to translate the financial statements of a foreign subsidiary into the home currency of the multinational firm. Although this may seem logical, it is incompatible with the historic cost principle, which, as we saw earlier, is a generally accepted accounting principle in many countries, including the United States. Consider the case of a U.S. firm that invests $100,000 in a Malaysian subsidiary. Assume the exchange rate at the time is $1 = 5$ Malaysian *ringgit*. The subsidiary converts the $100,000 into *ringgit*, which gives it 500,000 *ringgit*. It then purchases land with this money. Subsequently, the dollar depreciates against the *ringgit*, so that by year-end, $1 = 4$ *ringgit*. If this exchange rate is used to convert the value of the land back into U.S. dollars for preparing consolidated accounts, the land will be valued at $125,000. The piece of land would appear to have increased in value by $25,000, although in reality the increase would be simply a function of an exchange rate change. Thus, the consolidated accounts would present a somewhat misleading picture.

The Temporal Method

One way to avoid this problem is to use the temporal method to translate the accounts of a foreign subsidiary. The temporal method translates assets valued in a foreign currency into the home-country currency using the exchange rate that exists when the assets are purchased. Referring to our example, the exchange rate of $1 = 5$ *ringgit*, the rate on the day the Malaysian subsidiary purchased the land, would be used to convert the value of the land back into U.S. dollars at year-end. However, although the temporal method will ensure that the dollar value of the land does not fluctuate due to exchange rate changes, it has its own serious problem. Because the various assets of a foreign subsidiary will in all probability be acquired at different times and because exchange rates seldom remain stable for long, different exchange rates will probably have to be used to translate those foreign assets into the multinational's home currency. Consequently, the multinational's balance sheet may not balance!

Consider the case of a U.S. firm that on January 1, 2005, invests $100,000 in a new Japanese subsidiary. The exchange rate at that time is $1 = ¥100. The initial investment is therefore ¥10 million, and the Japanese subsidiary's balance sheet looks like this on January 1, 2005:

	Yen	Exchange Rate	U.S. Dollars
Cash	10,000,000	($1 = ¥100)	100,000
Owners' equity	10,000,000	($1 = ¥100)	100,000

Assume that on January 31, when the exchange rate is $1 = ¥95, the Japanese subsidiary invests ¥5 million in a factory (i.e., fixed assets). Then on February 15, when the exchange rate is $1 = ¥90, the subsidiary purchases ¥5 million of inventory. The balance sheet of the subsidiary will look like this on March 1, 2005:

	Yen	Exchange Rate	U.S. Dollars
Fixed assets	5,000,000	($1 = ¥95)	52,632
Inventory	5,000,000	($1 = ¥90)	55,556
Total	10,000,000		108,187
Owners' equity	10,000,000	($1 = ¥100)	100,000

Although the balance sheet balances in yen, it does not balance when the temporal method is used to translate the yen-denominated balance sheet figures back into dollars. In translation, the balance sheet debits exceed the credits by $8,187. The accounting profession has yet to adopt a satisfactory solution to the gap between debits and credits. The practice currently used in the United States is explained next.

CURRENT U.S. PRACTICE

U.S.-based multinational firms must follow the requirements of Statement 52, "Foreign Currency Translation," issued by the Financial Accounting Standards Board in 1981.[19] Under Statement 52, a foreign subsidiary is classified either as a self-sustaining, autonomous subsidiary or as integral to the activities of the parent company.[20] (A link can be made here with the material on strategy discussed in Chapter 12. Firms pursuing localization and international strategies are most likely to have self-sustaining subsidiaries, whereas firms pursuing global and transnational strategies are most likely to have integral subsidiaries.) According to Statement 52, the local currency of a self-sustaining foreign subsidiary is to be its functional currency. The balance sheet for such subsidiaries is translated into the home currency using the exchange rate in effect at the end of the firm's financial year, whereas the income statement is translated using the average exchange rate for the firm's financial year. But the functional currency of an integral subsidiary is to be U.S. dollars. The financial statements of such subsidiaries are translated at various historic rates using the temporal method (as we did in the example), and the dangling debit or credit increases or decreases consolidated earnings for the period.

Accounting Aspects of Control Systems

Corporate headquarters' role is to control subunits within the organization to ensure they achieve the best possible performance. In the typical firm, the control process is annual and involves three main steps:

1. Head office and subunit management jointly determine subunit goals for the coming year.

2. Throughout the year, the head office monitors subunit performance against the agreed goals.

3. If a subunit fails to achieve its goals, the head office intervenes in the subunit to learn why the shortfall occurred, taking corrective action when appropriate.

The accounting function plays a critical role in this process. Most of the goals for subunits are expressed in financial terms and are embodied in the subunit's budget for the coming year. The budget is the main instrument of financial control. The budget is typically prepared by the subunit, but it must be approved by headquarters management. During the approval process, headquarters and subunit managements debate the goals that should be incorporated in the budget. One function of headquarters management is to ensure a subunit's budget contains challenging but realistic performance goals. Once headquarters and the subunit agree on a budget, accounting information systems are used to collect data throughout the year so the subunit's performance can be evaluated against the goals contained in its budget.

In most international businesses, many of the firm's subunits are foreign subsidiaries. The performance goals for the coming year are thus set by negotiation between corporate management and the managers of foreign subsidiaries. According to one survey of control practices within multinational enterprises, the most important criterion for evaluating the performance of a foreign subsidiary is the subsidiary's actual profits compared to budgeted profits.[21] This is closely followed by a subsidiary's actual sales compared to budgeted sales and its return on investment. The same criteria were also useful in evaluating the performance of the subsidiary managers. We will discuss this point later in this section. First, however, we will examine two factors that can complicate the control process in an international business: exchange rate changes and transfer pricing practices.

EXCHANGE RATE CHANGES AND CONTROL SYSTEMS

Most international businesses require all budgets and performance data within the firm to be expressed in the "corporate currency," which is normally the home currency. Thus, the Malaysian subsidiary of a U.S. multinational would probably submit a budget prepared in U.S. dollars, rather than Malaysian *ringgit*, and performance data throughout the year would be reported to headquarters in U.S. dollars. This facilitates comparisons between subsidiaries in different countries, and it makes things easier for headquarters management. However, it also allows exchange rate changes during the year to introduce substantial distortions. For example, the Malaysian subsidiary may fail to achieve profit goals not because of any performance problems, but merely because of a decline in the value of the *ringgit* against the dollar. The opposite can occur, also, making a foreign subsidiary's performance look better than it actually is.

The Lessard–Lorange Model

According to research by Donald Lessard and Peter Lorange, a number of methods are available to international businesses for dealing with this problem.[22] Lessard and Lorange point out three exchange rates that can be used to translate foreign currencies

FIGURE 19.3

Possible Combinations
of Exchange Rates in
the Control Process

**Rate Used to Translate Actual Performance
for Comparison with Budget**

		Initial (I)	Projected (P)	Ending (E)
Rate Used for Translating Budget	Initial (I)	(II) Budget at Initial Actual at Initial	(IE) Budget at Initial Actual at Projected	(IE) Budget at Initial Actual at Ending
	Projected (P)	Budget at Projected Actual at Initial	(PP) Budget at Projected Actual at Projected	(PE) Budget at Projected Actual at Ending
	Ending (E)	Budget at Ending Actual at Initial	Budget at Ending Actual at Projected	(EE) Budget at Ending Actual at Ending

into the corporate currency in setting budgets and in the subsequent tracking of performance:

- The initial rate, the spot exchange rate when the budget is adopted.
- The projected rate, the spot exchange rate forecast for the end of the budget period (i.e., the forward rate).
- The ending rate, the spot exchange rate when the budget and performance are being compared.

These three exchange rates imply nine possible combinations (see Figure 19.3). Lessard and Lorange ruled out four of the nine combinations as illogical and unreasonable; they are shaded brown in Figure 19.3. For example, it would make no sense to use the ending rate to translate the budget and the initial rate to translate actual performance data. Any of the remaining five combinations might be used for setting budgets and evaluating performance.

With three of these five combinations—II, PP, and EE—the same exchange rate is used for translating both budget figures and performance figures into the corporate currency. All three combinations have the advantage that a change in the exchange rate during the year does not distort the control process. This is not true for the other two combinations, IE and PE. In those cases, exchange rate changes can introduce distortions. The potential for distortion is greater with IE; the ending spot exchange rate used to evaluate performance against the budget may be quite different from the initial spot exchange rate used to translate the budget. The distortion is less serious in the case of PE because the projected exchange rate takes into account future exchange rate movements.

Of the five combinations, Lessard and Lorange recommend that firms use the projected spot exchange rate to translate both the budget and performance figures into the corporate currency, combination PP. The projected rate in such cases will typically be the forward exchange rate as determined by the foreign exchange market (see Chapter 10 for the definition of forward rate) or some company-generated forecast of future spot rates, which Lessard and Lorange refer to as the **internal forward rate.** The internal forward rate may differ from the forward rate quoted by the foreign exchange market if the firm wishes to bias its business in favor of, or against, the particular foreign currency.

TRANSFER PRICING AND CONTROL SYSTEMS

In Chapter 12 we reviewed the various strategies that international businesses pursue. Two of these strategies, the global strategy and the transnational strategy, give rise to a globally dispersed web of productive activities. Firms pursuing these strategies disperse each value creation activity to its optimal location in the world. Thus, a product might be designed in one country, some of its components might be manufactured in a second country, other components might be manufactured in a third country, all might be assembled in a fourth country, and then the product could be sold worldwide.

The volume of intrafirm transactions in such firms is very high. The firms are continually shipping component parts and finished goods between subsidiaries in different countries. This poses a very important question: How should goods and services transferred between subsidiary companies in a multinational firm be priced? The price at which such goods and services are transferred is referred to as the transfer price.

The choice of transfer price can critically affect the performance of two subsidiaries that exchange goods or services. Consider this example: A French manufacturing subsidiary of a U.S. multinational imports a major component from Brazil. It incorporates this part into a product that it sells in France for the equivalent of $230 per unit. The product costs $200 to manufacture, of which $100 goes to the Brazilian subsidiary to pay for the component part. The remaining $100 covers costs incurred in France. Thus, the French subsidiary earns $30 profit per unit.

	Before Change in Transfer Price	After 20 Percent Increase in Transfer Price
Revenues per unit	$230	$230
Cost of component per unit	100	120
Other costs per unit	100	100
Profit per unit	$ 30	$ 10

Look at what happens if corporate headquarters decides to increase transfer prices by 20 percent ($20 per unit). The French subsidiary's profits will fall by two-thirds from $30 per unit to $10 per unit. Thus, the performance of the French subsidiary depends on the transfer price for the component part imported from Brazil, and corporate headquarters controls the transfer price. When setting budgets and reviewing a subsidiary's performance, corporate headquarters must keep in mind the distorting effect of transfer prices.

How should transfer prices be determined? We discuss this issue in detail in the next chapter. International businesses often manipulate transfer prices to minimize their worldwide tax liability, minimize import duties, and avoid government restrictions on capital flows. For now, however, it is enough to note that the transfer price must be considered when setting budgets and evaluating a subsidiary's performance.

SEPARATION OF SUBSIDIARY AND MANAGER PERFORMANCE

In many international businesses, the same quantitative criteria are used to assess the performance of both a foreign subsidiary and its managers. Many accountants, however, argue that although it is legitimate to compare subsidiaries against each other on the basis of return on investment (ROI) or other indicators of profitability, it may not be appropriate to use these for comparing and evaluating the managers of different subsidiaries. Foreign subsidiaries do not operate in uniform environments; their environments have widely different economic, political, and social conditions, all of which influence the costs of doing business in a country and hence the subsidiaries' profitability. Thus, the manager of a subsidiary in an adverse environment that has an ROI of 5 percent may be doing a better job than the manager of a subsidiary in a benign environment that has an ROI of 20 percent. Although the firm might want to pull out of a country where its ROI is only 5 percent, it may also want to recognize the manager's achievement.

Accordingly, it has been suggested that the evaluation of a subsidiary should be kept separate from the evaluation of its manager.[23] The manager's evaluation should consider how hostile or benign the country's environment is for that business. Further, managers should be evaluated in local currency terms after making allowances for those items over which they have no control (e.g., interest rates, tax rates, inflation rates, transfer prices, exchange rates).

CHAPTER SUMMARY

This chapter focused on financial accounting within the multinational firm. We explained why accounting practices and standards differ from country to country and surveyed the efforts under way to harmonize countries' accounting practices. We discussed the rationale behind consolidated accounts and looked at currency translation. We reviewed several issues related to the use of accounting-based control systems within international businesses. This chapter made the following points:

1. Accounting is the language of business: the means by which firms communicate their financial position to the providers of capital and to governments (for tax purposes). It is also the means by which firms evaluate their own performance, control their expenditures, and plan for the future.

2. Accounting is shaped by the environment in which it operates. Each country's accounting system has evolved in response to the local demands for accounting information.

3. Five main factors seem to influence the type of accounting system a country has: (a) the relationship between business and the providers of capital, (b) political and economic ties with other countries, (c) the level of inflation, (d) the level of a country's development, and (e) the prevailing culture in a country.

4. National differences in accounting and auditing standards have historically resulted in a general lack of comparability in countries' financial reports.

5. This lack of comparability has become a problem as transnational financing and transnational investment have grown rapidly in recent decades (a consequence of the globalization of capital markets). Due to the lack of comparability, a firm may have to explain to investors why its financial position looks very different on financial reports that are based on different accounting practices.

6. The most significant push for harmonization of accounting standards across countries has come from the International Accounting Standards Committee (IASC) and its successor, the International Accounting Standards Board (IASB).

7. Consolidated financial statements provide financial accounting information about a group of companies that recognizes the companies' economic interdependence.

8. Transactions among the members of a corporate family are not included on consolidated financial statements; only assets, liabilities, revenues, and expenses generated with external third parties are shown.

9. Foreign subsidiaries of a multinational firm normally keep their accounting records and prepare their financial statements in the currency of the country in which they are

located. When the multinational prepares its consolidated accounts, these financial statements must be translated into the currency of its home country.

10. Under the current rate translation method, the exchange rate at the balance sheet date is used to translate the financial statements of a foreign subsidiary into the home currency. This has the drawback of being incompatible with the historic cost principle.

11. Under the temporal method, assets valued in a foreign currency are translated into the home currency using the exchange rate that existed when the assets were purchased. A problem with this approach is that the multinational's balance sheet may not balance.

12. In most international businesses, the annual budget is the main instrument by which headquarters controls foreign subsidiaries. Throughout the year, headquarters compares a subsidiary's performance against the financial goals incorporated in its budget, intervening selectively in its operations when shortfalls occur.

13. Most international businesses require all budgets and performance data within the firm to be expressed in the corporate currency. This enhances comparability, but it distorts the control process if the relevant exchange rates change between the time a foreign subsidiary's budget is set and the time its performance is evaluated.

14. According to the Lessard–Lorange model, the best way to deal with this problem is to use a projected spot exchange rate to translate both budget figures and performance figures into the corporate currency.

15. Transfer prices also can introduce significant distortions into the control process and thus must be considered when setting budgets and evaluating a subsidiary's performance.

16. Foreign subsidiaries do not operate in uniform environments, and some environments are much tougher than others. Accordingly, it has been suggested that the evaluation of a subsidiary should be kept separate from the evaluation of the subsidiary manager.

Critical Thinking and Discussion Questions

1. Why do the accounting systems of different countries differ? Why do these differences matter?

2. Why are transactions among members of a corporate family not included in consolidated financial statements?

3. The following are selected amounts from the separate financial statements of a parent company (unconsolidated) and one of its subsidiaries

	Parent	**Subsidiary**
Cash	$ 180	$ 80
Receivables	380	200
Accounts payable	245	110
Retained earnings	790	680
Revenues	4,980	3,520
Rent income	0	200
Dividend income	250	0
Expenses	4,160	2,960

Notes:
i. Parent owes subsidiary $70.
ii. Parent owns 100 percent of subsidiary. During the year subsidiary paid parent a dividend of $250.
iii. Subsidiary owns the building that parent rents for $200.
iv. During the year parent sold some inventory to subsidiary for $2,200. It had cost parent $1,500. Subsidiary, in turn, sold the inventory to an unrelated party for $3,200.

Given this,

    a. What is the parent's (unconsolidated) net income?

    b. What is the subsidiary's net income?

    c. What is the consolidated profit on the inventory that the parent originally sold to the subsidiary?

    d. What are the amounts of consolidated cash and receivables?

4. Why might an accounting-based control system provide headquarters management with biased information about the performance of a foreign subsidiary? How can these biases best be corrected?

Research Task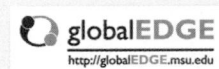

Use the globalEDGE™ site to complete the following exercises:

1. The globalEDGE™ site offers a "country comparator" tool that allows investigators to compare countries based on statistical indicators. Utilize this tool to identify in which of the following countries the historic cost principle of accounting cannot provide accurate results: Argentina, Bulgaria, Ecuador, Indonesia, Latvia, Malaysia, Mexico, Romania, Russia, and Senegal. Use the "rank countries" tool to identify other countries in which the historic cost principle would not provide valid results.

2. Deloitte hosts an International Accounting Standards (IAS) Web page called *IAS PLUS* that provides information and guidelines regarding accounting procedures approved by IASC. Locate the Web site, the section on Standards, and subsequently prepare a short description of the IAS approach for recording inventory levels.

CLOSING CASE

Adopting International Accounting Standards

Following a European Union mandate, from January 1, 2005, onward some 7,000 companies whose stock is publicly traded on European stock exchanges were required to issue all future financial accounts in a format agreed upon by the International Accounting Standards Board (IASB). In addition, some 65 countries outside of the EU have also committed to requiring that public companies issue accounts that conform to IASB rules. Even American accounting authorities, who historically have not been known for cooperating on international projects, have been trying to mesh their rules with those of the IASB.

Historically, different accounting practices made it very difficult for investors to compare the financial statements of firms based in different nations. For example, after the 1997 Asian crisis a United Nations analysis concluded that prior to the crisis two-thirds of the 73 largest East Asian banks hadn't disclosed problem loans and debt from related parties, such as loans between a parent and its subsidiary. About 85 percent of the banks didn't disclose their gains or losses from foreign currency translations or their net foreign currency exposures, and two-thirds failed to disclose the amounts they had

invested in derivatives. Had this accounting information been made available to the public—as it would have been under accounting standards prevailing at the time in many developed nations—it is possible that problems in the East Asian banking system would have come to light sooner, and the crisis that unfolded in 1997 might not have been as serious as it ultimately was.

In another example of the implications of differences in accounting standards, a Morgan Stanley research project found that country differences in the way corporate pension expenses are accounted for distorted the earnings statements of companies in the automobile industry. Most strikingly, while U.S. auto companies charged certain pension costs against earnings and funded them annually, Japanese auto companies took no charge against earnings for pension costs, and their pension obligations were largely unrecorded. By adjusting for these differences, Morgan Stanley found that the U.S. companies generally understated their earnings and had stronger balance sheets than commonly supposed, whereas Japanese companies had lower earnings and weaker balance sheets. By putting everybody on the same footing, the move toward common global accounting standards should eliminate such divergent practices, and make cross-national comparisons easier.

However, the road toward common accounting standards has some speed bumps on it. In November 2004, for example, Shell, the large oil company, announced that adopting international accounting standards would reduce the value of assets on its balance sheet by $4.9 billion. The reduction primarily came from a change in the way Shell must account for employee benefits, such as pensions. Similarly, following IASB standards, the net worth of the French cosmetics giant, L'Oreal, fell from 8.1 billion to 6.3 billion euros, primarily due to a change in the way certain classes of stock were classified. On the other hand, some companies will benefit from the shift. The UK-based mobile phone giant, Vodafone, for example, announced in early 2005 that under newly adopted IASB standards, its reported

profits for the last six months of 2004 would have been some $13 billion higher, primarily because the company would not have had to amortize goodwill associated with previous acquisitions against earnings.[24]

Case Discussion Questions

1. What are the benefits of adopting international accounting standards for (a) investors, and (b) business enterprises?

2. What are the potential risks associated with a move in a nation toward adoption of international accounting standards?

3. In which nation is the move to adoption of IASB standards likely to cause revisions in the reported financial performance of business enterprises, the United States or China? Why? (See the opening case for more details on China).

Notes

1. Sources: P. Practer, "Emerging Trends," *Accountancy*, May 2001, p. 1293; E. Yiu, "China Sees Benefits of Global Standards," *South China Morning Post*, November 20, 2004, p. 3; J. Baglole, "China's Listings Lose Steam," *The Wall Street Journal*, April 26, 2004, p. A13; "Skills Shortage a Hurdle to IAS," *The Standard*, December 2, 2003; E. McDonald, "Shanghai Surprise," *Forbes*, March 26, 2007, pp. 62–63; "Cultural Revolution: Chinese Accounting," *The Economist*, January 13, 2007, p. 63.

2. G. G. Mueller, H. Gernon, and G. Meek, *Accounting: An International Perspective* (Burr Ridge, IL: Richard D. Irwin, 1991).

3. S. J. Gary, "Towards a Theory of Cultural Influence on the Development of Accounting Systems Internationally," *Abacus* 3 (1988), pp. 1–15; and R. S. Wallace, O. Gernon, and H. Gernon, "Frameworks for International Comparative Financial Accounting," *Journal of Accounting Literature* 10 (1991), pp. 209–64.

4. K. M. Dunne and G. A. Ndubizu, "International Acquisition Accounting Method and Corporate Multinationalism," *Journal of International Business Studies* 26 (1995), pp. 361–77.

5. D. L. Holamn, "Convergence: Hurdles Remain," *Financial Executive*, November 2004, pp. 32–35.

6. W. A. Wallace and J. Walsh, "Apples to Apples: Profits Abroad," *Financial Executive*, May–June 1995, pp. 28–31.

7. Wallace, Gernon, and Gernon, "Frameworks for International Comparative Financial Accounting."

8. P. Walton, "Special Rules for a Special Case," *Financial Times*, September 18, 1997, p. 11.

9. Gary, "Towards a Theory of Cultural Influence on the Development of Accounting Systems Internationally"; and S. B. Salter and F. Niswander, "Cultural Influences on the Development of Accounting Systems Internationally," *Journal of International Business Studies* 26 (1995), pp. 379–97.

10. G. Hofstede, *Culture's Consequences: International Differences in Work Related Values* (Beverly Hills, CA: Sage Publications, 1980).

11. Salter and Niswander, "Cultural Influences on the Development of Accounting Systems Internationally."

12. Ibid.

13. Sources: S. F. O'Malley, "Accounting across Borders," *Financial Executive*, March/April 1992, pp. 28–31; L. Berton, "All Accountants May Soon Speak the Same Language," *The Wall Street Journal*, August 29, 1995, p. A15; "GAAP Reconciliations," *Company Reporting*, July 2001, pp. 3–6.

14. R. G. Barker, "Global Accounting Is Coming," *Harvard Business Review*, April 2003, pp. 2–3.

15. A current list can be accessed at www.iasb.org.uk. See also D. Tweedie, "Globalization, Here We

Come," *Financial Times*, February 1, 2001, p. 2.; and "Bean Counters, Unite!" *The Economist*, June 10, 1995, pp. 67–68.

16. P. D. Fleming, "The Growing Importance of International Accounting Standards," *Journal of Accountancy*, September 1991, pp. 100–06.

17. D. Reilly, "SEC to Consider Letting Companies Use International Accounting Rules," *The Wall Street Journal*, April 25, 2007, p. C3.

18. Sources: A. Jack, "Swiss Group Moves from Night to Day," *Financial Times*, March 30, 1994, p. 22; L. Berton, "All Accountants May Soon Speak the Same Language," *The Wall Street Journal*, August 29, 1995, p. A15; and A. Beard, "Novartis Steps Up the Pace of Its U.S. Charm Offensive," *Financial Times*, May 14, 2001, p. 23.

19. L. Henock, "The Value Relevance of the Foreign Translation Adjustment," *The Accounting Review* 78 (4) (October 2003), pp. 1027–48.

20. The statement can be accessed at http://www.fasb.org/st/summary/stsum52.shtml.

21. F. Choi and I. Czechowicz, "Assessing Foreign Subsidiary Performance: A Multinational Comparison," *Management International Review* 4, 1983, pp. 14–25.

22. D. Lessard and P. Lorange, "Currency Changes and Management Control: Resolving the Centralization/Decentralization Dilemma," *Accounting Review*, July 1977, pp. 628–37.

23. Mueller, Gernon, and Meek, *Accounting: An International Perspective*.

24. Sources: E. McDonald, "What Happened?" *The Wall Street Journal*, April 26, 1999, p. R6; P. Grant, "IFRS Boosts Vodafone Profits by Sterling 6.8 Billion," *Accountancy Age*, January 20, 2005; G. Hinks, "IFRS to Wipe $4.7 Billion Off Shell's Balance Sheet," *Accountancy Age*, November 23, 2004.

Global Treasury Management at Procter & Gamble

With hundreds of brands of paper, detergent, food, health, and cosmetics products sold in over 130 countries and over 60 percent of its revenues generated outside the United States, Procter & Gamble is the quintessential example of a global consumer products firm. Despite this global spread, P&G's treasury operations—which embrace investment, financing, money management, and foreign exchange decisions—were quite decentralized until the 1990s. Essentially, each major international subsidiary managed its own investments, borrowings, and foreign exchange trades, subject only to outside borrowing limits imposed by the international treasury group at P&G's headquarters in Cincinnati.

Today P&G operates with a much more centralized system in which a global treasury management function at corporate headquarters exercises close oversight over

the operations of different regional treasury centers around the world. This move was a response in part to the rise in the volume of P&G's international transactions and the resulting increase in foreign exchange exposures. Like many global firms, P&G has been trying to rationalize its global production system to realize cost economies by concentrating the production of certain products at specific locations, as opposed to producing those products in every major country in which it does business. As it has moved in this direction, the number and volume of raw materials and finished products that are being shipped across borders has been growing by leaps and bounds. This has led to a commensurate increase in the size of P&G's foreign exchange exposure, which at any one time now runs into billions of dollars. Also, more than one-third of P&G's foreign exchange

Financial Management in the International Business

LEARNING OBJECTIVES

After you have read this chapter you should be able to:

LO¹ Discuss how operating in different nations impacts investment decisions within the multinational enterprise.

LO² Discuss the different financing options available to the foreign subsidiary of a multinational enterprise.

LO³ Understand how money management in the international business can be used to minimize cash balances, transaction costs, and taxation.

LO⁴ Be familiar with the basic techniques for global money management.

---

exposure is now in non-dollar exposures, such as transactions that involve the exchange of euros into won or sterling into yen.

P&G believes that centralizing the overall management of the resulting foreign exchange transactions can help the company realize a number of important gains. First, because its international subsidiaries often accumulate cash balances in the currency of the country where they are based, P&G now trades currencies between its subsidiaries. By cutting banks out of the process, P&G saves on transaction costs. Second, P&G has found that many of its subsidiaries purchase currencies in relatively small lots of say $100,000. By grouping these lots into larger purchases, P&G can generally get a better price from foreign trade dealers. Third, P&G is pooling foreign exchange risks and purchasing an

"umbrella option" to cover the risks associated with various currency positions, which is cheaper than purchasing options to cover each position.

In addition to managing foreign exchange transactions, P&G's global treasury operation arranges for subsidiaries to invest their surplus funds in and to borrow money from other Procter & Gamble entities, instead of from local banks. Subsidiaries that have excess cash lend it to those that need cash, and the global treasury operation acts as a financial intermediary. P&G has cut the number of local banks that it does business with from 450 to about 200. Using intra-company loans instead of loans from local banks lowers the overall borrowing costs, which may result in annual savings on interest payments that run into tens if not hundreds of millions of dollars.[1]

Introduction

This chapter focuses on financial management in the international business. Included within the scope of financial management are three sets of related decisions:

- *Investment decisions*, decisions about what activities to finance.
- *Financing decisions*, decisions about how to finance those activities.
- *Money management decisions*, decisions about how to manage the firm's financial resources most efficiently.

The opening case describes Procter & Gamble's approach toward these decisions. By managing investing, financing, and money management decisions centrally through its global treasury function, P&G has realized considerable cost economies. These economies help P&G compete more effectively in the global marketplace.

In an international business, investment, financing, and money management decisions are complicated by the fact that countries have different currencies, different tax regimes, different regulations concerning the flow of capital across their borders, different norms regarding the financing of business activities, different levels of economic and political risk, and so on. Financial managers must consider all these factors when deciding which activities to finance, how best to finance those activities, how best to manage the firm's financial resources, and how best to protect the firm from political and economic risks (including foreign exchange risk).

Good financial management can be an important source of competitive advantage. For example, consider FMC, a Chicago-based producer of chemicals and farm equipment. FMC counts on overseas business for 40 percent of its sales. FMC attributes some of its success overseas to aggressive trading in the forward foreign exchange market. By trading in currency futures, FMC can provide overseas customers with stable long-term prices for three years or more, regardless of what happens to exchange rates. According to an FMC spokesman, "Some of our competitors change their prices on a relatively short-term basis depending on what is happening with their own exchange rate. We want to provide longer-term pricing as a customer service—they can plan their budgets knowing what the numbers will be—and we can hopefully maintain and build our customer base." FMC also offers its customers the option of paying in any of several currencies as a convenience to them and as an attempt to retain customers. If customers could pay only in dollars, they might give their business to a competitor that offered pricing in a variety of currencies. By adopting this policy, FMC deals with "the hassle of foreign exchange movements," says the spokesman, so its customers don't have to. By offering customers multicurrency pricing alternatives, FMC implicitly accepts the responsibility of managing foreign exchange risk for its business units that sell overseas. It has set up what amounts to an in-house bank to manage the operation, monitoring currency rates daily and managing its risks on a portfolio basis. This bank handles more than $1 billion in currency transactions annually, which means the company can often beat the currency prices quoted by commercial banks.[2]

Chapter 12 talked about the value chain and pointed out that creating a competitive advantage requires a firm to reduce its costs of value creation and/or add value by improving its customer service. Good financial management can help both reduce the costs of creating value and add value by improving customer service. By reducing the firm's cost of capital (as in the case of Gol, which will be discussed in the closing case of this chapter), eliminating foreign exchange losses, minimizing the firm's tax burden, minimizing the firm's exposure to unnecessarily risky activities, and managing the firm's cash flows and reserves in the most efficient manner, the finance function can reduce the costs of creating value. As the example of FMC illustrates, good financial management can also enhance customer service, thus adding value.

We begin this chapter by looking at investment decisions in an international business. We will be most concerned with the issue of capital budgeting. Our objective is to identify the factors that can complicate capital budgeting decisions in an international business, as opposed to a purely domestic business. Most important, we will discuss how such factors as political and economic risk complicate capital budgeting decisions.

Then we look at financing decisions in an international business. Here we shall discuss the rise of the global capital market in recent decades, and how this has given companies more options for raising funds and lowering their cost of capital.

Finally, we examine money management decisions in an international business. We will look at the objectives of global money management, the various ways businesses can move money across borders, and some techniques for managing the firm's financial resources efficiently. What we do not discuss in this chapter are policies for managing foreign exchange risk—even though they are a very important part of financial management in the international business—since we already covered the topic in Chapter 9 when we looked at the foreign exchange market and the forces that determine exchange rate movements. In that chapter, in the section that discussed the implications for managers of the foreign exchange market, we discussed the various tactics and strategies international businesses use to manage their foreign exchange risk.

Investment Decisions

A decision to invest in activities in a given country must consider many economic, political, cultural, and strategic variables. We have been discussing this issue throughout much of this book. We touched on it in Chapters 2 and 3 when we discussed how the political, economic, legal, and cultural environment of a country can influence the benefits, costs, and risks of doing business there and thus its attractiveness as an investment site. We returned to the issue in Chapter 6 with a discussion of the economic theory of foreign direct investment. We identified a number of factors that determine the economic attractiveness of a foreign investment opportunity. In Chapter 7, we looked at the political economy of foreign direct investment and we considered the role that government intervention can play in foreign investment. In Chapter 12, we pulled much of this material together when we considered how a firm can reduce its costs of value creation and/or increase its value added by investing in productive activities in other countries. We returned to the issue again in Chapter 14 when we considered the various modes for entering foreign markets.

One role of the financial manager in an international business is to try to quantify the various benefits, costs, and risks that are likely to flow from an investment in a given location. Capital budgeting techniques can accomplish that goal.

CAPITAL BUDGETING

Capital budgeting quantifies the benefits, costs, and risks of an investment. This enables top managers to compare, in a reasonably objective fashion, different investment alternatives within and across countries so they can make informed choices about where the firm should invest its scarce financial resources. Capital budgeting for a foreign project uses the same theoretical framework that domestic capital budgeting uses; that is, the firm must first estimate the cash flows associated with the project over time. In most cases, the cash flows will be negative at first, because the firm will be investing heavily in production facilities. After some initial period, however, the cash flows will become positive as investment costs decline and revenues grow. Once the cash flows have been estimated, they must be discounted to determine their net present value using an appropriate discount rate. The most commonly used discount rate is either the firm's cost of capital or some other required rate of return. If the net present value of the discounted cash flows is greater than zero, the firm should go ahead with the project.[3]

Although this might sound quite straightforward, capital budgeting is in practice a very complex and imperfect process. Among the factors complicating the process for an international business are these:

1. A distinction must be made between cash flows to the project and cash flows to the parent company.
2. Political and economic risks, including foreign exchange risk, can significantly change the value of a foreign investment.
3. The connection between cash flows to the parent and the source of financing must be recognized.

We look at the first two of these issues in this section and postpone discussion of the connection between cash flows and the source of financing until the next section, where we discuss the source of financing.

PROJECT AND PARENT CASH FLOWS

A theoretical argument exists for analyzing any foreign project from the perspective of the parent company because cash flows to the project are not necessarily the same thing as cash flows to the parent company. The project may not be able to remit all its cash flows to the parent for a number of reasons. For example, cash flows may be blocked from repatriation by the host-country government, they may be taxed at an unfavorable rate, or the host government may require a certain percentage of the cash flows generated from the project be reinvested within the host nation. While these restrictions don't affect the net present value of the project itself, they do affect the net present value of the project to the parent company because they limit the cash flows that can be remitted to it from the project.

When evaluating a foreign investment opportunity, the parent should be interested in the cash flows it will receive—as opposed to those the project generates—because those are the basis for dividends to stockholders, investments elsewhere in the world, repayment of worldwide corporate debt, and so on. Stockholders will not perceive blocked earnings as contributing to the value of the firm, and creditors will not count them when calculating the parent's ability to service its debt.

But the problem of blocked earnings is not as serious as it once was. The worldwide move toward greater acceptance of free market economics (discussed in Chapter 2) has reduced the number of countries in which governments are likely to prohibit the affiliates of foreign multinationals from remitting cash flows to their parent companies. In addition, as we will see later in the chapter, firms have a number of options for circumventing host-government attempts to block the free flow of funds from an affiliate.

ADJUSTING FOR POLITICAL AND ECONOMIC RISK

When analyzing a foreign investment opportunity, the company must consider the political and economic risks that stem from the foreign location.[4] We will discuss these risks before looking at how capital budgeting methods can be adjusted to take them into account.

Political Risk

We initially encountered the concept of political risk in Chapter 2. There we defined it as the likelihood that political forces will cause drastic changes in a country's business environment that hurt the profit and other goals of a business enterprise. Political risk tends to be greater in countries experiencing social unrest or disorder and countries where the underlying nature of the society makes the likelihood of social unrest high. When political risk is high, there is a high probability that a change will occur in the country's political environment that will endanger foreign firms there.

In extreme cases, political change may result in the expropriation of foreign firms' assets. This occurred to U.S. firms after the Iranian revolution of 1979. In recent decades,

Black Sea Energy Ltd.

In 1996, Black Sea Energy, Ltd., of Calgary, Canada, formed a 50–50 joint venture with the Tyumen Oil Company, then Russia's sixth-largest integrated oil company. The objective of the venture, know as the Tura Petroleum Company, was to explore the Tura oilfield in Western Siberia. At the time, the Russian government owned 90 percent of Tyumen; consequently Black Sea Ltd. negotiated directly with representatives of the Russian government when establishing the joint venture. The agreement called for both parties to contribute over $40 million to the formation of the venture, Black Sea in the form of cash, technology, and expertise, and Tyumen in the form of infrastructure and the licenses for oil exploration and production that it held in the region.

From an operational perspective, the venture proved to be a success. Following the injection of cash and technology from Black Sea Energy, production at the Tura field went from 4,000 barrels/day to nearly 12,000. However, Black Sea did not capture any of the economic profits flowing from this investment. In 1997, the Moscow-based Alfa Group, one of Russia's largest

private companies, purchased a controlling stake in Tyumen from the Russian government. The new owners of Tyumen quickly came to the conclusion that the Tura joint venture was not fair to them and demanded that it be canceled. Their argument was that the value of the assets Tyumen contributed to the joint venture was far in excess of $40 million, while the value of the technology and expertise Black Sea contributed was significantly less than $40 million. The new owners also found some conflicting legislation that seemed to indicate that Tura's licenses were in fact owned by Tyumen, and that Black Sea therefore had no right to the resulting production. Tyumen took the issue to court in Russia, and consistently won, despite the fact that the Russian government had originally negotiated the deal. At the end of the day, Black Sea Energy had little choice but to walk away. According to Black Sea, by legal maneuvering, Tyumen was able to expropriate Black Sea's investment in the Tura venture. In contrast, Tyumen's management claimed that it had behaved in a perfectly legal manner.[5]

the risk of outright expropriations has become almost zero. However, a lack of consistent legislation and proper law enforcement, and no willingness on the part of the government to enforce contracts and protect private property rights, can result in the de facto expropriation of the assets of a foreign multinational. The Management Focus provides an example from Russia during the late 1990s.

Political and social unrest may also result in economic collapse, which can render a firm's assets worthless. This occurred to many foreign companies' assets as a result of the bloody war following the breakup of the former Yugoslavia. In less extreme cases, political changes may result in increased tax rates, the imposition of exchange controls that limit or block a subsidiary's ability to remit earnings to its parent company, the imposition of price controls, and government interference in existing contracts. The likelihood of any of these events impairs the attractiveness of a foreign investment opportunity.

Many firms devote considerable attention to political risk analysis and to quantifying political risk. *Euromoney* magazine publishes an annual "country risk rating," and businesses widely use its assessments of political and other risks. The problem with all attempts to forecast political risk, however, is that they try to predict a future that can only be guessed at—and in many cases, the guesses are wrong. Few people foresaw the 1979 Iranian revolution, the collapse of communism in Eastern Europe, the dramatic breakup of the Soviet Union, or the terrorist attack on the World Trade Center in September 2001, yet all these events have had a profound impact on the business environments of many countries. This is not to say that political risk assessment is without value, but it is more art than science.

Economic Risk

Like political risk, we first encountered the concept of economic risk in Chapter 2. There we defined it as the likelihood that economic mismanagement will cause drastic changes in a country's business environment that hurt the profit and other goals of a business enterprise. In practice, the biggest problem arising from economic mismanagement has been inflation. Historically, many governments have expanded their domestic money supply in misguided attempts to stimulate economic activity. The result has often been too much money chasing too few goods, resulting in price inflation. As we saw in Chapter 9, price inflation is reflected in a drop in the value of a country's currency on the foreign exchange market. This can be a serious problem for a foreign firm with assets in that country because the value of the cash flows it receives from those assets will fall as the country's currency depreciates on the foreign exchange market. The likelihood of this occurring decreases the attractiveness of foreign investment in that country.

There have been many attempts to quantify countries' economic risk and long-term movements in their exchange rates. (*Euromoney*'s annual country risk rating also incorporates an assessment of economic risk in its calculation of each country's overall level of risk.) As we saw in Chapter 9, there have been extensive empirical studies of the relationship between countries' inflation rates and their currencies' exchange rates. These studies show that there is a long-run relationship between a country's relative inflation rates and changes in exchange rates. However, the relationship is not as close as theory would predict; it is not reliable in the short run and is not totally reliable in the long run. So, as with political risk, any attempts to quantify economic risk must be tempered with some healthy skepticism.

RISK AND CAPITAL BUDGETING

In analyzing a foreign investment opportunity, the additional risk that stems from its location can be handled in at least two ways. The first method is to treat all risk as a single problem by increasing the discount rate applicable to foreign projects in countries where political and economic risks are perceived as high. Thus, for example, a firm might apply a 6 percent discount rate to potential investments in Great Britain, the United States, and Germany, reflecting those countries' economic and political stability, and it might use a 20 percent discount rate for potential investments in Russia, reflecting the greater perceived political and economic risks in that country. The higher the discount rate, the higher the projected net cash flows must be for an investment to have a positive net present value.

Adjusting discount rates to reflect a location's riskiness seems to be fairly widely practiced. For example, several studies of large U.S. multinationals have found that many of them routinely add a premium percentage for risk to the discount rate they used in evaluating potential foreign investment projects.[6] However, critics of this method argue that it penalizes early cash flows too heavily and does not penalize distant cash flows enough.[7] They point out that if political or economic collapse were expected in the near future, the investment would not occur anyway. So for any investment decisions, the political and economic risk being assessed is not of immediate possibilities, but rather at some distance in the future. Accordingly, it can be argued that rather than using a higher discount rate to evaluate such risky projects, which penalizes early cash flows too heavily, it is better to revise future cash flows from the project downward to reflect the possibility of adverse political or economic changes sometime in the future. Surveys of actual practice within multinationals suggest that the practice of revising future cash flows downward is almost as popular as that of revising the discount rate upward.[8]

🌐 Financing Decisions

When considering its options for financing, an international business must consider two factors. The first is how the foreign investment will be financed. If external financing is required, the firm must decide whether to tap the global capital market for funds, or borrow from sources in the host country. The second factor is how the financial structure of the foreign affiliate should be configured.

SOURCE OF FINANCING

If the firm is going to seek external financing for a project, it will want to borrow funds from the lowest cost source of capital available. As we saw in Chapter 11, firms increasingly are turning to the global capital market to finance their investments. The cost of capital is typically lower in the global capital market, by virtue of its size and liquidity, than in many domestic capital markets, particularly those that are small and relatively illiquid. Thus, for example, a U.S. firm investing in Denmark may finance the investment by borrowing through the London-based Eurobond market rather than the Danish capital market.

However, despite the trends toward deregulation of financial services, in some cases host-country government restrictions may rule out this option. The governments of some countries require, or at least prefer, foreign multinationals to finance projects in their country by local debt financing or local sales of equity. In countries where liquidity is limited, this raises the cost of capital used to finance a project. Thus, in capital budgeting decisions, the discount rate must be adjusted upward to reflect this. However, this is not the only possibility. In Chapter 7, we saw that some governments court foreign investment by offering foreign firms low-interest loans, lowering the cost of capital. Accordingly, in capital budgeting decisions, the discount rate should be revised downward in such cases.

In addition to the impact of host-government policies on the cost of capital and financing decisions, the firm may wish to consider local debt financing for investments in countries where the local currency is expected to depreciate on the foreign exchange market. The amount of local currency required to meet interest payments and retire principal on local debt obligations is not affected when a country's currency depreciates. However, if foreign debt obligations must be served, the amount of local currency required to do this will increase as the currency depreciates, and this effectively raises the cost of capital. Thus, although the initial cost of capital may be greater with local borrowing, it may be better to borrow locally if the local currency is expected to depreciate on the foreign exchange market.

FINANCIAL STRUCTURE

There is a difference in the financial structures of firms based in different countries. By financial structure we mean the mix of debt and equity used to finance a business. It is well known, for example, that Japanese firms rely far more on debt financing than do most U.S. firms. One study of firms in 23 countries found that debt to equity ratios varied from a low of 0.34 in Singapore to 0.76 in Italy. The average ratio in the United States was 0.55. It was also 0.55 in the UK, and 0.62 in Germany.[9] Another study of more than 4,000 firms in five countries found that the ratio of long-term debt to assets was 0.185 in the United States, 0.155 in Japan, 0.98 in the UK, 0.88 in Germany, and 0.145 in France, suggesting again that reliance on debt financing varies from country to country.[10]

It is not clear why the financial structure of firms should vary so much across countries. One possible explanation is that different tax regimes determine the relative attractiveness of debt and equity in a country. For example, if interest income were taxed at a high rate, a preference for debt financing over equity financing would be expected. However, according to empirical research, country differences in financial structure do not seem related in any systematic way to country differences in tax structure.[11] Another possibility is that these country differences may reflect cultural norms.[12] This explanation may be valid, although the mechanism by which culture influences capital structure has not yet been explained.

The interesting question for the international business is whether it should conform to local capital structure norms. Should a U.S. firm investing in Italy adopt the higher debt ratio typical of Italian firms for its Italian subsidiary, or should it stick with its more conservative practice? There are few good arguments for conforming to local norms. One advantage claimed for conforming to host-country debt norms is that management can more easily evaluate its return on equity relative to local competitors in the same industry. However, this seems a weak rationale for what is an important decision. Another point often made is that conforming to higher host-country debt norms can improve the image of foreign affiliates that have been operating with too little debt and thus appear insensitive to local monetary policy. Just how important this point is, however, has not been established. The best recommendation is that an international business should adopt a financial structure for each foreign affiliate that minimizes its cost of capital, irrespective of whether that structure is consistent with local practice.

Global Money Management: The Efficiency Objective

Money management decisions attempt to manage the firm's global cash resources—its working capital—most efficiently. This involves minimizing cash balances and reducing transaction costs.

MINIMIZING CASH BALANCES

For any given period, a firm must hold certain cash balances. This is necessary for serving any accounts and notes payable during that period and as a contingency against unexpected demands on cash. The firm does not sit on its cash reserves. It typically invests them in money market accounts so it can earn interest on them. However, it must be able to withdraw its money from those accounts freely. Such accounts typically offer a relatively low rate of interest. In contrast, the firm could earn a higher rate of interest if it could invest its cash resources in longer-term financial instruments (e.g., six-month certificates of deposit). The problem with longer-term instruments, however, is that the firm cannot withdraw its money before the instruments mature without suffering a financial penalty.

Thus, the firm faces a dilemma. If it invests its cash balances in money market accounts (or the equivalent), it will have unlimited liquidity but earn a relatively low rate of interest. If it invests its cash in longer-term financial instruments (certificates of deposit, bonds, etc.), it will earn a higher rate of interest, but liquidity will be limited. In an ideal world, the firm would have minimal liquid cash balances. We will see later in the chapter that by managing its total global cash reserves through a centralized depository (as opposed to letting each affiliate manage its own cash reserves), an international business can reduce the amount of funds it must hold in liquid accounts and thereby increase its rate of return on its cash reserves.

REDUCING TRANSACTION COSTS

Transaction costs are the cost of exchange. Every time a firm changes cash from one currency into another currency it must bear a transaction cost—the commission fee it pays to foreign exchange dealers for performing the transaction. Most banks also charge a **transfer fee** for moving cash from one location to another; this is another transaction cost. The commission and transfer fees arising from intrafirm transactions can be substantial; according to the United Nations, 40 percent of international trade involves transactions between the different national subsidiaries of transnational corporations. As we will see later in the chapter, multilateral netting can reduce the number of transactions between the firm's subsidiaries, thereby reducing the total transactions costs arising from foreign exchange dealings and transfer fees.

Global Money Management: The Tax Objective

Different countries have different tax regimes. Table 20.1 illustrates top corporate income tax rates in 2006 for a selection of countries in a survey by KPMG, an international accounting firm.[13] As can be seen, the top rates for corporate income tax varied from a high of 40.69 percent in Japan to a low of 12.5 percent in Ireland. However, the picture is much more complex than the one Table 20.1 presents. For example, in Germany and Japan, the tax rate is lower on income distributed to stockholders as dividends (36 and 35 percent, respectively), whereas in France the tax on profits distributed to stockholders is higher (42 percent). In the United States, the rate varies from state to state. The top federal rate is 35 percent, but states also tax corporate income, with state and local taxes ranging from 1 percent to 12 percent, hence the average effective rate of 40 percent.

Many nations follow the worldwide principle that they have the right to tax income earned outside their boundaries by entities based in their country.[14] Thus, the U.S. government can tax the earnings of the German subsidiary of an enterprise incorporated in the United States. Double taxation occurs when both the host-country government and the parent company's home government tax the income of a foreign subsidiary. However, double taxation is mitigated to some extent by tax credits, tax treaties, and the deferral principle.

A **tax credit** allows an entity to reduce the taxes paid to the home government by the amount of taxes paid to the foreign government. A **tax treaty** between two countries is an agreement specifying what items of income will be taxed by the authorities of the country where the income is earned. For example, a tax treaty between the United States and Germany may specify that a U.S. firm need not pay tax in Germany on any earnings from its German subsidiary that are remitted to the United States in the form of dividends. A **deferral principle** specifies that parent companies are not taxed on foreign source income until they actually receive a dividend.

For the international business with activities in many countries, the various tax regimes and tax treaties have important implications for how the firm should structure its internal payments system among the foreign subsidiaries and the parent company. As we will see in the next section, the firm can use transfer prices and fronting loans to minimize its global tax liability. In addition, the form in which income is remitted from a foreign subsidiary to the parent company (e.g., royalty payments versus dividend payments) can be structured to minimize the firm's global tax liability.

Country	Top Corporate Income Tax Rate
Canada	36.1%
Chile	17.0
China	33.0
France	33.33
Germany	38.36
Ireland	12.5
Japan	40.69
Mexico	28.0
Singapore	20.0
United Kingdom	30.0
United States	40.0

TABLE 20.1

Corporate Income Tax Rates, 2006

Source: KPMG Corporate Tax Rates Survey, January 2007.

Some firms use **tax havens** such as the Bahamas and Bermuda to minimize their tax liability. A tax haven is a country with an exceptionally low, or even no, income tax. International businesses avoid or defer income taxes by establishing a wholly owned, nonoperating subsidiary in the tax haven. The tax haven subsidiary owns the common stock of the operating foreign subsidiaries. This allows all transfers of funds from foreign operating subsidiaries to the parent company to be funneled through the tax haven subsidiary. The tax levied on foreign source income by a firm's home government, which might normally be paid when a foreign subsidiary declares a dividend, can be deferred under the deferral principle until the tax haven subsidiary pays the dividend to the parent. This dividend payment can be postponed indefinitely if foreign operations continue to grow and require new internal financing from the tax haven affiliate. For U.S.-based enterprises, however, U.S. regulations tax U.S. shareholders on the firm's overseas income when it is earned, regardless of when the parent company in the United States receives it. This regulation eliminates U.S.-based firms' ability to use tax haven subsidiaries to avoid tax liabilities in the manner just described.

Moving Money across Borders: Attaining Efficiencies and Reducing Taxes

Pursuing the objectives of utilizing the firm's cash resources most efficiently and minimizing the firm's global tax liability requires the firm to be able to transfer funds from one location to another around the globe. International businesses use a number of techniques to transfer liquid funds across borders. These include dividend remittances, royalty payments and fees, transfer prices, and fronting loans. Some firms rely on more than one of these techniques to transfer funds across borders—a practice known as unbundling. By using a mix of techniques to transfer liquid funds from a foreign subsidiary to the parent company, unbundling allows an international business to recover funds from its foreign subsidiaries without piquing host-country sensitivities with large "dividend drains."

A firm's ability to select a particular policy is severely limited when a foreign subsidiary is owned in part either by a local joint venture partner or by local stockholders. Serving the legitimate demands of the local co-owners of a foreign subsidiary may limit the firm's ability to impose the kind of dividend policy, royalty payment schedule, or transfer pricing policy that would be optimal for the parent company.

DIVIDEND REMITTANCES

Payment of dividends is probably the most common method by which firms transfer funds from foreign subsidiaries to the parent company. The dividend policy typically varies with each subsidiary depending on such factors as tax regulations, foreign exchange risk, the age of the subsidiary, and the extent of local equity participation. For example, the higher the rate of tax the host government levies on dividends, the less attractive this option becomes relative to other options for transferring liquid funds. With regard to foreign exchange risk, firms sometimes require foreign subsidiaries based in "high-risk" countries to speed up the transfer of funds to the parent through accelerated dividend payments. This moves corporate funds out of a country whose currency is expected to depreciate significantly. The age of a foreign subsidiary influences dividend policy in that older subsidiaries tend to remit a higher proportion of their earnings in dividends to the parent, presumably because a subsidiary has fewer capital investment needs as it matures. Local equity participation is a factor because local co-owners' demands for dividends must be recognized.

ROYALTY PAYMENTS AND FEES

Royalties represent the remuneration paid to the owners of technology, patents, or trade names for the use of that technology or the right to manufacture and/or sell products under those patents or trade names. It is common for a parent company to charge its foreign subsidiaries royalties for the technology, patents, or trade names it has transferred to them. Royalties may be levied as a fixed monetary amount per unit of the product the subsidiary sells or as a percentage of a subsidiary's gross revenues.

A fee is compensation for professional services or expertise the parent company or another subsidiary supplies to a foreign subsidiary. Fees are sometimes differentiated into "management fees" for general expertise and advice and "technical assistance fees" for guidance in technical matters. Fees are usually levied as fixed charges for the particular services provided.

Royalties and fees have certain tax advantages over dividends, particularly when the corporate tax rate is higher in the host country than in the parent's home country. Royalties and fees are often tax-deductible locally (because they are viewed as an expense), so arranging for payment in royalties and fees will reduce the foreign subsidiary's tax liability. If the foreign subsidiary compensates the parent company by dividend payments, local income taxes must be paid before the dividend distribution, and withholding taxes must be paid on the dividend itself. Although the parent can often take a tax credit for the local withholding and income taxes it has paid, part of the benefit can be lost if the subsidiary's combined tax rate is higher than the parent's.

TRANSFER PRICES

Any international business normally involves a large number of transfers of goods and services between the parent company and foreign subsidiaries and between foreign subsidiaries. This is particularly likely in firms pursuing global and transnational strategies because these firms are likely to have dispersed their value creation activities to various "optimal" locations around the globe (see Chapter 12). As noted in Chapter 19, the price at which goods and services are transferred between entities within the firm is referred to as the **transfer price**.[15]

Transfer prices can be used to position funds within an international business. For example, funds can be moved out of a particular country by setting high transfer prices for goods and services supplied to a subsidiary in that country and by setting low transfer prices for the goods and services sourced from that subsidiary. Conversely, funds can be positioned in a country by the opposite policy: setting low transfer prices for goods and services supplied to a subsidiary in that country and setting high transfer prices for the goods and services sourced from that subsidiary. This movement of funds can be between the firm's subsidiaries or between the parent company and a subsidiary.

Benefits of Manipulating Transfer Prices

At least four gains can be derived by manipulating transfer prices:

1. The firm can reduce its tax liabilities by using transfer prices to shift earnings from a high-tax country to a low-tax one.

2. The firm can use transfer prices to move funds out of a country where a significant currency devaluation is expected, thereby reducing its exposure to foreign exchange risk.

3. The firm can use transfer prices to move funds from a subsidiary to the parent company (or a tax haven) when financial transfers in the form of dividends are restricted or blocked by host-country government policies.

4. The firm can use transfer prices to reduce the import duties it must pay when an ad valorem tariff is in force—a tariff assessed as a percentage of value. In this case, low transfer prices on goods or services being imported into the country are required. Since this lowers the value of the goods or services, it lowers the tariff.

Problems with Transfer Pricing

Significant problems are associated with pursuing a transfer pricing policy.[16] Few governments like it.[17] When transfer prices are used to reduce a firm's tax liabilities or import duties, most governments feel they are being cheated of their legitimate income. Similarly, when transfer prices are manipulated to circumvent government restrictions on capital flows (e.g., dividend remittances), governments perceive this as breaking the spirit—if not the letter—of the law. Many governments now limit international businesses' ability to manipulate transfer prices in the manner described. The United States has strict regulations governing transfer pricing practices. According to Section 482 of the Internal Revenue Code, the Internal Revenue Service (IRS) can reallocate gross income, deductions, credits, or allowances between related corporations to prevent tax evasion or to reflect more clearly a proper allocation of income. Under the IRS guidelines and subsequent judicial interpretation, the burden of proof is on the taxpayer to show that the IRS has been arbitrary or unreasonable in reallocating income. The correct transfer price, according to the IRS guidelines, is an arm's-length price—the price that would prevail between unrelated firms in a market setting. Such a strict interpretation of what is a correct transfer price theoretically limits a firm's ability to manipulate transfer prices to achieve the benefits we have discussed. Many other countries have followed the U.S. lead in emphasizing that transfer prices should be set on an arms-length basis.

Another problem associated with transfer pricing is related to management incentives and performance evaluation.[18] Transfer pricing is inconsistent with a policy of treating each subsidiary in the firm as a profit center. When the firm manipulates transfer prices and they deviate significantly from the arm's-length price, the subsidiary's performance may depend as much on transfer prices as it does on other pertinent factors, such as management effort. A subsidiary told to charge a high transfer price for a good supplied to another subsidiary will appear to be doing better than it actually is, while the subsidiary purchasing the good will appear to be doing worse. Unless this is recognized when performance is being evaluated, serious distortions in management incentive systems can occur. For example, managers in the selling subsidiary may be able to use high transfer prices to mask inefficiencies, while managers in the purchasing subsidiary may become disheartened by the effect of high transfer prices on their subsidiary's profitability.

Despite these problems, research suggests that not all international businesses use arm's-length pricing but instead use some cost-based system for pricing transfers among their subunits (typically cost plus some standard markup). A survey of 164 U.S. multinational firms found that 35 percent of the firms used market-based prices, 15 percent used negotiated prices, and 65 percent used a cost-based pricing method. (The figures add up to more than 100 percent because some companies use more than one method.)[19] Only market and negotiated prices could reasonably be interpreted as arm's-length prices. The opportunity for price manipulation is much greater with cost-based transfer pricing. Other more sophisticated research has uncovered indirect evidence that many corporations do manipulate transfer prices in order to reduce global tax liabilities.[20]

Although a firm may be able to manipulate transfer prices to avoid tax liabilities or circumvent government restrictions on capital flows across borders, this does not mean the firm should do so. Since the practice often violates at least the spirit of the law in many countries, the ethics of engaging in transfer pricing are dubious at best. Moreover, there are clear signs that tax authorities in many countries are increasing their scrutiny of this practice in order to stamp out abuses. A 2000 survey of some 600 multinationals by accountants Ernst & Young found that 75 percent of them believed they would be the subject of a transfer pricing audit by tax authorities in the next two years.[21] Some 61 percent of the multinationals in the survey stated that transfer pricing was the number one tax issue they faced.

FRONTING LOANS

A fronting loan is a loan between a parent and its subsidiary channeled through a financial intermediary, usually a large international bank. In a direct intrafirm loan, the parent

FIGURE 20.1

An Example of the Tax
Aspects of a Fronting
Loan

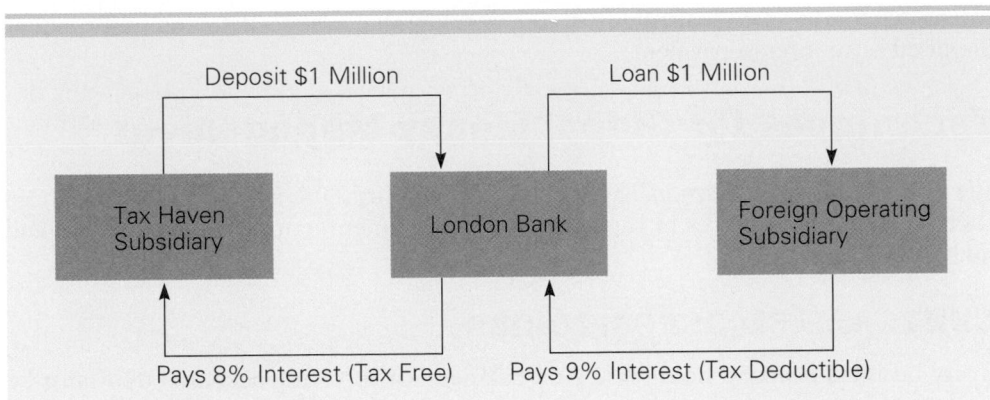

company lends cash directly to the foreign subsidiary, and the subsidiary repays it later. In a fronting loan, the parent company deposits funds in an international bank, and the bank then lends the same amount to the foreign subsidiary. Thus, a U.S. firm might deposit $100,000 in a London bank. The London bank might then lend that $100,000 to an Indian subsidiary of the firm. From the bank's point of view, the loan is risk free because it has 100 percent collateral in the form of the parent's deposit. The bank "fronts" for the parent, hence the name. The bank makes a profit by paying the parent company a slightly lower interest rate on its deposit than it charges the foreign subsidiary on the borrowed funds.

Firms use fronting loans for two reasons. First, fronting loans can circumvent host-country restrictions on the remittance of funds from a foreign subsidiary to the parent company. A host government might restrict a foreign subsidiary from repaying a loan to its parent in order to preserve the country's foreign exchange reserves, but it is less likely to restrict a subsidiary's ability to repay a loan to a large international bank. To stop payment to an international bank would hurt the country's credit image, whereas halting payment to the parent company would probably have a minimal impact on its image. Consequently, international businesses sometimes use fronting loans when they want to lend funds to a subsidiary based in a country with a fairly high probability of political turmoil that might lead to restrictions on capital flows (i.e., where the level of political risk is high).

A fronting loan can also provide tax advantages. For example, a tax haven (Bermuda) subsidiary that is 100 percent owned by the parent company deposits $1 million in a London-based international bank at 8 percent interest. The bank lends the $1 million to a foreign operating subsidiary at 9 percent interest. The country where the foreign operating subsidiary is based taxes corporate income at 50 percent (see Figure 20.1).

Under this arrangement, interest payments net of income tax will be as follows:

1. The foreign operating subsidiary pays $90,000 interest to the London bank. Deducting these interest payments from its taxable income results in a net after-tax cost of $45,000 to the foreign operating subsidiary.

2. The London bank receives the $90,000. It retains $10,000 for its services and pays $80,000 interest on the deposit to the Bermuda subsidiary.

3. The Bermuda subsidiary receives $80,000 interest on its deposit tax free.

The net result is that $80,000 in cash has been moved from the foreign operating subsidiary to the tax haven subsidiary. Because the foreign operating subsidiary's after-tax cost of borrowing is only $45,000, the parent company has moved an additional $35,000 out of the country by using this arrangement. If the tax haven subsidiary had made a direct loan to the foreign operating subsidiary, the host government may have disallowed the interest charge as a tax-deductible expense by ruling that it was a dividend to the parent disguised as an interest payment.

Techniques for Global Money Management

We now look at two money management techniques firms use in attempting to manage their global cash resources in the most efficient manner: centralized depositories and multilateral netting.

CENTRALIZED DEPOSITORIES

Every business needs to hold some cash balances for servicing accounts that must be paid and for insuring against unanticipated negative variation from its projected cash flows. The critical issue for an international business is whether each foreign subsidiary should hold its own cash balances or whether a centralized depository should hold them. In general, firms prefer to hold cash balances at a centralized depository for three reasons.

First, by pooling cash reserves centrally, the firm can deposit larger amounts. Cash balances are typically deposited in liquid accounts, such as overnight money market accounts. Because interest rates on such deposits normally increase with the size of the deposit, by pooling cash centrally, the firm should be able to earn a higher interest rate than it would if each subsidiary managed its own cash balances.

Second, if the centralized depository is located in a major financial center (e.g., London, New York, or Tokyo), it should have access to information about good short-term investment opportunities that the typical foreign subsidiary would lack. Also, the financial experts at a centralized depository should be able to develop investment skills and know-how that managers in the typical foreign subsidiary would lack. Thus, the firm should make better investment decisions if it pools its cash reserves at a centralized depository.

Third, by pooling its cash reserves, the firm can reduce the total size of the cash pool it must hold in highly liquid accounts, which enables the firm to invest a larger amount of cash reserves in longer-term, less liquid financial instruments that earn a higher interest rate. For example, a U.S. firm has three foreign subsidiaries—one in Korea, one in China, and one in Japan. Each subsidiary maintains a cash balance that includes an amount for dealing with its day-to-day needs plus a precautionary amount for dealing with unanticipated cash demands. The firm's policy is that the total required cash balance is equal to three standard deviations of the expected day-to-day-needs amount. The three-standard-deviation requirement reflects the firm's estimate that, in practice, there is a 99.87 percent probability that the subsidiary will have sufficient cash to deal with both day-to-day and unanticipated cash demands. Cash needs are assumed to be normally distributed in each country and independent of each other (e.g., cash needs in Japan do not affect cash needs in China).

The individual subsidiaries' day-to-day cash needs and the precautionary cash balances they should hold are as follows (in millions of dollars):

	Day-to-Day Cash Needs (A)	One Standard Deviation (B)	Required Cash Balance (A + 3 × B)
Korea	$10	$1	$13
China	6	2	12
Japan	12	3	21
Total	$28	$6	$46

Thus, the Korean subsidiary estimates that it must hold $10 million to serve its day-to-day needs. The standard deviation of this is $1 million, so it is to hold an additional $3 million as a precautionary amount. This gives a total required cash balance of $13 million. The total of the required cash balances for all three subsidiaries is $46 million.

Now consider what might occur if the firm decided to maintain all three cash balances at a centralized depository in Tokyo. Because variances are additive when probability distributions are independent of each other, the standard deviation of the combined precautionary account would be

$$\text{Square root of } (\$1,000,000^2 + 2,000,000^2 + 3,000,000^2)$$
$$= \text{Square root of } 14,000,000$$
$$= \$3,741,657$$

Therefore, if the firm used a centralized depository, it would need to hold $28 million for day-to-day needs plus (3 × $3,741,657) as a precautionary amount, or a total cash balance of $39,224,972. In other words, the firm's total required cash balance would be reduced from $46 million to $39,224,972, a saving of $6,775,028. This is cash that could be invested in less liquid, higher-interest accounts or in tangible assets. The saving arises simply due to the statistical effects of summing the three independent, normal probability distributions.

However, a firm's ability to establish a centralized depository that can serve short-term cash needs might be limited by government-imposed restrictions on capital flows across borders (e.g., controls put in place to protect a country's foreign exchange reserves). Also, the transaction costs of moving money into and out of different currencies can limit the advantages of such a system. Despite this, many firms hold at least their subsidiaries' precautionary cash reserves at a centralized depository, having each subsidiary hold its own day-to-day-needs cash balance. The globalization of the world capital market and the general removal of barriers to the free flow of cash across borders (particularly among advanced industrialized countries) are two trends likely to increase the use of centralized depositories.

MULTILATERAL NETTING

Multilateral netting allows a multinational firm to reduce the transaction costs that arise when many transactions occur between its subsidiaries. These transaction costs are the commissions paid to foreign exchange dealers for foreign exchange transactions and the fees banks charge for transferring cash between locations. The volume of such transactions is likely to be particularly high in a firm that has a globally dispersed web of interdependent value creation activities. Netting reduces transaction costs by reducing the number of transactions.

Multilateral netting is an extension of **bilateral netting.** Under bilateral netting, if a French subsidiary owes a Mexican subsidiary $6 million and the Mexican subsidiary simultaneously owes the French subsidiary $4 million, a bilateral settlement will be made with a single payment of $2 million from the French subsidiary to the Mexican subsidiary, the remaining debt being canceled.

Under **multilateral netting,** this simple concept is extended to the transactions between multiple subsidiaries within an international business. Consider a firm that wants to establish multilateral netting among four Asian subsidiaries based in Korea, China, Japan, and Taiwan. These subsidiaries all trade with each other, so at the end of each month a large volume of cash transactions must be settled. Figure 20.2A shows how the payment schedule might look at the end of a given month. Figure 20.2B is a payment matrix that summarizes the obligations among the subsidiaries. Note that $43 million needs to flow among the subsidiaries. If the transaction costs (foreign exchange

FIGURE 20.2A

Cash Flows before
Multilateral Netting

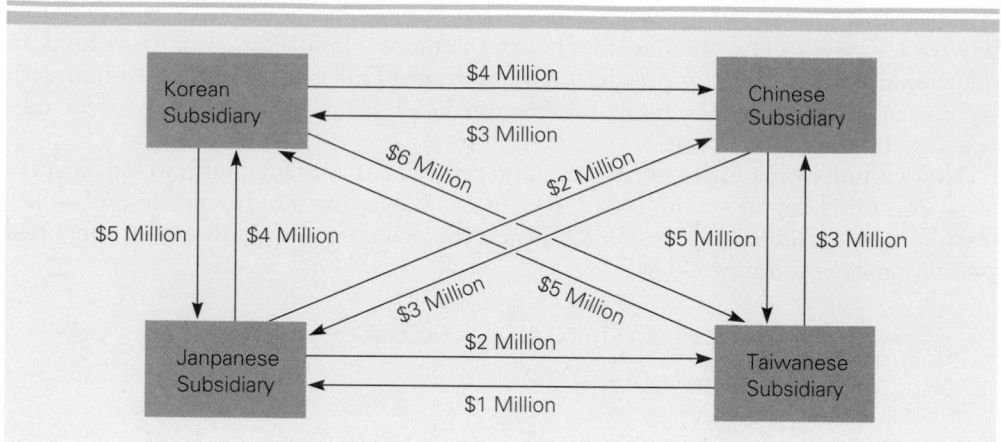

Paying Subsidiary

Receiving Subsidiary	Germany	France	Spain	Italy	Total Receipts	Net Receipts (payments)
Korean	—	$ 3	$4	$5	$12	($3)
Chinese	$ 4	—	2	3	9	(2)
Japanese	5	3	—	1	9	1
Taiwanese	6	5	2	—	13	4
Total payments	$15	$11	$8	$9		

FIGURE 20.2B

Calculation of Net Receipts (all amounts in millions)

FIGURE 20.2C

Cash Flows after
Multilateral Netting

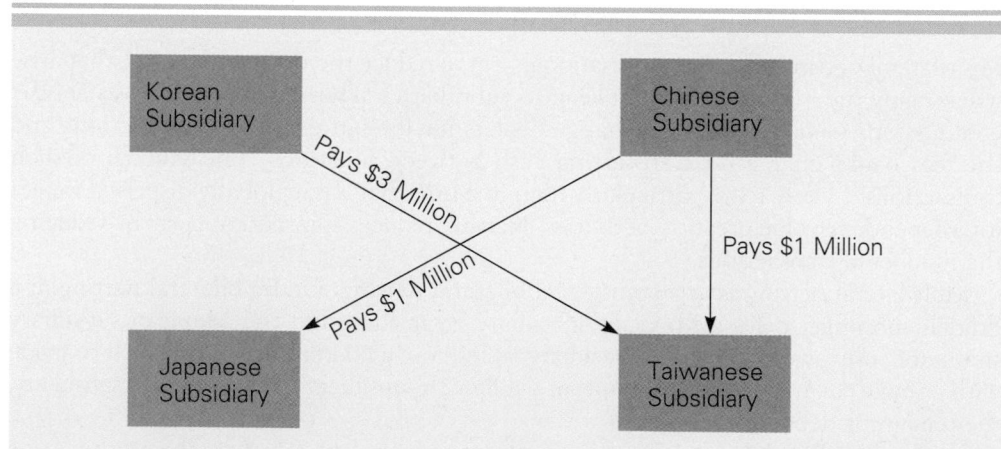

commissions plus transfer fees) amount to 1 percent of the total funds to be transferred, this will cost the parent firm $430,000. However, multilateral netting can reduce this amount. Using the payment matrix (Figure 20.2B), the firm can determine the payments that need to be made among its subsidiaries to settle these obligations. Figure 20.2C shows the results. By multilateral netting, the transactions depicted in Figure 20.2A are reduced to just three; the Korean subsidiary pays $3 million to the Taiwanese subsidiary, and the Chinese subsidiary pays $1 million to the Japanese subsidiary and $1 million to the Taiwanese subsidiary. The total funds that flow among the subsidiaries are reduced from $43 million to just $5 million, and the transaction costs are reduced from $430,000 to $50,000, a savings of $380,000 achieved through multilateral netting.

CHAPTER SUMMARY

This chapter was concerned with financial management in the international business. We discussed how investment decisions, financing decisions, and money management decisions are complicated by the fact that different countries have different currencies, different tax regimes, different levels of political and economic risk, and so on. Financial managers must account for all these factors when deciding which activities to finance, how best to finance those activities, how best to manage the firm's financial resources, and how best to protect the firm from political and economic risks (including foreign exchange risk). This chapter made the following points:

1. When using capital budgeting techniques to evaluate a potential foreign project, a distinction must be made between cash flows to the project and cash flows to the parent. The two will not be the same thing when a host-country government blocks the repatriation of cash flows from a foreign investment.

2. When using capital budgeting techniques to evaluate a potential foreign project, the firm needs to recognize the specific risks arising from its foreign location. These include political risks and economic risks (including foreign exchange risk).

3. Political and economic risks can be incorporated into the capital budgeting process either by using a higher discount rate to evaluate risky projects or by forecasting lower cash flows for such projects.

4. The cost of capital is typically lower in the global capital market than in domestic markets. Consequently, other things being equal, firms prefer to finance their investments by borrowing from the global capital market.

5. Borrowing from the global capital market may be restricted by host-government regulations or demands. In such cases, the discount rate used in capital budgeting must be revised upward.

6. The firm may want to consider local debt financing for investments in countries where the local currency is expected to depreciate.

7. The principal objectives of global money management are to utilize the firm's cash resources in the most efficient manner and to minimize the firm's global tax liabilities.

8. Firms use a number of techniques to transfer funds across borders, including dividend remittances, royalty payments and fees, transfer prices, and fronting loans.

9. Dividend remittances are the most common method used for transferring funds across borders, but royalty payments and fees have certain tax advantages over dividend remittances.

10. Firms sometimes manipulate transfer prices to move funds out of a country to minimize tax liabilities, hedge against foreign exchange risk, circumvent government restrictions on capital flows, and reduce tariff payments.

11. However, manipulating transfer prices in this manner runs counter to government regulations in many countries, it may distort incentive systems within the firm, and it has ethically dubious foundations.

12. Fronting loans involves channeling funds from a parent company to a foreign subsidiary through a third party, normally an international bank. Fronting loans can circumvent host-government restrictions on the remittance of funds and provide certain tax advantages.

13. By holding cash at a centralized depository, the firm may be able to invest its cash reserves more efficiently. It can reduce the total size of the cash pool that it needs to hold in highly liquid accounts, thereby freeing cash for investment in accounts with higher interest rates (less liquid accounts) or in tangible assets.

14. Multilateral netting reduces the transaction costs arising when a large number of transactions occur between a firm's subsidiaries in the normal course of business.

Critical Thinking and Discussion Questions

1. How can the finance function of an international business improve the firm's competitive position in the global marketplace?

2. What actions can a firm take to minimize its global tax liability? On ethical grounds, can such actions be justified?

3. You are the CFO of a U.S. firm whose wholly owned subsidiary in Mexico manufactures component parts for your U.S. assembly operations. The subsidiary has been financed by bank borrowings in the United States. One of your analysts told you that the Mexican peso is expected to depreciate by 30 percent against the dollar on the foreign exchange markets over the next year. What actions, if any, should you take?

4. You are the CFO of a Canadian firm that is considering building a $10 million factory in Russia to produce milk. The investment is expected to produce net cash flows of $3 million each year for the next 10 years, after which the investment will have to close down because of technological obsolescence. Scrap values will be zero. The cost of capital will be 6 percent if financing is arranged through the Eurobond market. However, you have an option to finance the project by borrowing funds from a Russian bank at 12 percent. Analysts tell you that due to high inflation in Russia, the Russian ruble is expected to depreciate against the Canadian dollar. Analysts also rate the probability of violent revolution occurring in Russia within the next 10 years as high. How would you incorporate these factors into your evaluation of the investment opportunity? What would you recommend the firm do?

Research Task

Use the globalEDGE™ site to complete the following exercises:

1. Tax rates in different countries can impact the level of spending income available to companies and people in different countries. The top management of your company requested a report regarding the tax policies of the following countries: Argentina, Belgium, Bulgaria, China, Czech Republic, Denmark, Egypt, Germany, Italy, and the United Kingdom. A tax colleague indicated over lunch that a resource called "Worldwide Tax" may assist you in completing your report. Prepare a table including the corporate and individual income tax rates and the value added tax rates (where applicable) for the countries on your list.

2. Country risk is an important issue for investors to consider prior to investing in foreign countries. One of the Marketing Potential Indicators for Emerging Markets is identified as country risk. Utilize the ranking provided by the globalEDGE™ Web site and identify five emerging markets that exhibit the least risk for foreign investors.

CLOSING CASE

Brazil's Gol

Brazil's *Gol Linhas Aereas Inteligentes* is a tropical version of JetBlue Airways and Ryanair, the low-cost no-frills carriers in the United States and Europe. Established in 2001, Gol adopted the low-cost model pioneered by Southwest Airlines and refined by the likes of JetBlue and Ryanair. Gol sells discount tickets, mainly over the Internet. It targets price sensitive business travelers, who account for 70 percent of all traffic in Brazil's rapidly growing market for air travel (demand for air travel in Brazil is growing at roughly twice the rate of growth in the country's gross domestic product). Gol is also going after Brazil's large bus market—in 2001 some 130 million people in Brazil traveled by interstate bus companies. Gol has standardized its fleet on a single aircraft model, Boeing's 737 series. There are no airport clubs or frequent flyer programs, cabins are a single class, and light snacks and beverages replace meals. The airline also offers Internet check-in and delivers a reliable product, with 95 percent of flights arriving on time. Gol's service has elicited a remarkable response from customers, with an independent market research survey finding that more than 90 percent of customers would continue to use the airline and recommend it to others.

From a standing start in January 2001, this business model enabled Gol to capture a 22 percent share of the Brazilian market by mid-2004. By then, Gol had a fleet of 25 aircraft and was already ranked as one of the fastest growing and most profitable airlines in the world, but its aspirations are much bigger. Gol wants to be the low-cost carrier in South America. To get to that point, it plans to expand its fleet to some 69 aircraft by 2010.

To help finance this expansion, Gol decided to tap into the global capital market. In mid-2004 the privately held company offered nonvoting preferred stock to investors on the São Paulo Bovespa and the New York Stock Exchange. The simultaneous offering was oversubscribed, with the underwriters lifting the offering price twice, and raised some $322 million. In explaining the decision to offer stock through the New York Stock Exchange, Gol's chief financial officer noted that "We wanted to get a solid group of long-term investors that understood the business. We've got that. We also wanted to get a group of research analysts that understood this sector and we now have seven analysts covering the stock. Southwest, JetBlue, Ryanair and Westjet are considered the tier one in terms of operating profitability and successes. We were able to put Gol right up in that group. Doing both the NYSE and Bovespa was part of

our strategy to sell shares to investors that have familiarity with low-cost carriers. The strategy works. If you look at the list of major investors in the company, the majority of them have high positions in trade of the equities of JetBlue, Southwest and Ryanair. For them, it was a very easy analysis to understand Gol's business model and how it makes money."

Aided by the financing, Gol was able to expand rapidly. By early 2007 it already had 65 aircraft and was operating 600 daily flights to 55 destinations, including seven international routes to five South American countries. Gol had domestic and Brazilian market shares of 37 percent and 13 percent respectively, its planes were 74 percent full on average, the best in Brazil, and it was the most punctual airline in Brazil.[22]

Case Discussion Questions

1. What were the benefits to Gol of a listing on the New York Stock Exchange in addition to the São Paulo Bovespa?

2. Why do you think the Gol stock offering was oversubscribed?

3. Do you think Gol would have raised as much money if it had just listed on the São Paulo exchange?

4. How might the joint listing of the New York and São Paulo stock exchanges affect Gol's ability to raise additional capital in the future?

Notes

1. Sources: R. C. Stewart, "Balancing on the Global High Wire," *Financial Executive*, September/October 1995, pp. 35–39; S. Lipin, F. R. Bleakley, and B. D. Granito, "Portfolio Poker," *The Wall Street Journal*, April 14, 1994, p. A1; and Procter & Gamble 10K report for 2000.

2. L. Quinn, "Currency Futures Trading Helps Firms Sharpen Competitive Edge," *Crain's Chicago Business*, March 2, 1992, p. 20.

3. For details of capital budgeting techniques, see R. A. Brealy and S. C. Myers, *Principles of Corporate Finance* (New York: McGraw-Hill, 1988).

4. D. J. Feils and F. M. Sabac, "The Impact of Political Risk on the Foreign Direct Investment Decision: A Capital Budgeting Analysis," *The Engineering Economist* 45, 2000, pp 129–34.

5. Sources: Feils and Sabac, "The Impact of Political Risk on the Foreign Direct Investment Decision"; S. Kukes, "Letters to the Editor: Tura Joint Venture," *The Wall Street Journal*, June 14, 1999, p. A21; and M. Whitehouse, "US Export–Import Bank Agrees to Give Russia's Tyumen Oil Loan Guarantee," *The Wall Street Journal*, May 25, 1999, p. A21.

6. See S. Block. "Integrating Traditional Capital Budgeting Concepts into an International Decision Making Environment," *The Engineering Economist* 45 (2000), pp. 309–25; J. C. Backer and L. J. Beardsley, "Multinational Companies' Use of Risk Evaluation and Profit Measurement for Capital Budgeting Decisions," *Journal of Business Finance*, Spring 1973, pp. 34–43.

7. For example, see D. K. Eiteman, A. I. Stonehill, and M. H. Moffett, *Multinational Business Finance* (Reading, MA: Addison-Wesley, 1992).

8. M. Stanley and S. Block, "An Empirical Study of Management and Financial Variables Influencing Capital Budgeting Decisions for Multinational Corporations in the 1980s," *Management International Review* 23 (1983), pp. 61–71.

9. W. S. Sekely and J. M. Collins, "Cultural Influences on International Capital Structure," *Journal of International Business Studies*, Spring 1988, pp. 87–100.

10. J. K. Wald. "How Firm Characteristics Affect Capital Structure: An International Comparison," *Journal of Financial Research* 22 (2), 1999, pp. 161–187.

11. J. Collins and W. S. Sekely, "The Relationship of Headquarters, Country, and Industry Classification to Financial Structure," *Financial Structure*, Autumn 1983, pp. 45–51; J. Rutterford, "An International Perspective on the Capital Structure Puzzle," *Midland Corporate Finance Journal*, Fall 1985, p. 72; R. G. Rajan and L. Zingales, "What Do We Know about Capital Structure," *Journal of Finance*, 50, 1995, pp. 1421–60; J. K. Wald, "How Firm Characteristics Affect Capital Structure: An International Comparison," *Journal of Financial Research* 22 (2), 1999, pp. 161–87.

12. Sekely and Collins, "Cultural Influences on International Capital Structure." See also A. C. W. Chui, A. E. Lloyd, and C. C. Y. Kwok, "The Determination of Capital Structure: Is National Culture the Missing Piece to the Puzzle?" *Journal of International Business Studies* 33, 2002, pp. 99–127.

13. KPMG, "KPMG Corporate and Indirect Tax Rate Survey—January 2007," http://www.kpmg .com/NR/rdonlyres/89E7B050-9654-4C7A-8A6E-A05158793CD5/0/CorporateTaxRate-Survey2007.pdf, accessed June 24, 2007.

14. "Taxing Questions," *The Economist*, May 22, 1993, p. 73.

15. S. Crow and E. Sauls, "Setting the Right Transfer Price," *Management Accounting*, December 1994, pp. 41–47.

16. V. H. Miesel, H. H. Higinbotham, and C. W. Yi. "International Transfer Pricing: Practical Solutions for Inter-company Pricing," *International Tax Journal* 28 (Fall 2002), pp. 1–22.

17. J. Kelly, "Administrators Prepare for a More Efficient Future," *Financial Times Survey: World Taxation*, February 24, 1995, p. 9.

18. S. Crow and E. Sauls, "Setting the Right Transfer Price."

19. M. F. Al-Eryani, P. Alam, and S. Akhter, "Transfer Pricing Determinants of U.S. Multinationals," *Journal of International Business Studies*, September 1990, pp. 409–25.

20. D. L. Swenson, "Tax Reforms and Evidence of Transfer Pricing," *National Tax Journal*, March 2001, 54, pp. 7–25.

21. "Transfer Pricing Survey Shows Multinationals Face Greater Scrutiny," *The CPA Journal*, March 2000, p. 10.

22. Sources: E. P. Lima, "Winning Gol!" *Air Transport World*, October 2004, pp. 22–26; G. Samor, "Brazil's Gol Faces Hurdles," *The Wall Street Journal*, August 9, 2004, p. C3; "Gol Launches $322 Million Flotation," *Airfinance Journal*, June 2004, p. 1; "Gol Commemorates Sixth Anniversary," *PR Newswire*, January 15, 2007.

part six
cases

Molex

Molex, a 70-year-old manufacturer of electronic components based in Chicago, is the world's second-largest manufacturer of electronic components. The company established an international division to coordinate exporting in 1967 and opened its first overseas plant in Japan in 1970 and a second in Ireland in 1971. From that base, Molex has evolved into a global business that generates about 61 percent of its $1.84 billion in revenues outside of the United States. The company operates some 50 manufacturing plants in 21 countries and employs more than 16,000 people worldwide, with only one-third of them located in the United States. Molex's competitive advantage is based on a strategy that emphasizes a combination of low costs, excellent customer service, and the mass production of standardized products that are sold globally. Manufacturing sites are located in countries where cost conditions are favorable and major customers are close. Since the 1970s, a key goal of Molex has been to build a truly global company that is at home wherever in the world it operates and that proactively shares valuable knowledge across operations in different countries. The human resource management function of Molex has always played a central role in meeting this goal.

As Molex grew rapidly overseas, the HRM function made sure that every new unit did the same basic things. Each new entity had to have an employee manual with policies and practices in writing, new employee orientation programs, salary administration with a consistent grading system, written job descriptions, written promotion and grievance procedures, standard performance appraisal systems that were written down, and so on. Beyond these things, however, Molex views HRM as the most localized of functions. Different legal systems, particularly with regard to employment law, different compensation norms, different cultural attitudes toward work, different norms regarding vacation, and so on all imply that policies and programs must be customized to the conditions prevailing in a country. To make sure this occurs, Molex's policy is to hire experienced HRM professionals from other companies in the same country in which it has operations. The idea is to hire people who know the language, have credibility, know the law, and know how to recruit in that country.

Molex's strategy for building a global company starts with its staffing policy for managers and engineers. The company frequently hires foreign nationals who are living in the United States, have just completed MBAs, and are willing to relocate if required. These individuals will typically work in the United States for a while, becoming familiar with the company's culture. Some of them will then be sent back to their home country to work there. Molex also carefully screens its American applicants, favoring those who are fluent in at least one other language. Molex is unusual for a U.S. company in this regard. However, with more than 15 languages spoken at its headquarters by native speakers, Molex is committed to multilingual competency. The company also hires a significant number of managers and engineers at the local level. Here, too, a willingness to relocate internationally and foreign language competency are important, although this time English is the preferred foreign language. In a sign of how multinational Molex's management has become, it is not unusual to see foreign nationals holding senior positions at company headquarters. In addition to Americans, individuals of Greek, German, Austrian, Japanese, and British origin have all sat on the company's executive committee, its top decision-making body.

To help build a global company, Molex moves people around the world to give them experience in other countries and to help them learn from each other. It has five categories of expatriates: (1) regular expatriates who live in a country other than their home country for three- to five-year assignments (there are approximately 50 of these at any one time), (2) "inpats" who come to the company's U.S. headquarters from other countries, (3) third-country nationals who move from one Molex entity to another (e.g., Singapore to Taiwan), (4) short-term transfers who go to another Molex entity for six to nine months to work on a specific project, and (5) medium-term transfers who go to another entity for 12 to 24 months, again to work on a specific project.

Having a high level of intracompany movement is costly. For an employee making $75,000 in base salary, the total cost of an expatriate assignment can run as high as $250,000 when additional employee benefits are added in, such as the provision of schooling and housing, adjustments for higher costs of living, adjustments for higher tax rates, and so on. Molex also insists on treating all expatriates the same, whatever their country of origin, so a Singapore expatriate living in Taiwan is likely to be living in the same apartment building and sending his child to the same school as an American expatriate in Taiwan. This boosts the overall costs, but Molex believes that its extensive use of expatriates pays dividends. It allows individuals to understand the challenges of doing business in different countries, it facilitates the sharing of useful knowledge across different business entities, and it helps lay the foundation for a common company culture that is global in its outlook.

Molex also makes sure that expatriates know why they are being sent to a foreign country, both in terms of their own career development and Molex's corporate goals. To prevent expatriates from becoming disconnected from their home office, the HRM department touches base with them on a regular basis through telephone, e-mail, and direct visits. The company also encourages expatriates to make home office visits so that they do not become totally disconnected from their base and feel like a stranger when they return. Upon return, they are debriefed and their knowledge gained abroad is put to use by, for example, placing the expatriates on special task forces.

A final component of Molex's strategy for building a cadre of globally minded managers is the company's in-house management development programs. These are open to a wide range of managers who have worked at Molex for three years or more. Molex uses these programs not just to educate its managers in finance, operations, strategy, and the like, but also to bring together managers from different countries to build a network of individuals who know each other and can work together in a cooperative fashion to solve business problems that transcend borders.

Case Discussion Questions

1. What multinational strategy is Molex pursuing: localization, international, global standardization, or transnational?

2. How would you characterize the approach to staffing used at Molex? Is this appropriate given its strategy?

3. Molex is successful in its use of expatriate managers. Why do you think this is the case? What can be learned from Molex's approach?

4. How does the human resource management function at Molex contribute to attaining its multinational strategy?

Sources

1. J. Laabs, "Molex Makes Global HR Look Easy," *Workforce*, March 1999, pp. 42–46.

2. C. M. Solomon, "Foreign Relations," *Workforce*, November 2000, pp. 50–56.

3. C. M. Solomon, "Navigating Your Search for Global Talent," *Personnel Journal*, May 1995, pp. 94–100.

4. A. C. Poe, "Welcome Back," *HR Magazine*, March 2000, pp. 94–105.

5. Molex SEC Form 10K, 2004.

Procter & Gamble in Japan

Procter & Gamble (P&G), the large U.S. consumer products company, has a well-earned reputation as one of the world's best marketers. P&G manufactures and markets more than 200 products that it sells in 130 countries around the world. Along with Unilever, P&G is a dominant global force in laundry detergents, cleaning products, personal care products, and pet food products. P&G expanded abroad after World War II by exporting its products, brands, and marketing policies to Western Europe, initially with considerable success. Over the next 30 years, this policy of developing new products and marketing strategies in the United States and then transferring them to other countries became entrenched. P&G's adaptation of marketing policies to accommodate country differences was minimal. In general, products were developed in the United States, manufactured locally, and sold using a marketing message created in Cincinnati.

The first signs that this policy was no longer effective emerged in the 1970s, when P&G suffered a number of major setbacks in Japan. By 1985, after 13 years in Japan, P&G was still losing $40 million a year there. It had introduced disposable diapers in Japan and at one time had commanded an 80 percent share of the market, but by the early 1980s it held a miserable 8 percent. Three large Japanese consumer products companies were dominating the market. P&G's diapers, developed in the United States, were too bulky for the tastes of Japanese consumers. Kao, a Japanese company, had developed a line of trim-fit diapers that appealed more to Japanese tastes. Kao introduced its product with a marketing blitz and was quickly rewarded with a 30 percent share of the market. P&G realized it would have to modify its diapers if it were to compete in Japan. It did, and the company now has a 30 percent share of the Japanese market. Plus, P&G's trim-fit diapers have become a best-seller in the United States.

P&G had a similar experience in marketing education in the Japanese laundry detergent market. In the early 1980s, P&G introduced its Cheer laundry detergent in Japan. Developed in the United States, Cheer was promoted in Japan with the U.S. marketing message—Cheer works in all temperatures and produces lots of rich suds. But many Japanese consumers wash their clothes in cold water, which made the claim of working in all temperatures irrelevant. Also, many Japanese add fabric softeners to their water, which reduces detergents' sudsing action, so Cheer did not suds up as advertised. After a disastrous launch, P&G knew it had to adapt its marketing message. Cheer is now promoted as a product that works effectively in cold water with fabric softeners added, and it is one of P&G's best-selling products in Japan.

P&G's experience with disposable diapers and laundry detergents in Japan forced the company to rethink its product development and marketing philosophy. The company decided that its U.S.-centered way of doing business did not work. For the last decade, P&G has been delegating more responsibility for new-product development and marketing to its major subsidiaries in Japan and Europe. The company is more responsive to local differences in consumer tastes and preferences and more willing to admit that good new products can be developed outside the United States.

Evidence that this new approach is working can again be found in the company's activities in Japan. Until 1995, P&G did not sell dish soap in Japan. By 1998, it had Japan's best-selling brand, Joy, which now has a 20 percent share of Japan's $400 million market for dish soap. It made major inroads against the products of two domestic firms, Kao and Lion Corp., each of which marketed multiple brands and controlled nearly 40 percent of the market before P&G's entry. P&G's success with Joy was because of its ability to develop a product formula that was targeted at the unmet needs of Japanese consumers, to design a packaging format that appealed to retailers, and to create a compelling advertising campaign.

In researching the market in the early 1990s, P&G discovered an odd habit: Japanese homemakers squirted out excessive amounts of detergent onto dirty dishes, a clear sign of dissatisfaction with existing products. On further inspection, P&G found that this behavior resulted from the changing eating habits of Japanese consumers. The Japanese are consuming more fried food, and existing dish soaps did not effectively remove grease. Armed with this knowledge, P&G researchers in Japan went to work to create a highly concentrated soap formula based on a new technology developed by the company's scientists in Europe that was highly effective in removing grease. The company also designed a novel package for the product. The packaging of existing products had a clear weakness: the long-neck bottles wasted space on supermarket shelves. P&G's dish soap containers were compact cylinders that took less space in stores, warehouses, and delivery trucks. This improved the efficiency of distribution and allowed supermarkets to use their shelf space more effectively, which made them receptive to

stocking Joy. P&G also devoted considerable attention to developing an advertising campaign for Joy. P&G's ad agency, Dentsu Inc., created commercials in which a famous comedian dropped in on homemakers unannounced with a camera crew to test Joy on the household's dirty dishes. The camera focused on a patch of oil in a pan full of water. After a drop of Joy, the oil dramatically disappeared.

With the product, packaging, and advertising strategy carefully worked out, P&G launched Joy throughout Japan in March 1996. The product almost immediately gained a 10 percent market share. Within three months the product's share had increased to 15 percent, and by year-end it was close to 18 percent. Because of strong demand, P&G was also able to raise prices as were the retailers that stocked the product, all of which translated into fatter margins for the retailers and helped consolidate Joy's position.

In the laundry detergent market too, P&G has been making inroads. Through market research, P&G found that Japanese consumers wanted detergents with stronger cleaning power, so the company developed and launched bleach-reinforced and antibacterial versions of its Ariel detergent in Japan. Both have been very successful, helping to take P&G's share of the Japanese laundry detergent market up to 20 percent by the early 2000s.

Case Discussion Questions

1. How would you characterize P&G's product development and marketing strategy toward Japan in the 1970s and 1980s. What were the advantages of this strategy? What were the drawbacks?

2. How would you characterize the strategy since the early 1990s? What are the advantages of this strategy? What are the potential drawbacks?

3. Which strategy has been more successful? Why?

4. What changes do you think P&G has had to make in its organization and company culture to implement this strategic shift?

5. What does P&G's experience teach us about the argument that consumer tastes and preferences across nations are converging and global markets are becoming more homogenous?

Sources

1. G. de Jonquieres and C. Bobinski, "Wash and Get into a Lather in Poland," *Financial Times*, May 28, 1992, p. 2.

2. "Perestroika in Soapland," *The Economist*, June 10, 1989, pp. 69–71.

3. "After Early Stumbles P&G Is Making Inroads Overseas," *The Wall Street Journal*, February 6, 1989, p. B1.

4. C. A. Bartlett and S. Ghoshal, *Managing across Borders: The Transnational Solution* (Boston: Harvard Business School Press, 1989).

5. N. Shirouzu, "P&G's Joy Makes an Unlikely Splash in Japan," *The Wall Street Journal*, December 10, 1997, p. B1.

6. A. Mollet, "Japan's Washaday Blues," *Chemical Week*, January 26, 2000, p. 26.

Merrill Lynch in Japan

Merrill Lynch is an investment banking titan. The U.S.-based financial services institution is the world's largest underwriter of debt and equity and the third largest mergers and acquisitions adviser behind Morgan Stanley and Goldman Sachs. Merrill Lynch's investment banking operations have long had a global reach. The company has a dominant presence in London and Tokyo. However, Merrill Lynch's international presence was limited to the investment banking side of its business until recently. In contrast, its private client business, which offers banking, financial advice, and stockbrokerage services to individuals, had historically been concentrated in the United States. This started to change in the mid-1990s. In 1995, Merrill Lynch purchased Smith New Court, the largest stockbrokerage in Great Britain. This was followed in 1997 by the acquisition of Mercury Asset Management, the United Kingdom's leading manager of mutual funds. Then in 1998, Merrill Lynch acquired Midland Walwyn, Canada's last major independent stockbrokerage. The company's boldest moves, however, have probably been in Japan.

Merrill Lynch started a private client business in Japan in the 1980s but met with limited success. At the time, it was the first foreign firm to enter Japan's private client investment market. The company found it extremely difficult to attract employee talent and customers away from Japan's big four stockbrokerages, which traditionally had monopolized the Japanese market. Plus, restrictive regulations made it almost impossible for Merrill Lynch to offer its Japanese private clients the range of services it offered clients in the United States. For example, foreign exchange regulations meant it was very difficult to sell non-Japanese stocks, bonds, and mutual funds to Japanese investors. In 1993, Merrill Lynch admitted defeat, closed its six retail branches in Kobe and Kyoto, and withdrew from the private client market in Japan.

Over the next few years, however, things changed. In the mid-1990s, Japan embarked on a wide ranging deregulation of its financial services industry. This led to the removal of many of the restrictions that had made it so difficult for Merrill Lynch to do business in Japan. For example, the relaxation of foreign exchange controls meant that by 1998, Japanese citizens could purchase foreign stocks, bonds, and mutual funds. Meanwhile, Japan's big four stockbrokerages continued to struggle with serious financial problems that resulted from the 1991 crash of that country's stock market. In November 1997, in what was a shock to many Japanese, one of these firms, Yamaichi Securities, declared it was bankrupt due to $2.2 billion in accumulated "hidden losses" and that it would shut its doors. Recognizing the country's financial system was strained and in need of fresh capital, know-how, and the stimulus of greater competition, the Japanese government signaled that it would adopt a more relaxed attitude to foreign entry into its financial services industry. This attitude underlay Japan's wholehearted endorsement of a 1997 deal brokered by the World Trade Organization to liberalize global financial services. Among other things, the WTO deal made it much easier for foreign firms to sell financial service products to Japanese investors.

By 1997, it had become clear to Merrill Lynch that the climate in Japan had changed significantly. The big attraction of the market was still the same: the financial assets owned by Japanese households are huge, amounting to ¥1,220 trillion in late 1997, only 3 percent of which were then invested in mutual funds (most are invested in low-yielding bank accounts and government bonds). In mid-1997, Merrill Lynch started to consider reentering the Japanese private client market.

The company initially considered a joint venture with Sanwa Bank to sell Merrill Lynch's mutual fund products to Japanese consumers through Sanwa's 400 retail branches. The proposed alliance would have allowed Merrill Lynch to leverage Sanwa's existing distribution system, rather than having to build its own distribution system. However, the long-run disadvantage of such a strategy was that it would not have given Merrill Lynch the presence that it believed it needed to build a solid financial services business in Japan. Top executives reasoned that it was important for them to make a major commitment to the Japanese market to establish the company's brand name as a premier provider of investment products and financial advice to individuals. This would enable Merrill Lynch to entrench itself as a major player before other foreign institutions entered the market—and before Japan's own stockbrokerages rose to the challenge.

At the same time, given their prior experience in Japan, Merrill Lynch executives were hesitant to go down this road because of the huge costs and risks involved.

The problem of how best to enter the Japanese market was solved by the bankruptcy of Yamaichi Securities. Suddenly Yamaichi's nationwide network of offices and 7,000 employees were up for grabs. In late December 1997, Merrill Lynch announced it would hire 2,000 of Yamaichi's employees and acquire 33 of Yamaichi's branch offices. The deal, which was enthusiastically endorsed by the Japanese government, significantly lowered Merrill Lynch's costs of establishing a retail network in Japan.

The company got off to a quick start. In February 1998, Merrill Lynch launched its first mutual fund in Japan and saw the value of its assets swell to $1 billion by April. By mid-2002, Merrill Lynch announced it had $12.9 billion under management in Japan. However, the collapse in global stock markets in 2001–02 hit Merrill's Japanese unit hard. After losing $500 million in Japan on its investment, in January 2002 the company fired 75 percent of its Japanese workforce and closed all but eight of its retail locations. Despite this costly downsizing, the company held onto almost all of the assets under management, continued to attract new accounts, and by mid-2002 was reportedly making a profit in Japan.

Case Discussion Questions

1. Given the changes that have occurred in the international capital markets during the past decade, does Merrill Lynch's strategy of expanding internationally make sense? Why?

2. What factors make Japan a suitable market for Merrill Lynch to enter?

3. Review Merrill Lynch's 1997 reentry into the Japanese private client market. Pay close attention to the timing and scale of entry and the nature of the strategic commitments Merrill Lynch is making in Japan. What are the potential benefits associated with this strategy? What are the costs and risks? Do you think the trade-off between benefits and risks and costs makes sense? Why?

4. The collapse in stock market values in 2001–2002 resulted in Merrill Lynch's Japanese unit incurring significant losses. In retrospect, was the Japanese expansion a costly blunder or did the company simply get hit by macroeconomic events that were difficult to predict and avoid?

5. Do you think Merrill Lynch should continue in Japan? Why?

Sources

1. "Japan's Big Bang. Enter Merrill," *The Economist*, January 3, 1998, p. 72.

2. J. P. Donlon, "Merrill Cinch," *Chief Executive*, March 1998, pp. 28–32.

3. D. Holley, "Merrill Lynch to Open 31 Offices throughout Japan," *Los Angeles Times*, February 13, 1998, p. D1.

4. A. Rowley, "Merrill Thunders into Japan," *The Banker*, March 1998, p. 6.

5. J. Singer, "Merrill Reports Profits for Operation in Japan," *The Wall Street Journal*, July 19, 2002, p. A9.

6. Merrill Lynch's Web site, www.ml.com.

GLOSSARY

A

absolute advantage A country has an absolute advantage in the production of a product when it is more efficient than any other country at producing it.

accounting standards Rules for preparing financial statements.

ad valorem tariff A tariff levied as a proportion of the value of an imported good.

administrative trade policies Administrative policies, typically adopted by government bureaucracies, that can be used to restrict imports or boost exports.

Andean Pact A 1969 agreement between Bolivia, Chile, Ecuador, Colombia, and Peru to establish a customs union.

antidumping policies Designed to punish foreign firms that engage in dumping and thus protect domestic producers from unfair foreign competition.

antidumping regulations Regulations designed to restrict the sale of goods for less than their fair market price.

arbitrage The purchase of securities in one market for immediate resale in another to profit from a price discrepancy.

Asia–Pacific Economic Cooperation (APEC) Made up of 21 member states whose goal is to increase multilateral cooperation in view of the economic rise of the Pacific nations.

Association of South East Asian Nations (ASEAN) Formed in 1967, an attempt to establish a free trade area between Brunei, Indonesia, Malaysia, the Philippines, Singapore, and Thailand.

auditing standards Rules for performing an audit.

B

backward vertical FDI Investing in an industry abroad that provides inputs for a firm's domestic processes.

balance-of-payments accounts National accounts that track both payments to and receipts from foreigners.

balance-of-trade equilibrium Reached when the income a nation's residents earn from exports equals money paid for imports.

bandwagon effect When traders move like a herd, all in the same direction and at the same time, in response to each others' perceived actions.

banking crisis A loss of confidence in the banking system that leads to a run on banks, as individuals and companies withdraw their deposits.

barriers to entry Factors that make it difficult or costly for firms to enter an industry or market.

barter The direct exchange of goods or services between two parties without a cash transaction.

basic research centers Centers for fundamental research located in regions where valuable scientific knowledge is being created; they develop the basic technologies that become new products.

bilateral netting Settlement in which the amount one subsidiary owes another can be canceled by the debt the second subsidiary owes the first.

bill of exchange An order written by an exporter instructing an importer, or an importer's agent, to pay a specified amount of money at a specified time.

bill of lading A document issued to an exporter by a common carrier transporting merchandise. It serves as a receipt, a contract, and a document of title.

Bretton Woods A 1944 conference in which representatives of 40 countries met to design a new international monetary system.

bureaucratic controls Achieving control through establishment of a system of rules and procedures.

business ethics The accepted principles of right or wrong governing the conduct of businesspeople.

buyback Agreement to accept percentage of a plant's output as payment for contract to build a plant.

C

capital account In the balance of payments, records transactions involving the purchase or sale of assets.

capital controls Restrictions on cross-border capital flows that segment different stock markets; limit amount of a firm's stock a foreigner can own; and limit a citizen's ability to invest outside the country.

capital flight Residents convert domestic currency into a foreign currency.

Caribbean Single Market and Economy (CSME) Unites six CARICOM members in agreeing to lower trade barriers and harmonize macroeconomic and monetary policies.

CARICOM An association of English-speaking Caribbean states that are attempting to establish a customs union.

caste system A system of social stratification in which social position is determined by the family into which a person is born, and change in that position is usually not possible during an individual's lifetime.

Central America Free Trade Agreement (CAFTA) The agreement of the member states of the Central American Common Market joined by the Dominican Republic to trade freely with the United States.

Central American Common Market A trade pact between Costa Rica, El Salvador, Guatemala, Honduras, and Nicaragua, which began in the early 1960s but collapsed in 1969 due to war.

centralized depository The practice of centralizing corporate cash balances in a single depository.

channel length The number of intermediaries that a product has to go through before it reaches the final consumer.

channel quality The expertise, competencies, and skills of established retailers in a nation, and their ability to sell and support the products of international businesses.

civil law system A system of law based on a very detailed set of written laws and codes.

class-consciousness A tendency for individuals to perceive themselves in terms of their class background.

class system A system of social stratification in which social status is determined by the family into which a person is born and by subsequent socioeconomic achievements. Mobility between classes is possible.

code of ethics A formal statement of the ethical priorities of a business or organization.

collectivism An emphasis on collective goals as opposed to individual goals.

COMECON Now-defunct economic association of Eastern European Communist states headed by the former Soviet Union.

command economy An economic system where the allocation of resources, including determination of what goods and services should be produced, and in what quantity, is planned by the government.

common law system A system of law based on tradition, precedent, and custom. When law courts interpret common law, they do so with regard to these characteristics.

common market A group of countries committed to (1) removing all barriers to the free flow of goods, services, and factors of production between each other and (2) the pursuit of a common external trade policy.

communist totalitarianism A version of collectivism advocating that socialism can be achieved only through a totalitarian dictatorship.

communists Those who believe socialism can be achieved only through revolution and totalitarian dictatorship.

comparative advantage The theory that countries should specialize in the production of goods and services they can produce most efficiently. A country is said to have a comparative advantage in the production of such goods and services.

competition policy Regulations designed to promote competition and restrict monopoly practices.

Confucian dynamism Theory that Confucian teachings affect attitudes toward time, persistence, ordering by status, protection of face, respect for tradition, and reciprocation of gifts and favors.

constant returns to specialization The units of resources required to produce a good are assumed to remain constant no matter where one is on a country's production possibility frontier.

contract Document that specifies conditions of an exchange and details rights and obligations of involved parties.

contract law Body of law that governs contract enforcement.

control systems Metrics used to measure performance of subunits.

controlling interest A firm has a controlling interest in another business entity when it owns more than 50 percent of that entity's voting stock.

controls The metrics used to measure the performance of subunits and make judgments about how well managers are running those subunits.

Convention on Combating Bribery of Foreign Public Officials in International Business Transactions OECD agreement to make the bribery of foreign public officials a criminal offense.

copyright Exclusive legal rights of authors, composers, playwrights, artists, and publishers to publish and dispose of their work as they see fit.

core competence Firm skills that competitors cannot easily match or imitate.

corporate culture The organization's norms and value systems.

cost of capital Price of money.

Council of the European Union Represents the interests of EU members and has authority to approve EU laws.

counterpurchase A reciprocal buying agreement.

countertrade The trade of goods and services for other goods and services.

countervailing duties Antidumping duties.

Court of Justice Supreme appeals court for EU law.

cross-cultural literacy Understanding how the culture of a country affects the way business is practiced.

cross-licensing agreement An arrangement in which a company licenses valuable intangible property to a foreign partner and receives a license for the partner's valuable knowledge; reduces risk of licensing.

cultural controls Achieving control by persuading subordinates to identify with the norms and value systems of the organization (self-control).

cultural relativism   Belief that ethics are culturally determined, and a firm should adopt the ethics of the culture in which it is operating.

culture   The complex whole that includes knowledge, belief, art, morals, law, custom, and other capabilities acquired by a person as a member of society.

currency board   Means of controlling a country's currency.

currency crisis   Occurs when a speculative attack on the exchange value of a currency results in a sharp depreciation in the value of the currency or forces authorities to expend large volumes of international currency reserves and sharply increase interest rates to defend the prevailing exchange rate.

currency speculation   Involves short-term movement of funds from one currency to another in hopes of profiting from shifts in exchange rates.

currency swap   Simultaneous purchase and sale of a given amount of foreign exchange for two different value dates.

currency translation   Converting the financial statements of foreign subsidiaries into the currency of the home country.

current account   In the balance of payments, records transactions involving the export or import of goods and services.

current account deficit   The current account of the balance of payments is in deficit when a country imports more goods and services than it exports.

current account surplus   The current account of the balance of payments is in surplus when a country exports more goods and services than it imports.

current cost accounting   Method that adjusts all items in a financial statement to factor out the effects of inflation.

current rate method   Using the exchange rate at the balance sheet date to translate the financial statements of a foreign subsidiary into the home currency.

customs union   A group of countries committed to (1) removing all barriers to the free flow of goods and services between each other and (2) the pursuit of a common external trade policy.

D

D'Amato Act   Act passed in 1996, similar to the Helms-Burton Act, aimed at Libya and Iran.

debt loan   Requires a corporation to repay loan at regular intervals.

deferral principle   Parent companies are not taxed on the income of a foreign subsidiary until they actually receive a dividend from that subsidiary.

democracy   Political system in which government is by the people, exercised either directly or through elected representatives.

deregulation   Removal of government restrictions concerning the conduct of a business.

diminishing returns to specialization   Applied to international trade theory, the more of a good that a country produces, the greater the units of resources required to produce each additional item.

dirty-float system   A system under which a country's currency is nominally allowed to float freely against other currencies, but in which the government will intervene, buying and selling currency, if it believes that the currency has deviated too far from its fair value.

draft   An order written by an exporter telling an importer what and when to pay.

drawee   The party to whom a bill of lading is presented.

dumping   Selling goods in a foreign market for less than their cost of production or below their "fair" market value.

E

eclectic paradigm   Argument that combining location-specific assets or resource endowments and the firm's own unique assets often requires FDI; it requires the firm to establish production facilities where those foreign assets or resource endowments are located.

e-commerce   Conducting business online through the Internet.

economic exposure   The extent to which a firm's future international earning power is affected by changes in exchange rates.

economic risk   The likelihood that events, including economic mismanagement, will cause drastic changes in a country's business environment that adversely affect the profit and other goals of a particular business enterprise.

economic union   A group of countries committed to (1) removing all barriers to the free flow of goods, services, and factors of production between each other, (2) the adoption of a common currency, (3) the harmonization of tax rates, and (4) the pursuit of a common external trade policy.

economies of scale   Cost advantages associated with large-scale production.

efficient market   A market where prices reflect all available information.

ending rate   The spot exchange rate when budget and performance are being compared.

entrepreneurs   Those who first commercialize innovations.

equity loan   Occurs when a corporation sells stock to an investor.

ethical dilemma   Situation in which no available alternative seems ethically acceptable.

ethical strategy A course of action that does not violate business ethics.

ethical systems Cultural beliefs about what is proper behavior and conduct.

ethics officer An individual hired by a company to be responsible for making sure that all employees are trained to be ethically aware, that ethical considerations enter the decision-making process, and that employees follow the company's code of ethics.

ethnocentric behavior Behavior that is based on the belief in the superiority of one's own ethnic group or culture; often shows disregard or contempt for the culture of other countries.

ethnocentric staffing A staffing approach within the MNE in which all key management positions are filled by parent-country nationals.

ethnocentrism Belief in the superiority of one's own ethnic group or culture.

eurobonds A bond placed in countries other than the one in whose currency the bond is denominated.

eurocurrency Any currency banked outside its country of origin.

eurodollar Dollar banked outside the United States.

European Commission Responsible for proposing EU legislation, implementing it, and monitoring compliance.

European Council Consists of the heads of state of EU members and the president of the European Commission.

European Free Trade Association (EFTA) A free trade association including Norway, Iceland, and Switzerland.

European Monetary System (EMS) EU system designed to create a zone of monetary stability in Europe, control inflation, and coordinate exchange rate policies of EU countries.

European Parliament Elected EU body that provides consultation on issues proposed by European Commission.

European Union (EU) An economic group of 25 European nations. Established as a customs union, it is now moving toward economic union. (Formerly the European Community.)

exchange rate The rate at which one currency is converted into another.

exchange rate mechanism (ERM) Mechanism for aligning the exchange rates of EU currencies against each other.

exclusive channel A distribution channel that outsiders find difficult to access.

expatriate A citizen of one country working in another country.

expatriate failure The premature return of an expatriate manager to the home country.

expatriate manager A national of one country appointed to a management position in another country.

experience curve Systematic production cost reductions that occur over the life of a product.

experience curve pricing Aggressive pricing designed to increase volume and help the firm realize experience curve economies.

Export–Import Bank (Eximbank) Agency of the U.S. government whose mission is to provide aid in financing and facilitate exports and imports.

export management company Export specialists who act as an export marketing department for client firms.

exporting Sale of products produced in one country to residents of another country.

external stakeholders All other individuals and groups, other than internal stakeholders, that have some claim on the business.

externalities Knowledge spillovers.

externally convertible currency Nonresidents can convert their holdings of domestic currency into foreign currency, but the ability of residents to convert the currency is limited in some way.

F

factor endowments A country's endowment with resources such as land, labor, and capital.

factors of production Inputs into the productive process of a firm, including labor, management, land, capital, and technological know-how.

Financial Accounting Standards Board (FASB) The body that writes the generally accepted accounting principles by which the financial statements of U.S. firms must be prepared.

financial structure Mix of debt and equity used to finance a business.

first-mover advantages Advantages accruing to the first to enter a market.

first-mover disadvantages Disadvantages associated with entering a foreign market before other international businesses.

Fisher Effect Nominal interest rates (i) in each country equal the required real rate of interest (r) and the expected rate of inflation over the period of time for which the funds are to be lent (I). That is, $i = r + I$.

fixed exchange rates A system under which the exchange rate for converting one currency into another is fixed.

fixed-rate bond Offers a fixed set of cash payoffs each year until maturity, when the investor also receives the face value of the bond in cash.

flexible machine cells Flexible manufacturing technology in which a grouping of various machine types, a common materials handler, and a centralized cell controller produce a family of products.

flexible manufacturing technologies Manufacturing technologies designed to improve job scheduling, reduce setup time, and improve quality control.

floating exchange rates A system under which the exchange rate for converting one currency into another is continuously adjusted depending on the laws of supply and demand.

flow of foreign direct investment The amount of foreign direct investment undertaken over a given time period (normally one year).

folkways Routine conventions of everyday life.

foreign bonds Bonds sold outside the borrower's country and denominated in the currency of the country in which they are issued.

Foreign Corrupt Practices Act U.S. law regulating behavior regarding the conduct of international business in the taking of bribes and other unethical actions.

foreign debt crisis Situation in which a country cannot service its foreign debt obligations, whether private-sector or government debt.

foreign direct investment (FDI) Direct investment in business operations in a foreign country.

foreign exchange exposure The risk that future changes in a country's exchange rate will hurt the firm.

foreign exchange market A market for converting the currency of one country into that of another country.

foreign exchange risk The risk that changes in exchange rates will hurt the profitability of a business deal.

foreign portfolio investment (FPI) Investments by individuals, firms, or public bodies (e.g., national and local governments) in foreign financial instruments (e.g., government bonds, foreign stocks).

forward exchange When two parties agree to exchange currency and execute a deal at some specific date in the future.

forward exchange rate The exchange rates governing forward exchange transactions.

forward vertical FDI Investing in an industry abroad that sells outputs of domestic processes.

franchising A specialized form of licensing in which the franchiser sells intangible property to the franchisee and insists on rules to conduct the business.

free trade The absence of barriers to the free flow of goods and services between countries.

free trade area A group of countries committed to removing all barriers to the free flow of goods and services between each other, but pursuing independent external trade policies.

freely convertible currency A country's currency is freely convertible when the government of that country allows both residents and nonresidents to purchase unlimited amounts of foreign currency with the domestic currency.

fronting loan A loan between a parent company and a foreign subsidiary that is channeled through a financial intermediary.

fundamental analysis Draws on economic theory to construct sophisticated econometric models for predicting exchange rate movements.

fundamental rights of stakeholders Basic rights of stakeholders, such as the right to information about products and working conditions, that should be considered when business decisions are made.

G

gains from trade The economic gains to a country from engaging in international trade.

General Agreement on Tariffs and Trade (GATT) International treaty that committed signatories to lowering barriers to the free flow of goods across national borders and led to the WTO.

geocentric staffing A staffing policy where the best people are sought for key jobs throughout an MNE, regardless of nationality.

global learning The flow of skills and product offerings from foreign subsidiary to home country and from foreign subsidiary to foreign subsidiary.

global matrix structure Horizontal differentiation proceeds along two dimensions: product divisions and areas.

global standardization strategy Strategy focusing on increasing profitability by reaping cost reductions from experience curve and location economies.

global web When different stages of the value chain are dispersed to those locations around the globe where value added is maximized or where costs of value creation are minimized.

globalization Trend away from distinct national economic units and toward one huge global market.

globalization of markets Moving away from an economic system in which national markets are distinct entities, isolated by trade barriers and barriers of distance, time, and culture, and toward a system in which national markets are merging into one global market.

globalization of production Trend by individual firms to disperse parts of their productive processes to different locations around the globe to take advantage of differences in cost and quality of factors of production.

gold par value The amount of currency needed to purchase one ounce of gold.

gold standard The practice of pegging currencies to gold and guaranteeing convertibility.

greenfield investment Establishing a new operation in a foreign country.

gross domestic product (GDP)   The market value of a country's output attributable to factors of production located in the country's territory.

gross fixed capital formation   Summarizes the total amount of capital invested in factories, stores, office buildings, and the like.

gross national income (GNI)   Measures the total annual income received by residents of a nation.

gross national product (GNP)   The market value of all the final goods and services produced by a national economy.

group   An association of two or more individuals who have a shared sense of identity and who interact with each other in structured ways on the basis of a common set of expectations about each other's behavior.

H

Heckscher-Ohlin theory   Countries will export those goods that make intensive use of locally abundant factors of production and import goods that make intensive use of locally scarce factors of production.

hedge fund   Investment fund that not only buys financial assets (stocks, bonds, currencies) but also sells them short.

hedging   The process of insuring one's business against foreign exchange risk by using forward exchanges or currency swaps.

Helms–Burton Act   Act passed in 1996 that allowed Americans to sue foreign firms that use Cuban property confiscated from them after the 1959 revolution.

historic cost principle   Accounting principle founded on the assumption that the currency unit used to report financial results is not losing its value due to inflation.

home country   The source country for foreign direct investment.

horizontal differentiation   The division of the firm into subunits.

horizontal foreign direct investment   Foreign direct investment in the same industry abroad as a firm operates in at home.

host country   Recipient country of inward investment by a foreign firm.

Human Development Index   An attempt by the United Nations to assess the impact of a number of factors on the quality of human life in a country.

human resource management   Activities an organization conducts to use its human resources effectively.

I

import quota   A direct restriction on the quantity of a good that can be imported into a country.

incentives   Devices used to reward managerial behavior.

individualism   An emphasis on the importance of guaranteeing individual freedom and self-expression.

individualism versus collectivism   Theory focusing on the relationship between the individual and his or her fellows. In individualistic societies, the ties between individuals are loose and individual achievement is highly valued. In societies where collectivism is emphasized, ties between individuals are tight, people are born into collectives, such as extended families, and everyone is supposed to look after the interests of his or her collective.

inefficient market   One in which prices do not reflect all available information.

infant industry argument   New industries in developing countries must be temporarily protected from international competition to help them reach a position where they can compete on world markets with the firms of developed nations.

inflows of FDI   Flow of foreign direct investment into a country.

initial rate   The spot exchange rate when a budget is adopted.

innovation   Development of new products, processes, organizations, management practices, and strategies.

integrating mechanisms   Mechanisms for achieving coordination between subunits within an organization.

intellectual property   Products of the mind, ideas (e.g., books, music, computer software, designs, technological know-how). Intellectual property can be protected by patents, copyrights, and trademarks.

internal forward rate   A company-generated forecast of future spot rates.

internal stakeholders   Individuals or groups who work for or own the business.

internalization theory   Marketing imperfection approach to foreign direct investment.

International Accounting Standards Board (IASB)   Organization of representatives of professional accounting organizations from many countries that is attempting to harmonize accounting standards across countries.

international business   Any firm that engages in international trade or investment.

international division   Division responsible for a firm's international activities.

International Fisher Effect   For any two countries, the spot exchange rate should change in an equal amount but in the opposite direction to the difference in nominal interest rates between countries.

International Monetary Fund (IMF)   International institution set up to maintain order in the international monetary system.

international monetary system   Institutional arrangements countries adopt to govern exchange rates.

international strategy Trying to create value by transferring core competencies to foreign markets where indigenous competitors lack those competencies.

international trade Occurs when a firm exports goods or services to consumers in another country.

ISO 9000 Certification process that requires certain quality standards that must be met.

J

joint venture A cooperative undertaking between two or more firms.

just distribution One that is considered fair and equitable.

just-in-time (JIT) Logistics systems designed to deliver parts to a production process as they are needed, not before.

justice theories Ethical approaches that focus on the attainment of a just distribution of economic goods and services.

K

Kantian ethics Belief that people should be treated as ends and never purely as means to the ends of others.

knowledge network Network for transmitting information within an organization that is based on informal contacts between managers within an enterprise and on distributed information systems.

L

lag strategy Delaying the collection of foreign currency receivables if that currency is expected to appreciate, and delaying payables if that currency is expected to depreciate.

late-mover advantages Benefits enjoyed by a company that is late to enter a new market, such as consumer familiarity with the product or knowledge gained about a market.

late-mover disadvantages Handicap that late entrants to a market suffer.

law of one price In competitive markets free of transportation costs and barriers to trade, identical products sold in different countries must sell for the same price when their price is expressed in the same currency.

lead market Market where products are first introduced.

lead strategy Collecting foreign currency receivables early when a foreign currency is expected to depreciate, and paying foreign currency payables before they are due when a currency is expected to appreciate.

lean production systems Flexible manufacturing technologies pioneered at Toyota and now used in much of the automobile industry.

learning effects Cost savings from learning by doing.

legal risk The likelihood that a trading partner will opportunistically break a contract or expropriate intellectual property rights.

legal system System of rules that regulate behavior and the processes by which the laws of a country are enforced and through which redress of grievances is obtained.

Leontief paradox The empirical finding that, in contrast to the predictions of the Heckscher-Ohlin theory, U.S. exports are less capital intensive than U.S. imports.

letter of credit Issued by a bank, indicating that the bank will make payments under specific circumstances.

licensing Occurs when a firm (the licensor) licenses the right to produce its product, use its production processes, or use its brand name or trademark to another firm (the licensee). In return for giving the licensee these rights, the licensor collects a royalty fee on every unit the licensee sells.

licensing agreement Arrangement in which a licensor grants the rights to intangible property to a licensee for a specified period and receives a royalty fee in return.

local content requirement A requirement that some specific fraction of a good be produced domestically.

localization strategy Plan focusing on increasing profitability by customizing the goods or services to match tastes in national markets.

location economies Cost advantages from performing a value creation activity at the optimal location for that activity.

location-specific advantages Advantages that arise from using resource endowments or assets that are tied to a particular foreign location and that a firm finds valuable to combine with its own unique assets (such as the firm's technological, marketing, or management know-how).

logistics The procurement and physical transmission of material through the supply chain, from suppliers to customers.

M

Maastricht Treaty Treaty agreed to in 1991, but not ratified until January 1, 1994, that committed the 12 member states of the European Community to a closer economic and political union.

make-or-buy decisions Decisions a company makes about whether to perform a value creation activity itself or to outsource it to another entity.

maker Person or business initiating a bill of lading (draft).

managed-float system System under which some currencies are allowed to float freely, but the majority are either managed by government intervention or pegged to another currency.

management network A network of informal contact between individual managers.

market economy The allocation of resources is determined by the invisible hand of the price system.

market imperfections Imperfections in the operation of the market mechanism.

market makers Financial service companies that connect investors and borrowers, either directly or indirectly.

market power Ability of a firm to exercise control over industry prices or output.

market segmentation Identifying groups of consumers whose purchasing behavior differs from others in important ways.

marketing mix Choices about product attributes, distribution strategy, communication strategy, and pricing strategy that a firm offers its targeted markets.

masculinity versus femininity Theory of the relationship between gender and work roles. In masculine cultures, sex roles are sharply differentiated and traditional "masculine values" such as achievement and the effective exercise of power determine cultural ideals. In feminine cultures, sex roles are less sharply distinguished, and little differentiation is made between men and women in the same job.

mass customization The production of a wide variety of end products at a unit cost that could once be achieved only through mass production of a standardized output.

materials management The activity that controls the transmission of physical materials through the value chain, from procurement through production and into distribution.

mercantilism An economic philosophy advocating that countries should simultaneously encourage exports and discourage imports.

MERCOSUR Pact between Argentina, Brazil, Paraguay, and Uruguay to establish a free trade area.

minimum efficient scale The level of output at which most plant-level scale economies are exhausted.

MITI Japan's Ministry of International Trade and Industry.

mixed economy Certain sectors of the economy are left to private ownership and free market mechanisms, while other sectors have significant government ownership and government planning.

money management Managing a firm's global cash resources efficiently.

Moore's Law The power of microprocessor technology doubles and its costs of production fall in half every 18 months.

moral hazard Arises when people behave recklessly because they know they will be saved if things go wrong.

moral imagination Standing in the shoes of a stakeholder and asking how a proposed decision will affect that stakeholder.

mores Norms seen as central to the functioning of a society and to its social life.

multidomestic strategy Emphasizing the need to be responsive to the unique conditions prevailing in different national markets.

Multilateral Agreement on Investment (MAI) An agreement that would make it illegal for signatory states to discriminate against foreign investors; would have liberalized rules governing FDI between OECD states.

multilateral netting A technique used to reduce the number of transactions between subsidiaries of the firm, thereby reducing the total transaction costs arising from foreign exchange dealings and transfer fees.

multinational enterprise (MNE) A firm that owns business operations in more than one country.

multipoint competition Arises when two or more enterprises encounter each other in different regional markets, national markets, or industries.

multipoint pricing Occurs when a pricing strategy in one market may have an impact on a rival's pricing strategy in another market.

N

naive immoralism Approach that accepts ignoring ethical norms if others do so too.

new trade theory The observed pattern of trade in the world economy may be due in part to the ability of firms in a given market to capture first-mover advantages.

noblesse oblige A French term referring to the honorable and benevolent behavior required of persons with noble birth.

nonconvertible currency A currency is not convertible when both residents and nonresidents are prohibited from converting their holdings of that currency into another currency.

norms Social rules and guidelines that prescribe appropriate behavior in particular situations.

North American Free Trade Agreement (NAFTA) Free trade area between Canada, Mexico, and the United States.

O

offset Agreement to purchase goods and services with a specified percentage of proceeds from an original sale in that country from any firm in the country.

offshore production FDI undertaken to serve the home market.

oligopoly An industry composed of a limited number of large firms.

operations The various value-creation activities a firm undertakes.

optimal currency area Region in which similarities in economic activity make a single currency and exchange rate feasible instruments of macroeconomic policy.

organization architecture   The totality of a firm's organization, including formal organizational structure, control systems and incentives, organizational culture, processes, and people.

organization culture   Norms and values shared by employees.

Organization for Economic Cooperation and Development (OECD)   A Paris-based intergovernmental organization of "wealthy" nations whose purpose is to provide its 29 member states with a forum in which governments can compare their experiences, discuss the problems they share, and seek solutions that can then be applied within their own national contexts.

organizational structure   The three-part structure of an organization, including its formal division into subunits such as product divisions, its location of decision-making responsibilities within that structure, and the establishment of integrating mechanisms to coordinate the activities of all subunits.

outflows of FDI   Flow of foreign direct investment out of a country.

output controls   Achieving control by setting goals for subordinates, expressing these goals in terms of objective criteria, and then judging performance by a subordinate's ability to meet these goals.

P

Paris Convention for the Protection of Industrial Property   International agreement to protect intellectual property; signed by 96 countries.

patent   Grants the inventor of a new product or process exclusive rights to the manufacture, use, or sale of that invention.

pegged exchange rate   Currency value is fixed relative to a reference currency.

people   Part of the organizational architecture that includes strategy used to recruit, compensate, and retain employees.

performance ambiguity   Occurs when the causes of good or bad performance are not clearly identifiable.

personal controls   Achieving control by personal contact with subordinates.

personal ethics   The generally accepted principles of right and wrong governing the conduct of individuals.

pioneering costs   Costs an early entrant bears that later entrants avoid, such as the time and effort in learning the rules, failure due to ignorance, and the liability of being a foreigner.

political economy   The study of how political factors influence the functioning of an economic system.

political risk   The likelihood that political forces will cause drastic changes in a country's business environment that will adversely affect the profit and other goals of a particular business enterprise.

political system   System of government in a nation.

political union   A central political apparatus coordinates economic, social, and foreign policy.

polycentric staffing   A staffing policy in an MNE in which host-country nationals are recruited to manage subsidiaries in their own country, while parent-country nationals occupy key positions at corporate headquarters.

positive-sum game   A situation in which all countries can benefit even if some benefit more than others.

power distance   Theory of how a society deals with the fact that people are unequal in physical and intellectual capabilities. High power distance cultures are found in countries that let inequalities grow over time into inequalities of power and wealth. Low power distance cultures are found in societies that try to play down such inequalities as much as possible.

predatory pricing   Reducing prices below fair market value as a competitive weapon to drive weaker competitors out of the market ("fair" being cost plus some reasonable profit margin).

price discrimination   The practice of charging different prices for the same product in different markets.

price elasticity of demand   A measure of how responsive demand for a product is to changes in price.

private action   Violation of property rights through theft, piracy, blackmail, and the like by private individuals or groups.

privatization   The sale of state-owned enterprises to private investors.

processes   Manner in which decisions are made and work is performed.

product liability   Involves holding a firm and its officers responsible when a product causes injury, death, or damage.

product life-cycle theory   The optimal location in the world to produce a product changes as the market for the product matures.

product safety laws   Set certain safety standards to which a product must adhere.

production   Activities involved in creating a product.

production possibility frontier (PPF)   The various output possibilities a country can produce from its resource pool.

profit   Difference between revenues and costs.

profit growth   The percentage increase in net profits over time.

profitability   A rate of return concept.

projected rate   The spot exchange rate forecast for the end of the budget period.

property rights   Bundle of legal rights over the use to which a resource is put and over the use made of any income that may be derived from that resource.

public action   Violation of property rights when public officials extort income, resources, or the property itself from property holders.

pull strategy   A marketing strategy emphasizing mass media advertising as opposed to personal selling.

purchasing power parity (PPP)   An adjustment in gross domestic product per capita to reflect differences in the cost of living.

push strategy   A marketing strategy emphasizing personal selling rather than mass media advertising.

Q

quota rent   Extra profit producers make when supply is artificially limited by an import quota.

R

regional economic integration   Agreements among countries in a geographic region to reduce and ultimately remove tariff and nontariff barriers to the free flow of goods, services, and factors of production between each other.

relatively efficient market   One in which few impediments to international trade and investment exist.

religion   A system of shared beliefs and rituals concerned with the sacred.

representative democracy   A political system in which citizens periodically elect individuals to represent them in government.

right-wing totalitarianism   A political system in which political power is monopolized by a party, group, or individual that generally permits individual economic freedom but restricts individual political freedom, including free speech, often on the grounds that it would lead to the rise of communism.

righteous moralism   Approach that one's own ethics are appropriate in all cultures.

rights theories   Ethical approaches that recognize that humans have fundamental rights that transcend national boundaries.

royalties   Remuneration paid to the owners of technology, patents, or trade names for the use of same.

S

short selling   Occurs when an investor places a speculative bet that the value of a financial asset will decline, and profits from that decline.

sight draft   A draft payable on presentation to the drawee.

Single European Act   A 1997 act, adopted by members of the European Community, that committed member countries to establishing an economic union.

Six Sigma   Statistically based philosophy to reduce defects, boost productivity, eliminate waste, and cut costs.

Smoot–Hawley Act   Enacted in 1930 by the U.S. Congress, this act erected a wall of tariff barriers against imports into the United States.

social democrats   Those committed to achieving socialism by democratic means.

social mobility   The extent to which individuals can move out of the social strata into which they are born.

social responsibility   Concept that businesspeople should consider the social consequences of economic actions when making business decisions.

social strata   Hierarchical social categories.

social structure   The basic social organization of a society.

socialism   A political philosophy advocating substantial public involvement, through government ownership, in the means of production and distribution.

society   Group of people who share a common set of values and norms.

sogo shosha   Japanese trading companies; a key part of the keiretsu, the large Japanese industrial groups.

sourcing decisions   Whether a firm should make or buy component parts.

specialized asset   An asset designed to perform a specific task, whose value is significantly reduced in its next-best use.

specific tariff   Tariff levied as a fixed charge for each unit of good imported.

spot exchange rate   The exchange rate at which a foreign exchange dealer will convert one currency into another that particular day.

staffing policy   Strategy concerned with selecting employees for particular jobs.

stakeholders   Individuals or groups that have an interest, claim, or stake in the company, in what it does, and in how well it performs.

state-directed economy   An economy in which the state plays a proactive role in influencing the direction and magnitude of private-sector investments.

stock of foreign direct investment   The total accumulated value of foreign-owned assets at a given time.

strategic alliances   Cooperative agreements between two or more firms.

strategic commitment   A decision that has a long-term impact and is difficult to reverse, such as entering a foreign market on a large scale.

strategic trade policy   Government policy aimed at improving the competitive position of a domestic industry and/or domestic firm in the world market.

strategy   Actions managers take to attain the firm's goals.

Structural Impediments Initiative   A 1990 agreement between the United States and Japan aimed at trying to decrease nontariff barriers restricting imports into Japan.

subsidy   Government financial assistance to a domestic producer.

Sullivan principles   A twofold approach to doing business in apartheid South Africa, comprising passive resistance to apartheid laws and attempts to influence the abolition of apartheid laws.

swaps   The simultaneous purchase and sale of a given amount of foreign exchange for two different value dates.

switch trading   Use of a specialized third-party trading house in a countertrade arrangement.

systematic risk   Movements in a stock portfolio's value that are attributable to macroeconomic forces affecting all firms in an economy, rather than factors specific to an individual firm (unsystematic risk).

T

tariff   A tax levied on imports.

tariff rate quota   Lower tariff rates applied to imports within the quota than those over the quota.

tax credit   Allows a firm to reduce the taxes paid to the home government by the amount of taxes paid to the foreign government.

tax haven   A country with exceptionally low, or even no, income taxes.

tax treaty   Agreement between two countries specifying what items of income will be taxed by the authorities of the country where the income is earned.

technical analysis   Uses price and volume data to determine past trends, which are expected to continue into the future.

temporal method   Translating assets valued in a foreign currency into the home currency using the exchange rate that existed when the assets were originally purchased.

theocratic law system   A system of law based on religious teachings.

theocratic totalitarianism   A political system in which political power is monopolized by a party, group, or individual that governs according to religious principles.

time draft   A promise to pay by the accepting party at some future date.

time-based competition   Competing on the basis of speed in responding to customer demands and developing new products.

timing of entry   Entry is early when a firm enters a foreign market before other foreign firms and late when a firm enters after other international businesses have established themselves.

total quality management   Management philosophy that takes as its central focus the need to improve the quality of a company's products and services.

totalitarianism   Form of government in which one person or political party exercises absolute control over all spheres of human life and opposing political parties are prohibited.

trade creation   Trade created due to regional economic integration; occurs when high-cost domestic producers are replaced by low-cost foreign producers within a free trade area.

trade deficit   See **current account deficit.**

trade diversion   Trade diverted due to regional economic integration; occurs when low-cost foreign suppliers outside a free trade area replace higher-cost suppliers within a free trade area.

Trade Related Aspects of Intellectual Property Rights   WTO agreement overseeing stricter intellectual property regulations.

trade surplus   See **current account surplus.**

trademarks   Designs and names, often officially registered, by which merchants or manufacturers designate and differentiate their products.

transaction costs   The costs of exchange.

transaction exposure   The extent to which income from individual transactions is affected by fluctuations in foreign exchange values.

transfer fee   A bank charge for moving cash from one location to another.

transfer price   The price at which goods and services are transferred between subsidiary companies of a corporation.

translation exposure   The extent to which the reported consolidated results and balance sheets of a corporation are affected by fluctuations in foreign exchange values.

transnational corporation   A firm that tries to simultaneously realize gains from experience curve economies, location economies, and global learning, while remaining locally responsive.

transnational financial reporting   The need for a firm headquartered in one country to report its results to citizens of another country.

transnational strategy   Plan to exploit experience-based cost and location economies, transfer core competencies with the firm, and pay attention to local responsiveness.

Treaty of Rome   The 1957 treaty that established the European Community.

tribal totalitarianism   A political system in which a party, group, or individual that represents the interests of a particular tribe (ethnic group) monopolizes political power.

turnkey project   A project in which a firm agrees to set up an operating plant for a foreign client and hand over the "key" when the plant is fully operational.

U

unbundling   Relying on more than one financial technique to transfer funds across borders.

uncertainty avoidance   Extent to which cultures socialize members to accept ambiguous situations and to tolerate uncertainty.

United Nations   International institution with 191 member countries created to preserve peace.

United Nations Convention on Contracts for the International Sale of Goods (CIGS)   Agreement establishing a uniform set of rules governing contracts between businesses in different nations.

Universal Declaration of Human Rights   An agreement that establishes basic principles that should be adhered to irrespective of the culture.

universal needs   Needs that are the same all over the world, such as steel, bulk chemicals, and industrial electronics.

utilitarian approach   Ethical approach that holds that the moral worth of actions is determined by their consequences.

V

value creation   Performing activities that increase the value of goods or services to consumers.

values   Abstract ideas about what a society believes to be good, right, and desirable.

vehicle currency   A currency that plays a central role in the foreign exchange market (e.g., the U.S. dollar and Japanese yen).

vertical differentiation   The centralization and decentralization of decision-making responsibilities.

vertical foreign direct investment   Foreign direct investment in an industry abroad that provides input into a firm's domestic operations, or foreign direct investment into an industry abroad that sells the outputs of a firm's domestic operations.

vertical integration   Extension of a firm's activities into adjacent stages of production (i.e., those providing the firm's inputs or those that purchase the firm's outputs).

voluntary export restraint (VER)   A quota on trade imposed from the exporting country's side, instead of the importer's; usually imposed at the request of the importing country's government.

W

wholly owned subsidiary   A subsidiary in which the firm owns 100 percent of the stock.

World Bank   International institution set up to promote general economic development in the world's poorer nations.

World Intellectual Property Organization   Group of 188 countries that have signed international treaties designed to protect intellectual property.

World Trade Organization (WTO)   The organization that succeeded the General Agreement on Tariffs and Trade (GATT) as a result of the successful completion of the Uruguay round of GATT negotiations.

worldwide area structure   Business organizational structure under which the world is divided into areas.

worldwide product division structure   Business organizational structure based on product divisions that have worldwide responsibility.

Z

zero-sum game   A situation in which an economic gain by one country results in an economic loss by another.

photo CREDITS

ORGANIZATION INDEX

NAME INDEX

SUBJECT INDEX